Wilma West

Chambers
Pocket
Thesaurus

Chambers
Pocket
Thesaurus

Managing Editor
Catherine Schwarz

Chambers

CHAMBERS
An imprint of Chambers Harrap Publishers Ltd
7 Hopetoun Crescent
Edinburgh, EH7 4AY

First published by W. R. Chambers Ltd 1992
Reprinted 1993, 1995, 1997, 1998

A catalogue record for this book is available
from the British Library

ISBN 0 550 10582 4

Typeset by Hower Text Composition Services, Edinburgh
Printed and bound in Great Britain by
Caledonian International Book Manufacturing Ltd, Glasgow

Contents

Abbreviations used in the *Pocket Thesaurus*

adj	adjective	*n*	noun
adv	adverb	*v*	verb
	® registered trademark		

Preface

Chambers Pocket Thesaurus is an easily accessible source, in A-Z form, of synonyms and antonyms. It provides words that mean the same as, and the opposite of, over 14 000 of the commonest words in the English language, in a handy easy-to-use format.

Drawn from Chambers English language database, the *Pocket Thesaurus* is up to date, authoritative and comprehensive, including as it does the vocabulary of recent medical and scientific advances, of national and international politics, of widening cultural horizons, of sport and of war.

The *Pocket Thesaurus* is essential for everyone who wants or needs to use language well, whether writing or speaking, at home, at work, or for fun. It jogs the memory, it opens doors, it solves problems; it is an indispensable language tool.

Used in conjunction with a dictionary—*Chambers Pocket Dictionary, Chambers Maxi Paperback Dictionary* or even the larger *Chambers English Dictionary*—the *Pocket Thesaurus* extends language appreciation and skills on every occasion.

A

abandon *v* abdicate, back-pedal, cede, chuck, desert, desist, discontinue, ditch, drop, evacuate, forgo, forsake, give up, jilt, leave, leave behind, leave in the lurch, quit, relinquish, renounce, repudiate, resign, scrap, sink, surrender, vacate, waive, withdraw from, yield. *antonyms* continue, persist, support.
n dash, recklessness, unrestraint, wantonness, wildness. *antonym* restraint.

abandoned *adj* cast aside, cast away, cast out, corrupt, debauched, depraved, derelict, deserted, desolate, discarded, dissipated, dissolute, dropped, forlorn, forsaken, jilted, left, neglected, outcast, profligate, rejected, relinquished, reprobate, scorned, sinful, unoccupied, vacant, wanton, wicked. *antonyms* cherished, restrained.

abase *v* belittle, cast down, debase, degrade, demean, discredit, disgrace, dishonour, downgrade, humble, humiliate, lower, malign, mortify, reduce, vitiate. *antonyms* elevate, honour.

abashed *adj* affronted, ashamed, astounded, bewildered, chagrined, confounded, confused, cowed, discomfited, discomposed, disconcerted, discountenanced, discouraged, dismayed, dum(b)founded, embarrassed, floored, humbled, humiliated, mortified, nonplussed, perturbed, shamefaced, taken aback. *antonyms* at ease, audacious, composed.

abate *v* alleviate, appease, attenuate, bate, decline, decrease, deduct, diminish, discount, dull, dwindle, ease, ebb, fade, faik, fall off, lessen, let up, mitigate, moderate, mollify, pacify, quell, rebate, reduce, relieve, remit, sink, slacken, slake, slow, subside, subtract, taper off, wane, weaken. *antonyms* increase, strengthen.

abbey *n* cloister, convent, friary, monastery, nunnery, priory, seminary.

abbreviate *v* abridge, abstract, clip, compress, condense, contract, curtail, cut, digest, epitomise, lessen, précis, reduce, shorten, shrink, summarise, trim, truncate. *antonyms* amplify, extend.

abbreviation *n* abridgement, abstract, abstraction, clipping, compendium, compression, condensation, contraction, curtailment, digest, epitome, précis, reduction, résumé, shortening, summarisation, summary, summation, synopsis, trimming, truncation. *antonyms* expansion, extension.

abdicate *v* abandon, abjure, abnegate, cede, demit, forgo, give up, quit, relinquish, renounce, repudiate, resign, retire, surrender, vacate, yield.

abdication *n* abandonment, abjuration, abnegation, cession, giving up, quitting, relinquishment, renunciation, resignation, retiral, retirement, surrender.

abdomen *n* belly, bread-basket, guts, hind-body, midriff, paunch, pot, stomach, tum, tummy, venter.

abduct *v* abduce, appropriate, carry off, kidnap, lay hold of, make off with, rape, run away with, run off with, seduce, seize, snatch, spirit away.

abducted *adj* appropriated, enlevé, kidnapped, seduced, seized, snatched, stolen.

abduction *n* appropriation, enlevement, kidnap, rape, seduction, seizure, theft.

aberration *n* aberrancy, abnormality, anomaly, defect, delusion, deviation, divergence, eccentricity, freak, hallucination, illusion, irregularity, lapse, nonconformity, oddity, peculiarity, quirk, rambling, rogue, straying, vagary, wandering. *antonym* conformity.

abet *v* aid, assist, back, condone, connive, egg on, encourage, goad, help, incite, promote, prompt, sanction, second, spur, succour, support, sustain, uphold, urge. *antonym* discourage.

abeyance *n* adjournment, deferral, discontinuation, inactivity, intermission, lull, postponement, recess, remission, reservation, suspension, waiting. *antonyms* activity, continuation.

abhor *v* abominate, despise, detest, execrate, hate, loathe, recoil from, shrink from, shudder at, spurn. *antonyms* adore, love.

abhorrence *n* abomination, animosity, aversion, detestation, disgust, distaste, enmity, execration, hate, hatred, horror, loathing, malice, odium, repugnance, revulsion. *antonyms* adoration, love.

abhorrent *adj* abominable, detestable, disgusting, distasteful, execrable, hated, hateful, heinous, horrible, horrid, loathsome, nauseating, obnoxious, odious, offensive, repellent, repugnant, repulsive, revolting. *antonym* attractive.

abide *v* accept, bear, brook, continue, endure, last, outlive, persist, put up with, remain, stand, stay, stomach, submit to, suffer, survive, tolerate. *antonyms* dispute, quit.

abide by acknowledge, acquiesce in, adhere to, agree to, carry out, comply with, conform to, discharge, follow, fulfil, go along with, hold to, keep to, obey, observe, stand by, submit to.

abiding *adj* constant, continual, continuing, continuous, durable, enduring, eternal, everlasting, fast, firm, immortal, immutable, lasting, permanent, persistent, persisting, stable, steadfast, surviving, tenacious, unchangeable, unchanging, unending. *antonyms* ephemeral, transient.

ability *n* adeptness, adroitness, aptitude, capability, capacity, competence, competency, deftness, dexterity, endowment, energy, expertise, expertness, facility, faculty, flair, forte, genius, gift, knack, know-how, long suit, nous, potentiality, power, proficiency, qualification, savoir-faire, savvy, skill, strength, talent, touch. *antonyms* inability, incompetence.

abject *adj* base, contemptible, cringing, debased, degenerate, degraded, deplorable, despicable, dishonourable, execrable, fawning, forlorn, grovelling, hopeless, humiliating, ignoble, ignominious, low, mean, miserable, outcast, pathetic, pitiable, servile, slavish, sordid, submissive, vile, worthless, wretched. *antonym* exalted.

abjure *v* abandon, abnegate, abstain from, deny, disavow, discard, disclaim, disown, eschew, forsake, forswear, give up, recant, refrain from, reject, relinquish, renegue on, renounce, retract. *antonyms* agree, assent, support.

ablaze *adj* afire, aflame, aglow, alight, angry, aroused, blazing, brilliant, burning, enthusiastic, excited, exhilarated, fervent, fiery, flaming, flashing, frenzied, fuming, furious, glaring, gleaming, glowing, ignited, illuminated, impassioned, incensed, lighted, on fire, passionate, radiant, raging, sparkling.

able *adj* accomplished, adept, adequate, adroit, capable, clever, competent, deft, dexterous, effective, efficient, experienced, expert, fit, gifted, ingenious, masterly, powerful, practised, proficient, qualified, skilful, skilled, strong, talented. *antonyms* incapable, incompetent.

able-bodied *adj* firm, fit, hale, hardy, healthy, hearty, powerful, robust, sound, stalwart, staunch, stout, strapping, strong, sturdy, tough, vigorous. *antonyms* delicate, infirm.

abnegate *v* abandon, abdicate, abjure, abstain from, acquiesce, concede, decline, deny, disallow, eschew, forbear, forgo, forsake, give up, refrain from, reject, relinquish, renounce, sacrifice, submit, surrender, yield.

abnormal *adj* aberrant, anomalous, atypical, curious, deviant, different, divergent, eccentric, erratic, exceptional, extraordinary, irregular, monstrous, odd, paranormal, peculiar, queer, singular, strange, uncanny, uncommon, unnatural, untypical, unusual, wayward, weird.

abnormality *n* aberration, anomaly, atypicalness, bizarreness, deformity, deviation, difference, divergence, eccentricity, exception, flaw, irregularity, monstrosity, oddity, peculiarity, queerness, singularity, strangeness, unusualness, weirdness.

abode *n* domicile, dwelling, dwelling-place, habitat, habitation, home, house, lodging, pad, place, quarters, residence.

abolish *v* abrogate, annihilate, annul, blot out, cancel, destroy, do away with, eliminate, end, eradicate, expunge, exterminate, extinguish, extirpate, get rid of, invalidate, nullify, obliterate, overthrow, overturn, put an end to, quash, repeal, repudiate, rescind, revoke, sink, stamp out, subvert, suppress, terminate, vitiate, wipe out. *antonym* retain.

abolition *n* abrogation, annihilation, annulment, cancellation, destruction, dissolution, elimination, end, ending, eradication, expunction, extermination, extinction, extirpation, invalidation, nullification, obliteration, overthrow, overturning, quashing, repeal, repudiation, revocation, subversion, suppression, termination, vitiation, withdrawal. *antonym* retention.

abominable *adj* abhorrent, accursed, appalling, atrocious, base, beastly, contemptible, despicable, detestable, disgusting, execrable, foul, hateful, heinous, hellish, horrible, horrid, loathsome, nauseating, nauseous, obnoxious, odious, repellent, reprehensible, repugnant, repulsive, revolting, terrible, vile, villainous, wretched. *antonym* delightful.

abomination *n* abhorrence, anathema, animosity, antipathy, aversion, curse, detestation, disgrace, disgust, distaste, evil, execration, hate, hatred, horror, hostility, loathing, odium, offence, plague, repugnance, revulsion, torment. *antonyms* adoration, delight.

aboriginal *adj* ancient, domestic, earliest, endemic, first, indigenous, native, original, primal, primary, primeval, primitive, primordial.

aborigine *n* aboriginal, native. *antonym* immigrant.

abort *v* arrest, call off, check, end, fail, frustrate, halt, miscarry, nullify, stop, terminate, thwart. *antonym* continue.

abortion *n* disappointment, failure, fiasco, freak, frustration, misadventure, misbirth, miscarriage, monster, monstrosity, termination, thwarting. *antonyms* continuation, success.

abortive *adj* barren, failed, failing, fruitless, futile, idle, ineffective, ineffectual, misborn, miscarried, sterile, unproductive, unsuccessful, useless, vain. *antonym* successful.

abound *v* be plentiful, brim over, crowd, exuberate, flourish, increase, infest, luxuriate, overflow, proliferate, run riot, superabound, swarm, swell, teem, thrive. *antonym* be in short supply.

about *prep* adjacent to, all over, around, as regards, beside, busy with, circa, close to, concerned with, concerning, connected with, encircling, encompassing, engaged on, in respect to, in the matter of, near, nearby, of, on, over, re, referring to, regarding, relating to, relative to, respecting, round, surrounding, through, throughout, with reference to, with regard to, with respect to.

adv active, almost, approaching, approximately, around, close to, from place to place, here and there, in motion, in the region of, more or less, nearing, nearly, present, roughly, stirring, to and fro.

about to all but, intending to, on the point of, on the verge of, preparing to, ready to.

about-turn *n* about-face, backtrack, reversal, right-about (face), turnabout, turn(a)round, U-turn, volte-face.

above *prep* before, beyond, exceeding, higher than, in excess of, on top of, over, prior to, superior to, surpassing, upon. *antonyms* below, under.

adv aloft, earlier, heavenwards, in heaven, on high, overhead. *antonym* below.

adj above-mentioned, above-stated, aforementioned, aforesaid, earlier, foregoing, preceding, previous, prior.

above suspicion above reproach, blameless, guiltless, honourable, innocent, irreproachable, pure, sinless, unimpeachable, virtuous.

above-board *adj* candid, fair, fair and square, forthright, frank, guileless, honest, honourable, legitimate, on the level, open, overt, reputable, square, straight, straightforward, true, trustworthy, truthful, upright, veracious. *antonyms* shady, underhand.

abrasion *n* abrading, chafe, chafing, erosion, friction, grating, graze, grinding, rubbing, scouring, scrape, scraping, scratch, scratching, scuff, scuffing, wearing away, wearing down.

abrasive *adj* annoying, biting, caustic, chafing, erosive, frictional, galling, grating, hurtful, irritating, nasty, rough, scraping, scratching, scratchy, scuffing, sharp, unpleasant.

abreast *adj* acquainted, au fait, conversant, familiar, in the picture, in touch, informed, knowledgeable, on the ball, up to date. *antonyms* out of touch, unaware.

abridge *v* abbreviate, abstract, clip, compress, concentrate, condense, contract, curtail, cut, cut down, decrease, digest, diminish, dock, lessen, précis, prune, reduce, shorten, summarise, trim, truncate. *antonyms* amplify, pad.

abroad *adv* about, at large, away, circulating, current, elsewhere, extensively, far, far and wide, forth, in circulation, in foreign parts, out, out of the country, out-of-doors, outside, overseas, publicly, widely.

abrogate *v* abolish, annul, cancel, countermand, discontinue, dissolve, end, invalidate, nullify, override, overrule, quash, recall, repeal, repudiate, rescind, retract, reverse, revoke, set aside, terminate, void, withdraw. *antonyms* establish, institute.

abrupt *adj* blunt, brief, brisk, brusque, curt, direct, discourteous, gruff, hasty, headlong, hurried, impolite, irregular, jerky, precipitate, precipitous, quick, rapid, rough, rude, sharp, sheer, short, snappy, steep, sudden, surprising, swift, terse, unceremonious, uncivil, uneven, ungracious. *antonyms* ceremonious, expansive, leisurely.

abscond *v* bolt, decamp, disappear, escape, flee, flit, fly, quit, run off, skive, take French leave.

absence *n* absenteeism, absent-mindedness, abstraction, dearth, default, defect, deficiency, distraction, inattention, lack, need, non-attendance, omission, paucity, preoccupation, reverie, scarcity, truancy, unavailability, vacancy, vacuity, want. *antonyms* existence, presence.

absent *adj* absent-minded, absorbed, abstracted, away, bemused, blank, day-dreaming, distracted, distrait(e), dreamy, elsewhere, empty, faraway, gone, heedless, inattentive, lacking, missing, musing, non-existent, not present, oblivious, out, preoccupied, truant, unavailable, unaware, unconscious, unheeding, unthinking, vacant, vague, wanting, wool-gathering. *antonyms* aware, present.

absent-minded *adj* dreaming, dreamy, engrossed, faraway, forgetful, heedless, inattentive, musing, oblivious, pensive, preoccupied, scatterbrained, unaware, unconscious, unheeding, unthinking, wool-gathering.

absolute *adj* actual, almighty, arbitrary, autocratic, autonomous, categorical, certain, complete, conclusive, consummate, decided, decisive, definite, definitive, despotic, dictatorial, downright, entire, exact, exhaustive, final, flawless, free, full, genuine, independent, infallible, omnipotent, out-and-out, outright, perfect, positive, precise, pure, sheer, sovereign, supreme, sure, thorough, total, totalitarian, tyrannical, unadulterated, unalloyed, unambiguous, unconditional, uncontrolled, undivided, unequivocal, unlimited, unmitigated, unmixed, unqualified, unquestionable, unrestricted, utter. *antonyms* conditional, partial.

absolutely *adv* actually, arbitrarily, autocratically, autonomously, bang, categorically, certainly, completely, conclusively, consummately, dead, decidedly, decisively, definitely, despotically, diametrically, dictatorially, entirely, exactly, exhaustively, finally, fully, genuinely, infallibly, perfectly, positively, precisely, purely, sovereignly, supremely, surely, thoroughly, totally, truly, tyrannically, unambiguously, unconditionally,

unequivocally, unquestionably, utterly, wholly.

absolve *v* acquit, clear, deliver, discharge, exculpate, excuse, exempt, exonerate, forgive, free, justify, let off, liberate, loose, pardon, redeem, release, remit, set free, vindicate. *antonym* charge.

absorb *v* adsorb, apprehend, assimilate, captivate, consume, devour, digest, drink in, engage, engross, engulf, enthral(l), exhaust, fascinate, fill (up), fix, grip, hold, immerse, incorporate, ingest, involve, monopolise, occupy, preoccupy, rivet, soak up, suck up, take in, understand. *antonyms* dissipate, exude.

absorbed *adj* captivated, concentrating, engaged, engrossed, enthralled, fascinated, fixed, gripped, held, immersed, obsessed, occupied, preoccupied, rapt, riveted. *antonyms* bored, distracted.

absorbing *adj* captivating, compulsive, diverting, engrossing, entertaining, enthralling, fascinating, gripping, interesting, intriguing, preoccupying, riveting, spellbinding, unputdownable. *antonyms* boring, off-putting.

absorption *n* adsorption, assimilation, attentiveness, captivation, concentration, consumption, digestion, fascination, holding, immersion, ingestion, intentness, occupation, osmosis, preoccupation, soaking up, sucking up.

abstain *v* avoid, cease, decline, deny, desist, eschew, forbear, forgo, give up, keep from, refrain, refuse, reject, renounce, resist, shun, stop, swear off, withhold. *antonym* indulge.

abstemious *adj* abstinent, disciplined, frugal, moderate, restrained, self-denying, self-disciplined, sober, sparing, temperate. *antonyms* gluttonous, intemperate, luxurious.

abstention *n* abstaining, abstinence, avoidance, forbearance, frugality, non-indulgence, refraining, refusal, restraint, self-control, self-denial, self-discipline, self-restraint, sobriety.

abstinence *n* abstemiousness, avoidance, forbearance, frugality, moderation, non-indulgence, refraining, self-denial, self-discipline, self-restraint, sobriety, teetotalism, temperance. *antonym* self-indulgence.

abstract *adj* abstruse, academic, arcane, complex, conceptual, deep, discrete, general, generalised, hypothetical, indefinite, intellectual, metaphysical, non-concrete, occult, philosophical, profound, recondite, separate, subtle, theoretical. **antonym** concrete.

n abbreviation, abridgement, compression, condensation, digest, epitome, essence, outline, précis, résumé, summary, synopsis.

v abbreviate, abridge, compress, condense, digest, dissociate, epitomise, extract, isolate, outline, précis, remove, separate, shorten, summarise. **antonyms** expand, insert.

abstruse *adj* abstract, arcane, complex, cryptic, dark, deep, devious, difficult, enigmatic, esoteric, hidden, incomprehensible, mysterious, mystical, obscure, occult, perplexing, profound, puzzling, recondite, subtle, tortuous, unfathomable. **antonyms** concrete, obvious.

absurd *adj* anomalous, comical, crazy, daft, derisory, fantastic, farcical, foolish, funny, humorous, idiotic, illogical, implausible, incongruous, irrational, laughable, ludicrous, meaningless, nonsensical, paradoxical, preposterous, ridiculous, senseless, silly, stupid, unreasonable, untenable. **antonyms** logical, rational, sensible.

abundance *n* affluence, amplitude, bonanza, bounty, fullness, milk and honey, munificence, opulence, plenitude, plenty, plethora, prodigality, profusion, riches, richness, wealth. **antonyms** dearth, scarcity.

abundant *adj* ample, bounteous, bountiful, copious, generous, in plenty, lavish, luxuriant, overflowing, plenteous, plentiful, prodigal, profuse, rich, teeming. **antonyms** scarce, sparse.

abuse *v* batter, castigate, curse, damage, deceive, defame, denigrate, disparage, exploit, harm, hurt, ill-treat, impose on, injure, insult, inveigh against, libel, malign, maltreat, manhandle, mar, misapply, misuse, molest, oppress, oppugn, revile, scold, slander, slate, smear, spoil, take advantage of, upbraid, vilify, violate, vituperate, wrong.

n affront, blame, calumny, castigation, censure, curses, cursing, damage, defamation, denigration, derision, disparagement, execration, exploitation, harm, hurt, ill-treatment, imposition, injury, insults, invective, libel, malediction, maltreatment, misapplication, misconduct, misdeed, misuse, offence, oppression, opprobrium, reproach, revilement, scolding, sin, slander, spoiling, swearing, traducement, upbraiding, vilification, violation, vitriol, vituperation.

abusive *adj* brutal, castigating, censorious, contumelious, cruel, defamatory, denigrating, derisive, derogatory, destructive, disparaging, harmful, hurtful, injurious, insulting, libellous, maligning, offensive, pejorative, reproachful, reviling, rough, rude, scathing, scolding, slanderous, upbraiding, vilifying, vituperative.

abyss *n* canyon, chasm, crater, crevasse, depth, fissure, gorge, gulf, pit, void.

academic *adj* bookish, collegiate, conjectural, donnish, educational, erudite, highbrow, hypothetical, impractical, instructional, learned, lettered, literary, notional, pedagogical, scholarly, scholastic, speculative, studious, theoretical, well-read.

n don, fellow, lecturer, man of letters, master, professor, savant, scholar, student, tutor.

accede *v* accept, acquiesce, admit, agree, assent, assume, attain, capitulate, comply, concede, concur, consent, defer, endorse, grant, inherit, submit, succeed (to), yield. **antonyms** demur, object.

accelerate *v* advance, expedite, facilitate, forward, further, hasten, hurry, pick up speed, precipitate, promote, quicken, speed, speed up, spur, step up, stimulate. **antonym** delay.

accent *n* beat, cadence, emphasis, enunciation, force, inflection, intonation, modulation, pitch, pronunciation, pulse, rhythm, stress, timbre, tonality, tone.

v accentuate, emphasise, stress, underline, underscore.

accentuate *v* accent, emphasise, highlight, italicise, spotlight, strengthen, stress, underline, underscore. **antonyms** play down, weaken.

accept *v* abide by, accede, acknowledge, acquiesce, acquire, admit, adopt, affirm, agree to, approve, assume, avow, bear, believe, bow to, brook, concur with, consent to, co-operate with, defer to, gain, get, have, jump at, obtain, put up with, receive, recognise, secure, stand, stomach, submit to, suffer, swallow, take, tolerate, undertake, wear, yield to. **antonyms** demur, reject.

acceptable *adj* adequate, admissible, agreeable, correct, delightful, desirable, done, moderate, passable, pleasant, pleasing, satisfactory, standard, suitable, tolerable, unexceptionable, unobjectionable, welcome.

acceptance n accedence, accepting, accession, acknowledgement, acquiescence, admission, adoption, affirmation, agreement, approbation, approval, assent, compliance, concession, concurrence, consent, credence, gaining, getting, having, obtaining, permission, ratification, receipt, recognition, seal of approval, securing, stamp of approval, tolerance, toleration, undertaking. **antonyms** dissent, refusal.

accepted adj acknowledged, admitted, agreed, agreed upon, approved, authorised, common, confirmed, conventional, correct, customary, established, normal, ratified, received, recognised, regular, sanctioned, standard, time-honoured, traditional, universal, usual. **antonym** unorthodox.

access n admission, admittance, approach, avenue, course, door, entrance, entry, gateway, increase, key, onset, passage, path, road, upsurge. **antonym** outlet.

accessible adj achievable, affable, approachable, at hand, attainable, available, come-at-able, conversable, cordial, exposed, friendly, handy, informal, liable, near, nearby, obtainable, on hand, open, reachable, ready, sociable, subject, user-friendly, vulnerable, wide-open. **antonym** inaccessible.

accession n acceptance, acquiescence, acquisition, addition, agreement, assumption, attainment, augmentation, concurrence, consent, entering upon, extension, increase, installation, purchase, submission, succession, taking over, yielding.

accessory n accompaniment, accomplice, addition, aid, appendage, assistant, associate, attachment, colleague, component, convenience, decoration, helper, partner, supplement. adj abetting, additional, ancillary, assisting, auxiliary, contributory, incidental, secondary, subordinate, subsidiary, supplementary.

accident n calamity, casualty, chance, collision, contingency, crash, disaster, fate, fluke, fortuity, fortune, happenstance, hazard, luck, misadventure, miscarriage, mischance, misfortune, mishap, pile-up, serendipity, shunt.

accidental adj casual, chance,

contingent, fluky, fortuitous, haphazard, inadvertent, incidental, random, unexpected, unforeseen, unintended, unintentional, unplanned, unpremeditated, unwitting. **antonyms** intentional, premeditated.

acclaim v applaud, approve, celebrate, cheer, clap, commend, crown, declare, exalt, extol, hail, honour, laud, praise, salute, welcome.
n applause, approbation, approval, celebration, cheering, commendation, eulogy, exaltation, honour, ovation, praise, welcome. **antonyms** brickbats, criticism, vituperation.

acclimatise v accommodate, accustom, adapt, adjust, attune, conform, familiarise, find one's legs, get used to, habituate, inure, naturalise.

accolade n award, honour, kudos, laurels, praise.

accommodate v acclimatise, accustom, adapt, adjust, afford, aid, assist, attune, billet, board, cater for, comply, conform, domicile, entertain, fit, furnish, harbour, help, house, lodge, modify, oblige, provide, put up, quarter, reconcile, serve, settle, shelter, supply.

accommodating adj complaisant, considerate, co-operative, friendly, helpful, hospitable, indulgent, kind, obliging, polite, sympathetic, unselfish, willing. **antonym** disobliging.

accommodation[1] n adaptation, adjustment, assistance, compliance, composition, compromise, conformity, fitting, help, modification, reconciliation, settlement.

accommodation[2] n bed and breakfast, billet, board, digs, domicile, dwelling, housing, lodgings, residence, shelter.

accompaniment n accessory, attendance, background, back-up, complement, concomitant, support.

accompany v attend, belong to, chaperon, co-exist, coincide, complement, conduct, consort, convoy, escort, follow, go with, occur with, supplement, usher.

accompanying adj accessory, added, additional, appended, associate, associated, attached, attendant, background, complementary, concomitant, concurrent, connected, fellow, joint, related, subsidiary, supplementary.

accomplice n accessory, ally, assistant, associate, collaborator, colleague, conspirator, helper, helpmate, henchman, partner.

accomplish v achieve, attain, bring about, bring off, carry out, complete, conclude, consummate, discharge, do, effect, effectuate, engineer, execute, finish, fulfil, manage, obtain, perform, produce, realise.

accomplished adj adept, adroit, consummate, expert, facile, gifted, masterly, polished, practised, professional, proficient, skilful, skilled, talented. **antonym** inexpert.

accomplishment n ability, achievement, act, aptitude, art, attainment, capability, carrying out, completion, conclusion, consummation, coup, deed, discharge, doing, effecting, execution, exploit, faculty, feat, finishing, forte, fruition, fulfilment, gift, management, perfection, performance, production, proficiency, realisation, skill, stroke, talent, triumph.

accord v agree, allow, assent, bestow, concede, concur, confer, conform, correspond, endow, fit, give, grant, harmonise, jibe, match, present, suit, tally, tender, vouchsafe.

n accordance, agreement, assent, concert, concurrence, conformity, consort, correspondence, harmony, rapport, symmetry, sympathy, unanimity, unity. **antonym** discord.

accordingly adv appropriately, as a result, as requested, consequently, correspondingly, fitly, hence, in accord with, in accordance, in consequence, properly, so, suitably, therefore, thus.

according to after, after the manner of, agreeably to, commensurate with, consistent with, in accordance with, in compliance with, in conformity with, in keeping with, in line with, in obedience to, in proportion, in relation to, in the light of, in the manner of, obedient to.

accost v address, approach, buttonhole, confront, detain, greet, hail, halt, importune, salute, solicit, stop, waylay.

account[1] n advantage, basis, benefit, cause, chronicle, concern, consequence, consideration, description, detail, distinction, esteem, estimation, explanation, ground, grounds, history, honour, import, importance, interest, memoir, merit, motive, narration, narrative, note, performance, portrayal, presentation, profit, rank, reason, recital, record, regard, relation, report, reputation, repute, sake, score, significance, sketch, standing, statement, story, tale, use, value, version, worth, write-up.

v adjudge, appraise, assess, believe, consider, count, deem, esteem, estimate, explain, gauge, hold, judge, rate, reckon, regard, think, value, weigh.

account for answer for, clarify, clear up, destroy, elucidate, explain, illuminate, incapacitate, justify, kill, put paid to, rationalise, vindicate.

account[2] n balance, bill, book, books, charge, check, computation, inventory, invoice, ledger, reckoning, register, score, statement, tab, tally, tick.

accountability n amenability, liability, responsibility.

accountable adj amenable, answerable, blamable, bound, charged with, liable, obligated, obliged, responsible.

accredit v appoint, approve, ascribe, assign, attribute, authorise, certificate, certify, commission, credit, depute, empower, enable, endorse, entrust, guarantee, license, okay, qualify, recognise, sanction, vouch for.

accredited adj appointed, approved, attested, authorised, certificated, certified, commissioned, deputed, deputised, empowered, endorsed, guaranteed, licensed, official, qualified, recognised, sanctioned, vouched for. **antonym** unauthorised.

accrue v accumulate, amass, arise, be added, build up, collect, emanate, enlarge, ensue, fall due, flow, follow, gather, grow, increase, issue, proceed, result, spring up.

accumulate v accrue, agglomerate, aggregate, amass, assemble, build up, collect, gather, grow, hoard, increase, multiply, pile up, stash, stockpile, store. **antonyms** diffuse, disseminate.

accurate adj authentic, careful, close, correct, exact, factual, faithful, faultless, just, letter-perfect, mathematical, meticulous, minute, nice, perfect, precise, proper, regular, right, rigorous, scrupulous, sound, spot-on, strict, true, truthful, unerring, veracious, well-aimed, well-directed, well-judged, word-perfect.

accursed adj abominable, bedevilled, bewitched, blighted, condemned, cursed, damned, despicable, detestable, doomed, execrable, foredoomed, hateful, hellish, hopeless, horrible, ill-fated, ill-omened, jinxed, luckless, ruined, star-crossed, undone, unfortunate, unholy, unlucky, wretched. **antonym** blessed.

accusation n allegation, arraignment, attribution, charge, citation, complaint, denunciation, impeachment, imputation, incrimination, indictment, plaint, recrimination.

accuse v allege, arraign, attaint, attribute, blame, censure, charge, cite, denounce, impeach, impugn, impute, incriminate, indict, inform against, recriminate, tax.

accustom v acclimatise, acquaint, adapt, adjust, discipline, exercise, familiarise, habituate, harden, inure, season, train.

accustomed adj acclimatised, acquainted, adapted, common, confirmed, conventional, customary, disciplined, established, everyday, exercised, expected, familiar, familiarised, fixed, general, given to, habitual, in the habit of, inured, normal, ordinary, prevailing, regular, routine, seasoned, set, traditional, trained, used, usual, wonted.

ace adj brilliant, champion, excellent, expert, fine, first-class, great, masterly, matchless, outstanding, superb, superlative, tiptop, virtuoso.

acerbic adj abrasive, acid, acrid, acrimonious, astringent, bitter, brusque, caustic, churlish, corrosive, harsh, incisive, mordant, nasty, rancorous, rude, sarcastic, severe, sharp, sour, stern, tart, trenchant, unfriendly, unkind. *antonym* mild.

ache v agonise, covet, crave, desire, grieve, hanker, hunger, hurt, itch, long, mourn, need, pain, pine, rack, smart, sorrow, suffer, throb, twinge, yearn.
n anguish, craving, desire, grief, hankering, hunger, hurt, itch, longing, misery, mourning, need, pain, pang, pining, smart, smarting, soreness, sorrow, suffering, throb, throbbing, yearning.

achieve v accomplish, acquire, attain, bring about, carry out, complete, consummate, do, earn, effect, effectuate, execute, finish, fulfil, gain, get, manage, obtain, perform, procure, produce, reach, realise, score, strike, succeed, win.

achievement n accomplishment, acquirement, act, attainment, completion, deed, effort, execution, exploit, feat, fruition, fulfilment, magnum opus, performance, production, qualification, realisation, stroke, success.

achiever n doer, goer, go-getter, performer, succeeder.

acid adj acerbic, acrid, astringent, biting, bitter, caustic, corrosive, cutting, harsh, hurtful, ill-natured, incisive, mordant, morose, pungent, sharp, sour, stinging, tart, trenchant, vinegarish, vinegary, vitriolic.

acid test experimentum crucis, proof of the pudding.

acidity n acerbity, asperity, astringency, bitterness, corrosiveness, harshness, hurtfulness, incisiveness, mordancy, pungency, sharpness, sourness, tartness, trenchancy.

acknowledge v accede, accept, acquiesce, address, admit, affirm, allow, answer, attest, avouch, concede, confess, confirm, declare, endorse, grant, greet, hail, notice, own, profess, react to, recognise, reply to, respond to, return, salute, vouch for, witness, yield.

acknowledged adj accepted, accredited, admitted, affirmed, answered, approved, attested, avowed, conceded, confessed, declared, endorsed, professed, recognised, returned.

acknowledgement n acceptance, accession, acquiescence, addressing, admission, affirmation, allowing, answer, appreciation, confession, credit, declaration, endorsement, gratitude, greeting, hail, hailing, honour, notice, profession, reaction, realisation, recognition, recompense, reply, response, return, salutation, salute, thanks, tribute, yielding.

acolyte n adherent, admirer, altar boy, assistant, attendant, follower, helper, lackey, slave.

acoustic adj auditory, aural.

acquaint v accustom, advise, announce, apprise, brief, disclose, divulge, enlighten, familiarise, inform, notify, reveal, tell.

acquaintance n associate, association, awareness, chum, cognisance, colleague, companionship, confrère, contact, conversance, conversancy, experience, familiarity, fellowship, intimacy, knowledge, relationship, understanding.

acquainted adj abreast, conversant, familiar, in the know, informed.

acquiesce v accede, accept, agree, allow, approve, assent, comply, concur, conform, consent, defer, give in, submit, yield. *antonyms* disagree, object.

acquiescence n acceptance, accession, agreement, approval, assent, compliance, concurrence, conformity, consent, deference, giving in, obedience, sanction, submission, yielding. *antonym* disagreement, rebelliousness.

acquire *v* achieve, amass, appropriate, attain, buy, collect, cop, earn, gain, gather, get, net, obtain, pick up, procure, realise, receive, secure, win. **antonyms** forfeit, forgo, relinquish.

acquisition *n* achievement, appropriation, attainment, buy, gain, gaining, learning, obtainment, possession, prize, procurement, property, purchase, pursuit, securing, take-over.

acquisitive *adj* avaricious, avid, covetous, grabbing, grasping, greedy, insatiable, mercenary, possessive, predatory, rapacious, voracious.

acquit *v* absolve, bear, behave, clear, comport, conduct, deliver, discharge, dismiss, exculpate, excuse, exonerate, free, fulfil, liberate, pay, pay off, perform, release, relieve, repay, reprieve, satisfy, settle, vindicate. **antonym** convict.

acquittal *n* absolution, clearance, deliverance, discharge, dismissal, dispensation, exculpation, excusing, exoneration, freeing, liberation, release, relief, reprieve, vindication. **antonym** conviction.

acrid *adj* acerbic, acid, acrimonious, astringent, biting, bitter, burning, caustic, cutting, harsh, incisive, irritating, malicious, mordant, nasty, pungent, sarcastic, sardonic, sharp, stinging, trenchant, venomous, virulent, vitriolic.

acridity *n* acidity, acrimony, astringency, bitterness, causticity, harshness, mordancy, sharpness, trenchancy.

acrimonious *adj* abusive, acerbic, astringent, biting, bitter, caustic, censorious, churlish, crabbed, cutting, ill-tempered, irascible, mordant, peevish, petulant, pungent, rancorous, sarcastic, severe, sharp, spiteful, splenetic, tart, testy, trenchant, virulent, waspish. **antonyms** kindly, peaceable.

acrobat *n* aerialist, balancer, contortionist, funambulist, gymnast, somersaulter, stunt-girl, stuntman, tumbler.

act *n* accomplishment, achievement, action, affectation, attitude, bill, blow, counterfeit, decree, deed, dissimulation, doing, edict, enactment, enterprise, execution, exertion, exploit, fake, feat, feigning, front, gest, gig, law, make-believe, manoeuvre, measure, move, operation, ordinance, performance, pose, posture, pretence, proceeding, resolution, routine, sham, show, sketch, spiel, stance, statute, step, stroke, transaction, turn, undertaking.

v acquit, act out, affect, assume, bear, behave, carry, carry out, characterise, comport, conduct, counterfeit, dissimulate, do, enact, execute, exert, feign, function, go about, imitate, impersonate, make, mime, mimic, move, operate, perform, personify, play, portray, pose, posture, pretend, put on, react, represent, seem, serve, sham, simulate, strike, take effect, undertake, work.

act up carry on, cause trouble, give bother, give trouble, horse around, make waves, malfunction, mess about, misbehave, muck about, play up, rock the boat.

act (up)on affect, alter, carry out, change, comply with, conform to, execute, follow, fulfil, heed, influence, modify, obey, sway, transform, yield to.

acting *adj* interim, pro tem, provisional, reserve, stand-by, stop-gap, substitute, supply, surrogate, temporary.

n affectation, assuming, bluff, characterisation, counterfeiting, dissimulation, dramatics, enacting, feigning, histrionics, imitating, imitation, impersonation, imposture, melodrama, performance, performing, play-acting, playing, portrayal, portraying, posing, posturing, pretence, pretending, putting on, seeming, shamming, stagecraft, theatre, theatricals.

action *n* accomplishment, achievement, act, activity, affray, agency, battle, case, cause, clash, combat, conflict, contest, deed, effect, effort, encounter, endeavour, energy, engagement, enterprise, exercise, exertion, exploit, feat, fight, fighting, force, fray, functioning, influence, lawsuit, litigation, liveliness, mechanism, motion, move, movement, operation, performance, power, proceeding, process, prosecution, skirmish, sortie, spirit, stop, stroke, suit, undertaking, vigour, vim, vitality, warfare, work, working, works.

actions *n* address, air, bearing, behaviour, comportment, conduct, demeanour, deportment, manners, ways.

activate *v* actuate, animate, arouse, bestir, energise, excite, fire, galvanise, impel, initiate, mobilise, motivate, move, prompt, propel, rouse, set in motion, set off, start, stimulate, stir, switch on, trigger. **antonyms** arrest, deactivate, stop.

active adj acting, activist, aggressive, agile, alert, ambitious, animated, assertive, assiduous, astir, bustling, busy, committed, deedy, devoted, diligent, effectual, energetic, engaged, enterprising, enthusiastic, forceful, forward, functioning, hard-working, in force, in operation, industrious, involved, light-footed, live, lively, militant, moving, nimble, occupied, on the go, on the move, operate, quick, running, sedulous, spirited, sprightly, spry, stirabout, stirring, strenuous, vibrant, vigorous, vital, vivacious, working, zealous. **antonyms** dormant, inert, passive.

activity n act, action, activeness, animation, avocation, bustle, commotion, deed, endeavour, enterprise, exercise, exertion, hobby, hurly-burly, hustle, industry, interest, job, kerfuffle, labour, life, liveliness, motion, movement, occupation, pastime, project, pursuit, scheme, stir, task, undertaking, venture, work.

actor n actress, agent, artist, comedian, doer, executor, functionary, guiser, ham, impersonator, masquerader, mime, mummer, operative, operator, participant, participator, performer, perpetrator, play-actor, player, practitioner, Thespian, tragedian, trouper, worker.

actual adj absolute, authentic, bona fide, categorical, certain, concrete, confirmed, corporeal, current, de facto, definite, existent, extant, factual, genuine, indisputable, indubitable, legitimate, live, living, material, physical, positive, present, present-day, prevailing, real, realistic, substantial, tangible, true, truthful, unquestionable, verified, veritable. **antonyms** apparent, imaginary, theoretical.

actually adv absolutely, as a matter of fact, de facto, essentially, in fact, in reality, in truth, indeed, literally, really, truly, verily, veritably.

acumen n acuteness, astuteness, cleverness, discernment, discrimination, gumption, ingenuity, insight, intelligence, intuition, judgement, judiciousness, keenness, penetration, perception, perceptiveness, perspicacity, perspicuity, quickness, sagacity, sharpness, shrewdness, smartness, wisdom, wit. **antonym** obtuseness.

acute[1] adj astute, canny, clever, critical, crucial, cutting, dangerous, decisive, discerning, discriminating, distressing, essential, excruciating, exquisite, extreme, fierce, grave, important, incisive, ingenious, insightful, intense, intuitive, judicious, keen, lancinating, observant, overpowering, overwhelming, penetrating, perceptive, perspicacious, piercing, poignant, pointed, powerful, sagacious, sapient, sensitive, serious, severe, sharp, shooting, shrewd, shrill, smart, stabbing, subtle, sudden, urgent, violent, vital. **antonyms** chronic, mild, obtuse.

acute[2] adj cuspate, needle-shaped, peaked, pointed, sharp, sharpened. **antonym** obtuse.

adage n aphorism, apophthegm, axiom, byword, dictum, gnome, maxim, motto, precept, proverb, saying, sentence.

adamant adj determined, firm, fixed, flinty, hard, immovable, impenetrable, indestructible, inexorable, inflexible, insistent, intransigent, obdurate, resolute, rigid, rock-like, rocky, set, steely, stiff, stony, stubborn, tough, unbending, unbreakable, uncompromising, unrelenting, unshakable, unyielding. **antonyms** flexible, pliant, yielding.

adapt v acclimatise, accommodate, adjust, alter, apply, change, comply, conform, convert, customise, familiarise, fashion, fit, habituate, harmonise, match, metamorphose, modify, prepare, proportion, qualify, refashion, remodel, shape, suit, tailor.

adaptable adj adjustable, alterable, amenable, changeable, compliant, conformable, convertible, easy-going, flexible, malleable, modifiable, plastic, pliant, resilient, tractable, variable, versatile. **antonyms** inflexible, refractory.

adaptation n acclimatisation, accommodation, adaption, adjustment, alteration, change, conversion, familiarisation, habituation, modification, naturalisation, refashioning, refitting, remodelling, reshaping, reworking, shift, transformation, variation, version.

add v adjoin, affix, amplify, annex, append, attach, augment, combine, compute, count, include, join, reckon, sum up, superimpose, supplement, tack on, tot up, total. **antonym** subtract.

add up add, amount, be consistent, be plausible, be reasonable, come to, compute, count, count up, hang together, hold water, imply, indicate, make sense mean, reckon, reveal, ring true, signify, stand to reason, sum up, tally, tot up, total.

added *adj* additional, adjective, adjunct, extra, fresh, further, increased, new, supplementary.

addict *n* acid-head, adherent, buff, devotee, dope-fiend, enthusiast, fan, fiend, follower, freak, head, hop-head, junkie, mainliner, nut, pillhead, pillpopper, pot-head, tripper, user.

addicted *adj* absorbed, accustomed, dedicated, dependent, devoted, disposed, enslaved, fond, habituated, hooked, inclined, obsessed, prone, spaced out.

addiction *n* craving, dependence, enslavement, habit, obsession.

addition *n* accession, accessory, accretion, addendum, adjoining, adjunct, affix, amplification, annexation, appendage, appendix, appurtenance, attachment, augmentation, computation, counting, enlargement, extension, extra, gain, inclusion, increase, increment, reckoning, summation, summing-up, supplement, totalling, totting-up.

additional *adj* added, affixed, appended, excrescent, extra, fresh, further, increased, more, new, other, spare, supplementary.

address¹ *n* abode, department, direction, domicile, dwelling, home, house, inscription, location, lodging, place, residence, situation, whereabouts.

address² *n* adroitness, air, application, art, bearing, declamation, deftness, dexterity, discourse, discretion, dispatch, dissertation, expedition, expertise, expertness, facility, harangue, ingenuity, lecture, manner, oration, sermon, skilfulness, skill, speech, tact, talk.

v accost, address (oneself) to, apply (oneself) to, approach, attend to, button-hole, concentrate on, devote (oneself) to, discourse, engage in, focus on, greet, hail, harangue, invoke, lecture, orate, salute, sermonise, speak, speak to, take care of, talk, talk to, turn to, undertake.

adept *adj* able, accomplished, ace, adroit, deft, dexterous, experienced, expert, masterful, masterly, nimble, polished, practised, proficient, skilful, skilled, versed. **antonyms** bungling, incompetent, inept.

n ace, dab hand, don, expert, genius, maestro, master, old hand, pastmaster, wizard. **antonyms** bungler, incompetent.

adequate *adj* able, acceptable, capable,

commensurate, competent, efficacious, enough, fair, fit, passable, presentable, requisite, respectable, satisfactory, serviceable, sufficient, suitable, tolerable. **antonyms** inadequate, insufficient.

adhere *v* abide by, agree, attach, cement, cleave, cleave to, cling, coalesce, cohere, combine, comply with, fasten, fix, follow, fulfil, glue, heed, hold, hold fast, join, keep, link, maintain, mind, obey, observe, paste, respect, stand by, stick, stick fast, support, unite.

adherent *n* admirer, advocate, aficionado, devotee, disciple, enthusiast, fan, follower, freak, hanger-on, henchman, nut, partisan, satellite, supporter, upholder, votary.

adhesion *n* allegiance, attachment, bond, cohesion, constancy, devotion, faithfulness, fidelity, fulfilment, grip, heed, holding fast, loyalty, obedience, observation, respect, sticking, support, union.

adhesive *adj* attaching, clinging, cohesive, gluey, glutinous, gummy, holding, mucilaginous, sticking, sticky, tacky, tenacious.

n cement, glue, gum, paste, tape.

adieu *n* bon voyage, cheerio, congé, departure, farewell, goodbye, leave-taking, parting, valediction.

adjacent *adj* abutting, adjoining, alongside, beside, bordering, close, conterminous, contiguous, juxtaposed, near, neighbouring, next, proximate, touching.

adjoin *v* abut, add, affix, annex, append, approximate, attach, border, combine, communicate with, connect, couple, impinge, interconnect, join, juxtapose, link, meet, neighbour, touch, unite, verge.

adjoining *adj* abutting, adjacent, bordering, connecting, contiguous, impinging, interconnecting, joined, juxtaposed, near, neighbouring, next, next door, proximate, touching, verging.

adjourn *v* continue, defer, delay, discontinue, interrupt, postpone, put off, recess, stay, suspend. **antonym** convene.

adjournment *n* break, deferment, deferral, delay, discontinuation, dissolution, interruption, pause, postponement, putting off, recess, stay, suspension.

adjudicate *v* adjudge, arbitrate, decide, determine, judge, pronounce, ref, referee, settle, umpire.

adjunct *n* accessory, addendum,

addition, appendage, appendix, appurtenance, auxiliary, complement, extension, supplement.

adjust v acclimatise, accommodate, accustom, adapt, alter, arrange, balance, change, compose, concert, conform, convert, dispose, fine-tune, fit, fix, harmonise, measure, modify, order, proportion, reconcile, rectify, redress, refashion, regulate, remodel, reshape, set, settle, shape, square, suit, temper, tune.

adjustable adj adaptable, alterable, flexible, malleable, modifiable, mouldable, movable, tractable. **antonym** fixed.

adjustment n acclimatisation, accommodation, adaptation, alteration, arrangement, arranging, conforming, conversion, fitting, fixing, harmonisation, modification, naturalisation, ordering, orientation, reconciliation, redress, refashioning, regulation, remodelling, setting, settlement, settling in, shaping, tuning.

ad-lib v extemporise, improvise, invent, make up.

adj extemporaneous, extempore, extemporised, impromptu, improvised, made up, off-the-cuff, spontaneous, unpremeditated, unprepared, unrehearsed. **antonym** prepared.

adv extemporaneously, extempore, impromptu, impulsively, off the cuff, off the top of one's head, spontaneously.

administer v apply, assign, conduct, contribute, control, direct, disburse, dispense, dispose, distribute, dole out, execute, give, govern, head, impose, lead, manage, measure out, mete out, officiate, organise, oversee, perform, preside over, provide, regulate, rule, run, superintend, supervise, supply.

administration n application, conduct, control, direction, directorship, disbursement, dispensation, disposal, distribution, execution, executive, governing, governing body, government, leadership, management, organisation, overseeing, performance, provision, regime, regulation, rule, ruling, running, settlement, superintendence, supervision, supply, term of office.

administrative adj authoritative, directorial, executive, governmental, legislative, management, managerial, organisational, regulatory, supervisory.

administrator n boss, controller, curator, custodian, director, factor,

governor, guardian, leader, manager, organiser, overseer, ruler, superintendent, supervisor, trustee.

admirable adj choice, commendable, creditable, deserving, estimable, excellent, exquisite, fine, laudable, meritorious, praiseworthy, rare, respected, superior, valuable, wonderful, worthy. **antonym** despicable.

admiration n adoration, affection, amazement, appreciation, approbation, approval, astonishment, awe, delight, esteem, pleasure, praise, regard, respect, reverence, surprise, veneration, wonder, wonderment, worship. **antonym** contempt.

admire v adore, applaud, appreciate, approve, esteem, idolise, laud, praise, prize, respect, revere, value, venerate, worship. **antonym** despise.

admirer n adherent, aficionado, beau, boyfriend, devotee, disciple, enthusiast, fan, follower, gallant, idoliser, lover, partisan, suitor, supporter, sweetheart, votary, wooer, worshipper. **antonym** critic.

admissible adj acceptable, allowable, allowed, equitable, justifiable, lawful, legitimate, passable, permissible, permitted, tolerable, tolerated.

admission n acceptance, access, acknowledgement, admittance, affirmation, allowance, avowal, concession, confession, declaration, disclosure, divulgence, entrance, entry, exposé, granting, inclusion, initiation, introduction, owning, profession, revelation. **antonyms** denial, exclusion.

admit v accept, acknowledge, affirm, agree, allow, allow to enter, avow, concede, confess, declare, disclose, divulge, give access, grant, initiate, introduce, let, let in, permit, profess, receive, recognise, reveal, take in. **antonyms** exclude, gainsay.

admittance n acceptance, access, allowing, entrance, entry, letting in, passage, reception.

admonish v advise, berate, caution, censure, check, chide, counsel, enjoin, exhort, forewarn, rebuke, reprehend, reprimand, reproach, reprove, scold, upbraid, warn.

admonition n advice, berating, caution, censure, counsel, rebuke, reprehension, reprimand, reproach, reproof, scolding, warning.

adolescence n boyhood, boyishness, childishness, development, girlhood, girlishness, immaturity, minority, puberty, puerility, teens, transition, youth, youthfulness. *antonym* senescence.

adolescent *adj* boyish, girlish, growing, immature, juvenile, maturing, puerile, teenage, young, youthful.

n bobbysoxer, halfling, juvenile, minor, teenager, youngster, youth.

adopt *v* accept, affect, appropriate, approve, assume, back, choose, embrace, endorse, espouse, follow, foster, maintain, ratify, sanction, select, support, take in, take on, take up. *antonyms* disown, repudiate.

adoption *n* acceptance, affectation, approbation, appropriation, approval, assumption, choice, embracing, endorsement, espousal, following, fostering, maintenance, ratification, sanction, selection, support.

adorable *adj* appealing, attractive, bewitching, captivating, charming, darling, dear, delightful, enchanting, fetching, lovable, pleasing, precious, winsome.

adoration *n* admiration, esteem, exaltation, glorification, honour, idolatry, idolisation, love, magnification, reverence, veneration, worship. *antonyms* abhorrence, detestation.

adore *v* admire, cherish, dote on, esteem, exalt, glorify, honour, idolise, love, magnify, revere, reverence, venerate, worship. *antonyms* abhor, hate.

adorn *v* array, beautify, bedeck, bejewel, crown, deck, decorate, doll up, embellish, emblazon, enhance, enrich, garnish, gild, grace, impearl, ornament, tart up, trim.

adornment *n* accessory, beautification, decorating, decoration, embellishment, flounce, frill, frippery, garnish, gilding, ornament, ornamentation, ornateness, trappings, trimming.

adrift *adj* aimless, amiss, anchorless, astray, at sea, directionless, goalless, insecure, off course, purposeless, rootless, rudderless, unsettled, wrong. *antonyms* anchored, stable.

adroit *adj* able, adept, apt, artful, clever, cunning, deft, dexterous, expert, ingenious, masterful, neat, nimble, proficient, quick, resourceful, skilful, skilled, slick. *antonyms* clumsy, inept, maladroit.

adulation *n* blandishment, bootlicking, fawning, flattery, idolatory, idolisation, personality cult, sycophancy, worship. *antonym* abuse.

adult *adj* developed, full-grown, fully grown, grown-up, mature, of age, ripe, ripened. *antonym* immature.

adulterate *v* attenuate, bastardise, contaminate, corrupt, dash, debase, defile, depreciate, deteriorate, devalue, dilute, doctor, infect, load, pollute, taint, thin, vitiate, water down, weaken. *antonym* refine.

advance *v* accelerate, adduce, allege, ameliorate, assist, benefit, bring forward, cite, elevate, expedite, facilitate, foster, furnish, further, go ahead, go forward, grow, hasten, improve, increase, lend, move on, multiply, offer, present, press on, proceed, proffer, profit, progress, promote, prosper, provide, raise, send forward, speed, submit, suggest, supply, thrive, upgrade. *antonyms* impede, retard, retreat.

n advancement, amelioration, betterment, breakthrough, credit, deposit, development, down payment, furtherance, gain, growth, headway, improvement, increase, loan, preferment, prepayment, profit, progress, promotion, retainer, rise, step. *antonym* recession.

adj beforehand, early, foremost, forward, in front, leading, preliminary, prior.

advanced *adj* ahead, avant-garde, extreme, foremost, forward, forward-looking, higher, imaginative, late, leading, original, precocious, progressive. *antonyms* backward, retarded.

advancement *n* amelioration, betterment, development, gain, growth, headway, improvement, maturation, onward movement, progress, promotion, rise. *antonyms* demotion, retardation.

advances *n* addresses, approaches, attentions, moves, overtures, proposals, proposition.

advantage *n* account, aid, ascendancy, asset, assistances, avail, benefit, blessing, boon, boot, convenience, dominance, edge, expediency, fruit, gain, good, help, hold, interest, lead, leverage, precedence, pre-eminence, profit, purchase, service, start, superiority, sway, upper hand, use, usefulness, utility, welfare. *antonyms* disadvantage, hindrance.

advantageous *adj* beneficial, convenient, favourable, gainful, helpful, opportune, profitable, propitious, remunerative, rewarding, superior, useful, valuable, worthwhile. *antonym* disadvantageous.

advent *n* accession, appearance, approach, arrival, coming, dawn, entrance, inception, introduction, occurrence, onset, visitation.

adventure *n* chance, contingency, enterprise, experience, exploit, hazard, incident, occurrence, risk, speculation, undertaking, venture.

adventurous *adj* audacious, bold, dangerous, daredevil, daring, doughty, enterprising, foolhardy, game, hazardous, headstrong, impetuous, intrepid, perilous, plucky, rash, reckless, risky, spunky, swashbuckling, temerarious, venturesome. *antonyms* cautious, chary, prudent.

adversary *n* antagonist, assailant, attacker, competitor, contestant, enemy, foe, opponent, rival. *antonyms* ally, supporter.

adverse *adj* antagonistic, conflicting, contrary, counter, counter-productive, detrimental, disadvantageous, hostile, hurtful, inauspicious, inexpedient, inimical, injurious, inopportune, negative, opposing, opposite, reluctant, repugnant, uncongenial, unfavourable, unfortunate, unfriendly, unlucky, unpropitious, untoward, unwilling. *antonyms* advantageous, propitious.

adversity *n* affliction, bad luck, calamity, catastrophe, disaster, distress, hard times, hardship, ill-fortune, ill-luck, mischance, misery, misfortune, mishap, reverse, sorrow, suffering, trial, tribulation, trouble, woe, wretchedness. *antonym* prosperity.

advertise *v* advise, announce, broadcast, declare, display, flaunt, herald, inform, make known, notify, plug, praise, proclaim, promote, promulgate, publicise, publish, push, tout.

advertisement *n* ad, advert, announcement, bill, blurb, circular, commercial, display, handbill, handout, hype, leaflet, notice, placard, plug, poster, promotion, propaganda, propagation, publicity, trumpet-blowing.

advice *n* admonition, caution, communication, counsel, direction, do's and don'ts, guidance, help, information, injunction, instruction, intelligence, memorandum, notice, notification, opinion, recommendation, suggestion, view, warning, wisdom, word.

advisable *adj* advantageous, appropriate, apt, beneficial, correct, desirable,

expedient, fit, fitting, judicious, politic, profitable, proper, prudent, recommended, seemly, sensible, sound, suggested, suitable, wise. *antonyms* inadvisable, injudicious.

advise *v* acquaint, apprise, caution, commend, counsel, enjoin, forewarn, guide, inform, instruct, make known, notify, recommend, report, suggest, teach, tell, tutor, urge, warn.

adviser *n* aide, authority, coach, confidant, consultant, counsel, counsellor, eminence grise, guide, helper, instructor, lawyer, mentor, monitor, preceptor, righthand man, solicitor, teacher, tutor.

advisory *adj* advising, consultative, consulting, counselling, helping, recommending.

advocate *v* adopt, advise, argue for, campaign for, champion, countenance, defend, encourage, endorse, espouse, favour, justify, patronise, plead for, press for, promote, propose, recommend, subscribe to, support, uphold, urge. *antonyms* deprecate, disparage, impugn. *n* apologist, apostle, attorney, backer, barrister, campaigner, champion, counsel, counsellor, defender, lawyer, mediator, patron, pleader, promoter, proposer, solicitor, speaker, spokesman, supporter, upholder, vindicator. *antonyms* critic, opponent.

aegis *n* advocacy, auspices, backing, championship, favour, guardianship, patronage, protection, shelter, sponsorship, support, wing.

affable *adj* agreeable, amiable, amicable, approachable, benevolent, benign, civil, congenial, cordial, courteous, expansive, free, friendly, genial, good-humoured, good-natured, gracious, kindly, mild, obliging, open, pleasant, sociable, suave, urbane, warm. *antonyms* cool, reserved, reticent, unfriendly.

affair *n* activity, adventure, amour, business, circumstance, concern, connection, episode, event, happening, incident, interest, intrigue, liaison, matter, occurrence, operation, organisation, party, proceeding, project, question, reception, relationship, responsibility, romance, subject, topic, transaction, undertaking.

affect¹ *v* act on, agitate, alter, apply to, attack, bear upon, change, concern, disturb, grieve, grip, impinge upon, impress, influence, interest, involve, modify, move, overcome, penetrate, pertain to, perturb, prevail over, regard, relate to, seize, stir, strike, sway, touch, transform, trouble, upset.

affect² *v* adopt, aspire to, assume, contrive, counterfeit, fake, feign, imitate, pretend, profess, put on, sham, simulate.

affectation *n* act, appearance, artificiality, façade, fakery, false display, imitation, insincerity, mannerism, pose, pretence, pretentiousness, sham, show, simulation, staginess, theatricality, unnaturalness. **antonyms** artlessness, ingenuousness.

affected¹ *adj* afflicted, agitated, altered, changed, concerned, damaged, distressed, gripped, hurt, impaired, impressed, influenced, injured, moved, perturbed, smitten, stimulated, stirred, swayed, touched, troubled, upset.

affected² *adj* artificial, assumed, bogus, conceited, contrived, counterfeit, fake, feigned, insincere, lah-di-dah, mannered, mincing, namby-pamby, phoney, pompous, precious, pretended, pretentious, put-on, sham, simulated, spurious, stiff, studied, unnatural. **antonyms** genuine, natural.

affection *n* attachment, care, desire, devotion, favour, feeling, fondness, friendliness, good will, inclination, kindness, liking, love, partiality, passion, penchant, predilection, predisposition, proclivity, propensity, regard, tenderness, warmth. **antonyms** antipathy, dislike.

affectionate *adj* amiable, amorous, attached, caring, cordial, devoted, doting, fond, friendly, kind, loving, passionate, responsive, solicitous, tender, warm, warm-hearted. **antonyms** cold, undemonstrative.

affiliate *v* ally, amalgamate, annex, associate, band together, combine, confederate, conjoin, connect, federate, incorporate, join, merge, syndicate, unite.

affinity *n* alliance, analogy, attraction, closeness, compatibility, connection, correspondence, fondness, inclination, kinship, leaning, likeness, liking, partiality, predisposition, proclivity, propensity, rapport, relation, relationship, resemblance, similarity, similitude, sympathy. **antonym** dissimilarity.

affirm *v* assert, asseverate, attest, aver, avow, certify, confirm, corroborate, declare, endorse, maintain, pronounce, ratify, state, swear, testify, witness.

affirmative *adj* affirmatory, agreeing, approving, assenting, concurring, confirming, consenting, corroborative, emphatic, positive. **antonyms** dissenting, negative.

affix *v* add, adjoin, annex, append, assign, attach, attribute, bind, connect, fasten, glue, join, paste, pin on, stick, tack, tag. **antonym** detach.

afflict *v* beset, burden, distress, grieve, harass, harm, harrow, hurt, oppress, pain, plague, smite, strike, torment, torture, trouble, try, visit, wound, wring. **antonyms** comfort, solace.

affliction *n* adversity, calamity, cross, curse, depression, disaster, disease, distress, grief, hardship, illness, misery, misfortune, ordeal, pain, plague, scourge, sickness, sorrow, suffering, torment, trial, tribulation, trouble, visitation, woe, wretchedness. **antonyms** comfort, consolation, solace.

affluent *adj* comfortable, flourishing, flush, loaded, moneyed, opulent, pecunious, prosperous, rich, wealthy, well-heeled, well-off, well-to-do. **antonyms** impecunious, impoverished, poor.

afford *v* bear, bestow, cope with, engender, furnish, generate, give, grant, impart, manage, offer, produce, provide, render, spare, stand, supply, sustain, yield.

affront *v* abuse, anger, annoy, displease, gall, incense, insult, irritate, nettle, offend, outrage, provoke, slight, snub, vex. **antonyms** appease, compliment. *n* abuse, discourtesy, disrespect, indignity, injury, insult, offence, outrage, provocation, rudeness, slap in the face, slight, slur, snub, vexation, wrong.

afoot *adv* about, abroad, astir, brewing, circulating, current, going about, in preparation, in progress, in the air, in the wind, up.

afraid *adj* alarmed, anxious, apprehensive, cowardly, diffident, distrustful, faint-hearted, fearful, frightened, intimidated, nervous, regretful, reluctant, scared, sorry, suspicious, timid, timorous, tremulous, unhappy. **antonyms** confident, unafraid.

after *adv, prep* afterwards, as a result of, behind, below, following, in consequence of, later, post, subsequent to, subsequently, succeeding, thereafter.

aftermath *n* after-effects, consequences, effects, end, fall-out, outcome, repercussion, results, upshot, wake.

again *adv* afresh, also, anew, another time, besides, bis, conversely, ditto, encore, furthermore, in addition, moreover, on the contrary, on the other hand, once more.

against *prep* abutting, across, adjacent to, close up to, confronting, counter to, facing, fronting, hostile to, in contact with, in contrast to, in defiance of, in exchange for, in opposition to, in the face of, on, opposed to, opposing, opposite to, resisting, touching, versus.

age *n* (a)eon, agedness, date, day, days, decline, decrepitude, dotage, duration, elderliness, epoch, era, generation, lifetime, majority, maturity, old age, period, senescence, senility, seniority, span, time, years. **antonyms** salad days, youth.

v decline, degenerate, deteriorate, grow old, mature, mellow, ripen, season.

aged *adj* advanced, age-old, ancient, antiquated, antique, decrepit, elderly, geriatric, grey, hoary, old, patriarchal, senescent, superannuated, time-worn, venerable, worn-out. **antonyms** young, youthful.

agency *n* action, activity, bureau, business, department, effect, finger, force, handling, influence, intervention, means, mechanism, mediation, medium, office, offices, operation, organisation, power, work, workings.

agenda *n* calendar, diary, list, menu, plan, programme, schedule, timetable.

agent *n* actor, agency, author, cause, channel, delegate, deputy, emissary, envoy, executor, factor, force, functionary, go-between, instrument, intermediary, means, middleman, negotiator, operative, operator, organ, performer, power, rep, representative, substitute, surrogate, vehicle.

aggravate *v* annoy, exacerbate, exaggerate, exasperate, harass, hassle, heighten, incense, increase, inflame, intensify, irk, irritate, magnify, needle, nettle, peeve, pester, provoke, tease, vex, worsen. **antonyms** alleviate, appease, mollify.

aggravation *n* annoyance, bore, drag, exacerbation, exaggeration, exasperation, hassle, heightening, increase, inflammation, intensification, irritant, irritation, magnification, provocation, teasing, thorn in the flesh, vexation, worsening.

aggregate *n* accumulation, agglomeration, aggregation, amount, body, bulk, collection, combination, entirety, generality, heap, herd, lump, mass, mixture, pile, sum, throng, total, totality, whole.

adj accumulated, added, assembled, collected, collective, combined, complete, composite, corporate, mixed, total, united. **antonyms** individual, particular.

v accumulate, add up, agglomerate, amass, amount to, assemble, cluster, collect, combine, conglomerate, heap, mix, pile, total.

aggression *n* aggressiveness, antagonism, assault, attack, bellicosity, belligerence, combativeness, destructiveness, encroachment, hostility, impingement, incursion, injury, intrusion, invasion, jingoism, militancy, offence, offensive, onslaught, provocation, pugnacity, raid.

aggressive *adj* argumentative, assertive, bare-knuckle, bellicose, belligerent, bold, combative, contentious, destructive, disputatious, dynamic, energetic, enterprising, forceful, go-ahead, hostile, intrusive, invasive, jingoistic, militant, offensive, provocative, pugnacious, pushy, quarrelsome, vigorous, zealous. **antonyms** peaceable, submissive.

aggressor *n* assailant, attacker, intruder, invader, offender, provoker. **antonym** victim.

aggrieved *adj* afflicted, affronted, distressed, disturbed, harmed, hurt, ill-used, injured, insulted, offended, pained, peeved, saddened, unhappy, woeful, wronged. **antonym** pleased.

aghast *adj* afraid, amazed, appalled, astonished, astounded, awestruck, confounded, dismayed, frightened, horrified, horror-struck, shocked, startled, stunned, stupefied, terrified, thunder-struck.

agile *adj* active, acute, adroit, alert, brisk, clever, fleet, flexible, limber, lissome, lithe, lively, mobile, nimble, prompt, quick, quick-witted, sharp, sprightly, spry, supple, swift. **antonyms** clumsy, stiff, torpid.

agitate *v* alarm, arouse, beat, churn, confuse, convulse, discompose, disconcert, disquiet, distract, disturb, excite, ferment, flurry, fluster, incite, inflame, perturb, rattle, rock, rouse, ruffle, shake, stimulate, stir, toss, trouble, unnerve, unsettle, upset, work up, worry. **antonyms** calm, tranquillise.

agitated *adj* anxious, distracted, dithery, feverish, flurried, flustered, in a lather, insecure, jumpy, nervous, perturbed, restive, restless, ruffled, twitchy, uneasy, unnerved, unsettled, upset, wrought-up. *antonyms* calm, composed.

agitation *n* agitprop, alarm, anxiety, churning, clamour, commotion, confusion, controversy, convulsion, disquiet, distraction, disturbance, excitement, ferment, flurry, fluster, hassle, incitement, outcry, rocking, shaking, solicitude, stimulation, stir, stirring, tail-spin, taking, tizz(y), tossing, trepidation, trouble, tumult, turbulence, turmoil, uneasiness, unrest, upset, worry. *antonyms* calm, tranquillity.

agitator *n* agent provocateur, demagogue, firebrand, inciter, instigator, mob orator, rabble-rouser, revolutionary, soap-box orator, stirrer, troublemaker, tub-thumper.

agog *adj* avid, breathless, curious, eager, enthralled, excited, expectant, impatient, keen, on tenterhooks. *antonyms* incurious, laid-back.

agonise *v* afflict, anguish, bleed, distress, excruciate, harrow, labour, pain, rack, strain, strive, struggle, suffer, toil, torment, torture, trouble, worry, wrestle, writhe.

agony *n* affliction, anguish, distress, misery, pain, pangs, paroxysm, spasm, suffering, throes, torment, torture, tribulation, woe, wretchedness.

agree *v* accede, accord, acquiesce, admit, allow, answer, assent, coincide, comply, concede, concord, concur, conform, consent, contract, correspond, covenant, engage, fit, fix, get on, grant, homologate, match, permit, promise, see eye to eye, settle, side with, square, suit, tally, yield. *antonyms* conflict, disagree.

agreeable *adj* acceptable, acquiescent, amenable, amicable, appropriate, approving, attractive, befitting, compatible, complying, concurring, conformable, congenial, consenting, consistent, delightful, enjoyable, fitting, gratifying, in accord, likeable, palatable, pleasant, pleasing, pleasurable, proper, responsive, satisfying, suitable, sympathetic, well-disposed, willing. *antonyms* disagreeable, distasteful, incompatible, nasty.

agreement[1] *n* acceptance, accord, accordance, adherence, affinity, analogy, closing, compact, compatibility, complaisance, compliance, concert, concord, concordat, concurrence, conformity, congruity, consistency, correspondence, harmony, modus vivendi, resemblance, similarity, suitableness, sympathy, unanimity, union, unison. *antonym* disagreement.

agreement[2] *n* arrangement, bargain, compact, concordat, contract, covenant, deal, pact, settlement, treaty, understanding.

agriculture *n* cultivation, culture, farming, husbandry, tillage.

ahead *adj, adv* advanced, along, at an advantage, at the head, before, earlier on, forwards, in advance, in front, in the forefront, in the lead, in the vanguard, leading, onwards, superior, to the fore, winning.

aid *v* abet, accommodate, assist, befriend, boost, ease, encourage, expedite, facilitate, favour, help, oblige, promote, rally round, relieve, serve, subsidise, succour, support, sustain. *antonyms* impede, obstruct.
n a leg up, assistance, assistant, benefit, contribution, donation, encouragement, favour, help, helper, patronage, prop, relief, service, sponsorship, subsidy, subvention, succour, support, supporter. *antonyms* impediment, obstruction.

aide *n* adjutant, adviser, advocate, aide de camp, assistant, attaché, confidant, disciple, follower, henchman, right-hand man, supporter.

ail *v* afflict, annoy, be indisposed, bother, decline, distress, droop, fail, irritate, languish, pain, pine, sicken, trouble, upset, weaken, worry. *antonyms* comfort, flourish.

ailing *adj* debilitated, diseased, feeble, frail, ill, indisposed, infirm, invalid, languishing, off-colour, out of sorts, peaky, poorly, sick, sickly, suffering, under the weather, unsound, unwell, weak, weakly. *antonyms* flourishing, healthy.

ailment *n* affliction, complaint, disability, disease, disorder, illness, indisposition, infection, infirmity, malady, sickness, weakness.

aim *v* address, aspire, attempt, beam, design, direct, endeavour, essay, intend, level, mean, plan, point, propose, purpose, resolve, seek, set one's sights on, sight, strive, take aim, target, train, try, want, wish, zero in on.
n ambition, aspiration, course, design, desire, direction, dream, end, goal, hope, intent, intention, mark, motive, object,

objective, plan, purpose, scheme, target, wish.

aimless *adj* chance, desultory, directionless, erratic, feckless, frivolous, goalless, haphazard, irresolute, pointless, purposeless, rambling, random, stray, undirected, unguided, unmotivated, unpredictable, vagrant, wayward. **antonyms** determined, positive, purposeful.

air *n* ambience, appearance, aria, atmosphere, aura, bearing, blast, breath, breeze, character, demeanour, draught, effect, ether, feeling, flavour, heavens, impression, lay, look, manner, melody, mood, motif, oxygen, puff, quality, sky, song, strain, style, theme, tone, tune, waft, whiff, wind.
v aerate, broadcast, circulate, communicate, declare, disclose, display, disseminate, divulge, exhibit, expose, express, freshen, give vent to, make known, make public, parade, proclaim, publicise, publish, reveal, tell, utter, vaunt, ventilate, voice.

airs *n* affectation, arrogance, artificiality, haughtiness, pomposity, posing, pretensions, pretentiousness, staginess, superciliousness, swank.

airy *adj* aerial, blithe, blowy, bodiless, breezy, buoyant, cheerful, cheery, debonair, delicate, disembodied, draughty, ethereal, fanciful, flimsy, fresh, frolicsome, gay, graceful, high-spirited, illusory, imaginary, immaterial, incorporeal, insubstantial, jaunty, light, light-hearted, lively, lofty, merry, nimble, nonchalant, offhand, open, roomy, spacious, spectral, sportive, sprightly, trifling, uncluttered, unreal, vaporous, visionary, weightless, well-ventilated, windy. **antonyms** close, heavy, oppressive, stuffy.

akin *adj* affiliated, alike, allied, analogous, cognate, comparable, connected, consanguineous, corresponding, kindred, like, parallel, related, similar.

alacrity *n* alertness, avidity, briskness, celerity, cheerfulness, dispatch, eagerness, enthusiasm, gaiety, liveliness, promptness, quickness, readiness, speed, sprightliness, swiftness, willingness, zeal.

alarm *v* affright, agitate, daunt, dismay, distress, frighten, give (someone) a turn, panic, put the wind up (someone), scare, startle, terrify, terrorise, unnerve. **antonyms** calm, reassure, soothe.
n alert, anxiety, apprehension, bell, bleeper, consternation, danger signal, dismay, distress, distress signal, fear, fright, horror, nervousness, panic, scare, siren, terror, trepidation, unease, uneasiness, warning. **antonym** composure.

alarming *adj* daunting, dismaying, distressing, disturbing, dreadful, frightening, ominous, scaring, shocking, startling, terrifying, threatening, unnerving. **antonym** reassuring.

albeit *conj* although, even if, even though, notwithstanding that, though.

alcohol *n* bev(v)y, booze, firewater, hard stuff, hooch, John Barleycorn, (jungle) juice, liquor, medicine, moonshine, mountain dew, rotgut, spirits.

alcoholic *adj* brewed, distilled, fermented, hard, intoxicating, strong, vinous.
n bibber, boozer, dipso, dipsomaniac, drunk, drunkard, hard drinker, lush, piss artist, soak, sot, sponge, tippler, wino.

alcove *n* bay, booth, carrel, compartment, corner, cubby-hole, cubicle, niche, nook, recess.

alert *adj* active, agile, attentive, brisk, careful, circumspect, heedful, lively, nimble, observant, on the ball, on the lookout, perceptive, prepared, quick, ready, sharp-eyed, sharp-witted, sprightly, streetwise, vigilant, wary, watchful, wide-awake. **antonyms** listless, slow.
n alarm, signal, siren, warning.
v alarm, forewarn, inform, notify, signal, tip off, warn.

alertness *n* agility, attention, attentiveness, briskness, circumspection, heedfulness, liveliness, nimbleness, perceptiveness, promptitude, readiness, sprightliness, vigilance, wakefulness, wariness, watchfulness.

alias *n* assumed name, false name, nickname, nom de guerre, nom de plume, pen name, pseudonym, soubriquet, stage name.

alibi *n* cover-up, defence, excuse, explanation, justification, plea, pretext, reason, story.

alien *adj* adverse, antagonistic, conflicting, contrary, estranged, exotic, extraneous, foreign, inappropriate, incompatible, incongruous, inimical, opposed, outlandish, remote, repugnant, separated, strange, unfamiliar.
n emigrant, foreigner, immigrant, newcomer, outlander, outsider, stranger. **antonym** native.

alienate *v* antagonise, disaffect, divert, divorce, estrange, separate, set against, turn away, turn off, withdraw.

alight¹ *v* come down, come to rest, descend, disembark, dismount, get down, get off, land, light, perch, settle, touch down. **antonyms** ascend, board, rise.

alight² *adj* ablaze, afire, aflame, aglow, blazing, bright, brilliant, burning, fiery, flaming, flaring, ignited, illuminated, lighted, lit, lit up, on fire, radiant, shining.

align *v* affiliate, agree, ally, arrange in line, associate, co-operate, co-ordinate, even up, join, line up, make parallel, order, range, regulate, side, straighten, sympathise.

alignment *n* adjustment, affiliation, agreement, alliance, arrangement, association, conformity, co-operation, co-ordination, line, order, sympathy, union.

alike *adj* akin, analogous, cognate, comparable, corresponding, duplicate, equal, equivalent, identical, parallel, resembling, similar, the same, uniform. **antonyms** different, unlike.
adv analogously, correspondingly, equally, identically, in common, similarly, uniformly.

alive *adj* active, alert, animate, animated, awake, breathing, brisk, cheerful, eager, energetic, existent, existing, extant, functioning, having life, in existence, in force, life-like, live, lively, living, operative, quick, real, spirited, sprightly, spry, subsisting, vibrant, vigorous, vital, vivacious, zestful.

alive with abounding in, bristling with, bustling with, buzzing with, crawling with, crowded with, infested with, overflowing with, overrun by, swarming with, teeming with, thronged with.

all *adj* complete, each, each and every, entire, every, every bit of, every one of, every single, full, greatest, gross, outright, perfect, the complete, the entire, the sum of, the total of, the totality of, the whole of, total, utter. **antonym** none.
adv altogether, completely, entirely, fully, totally, utterly, wholesale, wholly.
all being well God willing, if I'm spared.
all right *adj* acceptable, adequate, allowable, average, fair, hale, healthy, OK, passable, permissible, right as rain, safe, satisfactory, secure, sound, standard, unharmed, unhurt, unimpaired, uninjured, unobjectionable,

well, whole. **antonyms** unacceptable, injured.
adv acceptably, adequately, appropriately, OK, passably, reasonably, satisfactorily, suitably, unobjectionably, well enough. **antonyms** unacceptably, unsatisfactorily.
all the time always, constantly, continually, continuously, ever, everlastingly, perpetually, unceasingly.
all thumbs butter-fingered, cack-handed, clumsy, ham-fisted, inept, maladroit, unhandy.

allay *v* alleviate, appease, assuage, calm, check, compose, diminish, dull, ease, lessen, lull, mitigate, moderate, mollify, pacify, quell, quiet, reduce, relieve, slake, smooth, soften, soothe, subdue, tranquillise. **antonyms** exacerbate, intensify.

allegation *n* accusation, affirmation, assertion, asseveration, attestation, averment, avowal, charge, claim, declaration, deposition, plea, profession, statement, testimony.

allege *v* advance, affirm, assert, asseverate, attest, aver, avow, charge, claim, contend, declare, depose, hold, insist, maintain, plead, profess, put forward, state.

alleged *adj* affirmed, asserted, averred, claimed, declared, designated, doubtful, dubious, inferred, ostensible, professed, purported, reputed, so-called, stated, supposed, suspect, suspicious.

allegiance *n* adherence, constancy, devotion, duty, faithfulness, fidelity, friendship, homage, loyalty, obedience, obligation, support. **antonyms** disloyalty, enmity.

allegory *n* analogy, comparison, fable, metaphor, parable, symbol, symbolism.

allergic *adj* antipathetic, averse, disinclined, hostile, hypersensitive, loath, opposed, sensitised, sensitive, susceptible.

alleviate *v* abate, allay, assuage, check, cushion, deaden, diminish, dull, ease, lessen, lighten, mitigate, moderate, modify, mollify, palliate, quell, quench, quiet, reduce, relieve, slake, smooth, soften, soothe, subdue, temper. **antonym** aggravate.

alliance *n* affiliation, affinity, agreement, association, bloc, bond, cartel, coalition, combination, compact, concordat, confederacy, confederation, conglomerate, connection, consortium, faction, federation, guild, league, marriage, pact, partnership, syndicate, treaty, union. **antonyms** divorce, enmity, estrangement, hostility.

allied *adj* affiliated, amalgamated, associated, bound, combined, confederate, connected, correlate(d), hand in glove, in cahoots, in league, joined, joint, kindred, linked, married, related, unified, united, wed. **antonym** estranged.

allocate *v* allot, apportion, appropriate, assign, budget, designate, disperse, distribute, earmark, mete, ration, set aside, share out.

allot *v* allocate, apportion, appropriate, assign, budget, designate, dispense, distribute, earmark, grant, mete, render, set aside, share out.

all-out *adj* complete, determined, energetic, exhaustive, full, full-scale, intensive, maximum, no-holds-barred, optimum, powerful, resolute, supreme, thorough, thoroughgoing, total, undivided, unlimited, unremitting, unrestrained, utmost, vigorous, wholesale. **antonyms** half-hearted, perfunctory.

allow *v* accord, acknowledge, acquiesce, admit, allocate, allot, apportion, approve, assign, authorise, bear, brook, concede, confess, deduct, endure, give, give leave, grant, let, own, permit, provide, put up with, remit, sanction, spare, stand, suffer, tolerate. **antonyms** deny, forbid.

allow for arrange for, bear in mind, consider, foresee, include, keep in mind, keep in view, make allowances for, make concessions for, make provision for, plan for, provide for, take into account. **antonym** discount.

allowable *adj* acceptable, admissible, all right, appropriate, approved, apt, legal(ised), legitimate, permissible, sanctionable, sufferable, suitable, supportable, tolerable. **antonym** unacceptable.

allowance *n* admission, allocation, allotment, amount, annuity, concession, deduction, discount, grant, lot, measure, pension, portion, quota, ration, rebate, reduction, remittance, sanction, share, stint, stipend, subsidy, sufferance, tolerance, weighting.

alloy *n* admixture, amalgam, blend, coalescence, combination, composite, compound, fusion, hybrid, mix, mixture. *v* admix, amalgamate, blend, combine, compound, debase, fuse, impair, mix, qualify, temper.

allude *v* adumbrate, advert, cite, glance, hint, imply, infer, insinuate, intimate, mention, refer, remark, speak of, suggest, touch upon.

allure *n* appeal, attraction, captivation, charm, enchantment, enticement, fascination, glamour, lure, magnetism, persuasion, seductiveness, temptation.

alluring *adj* arousing, attractive, beguiling, bewitching, captivating, come-hither, enchanting, engaging, enticing, fascinating, fetching, intriguing, seductive, sensuous, sexy, tempting, voluptuous, winning. **antonym** repellant.

allusion *n* citation, glance, hint, implication, innuendo, insinuation, intimation, mention, observation, quotation, reference, remark, suggestion.

ally *n* accessory, accomplice, associate, collaborator, colleague, confederate, confrere, consort, co-worker, friend, helper, partner, side-kick. **antonyms** antagonist, enemy.

v affiliate, amalgamate, associate, band together, collaborate, combine, confederate, conjoin, connect, fraternise, join, join forces, marry, team up, unify, unite. **antonym** estrange.

almighty *adj* absolute, all-powerful, awful, desperate, enormous, excessive, great, intense, invincible, loud, omnipotent, overpowering, overwhelming, severe, supreme, terrible, unlimited. **antonyms** impotent, insignificant, weak.

almost *adv* about, all but, approaching, approximately, as good as, close to, just about, nearing, nearly, not far from, not quite, practically, towards, virtually, well-nigh.

alone *adj, adv* abandoned, apart, by itself, by oneself, deserted, desolate, detached, forlorn, forsaken, incomparable, isolated, just, lonely, lonesome, matchless, mere, on one's own, on one's tod, only, peerless, separate, simply, single, single-handed, singular, sole, solitary, unaccompanied, unaided, unassisted, unattended, uncombined, unconnected, unequalled, unescorted, unique, unparalleled, unsurpassed.

aloof *adj* chilly, cold, cool, detached, distant, forbidding, formal, haughty, inaccessible, indifferent, remote, reserved, reticent, stand-offish, supercilious, unapproachable, uncompanionable, unforthcoming, unfriendly, uninterested, unresponsive, unsociable, unsympathetic. **antonym** sociable.

already *adv* at present, before now,

beforehand, by now, by that time, by then, by this time, even now, heretofore, hitherto, just now, previously.

also *adv* additionally, along with, and, as well, as well as, besides, ditto, further, furthermore, in addition, including, moreover, plus, to boot, too.

alter *v* adapt, adjust, amend, castrate, change, convert, diversify, emend, metamorphose, modify, qualify, recast, reform, remodel, reshape, revise, shift, take liberties with, transform, transmute, transpose, turn, vary.

alteration *n* adaptation, adjustment, amendment, castration, change, conversion, difference, diversification, emendation, interchanging, metamorphosis, modification, reciprocation, reformation, remodelling, reshaping, revision, rotation, shift, transfiguration, transformation, transmutation, transposition, variance, variation.

altercation *n* argument, bickering, clash, contention, controversy, debate, disagreement, discord, dispute, dissension, fracas, quarrel, row, sparring, squabble, wrangle.

alternate *v* alter, change, fluctuate, follow one another, interchange, intersperse, oscillate, reciprocate, rotate, substitute, take turns, transpose, vary.
adj alternating, alternative, another, different, every other, every second, interchanging, reciprocal, reciprocating, reciprocative, rotating, second, substitute.

alternative *n* back-up, choice, option, other, preference, recourse, selection, substitute.
adj alternate, another, different, fallback, fringe, other, second, substitute, unconventional, unorthodox.

although *conj* admitting that, albeit, conceding that, even if, even supposing, even though, granted that, notwithstanding, though, while.

altogether *adv* absolutely, all in all, all told, as a whole, collectively, completely, entirely, fully, generally, in all, in general, in sum, in toto, on the whole, perfectly, quite, thoroughly, totally, utterly, wholesale, wholly.

altruism *n* generosity, humanity, philanthropy, public spirit, self-abnegation, self-sacrifice, social conscience, unselfishness. **antonym** selfishness.

altruistic *adj* benevolent, charitable, considerate, generous, humane, humanitarian, philanthropic, public-spirited, self-abnegating, self-sacrificing, unselfish.

always *adv* aye, consistently, constantly, continually, endlessly, eternally, ever, everlastingly, evermore, every time, forever, invariably, perpetually, regularly, repeatedly, unceasingly, unfailingly, without exception. **antonym** never.

amalgamate *v* alloy, ally, blend, coalesce, combine, commingle, compound, fuse, homogenise, incorporate, integrate, intermix, merge, mingle, synthesise, unify, unite. **antonym** separate.

amass *v* accumulate, agglomerate, agglutinate, aggregate, assemble, collect, compile, garner, gather, heap up, hoard, pile up, scrape together.

amateur *n* aficionado, buff, dabbler, do-it-yourselfer, fancier, ham, layman, non-professional. **antonym** professional.

amateurish *adj* amateur, clumsy, crude, hammy, incompetent, inept, inexpert, unaccomplished, unprofessional, unskilful, untrained. **antonyms** professional, skilled.

amaze *v* alarm, astonish, astound, bewilder, confound, daze, disconcert, dismay, dumbfound, electrify, flabbergast, floor, shock, stagger, startle, stun, stupefy, surprise.

amazement *n* admiration, astonishment, bewilderment, confusion, dismay, incomprehension, marvel, perplexity, shock, stupefaction, surprise, wonder, wonderment.

ambassador *n* agent, apostle, consul, deputy, diplomat, emissary, envoy, minister, nuncio, plenipotentiary, representative.

ambience *n* air, atmosphere, aura, character, climate, environment, feel, feeling, flavour, impression, milieu, mood, quality, setting, spirit, surroundings, tenor, tone, vibes, vibrations.

ambiguity *n* ambivalence, confusion, doubt, doubtfulness, dubiousness, enigma, equivocality, inconclusiveness, indefiniteness, indeterminateness, obscurity, puzzle, uncertainty, unclearness, vagueness, weasel word(s), woolliness. **antonym** clarity.

ambiguous *adj* ambivalent, confused, confusing, cryptic, double-barrelled, double-meaning, doubtful, dubious, enigmatic, equivocal, inconclusive, indefinite, indeterminate, multivocal, obscure, puzzling, uncertain, unclear, vague, woolly. **antonym** clear.

ambition n aim, aspiration, avidity, craving, design, desire, dream, drive, eagerness, end, enterprise, goal, hankering, hope, hunger, ideal, intent, longing, object, objective, purpose, push, striving, target, wish, yearning, zeal. **antonyms** apathy, diffidence.

ambitious adj arduous, aspiring, assertive, avid, bold, challenging, demanding, difficult, driving, eager, elaborate, energetic, enterprising, enthusiastic, exacting, fervid, formidable, go-ahead, grandiose, hard, hopeful, impressive, industrious, intent, keen, pretentious, purposeful, pushy, severe, strenuous, striving, zealous.

ambivalence n ambiguity, clash, conflict, confusion, contradiction, doubt, equivocation, fluctuation, hesitancy, inconsistency, indecision, instability, irresolution, opposition, uncertainty, vacillation, wavering. **antonym** certainty.

ambivalent adj ambiguous, clashing, conflicting, confused, contradictory, debatable, doubtful, equivocal, fluctuating, hesitant, inconclusive, inconsistent, irresolute, mixed, opposed, uncertain, undecided, unresolved, unsettled, unsure, vacillating, warring, wavering. **antonym** unequivocal.

amble v dawdle, drift, meander, mosey, perambulate, promenade, ramble, saunter, stroll, toddle, walk, wander. **antonyms** march, stride.

ameliorate v advance, alleviate, assuage, benefit, better, ease, elevate, enhance, improve, mend, mitigate, promote, raise, redress, reform, relieve. **antonyms** exacerbate, worsen.

amenable adj accountable, acquiescent, agreeable, answerable, biddable, complaisant, conformable, docile, flexible, liable, open, persuadable, responsive, submissive, susceptible, tractable. **antonym** intractable.

amend v adjust, alter, ameliorate, better, change, correct, emend, enhance, fix, improve, mend, modify, qualify, rectify, redress, reform, remedy, repair, revise. **antonyms** impair, worsen.

amendment n addendum, addition, adjunct, adjustment, alteration, amelioration, betterment, change, clarification, correction, emendation, enhancement, improvement, mending, modification, qualification, rectification,

redress, reform, remedy, repair, revision. **antonyms** deterioration, impairment.

amends n atonement, compensation, expiation, indemnification, indemnity, mitigation, quittance, recompense, redress, reparation, restitution, restoration, satisfaction.

amenity n advantage, attraction, beauty, charm, comfort, convenience, facility, pleasantness, refinement, service. **antonyms** eyesore, inconvenience.

amiable adj accessible, affable, agreeable, approachable, attractive, benign, biddable, charming, cheerful, companionable, complaisant, congenial, conversable, delightful, engaging, friendly, genial, good-humoured, good-natured, good-tempered, kind, kindly, likable, lovable, obliging, pleasant, pleasing, sociable, sweet, winning, winsome. **antonyms** hostile, unfriendly.

amicable adj amiable, brotherly, civil, civilised, cordial, courteous, easy, frank, fraternal, friendly, good-natured, harmonious, kind, kindly, neighbourly, open, peaceable, peaceful, polite, sociable, unreserved. **antonym** hostile.

amiss adj awry, defective, erroneous, fallacious, false, faulty, improper, inaccurate, inappropriate, incorrect, out of order, unsuitable, untoward, wonky, wrong.
adv ill, imperfect, imprecise, out of kilter. **antonyms** right, well.

amnesty n absolution, dispensation, forgiveness, immunity, indulgence, lenience, mercy, oblivion, pardon, remission, reprieve.

amok adv amuck, berserk, crazy, in a frenzy, in a fury, insane, like a madman, mad, wild.

among prep amid, amidst, amongst, between, in the middle of, in the midst of, in the thick of, midst, surrounded by, together with, with.

amoral adj abandoned, free-living, intemperate, lax, loose, uninhibited, unrestrained.

amorous adj affectionate, ardent, attached, doting, enamoured, erotic, fond, impassioned, in love, lovesick, loving, lustful, passionate, randy, tender. **antonyms** cold, indifferent.

amorphous adj chaotic, characterless, featureless, formless, indeterminate, indistinct, irregular, nebulous, nondescript, shapeless, undefined, unformed unshaped, unshapen, unstructured, vague. *antonyms* definite, distinctive.

amount *n* addition, aggregate, bulk, entirety, expanse, extent, lot, magnitude, mass, measure, number, quantity, quota, sum, sum total, supply, total, volume, whole.

amount to add up to, aggregate, approximate to, be equivalent to, be tantamount to, become, come to, equal, grow, mean, purport, run to, total.

ample *adj* abundant, big, bountiful, broad, capacious, commodious, considerable, copious, expansive, extensive, full, generous, goodly, great, handsome, large, lavish, liberal, munificent, plenteous, plentiful, plenty, profuse, rich, roomy, spacious, substantial, sufficient, unrestricted, voluminous, wide. *antonyms* insufficient, meagre.

amplify *v* add to, augment, boost, broaden, bulk out, deepen, develop, dilate, elaborate, enhance, enlarge, expand, expatiate, extend, fill out, heighten, increase, intensify, lengthen, magnify, raise, strengthen, supplement, widen. *antonym* reduce.

amplitude *n* abundance, ampleness, breadth, bulk, capaciousness, capacity, compass, completeness, copiousness, dimension, expanse, extent, fullness, greatness, hugeness, largeness, magnitude, mass, plenitude, plentifulness, plethora, profusion, range, reach, richness, scope, size, spaciousness, sweep, vastness, volume, width.

amputate *v* curtail, cut off, dock, excise, lop, remove, separate, sever, truncate.

amuse *v* absorb, beguile, charm, cheer, cheer up, delight, disport, divert, engross, enliven, entertain, enthral, gladden, interest, occupy, please, recreate, regale, relax, slay, tickle. *antonym* bore.

amusement *n* beguilement, delight, disportment, distraction, diversion, enjoyment, entertainment, fun, game, gladdening, hilarity, hobby, interest, joke, lark, laughter, merriment, mirth, pastime, pleasure, prank, recreation, sport. *antonyms* bore, boredom.

amusing *adj* charming, cheerful, cheering, comical, delightful, diverting, droll, enjoyable, entertaining, facetious, funny, gladdening, hilarious, humorous, interesting, jocular, jolly, killing, laughable, lively, ludicrous, merry, pleasant, pleasing, rib-tickling, sportive, witty. *antonym* boring.

an eye for an eye justice, reciprocation, repayment, reprisal, retaliation, retribution, revenge, tit for tat, vengeance.

anachronism *n* antique, archaism, back number, dinosaur, fogey, fossil.

anaemic *adj* ashen, bloodless, chalky, characterless, colourless, dull, enervated, feeble, frail, ineffectual, infirm, insipid, pale, pallid, pasty, peelie-wally, sallow, sickly, spiritless, wan, weak, whey-faced. *antonyms* full-blooded, ruddy, sanguine.

anaesthetic *n* analgesic, anodyne, narcotic, opiate, pain-killer, palliative, sedative, soporific.

anaesthetise *v* benumb, deaden, desensitise, dope, dull, etherise, lull, mull, numb, stupefy.

analogous *adj* agreeing, akin, alike, comparable, correlative, corresponding, equivalent, like, matching, parallel, reciprocal, related, resembling, similar. *antonym* disparate.

analogy *n* agreement, comparison, correlation, correspondence, equivalence, homologue, likeness, parallel, parallelism, relation, resemblance, semblance, similarity, similitude.

analyse *v* anatomise, assay, break down, consider, dissect, dissolve, divide, estimate, evaluate, examine, interpret, investigate, judge, reduce, resolve, review, scrutinise, separate, sift, study, test.

analysis *n* anatomisation, assay, breakdown, dissection, dissolution, division, enquiry, estimation, evaluation, examination, exegesis, explanation, explication, exposition, interpretation, investigation, judgement, opinion, reasoning, reduction, resolution, review, scrutiny, separation, sifting, study, test.

anarchic *adj* anarchical, chaotic, confused, disordered, disorganised, iconoclastic, lawless, libertarian, nihilist, rebellious, revolutionary, riotous, ungoverned. *antonyms* orderly, submissive.

anarchist *n* iconoclast, insurgent, libertarian, nihilist, rebel, revolutionary, terrorist.

anarchy *n* anarchism, bedlam, chaos, confusion, disorder, disorganisation, iconoclasm, insurrection, lawlessness, libertarianism, misgovernment, misrule, mutiny, nihilism, pandemonium, rebellion, revolution, riot, unrule. *antonyms* control, order, rule.

anathema *n* abhorrence, abomination,

aversion, ban, bane, bête noire, bugbear, condemnation, curse, damnation, denunciation, excommunication, execration, imprecation, malediction, object of loathing, pariah, proscription, taboo.

anatomy *n* analysis, build, composition, constitution, construction, dissection, frame, framework, make-up, structure, vivisection.

ancestor *n* antecedent, forebear, forefather, forerunner, precursor, predecessor. *antonym* descendant.

ancestral *adj* familial, genealogical, genetic, hereditary, lineal, parental.

ancestry *n* ancestors, antecedents, blood, derivation, descent, extraction, family, forebears, forefathers, genealogy, heredity, heritage, house, line, lineage, origin, parentage, pedigree, race, roots, stirps, stock.

anchor *n* grapnel, mainstay, mud-hook, pillar of strength, prop, security, staff, support.
v affix, attach, fasten, fix, make fast, moor.

ancient *adj* aged, age-old, antediluvian, antiquated, antique, archaic, bygone, early, fossilised, hoary, immemorial, obsolete, old, olden, old-fashioned, original, outmoded, out-of-date, prehistoric, primeval, primordial, superannuated, time-worn, venerable, world-old. *antonym* modern.

ancillary *adj* accessory, additional, auxiliary, contributory, extra, secondary, subordinate, subsidiary, supplementary.

androgynous *adj* bisexual, epicene, hermaphrodite.

angel *n* archangel, backer, benefactor, cherub, darling, divine messenger, fairy godmother, guardian spirit, ideal, paragon, saint, seraph, supporter, treasure. *antonyms* devil, fiend.

angelic *adj* adorable, beatific, beautiful, celestial, cherubic, divine, entrancing, ethereal, exemplary, heavenly, holy, innocent, lovely, pious, pure, saintly, seraphic, unworldly, virtuous. *antonyms* devilish, fiendish.

anger *n* annoyance, antagonism, bad blood, bile, bitterness, dander, displeasure, dudgeon, exasperation, fury, gall, indignation, ire, irritability, irritation, outrage, passion, pique, rage, rancour, resentment, spleen, temper, vexation, wrath. *antonym* forbearance.
v affront, aggravate, annoy, antagonise, bother, bug, displease, enrage, exasperate, fret, frustrate, gall, incense,

infuriate, irk, irritate, madden, miff, needle, nettle, offend, outrage, pique, provoke, rile, ruffle, vex. *antonyms* appease, calm, please.

angle *n* approach, aspect, bend, corner, crook, crotch, cusp, direction, edge, elbow, facet, hook, nook, outlook, perspective, point, point of view, position, side, slant, standpoint, turn, viewpoint.

angle for aim for, be after, be out for, contrive, fish for, have one's beady eye on, hunt, invite, scheme, seek, solicit.

angry *adj* aggravated, annoyed, antagonised, bitter, burned up, choked, chuffed, disgruntled, displeased, enraged, exasperated, furious, heated, hot, incensed, indignant, infuriated, irascible, irate, irked, irritable, irritated, mad, miffed, needled, nettled, outraged, passionate, piqued, provoked, raging, rancorous, ratty, red-headed, resentful, riled, shirty, splenetic, tumultuous, uptight, waxy, wrathful. *antonyms* calm, content.

angst *n* agony, anguish, anxiety, apprehension, depression, dread, foreboding, future shock, malaise, mid-life crisis, worry.

anguish *n* agony, angst, anxiety, desolation, distress, dole, dolour, grief, heartache, heartbreak, misery, pain, pang, rack, sorrow, suffering, torment, torture, tribulation, woe, wretchedness. *antonyms* happiness, solace.

anguished *adj* afflicted, agonised, angst-ridden, distressed, dolorous, harrowed, miserable, racked, stricken, suffering, tormented, tortured, wretched.

angular *adj* bony, gauche, gaunt, gawky, lanky, lean, rangy, rawboned, scrawny, skinny, spare, ungainly.

animal *n* barbarian, beast, brute, creature, cur, hound, mammal, monster, pig, savage, swine.
adj bestial, bodily, brutish, carnal, fleshly, gross, inhuman, instinctive, physical, piggish, savage, sensual, wild.

animate *v* activate, arouse, embolden, encourage, energise, enliven, excite, fire, galvanise, goad, impel, incite, inspire, inspirit, instigate, invest, invigorate, irradiate, kindle, move, quicken, reactivate, revive, rouse, spark, spur, stimulate, stir, suffuse, urge, vitalise. *antonyms* dull, inhibit.
adj alive, breathing, conscious, live, living, sentient. *antonyms* dull, spiritless.

animated *adj* active, airy, alive, ardent, brisk, buoyant, eager, ebullient, energetic, enthusiastic, excited, fervent, gay, glowing, impassioned, lively, passionate, quick, radiant, spirited, sprightly, vehement, vibrant, vigorous, vital, vivacious, vivid, zestful. *antonyms* inert, sluggish.

animation *n* action, activity, ardour, briskness, buoyancy, ebullience, elation, energy, enthusiasm, excitement, exhilaration, fervour, gaiety, high spirits, life, liveliness, passion, pep, radiance, sparkle, spirit, sprightliness, verve, vibrancy, vigour, vitality, vivacity, zeal, zest, zing. *antonyms* dullness, inertia.

animosity *n* acrimony, animus, antagonism, antipathy, bad blood, bitterness, enmity, feud, feuding, hate, hatred, hostility, ill-will, loathing, malevolence, malice, malignity, odium, rancour, resentment, spite. *antonym* goodwill.

annex *v* acquire, add, adjoin, affix, append, appropriate, attach, connect, conquer, expropriate, fasten, incorporate, join, occupy, purloin, seize, tack, take over, unite, usurp.
n addendum, addition, adjunct, appendix, attachment, supplement.

annexation *n* amalgamation, annexing, appropriation, augmentation, combination, conquest, expropriation, occupation, seizure, takeover, usurpation.

annihilate *v* abolish, assassinate, destroy, eliminate, eradicate, erase, exterminate, extinguish, extirpate, liquidate, murder, nullify, obliterate, raze, rub out, thrash, trounce, wipe out.

annotate *v* comment, commentate, elucidate, explain, gloss, interpret, marginalise, note.

annotation *n* comment, commentary, elucidation, exegesis, explanation, explication, footnote, gloss, interpretation, marginalia, note.

announce *v* advertise broadcast, declare, disclose, divulge, intimate, leak, make known, notify, proclaim, promulgate, propound, publicise, publish, report, reveal, state. *antonym* suppress.

announcement *n* advertisement, broadcast, bulletin, communiqué, declaration, disclosure, dispatch, divulgence, intimation, notification, proclamation, promulgation, publication, report, revelation, statement.

announcer *n* anchor man, broadcaster, commentator, compère, crier, harbinger, herald, messenger, newscaster, newsreader, reporter.

annoy *v* aggravate, anger, badger, bore, bother, bug, contrary, displease, disturb, exasperate, fash, gall, get, harass, harm, harry, hump, incommode, irk, irritate, madden, miff, molest, needle, nettle, peeve, pester, pique, plague, provoke, rile, ruffle, tease, trouble, vex. *antonyms* gratify, please.

annoyance *n* aggravation, anger, bind, bore, bother, displeasure, disturbance, exasperation, fash, harassment, headache, irritant, irritation, nuisance, pain, pest, pique, plague, provocation, tease, trouble, vexation. *antonym* pleasure.

annoyed *adj* bored, bugged, chagrined, displeased, exasperated, galled, harassed, irked, irritated, miffed, narked, peeved, piqued, provoked, shirty, vexed. *antonym* pleased.

annoying *adj* aggravating, boring, bothersome, displeasing, disturbing, exasperating, galling, harassing, irksome, irritating, maddening, offensive, peeving, pesky, plaguesome, provoking, teasing, troublesome, vexatious. *antonyms* pleasing, welcome.

annul *v* abolish, abrogate, cancel, cashier, countermand, invalidate, negate, nullify, quash, recall, repeal, rescind, retract, reverse, revoke, suspend, void. *antonyms* enact, restore.

annulment *n* abolition, abrogation, cancellation, cassation, countermanding, disannulment, invalidation, negation, nullification, quashing, recall, repeal, rescindment, rescission, retraction, reversal, revocation, suspension, voiding. *antonyms* enactment, restoration.

anodyne *adj* analgesic, bland, blunting, calmative, deadening, desensitising, dulling, inoffensive, narcotic, numbing, pain-killing, pain-relieving, palliative, sedative. *antonym* irritant.
n analgesic, narcotic, pain-killer, pain-reliever, palliative, sedative. *antonym* irritant.

anoint *v* bless, consecrate, daub, dedicate, embrocate, grease, hallow, lard, lubricate, oil, rub, sanctify, smear.

anomalous *adj* aberrant, abnormal, atypical, bizarre, deviant, eccentric, exceptional, freakish, incongruous, inconsistent, irregular, odd, peculiar, quirky, rare, singular, untypical, unusual.

anomaly *n* aberration, abnormality, departure, deviant, deviation, divergence, eccentricity, exception, freak, incongruity, inconsistency, irregularity, misfit, oddity, peculiarity, rarity.

anonymous *adj* characterless, faceless, impersonal, incognito, nameless, nondescript, unacknowledged, unattested, unauthenticated, uncredited, unexceptional, unidentified, unknown, unnamed, unsigned, unspecified. *antonyms* distinctive, identifiable, named.

answer *n* acknowledgement, apology, comeback, countercharge, defence, explanation, outcome, plea, reaction, rebuttal, reciprocation, refutation, rejoinder, reply, report, resolution, response, retaliation, retort, return, riposte, solution, vindication.
v acknowledge, agree, balance, conform, correlate, correspond, do, echo, explain, fill, fit, fulfil, match up to, meet, pass, qualify, react, reciprocate, refute, rejoin, reply, resolve, respond, retaliate, retort, return, satisfy, serve, solve, succeed, suffice, suit, work.

answer back argue, cheek, contradict, disagree, dispute, rebut, retaliate, retort, riposte, talk back. *antonym* acquiesce.

answerable¹ *adj* accountable, amenable, blameable, blameworthy, chargeable, liable, responsible, to blame.

answerable² *adj* defensible, deniable, disprovable, explicable, rebuttable, refutable, repudiable.

antagonise *v* alienate, anger, annoy, disaffect, embitter, estrange, incense, insult, irritate, offend, provoke, repel. *antonym* disarm.

antagonism *n* animosity, animus, antipathy, competition, conflict, contention, discord, dissension, friction, hostility, ill-feeling, ill-will, opposition, rivalry. *antonyms* rapport, sympathy.

antagonistic *adj* adverse, antipathetic, at variance, averse, bellicose, belligerent, conflicting, contentious, hostile, ill-disposed, incompatible, inimical, opposed, pugnacious, unfriendly. *antonyms* friendly, sympathetic.

antecedents *n* ancestors, ancestry, background, blood, descent, dossier, extraction, family, forebears, forefathers, genealogy, history, line, lineage, past, pedigree, record, stock.

anterior *adj* antecedent, earlier, foregoing, former, introductory, preceding, previous, prior. *antonym* subsequent.

anthology *n* choice, collection, compendium, compilation, digest, garland, miscellany, selection, treasury.

anticipate *v* antedate, apprehend, await, bank on, beat to it, count upon, expect, forecast, foredate, foresee, forestall, foretaste, foretell, forethink, hope for, intercept, look for, look forward to, predict, pre-empt, prevent.

anticipation *n* apprehension, awaiting, expectancy, expectation, foresight, foretaste, forethought, forewarning, hope, preconception, premonition, prescience, presentiment.

anticlimax *n* bathos, comedown, damp squib, disappointment, disenchantment, fiasco, let-down.

antics *n* buffoonery, capers, clowning, doings, escapades, foolery, foolishness, frolics, larks, mischief, monkey tricks, playfulness, pranks, silliness, skylarking, stunts, tomfoolery, tricks.

antidote *n* antitoxin, corrective, counter-agent, countermeasure, cure, detoxicant, neutraliser, preventive, remedy.

antipathetic *adj* abhorrent, allergic, antagonistic, averse, disgusting, distasteful, hateful, horrible, hostile, incompatible, inimical, invidious, loathsome, obnoxious, odious, offensive, repellent, repugnant, repulsive, revolting. *antonyms* agreeable, harmonious, sympathetic.

antipathy *n* abhorrence, allergy, animosity, animus, antagonism, aversion, bad blood, contrariety, disgust, dislike, distaste, enmity, hate, hatred, hostility, ill-will, incompatibility, loathing, odium, opposition, rancour, repugnance, repulsion, resentment. *antonyms* rapport, sympathy.

antiquary *n* antiquarian, archaeologist, archaist, bibliophile, collector.

antiquated *adj* anachronistic, ancient, antediluvian, antique, archaic, dated, elderly, fogeyish, fossilised, obsolete, old, old hat, old-fashioned, old-fogeyish, outdated, outmoded, out-of-date, outworn, passé, quaint, superannuated, unfashionable. *antonyms* forward-looking, modern.

antique *adj* aged, ancient, antiquarian, archaic, elderly, obsolete, old, old-fashioned, outdated, quaint, superannuated, vintage.
n antiquity, bygone, curio, curiosity,

heirloom, knick-knack, museum-piece, object of virtu, period piece, rarity, relic.

antiquity n age, agedness, ancient times, antique, distant past, elderliness, old age, olden days, time immemorial, venerableness. **antonyms** modernity, novelty.

antiseptic adj bactericidal, clean, disinfectant, germ-free, germicidal, hygienic, medicated, pure, sanitary, sanitised, sterile, uncontaminated, unpolluted.
n bactericide, cleanser, decontaminant, disinfectant, germicide, purifier.

antisocial adj alienated, anarchic, antagonistic, belligerent, disorderly, disruptive, hostile, menacing, misanthropic, rebellious, reserved, retiring, unacceptable, unapproachable, uncommunicative, unfriendly, unsociable, withdrawn. **antonyms** acceptable, sociable.

antithesis n contradiction, contrariety, contrary, contrast, converse, inverse, inversion, opposite, opposite extreme, opposition, polarity, reversal, reverse.

anxiety n angst, anxiousness, apprehension, care, concern, craving, disquiet, disquietude, distress, dread, eagerness, foreboding, fretfulness, impatience, keenness, misgiving, nervousness, presentiment, restlessness, solicitude, suspense, tension, torment, torture, unease, uneasiness, watchfulness, willingness, worriment, worry. **antonym** composure.

anxious adj afraid, angst-ridden, apprehensive, avid, careful, concerned, disquieted, distressed, disturbed, eager, expectant, fearful, fretful, impatient, in suspense, intent, itching, keen, nervous, on tenterhooks, overwrought, restless, solicitous, taut, tense, tormented, tortured, troubled, uneasy, unquiet, watchful, worried, yearning. **antonym** composed.

apart adv afar, alone, aloof, aside, asunder, away, by oneself, cut off, distant, distinct, divorced, excluded, in bits, in pieces, independent, independently, individually, into parts, isolated, on one's own, piecemeal, privately, separate, separated, separately, singly, to bits, to one side, to pieces.

apathetic adj cold, cool, dispassionate, emotionless, impassive, indifferent, listless, numb, passive, phlegmatic, sluggish, stoic, torpid, unambitious, unconcerned, unemotional, unfeeling,

uninterested, uninvolved, unmotivated, unmoved, unresponsive. **antonyms** concerned, responsive.

apathy n coldness, coolness, impassivity, incuriousness, indifference, inertia, insensibility, lethargy, listlessness, passiveness, passivity, phlegm, sluggishness, torpor, unconcern, unfeelingness, uninterestedness, unresponsiveness. **antonyms** concern, warmth.

ape v affect, caricature, copy, counterfeit, echo, imitate, mimic, mirror, mock, parody, parrot, take off.
n baboon, boor, brute, chimpanzee, gibbon, gorilla, monkey, oaf, orang-utan, savage.

aperture n breach, chink, cleft, crack, eye, eyelet, fissure, gap, hole, interstice, opening, orifice, passage, perforation, rent, rift, slit, slot, space, vent.

apex n acme, apogee, climax, consummation, crest, crown, crowning point, culmination, height, high point, peak, pinnacle, point, summit, tip, top, vertex, zenith. **antonym** nadir.

aphorism n adage, apothegm, axiom, dictum, epigram, gnome, maxim, precept, proverb, saying.

aplomb n assurance, audacity, balance, calmness, composure, confidence, coolness, equanimity, poise, sang-froid, savoir faire, self-assurance, self-confidence, self-possession. **antonym** discomposure.

apocalyptic adj ominous, portentous, prophetic, revelatory, signal, threatening.

apocryphal adj concocted, doubtful, dubious, equivocal, fabricated, fictitious, imaginary, legendary, mythical, phony, questionable, spurious, unauthenticated, unsubstantiated, unsupported, unverified. **antonym** true.

apogee n acme, apex, climax, consummation, crest, crown, culmination, height, high point, peak, pinnacle, summit, tip, top, vertex, zenith. **antonyms** nadir, perigee.

apologetic adj conscience-stricken, contrite, penitent, regretful, remorseful, repentant, rueful, sorry. **antonym** defiant.

apologist n advocate, champion, defender, endorser, justifier, pleader, seconder, spokesman, supporter, upholder, vindicator. **antonym** critic.

apology n acknowledgement, apologia, confession, defence, excuse, explanation, extenuation, justification, palliation, plea, semblance, substitute, travesty, vindication. **antonym** defiance.

apostle n advocate, champion, crusader, evangelist, exponent, herald, messenger, missionary, pioneer, preacher, promoter, propagandist, propagator, proponent.

apotheosis n deification, elevation, exaltation, glorification, idealisation, idolisation, immortalisation.

appal v alarm, astound, daunt, disconcert, disgust, dishearten, dismay, frighten, harrow, horrify, intimidate, outrage, petrify, scare, shock, terrify, unnerve. **antonyms** encourage, reassure.

appalling adj alarming, astounding, awful, daunting, dire, disheartening, dismaying, dreadful, fearful, frightening, frightful, ghastly, grim, harrowing, hideous, horrible, horrid, horrific, horrifying, intimidating, loathsome, petrifying, scaring, shocking, startling, terrible, terrifying, unnerving, wretched.

apparatus n appliance, bureaucracy, contraption, device, equipment, framework, gadget, gear, gismo, hierarchy, implements, machine, machinery, materials, means, mechanism, network, organisation, outfit, set-up, structure, system, tackle, tools, utensils.

apparel n accoutrements, array, attire, clothes, clothing, costume, dress, equipment, garb, garments, gear, guise, habit, outfit, rig-out, robes, suit, trappings, vestiture, vestments, wardrobe.

apparent adj clear, conspicuous, declared, discernible, distinct, evident, indubitable, manifest, marked, noticeable, obvious, on paper, open, ostensible, outward, overt, patent, perceptible, plain, seeming, specious, superficial, unmistakable, visible. **antonyms** obscure, real.

apparently adv clearly, manifestly, obviously, ostensibly, outwardly, patently, plainly, seemingly, speciously, superficially.

apparition n chimera, ghost, manifestation, materialisation, phantasm, phantom, presence, shade, spectre, spirit, spook, vision, visitation.

appeal[1] n adjuration, application, entreaty, invocation, petition, plea, prayer, request, solicitation, suit, supplication.

v address, adjure, apply, ask, beg, beseech, call, call upon, entreat, implore, invoke, petition, plead, pray, refer, request, resort to, solicit, sue, supplicate.

appeal[2] n allure, attraction, attractiveness, beauty, charisma, charm, enchantment, fascination, interest, magnetism, winsomeness.

v allure, attract, charm, draw, engage, entice, fascinate, interest, invite, lure, please, tempt.

appear v act, arise, arrive, attend, be published, bob up, come into sight, come into view, come out, come to light, crop up, develop, emerge, enter, issue, leak out, look, loom, materialise, occur, perform, play, rise, seem, show, show up, surface, take part, transpire, turn out, turn up. **antonym** disappear.

appearance n advent, air, appearing, arrival, aspect, bearing, brow, cast, character, coming, début, demeanour, emergence, expression, façade, face, favour, figure, form, front, guise, illusion, image, impression, introduction, look, looks, manner, mien, physiognomy, presence, pretence, seeming, semblance, show, the cut of one's jib. **antonyms** disappearance, reality.

appease v allay, assuage, blunt, calm, compose, conciliate, diminish, ease, give a sop to, humour, lessen, lull, mitigate, mollify, pacify, placate, propitiate, quell, quench, quiet, reconcile, satisfy, soften, soothe, subdue, tranquillise. **antonym** aggravate.

appeasement n acceding, accommodation, assuagement, compromise, concession, conciliation, humouring, lessening, mitigation, mollification, pacification, placation, propitiation, quelling, quieting, satisfaction, softening, sop. **antonyms** aggravation, resistance.

append v add, adjoin, affix, annex, attach, conjoin, fasten, join, tack on.

appendage n accessory, addendum, addition, adjunct, affix, ancillary, annexe, appendix, appurtenance, attachment, auxiliary, excrescence, extremity, limb, member, projection, prosthesis, protuberance, supplement, tab, tag.

appendix n addendum, addition, adjunct, appendage, codicil, epilogue, postscript, rider, supplement.

appertaining adj applicable, applying, belonging, characteristic, connected, germane, pertinent, related, relevant.

appetiser n antipasto, apéritif, canapé,

cocktail, foretaste, hors d'oeuvre, preview, sample, taste, taster, titbit.

appetising *adj* appealing, delicious, inviting, lip-smacking, mouthwatering, palatable, piquant, savoury, scrumptious, succulent, tasty, tempting, yummy. *antonym* disgusting.

appetite *n* craving, demand, desire, eagerness, hankering, hunger, inclination, keenness, liking, longing, passion, predilection, proclivity, propensity, relish, stomach, taste, willingness, yearning, zeal, zest. *antonym* distaste.

applaud *v* acclaim, approve, cheer, clap, commend, compliment, congratulate, encourage, eulogise, extol, laud, praise. *antonyms* censure, disparage.

applause *n* acclaim, acclamation, accolade, approbation, approval, cheering, cheers, commendation, congratulation, encomium, eulogies, eulogising, hand, laudation, ovation, plaudits, praise. *antonyms* censure, disparagement.

appliance *n* apparatus, contraption, contrivance, device, gadget, gismo, implement, instrument, machine, mechanism, tool.

applicable *adj* apposite, appropriate, apropos, apt, befitting, fit, fitting, germane, legitimate, pertinent, proper, related, relevant, suitable, suited, useful, valid. *antonym* inapplicable.

application[1] *n* appeal, apposition, assiduity, attention, attentiveness, claim, commitment, dedication, diligence, effort, exercise, function, germaneness, industry, inquiry, keenness, lesson, moral, perseverance, pertinence, petition, practice, purpose, reference, relevance, request, requisition, sedulity, solicitation, use, value.

application[2] *n* balm, cream, dressing, emollient, lotion, medication, ointment, poultice, preparation, salve, unguent.

apply[1] *v* administer, assign, bring into play, bring to bear, direct, employ, engage, execute, exercise, implement, ply, practise, resort to, set, use, utilise, wield.

apply[2] *v* be relevant, fit, have force, pertain, refer, relate, suit.

apply[3] *v* anoint, cover with, lay on, paint, place, put on, rub, smear, spread on, use.

apply[4] *v* appeal, ask for, claim, inquire, petition, put in, request, requisition, solicit, sue.

apply[5] *v* address, bend, buckle down, commit, concentrate, dedicate, devote, direct, give, persevere, settle down, study, throw.

appoint *v* allot, arrange, assign, charge, choose, command, commission, co-opt, decide, decree, delegate, designate, destine, detail, determine, devote, direct, elect, engage, enjoin, equip, establish, fit out, fix, furnish, install, name, nominate, ordain, outfit, provide, select, set, settle, supply. *antonyms* dismiss, reject.

appointed *adj* allotted, arranged, assigned, chosen, commanded, commissioned, co-opted, decided, decreed, delegated, designated, determined, directed, elected, enjoined, equipped, established, fitted out, fixed, furnished, installed, invested, named, nominated, ordained, preordained, provided, selected, set, settled, supplied.

appointment *n* allotment, arrangement, assignation, assignment, choice, choosing, commissioning, consultation, date, delegation, election, engagement, installation, interview, job, meeting, naming, nomination, office, place, position, post, rendezvous, selection, session, situation, station, tryst.

apportion *v* accord, admeasure, allocate, allot, assign, award, deal, dispense, distribute, divide, dole out, grant, measure out, mete, morsel, portion out, ration, share.

apposite *adj* applicable, appropriate, apropos, apt, befitting, condign, germane, in point, pertinent, proper, relevant, suitable, suited, to the point, to the purpose. *antonym* inapposite.

appraisal *n* appreciation, assay, assaying, assessment, estimate, estimation, evaluation, examination, inspection, judgement, once-over, opinion, pricing, rating, reckoning, review, sizing-up, survey, valuation.

appraise *v* assay, assess, estimate, evaluate, examine, gauge, inspect, judge, price, rate, review, size up, survey, valuate, value.

appreciable *adj* apparent, ascertainable, clear-cut, considerable, definite, detectable, discernible, distinguishable, evident, marked, material, measurable, noticeable, obvious, perceivable, perceptible, pronounced, recognisable, significant, substantial, undeniable, visible. *antonyms* imperceptible, negligible.

appreciate[1] *v* acknowledge, admire, be sensitive to, cherish, comprehend, dig, do justice to, enjoy, esteem, estimate, know, like, perceive, prize, realise, recognise, regard, relish, respect, savour, sympathise with, take kindly to, treasure, understand, value. **antonyms** despise, overlook.

appreciate[2] *v* enhance, gain, grow, improve, increase, inflate, mount, rise, strengthen. **antonym** depreciate.

appreciation *n* acknowledgement, admiration, appraisal, assessment, awareness, cognisance, comprehension, criticism, critique, enjoyment, esteem, estimation, gratefulness, gratitude, indebtedness, judgement, knowledge, liking, notice, obligation, perception, praise, realisation, recognition, regard, relish, respect, responsiveness, review, sensitivity, sympathy, thankfulness, thanks, tribute, understanding, valuation. **antonyms** ingratitude, neglect.

appreciative *adj* admiring, aware, beholden, cognisant, conscious, encouraging, enthusiastic, grateful, indebted, knowledgeable, mindful, obliged, perceptive, pleased, regardful, respectful, responsive, sensible, sensitive, supportive, sympathetic, thankful, understanding. **antonym** ungrateful.

apprehend[1] *v* arrest, bust, capture, catch, collar, detain, get, grab, nab, nick, pinch, run in, seize, take.

apprehend[2] *v* appreciate, believe, comprehend, conceive, consider, discern, grasp, imagine, know, perceive, realise, recognise, see, twig, understand.

apprehension[1] *n* arrest, capture, catching, seizure, taking.

apprehension[2] *n* alarm, anxiety, apprehensiveness, awareness, belief, comprehension, concept, conception, concern, conjecture, discernment, disquiet, doubt, dread, fear, foreboding, grasp, idea, impression, intellect, intelligence, ken, knowledge, misgiving, mistrust, nervousness, notion, opinion, perception, premonition, presentiment, qualm, sentiment, suspicion, thought, understanding, unease, uneasiness, uptake, view, worry.

apprehensive *adj* afraid, alarmed, anxious, concerned, disquieted, distrustful, disturbed, doubtful, fearful, mistrustful, nervous, solicitous, suspicious, uneasy, worried. **antonym** confident.

approach *v* advance, appeal to, apply to, approximate, be like, begin, broach, catch up, come close, come near to, commence, compare with, draw near, embark on, gain on, introduce, make advances, make overtures, meet, mention, near, reach, resemble, set about, sound out, undertake.

n access, advance, advent, appeal, application, approximation, arrival, attitude, avenue, course, doorway, entrance, gesture, invitation, landfall, likeness, manner, means, method, mode, modus operandi, motion, nearing, offer, overture, passage, procedure, proposal, proposition, resemblance, road, semblance, style, system, technique, threshold, way.

approachable *adj* accessible, affable, agreeable, attainable, congenial, cordial, easy, friendly, informal, open, reachable, sociable.

approbation *n* acceptance, acclaim, applause, approval, assent, commendation, congratulation, encouragement, endorsement, esteem, favour, kudos, laudation, praise, ratification, recognition, regard, sanction, support. **antonym** disapprobation.

appropriate *adj* applicable, apposite, apropos, apt, becoming, befitting, belonging, correct, felicitous, fit, fitting, germane, meet, merited, opportune, pertinent, proper, relevant, right, seasonable, seemly, spot-on, suitable, timely, to the point, well-chosen, well-suited, well-timed. **antonym** inappropriate.

v allocate, allot, annex, apportion, assign, assume, commandeer, confiscate, devote, earmark, embezzle, expropriate, filch, impound, misappropriate, pilfer, pocket, possess oneself of, pre-empt, purloin, seize, set apart, steal, take, usurp.

appropriation *n* allocation, allotment, annexation, assignment, assumption, commandeering, confiscation, dispensation, earmarking, expropriation, impoundment, misappropriation, pre-emption, seizure, setting apart, usurpation.

approval *n* acclaim, acclamation, acquiescence, admiration, adoption, agreement, applause, appreciation, approbation, assent, authorisation, blessing, certification, commendation, compliance, concurrence, confirmation, consent, countenance, endorsement, esteem, favour, go-ahead, good opinion, green light, honour, leave, licence, liking, mandate, OK, permission, plaudits praise, ratification, recommendation, regard, respect, sanction, support, thumbs-up, validation. **antonym** disapproval.

approve v accede to, accept, acclaim, admire, adopt, advocate, agree to, allow, applaud, appreciate, assent to, authorise, back, bless, commend, comply with, concur in, confirm, consent to, countenance, endorse, esteem, favour, like, mandate, OK, pass, permit, praise, ratify, recommend, regard, respect, rubber-stamp, sanction, second, support, take kindly to, uphold, validate. **antonym** disapprove.

approved adj acceptable, accepted, authorised, correct, favoured, official, permissible, permitted, preferred, proper, recognised, recommended, sanctioned. **antonym** unorthodox.

approximate adj ballpark, close, comparable, conjectural, estimated, extrapolated, guessed, inexact, like, loose, near, relative, rough, similar, verging on. **antonym** exact. v approach, be tantamount to, border on, resemble, verge on.

approximately adv about, almost, around, circa, close to, coming up to, in round numbers, in the region of, in the vicinity of, just about, loosely, more or less, nearly, not far off, pushing, relatively, roughly, round about, well-nigh. **antonym** exactly.

approximation n approach, conjecture, estimate, estimation, extrapolation, guess, guesstimate, guesswork, likeness, proximity, resemblance, rough calculation, rough idea, semblance. **antonyms** exactitude, precision.

apropos adj applicable, apposite, appropriate, apt, befitting, belonging, correct, fit, fitting, germane, meet, opportune, pertinent, proper, related, relevant, right, seemly, suitable, timely, to the point. **antonym** inappropriate. adv appositely, appropriately, aptly, by the bye, by the way, in passing, incidentally, opportunely, pat, pertinently, properly, relevantly, suitably, to the point. **antonym** inappropriately.

apropos of in connection with, in relation to, in respect of, on the subject of, re, regarding, respecting, with reference to, with regard to, with respect to.

apt adj accurate, adept, applicable, apposite, appropriate, apropos, astute, befitting, bright, clever, correct,

disposed, expert, fair, fit, fitting, germane, gifted, given, inclined, ingenious, intelligent, liable, likely, meet, pertinent, prompt, prone, proper, quick, ready, relevant, seasonable, seemly, sharp, skilful, smart, spot-on, suitable, talented, teachable, tending, timely. **antonym** inapt.

aptitude n ability, aptness, bent, capability, capacity, cleverness, disposition, facility, faculty, flair, gift, inclination, intelligence, knack, leaning, penchant, predilection, proclivity, proficiency, propensity, quickness, talent, tendency. **antonym** inaptitude.

arbiter n adjudicator, arbitrator, authority, controller, dictator, expert, intermediary, judge, master, mediator, negotiator, pundit, referee, ruler, umpire.

arbitrariness n absoluteness, capriciousness, despotism, dogmatism, fancifulness, high-handedness, imperiousness, inconsistency, irrationality, irresponsibility, peremptoriness, randomness, subjectivity, summariness, tyranny, unreasonableness, waywardness, whimsicality, wilfulness.

arbitrary adj absolute, autocratic, capricious, chance, despotic, dictatorial, discretionary, dogmatic, domineering, erratic, fanciful, high-handed, imperious, inconsistent, instinctive, magisterial, optional, overbearing, peremptory, personal, random, subjective, summary, tyrannical, unreasonable, unreasoned, unsupported, whimsical, wilful. **antonyms** circumspect, rational, reasoned.

arbitrate v adjudge, adjudicate, decide, determine, judge, pass judgement, referee, settle, umpire.

arbitration n adjudication, decision, determination, intervention, judgement, mediation, negotiation, settlement.

arbitrator n adjudicator, arbiter, intermediary, judge, mediator, moderator, negotiator, referee, umpire.

arcane adj abstruse, cabbalistic, cryptic, enigmatic, esoteric, hidden, mysterious, mystical, obscure, occult, profound, recondite, secret. **antonym** commonplace.

arch[1] n arc, archway, bend, bow, concave, cupola, curvature, curve, dome, semicircle, span, vault. v arc, bend, bow, camber, curve, embow, extend, vault.

arch[2] adj accomplished, chief, consummate, coy, egregious, expert, finished, first, first-class, foremost, greatest, highest, knowing, leading, main, major, master, mischievous, pert, playful, pre-eminent, primary, principal, provocative, roguish, saucy, sly, top, waggish, wily.

archaic *adj* ancient, antediluvian, antiquated, antique, bygone, obsolete, old, old hat, old-fashioned, outdated, outmoded, out-of-date, passé, primitive, quaint, superannuated. *antonym* modern.

archetype *n* classic, conception, exemplar, form, idea, ideal, model, original, paradigm, pattern, precursor, prototype, standard, type.

architect *n* artist, author, constructor, contriver, creator, designer, deviser, engineer, fabricator, fashioner, founder, instigator, inventor, maker, master builder, originator, planner, prime mover, shaper.

archives *n* annals, chronicles, deeds, documents, ledgers, memorabilia, memorials, papers, records, registers, roll.

ardent *adj* amorous, avid, devoted, eager, enthusiastic, fervent, fervid, fierce, fiery, hot, hot-blooded, impassioned, intense, keen, lusty, passionate, spirited, vehement, warm, zealous. *antonym* dispassionate.

ardour *n* animation, avidity, devotion, eagerness, earnestness, enthusiasm, feeling, fervour, fire, heat, intensity, keenness, lust, passion, spirit, vehemence, warmth, zeal, zest. *antonyms* coolness, indifference.

arduous *adj* backbreaking, burdensome, daunting, difficult, exhausting, fatiguing, formidable, gruelling, hard, harsh, herculean, laborious, onerous, punishing, rigorous, severe, strenuous, taxing, tiring, toilsome, tough, troublesome, trying, uphill, wearisome. *antonym* easy.

area *n* arena, bailiwick, ball-park, breadth, canvas, compass, department, district, domain, environs, expanse, extent, field, locality, neighbourhood, part, patch, portion, province, range, realm, region, scope, section, sector, size, sphere, stretch, terrain, territory, tract, width, zone.

arena *n* amphitheatre, area, battlefield, battleground, bowl, coliseum, field, ground, park, ring, scene, stadium, stage.

argue *v* altercate, assert, bicker, chop logic, claim, contend, convince, debate, demonstrate, denote, disagree, discuss, display, dispute, evidence, evince, exhibit, expostulate, fall out, fence, feud, fight, haggle, hold, imply, indicate, join issue, maintain, manifest, moot, persuade, plead, prevail upon, prove, quarrel, question, reason, remonstrate, show, squabble, suggest, talk into, wrangle.

argument *n* abstract, altercation, argumentation, assertion, barney, beef, bickering, case, claim, clash, contention, controversy, debate, defence, demonstration, dialectic, difference, disagreement, discussion, dispute, exposition, expostulation, feud, fight, gist, ground, logic, outline, plea, pleading, plot, polemic, quarrel, questioning, reason, reasoning, remonstrance, remonstration, row, set-to, shouting-match, squabble, story, story line, subject, summary, synopsis, theme, thesis, wrangle.

argumentative *adj* belligerent, captious, combative, contentious, contrary, disputatious, dissentious, litigious, opinionated, perverse, polemical, quarrelsome, wranglesome. *antonym* complaisant.

arid *adj* baked, barren, boring, colourless, desert, desiccated, dreary, dry, dull, empty, flat, infertile, lifeless, moistureless, monotonous, parched, spiritless, sterile, tedious, uninspired, uninteresting, unproductive, vapid, waste, waterless. *antonyms* fertile, lively.

arise *v* appear, ascend, begin, climb, come to light, commence, crop up, derive, emanate, emerge, ensue, flow, follow, get up, go up, grow, happen, issue, lift, mount, occur, originate, proceed, result, rise, set in, soar, spring, stand up, start, stem, tower, wake up.

aristocracy *n* élite, gentility, gentry, nobility, noblemen, noblesse, patricians, peerage, quality, ruling class, top drawer, upper class, upper crust. *antonym* the plebs.

aristocrat *n* grand seigneur, grande dame, grandee, lady, lord, lordling, nob, noble, nobleman, noblewoman, patrician, peer, peeress, swell, toff. *antonym* commoner.

aristocratic *adj* blue-blooded, courtly, dignified, elegant, élite, fine, gentle, gentlemanly, haughty, highborn, lordly, noble, patricianly, polished, refined, supercilious, thoroughbred, titled, upper class, upper-crust, well-born, well-bred. *antonyms* plebeian, vulgar.

arm¹ *n* appendage, authority, bough, branch, channel, department, detachment, division, estuary, extension, firth, inlet, limb, offshoot, projection, section, sector, sound, strait, sway, tributary, upper limb.

arm² *v* array, brace, equip, forearm, fortify, furnish, gird, issue with, munition, nuclearise, outfit, prepare, prime, protect, provide, reinforce, rig, steel, strengthen, supply.

armaments *n* ammunition, arms, artillery, cannon, guns, matériel, munitions, ordnance, weaponry, weapons.

armed *adj* armoured, arrayed, braced, briefed, equipped, fitted out, forearmed, fortified, furnished, girded, guarded, prepared, primed, protected, provided, steeled, strengthened, thorny. *antonym* unprepared.

army *n* armed force, array, cohorts, gang, horde, host, land forces, legions, military, militia, mob, multitude, pack, soldiers, soldiery, swarm, throng, troops.

aroma *n* bouquet, fragrance, odour, perfume, redolence, savour, scent, smell.

aromatic *adj* balmy, fragrant, perfumed, pungent, redolent, savoury, spicy, sweet-smelling. *antonym* acrid.

around *prep* about, approximately, circa, circling, encircling, enclosing, encompassing, environing, more or less, on all sides of, on every side of, roughly, surrounding.
adv about, abroad, all over, at hand, close, close by, everywhere, here and there, in all directions, in the air, near, nearby, nigh, on all sides, to and fro.

arouse *v* agitate, animate, awaken, bestir, call forth, disentrance, enliven, evoke, excite, foment, foster, galvanise, goad, incite, inflame, instigate, kindle, move, prompt, provoke, quicken, rouse, sharpen, spark, spur, startle, stimulate, stir up, summon up, wake up, waken, warm, whet, whip up. *antonyms* calm, lull, quieten.

arraign *v* accuse, attack, call to account, charge, denounce, impeach, impugn, incriminate, indict, prosecute.

arrange¹ *v* adjust, align, array, categorise, class, classify, collocate, concert, construct, contrive, co-ordinate, design, determine, devise, dispose, distribute, file, fix, form, format, group, lay out, marshal, order, organise, plan,

position, prepare, project, range, rank, regulate, schedule, set out, settle, sift, sort, sort out, stage-manage, style, swing, systematise, tidy, trim.

arrange² *v* adapt, harmonise, instrument, orchestrate, score, set.

arrangement¹ *n* adjustment, agreement, alignment, array, battery, classification, compact, compromise, construction, deal, design, display, disposition, form, grouping, layout, line-up, marshalling, method, modus vivendi, order, ordering, organisation, plan, planning, preconcert, preparation, provision, ranging, rank, schedule, scheme, settlement, set-up, spacing, structure, system, tabulation, taxis, terms.

arrangement² *n* adaptation, harmonisation, instrumentation, interpretation, orchestration, score, setting, version.

arrant *adj* absolute, atrocious, barefaced, blatant, brazen, complete, downright, egregious, extreme, flagrant, gross, incorrigible, infamous, monstrous, notorious, out-and-out, outright, rank, thorough, thoroughgoing, undisguised, unmitigated, unregenerate, utter, vile.

array *n* apparel, arrangement, assemblage, attire, battery, clothes, collection, display, disposition, dress, exhibition, exposition, finery, formation, garb, garments, line-up, marshalling, muster, order, parade, regalia, robes, show, supply.
v adorn, align, apparel, arrange, assemble, attire, bedeck, clothe, deck, decorate, display, dispose, draw up, dress, equip, exhibit, form up, garb, group, habilitate, line up, marshal, muster, order, outfit, parade, range, rig out, robe, show, supply, trick out, wrap.

arrest *v* absorb, apprehend, block, bust, capture, catch, check, collar, delay, detain, divert, end, engage, engross, fascinate, grip, halt, hinder, hold, impede, inhibit, interrupt, intrigue, lay, nab, nick, nip, obstruct, occupy, pinch, prevent, restrain, retard, run in, seize, slow, stall, stanch, stay, stem, stop, suppress.
n apprehension, blockage, bust, caption, capture, cessation, check, cop, delay, detention, end, halt, hindrance, inhibition, interruption, obstruction, prevention, restraint, seizure, stalling, stay, stoppage, suppression, suspension.

arresting *adj* amazing, conspicuous, engaging, extraordinary, impressive, notable, noteworthy, noticeable, outstanding, remarkable, striking, stunning, surprising. *antonyms* inconspicuous, unremarkable.

arrival *n* accession, advent, appearance, approach, caller, comer, coming, débutant(e), entrance, entrant, happening, incomer, landfall, newcomer, occurrence, visitant, visitor. *antonym* departure.

arrive *v* alight, appear, attain, befall, come, enter, fetch, get to the top, happen, land, make it, materialise, occur, reach, show, show up, succeed, turn up. *antonym* depart.

arrogance *n* airs, conceit, conceitedness, condescension, contempt, contemptuousness, disdain, disdainfulness, haughtiness, hauteur, high-handedness, hubris, imperiousness, insolence, loftiness, lordliness, presumption, presumptuousness, pretension, pretentiousness, pride, scorn, scornfulness, superciliousness, superiority, uppishness. *antonym* humility.

arrogant *adj* conceited, condescending, contemptuous, contumelious, disdainful, haughty, high and mighty, highhanded, hubristic, imperious, insolent, lordly, on the high ropes, overbearing, overweening, presumptuous, proud, scornful, supercilious, superior, uppish. *antonym* humble.

art *n* address, adroitness, aptitude, artfulness, artifice, artistry, artwork, astuteness, contrivance, craft, craftiness, craftsmanship, cunning, deceit, dexterity, draughtsmanship, drawing, expertise, facility, finesse, guile, ingenuity, knack, knowledge, mastery, method, métier, painting, profession, sculpture, skill, slyness, subtlety, trade, trick, trickery, virtu, virtuosity, visuals, wiliness.

artful *adj* adept, adroit, canny, clever, crafty, cunning, deceitful, designing, devious, dexterous, fly, foxy, ingenious, masterly, politic, resourceful, scheming, sharp, shrewd, skilful, sly, smart, subtle, tricksy, tricky, wily. *antonyms* artless, ingenuous, naïve.

article *n* account, bit, commodity, composition, constituent, detail, discourse, division, element, essay, feature, head, heading, item, matter, object, paper, paragraph, part, particular, piece, point, portion, report, review, section, story, thing, unit.

articulate¹ *adj* clear, coherent,

comprehensible, distinct, eloquent, expressive, facile, fluent, intelligible, lucid, meaningful, understandable, vocal, well-spoken.
v breathe, enunciate, express, pronounce, say, speak, state, talk, utter, verbalise, vocalise, voice.

articulate² *v* attach, connect, couple, fasten, fit together, hinge, interlock, join, joint, link.

articulation¹ *n* delivery, diction, enunciation, expression, pronunciation, saying, speaking, talking, utterance, verbalisation, vocalisation, voicing.

articulation² *n* conjunction, connection, coupling, hinge, interlinking, interlock, joint, jointing, juncture, link.

artifice *n* adroitness, artfulness, chicanery, cleverness, contrivance, craft, craftiness, cunning, deception, deftness, device, dodge, duplicity, expedient, facility, finesse, fraud, guile, hoax, invention, machination, manipulation, manoeuvre, ruse, scheme, shift, skill, slyness, stratagem, strategy, subterfuge, subtlety, tactic, trick, trickery, wile.

artificer *n* architect, artisan, builder, constructer, contriver, craftsman, creator, designer, deviser, fabricator, fashioner, inventor, maker, mechanic, originator.

artificial *adj* affected, assumed, bogus, contrived, counterfeit, ersatz, factitious, fake, false, feigned, forced, hyped up, imitation, insincere, made-up, man-made, mannered, manufactured, meretricious, mock, non-natural, phoney, plastic, pretended, pseudo, sham, simulated, specious, spurious, stagey, synthetic, unnatural. *antonyms* genuine, natural.

artistic *adj* aesthetic, beautiful, bohemian, creative, cultivated, cultured, decorative, elegant, exquisite, graceful, harmonious, imaginative, ornamental, refined, sensitive, skilled, stylish, talented, tasteful. *antonym* inelegant.

artistry *n* accomplishment, art, brilliance, craft, craftsmanship, creativity, deftness, expertise, finesse, flair, genius, mastery, proficiency, sensibility, sensitivity, skill, style, talent, taste, touch, virtuosity, workmanship. *antonym* ineptitude.

artless *adj* candid, childlike, direct, frank, genuine, guileless, honest, humble, ingenuous, innocent, naïf, naïve, naked, natural, open, plain, primitive, pure, simple, sincere, straightforward, true, trustful, trusting, unadorned, unaffected, uncontrived, undesigning, unpretentious, unsophisticated, unwary, unworldly. **antonym** artful.

as *conj, prep* because, being, considering that, for example, for instance, in that, in the character of, in the manner of, in the part of, in the role of, inasmuch as, like, seeing that, since, such as, that, to wit, what, when, which, while.

as a rule characteristically, customarily, generally, habitually, mainly, normally, ordinarily, regularly, typically, usually.

as for as regards, in connection with, in reference to, on the subject of, with reference to, with regard to, with relation to, with respect to.

as it were as it might be, in a manner of speaking, in a way, in some way, so to say, so to speak.

as long as assuming, on condition that, provided, supposing, with the provision that.

ascend *v* climb, float up, fly up, go up, lift off, mount, move up, rise, scale, slope upwards, soar, take off, tower. **antonym** descend.

ascendancy *n* authority, command, control, dominance, domination, dominion, edge, influence, leadership, lordship, mastery, power, predominance, pre-eminence, prestige, prevalence, reign, rule, sovereignty, superiority, supremacy, sway, upper hand. **antonyms** decline, subordination.

ascent *n* advancement, ascending, clamber, clambering, climb, climbing, elevation, escalation, gradient, hill, incline, mounting, ramp, rise, rising, scaling, slope. **antonym** descent.

ascertain *v* confirm, detect, determine, discover, establish, find out, fix, identify, learn, locate, make certain, settle, verify.

ascetic *n* abstainer, anchorite, celibate, flagellant, hermit, monk, nun, puritan, recluse, solitary, spartan. **antonym** voluptuary.
adj abstemious, abstinent, austere, celibate, frugal, harsh, plain, puritanical, rigorous, self-controlled, self-denying, self-disciplined, severe, spartan, stern, strict, temperate. **antonym** voluptuous.

asceticism *n* abstemiousness, abstinence, austerity, celibacy, frugality, harshness, moderation, monasticism, plainness, puritanism, rigorousness, rigour, self-abnegation, self-control, self-denial, self-discipline, temperance. **antonym** voluptuousness.

ascribe *v* accredit, assign, attribute, chalk up to, charge, credit, impute, put down.

ashamed *adj* abashed, apologetic, bashful, blushing, confused, conscience-stricken, discomfited, discomposed, distressed, embarrassed, guilty, hesitant, humbled, humiliated, modest, mortified, prudish, red in the face, redfaced, reluctant, remorseful, self-conscious, shamefaced, sheepish, shy, sorry, unwilling. **antonyms** defiant, shameless.

ashen *adj* anaemic, ashy, blanched, bleached, colourless, ghastly, grey, leaden, livid, pale, pallid, pasty, wan, white. **antonym** ruddy.

aside *adv* alone, apart, away, in isolation, in reserve, on one side, out of the way, privately, secretly, separately.
n departure, digression, excursion, excursus, interpolation, interposition, parenthesis, soliloquy, whisper.

asinine *adj* absurd, brainless, cretinous, daft, doltish, dunderheaded, fatuous, foolish, goofy, gormless, half-witted, idiotic, imbecile, imbecilic, inane, moronic, obstinate, potty, senseless, silly, stupid, witless. **antonyms** intelligent, sensible.

ask *v* appeal, apply, beg, beseech, bid, claim, clamour, crave, demand, enquire, entreat, implore, importune, indent, interrogate, invite, order, petition, plead, pray, press, query, question, quiz, request, require, seek, solicit, sue, summon, supplicate.

askance *adv* contemptuously, disapprovingly, disdainfully, distrustfully, doubtfully, dubiously, indirectly, mistrustfully, obliquely, sceptically, scornfully, sideways, suspiciously.

askew *adv, adj* aslant, asymmetric, awry, cock-eyed, crooked, crookedly, lopsided, oblique, off-centre, out of line, skew, skew-whiff, squint.

asleep *adj* comatose, dead to the world, dormant, dozing, fast asleep, inactive, inert, napping, reposing, sleeping, slumbering, snoozing, sound asleep, unconscious.

aspect *n* air, angle, appearance, attitude, bearing, condition, countenance, demeanour, direction, elevation, exposure, expression, face, facet, feature, look, manner, mien, outlook, physiognomy, point of view, position, prospect, scene, side, situation, standpoint, view, visage.

asperity *n* acerbity, acidity,

acrimony, astringency, bitterness, churlishness, harshness, irascibility, irritability, peevishness, roughness, severity, sharpness, sourness. *antonym* mildness.

aspersion *n* abuse, calumny, censure, criticism, defamation, denigration, derogation, detraction, disparagement, mud-slinging, obloquy, reproach, slander, slur, smear, traducement, vilification, vituperation. *antonyms* commendation, compliment.

aspiration *n* aim, ambition, craving, desire, dream, eagerness, endeavour, goal, hankering, hope, ideal, intent, longing, object, objective, purpose, wish, yearning.

aspire *v* aim, crave, desire, dream, hanker, hope, intend, long, purpose, pursue, seek, wish, yearn.

aspiring *adj* ambitious, aspirant, eager, endeavouring, enterprising, hopeful, keen, longing, optimistic, striving, wishful, would-be.

ass *n* blockhead, bonehead, cretin, dolt, dope, dunce, fool, half-wit, idiot, moron, nincompoop, ninny, nitwit, numskull, schmuck, simpleton, twerp, twit.

assail *v* abuse, assault, attack, belabour, berate, beset, bombard, charge, criticise, encounter, fall upon, impugn, invade, lay into, malign, maltreat, pelt, revile, set about, set upon, strike, vilify.

assailant *n* abuser, adversary, aggressor, assaulter, attacker, invader, opponent, reviler.

assassin *n* cut-throat, eliminator, executioner, hatchet man, hit-man, homicide, killer, liquidator, murderer, ninja, slayer, thug.

assassinate *v* dispatch, eliminate, hit, kill, liquidate, murder, rub out, slay.

assault *n* aggression, attack, blitz, charge, incursion, invasion, offensive, onset, onslaught, raid, storm, storming, strike.
v assail, attack, beset, charge, fall on, hit, invade, lay violent hands on, set upon, storm, strike.

assay *v* analyse, appraise, assess, estimate, evaluate, examine, inspect, investigate, prove, test, try, weigh.
n analysis, assaying, attempt, endeavour, essay, examination, inspection, investigation, test, trial, try, valuation, venture.

assemble *v* accumulate, amass, build, collect, compose, congregate, construct, convene, convocate, convoke, erect,

fabricate, flock, gather, group, join up, levy, make, manufacture, marshal, meet, mobilise, muster, muster (up), piece, rally, round up, set up, summon together. *antonym* disperse.

assembly *n* assemblage, body, building, collection, company, conclave, conference, congregation, congress, consistory, construction, convocation, council, crowd, diet, erection, fabrication, fitting, flock, gathering, group, joining, levy, manufacture, mass, meeting, multitude, rally, reception, setting up, soirée, synod, throng.

assent *v* accede, accept, acquiesce, agree, allow, approve, comply, concede, concur, consent, grant, permit, sanction, submit, subscribe, yield. *antonym* disagree.
n acceptance, accession, accord, acquiescence, agreement, approval, capitulation, compliance, concession, concurrence, consent, permission, sanction, submission.

assert *v* advance, affirm, allege, asseverate, attest, aver, avouch, avow, claim, constate, contend, declare, defend, dogmatise, insist, lay down, maintain, predicate, press, profess, promote, pronounce, protest, state, stress, swear, testify to, thrust forward, uphold, vindicate. *antonym* deny.

assertion *n* affirmation, allegation, attestation, averment, avowal, claim, contention, declaration, dictum, predication, profession, pronouncement, statement, vindication, word. *antonym* denial.

assertive *adj* aggressive, assuming, bold, bumptious, confident, decided, dogmatic, domineering, emphatic, firm, forceful, forward, insistent, opinionated, overbearing, presumptuous, pushy, self-assured, strong-willed. *antonym* diffident.

assess *v* appraise, compute, consider, demand, determine, estimate, evaluate, fix, gauge, impose, investigate, judge, levy, rate, review, size up, tax, value, weigh.

assessment *n* appraisal, calculation, consideration, determination, estimate, estimation, evaluation, gauging, judgement, opinion, rating, review, taxation, valuation.

asset *n* advantage, aid, benefit, blessing, help, plus, resource, service, strength, virtue. *antonym* liability.

assets *n* capital, estate, funds, goods,

holdings, means, money, possessions, property, reserves, resources, securities, wealth, wherewithal.

assiduous *adj* attentive, conscientious, constant, dedicated, devoted, diligent, hard-working, indefatigable, industrious, persevering, persistent, sedulous, steady, studious, unflagging, untiring. *antonym* negligent.

assign *v* accredit, adjudge, allocate, allot, apart, appoint, apportion, arrogate, ascribe, attribute, choose, consign, delegate, designate, determine, dispense, distribute, fix, give, grant, name, nominate, put down, select, set, specify, stipulate.

assignation *n* allocation, allotment, appointment, arrangement, date, engagement, meeting, rendezvous, tryst.

assignment *n* allocation, allotment, appointment, apportionment, ascription, attribution, charge, commission, consignment, delegation, designation, determination, dispensation, distribution, duty, errand, giving, grant, imposition, job, mission, nomination, position, post, responsibility, selection, specification, task.

assimilate *v* absorb, accept, acclimatise, accommodate, accustom, adapt, adjust, blend, conform, digest, fit, homogenise, imbibe, incorporate, ingest, intermix, learn, merge, mingle, take in, tolerate. *antonym* reject.

assist *v* abet, accommodate, aid, back, benefit, boost, collaborate, co-operate, enable, expedite, facilitate, further, help, rally round, reinforce, relieve, second, serve, succour, support, sustain. *antonym* thwart.

assistance *n* a leg up, accommodation, aid, backing, benefit, boost, collaboration, comfort, co-operation, furtherance, help, reinforcement, relief, succour, support, sustainment. *antonym* hindrance.

assistant *n* accessory, accomplice, adjutant, aide, ally, ancillary, associate, auxiliary, backer, collaborator, colleague, confederate, co-operator, Girl Friday, helper, henchman, Man Friday, partner, Person Friday, right-hand man, second, subordinate, subsidiary, supporter.

associate *v* accompany, affiliate, ally, amalgamate, combine, company, confederate, conjoin, connect, consort, correlate, couple, fraternise, hang around, hobnob, identify, join, league,

link, mingle, mix, pair, relate, socialise, unite.

n affiliate, ally, assistant, bedfellow, collaborator, colleague, companion, comrade, confederate, confrère, co-worker, fellow, follower, friend, mate, partner, peer, side-kick.

association *n* affiliation, alliance, analogy, band, blend, bloc, bond, cartel, clique, club, coalition, combination, combine, companionship, company, compound, comradeship, concomitance, confederacy, confederation, connection, consortium, conspiracy, co-operative, corporation, correlation, familiarity, federation, fellowship, fraternisation, fraternity, friendship, group, intimacy, joining, juxtaposition, league, linkage, mixture, organisation, pairing, partnership, relation, relations, relationship, resemblance, society, syndicate, syndication, tie, trust, union.

assorted *adj* different, differing, divergent, divers, diverse, diversified, heterogeneous, manifold, miscellaneous, mixed, motley, multifarious, multiform, several, sundry, varied, variegated, various.

assortment *n* arrangement, array, assemblage, categorisation, choice, classification, collection, disposition, distribution, diversity, farrago, grading, grouping, hotchpotch, jumble, medley, mélange, miscellany, mishmash, mixture, olio, pot-pourri, ranging, salad, selection, sift, sifting, sorting, variety.

assuage *v* allay, alleviate, appease, calm, dull, ease, lessen, lighten, lower, lull, mitigate, moderate, mollify, pacify, palliate, quench, quieten, reduce, relieve, satisfy, slake, soften, soothe, still, temper, tranquillise. *antonym* exacerbate.

assume *v* accept, acquire, adopt, affect, appropriate, arrogate, believe, commandeer, counterfeit, deduce, don, embrace, expect, expropriate, fancy, feign, guess, imagine, infer, opine, postulate, pre-empt, premise, presume, presuppose, pretend to, put on, seize, sham, shoulder, simulate, strike, suppose, surmise, suspect, take, take for granted, take on, take over, take up, think, understand, undertake, usurp.

assumed *adj* accepted, adopted, affected, bogus, conjectural, counterfeit, expected, fake, false, feigned, fictitious, hypothetical, made-up, phoney, presumed, presupposed, pretended, pseudonymous, seized, sham, simulated, specious, spurious, supposed, suppositional, surmised, usurped.

assumption n acceptance, acquisition, adoption, appropriation, arrogance, arrogation, audacity, belief, bumptiousness, conceit, conjecture, expectation, expropriation, fancy, guess, guesswork, hypothesis, impudence, inference, postulate, postulation, pre-emption, premise, premiss, presumption, presumptuousness, presupposition, pride, seizure, self-importance, supposition, surmise, suspicion, theory, understanding, undertaking, usurpation.

assurance n affirmation, aplomb, assertion, asseveration, assuredness, audacity, boldness, certainty, certitude, chutzpah, confidence, conviction, coolness, courage, declaration, firmness, gall, guarantee, nerve, oath, pledge, plerophory, poise, positiveness, profession, promise, protestation, security, self-confidence, self-reliance, sureness, vow, word. **antonym** uncertainty.

assure v affirm, attest, boost, certify, clinch, comfort, confirm, convince, embolden, encourage, ensure, guarantee, hearten, persuade, pledge, promise, reassure, seal, secure, soothe, strengthen, swear, tell, vow, warrant.

assured adj assertive, audacious, belt-and-braces, bold, certain, clinched, cocksure, confident, confirmed, definite, ensured, fixed, guaranteed, indisputable, indubitable, irrefutable, overconfident, pert, poised, positive, secure, self-assured, self-confident, self-possessed, settled, sure, unquestionable. **antonym** uncertain.

astonish v amaze, astound, baffle, bewilder, confound, daze, dumbfound, electrify, flabbergast, floor, nonplus, shock, stagger, startle, stun, stupefy, surprise, wow.

astonished adj amazed, astounded, baffled, bewildered, confounded, dazed, dumbfounded, flabbergasted, incredulous, staggered, startled, stunned, surprised, thunder-struck.

astonishing adj amazing, astounding, baffling, bewildering, breathtaking, dazzling, impressive, incredible, prodigious, staggering, startling, striking, stunning, stupefying, surprising.

astonishment n amazement, awe, bafflement, bewilderment, confusion, consternation, dismay, shock, stupefaction, surprise, wonder, wonderment.

astound v abash, amaze, astonish, baffle, bewilder, confound, daze, dumbfound, flabbergast, overwhelm, shake, shock, stagger, stun, stupefy, surprise, wow.

astounded adj abashed, amazed, baffled, bewildered, confounded, dazed, dumbfounded, flabbergasted, incredulous, overwhelmed, shaken, shocked, staggered, stunned, stupefied, wowed.

astounding adj amazing, astonishing, baffling, bewildering, breathtaking, impressive, incredible, overwhelming, shocking, staggering, striking, stunning, stupefying, surprising.

astringent adj acerbic, acid, austere, biting, caustic, contractive, exacting, grim, hard, harsh, puckery, restringent, rigorous, scathing, severe, stern, strict, stringent, styptic, trenchant. **antonym** bland.

astute adj acute, adroit, artful, calculating, canny, clever, crafty, cunning, discerning, fly, foxy, intelligent, keen, knowing, penetrating, perceptive, perspicacious, politic, prudent, sagacious, sharp, shrewd, sly, subtle, wily, wise. **antonym** stupid.

astuteness n acumen, acuteness, adroitness, artfulness, canniness, cleverness, craftiness, cunning, discernment, insight, intelligence, penetration, perceptiveness, perspicacity, sagacity, sharpness, shrewdness, slyness, subtlety, wiliness. **antonym** stupidity.

asylum n bedlam, cover, funny farm, harbour, haven, hospital, institution, loony-bin, madhouse, mental hospital, nuthouse, preserve, refuge, reserve, retreat, safety, sanctuary, shelter.

asymmetrical adj awry, crooked, disproportionate, irregular, unbalanced, unequal, uneven, unsymmetrical.

asymmetry n disproportion, imbalance, inequality, irregularity, misproportion, unevenness.

at a loss baffled, bewildered, confounded, confused, helpless, nonplussed, perplexed, puzzled, resourceless, stuck, stumped.

at bay caught, cornered, trapped, up against it, with one's back to the wall.

at fault accountable, answerable, blamable, blameworthy, culpable, guilty, responsible.

at first sight on first acquaintance, on the surface, prima facie, superficially, to the outsider.

at hand approaching, at one's elbow

available, close, handy, immediate, imminent, impending, near, nearby, on tap, ready.

at home at ease, comfortable, contented, conversant, experienced, familiar, knowledgeable, proficient, relaxed, skilled, well-versed.

at large at liberty, footloose, free, independent, liberated, on the loose, on the run, roaming, unconfined, unconstrained.

at last at length, at long last, eventually, finally, in conclusion, in due course, in the end, in time, ultimately.

at leisure at ease, at liberty, free, idle, off the hook.

at length at last, at long last, completely, eventually, exhaustively, finally, for ages, for hours, fully, in depth, in detail, in the end, in time, interminably, thoroughly, to the full, ultimately.

at liberty at large, at leisure, footloose, free, idle, not confined, on the loose, unconstrained, unrestricted.

at odds at daggers drawn, at enmity, at loggerheads, at one another's throats, at outs, at variance, feuding, in conflict, in dispute, opposed, quarrelling.

at once at one go, at the same time, directly, forthwith, immediately, in concert, in unison, incontinent, instantly, now, promptly, right away, simultaneously, straight away, this minute, together, unhesitatingly, without delay.

at one's wits' end at a loss, at the end of one's tether, baffled, bewildered, desperate, in despair, in dire straits, lost, resourceless, stuck, stumped.

at random accidentally, aimlessly, arbitrarily, casually, desultorily, fortuitously, haphazardly, indiscriminately, irregularly, purposelessly, randomly, unsystematically.

at rest asleep, at a standstill, calm, dead, idle, inactive, motionless, peaceful, resting, sleeping, still, stopped, tranquil, unmoving.

at sea adrift, astray, baffled, bewildered, confused, disoriented, insecure, lost, mystified, perplexed, puzzled, upset.

at the double at full speed, at once, briskly, immediately, in double-quick time, lickety-split, like lightning, posthaste, quickly, without delay.

atheism *n* free-thinking, godlessness, heathenism, impiety, infidelity, irreligion, non-belief, paganism, rationalism, scepticism, unbelief, ungodliness.

atheistic *adj* free-thinking, heathen, impious, irreligious, irreverent, rationalistic, sceptical, unbelieving, ungodly, unreligious. *antonym* religious.

athletic *adj* active, brawny, energetic, fit, husky, muscular, powerful, robust, sinewy, strapping, strong, sturdy, vigorous, well-proportioned, wiry. *antonym* puny.

atmosphere *n* air, ambience, aura, character, climate, environment, feel, feeling, flavour, heavens, milieu, mood, quality, sky, spirit, surroundings, tenor, tone, vibrations.

atom *n* bit, crumb, grain, hint, iota, jot, mite, molecule, morsel, particle, scintilla, scrap, shred, smidgen, speck, spot, tittle, trace, whit.

atone *v* compensate, expiate, make amends, make up for, offset, pay for, propitiate, recompense, reconcile, redeem, redress, remedy.

atonement *n* amends, compensation, expiation, indemnity, payment, penance, propitiation, recompense, redress, reparation, repayment, restitution, restoration, satisfaction.

atrocious *adj* abominable, barbaric, brutal, cruel, diabolical, execrable, fell, fiendish, ghastly, grievous, heinous, hideous, horrible, horrifying, infamous, infernal, inhuman, monstrous, ruthless, savage, shocking, terrible, vicious, vile, villainous, wicked.

atrocity *n* abomination, atrociousness, barbarity, barbarousness, brutality, crime, cruelty, enormity, evil, ghastliness, heinousness, hideousness, horror, infamy, inhumanity, monstrosity, monstrousness, outrage, ruthlessness, savagery, viciousness, vileness, villainy, wickedness.

atrophy *n* decay, decline, degeneration, deterioration, diminution, emaciation, shrivelling, wasting, withering.
v decay, decline, degenerate, deteriorate, diminish, dwindle, emaciate, fade, shrink, shrivel, waste, wither.

attach *v* add, adhere, affix, annex, append, articulate, ascribe, assign, associate, attract, attribute, belong, bind, captivate, combine, connect, couple, fasten, fix, impute, join, link, place, put, relate to, secure, stick, tie, unite, weld. *antonyms* detach, unfasten.

attached *adj* affectionate, affiliated, associated, connected, fond, loving.

attachment *n* accessory, accoutrement, adapter, addition, adhesion, adjunct, affection, affinity, appendage, attraction, bond, codicil, cohesion, confiscation, connection, connector, coupling, devotion, esteem, extension, extra, fastener, fastening, fidelity, fitting, fixture, fondness, friendship, joint, junction, liking, link, love, loyalty, partiality, predilection, regard, seizure, supplement, tenderness, tie.

attack n abuse, access, aggression, assailment, assault, battery, blitz, bombardment, bout, broadside, censure, charge, convulsion, criticism, fit, foray, impugnment, incursion, inroad, invasion, invective, offensive, onset, onslaught, paroxysm, raid, rush, seizure, spasm, spell, strike, stroke.
v abuse, assail, assault, belabour, berate, blame, censure, charge, chastise, criticise, denounce, do over, fake, fall on, flay, have one's knife in, impugn, invade, inveigh against, lash, lay into, light into, make at, malign, mob, put the boot in, raid, rate, revile, rush, set about, set on, snipe, storm, strafe, strike, vilify, visit, wade into.

attain v accomplish, achieve, acquire, arrive at, bag, compass, complete, earn, effect, fulfil, gain, get, grasp, net, obtain, procure, reach, realise, reap, secure, touch, win.

attainable adj accessible, achievable, available, feasible, manageable, obtainable, possible, potential, practicable, probable, reachable, realistic, within reach. **antonym** unattainable.

attainment n ability, accomplishment, achievement, acquirement, acquisition, aptitude, art, capability, competence, completion, consummation, facility, feat, fulfilment, gift, mastery, procurement, proficiency, reaching, realisation, skill, success, talent.

attempt n assault, assay, attack, bash, bid, crack, effort, endeavour, essay, experiment, go, move, push, shot, stab, struggle, trial, try, undertaking, venture.
v aspire, endeavour, essay, experiment, have a bash, have a crack, have a go, have a shot, seek, strive, tackle, try, try one's hand at, try one's luck at, undertake, venture.

attend v accompany, appear, arise from, assist, be all ears, be present, care for, chaperon, companion, convoy, escort, follow, frequent, give ear, guard, hear, hearken, heed, help, lend an ear, listen, look after, mark, mind, minister to, note, notice, nurse, observe, pay attention, pay

heed, pin back one's ears, regard, result from, serve, squire, succour, take care of, tend, usher, visit, wait upon, watch.
attend to concentrate on, control, cope with, deal with, direct, look after, manage, oversee, see to, supervise, take care of.

attendant adj accessory, accompanying, associated, attached, concomitant, consequent, incidental, related, resultant, subsequent.

attention n alertness, attentiveness, awareness, care, civility, concentration, concern, consciousness, consideration, contemplation, courtesy, deference, ear, gallantry, heed, heedfulness, intentness, mindfulness, ministration, notice, observation, politeness, recognition, regard, respect, service, thought, thoughtfulness, treatment, vigilance. **antonyms** disregard, inattention.

attentive adj accommodating, advertent, alert, awake, careful, civil, concentrating, conscientious, considerate, courteous, deferential, devoted, gallant, gracious, heedful, intent, kind, mindful, obliging, observant, polite, regardant, studious, thoughtful, vigilant, watchful. **antonyms** heedless, inattentive, inconsiderate.

attenuate v adulterate, debase, decrease, devaluate, dilute, diminish, draw out, elongate, enervate, enfeeble, extend, lengthen, rarefy, reduce, refine, sap, stretch out, taper, thin, thin out, water down, weaken. **antonyms** expand, intensify, thicken.

attenuated adj adulterated, debased, decreased, devalued, diluted, diminished, drawn out, elongated, enervated, enfeebled, extended, lengthened, rarefied, reduced, refined, sapped, slender, spun out, stretched out, tapering, thinned, watered down, weakened.

attest v affirm, assert, authenticate, aver, certify, confirm, corroborate, declare, demonstrate, depose, display, endorse, evidence, evince, exhibit, manifest, prove, ratify, seal, show, substantiate, swear, testify, verify, vouch, warrant, witness.

attestation n affirmation, asseveration, assurance, avowal, certification, confirmation, corroboration, declaration, deposition, endorsement, evidence, testification, testimony, vouch, witness.

attire n accoutrements, apparel, array, clothes, clothing, costume, dress finery, garb, garments, gear, get-up, habiliments, habit, outfit, raiment, rig-out, robes, togs, uniform, vestment, wear, weeds.

v adorn, apparel, array, clothe, costume, deck out, dress, equip, garb, habilitate, outfit, prepare, rig out, robe, turn out.

attitude *n* affectation, air, approach, aspect, bearing, carriage, condition, demeanour, disposition, feeling, manner, mien, mood, opinion, outlook, perspective, point of view, pose, position, posture, stance, view.

attract *v* allure, appeal to, bewitch, captivate, charm, decoy, draw, enchant, engage, entice, fascinate, incline, induce, interest, inveigle, invite, lure, pull, seduce, tempt. *antonym* repel.

attraction *n* allure, amenity, appeal, attractiveness, bait, captivation, charm, crowd-puller, draw, enchantment, entertainment, enticement, event, fascination, inducement, interest, invitation, lure, magnetism, pull, seduction, show, temptation. *antonym* repulsion.

attractive *adj* agreeable, alluring, appealing, beautiful, beddable, captivating, catching, catchy, charming, comely, enchanting, engaging, enticing, fair, fascinating, fetching, glamorous, good-looking, gorgeous, handsome, hunky, interesting, inviting, lovely, magnetic, nubile, personable, pleasant, pleasing, prepossessing, pretty, seductive, snazzy, stunning, tempting, voluptuous, winning, winsome. *antonym* repellent.

attribute *v* accredit, apply, arrogate, ascribe, assign, blame, charge, credit, impute, put down, refer.

n affection, aspect, character, characteristic, facet, feature, idiosyncrasy, mark, note, peculiarity, point, property, quality, quirk, sign, symbol, trait, virtue.

attune *v* acclimatise, accustom, adapt, adjust, assimilate, co-ordinate, familiarise, harmonise, modulate, reconcile, regulate, set, tune.

atypical *adj* aberrant, abnormal, anomalous, deviant, divergent, eccentric, exceptional, extraordinary, freakish, untypical, unusual.

au fait abreast of, acquainted, au courant, clued-up, conversant, hep, in the know, in the stream, in the swim, in touch, knowledgeable, on the ball, posted, up-to-date, well up, well-informed.

audacious *adj* adventurous, assuming, assured, bold, brave, brazen, cheeky, courageous, dare-devil, daring,

dauntless, death-defying, disrespectful, enterprising, fearless, forward, impertinent, impudent, insolent, intrepid, pert, plucky, presumptuous, rash, reckless, risky, rude, shameless, unabashed, valiant, venturesome. *antonyms* cautious, reserved, timid.

audacity *n* adventurousness, assurance, boldness, brass neck, bravery, brazenness, cheek, chutzpah, courage, daring, dauntlessness, defiance, derring-do, disrespectfulness, effrontery, enterprise, fearlessness, foolhardiness, forwardness, gall, guts, impertinence, impudence, insolence, intrepidity, nerve, pertness, presumption, rashness, recklessness, rudeness, shamelessness, valour. *antonyms* caution, reserve, timidity.

audible *adj* appreciable, clear, detectable, discernible, distinct, perceptible, recognisable.

audience *n* assemblage, assembly, auditorium, congregation, crowd, devotees, fans, following, gallery, gathering, hearing, house, interview, listeners, market, meeting, onlookers, public, ratings, reception, regulars, spectators, turn-out, viewers.

augment *v* add to, amplify, boost, dilate, eke out, enhance, enlarge, expand, extend, grow, heighten, increase, inflate, intensify, magnify, multiply, raise, reinforce, strengthen, supplement, swell. *antonym* decrease.

augur *v* auspicate, betoken, bode, forebode, foreshadow, foretoken, harbinger, herald, import, portend, predict, prefigure, presage, promise, prophesy, signify.

august *adj* dignified, exalted, glorious, grand, imposing, impressive, lofty, magnificent, majestic, monumental, noble, portentous, regal, revered, solemn, splendid, stately, venerable.

aura *n* air, ambience, aroma, atmosphere, emanation, feel, feeling, hint, mood, nimbus, odour, quality, scent, suggestion, vibes, vibrations.

auspices *n* aegis, authority, backing, care, championship, charge, control, guidance, influence, patronage, protection, responsibility, sponsorship, superintendence, supervision, support, tutelage.

auspicious *adj* bright, cheerful, encouraging, favourable, felicitous, fortunate, happy, hopeful, lucky, opportune, optimistic, promising, propitious, prosperous, rosy, white. *antonyms* inauspicious, ominous.

austere *adj* abstemious, abstinent, ascetic, astringent, bitter, bleak, chaste, cold, conservative, continent, economical, exacting, forbidding, formal, grave, grim, hard, harsh, plain, puritanical, restrained, rigid, rigorous, self-denying, self-disciplined, serious, severe, simple, sober, solemn, sour, spare, spartan, stark, stern, strict, stringent, unadorned, unembellished, unornamented, unrelenting. *antonyms* elaborate, extravagant, genial.

austerity *n* abstemiousness, abstinence, asceticism, chasteness, chastity, coldness, continence, economy, formality, gravity, grimness, hardness, harshness, inflexibility, plainness, puritanism, reserve, restraint, rigidity, rigour, self-control, self-denial, self-discipline, seriousness, severity, simplicity, sobriety, solemnity, spareness, spartanism, starkness, sternness, strictness. *antonyms* elaborateness, geniality.

authentic *adj* accurate, actual, authoritative, bona fide, certain, dependable, dinkum, factual, faithful, genuine, honest, kosher, legitimate, original, pure, real, reliable, true, true-to-life, trustworthy, valid, veracious, veritable. *antonyms* counterfeit, spurious.

authenticate *v* accredit, attest, authorise, avouch, certify, confirm, corroborate, endorse, guarantee, validate, verify, vouch for, warrant.

authenticity *n* accuracy, actuality, authoritativeness, certainty, correctness, dependability, factualness, faithfulness, fidelity, genuineness, honesty, legitimacy, purity, reality, realness, reliability, trustworthiness, truth, truthfulness, validity, veracity, veritableness, verity. *antonyms* invalidity, spuriousness.

author *n* architect, begetter, composer, creator, designer, fabricator, fashioner, father, forger, founder, initiator, inventor, maker, mover, originator, paper-stainer, parent, pen, penman, penwoman, planner, prime mover, producer, volumist, writer.

authorise *v* accredit, allow, approve, commission, confirm, consent to, countenance, empower, enable, entitle, legalise, license, permit, ratify, sanction, validate, warrant.

authoritarian *adj* absolute, autocratic,

despotic, dictatorial, disciplinarian, doctrinaire, dogmatic, domineering, harsh, heavy, imperious, inflexible, oppressive, repressive, rigid, severe, strict, tyrannical, unyielding. *antonym* liberal.

n absolutist, autocrat, despot, dictator, disciplinarian, fascist, Hitler, tyrant.

authoritative *adj* accepted, accurate, approved, assured, authentic, authorised, commanding, confident, convincing, decisive, definitive, dependable, factual, faithful, learned, legitimate, magisterial, masterly, official, reliable, sanctioned, scholarly, sound, sovereign, true, trustworthy, truthful, valid, veritable. *antonym* unreliable.

authority[1] *n* administration, ascendancy, attestation, authorisation, avowal, charge, command, control, declaration, domination, dominion, evidence, force, government, influence, jurisdiction, justification, licence, management, might, officialdom, permission, permit, power, prerogative, profession, right, rule, sanction, sovereignty, statement, strength, supremacy, sway, testimony, textbook, warrant, weight, word.

authority[2] *n* arbiter, bible, connoisseur, expert, judge, master, professional, pundit, sage, scholar, specialist.

autocracy *n* absolutism, authoritarianism, despotism, dictatorship, fascism, Hitlerism, totalitarianism, tyranny. *antonym* democracy.

autocrat *n* absolutist, authoritarian, Caesar, despot, dictator, fascist, Hitler, panjandrum, totalitarian, tyrant.

autocratic *adj* absolute, all-powerful, authoritarian, despotic, dictatorial, dictatory, domineering, imperious, overbearing, totalitarian, tyrannical. *antonyms* democratic, liberal.

automatic *adj* automated, certain, habitual, inescapable, inevitable, instinctive, involuntary, mechanical, mechanised, natural, necessary, perfunctory, push-button, reflex, robot, robot-like, routine, self-acting, self-activating, self-moving, self-propelling, self-regulating, spontaneous, unavoidable, unbidden, unconscious, unthinking, unwilled.

autonomous *adj* free, independent, self-determining, self-governing, sovereign, voluntary. *antonym* subject.

autonomy *n* autarky, free will, freedom, home rule, independence, self-determination, self-government, self-rule, sovereignty. **antonyms** compulsion, subjection.

auxiliary adj accessory, aiding, ancillary, assistant, assisting, back-up, emergency, helping, reserve, secondary, subsidiary, substitute, supplementary, supporting, supportive.

n accessory, accomplice, ally, ancillary, assistant, associate, companion, confederate, helper, partner, reserve, subordinate, supporter.

avail v advance, advantage, aid, assist, benefit, boot, dow, exploit, help, make the most of, profit, serve, work.

n advantage, aid, assistance, benefit, good, help, profit, purpose, service, use, value.

avail oneself of capitalise on, make use of, profit by, profit from, take advantage of, turn to account, use, utilise.

available adj accessible, at hand, attainable, convenient, disengaged, free, handy, obtainable, on hand, on tap, procurable, ready, to hand, vacant, within reach.

avalanche n barrage, cascade, cataclysm, deluge, flood, inundation, landslide, landslip, torrent.

avant-garde adj advanced, enterprising, experimental, far-out, forward-looking, innovative, inventive, pioneering, progressive, unconventional, way-out. **antonyms** conservative, dyed-in-the-wool.

avarice n acquisitiveness, cheese-paring, covetousness, cupidity, greed, greediness, meanness, miserliness, niggardliness, parsimony, penny-pinching, penuriousness, rapacity, stinginess, tight-fistedness. **antonym** generosity.

avaricious adj acquisitive, cheese-paring, covetous, grasping, greedy, mean, miserable, miserly, money-grubbing, niggardly, parsimonious, penny-pinching, penurious, rapacious, stingy, tight-fisted. **antonym** generous.

avenge v punish, repay, requite, take revenge for, take vengeance for, vindicate.

avenging adj retaliatory, retributive, vengeful, vindictive.

avenue n access, alley, approach, boulevard, channel, course, drive, driveway, entrance, entrée, entry, means, pass, passage, path, pathway, road, route, street, thoroughfare, vista, walk, way.

aver v affirm, allege, assert, asseverate, attest, avow, declare, insist, maintain, proclaim, profess, pronounce, protest, say, state, swear, testify, witness.

average n mean, mediocrity, medium, midpoint, norm, par, rule, run, standard. **antonyms** exception, extreme.

adj common, commonplace, everyday, fair, general, indifferent, intermediate, mean, mediocre, medium, middle, middling, moderate, normal, ordinary, passable, regular, run-of-the-mill, satisfactory, so-so, standard, tolerable, typical, undistinguished, unexceptional, unremarkable, usual. **antonyms** exceptional, extreme.

averse adj antagonistic, antipathetic, disapproving, disinclined, hostile, ill-disposed, inimical, loath, opposed, reluctant, unfavourable, unwilling. **antonyms** sympathetic, willing.

aversion n abhorrence, abomination, anathema, animosity, antagonism, antipathy, detestation, disapproval, disgust, disinclination, dislike, distaste, hate, hatred, horror, hostility, loathing, odium, opposition, phobia, reluctance, repugnance, repulsion, revulsion, unwillingness. **antonyms** liking, sympathy.

avert v avoid, deflect, evade, fend off, forestall, frustrate, obviate, parry, preclude, prevent, stave off, turn, turn aside, turn away, ward off.

avid adj acquisitive, ardent, avaricious, covetous, dedicated, devoted, eager, earnest, enthusiastic, fanatical, fervent, grasping, greedy, hungry, insatiable, intense, keen, passionate, rapacious, ravenous, thirsty, voracious, zealous. **antonym** indifferent.

avocation n business, calling, distraction, diversion, employment, hobby, interest, job, occupation, pastime, profession, pursuit, recreation, relaxation, sideline, trade, vocation, work.

avoid v abstain from, avert, balk, bypass, circumvent, dodge, duck, elude, escape, eschew, evade, evite, get out of, obviate, prevent, refrain from, shirk, shun, side-step, steer clear of.

avoidable adj avertible, eludible, escapable, evadable, preventable. **antonym** inevitable.

avoidance n abstention, abstinence, circumvention, dodge, dodging, eluding, elusion, escape, eschewal, evasion, prevention, refraining, shunning, shunning.

avow v acknowledge, admit, affirm, allege, assert, asseverate, attest, aver, confess, declare, maintain, own, proclaim, profess, recognise, state, swear, testify.

avowal n acknowledgment, admission, affirmation, allegation, assertion, asseveration, attestation, averment, confession, declaration, oath, proclamation, profession, recognition, statement, swearing, testimony.

avowed adj acknowledged, admitted, confessed, declared, open, overt, professed, self-confessed, self-proclaimed, sworn.

await v anticipate, attend, be in store for, expect, hope for, lie in wait, look for, look forward to, wait for.

awake v arouse, awaken, rouse, wake, wake up.
adj alert, alive, aroused, astir, attentive, awakened, aware, conscious, heedful, observant, sensitive, vigilant, wakeful, waking, watchful, wide-awake.

awaken v activate, alert, animate, arouse, awake, call forth, enliven, evoke, excite, fan, kindle, prompt, provoke, revive, rouse, stimulate, stir up, vivify, wake, waken. **antonyms** lull, quell, quench.

awakening n activation, animating, arousal, birth, enlivening, evocation, kindling, prompting, provocation, revival, rousing, stimulation.

award v accord, adjudge, allot, allow, apportion, assign, bestow, confer, determine, dispense, distribute, endow, gift, give, grant, present.
n adjudication, allotment, allowance, bestowal, conferment, conferral, decision, decoration, dispensation, endowment, gift, grant, judgement, order, presentation, prize, trophy.

aware adj acquainted, alive to, appreciative, attentive, au courant, cognisant, conscious, conversant, enlightened, familiar, heedful, hep, hip, informed, knowing, knowledgeable, mindful, observant, on the ball, sensitive, sentient, sharp, shrewd. **antonym** insensitive.

awareness n acquaintance, appreciation, attention, cognisance, consciousness, enlightenment, familiarity, knowledge, observation, perception, realisation, recognition, sensibility, sensitivity, sentience, understanding. **antonym** insensitivity.

awe n admiration, amazement, apprehension, astonishment, dread, fear, respect, reverence, terror, veneration, wonder, wonderment. **antonym** contempt.
v amaze, astonish, cow, daunt, frighten, horrify, impress, intimidate, overwhelm, stun, terrify.

awesome adj alarming, amazing, astonishing, august, awe-inspiring, awful, breathtaking, daunting, dread, dreadful, fearful, fearsome, formidable, frightening, imposing, impressive, intimidating, magnificent, majestic, moving, overwhelming, redoubtable, solemn, stunning, stupefying, stupendous, terrible, terrifying, wonderful, wondrous.

awe-struck adj afraid, amazed, astonished, awed, awe-inspired, awe-stricken, cowed, daunted, dumbfounded, fearful, frightened, impressed, intimidated, speechless, struck dumb, stunned, terrified, wonder-struck.

awful adj abysmal, alarming, amazing, atrocious, august, awe-inspiring, awesome, blood-curdling, dire, dread, dreadful, fearful, fearsome, frightful, ghastly, gruesome, harrowing, hideous, horrendous, horrible, horrific, horrifying, majestic, nasty, portentous, shocking, solemn, spine-chilling, terrible, tremendous, ugly, unpleasant.

awfully adv abysmally, badly, disgracefully, disputably, dreadfully, exceedingly, exceptionally, excessively, extremely, greatly, immensely, inadequately, quite, reprehensibly, shockingly, shoddily, terribly, unforgivably, unpleasantly, very, wickedly, woefully, wretchedly.

awkward adj annoying, bloody-minded, blundering, bungling, clownish, clumsy, coarse, compromising, cumbersome, delicate, difficult, disobliging, embarrassed, embarrassing, exasperating, fiddly, gauche, gawky, graceless, ham-fisted, hazardous, ill at ease, inconvenient, inelegant, inept, inexpedient, inexpert, inopportune, intractable, intransigent, irritable, left-handed, maladroit, obstinate, painful, perplexing, perverse, prickly, risky, rude, spastic, sticky, stubborn, thorny, ticklish, touchy, troublesome, trying, uncomfortable, unco-operative, unco-ordinated, uncouth, ungainly, ungraceful, unhandy, unhelpful, unmanageable, unpleasant, unrefined, unskilful, untimely, untoward, unwieldy, vexatious, vexing. **antonyms**

amenable, convenient, elegant, graceful, straightforward.

awry *adv, adj* amiss, askew, asymmetrical, cock-eyed, crooked, misaligned, oblique, off-centre, out of kilter, skew-whiff, twisted, uneven, unevenly, wonky, wrong. *antonyms* straight, symmetrical.

axe *v* cancel, chop, cleave, cut, cut down, discharge, discontinue, dismiss, eliminate, fell, fire, get rid of, hew, remove, sack, split, terminate, throw out, withdraw.

axiom *n* adage, aphorism, apophthegm, byword, dictum, fundamental, gnome, maxim, postulate, precept, principle, truism, truth.

axiomatic *adj* absolute, accepted, aphoristic, assumed, certain, fundamental, given, gnomic, granted, indubitable, manifest, presupposed, proverbial, self-evident, understood, unquestioned.

axis *n* alliance, arbor, axle, bloc, centre-line, coalition, compact, entente, league, longitude, pact, pivot, plumb-line, shaft, spindle, vertical.

B

babble *v* blab, burble, cackle, chatter, gabble, gibber, gurgle, jabber, mumble, murmur, mutter, prate, prattle.
n burble, clamour, drivel, gabble, gibberish, murmur.

babbling *adj* burbling, cackling, chattering, drivelling, drooling, gabbling, gibbering, gurgling, incoherent, jabbering, long-tongued, murmuring, prattling, rambling, unco-ordinated, unintelligible.

baby *n* babe, bairn, child, infant, nursling, papoose, suckling, tiny, toddler.
adj diminutive, dwarf, little, midget, mini, miniature, minute, pygmy, small, small-scale, tiny, toy, wee.
v coddle, cosset, humour, indulge, mollycoddle, overindulge, pamper, pander to, pet, spoil, spoon-feed.

babyish *adj* baby, childish, foolish, immature, infantile, juvenile, naïve, namby-pamby, puerile, silly, sissy, soft, spoilt. **antonyms** mature, precocious.

back¹ *v* advocate, assist, boost, buttress, champion, countenance, countersign, encourage, endorse, favour, finance, sanction, second, side with, sponsor, subsidise, support, sustain, underwrite. **antonym** discourage.

back up aid, assist, bolster, champion, confirm, corroborate, endorse, reinforce, second, substantiate, support. **antonym** let down.

back² *n* backside, end, hind part, hindquarters, posterior, rear, reverse, stern, tail, tail end, verso.
adj end, hind, hindmost, posterior, rear, reverse, tail.

back³ *v* backtrack, recede, recoil, regress, retire, retreat, reverse, withdraw.

back down accede, back-pedal, concede, give in, retreat, submit, surrender, withdraw, yield.

back out abandon, bunk off, cancel, chicken out, give up, go back on, recant, renegue, resign, withdraw.

back⁴ *adj* delayed, earlier, elapsed, former, outdated, overdue, past, previous, prior, superseded.

backbiting *n* abuse, aspersion, bitchiness, calumniation, calumny, cattiness, criticism, defamation, denigration, detraction, disparagement, gossip, malice, revilement, scandalmongering, slagging, slander, spite, spitefulness, vilification, vituperation. **antonym** praise.

backbone *n* basis, bottle, character, core, courage, determination, firmness, foundation, grit, mainstay, mettle, nerve, pluck, power, resolution, resolve, spine, stamina, staunchness, steadfastness, strength, support, tenacity, toughness, vertebral column, will. **antonyms** spinelessness, weakness.

backbreaking *adj* arduous, crushing, exhausting, gruelling, hard, heavy, killing, laborious, punishing, strenuous, tiring, toilsome, wearing, wearisome.

backer *n* advocate, benefactor, bottle-holder, champion, funder, patron, promoter, second, seconder, sponsor, subscriber, supporter, underwriter, well-wisher.

background *n* breeding, circumstances, credentials, culture, dossier, education, environment, experience, grounding, history, milieu, preparation, record, surroundings, tradition, upbringing.

backing *n* accompaniment, advocacy, aid, assistance, championing, championship, encouragement, endorsement, favour, funds, grant, helpers, moral support, patronage, sanction, seconding, sponsorship, subsidy, support.

backlash *n* backfire, boomerang, counterblast, kickback, reaction, recoil, repercussion, reprisal, resentment, response, retaliation.

backlog *n* accumulation, excess, hoard, mountain, reserve, reserves, resources, stock, supply.

backslide *v* default, defect, fall from grace, lapse, regress, relapse, renegue, retrogress, revert, sin, slip, stray, weaken. **antonym** persevere.

backward *adj* bashful, behind, behindhand, diffident, dull, hesitant, hesitating, immature, late, reluctant, retarded, shy, slow, sluggish, stupid, subnormal, tardy, underdeveloped, unwilling, wavering. **antonyms** forward, precocious.

bad *adj* adverse, ailing, base, blameworthy, conscience-stricken, contrite, corrupt, criminal, damaging, dangerous, decayed, defective, deficient, deleterious, delinquent, despondent, detrimental, disastrous, discouraged, discouraging, diseased, disobedient, distressed, distressing, evil, fallacious, faulty, gloomy, grave, grim, grotty, guilty, harmful, harsh, ill, illaudable, immoral, imperfect, inadequate, incorrect, inferior, injurious, mean, melancholy, mischievous, mouldy, naughty, no-good, noxious, off, offensive, painful, poor, putrid, rancid, regretful, remorseful, ropy, rotten, rueful, ruinous, sad, serious, severe, shoddy, sick, sinful, sombre, sorry, sour, spoilt, stormy, substandard, terrible, troubled, unfortunate, unhealthy, unpleasant, unruly, unsatisfactory, unwell, upset, vile, wicked, wrong.

bad blood acrimony, anger, animosity, antagonism, bad feeling, dislike, distrust, enmity, feud, hatred, hostility, malevolence, malice, nastiness, odium, rancour, resentment, upset, vendetta.

bad form bad style, barbarism, gaucherie, impropriety, inelegance, solecism.

bad luck adversity, blow, hard cheese, hard lines, hard luck, hoodoo, mischance, misfortune, reverse, setback. *antonym* luck.

bad manners boorishness, coarseness, discourtesy, disrespect, impoliteness, incivility, inconsideration, indelicacy, unmannerliness. *antonym* politeness.

bad taste coarseness, crudeness, grossness, indecency, indelicacy, obscenity, offensiveness, poor taste, smuttiness, tactlessness, tastelessness, vulgarity. *antonyms* delicacy, tastefulness.

bad time agony, going-over, grilling, nasty moment, suspense, third degree, torture.

badge *n* brand, device, emblem, identification, insignia, logo, mark, sign, stamp, token, trademark.

badger *v* bait, bully, chivvy, goad, harass, harry, hassle, hound, importune, nag, pester, plague, torment.

badly¹ *adv* carelessly, criminally, defectively, faultily, immorally, imperfectly, improperly, inadequately, incompetently, incorrectly, ineptly, negligently, poorly, shamefully, shoddily, unethically, unfairly, unfavourably, unfortunately, unsatisfactorily, unsuccessfully, wickedly, wrong, wrongly.

badly² *adv* acutely, bitterly, critically, crucially, deeply, desperately, exceedingly, extremely, gravely, greatly, intensely, painfully, seriously, severely.

bad-tempered *adj* cantankerous, captious, crabbed, cross, crotchety, dyspeptic, fractious, impatient, irascible, irritable, peevish, petulant, querulous, snappy, splenetic, stroppy, testy. *antonyms* equable, genial.

baffle *v* amaze, astound, bamboozle, bemuse, bewilder, check, confound, confuse, daze, defeat, disconcert, dumbfound, flabbergast, floor, flummox, foil, frustrate, hinder, mystify, nonplus, perplex, puzzle, stump, stun, stymie, thwart, upset. *antonym* enlighten.

baffling *adj* amazing, astounding, bemusing, confusing, extraordinary, frustrating, mysterious, perplexing, stupefying, surprising, thwarting, unfathomable. *antonyms* enlightening, explanatory.

bag *v* acquire, appropriate, capture, catch, commandeer, corner, gain, get, grab, kill, land, obtain, reserve, shoot, take, trap.

baggage *n* accoutrements, bags, belongings, equipment, gear, luggage, paraphernalia, suit-cases, things.

baggy *adj* billowing, bulging, droopy, flaccid, floppy, ill-fitting, loose, oversize, roomy, sagging, slack. *antonyms* firm, tight.

bait *n* allurement, attraction, bribe, carrot, decoy, enticement, inducement, lure, temptation. *antonym* disincentive. *v* annoy, gall, goad, harass, hound, irk, irritate, needle, persecute, provoke, tease, torment.

balance *v* adjust, assess, calculate, compare, compute, consider, counteract, counterbalance, counterpoise, deliberate, equalise, equate, estimate, evaluate, level, match, neutralise, offset, parallel, poise, settle, square, stabilise, steady, tally, total, weigh.
n composure, correspondence, difference, equality, equanimity, equilibrium, equipoise, equity, equivalence, evenness, parity, poise, remainder, residue, rest, self-possession, stability, stasis, steadiness, surplus, symmetry. *antonyms* imbalance, instability.

balanced *adj* calm, equitable, even-handed, fair, impartial, just, self-possessed, sensible, unbiased, unprejudiced, well-rounded. *antonym* prejudiced.

bald *adj* bare, barren, bleak, direct, downright, exposed, forthright, naked, outright, plain, severe, simple, stark, straight, straightforward, treeless, unadorned, uncompromising, uncovered, undisguised, unvarnished. *antonym* adorned.

baleful *adj* deadly, destructive, evil, fell, harmful, hurtful, injurious, malevolent, malignant, menacing, mournful, noxious, ominous, pernicious, ruinous, sad, sinister, venomous, woeful. *antonyms* auspicious, favourable.

balk, baulk *v* baffle, bar, boggle, check, counteract, defeat, demur, disconcert, dodge, evade, flinch, foil, forestall, frustrate, hesitate, hinder, jib, make difficulties, obstruct, prevent, recoil, refuse, resist, shirk, shrink, stall, thwart.

ball¹ *n* bauble, bobble, bullet, clew, conglomeration, drop, globe, globule, orb, pellet, pill, shot, slug, sphere, spheroid.

ball² *n* assembly, carnival, dance, dinner-dance, hop, masquerade, party.

balloon *v* bag, belly, billow, blow up, bulge, dilate, distend, enlarge, expand, inflate, puff out, swell.

ballot *n* election, plebiscite, poll, polling, referendum, vote, voting.

ballyhoo *n* agitation, clamour, commotion, disturbance, excitement, fuss, hubbub, hue and cry, hullabaloo, hype, noise, promotion, propaganda, publicity, racket, tumult.

balm *n* anodyne, balsam, bromide, calmative, comfort, consolation, cream, curative, embrocation, emollient, lotion, ointment, palliative, restorative, salve, sedative, solace, unguent. *antonyms* irritant, vexation.

balmy¹ *adj* clement, gentle, mild, pleasant, soft, summery, temperate. *antonym* inclement.

balmy² *adj* barmy, crazy, daft, dippy, dotty, foolish, idiotic, insane, loony, mad, nuts, nutty, odd, round the bend, silly, stupid. *antonyms* rational, sane, sensible.

bamboozle *v* baffle, befuddle, bemuse, cheat, con, confound, confuse, deceive, defraud, delude, dupe, fool, hoax, hoodwink, mystify, perplex, puzzle, stump, swindle, trick.

ban *v* banish, bar, debar, disallow, exclude, forbid, interdict, ostracise, outlaw, prohibit, proscribe, restrict, suppress. *antonym* permit.
n boycott, censorship, condemnation, curse, denunciation, embargo, interdiction, prohibition, proscription, restriction, stoppage, suppression, taboo. *antonyms* dispensation, permission.

banal *adj* boring, clichéd, cliché-ridden, commonplace, corny, empt[y], everyday, hackneyed, humdrum, old ha[t], ordinary, pedestrian, platitudinous, stal[e], stereotyped, stock, threadbare, tire[d], trite, unimaginative, unoriginal, vapid. *antonym* original.

banality *n* bromide, cliché, commonplace, dullness, platitud[e], triteness, triviality, truism, vapidity. *antonym* originality.

band *n* association, body, cliqu[e], club, combo, company, coterie, crew, ensemble, flock, gang, group, her[d], horde, orchestra, party, range, societ[y], troop, waits.
v affiliate, ally, amalgamat[e], collaborate, consolidate, federate, gathe[r], group, join, merge, unite. *antonym* disband, disperse.

bandage *n* compress, dressing, gauz[e], ligature, plaster, swaddle, swath[e], tourniquet.
v bind, cover, dress, swaddle, swathe.

bandit *n* brigand, buccanee[r], cowboy, desperado, freebooter, gangste[r], gunman, highwayman, hijacke[r], marauder, outlaw, pirate, racketee[r], robber, ruffian, thief.

bane *n* adversity, affliction, annoyanc[e], bête noire, blight, burden, calamit[y], curse, despair, destruction, disaste[r], distress, downfall, evil, irritation, miser[y], misfortune, nuisance, ordeal, pes[t], pestilence, plague, ruin, scourge, sorrow, torment, trial, trouble, vexation, woe. *antonym* blessing.

bang *n* blow, boom, box, bum[p], clang, clap, clash, collision, crash, cuf[f], detonation, explosion, hit, knock, nois[e], peal, pop, punch, report, shot, slan[?], smack, stroke, thud, thump, wallo[p], whack.
v bash, boom, bump, burst, clang, clatter, crash, detonate, drum, ech[o], explode, hammer, knock, peal, poun[d], pummel, rap, resound, slam, stamp, strike, thump, thunder.
adv directly, hard, headlong, noisil[y], plumb, précisely, right, slap, smack, straight, suddenly.

banish *v* ban, bar, blacklist, deba[r], deport, discard, dislodge, dismiss, dispe[l], eject, eliminate, eradicate, evict, exclud[e], excommunicate, exile, expatriate, expe[l], get rid of, ostracise, oust, outlaw, remove, shut out, transport. *antonym* recall, welcome.

bank¹ *n* accumulation, cache, depository

fund, hoard, pool, repository, reserve, reservoir, savings, stock, stockpile, store, storehouse, treasury.

v accumulate, deposit, keep, save, stockpile, store. *antonym* spend.

bank² *n* banking, brink, earthwork, edge, embankment, heap, margin, mass, mound, pile, rampart, ridge, shallow, shoal, shore, side, slope, tilt.

v accumulate, aggrade, amass, camber, drift, heap, incline, mass, mound, pile, pitch, slant, slope, stack, tilt, tip.

bank³ *n* array, bench, file, group, line, rank, row, sequence, series, succession, tier, train.

bankrupt *adj* beggared, broke, depleted, destitute, exhausted, failed, impecunious, impoverished, insolvent, lacking, penurious, ruined, spent. *antonyms* solvent, wealthy.

n debtor, insolvent, pauper.

bankruptcy *n* beggary, disaster, exhaustion, failure, indebtedness, insolvency, lack, liquidation, penury, ruin, ruination. *antonyms* solvency, wealth.

banter *n* badinage, chaff, chaffing, cross-talk, derision, jesting, joking, kidding, mockery, persiflage, pleasantry, quiz, raillery, repartee, ribbing, ridicule, word play.

baptise *v* admit, call, christen, cleanse, dub, enrol, immerse, initiate, introduce, name, purify, recruit, sprinkle, style, term, title.

baptism *n* beginning, christening, début, dedication, immersion, initiation, introduction, launch, launching, purification, sprinkling.

bar¹ *n* barricade, barrier, batten, check, cross-piece, deterrent, deterrment, hindrance, impediment, obstacle, obstruction, pole, preventive, rail, railing, rod, shaft, stake, stanchion, stick, stop.

v ban, barricade, blackball, bolt, debar, exclude, fasten, forbid, hinder, latch, lock, obstruct, preclude, prevent, prohibit, restrain, secure.

bar² *n* boozer, canteen, counter, dive, exchange, gin-palace, honky-tonk, inn, joint, lounge, nineteenth hole, pub, public house, saloon, tavern, vaults, watering-hole.

bar³ *n* advocates, attorneys, barristers, bench, counsel, court, courtroom, dock, law court, tribunal.

bar⁴ *n* block, chunk, ingot, lump, nugget, slab, wedge.

barbarian *n* ape, boor, brute, clod, hooligan, ignoramus, illiterate, lout, lowbrow, oaf, philistine, ruffian, savage, vandal, yahoo.

adj boorish, brutish, coarse, crude, lowbrow, philistine, rough, tramontane, uncivilised, uncouth, uncultivated, uncultured, unsophisticated, vulgar.

barbaric *adj* barbarous, boorish, brutal, brutish, coarse, crude, cruel, ferocious, fierce, inhuman, primitive, rude, savage, uncivilised, uncouth, vulgar, wild. *antonyms* civilised, humane.

barbarism *n* abuse, atrocity, barbarity, brutishness, coarseness, corruption, crudity, cruelty, enormity, misuse, outrage, savagery, solecism, vulgarism.

barbarity *n* barbarousness, boorishness, brutality, brutishness, cruelty, ferocity, inhumanity, rudeness, ruthlessness, savagery, viciousness, wildness. *antonyms* civilisation, civility, humanity.

barbarous *adj* barbarian, barbaric, brutal, brutish, coarse, crude, cruel, ferocious, heartless, ignorant, inhuman, monstrous, philistine, primitive, rough, rude, ruthless, savage, uncivilised, uncouth, uncultured, unrefined, vicious, vulgar, wild. *antonyms* civilised, cultured.

barbed *adj* acerbic, acid, catty, caustic, critical, cutting, hooked, hostile, hurtful, jagged, nasty, pointed, prickly, pronged, snide, spiked, spiny, thorny, toothed, unkind.

bare *adj* austere, bald, barren, basic, blank, defoliate, denuded, empty, essential, explicit, exposed, hard, lacking, literal, mean, naked, nude, open, plain, poor, scanty, scarce, severe, sheer, shorn, simple, spare, stark, stripped, unadorned, unarmed, unclad, unclothed, uncovered, undisguised, undressed, unembellished, unfurnished, unprovided, unsheathed, unvarnished, vacant, void, wanting, woodless.

barefaced *adj* arrant, audacious, bald, blatant, bold, brash, brazen, flagrant, glaring, impudent, insolent, manifest, naked, obvious, open, palpable, patent, shameless, transparent, unabashed, unconcealed.

barely¹ *adv* almost, hardly, just, scarcely, sparingly, sparsely.

barely² *adv* explicitly, nakedly, openly, plainly.

bargain *n* agreement, arrangement, compact, contract, discount, giveaway, negotiation, pact, pledge, promise, reduction, snip, steal, stipulation, transaction, treaty, understanding.

v agree, barter, broke, buy, contract, covenant, deal, haggle, negotiate, promise, sell, stipulate, trade, traffic, transact.

bargain for anticipate, consider, contemplate, expect, foresee, imagine, include, look for, plan for, reckon on.

bargaining *n* barter, bartering, dealing, haggling, horse-trading, negotiation, trading, trafficking, wheeler-dealing.

barge *v* bump, butt in, cannon, collide, elbow, encroach, gatecrash, hit, impinge, interfere, interrupt, intrude, muscle in, push, push in, shove.

bark *n* bawl, bay, growl, shout, snap, snarl, woof, yap, yell, yelp.

v bawl, bay, bluster, cough, growl, shout, snap, snarl, yap, yell, yelp.

barmy *adj* balmy, crazy, daft, dippy, dotty, foolish, idiotic, insane, loony, mad, nuts, nutty, odd, silly, stupid. *antonyms* rational, sane, sensible.

baroque *adj* bizarre, bold, convoluted, elaborate, extravagant, exuberant, fanciful, fantastic, flamboyant, florid, grotesque, ornate, overdecorated, vigorous, whimsical. *antonym* plain.

barrage *n* assault, attack, battery, bombardment, broadside, burst, cannonade, deluge, fusillade, gunfire, hail, mass, onset, onslaught, plethora, profusion, rain, salvo, shelling, shower, storm, stream, torrent, volley.

barred *adj* banned, blackballed, disallowed, excluded, forbidden, outlawed, prohibited, proscribed, taboo. *antonym* permissible.

barren *adj* arid, boring, childless, desert, desolate, dry, dull, empty, flat, fruitless, infertile, lacklustre, pointless, profitless, stale, sterile, uninformative, uninspiring, uninstructive, uninteresting, unproductive, unrewarding, useless, vapid, waste. *antonyms* fertile, productive, useful.

barricade *n* barrier, blockade, bulwark, fence, obstruction, palisade, protection, rampart, screen, stockade.

v bar, block, blockade, defend, fortify, obstruct, palisade, protect, screen.

barrier *n* bail, bar, barricade, blockade, boom, boundary, bulkhead, check, difficulty, ditch, drawback, fence, fortification, handicap, hindrance, hurdle, impediment, limitation, obstacle, obstruction, railing, rampart, restriction, stop, stumbling-block, transverse, wall.

barter *v* bargain, deal, exchange, haggle, negotiate, sell, swap, trade, traffic, truck.

base¹ *n* basis, bed, bottom, camp, centre, core, essence, essential, foot, foundation, fundamental, groundwork, headquarters, heart, home, key, keystone, origin, pedestal, plinth, post, principal, rest, root, settlement, source, stand, standard, starting-point, station, substructure, support, underpinning, understructure.

v build, construct, depend, derive, establish, found, ground, hinge, locate, station.

base² *adj* abject, contemptible, corrupt, counterfeit, depraved, disgraceful, disreputable, evil, grovelling, humble, ignoble, ignominious, immoral, infamous, low, lowly, low-minded, low-thoughted, mean, menial, miserable, paltry, pitiful, poor, scandalous, servile, shameful, slavish, sordid, sorry, valueless, vile, villainous, vulgar, wicked, worthless, wretched.

base³ *adj* adulterated, alloyed, artificial, bastard, counterfeit, debased, fake, forged, fraudulent, impure, inferior, spurious.

baseless *adj* gratuitous, groundless, unattested, unauthenticated, uncalled-for, unconfirmed, uncorroborated, unfounded, ungrounded, unjustifiable, unjustified, unsubstantiated, unsupported. *antonym* justifiable.

baseness *n* contemptibility, degradation, depravity, ignominy, infamy, knavery, lowliness, meanness, misery, poverty, servility, slavishness, sordidness, sorriness, subservience, turpitude, vileness, villainy, worthlessness, wretchedness.

bash *v* belt, biff, break, crash, crush, dunt, hit, punch, slosh, slug, smack, smash, sock, strike, swipe, wallop.

n attempt, crack, go, shot, stab, try, turn, whirl.

bashful *adj* abashed, backward, blushing, confused, coy, diffident, embarrassed, hesitant, inhibited, modest, nervous, reserved, reticent, retiring, self-conscious, self-effacing, shamefaced, sheepish, shrinking, shy, timid, timorous, unforthcoming. *antonym* confident.

bashfulness *n* coyness, diffidence, embarrassment, hesitancy, inhibition, modesty, reserve, self-consciousness, shamefacedness, sheepishness, shyness, timidity, timorousness. *antonym* confidence.

basic *adj* central, elementary, essential, fundamental, important, indispensable, inherent, intrinsic, key, necessary, primary, radical, root, underlying, vital. *antonyms* inessential, peripheral.

basically *adv* at bottom, at heart, essentially, fundamentally, inherently, intrinsically, primarily, principally, radically.

basics *n* bedrock, brass tacks, core, essentials, facts, fundamentals, grass roots, necessaries, nitty-gritty, nuts and bolts, practicalities, principles, rock bottom, rudiments.

basis *n* approach, base, bottom, core, essential, fond, footing, foundation, fundamental, ground, groundwork, heart, keynote, pedestal, premise, principle, support, thrust.

bask *v* delight in, enjoy, laze, lie, lounge, luxuriate, relax, relish, revel, savour, sunbathe, wallow.

bastard *n* git, love child, love-child, mother-fucker, natural child, whoreson. *adj* abnormal, adulterated, anomalous, artificial, base, baseborn, counterfeit, false, illegitimate, imperfect, impure, inferior, irregular, misbegotten, sham, spurious, synthetic. *antonyms* genuine, legitimate.

bastardise *v* adulterate, cheapen, corrupt, debase, defile, degrade, demean, depreciate, devalue, distort, pervert, vitiate.

bastion *n* bulwark, citadel, defence, fastness, fortress, mainstay, pillar, prop, rock, stronghold, support, tower of strength.

batch *n* amount, assemblage, assortment, bunch, collection, consignment, contingent, group, lot, pack, parcel, quantity, set.

bathe *v* cleanse, cover, dunk, flood, immerse, moisten, rinse, soak, steep, stew, suffuse, swim, wash, wet. *n* dip, rinse, soak, swim, wash.

batter *v* abuse, assault, bash, beat, belabour, bruise, buffet, crush, dash, deface, demolish, destroy, disfigure, distress, hurt, injure, lash, mangle, manhandle, mar, maul, pelt, pound, pummel, ruin, shatter, smash, thrash, wallop.

battered *adj* abused, beaten, bruised, crumbling, crushed, damaged, dilapidated, ill-treated, injured, ramshackle, tumbledown, weather-beaten.

battery *n* artillery, assault, attack, barrage, beating, cannon, guns, mayhem, onslaught, progression, sequence, series, set, thrashing, violence.

battle *n* action, attack, campaign, clash, combat, conflict, contest, controversy, crusade, debate, disagreement, dispute, encounter, engagement, fight, fray, hostilities, row, skirmish, stour, strife, struggle, war, warfare. *v* agitate, argue, campaign, clamour, combat, contend, contest, crusade, dispute, feud, fight, strive, struggle, war.

battle-axe *n* disciplinarian, harridan, martinet, Tartar, termagant, virago.

battle-cry *n* catchword, motto, slogan, war cry, warsong, watchword.

batty *adj* barmy, bats, bonkers, cracked, crackers, crazy, daffy, daft, demented, dippy, dotty, eccentric, idiotic, insane, loony, lunatic, mad, nuts, nutty, odd, off one's rocker, peculiar, potty, queer, screwy, touched. *antonym* sane.

bauble *n* bagatelle, gewgaw, gimcrack, knick-knack, plaything, toy, trifle, trinket.

baulk, balk *v* baffle, bar, boggle, check, counteract, defeat, demur, disconcert, dodge, evade, flinch, foil, forestall, frustrate, hesitate, hinder, jib, make difficulties, obstruct, prevent, recoil, refuse, resist, shirk, shrink, stall, thwart.

bawdy *adj* blue, coarse, dirty, erotic, gross, improper, indecent, indecorous, indelicate, lascivious, lecherous, lewd, libidinous, licentious, lustful, obscene, pornographic, prurient, ribald, risqué, rude, salacious, smutty, suggestive, vulgar. *antonyms* chaste, clean.

bawl *v* bellow, blubber, call, caterwaul, clamour, cry, halloo, howl, roar, shout, sob, squall, vociferate, wail, weep, yell.

be *v* abide, arise, befall, breathe, come about, come to pass, continue, develop, dwell, endure, exist, happen, inhabit, inhere, last, live, obtain, occur, persist, prevail, remain, reside, stand, stay, survive, take place.

beach *n* coast, foreshore, lido, littoral, margin, sand, sands, seaboard, seashore, seaside, shingle, shore, strand, water's edge.

beam *n* arbor, bar, boom, girder, gleam, glimmer, glint, glow, joist, plank, radiation, rafter, ray, shaft, spar, stanchion, stream, support, timber, transom. *v* broadcast, emit, glare, glimmer, glitter, glow, grin, laugh, radiate, shine, smile, transmit.

beaming *adj* beautiful, bright, brilliant, cheerful, effulgent, flashing, gleaming, glistening, glittering, glowing, grinning, happy, joyful, lambent, radiant, scintillating, shining, smiling, sparkling, sunny. *antonyms* lowering, sullen.

bear[1] *v* abide, admit, allow, beget, bring, brook, carry, cherish, convey, endure, entertain, exhibit, hack, harbour, have, hold, maintain, move, permit, possess, put up with, shoulder, stomach, suffer, support, sustain, take, tolerate, tote, transport, undergo, uphold, weather, weigh upon.

bear down advance on, approach, attack, burden, close in, compress, converge on, encumber, near, oppress, press down, push, strain, weigh down.

bear in mind be cognisant of, be mindful of, beware, consider, heed, include, mind out for, note, remember.

bear on affect, appertain to, concern, connect with, involve, pertain to, refer to, relate to, touch on.

bear oneself acquit oneself, act, behave, comport oneself, demean oneself, deport oneself, perform.

bear out confirm, corroborate, demonstrate, endorse, justify, prove, substantiate, support, testify, uphold, vindicate.

bear up carry on, endure, keep one's pecker up, persevere, soldier on, suffer, withstand.

bear with be patient with, endure, forbear, make allowances for, put up with, suffer, tolerate.

bear witness attest, confirm, corroborate, demonstrate, depose, evidence, evince, prove, show, testify, testify to, vouch for.

bear[2] *v* breed, bring forth, develop, drop, engender, generate, give birth to, give up, produce, propagate, yield.

bearable *adj* acceptable, endurable, livable(-with), manageable, sufferable, supportable, sustainable, tolerable.

bearded *adj* bewhiskered, bristly, bushy, hairy, hirsute, shaggy, tufted, unshaven, whiskered. *antonyms* beardless, clean-shaven, smooth.

bearer *n* beneficiary, carrier, conveyor, courier, holder, messenger, payee, porter, possessor, post, runner, servant.

bearing *n* air, application, aspect, attitude, behaviour, carriage, comportment, connection, course, demeanour, deportment, direction, import, manner, pertinence, poise, posture, presence, reference, relation, relevance, significance.

beast *n* animal, ape, barbarian, brute, creature, devil, fiend, monster, pig, sadist, savage, swine.

beastly *adj* barbarous, bestial, brutal, brutish, coarse, cruel, depraved, disagreeable, foul, inhuman, mean, monstrous, nasty, repulsive, rotten, sadistic, savage, sensual, swinish, terrible, unpleasant, vile.

beat[1] *v* bang, bash, baste, batter, belabour, bludgeon, bruise, buffet, cane, contuse, cudgel, drub, dunt, fashion, flog, forge, form, hammer, hit, impinge, knobble, knock, knout, lash, lay into, maul, mill, model, pelt, pound, punch, shape, slat, strap, strike, swipe, tan, thrash, thwack, trounce, warm, welt, whale, wham, whip, work.

n blow, hit, lash, punch, shake, slap, strike, swing, thump.

adj exhausted, fatigued, jiggered, tired, wearied, worn out, zonked.

beat it go away, hop it, leave, scarper, scram, shoo, skedaddle, vamoose.

beat up assault, attack, batter, do over, duff up, fill in, hammer, knock about, knock around, thrash.

beat[2] *v* conquer, defeat, excel, hammer, outdo, outrun, outstrip, overcome, overwhelm, slaughter, subdue, surpass, trounce, vanquish.

beat[3] *v* flutter, palpitate, patter, pound, pulsate, pulse, quake, quiver, race, shake, throb, thump, tremble, vibrate.

n accent, cadence, flutter, measure, metre, palpitation, pulsation, pulse, rhyme, rhythm, stress, throb, time.

beat[4] *n* circuit, course, journey, path, round, rounds, route, territory, way.

beaten[1] *adj* baffled, cowed, defeated, disappointed, disheartened, frustrated, overcome, ruined, surpassed, thwarted, vanquished.

beaten[2] *adj* fashioned, forged, formed, hammered, shaped, stamped, worked.

beatify *v* bless, exalt, glorify, sanctify.

beating *n* belting, caning, chastisement, conquest, corporal punishment, defeat, downfall, dressing, drubbing, flogging, laldie, overthrow, rout, ruin, slapping, smacking, thrashing, warming, whaling, whipping.

adj pounding, pulsating, pulsing, racing, throbbing, thumping.

beatitude *n* beatification, blessedness, bliss, ecstasy, exaltation, felicity, happiness, holiness, joy, saintliness, sanctity.

beau *n* admirer, Adonis, boyfriend, escort, fancy man, fiancé, ladies' man, lover, suitor, sweetheart, swell.

beautiful *adj* alluring, appealing, attractive, beauteous, charming, comely, delightful, exquisite, fair, fine, good-looking, gorgeous, graceful, handsome, lovely, pleasing, radiant, ravishing, stunning. **antonyms** plain, ugly.

beautify *v* adorn, array, bedeck, deck, decorate, embellish, enhance, garnish, gild, glamorise, grace, improve, ornament, tart up, titivate. **antonyms** disfigure, spoil.

beauty¹ *n* allure, attractiveness, bloom, charm, comeliness, elegance, excellence, exquisiteness, fairness, glamour, grace, handsomeness, loveliness, pleasure, seemliness, symmetry. **antonym** ugliness.

beauty² *n* belle, charmer, corker, cracker, femme fatale, goddess, good-looker, knockout, lovely, siren, stunner. **antonym** frump.

because *conj* as, by reason of, for, forasmuch, in that, inasmuch as, on account of, owing to, since, thanks to.

beckon *v* allure, attract, bid, call, coax, decoy, draw, entice, gesticulate, gesture, invite, lure, motion, nod, pull, signal, summon, tempt, waft.

become *v* befit, behove, embellish, enhance, fit, flatter, grace, harmonise, ornament, set off, suit.

becoming *adj* appropriate, attractive, befitting, charming, comely, compatible, decent, decorous, enhancing, fit, fitting, flattering, graceful, maidenly, meet, neat, pretty, proper, seemly, suitable, tasteful, worthy.

bedeck *v* adorn, array, beautify, decorate, embellish, festoon, garnish, ornament, trick out, trim. **antonym** strip.

bedevil *v* afflict, annoy, besiege, confound, distress, fret, frustrate, harass, irk, irritate, pester, plague, tease, torment, torture, trouble, vex, worry.

bedlam *n* anarchy, babel, chaos, clamour, commotion, confusion, furore, hubbub, hullabaloo, madhouse, noise, pandemonium, tumult, turmoil, uproar. **antonym** calm.

bedraggled *adj* dirty, dishevelled, disordered, messy, muddied, muddy, scruffy, slovenly, sodden, soiled, stained, sullied, unkempt, untidy. **antonym** tidy.

beef¹ *n* beefiness, brawn, bulk, flesh, fleshiness, heftiness, muscle, robustness, sinew, strength.

beef² *n* complaint, criticism, dispute, dissatisfaction, grievance, gripe, grouse, grumble, objection, protest.
v complain, criticise, gripe, grumble, moan, object. **antonym** approve.

beefy *adj* brawny, bulky, burly, corpulent, fat, fleshy, heavy, hefty, hulking, muscular, plump, podgy, pudgy, rotund, stalwart, stocky, strapping, sturdy. **antonym** slight.

beetle *v* dash, hurry, nip, run, rush, scamper, scoot, scurry, tear, zip.

beetling *adj* jutting, overhanging, pendent, poking, projecting, prominent, protruding.

befall *v* arrive, betide, chance, ensue, fall, follow, happen, materialise, occur, take place.

befitting *adj* appropriate, becoming, correct, decent, fit, fitting, meet, proper, right, seemly, suitable. **antonym** unbecoming.

before *adv* ahead, earlier, formerly, in advance, in front, previously, sooner. **antonyms** after, later.
prep ahead of, earlier than, in advance of, in anticipation of, in front of, in preparation for, previous to, prior to, sooner than.
conj in case, rather than.

beforehand *adv* already, before, earlier, in advance, preliminarily, previously, sooner.

befriend *v* aid, assist, back, benefit, comfort, encourage, favour, help, patronise, stand by, succour, support, sustain, take a liking to, take under one's wing, uphold, welcome. **antonym** neglect.

befuddled *adj* baffled, bewildered, confused, dazed, fuddled, groggy, hazy, inebriated, intoxicated, muddled, woozy. **antonym** lucid.

beg *v* beseech, cadge, crave, desire, entreat, implore, importune, petition, plead, pray, request, require, scrounge, solicit, sponge on, supplicate, touch.
beg the question avoid, dodge, duck, equivocate, evade, hedge, shirk, shun, side-step, take for granted.

beget *v* breed, bring, cause, create, effect, engender, father, generate, get, give rise to, occasion, procreate, produce, propagate, result in, sire, spawn.

beggar¹ *n* cadger, down-and-out, mendicant, pauper, scrounger, sponger, starveling, supplicant, toe-rag, tramp, vagrant.

beggar² v baffle, challenge, defy, exceed, surpass, transcend.

beggarly adj abject, contemptible, despicable, destitute, impoverished, inadequate, indigent, low, meagre, mean, miserly, needy, niggardly, paltry, pathetic, penurious, pitiful, poor, poverty-stricken, stingy, vile, wretched. *antonyms* affluent, generous.

begging adj beseeching, entreating, imploring, pleading.
n cadging, entreaty, mendicancy, mendicity, petitioning, prayers, scrounging, soliciting, sponging, supplication.

begin v activate, actuate, appear, arise, commence, crop up, dawn, emerge, happen, inaugurate, initiate, instigate, institute, introduce, originate, prepare, set about, set in, spring, start. *antonyms* end, finish.

beginner n amateur, apprentice, fledgling, freshman, greenhorn, initiate, learner, novice, recruit, rookie, rooky, starter, student, trainee. *antonyms* expert, old hand, veteran.

beginning n birth, commencement, embryo, establishment, fountainhead, germ, inauguration, inception, initiation, introduction, onset, opening, origin, outset, preface, prelude, prime, rise, root, rudiments, seed, source, start, starting point. *antonyms* end, finish.
adj early, elementary, inaugural, incipient, initial, introductory, nascent, primal, primary, primeval.

beguile v amuse, charm, cheat, cheer, cozen, deceive, delight, delude, distract, divert, dupe, engross, entertain, fool, hoodwink, mislead, occupy, pass, solace, trick, wile.

beguiling adj alluring, appealing, attractive, bewitching, captivating, charming, diverting, enchanting, entertaining, enticing, interesting, intriguing. *antonyms* offensive, repulsive.

behave v acquit, act, bear, comport, conduct, demean, deport, function, operate, perform, react, respond, run, work.

behaviour n action, actions, bearing, carriage, comportment, conduct, dealings, demeanour, deportment, doings, functioning, habits, manner, manners, operation, performance, reaction, response, ways.

behest n authority, bidding, charge, command, commandment, decre, dictate, direction, fiat, injunctio, instruction, mandate, order, ordinanc, precept, wish.

behind prep after, backing, causin, following, for, initiating, instigatin, later than, responsible for, supporting.
adv after, afterwards, behindhan, following, in arrears, in debt, in the wal, of, next, overdue, subsequently.
n backside, bottom, butt, buttock, derrière, posterior, rear, rump, seat, tail
behind one's back covertl, deceitfully, secretly, sneakil, surreptitiously, treacherously.
behind the times antiquated, date, obsolete, old hat, old-fashioned, out date, outdated, outmoded, passé, square

behold v consider, contemplate, discer, espy, eye, look at, note, observ, perceive, regard, scan, survey, view, watch, witness.
interj lo, look, mark, observe, se, watch.

beholden adj bound, grateful, indebte, obligated, obliged, owing, thankful.

behove v advance, be to one, advantage, befit, benefit, beseem, profi

beige adj biscuit, buff, camel, coffe, cream, ecru, fawn, mushroom, neutra, oatmeal, sand.

being¹ n actuality, animation, entity, essence, existence, life, living, natur, reality, soul, spirit, substance.

being² n animal, beast, body, creature, human being, individual, morta, sentient, thing.

belabour v attack, bash, batter, bea, belt, berate, castigate, censure, chastis, criticise, flay, flog, lambast, lay int, thrash, whip.

belated adj behind-hand, delayed, late, overdue, retarded, tardy, unpunctual. *antonyms* punctual, timely.

beleaguered adj badgered, bese, besieged, bothered, harassed, hedge, about, hedged in, persecuted, plague, surrounded, vexed, worried.

belie v conceal, confute, contradic, deceive, deny, disguise, disprove, falsif, gainsay, mislead, misrepresent, negate, refute, repudiate, run counter t, understate. *antonym* attest.

belief n assurance, confidence, conviction, credence, credit, credo, creed, doctrine, dogma, expectation, faith, feeling, ideology, impression, intuition, ism, judgement, notion, opinion, persuasion, presumption principle, principles, reliance, sureness, tenet, theory, trust, view. **antonym** disbelief.

believable adj acceptable, authentic, authoritative, conceivable, credible, creditable, imaginable, likely, plausible, possible, probable, reliable, thinkable, trustworthy. **antonym** unconvincing.

believe v accept, assume, be under the impression, conjecture, consider, count on, credit, deem, depend on, gather, guess, hold, imagine, judge, maintain, postulate, presume, reckon, rely on, speculate, suppose, swallow, swear by, think, trust, wear. **antonym** disbelieve.

believer n adherent, convert, devotee, disciple, follower, supporter, upholder. **antonyms** apostate, sceptic, unbeliever.

belittle v decry, deprecate, depreciate, deride, derogate, detract, diminish, dismiss, disparage, downgrade, lessen, minimise, ridicule, run down, scorn, underestimate, underrate, undervalue. **antonym** exaggerate.

bellicose adj aggressive, antagonistic, argumentative, belligerent, combative, contentious, defiant, hawkish, hostile, jingoistic, militant, militaristic, provocative, pugnacious, quarrelsome, sabre-rattling, warlike, war-loving, warmongering. **antonym** peaceable.

belligerent adj aggressive, antagonistic, argumentative, bellicose, bullying, combative, contentious, forceful, militant, pugnacious, quarrelsome, violent, warlike, warring. **antonym** peaceable.

belong v attach to, be connected with, be part of, be relevant to, be tied to, fit, go with, inhere, link up with, pertain to, relate to, tie up with.

belonging n acceptance, affinity, association, attachment, closeness, compatibility, fellow-feeling, fellowship, inclusion, kinship, link, linkage, loyalty, rapport, relationship. **antonym** antipathy.

belonging to affiliated to, associated with, essential to, held by, included in, inherent in, intrinsic to, native to, owned by. **antonym** alien to.

belongings n accoutrements, chattels, effects, gear, goods, paraphernalia, possessions, stuff, things.

beloved adj admired, adored, cherished, darling, dear, dearest, favourite, loved, pet, precious, prized, revered, sweet, treasured.

n adored, darling, dear, dearest, favourite, lover, pet, precious, sweet, sweetheart.

below adv beneath, down, infra, lower, lower down, under, underneath.

prep inferior to, lesser than, subject to, subordinate to, under, underneath, unworthy of.

below par below average, imperfect, inferior, lacking, not oneself, off, off-colour, off-form, poor, poorly, second-rate, substandard, under the weather, unfit, unhealthy, wanting.

below the belt cowardly, dirty, dishonest, foul, unfair, unjust, unscrupulous, unsporting, unsportsmanlike.

belt[1] n area, band, cincture, district, girdle, girth, layer, region, strait, stretch, strip, tract, waistband, zone.

v circle, encircle, girdle, ring, surround.

belt up be quiet, cut it out, leave it out, put a sock in it, shut one's mouth, shut up, stow it.

belt[2] v bolt, career, charge, dash, hurry, race, rush, speed.

bemoan v bewail, deplore, grieve for, lament, mourn, regret, rue, sigh for, sorrow over, weep for. **antonym** gloat.

bemused adj absent-minded, befuddled, bewildered, confused, dazed, distracted, engrossed, fuddled, muddled, mused, perplexed, stunned, stupefied. **antonyms** clear, clear-headed, lucid.

benchmark n criterion, example, level, model, norm, reference, reference-point, standard, touchstone, yardstick.

bend v aim, bow, brace, buckle, compel, constrain, contort, couch, crankle, crimp, crouch, curve, deflect, direct, dispose, diverge, dog-leg, fasten, flex, incline, influence, lean, mould, nerve, persuade, shape, stoop, string, subdue, submit, sway, swerve, turn, twist, veer, warp, yield.

n angle, arc, bight, bow, corner, crook, curvature, curve, dog-leg, elbow, hook, loop, turn, twist, zigzag.

beneath adv below, lower, lower down, under, underneath.

prep below, inferior to, infra dig(nitatem), lower than, subject to, subordinate to, unbefitting, under, underneath, unworthy of.

benediction n beatitude, blessing, consecration, favour, grace, invocation, prayer, thanksgiving. **antonyms** anathema, curse, execration.

benefactor n angel, backer, contributor, donor, endower, friend, helper, patron, philanthropist, promoter, provider, sponsor, subscriber, subsidiser, supporter, well-wisher. **antonyms** opponent, persecutor.

beneficent *adj* altruistic, benevolent, benign, bounteous, bountiful, charitable, compassionate, generous, helpful, kind, liberal, munificent, unselfish. **antonym** mean.

beneficial *adj* advantageous, benign, edifying, favourable, gainful, healthful, helpful, improving, nourishing, nutritious, profitable, restorative, rewarding, salubrious, salutary, serviceable, useful, valuable, wholesome. **antonym** harmful.

beneficiary *n* assignee, heir, heiress, inheritor, legatee, payee, receiver, recipient, successor.

benefit *n* advantage, aid, asset, assistance, avail, betterment, blessing, boon, favour, gain, good, help, interest, plus, profit, service, use, welfare. **antonym** harm.

v advance, advantage, aid, ameliorate, amend, assist, avail, better, enhance, further, improve, profit, promote, serve. **antonyms** harm, hinder, undermine.

benefits *n* advantages, bonuses, extras, freebies, perks, perquisites, pluses. **antonym** disadvantages.

benevolence *n* altruism, bounty, charity, compassion, fellow-feeling, generosity, goodness, goodwill, humanity, kind-heartedness, kindliness, kindness, munificence, sympathy. **antonym** meanness.

benevolent *adj* altruistic, beneficent, benign, bounteous, bountiful, caring, charitable, compassionate, considerate, generous, good-will, humane, humanitarian, kind, kind-hearted, kindly, liberal, loving, philanthropic, solicitous, well-disposed. **antonym** mean.

benign *adj* advantageous, amiable, auspicious, balmy, beneficent, beneficial, benevolent, complaisant, curable, curative, encouraging, favourable, friendly, generous, genial, gentle, good, gracious, harmless, healthful, kind, kindly, liberal, lucky, mild, obliging, propitious, refreshing, restorative, salubrious, salutary, sympathetic, temperate, warm, wholesome. **antonyms** harmful, hostile, malign, malignant.

bent *adj* angled, arched, bowed, criminal, crooked, curved, dishonest, doubled, folded, homosexual, hunched, retorted, stolen, stooped, twisted, untrustworthy. **antonym** straight.

n ability, aptitude, capacity, facility, faculty, flair, forte, gift, inclination, knack, leaning, penchant, preference, proclivity, propensity, talent, tendency.

bent on determined, disposed, fixed, heading for, inclined, insistent, resolved, set on.

bequeath *v* assign, bestow, commit, devise, endow, entrust, gift, give, grant, hand down, impart, pass on, settle, transmit, will.

bequest *n* bestowal, donation, dower, endowment, estate, gift, heritage, inheritance, legacy, patrimony, settlement, trust.

berate *v* castigate, censure, chastise, chide, criticise, jump down the throat of, rail at, rebuke, reprimand, reproach, reprove, revile, scold, tell off, upbraid. **antonym** praise.

bereft *adj* denuded, deprived, despoiled, destitute, devoid, lacking, minus, robbed, shorn, stripped, wanting.

berserk *adj* amok, crazy, demented, deranged, enraged, frantic, frenetic, frenzied, furious, insane, mad, maniacal, manic, rabid, raging, raving, uncontrollable, violent, wild. **antonym** calm, sane.

berth *n* anchorage, bed, billet, bunk, cot, dock, hammock, harbour, harbourage, haven, landfall, pier, port, quay, shelter, slip, wharf.

v anchor, dock, drop anchor, land, moor, tie up. **antonym** weigh anchor.

beseech *v* adjure, ask, beg, call on, conjure, crave, desire, entreat, implore, importune, petition, plead, pray, solicit, sue, supplicate.

beset *v* assail, attack, badger, bamboozle, bedevil, besiege, embarrass, encircle, enclose, encompass, entangle, environ, faze, harass, hassle, hem in, perplex, pester, plague, surround.

beside *prep* abreast of, abutting on, adjacent, bordering on, close to, near, neighbouring, next door to, next to, overlooking, upsides with.

beside oneself berserk, crazed, delirious, demented, deranged, distracted, distraught, frantic, frenetic, frenzied, furious, insane, mad, unbalanced, unhinged.

beside the point extraneous, immaterial, inapplicable, incidental, inconsequential, irrelevant, pointless, unimportant, unrelated. **antonym** relevant.

besides *adv* additionally, also, as well

extra, further, furthermore, in addition, into the bargain, moreover, otherwise, to boot, too.

prep apart from, in addition to, other than, over and above.

besiege *v* assail, badger, belay, beleaguer, beset, blockade, bother, confine, encircle, encompass, environ, harass, harry, hound, importune, nag, pester, plague, surround, trouble.

besmirch *v* daub, defame, defile, dirty, dishonour, muddy, slander, smear, soil, spatter, stain, sully, tarnish. **antonym** enhance.

besotted *adj* befuddled, bewitched, confused, doting, foolish, hypnotised, infatuated, intoxicated, muddled, obsessed, smitten. **antonyms** disenchanted, indifferent, sober.

best *adj* advantageous, apt, correct, excellent, finest, first, first-class, first-rate, foremost, greatest, highest, incomparable, largest, leading, matchless, optimal, optimum, outstanding, perfect, pre-eminent, preferable, principal, right, superlative, supreme, transcendent, unequalled, unsurpassed. **antonym** worst.

adv excellently, exceptionally, extremely, greatly, superlatively, surpassingly. **antonym** worst.

n choice, cream, crème de la crème, élite, favourite, finest, first, flower, hardest, pick, prime, the tops, top, utmost. **antonym** worst.

v beat, conquer, defeat, get the better of, have the laugh of, lick, outclass, outdo, outwit, surpass, thrash, trounce, vanquish, worst.

bestial *adj* animal, barbaric, barbarous, beastly, brutal, brutish, carnal, degraded, depraved, gross, inhuman, savage, sensual, sordid, subhuman, vile. **antonyms** civilised, humane.

bestir *v* activate, actuate, animate, arouse, awaken, energise, exert, galvanise, incite, motivate, rouse, stimulate. **antonyms** calm, lull, quell.

bestow *v* accord, allot, apportion, award, bequeath, commit, confer, donate, dower, endow, entrust, give, grant, impart, lavish, lend, present, transmit. **antonym** deprive.

bet *n* accumulator, ante, bid, flutter, gamble, hazard, pledge, risk, speculation, stake, venture, wager.

v ante, bid, chance, gamble, hazard, lay, pledge, punt, risk, speculate, stake, venture, wager.

betide *v* bechance, befall, chance, develop, ensue, happen, occur, overtake.

betimes *adv* early, expeditiously, punctually, seasonably, soon, speedily. **antonym** late.

betoken *v* augur, bode, declare, denote, evidence, forebode, import, indicate, manifest, mark, portend, presage, prognosticate, promise, represent, signify, suggest.

betray *v* abandon, beguile, corrupt, deceive, delude, desert, disclose, discover, divulge, double-cross, dupe, ensnare, entrap, evince, expose, forsake, give away, grass, inform on, jilt, manifest, mislead, reveal, seduce, sell, sell down the river, sell out, shop, show, tell, turn Queen's (King's) evidence, undo. **antonyms** defend, fulfil, protect.

betrayal *n* deception, disclosure, discovery, disloyalty, divulgence, double-dealing, duplicity, exposure, falseness, Judas-kiss, perfidy, ratting, revelation, sell-out, treachery, treason, trickery, unfaithfulness. **antonyms** loyalty, protection.

betroth *v* affiance, contract, espouse, plight one's troth, promise.

better *adj* bigger, cured, finer, fitter, greater, healthier, improving, larger, longer, on the mend, preferable, progressing, recovered, recovering, restored, stronger, superior, surpassing, worthier. **antonym** worse.

v advance, ameliorate, amend, beat, cap, correct, enhance, exceed, excel, forward, further, go one further than, improve, improve on, increase, mend, outdo, outstrip, overtake, promote, raise, rectify, redress, reform, strengthen, surpass, top, transcend. **antonyms** deteriorate, worsen.

betterment *n* advancement, amelioration, edification, enhancement, furtherance, improvement. **antonyms** deterioration, impairment.

between *prep* amidst, among, amongst, betwixt, inter-, mid.

between ourselves entre nous, in confidence, in secret, privately, within these four walls.

bevy *n* band, bunch, collection, company, crowd, flock, gaggle, gathering, group, pack, throng, troupe.

bewail *v* bemoan, cry over, deplore, greet, grieve for, keen, lament, moan, mourn, regret, repent, rue, sigh over, sorrow over. **antonyms** gloat, glory, vaunt.

beware v avoid, give a wide berth to, guard against, heed, look out, mind, shun, steer clear of, take heed, watch out. **antonym** court.

bewilder v baffle, bamboozle, befuddle, bemuse, confound, confuse, daze, disconcert, disorient, fuddle, maze, muddle, mystify, perplex, puzzle, stupefy, tie in knots.

bewildered adj awed, baffled, bamboozled, bemused, confused, disconcerted, disoriented, dizzy, giddy, muddled, mystified, nonplussed, perplexed, puzzled, stunned, surprised, uncertain. **antonyms** collected, unperturbed.

bewitch v allure, attract, beguile, captivate, charm, enchant, enrapture, entrance, fascinate, hypnotise, jinx, obsess, possess, spellbind.

bewitched adj charmed, enchanted, enthralled, entranced, fascinated, jinxed, mesmerised, obsessed, possessed, spellbound, transfixed, transformed.

bewitching adj beguiling, charming, enchanting, entrancing, fascinating, glamorous, hypnotic, intriguing, seductive, tantalising, witching. **antonym** repellent.

beyond prep above, across, apart from, away from, before, further than, out of range, out of reach of, over, past, remote from, superior to, yonder.

beyond price inestimable, invaluable, irreplaceable, precious, priceless.

bias n angle, bent, bigotry, distortion, favouritism, inclination, intolerance, leaning, one-sidedness, partiality, predilection, predisposition, prejudice, proclivity, proneness, propensity, slant, tendency, tendentiousness, turn, unfairness, viewiness. **antonyms** fairness, impartiality.
v angle, distort, influence, jaundice, load, load the dice, predispose, prejudice, slant, sway, twist, warp, weight.

biased adj angled, bigoted, blinkered, distorted, embittered, jaundiced, loaded, one-sided, partial, predisposed, prejudiced, slanted, swayed, tendentious, twisted, unfair, warped, weighted. **antonyms** fair, impartial.

bicker v altercate, argue, clash, disagree, dispute, feud, fight, quarrel, row, scrap, spar, squabble, wrangle. **antonym** agree.

bid v ask, call, charge, command, desire, direct, enjoin, greet, instruct, invite, offer, proclaim, propose, request, require, say, solicit, summon, tell, wish.
n advance, amount, ante, attempt, crack, effort, endeavour, go, offer, price, proposal, proposition, submission, sum, tender, try, venture.

biddable adj acquiescent, agreeable, amenable, complaisant, co-operative, docile, obedient, responsive, teachable, tractable. **antonym** recalcitrant.

bidding n behest, call, charge, command, demand, dictate, direction, injunction, instruction, invitation, order, request, requirement, summons.

big adj adult, altruistic, beefy, benevolent, boastful, bombastic, bulky, burly, buxom, colossal, considerable, corpulent, elder, elephantine, eminent, enormous, extensive, gargantuan, generous, gigantic, gracious, great, grown, grown-up, heroic, huge, hulking, immense, important, influential, large, leading, lofty, magnanimous, main, mammoth, man-sized, massive, mature, momentous, noble, paramount, ponderous, powerful, prime, principal, prodigious, prominent, serious, significant, sizable, spacious, stout, substantial, titanic, tolerant, unselfish, valuable, vast, voluminous, weighty. **antonyms** little, small.

big shot big noise, bigwig, celebrity, dignitary, heavyweight, mogul, nob, notable, panjandrum, personage, somebody, VIP. **antonym** nonentity.

bigot n chauvinist, dogmatist, fanatic, racist, sectarian, sexist, zealot. **antonyms** humanitarian, liberal.

bigoted adj biased, blinkered, chauvinist, closed, dogmatic, illiberal, intolerant, narrow, narrow-minded, obstinate, opinionated, prejudiced, sectarian, twisted, verkrampte, warped. **antonyms** broad-minded, enlightened, liberal.

bigotry n bias, chauvinism, discrimination, dogmatism, fanaticism, ignorance, illiberality, injustice, intolerance, jingoism, mindlessness, narrow-mindedness, prejudice, racialism, racism, sectarianism, sexism.

bigwig n big gun, big noise, big shot, celebrity, dignitary, heavyweight, mogul, nob, notable, panjandrum, personage, somebody, VIP. **antonym** nobody.

bile n anger, bitterness, gall, ill-humour, irascibility, irritability, peevishness, rancour, spleen, testiness.

bill *n* account, advertisement, broadsheet, bulletin, card, catalogue, charges, chit, circular, greenback, handbill, hand-out, inventory, invoice, leaflet, legislation, list, listing, measure, note, notice, placard, playbill, poster, programme, proposal, reckoning, roster, schedule, score, sheet, statement, syllabus, tab, tally.
v advertise, announce, charge, debit, invoice, list, post, reckon, record.

billow *v* balloon, belly, expand, fill out, heave, puff out, roll, seethe, spread, surge, swell, undulate.

bind *v* attach, bandage, border, clamp, compel, complain, confine, constipate, constrain, cover, detain, dress, edge, encase, engage, fasten, finish, force, glue, hamper, harden, hinder, hitch, lash, necessitate, obligate, oblige, prescribe, require, restrain, restrict, rope, seal, secure, stick, strap, swathe, tie, trim, truss, wrap.
n bore, difficulty, dilemma, embarrassment, hole, impasse, nuisance, predicament, quandary.

binding *adj* compulsory, conclusive, imperative, indissoluble, irrevocable, mandatory, necessary, obligatory, permanent, requisite, strict, unalterable, unbreakable.
n bandage, border, covering, edging, stricture, tape, trimming, wrapping.

binge *n* banquet, beano, bender, bout, do, feast, fling, guzzle, orgy, spree. *antonym* fast.

biography *n* account, adventures, autobiography, biopic, curriculum vitae, exposé, fortunes, history, life, life story, memoir, memoirs, recollections, record.

birth *n* ancestry, background, beginning, birthright, blood, breeding, childbirth, delivery, derivation, descent, emergence, extraction, family, genealogy, genesis, line, lineage, nativity, nobility, origin, parentage, pedigree, race, rise, source, stock, strain.

birthplace *n* fount, incunabula, native country, native town, place of origin, provenance, roots, source.

bisexual *adj* androgynous, epicene, hermaphrodite. *antonyms* heterosexual, homosexual.

bit *n* atom, chip, crumb, fragment, grain, instant, iota, jiffy, jot, minute, mite, moment, morsel, part, period, piece, scrap, second, segment, sippet, slice, snippet, speck, spell, tick, time, while, whit.

bit by bit gradually, insidiously, little by little, piecemeal, step by step. *antonym* wholesale.

bitchy *adj* back-biting, catty, cruel, malicious, mean, nasty, poisonous, snide, spiteful, venomous, vicious, vindictive, waspish. *antonym* kind.

bite *v* burn, champ, chew, clamp, corrode, crunch, crush, cut, gnaw, nibble, nip, pierce, pinch, rend, seize, smart, snap, sting, tear, tingle, wound.
n edge, food, grip, kick, morsel, mouthful, nip, piece, pinch, piquancy, prick, punch, pungency, refreshment, smarting, snack, spice, sting, taste, wound.

bite the dust crumple, die, drop, drop dead, fall, perish.

biting *adj* astringent, bitter, blighting, caustic, cold, cutting, cynical, freezing, harsh, hurtful, incisive, mordant, nipping, penetrating, piercing, raw, sarcastic, scathing, severe, sharp, stinging, tart, trenchant, withering. *antonyms* bland, mild.

bitter *adj* acerbic, acid, acrid, acrimonious, astringent, begrudging, biting, calamitous, crabbed, cruel, cynical, dire, distressing, embittered, fierce, freezing, galling, grievous, harsh, hateful, heartbreaking, hostile, intense, ironic, jaundiced, merciless, morose, odious, painful, poignant, rancorous, raw, resentful, ruthless, sarcastic, savage, severe, sharp, sore, sour, stinging, sullen, tart, unsweetened, vexatious, vinegary, waspish. *antonyms* contented, genial, sweet.

bitterness *n* acerbity, acidity, acrimoniousness, animosity, asperity, astringency, causticity, grudge, hostility, irony, mordancy, pique, rancour, resentment, sarcasm, sharpness, sourness, tartness, venom, virulence. *antonyms* contentment, geniality, sweetness.

bizarre *adj* abnormal, comical, curious, deviant, eccentric, extraordinary, extravagant, fantastic, freakish, grotesque, ludicrous, odd, off-beat, outlandish, peculiar, quaint, queer, ridiculous, strange, unusual, way-out, weird. *antonym* normal.

blab *v* blurt, disclose, divulge, gossip, leak, reveal, squeal, tell. *antonyms* hide, hush up.

blabber *v* blether, chatter, chinwag, earbash, gab, gabble, jabber, natter, prattle, whitter.

black *adj* angry, atrocious, bad, coal-black, dark, depressing, dingy, dirty, dismal, doleful, dusky, ebony, evil, filthy, funereal, furious, gloomy, grim, grimy, grubby, hopeless, horrible, hostile, inky, jet, jet-black, jetty, lugubrious, menacing, moonless, mournful, murky, nefarious, ominous, overcast, pitchy, raven, resentful, sable, sad, soiled, sombre, sooty, stained, starless, sullen, swarthy, threatening, thunderous, villainous, wicked.

v ban, bar, blacklist, boycott, taboo.

black magic black art, devil-worship, diabolism, hoodoo, necromancy, sorcery, voodoo, witchcraft, wizardry.

black out censor, collapse, conceal, cover up, darken, eclipse, extinguish, faint, flake out, gag, keel over, obfuscate, obliterate, pass out, shade, suppress, swoon, withhold.

black sheep disgrace, drop-out, ne'er-do-well, outcast, pariah, prodigal, reject, renegade, reprobate, wastrel. *antonym* pride.

blackball *v* ban, bar, blacklist, debar, exclude, expel, ostracise, oust, reject, repudiate, snub, veto.

blacken *v* befoul, begrime, besmirch, calumniate, cloud, darken, decry, defame, defile, denigrate, detract, dishonour, malign, revile, slander, smear, smirch, smudge, soil, stain, sully, taint, tarnish, traduce, vilify. *antonyms* enhance, praise.

blacklist *v* ban, bar, blackball, boycott, debar, disallow, exclude, expel, ostracise, preclude, proscribe, reject, repudiate, snub, taboo, veto. *antonyms* accept, allow.

blackmail *n* blood-sucking, extortion, hush money, intimidation, milking, pay-off, protection, ransom.

v bleed, bribe, coerce, compel, demand, force, hold to ransom, lean on, milk, squeeze, threaten.

blackness *n* darkness, duskiness, filthiness, gloom, griminess, inkiness, murkiness, wickedness.

blackout *n* censorship, coma, concealment, cover-up, faint, oblivion, power cut, secrecy, suppression, swoon, unconsciousness.

blade *n* dagger, edge, knife, rapier, scalpel, sword, vane.

blame *n* accountability, accusation, castigation, censure, charge, complaint, condemnation, criticism, culpability, fault, guilt, incrimination, liability, onus, rap, recrimination, reprimand, reproach, reproof, responsibility, stick, stricture.

v accuse, admonish, censure, charge, chide, condemn, criticise, disapprove, discommend, dispraise, find fault with, rebuke, reprehend, reprimand, reproach, reprove, tax, upbraid. *antonym* exonerate.

blameless *adj* above reproach, clean, clear, faultless, guiltless, immaculate, impeccable, inculpable, innocent, irreproachable, irreprovable, perfect, sinless, stainless, unblamable, unblemished, unimpeachable, unsullied, untarnished, upright, virtuous. *antonym* guilty.

blameworthy *adj* censurable, culpable, discreditable, disreputable, guilty, indefensible, inexcusable, reprehensible, reproachable, shameful, unworthy. *antonym* blameless.

bland *adv* affable, amiable, balmy, boring, calm, characterless, congenial, courteous, dull, fair-spoken, flat, friendly, gentle, gracious, humdrum, impassive, inscrutable, insipid, mild, mollifying, monotonous, nondescript, non-irritant, smooth, soft, soothing, suave, tasteless, tedious, temperate, unexciting, uninspiring, uninteresting, urbane, vapid, weak. *antonyms* piquant, sharp.

blandishments *n* blarney, cajolery, coaxing, compliments, enticements, fawning, flattery, inducements, ingratiation, inveiglement, persuasiveness, soft soap, sweet talk, sycophancy, wheedling.

blank *adj* apathetic, bare, bewildered, clean, clear, confounded, confused, deadpan, disconcerted, dull, dumbfounded, empty, expressionless, featureless, glazed, hollow, immobile, impassive, inane, inscrutable, lifeless, muddled, nonplussed, plain, poker-faced, sheer, spotless, staring, uncomprehending, unfilled, unmarked, unrhymed, vacant, vacuous, vague, void, white.

n break, emptiness, gap, nothingness, space, vacancy, vacuity, vacuum, void.

blanket *n* carpet, cloak, coat, coating, cover, covering, coverlet, envelope, film, layer, mantle, rug, sheet, wrapper, wrapping.

adj across-the-board, all-embracing, all-inclusive, comprehensive, inclusive, overall, sweeping, wide-ranging.

v cloak, cloud, coat, conceal, cover, deaden, eclipse, hide, mask, muffle, obscure, surround.

blankness *n* abstraction, bareness,

emptiness, immobility, impassivity, inanity, incomprehension, indifference, inscrutability, obliviousness, vacancy, vacuity, void.

blare v blast, boom, clamour, clang, honk, hoot, peal, resound, ring, roar, scream, shriek, toot, trumpet.

blasé adj apathetic, bored, dulled, indifferent, jaded, nonchalant, offhand, unconcerned, unexcited, unimpressed, unimpressible, uninspired, uninterested, unmoved, weary, world-weary. **antonyms** enthusiastic, excited.

blaspheme v abuse, curse, damn, defile, desecrate, execrate, imprecate, profane, revile, swear.

blasphemous adj godless, impious, imprecatory, irreligious, irreverent, profane, sacrilegious, ungodly.

blasphemy n curse, cursing, defilement, desecration, execration, expletive, impiety, impiousness, imprecation, irreverence, outrage, profanation, profanity, sacrilege, swearing, violation.

blast[1] n, v blare, blow, boom, honk, hoot, peal, roar, scream, shriek, sound, wail.

blast[2] n bang, bluster, burst, clap, crack, crash, detonation, discharge, draught, eruption, explosion, gale, gust, hail, outburst, salvo, squall, storm, tempest, volley.
v assail, attack, blight, blow up, burst, castigate, demolish, destroy, explode, flay, kill, lash, ruin, shatter, shrivel, storm at, wither.

blatant adj arrant, bald, barefaced, brazen, clamorous, conspicuous, egregious, flagrant, flaunting, glaring, harsh, loud, naked, noisy, obtrusive, obvious, ostentatious, outright, overt, prominent, pronounced, sheer, unmitigated.

blaze n blast, bonfire, brilliance, burst, conflagration, eruption, explosion, fire, flame, flames, flare, flare-up, flash, fury, glare, gleam, glitter, glow, light, outbreak, outburst, radiance, rush, storm.
v beam, burn, burst, erupt, explode, fire, flame, flare, flare up, flash, fume, glare, gleam, glow, seethe, shine.

bleak adj bare, barren, blasted, cheerless, chilly, cold, colourless, comfortless, delightless, depressing, desolate, discouraging, disheartening, dismal, dreary, empty, exposed, gaunt, gloomy, grim, hopeless, joyless, leaden, loveless, open, raw, sombre, unsheltered, weather-beaten, windswept, windy. **antonyms** cheerful, congenial.

bleary adj blurred, blurry, cloudy, dim, fogged, foggy, fuzzy, hazy, indistinct, misty, muddy, murky, obscured, rheumy, watery.

bleed v blackmail, deplete, drain, exhaust, exploit, exsanguinate, extort, extract, exude, fleece, flow, gush, haemorrhage, leech, milk, ooze, run, sap, seep, spurt, squeeze, suck dry, trickle, weep.

blemish n birthmark, blot, blur, botch, defect, deformity, disfigurement, disgrace, dishonour, fault, flaw, imperfection, macula, mark, naevus, smudge, speck, spot, stain, taint.
v besmirch, blot, blotch, blur, damage, deface, disfigure, flaw, impair, injure, mar, mark, smudge, spoil, spot, stain, sully, taint, tarnish.

blend v amalgamate, coalesce, combine, complement, compound, contemper, fit, fuse, harmonise, intermix, meld, merge, mingle, mix, synthesise, unite. **antonym** separate.
n alloy, amalgam, amalgamation, combination, composite, compound, concoction, fusion, meld, mix, mixture, synthesis, union.

bless v anoint, approve, bestow, consecrate, countenance, dedicate, endow, exalt, extol, favour, glorify, grace, hallow, magnify, ordain, praise, provide, sanctify, thank. **antonyms** condemn, curse.

blessed adj adored, beatified, blissful, contented, divine, endowed, favoured, fortunate, glad, hallowed, happy, holy, joyful, joyous, lucky, prosperous, revered, sacred, sanctified, seely. **antonym** cursed.

blessing n advantage, approbation, approval, authority, backing, benediction, benefit, boon, bounty, commendation, concurrence, consecration, consent, countenance, dedication, favour, gain, gift, godsend, grace, help, invocation, kindness, leave, permission, profit, sanction, service, support, thanksgiving, windfall. **antonyms** blight, condemnation, curse.

blight n affliction, bane, cancer, canker, contamination, corruption, curse, decay, depression, disease, evil, fungus, infestation, mildew, pest, pestilence, plague, pollution, rot, scourge, set-back, woe. **antonyms** blessing, boon.
v annihilate, blast, crush, dash, destroy, disappoint, frustrate, injure, mar, ruin, shatter, shrivel, spoil, undermine, wither, wreck. **antonym** bless.

blind *adj* blinkered, careless, closed, concealed, dark, dim, eyeless, hasty, heedless, hidden, ignorant, impetuous, inattentive, inconsiderate, indifferent, indiscriminate, injudicious, insensitive, irrational, mindless, neglectful, oblivious, obscured, obstructed, prejudiced, rash, reckless, senseless, sightless, thoughtless, unaware, uncontrollable, uncritical, undiscerning, unobservant, unobserving, unreasoning, unseeing, unsighted, unthinking, violent, visionless, wild. **antonyms** aware, clear, sighted.

n camouflage, cloak, cover, cover-up, distraction, façade, feint, front, mask, masquerade, screen, smoke-screen.

blindly *adv* aimlessly, carelessly, confusedly, frantically, headlong, heedlessly, impetuously, impulsively, incautiously, inconsiderately, indiscriminately, madly, passionately, precipitately, purposelessly, recklessly, regardlessly, senselessly, thoughtlessly, wilfully. **antonym** cautiously.

blindness *n* ignorance, indifference, insensitivity, narrow-mindedness, neglect, prejudice, sightlessness, unawareness. **antonyms** awareness, sight, sightedness.

blink *v* bat, condone, connive at, disregard, flash, flicker, flutter, gleam, glimmer, glimpse, ignore, overlook, peer, scintillate, shine, sparkle, squint, twinkle, wink.

bliss *n* beatitude, blessedness, blissfulness, ecstasy, euphoria, felicity, gladness, happiness, heaven, joy, nirvana, paradise, rapture. **antonyms** damnation, misery.

blissful *adj* beatific, delighted, ecstatic, elated, enchanted, enraptured, euphoric, happy, heavenly, joyful, joyous, rapturous. **antonym** wretched.

blistering *adj* cruel, excoriating, hot, intense, sarcastic, savage, scathing, scorching, strenuous, vicious, virulent, withering. **antonym** mild.

blithe *adj* animated, buoyant, carefree, careless, casual, cheerful, cheery, debonair, gay, happy, heedless, jaunty, light-hearted, lively, merry, mirthful, nonchalant, sprightly, sunny, thoughtless, unconcerned, untroubled, vivacious. **antonym** morose.

bloated *adj* blown up, bombastic, dilated, distended, enlarged, expanded, inflated, swollen. **antonyms** shrivelled, shrunken, thin.

blob *n* ball, bead, bubble, dab, dew-drop, drop, droplet, glob, globule, gob, lump, mass, pearl, spot.

block *n* bar, barrier, blockage, brick, cake, chunk, cube, delay, hang-up, hindrance, hunk, impediment, ingot, jam, lump, mass, obstacle, obstruction, piece, resistance, square, stoppage, tranche.

v arrest, bar, check, choke, clog, close, dam up, deter, halt, hinder, impede, obstruct, plug, scotch, stonewall, stop, stop up, thwart, trig.

blockade *n* barricade, barrier, closure, encirclement, obstruction, restriction, siege, stoppage.

blockage *n* block, blocking, clot, embolism, hindrance, impediment, jam, log-jam, obstruction, occlusion, stoppage.

blockhead *n* bonehead, chump, dolt, dullard, dunce, fool, idiot, ignoramus, numskull, pinhead, thickhead. **antonyms** brain, genius.

bloke *n* bastard, bod, body, bugger, chap, character, cove, customer, fellow, individual, Johnny, punter.

blood *n* ancestry, anger, birth, bloodshed, consanguinity, descendants, descent, extraction, family, kindred, kinship, lineage, murder, relations, relationship, temper, temperament.

bloodcurdling *adj* appalling, chilling, dreadful, fearful, frightening, hair-raising, horrendous, horrible, horrid, horrifying, scaring, spine-chilling, terrifying.

bloodless *adj* anaemic, ashen, chalky, cold, colourless, drained, feeble, insipid, languid, lifeless, listless, pale, pallid, passionless, pasty, sallow, sickly, spiritless, torpid, unemotional, unfeeling, wan. **antonyms** bloody, ruddy, vigorous.

bloodshed *n* bloodletting, butchery, carnage, gore, killing, massacre, murder, slaughter, slaying.

bloodthirsty *adj* barbaric, barbarous, brutal, cruel, ferocious, inhuman, murderous, ruthless, sanguinary, savage, slaughterous, vicious, warlike.

bloody *adj* bleeding, bloodstained, blooming, brutal, cruel, ferocious, fierce, gaping, murderous, raw, sanguinary, sanguine, savage.

bloom *n* beauty, blossom, blossoming, blow, blush, bud, efflorescence, florescence, flourishing, flower, flush, freshness, glow, health, heyday, lustre, perfection, prime, radiance, rosiness, vigour.

v blossom, blow, bud, burgeon, develop, flourish, grow, open, prosper, sprout, succeed, thrive, wax. *antonym* wither.

blooming *adj* blossoming, bonny, florescent, flowering, healthful, healthy, rosy, ruddy. *antonym* ailing.

blossom *n* bloom, bud, floret, flower, flowers.

v bloom, blow, burgeon, develop, effloresce, flourish, flower, grow, mature, progress, prosper, thrive. *antonym* wither.

blot *n* blemish, blotch, defect, disgrace, fault, flaw, macula, mark, patch, smear, smudge, speck, splodge, spot, stain, taint.
v bespatter, blur, disfigure, disgrace, mar, mark, smudge, spoil, spot, stain, sully, taint, tarnish.

blot out cancel, darken, delete, destroy, eclipse, efface, erase, expunge, obliterate, obscure, shadow.

blow¹ *v* bear, blare, blast, breathe, buffet, drive, exhale, fan, fling, flow, flutter, mouth, pant, pipe, play, puff, rush, sound, stream, sweep, toot, trumpet, vibrate, waft, whirl, whisk, wind.
n blast, draught, flurry, gale, gust, puff, squall, tempest, wind.

blow over cease, die down, disappear, dissipate, end, finish, fizzle out, pass, peter out, subside, vanish.

blow up balloon, belly out, bloat, dilate, distend, enlarge, exaggerate, expand, fill, fill out, heighten, inflate, magnify, overstate, puff up, pump up, swell.

blow² *n* affliction, bang, bash, bat, belt, biff, bombshell, bop, box, buff, buffet, calamity, catastrophe, clap, clip, clout, clump, comedown, concussion, counterbluff, disappointment, disaster, douse, fourpenny one, haymaker, jolt, knock, knuckle sandwich, misfortune, oner, punch, rap, reverse, setback, shock, slap, smack, sock, souse, stroke, swat, swipe, thump, upset, wallop, welt, whack, whang.

blow up blast, blow one's top, bomb, burst, castigate, detonate, dynamite, erupt, explode, go off, go off the deep end, hit the roof, lose one's cool, lose one's rag, lose one's temper, rage, reprimand, rupture, scold, shatter.

blow-out *n* beanfeast, binge, blast, burst, carousal, detonation, eruption, escape, explosion, feast, fuse, leak, party, puncture, rupture, spree, tear.

blowzy *adj* bedraggled, dishevelled, messy, slatternly, slipshod, sloppy, slovenly, sluttish, tousled, ungroomed, unkempt, untidy. *antonyms* neat, smart.

bludgeon *n* baton, club, cosh, cudgel, night-stick, shillelagh, truncheon.
v badger, batter, beat, browbeat, bulldoze, bully, club, coerce, cosh, cudgel, force, harass, hector, intimidate, sap, steam-roller, strike, terrorise, torment.

blue¹ *adj* aquamarine, azure, cerulean, cobalt, cyan, indigo, navy, sapphire, turquoise, ultramarine.

blue² *adj* black, bleak, dejected, depressed, despondent, dismal, dispirited, doleful, down in the dumps, downcast, down-hearted, fed up, gloomy, glum, low, melancholy, miserable, morose, sad, unhappy. *antonym* cheerful.

blue³ *adj* bawdy, coarse, dirty, improper, indecent, lewd, naughty, near the bone, near the knuckle, obscene, offensive, pornographic, risqué, smutty, vulgar. *antonym* decent.

blueprint *n* archetype, design, draft, guide, model, outline, pattern, pilot, plan, prototype, sketch.

blues *n* dejection, depression, despondency, doldrums, dumps, gloom, gloominess, glumness, melancholy, miseries, moodiness. *antonym* euphoria.

bluff¹ *adj* affable, blunt, candid, direct, downright, frank, genial, good-natured, hearty, open, outspoken, plain-spoken, straightforward. *antonyms* diplomatic, refined.

bluff² *v* bamboozle, blind, deceive, defraud, delude, fake, feign, grift, hoodwink, humbug, lie, mislead, pretend, sham.
n bluster, boast, bravado, deceit, deception, fake, feint, fraud, grift, humbug, idle boast, lie, pretence, sham, show, subterfuge, trick.

blunder *n* bloomer, boob, booboo, clanger, clinker, error, fault, faux pas, fluff, gaffe, goof, howler, impropriety, inaccuracy, indiscretion, mistake, oversight, slip, slip-up, solecism.
v blow it, botch, bumble, bungle, err, flounder, fluff, fumble, goof, miscalculate, misjudge, mismanage, muff it, slip up, stumble.

blunt *adj* abrupt, bluff, brusque, candid, curt, direct, discourteous, downright, dull, dulled, edgeless, explicit, forthright, frank, honest, impolite, insensitive, obtuse, outspoken, plain-spoken, pointless,

rounded, rude, straightforward, stubbed, stumpy, tactless, thick, trenchant, unceremonious, uncivil, unpolished, unsharpened. **antonyms** sharp, tactful.
v abate, allay, alleviate, anaesthetise, bate, dampen, deaden, dull, numb, palliate, rebate, soften, stupefy, weaken. **antonyms** intensify, sharpen.

blur v becloud, befog, blear, blemish, blot, blotch, cloud, darken, dim, fog, mask, obfuscate, obscure, smear, soften, spot, stain.
n blear, blot, blotch, cloudiness, confusion, dimness, fog, fuzziness, haze, indistinctness, muddle, obscurity, smear, smudge, spot, stain.

blurred adj bleary, blurry, clouded, confused, dim, faint, foggy, fuzzy, hazy, ill-defined, indistinct, misty, nebulous, unclear, vague. **antonym** distinct.

blurt v babble, blab, cry, disclose, divulge, ejaculate, exclaim, gush, leak, let slip, let the cat out of the bag, reveal, spill, spill the beans, spout, utter. **antonym** hush up.

blush v colour, flush, glow, mantle, redden. **antonym** blanch.
n colour, flush, glow, reddening, rosiness, ruddiness, suffusion.

blushing adj confused, discomfited, embarrassed, flushed, glowing, red, rosy, suffused. **antonyms** composed, pale.

bluster v boast, brag, bully, domineer, hector, rant, roar, roist, roister, storm, strut, swagger, swell, talk big, vapour, vaunt.
n bluff, boasting, bombast, bragging, bravado, crowing, parade, racket, swagger, swaggering, vapour.

blustery adj boisterous, gusty, noisy, squally, stormy, tempestuous, tumultuous, violent, wild, windy. **antonym** calm.

boast v be all mouth, blow, bluster, bounce, brag, claim, crow, exaggerate, exhibit, possess, puff, show off, strut, swagger, talk big, trumpet, vaunt. **antonym** deprecate.
n avowal, brag, claim, joy, pride, swank, treasure, vaunt.

boastful adj bragging, cocky, conceited, crowing, egotistical, proud, puffed-up, self-glorious, swaggering, swanky, swollen-headed, vain, vainglorious, vaunting, windy. **antonym** modest.

boasting n bluster, bragging, conceit, ostentation, swagger, swank, vaingloriousness, vainglory, vaunting, windiness. **antonym** modesty.

boat n canoe, dinghy, gondola, ketch, punt, rowing-boat, speed-boat, watercraft.

bob v bounce, duck, hop, jerk, jolt, jounce, jump, leap, nod, oscillate, quiver, shake, skip, spring, twitch, waggle, weave, wobble.

bob up appear, arise, arrive, crop up, emerge, materialise, pop up, rise, show up, spring up, surface.

bode v augur, betoken, forebode, foreshadow, foreshow, foretell, forewarn, import, indicate, intimate, omen, portend, predict, presage, prophesy, signify, threaten, warn.

bodily adj actual, carnal, concrete, corporal, corporeal, earthly, fleshly, incarnate, material, physical, real, substantial, tangible. **antonym** spiritual.
adv altogether, as a whole, bag and baggage, collectively, completely, en masse, entirely, fully, in toto, totally, wholly. **antonym** piecemeal.

body[1] n being, bod, build, bulk, cadaver, carcass, consistency, corpse, corpus, creature, density, essence, figure, firmness, form, frame, human, individual, mass, material, matter, mortal, opacity, person, physique, relics, remains, richness, shape, solidity, stiff, substance, substantiality, tabernacle, torso, trunk.

body[2] n association, band, bevy, bloc, cartel, collection, company, confederation, congress, corporation, crowd, group, horde, majority, mass, mob, multitude, society, syndicate, throng.

boffin n backroom-boy, brain, designer, egghead, engineer, genius, intellect, intellectual, inventor, mastermind, planner, scientist, thinker, wizard.

bog n fen, marsh, marshland, mire, morass, moss, quagmire, quicksands, slough, swamp, swampland, wetlands.

bog down delay, deluge, halt, hinder, impede, overwhelm, retard, sink, slow down, slow up, stall, stick.

boggle v demur, dither, doubt, equivocate, falter, fight shy, flinch, funk, hang back, hesitate, hover, jib, jump, pause, recoil, shrink, shy, stagger, start, startle, vacillate, waver.

boggy adj fennish, fenny, marshy, miry, morassy, muddy, oozy, quaggy, soft, spongy, swampy, waterlogged. **antonym** arid.

bogus adj artificial, counterfeit, dummy, ersatz, fake, false, forged, fraudulent, imitation, phoney, pseudo, sham, spoof, spurious, unauthentic. **antonym** genuine.

bohemian *adj* alternative, artistic, arty, bizarre, eccentric, exotic, irregular, left-bank, nonconformist, offbeat, unconventional, unorthodox, way-out. **antonyms** bourgeois, conventional. *n* beatnik, drop-out, hippie, nonconformist. **antonyms** bourgeois, conformist.

boil *v* agitate, brew, bubble, churn, decoct, effervesce, erupt, explode, fizz, foam, froth, fulminate, fume, gurgle, rage, rave, seethe, simmer, sizzle, spume, steam, stew, storm.

boil down abridge, abstract, concentrate, condense, decrease, digest, distil, epitomise, reduce, summarise, synopsise.

boiling *adj* angry, baking, blistering, bubbling, enraged, flaming, fuming, furious, gurgling, hot, incensed, indignant, infuriated, roasting, scorching, seething, torrid, turbulent.

boisterous *adj* bouncy, clamorous, disorderly, exuberant, impetuous, loud, noisy, obstreperous, rackety, raging, riotous, roisting, rollicking, rough, rowdy, rumbustious, tempestuous, tumultous, turbulent, unrestrained, unruly, uproarious, vociferous, wild. **antonyms** calm, quiet, restrained.

bold *adj* adventurous, audacious, brash, brave, brazen, bright, cheeky, colourful, confident, conspicuous, courageous, daring, dauntless, enterprising, extrovert, eye-catching, fearless, flamboyant, flashy, forceful, forward, fresh, gallant, heroic, impudent, insolent, intrepid, jazzy, lively, loud, outgoing, pert, plucky, prominent, pronounced, saucy, shameless, showy, spirited, striking, strong, unabashed, unashamed, valiant, valorous, vivid. **antonyms** diffident, restrained.

bolster *v* aid, assist, augment, boost, brace, buoy up, buttress, firm up, help, maintain, prop, reinforce, shore up, stay, stiffen, strengthen, supplement, support. **antonym** undermine.

bolt *n* arrow, bar, bound, catch, dart, dash, elopement, escape, fastener, flight, flit, latch, lock, missile, peg, pin, projectile, rivet, rod, rush, shaft, sneck, sprint, thunderbolt. *v* abscond, bar, bound, cram, dart, dash, devour, discharge, elope, escape, expel, fasten, fetter, flee, fly, gobble, gorge,

gulp, guzzle, hurtle, jump, latch, leap, lock, run, rush, secure, spring, sprint, stuff, wolf.

bomb *v* attack, blow up, bombard, collapse, come a cropper, come to grief, destroy, fail, flop, misfire, shell, strafe, torpedo.

bombard *v* assail, assault, attack, barrage, batter, beset, besiege, blast, blitz, bomb, cannonade, harass, hound, importune, pelt, pester, pound, shell, strafe.

bombardment *n* air-raid, assault, attack, barrage, blitz, bombing, cannonade, fire, flak, salvo, shelling, strafe.

bombast *n* bluster, brag, euphuism, grandiloquence, grandiosity, heroics, magniloquence, pomposity, pretentiousness, rant, verbosity, wordiness. **antonyms** reserve, restraint.

bombastic *adj* bloated, declamatory, euphuistic, grandiloquent, grandiose, high-flown, histrionic, inflated, magniloquent, pompous, turgid, verbose, windy, wordy.

bona fide actual, authentic, genuine, honest, kosher, lawful, legal, legitimate, real, true, valid. **antonym** bogus.

bond *n* affiliation, affinity, agreement, attachment, band, binding, chain, compact, connection, contract, cord, covenant, fastening, fetter, ligature, link, manacle, obligation, pledge, promise, relation, shackle, tie, union, word. *v* bind, connect, fasten, fuse, glue, gum, paste, seal, unite.

bondage *n* captivity, confinement, durance, duress, enslavement, enthralment, imprisonment, incarceration, restraint, serfdom, servitude, slavery, subjection, subjugation, subservience, thraldom, vassalage, yoke. **antonyms** freedom, independence.

bonny *adj* attractive, beautiful, blithe, blooming, bouncing, buxom, cheerful, cheery, chubby, comely, fair, fine, gay, goodly, handsome, joyful, lovely, merry, pretty, shapely, sunny, sweet, wholesome, winsome.

bonus *n* advantage, benefit, bounty, bribe, commission, dividend, extra, freebie, gift, gratuity, hand-out, honorarium, perk, perquisite, plus, premium, prize, profit, reward, tip. **antonyms** disadvantage, disincentive, liability.

bony *adj* angular, drawn, emaciated, gangling, gaunt, gawky, knobbly, lanky, lean, osseous, scrawny, skinny, thin. *antonym* plump.

boob *n* balls-up, blunder, botch, clanger, error, fault, faux pas, gaffe, howler, inaccuracy, indiscretion, mistake, oversight, slip, slip-up, solecism.

book *n* album, booklet, companion, diary, jotter, manual, manuscript, notebook, pad, paperback, publication, roll, scroll, textbook, tome, tract, volume, work.
v arrange, arrest, bag, charter, engage, enter, insert, list, log, note, organise, post, procure, programme, record, register, reserve, schedule. *antonym* cancel.

bookish *adj* academic, cultured, donnish, erudite, highbrow, intellectual, learned, lettered, literary, pedantic, scholarly, scholastic, studious, well-read. *antonyms* lowbrow, unlettered.

boom¹ *v* bang, blare, blast, crash, explode, resound, reverberate, roar, roll, rumble, sound, thunder.
n bang, blast, burst, clang, clap, crash, explosion, reverberation, roar, rumble, thunder.

boom² *v* develop, escalate, expand, explode, flourish, gain, go from strength to strength, grow, increase, intensify, prosper, spurt, strengthen, succeed, swell, thrive. *antonyms* collapse, fail.
n advance, boost, development, escalation, expansion, explosion, gain, growth, improvement, increase, jump, spurt, upsurge, upturn. *antonyms* collapse, failure.

boon *n* advantage, benefaction, benefit, blessing, donation, favour, gift, godsend, grant, gratification, gratuity, kindness, petition, present, windfall. *antonyms* blight, disadvantage.

boor *n* barbarian, brute, churl, clodhopper, hog, lout, oaf, philistine, vulgarian. *antonyms* aesthete, charmer.

boorish *adj* barbaric, bearish, churlish, coarse, crude, gross, gruff, ill-bred, loutish, rude, rustic, uncivilised, uncouth, uneducated, unrefined, vulgar. *antonyms* cultured, polite, refined.

boost *n* addition, advancement, ego-trip, encouragement, enhancement, expansion, fillip, heave, help, hoist, hype, improvement, increase, increment, jump, lift, praise, promotion, push, rise, supplement, thrust. *antonyms* blow, setback.
v advance, advertise, aid, amplify, assist, augment, bolster, develop, elevate,

encourage, enhance, enlarge, expan foster, further, heave, heighten, hoi improve, increase, inspire, jack u lift, plug, praise, promote, push, rais supplement, support, sustain, thrust *antonyms* hinder, undermine.

booth *n* bay, carrel, compartment, h kiosk, stall, stand, ticket-office.

bootlicking *n* arse-licking, bac scratching, crawling, deferenc fawning, flattery, grovellin ingratiation, lackeying, obsequiousness servility, sycophancy, toadying.

booty *n* gains, haul, loot, picking pillage, plunder, spoil, spoils, swa takings, winnings.

border *n* borderline, boundary, bound brim, brink, circumference, confin confines, demarcation, edge, fring frontier, hem, limit, limits, lip, li march, margin, perimeter, peripher rim, skirt, surround, trimming, valanc verge.
adj boundary, circumscriptiv dividing, frontier, limitary, margina perimeter, separating, side.

border on abut, adjoin, appear lik approach, approximate, communica with, connect, contact, impinge, joi march, neighbour, resemble, touch, verg on.

bordered *adj* bounded, circumscribe edged, fringed, hemmed, margine rimmed, skirted, surrounded, trimmed.

borderline *adj* ambivalent, doubtfu iffy, indecisive, indefinite, indeterm nate, marginal, problematic, uncertain. *antonyms* certain, definite.

bore¹ *v* burrow, countermine, dri gouge, mine, penetrate, perforate, pierc sink, thirl, thrill, tunnel, undermine.

bore² *v* annoy, bother, bug, fatigu irk, irritate, jade, pester, tire, trouble vex, weary, worry. *antonyms* charm interest.
n annoyance, bind, bother, dra headache, nuisance, pain, pain in th neck, pest, trial, turn-off, vexatio yawn. *antonym* pleasure.

boredom *n* apathy, dullness, ennu flatness, irksomeness, listlessnes monotony, sameness, tediousnes tedium, weariness, wearisomeness world-weariness. *antonym* interest.

boring *adj* commonplace, dea dreary, dry, dull, ennuying, fla ho-hum, humdrum, insipid, irksom monotonous, repetitious, routine, stal stupid, tedious, tiresome, tiring, trit unamusing, undiverting, unedifying, uneventful, unexciting, unfunny, unimaginative, uninspired, uninteresting, unvaried, unwitty, vapid, wearisome. *antonyms* interesting, original.

borrow v adopt, ape, appropriate, cadge, copy, crib, derive, draw, echo, filch, imitate, list, mimic, obtain, pilfer, plagiarise, scrounge, sponge, steal, take, use, usurp.

bosom n breast, bust, centre, chest, circle, core, heart, midst, protection, sanctuary, shelter.
adj boon, cherished, close, confidential, dear, favourite, inseparable, intimate.

boss n administrator, baron, captain, chief, director, employer, executive, foreman, gaffer, governor, head, leader, manager, master, overseer, owner, superintendent, supervisor, supremo.
v administrate, command, control, direct, employ, manage, oversee, run, superintend, supervise.
boss around browbeat, bulldoze, bully, dominate, domineer, dragoon, hector, oppress, order about, overbear, push around, tyrannise.

bossy *adj* arrogant, authoritarian, autocratic, demanding, despotic, dictatorial, domineering, exacting, hectoring, highhanded, imperious, insistent, lordly, oppressive, overbearing, tyrannical. *antonym* unassertive.

botch v balls up, blunder, bungle, cobble, cock up, fuck up, fudge, fumble, goof, louse up, mar, mend, mess, mismanage, muff, patch, ruin, screw up, spoil. *antonyms* accomplish, succeed.
n balls-up, blunder, bungle, cock-up, failure, farce, hash, mess, miscarriage, muddle, shambles. *antonym* success.

bother v alarm, annoy, bore, chivvy, concern, dismay, distress, disturb, dog, harass, harry, hassle, inconvenience, irk, irritate, molest, nag, pester, plague, pother, trouble, upset, vex, worry.
n aggravation, annoyance, bustle, consternation, difficulty, flurry, fuss, hassle, inconvenience, irritation, kerfuffle, molestation, nuisance, palaver, perplexity, pest, pother, problem, shtook, strain, trouble, vexation, worry.

bothersome *adj* aggravating, annoying, boring, distressing, exasperating, inconvenient, infuriating, irksome, irritating, laborious, tedious, tiresome, troublesome, vexatious, vexing, wearisome.

bottle n carafe, dead-man, decanter, demijohn, flacon, flagon, flask, jar, phial, vial.
bottle up check, conceal, contain, curb, enclose, hide, hold in, inhibit, quell, restrain, restrict, suppress. *antonyms* unbosom, unburden.

bottom n arse, backside, base, basis, bed, behind, bum, butt, buttocks, core, depths, derrière, essence, floor, foot, foundation, fundament, fundus, ground, groundwork, heart, jacksie, nadir, origin, pedestal, plinth, posterior, principle, rear, rear end, root, rump, seat, sit-upon, sole, source, substance, substratum, substructure, support, tail, underneath, underside.

bottomless *adj* abysmal, abyssal, boundless, deep, fathomless, immeasurable, inexhaustible, infinite, limitless, measureless, profound, unfathomable, unfathomed, unlimited, unplumbed. *antonym* shallow.
bottomless pit abyss, chasm, crevasse, fire and brimstone, gulf, Hades, Hell, hellfire, infernal regions, inferno.

bounce v bob, bound, bump, dismiss, eject, jounce, jump, kick out, leap, oust, rebound, recoil, resile, ricochet, spring, stot, throw out.
n animation, bound, dynamism, ebullience, elasticity, energy, exuberance, give, go, life, liveliness, pep, rebound, recoil, resilience, spring, springiness, vigour, vitality, vivacity, zip.

bouncing *adj* blooming, bonny, healthy, lively, robust, strong, thriving, vigorous.

bound[1] *adj* bandaged, beholden, cased, certain, chained, committed, compelled, constrained, destined, doomed, dutybound, fastened, fated, fixed, forced, held, liable, manacled, obligated, obliged, pledged, required, restricted, secured, sure, tied, tied up.

bound[2] v bob, bounce, caper, frisk, gambol, hurdle, jump, leap, lope, lunge, pounce, prance, skip, spring, vault.
n bob, bounce, caper, dance, frisk, gambol, jump, leap, lope, lunge, pounce, prance, scamper, skip, spring, vault.

boundary n abuttal, barrier, border, borderline, bounds, brink, confines, demarcation, edge, extremity, fringe, frontier, junction, limits, line, march, margin, perimeter, termination, verge.
adj border, demarcation, frontier, perimeter.

bounded *adj* bordered, circumscribed, confined, controlled, defined, demarcated, edged, encircled, enclosed, encompassed, hemmed in, limited, restrained, restricted, surrounded, terminated.

boundless *adj* countless, endless, illimitable, immeasurable, immense, incalculable, indefatigable, inexhaustible, infinite, interminable, interminate, limitless, measureless, prodigious, unbounded, unconfined, unending, unflagging, unlimited, untold, vast. *antonym* limited.

bounds *n* borders, boundaries, circumference, confines, edges, extremities, fringes, frontiers, limits, marches, margins, periphery, rim, verges.

bountiful *adj* abundant, ample, boundless, bounteous, copious, exuberant, generous, lavish, liberal, luxuriant, magnanimous, munificent, open-handed, overflowing, plenteous, plentiful, princely, profuse, prolific, ungrudging, unstinting. *antonyms* meagre, mean, sparse.

bounty *n* allowance, assistance, beneficence, benevolence, bonus, charity, donation, generosity, gift, grace, grant, gratuity, kindness, largesse, liberality, philanthropy, premium, present, recompense, reward.

bourgeois *adj* conformist, conservative, conventional, dull, hide-bound, humdrum, materialistic, middle-class, pedestrian, tawdry, traditional, trite, trivial, unadventurous, unimaginative, uninspired, unoriginal. *antonyms* bohemian, original, unconventional.

bout *n* battle, competition, contest, course, encounter, engagement, fight, fit, go, heat, match, period, round, run, session, set-to, spell, spree, stint, stretch, struggle, term, time, turn, venue.

bow *v* accept, acquiesce, bend, capitulate, comply, concede, conquer, consent, crush, curtsey, defer, droop, genuflect, give in, incline, kowtow, nod, overpower, stoop, subdue, subjugate, submit, surrender, vanquish, yield.
n acknowledgement, bending, curtsey, genuflexion, inclination, kowtow, nod, obeisance, salaam, salutation.

bow out abandon, back out, bunk off, chicken out, defect, desert, give up, opt out, pull out, quit, resign, retire, stand down, step down, withdraw.

bowdlerise *v* blue-pencil, censor, clean up, cut, edit, expurgate, launder, modify, mutilate, purge, purify.

bowels *n* belly, centre, core, depths, entrails, guts, heart, hold, innards, inside,

insides, interior, intestines, middle, viscera.

bower *n* alcove, arbour, bay, belvedere, boudoir, dwelling, gazebo, grotto, hideaway, recess, retreat, sanctuary, shelter, summer-house.

bowl *v* fling, hurl, pitch, revolve, roll, rotate, spin, throw, trundle, whirl.

bowl over amaze, astonish, astound, dumbfound, fell, flabbergast, floor, stagger, startle, stun, surprise, topple, unbalance.

box[1] *n* carton, case, casket, chest, coffer, coffin, consignment, container, coop, fund, pack, package, portmanteau, present, receptacle, trunk.
v case, encase, pack, package, wrap.

box in cage, circumscribe, confine, contain, coop up, cordon off, corner, enclose, hem in, imprison, restrict, surround, trap.

box[2] *v* buffet, butt, clout, cuff, fight, hit, punch, slap, sock, spar, strike, thwack, wallop, whack, wham, whang.
n blow, buffet, clout, cuff, punch, slap, stroke, thump, wallop, wham, whang.

boy *n* cub, fellow, halfling, imp, junior, kid, lad, man-child, nipper, puppy, schoolboy, stripling, urchin, whippersnapper, youngster, youth.

boycott *v* ban, bar, black, blackball, blacklist, cold-shoulder, disallow, embargo, exclude, ignore, ostracise, outlaw, prohibit, proscribe, refuse, reject, spurn. *antonyms* encourage, support.

boyfriend *n* admirer, beau, date, fancy, man, lover, man, suitor, sweetheart, young man.

boyish *adj* adolescent, childish, gamine, immature, innocent, juvenile, puerile, tomboy, unfeminine, young, youthful.

brace *v* bandage, bind, bolster, buttress, fasten, fortify, prop, reinforce, shore (up), steady, strap, strengthen, support, tie, tighten.

bracing *adj* brisk, crisp, energetic, energising, enlivening, exhilarating, fortifying, fresh, invigorating, refreshing, restorative, reviving, rousing, stimulating, strengthening, tonic, vigorous. *antonym* debilitating.

brag *v* bluster, boast, crow, swagger, talk big, trumpet, vaunt. *antonym* deprecate.

bragging *n* bluster, boastfulness, boasting, bravado, exaggeration, showing off, strutting, swagger, swank, talk. *antonyms* modesty, unobtrusiveness.

brainless adj crazy, daft, foolish, half-witted, idiotic, incompetent, inept, mindless, senseless, stupid, thoughtless, unintelligent, witless. *antonyms* sensible, shrewd, wise.

brains n capacity, common sense, grey matter, head, intellect, intelligence, mind, nous, reason, sagacity, savvy, sense, shrewdness, understanding, wit.

brain-teaser n conundrum, mind-bender, poser, problem, puzzle, riddle.

brainwash v alter, bludgeon, condition, grill, indoctrinate, persuade, pressure, pressurise.

brainwashing n conditioning, double-think, grilling, indoctrination, mind-bending, persuasion, pressure, pressurisation, unlearning.

brainy adj bright, brilliant, clever, intellectual, intelligent, smart. *antonym* dull.

brake n check, constraint, control, curb, drag, rein, restraint, restriction, retardment.
v check, decelerate, drag, halt, moderate, pull up, retard, slacken, slow, stop. *antonym* accelerate.

branch n arm, bough, chapter, department, division, grain, limb, lodge, office, offshoot, part, prong, ramification, section, shoot, sprig, subdivision, subsection, whip, wing, witty.

branch out bifurcate, broaden out, develop, divaricate, diversify, enlarge, expand, extend, increase, move on, multiply, proliferate, vary.

brand n brand-name, class, emblem, grade, hallmark, kind, label, line, logo, make, mark, marker, marque, quality, sign, sort, species, stamp, symbol, trademark, type, variety.
v burn, censure, denounce, discredit, disgrace, label, mark, scar, stain, stamp, stigmatise, taint, type.

brandish v display, exhibit, flash, flaunt, flourish, parade, raise, shake, swing, wave, wield.

brash adj assuming, assured, audacious, bold, brazen, bumptious, cocky, foolhardy, forward, hasty, heedless, impertinent, impetuous, impudent, impulsive, incautious, indiscreet, insolent, precipitate, rash, reckless, rude. *antonyms* cautious, reserved, unobtrusive.

brass n assurance, audacity, brass neck, brazenness, cheek, effrontery, gall, impertinence, impudence, insolence, nerve, presumption, rudeness, self-assurance, temerity. *antonyms* circumspection, timidity.

brassy adj blaring, blatant, bold, brash, brazen, cheap, dissonant, flamboyant, flashy, forward, garish, gaudy, grating, hard, harsh, jangling, jarring, jazzy, loud, loud-mouthed, meretricious, noisy, obtrusive, pert, piercing, raucous, saucy, showy, shrill, strident, tawdry, vulgar.

brat n cub, get, guttersnipe, jackanapes, kid, nipper, puppy, rascal, ruffian, toe-rag, urchin, varmint, whippersnapper, youngster.

bravado n boast, boastfulness, boasting, bombast, brag, bragging, parade, pretence, show, showing off, swagger, swaggering, swank, swashbuckling, talk, vaunting. *antonyms* modesty, restraint.

brave adj audacious, bold, courageous, daring, dauntless, doughty, fearless, fine, gallant, game, glorious, hardy, heroic, indomitable, intrepid, plucky, resolute, splendid, stalwart, stoic, stoical, stout-hearted, unafraid, undaunted, unflinching, valiant. *antonyms* cowardly, timid.
v accost, bear, beard, challenge, confront, dare, defy, encounter, endure, face, face up to, stand up to, suffer, withstand. *antonyms* capitulate, crumple.

bravely adv courageously, dauntlessly, fearlessly, gallantly, gamely, heroically, intrepidly, manfully, pluckily, resolutely, splendidly, stoically, unflinchingly, valiantly, womanfully. *antonym* cravenly.

bravery n audacity, boldness, courage, daring, dauntlessness, doughtiness, fearlessness, fortitude, gallantry, grit, guts, hardihood, hardiness, heroism, mettle, pluck, pluckiness, resoluteness, resolution, spirit, spunk, stalwartness, stoicism, stout-heartedness, valiance, valour. *antonyms* cowardice, timidity.

bravura n animation, audacity, boldness, brilliance, daring, dash, display, élan, energy, exhibitionism, extravagance, flamboyance, liveliness, ostentation, panache, pizzazz, punch, spirit, verve, vigour, virtuosity. *antonym* restraint.

brawl n affray, altercation, argument, bagarre, battle, broil, bust-up, clash, disorder, dispute, dog-fight, dust-up, fight, fracas, fray, free-for-all, mêlée, punch-up, quarrel, row, ruckus, rumpus, scrap, scuffle, squabble, tumult, uproar, wrangle.

v altercate, argue, argy-bargy, battle, dispute, fight, quarrel, row, scrap, scuffle, squabble, tussle, wrangle, wrestle.

brawny *adj* athletic, beefy, bulky, burly, fleshy, hardy, hefty, herculean, hulking, husky, lusty, massive, muscular, powerful, robust, sinewy, solid, stalwart, strapping, strong, sturdy, vigorous, well-built. *antonyms* frail, slight.

brazen *adj* assured, audacious, barefaced, blatant, bold, brash, brassy, defiant, flagrant, forward, immodest, impudent, insolent, pert, saucy, shameless, unabashed, unashamed. *antonym* shamefaced.

breach *n* alienation, aperture, break, break-up, chasm, cleft, contravention, crack, crevice, difference, disaffection, disagreement, discontinuity, disobedience, disruption, dissension, dissociation, division, estrangement, fissure, gap, hole, infraction, infringement, lapse, offence, opening, parting, quarrel, rent, rift, rupture, schism, secession, separation, severance, split, transgression, trespass, variance, violation.

breadth *n* amplitude, area, beam, broadness, bulk, compass, comprehensiveness, dimension, expanse, extensiveness, extent, latitude, magnitude, measure, range, reach, scale, scope, size, space, span, spread, sweep, thickness, vastness, volume, wideness, width.

break *v* abandon, absorb, announce, appear, bankrupt, batter, beat, better, breach, burst, bust, contravene, cow, crack, crash, cripple, cushion, cut, dash, defeat, degrade, demolish, demoralise, destroy, diminish, discharge, disclose, discontinue, disintegrate, disobey, dispirit, disregard, divide, divulge, emerge, enervate, enfeeble, erupt, escape, exceed, excel, explode, flee, flout, fly, fracture, fragment, happen, humiliate, impair, impart, incapacitate, inform, infract, infringe, interrupt, jigger, knacker, lessen, moderate, modify, occur, outdo, outstrip, part, pause, proclaim, reduce, rend, rest, retard, reveal, ruin, separate, sever, shatter, shiver, smash, snap, soften, splinter, split, stave, stop, subdue, surpass, suspend, tame, tear, tell, transgress, undermine, undo, violate, weaken, worst.

n advantage, alienation, breach, breather, chance, cleft, crack,

crevice, disaffection, discontinuity, dispute, disruption, divergence, division, estrangement, fissure, fortune, fracture, gap, gash, halt, hiatus, hole, interlude, intermission, interruption, interval, lapse, let-up, lull, opening, opportunity, pause, quarrel, recess, rent, respite, rest, rift, rupture, schism, separation, split, suspension, tear, time-out.

break away depart, detach, escape, flee, fly, leave, part company, quit, renegue, revolt, run away, secede, separate, split.

break down analyse, anatomise, collapse, conk out, crack up, crush, demolish, dissect, fail, give way, seize up, stop.

break in burgle, encroach, impinge, interfere, interject, interpose, interrupt, intervene, intrude, invade.

break off cease, desist, detach, disconnect, discontinue, divide, end, finish, halt, interrupt, part, pause, separate, sever, snap off, splinter, stop, suspend, terminate.

break out abscond, arise, begin, bolt, burst, commence, emerge, erupt, escape, flare up, flee, happen, occur, start.

break the ice begin, lead the way, relax, set at ease, start the ball rolling, unbend.

break through achieve, emerge, gain ground, leap forward, make headway, pass, penetrate, progress, succeed.

break up adjourn, analyse, anatomise, demolish, destroy, disband, dismantle, disperse, disrupt, dissolve, divide, divorce, part, scatter, separate, sever, split, stop, suspend, terminate.

break with ditch, drop, finish with, jilt, part with, reject, renounce, repudiate, separate.

breakdown *n* analysis, categorisation, classification, collapse, disintegration, disruption, dissection, failure, interruption, itemisation, mishap, stoppage.

breakthrough *n* advance, development, discovery, find, finding, gain, headway, improvement, invention, leap, progress, step.

break-up *n* breakdown, crack-up, crumbling, disintegration, dispersal, dissolution, divorce, finish, parting, rift, separation, split, splitting, termination.

breasts *n* boobs, bristols, bust, cans, dugs, knockers, paps, teats, tits.

breath *n* air, animation, aroma, breathing, breeze, energy, exhalation, existence, flutter, gasp, gulp, gust, hint, inhalation, life, murmur, odour, pant, puff, respiration, sigh, smell, spirit, suggestion, suspicion, undertone, vapour, vitality, waft, wheeze, whiff, whisper.

breathe v articulate, exercise, exhale, expire, express, imbue, impart, infuse, inhale, inject, inspire, instil, live, murmur, pant, puff, respire, say, sigh, tire, transfuse, utter, voice, whisper.

breathless adj agog, anxious, avid, choking, eager, excited, exhausted, expectant, gasping, gulping, hushed, impatient, panting, puffing, short-winded, spent, wheezing, wheezy, winded.

breathtaking adj affecting, amazing, astonishing, awe-inspiring, awesome, exciting, impressive, magnificent, moving, overwhelming, stirring, stunning, thrilling.

breed v arouse, bear, beget, bring forth, bring up, cause, create, cultivate, develop, discipline, educate, engender, foster, generate, hatch, induce, instruct, make, multiply, nourish, nurture, occasion, originate, procreate, produce, propagate, raise, rear, reproduce, train.
n family, ilk, kind, line, lineage, pedigree, progeny, race, sort, species, stamp, stock, strain, type, variety.

breeding n ancestry, background, civility, courtesy, cultivation, culture, development, education, gentility, lineage, manners, nurture, polish, politeness, raising, rearing, refinement, reproduction, stock, strain, training, upbringing, urbanity. **antonym** vulgarity.

breeding-ground n hotbed, nest.

breeze n air, breath, draught, flurry, gale, gust, waft, whiff, wind, zephyr.
v flit, glide, hurry, sail, sally, sweep, trip, wander.

breezy adj airy, animated, blithe, blowing, blowy, blustery, bright, buoyant, carefree, careless, casual, cheerful, debonair, easy-going, exhilarating, fresh, gusty, informal, insouciant, jaunty, light, light-hearted, lively, nonchalant, sprightly, squally, sunny, untroubled, vivacious, windy. **antonyms** calm, staid.

brevity n abruptness, briefness, brusqueness, conciseness, concision, crispness, curtness, economy, evanescence, impermanence, incisiveness, pithiness, shortness, succinctness, summariness, terseness, transience, transitoriness.

antonyms longevity, permanence, verbosity.

brew v boil, build up, concoct, contrive, cook, decoct, develop, devise, excite, ferment, foment, gather, hatch, infuse, mix, plan, plot, prepare, project, scheme, seethe, soak, steep, stew.
n beverage, blend, broth, concoction, distillation, drink, fermentation, gruel, infusion, liquor, mixture, potion, preparation, stew.

bribe n allurement, back-hander, enticement, graft, grease, hush money, incentive, inducement, pay-off, payola, protection money, slush fund, sweetener.
v buy off, buy over, corrupt, reward, square, suborn.

bribery n corruption, graft, greasing, inducement, lubrication, palm-greasing, payola, protection, subornation.

brick n block, breeze block, brickbat, clanger, faux pas, firebrick, gaffe.

bridal adj conjugal, connubial, marital, marriage, matrimonial, nuptial, wedding.

bridge n arch, band, bond, causeway, connection, flyover, link, overpass, pontoon bridge, span, tie, viaduct, yoke.
v attach, bind, connect, couple, cross, fill, join, link, span, traverse, unite, yoke.

bridle v check, contain, control, curb, govern, master, moderate, rein in, repress, restrain, subdue.

brief adj abrupt, aphoristic, blunt, brusque, compendious, compressed, concise, crisp, cursory, curt, ephemeral, fast, fleeting, hasty, limited, momentary, passing, pithy, quick, sharp, short, short-lived, succinct, surly, swift, temporary, terse, transient, transitory. **antonyms** long, long-lived, verbose.
n advice, argument, briefing, case, contention, data, defence, demonstration, directions, directive, dossier, instructions, mandate, orders, outline, précis, remit, summary.
v advise, direct, explain, fill in, gen up, guide, inform, instruct, prepare, prime.

briefly adv abruptly, brusquely, concisely, cursorily, curtly, fleetingly, hastily, hurriedly, momentarily, précisely, quickly, shortly, summarily, temporarily, tersely. **antonyms** fully, permanently.

bright adj ablaze, acute, astute, auspicious, beaming, blazing, brainy, breezy, brilliant, burnished, cheerful, clear, clear-headed, clever, cloudless, dazzling, effulgent, encouraging, excellent, favourable, flashing, gay, genial, glad, glaring, gleaming, glistening, glittering, glorious, glowing, golden, happy, hopeful, illuminated, illustrious, ingenious, intelligent, intense, inventive, jolly, joyful, joyous, keen, lambent, light-hearted, limpid, lively, lucid, luminous, lustrous, magnificent, merry, observant, optimistic, perceptive, perspicacious, polished, promising, propitious, prosperous, quick, quick-witted, radiant, resplendent, rosy, scintillating, sharp, shimmering, shining, smart, sparkling, splendid, sunny, translucent, transparent, twinkling, unclouded, undulled, untarnished, vivacious, vivid, wide-awake. *antonyms* depressing, dull, stupid.

brighten *v* burnish, cheer up, clear up, encourage, enliven, flash, gladden, gleam, glow, hearten, illuminate, light up, lighten, perk up, polish, rub up, shine. *antonyms* darken, dull, tarnish.

brightness *n* blaze, brains, breeziness, brilliance, cheer, cheerfulness, cleverness, effulgence, gladness, glare, glitter, glory, hopefulness, illumination, joy, liveliness, luminosity, lustre, magnificence, optimism, promise, propitiousness, radiance, resplendence, sheen, sparkle, splendour, vivacity, vividness. *antonyms* cheerlessness, darkness, dullness.

brilliance *n* animation, aptitude, blaze, bravura, brightness, cleverness, dazzle, distinction, éclat, effulgence, excellence, gaiety, genius, giftedness, glamour, glare, gleam, glitter, glory, gloss, gorgeousness, grandeur, greatness, illustriousness, intensity, inventiveness, luminosity, lustre, magnificence, pizzazz, radiance, resplendence, scintillation, sheen, sparkle, splendour, talent, vivacity, vividness, wit.

brilliant *adj* ablaze, accomplished, adroit, animated, astute, blazing, brainy, bright, celebrated, clever, dazzling, effulgent, eminent, exceptional, expert, famous, gifted, glaring, glittering, glorious, glossy, illustrious, ingenious, intellectual, intelligent, intense, inventive, lambent, luminous, magnificent, masterly, outstanding, quick, scintillating, shining, showy, skilful, sparkling, splendid, star, star-like, superb, talented, vivacious, vivid, witty. *antonyms* dull, restrained, stupid, undistinguished.

brim *n* border, brink, circumference, edge, lip, marge, margin, perimeter, periphery, rim, skirt, verge.

bring *v* accompany, accustom, add, attract, bear, carry, cause, command, conduct, convey, convince, create, deliver, dispose, draw, earn, effect, engender, escort, fetch, force, gather, generate, get beget, gross, guide, induce, inflict, influence, introduce, lead, make, move, net, occasion, persuade, produce, prompt, return, sway, take, transfer, transport, usher, wreak, yield.

bring about accomplish, achieve, cause, compass, create, effect, effectuate, engender, engineer, fulfil, generate, manage, manipulate, manoeuvre, occasion, produce, realise.

bring down abase, break, debase, degrade, fell, floor, humble, lay low, level, lower, overthrow, overturn, reduce, ruin, shoot, topple, undermine.

bring forth afford, bear, beget, engender, furnish, generate, produce, provide, supply, yield.

bring home to convince, drive home, emphasise, impress upon, persuade, prove.

bring in accrue, earn, fetch, gross, introduce, net, produce, profit, realise, return, yield.

bring off accomplish, achieve, bring about, compass, discharge, execute, fulfil, perform, rescue.

bring on accelerate, advance, cause, expedite, generate, give rise to, induce, inspire, lead to, occasion, precipitate, prompt, provoke. *antonym* inhibit.

bring out draw out, emphasise, enhance, highlight, introduce, issue, print, publish, utter.

bring to light dig up, disclose, discover, expose, reveal, show, uncover, unearth, unveil.

bring to nothing destroy, knock the bottom out of, mar, nullify, ruin, scupper, spoil, undermine, vitiate.

bring up advance, broach, disgorge, educate, form, foster, introduce, mention, nurture, propose, puke, raise, rear, regurgitate, submit, succeed, succour, support, teach, throw up, train, vomit.

brink *n* bank, border, boundary, brim, edge, extremity, fringe, limit, lip, marge, margin, point, rim, skirt, threshold, verge, waterside.

brisk *adj* active, agile, alert, bracing, bright, bustling, busy, crisp, effervescing, energetic, exhilarating, expeditious, fresh, invigorating, keen, lively, nimble, nippy, no-nonsense, prompt, quick, refreshing, sharp, snappy, speedy, spirited, sprightly, spry, stimulating, vigorous. *antonym* sluggish.

bristling *adj* abounding, crawling, humming, incensed, indignant, seething, spitting, swarming, teeming.

brittle *adj* breakable, crackly, crisp, crumbling, crumbly, curt, delicate, edgy, fragile, frail, irritable, nervous, nervy, shattery, shivery, short, tense. *antonyms* durable, resilient, sturdy.

broach *v* crack open, introduce, launch into, mention, pierce, propose, puncture, raise, start, suggest, tap, uncork, utter.

broad *adj* all-embracing, ample, beamy, blue, capacious, catholic, coarse, comprehensive, eclectic, encyclopaedic, enlightened, expansive, extensive, far-reaching, general, generous, gross, improper, inclusive, indecent, indelicate, large, roomy, spacious, square, sweeping, tolerant, universal, unlimited, unrefined, vast, voluminous, vulgar, wide, wide-ranging, widespread. *antonym* narrow.

broadcast *v* advertise, air, announce, beam, cable, circulate, disseminate, proclaim, promulgate, publicise, publish, radio, relay, report, show, spread, televise, transmit.

broaden *v* augment, branch out, develop, diversify, enlarge, enlighten, expand, extend, increase, open up, spread, stretch, supplement, swell, thicken, widen.

broad-minded *adj* catholic, cosmopolitan, dispassionate, enlightened, flexible, free-thinking, indulgent, liberal, open-minded, permissive, receptive, tolerant, unbiased, unprejudiced, verligte.

broadside *n* assault, attack, battering, blast, bombardment, brickbat, cannonade, counterblast, denunciation, diatribe, harangue, invective.

broke *adj* bankrupt, bust, destitute, impecunious, impoverished, insolvent, penniless, penurious, ruined, skint, stony-broke, strapped. *antonyms* affluent, solvent.

broken *adj* bankrupt, beaten, betrayed, browbeaten, burst, crippled, crushed, defeated, defective, demolished, demoralised, destroyed, disconnected, discontinuous, dishonoured, disjointed, dismantled, dispersed, disregarded, disturbed, down, dud, duff, erratic, exhausted, faulty, feeble, forgotten, fractured, fragmentary, fragmented, halting, hesitating, humbled, ignored, imperfect, incoherent, incomplete, infirm, infringed, intermittent, interrupted, isolated, jiggered, kaput, knackered, oppressed, out of order, overpowered, rent, routed, ruined, run-down, ruptured, separated, severed, shattered, shivered, spasmodic, spent, stammering, subdued, tamed, transgressed, uncertain, vanquished, variegated, weak.

broken-down *adj* collapsed, decayed, dilapidated, disintegrated, inoperative, kaput, out of order, ruined.

broken-hearted *adj* crestfallen, dejected, desolate, despairing, despondent, devastated, disappointed, disconsolate, grief-stricken, hard-hit, heartbroken, inconsolable, miserable, mournful, prostrated, sorrowful, unhappy, wretched.

broker *n* agent, dealer, handler, intermediary, middleman, negotiator, stockbroker.

brood *v* agonise, cover, dwell on, fret, go over, hatch, incubate, meditate, mope, mull over, muse, ponder, rehearse, repine, ruminate.

brook *v* abide, accept, allow, bear, countenance, endure, permit, stand, stomach, submit to, suffer, support, swallow, tolerate, withstand.

brothel *n* bawdy-house, bordello, cathouse, house of ill fame, house of ill repute, knocking-shop, vaulting-house, whorehouse.

brother *n* associate, blood-brother, brer, chum, colleague, companion, comrade, confrère, cousin, fellow, friar, friend, kin, kinsman, mate, monk, pal, partner, relation, relative, sibling.

brotherhood *n* affiliation, alliance, association, clan, clique, community, confederacy, confederation, confraternity, coterie, fraternity, guild, league, society, union.

brotherly *adj* affectionate, amicable, benevolent, caring, concerned, cordial, fraternal, friendly, kind, loving, neighbourly, philanthropic, supervisory, sympathetic. *antonym* callous.

brow *n* appearance, aspect, bearing, brink, cliff, countenance, crown, edge, eyebrow, face, forehead, front, mien, peak, ridge, rim, summit, temples, tip, top, verge, visage.

browbeat *v* awe, batter, bludgeon, bulldoze, bully, coerce, cow, domineer, dragoon, hector, hound, intimidate, oppress, overbear, threaten, tyrannise. *antonym* coax.

brown *adj* auburn, bay, brick, bronze, bronzed, browned, brunette, chestnut, chocolate, coffee, dark, donkey, dun, dusky, ginger, hazel, mahogany, russet, rust, rusty, sunburnt, tan, tanned, tawny, toasted, umber.

brown study absence, absent-mindedness, absorption, abstraction, contemplation, meditation, musing, pensiveness, preoccupation, reflection, reverie, rumination.

browned off bored, bored stiff, brassed off, cheesed off, discontented, discouraged, disgruntled, disheartened, fed up, pissed off, weary. *antonyms* fascinated, interested.

browse *v* crop, dip into, eat, feed, flick through, graze, leaf through, nibble, pasture, peruse, scan, skim, survey.

bruise *v* blacken, blemish, contuse, crush, discolour, grieve, hurt, injure, insult, mar, mark, offend, pound, pulverise, stain, wound.
n blemish, contusion, discoloration, injury, mark, shiner, swelling.

brunt *n* burden, force, impact, impetus, pressure, shock, strain, stress, thrust, violence, weight.

brush[1] *v* buff, burnish, caress, clean, contact, flick, glance, graze, kiss, paint, polish, rub, scrape, shine, stroke, sweep, touch, wash.

brush aside belittle, dismiss, disregard, flout, ignore, override, pooh-pooh.

brush off cold-shoulder, discourage, disdain, dismiss, disown, disregard, ignore, rebuff, refuse, reject, repudiate, repulse, scorn, slight, snub, spurn. *antonyms* cultivate, encourage.

brush up cram, freshen up, improve, read up, refresh, relearn, revise, study, swot.

brush[2] *n* clash, conflict, confrontation, dust-up, encounter, fight, fracas, incident, run-in, scrap, set-to, skirmish, tussle.

brush-off *n* cold shoulder, discouragement, dismissal, go-by, rebuff, refusal, rejection, repudiation, repulse, slight, snub. *antonym* encouragement.

brusque *adj* abrupt, blunt, curt, discourteous, gruff, hasty, impolite, sharp, short, surly, tactless, tart, terse, uncivil, undiplomatic. *antonyms* courteous, tactful.

brutal *adj* animal, barbarous, bearish, beastly, bestial, bloodthirsty, boarish, brute, brutish, callous, coarse, crude, cruel, ferocious, gruff, harsh, heartless, impolite, inhuman, inhumane, insensitive, merciless, pitiless, remorseless, rough, rude, ruthless, savage, sensual, severe, uncivil, uncivilised, unfeeling, unmannerly, unsympathetic, vicious. *antonyms* humane, kindly.

brutality *n* atrocity, barbarism, barbarity, bloodthirstiness, brutishness, callousness, coarseness, cruelty, ferocity, inhumanity, roughness, ruthlessness, savageness, savagery, viciousness. *antonyms* gentleness, kindness.

brute *n* animal, barbarian, beast, boor, creature, devil, fiend, lout, monster, ogre, sadist, savage, swine. *antonym* gentleman.
adj bestial, coarse, depraved, gross, instinctive, mindless, physical, senseless, unthinking. *antonym* refined.

brutish *adj* barbarian, barbaric, barbarous, boorish, coarse, crass, crude, cruel, gross, loutish, savage, stupid, subhuman, swinish, uncouth, vulgar. *antonym* refined.

bubble *n* ball, bead, bladder, blister, blob, drop, droplet, globule, vesicle.
v babble, boil, burble, effervesce, fizz, foam, froth, gurgle, murmur, percolate, purl, ripple, seethe, sparkle, trickle, trill, wallop.

bubbly *adj* animated, bouncy, carbonated, curly, effervescent, elated, excited, fizzy, happy, lively, merry, sudsy. *antonym* flat.

buck *v* bound, cheer, dislodge, encourage, gladden, gratify, hearten, inspirit, jerk, jump, leap, please, prance, spring, start, throw, unseat, vault.

buck up brighten, cheer, cheer up, encourage, hearten, improve, inspirit, perk up, rally, stimulate, take heart. *antonym* dishearten.

buckle *n* bend, bulge, catch, clasp, clip, contortion, distortion, fastener, hasp, kink, twist, warp.
v bend, bulge, catch, cave in, clasp, close, collapse, connect, contort, crumple, distort, fasten, fold, hitch, hook, secure, twist, warp, wrinkle.

budding *adj* burgeoning, developing, embryonic, fledgling, flowering, germinal, growing, hopeful, incipient, intending, nascent, potential, promising. *antonym* experienced.

budge *v* bend, change, convince,

dislodge, give (way), inch, influence, move, persuade, propel, push, remove, roll, shift, slide, stir, sway, yield.

budget *n* allocation, allotment, allowance, cost, estimate, finances, funds, means, resources.
v allocate, apportion, cost, estimate, plan, ration.

buff *n* addict, admirer, aficionado, bug, cognoscente, connoisseur, devotee, enthusiast, expert, fan, fiend, freak.

buffer *n* bulwark, bumper, cushion, fender, intermediary, pad, pillow, safeguard, screen, shield, shock-absorber.

buffet *v* bang, batter, beat, box, bump, clobber, clout, cuff, flail, hit, jar, knock, pound, pummel, push, rap, shove, slap, strike, thump, wallop.
n bang, blow, box, bump, clout, cuff, jar, jolt, knock, push, rap, shove, slap, smack, thump, wallop.

buffoon *n* clown, comedian, comic, droll, fool, harlequin, jester, joker.

bug *n* addict, admirer, bacterium, blemish, buff, catch, craze, defect, disease, enthusiast, error, fad, failing, fan, fault, fiend, flaw, freak, germ, gremlin, imperfection, infection, mania, micro-organism, obsession, rage, snarl-up, virus.
v annoy, badger, bother, disturb, get, harass, irk, irritate, needle, nettle, pester, plague, vex.

bugbear *n* anathema, bane, bête noire, bloody-bones, bogey, devil, dread, fiend, horror, nightmare, pet hate.

build *v* assemble, augment, base, begin, big, constitute, construct, develop, edify, enlarge, erect, escalate, establish, extend, fabricate, form, formulate, found, improve, inaugurate, increase, initiate, institute, intensify, knock together, make, originate, raise, strengthen. *antonyms* destroy, knock down, lessen, weaken.
n body, figure, form, frame, physique, shape, size, structure.

build up advertise, amplify, assemble, boost, develop, enhance, expand, extend, fortify, heighten, hype, improve, increase, intensify, plug, promote, publicise, reinforce, strengthen. *antonyms* lessen, weaken.

building *n* architecture, construction, domicile, dwelling, edifice, erection, fabric, fabrication, house, pile, structure. *antonym* destruction.

build-up *n* accretion, accumulation, ballyhoo, development, enlargement, escalation, expansion, gain, growth, heap, hype, increase, load, mass, plug, promotion, publicity, puff, stack, stockpile, store. *antonyms* decrease, reduction.

built-in *adj* essential, fundamental, implicit, in-built, included, incorporated, inherent, inseparable, integral, intrinsic, necessary.

bulbous *adj* bellied, bellying, bloated, bulging, convex, distended, rounded, swelling, swollen.

bulge *n* belly, boost, bump, distension, hump, increase, intensification, lump, projection, protrusion, protuberance, rise, surge, swelling, upsurge.
v bag, belly, dilate, distend, enlarge, expand, hump, project, protrude, sag, swell.

bulk *n* amplitude, bigness, body, dimensions, extensity, extent, generality, immensity, largeness, magnitude, majority, mass, most, plurality, preponderance, size, substance, volume, weight.

bulky *adj* big, colossal, cumbersome, enormous, heavy, hefty, huge, hulking, immense, large, lumping, mammoth, massive, ponderous, substantial, unmanageable, unwieldy, voluminous, weighty. *antonyms* handy, insubstantial, small.

bulldoze *v* browbeat, bully, clear, coerce, cow, demolish, drive, flatten, force, hector, intimidate, knock down, level, propel, push, push through, raze, shove, thrust.

bulletin *n* announcement, communication, communiqué, dispatch, message, newsflash, notification, report, statement.

bully *n* bouncer, browbeater, bully-boy, intimidator, oppressor, persecutor, ruffian, tormentor, tough, tyrant.
v bluster, browbeat, bulldoze, coerce, cow, domineer, hector, intimidate, oppress, overbear, persecute, push around, swagger, terrorise, tyrannise. *antonyms* coax, persuade.

bulwark *n* bastion, buffer, buttress, defence, embankment, fortification, guard, mainstay, outwork, partition, rampart, safeguard, security, support.

bumbling *adj* awkward, blundering, botching, bungling, clumsy, incompetent, inefficient, inept, lumbering, maladroit, muddled, stumbling. *antonyms* competent, efficient.

bump v bang, bounce, budge, collide
(with), crash, dislodge, displace, hit, jar,
jerk, jolt, jostle, jounce, knock, move,
rattle, remove, shake, shift, slam, strike.
n bang, blow, bulge, collision,
contusion, crash, hit, hump, impact, jar,
jolt, knob, knock, knot, lump, node,
nodule, protuberance, rap, shock, smash,
swelling, thud, thump.
bump off assassinate, dispatch, do
in, eliminate, kill, liquidate, murder,
remove, rub out, top.

bumper adj abundant, bountiful,
enormous, excellent, exceptional, great,
huge, jumbo, large, massive, prodigal,
spanking, teeming, unusual, whacking,
whopping. **antonyms** miserly, small.

bumpkin n hick, hillbilly, peasant,
provincial, rustic, yokel.

bumptious adj arrogant, boastful,
brash, cocky, conceited, egotistic,
forward, full of oneself, impudent,
overbearing, over-confident, pompous,
presumptuous, pushy, self-assertive,
self-important, showy, swaggering,
vainglorious, vaunting. **antonyms**
humble, modest.

bumpy adj bouncy, choppy, irregular,
jarring, jerky, jolting, jolty, knobbly,
knobby, lumpy, rough, rutted, uneven.
antonym smooth.

bunch n assortment, band, batch,
bouquet, bundle, clump, cluster,
collection, crew, crowd, flock, gang,
gathering, heap, lot, mass, mob,
multitude, number, parcel, party, pile,
quantity, sheaf, spray, stack, swarm,
team, troop, tuft.
v assemble, bundle, cluster, collect,
congregate, crowd, flock, group, herd,
huddle, mass, pack. **antonyms** scatter,
spread out.

bundle n accumulation, assortment,
bag, bale, batch, box, bunch, carton,
collection, consignment, crate, drum,
group, heap, mass, pack, package,
packet, pallet, parcel, pile, quantity, roll,
shock, stack, swag.
v bale, bind, fasten, pack, tie, truss,
wrap.

bungle v blunder, bodge, boob, botch,
bumble, cock up, duff, flub, footle,
foozle, foul up, fuck up, fudge, goof,
louse up, mar, mess up, miscalculate,
mismanage, muff, mull, ruin, screw
up, spoil.
n blunder, boob, booboo, botch-up,
cock-up, foul-up, mull.

bunkum n balderdash, baloney,

bilge, bosh, bunk, garbage,
hooey, horsefeathers, nonsense, piffle,
poppycock, rot, rubbish, stuff and
nonsense, tommyrot, tosh, trash, tripe,
twaddle. **antonym** sense.

buoyant adj afloat, animated, blithe,
bouncy, breezy, bright, bullish, carefree,
cheerful, debonair, floating, happy,
jaunty, joyful, light, light-hearted, lively,
peppy, sprightly, sunny, weightless.
antonym depressed.

burble n babble, gurgle, lapping,
murmur, purl, purling.
v babble, gurgle, lap, murmur, purl.

burden n affliction, anxiety, bear, care,
cargo, clog, dead weight, encumbrance,
grievance, load, millstone, obligation,
obstruction, onus, responsibility, sorrow,
strain, stress, trial, trouble, weight,
worry.
v bother, encumber, handicap, lade, lie
hard on, lie heavy on, load, oppress,
overload, overwhelm, strain, tax, worry.
antonyms disburden, lighten, relieve.

burdensome adj crushing, difficult,
distressing, exacting, heavy, irksome,
onerous, oppressive, taxing, troublesome, trying, wearisome, weighty.
antonyms easy, light.

bureaucracy n administration, city hall,
civil service, directorate, government,
ministry, officialdom, officialese,
officials, red tape, regulations, the
authorities, the system.

bureaucrat n administrator,
apparatchik, civil servant, functionary,
mandarin, minister, official.

burial n burying, entombment,
exequies, funeral, inhumation, interment,
obsequies, sepulchre.

burlesque n caricature, mickey-taking,
mock, mockery, parody, ridicule, satire,
send-up, spoof, take-off, travesty.
adj comic, derisive, droll, farcical,
mocking, parodying, satirical. **antonym**
serious.
v ape, caricature, exaggerate, imitate,
lampoon, mock, parody, ridicule,
satirise, send up, spoof, take off,
travesty.

burly adj athletic, beefy, big, brawny,
bulky, heavy, hefty, hulking, husky,
muscular, powerful, stocky, stout,
strapping, strong, sturdy, thickset, well-
built. **antonyms** puny, slim, small,
thin.

burn v bite, blaze, brand, calcine,
cauterise, char, combust, conflagrate,
consume, corrode, deflagrate, desire,

expend, flame, flare, flash, flicker, fume, glow, hurt, ignite, incinerate, kindle, light, oxidise, pain, parch, scorch, seethe, shrivel, simmer, singe, smart, smoke, smoulder, sting, tingle, toast, use, wither, yearn.

urning *adj* acrid, acute, alight, ardent, biting, blazing, caustic, compelling, consuming, corrosive, critical, crucial, eager, earnest, essential, excessive, fervent, fiery, flaming, flashing, frantic, frenzied, gleaming, glowing, hot, illuminated, impassioned, important, intense, irritating, painful, passionate, piercing, pressing, prickling, pungent, scorching, significant, smarting, smouldering, stinging, tingling, urgent, vehement, vital, zealous. **antonyms** apathetic, cold, mild, unimportant.

urrow *n* den, earth, hole, lair, retreat, set(t), shelter, tunnel, warren.
v delve, dig, earth, excavate, mine, tunnel, undermine.

urst *v* barge, blow up, break, crack, disintegrate, erupt, explode, fragment, gush, puncture, run, rupture, rush, shatter, shiver, split, spout, tear.
n bang, blast, blasting, blow-out, blow-up, breach, break, crack, discharge, eruption, explosion, fit, gallop, gush, gust, outbreak, outburst, outpouring, rupture, rush, spate, split, spurt, surge, torrent.
adj broken, flat, kaput, punctured, ruptured, split, torn.

ury *v* absorb, conceal, cover, embed, enclose, engage, engross, engulf, enshroud, entomb, hide, immerse, implant, inhume, inter, interest, lay to rest, occupy, secrete, shroud, sink, submerge. **antonyms** disinter, uncover.

ushy *adj* bristling, bristly, fluffy, fuzzy, luxuriant, rough, shaggy, spreading, stiff, thick, unruly, wiry. **antonyms** neat, tidy, trim, well-kept.

usily *adv* actively, assiduously, briskly, diligently, earnestly, energetically, hard, industriously, intently, purposefully, speedily, strenuously.

usiness *n* affair, assignment, bargaining, calling, career, commerce, company, concern, corporation, craft, dealings, duty, employment, enterprise, establishment, firm, function, industry, issue, job, line, manufacturing, matter, merchandising, métier, occupation, organisation, palaver, point, problem, profession, pursuit, question, responsibility, selling, subject, task, topic, trade, trading, transaction(s), venture, vocation, work.

business-like *adj* correct, efficient, formal, impersonal, matter-of-fact, methodical, orderly, organised, practical, précise, professional, regular, routine, systematic, thorough, well-ordered. **antonyms** disorganised, inefficient.

bustle *v* dash, fuss, hasten, hurry, rush, scamper, scramble, scurry, scuttle, stir, tear.
n activity, ado, agitation, commotion, excitement, flurry, fuss, haste, hurly-burly, hurry, palaver, stir, to-do, toing and froing, tumult.

bustling *adj* active, astir, busy, buzzing, crowded, energetic, eventful, full, humming, lively, restless, rushing, stirring, swarming, teeming, thronged. **antonym** quiet.

busy *adj* active, assiduous, brisk, diligent, employed, energetic, engaged, engrossed, exacting, full, fussy, hectic, industrious, inquisitive, interfering, lively, meddlesome, meddling, nosy, occupied, officious, persevering, prying, restless, slaving, stirring, strenuous, tireless, tiring, troublesome, working. **antonyms** idle, quiet.
v absorb, bother, concern, employ, engage, engross, immerse, interest, occupy.

busybody *n* eavesdropper, gossip, intriguer, intruder, meddler, nosey parker, prodnose, pry, scandalmonger, snoop, snooper, troublemaker.

butcher *v* assassinate, botch, carve, clean, cut, destroy, exterminate, kill, liquidate, massacre, mutilate, ruin, slaughter, slay, spoil, wreck.

butt[1] *n* base, end, foot, haft, handle, hilt, shaft, shank, stock, stub, tail, tip.

butt[2] *n* dupe, laughing-stock, object, point, subject, target, victim.

butt[3] *v, n* buck, buffet, bump, hit, jab, knock, poke, prod, punch, push, ram, shove, thrust.

butt in cut in, interfere, interpose, interrupt, intrude, meddle.

butter up blarney, cajole, coax, flatter, soft-soap, wheedle.

buttocks *n* arse, backside, beam end, behind, bottom, breach, bum, derrière, fanny, fud, haunches, hinder-end, hindquarters, posterior, prat, rear, rump, seat.

buttonhole *v* accost, bore, catch, detain, grab, importune, nab, pin, waylay.

buttress *n* brace, mainstay, pier, prop,

reinforcement, shore, stanchion, stay, strut, support.

v bolster up, brace, hold up, prop up, reinforce, shore up, strengthen, support, sustain, uphold. *antonym* weaken.

buxom *adj* ample, bosomy, busty, chesty, comely, hearty, jolly, lively, lusty, merry, plump, robust, voluptuous, well-rounded, winsome. *antonyms* petite, slim, small.

buy *v* acquire, bribe, corrupt, fix, get, obtain, procure, purchase, square, suborn. *antonym* sell.

n acquisition, bargain, deal, purchase.

buzz *n* buzzing, drone, gossip, hearsay, hiss, hum, murmur, news, purr, report, ring, ringing, rumour, scandal, whir(r), whisper, whizz.

v drone, hum, murmur, reverberate, ring, whir(r), whisper, whizz.

by *prep* along, beside, near, next to, over, past, through, via.

adv aside, at hand, away, beyond, close, handy, near, past.

by all means absolutely, certainly, doubtlessly, of course, positively, surely.

by any means anyhow.

by chance perchance.

by degrees bit by bit, gently, gradually, imperceptibly, inch by inch, little by little, slowly, step by step. *antonyms* all at one go, quickly, suddenly.

by far by a long chalk, by a long

shot, easily, far and away, immeasurably incomparably, much.

by fits and starts erratically, fitfully intermittently, irregularly, now and again, on and off, spasmodically, spo radically, unsystematically. *antonym.* constantly, continuously.

by halves imperfectly, incompletely scrappily, skimpily. *antonym* completely, totally.

by heart by rote, memoriter, off pat parrot-fashion, pat, word for word.

by mistake in error, mistakenly.

by no means in no way, not at all not in the least, not the least bit, on n account.

bygone *adj* ancient, antiquated departed, erstwhile, forgotten, former lost, olden, past, previous. *antonym* modern, recent.

n antique, oldie.

bypass *v* avoid, circumvent, ignore neglect, outflank.

n detour, ring road.

by-product *n* after-effect, consequence fall-out, repercussion, result, side-effec

bystander *n* eye-witness, looker-on observer, onlooker, passer-by, spectator watcher, witness.

byword *n* adage, aphorism apophthegm, catch-word, dictum epithet, gnome, maxim, motto, precep proverb, saying, slogan.

cabal *n* caucus, clique, coalition, conclave, confederacy, conspiracy, coterie, faction, intrigue, junta, league, machination, party, plot, plotters, scheme, set.

cabin *n* berth, bothy, chalet, compartment, cottage, deck-house, hovel, hut, lodge, quarters, room, shack, shanty, shed.

cache *n* accumulation, fund, garner, hoard, repository, reserve, stockpile, store, storehouse, supply, treasure-store. *v* bury, conceal, hide, secrete, stash, store, stow.

cackle *v, n* babble, chatter, chuckle, crow, gabble, giggle, jabber, laugh, prattle, snicker, snigger, titter.

cacophony *n* caterwauling, discord, disharmony, dissonance, stridency. *antonym* harmony.

cad *n* blackguard, bounder, churl, cur, heel, knave, rat, rotter, skunk, swine, worm. *antonym* gentleman.

cadence *n* accent, beat, inflection, intonation, lilt, measure, metre, modulation, pattern, pulse, rate, rhythm, stress, swing, tempo, throb.

cadge *v* beg, bum, freeload, hitch, scrounge, sponge.

cafe *n* cafeteria, coffee bar, coffee shop, greasy spoon, restaurant, snack bar, tea-room.

cage *v* confine, coop up, fence in, immure, impound, imprison, incarcerate, lock up, restrain, shut up. *antonyms* free, let out. *n* aviary, coop, corral, enclosure, pen, pound.

cag(e)y *adj* careful, chary, circumspect, discreet, guarded, non-committal, secretive, shrewd, wary, wily. *antonyms* frank, indiscreet, open.

cajole *v* beguile, blandish, blarney, coax, decoy, dupe, entice, entrap, flatter, inveigle, lure, manoeuvre, mislead, seduce, soothe, sweet-talk, tempt, wheedle. *antonyms* bully, force.

cake *v* bake, cement, coagulate, coat, condense, congeal, consolidate, cover, dry, encrust, harden, ossify, solidify, thicken.

calamitous *adj* cataclysmic, catastrophic, deadly, devastating, dire, disastrous, dreadful, fatal, ghastly, grievous, pernicious, ruinous, tragic, woeful. *antonyms* fortunate, happy.

calamity *n* adversity, affliction, cataclysm, catastrophe, desolation, disaster, distress, downfall, misadventure, mischance, misfortune, mishap, reverse, ruin, scourge, tragedy, trial, tribulation, woe, wretchedness. *antonyms* blessing, godsend.

calculate *v* aim, compute, consider, count, determine, enumerate, estimate, figure, gauge, intend, judge, plan, rate, reckon, value, weigh, work out.

calculated *adj* considered, deliberate, intended, intentional, planned, premeditated, purposed, purposeful, wilful. *antonyms* unintended, unplanned.

calculating *adj* canny, cautious, contriving, crafty, cunning, designing, devious, Machiavellian, manipulative, politic, scheming, sharp, shrewd, sly. *antonyms* artless, naïve, open.

calculation *n* answer, caution, ciphering, circumspection, computation, deliberation, estimate, estimation, figurework, figuring, forecast, foresight, forethought, judgement, planning, precaution, reckoning, result.

calibre *n* ability, bore, capacity, character, diameter, distinction, endowment, faculty, force, gauge, gifts, league, measure, merit, parts, quality, scope, size, stature, strength, talent, worth.

call *v* announce, appoint, arouse, assemble, awaken, bid, christen, collect, consider, contact, convene, convoke, cry, declare, decree, denominate, designate, dub, elect, entitle, estimate, gather, hail, halloo, invite, judge, label, muster, name, ordain, order, phone, proclaim, rally, regard, rouse, shout, style, summon, telephone, term, think, waken, yell.
n announcement, appeal, cause, claim, command, cry, demand, excuse, grounds, hail, invitation, justification, need, notice, occasion, order, plea, reason, request, right, ring, scream, shout, signal, summons, supplication, urge, visit, whoop, yell.

call for¹ demand, entail, involve, necessitate, need, occasion, require, suggest.

call for² collect, fetch, pick up, uplift.

call it a day finish, knock off, leave off,

pack it in, pack up, shut up shop, stop, throw in the towel.

call off abandon, break off, cancel, desist, discontinue, drop, withdraw.

call on appeal, appeal to, ask, bid, call round, entreat, go and see, invite, invoke, request, summon, supplicate, visit.

call the tune call the shots, command, dictate, give the orders, govern, lead, rule, rule the roost.

calling n business, career, employment, field, job, line, line of country, métier, mission, occupation, profession, province, pursuit, trade, vocation, work.

callous adj case-hardened, cold, hard-bitten, hard-boiled, hardened, hard-hearted, heartless, indifferent, insensitive, inured, obdurate, soulless, thick-skinned, uncaring, unfeeling, unresponsive, unsouled, unsusceptible, unsympathetic. **antonyms** kind, sensitive, sympathetic.

callow adj fledgling, green, guileless, immature, inexperienced, juvenile, naïve, puerile, raw, unfledged, uninitiated, unsophisticated. **antonym** experienced.

calm adj balmy, collected, composed, cool, dispassionate, equable, halcyon, impassive, imperturbable, laid back, mild, pacific, passionless, peaceful, placid, quiet, relaxed, restful, sedate, self-collected, self-possessed, serene, smooth, still, stilly, tranquil, unclouded, undisturbed, unemotional, uneventful, unexcitable, unexcited, unflappable, unflustered, unmoved, unperturbed, unruffled, untroubled, windless. **antonyms** excitable, rough, stormy, wild, worried.

v compose, hush, mollify, pacify, placate, quieten, relax, soothe. **antonyms** excite, irritate, worry.

n calmness, dispassion, hush, peace, peacefulness, quiet, repose, serenity, stillness. **antonyms** restlessness, storminess.

calmness n calm, composure, cool, coolness, dispassion, equability, equanimity, hush, impassiveness, impassivity, motionless, peace, peacefulness, poise, quiet, repose, restfulness, sang-froid, self-possession, serenity, smoothness, stillness, tranquillity, unexcitableness, unflappableness. **antonyms** excitability, restlessness, storminess.

calumny n abuse, aspersion, backbiting, defamation, denigration, derogation, disparagement, insult, libel, lying, misrepresentation, obloquy, revilement, slander, smear, stigma, vilification, vituperation.

camaraderie n brotherhood, brotherliness, companionship, comradeship, esprit de corps, fellowship, fraternisation, good-fellowship, intimacy, togetherness.

camouflage n cloak, concealment, cover, covering, deception, disguise, front, guise, mask, masquerade, screen, subterfuge.

v cloak, conceal, cover, disguise, hide, mask, obfuscate, obscure, screen, veil. **antonyms** reveal, uncover.

camp adj affected, artificial, effeminate, exaggerated, homosexual, mannered, ostentatious, over the top, poncy, posturing, theatrical.

campaign n attack, crusade, drive, excursion, expedition, movement, offensive, operation, promotion, push.

v advocate, attack, crusade, fight, promote, push.

cancel v abolish, abort, abrogate, annul, compensate, counterbalance, countermand, delete, efface, eliminate, erase, expunge, neutralise, nullify, obliterate, offset, quash, redeem, repeal, repudiate, rescind, revoke, scrub, strike.

cancellation n abandoning, abandonment, abolition, annulment, deletion, elimination, neutralisation, nullifying, quashing, repeal, revocation.

cancer n blight, canker, carcinoma, corruption, evil, growth, malignancy, melanoma, pestilence, rot, sickness, tumour.

candid adj blunt, clear, fair, forthright, frank, free, guileless, ingenuous, just, open, outspoken, plain, sincere, straightforward, truthful, unbiased, uncontrived, unequivocal, unposed, unprejudiced, upfront. **antonyms** cagey, devious, evasive.

candidate n applicant, aspirant, claimant, competitor, contender, contestant, entrant, nominee, possibility, pretender, runner.

candour n artlessness, directness, fairness, forthrightness, frankness, guilelessness, honesty, ingenuousness, naïvety, openness, outspokenness, plain-dealing, simplicity, sincerity, straightforwardness, truthfulness, unequivocalness. **antonyms** cageyness, deviousness, evasiveness.

canker n bane, blight, boil, cancer,

corrosion, corruption, infection, lesion, rot, scourge, sore, ulcer.

canny *adj* acute, artful, astute, careful, cautious, circumspect, clever, comfortable, gentle, harmless, innocent, judicious, knowing, lucky, perspicacious, prudent, sagacious, sharp, shrewd, skilful, sly, subtle, wise, worldly-wise. **antonyms** foolish, imprudent.

canonical *adj* accepted, approved, authorised, authoritative, orthodox, recognised, regular, sanctioned. **antonym** uncanonical.

cant *n* argot, humbug, hypocrisy, insincerity, jargon, lingo, pretentiousness, sanctimoniousness, slang, vernacular.

cantankerous *adj* bad-tempered, captious, contrary, crabbed, crabby, crotchety, crusty, difficult, disagreeable, feisty, grouchy, grumpy, ill-humoured, ill-natured, irascible, irritable, peevish, perverse, piggish, quarrelsome, testy. **antonyms** good-natured, pleasant.

canvass *v* agitate, analyse, ask for, campaign, debate, discuss, dispute, electioneer, examine, inspect, investigate, poll, scan, scrutinise, seek, sift, solicit, study.
n examination, investigation, poll, scrutiny, survey, tally.

cap *v* beat, better, complete, cover, crown, eclipse, exceed, excel, finish, outdo, outstrip, surpass, top, transcend.

capability *n* ability, capacity, competence, facility, faculty, means, potential, potentiality, power, proficiency, qualification, skill, talent.

capable *adj* able, accomplished, adept, adequate, apt, clever, competent, disposed, efficient, experienced, fitted, gifted, intelligent, liable, masterly, proficient, qualified, skilful, suited, talented. **antonyms** incapable, incompetent, useless.

capacious *adj* ample, big, broad, comfortable, commodious, comprehensive, expansive, extensive, generous, huge, large, liberal, roomy, sizable, spacious, substantial, vast, voluminous, wide. **antonyms** cramped, small.

capacity *n* ability, amplitude, appointment, aptitude, aptness, brains, calibre, capability, cleverness, competence, dimensions, efficiency, extent, facility, faculty, forte, function, genius, gift, intelligence, magnitude, office, position, post, power, province, range, readiness, role, room, scope, service, size, space, sphere, strength, volume.

caper *v* bounce, bound, cavort, dance, frisk, frolic, gambol, hop, jump, leap, romp, skip, spring.
n affair, antic, business, escapade, gambol, high jinks, hop, jape, jest, jump, lark, leap, mischief, prank, revel, sport, stunt.

capital[1] *adj* cardinal, central, chief, controlling, essential, excellent, fine, first, first-rate, foremost, great, important, leading, main, major, overruling, paramount, pre-eminent, primary, prime, principal, splendid, superb, upper-case. **antonyms** minor, sad, unfortunate.

capital[2] *n* assets, cash, finance, finances, financing, funds, investment(s), means, money, principal, property, resources, stock, wealth, wherewithal.

capitulate *v* give in, relent, submit, succumb, surrender, throw in the towel/sponge, yield. **antonym** fight on.

capitulation *n* accedence, submission, surrender, yielding.

caprice *n* changeableness, fad, fancy, fantasy, fickleness, fitfulness, freak, impulse, inconstancy, notion, quirk, vagary, whim, whimsy.

capricious *adj* changeable, crotchety, erratic, fanciful, fickle, fitful, freakish, impulsive, inconstant, mercurial, odd, queer, quirky, uncertain, unpredictable, variable, wayward, whimsical. **antonyms** sensible, steady.

capsize *v* invert, keel over, overturn, turn over, turn turtle, upset.

captain *n* boss, chief, chieftain, commander, head, leader, master, officer, pilot, skip, skipper.

captious *adj* acrimonious, cantankerous, carping, censorious, crabbed, critical, cross, disparaging, fault-finding, irritable, nagging, narky, nit-picking, peevish, testy, touchy. **antonyms** amiable, good-natured, pleasant.

captivate *v* allure, attract, beguile, besot, bewitch, charm, dazzle, enamour, enchain, enchant, enrapture, enslave, ensnare, enthrall, entrance, fascinate, hypnotise, infatuate, lure, mesmerise, seduce, win. **antonyms** appal, repel.

captive *n* convict, detainee, hostage, internee, prisoner, slave.
adj caged, confined, enchained, enslaved, ensnared, imprisoned, incarcerated, restricted, subjugated. **antonym** free.

captivity *n* bondage, confinement,

custody, detention, duress, enchainment, enthralment, imprisonment, incarceration, internment, restraint, servitude, slavery. **antonym** freedom.

capture v apprehend, arrest, bag, catch, collar, cop, feel someone's collar, lift, nab, secure, seize, snaffle, take.
n apprehension, arrest, catch, imprisonment, seizure, taking, trapping.

cardinal adj capital, central, chief, essential, first, foremost, fundamental, greatest, highest, important, key, leading, main, paramount, pre-eminent, primary, prime, principal.

care n affliction, anxiety, attention, burden, carefulness, caution, charge, circumspection, concern, consideration, control, custody, direction, disquiet, forethought, guardianship, hardship, heed, interest, keeping, management, meticulousness, ministration, pains, pressure, protection, prudence, regard, responsibility, solicitude, stress, supervision, tribulation, trouble, vexation, vigilance, ward, watchfulness, woe, worry. **antonyms** carelessness, inattention, thoughtlessness.

care for attend, delight in, desire, enjoy, foster, like, love, mind, nurse, prize, protect, take pleasure in, tend, want, watch over.

career n calling, course, employment, job, life-work, livelihood, occupation, passage, path, procedure, progress, pursuit, race, vocation, walk.
v bolt, dash, gallop, hurtle, race, run, rush, shoot, speed, tear.

carefree adj blithe, breezy, buoyant, careless, cheerful, cheery, easy-going, happy, happy-go-lucky, jaunty, laid-back, light-hearted, radiant, sunny, untroubled, unworried. **antonyms** anxious, worried.

careful adj accurate, alert, attentive, cautious, chary, circumspect, concerned, conscientious, discreet, fastidious, heedful, judicious, meticulous, mindful, painstaking, particular, precise, protective, prudent, punctilious, scrupulous, softly-softly, solicitous, thoughtful, thrifty, vigilant, wary, watchful. **antonyms** careless, inattentive, thoughtless.

carefully adv cautiously, painstakingly, punctiliously, warily. **antonym** carelessly.

careless adj absent-minded, casual, cursory, derelict, forgetful, heedless, hit-or-miss, inaccurate, incautious, inconsiderate, indiscreet, irresponsible, lackadaisical, messy, neglectful, negligent, nonchalant, offhand, perfunctory, regardless, remiss, slap-dash, slipshod, sloppy, thoughtless, uncaring, unconcerned, unguarded, unmindful, unstudied, unthinking. **antonyms** accurate, careful, meticulous, thoughtful.

carelessness n absent-mindedness, heedlessness, inaccuracy, inattention, inconsiderateness, indiscretion, irresponsibility, messiness, neglect, negligence, omission, remissness, slackness, slipshodness, sloppiness, thoughtlessness. **antonyms** accuracy, care, thoughtfulness.

caress v canoodle, cuddle, embrace, fondle, hug, kiss, nuzzle, paw, pet, rub, stroke, touch.
n cuddle, embrace, fondle, hug, kiss, pat, stroke.

careworn adj exhausted, fatigued, gaunt, haggard, tired, weary, worn, worn-out. **antonyms** lively, sprightly.

cargo n baggage, consignment, contents, freight, goods, haul, lading, load, merchandise, pay-load, shipment, tonnage, ware.

carnage n blood-bath, bloodshed, butchery, havoc, holocaust, massacre, murder, shambles, slaughter.

carnal adj animal, bodily, erotic, fleshly, impure, lascivious, lecherous, lewd, libidinous, licentious, lustful, physical, profane, prurient, salacious, sensual, sensuous, sexual, unchaste, unregenerate, voluptuous, wanton, worldly. **antonyms** chaste, pure, spiritual.

carnival n celebration, fair, festival, fête, fiesta, gala, holiday, jamboree, jubilee, merrymaking, revelry.

carp v censure, complain, criticise, knock, nag, quibble, reproach. **antonym** praise.

carping adj biting, bitter, captious, critical, fault-finding, grouchy, nagging, nit-picking, picky, reproachful.
n censure, complaints, criticism, disparagement, knocking, reproofs. **antonyms** compliments, praise.

carriage n air, bearing, behaviour, cab, carrying, coach, comportment, conduct, conveyance, conveying, delivery, demeanour, deportment, freight, gait, manner, posture, presence, transport, transportation, vehicle, wagon.

carrier n bearer, conveyor, delivery-man,

arry v accomplish, bear, bring, broadcast, capture, chair, communicate, conduct, convey, display, disseminate, drive, effect, fetch, gain, give, haul, hip, impel, influence, lift, lug, maintain, motivate, move, offer, publish, relay, release, secure, shoulder, spur, stand, stock, suffer, support, sustain, take, tote, transfer, transmit, transport, underpin, uphold, urge, win.

carry on administer, continue, endure, flirt, last, maintain, manage, misbehave, operate, perpetuate, persevere, persist, proceed, run.

carry out accomplish, achieve, bring off, discharge, do, effect, execute, fulfil, implement, perform, realise.

art v bear, carry, convey, haul, hump, humph, lug, move, transport.

artoon n animation, caricature, comic strip, drawing, representation, sketch, take-off.

arve v chip, chisel, cut, divide, engrave, etch, fashion, form, hack, hew, incise, indent, make, mould, sculp(t), sculpture, slash, slice, tool, whittle.

ascade n avalanche, cataract, deluge, falls, flood, force, fountain, outpouring, rush, shower, torrent, waterfall. *antonym* trickle.

v descend, flood, gush, overflow, pitch, plunge, pour, rush, shower, spill, surge, tumble.

ase[1] n box, cabinet, canister, capsule, carton, cartridge, casing, casket, chest, compact, container, cover, covering, crate, envelope, folder, holder, jacket, receptacle, sheath, shell, showcase, suit-case, tray, trunk, wrapper, wrapping.

v encase, enclose, skin.

ase[2] n argument, circumstances, condition, context, contingency, dilemma, event, example, illustration, instance, occasion, occurrence, plight, point, position, predicament, situation, specimen, state.

v investigate, reconnoitre.

ase[3] n action, argument, cause, dispute, lawsuit, proceedings, process, suit, trial.

ash n bank-notes, bread, bullion, change, coin, coinage, currency, dough, funds, hard currency, hard money, money, notes, payment, readies, ready, ready money, resources, wherewithal.

v encash, liquidate, realise.

ast[1] v abandon, add, allot, appoint, assign, bestow, calculate, categorise, choose, chuck, compute, deposit, diffuse, distribute, drive, drop, emit, figure, fling, forecast, form, found, give, hurl, impel, launch, lob, model, mould, name, pick, pitch, project, radiate, reckon, reject, scatter, select, set, shape, shed, shy, sling, spread, throw, thrust, toss, total.

n air, appearance, complexion, demeanour, fling, form, lob, look, manner, quality, semblance, shade, stamp, style, throw, thrust, tinge, tone, toss, turn.

cast down crush, deject, depress, desolate, discourage, dishearten, dispirit, sadden. *antonyms* encourage, lift up.

cast[2] n actors, artistes, characters, company, dramatis personae, entertainers, performers, players, troupe.

caste n class, degree, estate, grade, lineage, order, position, race, rank, species, station, status, stratum.

castigate v beat, berate, cane, censure, chastise, chide, correct, discipline, flail, flay, flog, lash, rebuke, reprimand, scold, scourge, whip.

castle n casbah (kasba, kasbah), château, citadel, donjon, fastness, fortress, keep, mansion, palace, schloss, stronghold, tower.

castrate v emasculate, geld, neuter, unman, unsex.

casual adj accidental, apathetic, blasé, chance, contingent, cursory, fortuitous, incidental, indifferent, informal, irregular, lackadaisical, negligent, nonchalant, occasional, offhand, perfunctory, random, relaxed, serendipitous, stray, unceremonious, uncertain, unconcerned, unexpected, unforeseen, unintentional, unpremeditated. *antonyms* deliberate, painstaking, planned.

casualty n death, injured, injury, loss, sufferer, victim, wounded.

cataclysm n blow, calamity, catastrophe, collapse, convulsion, debacle (débâcle), devastation, disaster, upheaval.

catacomb n burial-vault, crypt, ossuary, tomb, vault.

catalogue n directory, gazetteer, index, inventory, list, litany, record, register, roll, roster, schedule, table.

v alphabetise, classify, file, index, inventory, list, record, register.

catapult v heave, hurl, hurtle, launch, pitch, plunge, propel, shoot, throw, toss.

cataract n cascade, deluge, downpour, falls, force, rapids, torrent, waterfall.

catastrophe n adversity, affliction,

blow, calamity, cataclysm, conclusion, culmination, curtain, debacle (débâcle), devastation, disaster, end, failure, fiasco, ill, mischance, misfortune, mishap, reverse, ruin, tragedy, trial, trouble, upheaval, winding-up.

catch v apprehend, arrest, benet, bewitch, captivate, capture, charm, clutch, contract, cop, delight, detect, develop, discern, discover, enchant, enrapture, ensnare, entangle, entrap, expose, fascinate, feel, follow, grab, grasp, grip, hear, incur, nab, nail, perceive, recognise, seize, sense, snare, snatch, surprise, take, twig, unmask. **antonyms** drop, free, miss.
n bolt, clasp, clip, disadvantage, drawback, fastener, hasp, hitch, hook, latch, obstacle, snag, sneck, trap, trick.
catch sight of espy, glimpse, notice, recognise, spot, view.
catch up draw level with, gain on, overtake.

catching adj attractive, captivating, charming, communicable, contagious, enchanting, fascinating, fetching, infectious, taking, transferable, transmissible, transmittable, winning, winsome. **antonyms** boring, ugly, unattractive.

catchword n byword, catch-phrase, motto, password, refrain, slogan, watchword.

catchy adj attractive, captivating, haunting, memorable, popular. **antonyms** boring, dull.

categorical adj absolute, clear, direct, downright, emphatic, explicit, express, positive, total, unambiguous, unconditional, unequivocal, unqualified, unquestionable, unreserved. **antonyms** qualified, tentative, vague.

categorise v class, classify, grade, group, list, order, pigeonhole, rank, sort.

category n chapter, class, classification, department, division, grade, grouping, head, heading, list, order, rank, section, sort, type.

cater v furnish, humour, indulge, outfit, pander, provide, provision, purvey, supply.

catholic adj all-embracing, all-inclusive, broad, broad-minded, charitable, comprehensive, eclectic, ecumenical, general, global, inclusive, liberal, tolerant, universal, whole, wide, wide-ranging, world-wide. **antonyms** narrow, narrow-minded.

catty adj back-biting, bitchy, ill-natured,

malevolent, malicious, mean, rancorous, spiteful, venomous, vicious. **antonyms** kind, pleasant.

cause n account, agency, agent, aim, attempt, basis, beginning, belief, causation, consideration, conviction, creator, end, enterprise, genesis, grounds, ideal, impulse, incentive, inducement, mainspring, maker, motivation, motive, movement, object, origin, originator, producer, purpose, reason, root, source, spring, stimulus, undertaking. **antonyms** effect, result.
v begin, compel, create, effect, engender, gar, generate, give rise to, incite, induce, motivate, occasion, precipitate, produce, provoke, result in.

caustic adj acidulous, acrid, acrimonious, astringent, biting, bitter, burning, corroding, corrosive, cutting, keen, mordant, pungent, sarcastic, scathing, severe, stinging, trenchant, virulent, waspish. **antonyms** mild, soothing.

caution n admonition, advice, alertness, care, carefulness, circumspection, counsel, deliberation, discretion, forethought, heed, heedfulness, injunction, prudence, vigilance, wariness, warning, watchfulness.
v admonish, advise, urge, warn.

cautious adj alert, cagey, careful, chary, circumspect, discreet, guarded, heedful, judicious, prudent, scrupulous, softly softly, tentative, unadventurous, vigilant, wary, watchful. **antonyms** heedless, imprudent, incautious.

cavalcade n array, march-past, parade, procession, retinue, spectacle, train, troop.

cavalier n attendant, beau, blade, chevalier, equestrian, escort, gallant, gentleman, horseman, knight, partner, royalist.
adj arrogant, cavalierish, condescending, curt, disdainful, free-and-easy, gay, haughty, insolent, lofty, lordly, misproud, off-hand, scornful, supercilious, swaggering.

cave n cavern, cavity, den, grotto, hollow, pothole.
cave in collapse, fall, give way, slip, subside, yield.

cavern n cave, cavity, den, grotto, hollow, pothole, vault.

cavernous adj deep, deep-set, echoing, gaping, hollow, resonant, reverberant, sunken, yawning.

avity *n* caries, crater, dent, gap, hole, hollow, pit, pot-hole, well.

avort *v* caper, dance, frisk, frolic, gambol, hop, prance, romp, skip, sport.

ease *v* call a halt, call it a day, conclude, culminate, desist, die, discontinue, end, fail, finish, halt, pack in, poop out, refrain, stay, stop, terminate. **antonyms** begin, start.

easeless *adj* constant, continual, continuous, endless, eternal, everlasting, incessant, indefatigable, interminable, never-ending, non-stop, perennial, perpetual, persistent, unending, unremitting, untiring. **antonyms** irregular, occasional.

ede *v* abandon, abdicate, allow, concede, convey, give up, grant, relinquish, renounce, resign, surrender, transfer, yield.

elebrate *v* bless, commemorate, commend, eulogise, exalt, extol, glorify, honour, keep, laud, live it up, observe, perform, praise, proclaim, publicise, rejoice, reverance, solemnise, toast, wassail, whoop it up.

celebrated *adj* acclaimed, big, distinguished, eminent, exalted, famed, famous, glorious, illustrious, lionised, notable, outstanding, popular, pre-eminent, prominent, renowned, revered, well-known. **antonyms** obscure, unknown.

elebration *n* anniversary, carousal, commemoration, festival, festivity, gala, honouring, jubilee, merrymaking, observance, orgy, party, performance, rave-up, rejoicings, remembrance, revelry, shindig, solemnisation.

celebrity *n* big name, big shot, bigwig, celeb, dignitary, distinction, eminence, fame, glory, honour, lion, luminary, name, notability, personage, personality, popularity, pre-eminence, prestige, prominence, renown, reputation, repute, star, stardom, superstar, VIP. **antonyms** nobody, obscurity.

celerity *n* dispatch, expedition, haste, promptness, quickness, rapidity, speed, swiftness, velocity. **antonyms** sloth, slowness.

celestial *adj* angelic, astral, divine, eternal, ethereal, godlike, heavenly, immortal, seraphic, spiritual, starry, sublime, supernatural, transcendental. **antonyms** earthly, mundane.

cement *v* attach, bind, bond, cohere, combine, fix together, glue, gum, join, plaster, seal, solder, stick, unite, weld.

cemetery *n* boneyard, burial-ground, churchyard, God's acre, graveyard, necropolis.

censor *v* amend, blue-pencil, bowdlerise, cut, edit, expurgate.

censorious *adj* captious, carping, condemnatory, critical, disapproving, disparaging, fault-finding, severe. **antonyms** approving, complimentary, laudatory.

censure *n* admonition, blame, castigation, condemnation, criticism, disapproval, obloquy, rebuke, remonstrance, reprehension, reprimand, reproach, reprobation, reproof, stricture, telling-off, vituperation. **antonyms** approval, compliments, praise.
v abuse, admonish, berate, blame, castigate, chide, condemn, criticise, decry, denounce, inveigh against, jump on, rebuke, reprehend, reprimand, reproach, reprobate, reprove, scold, slam, tell off, upbraid. **antonyms** approve, compliment, praise.

central *adj* chief, essential, focal, fundamental, important, inner, interior, key, main, mean, mid, middle, pivotal, primary, principal, vital. **antonyms** minor, peripheral.

centralise *v* amalgamate, compact, concentrate, condense, converge, gather together, incorporate, rationalise, streamline, unify. **antonym** decentralise.

centre *n* bull's-eye, core, crux, focus, heart, hub, Mecca, mid, middle, mid-point, nave, nucleus, pivot. **antonyms** edge, outskirts, periphery.
v cluster, concentrate, converge, focus, gravitate, hinge, pivot, revolve.

ceremonial *adj* dress, formal, liturgical, ritual, ritualistic, solemn, stately. **antonym** informal.
n ceremony, formality, protocol, rite, ritual, solemnity.

ceremonious *adj* civil, courteous, courtly, dignified, exact, formal, grand, polite, pompous, precise, punctilious, ritual, solemn, starchy, stately, stiff. **antonyms** informal, relaxed.

ceremony *n* celebration, ceremonial, commemoration, etiquette, event, form, formality, function, niceties, observance, parade, pomp, propriety, protocol, rite, ritual, service, show, solemnities.

certain *adj* ascertained, assured, bound, conclusive, confident, constant, convinced, convincing, decided, definite, dependable, destined, determinate, established, express, fated, fixed, incontrovertible, individual, indubitable, ineluctable, inescapable, inevitable, inexorable, irrefutable, known, one, particular, plain, positive, precise, regular, reliable, resolved, satisfied, settled, some, special, specific, stable, steady, sure, true, trustworthy, undeniable, undoubted, unequivocal, unfailing, unmistakable, unquestionable, valid. *antonyms* doubtful, hesitant, unsure.

certainly *adv* doubtlessly, naturally, of course, without question.

certainty *n* assurance, authoritativeness, certitude, confidence, conviction, fact, faith, inevitability, positiveness, reality, sure thing, sureness, surety, trust, truth, validity. *antonyms* doubt, hesitation.

certificate *n* attestation, authorisation, award, coupon, credentials, diploma, document, endorsement, guarantee, licence, pass, qualification, testimonial, validation, voucher, warrant.

certify *v* ascertain, assure, attest, authenticate, authorise, aver, avow, confirm, corroborate, declare, endorse, evidence, guarantee, notify, show, testify, validate, verify, vouch, witness.

cessation *n* abeyance, arresting, break, ceasing, desistance, discontinuation, end, ending, halt, halting, hiatus, intermission, interruption, interval, let-up, pause, recess, remission, respite, rest, standstill, stay, stoppage, stopping, suspension, termination. *antonym* commencement.

chafe *v* abrade, anger, annoy, enrage, exasperate, fret, fume, gall, get, grate, heat, incense, inflame, irritate, offend, provoke, rage, rasp, rub, scrape, scratch, vex, wear, worry.

chaff *n* badinage, banter, jesting, jokes, joking, raillery, teasing.
v banter, deride, jeer, laugh at, mock, pull (someone's) leg, rib, ridicule, scoff, taunt, tease.

chagrin *n* annoyance, discomfiture, discomposure, displeasure, disquiet, dissatisfaction, embarrassment, exasperation, fretfulness, humiliation, indignation, irritation, mortification, peevishness, spleen, vexation. *antonyms* delight, pleasure.
v annoy, displease, disquiet, dissatisfy, embarrass, exasperate, humiliate, irk, irritate, mortify, peeve, vex.

chain *n* bond, coupling, fetter, fob, link, manacle, progression, restraint, sequence, series, set, shackle, string, succession, train, union.
v bind, confine, enslave, fasten, fetter, handcuff, manacle, restrain, secure, shackle, tether, trammel. *antonyms* free, release.

chalk up accumulate, achieve, ascribe, attain, attribute, charge, credit, enter, gain, log, mark, record, register, score, tally, win.

chalky *adj* ashen, calcareous, pale, pallid, powdery, wan, white.

challenge *v* accost, beard, brave, confront, dare, defy, demand, dispute, impugn, provoke, query, question, stimulate, summon, tax, test, throw down the gauntlet, try.
n confrontation, dare, defiance, gauntlet, hurdle, interrogation, obstacle, poser, provocation, question, test, trial, ultimatum.

chamber *n* apartment, assembly, bed, chamber, bedroom, boudoir, camera, cavity, closet, compartment, council, cubicle, enclosure, hall, legislature, parliament, room, vault.

champion *n* backer, challenger, conqueror, defender, guardian, hero, patron, protector, upholder, victor, vindicator, warrior, winner.
v advocate, back, defend, espouse, maintain, promote, stand up for, support, uphold.

chance *n* accident, act of God, coincidence, contingency, destiny, fate, fortuity, fortune, gamble, happenstance, hazard, jeopardy, liability, likelihood, luck, misfortune, occasion, odds, opening, opportunity, peril, possibility, probability, prospect, providence, risk, scope, speculation, time, uncertainty. *antonyms* certainty, law, necessity.
v befall, gamble, happen, hazard, occur, risk, stake, transpire, try, venture, wager.
adj accidental, casual, contingent, fortuitous, inadvertent, incidental, random, serendipitous, unforeseeable, unforeseen, unintended, unintentional, unlooked-for. *antonyms* certain, deliberate, intentional.

chancy *adj* dangerous, dicey, dodgy, fraught, hazardous, problematical, risky, speculative, tricky, uncertain. *antonyms* safe, secure.

change *v* alter, alternate, barter, convert, displace, diversify, exchange, fluctuate, interchange, metamorphose, moderate, modify, mutate, reform, remodel, remove, reorganise, replace, restyle, shift, substitute, swap, take liberties with, trade, transfigure, transform, transmit, transmute, transpose, vacillate, vary, veer.

n alteration, break, chop, conversion, difference, diversion, exchange, innovation, interchange, metamorphosis, modification, mutation, novelty, permutation, revolution, satisfaction, sea-change, shift, substitution, trade, transformation, transition, transmutation, transposition, upheaval, variation, variety, vicissitude.

changeable *adj* capricious, changeful, erratic, fickle, fitful, fluid, inconstant, irregular, mercurial, mobile, mutable, protean, shifting, uncertain, unpredictable, unreliable, unsettled, unstable, unsteady, vacillating, variable, vicissitudinous, volatile, wavering, windy. *antonyms* constant, reliable, unchangeable.

changing *adj* different, diverse, fluctuating, fluid, inconstant, mobile, unstable, various, varying.

channel *n* approach, artery, avenue, canal, chamber, chamfer, communication, conduit, course, duct, flume, fluting, furrow, groove, gullet, gutter, main, means, medium, overflow, passage, path, route, sound, start, strait, trough, watercourse, waterway, way.

v conduct, convey, direct, force, furrow, guide, send, transmit.

chaos *n* anarchy, bedlam, confusion, disorder, disorganisation, lawlessness, mayhem, pandemonium, tumult. *antonym* order.

chaotic *adj* anarchic, confused, deranged, disordered, disorganised, lawless, purposeless, riotous, shambolic, topsy-turvy, tumultous, uncontrolled. *antonyms* organised, purposive.

chap *n* bloke, buffer, character, codger, cove, customer, fellow, guy, individual, Johnny, person, punter, sort, type.

chapter *n* assembly, branch, chapel, clause, division, episode, part, period, phase, section, stage, topic.

character¹ *n* attributes, bent, calibre, cast, complexion, constitution, disposition, feature, honour, individuality, integrity, kidney, make-up, nature, peculiarity, personality, position, quality, rank, reputation, stamp, status, strength, temper, temperament, type.

character² *n* card, cove, customer, eccentric, fellow, guy, individual, oddball, oddity, part, person, persona, portrayal, role, sort, type.

character³ *n* cipher, device, emblem, figure, hieroglyph, ideogram, ideograph, letter, logo, mark, rune, sign, symbol, type.

characterise *v* brand, distinguish, identify, indicate, inform, mark, represent, stamp, typify.

characteristic *adj* discriminative, distinctive, distinguishing, idiosyncratic, individual, peculiar, representative, singular, special, specific, symbolic, symptomatic, typical, vintage.

n attribute, faculty, feature, hallmark, idiosyncrasy, lineament, mannerism, mark, peculiarity, property, quality, symptom, thing, trait.

charge *v* accuse, adjuration, afflict, arraign, ask, assail, assault, attack, behest, bid, blame, burden, command, commit, count, demand, enjoin, entrust, exact, exhort, fill, impeach, incriminate, inculpate, indict, instil, instruct, involve, lade, load, onset, order, require, rush, storm, suffuse, tax, terms.

n accusation, allegation, amount, assault, attack, burden, care, command, concern, cost, custody, damage, demand, dictate, direction, duty, exhortation, expenditure, expense, imputation, indictment, injunction, instruction, mandate, office, onset, onslaught, order, outlay, payment, precept, price, rate, responsibility, rush, safekeeping, sortie, trust, ward.

charitable *adj* accommodating, beneficent, benevolent, benign, bountiful, clement, compassionate, considerate, favourable, forgiving, generous, gracious, humane, indulgent, kind, kindly, lavish, lenient, liberal, magnanimous, mild, philanthropic, sympathetic, tolerant, understanding. *antonym* unforgiving.

charity *n* affection, altruism, assistance, benefaction, beneficence, benevolence, bountifulness, bounty, clemency, compassion, endowment, fund, generosity, gift, goodness, handout, humanity, indulgence, love, philanthropy, relief, tender-heartedness.

charlatan *n* cheat, con man, fake, fraud, impostor, mountebank, phoney, pretender, quack, swindler, trickster.

charm *v* allure, attract, beguile, bewitch, cajole, captivate, delight, enamour, enchant, enrapture, entrance, fascinate, mesmerise, please, win.

n allure, allurement, amulet, appeal, attraction, attractiveness, desirability, enchantment, fascination, idol, ju-ju, magic, magnetism, mascot, medicine, sorcery, spell, talisman, trinket.

charming *adj* appealing, attractive, bewitching, captivating, delectable, delightful, engaging, eye-catching, fetching, irresistible, lovely, pleasant, pleasing, seductive, sweet, winning, winsome. *antonyms* ugly, unattractive.

chart *n* blueprint, diagram, graph, map, plan, table, tabulation.
v delineate, draft, draw, graph, map out, mark, outline, place, plot, shape, sketch.

charter *n* authorisation, bond, concession, contract, deed, document, franchise, licence, permit, prerogative, privilege, right.
v authorise, commission, employ, engage, hire, lease, rent, sanction.

chary *adj* careful, cautious, circumspect, guarded, heedful, prudent, reluctant, slow, suspicious, uneasy, unwilling, wary. *antonyms* heedless, unwary.

chase *v* course, drive, expel, follow, hunt, hurry, pursue, rush, track.
n coursing, hunt, hunting, pursuit, race, run, rush.

chasm *n* abysm, abyss, breach, canyon, cavity, cleft, crater, crevasse, fissure, gap, gorge, gulf, hollow, opening, ravine, rent, rift, split, void.

chaste *adj* austere, decent, decorous, elegant, immaculate, incorrupt, innocent, maidenly, modest, moral, neat, pure, refined, restrained, simple, unaffected, undefiled, unsullied, vestal, virginal, virtuous, wholesome. *antonyms* indecorous, lewd.

chastise *v* beat, berate, castigate, censure, correct, discipline, flog, lash, punish, reprove, scold, scourge, smack, spank, upbraid, whip.

chastity *n* abstinence, celibacy, continence, innocence, maidenhood, modesty, purity, restraint, self-restraint, temperateness, virginity, virtue.

chat *n* chatter, chinwag, confab, crack, gossip, heart-to-heart, natter, talk, tête-à-tête, visit.
v chatter, chew the fat, gossip, jaw, natter, rabbit (on), talk, yackety-yak.

chatter *n* babble, blether, chat, chinwag, gossip, jabber, natter, prattle, twaddle.
v babble, blether, chat, gab, gossip, jabber, natter, prattle, yackety-yak.

chatty *adj* colloquial, familiar, friendly, gossipy, informal, talkative.

cheap *adj* bargain, base, budget, common, contemptible, cut-price, despicable, dirt-cheap, economical, economy, inexpensive, inferior, keen, knock-down, low, low-cost, low-priced, mean, paltry, poor, reasonable, reduced, sale, second-rate, shoddy, sordid, tatty, tawdry, vulgar, worthless. *antonyms* costly, excellent, noble, superior.

cheapen *v* belittle, debase, degrade, demean, denigrate, depreciate, derogate, devalue, discredit, disparage, downgrade, lower, prostitute. *antonym* enhance.

cheat *v* baffle, bamboozle, beguile, bilk, check, chisel, con, cozen, deceive, defeat, defraud, deprive, diddle, do, double-cross, dupe, fleece, fob, foil, fool, frustrate, fudge, grift, gull, hand (someone) a lemon, hoax, hoodwink, mislead, prevent, rip off, screw, short change, skin, smouch, swindle, thwart, touch, trick, trim, victimise.
n artifice, charlatan, cheater, cogger, con man, deceiver, deception, dodger, double-crosser, extortioner, fraud, grifter, impostor, imposture, knave, rip off, rogue, shark, sharp, sharper, swindle, swindler, trickery, trickster, welsher.

check[1] *v* compare, confirm, examine, give the once-over, inspect, investigate, monitor, note, probe, research, scrutinise, study, test, verify.
n audit, examination, inspection, investigation, research, scrutiny, test.
check out examine, investigate, test.

check[2] *v* arrest, bar, blame, bridle, chide, control, curb, damp, delay, halt, hinder, impede, inhibit, limit, obstruct, pause, rebuke, repress, reprimand, reprove, restrain, retard, scold, stop, thwart.
n blow, constraint, control, curb, damp, damper, disappointment, frustration, hindrance, impediment, inhibition, limitation, obstruction, rejection, restraint, reverse, setback, stoppage.

cheek[1] *n* audacity, brass, brass neck, brazenness, brazenry, disrespect, effrontery, gall, impertinence, impudence, insolence, lip, nerve, sauce, temerity.

cheek[2] *n* chap, face, gena, jowl.

cheeky *adj* audacious, disrespectful, forward, impertinent, impudent, insolent, insulting, lippy, pert, saucy. *antonyms* polite, respectful.

cheer *v* acclaim, animate, applaud, brighten, clap, comfort, console, elate, elevate, encourage, enhearten, enliven, exhilarate, gladden, hail, hearten, incite, inspirit, solace, uplift, warm. *antonyms* boo, dishearten, jeer.

n animation, applause, bravo, buoyancy, cheerfulness, comfort, gaiety, gladness, glee, hopefulness, joy, liveliness, merriment, merry-making, mirth, optimism, ovation, plaudits, solace.

cheerful *adj* animated, blithe, bright, buoyant, cheery, chipper, chirpy, contented, enlivening, enthusiastic, gay, gaysome, genial, glad, happy, hearty, jaunty, jolly, jovial, joyful, joyous, light-hearted, light-spirited, merry, optimistic, perky, pleasant, sparkling, sprightly, sunny, upbeat, winsome. **antonym** sad.

cheerfulness *n* blitheness, buoyancy, cheeriness, exuberance, gaiety, geniality, gladness, happiness, jauntiness, joyfulness, joyousness, light-heartedness, sprightliness. **antonym** sadness.

cheering *adj* auspicious, bright, comforting, encouraging, heartening, inspiring, promising, propitious, reassuring. **antonyms** depressing, disheartening.

cheerless *adj* austere, barren, bleak, cold, comfortless, dank, dark, dejected, depressed, desolate, despondent, dingy, disconsolate, dismal, dolorous, drab, dreary, dull, forlorn, gloomy, grim, joyless, lonely, melancholy, miserable, mournful, sad, sombre, sorrowful, sullen, sunless, unhappy, uninviting, woebegone, woeful. **antonyms** bright, cheerful.

cheers *interj* bottoms up, prosit, skol, slàinte.

cheery *adj* blithe, breezy, bright, carefree, cheerful, chipper, gay, good-humoured, happy, jovial, lightsome, light-spirited, lively, merry, pleasant, sparkling, sunny. **antonyms** downcast, sad.

cherish *v* comfort, cosset, encourage, entertain, foster, harbour, make much of, nourish, nurse, nurture, prize, shelter, support, sustain, tender, treasure, value.

chew *v* champ, crunch, gnaw, grind, masticate, munch.

chic *adj* à la mode, elegant, fashionable, modish, smart, stylish, trendy. **antonyms** out-moded, unfashionable.

chicanery *n* artifice, cheating, deception, deviousness, dodge, double-dealing, duplicity, intrigue, jiggery-pokery, sharp practice, skulduggery, sophistry, stratagems, subterfuge, trickery, underhandedness, wiles.

chide *v* admonish, berate, blame, censure, check, criticise, lecture,

objurgate, rate, rebuke, reprehend, reprimand, reproach, reprove, scold, tell off, upbraid. **antonym** praise.

chief *adj* capital, cardinal, central, especial, essential, foremost, grand, highest, key, leading, main, outstanding, paramount, predominant, pre-eminent, premier, prevailing, primal, primary, prime, principal, superior, supreme, uppermost, vital. **antonyms** junior, minor, unimportant.

n boss, captain, chieftain, commander, director, gaffer, governor, head, leader, lord, manager, master, principal, ringleader, ruler, superintendent, superior, supremo.

chiefly *adv* especially, essentially, for the most part, generally, mainly, mostly, predominantly, primarily, principally, usually.

child *n* babe, baby, bairn, bambino, brat, descendant, get, git, infant, issue, juvenile, kid, kiddiewinkie, kiddywink, minor, nipper, nursling, offspring, papoose, progeny, sprog, suckling, toddler, tot, wean, youngling, youngster.

childish *adj* boyish, foolish, frivolous, girlish, immature, infantile, juvenile, puerile, silly, simple, young. **antonyms** adult, sensible.

childlike *adj* artless, credulous, guileless, ingenuous, innocent, naïve, natural, simple, trustful, trusting.

chill *adj* biting, bleak, chilly, cold, cool, depressing, distant, freezing, frigid, hostile, parky, raw, sharp, stony, unfriendly, unresponsive, unwelcoming, wintry. **antonyms** friendly, warm.

v congeal, cool, dampen, depress, discourage, dishearten, dismay, freeze, frighten, refrigerate, terrify.

n bite, cold, coldness, coolness, coolth, crispness, frigidity, nip, rawness, sharpness.

chilly *adj* blowy, breezy, brisk, cold, cool, crisp, draughty, fresh, frigid, hostile, nippy, parky, penetrating, sharp, stony, un-friendly, unresponsive, unsympathetic, unwelcoming. **antonyms** friendly, warm.

chime *v* clang, dong, jingle, mark, peal, ping, ring, sound, strike, tell, tinkle, tintinnabulate, toll.

chimera *n* bogy, delusion, dream, fancy, fantasy, figment, hallucination, idle fancy, illusion, monster, monstrosity, spectre, will-o'-the-wisp.

chink¹ *n* aperture, cleft, crack, crevice, cut, fissure, flaw, gap, opening, rift, slot, space.

chink² *n* clink, ding, jangle, jingle, ping, ring, tinkle.

chip *n* dent, flake, flaw, fragment, nick, notch, scrap, scratch, shard, shaving, sliver, wafer.
v chisel, damage, gash, nick, notch, whittle.
chip in contribute, donate, interpose, interrupt, participate, pay, subscribe.

chirp *v, n* cheep, chirrup, peep, pipe, tweet, twitter, warble, whistle.

chirpy *adj* blithe, bright, cheerful, cheery, chipper, gay, happy, jaunty, merry, perky, sunny. **antonyms** downcast, sad.

chivalrous *adj* bold, brave, courageous, courteous, courtly, gallant, gentlemanly, heroic, honourable, knightly, polite, true, valiant. **antonyms** cowardly, ungallant.

chivvy *v* badger, harass, hassle, hound, importune, nag, pester, plague, pressure, prod, torment.

choice *n* alternative, choosing, decision, dilemma, discrimination, election, espousal, opting, option, pick, preference, say, selection, variety.
adj best, elect, élite, excellent, exclusive, exquisite, hand-picked, nice, plum, precious, prime, prize, rare, select, special, superior, valuable. **antonym** inferior.

choke *v* asphyxiate, bar, block, clog, close, congest, constrict, dam, gag, obstruct, occlude, overpower, reach, retch, smother, stifle, stop, strangle, suffocate, suppress, throttle.

choose *v* adopt, cull, designate, desire, elect, espouse, fix on, opt for, pick, plump for, predestine, see fit, select, settle on, single out, take, vote for, wish.

choosy *adj* discriminating, exacting, faddy, fastidious, finicky, fussy, particular, picky, selective. **antonym** undemanding.

chop *v* cleave, cut, divide, fell, hack, hew, lop, sever, shear, slash, slice, truncate.
chop up cube, cut up, dice, divide, fragment, mince, slice (up).

choppy *adj* blustery, broken, rough, ruffled, squally, stormy, tempestuous, wavy, white. **antonym** calm.

chore *n* burden, duty, errand, fag, job, stint, task, trouble.

chorus *n* burden, call, choir, choristers, ensemble, refrain, response, shou singers, strain, vocalists.

chosen *adj* elect, élite, peculia predilected, selected.

christen *v* baptise, call, designate, dub inaugurate, name, style, term, title, use.

chronic *adj* appalling, atrocious awful, confirmed, deep-rooted, deep seated, dreadful, habitual, incessan incurable, ineradicable, ingrained inveterate, persistent, terrible. **antonyn** temporary.

chronicle *n* account, annals, diary epic, history, journal, narrative, record register, saga, story.
v enter, list, narrate, record, recoun register, relate, report, tell, write down.

chubby *adj* buxom, flabby, fleshy paunchy, plump, podgy, portly, rotund round, stout, tubby. **antonyms** skinny slim.

chuck *v* cast, discard, fling, heave hurl, jettison, pitch, reject, shy, sling throw, toss.

chuckle *v* chortle, crow, exult, giggle laugh, snigger, snort, titter.

chum *n* china, cobber, companion comrade, crony, friend, mate, pal. **antonym** enemy.

chummy *adj* affectionate, close friendly, intimate, matey, pally, sociable thick.

chunk *n* block, chuck, dod, dollop, hunk lump, mass, piece, portion, slab, wad wodge.

chunky *adj* beefy, brawny, dumpy, fat, square, stocky, stubby, thick, thickset. **antonym** slim.

churlish *adj* boorish, brusque, crabbed, harsh, ill-tempered, impolite, loutish, morose, oafish, rude, sullen, surly, uncivil, unmannerly, unneighbourly, unsociable, vulgar. **antonyms** polite, urbane.

churn *v* agitate, beat, boil, convulse, foam, froth, knot, seethe, swirl, toss, writhe.

cigarette *n* cancer-stick, cig, ciggy, coffin-nail, fag, gasper, joint, smoke, snout, whiff.

cinch *n* doddle, piece of cake, snip, stroll, walk-over.

cipher *n* character, code, cryptograph, device, digit, figure, logo, mark, monogram, nil, nobody, nonentity, nothing, nought, number, numeral, symbol, zero.

circle *n* area, assembly, band, bounds, circuit, circumference, class, clique.

club, coil, company, compass, cordon, coterie, crowd, cycle, disc, domain, enclosure, fellowship, field, fraternity, globe, group, lap, loop, orb, orbit, perimeter, periphery, province, range, realm, region, revolution, ring, round, roundance, roundel, scene, school, set, society, sphere, turn.

v belt, circumnavigate, circumscribe, coil, compass, curl, curve, encircle, enclose, encompass, envelop, gird, girdle, hem in, loop, pivot, revolve, ring, rotate, surround, tour, whirl.

circuit *n* ambit, area, boundary, bounds, circumference, compass, course, district, journey, lap, limit, orbit, range, region, revolution, round, route, tour, track, tract.

circuitous *adj* cagey, devious, indirect, labyrinthine, meandering, oblique, periphrastic, rambling, roundabout, tortuous, winding. **antonyms** direct, straight.

circular *adj* annular, disc-shaped, hoop-shaped, ring-shaped, round.

n advert, announcement, handbill, leaflet, letter, notice, pamphlet.

circulate *v* broadcast, diffuse, disseminate, distribute, flow, go around, go the rounds, gyrate, issue, promulgate, propagate, publicise, publish, radiate, revolve, rotate, spread, spread abroad, swirl, whirl.

circulation *n* blood-flow, circling, currency, dissemination, distribution, flow, motion, rotation, spread, spreading, transmission.

circumference *n* border, boundary, bounds, circuit, edge, extremity, fringe, limits, margin, outline, perimeter, periphery, rim, verge.

circumspect *adj* attentive, canny, careful, cautious, chary, deliberate, discreet, discriminating, guarded, heedful, judicious, observant, politic, sagacious, sage, vigilant, wary, watchful. **antonyms** unguarded, unwary.

circumspection *n* canniness, care, caution, chariness, deliberation, discretion, guardedness, prudence, wariness.

circumstance *n* accident, condition, contingency, detail, element, event, fact, factor, happening, happenstance, incident, item, occurrence, particular, position, respect, situation.

circumstances *n* conditions, lifestyle, means, position, resources, situation, state, state of affairs, station, status, times.

circumstantial *adj* conjectural, contingent, detailed, evidential, exact, hearsay, incidental, indirect, inferential, minute, particular, presumptive, provisional, specific. **antonyms** hard, inexact, vague.

circumvent *v* beguile, bypass, deceive, dupe, elude, ensnare, entrap, evade, get out of, get past, hoodwink, mislead, outflank, outwit, overreach, sidestep, steer clear of, thwart, trick.

citation *n* award, commendation, cutting, excerpt, illustration, mention, passage, quotation, quote, reference, source.

cite *v* accite, adduce, advance, call, enumerate, evidence, extract, mention, name, quote, specify, subpoena, summon.

civil *adj* accommodating, affable, civic, civilised, complaisant, courteous, courtly, domestic, home, interior, internal, internecine, lay, municipal, obliging, polished, polite, political, refined, secular, urbane, well-bred, well-mannered.

civilisation *n* advancement, cultivation, culture, development, education, enlightenment, progress, refinement, sophistication, urbanity. **antonyms** barbarity, primitiveness.

civilise *v* ameliorate, cultivate, educate, enlighten, humanise, improve, perfect, polish, refine, sophisticate, tame.

civilised *adj* advanced, cultured, educated, enlightened, humane, polite, refined, sophisticated, tolerant, urbane. **antonyms** barbarous, primitive.

civility *n* affability, amenity, amiability, attention, breeding, comity, complaisance, cordiality, courteousness, courtesy, graciousness, politeness, politesse, tact, urbanity. **antonyms** rudeness, uncouthness.

claim *v* affirm, allege, arrogate, ask, assert, challenge, collect, demand, exact, hold, insist, maintain, need, profess, request, require, state, take, uphold.

n affirmation, allegation, application, assertion, call, demand, insistence, petition, pretension, privilege, protestation, request, requirement, right, title.

clairvoyant *adj* extra-sensory, oracular, prescient, prophetic, psychic, second-sighted, telepathic, visionary.

n augur, diviner, fortune-teller, oracle, prophet, seer, soothsayer, telepathist, visionary.

clammy *adj* close, damp, dank, heavy, moist, muggy, pasty, slimy, sticky, sweating, sweaty.

clamorous *adj* blaring, deafening, insistent, noisy, riotous, tumultuous, uproarious, vehement, vociferous. *antonym* silent.

clamour *n* agitation, babel, blare, commotion, complaint, din, exclamation, hubbub, hue, hullabaloo, noise, outcry, racket, shouting, uproar, vociferation. *antonym* silence.

clamp *n* brace, bracket, fastener, grip, press, vice.
v brace, clinch, fasten, fix, impose, secure.

clan *n* band, brotherhood, clique, confraternity, coterie, faction, family, fraternity, group, house, race, sect, set, society, tribe.

clandestine *adj* backroom, behind-door, cloak-and-dagger, closet, concealed, covert, furtive, hidden, private, secret, sly, sneaky, stealthy, surreptitious, underground, underhand, under-the-counter. *antonym* open.

clang *v* bong, chime, clank, clash, jangle, peal, resound, reverberate, ring, toll.
n bong, clank, clash, clatter, jangle, peal.

clannish *adj* cliqu(e)y, close, exclusive, insular, narrow, parochial, sectarian, select, unfriendly. *antonyms* friendly, open.

claptrap *n* affectation, balderdash, blarney, bombast, bunk, bunkum, codswallop, drivel, flannel, guff, hokum, hot air, humbug, nonsense, rubbish, tripe.

clarification *n* definition, elucidation, explanation, exposition, gloss, illumination, interpretation, simplification. *antonym* obfuscation.

clarify *v* cleanse, define, elucidate, explain, gloss, illuminate, purify, refine, resolve, shed/throw light on, simplify. *antonym* obscure.

clarity *n* comprehensibility, definition, explicitness, intelligibility, lucidity, obviousness, precision, simplicity, transparency, unambiguousness. *antonyms* obscurity, vagueness.

clash *v* bang, clang, clank, clatter, conflict, crash, disagree, feud, fight, grapple, jangle, jar, quarrel, rattle, war, wrangle.
n brush, clank, clatter, collision, conflict, confrontation, disagreement, fight, jangle, jar, noise, show-down.

clasp *n* brooch, buckle, catch, clip, embrace, fastener, fastening, grasp, grip, hasp, hold, hook, hug, pin.
v attach, clutch, connect, embrace, enclasp, enfold, fasten, grapple, grasp, grip, hold, hug, press, seize, squeeze.

class¹ *n* calibre, caste, category, classification, collection, denomination, department, description, division, genre, genus, grade, group, grouping, ilk, kidney, kind, kingdom, league, order, phylum, quality, rank, section, set, sort, species, sphere, status, style, type, value.
v assort, brand, categorise, classify, codify, designate, grade, group, rank, rate.

class² *n* course, lecture, seminar, tutorial.

classic *adj* abiding, ageless, archetypal, best, characteristic, chaste, consummate, definitive, enduring, established, excellent, exemplary, finest, first-rate, ideal, immortal, lasting, master, masterly, model, quintessential, refined, regular, standard, time-honoured, traditional, typical, usual. *antonym* second-rate.
n masterpiece, masterwork, model, pièce de résistance, prototype, standard.

classification *n* analysis, arrangement, cataloguing, categorisation, digestion, grading, pigeon-holing, sorting, taxonomy.

classify *v* arrange, assort, catalogue, categorise, digest, distribute, file, grade, pigeon-hole, rank, sort, systematise, tabulate.

classy *adj* elegant, exclusive, exquisite, fine, gorgeous, grand, high-class, posh, select, stylish, superior, swanky, up-market. *antonyms* dowdy, plain, unstylish.

clause *n* article, chapter, condition, demand, heading, item, paragraph, part, passage, point, provision, proviso, section, specification, stipulation, subsection.

clean *adj* antiseptic, chaste, clarified, complete, conclusive, decent, decisive, decontaminated, delicate, elegant, entire, exemplary, faultless, final, flawless, fresh, good, graceful, guiltless, honest, honourable, hygienic, immaculate, innocent, laundered, moral, natural, neat, perfect, pure, purified, respectable, sanitary, simple, spotless, sterile, sterilised, thorough, tidy, total, trim, unblemished, unadulterated, uncluttered, uncontaminated, undefiled, unimpaired, unpolluted, unsoiled, unstained, unsullied, upright, virtuous, washed, whole. *antonyms* dirty, indecent, polluted, unsterile.

v bath, cleanse, deodorise, disinfect, dust, launder, mop, purge, purify, rinse, sanitise, scour, scrub, sponge, swab, sweep, vacuum, wash, wipe. *antonyms* defile, dirty.

cleanse *v* absolve, clean, clear, detoxify, porge, purge, purify, rinse, scour, scrub, wash. *antonyms* defile, dirty.

clear *adj* apparent, audible, bright, certain, clean, cloudless, coherent, comprehensible, conspicuous, convinced, crystalline, decided, definite, diaphanous, disengaged, distinct, empty, evident, explicit, express, fair, fine, free, glassy, guiltless, halcyon, immaculate, incontrovertible, innocent, intelligible, light, limpid, lucid, luminous, manifest, obvious, open, palpable, patent, perceptible, plain, positive, pronounced, pure, recognisable, resolved, satisfied, see-through, serene, sharp, shining, smooth, stainless, sunny, sure, translucent, transparent, unambiguous, unblemished, unclouded, undefiled, undimmed, undulled, unequivocal, unhampered, unhindered, unimpeded, unlimited, unmistakable, unobstructed, unquestionable, untarnished, untroubled, well-defined. *antonyms* cloudy, fuzzy, guilty, vague.

v absolve, acquire, acquit, brighten, clarify, clean, cleanse, decode, decongest, disengage, disentangle, earn, emancipate, erase, excuse, exonerate, extricate, fix, free, gain, jump, justify, leap, liberate, lighten, loosen, make, miss, open, pass over, purify, reap, refine, rid, secure, strip, tidy, unblock, unclog, uncloud, unload, unpack, unscramble, vault, vindicate, wipe. *antonyms* block, condemn, defile, dirty.

clear out beat it, clear off, decamp, depart, empty, exhaust, leave, retire, sort, throw out, withdraw.

clear up answer, clarify, elucidate, explain, fix, order, rearrange, remove, resolve, solve, sort, tidy, unravel.

clearance *n* allowance, authorisation, consent, endorsement, gap, go-ahead, headroom, leave, margin, OK, permission, sanction, space, the green light.

clear-cut *adj* clear, definite, distinct, explicit, plain, precise, specific, straightforward, unambiguous, unequivocal, well-defined. *antonyms* ambiguous, vague.

clearly *adv* distinctly, evidently, incontestably, incontrovertibly, manifestly, markedly, obviously, openly, plainly, undeniably, undoubtedly. *antonyms* indistinctly, vaguely.

clearness *n* audibility, brightness, clarity, coherence, distinctness, explicitness, intelligibility, limpidity, lucidity, luminosity, transparency, unambiguousness.

cleft *n* breach, break, chasm, chink, crack, cranny, crevice, fissure, fracture, gap, opening, rent, split.

adj cloven, divided, parted, rent, riven, ruptured, separated, split, torn. *antonym* solid.

clement *adj* balmy, calm, compassionate, fair, fine, forbearing, forgiving, generous, gentle, humane, indulgent, kind, kind-hearted, lenient, magnanimous, merciful, mild, soft-hearted, temperate, tender. *antonyms* harsh, ruthless.

clench *v* clasp, close, clutch, grasp, grip, grit, hold.

clergyman *n* chaplain, churchman, cleric, curate, deacon, dean, father, man of God, minister, padre, parson, pastor, priest, rabbi, rector, reverend, vicar.

clever *adj* able, adroit, apt, astute, brainy, bright, canny, capable, cunning, deep, dexterous, discerning, elegant, expert, gifted, good-natured, habile, ingenious, intelligent, inventive, keen, knowing, knowledgeable, quick, quick-witted, rational, resourceful, sagacious, sensible, shrewd, skilful, smart, talented, witty. *antonyms* foolish, naïve, senseless.

clever dick smart Alec, smart-ass, smartypants.

cleverness *n* ability, adroitness, astuteness, brains, brightness, canniness, cunning, dexterity, flair, gift, gumption, ingenuity, intelligence, nous, quickness, resourcefulness, sagacity, sense, sharpness, shrewdness, smartness, talent, wit. *antonyms* foolishness, naïvety, senselessness.

click *n, v* beat, clack, snap, snick, snip, tick.

clientèle *n* business, clients, customers, following, market, patronage, patrons, regulars, trade.

climactic *adj* critical, crucial, decisive, exciting, orgasmic, paramount. *antonyms* bathetic, trivial.

climate *n* ambience, atmosphere, clime, country, disposition, feeling, milieu, mood, region, setting, temper, temperature, tendency, trend, weather.

climax *n* acme, apogee, culmination, head, height, high point, highlight, orgasm, peak, summit, top, zenith. ***antonyms*** bathos, low point, nadir.

climb *v* ascend, clamber, mount, rise, scale, shin up, soar, swarm (up), top.

climb down back down, clamber down, descend, dismount, eat one's words, retract, retreat.

clinch *v* assure, bolt, cap, clamp, conclude, confirm, cuddle, decide, determine, embrace, fasten, fix, grasp, hug, nail, neck, rivet, seal, secure, settle, squeeze, verify.

cling *v* adhere, clasp, cleave, clutch, embrace, fasten, grasp, grip, hug, stick.

clinical *adj* analytic, business-like, cold, detached, disinterested, dispassionate, emotionless, impersonal, objective, scientific, unemotional. ***antonyms*** biased, subjective.

clique *n* bunch, circle, clan, coterie, crew, crowd, faction, gang, group, mates, mob, pack, set.

cloak *n* blind, cape, coat, cover, front, mantle, mask, pretext, shield, wrap.
v camouflage, conceal, cover, disguise, hide, mask, obscure, screen, veil.

clog *v* ball, block, burden, congest, dam up, hamper, hinder, impede, jam, obstruct, occlude, shackle, stop up, stuff. ***antonym*** unblock.
n burden, dead-weight, drag, encumbrance, hindrance, impediment, obstruction.

cloistered *adj* confined, enclosed, hermitic, insulated, protected, reclusive, restricted, secluded, sequestered, sheltered, shielded, withdrawn. ***antonyms*** open, urbane.

close¹ *v* bar, block, cease, choke, clog, complete, conclude, confine, connect, cork, couple, culminate, discontinue, end, fill, finish, fuse, grapple, join, lock, mothball, obstruct, plug, seal, secure, shut, stop, terminate, unite, wind up.
n cessation, completion, conclusion, culmination, dénouement, end, ending, finale, finish, junction, pause, stop, termination, wind-up.

close² *adj* accurate, adjacent, adjoining, airless, alert, approaching, approximative, assiduous, at hand, attached, attentive, careful, compact, concentrated, confidential, confined, congested, conscientious, cramped,

cropped, crowded, dear, dense, detailed, devoted, dogged, earnest, exact, faithful, familiar, fixed, frowsty, handy, hard by, heavy, hidden, humid, illiberal, imminent, impending, impenetrable, inseparable, intense, intent, intimate, jam-packed, keen, literal, loving, mean, mingy, minute, miserly, muggy, narrow, near, near-by, neighbouring, niggardly, nigh, oppressive, packed, painstaking, parsimonious, penurious, precise, private, reserved, reticent, retired, rigorous, searching, secluded, secret, secretive, short, solid, stale, stifling, stingy, strict, stuffy, suffocating, sweltering, taciturn, thick, thorough, tight, tight-fisted, uncommunicative, un-forthcoming, ungenerous, unventilated. ***antonyms*** careless, cool, far, unfriendly.

closed *adj* concluded, decided, ended, exclusive, fastened, finished, locked, over, resolved, restricted, sealed, settled, shut, terminated, wound-up. ***antonyms*** open, unfastened, unsettled.

closure *n* cap, cessation, closing, conclusion, end, finish, guillotine, lid, plug, seal, stoppage, stopper, stricture, winding-up. ***antonym*** opening.

clot¹ *n* clotting, coagulation, curdling, embolism, gob, lump, mass, occlusion, thrombus.
v coagulate, congeal, curdle, jell, thicken.

clot² *n* ass, buffoon, dolt, dunderhead, fathead, fool, idiot, nincompoop, nit, nitwit, numskull, twerp.

clothe *v* array, attire, cover, deck, drape, dress, endow, equip, outfit, rig, robe, swathe. ***antonyms*** unclothe, undress.

clothes *n* apparel, attire, clobber, clothing, costume, dress, duds, ensemble, garb, garments, gear, get-up, habit(s), outfit, rig-out, threads, togs, vestments, wardrobe, wear, weeds.

cloud *n* billow, crowd, darkness, flock, fog, gloom, haze, horde, host, mist, multitude, murk, obscurity, vapour.
v confuse, darken, dim, disorient, distort, dull, eclipse, impair, muddle, obfuscate, obscure, overcast, overshadow, shade, shadow, stain, veil. ***antonym*** clear.

cloudy *adj* blurred, blurry, confused, dark, dim, dismal, dull, emulsified, hazy, indistinct, leaden, lightless, lowering, muddy, murky, nebulous, obscure, opaque, overcast, sombre, sullen, sunless. ***antonyms*** clear, sunny.

clout v box, clobber, cuff, hit, skelp, slap, smack, sock, strike, thump, wallop, whack, wham.
  n authority, cuff, influence, power, prestige, pull, skelp, slap, smack, sock, standing, thump, wallop, weight, whack.

cloy v choke, disgust, glut, gorge, nauseate, sicken, surfeit, tire, weary. **antonyms** please, whet.

cloying adj excessive, nauseating, oversweet, sickening, sickly.

club[1] n bat, bludgeon, cosh, cudgel, mace, mere, stick, truncheon.
  v bash, baste, batter, beat, bludgeon, clobber, clout, cosh, hammer, hit, pummel, strike.

club[2] n association, bunch, circle, clique, combination, company, fraternity, group, guild, lodge, order, set, society, union.

clue n evidence, hint, idea, indication, inkling, intimation, lead, notion, pointer, sign, suggestion, suspicion, tip, tip-off, trace.

clump n bunch, bundle, cluster, mass, shock, thicket, tuffet, tuft.
  v clomp, lumber, plod, stamp, stomp, stump, thud, thump, tramp, tread.

clumsy adj awkward, blundering, bumbling, bungling, cack-handed, clumping, crude, gauche, gawky, ham-fisted, heavy, hulking, inept, inexpert, lumbering, rough, shapeless, spastic, unco-ordinated, uncouth, ungainly, ungraceful, unskilful, unwieldy. **antonym** graceful.

cluster n assemblage, batch, bunch, clump, collection, gathering, glomeration, group, knot, mass.
  v assemble, bunch, collect, flock, gather, group.

clutch v catch, clasp, embrace, fasten, grab, grapple, grasp, grip, hang on to, seize, snatch.

clutter n confusion, disarray, disorder, hotchpotch, jumble, litter, mess, muddle, untidiness.
  v cover, encumber, fill, litter, scatter, strew.

coach v cram, drill, instruct, prepare, teach, train, tutor.

coagulate v clot, congeal, curdle, jell, solidify, thicken. **antonym** melt.

coalesce v amalgamate, blend, cohere, combine, commingle, consolidate, fuse, incorporate, integrate, merge, mix, unite.

coalition n affiliation, alliance, amalgam, amalgamation, association, bloc, combination, compact, confederacy, confederation, conjunction, federation, fusion, integration, league, merger, union.

coarse adj barrack-room, bawdy, blowzy, boorish, brutish, coarse-grained, crude, earthly, foul-mouthed, immodest, impolite, improper, impure, indelicate, inelegant, loutish, mean, offensive, porterly, ribald, rough, rude, smutty, uncivil, unfinished, unpolished, unprocessed, unpurified, unrefined, vulgar. **antonyms** fine, polite, refined, sophisticated.

coast n coastline, littoral, seaboard, seaside, shore.
  v cruise, drift, free-wheel, glide, sail.

coating n blanket, coat, covering, dusting, film, finish, fur, glaze, lamination, layer, membrane, sheet, skin, varnish, veneer, wash.

coax v allure, beguile, cajole, decoy, entice, flatter, inveigle, persuade, soft-soap, sweet-talk, wheedle. **antonym** force.

cobble v botch, bungle, knock up, mend, patch, put together, tinker.

cock-eyed adj absurd, askew, asymmetrical, awry, crazy, crooked, daft, lop-sided, ludicrous, nonsensical, preposterous, skew-whiff, squint. **antonyms** sensible, sober.

cocky adj arrogant, brash, cocksure, conceited, egotistical, swaggering, swollen-headed, vain.

cocoon v cover, cushion, envelop, insulate, pad, preserve, protect, sheathe, swaddle, swathe, wrap.

coddle v baby, cosset, humour, indulge, mollycoddle, nurse, pamper, pet, spoil.

code n canon, cipher, convention, cryptograph, custom, ethics, etiquette, manners, maxim, regulations, rules, system.
  v encipher, encode.

coerce v bludgeon, browbeat, bulldoze, bully, compel, constrain, dragoon, drive, drum, force, intimidate, press-gang, pressurise. **antonyms** coax, persuade.

coercion n browbeating, bullying, compulsion, constraint, direct action, duress, force, intimidation, pressure, threats. **antonym** persuasion.

co-existent adj coeval, co-existing, concomitant, contemporaneous, contemporary.

cogent adj compelling, conclusive, convincing, effective, forceful, forcible, influential, irresistible, persuasive, potent, powerful, strong, unanswerable, urgent. **antonyms** ineffective, unsound.

cogitate *v* cerebrate, consider, contemplate, deliberate, meditate, muse, ponder, reflect, ruminate, think.

cognate *adj* affiliated, akin, alike, allied, analogous, associated, connected, kindred, related, similar. **antonym** unconnected.

cognisant *adj* acquainted, aware, conscious, conversant, familiar, informed, knowledgeable, versed, witting. **antonym** unaware.

coherent *adj* articulate, comprehensible, consistent, intelligible, logical, lucid, meaningful, orderly, organised, rational, reasoned, sensible, systematic.

cohort *n* accomplice, assistant, associate, band, companion, company, comrade, contingent, crony, division, follower, henchman, legion, mate, partner, regiment, sidekick, squadron, supporter, troop.

coil *v* convolute, curl, entwine, loop, snake, spiral, twine, twist, wind, wreathe, writhe.
n bight, convolution, curl, loop, spiral, twist.

coin *v* conceive, create, devise, fabricate, forge, form, formulate, frame, introduce, invent, make up, mint, mould, originate, produce, think up.
n bit, cash, change, copper, loose change, money, piece, silver, small change, specie.

coincide *v* accord, agree, co-exist, concur, correspond, harmonise, match, square, tally.

coincidence *n* accident, chance, concomitance, concurrence, conjunction, correlation, correspondence, eventuality, fluke, fortuity, luck.

coincidental *adj* casual, chance, coincident, concomitant, concurrent, fluky, fortuitous, lucky, simultaneous, unintentional, unplanned. **antonyms** deliberate, planned.

cold *adj* aloof, apathetic, arctic, benumbed, biting, bitter, bleak, chill, chilled, chilly, cold-blooded, cool, dead, distant, freezing, frigid, frosty, frozen, glacial, icy, inclement, indifferent, inhospitable, lukewarm, numbed, parky, passionless, raw, reserved, shivery, spiritless, stand-offish, stony, undemonstrative, unfeeling, unfriendly, unheated, unmoved, unresponsive, unsympathetic, wintry. **antonyms** friendly, warm.
n catarrh, chill, chilliness, frigidity, frostiness, hypothermia, iciness, inclemency. **antonyms** friendlines warmth.

cold-blooded *adj* barbaric, barbarou brutal, callous, cruel, dispassionate, fe flinty, heartless, inhuman, merciles obdurate, pitiless, ruthless, savag steely, stony-hearted, uncompassiona unemotional, unfeeling, unmoved **antonyms** compassionate, merciful.

cold-hearted *adj* callous, col detached, frigid, frozen, heartles indifferent, inhuman, insensitive, ston hearted, uncaring, uncompassionat unfeeling, unkind, unsympathetic **antonym** warm-hearted.

collaborate *v* coact, collude, conspir co-operate, co-produce, fraternis participate, team up.

collaborator *n* assistant, associat colleague, confederate, co-worke fellow-traveller, partner, quisling, tean mate, traitor, turncoat.

collapse *v* crumple, fail, faint, fall, fol founder, peg out, sink, subside.
n breakdown, cave-in, debac (débâcle), disintegration, downfal exhaustion, failure, faint, flo subsidence.

collar *v* apprehend, appropriate, arres capture, catch, grab, nab, nick, seize.

collate *v* arrange, collect, compar compose, gather, sort.

collateral *n* assurance, deposit, fund guarantee, pledge, security, surety.

colleague *n* aide, ally, assistan associate, auxiliary, bedfellow collaborator, companion, comrad confederate, confrère, helper, partne team-mate, workmate.

collect *v* accumulate, acquire, aggregat amass, assemble, cluster, congregat convene, converge, gather, gathe together, heap, hoard, muster, obtai raise, rally, save, secure, stockpile, uplif

collected *adj* assembled, calm composed, confident, cool, efficien gathered, imperturbable, placid, poise self-possessed, serene, togethe unperturbed, unruffled. **antonym** disorganised, dithery, worried.

collection *n* accumulation, antholog assemblage, assembly, assortmen caboodle, cluster, company, compilatio conglomerate, conglomeration, congre gation, convocation, crowd, gatherin group, harvesting, heap, hoard, job lot, mass, pile, set, stockpile, store whip-round.

collective *adj* aggregate, combined

common, composite, concerted, congregated, co-operative, corporate, cumulative, joint, shared, unified, united.
n aggregate, assemblage, corporation, gathering, group.

collision *n* accident, bump, clash, clashing, conflict, confrontation, crash, encounter, impact, opposition, pile-up, prang, skirmish, smash.

colloquial *adj* conversational, everyday, familiar, idiomatic, informal, vernacular. **antonym** formal.

collusion *n* artifice, cahoots, complicity, connivance, conspiracy, deceit, intrigue.

colossal *adj* elephantine, enormous, gargantuan, gigantic, herculean, heroic, huge, immense, leviathan, mammoth, massive, monstrous, monumental, mountainous, prodigious, titanic, vast. **antonym** tiny.

colour *n* animation, appearance, bloom, blush, brilliance, colorant, coloration, complexion, disguise, dye, façade, flush, glow, guise, hue, liveliness, paint, pigment, pigmentation, plausibility, pretence, pretext, race, reason, rosiness, ruddiness, semblance, shade, timbre, tinge, tint, variety, vividness, wash, water-colour.
v blush, burn, colourwash, disguise, distort, dye, embroider, encolour, exaggerate, falsify, flush, misrepresent, paint, pervert, prejudice, redden, slant, stain, strain, taint, tinge, tint.

colourful *adj* bright, brilliant, distinctive, graphic, intense, interesting, jazzy, kaleidoscopic, lively, motley, multicoloured, psychedelic, rich, stimulating, unusual, variegated, vibrant, vivid. **antonyms** colourless, drab, plain.

colourless *adj* anaemic, ashen, bleached, characterless, drab, dreary, faded, insipid, lacklustre, neutral, pale, sickly, tame, transparent, uninteresting, unmemorable, vacuous, vapid, wan, washed out. **antonym** colourful.

colours *n* banner, colour, emblem, ensign, flag, standard.

column *n* cavalcade, file, line, list, obelisk, pilaster, pillar, post, procession, queue, rank, row, shaft, string, support, train, upright.

comatose *adj* cataleptic, drowsy, insensible, lethargic, sleepy, sluggish, somnolent, stupefied, torpid, unconscious. **antonym** conscious.

comb *v* hunt, rake, ransack, rummage, scour, screen, search, sift, sweep.

combat *n* action, battle, bout, clash, conflict, contest, duel, encounter, engagement, fight, hostilities, j(i)u-jitsu, judo, karate, kendo, kung fu, skirmish, struggle, war, warfare.
v battle, contend, contest, defy, engage, fight, oppose, resist, strive, struggle, withstand.

combatant *n* adversary, antagonist, contender, enemy, fighter, opponent, serviceman, soldier, warrior.
adj active, battling, belligerent, contending, fighting, opposing, warring.

combative *adj* aggressive, antagonistic, argumentative, bellicose, belligerent, contentious, militant, pugnacious, quarrelsome, truculent, warlike. **antonyms** pacific, peaceful.

combination *n* alliance, amalgam, amalgamation, association, blend, coalition, combine, composition, compound, confederacy, confederation, conjunction, connection, consortium, conspiracy, federation, meld, merger, mix, mixture, syndicate, unification, union.

combine *v* amalgamate, associate, bind, blend, bond, compound, conjoin, connect, cooperate, fuse, incorporate, integrate, join, link, marry, meld, merge, mix, pool, synthesise, unify, unite. **antonym** separate.

come *v* advance, appear, approach, arrive, attain, become, draw near, ejaculate, enter, happen, materialise, move, near, occur, originate, reach. **antonyms** depart, go, leave.

come about arise, befall, come to pass, happen, occur, result, transpire.

come across bump into, chance upon, discover, encounter, find, happen on, meet, notice, unearth.

come along arise, arrive, develop, happen, improve, mend, progress, rally, recover, recuperate.

come apart break, crumble, disintegrate, fall to bits, separate, split, tear.

come between alienate, disunite, divide, estrange, interfere, part, separate, split up.

come by acquire, get, obtain, procure, secure. **antonyms** give, lose.

come clean acknowledge, admit, confess, own, own up, reveal, spill the beans.

come down decline, degenerate, descend, deteriorate, fall, reduce, worsen.

come in appear, arrive, enter, finish, show up.

come on advance, appear, begin, develop, improve, proceed, progress, take place, thrive.

come out conclude, emerge, end, result, terminate.

come out with affirm, declare, disclose, divulge, own, say, state.

come round accede, acquiesce, allow, awake, awaken, concede, grant, mellow, recover, relent, revive, wake, waken, yield.

come through accomplish, achieve, endure, prevail, succeed, survive, triumph, withstand.

come to grief bomb, come unstuck, fail, miscarry. **antonyms** succeed, triumph.

come to light appear, come out, transpire, turn up.

come up with advance, create, discover, find, furnish, offer, present, produce, propose, provide, submit, suggest, think of, think out.

come-back n quip, rally, rebound, recovery, rejoinder, reply, response, resurgence, retaliation, retort, return, revival, riposte.

comedian n card, clown, comic, funny man, humorist, jester, joker, laugh, wag, wit.

come-down n anticlimax, blow, decline, deflation, degradation, demotion, descent, disappointment, humiliation, let-down, reverse.

comedy n clowning, drollery, facetiousness, farce, fun, hilarity, humour, jesting, joking, sitcom, slapstick, wisecracking, witticisms.

comely adj attractive, beautiful, becoming, blooming, bonny, buxom, decent, decorous, fair, fit, fitting, good-looking, graceful, handsome, lovely, pleasing, pretty, proper, seemly, suitable, wholesome, winsome.

comfort v alleviate, assuage, cheer, console, ease, encheer, encourage, enliven, gladden, hearten, inspirit, invigorate, reassure, refresh, relieve, solace, soothe, strengthen.

n aid, alleviation, cheer, compensation, consolation, cosiness, ease, easy street, encouragement, enjoyment, help, luxury, opulence, relief, satisfaction, snugness, succour, support, well-being. **antonyms** distress, torment.

comfortable adj adequate, affluent, agreeable, ample, commodious, contented, convenient, cosy, delightful, easy, enjoyable, gratified, happy,

homely, loose, loose-fitting, pleasant, prosperous, relaxed, relaxing, restful, roomy, serene, snug, well-off, well-to-do. **antonyms** poor, uncomfortable.

comforting adj cheering, consoling, encouraging, heart-warming, reassuring, soothing. **antonym** worrying.

comic adj amusing, comical, droll, facetious, farcical, funny, humorous, jocular, joking, light, waggish, witty. **antonyms** serious, tragic, unfunny.

n buffoon, clown, comedian, gagster, humorist, jester, joker, wag, wit.

comical adj absurd, amusing, comic, diverting, droll, entertaining, farcical, funny, hilarious, humorous, laughable, ludicrous, priceless, ridiculous, side-splitting, silly, whimsical. **antonyms** sad, unamusing.

coming adj approaching, aspiring, due, forthcoming, future, imminent, impending, near, next, nigh, promising, rising, up-and-coming.

n accession, advent, approach, arrival.

command v bid, charge, compel, control, demand, direct, dominate, enjoin, govern, head, lead, manage, order, reign over, require, rule, supervise, sway.

n authority, behest, bidding, charge, commandment, control, decree, dictation, diktat, direction, directive, domination, dominion, edict, fiat, government, grasp, injunction, instruction, management, mandate, mastery, order, power, precept, requirement, rule, supervision, sway, ultimatum.

commandeer v appropriate, confiscate, expropriate, hijack, requisition, seize, sequestrate, usurp.

commanding adj advantageous, assertive, authoritative, autocratic, compelling, controlling, decisive, dominant, dominating, forceful, imposing, impressive, peremptory, superior.

commemorate v celebrate, honour, immortalise, keep, memorialise, observe, remember, salute, solemnise.

commence v begin, embark on, inaugurate, initiate, open, originate, start. **antonyms** cease, finish.

commend v acclaim, applaud, approve, commit, compliment, confide, consign, deliver, entrust, eulogise, extol, praise, recommend, yield. **antonym** criticise.

commendable adj admirable, creditable, deserving, estimable, excellent, exemplary, laudable, meritorious, noble, praiseworthy, worthy. *antonyms* blameworthy, poor.

commendation *n* acclaim, accolade, applause, approbation, approval, credit, encouragement, praise, recommendation. *antonyms* blame, criticism.

commensurate *adj* acceptable, adequate, appropriate, comparable, compatible, consistent, corresponding, due, equivalent, fitting, just, meet, proportionate, sufficient. *antonym* inappropriate.

comment *v* annotate, criticise, elucidate, explain, gloss, interpose, interpret, mention, note, observe, opine, remark, say.
n annotation, commentary, criticism, elucidation, explanation, exposition, footnote, illustration, marginal note, marginalia, note, observation, remark, statement.

commentary *n* analysis, critique, description, elucidation, exegesis, explanation, narration, notes, review, treatise, voice-over.

commerce *n* business, communication, dealing(s), exchange, intercourse, merchandising, relations, trade, traffic.

commercial *adj* business, marketable, materialistic, mercantile, mercenary, monetary, pecuniary, popular, profitable, profit-making, saleable, sales, sellable, trade, trading.

commiseration *n* compassion, condolence, consolation, pity, sympathy.

commission *n* allowance, appointment, authority, board, brokerage, charge, committee, compensation, cut, delegation, deputation, duty, employment, errand, fee, function, mandate, mission, percentage, rake-off, representative, task, trust, warrant.
v appoint, ask for, authorise, contract, delegate, depute, empower, engage, nominate, order, request, select, send.

commit *v* align, bind, commend, compromise, confide, confine, consign, deliver, deposit, do, enact, endanger, engage, entrust, execute, give, imprison, involve, obligate, perform, perpetrate, pledge.
commit oneself bind oneself, decide, promise, take the plunge, undertake.

commitment *n* adherence, assurance, dedication, devotion, duty, engagement, guarantee, involvement, liability, loyalty, obligation, pledge, promise, responsibility, tie, undertaking, vow, word.

committed *adj* active, card-carrying, fervent, red-hot. *antonym* apathetic.

committee *n* advisory group, board, cabinet, commission, council, jury, panel, table, task force, think-tank, working party.

commodities *n* goods, merchandise, output, produce, products, stock, things, wares.

common *adj* accepted, average, coarse, collective, commonplace, communal, conventional, customary, daily, everyday, familiar, flat, frequent, general, habitual, hackneyed, humdrum, inferior, low, mutual, obscure, ordinary, pedestrian, plain, plebby, plebeian, popular, prevailing, prevalent, public, regular, routine, run-of-the-mill, simple, social, stale, standard, stock, trite, undistinguished, unexceptional, universal, usual, vulgar, widespread, workaday. *antonym* noteworthy.

common sense gumption, judgement, level-headedness, nous, practicality, prudence, soundness.

commonplace *adj* common, customary, everyday, humdrum, obvious, ordinary, pedestrian, quotidian, stale, threadbare, trite, uninteresting, widespread, worn out. *antonyms* exceptional, rare.
n banality, cliché, platitude, truism.

common-sense *adj* astute, common-sensical, down-to-earth, hard-headed, judicious, level-headed, matter-of-fact, practical, pragmatic, realistic, reasonable, sane, savvy, sensible, shrewd, sound. *antonym* foolish.

commotion *n* ado, agitation, ballyhoo, burst-up, bustle, bust-up, disorder, disturbance, excitement, ferment, fracas, furore, fuss, hoo-ha, hubbub, hullabaloo, hurly-burly, pother, racket, riot, rumpus, to-do, toss, tumult, turmoil, uproar.

communal *adj* collective, common, community, general, joint, public, shared. *antonyms* personal, private.

commune *n* collective, colony, community, co-operative, encampment, fellowship, kibbutz, settlement.
v communicate, confer, converse, discourse, make contact with.

communicate *v* acquaint, announce, bestow, connect, contact, convey, correspond, declare, diffuse, disclose, disseminate, divulge, fax, impart, inform, intimate, notify, proclaim, promulgate, publish, report, reveal, signify, spread, telex, transmit, unfold.

communication *n* announcement, bulletin, communiqué, connection, contact, conversation, converse, correspondence, disclosure, dispatch, dissemination, fax, information, intelligence, intercourse, intimation, message, news, promulgation, report, statement, telex, transmission, word.

communicative *adj* candid, chatty, expansive, extrovert, forthcoming, frank, free, friendly, informative, loquacious, open, outgoing, sociable, talkative, unreserved, voluble. *antonym* reticent.

communion *n* accord, affinity, agreement, closeness, communing, concord, converse, empathy, Eucharist, fellow-feeling, fellowship, harmony, Holy Communion, intercourse, Lord's Supper, Mass, participation, rapport, Sacrament, sympathy, togetherness, unity.

communism *n* Bolshevism, collectivism, Leninism, Marxism, socialism, sovietism, Stalinism, totalitarianism, Trotskyism.

community *n* affinity, agreement, association, body politic, brotherhood, colony, commonness, commonwealth, company, concurrence, confraternity, confrèrie, correspondence, district, fellowship, fraternity, identity, kibbutz, kindredness, likeness, locality, nest, people, populace, population, public, residents, sameness, similarity, society, state.

commute *v* adjust, alter, curtail, decrease, lighten, mitigate, modify, reduce, remit, shorten, soften.

commuter *n* exurbanite, strap-hanger, suburbanite, traveller.

compact *adj* brief, close, compendious, compressed, concise, condensed, dense, firm, impenetrable, solid, stocky, succinct, thick. *antonyms* diffuse, rambling, rangy.
v compress, condense, consolidate, cram, flatten, ram, squeeze, tamp.

companion *n* accomplice, aide, ally, assistant, associate, attendant, buddy, chaperon, cohort, colleague, complement, comrade, confederate, confidant, confidante, consort, counterpart, crony, escort, fellow, follower, friend, intimate, mate, partner, shadow, twin.

companionable *adj* affable, amiable, approachable, congenial, conversable, convivial, extrovert, familiar, friendly, genial, gregarious, informal, neighbourly, outgoing, sociable, sympathetic. *antonym* unfriendly.

companionship *n* camaraderie, company, comradeship, confraternity, conviviality, esprit de corps, fellowship, fraternity, friendship, rapport, support, sympathy, togetherness.

company[1] *n* assemblage, assembly, association, band, body, business, cartel, circle, collection, community, concern, consortium, convention, corporation, coterie, crew, crowd, ensemble, establishment, firm, fraternity, gathering, group, house, league, line, partnership, party, set, syndicate, throng, troop, troupe.

company[2] *n* attendance, callers, companionhood, companionship, fellowship, guests, party, presence, society, support, visitors.

comparable *adj* akin, alike, analogous, cognate, commensurate, corresponding, equal, equivalent, kindred, parallel, proportionate, related, similar, tantamount. *antonym* unlike.

compare *v* balance, collate, confront, contrast, correlate, equal, equate, juxtapose, liken, match, parallel, resemble, weigh.

comparison *n* analogy, collation, comparability, contrast, correlation, distinction, juxtaposition, likeness, parallel, parallelism, resemblance, similarity, similitude.

compartment *n* alcove, area, bay, berth, booth, box, carrel, carriage, category, cell, chamber, cubby-hole, cubicle, department, division, locker, niche, pigeon-hole, section, stall, subdivision.

compass *n* area, boundary, bounds, circle, circuit, circumference, enclosure, extent, field, gamut, girth, limit, range, reach, realm, round, scale, scope, space, sphere, stretch, zone.
v accomplish, achieve, beset, besiege, blockade, circumscribe, contrive, devise, effect, encircle, enclose, encompass, environ, manage, realise, surround.

compassion *n* charity, clemency, commiseration, concern, condolence, fellow-feeling, heart, humanity, kindness, loving-kindness, mercy, pity, sorrow, sympathy, tenderness, understanding. *antonym* indifference.

compassionate *adj* benevolent, caring, charitable, clement, humane, humanitarian, indulgent, kind-hearted, kindly, lenient, merciful, piteous, pitying, supportive, sympathetic, tender, tender-hearted, understanding, warm-hearted. **antonym** indifferent.

compatibility *n* accord, affinity, agreement, concord, congeniality, consistency, consonance, correspondence, empathy, fellowship, harmony, like-mindedness, rapport, reconcilability, sympathy, understanding, unity. **antonyms** antagonism, antipathy, incompatibility.

compatible *adj* accordant, adaptable, agreeable, conformable, congenial, congruent, congruous, consistent, consonant, harmonious, kindred, like-minded, reconcilable, suitable, sympathetic. **antonyms** antagonistic, antipathetic, incompatible.

compel *v* browbeat, bulldoze, bully, coact, coerce, constrain, dragoon, drive, enforce, exact, force, hustle, impel, make, necessitate, obligate, oblige, press-gang, pressurise, strongarm, urge.

compelling *adj* binding, coercive, cogent, compulsive, conclusive, convincing, enchanting, enthralling, forceful, gripping, hypnotic, imperative, incontrovertible, irrefutable, irresistible, mesmeric, overriding, peremptory, persuasive, powerful, pressing, spellbinding, telling, unanswerable, unavoidable, unputdownable, urgent, weighty.

compendium *n* abbreviation, abridgement, abstract, brief, companion, condensation, digest, encapsulation, handbook, manual, précis, recapitulation, summary, synopsis.

compensate *v* atone, balance, cancel, counteract, counterbalance, countervail, expiate, indemnify, offset, recompense, recover, recuperate, redeem, redress, refund, reimburse, remunerate, repay, requite, restore, reward, satisfy.

compensation *n* amends, atonement, comfort, consolation, damages, indemnification, indemnity, payment, quittance, recompense, redress, refund, reimbursement, remuneration, reparation, repayment, requital, restitution, restoration, return, reward, satisfaction.

compete *v* battle, challenge, contend, contest, duel, fight, oppose, rival, strive, struggle, tussle, vie.

competence *n* ability, adequacy, appropriateness, aptitude, capability, capacity, competency, experience, expertise, facility, fitness, proficiency, skill, suitability, technique. **antonym** incompetence.

competent *adj* able, adapted, adequate, appropriate, belonging, capable, clever, efficient, endowed, equal, fit, legitimate, masterly, pertinent, proficient, qualified, satisfactory, strong, sufficient, suitable, trained, well-qualified. **antonym** incompetent.

competition *n* challenge, challengers, championship, combativeness, competitiveness, competitors, contention, contest, corrivalry, cup, event, field, match, opposition, quiz, race, rivalry, rivals, series, strife, struggle, tournament, tourney, trial.

competitive *adj* aggressive, ambitious, antagonistic, combative, contentious, cut-throat, keen, pushy, vying. **antonyms** sluggish, unambitious.

competitiveness *n* aggression, aggressiveness, ambition, ambitiousness, antagonism, assertiveness, challenge, combativeness, contention, contentiousness, keenness, pushiness, rivalry, self-assertion. **antonyms** backwardness, sluggishness.

competitor *n* adversary, agonist, antagonist, challenger, competition, contender, contestant, corrival, emulator, entrant, opponent, opposition, rival.

compilation *n* accumulation, anthology, arrangement, assemblage, assortment, collection, composition, selection, thesaurus, treasury, work.

compile *v* accumulate, amass, anthologise, arrange, assemble, collect, compose, cull, garner, gather, marshal, organise.

complacent *adj* contented, gloating, gratified, pleased, proud, satisfied, self-assured, self-congratulatory, self-contented, self-righteous, self-satisfied, smug, unconcerned. **antonyms** diffident, discontented.

complain *v* beef, belly-ache, bemoan, bewail, bind, bitch, bleat, carp, deplore, fuss, girn, grieve, gripe, groan, grouse, growl, grumble, lament, moan, protest, squeal, whine, whinge.

complaint[1] *n* accusation, annoyance, beef, belly-ache, censure, charge, criticism, dissatisfaction, fault-finding, girn, grievance, gripe, grouse, grumble, lament, moan, nit-picking, plaint, protest, remonstrance, stricture, wail, whinge, winge.

complaint[2] *n* affliction, ailment,

disease, disorder, illness, indisposition, malady, malaise, sickness, trouble, upset.

complement n aggregate, capacity, companion, completion, consummation, counterpart, entirety, fellow, quota, sum, supplement, total, totality, wholeness.

complementary adj companion, correlative, corresponding, dove-tailed, fellow, interdependent, interrelated, interrelating, interwoven, matched, reciprocal.

complete adj absolute, accomplished, achieved, all, concluded, consummate, ended, entire, equipped, faultless, finished, full, intact, integral, integrate, out-and-out, perfect, plenary, root-and-branch, self-contained, thorough, thoroughgoing, thorough-paced, total, unabbreviated, unabridged, unbroken, uncut, undivided, unedited, unexpurgated, unimpaired, utter, whole, whole-hog. *antonyms* imperfect, incomplete.

v accomplish, achieve, cap, clinch, close, conclude, consummate, crown, discharge, do, effect, end, execute, finalise, finish, fulfil, perfect, perform, realise, settle, terminate, wind up.

completely adv absolutely, altogether, diametrically, en bloc, en masse, entirely, every inch, from first to last, fully, heart and soul, in full, in toto, lock stock and barrel, perfectly, quite, root and branch, solidly, thoroughly, totally, utterly, wholly.

completion n accomplishment, achievement, attainment, close, conclusion, consummation, crowning, culmination, discharge, end, expiration, finalisation, finish, fruition, fulfilment, perfection, plenitude, realisation, settlement, termination.

complex adj circuitous, complicated, composite, compound, compounded, convoluted, diverse, elaborate, heterogeneous, intricate, involved, knotty, labyrinthine, manifold, mingled, mixed, multifarious, multiple, tangled, tortuous. *antonym* simple.

n aggregate, composite, establishment, fixation, hang-up, idée fixe, institute, network, obsession, organisation, phobia, preoccupation, scheme, structure, syndrome, synthesis, system.

complexion n appearance, aspect, cast, character, colour, colouring, composition, countenance, disposition, guise, hue, kind, light, look, make-up, nature, pigmentation, skin, stamp, temperament, type.

complexity n complication, convolution, deviousness, diversity, elaboration, entanglement, intricacy, involvement, multifariousness, multiplicity, tortuousness, variation, variety. *antonym* simplicity.

compliance n acquiescence, agreement, assent, complaisance, concession, concurrence, conformability, conformity, consent, co-operation, deference, obedience, observance, passivity, submission, submissiveness, yielding. *antonyms* defiance, disobedience.

compliant adj accommodating, acquiescent, agreeable, amenable, biddable, complaisant, conformable, deferential, docile, obedient, obliging, passive, submissive, tractable, yielding. *antonyms* disobedient, intractable.

complicate v complexity, compound, confuse, elaborate, embroil, entangle, foul up, involve, mix up, muddle, tangle. *antonym* simplify.

complicated adj ambivalent, baroque, complex, convoluted, devious, difficult, elaborate, entangled, Heath-Robinson, intricate, involved, labyrinthine, perplexing, problematic, puzzling, tangled, tortuous, troublesome. *antonyms* easy, simple.

complication n aggravation, complexification, complexity, complicatedness, confusion, difficulty, drawback, elaboration, embarrassment, entanglement, factor, intricacy, mixture, obstacle, problem, ramification, repercussion, snag, web.

complicity n agreement, approval, collaboration, collusion, concurrence, connivance, involvement, knowledge. *antonyms* ignorance, innocence.

compliment n accolade, admiration, commendation, congratulations, courtesy, eulogy, favour, felicitation, flattery, honour, plaudit, praise, tribute. *antonyms* criticism, insult.

v admire, applaud, commend, congratulate, eulogise, extol, felicitate, flatter, laud, praise, salute. *antonym* condemn, insult.

complimentary adj admiring, appreciative, approving, commendatory, congratulatory, courtesy, favourable, flattering, free, gratis, honorary, laudatory. *antonyms* critical, insulting, unflattering.

compliments n best wishes,

congratulations, greetings, regards, remembrances, respects, salutation.

omply v accede, accommodate, accord, acquiesce, agree, assent, conform, consent, defer, discharge, fall in, follow, fulfil, obey, oblige, observe, perform, respect, satisfy, submit, yield. **antonyms** disobey, resist.

omponent n bit, constituent, element, factor, ingredient, item, part, piece, spare part, unit.

ompose v adjust, arrange, build, calm, collect, compound, comprise, constitute, construct, contrive, control, create, devise, fashion, form, frame, govern, imagine, invent, make, pacify, produce, quell, quiet, recollect, reconcile, regulate, resolve, settle, soothe, still, structure, tranquillise, write.

omposed adj calm, collected, complacent, confident, cool, imperturbable, level-headed, placid, poised, relaxed, self-possessed, serene, together, tranquil, unflappable, unruffled, unworried. **antonym** agitated.

omposition n arrangement, balance, combination, compilation, compromise, concord, confection, configuration, congruity, consonance, constitution, creation, design, essay, exercise, form, formation, formulation, harmony, invention, lay-out, make-up, making, mixture, opus, organisation, piece, placing, production, proportion, structure, study, symmetry, work, writing.

omposure n aplomb, assurance, calm, calmness, confidence, cool, coolness, dignity, dispassion, ease, equanimity, impassivity, imperturbability, placidity, poise, sang-froid, savoir-faire, sedateness, self-assurance, self-possession, serenity, tranquillity. **antonym** discomposure.

ompound v aggravate, alloy, amalgamate, augment, blend, coalesce, combine, complicate, compose, concoct, exacerbate, fuse, heighten, increase, intensify, intermingle, magnify, mingle, mix, synthesise, unite, worsen.
n alloy, amalgam, amalgamation, blend, combination, composite, composition, confection, conglomerate, conglomeration, fusion, medley, mixture, synthesis.
adj complex, complicated, composite, conglomerate, intricate, mixed, multiple.

omprehend v appreciate, apprehend, assimilate, compass, comprise, conceive, cover, discern, embrace, encompass, fathom, grasp, include, know, penetrate, perceive, see, twig, understand. **antonym** misunderstand.

comprehensible adj clear, coherent, conceivable, explicit, graspable, intelligible, knowable, lucid, plain, rational, simple, straightforward, understandable. **antonym** incomprehensible.

comprehension n appreciation, apprehension, capacity, conception, discernment, grasp, intellection, intelligence, intension, judgement, knowledge, perception, realisation, sense, understanding. **antonym** incomprehension.

comprehensive adj across-the-board, all-embracing, all-inclusive, blanket, broad, catholic, compendious, complete, encyclopaedic, exhaustive, extensive, full, general, inclusive, omnibus, sweeping, thorough, wide. **antonyms** incomplete, selective.

compress v abbreviate, compact, concentrate, condense, constrict, contract, cram, crowd, crush, flatten, impact, jam, précis, press, shorten, squash, squeeze, stuff, summarise, synopsise, telescope, wedge. **antonyms** diffuse, expand, separate.

comprise v comprehend, consist of, contain, cover, embody, embrace, encompass, include, incorporate, involve, subsume.

compromise[1] v adapt, adjust, agree, arbitrate, bargain, concede, make concessions, negotiate, retire, retreat, settle. **antonyms** differ, quarrel.
n accommodation, accord, adjustment, agreement, bargain, concession, co-operation, settlement, trade-off. **antonyms** disagreement, intransigence.

compromise[2] v discredit, dishonour, embarrass, embroil, expose, hazard, imperil, implicate, involve, jeopardise, prejudice, undermine, weaken.

compulsion n coercion, constraint, demand, distress, drive, duress, force, impulse, necessity, need, obligation, obsession, preoccupation, pressure, pressurisation, urge, urgency. **antonyms** freedom, liberty.

compulsive adj besetting, compelling, driving, hardened, hopeless, incorrigible, incurable, irredeemable, irresistible, obsessive, overmastering, overpowering, overwhelming, uncontrollable, unputdownable, urgent.

compulsory adj binding, de

rigueur, forced, imperative, mandatory, obligatory, required, requisite, stipulated, stipulatory. **antonyms** optional, voluntary.

compunction n contrition, hesitation, misgiving, penitence, qualm, regret, reluctance, remorse, repentance, sorrow, unease, uneasiness. **antonyms** callousness, defiance.

compute v assess, calculate, count, enumerate, estimate, evaluate, figure, measure, rate, reckon, sum, tally, total.

comrade n ally, associate, brother, buddy, china, cobber, colleague, companion, compatriot, confederate, co-worker, crony, fellow, friend, mate, pal, partner, sidekick.

con v bamboozle, beguile, bilk, bluff, bunko, cheat, cozen, deceive, defraud, double-cross, dupe, fiddle, grift, gull, hoax, hoodwink, humbug, inveigle, mislead, racket, rip off, rook, swindle, trick.
n bluff, deception, fraud, grift, kidology, scam, swindle, trick.

concave adj cupped, depressed, hollow, hollowed, incurved, indented, scooped, sunken. **antonym** convex.

conceal v bury, camouflage, cloak, cover, disguise, dissemble, hide, keep dark, mask, obscure, screen, secrete, shelter, sink, smother, submerge, suppress, veil. **antonym** reveal.

concealed adj clandestine, covered, covert, disguised, hidden, masked, screened, secret, secreted, ulterior, unseen, veiled. **antonyms** clear, plain.

concealment n ambush, camouflage, cloak, cover, disguise, hide-away, hideout, hiding, protection, screen, secrecy, shelter. **antonyms** openness, revelation.

concede v accept, acknowledge, admit, allow, cede, confess, forfeit, grant, own, recognise, relinquish, sacrifice, surrender, yield. **antonyms** deny, dispute.

conceit n arrogance, assumption, cockiness, complacency, conceitedness, egotism, narcissism, pride, self-assumption, self-importance, self-love, self-pride, self-satisfaction, swagger, vainglory, vainness, vanity. **antonyms** diffidence, modesty.

conceited adj arrogant, assuming, bigheaded, cocky, complacent, egotistical, hoity-toity, immodest, narcissistic, overweening, self-important, self-

satisfied, stuck-up, swell-headed, swollen-headed, toffee-nose(d), uppity, vain, vainglorious, windy. **antonyms** diffident, modest.

conceivable adj believable, credible, imaginable, likely, possible, probable, supposable, tenable, thinkable. **antonym** inconceivable.

conceive v appreciate, apprehend, believe, comprehend, contrive, create, design, develop, devise, envisage, fancy, form, formulate, germinate, grasp, imagine, invent, originate, produce, project, purpose, realise, suppose, think, understand, visualise.

concentrate v absorb, accumulate, attend, attract, centre, cluster, collect, condense, congregate, converge, crowd, draw, engross, focus, gather, huddle, intensify. **antonyms** disperse, distract, separate.
n decoction, distillate, essence, extract, juice, quintessence.

concentrated adj all-out, compact, condensed, deep, dense, evaporated, hard, intense, intensive, reduced, rich, thickened, undiluted. **antonyms** desultory, diffuse, diluted.

concentration n absorption, accumulation, agglomeration, aggregation, application, centralisation, centring, cluster, collection, combination, compression, conglomeration, consolidation, convergence, crowd, denseness, focusing, grouping, horde, intensification, intensity, mass, single-mindedness. **antonyms** dilution, dispersal, distraction.

concept n abstraction, conception, conceptualisation, construct, hyphothesis, idea, image, impression, invention, notion, pattern, picture, plan, theory, type, view, visualisation.

conception n appreciation, beginning, birth, clue, comprehension, concept, design, envisagement, fertilisation, formation, germination, idea, image, impression, inauguration, inception, initiation, inkling, invention, knowledge, launching, notion, origin, outset, perception, picture, plan, understanding, visualisation.

concern v affect, bother, disquiet, distress, disturb, interest, involve, pertain to, perturb, refer to, regard, relate to, touch, trouble, upset, worry.
n affair, anxiety, apprehension, attention, bearing, burden, business, care, charge, company, consideration,

corporation, disquiet, disquietude, distress, enterprise, establishment, field, firm, heed, house, importance, interest, involvement, job, matter, mission, occupation, organisation, reference, relation, relevance, responsibility, solicitude, stake, task, transaction, unease, uneasiness, worry. *antonym* unconcern.

concerned *adj* active, anxious, apprehensive, attentive, bothered, caring, connected, disquieted, distressed, disturbed, exercised, implicated, interested, involved, perturbed, solicitous, troubled, uneasy, unhappy, upset, worried. *antonym* unconcerned.

concerning *prep* about, apropos of, as regards, germane to, in regard to, in the matter of, re, regarding, relating to, relevant to, respecting, touching, with reference to, with regard to.

concerted *adj* collaborative, collective, combined, co-ordinated, joint, organised, planned, prearranged, shared, united. *antonyms* disorganised, separate, unco-ordinated.

concession *n* acknowledgement, adjustment, admission, allowance, assent, boon, compromise, exception, favour, grant, indulgence, permit, privilege, relaxation, sacrifice, surrender, yielding.

conciliation *n* appeasement, indulgence, mollification, pacification, peace-making, placation, reconciliation, satisfaction. *antonyms* alienation, antagonisation.

concise *adj* abbreviated, abridged, aphoristic, brief, compact, compendious, compressed, condensed, pithy, short, succinct, summary, terse. *antonyms* diffuse, expansive.

conclude *v* accomplish, assume, cease, clinch, close, complete, consummate, culminate, decide, deduce, determine, effect, end, establish, finish, fix, gather, infer, judge, opine, reckon, resolve, settle, suppose, surmise, terminate.

concluding *adj* closing, final, last, terminal, ultimate. *antonym* introductory.

conclusion *n* answer, assumption, clincher, close, come-off, completion, consequence, consummation, conviction, culmination, decision, finale, finish, inference, issue, judgement, opinion, outcome, resolution, result, settlement, solution, termination, upshot, verdict.

conclusive *adj* clear, clinching,

convincing, decisive, definite, definitive, final, incontrovertible, irrefutable, manifest, ultimate, unanswerable, unarguable, undeniable.

concoct *v* brew, contrive, decoct, design, develop, devise, digest, fabricate, form, formulate, hatch, invent, mature, plan, plot, prepare, project, refine.

concomitant *adj* accompanying, attendant, co-existent, coincidental, complementary, concurrent, contributing, incidental, simultaneous. *antonyms* accidental, unrelated.

concord *n* accord, agreement, amicability, brotherliness, compact, concordat, consensus, consonance, convention, entente, friendship, harmony, peace, protocol, rapport, treaty, unanimity, unison. *antonym* discord.

concourse *n* assemblage, assembly, collection, confluence, convergence, crowd, crush, entrance, foyer, gathering, hall, lobby, lounge, meeting, multitude, piazza, plaza, swarm, throng.

concrete *adj* actual, compact, compressed, conglomerated, consolidated, definite, explicit, factual, firm, material, perceptible, physical, real, sensible, solid, solidified, specific, substantial, tactile, tangible, touchable, visible. *antonym* abstract.

concur *v* accede, accord, acquiesce, agree, approve, assent, coincide, combine, comply, consent, co-operate, harmonise, join, meet, unite. *antonym* disagree.

concurrence *n* acquiescence, agreement, assent, association, co-existence, coincidence, common ground, community, concomitance, conjunction, consilience, convergence, juxtaposition, simultaneity. *antonyms* difference, disagreement.

concurrent *adj* co-existing, coincident, coinciding, concomitant, confluent, contemporaneous, convergent, converging, simultaneous, uniting.

condemn *v* ban, blame, castigate, censure, convict, damn, decry, denounce, disapprove, disparage, doom, pan, proscribe, reprehend, reproach, reprove, revile, sentence, slam, slate, upbraid. *antonyms* approve, praise.

condemnation *n* ban, blame, castigation, censure, conviction, damnation, denouncement, denunciation, disapproval, disparagement, judgement, proscription, reproach, reprobation, reproof, sentence, slating, stricture, thumbs-down. *antonyms* approval, praise.

condense *v* abbreviate, abridge, coagulate, compact, compress, concentrate, contract, crystallise, curtail, decoct, distil, encapsulate, epitomise, evaporate, precipitate, précis, reduce, shorten, solidify, summarise, thicken. *antonyms* dilute, expand.

condensed *adj* abbreviated, abridged, abstracted, clotted, coagulated, compact, compressed, concentrated, concise, contracted, crystallised, curtailed, distilled, epitomised, evaporated, precipitated, reduced, shortened, shrunken, summarised, thickened. *antonyms* diluted, expanded.

condescend *v* bend, deign, patronise, see fit, stoop, submit, unbend, vouchsafe.

condescending *adj* disdainful, gracious, haughty, imperious, lofty, lordly, patronising, snooty, stooping, supercilious, superior, unbending. *antonyms* approachable, humble.

condition *n* ailment, arrangement, article, case, caste, circumstances, class, complaint, defect, demand, disease, disorder, estate, fettle, fitness, grade, health, infirmity, level, liability, limitation, malady, modification, nick, obligation, order, plight, position, predicament, prerequisite, problem, provision, proviso, qualification, rank, requirement, requisite, restriction, rule, shape, situation, state, status, stipulation, stratum, terms, trim, understanding, weakness.
v accustom, adapt, adjust, attune, determine, educate, equip, groom, habituate, hone, indoctrinate, inure, limit, prepare, prime, ready, restrict, season, temper, train, tune.

conditional *adj* contingent, dependent, limited, provisional, qualified, relative, restricted, tied. *antonym* unconditional.

conditioned *adj* acclimatised, accustomed, adapted, adjusted, attuned, familiarised, groomed, habituated, honed, indoctrinated, inured, prepared, primed, seasoned, tempered, trained, tuned, used.

conditioning *n* adjustment, education, familiarisation, grooming, hardening, honing, indoctrination, inurement, preparation, priming, reorientation, seasoning, tempering, training, tuning.

conditions *n* atmosphere, background, circumstances, context, environment, habitat, medium, milieu, setting, situation, state, surroundings.

condolence *n* commiseration, compassion, condolences, consolation, pity, support, sympathy. *antonym* congratulation.

condone *v* allow, brook, disregard, excuse, forgive, ignore, indulge, overlook, pardon, tolerate. *antonym* censure, disallow.

conducive *adj* advantageous, beneficial, contributory, encouraging, favourable, helpful, leading, productive, promotive, stimulative, tending. *antonym* adverse, unfavourable.

conduct *n* actions, administration, attitude, bearing, behaviour, carriage, comportment, control, co-ordination, demeanour, deportment, direction, discharge, escort, guidance, guide, leadership, management, manners, mien, orchestration, organisation, running, supervision, ways.
v accompany, acquit, act, administer, attend, bear, behave, carry, chair, comport, control, convey, demean, deport, direct, escort, govern, guide, handle, lead, manage, orchestrate, organise, pilot, regulate, run, solicit, steer, supervise, transact, usher.

confederate *adj* allied, associated, combined, federal, federated.
n accessory, accomplice, ally, assistant, associate, collaborator, colleague, conspirator, friend, leaguer, partner, practisant, supporter.
v ally, amalgamate, associate, bind, combine, federate, join, merge, unite, weld.

confer *v* accord, award, bestow, consult, converse, deliberate, discourse, discuss, give, grant, impart, lay heads together, lend, parley, powwow, present, talk, vouchsafe.

conference *n* confab, confabulation, congress, consultation, convention, convocation, debate, discussion, forum, meeting, powwow, seminar, symposium, synod, teach-in.

confess *v* acknowledge, admit, affirm, allow, assert, attest, aver, betray, concede, confide, confirm, declare, disclose, divulge, expose, grant, manifest, own, own up, profess, prove, recognise, reveal, show. *antonyms* conceal, deny.

confession *n* acknowledgement, admission, affirmation, assertion, attestation, averment, avowal, confidences, declaration, disclosure, divulgence, exposé, exposure, profession, revelation, unbosoming, unburdening, verbal. **antonyms** concealment, denial.

confide v admit, breathe, confess, disclose, divulge, impart, reveal, unburden, whisper. **antonyms** hide, suppress.

confidence n aplomb, assurance, belief, boldness, calmness, communication, composure, confession, coolness, courage, credence, dependence, disclosure, divulgence, faith, firmness, morale, nerve, reliance, savoir-faire, secret, self-assurance, self-confidence, self-possession, self-reliance, trust. **antonyms** diffidence, distrust.

confident adj assured, bold, certain, composed, convinced, cool, dauntless, fearless, persuaded, positive, sanguine, satisfied, secure, self-assured, self-confident, self-possessed, self-reliant, sure, unabashed, unbashful, unselfconscious. **antonyms** diffident, sceptical.

confidential adj classified, close, closed, faithful, familiar, hush-hush, in camera, intimate, private, privy, secret, tête-à-tête, trusted, trustworthy, trusty. **antonyms** common, public.

confidentially adv behind closed doors, between you me and the bed-post (lamp-post, gate-post), in camera, in confidence, in private, in secret, on the quiet, personally, privately, under the rose, within these four walls. **antonym** openly.

confine v bind, bound, cage, circumscribe, constrain, cramp, crib, enclose, immure, imprison, incarcerate, inhibit, intern, keep, keep prisoner, limit, mew, repress, restrain, restrict, shackle, shut up, trammel. **antonym** free.

confines n border, boundaries, bounds, circumference, edge, frontier, limits, perimeter, periphery, precincts.

confirm v approve, assure, attest, authenticate, back, buttress, clinch, corroborate, endorse, establish, evidence, fix, fortify, homologate, prove, ratify, reinforce, sanction, settle, strengthen, substantiate, support, validate, verify. **antonym** deny.

confirmation n acceptance, agreement, approval, assent, attestation, authentication, backing, corroboration, endorsement, evidence, proof, ratification, sanction, substantiation, support, testimony, validation, verification, witness. **antonym** denial.

confirmed adj authenticated, committed, corroborated, dyed-in-the-wool, entrenched, established, habitual, hardened, incorrigible, incurable, in-grained, inured, inveterate, irredeemable, long-established, long-standing, proved, proven, rooted, seasoned, substantiated.

confiscate v appropriate, commandeer, distrain, expropriate, impound, remove, seize, sequestrate. **antonym** restore.

conflict n agony, ambivalence, antagonism, antipathy, Armageddon, battle, brawl, clash, collision, combat, confrontation, contention, contest, difference, disagreement, discord, dissension, encounter, engagement, feud, fight, fracas, friction, hostility, interference, opposition, quarrel, set-to, skirmish, strife, turmoil, unrest, variance, war, warfare. **antonyms** agreement, concord.

v battle, clash, collide, combat, contend, contest, contradict, differ, disagree, fight, interfere, oppose, strive, struggle, war, wrangle. **antonym** agree.

conflicting adj ambivalent, antagonistic, clashing, contradictory, contrary, discordant, inconsistent, opposed, opposing, opposite, paradoxical, turbulent, warring. **antonym** compatible.

conform v accommodate, accord, adapt, adjust, agree, assimilate, comply, correspond, follow, harmonise, match, obey, square, suit, tally, yield. **antonym** differ.

conformity n affinity, agreement, allegiance, compliance, congruity, conventionalism, conventionality, correspondence, harmony, likeness, observance, orthodoxy, resemblance, similarity, traditionalism.

confound v abash, amaze, astonish, astound, baffle, bamboozle, bewilder, confuse, contradict, demolish, destroy, dismay, dumbfound, flabbergast, mystify, nonplus, overthrow, overwhelm, perplex, ruin, startle, stupefy, surprise, thwart, upset.

confounded adj arrant, astounded, baffled, bewildered, confused, consummate, cursed, discomfited, dismayed, dumbfounded, egregious, embarrassed, flabbergasted, frustrated, insufferable, mystified, nonplussed, notorious, outrageous, perplexed, rank, thwarted.

confront v accost, address, beard, brave,

challenge, defy, encounter, eyeball, face, front, oppose. *antonym* evade.

confrontation *n* battle, collision, conflict, contest, crisis, disagreement, encounter, engagement, face-off, fight, quarrel, set-to, showdown.

confuse *v* abash, addle, baffle, befuddle, bemuse, bewilder, confound, darken, demoralise, disarrange, discomfit, discompose, disconcert, discountenance, disorder, disorient, disorientate, embarrass, flummox, fluster, intermingle, involve, jumble, maze, mingle, mistake, mix up, mortify, muddle, mystify, nonplus, obscure, perplex, puzzle, rattle, shame, tangle, tie in knots, upset. *antonyms* clarify, enlighten, reassure.

confused *adj* addle(d), baffled, bewildered, chaotic, dazed, disarranged, disordered, disorderly, disorganised, disorientated, distracted, embarrassed, flummoxed, fuddled, jumbled, mistaken, misunderstood, muddled, muddle-headed, nonplussed, perplexed, puzzled, topsy-turvy, upset. *antonym* clear.

confusing *adj* ambiguous, baffling, bewildering, complicated, contradictory, cryptic, difficult, inconclusive, inconsistent, involved, misleading, muddling, perplexing, puzzling, tortuous, unclear. *antonyms* clear, definite.

confusion *n* abashment, balls-up, bemusement, bewilderment, bustle, chagrin, chaos, clutter, cock-up, commotion, disarrangement, disorder, disorganisation, disorientation, distraction, dudder, embarrassment, embroglio, embroilment, fluster, hotchpotch, imbroglio, jumble, mess, mix-up, muddle, mystification, overthrow, palaver, perplexity, puzzlement, shambles, shame, tangle, tizz(y), turmoil, untidiness, upheaval, welter. *antonyms* clarity, composure, order.

confute *v* annihilate, confound, controvert, disprove, give the lie to, impune, invalidate, nullify, oppugn, overthrow, overturn, rebut, refute, vitiate. *antonyms* confirm, prove.

congeal *v* clot, coagulate, coalesce, condense, curdle, freeze, fuse, harden, jell, set, solidify, stiffen, thicken. *antonyms* dissolve, melt, separate.

congenial *adj* agreeable, companionable, compatible, complaisant, cosy, delightful, favourable, friendly, genial, homely, kindly, kindred, like-minded, pleasant, pleasing, relaxing, suitable,

sympathetic, well-suited. *antonym* disagreeable.

congenital *adj* complete, hereditary, inborn, inbred, inherent, inherited, innate, inveterate, natural, thorough, utter.

congested *adj* blocked, clogged, crammed, engorged, full, jammed, overcharged, overcrowded, overfilled, overflowing, overfull, packed, saturated, stuffed, swollen, teeming. *antonym* clear.

congestion *n* bottle-neck, clogging, engorgement, jam, log-jam, mass, overcrowding, snarl-up, traffic-jam.

conglomerate *v* accumulate, agglomerate, agglutinate, aggregate, amass, assemble, clump, cohere, collect, congregate, foregather, gather, mass. *antonym* separate.

congratulate *v* compliment, felicitate. *antonym* commiserate.

congratulations *n* compliments, felicitations, good wishes, greetings. *antonyms* commiserations, condolences.

congregate *v* accumulate, assemble, bunch, clump, cluster, collect, concentrate, conglomerate, convene, converge, convoke, crowd, flock, foregather, gather, mass, meet, muster, rally, throng. *antonyms* dismiss, disperse.

congregation *n* assemblage, assembly, brethren, crowd, fellowship, flock, host, laity, multitude, parish, parishioners, throng.

congress *n* assembly, conclave, conference, convention, convocation, council, diet, forum, legislature, meeting, parliament, synod.

conjectural *adj* academic, assumed, hypothetical, posited, postulated, speculative, supposed, suppositional, surmised, tentative, theoretical. *antonyms* factual, real.

conjecture *v* assume, estimate, extrapolate, fancy, guess, hypothesise, imagine, infer, opine, reckon, speculate, suppose, surmise, suspect, theorise.
n assumption, conclusion, estimate, extrapolation, fancy, guess, guesstimate, guesswork, hypothesis, inference, notion, opinion, presumption, projection, speculation, supposition, surmise, theorising, theory.

conjugal *adv* bridal, connubial, marital, married, matrimonial, nuptial, wedded.

conjunction *n* amalgamation,

association, coincidence, combination, concurrence, juxtaposition, unification, union, unition.

conjure v adjure, beseech, bewitch, charm, compel, crave, enchant, entreat, fascinate, implore, importune, invoke, juggle, pray, raise, rouse, summon, supplicate.

conjure up awaken, contrive, create, evoke, excite, produce, recall, recollect.

conjuror, conjurer n illusionist, magician, prestidigitator, sorcerer, wizard.

connect v affix, ally, associate, cohere, combine, couple, fasten, join, link, relate, unite. **antonym** disconnect.

connected adj affiliated, akin, allied, associate, associated, combined, confederate, coupled, joined, linked, related, united. **antonyms** disconnected, unconnected.

connection n acquaintance, affinity, alliance, ally, associate, association, attachment, bond, coherence, commerce, communication, conjunction, contact, context, correlation, correspondence, coupling, fastening, friend, hook-up, intercourse, interrelation, intimacy, junction, kin, kindred, kinsman, kith, link, marriage, reference, relation, relationship, relative, relevance, sponsor, tie, tie-in, union. **antonym** disconnection.

connive v collude, complot, conspire, intrigue, plot, scheme.

connive at abet, aid, condone, disregard, let go, overlook, turn a blind eye to, wink at.

connoisseur n aficionado, authority, buff, cognoscente, devotee, expert, judge, savant, specialist, virtuoso.

connotation n association, colouring, hint, implication, nuance, overtone, significance, suggestion, undertone.

connote v betoken, hint at, imply, import, indicate, intimate, involve, purport, signify, suggest.

connubial adj conjugal, marital, married, matrimonial, nuptial, wedded.

conquer v acquire, annex, beat, best, checkmate, crush, defeat, discomfit, get the better of, humble, master, obtain, occupy, overcome, overpower, overrun, overthrow, prevail, quell, rout, seize, subdue, subjugate, succeed, surmount, triumph, vanquish, win, worst. **antonyms** surrender, yield.

conquest n acquisition, annexation, appropriation, captivation, coup, defeat, enchantment, invasion, inveiglement, mastery, occupation, overthrow, rout, seduction, subjection, subjugation, takeover, triumph, vanquishment, victory.

conscience-stricken adj ashamed, contrite, disturbed, guilt-ridden, guilty, penitent, regretful, remorseful, repentant, sorry, troubled. **antonyms** unashamed, unrepentant.

conscientious adj careful, diligent, exact, faithful, hard-working, high-principled, honest, honourable, incorruptible, just, meticulous, moral, painstaking, particular, punctilious, responsible, scrupulous, solicitous, straightforward, strict, thorough, upright. **antonyms** careless, irresponsible.

conscious adj alert, alive, awake, aware, calculated, cognisant, deliberate, heedful, intentional, knowing, mindful, percipient, premeditated, rational, reasoning, reflective, regardful, responsible, responsive, self-conscious, sensible, sentient, studied, wilful, witting.

consciousness n apprehension, awareness, intuition, knowledge, realisation, recognition, sensibility, sentience. **antonym** unconciousness.

consecrate v beatify, dedicate, devote, exalt, hallow, ordain, revere, sanctify, venerate.

consecutive adj chronological, continuous, following, running, sequential, succeeding, successive, unbroken, uninterrupted. **antonym** discontinuous.

consensus n agreement, concord, concurrence, consent, harmony, unanimity, unity. **antonym** disagreement.

consent v accede, acquiesce, admit, agree, allow, approve, assent, comply, concede, concur, grant, homologate, permit, yield. **antonyms** oppose, refuse. n accordance, acquiescence, agreement, approval, assent, compliance, concession, concurrence, go-ahead, green light, permission, sanction. **antonyms** opposition, refusal.

consequence n account, concern, distinction, effect, eminence, end, event, fall-out, import, importance, interest, issue, moment, notability, note, outcome, portent, rank, repercussion, repute, result, side effect, significance, standing, status, upshot, value, weight. **antonym** cause.

consequent adj ensuing, following,

resultant, resulting, sequent, sequential, subsequent, successive.

consequential *adj* arrogant, bumptious, conceited, consequent, eventful, far-reaching, grave, important, impressive, indirect, inflated, momentous, noteworthy, pompous, pretentious, resultant, self-important, serious, significant, supercilious, vainglorious, weighty. *antonyms* inconsequential, unimportant.

consequently *adv* accordingly, consequentially, ergo, hence, necessarily, subsequently, therefore, thus.

conservation *n* custody, economy, guardianship, husbandry, keeping, maintenance, preservation, protection, safeguarding, safe-keeping, saving, upkeep. *antonyms* destruction, neglect, waste.

conservative *adj* cautious, conventional, die-hard, establishmentarian, guarded, moderate, quiet, reactionary, right-wing, sober, Tory, traditional, unprogressive. *antonyms* left-wing, radical.
n diehard, moderate, reactionary, right-winger, stick-in-the-mud, Tory, traditionalist. *antonyms* left-winger, radical.

conserve *v* guard, hoard, husband, keep, maintain, nurse, preserve, protect, save. *antonyms* squander, use, waste.

consider *v* believe, cogitate, consult, contemplate, count, deem, deliberate, discuss, examine, judge, meditate, mull over, muse, perpend, ponder, rate, reflect, regard, remember, respect, revolve, ruminate, study, think, weigh. *antonym* ignore.

considerable *adj* abundant, ample, appreciable, big, comfortable, distinguished, goodly, great, important, influential, large, lavish, marked, much, noteworthy, noticeable, plentiful, reasonable, renowned, significant, siz(e)able, substantial, tidy, tolerable, venerable. *antonyms* insignificant, slight.

considerate *adj* attentive, charitable, circumspect, concerned, discreet, forbearing, gracious, kind, kindly, mindful, obliging, patient, solicitous, tactful, thoughtful, unselfish. *antonyms* selfish, thoughtless.

consideration *n* analysis, attention, cogitation, concern, considerateness, contemplation, deliberation, discussion, examination, factor, fee, friendliness, issue, kindliness, kindness, meditation, payment, perquisite, point, recompense, reflection, regard, remuneration, respect, review, reward, rumination, scrutiny, solicitude, study, tact, thought, thoughtfulness, tip. *antonyms* disdain, disregard.

consist of amount to, comprise, contain, embody, embrace, include, incorporate, involve.

consist in inhere, lie, reside.

consistency *n* accordance, agreement, coherence, compactness, compatibility, concordance, congruity, constancy, correspondence, density, evenness, firmness, harmony, identity, regularity, sameness, steadfastness, steadiness, thickness, uniformity, viscosity. *antonym* inconsistency.

consistent *adj* accordant, agreeing, coherent, compatible, congruous, consonant, constant, dependable, harmonious, logical, of a piece, regular, steady, unchanging, undeviating, unfailing, uniform. *antonyms* erratic, inconsistent.

consolation *n* aid, alleviation, cheer, comfort, ease, encouragement, help, relief, solace, succour, support. *antonym* discouragement.

console *v* assuage, calm, cheer, comfort, encourage, hearten, solace, soothe. *antonyms* agitate, upset.

consolidate *v* affiliate, amalgamate, cement, combine, compact, condense, confederate, conjoin, federate, fortify, fuse, harden, join, reinforce, secure, solidify, stabilise, strengthen, thicken, unify, unite.

consort *n* associate, companion, fellow, helpmate, husband, partner, spouse, wife.
v accord, agree, associate, correspond, fraternise, harmonise, jibe, mingle, mix, square, tally.

conspicuous *adj* apparent, blatant, clear, evident, flagrant, glaring, manifest, noticeable, obvious, patent, perceptible, remarked, showy, visible. *antonym* inconspicuous.

conspiracy *n* cabal, collusion, confederacy, fix, frame-up, intrigue, league, machination, plot, scheme, treason.

conspire *v* collude, combine, concur, confederate, contribute, contrive, co-operate, devise, hatch, intrigue, machinate, manoeuvre, plot, scheme, treason.

constancy *n* determination, devotion, faithfulness, fidelity, firmness, loyalty, permanence, perseverance, regularity, resolution, stability, steadfastness, steadiness, tenacity, uniformity. *antonyms* inconstancy, irregularity.

constant *adj* attached, ceaseless, changeless, continual, continuous, dependable, determined, devoted, dogged, endless, eternal, even, everlasting, faithful, firm, fixed, habitual, immutable, incessant, interminable, invariable, loyal, never-ending, non-stop, permanent, perpetual, persevering, persistent, regular, relentless, resolute, stable, staunch, steadfast, steady, sustained, true, trustworthy, trusty, unalterable, unbroken, unchangeable, unfailing, unflagging, uniform, uninterrupted, unrelenting, unremitting, unshaken, unvarying, unwavering. *antonyms* fickle, fitful, irregular, occasional, variable.

constantly *adv* always, continually, continuously, endlessly, everlastingly, incessantly, interminably, invariably, non-stop, perpetually, relentlessly, steadfastly, uniformly. *antonym* occasionally.

consternation *n* alarm, amazement, anxiety, awe, bewilderment, confusion, dismay, disquietude, distress, dread, fear, fright, horror, panic, shock, terror, trepidation. *antonym* composure.

constituent *adj* basic, component, elemental, essential, inherent, integral, intrinsic.
n bit, component, element, essential, factor, ingredient, part, portion, principle, section, unit. *antonym* whole.

constitute *v* appoint, authorise, commission, compose, comprise, create, delegate, depute, empower, enact, establish, fix, form, found, inaugurate, make, name, nominate, ordain.

constitution *n* build, character, composition, configuration, construction, disposition, establishment, form, formation, habit, health, make-up, nature, organisation, physique, structure, temper, temperament.

constitutional *adj* chartered, congenital, immanent, inborn, inherent, innate, intrinsic, organic, statutory.

constrain *v* bind, bulldoze, chain, check, coerce, compel, confine, constrict, curb, drive, force, impel, necessitate, oblige, pressure, pressurise, railroad, restrain, urge.

constrained *adj* embarrassed, forced, guarded, inhibited, reserved, reticent, stiff, subdued, uneasy, unnatural. *antonyms* free, relaxed.

constraint *n* check, coercion, compulsion, curb, damper, deterrent, duress, force, hindrance, limitation, necessity, pressure, restraint, restriction.

constrict *v* choke, compact, compress, contract, cramp, inhibit, limit, narrow, pinch, restrict, shrink, squeeze, strangle, strangulate, tighten. *antonym* expand.

constriction *n* blockage, compression, constraint, cramp, impediment, limitation, narrowing, pressure, reduction, restriction, squeezing, stricture, tightening, tightness. *antonym* expansion.

construct *v* assemble, build, compose, create, design, elevate, engineer, erect, establish, fabricate, fashion, form, formulate, found, frame, knock together, make, manufacture, model, organise, raise, shape. *antonyms* demolish, destroy.

construction *n* assembly, building, composition, constitution, creation, edifice, erection, fabric, fabrication, figure, form, formation, model, organisation, shape, structure. *antonym* destruction.

constructive *adj* advantageous, beneficial, helpful, positive, practical, productive, useful, valuable. *antonyms* destructive, negative, unhelpful.

construe *v* analyse, decipher, deduce, explain, expound, infer, interpret, read, take, translate.

consult *v* ask, commune, confer, consider, debate, deliberate, interrogate, parley, powwow, question, regard, respect.

consultation *n* appointment, conference, council, deliberation, dialogue, discussion, examination, hearing, interview, meeting, session.

consume *v* absorb, annihilate, decay, demolish, deplete, destroy, devastate, devour, discuss, dissipate, drain, eat, employ, engulf, envelop, exhaust, expend, gobble, guzzle, lessen, ravage, spend, squander, swallow, use (up), utilise, vanish, waste, wear out.

consuming *adj* absorbing, compelling, devouring, dominating, engrossing, excruciating, gripping, immoderate, monopolising, overwhelming, tormenting.

consummate *v* accomplish, achieve, cap, compass, complete, conclude, crown, effectuate, end, finish, fulfil, perfect, perform, terminate.

adj absolute, accomplished, complete, distinguished, finished, matchless, perfect, polished, practised, skilled, superb, superior, supreme, total, ultimate, unqualified, utter. **antonym** imperfect.

consumption *n* consuming, decay, decline, decrease, depletion, destruction, diminution, dissipation, exhaustion, expenditure, loss, TB, tuberculosis, use, utilisation, waste.

contact *n* acquaintance, association, communication, connection, contiguity, contingence, impact, junction, juxtaposition, meeting, touch, union.
v approach, call, get hold of, notify, phone, reach, ring.

contagious *adj* catching, communicable, epidemic, infectious, pestilential, spreading, transmissible.

contain *v* accommodate, check, comprehend, comprise, control, curb, embody, embrace, enclose, hold, include, incorporate, involve, limit, repress, restrain, seat, stifle. **antonym** exclude.

contaminate *v* adulterate, besmirch, corrupt, debase, defile, deprave, infect, pollute, soil, stain, sully, taint, tarnish, vitiate. **antonym** purify.

contemplate *v* behold, consider, deliberate, design, envisage, examine, expect, eye, foresee, inspect, intend, mean, meditate, mull over, observe, plan, ponder, propose, reflect on, regard, ruminate, scrutinise, study, survey, view.

contemporary *adj* co-existing, concurrent, contemporaneous, current, latest, modern, present, present-day, recent.

contempt *n* condescension, derision, detestation, disdain, disgrace, dishonour, disregard, disrespect, humiliation, loathing, mockery, neglect, scorn, shame, slight. **antonyms** admiration, regard.

contemptible *adj* abject, base, cheap, degenerate, despicable, detestable, ignominious, loathsome, low, low-down, mean, paltry, pitiful, scurvy, shabby, shameful, vile, worthless, wretched. **antonyms** admirable, honourable.

contemptuous *adj* arrogant, cavalier, condescending, cynical, derisive, disdainful, haughty, high and mighty, insolent, insulting, scornful, sneering, supercilious. **antonyms** humble, polite, respectful.

contend *v* affirm, allege, argue, assert, aver, avow, clash, compete, contest, cope, debate, declare, dispute, grapple, hold, jostle, maintain, skirmish, strive, struggle, vie, wrestle.

content¹ *v* appease, delight, gladden, gratify, humour, indulge, mollify, pacify, placate, please, reconcile, satisfy, suffice. **antonym** displease.
n comfort, contentment, delight, ease, gratification, happiness, peace, pleasure, satisfaction. **antonym** discontent.
adj agreeable, comfortable, contented, fulfilled, pleased, satisfied, untroubled. **antonym** dissatisfied.

content² *n* burden, capacity, essence, gist, ideas, load, matter, meaning, measure, significance, size, subject matter, substance, text, thoughts, volume.

contention *n* affirmation, allegation, argument, assertion, belief, claim, competition, contest, controversy, debate, declaration, discord, dispute, dissension, enmity, feuding, ground, hostility, idea, opinion, position, profession, rivalry, stand, strife, struggle, thesis, view, wrangling.

contentious *adj* antagonistic, argumentative, bickering, captious, combative, controversial, cross, debat(e)able, disputatious, factious, hostile, peevish, perverse, pugnacious, quarrelsome, querulous, wrangling. **antonyms** co-operative, peaceable, uncontroversial.

contentment *n* comfort, complacency, content, ease, equanimity, fulfilment, gladness, gratification, happiness, peace, peacefulness, placidity, pleasure, satisfaction. **antonym** dissatisfaction.

contest *n* affray, altercation, battle, combat, competition, concours, conflict, controversy, debate, dispute, encounter, fight, game, match, set-to, shock, struggle, tournament, trial.
v argue against, challenge, compete, contend, debate, deny, dispute, doubt, fight, oppose, question, refute, vie.

context *n* ambience, associations, background, circumstances, conditions, connection, frame of reference, framework, relation, situation.

contingency *n* accident, arbitrariness, chance, emergency, event, eventuality, fortuity, happening, incident, possibility, randomness, uncertainty.

contingent *n* batch, body, bunch, company, complement, deputation, detachment, group, mission, quota, section, set.

continual *adj* ceaseless, constant, continuous, endless, eternal, everlasting, frequent, incessant, interminable, oft-repeated, perpetual, recurrent, regular, repeated, repetitive, unbroken, unceasing, uninterrupted, unremitting. *antonyms* intermittent, occasional, temporary.

continuation *n* addition, appendix, epilogue, extension, furtherance, maintenance, perpetuation, postscript, prolongation, resumption, sequel, supplement. *antonyms* cessation, termination.

continue *v* abide, adjourn, carry on, endure, extend, go on, last, lengthen, maintain, persevere, persist, proceed, project, prolong, pursue, reach, recommence, remain, rest, resume, stay, stick at, survive, sustain. *antonyms* discontinue, stop.

continuity *n* cohesion, connection, extension, flow, interrelationship, linkage, progression, sequence, succession.

continuous *adj* connected, consecutive, constant, continued, extended, non-stop, prolonged, unbroken, unceasing, undivided, uninterrupted. *antonyms* discontinuous, intermittent, sporadic.

contort *v* convolute, deform, disfigure, distort, gnarl, knot, misshape, squirm, twist, warp, wrench, wriggle, writhe.

contract *v* abbreviate, abridge, acquire, agree, arrange, bargain, catch, clinch, close, compress, condense, confine, constrict, constringe, covenant, curtail, develop, dwindle, engage, incur, lessen, narrow, negotiate, pledge, purse, reduce, shrink, shrivel, stipulate, tighten, wither, wrinkle. *antonyms* enlarge, expand, lengthen.
n agreement, arrangement, bargain, bond, commission, commitment, compact, concordat, convention, covenant, deal, engagement, instrument, pact, settlement, stipulation, transaction, treaty, understanding.

contraction *n* abbreviation, astringency, compression, constriction, cramp, diminution, elision, narrowing, reduction, shortening, shrinkage, shrivelling, tensing, tightening. *antonyms* expansion, growth.

contradict *v* belie, challenge, contravene, controvert, counter, counteract, deny, disaffirm, dispute, gainsay, impugn, negate, oppose. *antonyms* agree, confirm, corroborate.

contradiction *n* conflict, confutation, contravention, denial, inconsistency, negation, opposite. *antonyms* agreement, confirmation, corroboration.

contradictory *adj* antagonistic, antithetical, conflicting, contrary, dissident, incompatible, inconsistent, irreconcilable, opposed, opposite, paradoxical, repugnant, unreconciled. *antonym* consistent.

contraption *n* apparatus, contrivance, device, gadget, gizmo, mechanism, rig, thingumajig, widget.

contrary *adj* adverse, antagonistic, awkward, balky, cantankerous, clashing, contradictory, counter, cross-grained, difficult, discordant, disobliging, hostile, inconsistent, inimical, intractable, intractible, obstinate, opposed, opposite, paradoxical, perverse, stroppy, unaccommodating, wayward, wilful. *antonyms* like, obliging, similar.
n antithesis, converse, opposite, reverse.

contrast *n* comparison, counter-view, difference, differentiation, disparity, dissimilarity, distinction, divergence, foil, opposition, set-off. *antonym* similarity.
v compare, differ, differentiate, discriminate, distinguish, oppose, set off.

contravene *v* break, contradict, counteract, cross, disobey, hinder, infringe, interfere, oppose, refute, thwart, transgress, trespass, violate. *antonym* uphold.

contribute *v* add, afford, bestow, donate, furnish, give, help, lead, provide, subscribe, supply, tend. *antonyms* subtract, withhold.

contribution *n* addition, donation, gift, grant, gratuity, handout, input, offering, subscription.

contrition *n* compunction, humiliation, penitence, remorse, repentance, sack-cloth and ashes, self-reproach, sorrow.

contrivance *n* apparatus, appliance, contraption, design, device, dodge, equipment, expedient, fabrication, gadget, gear, implement, intrigue, invention, inventiveness, machination, machine, mechanism, plan, plot, project, ruse, scheme, stratagem, trick.

contrive *v* arrange, compass, concoct, construct, create, design, devise, effect, engineer, excogitate, fabricate, frame, improvise, invent, manage, manoeuvre, plan, plot, scheme, wangle.

contrived *adj* artificial, elaborate, false, forced, laboured, mannered, overdone, planned, strained, unnatural. *antonym* natural.

control *v* boss, bridle, check, command, conduct, confine, constrain, contain, curb, determine, direct, dominate, govern, lead, limit, manage, manipulate, master, monitor, oversee, pilot, regiment, regulate, repress, restrain, rule, run, stage-manage, steer, subdue, superintend, supervise, suppress, verify. *n* authority, brake, charge, check, clutches, command, curb, direction, discipline, governance, government, guidance, jurisdiction, leash, limitation, management, mastery, regulation, rule, superintendence, supervision, supremacy.

controversial *adj* attacking, contentious, debatable, disputable, disputed, doubtful, polemic, polemical, questionable.

controversy *n* altercation, argument, contention, debate, disagreement, discussion, dispute, dissension, polemic, quarrel, squabble, strife, war of words, wrangle, wrangling. *antonyms* accord, agreement.

contusion *n* bruise, bump, discolour-ation, injury, knock, lump, swelling.

convalescence *n* improvement, recovery, recuperation, rehabilitation, restoration.

convene *v* assemble, call, collect, congregate, convoke, gather, meet, muster, rally, summon.

convenience *n* accessibility, accommodation, advantage, amenity, appliance, appropriateness, availability, benefit, chance, comfort, ease, enjoyment, facility, fitness, handiness, help, leisure, satisfaction, service, suitability, timeliness, use, usefulness, utility.

convenient *adj* accessible, adapted, appropriate, at hand, available, beneficial, commodious, fit, fitted, handy, helpful, labour-saving, nearby, opportune, suitable, suited, timely, useful, well-timed. *antonyms* awkward, inconvenient.

convention *n* agreement, assembly, bargain, code, compact, conclave, concordat, conference, congress, contract, convocation, council, custom, delegates, etiquette, formality, matter of form, meeting, pact, practice, propriety, protocol, representatives, stipulation, synod, tradition, treaty, understanding, usage.

conventional *adj* accepted, arbitrary, bourgeois, common, commonplace, copybook, correct, customary, decorous, expected, formal, formalist, habitual, hackneyed, normal, ordinary, orthodox, pedestrian, prevailing, prevalent, proper, prosaic, regular, ritual, routine, run-of-the-mill, standard, stereotyped, straight, stylised, traditional, unoriginal, usual, wonted. *antonyms* exotic, unconventional, unusual.

converge *v* approach, coincide, combine, concentrate, concur, focus, gather, join, meet, merge, mingle. *antonyms* disperse, diverge.

conversant with acquainted with, au fait with, experienced in, familiar with, informed about, knowledgeable about, practised in, proficient in, skilled in, versed in.

conversation *n* chat, chinwag, chitchat, communication, confab, confabulation, conference, dialogue, discourse, discussion, exchange, gossip, intercourse, interlocution, powwow, talk, tête-à-tête.

conversion *n* adaptation, alteration, change, metamorphosis, modification, rebirth, reconstruction, reformation, regeneration, remodelling, reorganisa-tion, transfiguration, transformation, transmutation.

convert *v* adapt, alter, apply, appropriate, baptise, change, convince, interchange, metamorphose, modify, reform, regenerate, remodel, reorganise, restyle, revise, save, transform, transmute, transpose, turn.

convey *v* bear, bequeath, bring, carry, cede, communicate, conduct, deliver, demise, devolve, disclose, fetch, forward, grant, guide, impart, lease, move, relate, reveal, send, steal, support, tell, transfer, transmit, transport, will.

conviction *n* assurance, belief, certainty, certitude, confidence, creed, earnestness, faith, fervour, firmness, opinion, persuasion, principle, reliance, tenet, view.

convince *v* assure, confirm, persuade, reassure, satisfy, sway, win over.

convincing *adj* cogent, conclusive, credible, impressive, incontrovertible, likely, persuasive, plausible, powerful, probable, telling. *antonyms* dubious, improbable.

convivial *adj* cheerful, festive, friendly

gay, genial, hearty, jolly, jovial, lively, merry, mirthful, sociable. *antonym* taciturn.

convoke v assemble, collect, convene, gather, muster, rally, round up, summon.

convoluted adj complex, complicated, involved, meandering, tangled, twisting, winding. *antonym* straightforward.

convolution n coil, coiling, complexity, contortion, helix, intricacy, loop, sinousness, sinuosity, spiral, tortuousness, twist, whorl, winding.

convulsion n agitation, commotion, contortion, contraction, cramp, disturbance, eruption, fit, furore, outburst, paroxysm, seizure, shaking, spasm, throe, tremor, tumult, turbulence, upheaval.

cook v bake, boil, braise, broil, fry, grill, heat, prepare, roast, sauté, simmer, steam, stew, toast.

cook up brew, concoct, contrive, devise, fabricate, improvise, invent, plan, plot, prepare, scheme.

cool adj aloof, apathetic, audacious, bold, brazen, calm, cheeky, chilled, chilling, chilly, coldish, collected, composed, cosmopolitan, deliberate, dispassionate, distant, down-beat, elegant, frigid, impertinent, imperturbable, impudent, incurious, indifferent, laid-back, level-headed, lukewarm, nippy, offhand, placid, pleasant, presumptuous, quiet, refreshing, relaxed, reserved, satisfying, self-controlled, self-possessed, serene, shameless, sophisticated, stand-offish, together, uncommunicative, unconcerned, unemotional, unenthusiastic, unexcited, unfriendly, unheated, uninterested, unresponsive, unruffled, unwelcoming, urbane. *antonyms* excited, friendly, hot, warm.

v abate, allay, assuage, calm, chill, dampen, defuse, fan, freeze, lessen, moderate, quiet, refrigerate, temper. *antonyms* excite, heat, warm.

n calmness, collectedness, composure, control, poise, sangfroid, self-control, self-discipline, self-possession, temper.

co-operate v abet, aid, assist, collaborate, combine, concur, conspire, contribute, co-ordinate, help, play along, play ball.

co-operation n assistance, collaboration, concurrence, give-and-take, helpfulness, participation, responsiveness, teamwork, unity.

co-operative adj accommodating, coactive, collective, combined, concerted, co-ordinated, helpful, joint, obliging, responsive, shared, supportive, unified, united.

co-ordinate v correlate, grade, graduate, harmonise, integrate, match, mesh, organise, relate, synchronise, systematise, tabulate.

adj correlative, correspondent, equal, equivalent, parallel, reciprocal.

cop out abandon, desert, dodge, evade, quit, renege, renounce, revoke, shirk, skip, skive, withdraw.

cope v carry on, get by, make do, manage, survive.

cope with contend with, deal with, encounter, grapple with, handle, manage, struggle with, tangle with, tussle with, weather, wrestle with.

copulate v bonk, enjoy, fuck, know, make love, mate, serve.

copy n borrowing, carbon copy, counterfeit, crib, duplicate, exemplar, facsimile, fax, forgery, image, imitation, likeness, model, pattern, photocopy, Photostat®, plagiarisation, print, replica, representation, reproduction, tracing, transcript, transcription, Xerox®. *antonym* original.

v ape, borrow, counterfeit, crib, duplicate, echo, emulate, engross, exemplify, extract, facsimile, follow, imitate, mimic, mirror, parrot, photocopy, Photostat®, plagiarise, repeat, replicate, reproduce, simulate, transcribe, Xerox®.

coquettish adj amorous, come-hither, coy, flighty, flirtatious, flirty, inviting, teasing, vampish.

cordial adj affable, affectionate, agreeable, cheerful, earnest, friendly, genial, heartfelt, hearty, invigorating, pleasant, sociable, warm, warm-hearted, welcoming. *antonyms* aloof, cool, hostile.

core n centre, crux, essence, gist, heart, kernel, nitty-gritty, nub, nucleus, pith. *antonyms* exterior, perimeter, surface.

corner n angle, bend, cavity, cranny, crook, hide-away, hideout, hidey-hole, hole, joint, niche, nook, pickle, predicament, recess, retreat, spot.

corny adj banal, clichéd, commonplace, dull, feeble, hackneyed, maudlin, mawkish, old-fashioned, platitudinous, sentimental, stale, stereotyped, trite. *antonyms* new, original.

corollary n conclusion, consequence, deduction, fall-out, inference, result, upshot.

corporal *adj* anatomical, bodily, carnal, concrete, corporeal, fleshly, material, physical, tangible. *antonym* spiritual.

corporate *adj* allied, amalgamated, collaborative, collective, combined, communal, concerted, joint, merged, pooled, shared, united.

corporation *n* association, authorities, body, combine, conglomerate, council, society.

corporeal *adj* actual, bodily, fleshly, human, material, mortal, physical, substantial, tangible. *antonym* spiritual.

corpulent *adj* beefy, bulky, burly, fat, fattish, fleshly, large, obese, overweight, plump, podgy, portly, pot-bellied, pudgy, roly-poly, rotund, stout, tubby, well-padded. *antonym* thin.

correct *v* adjust, admonish, amend, blue-pencil, chasten, chastise, chide, counterbalance, cure, discipline, emend, emendate, improve, punish, rectify, redress, reform, regulate, remedy, reprimand, reprove, right.
adj acceptable, accurate, appropriate, diplomatic, equitable, exact, faultless, fitting, flawless, just, OK, precise, proper, regular, right, seemly, standard, strict, true, well-formed, word-perfect. *antonyms* inaccurate, incorrect, wrong.

correction *n* adjustment, admonition, alteration, amendment, castigation, chastisement, discipline, emendation, improvement, modification, punishment, rectification, reformation, reproof, righting.

corrective *adj* curative, disciplinary, medicinal, palliative, penal, punitive, rehabilitative, remedial, restorative, therapeutic.

correctly *adv* accurately, aright, faithfully, faultlessly, perfectly, precisely, properly, right, rightly. *antonym* wrongly.

correlate *v* associate, compare, connect, co-ordinate, correspond, equate, interact, link, parallel, relate, tie in.

correlation *n* correspondence, equivalence, interaction, interchange, interdependence, interrelationship, link, reciprocity, relationship.

correspond *v* accord, agree, answer, coincide, communicate, complement, concur, conform, correlate, dovetail, fit, harmonise, match, square, tally, write.

correspondence *n* agreement, analogy, coincidence, communication, comparability, comparison, concurrence, conformity, congruity, correlation, equivalence, fitness, harmony, letters, mail, match, post, relation, resemblance, similarity, writing. *antonyms* divergence, incongruity.

corresponding *adj* analogous, answering, complementary, correlative, equivalent, identical, interrelated, matching, reciprocal, similar, synonymous.

corroborate *v* authenticate, bear out, confirm, document, endorse, establish, prove, ratify, substantiate, support, sustain, underpin, validate. *antonym* contradict.

corrode *v* canker, consume, corrupt, crumble, deteriorate, disintegrate, eat away, erode, fret, impair, oxidise, rust, waste, wear away.

corrosive *adj* abrasive, acid, acrid, biting, caustic, consuming, cutting, incisive, mordant, sarcastic, trenchant, venomous, virulent, wasting, wearing.

corrugated *adj* channelled, creased, crinkled, fluted, furrowed, grooved, puckered, ribbed, ridged, rumpled, striate(d), wrinkled.

corrupt *adj* abandoned, adulterate(d), altered, bent, bribed, contaminated, crooked, debased, decayed, defiled, degenerate, demoralised, depraved, dishonest, dishonoured, dissolute, distorted, doctored, falsified, fraudulent, infected, polluted, profligate, rotten, shady, tainted, unethical, unprincipled, unscrupulous, venal, vicious. *antonyms* honest, trustworthy, upright.
v adulterate, barbarise, bribe, canker, contaminate, debase, debauch, defile, demoralise, deprave, doctor, empoison, entice, fix, infect, lure, pervert, putrefy, seduce, spoil, square, suborn, subvert, taint, vitiate. *antonym* purify.

corruption *n* adulteration, baseness, bribery, bribing, crookedness, debasement, decadence, decay, defilement, degeneration, degradation, demoralisation, depravity, dishonesty, distortion, doctoring, evil, extortion, falsification, fiddling, foulness, fraud, fraudulence, fraudulency, immorality, impurity, infection, iniquity, perversion, pollution, profiteering, profligacy, rottenness, shadiness, sinfulness, turpitude, ulcer, unscrupulousness, vice, viciousness, virus, wickedness. *antonyms* honesty, purification.

cosmetic *adj* non-essential, superficial, surface. *antonym* essential.

cosmic *adj* boundless, grandiose, huge,

illimitable, immense, infinite, limitless, measureless, universal, vast.

cosmopolitan *adj* catholic, international, sophisticated, universal, unprejudiced, urbane, well-travelled, worldly, worldy-wise. *antonyms* insular, parochial, rustic.

cosset *v* baby, cherish, coddle, cuddle, mollycoddle, pamper, pet.

cost *n* amount, charge, damage, deprivation, detriment, disbursement, expenditure, expense, figure, harm, hurt, injury, loss, outlay, payment, penalty, price, rate, sacrifice, worth.

costly *adj* catastrophic, damaging, dear, deleterious, disastrous, excessive, exorbitant, expensive, extortionate, harmful, highly-priced, lavish, loss-making, luxurious, opulent, precious, priceless, pricy, rich, ruinous, splendid, steep, sumptuous, valuable. *antonyms* cheap, inexpensive.

costs *n* budget, expenses, outgoings, overheads.

costume *n* apparel, attire, clothing, dress, ensemble, garb, get-up, livery, outfit, robes, uniform, vestment.

cosy *adj* comfortable, comfy, homelike, homely, intimate, secure, sheltered, snug, warm. *antonyms* cold, uncomfortable.

coterie *n* camp, caucus, circle, clique, gang, group, outfit, set.

cottage *n* bothy, bungalow, but-and-ben, cabin, chalet, cot, hut, lodge, shack.

couch *v* bear, cradle, express, frame, phrase, support, utter, word.
n bed, chaise-longue, chesterfield, divan, lounge, settee, sofa.

cough up deliver, fork out, give, hand over, pay, pay out, shell out, surrender.

council *n* assembly, board, cabinet, chamber, committee, conclave, conference, congress, consult, convention, convocation, ministry, panel, parliament, soviet, syndicate, synod.

counsel *n* advice, advocate, attorney, barrister, caution, consideration, consultation, deliberation, direction, forethought, guidance, information, lawyer, plan, purpose, recommendation, solicitor, suggestion, warning.
v admonish, advise, advocate, caution, direct, exhort, guide, instruct, recommend, suggest, urge, warn.

count *v* add, ascribe, calculate, check, compute, consider, deem, enumerate, esteem, estimate, hold, impute, include, judge, list, matter, number, rate, reckon, regard, score, signify, tally, tell, think, tot up, total, weigh.
n addition, calculation, computation, enumeration, numbering, poll, reckoning, sum, tally, total.

count for nothing cut no ice, make no difference.

count on bank on, believe, depend on, expect, reckon on, rely on, trust.

count out exclude, include out. *antonym* include.

countenance *n* acquiescence, aid, air, appearance, approval, aspect, assistance, backing, demeanour, endorsement, expression, face, favour, features, help, look, physiognomy, sanction, support, visage.
v abet, acquiesce, agree to, aid, approve, back, brook, champion, condone, encourage, endorse, endure, help, sanction, support, tolerate.

counter *adv* against, contrarily, conversely, in opposition.
adj adverse, against, antithetical, conflicting, contradictory, contrary, contrasting, obverse, opposed, opposing, opposite. *antonyms* concurring, corroborating.
v answer, meet, offset, parry, resist, respond, retaliate, retort, return.

counteract *v* act against, annul, check, contravene, counterbalance, cross, defeat, foil, frustrate, hinder, invalidate, negate, neutralise, offset, oppose, resist, thwart, undo. *antonyms* assist, support.

counterbalance *v* balance, compensate for, counterpoise, countervail, equalise, neutralise, offset.

counterfeit *v* copy, fabricate, fake, feign, forge, imitate, impersonate, pretend, simulate.
adj bogus, copied, ersatz, faked, false, feigned, forged, fraudulent, imitation, phoney, pretend(ed), pseudo, sham, simulate(d), spurious. *antonym* genuine.
n copy, fake, forgery, fraud, imitation, phoney, reproduction, sham.

counterpart *n* complement, copy, correlative, duplicate, equal, fellow, match, mate, opposite number, supplement, twin.

countless *adj* endless, immeasurable, incalculable, infinite, innumerable, legion, limitless, measureless, multitudinous, myriad, numberless, unnumbered, untold. *antonym* limited.

countrified *adj* arcadian, bucolic, hick,

homespun, idyllic, pastoral, provincial, rural, rustic. *antonyms* oppidan, urban.

country *n* backwoods, citizenry, citizens, clime, commonwealth, community, countryside, electors, farmland, fatherland, green belt, homeland, inhabitants, kingdom, land, motherland, nation, nationality, outback, outdoors, part, people, populace, provinces, public, realm, region, society, sovereign state, state, sticks, terrain, territory, voters.

adj agrarian, agrestic, arcadian, bucolic, pastoral, provincial, rural, rustic. *antonyms* oppidan, urban.

countryman *n* bumpkin, compatriot, farmer, fellow countryman, peasant, provincial, rustic, yokel.

coup *n* accomplishment, action, blow, coup d'état, deed, exploit, feat, manoeuvre, masterstroke, putsch, revolution, stratagem, stroke, stunt, tour de force.

coup d'état coup, overthrow, palace revolution, putsch, rebellion, revolt, revolution, takeover, uprising.

couple *n* brace, Darby and Joan, duo, pair, team, twosome.

v accompany, buckle, clasp, connect, copulate, fornicate, hitch, join, link, marry, pair, unite, wed, yoke.

courage *n* boldness, bottle, bravery, daring, dauntlessness, fearlessness, firmness, fortitude, gallantry, grit, guts, heroism, mettle, nerve, pluck, resolution, spirit, spunk, stomach, valour. *antonym* cowardice.

courageous *adj* audacious, bold, brave, daring, dauntless, dreadless, fearless, gallant, gutsy, hardy, heroic, high-hearted, indomitable, intrepid, lion-hearted, plucky, resolute, stout-hearted, valiant, valorous. *antonym* cowardly.

courier *n* bearer, carrier, emissary, envoy, guide, herald, messenger, representative, runner.

course *n* advance, advancement, channel, circuit, circus, classes, continuity, current, curriculum, development, direction, duration, flight-path, flow, furtherance, hippodrome, lap, lectures, line, march, method, mode, movement, orbit, order, passage, passing, path, piste, plan, policy, procedure, programme, progress, progression, race, race-course, race-track, regimen, road, round, route, schedule, sequence, series, studies, succession, sweep, syllabus, tack, term, time, track, trail, trajectory, unfolding, vector, voyage, way, wheel.

v chase, dash, flow, follow, gush, hunt, move, pour, pursue, race, run, scud, scurry, speed, stream, surge, tumble.

court *n* attendants, bailey, bar, bench, cloister, cortège, courtyard, entourage, hall, law-court, manor, palace, piazza, plaza, quad, quadrangle, retinue, square, suite, train, tribunal, yard.

v attract, chase, cultivate, date, flatter, incite, invite, lionise, pander to, prompt, provoke, pursue, seek, serenade, solicit, woo.

courteous *adj* affable, attentive, ceremonious, civil, considerate, courtly, debonair, elegant, gallant, gracious, mannerly, obliging, polished, polite, refined, respectful, urbane, well-bred, well-mannered. *antonyms* discourteous, rude.

courtesan *n* call girl, harlot, kept woman, mistress, paramour, prostitute, scarlet woman, whore, woman of easy virtue, woman of the night, woman of the town.

courtesy *n* affability, attention, benevolence, breeding, civility, consideration, courteousness, courtliness, elegance, favour, gallantness, gallantry, generosity, graciousness, indulgence, kindness, manners, polish, politeness, urbanity. *antonyms* discourtesy, rudeness.

courtier *n* attendant, follower, henchman, lady, lord, noble, nobleman, page, squire, steward, sycophant, toady.

courtly *adj* affable, aristocratic, ceremonious, chivalric, chivalrous, civil, decorous, dignified, elegant, flattering, formal, gallant, high-bred, lordly, obliging, polished, polite, refined, stately. *antonyms* inelegant, provincial, rough.

covenant *n* arrangement, bargain, bond, commitment, compact, concordat, contract, convention, deed, engagement, pact, pledge, promise, stipulation, treaty, trust, undertaking.

v agree, bargain, contract, engage, pledge, promise, stipulate, undertake.

cover *v* balance, camouflage, canopy, clad, cloak, clothe, coat, compensate, comprehend, comprise, conceal, consider, contain, counterbalance, curtain, daub, defend, describe, detail, disguise, dress, eclipse, embody, embrace, encase, encompass, enshroud, envelop, examine, guard, hide, hood, house, include, incorporate, insure, invest, investigate, involve, layer, mantle, mask, narrate, obscure, offset, overlay, overspread, protect, recount, reinforce, relate, report, screen, secrete, shade, sheathe, shelter, shield, shroud, suffuse, survey, veil.

n bedspread, binding, camouflage, canopy, cap, case, cloak, clothing, coating, compensation, concealment, confederate, covering, cover-up, defence, disguise, dress, envelope, façade, front, guard, indemnity, insurance, jacket, lid, mask, payment, pretence, pretext, protection, refuge, reimbursement, sanctuary, screen, sheath, shelter, shield, smoke, spread, top, undergrowth, veil, woods, wrapper.

cover up coat, conceal, cover, dissemble, dissimulate, encrust, envelop, hide, hush up, plaster, repress, stonewall, suppress, swathe, whitewash. **antonym** uncover.

coverage *n* analysis, assurance, description, insurance, protection, reportage, reporting, treatment.

covering *n* blanket, casing, cloak, clothing, coating, cocoon, cover, housing, layer, mask, masking, overlay, protection, sheath, shelter, top, umbrella, wash, wrap, wrapper, wrapping.

adj accompanying, descriptive, explanatory, introductory, masking, obscuring, protective.

covert *adj* clandestine, concealed, disguised, dissembled, hidden, private, secret, sneaky, stealthy, surreptitious, ulterior, under the table, underhand, unsuspected, veiled. **antonym** open.

cover-up *n* complicity, concealment, conspiracy, dissemblance, dissimulation, front, pretence, smoke-screen, whitewash.

covet *v* begrudge, crave, desire, envy, fancy, hanker, long for, lust after, thirst for, want, yearn for, yen for. **antonym** abjure.

covetous *adj* acquisitive, avaricious, close-fisted, envious, grasping, greedy, jealous, mercenary, rapacious, thirsting, yearning. **antonyms** generous, temperate.

cow *v* break, browbeat, bulldoze, bully, daunt, dishearten, dismay, domineer, frighten, intimidate, scare, subdue, terrorise, unnerve. **antonym** encourage.

coward *n* chicken, craven, faint-heart, renegade, scaredy-cat, skulker, sneak, yellow-belly, yellow-dog. **antonym** hero.

cowardly *adj* base, chicken, chicken-hearted, chicken-livered, craven, dastard(ly), faint-hearted, fearful, gutless, lily-livered, nesh, pusillanimous, scared, shrinking, soft, spineless, timorous, unheroic, weak, weak-kneed, yellow, yellow-bellied. **antonym** courageous.

cowboy *n* bronco-buster, buckaroo, cattleman, cowhand, cowpoke, cowpuncher, drover, gaucho, herder, herdsman, rancher, ranchero, stockman, vaquero, wrangler.

cower *v* cringe, crouch, flinch, grovel, quail, shake, shiver, shrink, skulk, tremble.

coy *adj* arch, bashful, coquettish, demure, diffident, flirtatious, kittenish, maidenly, modest, prudish, reserved, retiring, self-effacing, shrinking, shy, timid, virginal. **antonyms** forward, impudent, sober.

cozen *v* bamboozle, bilk, cheat, circumvent, con, deceive, diddle, double-cross, dupe, gull, hoodwink, inveigle, swindle, trick.

crack *v* break, buffet, burst, chap, chip, chop, cleave, clip, clout, collapse, crackle, crash, craze, cuff, decipher, detonate, explode, fathom, fracture, pop, ring, slap, snap, solve, splinter, succumb, thump, wallop, whack, yield.

n attempt, blow, breach, break, buffet, burst, chap, chink, chip, clap, cleft, clip, clout, cranny, crash, craze, crevasse, crevice, cuff, dig, explosion, fent, fissure, flaw, fracture, gag, gap, go, insult, interstice, jibe, joke, moment, opportunity, pop, quip, report, rift, slap, smack, snap, stab, thump, try, wallop, whack, wisecrack, witticism.

adj ace, choice, élite, excellent, first-class, first-rate, hand-picked, superior, top-notch.

crack down on act against, check, clamp down on, end, put a stop to, stop.

crack up break down, collapse, go crackers, go crazy, go to pieces.

cracked *adj* bats, batty, broken, chipped, crackpot, crazed, crazy, daft, damaged, defective, deranged, eccentric, faulty, flawed, imperfect, insane, loony, nuts, nutty, rent, split, torn. **antonyms** flawless, perfect, sane.

crackers *adj* cracked, crazy, daft, foolish, idiotic, loony, mad, nuts. **antonym** sane.

crackpot *n* idiot, loony, nut, nutter..

cradle *v* bear, couch, hold, lull, nestle, nurse, rock, support, tend.

craft *n* ability, aircraft, aptitude,

art, artfulness, artifice, artistry, boat, business, calling, cleverness, contrivance, craftiness, cunning, deceit, dexterity, duplicity, employment, expertise, expertness, guile, handicraft, handiwork, ingenuity, know-how, occupation, plane, pursuit, ruse, scheme, ship, shrewdness, skill, spacecraft, spaceship, stratagem, subterfuge, technique, trade, trickery, vessel, vocation, wiles, work, workmanship. *antonyms* naïvety, openness.

craftiness *n* artfulness, astuteness, canniness, cunning, deceit, deviousness, double-dealing, duplicity, guile, shrewdness, slyness, subtlety, trickiness, underhandedness, wiliness. *antonyms* naïvety, openness.

crafty *adj* artful, astute, calculating, canny, cunning, deceitful, designing, devious, duplicitous, fraudulent, guileful, insidious, knowing, machiavellian, scheming, sharp, shrewd, sly, subtle, tricksy, tricky, wily. *antonyms* naïve, open.

craggy *adj* broken, cragged, jagged, jaggy, precipitous, rocky, rough, rugged, stony, uneven. *antonyms* pleasant, smooth.

cram *v* bag, compact, compress, crowd, crush, force, glut, gorge, grind, guzzle, jam, mug up, overcrowd, overeat, overfeed, overfill, pack, press, ram, satiate, shove, squeeze, stodge, study, stuff, swot.

cramp[1] *v* check, clog, confine, constrain, encumber, frustrate, hamper, hamstring, handicap, hinder, impede, inhibit, obstruct, restrict, shackle, stymie, thwart, tie.

cramp[2] *n* ache, contraction, convulsion, crick, pain, pang, pins and needles, spasm, stiffness, stitch, twinge.

cramped *adj* awkward, confined, congested, crowded, jam-packed, narrow, overcrowded, packed, restricted, riggling, squashed, squeezed, tight, uncomfortable. *antonym* spacious.

cranky *adj* bizarre, capricious, crabbed, cross, crotchety, dotty, eccentric, erratic, freakish, freaky, funny, idiosyncratic, irritable, odd, peculiar, prickly, queer, quirky, strange, surly, wacky. *antonyms* normal, placid, sensible.

cranny *n* chink, cleavage, cleft, crack, crevice, fissure, gap, hole, interstice, nook, opening.

crash *n* accident, bang, bankruptcy, boom, bump, clang, clash, clatter, clattering, collapse, collision, debacle (débâcle), depression, din, downfall, failure, jar, jolt, pile-up, prang, racket, ruin, smash, smashing, smash-up, thud, thump, thunder, wreck.

v bang, break, bump, collapse, collide, dash, disintegrate, fail, fall, fold (up), fracture, fragment, go bust, go under, hurtle, lurch, overbalance, pitch, plunge, prang, shatter, shiver, smash, splinter, sprawl, topple.

adj concentrated, emergency, immediate, intensive, round-the-clock, urgent.

crass *adj* asinine, blundering, boorish, bovine, coarse, dense, doltish, gross, indelicate, insensitive, oafish, obtuse, stupid, tactless, unrefined, unsubtle, witless. *antonyms* refined, sensitive.

crave *v* ask, beg, beseech, desire, entreat, fancy, hanker after, hunger after, implore, long for, need, petition, pine for, require, seek, solicit, supplicate, thirst for, want, yearn for, yen for. *antonyms* dislike, spurn.

craven *adj* chicken-hearted, cowardly, dastardly, fearful, lily-livered, mean-spirited, pusillanimous, scared, spiritless, timorous, unheroic, weak, yellow. *antonym* courageous.

craving *n* appetite, desire, hankering, hunger, longing, lust, thirst, urge, yearning, yen. *antonyms* dislike, distaste.

crawl *v* creep, cringe, drag, eat crow, eat dirt, eat humble pie, fawn, grovel, inch, slither, swarm, teem, toady, wriggle, writhe.

craze *n* enthusiasm, fad, fashion, frenzy, infatuation, mania, mode, novelty, obsession, passion, preoccupation, rage, thing, trend, vogue.

v bewilder, confuse, dement, derange, distemper, distract, enrage, infatuate, inflame, madden, unbalance, unhinge.

crazy *adj* absurd, ardent, bananas, barmy, bats, batty, berserk, bird-brained, bizarre, bonkers, cockeyed, cracked, crazed, cuckoo, daffy, daft, delirious, demented, deranged, derisory, devoted, dippy, eager, eccentric, enamoured, enthusiastic, fanatical, fantastic, fatuous, foolhardy, foolish, fruity, half-baked, hysterical, idiotic, ill-conceived, impracticable, imprudent, inane, inappropriate, infatuated, insane, irresponsible, ludicrous, lunatic, mad, maniacal, mental, nonsensical, nuts, nutty, odd, off one's rocker, outrageous, passionate, peculiar, potty, preposterous, quixotic, ridiculous, scatty, senseless, short-sighted, silly, smitten, strange, touched, unbalanced, unhinged, unrealistic, unwise, unworkable, up the pole, wacky, weird, wild, zany, zealous. *antonyms* sane, sensible.

creak v grate, grind, groan, rasp, scrape, scratch, screak, screech, squeak, squeal.

cream n best, cosmetic, crème de la crème, élite, emulsion, essence, flower, liniment, lotion, oil, ointment, paste, pick, prime, salve, unguent.

creamy adj buttery, cream-coloured, creamed, lush, milky, off-white, oily, rich, smooth, soft, velvety.

crease v corrugate, crimp, crinkle, crumple, fold, pucker, ridge, rumple, wrinkle.
n bulge, corrugation, crumple, fold, groove, line, overlap, pucker, ridge, ruck, rumple, tuck, wrinkle.

create v appoint, beget, cause, coin, compose, concoct, constitute, design, develop, devise, engender, establish, form, formulate, found, generate, hatch, initiate, install, institute, invent, invest, make, occasion, originate, produce, set up, sire, spawn. *antonym* destroy.

creation n achievement, brainchild, chef d'oeuvre, concept, conception, concoction, constitution, cosmos, development, establishment, formation, foundation, generation, genesis, handiwork, inception, institution, invention, life, magnum opus, making, nature, origination, pièce de résistance, procreation, production, siring, universe, world. *antonym* destruction.

creative adj adept, artistic, clever, fertile, gifted, imaginative, ingenious, inspired, inventive, original, productive, resourceful, stimulating, talented, visionary. *antonym* unimaginative.

creativity n artistry, cleverness, fecundity, fertility, imagination, imaginativeness, ingenuity, inspiration, inventiveness, originality, resourcefulness, talent, vision. *antonym* unimaginativeness.

creator n architect, auteur, author, begetter, designer, father, God, initiator, inventor, maker, originator.

creature n animal, beast, being, body, brute, character, critter, dependant, fellow, hanger-on, henchman, hireling, individual, instrument, lackey, man, minion, mortal, person, puppet, soul, toady, tool, woman, wretch.

credentials n authorisation, card, certificate, deed, diploma, docket, endorsement, letters of credence, licence, missive, passport, permit, recommendation, reference, testament, testimonial, title, voucher, warrant.

credibility n integrity, likeliness, plausibility, probability, reliability, tenability, trustworthiness. *antonym* implausibility.

credible adj believable, conceivable, convincing, dependable, honest, imaginable, likely, persuasive, plausible, possible, probable, reasonable, reliable, sincere, supposable, tenable, thinkable, trustworthy, trusty. *antonyms* implausible, unreliable.

credit n acclaim, acknowledgement, approval, belief, character, clout, commendation, confidence, credence, distinction, esteem, estimation, faith, fame, glory, honour, influence, kudos, merit, position, praise, prestige, recognition, regard, reliance, reputation, repute, standing, status, thanks, tribute, trust. *antonym* discredit.
v accept, believe, buy, subscribe to, swallow, trust. *antonym* disbelieve.

creditable adj admirable, commendable, deserving, estimable, excellent, exemplary, good, honourable, laudable, meritorious, praiseworthy, reputable, respectable, sterling, worthy. *antonyms* blameworthy, shameful.

credulity n credulousness, gullibility, naïvety, silliness, simplicity, stupidity. *antonym* scepticism.

credulous adj green, gullible, naïve, trusting, uncritical, unsuspecting, unsuspicious, wide-eyed. *antonym* sceptical.

creed n articles, belief, canon, catechism, confession, credo, doctrine, dogma, faith, persuasion, principles, tenets.

creep v bootlick, cower, crawl, cringe, dawdle, drag, edge, fawn, grovel, inch, insinuate, kowtow, scrape, skulk, slink, slither, snail, sneak, squirm, steal, tiptoe, toady, worm, wriggle, writhe.
n bootlicker, jerk, sneak, sycophant, toady.

creepy adj awful, disturbing, eerie, frightening, ghoulish, gruesome, hair-raising, horrible, macabre, menacing, nightmarish, ominous, scary, sinister, spookish, spooky, terrifying, threatening, unearthly, unpleasant, weird. *antonyms* normal, pleasant.

crest n apex, badge, comb, crown, device, emblem, head, height, insignia, mane, peak, pinnacle, plume, ridge, summit, symbol, top, topknot, tuft.

crestfallen *adj* dejected, depressed, despondent, disappointed, disconsolate, discouraged, disheartened, dispirited, downcast, downhearted, woebegone. **antonym** elated.

crevice *n* chink, cleavage, cleft, crack, cranny, fissure, fracture, gap, hole, interstice, opening, rent, rift, slit, split.

crew *n* assemblage, band, bunch, company, complement, crowd, gang, hands, henchmen, herd, horde, lot, mob, pack, party, posse, set, squad, swarm, team, troop.

crib *v* borrow, cheat, copy, pinch, plagiarise, purloin, steal.

crime *n* atrocity, corruption, delinquency, fault, felony, guilt, illegality, iniquity, law-breaking, malfeasance, misconduct, misdeed, misdemeanour, offence, outrage, sin, transgression, trespass, vice, villainy, violation, wickedness, wrong, wrong-doing.

criminal *n* con, convict, crook, culprit, delinquent, evil-doer, felon, jail-bird, law-breaker, malefactor, offender, sinner, transgressor.
adj bent, corrupt, crooked, culpable, deplorable, felonious, foolish, illegal, immoral, indictable, iniquitous, lawless, malfeasant, nefarious, preposterous, ridiculous, scandalous, senseless, unlawful, vicious, villainous, wicked, wrong. **antonyms** honest, upright.

cringe *v* bend, blench, bootlick, bow, cower, crawl, creep, crouch, fawn, flinch, grovel, kneel, kowtow, quiver, recoil, shrink, shy, sneak, start, stoop, submit, toady, tremble, wince.

crinkle *n* curl, fold, pucker, ruffle, rumple, rustle, scallop, twist, wave, wrinkle.
v crimp, crimple, crumple, curl, fold, pucker, ruffle, rumple, rustle, scallop, twist, wrinkle.

crinkly *adj* curly, fluted, frizzy, furrowed, gathered, kinky, puckered, ruffled, scalloped, wrinkled, wrinkly. **antonyms** smooth, straight.

cripple *v* cramp, damage, debilitate, destroy, disable, enfeeble, halt, hamstring, impair, incapacitate, lame, maim, mutilate, paralyse, ruin, sabotage, spoil, vitiate, weaken.

crippled *adj* deformed, disabled, enfeebled, handicapped, incapacitated, invalid, lame, paralysed.

crisis *n* calamity, catastrophe, climax, confrontation, crunch, crux, culmination, difficulty, dilemma, disaster, emergency, extremity, height, impasse, mess, pinch, plight, predicament, quandary, strait, trouble.

crisp *adj* bracing, brief, brisk, brittle, brusque, clear, crispy, crumbly, crunchy, decisive, firm, forthright, fresh, incisive, invigorating, neat, orderly, pithy, refreshing, short, smart, snappy, spruce, succinct, tart, terse, tidy, vigorous. **antonyms** flabby, limp, vague.

criterion *n* bench-mark, canon, gauge, measure, norm, precedent, principle, proof, rule, standard, test, touchstone, yardstick.

critical *adj* accurate, all-important, analytical, censorious, crucial, dangerous, deciding, decisive, derogatory, diagnostic, disapproving, discerning, discriminating, disparaging, fastidious, fault-finding, grave, hairy, high-priority, judgemental, judicious, momentous, nagging, niggling, nit-picking, penetrating, perceptive, perilous, pivotal, precarious, precise, pressing, psychological, risky, serious, sharp-tongued, uncomplimentary, urgent, vital. **antonyms** uncritical, unimportant.

criticise *v* analyse, appraise, assess, badmouth, blame, censure, condemn, decry, disparage, evaluate, excoriate, judge, knock, pan, review, roast, scarify, slag, slam, slash, slate, snipe. **antonym** praise.

criticism *n* analysis, appraisal, appreciation, assessment, blame, brickbat, censure, comment, commentary, critique, disapproval, disparagement, elucidation, evaluation, fault-finding, flak, judgement, knocking, notice, panning, review, slating, stick, stricture. **antonym** praise.

croak *v* caw, die, expire, gasp, grunt, kick the bucket, pass away, perish, snuff it, squawk, wheeze.

crony *n* accomplice, ally, associate, buddy, china, chum, colleague, companion, comrade, follower, friend, henchman, mate, pal, sidekick.

crook *n* cheat, criminal, knave, racketeer, robber, rogue, shark, shyster, swindler, thief, villain.

crooked[1] *adj* bent, corrupt, crafty, criminal, deceitful, discreditable, dishonest, dishonourable, dubious, fraudulent, illegal, nefarious, questionable, shady, shifty, treacherous, underhand, unethical, unlawful, unprincipled, unscrupulous. **antonym** honest.

crooked² *adj* angled, askew, asymmetric, awry, bent, bowed, cranky, crippled, curved, deformed, deviating, disfigured, distorted, hooked, irregular, lopsided, meandering, misshapen, off-centre, skew-whiff, slanted, slanting, squint, tilted, tortuous, twisted, twisting, uneven, warped, winding, zigzag. **antonym** straight.

crop *n* fruits, gathering, growth, harvest, produce, vintage, yield.
v browse, clip, collect, curtail, cut, garner, gather, graze, harvest, lop, mow, nibble, pare, pick, prune, reap, reduce, shear, shingle, shorten, snip, top, trim, yield.

crop up appear, arise, arrive, emerge, happen, occur.

cross *adj* adverse, angry, annoyed, cantankerous, captious, churlish, contrary, cranky, crosswise, crotchety, crusty, disagreeable, displeased, fractious, fretful, grouchy, grumpy, hybrid, ill-humoured, ill-tempered, impatient, interchanged, intersecting, irascible, irritable, oblique, opposed, opposing, opposite, peeved, peevish, petulant, querulous, reciprocal, shirty, short, snappish, snappy, splenetic, sullen, surly, testy, transverse, unfavourable, vexed, waspish. **antonyms** calm, placid, pleasant.
v annoy, bestride, blend, block, bridge, cancel, criss-cross, crossbreed, cross-fertilise, cross-pollinate, deny, foil, ford, frustrate, hinder, hybridise, impede, interbreed, intercross, interfere, intersect, intertwine, lace, meet, mix, mongrelise, obstruct, oppose, resist, span, thwart, traverse, zigzag.
n affliction, amalgam, blend, burden, combination, crossbreed, crossing, crossroads, crucifix, holy-rood, hybrid, hybridisation, intersection, load, misery, misfortune, mixture, mongrel, rood, trial, tribulation, trouble, woe, worry.

cross swords argue, dispute, fight, spar, take issue, wrangle.

cross-examine *v* catechise, give (someone) the third degree, grill, interrogate, pump, question, quiz.

crosswise *adv* across, aslant, athwart, awry, crisscross, crossways, diagonally, over, sideways, transversely.

crotchety *adj* awkward, bad-tempered, cantankerous, contrary, crabbed, crabby, cross, crusty, difficult, disagreeable,

fractious, grumpy, irascible, irritable, obstreperous, peevish, prickly, surly, testy. **antonyms** clam, placid, pleasant.

crouch *v* bend, bow, cower, cringe, duck, hunch, kneel, ruck, squat, stoop.

crow *v* bluster, boast, brag, exult, flourish, gloat, prate, rejoice, triumph, vaunt.

crowd *n* army, assembly, attendance, audience, bunch, caboodle, circle, clique, company, concourse, flock, gate, group, herd, hoi polloi, horde, host, house, lot, mass, masses, mob, multitude, pack, people, populace, press, proletariat, public, rabble, riff-raff, set, spectators, squash, swarm, the many, throng, troupe.
v bundle, cluster, compress, congest, congregate, cram, elbow, flock, gather, huddle, jostle, mass, muster, pack, pile, press, push, shove, squeeze, stream, surge, swarm, throng.

crowded *adj* busy, congested, cramped, crushed, filled, full, huddled, jammed, jam-packed, mobbed, overflowing, packed, populous, swarming, teeming, thronged. **antonym** empty.

crown *n* acme, apex, circlet, coronet, crest, distinction, forehead, garland, head, honour, kudos, laurel wreath, laurels, monarch, monarchy, pate, perfection, pinnacle, prize, royalty, ruler, skull, sovereign, sovereignty, summit, tip, top, trophy, ultimate, zenith.
v adorn, biff, box, cap, clout, complete, consummate, cuff, dignify, finish, fulfil, honour, instal, perfect, punch, reward, surmount, terminate, top.

crowning *adj* climactic, consummate, culminating, final, paramount, perfect, sovereign, supreme, top, ultimate, unmatched, unsurpassed.

crucial *adj* central, critical, decisive, essential, important, key, momentous, pivotal, pressing, psychological, searching, testing, trying, urgent, vital. **antonym** unimportant.

crude *adj* amateurish, blue, boorish, clumsy, coarse, crass, dirty, earthy, gross, half-baked, immature, inartistic, indecent, lewd, makeshift, natural, obscene, outline, primitive, raw, rough, rough-hewn, rude, rudimentary, sketchy, smutty, tactless, tasteless, uncouth, undeveloped, undigested, unfinished, unformed, unpolished, unprepared, unprocessed, unrefined, unsubtle, vulgar. **antonyms** finished, polite, refined, tasteful.

cruel *adj* atrocious, barbarous, bitter,

bloodthirsty, brutal, brutish, butcherly, callous, cold-blooded, cutting, depraved, excruciating, fell, ferocious, fierce, flinty, grim, hard, hard-hearted, harsh, heartless, heathenish, hellish, inclement, inexorable, inhuman, inhumane, malevolent, marble-breasted, merciless, murderous, painful, pitiless, poignant, ravening, raw, relentless, remorseless, ruthless, sadistic, sanguinary, savage, severe, spiteful, stony-hearted, unfeeling, unkind, unmerciful, unnatural, unrelenting, vengeful, vicious. *antonyms* compassionate, kind, merciful.

cruelty *n* barbarity, bestiality, brutality, brutishness, callousness, depravity, ferocity, fiendishness, hard-heartedness, harshness, heartlessness, inhumanity, murderousness, ruthlessness, sadism, savagery, severity, spite, spitefulness, tyranny, venom, viciousness. *antonyms* compassion, kindness, mercy.

crumb *n* atom, bit, grain, iota, jot, mite, morsel, particle, scrap, shred, sliver, snippet, soupçon, speck.

crumble *v* break up, collapse, crumb, crush, decay, decompose, degenerate, deteriorate, disintegrate, fragment, granulate, grind, moulder, perish, pound, powder, pulverise.

crummy *adj* cheap, contemptible, grotty, half-baked, inferior, miserable, pathetic, poor, rotten, rubbishy, second-rate, shoddy, third-rate, trashy, useless, weak, worthless. *antonym* excellent.

crumple *v* collapse, crease, crush, fall, pucker, raffle, rumple, wrinkle.

crunch *v* champ, chomp, grind, masticate, munch.

n crisis, crux, emergency, pinch, test.

crush *v* abash, break, browbeat, bruise, chagrin, champ, comminute, compress, conquer, contuse, crease, crumble, crumple, crunch, embrace, extinguish, hug, humiliate, mash, mortify, overcome, overpower, overwhelm, pound, press, pulverise, quash, quell, rumple, shame, smash, squeeze, squelch, steam-roller, subdue, vanquish, wrinkle.

n check, crowd, huddle, jam.

crust *n* caking, coat, coating, concretion, covering, exterior, film, heel, impertinence, incrustation, layer, outside, rind, scab, shell, skin, surface.

crusty *adj* brittle, brusque, cantankerous, captious, choleric, crabbed, crabby, crisp, crispy, cross, curt, friable, grouchy, gruff, hard, ill-humoured, irritable,

peevish, prickly, short, short-tempered, snappish, snappy, snarling, splenetic, surly, testy, touchy. *antonyms* calm, pleasant, soft, soggy.

crux *n* core, essence, heart, nub.

cry *v* advertise, announce, bark, bawl, beg, bellow, beseech, bewail, blubber, boo-hoo, broadcast, call, caterwaul, clamour, ejaculate, entreat, exclaim, greet, hail, halloo, hawk, holler, howl, implore, lament, plead, pray, proclaim, promulgate, roar, scream, screech, shout, shriek, snivel, sob, squall, squeal, trumpet, vociferate, wail, weep, whimper, whine, whinge, whoop, yell, yowl.

n announcement, appeal, battle-cry, bawl(ing), bellow, blubber(ing), call, caterwaul, ejaculation, entreaty, exclamation, greet, holler, hoot, howl, lament, lamentation, outcry, petition, plea, prayer, proclamation, report, roar, rumour, scream, screech, shriek, slogan, snivel(ling), sob(bing), sorrowing, squall, squawk, squeal, supplication, utterance, wail(ing), watch-word, weep(ing), whoop, yell, yelp.

cry-baby *n* cissy, mardy, softy.

cryptic *adj* abstruse, ambiguous, apocryphal, arcane, bizarre, cabbalistic, dark, enigmatic, equivocal, esoteric, hidden, mysterious, obscure, occult, perplexing, puzzling, recondite, secret, strange, vague, veiled. *antonyms* clear, obvious, straightforward.

crystallise *v* appear, coalesce, emerge, form, harden, materialise, solidify.

cuddle *v* canoodle, clasp, cosset, embrace, fondle, hug, nestle, pet, snuggle.

cudgel *v* bang, baste, batter, beat, bludgeon, cane, clobber, cosh, drub, maul, pound, pummel, thrash, thump, thwack.

cue *n* catchword, hint, feed-line, incentive, key, nod, prompt(ing), reminder, sign, signal, stimulus, suggestion.

cuff *v* bat, beat, belt, biff, box, buffet, clap, clobber, clout, knock, pummel, punch, slap, smack, smite, strike, thump, whack.

n belt, biff, blow, box, buffet, clout, knock, punch, rap, slap, smack, swat, thump, whack.

cull *v* amass, choose, collect, decimate, destroy, gather, glean, kill, pick, pick out, pluck, select, sift, thin, winnow.

culminate *v* climax, close, conclude,

consummate, end (up), finish, peak, terminate. *antonyms* begin, start.

culmination *n* acme, apex, apogee, climax, completion, conclusion, consummation, crown, finale, height, peak, perfection, pinnacle, summit, top, zenith. *antonyms* beginning, start.

culpable *adj* answerable, blam(e)able, blameworthy, guilty, liable, offending, reprehensible, sinful, to blame, wrong. *antonyms* blameless, innocent.

cult *n* admiration, believers, body, clique, craze, denomination, devotion, faith, following, idolisation, party, religion, reverence, school, sect, veneration, worship.

cultivate *v* aid, ameliorate, better, cherish, civilise, court, develop, discipline, elevate, encourage, enrich, farm, fertilise, forward, foster, further, harvest, help, improve, plant, plough, polish, prepare, promote, pursue, refine, school, support, tend, till, train, work. *antonym* neglect.

cultivation *n* advancement, advocacy, breeding, civilisation, civility, culture, development, discernment, discrimination, education, encouragement, enhancement, enlightenment, farming, fostering, furtherance, gardening, gentility, help, husbandry, learning, letters, manners, nurture, planting, ploughing, polish, promotion, pursuit, refinement, schooling, study, support, taste, tillage, tilling, tilth, working.

cultural *adj* aesthetic, artistic, arty, broadening, civilising, developmental, edifying, educational, educative, elevating, enlightening, enriching, humane, humanising, liberal.

culture *n* accomplishment, aestheticism, agriculture, art, breeding, civilisation, cultivation, customs, education, elevation, enlightenment, erudition, farming, gentility, husbandry, improvement, lifestyle, mores, polish, politeness, refinement, society, taste, the arts, urbanity.

cultured *adj* accomplished, advanced, aesthetic, arty, civilised, educated, enlightened, erudite, genteel, highbrow, knowledgeable, polished, refined, scholarly, urbane, versed, well-bred, well-informed, well-read.

cumbersome *adj* awkward, bulky, burdensome, clumsy, cumbrous, embarrassing, heavy, hefty, incommodious, inconvenient, onerous, oppressive, ponderous, unmanageable, unwieldy, weighty. *antonyms* convenient, manageable.

cunning *adj* adroit, arch, artful, astute, canny, crafty, deft, devious, dexterous, guileful, imaginative, ingenious, knowing, Machiavellian, sharp, shifty, shrewd, skilful, sneaky, subtle, tricky, wily. *antonyms* gullible, naïve.
n ability, adroitness, art, artfulness, artifice, astuteness, cleverness, craftiness, deceitfulness, deftness, deviousness, dexterity, finesse, guile, ingenuity, policy, shrewdness, skill, slyness, subtlety, trickery, wiliness. *antonyms* openness, simplicity.

curative *adj* corrective, healing, healthful, health-giving, medicinal, remedial, restorative, salutary, therapeutic, tonic.

curb *v* bit, bridle, check, constrain, contain, control, hamper, hinder, hobble, impede, inhibit, moderate, muzzle, repress, restrain, restrict, retard, subdue, suppress. *antonyms* encourage, foster, goad.
n brake, bridle, check, control, deterrent, hamper, hobble, limitation, rein, restraint.

curdle *v* clot, coagulate, condense, congeal, ferment, sour, thicken, turn.

cure[1] *v* alleviate, correct, ease, heal, help, mend, rehabilitate, relieve, remedy, restore.
n alleviation, antidote, corrective, detoxicant, healing, medicine, panacea, recovery, remedy, restorative, specific, treatment, vulnerary.

cure[2] *v* dry, kipper, pickle, preserve, salt, smoke.

curiosity *n* bygone, curio, freak, inquisitiveness, interest, knick-knack, marvel, nosiness, novelty, object of virtu, objet d'art, objet de vertu, oddity, phenomenon, prying, rarity, sight, snooping, spectacle, trinket, wonder.

curious *adj* bizarre, enquiring, exotic, extraordinary, funny, inquisitive, interested, marvellous, meddling, mysterious, nosy, novel, odd, peculiar, peeping, peering, prying, puzzled, puzzling, quaint, queer, questioning, rare, searching, singular, snoopy, strange, unconventional, unexpected, unique, unorthodox, unusual, wonderful. *antonyms* incurious, indifferent, normal, ordinary, uninterested.

curl *v* bend, coil, convolute, corkscrew, crimp, crimple, crinkle, crisp, curve, entwine, frizz, loop, meander, ripple, scroll, spiral, turn, twine, twirl, wind, wreathe, writhe. **antonym** uncurl.

n coil, kink, ringlet, spiral, swirl, tress, twist, whorl.

curly *adj* corkscrew, crimped, crimpy, crinkly, curled, curling, frizzy, fuzzy, kinky, spiralled, waved, wavy, whorled, winding. **antonym** straight.

currency *n* acceptance, bills, circulation, coinage, coins, exposure, legal tender, money, notes, popularity, prevalence, publicity, reign, transmission, vogue.

current *adj* accepted, circulating, common, contemporary, customary, extant, fashionable, general, on-going, popular, present, present-day, prevailing, prevalent, reigning, rife, trendy, up-to-date, up-to-the-minute, widespread. **antonyms** antiquated, old-fashioned.

n atmosphere, course, draught, drift, feeling, flow, inclination, jet, juice, mood, progression, river, stream, tendency, thermal, tide, trend, undercurrent.

curse *n* affliction, anathema, ban, bane, blasphemy, burden, calamity, cross, damn, denunciation, disaster, evil, excommunication, execration, expletive, imprecation, jinx, malediction, malison, misfortune, oath, obscenity, ordeal, plague, scourge, swearing, swear-word, torment, tribulation, trouble, vexation, woe. **antonyms** advantage, blessing.

v accurse, afflict, anathematise, blaspheme, blight, blind, blow, burden, cuss, damn, destroy, doom, excommunicate, execrate, fulminate, imprecate, plague, scourge, swear, torment, trouble, vex. **antonym** bless.

cursed *adj* abominable, accursed, bedevilled, bewitched, blessed, blighted, confounded, damnable, damned, destestable, devilish, doomed, excommunicate, execrable, fell, fey, fiendish, foredoomed, hateful, ill-fated, infamous, infernal, loathsome, odious, pernicious, star-crossed, unholy, unsanctified, vile, villainous.

cursory *adj* brief, careless, casual, desultory, fleeting, hasty, hurried, offhand, passing, perfunctory, quick, rapid, slap-dash, slight, summary, superficial. **antonyms** painstaking, thorough.

curt *adj* abrupt, blunt, brief, brusque, concise, gruff, laconic, offhand, pithy, rude, sharp, short, short-spoken, snappish, succinct, summary, tart, terse,

unceremonious, uncivil, ungracious. **antonym** voluble.

curtail *v* abbreviate, abridge circumscribe, contract, cut, decrease dock, lessen, lop, pare, prune reduce, restrict, retrench, shorten, trim truncate. **antonyms** extend, lengthen prolong.

curtain *v* conceal, drape, hide, screen shield, shroud, shutter, veil.

n arras, backdrop, drapery, hanging tapestry.

curvaceous *adj* bosomy, buxom comely, curvy, shapely, voluptuous well-proportioned, well-rounded, well stacked.

curve *v* arc, arch, bend, bow, coil, hook inflect, spiral, swerve, turn, twist, wind. *n* arc, bend, camber, curvature, half moon, loop, trajectory, turn.

curved *adj* arched, bent, bowed crooked, humped, rounded, serpentine sinuous, sweeping, turned, twisted. **antonym** straight.

cushion *v* allay, bolster, buttress cradle, dampen, deaden, lessen, mitigate muffle, pillow, protect, soften, stifle support, suppress.

cushy *adj* comfortable, easy, jammy plum, soft, undemanding. **antonym.** demanding, tough.

custodian *n* caretaker, chatelaine curator, guardian, keeper, overseer protector, superintendent, warden warder, watch-dog, watchman.

custody *n* arrest, care, charge confinement, custodianship, detention duress, guardianship, holding imprisonment, incarceration, keeping observation, possession, preservation protection, retention, safe-keeping supervision, trusteeship, ward, wardship watch.

custom *n* convention, customers etiquette, fashion, form, formality, habit habitualness, habitude, manner, mode observance, observation, patronage policy, practice, procedure, ritual routine, rule, style, trade, tradition, usage use, way, wont.

customarily *adv* commonly, generally habitually, normally, ordinarily, popularly, regularly, routinely, traditionally usually. **antonyms** occasionally, rarely

customary *adj* accepted, accustomed acknowledged, common, confirmed conventional, established, everyday familiar, fashionable, favourite, general habitual, normal, ordinary, popular prevailing, regular, routine, traditional, usual, wonted. **antonyms** occasional, rare, unusual.

customer n buyer, client, consumer, patron, punter, purchaser, regular, shopper.

cut v abbreviate, abridge, avoid, bisect, carve, castrate, chip, chisel, chop, cleave, clip, cold-shoulder, condense, contract, crop, cross, curtail, decrease, delete, dissect, divide, dock, edit, engrave, excise, fashion, fell, form, gash, gather, grieve, hack, harvest, hew, hurt, ignore, incise, insult, interrupt, intersect, lacerate, lop, lower, mow, nick, notch, pain, pare, part, penetrate, pierce, précis, prune, rationalise, reap, reduce, saw, scissor, score, sculpt, sculpture, segment, sever, shape, share, shave, shorten, slash, slice, slight, slim, slit, snub, split, spurn, sting, trim, truncate, whittle, wound.
n blow, chop, configuration, cutback, decrease, diminution, division, economy, fall, fashion, form, gash, graze, groove, incision, incisure, insection, kickback, laceration, lowering, mode, nick, percentage, piece, portion, rake-off, reduction, rent, rip, saving, section, shape, share, slash, slice, slit, snick, stroke, style, wound.

cut and dried automatic, fixed, organised, prearranged, predetermined, settled, sewn up.

cut back check, crop, curb, decrease, economise, lessen, lop, lower, prune, reduce, retrench, slash, trim.

cut down decrease, diminish, dispatch, fell, hew, kill, lessen, level, lop, lower, massacre, raze, reduce, slaughter, slay.

cut in interject, interpose, interrupt, intervene, intrude.

cut off block, disconnect, discontinue, disinherit, disown, end, excise, halt, intercept, interrupt, intersect, isolate, obstruct, renounce, separate, sever, stop, suspend.

cut out cease, contrive, debar, delete, displace, eliminate, excise, exclude, exsect, extract, oust, remove, sever, shape, stop, supersede, supplant.

cut out for adapted, adequate, competent, designed, equipped, fitted, made, qualified, right, suitable, suited.

cut short abbreviate, abort, arrest, check, crop, curtail, dock, halt, interrupt, postpone, prune, reduce, stop, terminate. **antonym** prolong.

cut up carve, chop, criticise, crucify, dice, divide, injure, knife, lacerate, mince, pan, ridicule, slash, slate, slice, vilify, wound.

cutback n cut, decrease, economy, lessening, reduction, retrenchment.

cut-price adj bargain, cheap, cut-rate, low-priced, reduced, sale.

cut-throat n assassin, butcher, executioner, hatchet man, hit-man, killer, liquidator, murderer, slayer, thug.
adj barbarous, bloodthirsty, bloody, brutal, competitive, cruel, dog-eat-dog, ferocious, fierce, homicidal, murderous, relentless, ruthless, savage, thuggish, unprincipled, vicious, violent.

cutting adj acid, acrimonious, barbed, biting, bitter, caustic, chill, hurtful, incisive, keen, malicious, mordant, numbing, penetrating, piercing, pointed, raw, sarcastic, sardonic, scathing, severe, sharp, stinging, trenchant, wounding.
n bit, cleavage, clipping, piece, slice.

cycle n aeon, age, circle, epoch, era, period, phase, revolution, rotation, round, sequence.

cyclone n hurricane, monsoon, tempest, tornado, twister, typhoon, whirlwind.

cylinder n barrel, bobbin, column, drum, reel, spindle, spool, trunk.

cynical adj contemptuous, derisive, distrustful, ironic, misanthropic(al), mocking, mordant, pessimistic, sarcastic, sardonic, sceptical, scoffing, scornful, sharp-tongued, sneering, streetwise.

cynicism n disbelief, distrust, doubt, misanthropy, pessimism, sarcasm, scepticism.

D

dab[1] *v* blot, daub, pat, stipple, swab, tap, touch, wipe.
n bit, dollop, drop, fingerprint, fleck, flick, pat, peck, smear, smidgen, smudge, speck, spot, stroke, tap, touch, trace.

dab[2] *n* ace, adept, dab hand, expert, pastmaster, wizard.

daft *adj* absurd, asinine, berserk, besotted, crackers, crazy, daffy, delirious, demented, deranged, dop(e)y, doting, dotty, foolish, giddy, hysterical, idiotic, inane, infatuated, insane, lunatic, mad, mental, nuts, nutty, potty, scatty, screwy, silly, simple, stupid, touched, unhinged, witless. **antonyms** bright, sane.

daily *adj* common, commonplace, customary, day-to-day, diurnal, everyday, normal, ordinary, quotidian, regular, routine.

dainty *adj* charming, choice, choos(e)y, delectable, delicate, delicious, dinky, elegant, exquisite, fastidious, fine, finicky, fussy, graceful, meticulous, mincing, neat, nice, palatable, particular, petite, pretty, refined, savoury, scrupulous, tasty, tender. **antonyms** clumsy, gross.

dam *n* barrage, barrier, blockage, embankment, hindrance, obstruction, wall.
v barricade, block, check, choke, confine, obstruct, restrict, staunch, stem.

damage *n* destruction, detriment, devastation, harm, hurt, impairment, injury, loss, mischief, mutilation, suffering. **antonym** repair.
v deface, harm, hurt, impair, incapacitate, injure, mar, mutilate, play havoc with, play hell with, ruin, spoil, tamper with, weaken, wreck. **antonyms** fix, repair.

damages *n* compensation, fine, indemnity, reimbursement, reparation, satisfaction.

damaging *adj* deleterious, detrimental, disadvantageous, harmful, hurtful, injurious, pernicious, prejudicial, ruinous, unfavourable. **antonyms** favourable, helpful.

damn *v* abuse, blaspheme, blast, castigate, censure, condemn, criticise, curse, darn, dash, denounce, denunciate, doom, excoriate, execrate, imprecate, pan, revile, sentence, slam, slate, swear.
antonym bless.
n brass farthing, darn, dash, hoot, iota, jot, monkey's, tinker's cuss, two hoots, whit.

damnable *adj* abominable, accursed, atrocious, culpable, cursed, despicable, detestable, execrable, hateful, horrible, iniquitous, offensive, sinful, wicked. **antonyms** admirable, praiseworthy.

damnation *n* anathema, ban, condemnation, denunciation, doom, excommunication, objurgation, perdition, proscription.

damned *adj* accursed, condemned, confounded, danged, darned, dashed, despicable, detestable, deuced, doggone(d), doomed, dratted, effing, flipping, fucking, goddam(n), goddamned, hateful, infamous, infernal, loathsome, lost, reprobate, revolting, unhappy. **antonym** blessed.

damp *n* clamminess, dampness, dankness, dew, drizzle, fog, humidity, mist, moisture, mugginess, vapour, wet. **antonym** dryness.
adj clammy, dank, dewy, dripping, drizzly, humid, misty, moist, muggish, muggy, sodden, soggy, sopping, wet. **antonyms** arid, dry.
v allay, check, chill, cool, curb, dampen, dash, deaden, deject, depress, diminish, discourage, dispirit, dull, inhibit, moderate, moisten, restrain, stifle, wet. **antonym** dry.

dampen *v* check, dash, deaden, decrease, depress, deter, diminish, dishearten, dismay, dull, lessen, moderate, moisten, muffle, reduce, restrain, smother, spray, stifle, wet. **antonyms** dry, encourage.

dance *v* caper, frolic, gambol, hoof it, hop, jig, jive, juke, prance, rock, skip, spin, stomp, sway, swing, tread a measure, whirl.

danger *n* hazard, insecurity, jeopardy, liability, menace, peril, precariousness, risk, threat, trouble, venture, vulnerability. **antonyms** safety, security.

dangerous *adj* alarming, breakneck, chancy, critical, daring, exposed, grave, hairy, harmful, hazardous, insecure, menacing, nasty, perilous, precarious, reckless, risky, serious, severe, threatening, treacherous, ugly, unsafe.

vulnerable. *antonyms* harmless, safe, secure.

dangle *v* droop, flap, flaunt, flourish, hang, lure, sway, swing, tantalise, tempt, trail, wave.

dank *adj* chilly, clammy, damp, dewy, dripping, moist, rheumy, slimy, soggy. *antonym* dry.

dapper *adj* active, brisk, chic, dainty, natty, neat, nimble, smart, spiffy, spruce, spry, stylish, trim, well-dressed, well-groomed. *antonyms* dishevelled, dowdy, scruffy, shabby, sloppy.

dappled *adj* brindled, checkered, dotted, flecked, freckled, mottled, piebald, pied, speckled, spotted, stippled, variegated.

dare *v* adventure, brave, challenge, defy, endanger, gamble, goad, have the gall, hazard, presume, provoke, risk, stake, taunt, venture.
n challenge, gauntlet, provocation, taunt.

daring *adj* adventurous, audacious, bold, brave, brazen, dauntless, fearless, game, impulsive, intrepid, plucky, rash, reckless, valiant, venturesome. *antonyms* afraid, timid.
n audacity, boldness, bottle, bravery, bravura, courage, defiance, derring-do, fearlessness, gall, grit, guts, nerve, pluck, prowess, rashness, spirit, spunk, temerity. *antonyms* cowardice, timidity.

dark *adj* abstruse, angry, arcane, atrocious, black, bleak, brunette, cheerless, cloudy, concealed, cryptic, damnable, darkling, dark-skinned, darksome, deep, dim, dingy, dismal, doleful, dour, drab, dusky, ebony, enigmatic, evil, forbidding, foul, frowning, gloomy, glowering, glum, grim, hellish, hidden, horrible, ignorant, indistinct, infamous, infernal, joyless, lightless, midnight, mirk, mirky, morbid, morose, mournful, murk, murky, mysterious, mystic, nefarious, obscure, occult, ominous, overcast, pitch-black, puzzling, recondite, satanic, scowling, secret, shadowy, shady, sinful, sinister, sombre, sulky, sullen, sunless, swarthy, tenebr(i)ous, threatening, uncultivated, unenlightened, unillumed, unilluminated, unlettered, unlit, vile, wicked. *antonyms* bright, happy, light, lucid.
n concealment, darkness, dimness, dusk, evening, gloom, ignorance, mirk, mirkiness, murk, murkiness, night, nightfall, night-time, obscurity, secrecy,

twilight. *antonyms* brightness, light.

darken *v* blacken, cloud, cloud over, deepen, deject, depress, dim, disilluminate, dispirit, eclipse, obscure, overshade, overshadow, sadden, shade, shadow. *antonyms* brighten, lighten.

darkness *n* blackness, blindness, concealment, dark, dimness, dusk, duskiness, gloom, ignorance, mirk, mirkiness, murk, murkiness, mystery, nightfall, obscurity, privacy, secrecy, shade, shadiness, shadows. *antonyms* brightness, daylight, lightness.

dart *v* bound, cast, dash, flash, fling, flit, fly, hurl, launch, propel, race, run, rush, scoot, send, shoot, sling, spring, sprint, start, tear, throw, whistle, whiz.
n arrow, barb, bolt, flight, shaft.

dash¹ *v* abash, blight, break, cast, chagrin, confound, crash, dampen, destroy, ding, disappoint, discomfort, discourage, fling, foil, frustrate, hurl, ruin, shatter, shiver, slam, sling, smash, splinter, spoil, throw, thwart.
n bit, bravura, drop, élan, flair, flavour, flourish, hint, little, panache, pinch, smack, soupçon, spirit, sprinkling, style, suggestion, tinge, touch, verve, vigour, vivacity.

dash² *v* be off like a shot, bolt, bound, dart, fly, haste(n), hurry, race, run, rush, speed, spring, sprint, tear.
n bolt, dart, race, run, rush, sprint, spurt.

dashing *adj* bold, dapper, daring, dazzling, debonair, elegant, exuberant, flamboyant, gallant, impressive, jaunty, lively, plucky, showy, smart, spirited, sporty, stylish, swashbuckling, swish. *antonym* drab.

dastardly *adj* base, contemptible, cowardly, craven, despicable, faint-hearted, lily-livered, low, mean, pusillanimous, sneaking, sneaky, spiritless, timorous, underhand, vile. *antonyms* heroic, noble.

data *n* details, documents, dope, facts, figures, info, information, input, materials, statistics.

date¹ *n* age, epoch, era, period, point, point in time, stage, time.

date² *n* appointment, assignation, engagement, escort, friend, meeting, partner, rendezvous, steady, tryst.

dated *adj* antiquated, archaic, obsolescent, obsolete, old hat, old-fashioned, out, outdated, outmoded, out-of-date, passé, superseded, unfashionable. *antonyms* fashionable, up-to-the-minute.

daub v blur, coat, cover, deface, dirty, grime, paint, plaster, smear, smirch, smudge, spatter, splatter, stain, sully.
n blot, blotch, smear, splash, splodge, splotch, spot, stain.

daunt v alarm, appal, cow, deter, discourage, dishearten, dismay, dispirit, frighten, intimidate, overawe, put off, scare, shake, subdue, terrify, unnerve.
antonyms encourage, hearten.

daunted adj alarmed, cowed, demoralised, deterred, discouraged, disheartened, disillusioned, dismayed, dispirited, downcast, frightened, hesitant, intimidated, overcome, put off, unnerved. **antonyms** encouraged, heartened.

dauntless adj bold, brave, courageous, daring, doughty, fearless, gallant, game, heroic, indomitable, intrepid, lion-hearted, plucky, resolute, stout-hearted, undaunted, unflinching, valiant, valorous. **antonyms** discouraged, disheartened.

dawdle v dally, delay, dilly-dally, fiddle, hang about, idle, lag, loaf, loiter, potter, shilly-shally, trail. **antonym** hurry.

dawn n advent, aurora, beginning, birth, cockcrow(ing), dawning, daybreak, daylight, emergence, genesis, inception, morning, onset, origin, outset, rise, start, sunrise, sun-up. **antonyms** dusk, sundown, sunset.
v appear, begin, break, brighten, develop, emerge, gleam, glimmer, hit, initiate, lighten, occur, open, originate, register, rise, strike, unfold.

day n age, ascendancy, childhood, cycle, date, daylight, daytime, epoch, era, generation, height, heyday, period, prime, time, young days, youth, zenith. **antonym** night.

day after day continually, endlessly, forever, monotonously, perpetually, persistently, regularly, relentlessly.

day by day daily, gradually, progressively, slowly but surely, steadily.

daybreak n break of day, cockcrow(ing), crack of dawn, dawn, first light, morning, sunrise, sun-up. **antonyms** sundown, sunset.

daydream n castles in Spain, castles in the air, dream, fantasy, figment, fond hope, imagining, musing, phantasm, pipe dream, reverie, star-gazing, vision, wish, wool-gathering.
v dream, fancy, fantasise, hallucinate, imagine, muse, stargaze.

daze v amaze, astonish, astound, bewilder, blind, confuse, dazzle, dumbfound, flabbergast, numb, paralyse, perplex, shock, stagger, startle, stun, stupefy, surprise.
n bewilderment, confusion, distraction, shock, stupor, trance.

dazed adj baffled, bemused, bewildered, confused, disorien(ta)ted, dizzy, dop(e)y, dumbstruck, flabbergasted, fuddled, groggy, light-headed, muddled, nonplussed, numbed, perplexed, punch-drunk, shocked, staggered, stunned, stupefied, woozy.

dazzle v amaze, astonish, awe, blind, blur, confuse, daze, fascinate, hypnotise, impress, overawe, overpower, overwhelm, scintillate, sparkle, stupefy.
n brilliance, glitter, magnificence, razzle-dazzle, razzmatazz, scintillation, sparkle, splendour.

dazzling adj brilliant, glaring, glary, glittering, glorious, radiant, ravishing, scintillating, sensational, shining, sparkling, splendid, stunning, sublime, superb, virtuoso.

de luxe choice, costly, elegant, exclusive, expensive, grand, luxurious, opulent, palatial, plush, rich, select, special, splendid, sumptuous, superior.

de rigueur conventional, correct, decent, decorous, done, fitting, necessary, proper, required, right, the done thing.

dead¹ adj apathetic, barren, boring, breathless, callous, cold, dead-beat, deceased, defunct, departed, dull, exhausted, extinct, flat, frigid, glassy, glazed, gone, inactive, inanimate, indifferent, inert, inoperative, insipid, late, lifeless, lukewarm, numb, obsolete, paralysed, perished, spent, spiritless, stagnant, stale, sterile, stiff, still, tasteless, tired, torpid, unemployed, uninteresting, unprofitable, unresponsive, useless, vapid, wooden, worn out. **antonyms** active, alive, animated.

dead² adj absolute, complete, downright, entire, outright, perfect, thorough, total, unqualified, utter.
adv absolutely, completely, entirely, exactly, perfectly, quite, totally.

deaden v abate, allay, alleviate, anaesthetise, blunt, check, cushion, damp, dampen, desensitise, diminish, dull, hush, impair, lessen, muffle, mute, numb, paralyse, quieten, reduce, smother, stifle, suppress, weaken. **antonym** enliven.

deadlock n halt, impasse, stalemate, standstill.

deadly adj accurate, ashen, baleful, baneful, boring, cruel, dangerous, death-dealing, deathful, deathlike, deathly, destructive, devastating, dull, effective, exact, fatal, ghastly, ghostly, grim, implacable, lethal, malignant, monotonous, mortal, noxious, pallid, pernicious, pestilent, poisonous, precise, ruthless, savage, sure, tedious, true, unerring, unfailing, uninteresting, unrelenting, venomous, wearisome, white. **antonyms** harmless, healthy.

deadpan adj blank, dispassionate, empty, expressionless, impassive, inexpressive, inscrutable, poker-faced, straight-faced, unexpressive.

deafening adj booming, ear-piercing, ear-splitting, fortissimo, piercing, resounding, ringing, roaring, thunderous. **antonyms** pianissimo, quiet.

deal v allot, apportion, assign, bargain, bestow, dispense, distribute, divide, dole out, give, mete out, negotiate, reward, sell, share, stock, trade, traffic, treat.
n agreement, amount, arrangement, bargain, buy, contract, degree, distribution, extent, hand, pact, portion, quantity, round, share, transaction, understanding.

deal with attend to, concern, consider, cope with, handle, manage, oversee, see to, treat.

dear adj beloved, cherished, close, costly, darling, esteemed, expensive, familiar, favourite, high-priced, intimate, loved, overpriced, precious, pric(e)y, prized, respected, treasured, valued. **antonyms** cheap, hateful.
n angel, beloved, darling, dearie, deary, loved one, precious, treasure.

dearly adv affectionately, devotedly, extremely, fondly, greatly, lovingly, profoundly, tenderly.

dearth n absence, barrenness, deficiency, famine, inadequacy, insufficiency, lack, need, paucity, poverty, scantiness, scarcity, shortage, sparseness, sparsity, want. **antonyms** abundance, excess.

death n annihilation, bane, bereavement, cessation, curtains, decease, demise, departure, destruction, dissolution, downfall, dying, end, eradication, exit, expiration, extermination, extinction, fatality, finish, grave, loss, obliteration, passing, quietus, release, ruin, ruination, undoing. **antonyms** birth, life.

deathly adj ashen, cadaverous, deadly, deathlike, fatal, gaunt, ghastly, grim, haggard, intense, mortal, pale, pallid, terrible, wan.

débâcle, debacle n cataclysm, catastrophe, collapse, defeat, devastation, disaster, downfall, farce, fiasco, havoc, overthrow, reversal, rout, ruin, ruination, stampede.

debar v bar, blackball, deny, eject, exclude, expel, hamper, hinder, obstruct, preclude, prevent, prohibit, restrain, segregate, shut out, stop. **antonym** admit.

debase v abase, adulterate, allay, bastardise, cheapen, contaminate, corrupt, defile, degrade, demean, depreciate, devalue, diminish, disgrace, dishonour, humble, humiliate, impair, lower, pollute, reduce, shame, taint, vitiate. **antonyms** elevate, upgrade.

debased adj abandoned, adulterated, base, corrupt, debauched, degenerate, degraded, depraved, depreciated, devalued, diminished, fallen, impure, low, lowered, mixed, perverted, polluted, reduced, sordid, vile. **antonyms** elevated, pure.

debatable adj arguable, borderline, contentious, contestable, controversial, disputable, doubtful, dubious, moot, open to question, problematical, questionable, uncertain, undecided, unsettled. **antonyms** certain, questionable.

debate v argue, cogitate, consider, contend, contest, controvert, deliberate, discuss, dispute, meditate on, mull over, ponder, question, reflect, revolve, ruminate, weigh, wrangle. **antonym** agree.
n altercation, argument, cogitation, consideration, contention, controversy, deliberation, discussion, disputation, dispute, meditation, polemic, reflection. **antonym** agreement.

debauch v corrupt, deflower, demoralise, deprave, over-indulge, pervert, pollute, ravish, ruin, seduce, subvert, violate, vitiate. **antonyms** cleanse, purge, purify.
n bacchanalia, bender, bevvy, binge, booze-up, bout, fling, orgy, pub-crawl, saturnalia, spree, wet.

debauched adj abandoned, corrupt, corrupted, debased, degenerate, degraded, depraved, dissipated, dissolute, immoral, intemperate, lewd, licentious, perverted, profligate, wanton. **antonyms** decent, pure, virtuous.

debauchery n carousal, depravity, dissipation, dissoluteness, excess, gluttony, immorality, indulgence, intemperance, lewdness, licentiousness, lust, orgy, overindulgence, revel, wantonness.

debilitate v devitalise, enervate, enfeeble, exhaust, impair, incapacitate, prostrate, relax, sap, undermine, unman, weaken, wear out. **antonyms** energise, invigorate, strengthen.

debilitating adj enervating, enfeebling, exhausting, fatiguing, tiring, weakening. **antonyms** invigorating, strengthening.

debonair adj affable, breezy, buoyant, charming, cheerful, courteous, dashing, elegant, gay, jaunty, light-hearted, refined, smooth, sprightly, suave, urbane, well-bred.

debris n bits, detritus, drift, dross, fragments, litter, pieces, remains, rubbish, rubble, ruins, sweepings, trash, waste, wreckage.

debt n arrears, bill, claim, commitment, debit, due, duty, indebtedness, liability, obligation, score, sin. **antonyms** asset, credit.

debut n appearance, beginning, bow, entrance, inauguration, initiation, introduction, launching, première, presentation.

decadence n corruption, debasement, decay, decline, degenerateness, degeneration, deterioration, dissipation, dissolution, fall, perversion, retrogression, symbolism. **antonyms** flourishing, rise.

decadent adj corrupt, debased, debauched, decaying, declining, degenerate, degraded, depraved, dissolute, effete, fin-de-siècle, immoral, self-indulgent, symbolist. **antonym** moral.

decamp v abscond, bolt, desert, do a bunk, escape, flee, flit, fly, guy, hightail it, make off, run away, scarper, skedaddle.

decay v atrophy, canker, corrode, crumble, decline, decompose, degenerate, deteriorate, disintegrate, dissolve, dote, dwindle, mortify, moulder, perish, putrefy, rot, shrivel, sink, spoil, wane, waste away, wear away, wither. **antonyms** flourish, grow, ripen.

n atrophy, caries, collapse, decadence, decline, decomposition, decrepitude, degeneracy, degeneration, deterioration, disintegration, dying, fading, failing, gangrene, mortification, perishing, putrefaction, rot, rotting, wasting, withering.

decayed adj bad, carrion, corroded, decomposed, off, perished, putrefied, putrid, rank, rotten, spoiled, wasted, withered.

decaying adj crumbling, decrepit, deteriorating, disintegrating, doty, gangrenous, perishing, rotting.

deceased adj dead, defunct, departed, expired, extinct, finished, former, gone, late, lifeless, lost.

n dead, decedent, departed.

deceit n abuse, artifice, cheat, cheating, chicanery, con, cozenage, craftiness, cunning, deceitfulness, deception, dissimulation, double-dealing, duplicity, fake, feint, fraud, fraudulence, guile, hypocrisy, misrepresentation, pretence, ruse, sham, shift, slyness, stratagem, subterfuge, swindle, treachery, trick, trickery, underhandedness, wile. **antonyms** honesty, openness.

deceitful adj collusive, counterfeit, crafty, deceiving, deceptive, designing, dishonest, disingenuous, double-dealing, duplicitous, fallacious, false, fraudulent, guileful, hypocritical, illusory, insincere, knavish, prestigious, sneaky, treacherous, tricky, two-faced, underhand, untrustworthy. **antonyms** honest, open, trustworthy.

deceive v abuse, bamboozle, befool, beguile, betray, camouflage, cheat, con, cozen, delude, diddle, disappoint, dissemble, dissimulate, double-cross, dupe, ensnare, entrap, flam, fool, gag, gammon, gloze, gull, have on, hoax, hoodwink, impose upon, lead on, mislead, outwit, swindle, take for a ride, take in, trick, two-time. **antonym** enlighten.

decency n appropriateness, civility, correctness, courtesy, decorum, etiquette, fitness, good form, good manners, helpfulness, modesty, propriety, respectability, seemliness, thoughtfulness. **antonyms** discourtesy, indecency.

decent adj acceptable, accommodating, adequate, ample, appropriate, average, becoming, befitting, chaste, comely, competent, courteous, decorous, delicate, fair, fit, fitting, friendly, generous, gracious, helpful, kind, modest, nice, obliging, passable, polite, presentable, proper, pure, reasonable, respectable, satisfactory, seemly, sufficient, suitable, thoughtful, tolerable. **antonyms** disobliging, indecent, poor.

deception *n* artifice, bluff, cheat, conning, craftiness, cunning, deceifulness, deceit, deceptiveness, decoy, dissembling, dissimulation, duplicity, false-pretences, feint, flim-flam, fraud, fraudulence, guile, hoax, hypocrisy, illusion, insincerity, leg-pull, lie, ruse, sham, snare, stratagem, subterfuge, take-in, treachery, trick, trickery, wile. **antonyms** artlessness, openness.

deceptive *adj* ambiguous, catchy, dishonest, fake, fallacious, false, fraudulent, illusory, misleading, mock, specious, spurious, unreliable. **antonyms** artless, genuine, open.

decide *v* adjudge, adjudicate, choose, conclude, decree, determine, elect, end, fix, judge, opt, purpose, reach a decision, resolve, settle.

decided *adj* absolute, assertive, categorical, certain, clear-cut, decisive, definite, deliberate, determined, distinct, emphatic, express, firm, forthright, indisputable, marked, noticeable, positive, pronounced, resolute, strong-willed, unambiguous, undeniable, undisputed, unequivocal, unfaltering, unhesitating, unmistakable, unquestionable. **antonyms** indecisive, undecided.

decidedly *adv* absolutely, certainly, clearly, decisively, definitely, distinctly, downright, positively, quite, unequivocally, unmistakably, very.

deciding *adj* chief, conclusive, critical, crucial, crunch, decisive, determining, final, influential, prime, principal, significant, supreme. **antonym** insignificant.

decipher *v* construe, crack, decode, deduce, explain, figure out, interpret, make out, read, solve, transliterate, understand, unfold, unravel, unscramble. **antonym** encode.

decision *n* arbitration, conclusion, decisiveness, determination, finding, firmness, judgement, outcome, purpose, purposefulness, resoluteness, resolution, resolve, result, ruling, settlement, verdict.

decisive *adj* absolute, conclusive, critical, crucial, crunch, decided, definite, definitive, determinate, determined,

fateful, final, firm, forceful, forthright, incisive, influential, momentous, positive, resolute, significant, strong-minded, supreme, trenchant. **antonyms** indecisive, insignificant.

deck *v* adorn, apparel, array, attire, beautify, clothe, decorate, doll up, dress, embellish, festoon, garland, grace, ornament, prettify, pretty up, rig out, smarten, titivate, tog out, tog up, trick out, trim.

declaim *v* hold forth, lecture, mouth, orate, preach, proclaim, rant, recite, speak, speechify, spiel, spout, tub-thump.

declamatory *adj* bombastic, discursive, grandiloquent, grandiose, high-flown, inflated, magniloquent, oratorical, overblown, pompous, rhetorical, stagy, stilted, theatrical, turgid.

declaration *n* acknowledgement, affirmation, announcement, assertion, asseveration, attestation, averment, avowal, deposition, disclosure, edict, manifesto, notification, proclamation, profession, promulgation, pronounce-ment, protestation, revelation, statement, testimony.

declare *v* affirm, announce, assert, attest, aver, avow, certify, claim, confess, confirm, convey, disclose, maintain, manifest, proclaim, profess, pronounce, reveal, show, state, swear, testify, validate, witness.

decline *v* avoid, balk, decay, decrease, degenerate, deny, deteriorate, deviate, diminish, droop, dwindle, ebb, fade, fail, fall, fall off, flag, forgo, languish, lessen, pine, refuse, reject, shrink, sink, turn down, wane, weaken, worsen.
n abatement, consumption, decay, decrepitude, degeneration, deterioration, deviation, diminution, downturn, dwindling, failing, falling-off, lessening, recession, senility, slump, weakening, worsening.

decode *v* decipher, interpret, translate, transliterate, uncipher, unscramble. **antonym** encode.

decompose *v* analyse, atomise, break down, break up, crumble, decay, decompound, degrade, disintegrate, dissolve, distil, fall apart, fester, putrefy, rot, separate, spoil. **antonyms** combine, unite.

decorate *v* adorn, beautify, colour, deck, do up, embellish, enrich, grace, ornament, paint, paper, prettify, renovate, tart up, trick out, trim, wallpaper.

decoration¹ n adornment, bauble, beautification, elaboration, embellishment, enrichment, flounce, flourish, frill, garnish, ornament, ornamentation, scroll, spangle, trimming, trinket.

decoration² n award, badge, colours, crown, emblem, garland, garter, laurel, laurel-wreath, medal, order, ribbon, star.

decorative adj adorning, beautifying, embellishing, enhancing, fancy, nonfunctional, ornamental, ornate, pretty, superfluous. **antonyms** plain, ugly.

decorous adj appropriate, becoming, befitting, comely, correct, courtly, decent, dignified, fit, maidenly, mannerly, modest, polite, proper, refined, sedate, seemly, staid, suitable, well-behaved. **antonym** indecorous.

decorum n behaviour, breeding, courtliness, decency, deportment, dignity, etiquette, gentility, good manners, grace, gravity, modesty, politeness, propriety, protocol, punctilio, respectability, restraint, seemliness.

decoy n attraction, bait, ensnarement, enticement, inducement, lure, pretence, trap.
v allure, attract, bait, beguile, deceive, draw, ensnare, entice, entrap, inveigle, lead, lure, seduce, tempt.

decrease v abate, contract, curtail, cut down, decline, diminish, drop, dwindle, ease, fall off, lessen, lower, peter out, reduce, shrink, slacken, slim, subside, taper, wane. **antonym** increase.
n contraction, cutback, decline, diminution, downturn, dwindling, ebb, falling-off, lessening, loss, reduction, shrinkage, step-down, subsidence. **antonym** increase.

decree n act, command, dictum, edict, enactment, law, mandate, order, ordinance, precept, proclamation, regulation, ruling, statute.
v command, decide, determine, dictate, enact, lay down, ordain, order, prescribe, proclaim, pronounce, rule.

decrepit adj aged, antiquated, battered, broken-down, crippled, debilitated, deteriorated, dilapidated, doddering, doddery, feeble, frail, incapacitated, infirm, ramshackle, rickety, run-down, superannuated, tumble-down, wasted, weak, worn-out. **antonyms** fit, well-cared-for, youthful.

decry v abuse, belittle, blame, censure, condemn, criticise, cry down, declaim against, denounce, depreciate, derogate,

detract, devalue, discredit, disparage, inveigh against, rail against, run down, traduce, underestimate, underrate, undervalue. **antonyms** praise, value.

dedicate v address, assign, bless, commit, consecrate, devote, give over to, hallow, inscribe, offer, pledge, present, sacrifice, sanctify, set apart, surrender.

dedicated adj committed, devoted, enthusiastic, given over to, purposeful, single-hearted, single-minded, sworn, whole-hearted, zealous. **antonyms** apathetic, uncommitted.

dedication n adherence, allegiance, attachment, commitment, devotion, faithfulness, loyalty, self-sacrifice, single-mindedness, whole-heartedness. **antonym** apathy.

deduce v conclude, derive, draw, gather, glean, infer, reason, surmise, understand.

deduct v decrease by, knock off, reduce by, remove, subtract, take away, withdraw. **antonym** add.

deduction¹ n assumption, conclusion, corollary, finding, inference, reasoning, result.

deduction² n abatement, allowance, decrease, diminution, discount, reduction, subtraction, withdrawal. **antonyms** addition, increase.

deed n achievement, act, action, exploit, fact, factum, feat, performance, reality, truth.

deem v account, adjudge, believe, conceive, consider, esteem, estimate, hold, imagine, judge, reckon, regard, suppose, think.

deep adj absorbed, abstract, abstruse, acute, arcane, bass, booming, bottomless, broad, cryptic, dark, engrossed, esoteric, extreme, far, fathomless, full-toned, grave, great, hidden, immersed, inmost, inner, innermost, insidious, intense, knowing, learned, lost, low, low-pitched, mysterious, obscure, penetrating, preoccupied, profound, rapt, recondite, resonant, rich, sagacious, scheming, secret, shrewd, sonorous, strong, unfathomable, unfathomed, unplumbed, vivid, wide, wise, yawning. **antonyms** open, shallow.
n briny, drink, high seas, main, ocean, sea.

deepen v dredge, excavate, grow, hollow, increase, intensify, magnify, reinforce, scoop out, strengthen. **antonym** fill in.

deeply adv acutely, affectingly, completely, distressingly, feelingly, gravely, intensely, mournfully, movingly, passionately, profoundly, sadly, seriously, severely, thoroughly, to the quick, very much. *antonym* slightly.

deep-seated *adj* confirmed, deep, deep-rooted, entrenched, fixed, ineradicable, ingrained, inveterate, rooted, settled, subconscious, unconscious. *antonyms* eradicable, temporary.

deface *v* blemish, damage, deform, destroy, disfigure, impair, injure, mar, mutilate, obliterate, spoil, sully, tarnish, vandalise. *antonym* repair.

defamation *n* aspersion, calumny, denigration, derogation, disparagement, innuendo, libel, mud-slinging, obloquy, opprobrium, scandal, slander, slur, smear, vilification. *antonym* praise.

defamatory *adj* abusive, calumnious, contumelious, denigrating, derogatory, disparaging, injurious, insulting, libellous, pejorative, slanderous, vilifying, vituperative. *antonym* complimentary.

default *n* absence, defect, deficiency, dereliction, failure, fault, lack, lapse, neglect, non-payment, omission, want.
v backslide, bilk, defraud, dodge, evade, fail, neglect, rat, renegue, swindle, welsh.

defeat *v* baffle, balk, beat, best, checkmate, clobber, confound, conquer, counteract, crush, disappoint, discomfit, down, foil, frustrate, get the better of, overpower, overthrow, overwhelm, psych out, quell, repulse, rout, ruin, stump, subdue, subjugate, tank, thump, thwart, trounce, vanquish, vote down, whop.
n beating, conquest, débâcle, disappointment, discomfiture, failure, frustration, overthrow, rebuff, repulse, reverse, rout, setback, thwarting, trouncing, vanquishment, Waterloo.

defeated *adj* balked, beaten, bested, checkmated, confounded, conquered, crushed, licked, nonplussed, overcome, overpowered, overwhelmed, routed, thrashed, thwarted, trounced, vanquished. *antonyms* conquering, triumphant.

defeatist *adj* cynical, despairing, despondent, fatalistic, gloomy, helpless, hopeless, pessimistic, resigned, resourceless. *antonym* optimistic.

defect *n* absence, blemish, bug, default, deficiency, error, failing, fault, flaw, frailty, imperfection, inadequacy, lack, mistake, shortcoming, spot, taint, want, weakness.

v break faith, desert, rebel, renegue, revolt.

defective *adj* abnormal, broken, deficient, faulty, flawed, imperfect, inadequate, incomplete, insufficient, kaput, out of order, scant, short, subnormal. *antonyms* normal, operative.

defence[1] *n* aegis, armament, barricade, bastion, buckler, bulwark, buttress, cover, deterrence, fastness, fortification, guard, immunity, munition, protection, rampart, resistance, safeguard, security, shelter, shield. *antonym* attack.

defence[2] *n* alibi, apologia, apology, argument, case, declaration, denial, excuse, exoneration, explanation, extenuation, justification, palliation, plea, pleading, rebuttal, testimony, vindication.

defenceless *adj* endangered, exposed, helpless, imperilled, naked, powerless, unarmed, undefended, unguarded, unprotected, unshielded, vulnerable, wide open. *antonym* protected.

defend *v* assert, champion, contest, cover, endorse, espouse, fortify, guard, justify, maintain, plead, preserve, protect, safeguard, screen, secure, shelter, shield, speak up for, stand by, stand up for, support, sustain, uphold, vindicate, watch over. *antonym* attack.

defender *n* advocate, bodyguard, champion, counsel, escort, guard, patron, protector, sponsor, supporter, vindicator. *antonym* attacker.

defensible *adj* arguable, holdable, impregnable, justifiable, pardonable, permissible, plausible, safe, secure, tenable, unassailable, valid, vindicable. *antonyms* indefensible, insecure.

defensive *adj* apologetic, averting, cautious, defending, opposing, protective, safeguarding, self-justifying, wary, watchful. *antonym* bold.

defer[1] *v* adjourn, delay, hold over, postpone, procrastinate, put off, put on ice, shelve, suspend, waive.

defer[2] *v* accede, bow, capitulate, comply, give way, kowtow, respect, submit, yield.

deference *n* acquiescence, attention, capitulation, civility, complaisance, compliance, consideration, courtesy, esteem, homage, honour, obedience, obsequiousness, politeness, regard, respect, reverence, submission, submissiveness, thoughtfulness, veneration, yielding.

deferential *adj* civil, complaisant, considerate, courteous, dutiful, ingratiating, obedient, obsequious, polite, regardful, respectful, reverential, submissive. **antonyms** arrogant, immodest.

defiance *n* challenge, confrontation, contempt, disobedience, disregard, insolence, insubordination, obstinacy, opposition, provocation, rebelliousness, recalcitrance, spite. **antonyms** acquiescence, submissiveness.

defiant *adj* aggressive, audacious, bold, challenging, daring, disobedient, insolent, insubordinate, intransigent, mutinous, obstinate, provocative, rebellious, recalcitrant, refractory, truculent, unco-operative. **antonyms** acquiescent, submissive.

deficiency *n* absence, dearth, defect, deficit, demerit, failing, fault, flaw, frailty, imperfection, inadequacy, insufficiency, lack, paucity, scantiness, scarcity, shortage, shortcoming, want, wantage, weakness. **antonym** superfluity.

deficient *adj* defective, faulty, flawed, impaired, imperfect, inadequate, incomplete, inferior, insufficient, lacking, meagre, scanty, scarce, short, skimpy, unsatisfactory, wanting, weak. **antonyms** excessive, superfluous.

deficit *n* arrears, default, deficiency, lack, loss, shortage, shortfall. **antonym** excess.

defile *v* abuse, befoul, besmirch, contaminate, corrupt, debase, deflower, defoul, degrade, desecrate, dirty, disgrace, dishonour, make foul, molest, pollute, profane, rape, ravish, seduce, smear, soil, stain, sully, taint, tarnish, violate, vitiate. **antonym** cleanse.

definable *adj* ascertainable, definite, describable, determinable, explicable, perceptible, specific. **antonym** indefinable.

define *v* bound, characterise, circumscribe, delimit, delineate, demarcate, describe, designate, detail, determine, explain, expound, interpret, limit, mark out, outline, specify, spell out.

definite *adj* assured, certain, clear, clear-cut, decided, determined, exact, explicit, express, fixed, guaranteed, marked, obvious, particular, positive, precise, settled, specific, substantive, sure. **antonyms** indefinite, vague.

definitely *adv* absolutely, beyond doubt, categorically, certainly, clearly, decidedly, doubtless, doubtlessly, easily, finally, indeed, indubitably, obviously,

plainly, positively, surely, undeniably, unequivocally, unmistakably, unquestionably, without doubt, without fail.

definition[1] *n* clarification, delimitation, delineation, demarcation, description, determination, elucidation, explanation, exposition, interpretation, outlining, settling.

definition[2] *n* clarity, clearness, contrast, distinctness, focus, precision, sharpness.

definitive *adj* absolute, authoritative, complete, conclusive, correct, decisive, exact, exhaustive, final, perfect, reliable, standard, ultimate. **antonym** interim.

deflate[1] *v* chasten, collapse, contract, dash, debunk, disconcert, dispirit, empty, exhaust, flatten, humble, humiliate, mortify, press, puncture, put down, shrink, squash, squeeze, void. **antonym** inflate.

deflate[2] *v* decrease, depreciate, depress, devalue, diminish, lessen, lower, reduce. **antonym** increase.

deflect *v* avert, bend, deviate, diverge, glance off, ricochet, shy, sidetrack, slew, swerve, turn, turn aside, twist, veer, wind.

deflection *n* aberration, bend, bending, declination, deviation, divergence, drift, refraction, swerve, turning, veer.

deflower *v* assault, defile, desecrate, despoil, force, harm, mar, molest, rape, ravish, ruin, seduce, spoil, violate.

deform *v* corrupt, disfigure, distort, mangle, mar, pervert, ruin, spoil, twist, warp.

deformed *adj* bent, blemished, buckled, contorted, corrupted, crippled, crooked, defaced, depraved, disfigured, distorted, gnarled, maimed, malformed, mangled, marred, misshapen, mutilated, perverted, ruined, spoilt, twisted, warped.

deformity *n* abnormality, corruption, defect, depravity, disfigurement, distortion, irregularity, malformation, misshapenness, ugliness.

defraud *v* beguile, bilk, cheat, con, cozen, deceive, delude, diddle, do, dupe, embezzle, fleece, gull, outwit, rip off, rob, sting, swindle, trick.

defray *v* clear, cover, discharge, foot, meet, pay, refund, repay, settle. **antonym** incur.

deft *adj* able, adept, adroit, agile, clever, dexterous, expert, habile, handy, neat, nifty, nimble, proficient, skilful. **antonym** clumsy.

defunct *adj* dead, deceased, departed, expired, extinct, gone, invalid, kaput, non-existent, obsolete. *antonyms* alive, live, operative.

defy *v* baffle, beard, beat, brave, challenge, confront, contemn, dare, defeat, despise, disregard, elude, face, flout, foil, frustrate, outdare, provoke, repel, repulse, resist, scorn, slight, spurn, thwart, withstand. *antonyms* flinch, quail, yield.

degenerate *adj* base, corrupt, debased, debauched, decadent, degraded, depraved, deteriorated, dissolute, effete, fallen, immoral, low, mean, perverted. *antonyms* upright, virtuous.
v age, decay, decline, decrease, deteriorate, fall off, lapse, regress, retrogress, rot, sink, slip, worsen. *antonym* improve.

degradation *n* abasement, decadence, decline, degeneracy, degeneration, destitution, deterioration, discredit, disgrace, dishonour, humiliation, ignominy, mortification, perversion, shame. *antonyms* enhancement, virtue.

degrade *v* abase, adulterate, break, brutalise, cashier, cheapen, corrupt, debase, declass, demean, demote, depose, deprive, deteriorate, discredit, disennoble, disgrace, disgrade, dishonour, disrank, disrate, downgrade, embase, humble, humiliate, impair, injure, lower, pervert, shame, unfrock, ungown, vitiate, weaken. *antonyms* enhance, improve.

degraded *adj* abandoned, abased, base, corrupt, debased, debauched, decadent, déclassé, depraved, despicable, disgraced, disreputable, dissolute, low, mean, profligate, sordid, vicious, vile. *antonyms* moral, upright.

degrading *adj* base, cheapening, contemptible, debasing, demeaning, disgraceful, dishonourable, humiliating, ignoble, infra dig, lowering, shameful, undignified, unworthy.

degree *n* calibre, class, division, doctorate, extent, gradation, grade, intensity, interval, level, limit, mark, measure, notch, order, point, position, proportion, quality, quantity, range, rank, rate, ratio, run, scale, scope, severity, stage, standard, standing, station, status, step, unit.

deify *v* elevate, ennoble, enthrone, exalt, extol, glorify, idealise, idolise, immortalise, venerate, worship.

deign *v* condescend, consent, demean oneself, lower oneself, stoop, vouchsafe.

deity *n* demigod, demigoddess, divinity,

god, goddess, godhead, godhood, idol, immortal, power.

dejected *adj* blue, cast down, crestfallen, depressed, despondent, disconsolate, disheartened, dismal, doleful, down, downcast, downhearted, gloomy, glum, low, lowspirited, melancholy, miserable, morose, sad, spiritless, woebegone, wretched. *antonyms* bright, happy, high-spirited.

dejection *n* blues, depression, despair, despondency, disconsolateness, disconsolation, doldrums, downheartedness, dumps, gloom, gloominess, low spirits, melancholy, sadness, sorrow, unhappiness. *antonyms* happiness, high spirits.

delay *v* arrest, bog down, check, dawdle, defer, detain, dilly-dally, drag, halt, hinder, hold back, hold over, hold up, impede, lag, linger, loiter, obstruct, play for time, postpone, procrastinate, prolong, protract, put off, retard, set back, shelve, stall, stave off, stop, suspend, table, tarry, temporise. *antonyms* accelerate, expedite, hurry.
n check, dawdling, deferment, detention, dilly-dallying, hindrance, hold-up, impediment, interruption, interval, lingering, loitering, obstruction, postponement, procrastination, setback, stay, stoppage, suspension, tarrying, wait. *antonyms* hastening, hurry.

delectable *adj* adorable, agreeable, ambrosian, appetising, charming, dainty, delicious, delightful, enjoyable, enticing, flavoursome, gratifying, inviting, luscious, lush, palatable, pleasant, pleasurable, satisfying, scrumptious, tasty, yummy. *antonyms* horrid, unpleasant.

delectation *n* amusement, comfort, contentment, delight, diversion, enjoyment, entertainment, gratification, happiness, pleasure, refreshment, relish, satisfaction. *antonym* distaste.

delegate *n* agent, ambassador, commissioner, deputy, envoy, messenger, representative.
v accredit, appoint, assign, authorise, charge, commission, consign, depute, designate, devolve, empower, entrust, give, hand over, mandate, name, nominate, pass on, relegate, transfer.

delegation *n* commission, contingent, deputation, embassy, mission.

delete *v* blot out, blue-pencil, cancel, cross out, dele, edit, edit out, efface, erase, expunge, obliterate, remove, rub out, strike, strike out. **antonym** add in.

deleterious *adj* bad, damaging, destructive, detrimental, harmful, hurtful, injurious, noxious, pernicious, prejudicial, ruinous. **antonyms** enhancing, helpful.

deliberate *v* cogitate, consider, consult, debate, discuss, meditate, mull over, ponder, reflect, ruminate, think, weigh. *adj* advised, calculated, careful, cautious, circumspect, conscious, considered, designed, heedful, intentional, measured, methodical, planned, ponderous, prearranged, premeditated, prudent, purposeful, slow, studied, thoughtful, unhurried, wary, wilful, willed, witting. **antonyms** chance, unintentional.

deliberately *adv* by design, calculatingly, consciously, determinedly, emphatically, in cold blood, intentionally, knowingly, on purpose, pointedly, resolutely, wilfully, with malice aforethought, wittingly. **antonym** unintentionally.

deliberation *n* calculation, canniness, care, carefulness, caution, circumspection, cogitation, conference, consideration, consultation, coolness, debate, discussion, forethought, meditation, prudence, purpose, reflection, rumination, speculation, study, thought, wariness.

delicacy *n* accuracy, daintiness, discrimination, elegance, exquisiteness, fastidiousness, fineness, finesse, lightness, luxury, niceness, nicety, precision, purity, refinement, relish, savoury, sensibility, sensitiveness, sensitivity, subtlety, sweetmeat, tact, taste, titbit, treat. **antonyms** indelicacy, tactlessness.

delicate *adj* accurate, ailing, careful, choice, considerate, critical, dainty, debilitated, deft, delicious, detailed, diaphanous, difficult, diplomatic, discreet, discriminating, eggshell, elegant, elfin, exquisite, faint, fastidious, fine, flimsy, fragile, frail, gauzy, graceful, hazardous, kid-glove, minute, muted, nesh, pastel, precarious, precise, prudish, pure, refined, risky, savoury, scrupulous, sensible, sensitive, sickly, skilled, slender, slight, soft, softly-softly, squeamish, sticky, subdued, subtle, tactful, tender, ticklish, touchy, weak. **antonyms** harsh, imprecise, strong.

delicious *adj* agreeable, ambrosian, appetising, charming, choice, dainty, delectable, delightful, enjoyable, entertaining, exquisite, flavoursome, lip-smacking, luscious, mouthwatering, palatable, pleasant, pleasing, savoury, scrummy, scrumptious, tasty, yummy. **antonym** unpleasant.

delight *n* bliss, ecstasy, enjoyment, felicity, gladness, gratification, happiness, heaven, joy, jubilation, pleasure, rapture, transport. **antonyms** dismay, displeasure. *v* amuse, charm, cheer, divert, enchant, gladden, gratify, please, ravish, rejoice, satisfy, thrill, tickle. **antonyms** dismay, displease.

delight in appreciate, enjoy, gloat over, glory in, indulge in, like, love, relish, revel in, savour, take pride in.

delighted *adj* captivated, charmed, cock-a-hoop, ecstatic, elated, enchanted, gladdened, happy, joyous, jubilant, overjoyed, pleased, pleased as Punch, thrilled. **antonyms** dismayed, displeased.

delightful *adj* agreeable, amusing, captivating, charming, congenial, delectable, delightsome, enchanting, engaging, enjoyable, entertaining, fascinating, fetching, gratifying, heavenly, pleasant, pleasing, pleasurable, rapturous, ravishing, scrummy, scrumptious, sweet, thrilling, wizard. **antonym** horrible.

delineate *v* characterise, chart, depict, describe, design, draw, figure, outline, paint, picture, portray, render, represent, sketch, trace.

delinquency *n* crime, criminality, fault, law-breaking, misbehaviour, misconduct, misdeed, misdemeanour, offence, wrong-doing.

delinquent *n* criminal, culprit, defaulter, hooligan, law-breaker, malefactor, miscreant, offender, rough, tough, wrong-doer, young offender. *adj* careless, culpable, guilty, neglectful, negligent, remiss. **antonyms** blameless, careful.

delirious *adj* beside oneself, crazy, demented, deranged, ecstatic, excited, frantic, frenzied, hysterical, incoherent, insane, light-headed, mad, raving, unhinged, wild. **antonym** sane.

delirium *n* derangement, ecstasy, fever, frenzy, fury, hallucination, hysteria, insanity, lunacy, madness, passion, rage, raving.

deliver *v* acquit, administer, aim, announce, bear, bring, carry, cart, cede, commit, convey, deal, declare, direct, discharge, dispense, distribute, emancipate, feed, free, give, give forth, give up, grant, hand over, inflict, launch, liberate, loose, make over, pass, present, proclaim, pronounce, publish, ransom, read, redeem, release, relinquish, rescue, resign, save, strike, supply, surrender, throw, transfer, transport, turn over, utter, yield.

deliverance n emancipation, escape, extrication, liberation, ransom, redemption, release, rescue, salvation.

delivery¹ n consignment, conveyance, dispatch, distribution, shipment, surrender, transfer, transmission, transmittal, transport.

delivery² n articulation, elocution, enunciation, intonation, presentation, speech, utterance.

delude v bamboozle, beguile, cheat, con, cozen, deceive, dupe, fool, gull, hoax, hoodwink, impose on, misguide, misinform, mislead, snow, take in, trick.

deluge n avalanche, barrage, cataclysm, downpour, flood, hail, inundation, rush, spate, torrent.
v bury, douse, drench, drown, engulf, flood, inundate, overload, overrun, overwhelm, soak, submerge, swamp.

delusion n deception, error, fallacy, fancy, hallucination, illusion, mirage, misapprehension, misbelief, misconception, mistake, phantasm.

delve v burrow, dig into, examine, explore, investigate, poke, probe, ransack, research, root, rummage, search.

demand v ask, call for, challenge, claim, exact, expect, inquire, insist on, interrogate, involve, necessitate, need, order, question, request, require, take, want. **antonyms** cede, supply.
n bidding, call, charge, claim, desire, inquiry, interrogation, necessity, need, order, question, request, requirement, requisition, want. **antonym** supply.

demanding adj back-breaking, challenging, clamorous, difficult, exacting, exhausting, exigent, fatiguing, hard, imperious, importunate, insistent, nagging, pressing, taxing, tough, trying, urgent, wearing. **antonyms** easy, easy-going, undemanding.

demarcation n bound, boundary, confine, delimitation, differentiation, distinction, division, enclosure, limit, line, margin, pale, separation.

demean v abase, condescend, debase, degrade, deign, descend, humble, lower, stoop. **antonym** enhance.

demeanour n air, bearing, behaviour, carriage, comportment, conduct, deportment, manner.

demented adj crazed, crazy, deranged, distracted, distraught, dotty, foolish, frenzied, idiotic, insane, lunatic, mad, maniacal, manic, non compos mentis, nutty, unbalanced, unhinged. **antonym** sane.

demise n collapse, death, decease, departure, dissolution, downfall, end, expiration, failure, fall, passing, ruin, termination.

democracy n autonomy, commonwealth, populism, republic, self-government.

democratic adj autonomous, egalitarian, popular, populist, representative, republican, self-governing.

demolish v annihilate, bulldoze, consume, defeat, delapidate, destroy, devour, dismantle, down, eat, flatten, gobble, gulp, guzzle, knock down, level, overthrow, overturn, pull down, pulverize, raze, ruin, tear down, undo, wreck. **antonym** build up.

demon¹ n devil, evil spirit, fallen angel, fiend, genius, goblin, guardian spirit, incubus, monster, numen, succubus, villain, warlock.

demon² n ace, addict, dab hand, fanatic, fiend, master, pastmaster, wizard.

demonstrable adj arguable, attestable, axiomatic, certain, clear, evident, incontrovertible, indubitable, irrefutable, obvious, palpable, positive, provable, self-evident, substantiable, undeniable, unmistakable, verifiable. **antonyms** untestable, unverifiable.

demonstrate¹ v describe, display, establish, evidence, evince, exhibit, explain, expound, illustrate, indicate, manifest, prove, show, substantiate, teach, testify to.

demonstrate² v march, parade, picket, protest, rally, sit in.

demonstration¹ n affirmation, confirmation, description, display, evidence, exhibition, explanation, exposition, expression, illustration, manifestation, presentation, proof, substantiation, test, testimony, trial, validation.

demonstration² n demo, march, parade, picket, protest, rally, sit-in, work-in.

demonstrative adj affectionate, effusive, emotional, expansive, explanatory, expository, expressive, illustrative, indicative, loving, open, symptomatic, unreserved, unrestrained. *antonyms* cold, undemonstrative.

demoralisation *n* agitation, corruption, crushing, debasement, dejection, depravation, depression, despondency, devitalisation, discomfiture, enervation, lowering, panic, perturbation, perversion, trepidation, unmanning, vitiation, weakening. *antonym* encouragement.

demoralise *v* corrupt, cripple, crush, daunt, debase, debauch, deject, deprave, depress, disconcert, discourage, dishearten, dispirit, enfeeble, lower, panic, pervert, rattle, sap, shake, undermine, unnerve, vitiate, weaken. *antonym* encourage.

demoralised *adj* bad, base, broken, corrupt, crushed, degenerate, dejected, depraved, depressed, despondent, discouraged, disheartened, dispirited, dissolute, downcast, immoral, low, reprobate, sinful, subdued, unmanned, unnerved, weakened, wicked. *antonyms* encouraged, heartened.

demote *v* declass, degrade, downgrade, reduce, relegate. *antonyms* promote, upgrade.

demur *v* balk, disagree, dispute, dissent, doubt, hesitate, object, pause, protest, refuse, take exception, waver.
n compunction, dissent, hesitation, misgiving, objection, protest, qualm, reservation, scruple.

demure *adj* coy, decorous, diffident, grave, maidenly, modest, priggish, prim, prissy, prudish, reserved, reticent, retiring, sedate, shy, sober, staid, strait-laced. *antonym* forward.

den *n* cave, cavern, cloister, cubby-hole, earth, haunt, hide-away, hide-out, hole, lair, retreat, sanctuary, sanctum, set(t), shelter, study.

denial *n* abjuration, abnegation, contradiction, denegation, disaffirmation, disavowal, disclaimer, dismissal, dissent, gainsay, negation, prohibition, rebuff, refusal, rejection, renunciation, repudiation, repulse, retraction, veto.

denigrate *v* abuse, assail, belittle, besmirch, blacken, calumniate, criticise, decry, defame, disparage, impugn, malign, revile, run down, slander, vilify, *antonym* praise.

denigration *n* aspersion, backbiting, defamation, derogation, detraction, disparagement, mud-slinging, obloquy, scandal, scurrility, slander, vilification. *antonym* praise.

denomination *n* appellation, belief, body, category, class, classification, communion, creed, designation, grade, group, label, name, persuasion, religion, school, sect, size, style, term, title, unit, value.

denote *v* betoken, designate, express, imply, import, indicate, mark, mean, show, signify, stand for, symbolise, typify.

dénouement *n* climax, close, conclusion, culmination, finale, finish, outcome, pay-off, resolution, solution, termination, upshot.

denounce *v* accuse, arraign, assail, attack, brand, castigate, censure, condemn, declaim against, decry, denunciate, fulminate, impugn, inveigh against, proscribe, revile, stigmatise, vilify. *antonym* praise.

dense *adj* close, close-knit, compact, compressed, condensed, crowded, dull, heavy, impenetrable, jam-packed, obtuse, opaque, packed, slow, slow-witted, solid, stolid, stupid, substantial, thick, thickset, thick-witted. *antonyms* clever, sparse.

density *n* body, bulk, closeness, compactness, consistency, denseness, impenetrability, mass, solidity, solidness, thickness, tightness. *antonym* sparseness.

dent *n* bang, chip, concavity, crater, depression, dimple, dint, dip, dunt, hollow, impression, indentation, pit.
v depress, dint, gouge, indent, push in.

denude *v* bare, defoliate, deforest, divest, expose, strip, uncover. *antonym* cover.

denunciation *n* accusation, assailment, castigation, censure, condemnation, criticism, decrying, denouncement, fulmination, incrimination, invective, obloquy, stigmatisation. *antonyms* compliment, praise.

deny *v* abjure, begrudge, contradict, decline, disaffirm, disagree with, disallow, disavow, discard, disclaim, disown, disprove, forbid, gainsay, oppose, rebuff, recant, refuse, refute, reject, renounce, repudiate, revoke, traverse, turn down, veto, withhold. *antonyms* admit, allow.

depart *v* absent oneself, decamp, deviate, differ, digress, disappear, diverge, escape, exit, go, leave, make off, migrate, quit, remove, retire, retreat, set forth, stray, swerve, take one's leave, toddle, vanish, vary, veer, withdraw. **antonyms** arrive, keep to.

departed *adj* dead, deceased, defunct, expired, late.

department *n* area, branch, bureau, district, division, domain, field, function, line, office, province, realm, region, responsibility, section, sector, speciality, sphere, station, subdivision, unit.

departure *n* abandonment, branching, branching out, change, decession, deviation, difference, digression, divergence, exit, exodus, going, innovation, leave-taking, leaving, lucky, novelty, removal, retirement, shift, variation, veering, withdrawal. **antonym** arrival.

depend on anticipate, bank on, calculate on, count on, expect, hang on, hinge on, lean on, reckon on, rely upon, rest on, revolve around, trust in, turn to.

dependable *adj* certain, conscientious, faithful, gilt-edged, honest, reliable, responsible, steady, sure, trustworthy, trusty, unfailing. **antonym** unreliable.

dependence *n* addiction, assurance, attachment, belief, confidence, craving, dependency, expectation, faith, helplessness, hope, need, reliance, subordination, subservience, trust, vulnerability, weakness.

dependent *adj* adjective, conditional, contingent, defenceless, depending, determined by, helpless, immature, liable to, relative, reliant, relying on, subject, subject to, subordinate, tributary, vulnerable, weak.

depict *v* caricature, characterise, delineate, describe, detail, draw, illustrate, narrate, outline, paint, picture, portray, render, reproduce, sculpt, sketch, trace.

depiction *n* caricature, delineation, description, drawing, illustration, image, likeness, outline, picture, portrayal, representation, sketch.

deplete *v* attenuate, bankrupt, consume, decrease, drain, empty, evacuate, exhaust, expend, impoverish, lessen, reduce, use up.

depleted *adj* attenuated, consumed, decreased, depreciated, drained, emptied, exhausted, lessened, reduced, spent, wasted, weakened, worn out. **antonyms** augmented, increased.

depletion *n* attenuation, consumption, decimation, decrease, deficiency, diminution, dwindling, exhaustion, expenditure, lessening, lowering, reduction, shrinkage. **antonyms** increase, supply.

deplorable *adj* blameworthy, calamitous, dire, disastrous, disgraceful, dishonourable, disreputable, distressing, execrable, grievous, heartbreaking, lamentable, melancholy, miserable, opprobrious, pitiable, regrettable, reprehensible, sad, scandalous, shameful, unfortunate, wretched. **antonyms** excellent, praiseworthy.

deplore *v* abhor, bemoan, bewail, censure, condemn, denounce, deprecate, grieve for, lament, mourn, regret, repent of, rue. **antonym** praise.

deploy *v* arrange, dispose, distribute, embattle, extend, position, station, use, utilise.

deportation *n* banishment, eviction, exile, expatriation, expulsion, extradition, ostracism, transportation.

deportment *n* air, appearance, aspect, bearing, behaviour, carriage, cast, comportment, conduct, demeanour, etiquette, manner, pose, posture, stance.

depose *v* break, cashier, decrown, degrade, demote, dethrone, disestablish, dismiss, displace, downgrade, oust, topple.

deposit¹ *v* drop, dump, lay, locate, park, place, precipitate, put, settle, sit.
n accumulation, alluvium, deposition, dregs, precipitate, sediment, silt.

deposit² *v* amass, bank, consign, entrust, file, hoard, lodge, reposit, save, store.
n down payment, instalment, money, part payment, pledge, retainer, security, stake, warranty.

deposition¹ *n* dethronement, dismissal, displacement, ousting, removal, toppling.

deposition² *n* affidavit, declaration, denunciation, evidence, information, statement, testimony.

depot *n* arsenal, bond, depository, dump, garage, receiving-house, repository, station, storehouse, terminus, warehouse.

deprave *v* brutalise, contaminate, corrupt, debase, debauch, degrade, demoralise, infect, pervert, seduce, subvert, vitiate. **antonym** improve.

depraved *adj* abandoned, base, corrupt, debased, debauched, degenerate, degraded, dissolute, evil, immoral, lewd, libertine, licentious, perverted, profligate, reprobate, shameless, sinful, vicious, vile, wicked. **antonym** upright.

depravity *n* baseness, contamination, corruption, criminality, debasement, debauchery, degeneracy, degradation, dissoluteness, evil, immorality, iniquity, lewdness, licence, perversion, profligacy, reprobacy, sinfulness, turpitude, vice, viciousness, vileness, wickedness. **antonym** uprightness.

deprecate v condemn, deplore, disapprove of, disparage, object to, protest at, reject. **antonyms** approve, commend.

deprecation n condemnation, deploration, disapproval, dismissal, disparagement, protestation, rejection. **antonyms** commendation, encouragement.

deprecatory adj apologetic, censorious, condemnatory, disapproving, dismissive, protesting, regretful, reproachful. **antonyms** commendatory, encouraging.

depreciate v belittle, decrease, decry, deflate, denigrate, deride, derogate, detract, devaluate, devalue, disparage, downgrade, drop, fall, lessen, lower, minimise, reduce, ridicule, scorn, slump, traduce, underestimate, underrate, undervalue. **antonyms** appreciate, overrate, praise.

depreciation n belittlement, deflation, depression, derogation, detraction, devaluation, disparagement, downgrading, drop, fall, misprising, misprision, pejoration, slump. **antonyms** appreciation, exaggeration, praise.

depress v burden, cheapen, chill, damp, daunt, debilitate, deject, depreciate, devaluate, devalue, devitalise, diminish, discourage, dishearten, dispirit, downgrade, drain, enervate, exhaust, flatten, hip, impair, lessen, level, lower, oppress, overburden, press, reduce, sadden, sap, squash, tire, undermine, upset, weaken, weary. **antonym** cheer.

depressed[1] adj blue, cast down, crestfallen, debilitated, dejected, deprived, despondent, desponding, destitute, disadvantaged, discouraged, disheartened, dispirited, distressed, down, down-beat, downcast, downhearted, fed up, glum, low, low-spirited, melancholy, miserable, moody, morose, pessimistic, poor, sad, unhappy. **antonym** cheerful.

depressed[2] adj concave, dented, dinted, dished, hollow, indented, recessed, sunken. **antonyms** convex, prominent, protuberant.

depressing adj black, bleak, cheerless, daunting, dejecting, discouraging, disheartening, dismal, dispiriting, distressing, dreary, gloomy, grey, heartbreaking, hopeless, lugubrious, melancholy, sad, saddening, sombre. **antonym** encouraging.

depression[1] n blues, decline, dejection, despair, despondency, doldrums, dolefulness, downheartedness, dullness, dumps, exanimation, gloominess, glumness, hard times, heart-heaviness, hopelessness, inactivity, low spirits, lowness, melancholia, melancholy, panophobia, recession, sadness, slump, stagnation. **antonyms** cheerfulness, prosperity.

depression[2] n basin, bowl, cavity, concavity, dent, dimple, dint, dip, dish, excavation, hollow, hollowness, impression, indentation, pit, sag, sink, valley. **antonyms** convexity, prominence, protuberance.

deprivation n degradation, denial, denudation, despoliation, destitution, disadvantage, dispossession, distress, divestment, expropriation, hardship, need, privation, removal, want, withdrawal, withholding. **antonym** bestowal.

deprive v bereave, denude, deny, despoil, dispossess, divest, expropriate, rob, starve, strip. **antonym** bestow.

deprived adj bereft, denuded, depressed, destitute, disadvantaged, forlorn, impoverished, lacking, necessitous, needy, poor. **antonyms** fortunate, prosperous.

depth n abstruseness, abyss, complexity, deepness, discernment, drop, exhaustiveness, extent, gulf, insight, intensity, measure, obscurity, penetration, pit, profundity, richness, sagacity, shrewdness, strength, thoroughness, wisdom.

deputation n appointment, assignment, commission, delegates, delegation, deputies, deputing, designation, embassy, mission, nomination, representatives.

deputise v commission, delegate, depute, double, replace, represent, stand in for, substitute, understudy.

deputy n agent, alternate, ambassador, commissary, commissioner, delegate, henchman, lieutenant, proxy, representative, second-in-command, substitute, surrogate, vicar, vicegerent. adj assistant, depute, subordinate.

derange v confound, confuse, craze, dement, disarrange, disarray, discompose, disconcert, disorder, displace, disturb, drive crazy, madden, ruffle, unbalance, unhinge, unsettle, upset.

deranged *adj* aberrant, batty, berserk, brainsick, confused, crazed, crazy, delirious, demented, disarranged, disordered, distracted, distraught, disturbed, frantic, frenzied, insane, irrational, loony, lunatic, mad, maddened, nutty, unbalanced, unhinged. **antonyms** calm, sane.

derelict *adj* abandoned, deserted, desolate, dilapidated, discarded, forlorn, forsaken, neglected, ruined.
n dosser, down-and-out, drifter, hobo, outcast, toe-rag, tramp, vagrant, wastrel.

dereliction *n* abandonment, abdication, betrayal, delinquency, desertion, evasion, failure, faithlessness, fault, forsaking, neglect, negligence, relinquishment, remissness, renegation, renunciation. **antonyms** devotion, faithfulness, fulfilment.

deride *v* belittle, condemn, detract, disdain, disparage, flout, gibe, insult, jeer, knock, mock, pillory, pooh-pooh, rail at, ridicule, satirise, scoff, scorn, sneer, taunt, vilipend. **antonym** praise.

derision *n* contempt, dicacity, disdain, disparagement, disrespect, insult, laughter, mockery, raillery, ridicule, satire, scoffing, scorn, sneering. **antonym** praise.

derisive *adj* contemptuous, disdainful, disrespectful, irreverent, jeering, mocking, scornful, taunting. **antonyms** appreciative, flattering.

derisory *adj* absurd, contemptible, insulting, laughable, ludicrous, mockable, outrageous, paltry, preposterous, ridiculous.

derivation *n* acquisition, ancestry, basis, beginning, deduction, descent, etymology, extraction, foundation, genealogy, inference, origin, root, source.

derivative *adj* acquired, borrowed, copied, cribbed, daughter, derived, hackneyed, imitative, inferred, obtained, plagiarised, plagiaristic, procured, regurgitated, rehashed, secondary, second-hand, transmitted, trite, unadventurous, uninventive, unoriginal.
n branch, by-product, derivation, descendant, development, formative, offshoot, outgrowth, product, refinement, spin-off.

derive *v* acquire, arise, borrow, collect, crib, deduce, descend, develop, draw, elicit, emanate, extract, flow, follow, gain, gather, get, glean, grow, infer, issue, lift, obtain, originate, proceed, procure, receive, spring, stem, trace.

derogate *v* belittle, decry, defame, denigrate, depreciate, detract, devalue, diminish, disparage, insult, lessen, slight, take away from. **antonyms** add to, appreciate, praise.

derogatory *adj* belittling, critical, damaging, defamatory, depreciative, destructive, disparaging, injurious, insulting, offensive, pejorative, slighting, snide, uncomplimentary, unfavourable, unflattering. **antonyms** appreciative, favourable, flattering.

descend *v* alight, arrive, assail, assault, attack, condescend, degenerate, deign, derive, deteriorate, develop, dip, dismount, drop, fall, gravitate, incline, invade, issue, leap, originate, plummet, plunge, pounce, proceed, raid, sink, slant, slope, spring, stem, stoop, subside, swoop, tumble.

descendants *n* children, family, issue, line, lineage, offspring, posterity, progeny, race, scions, seed, sons and daughters, successors.

descent *n* ancestry, assault, attack, comedown, debasement, decadence, declination, decline, declivity, degradation, deterioration, dip, drop, extraction, fall, family tree, genealogy, heredity, incline, invasion, lineage, origin, parentage, plunge, pounce, raid, slant, slope, stoop, swoop. **antonyms** ascent, improvement.

describe *v* characterise, define, delineate, depict, detail, draw, enlarge on, explain, express, illustrate, mark out, narrate, outline, portray, present, recount, relate, report, sketch, specify, tell, trace.

description *n* account, brand, breed, category, characterisation, class, delineation, depiction, detail, explanation, exposition, genre, genus, hypotyposis, ilk, kidney, kind, narration, narrative, order, outline, portrayal, presentation, report, representation, sketch, sort, species, specification, type, variety, word-painting, word-picture.

descriptive *adj* blow-by-blow, circumstantial, colourful, depictive, detailed, explanatory, expressive, graphic, illustrative, immediate, pictorial, specific, vivid. **antonyms** cursory, laconic.

desecrate *v* abuse, blaspheme, contaminate, debase, defile, despoil, dishallow, dishonour, insult, invade, pervert, pollute, profane, vandalise, violate.

desecration n blasphemy, debasement, defilement, dishonouring, impiety, insult, invasion, pollution, profanation, sacrilege, violation.

desert[1] n solitude, vacuum, vast, void, waste, wasteland, wilderness, wilds. *adj* arid, bare, barren, desolate, droughty, dry, infertile, lonely, solitary, sterile, uncultivated, uninhabited, unproductive, untilled, waste, waterless, wild.

desert[2] v abandon, abscond, backslide, betray, decamp, deceive, defect, forsake, give up, jilt, leave, leave in the lurch, maroon, quit, rat on, relinquish, renegue, renounce, resign, strand, vacate.

desert[3] n come-uppance, demerit, deserts, due, meed, merit, payment, recompense, remuneration, requital, retribution, return, reward, right, virtue, worth.

deserted *adj* abandoned, bereft, betrayed, derelict, desolate, empty, forlorn, forsaken, friendless, godforsaken, isolated, left in the lurch, lonely, neglected, solitary, stranded, underpopulated, unfriended, unoccupied, unpopulous, vacant, vacated. *antonym* populous.

desertion n abandonment, absconding, apostasy, betrayal, defection, delinquency, departure, dereliction, escape, evasion, flight, forsaking, relinquishment, renegation, tergiversation, truancy.

deserve v ask for, earn, gain, incur, justify, merit, procure, rate, warrant, win.

deserved *adj* apposite, appropriate, apt, condign, due, earned, fair, fitting, just, justifiable, justified, legitimate, meet, merited, proper, right, rightful, suitable, warranted, well-earned. *antonyms* gratuitous, undeserved.

deserving *adj* admirable, commendable, creditable, estimable, exemplary, laudable, meritorious, praiseworthy, righteous, worthy. *antonyms* undeserving, unworthy.

desiccated *adj* arid, dead, dehydrated, drained, dried, dry, lifeless, parched, passionless, powdered, spiritless, sterile.

design n aim, arrangement, blueprint, composition, configuration, conformation, conspiracy, construction, contrivance, delineation, draft, drawing, end, enterprise, exemplar, figure, form, goal, guide, intent, intention, intrigue, logo, machination, manoeuvre, meaning, model, motif, object, objective, organisation, outline, pattern, plan, plot, project, prototype, purpose, schema, scheme, shape, sketch, structure, style, target, undertaking.

v aim, conceive, construct, contrive, create, delineate, describe, destine, develop, devise, draft, draw, draw up, fabricate, fashion, form, intend, invent, make, mean, model, originate, outline, plan, project, propose, purpose, scheme, shape, sketch, structure, tailor, trace.

designate v allot, appoint, assign, bill, call, characterise, choose, christen, code-name, deem, define, delegate, denominate, denote, depute, describe, docket, dub, earmark, entitle, indicate, label, name, nickname, nominate, select, show, specify, stipulate, style, term, ticket, title.

designer n architect, artificer, author, contriver, couturier, creator, deviser, fashioner, inventor, maker, originator, stylist.

designing *adj* artful, conniving, conspiring, contriving, crafty, cunning, deceitful, devious, disingenuous, guileful, insidious, intriguing, Machiavellian, plotting, scheming, sharp, shrewd, sly, treacherous, tricky, underhand, unscrupulous, wily. *antonym* artless.

desirability n advantage, advisability, attraction, attractiveness, beauty, benefit, merit, profit, seductiveness, usefulness, value, worth. *antonyms* disadvantage, inadvisability, undesirability.

desirable *adj* adorable, advantageous, advisable, agreeable, alluring, appetible, appropriate, attractive, beneficial, captivating, covetable, eligible, enviable, expedient, fascinating, fetching, good, nubile, pleasing, plummy, preferable, profitable, seductive, sexy, tempting, worthwhile. *antonym* undesirable.

desire v ask, aspire to, beg, covet, crave, entreat, fancy, hanker after, hunger for, importune, lack, long for, need, petition, request, solicit, want, wish for, yearn for. n appeal, appetite, ardour, aspiration, covetousness, craving, entreaty, greed, hankering, importunity, lasciviousness, lechery, libido, longing, lust, lustfulness, need, passion, petition, request, solicitation, supplication, want, wish, yearning, yen.

desired *adj* accurate, appropriate, correct, exact, expected, express, fitting, longed-for, looked-for, necessary, particular, proper, required, right, sought-after, wanted, wished-for. *antonyms* undesired, unintentional.

desirous *adj* ambitious, anxious, aspiring, avid, burning, craving, eager, enthusiastic, hopeful, hoping, itching, keen, longing, ready, willing, wishing, yearning. *antonyms* reluctant, unenthusiastic.

desist *v* abstain, break off, cease, come to a halt, discontinue, end, forbear, give over, give up, halt, leave off, pause, peter out, refrain, remit, stop, suspend. *antonyms* continue, resume.

desolate *adj* abandoned, arid, bare, barren, bereft, bleak, cheerless, comfortless, companionless, dejected, depopulated, depressed, depressing, desert, despondent, disconsolate, disheartened, dismal, dismayed, distressed, downcast, dreary, forlorn, forsaken, gloomy, godforsaken, grieved, lonely, melancholy, miserable, ravaged, ruined, solitary, unfrequented, uninhabited, unpopulous, unsolaced. waste, wild, wretched. *antonym* cheerful.
v denude, depopulate, despoil, destroy, devastate, lay waste, pillage, plunder, ravage, ruin, spoil, waste, wreck.

desolation *n* anguish, barrenness, bleakness, dejection, depopulation, desolateness, despair, desperation, despondency, destruction, devastation, disconsolateness, distress, emptiness, forlornness, gloom, gloominess, grief, havoc, isolation, loneliness, melancholy, misery, ravages, ruin, ruination, sadness, solitariness, solitude, sorrow, unhappiness, wildness, woe, wretchedness.

despair *v* capitulate, collapse, crumple, despond, give in, give up, lose heart, lose hope, quit, surrender. *antonym* hope.
n anguish, dejection, depression, desperation, despond, despondency, emptiness, gloom, hopelessness, melancholy, misery, ordeal, pain, resourcelessness, sorrow, trial, tribulation, wretchedness. *antonyms* cheerfulness, resilience.

despairing *adj* anxious, broken-hearted, dejected, depressed, desolate, desperate, despondent, disconsolate, disheartened, distracted, distraught, downcast, frantic, grief-stricken, hopeless, inconsolable, melancholy, miserable, sorrowful, suicidal, wretched. *antonyms* cheerful, resilient.

despatch *see* **dispatch**.

desperado *n* bandit, brigand, criminal, cut-throat, gangster, gunman, heavy, hood, hoodlum, law-breaker, mugger, outlaw, ruffian, thug.

desperate *adj* grave, abandoned, acute, audacious, critical, dangerous, daring, despairing, despondent, determined, dire, do-or-die, drastic, extreme, foolhardy, forlorn, frantic, frenzied, furious, great, hasty, hazardous, headlong, headstrong, hopeless, impetuous, inconsolable, irremediable, irretrievable, madcap, precipitate, rash, reckless, risky, serious, severe, urgent, violent, wild, wretched.

desperately *adv* appallingly, badly, critically, dangerously, distractedly, fearfully, frantically, frenziedly, frightfully, gravely, hopelessly, perilously, seriously, severely, shockingly.

desperation *n* agony, anguish, anxiety, defiance, despair, despondency, disconsolateness, distraction, distress, foolhardiness, franticness, frenzy, hastiness, heedlessness, hoplessness, madness, misery, pain, rashness, recklessness, sorrow, trouble, unhappiness, worry.

despicable *adj* abhorrent, abject, base, cheap, contemptible, degrading, detestable, disgraceful, disgusting, disreputable, hateful, ignoble, ignominious, infamous, low, mean, reprehensible, reprobate, shameful, sordid, unprincipled, vile, worthless, wretched. *antonyms* laudable, noble.

despise *v* abhor, condemn, deplore, deride, detest, disdain, dislike, disregard, ignore, loathe, revile, scorn, slight, spurn, undervalue. *antonyms* appreciate, prize.

despite *prep* against, defying, heedless of, in spite of, in the face of, in the teeth of, notwithstanding, regardless of, undeterred by.

despoil *v* bereave, denude, deprive, destroy, devastate, dispossess, divest, loot, pillage, plunder, ransack, ravage, rifle, rob, strip, vandalise, wreck. *antonyms* adorn, enrich.

despondent *adj* blue, broken-hearted, dejected, depressed, despairing, disconsolate, discouraged, disheartened, dispirited, doleful, down, downcast, downhearted, gloomy, glum, hopeless, inconsolable, low, low-spirited, melancholy, miserable, morose, mournful, overwhelmed, sad, sorrowful, woebegone, wretched. *antonyms* cheerful, hopeful.

despot *n* absolutist, autocrat, boss, dictator, Hitler, monocrat, oppressor, tyrant. *antonyms* democrat, egalitarian, liberal.

despotic *adj* absolute, absolutist, arbitrary, arrogant, authoritarian, autocratic, bossy, dictatorial, domineering, imperious, monocratic, oppressive, overbearing, peremptory, tyrannical. *antonyms* democratic, egalitarian, liberal, tolerant.

despotism *n* absolutism, autarchy, autocracy, dictatorship, monarchism, monocracy, oppression, repression, totalitarianism, tyranny. *antonyms* democracy, egalitarianism, liberalism, tolerance.

destination *n* aim, ambition, aspiration, design, end, end in view, goal, harbour, haven, intention, journey's end, object, objective, port of call, purpose, station, stop, target, terminus.

destine *v* allot, appoint, assign, consecrate, decree, design, designate, devote, doom, earmark, fate, foredoom, head, intend, mark out, mean, ordain, predetermine, preordain, purpose, reserve.

destined *adj* assigned, booked, bound, certain, designed, directed, doomed, en route, fated, headed, heading, ineluctable, inescapable, inevitable, intended, meant, ordained, predestined, predetermined, preordained, routed, scheduled, unavoidable.

destitute *adj* bankrupt, beggared, bereft, deficient, depleted, deprived, devoid of, distressed, down and out, impecunious, impoverished, indigent, innocent of, insolvent, lacking, necessitous, needy, penniless, penurious, poor, poverty-stricken, skint, strapped, wanting. *antonyms* prosperous, wealthy.

destitution *n* bankruptcy, beggary, distress, impecuniousness, neediness, pennilessness, penury, poverty, privation, starvation, straits, want. *antonyms* prosperity, wealth.

destroy *v* annihilate, banjax, break, crush, demolish, destruct, devastate, dismantle, dispatch, eliminate, eradicate, extinguish, extirpate, gut, kill, level, nullify, overthrow, ravage, raze, ruin, sabotage, scuttle, shatter, slay, slight, smash, thwart, torpedo, undermine, undo, vaporise, waste, wreck, zap. *antonym* create.

destruction *n* annihilation, bane, confutation, crushing, defeat, demolition, depopulation, desolation, devastation, downfall, elimination, end, eradication, extermination, extinction, extirpation, havoc, liquidation, massacre, nullification, overthrow, ravagement, ruin, ruination, shattering, slaughter, undoing, wastage, wrack, wreckage. *antonym* creation.

destructive *adj* adverse, antagonistic, baleful, baneful, calamitous, cataclysmic, catastrophic, contrary, damaging, deadly, deathful, deleterious, derogatory, detrimental, devastating, disastrous, discouraging, disparaging, disruptive, fatal, harmful, hostile, hurtful, injurious, invalidating, lethal, malignant, mischievous, negative, noxious, nullifying, pernicious, pestilent, ruinous, slaughterous, subversive, undermining, vexatious, vicious. *antonyms* creative, positive, productive.

desultory *adj* aimless, capricious, cursory, disconnected, disorderly, disorganised, erratic, fitful, haphazard, inconsistent, inconstant, inexact, irregular, loose, maundering, random, spasmodic, unco-ordinated, undirected, unmethodical, unsystematic. *antonyms* concerted, methodical, systematic.

detach *v* abstract, alienate, cut off, disconnect, disengage, disentangle, disjoin, dissociate, disunite, divide, estrange, free, isolate, loosen, remove, segregate, separate, sever, uncouple, undo, unfasten, unfix, unhitch. *antonym* attach.

detached *adj* aloof, disconnected, discrete, disinterested, disjoined, dispassionate, dissociated, divided, free, free-standing, impartial, impassive, impersonal, independent, loosened, neutral, objective, reserved, separate, severed, unattached, unbiased, uncommitted, unconcerned, unconnected, unimpassioned, uninvolved, unprejudiced. *antonyms* concerned, connected, involved.

detachment *n* aloofness, coolness, disconnection, disengagement, disinterestedness, disjoining, fairness, impartiality, impassivity, indifference, laissez-faire, neutrality, non-partisanship, objectivity, remoteness, separation, severance, severing, unconcern. *antonym* concern.

detail *n* aspect, attribute, complexity, complication, component, count, elaborateness, elaboration, element, fact, factor, feature, ingredient, intricacy, item, meticulousness, nicety, particular, particularity, point, refinement, respect, specific, specificity, technicality, thoroughness, triviality.

v allocate, appoint, assign, catalogue, charge, commission, delegate, delineate, depict, depute, describe, detach, enumerate, individualise, itemise, list, narrate, particularise, portray, recount, rehearse, relate, send, specify.

detailed *adj* blow-by-blow, circumstantial, complex, complicated, comprehensive, descriptive, elaborate, exact, exhaustive, fine, full, intricate, itemised, meticulous, minute, particular, particularised, refined, specific, thorough. **antonyms** brief, cursory, summary.

details *n* complexities, complications, ins and outs, intricacies, minutiae, niceties, particularities, particulars, specifics, trivia, trivialities.

detain *v* arrest, buttonhole, check, confine, delay, hinder, hold, hold up, impede, intern, keep, prevent, restrain, retard, slow, stay, stop. **antonym** release.

detect *v* ascertain, catch, descry, discern, disclose, discover, distinguish, espy, expose, find, identify, note, notice, observe, perceive, recognise, reveal, scent, sight, spot, spy, track down, uncover, unmask.

detection *n* discernment, discovery, exposé, exposure, identification, revelation, smelling out, sniffing out, tracking down, uncovering, unearthing, unmasking.

detective *n* busy, constable, cop, copper, dick, gumshoe, investigator, private dick, private eye, private investigator, sleuth, tec.

detention *n* confinement, constraint, custody, delay, detainment, duress, hindrance, holding back, imprisonment, incarceration, quarantine, restraint, withholding. **antonym** release.

deter *v* caution, check, damp, daunt, debar, discourage, disincline, dissuade, frighten, hinder, inhibit, intimidate, prevent, prohibit, put off, repel, restrain, stop, turn off, warn. **antonym** encourage.

deteriorate *v* backslide, crumble, decay, decline, decompose, degenerate, depreciate, disintegrate, ebb, fade, fail, fall off, go downhill, lapse, relapse, slide, slip, weaken, worsen. **antonym** improve.

deterioration *n* atrophy, corrosion, debasement, decline, degeneration, degradation, depreciation, descent, dilapidation, disintegration, downturn, drop, failing, fall, falling-off, lapse, retrogression, slump, vitiation, wastage, worsening. **antonym** improvement.

determination *n* backbone, conclusion, constancy, conviction, decision, dedication, doggedness, drive, firmness, fortitude, indomitability, insistence, intention, judgement, obstinacy, perseverance, persistence, pertinacity, purpose, resoluteness, resolution, resolve, result, settlement, single-mindedness, solution, steadfastness, stubbornness, tenacity, verdict, will, will-power. **antonym** irresolution.

determine *v* affect, arbitrate, ascertain, certify, check, choose, conclude, control, decide, detect, dictate, direct, discover, elect, end, establish, finish, fix, govern, guide, identify, impel, impose, incline, induce, influence, intend, lead, learn, modify, ordain, point, purpose, regulate, resolve, rule, settle, shape, terminate, undertake, verify.

determined *adj* bent, constant, convinced, decided, dogged, firm, fixed, indivertible, insistent, intent, obstinate, persevering, persistent, pertinacious, purposeful, resolute, set, single-minded, steadfast, strong-minded, strong-willed, stubborn, tenacious, tough-minded, unflinching, unhesitating, unwavering. **antonym** irresolute.

deterrent *n* bar, barrier, check, curb, difficulty, discouragement, disincentive, hindrance, impediment, obstacle, obstruction, repellent, restraint, turn-off. **antonym** incentive.

detest *v* abhor, abominate, deplore, despise, dislike, execrate, hate, loathe, recoil from. **antonym** adore.

detestable *adj* abhorred, abhorrent, abominable, accursed, despicable, disgusting, execrable, foul, hated, hateful, heinous, loathsome, nauseating, obnoxious, odious, offensive, repellent, repugnant, repulsive, revolting, rotten, shocking, sordid, swinish, vile, villainous. **antonyms** admirable, adorable, pleasant.

detonate *v* blast, blow up, discharge, explode, ignite, kindle, set off, spark off.

detour *n* bypass, byway, deviation, digression, diversion, excursus.

detract *v* belittle, depreciate, derogate, devaluate, diminish, lessen, lower, negate, nullify, reduce, vitiate. **antonyms** add to, praise.

detraction *n* abuse, aspersion, belittlement, calumniation, calumny, defamation, denigration, depreciation, derogation, disparagement, innuendo, insinuation, misrepresentation, muckraking, revilement, scandalmongering, scurrility, slander, vituperation. **antonyms** appreciation, praise.

detriment *n* damage, disadvantage, disservice, evil, harm, hurt, ill, impairment, injury, loss, mischief, prejudice. **antonym** advantage.

detrimental *adj* adverse, baleful, damaging, deleterious, destructive, disadvantageous, harmful, hurtful, inimical, injurious, mischievous, noxious, pernicious, prejudicial, unfavourable, untoward. **antonym** advantageous.

devalue *v* decrease, deflate, devaluate, lower, reduce.

devastate *v* confound, demolish, desolate, despoil, destroy, discomfit, discompose, disconcert, floor, lay waste, level, nonplus, overwhelm, pillage, plunder, ransack, ravage, raze, ruin, sack, spoil, spoliate, waste, wreck.

devastation *n* annihilation, demolition, denudation, desolation, despoliation, destruction, havoc, pillage, plunder, ravages, ruin, ruination, spoliation, wrack, wreckage.

develop *v* acquire, advance, amplify, augment, begin, bloom, blossom, branch out, breed, broaden, commence, contract, cultivate, diversify, elaborate, engender, enlarge, ensue, establish, evolve, expand, flourish, follow, form, foster, generate, grow, happen, invent, make headway, mature, move on, originate, pick up, progress, promote, prosper, result, ripen, sprout, start, unfold.

development *n* advance, advancement, blooming, blossoming, change, circumstance, detail, elaboration, event, evolution, expansion, extension, furtherance, growth, happening, improvement, incident, increase, issue, maturation, maturity, occurrence, outcome, phenomenon, progress, progression, promotion, refinement, result, ripening, situation, spread, unfolding, unravelling, upbuilding, upshot.

deviant *adj* aberrant, abnormal, anomalous, bent, bizarre, divergent, freakish, freaky, heretical, irregular, kinky, perverse, perverted, queer, twisted, wayward. **antonym** normal. *n* freak, kook, misfit, oddball, pervert, queer. **antonym** straight.

deviate *v* depart, differ, digress, diverge, drift, err, go astray, go off the rails, part, stray, swerve, turn, turn aside, vary, veer, wander, yaw.

deviation *n* aberration, abnormality, alteration, anomaly, change, deflection, departure, detour, digression, discrepancy, disparity, divergence, eccentricity, fluctuation, freak, inconsistency, irregularity, kinkiness, quirk, shift, variance, variation, wandering. **antonym** conformity.

device *n* apparatus, appliance, artifice, badge, contraption, contrivance, crest, design, dodge, emblem, expedient, figure, gadget, gambit, gimmick, gismo, implement, improvisation, insignia, instrument, invention, logo, machination, manoeuvre, motif, motto, plan, plot, ploy, project, ruse, scheme, shield, shift, stratagem, strategy, stunt, symbol, tactic, token, tool, trick, utensil, wile.

devil *n* arch-fiend, bastard, beast, Beelzebub, Belial, bog(e)y-man, brute, bugger, cad, creature, deil, demon, enthusiast, fiend, Hornie, imp, incubus, jumpy, Lucifer, man of sin, Mephisto, Mephistopheles, monkey, monster, ogre, Old Harry, Old Nick, Prince of Darkness, rascal, rogue, rotter, Satan, savage, scamp, scoundrel, succubus, swine, terror, unfortunate, villain, wretch.

devilish *adj* accursed, black-hearted, damnable, diabolic, diabolical, execrable, fiendish, hellish, impious, infernal, iniquitous, mischievous, monstrous, nefarious, satanic, wicked.

devil-may-care *adj* careless, casual, cavalier, easy-going, flippant, frivolous, happy-go-lucky, heedless, jaunty, lackadaisical, nonchalant, reckless, swaggering, swashbuckling, unconcerned, unworried.

devilment *n* devilry, mischief, mischievousness, naughtiness, roguishness, sport, teasing.

devilry *n* black magic, chicanery, cruelty, devilment, diabolism, evil, jiggery-pokery, malevolence, malice, mischief, mischievousness, monkey-business, sorcery, vice, viciousness, villainy, wickedness.

devious *adj* calculating, circuitous, confusing, crooked, cunning, deceitful, deviating, dishonest, disingenuous, double-dealing, erratic, evasive, excursive, indirect, insidious, insincere, misleading, rambling, roundabout, scheming, slippery, sly, subtle, surreptitious, tortuous, treacherous, tricky, underhand, wandering, wily, winding. **antonyms** artless, candid, straightforward.

deviousness n cunning, deceit, dishonesty, disingenuity, evasion, evasiveness, indirectness, insincerity, slipperiness, slyness, subtlety, trickiness. **antonyms** artlessness, openness.

devise v arrange, compass, compose, conceive, concoct, construct, contrive, design, excogitate, forge, form, formulate, frame, imagine, invent, plan, plot, prepare, project, scheme, shape.

devoid adj barren, bereft, deficient, denuded, destitute, empty, free, innocent, lacking, sans, vacant, void, wanting, without. **antonyms** blessed, endowed.

devote v allocate, allot, apply, appropriate, assign, commit, consecrate, dedicate, enshrine, give, oneself, pledge, reserve, sacrifice, set apart, set aside, surrender.

devoted adj ardent, attentive, caring, committed, concerned, constant, dedicated, devout, faithful, fond, loving, loyal, staunch, steadfast, tireless, true, unremitting, unswerving. **antonyms** inconstant, indifferent, negligent.

devotee n addict, adherent, admirer, aficionado, buff, devil, disciple, enthusiast, fan, fanatic, fiend, follower, hound, merchant, supporter, votary, zealot. **antonyms** adversary, sceptic.

devotion n adherence, adoration, affection, allegiance, ardour, assiduity, attachment, commitment, consecration, constancy, dedication, devoutness, earnestness, faith, faithfulness, fervour, fidelity, fondness, godliness, holiness, indefatigability, love, loyalty, partiality, passion, piety, prayer, regard, religiousness, reverence, sanctity, sedulousness, spirituality, steadfastness, support, worship, zeal. **antonyms** inconstancy, negligence.

devotional adj devout, dutiful, holy, pious, religious, reverential, sacred, solemn, spiritual.

devour v absorb, annihilate, bolt, consume, cram, destroy, dispatch, down, eat, engulf, feast on, feast one's eyes on, gluttonise, gobble, gorge, gulp, guzzle, polish off, ravage, relish, revel in, spend, stuff, swallow, waste, wolf.

devout adj ardent, constant, deep, devoted, earnest, faithful, fervent, genuine, godly, heartfelt, holy, intense, orthodox, passionate, pious, prayerful, profound, pure, religious, reverent, saintly, serious, sincere, staunch, steadfast, unswerving, wholehearted, zealous. **antonyms** insincere, uncommitted.

dexterity n ability, address, adroitness, agility, aptitude, art, artistry, cleverness, cunning, deftness, effortlessness, expertise, expertness, facility, finesse, handiness, ingenuity, knack, mastery, neatness, nimbleness, proficiency, readiness, skilfulness, skill, smoothness, tact, touch. **antonyms** clumsiness, ineptitude.

dexterous adj able, active, acute, adept, adroit, agile, apt, clever, cunning, deft, expert, feat, handy, ingenious, lighthanded, masterly, neat, neat-handed, nifty, nimble, nimble-fingered, proficient, skilful. **antonyms** clumsy, inept.

diabolical adj damnable, devilish, difficult, disastrous, dreadful, excruciating, fiendish, hellish, infernal, nasty, outrageous, shocking, unpleasant, vile, villainous, wicked.

diagnose v analyse, determine, distinguish, explain, identify, interpret, investigate, isolate, pinpoint, pronounce, recognise.

diagnosis n analysis, answer, conclusion, examination, explanation, identification, interpretation, investigation, isolation, opinion, pronouncement, scrutiny, verdict.

diagnostic adj analytical, demonstrative, distinctive, distinguishing, idiosyncratic, indicative, interpretative, interpretive, particular, peculiar, recognisable, symptomatic.

diagonal adj angled, cater-cornered, cornerways, crooked, cross, crossways, crosswise, oblique, slanting, slantwise, sloping.

diagonally adv aslant, at an angle, cornerwise, crosswise, obliquely, on the bias, on the cross, on the slant, slantwise.

diagram n abac, chart, drawing, figure, graph, illustration, lay-out, outline, picture, plan, representation, schema, sketch, table.

dialect n accent, diction, idiom, jargon, language, lingo, localism, patois, pronunciation, provincialism, regionalism, speech, tongue, vernacular.

dialectic n analysis, argumentation, contention, debate, deduction, dialectics, discussion, disputation, logic, polemics, rationale, reasoning.

dialogue n colloquy, communication, confabulation, conference, conversation, converse, debate, discourse, discussion, exchange, interchange, interlocution, lines, script, table talk, talk.

diametric adj antipodal, antithetical, contrary, contrasting, counter, diametrical, opposed, opposite.

diaphanous adj cobwebby, delicate, filmy, fine, gauzy, gossamer, gossamery, light, see-through, sheer, thin, translucent, transparent, veily. **antonyms** heavy, opaque, thick.

diarrhoea n dysentery, gippy tummy, holiday tummy, looseness, Montezuma's revenge, Spanish tummy, the runs, the trots. **antonym** constipation.

diary n appointment book, chronicle, day-book, engagement book, journal, logbook, year-book.

diatribe n abuse, attack, castigation, criticism, denunciation, harangue, insult, invective, onslaught, reviling, stricture, tirade, upbraiding, vituperation. **antonyms** bouquet, encomium, praise.

dicey adj chancy, dangerous, difficult, dubious, hairy, iffy, problematic, risky, ticklish, tricky. **antonyms** certain, easy.

dicky adj ailing, frail, infirm, queer, shaky, unreliable, unsound, unsteady, weak. **antonyms** healthy, robust.

dictate v announce, command, decree, direct, enjoin, impose, instruct, ordain, order, prescribe, pronounce, rule, say, speak, transmit, utter.
n behest, bidding, code, command, decree, dictation, dictum, direction, edict, fiat, injunction, law, mandate, order, ordinance, precept, principle, requirement, rule, ruling, statute, ultimatum, word.

dictator n autarch, autocrat, Big Brother, boss, despot, Hitler, supremo, tyrant.

dictatorial adj absolute, almighty, arbitrary, autarchic, authoritarian, autocratic, bossy, despotic, dogmatic, domineering, imperious, magisterial, oppressive, overbearing, peremptory, repressive, totalitarian, tyrannical. **antonyms** democratic, egalitarian, liberal, tolerant.

dictatorship n absolute rule, absolutism, autarchy, authoritarianism, autocracy, despotism, fascism, Hitlerism, totalitarianism, tyranny. **antonyms** democracy, egalitarianism.

diction n articulation, delivery, elocution, enunciation, expression, fluency, idiom, inflection, intonation, language, phraseology, phrasing, pronunciation, speech, style, terminology, usage, vocabulary, wording.

dictionary n concordance, encyclopaedia, glossary, lexicon, thesaurus, vocabulary, wordbook.

dictum n adage, axiom, command, decree, dictate, edict, fiat, gnome, maxim, order, precept, pronouncement, proverb, ruling, saw, saying, utterance.

didactic adj educational, educative, instructive, moral, moralising, pedagogic, prescriptive.

die v breathe one's last, croak, decay, decease, decline, depart, desire, disappear, dwindle, ebb, end, expire, fade, finish, fizzle out, go over to the majority, go to one's (long) account, hunger, kick in, kick it, kick the bucket, languish, lapse, long for, pass, pass away, pass over, peg out, perish, peter out, pine for, pop off, run down, sink, slip the cable, snuff it, starve, stop, subside, succumb, suffer, vanish, wane, wilt, wither, yearn.

die-hard n blimp, Colonel Blimp, fanatic, fogey, hardliner, intransigent, reactionary, rightist, stick-in-the-mud, ultra-conservative, zealot.
adj blimpish, confirmed, dyed-in-the-wool, entrenched, hardcore, hardline, immovable, incorrigible, incurable, inflexible, intransigent, irreconcilable, obstinate, reactionary, rigid, stubborn, ultra-conservative, uncompromising, unyielding. **antonyms** enlightened, flexible, progressive.

diet n abstinence, aliment, board, comestibles, edibles, fare, fast, food, foodstuffs, nourishment, nutrition, provisions, rations, regime, regimen, subsistence, sustenance.
v abstain, fast, lose weight, reduce, slim, weight-watch.

differ v argue, be at odds with, clash, conflict, contend, contradict, contrast, debate, demur, depart from, deviate, disagree, dispute, dissent, diverge, fall out, oppose, part company with, quarrel, take issue, vary. **antonyms** agree, conform.

difference n alteration, argument, balance, change, clash, conflict, contention, contrariety, contrast, contretemps, controversy, debate, deviation, differentia, differentiation, disagreement, discordance, discrepancy, discreteness, disparateness, disparity, dispute, dissimilarity, distinction, distinctness, divergence, diversity, exception, idiosyncrasy, nuance, particularity, peculiarity, quarrel, remainder, rest, set-to, singularity, strife, tiff, unlikeness, variation, variety, wrangle. *antonyms* agreement, conformity, uniformity.

different *adj* altered, anomalous, assorted, at odds, at variance, atypical, bizarre, changed, clashing, contrasting, deviating, discrepant, discrete, disparate, dissimilar, distinct, distinctive, divergent, divers, diverse, eccentric, extraordinary, inconsistent, individual, manifold, many, miscellaneous, multifarious, numerous, opposed, original, other, peculiar, rare, separate, several, singular, special, strange, sundry, unalike, uncommon, unconventional, unique, unlike, unusual, varied, various. *antonyms* conventional, normal, same, similar, uniform.

differentiate *v* adapt, alter, change, contrast, convert, demarcate, discern, discriminate, distinguish, individualise, mark off, modify, nuance, particularise, separate, tell apart, transform. *antonyms* assimilate, associate, confuse, link.

differentiation *n* contrast, demarcation, differentia, discrimination, distinction, distinguishing, individualisation, modification, particularisation, separation. *antonyms* assimilation, association, confusion, connection.

difficult *adj* abstract, abstruse, arduous, awkward, baffling, burdensome, captious, complex, complicated, dark, delicate, demanding, difficile, disruptive, enigmatical, fastidious, formidable, fractious, fussy, grim, hard, herculean, iffy, intractable, intricate, involved, knotty, laborious, obscure, obstinate, obstreperous, onerous, painful, perplexing, perverse, problematic, problematical, recalcitrant, refractory, rigid, steep, sticky, stiff, straitened, strenuous, stubborn, thorny, ticklish, tiresome, toilsome, tough, troublesome, trying, unamenable, unco-operative, unmanageable, uphill, wearisome. *antonyms* easy, straightforward.

difficulty *n* a bad patch, arduousness, awkwardness, block, complication, dilemma, distress, embarrassment, fix, hang-up, hardship, hiccup, hindrance, hole, hurdle, impediment, jam, laboriousness, labour, mess, nineholes, objection, obstacle, opposition, pain, painfulness, perplexity, pickle, pinch, pitfall, plight, predicament, problem, protest, quandary, scruple, spot, strain, strait, straits, strenuousness, stumbling-block, trial, tribulation, trouble, vexed question. *antonyms* advantage, ease.

diffident *adj* abashed, backward, bashful, constrained, distrustful, doubtful, hesitant, inhibited, insecure, meek, modest, reluctant, reserved, self-conscious, self-effacing, shamefaced, sheepish, shrinking, shy, suspicious, tentative, timid, timorous, unadventurous, unassertive, unassuming, unobtrusive, unsure, withdrawn. *antonym* confident.

diffuse *adj* circuitous, circumlocutory, copious, diffused, digressive, disconnected, discursive, dispersed, long-winded, loose, meandering, prolix, rambling, scattered, unconcentrated, unco-ordinated, vague, verbose, waffling, wordy. *antonyms* concentrated, succinct.
v circulate, dispense, disperse, disseminate, dissipate, distribute, propagate, scatter, spread, winnow. *antonyms* concentrate, suppress.

dig[1] *v* burrow, delve, drive, excavate, go into, gouge, graft, grub, hoe, howk, investigate, jab, mine, penetrate, pierce, poke, probe, prod, punch, quarry, research, scoop, search, spit, thrust, till, tunnel.
n aspersion, barb, crack, cut, gibe, insinuation, insult, jab, jeer, poke, prod, punch, quip, sneer, taunt, thrust, wisecrack. *antonym* compliment.
dig up discover, disinter, dredge, exhume, expose, extricate, find, retrieve, track down, uncover, unearth. *antonyms* bury, obscure.

dig[2] *v* adore, appreciate, be into, enjoy, fancy, follow, get a kick out of, get off on, go a bundle on, go for, go overboard about, have the hots for, like, love, understand, warm to. *antonym* hate.

digest *v* abridge, absorb, arrange, assimilate, classify, codify, compress, condense, consider, contemplate, dispose, dissolve, grasp, incorporate, ingest, macerate, master, meditate, ponder, process, reduce, shorten, stomach, study, summarise, systematise, tabulate, take in, understand.

n abbreviation, abridgement, abstract, compendium, compression, condensation, epitome, précis, reduction, résumé, summary, synopsis.

dignified *adj* august, decorous, distinguished, exalted, formal, grave, honourable, imposing, impressive, lofty, lordly, majestic, noble, reserved, solemn, stately, upright. *antonym* undignified.

dignify *v* adorn, advance, aggrandise, distinguish, elevate, ennoble, exalt, glorify, honour, promote, raise. *antonyms* degrade, demean.

dignitary *n* bigwig, celeb, celebrity, dignity, high-up, notability, notable, personage, pillar of society, VIP, worthy.

dignity *n* courtliness, decorum, elevation, eminence, excellence, glory, grandeur, gravitas, gravity, greatness, hauteur, honour, importance, loftiness, majesty, nobility, nobleness, pride, propriety, rank, respectability, self-esteem, self-importance, self-possession, self-regard, self-respect, solemnity, standing, stateliness, station, status.

digress *v* depart, deviate, diverge, drift, excurse, expatiate, go off at a tangent, ramble, stray, wander.

digression *n* apostrophe, aside, departure, detour, deviation, divergence, diversion, evagation, excursion, footnote, parenthesis, straying, vagary, wandering.

dilapidated *adj* battered, broken-down, crumbling, decayed, decaying, decrepit, mouldering, neglected, ramshackle, rickety, ruined, ruinous, run-down, shabby, shaky, tumble-down, uncared-for, worn-out.

dilate *v* amplify, broaden, descant, detail, develop, distend, dwell on, elaborate, enlarge, expand, expatiate, expound, extend, increase, puff out, spin out, stretch, swell, widen. *antonyms* abbreviate, constrict, curtail.

dilatory *adj* backward, behind-hand, dallying, delaying, indolent, lackadaisical, laggard, lingering, loitering, procrastinating, slack, slothful, slow, sluggish, tardy, tarrying. *antonym* diligent.

dilemma *n* bind, corner, difficulty, embarrassment, fix, jam, mess, perplexity, pickle, pinch, plight, predicament, problem, puzzle, quandary, spot, strait.

diligence *n* activity, application, assiduity, assiduousness, attention, attentiveness, care, constancy, earnestness, heedfulness, industry, intentness, laboriousness, perseverance, pertinacity, sedulousness. *antonym* laziness.

diligent *adj* active, assiduous, attentive, busy, careful, conscientious, constant, dogged, earnest, hard-working, indefatigable, industrious, laborious, painstaking, persevering, persistent, pertinacious, sedulous, studious, tireless. *antonyms* dilatory, lazy.

dilute *v* adulterate, allay, attenuate, cut, dash, decrease, diffuse, diminish, lessen, mitigate, reduce, temper, thin (out), water down, weaken. *antonym* concentrate.

dim *adj* bleary, blurred, caliginous, cloudy, confused, dark, darkish, dense, depressing, dingy, discouraging, dull, dumb, dusky, faint, feeble, foggy, fuzzy, gloomy, grey, hazy, ill-defined, imperfect, indistinct, intangible, lack-lustre, misty, muted, obscure, obscured, obtuse, opaque, overcast, pale, remote, shadowy, slow, sombre, stupid, sullied, tarnished, tenebrious, thick, unclear, unfavourable, unilluminated, unpromising, vague, weak. *antonyms* bright, distinct.

v blear, blur, cloud, darken, dull, fade, lower, obscure, tarnish. *antonyms* brighten, illuminate.

dimension(s) *n* amplitude, bulk, capacity, extent, greatness, importance, largeness, magnitude, measure, range, scale, scope, size.

diminish *v* abate, belittle, cheapen, contract, curtail, cut, deactivate, decline, decrease, de-emphasise, demean, depreciate, devalue, dwindle, ebb, fade, lessen, lower, minify, peter out, recede, reduce, retrench, shrink, shrivel, sink, slacken, subside, taper off, wane, weaken. *antonyms* enhance, enlarge, increase.

diminutive *adj* bantam, dinky, Lilliputian, little, midget, mini, miniature, minute, petite, pint-size(d), pocket(-sized), pygmy, small, tiny, undersized, wee. *antonyms* big, great, huge, large.

dimwit *n* blockhead, bonehead, dullard, dunce, dunderhead, ignoramus, nitwit, numskull, thick, twit.

din *n* babble, clamour, clangour, clash, clatter, commotion, crash, hubbub, hullabaloo, noise, outcry, pandemonium, racket, row, shout, uproar. **antonyms** calm, quiet.

dine v banquet, break bread, eat, feast, feed, lunch, sup.

dine on banquet, consume, dine off, eat, feast, feed, regale oneself.

dingy adj colourless, dark, dim, dirty, discoloured, drab, dreary, dull, dusky, faded, gloomy, grimy, murky, obscure, rundown, seedy, shabby, soiled, sombre, tacky, worn. **antonyms** bright, clean.

dip v bathe, decline, descend, disappear, dook, dop, douse, droop, drop, duck, dunk, fade, fall, immerse, ladle, lower, plunge, rinse, sag, scoop, set, sink, slope, slump, souse, spoon, subside, tilt.

n basin, bathe, concavity, concoction, decline, depression, dilution, dive, dook, douche, drenching, ducking, fall, hole, hollow, immersion, incline, infusion, lowering, mixture, plunge, preparation, sag, slip, slope, slump, soaking, solution, suspension, swim.

dip into browse, dabble, peruse, sample, skim, try.

diplomacy n artfulness, craft, delicacy, discretion, finesse, manoeuvring, savoir-faire, skill, statesmanship, subtlety, tact, tactfulness.

diplomatic adj discreet, judicious, polite, politic, prudent, sagacious, sensitive, subtle, tactful. **antonyms** rude, tactless, thoughtless.

dire adj alarming, appalling, awful, calamitous, cataclysmic, catastrophic, critical, crucial, cruel, crying, desperate, disastrous, dismal, distressing, drastic, dreadful, exigent, extreme, fearful, gloomy, grave, grim, horrible, horrid, ominous, portentous, pressing, ruinous, terrible, urgent, woeful.

direct[1] v address, administer, advise, aim, bid, case, charge, command, conduct, control, dictate, dispose, enjoin, fix, focus, govern, guide, handle, indicate, instruct, intend, label, lead, level, mail, manage, mastermind, mean, order, oversee, point, regulate, route, rule, run, send, show, stage-manage, superintend, superscribe, supervise, train, turn.

direct[2] adj absolute, blunt, candid, categorical, downright, explicit, express, face-to-face, first-hand, frank, head-on, honest, immediate, man-to-man, matter-of-fact, non-stop, open, outright, outspoken, personal, plain, plain-spoken, point-blank, shortest, sincere, straight,

straightforward, through, unambiguous, unbroken, undeviating, unequivocal, uninterrupted. **antonyms** crooked, devious, indirect.

direction n address, administration, aim, approach, bearing, bent, bias, charge, command, control, course, current, drift, end, government, guidance, label, leadership, line, management, mark, order, orientation, oversight, path, proclivity, purpose, road, route, superintendence, superscription, supervision, tack, tendency, tenor, track, trend, way.

directions n briefing, guidance, guidelines, indication, instructions, orders, plan, recipe, recommendations, regulations.

directive n charge, command, decree, dictate, diktat, edict, fiat, imperative, injunction, instruction, mandate, notice, order, ordinance, regulation, ruling.

directly adv bluntly, candidly, dead, due, exactly, face-to-face, forthwith, frankly, honestly, immediately, instantaneously, instantly, openly, personally, plainly, point-blank, precisely, presently, promptly, pronto, quickly, right away, soon, speedily, straight, straightaway, straightforwardly, truthfully, unequivocally, unerringly, unswervingly.

director n administrator, auteur, boss, chairman, chief, conductor, controller, corrector, executive, governor, head, leader, manager, monitor, organiser, principal, producer, supervisor.

dirt n clay, crud, dust, earth, excrement, filth, grime, impurity, indecency, loam, mire, muck, mud, obscenity, pornography, slime, smudge, smut, soil, stain, tarnish, vomit, yuck. **antonyms** cleanliness, cleanness.

dirty adj angry, base, beggarly, bitter, blue, clouded, contemptible, corrupt, cowardly, crooked, cruddy, dark, despicable, dishonest, dull, filthy, foul, fraudulent, grimy, grubby, ignominious, illegal, indecent, low, low-down, manky, mean, messy, miry, mucky, muddy, nasty, obscene, off-colour, piggish, polluted, pornographic, risqué, salacious, scruffy, shabby, sluttish, smutty, soiled, sordid, squalid, sullied, treacherous, unclean, unfair, unscrupulous, unsporting, unsterile, unswept, vile, vulgar, yucky. **antonyms** clean, spotless.

v besmirch, blacken, defile, foul, mess

up, muddy, pollute, smear, smirch, smudge, soil, spoil, stain, sully. **antonyms** clean, cleanse.

disability n affliction, ailment, complaint, defect, disablement, disorder, disqualification, handicap, impairment, impotency, inability, incapacitation, incapacity, infirmity, malady, unfitness, weakness.

disable v cripple, damage, debilitate, disqualify, enfeeble, hamstring, handicap, immobilise, impair, incapacitate, invalidate, lame, paralyse, prostrate, unfit, unman, weaken.

disabled adj bedridden, crippled, handicapped, immobilised, incapacitated, infirm, lame, maimed, mangled, mutilated, paralysed, weak, weakened, wrecked. **antonyms** able, able-bodied.

disadvantage n burden, damage, debit, detriment, disservice, drawback, flaw, fly in the ointment, handicap, hardship, harm, hindrance, hurt, impediment, inconvenience, injury, liability, loss, minus, nuisance, prejudice, privation, snag, trouble, unfavourableness, weakness. **antonym** benefit.
v hamper, handicap, hinder, inconvenience, wrong-foot. **antonyms** aid, help.

disadvantaged adj deprived, handicapped, hindered, impeded, impoverished, struggling, underprivileged. **antonym** privileged.

disadvantageous adj adverse, burdensome, damaging, deleterious, detrimental, harmful, hurtful, ill-timed, inauspicious, inconvenient, inexpedient, injurious, inopportune, prejudicial, unfavourable. **antonym** advantageous.

disaffected adj alienated, antagonistic, antipathetic(al), discontented, disgruntled, disloyal, dissatisfied, estranged, hostile, mutinous, rebellious, seditious. **antonym** contented.

disaffection n alienation, animosity, antagonism, antipathy, aversion, breach, coolness, disagreement, discontentment, discord, disharmony, dislike, disloyalty, dissatisfaction, estrangement, hostility, ill-will, repugnance, resentment, unfriendliness. **antonym** contentment.

disagree v altercate, argue, bicker, bother, clash, conflict, contend, contest, contradict, counter, depart, deviate, differ, disaccord, discomfort, dissent, distress, diverge, fall out, hurt, nauseate, object, oppose, quarrel, run counter to, sicken, spat, squabble, take issue with,

tiff, trouble, upset, vary, wrangle. **antonym** agree.

disagreeable adj bad-tempered, brusque, churlish, contrary, cross, difficult, disgusting, disobliging, displeasing, distasteful, irritable, nasty, objectionable, obnoxious, offensive, peevish, repellent, repugnant, repulsive, rude, surly, unappetising, unfriendly, ungracious, uninviting, unpalatable, unpleasant, unsavoury. **antonyms** friendly, pleasant.

disagreement n altercation, argument, clash, conflict, debate, difference, disaccord, discord, discrepancy, disparity, dispute, dissent, dissimilarity, dissimilitude, divergence, diversity, division, falling-out, incompatibility, incongruity, misunderstanding, quarrel, squabble, strife, tiff, unlikeness, variance, wrangle.

disallow v abjure, ban, cancel, chalk off, debar, disaffirm, disavow, disclaim, dismiss, disown, embargo, forbid, prohibit, proscribe, rebuff, refuse, reject, repudiate, veto. **antonym** permit.

disallowed adj debarred, excepted, excluded, forbidden, impermissible, interdicted, prohibited, proscribed, rejected. **antonym** permissible.

disappear v cease, dematerialise, depart, dissolve, ebb, end, escape, evanesce, evaporate, expire, fade, flee, fly, go, pass, perish, recede, retire, scarper, vamoose, vanish, wane, withdraw. **antonym** appear.

disappearance n dematerialisation, departure, desertion, disappearing, dispersal, dispersion, dissipation, eclipse, evanescence, evaporation, fading, flight, going, loss, melting, passing, vanishing. **antonym** appearance.

disappoint v baffle, balk, chagrin, dash, deceive, defeat, delude, disconcert, disenchant, disgruntle, dishearten, disillusion, dismay, dissatisfy, fail, foil, frustrate, hamper, hinder, let down, miff, sadden, thwart, vex. **antonyms** delight, please, satisfy.

disappointed adj balked, depressed, despondent, discontented, discouraged, disenchanted, disgruntled, disillusioned, dissatisfied, distressed, down-hearted, foiled, frustrated, let down, miffed, saddened, thwarted, upset. **antonyms** delighted, pleased, satisfied.

disappointing adj anti-climactic, depressing, disagreeable, disconcerting, discouraging, inadequate, inferior, insufficient, pathetic, sad, sorry, unhappy, unsatisfactory, unworthy. **antonyms** encouraging, pleasant, satisfactory.

disappointment[1] *n* bafflement, chagrin, discontent, discouragement, disenchantment, disillusionment, displeasure, dissatisfaction, distress, failure, frustration, mortification, regret. **antonyms** delight, pleasure, satisfaction.

disappointment[2] *n* blow, calamity, comedown, disaster, drop, failure, fiasco, let-down, misfortune, setback, swiz, swizzle. **antonyms** boost, success.

disapprobation *n* blame, censure, condemnation, denunciation, disapproval, disfavour, dislike, displeasure, dissatisfaction, objection, reproach, reproof. **antonyms** approbation, approval.

disapproval *n* censure, condemnation, criticism, denunciation, deprecation, disapprobation, disfavour, dislike, disparagement, displeasure, dissatisfaction, objection, reproach, thumbs-down. **antonyms** approbation, approval, thumbs-up.

disapprove of blame, censure, condemn, denounce, deplore, deprecate, disallow, discountenance, dislike, disparage, object to, reject, spurn, take exception to. **antonym** approve of.

disapproving *adj* censorious, condemnatory, critical, deprecatory, disapprobatory, disparaging, reproachful.

disarm[1] *v* deactivate, demilitarise, demobilise, disable, disband.

disarm[2] *v* appease, conciliate, modify, persuade, win over.

disarming *adj* charming, conciliatory, irresistible, likeable, mollifying, persuasive, winning.

disarrange *v* confuse, derange, disarray, discompose, dislocate, disorder, disorganise, disrank, disturb, jumble, muss(e), shuffle, unsettle, untidy. **antonym** arrange.

disarray *n* chaos, clutter, confusion, discomposure, disharmony, dishevelment, dislocation, dismay, disorder, disorderliness, disorganisation, displacement, disunity, guddle, indiscipline, jumble, mess, muddle, shambles, tangle, unruliness, untidiness, upset. **antonyms** array, order.

disaster *n* accident, act of God, blow, calamity, cataclysm, catastrophe, curtains, debacle, melt, misadventure, mischance, misfortune, mishap, reverse, ruin, ruination, stroke, tragedy, trouble. **antonyms** success, triumph.

disastrous *adj* adverse, calamitous, cataclysmic, catastrophic, destructive, detrimental, devastating, dire, dreadful, fatal, grievous, hapless, harmful, ill-fated, ill-starred, miserable, ruinous, terrible, tragic, unfortunate, unlucky. **antonyms** successful, triumphant.

disband *v* break up, demobilise, dismiss, disperse, dissolve, part company, retire, scatter, separate. **antonyms** assemble, band, combine.

disbelief *n* distrust, doubt, dubiety, incredulity, mistrust, rejection, scepticism, suspicion, unbelief. **antonym** belief.

discard *v* abandon, cashier, cast aside, dispense with, dispose of, ditch, drop, dump, jettison, leave off, reject, relinquish, remove, repudiate, scrap, shed. **antonyms** adopt, embrace, espouse.

discern *v* ascertain, behold, descry, detect, determine, differentiate, discover, discriminate, distinguish, espy, judge, make out, notice, observe, perceive, recognise, see, wot.

discernible *adj* apparent, appreciable, clear, detectable, discoverable, distinct, distinguishable, manifest, noticeable, observable, obvious, patent, perceptible, plain, recognisable, sensible, visible. **antonym** invisible.

discerning *adj* acute, astute, clear-sighted, critical, discriminating, eagle-eyed, ingenious, intelligent, judicious, knowing, penetrating, perceptive, perspicacious, piercing, sagacious, sensitive, sharp, shrewd, subtle, wise. **antonym** obtuse.

discernment *n* acumen, acuteness, ascertainment, astuteness, awareness, clear-sightedness, cleverness, discrimination, ingenuity, insight, intelligence, judgement, keenness, penetration, perception, perceptiveness, perspicacity, sagacity, sharpness, understanding, wisdom.

discharge *v* absolve, accomplish, acquit, carry out, cashier, clear, detonate, disburden, discard, dismiss, dispense, drum out, effectuate, eject, emit, empty, excrete, execute, exonerate, expel, explode, exude, fire, free, fulfil, give off, gush, honour, leak, let off, liberate, meet, offload, ooze, oust, pardon, pay, perform, release, relieve, remove, sack, satisfy, set off, settle, shoot, unburden, unload, vent, void, volley. *antonyms* employ, engage, hire.

n accomplishment, achievement, acquittal, acquittance, blast, burst, clearance, conge, defluxion, demobilisation, detonation, disburdening, discharging, dismissal, effluent, ejection, emission, emptying, excretion, execution, exoneration, explosion, firing, flight, flow, flux, fluxion, fulfilment, fusillade, liberation, observance, ooze, pardon, payment, performance, pus, quietus, quittance, release, remittance, report, salvo, satisfaction, secretion, seepage, settlement, shot, suppuration, the boot, the sack, unburdening, unloading, vent, voidance, voiding, volley, whiff.

disciple *n* acolyte, adherent, apostle, believer, catechumen, convert, devotee, follower, learner, partisan, pupil, student, supporter, votary.

discipline *n* castigation, chastisement, conduct, control, correction, course, curriculum, drill, exercise, method, orderliness, practice, punishment, regimen, regulation, restraint, self-control, speciality, strictness, subject, training. *antonyms* carelessness, negligence.

v break in, castigate, chasten, chastise, check, control, correct, drill, educate, exercise, form, govern, habituate, instruct, inure, penalise, prepare, punish, regulate, reprimand, reprove, restrain, toughen, train.

disclaim *v* abandon, abjure, abnegate, decline, deny, disaffirm, disallow, disavow, disown, forswear, reject, renounce, repudiate. *antonyms* accept, acknowledge.

disclaimer *n* abjuration, abnegation, contradiction, denial, disavowal, disownment, rejection, renunciation, repudiation, retraction.

disclose *v* broadcast, communicate, confess, discover, divulge, exhibit, expose, impart, lay, lay bare, leak, let slip, publish, relate, reveal, show, tell, unbare, unbosom, unburden, uncover, unfold, unveil, utter. *antonyms* conceal, hide.

discolour *v* disfigure, fade, mar, mark, rust, soil, stain, streak, tarnish, tinge, weather.

discomfit *v* abash, baffle, balk, beat, checkmate, confound, confuse, defeat, demoralise, discompose, disconcert, embarrass, faze, flurry, fluster, foil, frustrate, humble, humiliate, outwit, overcome, perplex, perturb, rattle, ruffle, thwart, trump, unsettle, vanquish, worry, worst.

discomfiture *n* abashment, beating, chagrin, confusion, defeat, demoralisation, disappointment, discomposure, embarrassment, failure, frustration, humiliation, overthrow, repulse, rout, ruin, shame, undoing, unease, vanquishment.

discomfort *n* ache, annoyance, disquiet, distress, hardship, hurt, irritant, irritation, malaise, trouble, uneasiness, unpleasantness, vexation. *antonyms* comfort, ease.

disconcert *v* abash, agitate, baffle, balk, bewilder, confuse, discomfit, discompose, disturb, flurry, fluster, frustrate, hinder, nonplus, perplex, perturb, put someone's nose out of joint, rattle, ruffle, thwart, trouble, unbalance, undo, unsettle, upset, worry.

disconcerted *adj* annoyed, bewildered, confused, discomfited, distracted, disturbed, embarrassed, fazed, flurried, flustered, mixed-up, nonplussed, perturbed, rattled, ruffled, taken aback, thrown, troubled, unsettled, upset.

disconcerting *adj* alarming, awkward, baffling, bewildering, bothersome, confusing, dismaying, distracting, disturbing, embarrassing, off-putting, perplexing, upsetting.

disconnect *v* cut off, detach, disengage, divide, part, separate, sever, uncouple, unhitch, unhook, unplug. *antonyms* attach, connect, engage.

disconnected *adj* confused, disjointed, free, garbled, illogical, incoherent, irrational, jumbled, loose, rambling, unco-ordinated, unintelligible, wandering. *antonyms* attached, coherent.

disconsolate *adj* crushed, dejected, desolate, despairing, dispirited, forlorn, gloomy, grief-stricken, heartbroken, heavy-hearted, hopeless, inconsolable, melancholy, miserable, sad, unhappy, unsolaced, woeful, wretched. *antonyms* cheerful, cheery.

discontent *n* discontentment, displeasure, disquiet, dissatisfaction, envy, fretfulness, impatience, regret, restlessness, uneasiness, unhappiness, unrest, vexation.

discontented *adj* brassed off, browned off, cheesed off, complaining, disaffected, disgruntled, displeased, dissatisfied, exasperated, fed up, fretful, impatient, miserable, scunnered, unhappy, vexed. **antonyms** happy, satisfied.

discontinue v abandon, break off, cancel, cease, drop, end, finish, halt, interrupt, pause, quit, stop, suspend, terminate.

discord n cacophony, clashing, conflict, contention, difference, din, disagreement, discordance, disharmony, dispute, dissension, dissonance, disunity, division, friction, harshness, incompatibility, jangle, jarring, opposition, racket, rupture, split, strife, tumult, variance, wrangling. **antonyms** agreement, concord, harmony.

discordant adj at odds, cacophonous, clashing, conflicting, contradictory, contrary, different, disagreeing, dissonant, grating, harsh, incompatible, incongruous, inconsistent, inharmonious, jangling, jarring, opposite, shrill, strident, unmelodious. **antonyms** concordant, harmonious.

discount[1] v disbelieve, disregard, gloss over, ignore, overlook.

discount[2] n allowance, concession, cut, deduction, mark-down, rebate, reduction.

discourage v abash, awe, check, chill, cow, curb, damp, dampen, dash, daunt, deject, demoralise, deprecate, depress, deter, discountenance, disfavour, dishearten, dismay, dispirit, dissuade, frighten, hinder, inhibit, intimidate, overawe, prevent, put off, restrain, scare, unman, unnerve. **antonyms** encourage, favour, hearten, inspire.

discouraged adj crestfallen, dashed, daunted, depressed, deterred, disheartened, dismayed, dispirited, downcast, glum, pessimistic. **antonyms** encouraged, heartened.

discouragement n constraint, curb, damp, damper, dejection, depression, despair, despondency, deterrent, disappointment, discomfiture, disincentive, dismay, hindrance, hopelessness, impediment, obstacle, opposition, pessimism, rebuff, restraint, setback. **antonyms** encouragement, incentive.

discouraging adj dampening, daunting, depressing, disappointing, disheartening, dispiriting, dissuasive, inauspicious, off-putting, unfavourable, unpropitious. **antonyms** encouraging, heartening.

discourse n address, chat, communication, conversation, converse, dialogue, discussion, dissertation, essay, homily, lecture, oration, sermon, speech, talk, treatise.
v confer, converse, debate, declaim, descant, discuss, dissent, dissertate, expatiate, jaw, lecture, talk.

discourteous adj abrupt, bad-mannered, boorish, brusque, curt, disrespectful, ill-bred, ill-mannered, impolite, insolent, offhand, rude, slighting, unceremonious, uncivil, uncourteous, ungracious, unmannerly. **antonyms** polite, respectful.

discourtesy n affront, bad manners, disrespectfulness, ill-breeding, impertinence, impoliteness, incivility, indecorousness, indecorum, insolence, insult, rebuff, rudeness, slight, snub, ungraciousness, unmannerliness. **antonym** politeness.

discover v ascertain, conceive, contrive, descry, design, detect, determine, devise, dig up, discern, disclose, espy, find, invent, learn, light on, locate, notice, originate, perceive, pioneer, realise, recognise, reveal, see, spot, suss out, uncover, unearth. **antonyms** conceal, hide.

discovery n ascertainment, breakthrough, coup, detection, disclosure, espial, exploration, find, finding, innovation, introduction, invention, locating, location, origination, revelation, uncovering. **antonym** concealment.

discredit v blame, censure, challenge, defame, degrade, deny, disbelieve, discount, disgrace, dishonour, disparage, dispute, distrust, doubt, explode, mistrust, question, reproach, slander, slur, smear, vilify. **antonyms** believe, credit.
n aspersion, blame, censure, disgrace, dishonour, disrepute, distrust, doubt, ignominy, ill-repute, imputation, mistrust, odium, opprobrium, question, reproach, scandal, scepticism, shame, slur, smear, stigma, suspicion. **antonym** credit.

discreditable adj blameworthy, degrading, disgraceful, dishonourable, humiliating, ignoble, ignominious, improper, infamous, reprehensible, scandalous, shameful, unbecoming, unprincipled, unworthy. **antonym** worthy.

discreet adj careful, cautious, circumspect, considerate, delicate, diplomatic, discerning, guarded, judicious, politic, prudent, reserved, sagacious, sensible, softly-softly, tactful, wary. **antonyms** careless, indiscreet, tactless.

discrepancy n conflict, contrariety, difference, disagreement, discordance, disparity, dissimilarity, dissonance, divergence, imparity, incongruity, inconsistency, inequality, variance, variation.

discrete adj detached, disconnected, discontinuous, disjoined, distinct, individual, separate, unattached.

discretion n acumen, care, carefulness, caution, choice, circumspection, consideration, diplomacy, discernment, disposition, heedfulness, inclination, judgement, judiciousness, liking, maturity, mind, option, pleasure, predilection, preference, prudence, responsibility, sagacity, tact, volition, wariness, will, wisdom, wish. **antonym** indiscretion.

discriminate¹ v assess, differentiate, discern, distinguish, evaluate, make a distinction, segregate, separate, sift, tell apart. **antonyms** confound, confuse.

discriminate² (against) v be biased, be prejudiced, disfavour, victimise.

discriminating adj acute, astute, critical, cultivated, discerning, discriminant, fastidious, nasute, particular, perceptive, selective, sensitive, tasteful.

discrimination¹ n bias, bigotry, favouritism, inequity, intolerance, prejudice, unfairness.

discrimination² n acumen, acuteness, discernment, insight, judgement, keenness, penetration, perception, percipience, refinement, sagacity, subtlety, taste.

discriminatory¹ adj biased, favouring, inequitable, loaded, one-sided, partial, partisan, preferential, prejudiced, prejudicial, unfair, unjust, weighted. **antonyms** fair, impartial, unbiased.

discriminatory² adj analytical, astute, differentiating, discerning, discriminating, perceptive, perspicacious.

discursive adj circuitous, desultory, diffuse, digressive, erratic, long-winded, loose, meandering, prolix, rambling, wide-ranging. **antonyms** brief, short.

discuss v argue, confer, consider, consult, converse, debate, deliberate, examine, lay heads together, rap.

discussion n analysis, argument, colloquy, confabulation, conference, consideration, consultation, conversation, debate, deliberation, dialogue, discourse, examination, exchange, moot, rap, review, scrutiny, seminar, symposium, talk-in.

disdain v belittle, contemn, deride, despise, disavow, disregard, pooh-pooh, rebuff, reject, scorn, slight, sneer at, spurn, undervalue. **antonyms** admire, respect.

n arrogance, contempt, deprecation, derision, dislike, haughtiness, hauteur, imperiousness, indifference, scorn, sneering, snobbishness, superciliousness. **antonyms** admiration, respect.

disdainful adj aloof, arrogant, contemptuous, derisive, haughty, hoity-toity, imperious, insolent, proud, scornful, sneering, supercilious, superior, uppish. **antonyms** admiring, respectful.

disease n affection, affliction, ailment, blight, cancer, canker, complaint, condition, contagion, contamination, disorder, distemper, epidemic, ill-health, illness, indisposition, infection, infirmity, lurgy, malady, malaise, pest, plague, sickness, upset. **antonym** health.

diseased adj ailing, contaminated, distemperate, infected, poisoned, rotten, sick, sickly, tainted, unhealthy, unsound, unwell, unwholesome. **antonym** healthy.

disembodied adj bodiless, ghostly, immaterial, incorporeal, intangible, phantom, spectral, spiritual.

disenchanted adj blasé, cynical, disappointed, disillusioned, fed up, indifferent, jaundiced, scunnered, soured, undeceived.

disengage v detach, disconnect, disentangle, disjoin, disunite, divide, ease, extricate, free, liberate, loosen, release, separate, undo, unloose, untie, untwine, withdraw. **antonyms** attach, connect.

disentangle v clarify, detach, disconnect, disengage, extricate, free, loose, ravel out, resolve, separate, sever, simplify, unfold, unravel, unsnarl, untangle, untwine, untwist.

disfavour n disapprobation, disapproval, discredit, disgrace, disgust, dislike, displeasure, unpopularity. **antonym** favour.

disfigure v blemish, damage, deface, deform, disfeature, distort, injure, maim, mar, mutilate, scar, spoil, uglify. **antonym** adorn.

disgorge *v* belch, discharge, effuse, eject, empty, expel, regurgitate, relinquish, renounce, spew, spout, surrender, throw up, vomit.

disgrace *n* aspersion, baseness, blemish, blot, contempt, defamation, degradation, discredit, disesteem, disfavour, dishonour, disrepute, dog-house, ignominy, infamy, obloquy, odium, opprobrium, reproach, scandal, shame, slur, stain, stigma. *antonyms* esteem, honour, respect.
v abase, defame, degrade, discredit, disfavour, dishonour, disparage, humiliate, reproach, scandalise, shame, slur, stain, stigmatise, sully, taint. *antonyms* honour, respect.

disgraced *adj* branded, degraded, discredited, dishonoured, humiliated, in the doghouse, stigmatised. *antonyms* honoured, respected.

disgraceful *adj* appalling, blameworthy, contemptible, degrading, detestable, discreditable, dishonourable, disreputable, dreadful, ignominious, infamous, low, mean, opprobrious, scandalous, shameful, shocking, unworthy. *antonyms* honourable, respectable.

disgruntled *adj* annoyed, brassed off, browned off, cheesed off, discontented, displeased, dissatisfied, grumpy, irritated, malcontent, peeved, peevish, petulant, put out, scunnered, sulky, sullen, testy, vexed. *antonyms* pleased, satisfied.

disguise *v* camouflage, cloak, conceal, cover, deceive, dissemble, dissimulate, dress up, explain away, fake, falsify, fudge, hide, mask, misrepresent, screen, secrete, shroud, veil. *antonyms* expose, reveal, uncover.
n camouflage, cloak, concealment, costume, cover, couverture, deception, dissimulation, façade, front, get-up, mask, masquerade, pretence, screen, semblance, travesty, trickery, veil, veneer, visor.

disguised *adj* camouflaged, cloaked, covert, fake, false, feigned, incognito, made up, masked, undercover, unrecognisable.

disgust *v* displease, nauseate, offend, outrage, put off, repel, revolt, scandalise, scunner, sicken. *antonyms* delight, gratify, tempt.
n abhorrence, abomination, antipathy, aversion, detestation, dislike, disrelish, distaste, hatefulness, hatred, loathing, nausea, odium, repugnance, repulsion, revulsion. *antonyms* admiration, liking.

disgusted *adj* appalled, nauseated, offended, outraged, repelled, repulsed, scandalised, scunnered, sick (and tired), sickened. *antonyms* attracted, delighted.

disgusting *adj* abominable, detestable, distasteful, foul, gross, hateful, loathsome, nasty, nauseating, nauseous, objectionable, obnoxious, obscene, odious, offensive, repellent, repugnant, revolting, shameless, sickening, stinking, unappetising, vile, vulgar. *antonyms* attractive, delightful, pleasant.

dishearten *v* cast down, crush, damp, dampen, dash, daunt, deject, depress, deter, discourage, dismay, dispirit, frighten, weary. *antonyms* encourage, hearten.

disheartened *adj* crestfallen, crushed, daunted, dejected, depressed, disappointed, discouraged, dismayed, dispirited, downcast, downhearted, frightened, weary. *antonyms* encouraged, heartened.

dishevelled *adj* bedraggled, blowsy, disarranged, disordered, frowsy, messy, ruffled, rumpled, slovenly, tousled, uncombed, unkempt, untidy. *antonyms* neat, spruce, tidy.

dishonest *adj* bent, cheating, corrupt, crafty, crooked, deceitful, deceiving, deceptive, designing, disreputable, double-dealing, false, fraudulent, guileful, immoral, lying, mendacious, perfidious, shady, snide, swindling, treacherous, unethical, unfair, unprincipled, unscrupulous, untrustworthy, untruthful, wrongful. *antonyms* fair, honest, scrupulous, trustworthy.

dishonesty *n* cheating, chicanery, corruption, craft, criminality, crookedness, deceit, duplicity, falsehood, falsity, fraud, fraudulence, immorality, improbity, insincerity, mendacity, perfidy, stealing, treachery, trickery, unscrupulousness, wiliness. *antonyms* honesty, truthfulness.

dishonour *v* abase, blacken, corrupt, debase, debauch, defame, defile, deflower, degrade, demean, discredit, disgrace, disparage, pollute, rape, ravish, seduce, shame, sully.
n abasement, abuse, affront, aspersion, degradation, discourtesy, discredit, disfavour, disgrace, disrepute, ignominy, imputation, indignity, infamy, insult, obloquy, odium, offence, opprobrium,

outrage, reproach, scandal, shame, slight, slur.

dishonourable *adj* base, blackguardly, contemptible, corrupt, despicable, discreditable, disgraceful, disreputable, ignoble, ignominious, infamous, scandalous, shameful, shameless, treacherous, unethical, unprincipled, unscrupulous, untrustworthy, unworthy.

disillusioned *adj* disabused, disappointed, disenchanted, enlightened, indifferent, undeceived, unenthusiastic.

disincentive *n* barrier, constraint, damper, deterrent, discouragement, dissuasion, hindrance, impediment, obstacle, repellent, restriction, turn-off. **antonym** encouragement.

disinclined *adj* antipathetic, averse, hesitant, indisposed, loath, opposed, reluctant, resistant, undisposed, unenthusiastic, unwilling. **antonym** willing.

disingenuous *adj* artful, cunning, deceitful, designing, devious, dishonest, duplicitous, guileful, insidious, insincere, shifty, two-faced, wily. **antonyms** artless, frank, ingenuous, naive.

disintegrate *v* break up, crumble, decompose, disunite, fall apart, moulder, rot, separate, shatter, splinter. **antonyms** combine, merge, unite.

disinterest *n* candidness, detachment, disinterestedness, dispassionateness, equitableness, equity, fairness, impartiality, justice, neutrality, unbiasedness.

disinterested *adj* candid, detached, dispassionate, equitable, even-handed, impartial, impersonal, neutral, open-minded, unbiased, uninvolved, unprejudiced, unselfish. **antonyms** biased, concerned, prejudiced.

disjointed *adj* aimless, broken, confused, disarticulated, disconnected, dislocated, disordered, displaced, disunited, divided, fitful, incoherent, loose, rambling, separated, spasmodic, split, unconnected, unjointed. **antonym** coherent.

dislike *n* animosity, animus, antagonism, antipathy, aversion, detestation, disapprobation, disapproval, disgust, disinclination, displeasure, distaste, enmity, hatred, hostility, loathing, repugnance. **antonyms** attachment, liking, predilection.
v abhor, abominate, despise, detest, disapprove, disfavour, hate, loathe, scorn, shun. **antonyms** favour, prefer.

dislocate *v* derange, disarray, disarticulate, disconnect, disengage, disjoint, disorder, displace, disrupt, disturb, disunite, misplace, shift, unhinge.

dislocation *n* derangement, disarray, disarticulation, disconnection, disengagement, disorder, disorganisation, disruption, disturbance, misarrangement, unhinging. **antonym** order.

disloyal *adj* disaffected, faithless, false, perfidious, seditious, subversive, traitorous, treacherous, treasonable, two-faced, unfaithful, unpatriotic, untrustworthy.

disloyalty *n* betrayal, double-dealing, falseness, falsity, inconstancy, infidelity, lese-majesty, perfidy, sedition, treachery, treason, unfaithfulness.

dismal *adj* black, bleak, cheerless, dark, depressing, despondent, discouraging, doleful, dolorous, dreary, dreich, forlorn, funereal, ghostful, gloomy, gruesome, hopeless, incompetent, inept, lonesome, long-faced, lowering, low-spirited, lugubrious, melancholy, poor, sad, sepulchral, sombre, sorrowful, stupid, thick, useless. **antonyms** bright, cheerful.

dismantle *v* demolish, disassemble, dismount, raze, strike, strip, unrig. **antonym** assemble.

dismay *v* alarm, appal, consternate, daunt, depress, disappoint, disconcert, discourage, dishearten, disillusion, dispirit, distress, frighten, horrify, paralyse, put off, scare, terrify, unnerve, unsettle. **antonym** encourage.
n agitation, alarm, anxiety, apprehension, consternation, disappointment, distress, dread, fear, fright, funk, horror, panic, terror, trepidation, upset. **antonyms** boldness, encouragement.

dismiss *v* axe, banish, bounce, bowler-hat, cashier, chassé, chuck, disband, discharge, discount, dispel, disperse, disregard, dissolve, drop, fire, free, give (someone) the push, lay off, let go, oust, pooh-pooh, reject, release, relegate, remove, repudiate, sack, send packing, set aside, shelve, spurn. **antonyms** accept, appoint.

dismissal *n* adjournment, cards, congé, dear John letter, discharge, dismission, end, expulsion, marching orders, notice, release, removal, the boot, the bum's rush, the elbow, the mitten, the push, sack. **antonym** appointment.

dismissive *adj* contemptuous,

disdainful, off-hand, scornful, sneering. **antonyms** concerned, interested.

disobedient *adj* contrary, defiant, disorderly, insubordinate, intractable, mischievous, naughty, obstreperous, refractory, unruly, wayward, wilful.

disobey *v* contravene, defy, disregard, flout, ignore, infringe, overstep, rebel, resist, transgress, violate.

disorder *n* affliction, ailment, brawl, chaos, clamour, clutter, commotion, complaint, confusion, derangement, disarray, disease, disorderliness, disorganisation, disturbance, fight, fracas, hubbub, hullabaloo, illness, indisposition, irregularity, jumble, malady, mess, misarrangement, misarray, misorder, misrule, muddle, quarrel, riot, rumpus, shambles, sickness, tumult, untidiness, uproar.

v clutter, confound, confuse, derange, disarrange, discompose, disorganise, disturb, jumble, mess up, mix up, muddle, scatter, unsettle, upset. **antonyms** arrange, organise.

disordered *adj* confused, deranged, disarranged, dislocated, disorganised, displaced, higgledy-piggledy, jumbled, out of kilter, untidy. **antonyms** tidy.

disorderly *adj* chaotic, confused, disordinate, disorganised, disruptive, higgledy-piggledy, indiscriminate, irregular, jumbled, lawless, messy, obstreperous, rebellious, refractory, riotous, rowdy, shambolic, stormy, tumultuous, turbulent, undisciplined, ungovernable, unlawful, unmanageable, unruly, unsystematic, untidy. **antonyms** tidy, well-behaved.

disorganise *v* break up, confuse, derange, destroy, disarrange, discompose, disorder, disrupt, disturb, jumble, muddle, play havoc with, play hell with, unsettle, upset.

disorganised *adj* chaotic, confused, disordered, haphazard, jumbled, muddled, shambolic, shuffled, topsy-turvy, unmethodical, unorganised, unregulated, unsifted, unsorted, unstructured, unsystematic, unsystematised. **antonym** tidy.

disorientate *v* confuse, dislocate, disorient, faze, mislead, muddle, perplex, puzzle, upset.

disorientated *adj* adrift, astray, at sea, bewildered, confused, disoriented, lost, mixed up, muddled, perplexed, puzzled, unbalanced, unsettled, upset.

disown *v* abandon, abnegate, cast off, deny, disallow, disavow, disclaim, reject, renounce, repudiate. **antonym** accept.

disparage *v* belittle, criticise, decry, defame, degrade, denigrate, deprecate, depreciate, deride, derogate, detract from, discredit, disdain, dishonour, dismiss, malign, minimise, ridicule, run down, scorn, slander, traduce, underestimate, underrate, undervalue, vilify. **antonym** praise.

disparate *adj* contrary, contrasting, different, discordant, discrepant, dissimilar, distinct, diverse, unequal, unlike. **antonyms** equal, similar.

dispassionate *adj* calm, candid, collected, composed, cool, detached, disinterested, fair, impartial, impersonal, imperturbable, indifferent, moderate, neutral, objective, quiet, serene, sober, temperate, unbiased, unemotional, unexcitable, unexcited, uninvolved, unmoved, unprejudiced, unruffled. **antonyms** biased, emotional.

dispatch[1], **despatch** *v* accelerate, conclude, discharge, dismiss, dispose of, expedite, finish, hasten, hurry, perform, quicken, settle. **antonym** impede.

n alacrity, celerity, expedition, haste, precipitateness, promptitude, promptness, quickness, rapidity, speed, swiftness. **antonym** slowness.

dispatch[2], **despatch** *v* consign, express, forward, remit, send, transmit.

n account, bulletin, communication, communiqué, document, instruction, item, letter, message, missive, news, piece, report, story.

dispatch[3], **despatch** *v* assassinate, bump off, execute, kill, murder, rub out, slaughter, slay, waste.

dispel *v* allay, banish, discuss, dismiss, disperse, dissipate, drive off, eliminate, expel, melt away, resolve, rout, scatter. **antonym** give rise to.

dispensable *adj* disposable, expendable, inessential, needless, non-essential, replaceable, superfluous, unnecessary, useless. **antonym** indispensable.

dispensation *n* administration, allotment, appointment, apportionment, award, bestowal, conferment, consignment, derogation, direction, disbursement, distribution, dole, economy, endowment, exception, exemption, immunity, indulgence, licence, management, part, permission, plan, portion, privilege, quota, regulation, relaxation, relief, remission, reprieve, scheme, share, stewardship, supplying, system.

dispense v administer, allocate, allot, apply, apportion, assign, deal out, direct, disburse, discharge, distribute, dole out, enforce, except, excuse, execute, exempt, exonerate, implement, let off, measure, mete out, mix, operate, prepare, release, relieve, reprieve, share, supply, undertake.

dispense with abolish, cancel, dispose of, disregard, forgo, ignore, omit, pass over, relinquish, waive. **antonyms** accept, use.

disperse v broadcast, circulate, diffuse, disappear, disband, dismiss, dispel, disseminate, dissipate, dissolve, distribute, drive off, evanesce, melt away, rout, scatter, separate, spread, strew, vanish. **antonym** gather.

dispirit v damp, dampen, dash, deject, depress, deter, discourage, dishearten, put a damper on, sadden. **antonym** encourage.

dispirited adj brassed off, browned off, crestfallen, dejected, depressed, despondent, discouraged, disheartened, down, downcast, fed up, gloomy, glum, low, morose, sad. **antonym** encouraged.

displace v cashier, crowd out, depose, derange, disarrange, discard, discharge, dislocate, dislodge, dismiss, dispossess, disturb, eject, evict, fire, move, oust, remove, replace, sack, shift, succeed, supersede, supplant, transpose, unsettle.

display v betray, boast, demonstrate, disclose, evidence, evince, exhibit, expand, expose, extend, flash, flaunt, flourish, manifest, model, parade, present, reveal, show, show off, showcase, splash, sport, unfold, unfurl, unveil, vaunt, wear. **antonym** hide.
n array, demonstration, étalage, exhibition, exposition, exposure, flourish, manifestation, ostentation, pageant, parade, pomp, presentation, revelation, show, spectacle, splurge.

displease v aggravate, anger, annoy, disgust, dissatisfy, exasperate, gall, get, incense, infuriate, irk, irritate, nettle, offend, peeve, provoke, put out, rile, upset, vex. **antonyms** calm, please.

displeased n aggravated, angry, annoyed, dischuffed, exasperated, furious, irritated, peeved, piqued, put out, upset. **antonym** pleased.

displeasure n anger, annoyance, disapprobation, disapproval, discontent,

disfavour, disgruntlement, dudgeon, huff, indignation, irritation, offence, pique, resentment, vexation, wrath. **antonyms** gratification, pleasure.

disport v amuse, bound, caper, cavort, cheer, delight, divert, entertain, frisk, frolic, gambol, play, revel, romp, sport.

disposal n arrangement, array, assignment, authority, bequest, bestowal, clearance, conduct, consignment, control, conveyance, determination, direction, discarding, discretion, dispensation, disposition, distribution, dumping, ejection, gift, government, jettisoning, management, ordering, position, regulation, relinquishment, removal, responsibility, riddance, scrapping, settlement, transfer. **antonym** provision.

dispose v actuate, adapt, adjust, align, arrange, array, bias, condition, determine, dispone, distribute, fix, group, incline, induce, influence, lay, lead, marshal, motivate, move, order, place, position, predispose, prompt, put, range, rank, regulate, set, settle, situate, stand, tempt.

dispose of bestow, deal with, decide, destroy, determine, discard, dump, end, get rid of, give, jettison, make over, put the kibosh on, scrap, sell, settle, transfer, unload. **antonym** provide.

disposed adj apt, given, inclined, liable, likely, minded, moved, predisposed, prone, ready, subject, willing. **antonym** disinclined.

disposition n adjustment, arrangement, bent, bias, character, classification, constitution, control, direction, disposal, distribution, grain, grouping, habit, inclination, kidney, leaning, make-up, management, nature, ordering, organisation, placement, predisposition, proclivity, proneness, propensity, readiness, regulation, spirit, temper, temperament, tendency.

dispossess v deprive, dislodge, divest, eject, evict, expel, expropriate, oust, rob, strip, unhouse. **antonyms** give, provide.

disproportionate adj excessive, inappropriate, incommensurate, inordinate, unbalanced, unequal, uneven, unreasonable. **antonyms** appropriate, balanced.

disprove v answer, confute, contradict, controvert, discredit, explode, expose, invalidate, negate, rebut, refute. **antonym** prove.

disputable adj arguable, controversial,

debatable, doubtful, dubious, moot, questionable, uncertain. **antonym** indisputable.

disputatious *adj* argumentative, cantankerous, captious, contentious, polemical, pugnacious, quarrelsome.

dispute *v* altercate, argue, brawl, challenge, clash, contend, contest, contradict, controvert, debate, deny, discuss, doubt, gainsay, impugn, oppugn, quarrel, question, spar, squabble, traverse, wrangle. **antonym** agree.
n altercation, argument, brawl, conflict, contention, controversy, debate, disagreement, discord, discussion, dissension, disturbance, feud, friction, quarrel, spar, squabble, strife, wrangle. **antonym** agreement.

disqualify *v* debar, disable, disentitle, incapacitate, invalidate, preclude, prohibit, rule out, unfit. **antonyms** accept, allow.

disquiet *n* alarm, angst, anxiety, concern, distress, disturbance, fear, foreboding, fretfulness, nervousness, restlessness, trouble, uneasiness, unrest, worry. **antonym** calmness.
v agitate, annoy, bother, concern, discompose, distress, disturb, fret, harass, hassle, incommode, perturb, pester, plague, shake, trouble, unsettle, upset, vex, worry. **antonym** calm.

disquieting *adj* annoying, bothersome, disconcerting, distressing, disturbing, irritating, perturbing, troubling, unnerving, unsettling, upsetting, vexing, worrying. **antonym** calming.

disregard *v* brush aside, cold-shoulder, contemn, despise, discount, disdain, disobey, disparage, ignore, laugh off, make light of, neglect, overlook, pass over, pooh-pooh, slight, snub, turn a blind eye to. **antonyms** note, pay attention to.
n brush-off, contempt, disdain, disesteem, disrespect, heedlessness, ignoring, inattention, indifference, neglect, negligence, oversight, slight. **antonym** attention.

disrepair *n* collapse, decay, deterioration, dilapidation, ruin, ruination, shabbiness, unrepair. **antonyms** good repair, restoration.

disreputable *adj* base, contemptible, derogatory, discreditable, disgraceful, dishonourable, disorderly, disrespectable, ignominious, infamous, louche, low, mean, notorious, opprobrious, scandalous, seedy, shady, shameful, shocking, unprincipled. **antonyms** decent, honourable.

disrepute *n* discredit, disesteem, disfavour, disgrace, dishonour, disreputation, ignominy, infamy, obloquy, shame. **antonyms** esteem, honour.

disrespect *n* cheek, contempt, discourtesy, dishonour, disregard, impertinence, impoliteness, impudence, incivility, insolence, irreverence, rudeness, unmannerliness.

disrupt *v* agitate, break into, break up, confuse, derange, dislocate, disorder, disorganise, disturb, interrupt, intrude, obstruct, spoil, unsettle, upset.

disruption *n* burst-up, bust-up, cataclasm, confusion, disarray, disorder, disorderliness, dissolution, disturbance, interference, interruption, stoppage, upheaval.

disruptive *adj* boisterous, disorderly, distracting, disturbing, obstreperous, troublesome, turbulent, undisciplined, unruly, unsettling, upsetting. **antonym** well-behaved.

dissatisfaction *n* annoyance, chagrin, disappointment, discomfort, discontent, dislike, dismay, displeasure, distress, exasperation, frustration, irritation, non-fulfilment, regret, resentment, unfulfilment, unhappiness. **antonym** fulfilment.

dissatisfied *adj* disappointed, discontented, disgruntled, displeased, fed up, frustrated, unfulfilled, unhappy. **antonym** fulfilled.

dissect *v* analyse, anatomise, break down, dismember, examine, explore, inspect, investigate, pore over, scrutinise, study.

dissection *n* analysis, anatomisation, autopsy, breakdown, dismemberment, examination, inspection, investigation, scrutiny, study.

dissemble *v* affect, camouflage, cloak, conceal, counterfeit, cover up, disguise, dissimulate, fake, falsify, feign, hide, mask, play possum, pretend, sham, simulate. **antonym** admit.

disseminate *v* broadcast, circulate, diffuse, disperse, dissipate, distribute, evangelise, proclaim, promulgate, propagate, publicise, publish, scatter, sow, spread.

dissension *n* conflict, contention, difference, disagreement, discord, dispute, dissent, friction, quarrel, strife, variance. **antonyms** agreement, peace.

dissent v decline, differ, disagree, disconsent, object, protest, quibble, refuse. *antonyms* agree, consent.
n difference, disagreement, discord, dissension, nonconformity, objection, opposition, quibble, refusal, resistance. *antonym* agreement.

dissertation n critique, discourse, essay, exposition, monograph, paper, thesis, treatise.

disservice n bad turn, disfavour, harm, injury, injustice, unkindness, wrong. *antonym* favour.

dissident adj differing, disagreeing, discordant, dissenting, heterodox, nonconformist, schismatic. *antonyms* acquiescent, agreeing.
n agitator, dissenter, protestor, rebel, refus(e)nik, schismatic. *antonym* assenter.

dissimilar adj different, disparate, divergent, diverse, heterogeneous, incompatible, mismatched, unlike, unrelated, various. *antonym* compatible.

dissimilarity n difference, discrepancy, disparity, dissimilitude, distinction, divergence, diversity, incomparability, incompatibility, unlikeness, unrelatedness. *antonym* compatibility.

dissimulate v camouflage, cloak, conceal, disguise, dissemble, fake, feign, hide, mask, pretend.

dissimulation n act, affectation, concealment, deceit, deception, dissembling, double-dealing, duplicity, feigning, hypocrisy, play-acting, pretence, sham, wile. *antonym* openness.

dissipate v burn up, consume, deplete, disappear, dispel, disperse, dissolve, evaporate, expend, fritter away, lavish, scatter, spend, squander, vanish, waste. *antonym* accumulate.

dissipated adj abandoned, consumed, debauched, destroyed, dissolute, exhausted, intemperate, profligate, rakish, scattered, squandered, wasted. *antonyms* conserved, virtuous.

dissipation n abandonment, debauchery, disappearance, disintegration, dispersion, dissemination, dissoluteness, dissolution, excess, extravagance, intemperance, prodigality, profligacy, rakishness, scattering, squandering, vanishing, wantonness, waste. *antonyms* conservation, virtue.

dissociate v break off, detach, disband, disconnect, disrupt, distance, divorce, isolate, leave, quit, segregate, separate. *antonyms* attach, share.

dissociation n break, detachment, disconnection, disengagement, dissevering, distancing, disunion, division, divorce, isolation, segregation, separation, severance, severing, split. *antonyms* association, union.

dissolute adj abandoned, corrupt, debauched, degenerate, depraved, dissipated, immoral, lax, lewd, libertine, licentious, loose, profligate, rakish, unrestrained, vicious, wanton, wide, wild. *antonym* virtuous.

dissoluteness n abandon, corruption, debauchery, degeneracy, depravity, dissipation, immorality, lewdness, licence, licentiousness, profligacy, vice, wantonness. *antonym* virtue.

dissolution n adjournment, break-up, conclusion, death, decay, decomposition, demise, destruction, disappearance, disbandment, discontinuation, disintegration, dismissal, dispersal, disruption, dissembly, division, divorce, end, ending, evaporation, extinction, finish, liquefaction, melting, overthrow, parting, resolution, ruin, separation, solution, suspension, termination. *antonym* unification.

dissolve v break up, crumble, decompose, destroy, diffuse, disappear, discontinue, disintegrate, dismiss, disorganise, disperse, dissipate, disunite, divorce, dwindle, end, evanesce, evaporate, fade, flux, fuse, liquefy, loose, melt, overthrow, perish, ruin, separate, sever, soften, suspend, terminate, thaw, vanish, wind up.

dissonant adj anomalous, cacophonous, different, differing, disagreeing, discordant, discrepant, disharmonious, grating, harsh, incompatible, incongruous, inconsistent, inharmonious, irreconcilable, irregular, jangling, jarring, raucous, strident, tuneless, unmelodious. *antonyms* compatible, harmonious.

dissuade v dehort, deter, discourage, disincline, divert, expostulate, put off, remonstrate, warn. *antonym* persuade.

dissuasion n caution, determent, deterrence, deterring, discouragement, expostulation, remonstrance, remonstration, setback. *antonym* persuasion.

distance n absence, aloofness, coldness, coolness, extent, frigidity, gap, interval, isolation, lapse, length, range, reach, remoteness, remove, reserve

distant *adj* abroad, afar, aloof, apart, ceremonious, cold, cool, disparate, dispersed, distinct, faint, far, faraway, far-flung, far-off, formal, haughty, indirect, indistinct, isolated, obscure, outlying, out-of-the-way, remote, removed, reserved, restrained, reticent, scattered, separate, slight, stand-offish, stiff, unapproachable, uncertain, unfriendly, withdrawn. **antonyms** close, friendly.

distaste *n* abhorrence, antipathy, aversion, detestation, discontent, discontentment, disfavour, disgust, disinclination, dislike, displeasure, disrelish, dissatisfaction, horror, loathing, repugnance, revulsion. **antonym** inclination.

distasteful *adj* abhorrent, aversive, disagreeable, displeasing, dissatisfying, loathsome, nasty, nauseous, objectionable, obnoxious, offensive, repugnant, repulsive, undesirable, uninviting, unpalatable, unpleasant, unsavoury. **antonym** pleasing.

distended *adj* bloated, dilated, enlarged, expanded, inflated, puffed-out, puffy, stretched, swollen, varicose. **antonym** deflated.

distinct *adj* apparent, clear, clear-cut, decided, definite, detached, different, discrete, dissimilar, evident, individual, lucid, manifest, marked, noticeable, obvious, palpable, patent, plain, recognisable, separate, several, sharp, unambiguous, unconnected, unmistakable, well-defined. **antonyms** fuzzy, hazy, indistinct.

distinction¹ *n* characteristic, contradistinction, contrast, difference, differential, differentiation, discernment, discrimination, dissimilarity, distinctiveness, division, feature, individuality, mark, nuance, particularity, peculiarity, penetration, perception, quality, separation.

distinction² *n* account, celebrity, consequence, credit, eminence, excellence, fame, glory, greatness, honour, importance, merit, name, note, prestige, prominence, quality, rank, renown, reputation, repute, significance, superiority, worth. **antonym** insignificance.

distinctive *adj* characteristic, different, discriminative, discriminatory, distinguishing, extraordinary, idiosyncratic, individual, inimitable, original, peculiar, singular, special, typical, uncommon, unique. **antonym** common.

distinctness *n* clarity, clearness, difference, discreteness, disparateness, dissimilarity, dissociation, distinctiveness, individuality, lucidity, obviousness, plainness, sharpness, vividness. **antonyms** fuzziness, haziness, indistinctness.

distinguish *v* ascertain, categorise, celebrate, characterise, classify, decide, determine, differentiate, dignify, discern, discriminate, honour, immortalise, individualise, judge, know, make out, mark, perceive, pick out, recognise, see, separate, tell, tell apart.

distinguishable *adj* appreciable, clear, conspicuous, discernible, evident, manifest, noticeable, observable, obvious, perceptible, plain, recognisable.

distinguished *adj* acclaimed, celebrated, conspicuous, eminent, extraordinary, famed, famous, illustrious, marked, notable, noted, outstanding, renowned, signal, striking, well-known. **antonyms** insignificant, ordinary.

distinguishing *adj* characteristic, different, differentiating, distinctive, individual, individualistic, marked, peculiar, typical, unique.

distort *v* bend, bias, buckle, colour, contort, deform, disfigure, falsify, garble, miscolour, misrepresent, misshape, pervert, slant, torture, twist, warp, wrench, wrest, wring.

distorted *adj* awry, biased, deformed, false, misshapen, skewed, twisted, warped, wry. **antonym** straight.

distortion *n* bend, bias, buckle, colouring, contortion, crookedness, deformity, falsification, malformation, misrepresentation, obliquity, perversion, skew, slant, twist, warp.

distract *v* agitate, amuse, beguile, bewilder, confound, confuse, derange, discompose, disconcert, disturb, divert, engross, entertain, faze, harass, madden, occupy, perplex, puzzle, sidetrack, torment, trouble.

distracted *adj* agitated, bemused, bewildered, confounded, confused, crazy, deranged, distraught, flustered, frantic, frenzied, grief-stricken, harassed, hassled, insane, mad, maddened, overwrought, perplexed, puzzled, raving, troubled, wild, worked up, wrought up. **antonyms** calm, untroubled.

distracting *adj* annoying, bewildering,

confusing, disconcerting, disturbing, irritating, off-putting, perturbing.

distraction *n* aberration, abstraction, agitation, alienation, amusement, beguilement, bewilderment, commotion, confusion, delirium, derangement, desperation, discord, disorder, disturbance, diversion, divertissement, entertainment, frenzy, hallucination, harassment, incoherence, insanity, interference, interruption, mania, pastime, recreation.

distraught *adj* agitated, anxious, beside oneself, crazed, crazy, distracted, distressed, frantic, hysterical, mad, overwrought, raving, wild, worked up, wrought up. *antonyms* calm, untroubled.

distress *n* adversity, affliction, agony, anguish, anxiety, calamity, depravation, desolation, destitution, difficulties, discomfort, grief, hardship, heartache, indigence, misery, misfortune, need, pain, poverty, privation, sadness, sorrow, strait(s), suffering, torment, torture, trial, trouble, woe, worry, wretchedness. *antonyms* comfort, ease, security.

v afflict, agonise, bother, constrain, cut up, disturb, grieve, harass, harrow, pain, perplex, sadden, straiten, torment, trouble, upset, worry, wound. *antonyms* assist, comfort.

distressed *adj* afflicted, agitated, anxious, cut up, destitute, distracted, distraught, indigent, needy, poor, poverty-stricken, saddened, straitened, tormented, troubled, upset, worried, wretched. *antonyms* calm, untroubled.

distressing *adj* affecting, afflicting, afflictive, disquieting, distressful, disturbing, grievous, heart-breaking, hurtful, lamentable, nerve-racking, painful, perturbing, sad, trying, unnerving, upsetting, worrying. *antonyms* assuaging, pleasant.

distribute *v* administer, allocate, allot, apportion, arrange, assign, assort, bestow, carve up, categorise, circulate, class, classify, convey, deal, deliver, diffuse, dish out, dispense, disperse, dispose, disseminate, divide, dole, file, give, group, hand out, mete, scatter, share, spread, strew. *antonyms* collect, gather in.

distribution *n* allocation, allotment, apportionment, arrangement, assortment, circulation, classification, dealing, delivery, diffusion, dispensation, dispersal, dispersion, dissemination, division, handling, location, mailing, marketing, partition, placement, propagation, scattering, sharing, spreading, trading, transport, transportation. *antonyms* collection, gathering.

district *n* area, canton, community, locale, locality, neighbourhood, parish, precinct, quarter, region, sector, vicinity, ward.

distrust *v* disbelieve, discredit, doubt, mistrust, question, suspect.

n disbelief, doubt, misgiving, mistrust, qualm, question, scepticism, suspicion, wariness.

distrustful *adj* chary, cynical, disbelieving, distrusting, doubtful, doubting, dubious, mistrustful, sceptical, suspicious, uneasy, wary. *antonym* unsuspecting.

disturb *v* affray, agitate, alarm, annoy, bother, confound, confuse, derange, disarrange, discompose, disorder, disorganise, disrupt, distract, distress, excite, fluster, harass, interrupt, muddle, perturb, pester, rouse, ruffle, shake, startle, trouble, unsettle, upset, worry. *antonyms* calm, quiet, reassure.

disturbance *n* agitation, annoyance, bother, brawl, breeze, burst-up, bust-up, commotion, confusion, derangement, disorder, distraction, fracas, fray, hindrance, hubbub, interruption, intrusion, kick-up, molestation, perturbation, riot, ruckus, ruction, shake-up, stour, stramash, tumult, turmoil, unrest, upheaval, uproar, upset, upturn. *antonyms* peace, quiet.

disturbed *adj* agitated, anxious, apprehensive, bothered, concerned, confused, disordered, disquieted, flustered, maladjusted, neurotic, troubled, unbalanced, uneasy, upset, worried. *antonyms* calm, sane.

disturbing *adj* agitating, alarming, disconcerting, discouraging, dismaying, disquieting, distressful, distressing, frightening, perturbing, startling, threatening, troubling, unsettling, upsetting, worrying. *antonym* reassuring.

disuse *n* abandonment, decay, idleness, neglect. *antonym* use.

ditch *n* channel, drain, dyke, furrow, gully, ha-ha, level, moat, trench, watercourse.

v abandon, discard, dispose of, drop, dump, jettison, scrap.

dither *v* faff about, falter, footer, haver, hesitate, oscillate, shilly-shally, swither, teeter, vacillate, waver. *antonym* decide.

n bother, flap, fluster, flutter, indecision, panic, pother, stew, tizzy, twitter. **antonym** decision.

dive *v* descend, dip, drop, duck, fall, jump, leap, nose-dive, pitch, plummet, plunge, rush, sound, submerge, swoop.
n dash, header, jump, leap, lunge, nose-dive, plunge, rush, spring, swoop.

diverge *v* bifurcate, branch, conflict, depart, deviate, differ, digress, disagree, dissent, divide, fork, part, radiate, separate, split, spread, stray, vary, wander. **antonyms** agree, come together, join.

divergent *adj* conflicting, deviating, different, differing, disagreeing, dissimilar, diverging, diverse, forking, parting, radial, radiating, separate, spreading, variant, varying. **antonym** convergent.

divers *adj* different, manifold, many, miscellaneous, multifarious, numerous, several, some, sundry, varied, various.

diverse *adj* assorted, different, differing, discrete, disparate, dissimilar, distinct, divergent, diversified, heterogeneous, manifold, many, miscellaneous, multifarious, multiform, numerous, separate, several, some, sundry, unlike, varied, various, varying. **antonym** identical.

diversify *v* alter, assort, branch out, change, expand, mix, spread out, variegate, vary.

diversion *n* alteration, amusement, change, deflection, delight, departure, detour, deviation, digression, disportment, distraction, enjoyment, entertainment, game, gratification, pastime, play, pleasure, recreation, relaxation, sport, variation.

diversity *n* assortment, difference, dissimilarity, distinctiveness, divergence, diverseness, diversification, medley, multifariousness, multiplicity, range, unlikeness, variance, variegation, variety. **antonyms** sameness, similarity.

divert *v* amuse, avert, deflect, delight, detract, distract, entertain, gratify, hive off, recreate, redirect, regale, side-track, switch, tickle. **antonyms** direct, irritate.

divide *v* alienate, allocate, allot, apportion, arrange, bisect, break up, categorise, classify, cleave, cut, deal out, departmentalise, detach, disconnect, dispense, distribute, disunite, divvy, estrange, grade, group, part, partition, portion, segment, segregate, separate,

sever, share, shear, sort, split, subdivide, sunder. **antonyms** collect, gather, join.

divide out allocate, allot, apportion, dole out, measure out, parcel out, share, share out.

dividend *n* bonus, cut, divvy, extra, gain, gratuity, interest, plus, portion, share, surplus, whack.

divine *adj* angelic, beatific, beautiful, blissful, celestial, consecrated, exalted, excellent, glorious, godlike, heavenly, holy, marvellous, mystical, perfect, rapturous, religious, sacred, sanctified, spiritual, splendid, superhuman, superlative, supernatural, supreme, transcendent, transcendental, wonderful.
n churchman, clergyman, cleric, ecclesiastic, minister, parson, pastor, prelate, priest, reverend.
v apprehend, conjecture, deduce, foretell, guess, infer, intuit, perceive, prognosticate, suppose, surmise, suspect, understand.

divinity *n* deity, genius, god, goddess, godhead, godhood, godliness, holiness, sanctity, spirit.

division *n* allotment, apportionment, bisection, border, boundary, branch, breach, category, class, compartment, cutting, demarcation, department, detaching, dichotomy, disagreement, discord, distribution, disunion, divide, divider, dividing, estrangement, feud, group, head, part, partition, portion, rupture, schism, scission, section, sector, segment, separation, sept, sharing, side, split, splitting, stream, variance, ward, watershed, wing. **antonyms** agreement, multiplication, unification.

divorce *n* annulment, breach, break, break-up, decree nisi, dissolution, disunion, rupture, separation, severance, split-up.
v annul, cancel, disconnect, dissever, dissociate, dissolve, disunite, divide, part, separate, sever, split up. **antonyms** marry, unify.

divulge *v* betray, broadcast, communicate, confess, declare, disclose, exhibit, expose, impart, leak, let slip, proclaim, promulgate, publish, reveal, spill, tell, uncover.

divvy *n* bit, cut, dividend, percentage, portion, quota, share, whack.
v apportion, cut, distribute, divide, parcel out, share, share out, split.

dizzy *adj* befuddled, bemused, bewildered, capricious, confused, dazed, dazzled, faint, fickle, flighty, foolish, frivolous, giddy, light-headed, lofty, muddled, reeling, scatter-brained, shaky, staggering, steep, swimming, vertiginous, wobbly, woozy.

do *v* accomplish, achieve, act, adapt, answer, arrange, behave, carry out, cause, cheat, complete, con, conclude, cover, cozen, create, deceive, decipher, decode, defraud, discharge, dupe, effect, end, execute, explore, fare, fix, fleece, give, hoax, implement, make, manage, organise, pass muster, perform, prepare, present, proceed, produce, put on, render, resolve, satisfy, serve, solve, suffice, suit, swindle, tour, transact, translate, transpose, travel, trick, undertake, visit, work, work out.
n affair, event, function, gathering, occasion, party.

do away with abolish, bump off, destroy, discard, discontinue, do in, eliminate, exterminate, get rid of, kill, liquidate, murder, remove, slay.

do for defeat, destroy, finish (off), kill, ruin, shatter, slay.

do in butcher, dispatch, eliminate, execute, exhaust, fag, fatigue, kill, knacker, liquidate, murder, rub out, shatter, slaughter, slay, tire, waste, wear out, weary.

do out of balk, bilk, cheat, con, deprive, diddle, fleece, rook, swindle, trick.

do's and don'ts code, customs, etiquette, instructions, niceties, p's and q's, regulations, rules, standards.

do without abstain from, dispense with, forgo, give up, relinquish, waive.

docile *adj* amenable, biddable, complaisant, compliant, ductile, manageable, obedient, obliging, pliable, pliant, submissive, teachable, tractable, unmurmuring, unprotesting, unquestioning. *antonyms* truculent, unco-operative.

dock[1] *n* boat-yard, harbour, marina, pier, quay, waterfront, wharf.
v anchor, berth, drop anchor, join up, land, link up, moor, put in, rendezvous, tie up, unite.

dock[2] *v* clip, crop, curtail, cut, decrease, deduct, diminish, lessen, reduce, shorten, subtract, truncate, withhold.

docket *n* bill, certificate, chit, chitty, counterfoil, label, receipt, tab, tag, tally, ticket.
v catalogue, file, index, label, mark, register, tab, tag, ticket.

doctor *n* clinician, general practitioner, GP, internist, medic, medical officer, medical practitioner, medico, physician.

v adulterate, alter, botch, change, cobble, cook, cut, dilute, disguise, falsify, fix, fudge, hocus, load, medicate, mend, misrepresent, patch, pervert, repair, spike, tamper with, treat.

doctrinaire *adj* biased, doctrinarian, dogmatic, fanatical, hypothetical, ideological, impractical, inflexible, insistent, opinionated, pedantic, rigid, speculative, theoretical, unrealistic. *antonym* flexible.

doctrine *n* belief, canon, concept, conviction, creed, dogma, ism, opinion, precept, principle, teaching, tenet.

document *n* certificate, deed, form, instrument, paper, parchment, record, report.
v authenticate, back, certify, cite, corroborate, detail, enumerate, instance, list, particularise, prove, substantiate, support, validate, verify.

doddery *adj* aged, decrepit, doddering, faltering, feeble, infirm, rambling, senile, shaky, shambling, tottery, trembly, unsteady, weak. *antonyms* hale, youthful.

dodge *v* avoid, dart, deceive, duck, elude, equivocate, evade, fend off, fudge, hedge, parry, shift, shirk, shuffle, side-step, skive, swerve, swing the lead, trick.
n contrivance, device, feint, machination, manoeuvre, ploy, ruse, scheme, stratagem, subterfuge, trick, wheeze, wile.

dodgy *adj* chancy, dangerous, delicate, dicey, dicky, difficult, problematical, risky, ticklish, tricky, uncertain, unreliable, unsafe. *antonyms* easy, safe.

doff *v* discard, lift, raise, remove, shed, take off, throw off, tip, touch, undress. *antonym* don.

dog *n* beast, bitch, blackguard, bowwow, canine, cur, heel, hound, knave, mongrel, mutt, pooch, pup, puppy, scoundrel, tyke, villain.
v harry, haunt, hound, plague, pursue, shadow, tail, track, trail, trouble, worry.

dogged *adj* determined, firm, indefatigable, indomitable, obstinate, persevering, persistent, pertinacious, relentless, resolute, single-minded, staunch, steadfast, steady, stubborn, tenacious, unflagging, unshakable, unyielding. *antonym* irresolute.

dogma *n* article, article of faith, belief, conviction, credo, creed, doctrine, opinion, precept, principle, teaching, tenet.

dogmatic *adj* affirmative, arbitrary, assertive, authoritative, canonical, categorical, dictatorial, didactic, doctrinaire, doctrinal, downright, emphatic, ex cathedra, imperious, magisterial, obdurate, opinionated, oracular, overbearing, peremptory, pontific(al), positive.

dogsbody *n* doormat, drudge, factotum, galley-slave, lackey, menial, skivvy, slave.

doings *n* actions, activities, acts, adventures, affairs, concerns, dealings, deeds, events, exploits, goings-on, handiwork, happenings, proceedings, transactions.

doldrums *n* apathy, blues, boredom, depression, dullness, dumps, ennui, gloom, inertia, lassitude, listlessness, malaise, stagnation, tedium, torpor.

dole *n* allocation, allotment, allowance, alms, apportionment, benefit, dispensation, dispersal, distribution, division, donation, gift, grant, gratuity, issuance, parcel, pittance, portion, quota, share.
dole out administer, allocate, allot, apportion, assign, deal, dispense, distribute, divide, give, hand out, issue, mete, ration, share.

doleful *adj* blue, cheerless, depressing, dismal, distressing, dolorous, dreary, forlorn, funereal, gloomy, lugubrious, melancholy, mournful, painful, pathetic, pitiful, rueful, sad, sombre, sorrowful, woebegone, woeful, wretched. **antonym** cheerful.

dollop *n* ball, blob, bunch, clump, glob, gob, gobbet, lump.

dolorous *adj* anguished, distressing, doleful, grievous, harrowing, heart-rending, lugubrious, melancholy, miserable, mournful, painful, rueful, sad, sombre, sorrowful, woebegone, woeful, wretched. **antonym** happy.

dolour *n* anguish, distress, grief, heartache, heartbreak, lamentation, misery, mourning, sadness, sorrow, suffering. **antonym** beatitude.

dolt *n* ass, beetlebrain, blockhead, bonehead, chump, clod, clodhopper, clot, dimwit, dope, dullard, dunce, fool, half-wit, idiot, ignoramus, leather-head, mutt, mutton-head, nitwit, nutcase, palooka, sheep's-head, simpleton, turnip.

domain *n* area, authority, bailiwick, business, concern, demesne, department, discipline, dominion, empire, estate, field, jurisdiction, kingdom, lands, orbit, policies, power, province, realm, region, scope, speciality, sphere, sway, territory.

domestic *adj* domesticated, domiciliary, family, home, home-bred, home-loving, homely, house, household, house-trained, housewifely, indigenous, internal, native, pet, private, stay-at-home, tame, trained.
n au pair, char, charwoman, daily, daily help, help, maid, scullery maid, servant, woman.

domesticate *v* acclimatise, accustom, break, familiarise, habituate, house-train, naturalise, tame, train.

domesticated *adj* broken (in), domestic, home-loving, homely, house-proud, housewifely, naturalised, tame, tamed. **antonyms** feral, wild.

domicile *n* abode, dwelling, habitation, home, house, lodging(s), mansion, quarters, residence, residency, settlement.

dominant *adj* ascendant, assertive, authoritative, besetting, chief, commanding, controlling, governing, influential, leading, main, outstanding, paramount, predominant, pre-eminent, presiding, prevailing, prevalent, primary, prime, principal, prominent, ruling, superior, supreme. **antonym** subordinate.

dominate *v* bestride, control, direct, domineer, dwarf, eclipse, govern, have the whip hand, keep under one's thumb, lead, master, monopolise, outshine, overbear, overgang, overlook, overrule, overshadow, predominate, prevail, rule, tyrannise.

domination *n* ascendancy, authority, command, control, despotism, dictatorship, hegemony, influence, leadership, mastery, oppression, power, repression, rule, subjection, subordination, superiority, suppression, supremacy, sway, tyranny.

domineer *v* bluster, boss, browbeat, bully, command, hector, intimidate, jackboot, lord it over, menace, overbear, ride roughshod, rule, swagger, threaten, tyrannise.

domineering *adj* arrogant, authoritarian, autocratic, bossy, coercive, despotic, dictatorial, harsh, high-handed, imperious, iron-handed, magisterial, masterful, oppressive, overbearing, severe, tyrannical. **antonyms** meek, obsequious, servile.

dominion *n* ascendancy, authority, colony, command, control, country, domain, domination, empire, government, hegemony, jurisdiction, kingdom, lordship, mastery, power, province, realm, region, rule, sovereignty, supremacy, sway, territory.

don *v* affect, assume, clothe oneself in, dress in, get into, put on. **antonym** doff.

donate *v* bequeath, bestow, chip in, confer, contribute, cough up, fork out, gift, give, impart, present, proffer, subscribe.

donation *n* alms, benefaction, boon, conferment, contribution, gift, grant, gratuity, largess(e), offering, present, presentation, subscription.

done *adj* acceptable, accomplished, advised, agreed, completed, concluded, consummated, conventional, cooked, cooked to a turn, de rigueur, depleted, drained, ended, executed, exhausted, fatigued, finished, OK, over, perfected, proper, ready, realised, settled, spent, terminated, through, U, used up.

done for beaten, broken, dashed, defeated, destroyed, doomed, finished, foiled, for the high jump, lost, ruined, undone, vanquished, wrecked.

done in all in, bushed, dead, dead beat, dog-tired, exhausted, fagged, jiggered, knackered, pooped, worn to a frazzle, zonked.

donnish *adj* academic, bookish, erudite, learned, scholarly, scholastic.

donor *n* benefactor, contributor, donator, fairy godmother, giver, granter, philanthropist, provider. **antonym** beneficiary.

doom *n* Armageddon, catastrophe, condemnation, death, death-knell, decision, decree, destiny, destruction, Doomsday, downfall, fate, fortune, judgement, Judgement Day, kismet, lot, portion, ruin, sentence, the Last Judgement, verdict.
v condemn, consign, damn, decree, destine, judge, predestine, preordain, sentence, threaten.

doomed *adj* accursed, bedevilled, bewitched, condemned, cursed, fated, fey, hopeless, ill-fated, ill-omened, ill-starred, luckless, star-crossed.

dope[1] *n* details, drugs, facts, gen, hallucinogen, info, information, low-down, narcotic, news, opiate, tip.
v anaesthetise, doctor, drug, inject, load, medicate, narcotise, sedate, stupefy.

dope[2] *n* blockhead, bonehead, clot, dimwit, dolt, dullard, dunce, fool, half-wit, idiot, simpleton.

dop(e)y *adj* dazed, dense, doltish, dozy, drowsy, drugged, dumb, foolish, groggy, hazy, idiotic, muzzy, senseless, silly, simple, slow, stupefied, stupid, thick, woozy. **antonyms** alert, bright.

dormant *adj* asleep, comatose, fallow, hibernating, inactive, inert, inoperative, latent, quiescent, sleeping, sluggish, slumbering, suspended, torpid, undeveloped, unrealised. **antonym** active.

dot *n* atom, circle, dab, decimal point, dit, fleck, full stop, iota, jot, mark, mite, mote, pin-point, point, speck, spot.
v dab, dabble, fleck, punctuate, spot, sprinkle, stipple, stud.

dotage *n* decrepitude, feebleness, imbecility, old age, second childhood, senility, weakness. **antonym** youth.

dote on admire, adore, idolise, indulge, pamper, prize, spoil, treasure.

doting *adj* adoring, devoted, fond, foolish, indulgent, lovesick, soft.

dotty *adj* batty, crazy, eccentric, feeble-minded, loopy, peculiar, potty, touched, weird. **antonym** sensible.

double *adj* bifold, coupled, doubled, dual, duple, duplex, duplicate, paired, twice, twin, twofold.
v duplicate, enlarge, fold, grow, increase, magnify, multiply, repeat.
n clone, copy, counterpart, dead ringer, dead spit, doppelgänger, duplicate, fellow, image, lookalike, mate, replica, ringer, spitting image, twin.

double back backtrack, circle, dodge, evade, loop, retrace one's steps, return, reverse.

double entendre ambiguity, double meaning, innuendo, play on words, pun, suggestiveness, word-play.

double-cross *v* betray, cheat, con, cozen, defraud, hoodwink, mislead, swindle, trick, two-time.

double-dealing *n* bad faith, betrayal, cheating, deceit, deception, dishonesty, duplicity, foul play, hypocrisy, Machiavellianism, mendacity, perfidy, treachery, trickery, two-timing.
adj cheating, crooked, deceitful, dishonest, duplicitous, fraudulent, hypocritical, lying, Machiavellian, perfidious, scheming, shifty, sneaky, swindling, treacherous, tricky, two-faced, two-timing, underhanded, unscrupulous, untrustworthy, wily.

doubt *v* be dubious, be uncertain, demur, discredit, distrust, dubitate, fear, fluctuate, hesitate, misgive, mistrust, query, question, scruple, suspect, vacillate, waver. **antonyms** believe, trust.

n ambiguity, apprehension, arrière pensée, confusion, difficulty, dilemma, disquiet, distrust, dubiety, fear, hesitancy, hesitation, incredulity, indecision, irresolution, misgiving, mistrust, perplexity, problem, qualm, quandary, reservation, scepticism, suspense, suspicion, uncertainty, vacillation. **antonyms** belief, certainty, confidence, trust.

doubtful *adj* ambiguous, debatable, disreputable, distrustful, dubious, equivocal, hazardous, hesitant, hesitating, iffy, inconclusive, indefinite, indeterminate, irresolute, obscure, perplexed, precarious, problematic, problematical, questionable, sceptical, shady, suspect, suspicious, tentative, uncertain, unclear, unconfirmed, unconvinced, undecided, unresolved, unsettled, unsure, vacillating, vague, wavering. **antonyms** certain, definite.

doubtless *adv* apparently, assuredly, certainly, clearly, indisputably, most likely, of course, ostensibly, precisely, presumably, probably, questionless, seemingly, supposedly, surely, truly, undoubtedly, unquestionably, without doubt.

doughty *adj* able, bold, brave, courageous, daring, dauntless, fearless, gallant, game, hardy, heroic, intrepid, redoubtable, resolute, stout-hearted, strong, valiant, valorous. **antonyms** cowardly, weak.

dour *adj* austere, dismal, forbidding, gloomy, grim, hard, humourless, inflexible, morose, obstinate, rigid, rigorous, severe, sour, strict, sullen, uncompromising, unfriendly, unyielding. **antonyms** bright, cheery, easy-going.

douse, dowse *v* blow out, dip, drench, duck, dunk, extinguish, immerge, immerse, plunge, put out, saturate, smother, snuff, soak, souse, steep, submerge.

dowdy *adj* dingy, drab, frumpish, frumpy, ill-dressed, old-fashioned, shabby, slovenly, tacky, tatty, unfashionable, unmodish, unsmart. **antonyms** dressy, smart, spruce.

down[1] *n* bloom, fluff, fuzz, nap, pile, shag, thistledown, wool.

down[2] *v* drink, fell, floor, gulp, knock back, swallow, throw, topple, toss off.

down and out derelict, destitute, impoverished, on one's uppers, penniless, ruined.

down at heel dowdy, impoverished, out at elbows, run-down, seedy, shabby, slipshod, slovenly, slummy, worn.

down in the mouth blue, crestfallen, dejected, depressed, disheartened, dispirited, down, down in the dumps, downcast, in low spirits, in the doldrums, melancholy, sad, unhappy.

down the drain lost, out of the window, ruined, up the spout, wasted.

down with away with, exterminate, get rid of.

down-and-out *n* beggar, bum, derelict, dosser, loser, outcast, pauper, tramp, vagabond, vagrant.

downcast *adj* cheerless, crestfallen, daunted, dejected, depressed, despondent, disappointed, disconsolate, discouraged, disheartened, dismayed, dispirited, down, miserable, sad, unhappy. **antonyms** cheerful, elated, happy.

downfall *n* breakdown, cloudburst, collapse, comedown, come-uppance, débâcle, deluge, descent, destruction, disgrace, downpour, failure, fall, humiliation, overthrow, rainstorm, ruin, undoing, Waterloo.

downgrade *v* belittle, decry, degrade, demote, denigrate, detract from, disparage, humble, lower, reduce in rank, run down. **antonyms** improve, upgrade.

downhearted *adj* blue, crestfallen, dejected, depressed, despondent, discouraged, disheartened, dismayed, dispirited, downcast, gloomy, glum, jaw-fallen, low-spirited, sad, sorrowful, unhappy. **antonyms** cheerful, enthusiastic, happy.

downright *adj* absolute, blatant, blunt, candid, categorical, clear, complete, explicit, forthright, frank, honest, open, out-and-out, outright, outspoken, plain, positive, simple, sincere, straightforward, thoroughgoing, total, undisguised, unequivocal, unqualified, utter, wholesale.

down-to-earth *adj* commonsense, commonsensical, hard-headed, matter-of-fact, mundane, no-nonsense, plain-spoken, practical, realistic, sane, sensible, unsentimental. **antonyms** fantastic, impractical.

down-trodden *adj* abused, afflicted, distressed, exploited, helpless, oppressed, subjugated, subservient, trampled on, trampled underfoot, tyrannised, victimised.

downward *adj* declining, descending, downhill. *antonym* upward.

dowse *see* **douse**.

doze *v* catnap, dover, drop off, drowse, kip, nap, nod, nod off, sleep, slumber, snooze.

n catnap, forty winks, kip, nap, shut-eye, siesta, snooze.

drab *adj* cheerless, colourless, dingy, dismal, dreary, dull, flat, gloomy, grey, lack-lustre, shabby, sombre, uninspired, vapid. *antonym* bright.

draft *v* compose, delineate, design, draw, draw up, formulate, outline, plan, sketch.

n abstract, delineation, outline, plan, protocol, rough, sketch, version.

drag *v* crawl, creep, dawdle, draggle, draw, hale, harl, haul, inch, lag, linger, loiter, lug, pull, shamble, shuffle, straggle, sweep, tow, trail, tug, yank.

n annoyance, bore, bother, brake, nuisance, pain, pest, pill.

drag on, drag out draw out, extend, hang on, lengthen, persist, prolong, protract, spin out.

drag one's feet delay, obstruct, procrastinate, stall.

dragoon *v* browbeat, bully, coact, coerce, compel, constrain, drive, force, impel, intimidate, strong-arm.

drain *v* bleed, consume, deplete, discharge, dissipate, down, draw off, drink up, dry, empty, evacuate, exhaust, finish, flow out, lade, leak, milk, ooze, quaff, remove, sap, seep, strain, swallow, tap, tax, trickle, use up, weary, withdraw. *antonym* fill.

n channel, conduit, depletion, ditch, duct, exhaustion, expenditure, outlet, pipe, reduction, sap, sewer, sink, stank, strain, trench, watercourse, withdrawal.

dram *n* drop, glass, measure, shot, slug, snifter, snort, tot.

drama *n* acting, crisis, dramatics, dramatisation, dramaturgy, excitement, histrionics, melodrama, play, scene, show, spectacle, stage-craft, theatre, theatricals, Thespian art, turmoil.

dramatic *adj* affecting, breathtaking, climactic, effective, electrifying, emotional, exciting, expressive, graphic, impressive, meaningful, melodramatic, moving, powerful, sensational, startling, striking, sudden, suspenseful, tense, theatrical, Thespian, thrilling, vivid. *antonyms* normal, ordinary.

dramatise *v* act, exaggerate, overdo, overstate, play-act, put on, stage.

drape *v* adorn, array, cloak, cover, dangle, droop, drop, enrap, fold, hang, suspend, swathe, vest, wrap.

drastic *adj* desperate, dire, draconian, extreme, far-reaching, forceful, harsh, heroic, radical, severe, strong. *antonym* mild.

draught *n* cup, current, dose, dragging, drawing, drench, drink, flow, haulage, influx, movement, portion, puff, pulling, quantity, traction.

draw¹ *v* allure, attenuate, attract, borrow, breathe in, bring forth, choose, deduce, delineate, depict, derive, design, drag, drain, elicit, elongate, engage, entice, entrain, evoke, extend, extort, extract, get, haul, induce, infer, influence, inhale, inspire, invite, lengthen, make, map out, mark out, outline, paint, pencil, persuade, pick, portray, puff, pull, respire, select, sketch, stretch, suck, take, tow, trace, tug, unsheathe. *antonyms* propel, push.

n appeal, attraction, bait, enticement, interest, lure, pull.

draw back recoil, resile, retract, retreat, shrink, start back, withdraw.

draw lots choose, decide, draw straws, pick, select, spin a coin, toss up.

draw on employ, exploit, extract, make use of, quarry, rely on, take from, use.

draw out drag out, elongate, extend, lengthen, prolong, protract, spin out, stretch, string out. *antonym* curtail.

draw the line lay down the law, object, put one's foot down, restrict, say no, set a limit.

draw up compose, draft, formulate, frame, halt, prepare, pull up, stop, stop short, write out.

draw² *v* be equal, be even, be neck and neck, tie.

n dead-heat, deadlock, impasse, stalemate, tie.

drawback *n* block, defect, deficiency, detriment, difficulty, disability, disadvantage, fault, flaw, fly in the ointment, handicap, hindrance, hitch, impediment, imperfection, nuisance, obstacle, pull-back, snag, stumbling, trouble. *antonym* advantage.

drawing *n* cartoon, delineation, depiction, graphic, illustration, outline, picture, portrait, portrayal, representation, sketch, study.

drawn *adj* fatigued, fraught, haggard,

harassed, harrowed, hassled, pinched, sapped, strained, stressed, taut, tense, tired, worn.

dread v cringe at, fear, flinch, quail, shrink from, shudder, shy, tremble.

n alarm, apprehension, aversion, awe, dismay, disquiet, fear, fright, funk, heebie-jeebies, horror, misgiving, terror, trepidation, worry. **antonyms** confidence, security.

adj alarming, awe-inspiring, awful, dire, dreaded, dreadful, frightening, frightful, ghastly, grisly, gruesome, horrible, terrible, terrifying.

dreadful adj alarming, appalling, awful, dire, distressing, fearful, formidable, frightful, ghastly, grievous, grisly, gruesome, harrowing, hideous, horrendous, horrible, monstrous, shocking, terrible, tragic, tremendous. **antonym** comforting.

dream n ambition, aspiration, beauty, castle in Spain, castle in the air, daydream, delight, delusion, design, desire, fantasy, goal, hallucination, hope, illusion, imagination, joy, marvel, notion, phantasm, pipe-dream, pleasure, reverie, speculation, trance, treasure, vagary, vision, wish.

v conjure, daydream, envisage, fancy, fantasise, hallucinate, imagine, muse, star-gaze, think, visualise.

dream up conceive, concoct, contrive, cook up, create, devise, hatch, imagine, invent, spin, think up.

dreamy absent, abstracted, daydreaming, dreamlike, fanciful, fantastic, faraway, gentle, imaginary, impractical, intangible, misty, musing, pensive, phantasmagorical, preoccupied, quixotic, romantic, speculative, unreal, vague, visionary. **antonyms** down-to-earth, realistic.

dreary adj bleak, boring, cheerless, colourless, comfortless, commonplace, depressing, dismal, doleful, downcast, drab, drear, dreich, dull, forlorn, gloomy, glum, humdrum, joyless, lifeless, lonely, lonesome, melancholy, monotonous, mournful, routine, sad, solitary, sombre, sorrowful, tedious, trite, uneventful, uninteresting, wearisome, wretched. **antonyms** bright, interesting.

dredge v dig up, discover, drag up, draw up, expose, fish up, raise, rake up, scoop up, uncover, unearth.

dregs n canaille, deposit, dross, excrement, faeces, fag-end, grounds, lees, left-overs, outcasts, rabble, residue, riff-raff, scourings, scum, sediment, trash, waste.

drench v douse, drown, duck, flood, imbue, immerse, inundate, saturate, soak, souse, steep, wet.

dress n apparel, attire, clothes, clothing, costume, ensemble, frock, garb, garment, garments, gear, get-up, gown, guise, habit, outfit, rig-out, robe, suit, togs, vestment.

v adjust, adorn, align, arrange, array, attire, bandage, bedeck, bind up, change, clothe, deck, decorate, dispose, don, drape, embellish, fit, furbish, garb, garnish, groom, ornament, plaster, prepare, put on, rig, robe, set, straighten, tend, treat, trim. **antonyms** disrobe, strip, undress.

dress down berate, carpet, castigate, chide, haul over the coals, rebuke, reprimand, reprove, scold, tear off a strip, tell off, upbraid.

dress up adorn, beautify, dandify, deck, disguise, doll up, embellish, gild, improve, play-act, tart up, titivate, trick out.

dressy adj classy, elaborate, elegant, formal, natty, ornate, ritzy, smart, stylish, swanky, swish. **antonyms** dowdy, scruffy.

dribble v drip, drivel, drool, drop, leak, ooze, run, seep, slaver, slobber, sprinkle, trickle.

n drip, droplet, gobbet, leak, seepage, sprinkling, trickle.

drift v accumulate, amass, coast, drive, float, freewheel, gather, meander, pile up, stray, waft, wander.

n accumulation, aim, bank, course, current, design, direction, dune, flow, gist, heap, implication, import, impulse, intention, mass, meaning, mound, movement, object, pile, purport, ridge, rush, scope, significance, sweep, tendency, tenor, thrust, trend.

drifter n hobo, intinerant, rolling stone, rover, tramp, vagabond, vagrant, wanderer.

drill[1] v coach, discipline, exercise, instruct, practise, rehearse, teach, train, tutor.

n coaching, discipline, exercise, instruction, practice, preparation, repetition, training, tuition.

drill[2] v bore, penetrate, perforate, pierce, puncture.

n awl, bit, borer, gimlet.

drink v absorb, bib, booze, carouse, down, drain, dram, gulp, guzzle, hit the bottle, imbibe, indulge, knock back, liquefy, liquor up, partake of, quaff, revel, sip, suck, sup, swallow, swig, swill, tank up, tipple, tope, wassail, water.

n alcohol, ambrosia, beverage, bev(v)y, booze, deoch-an-doris, dose, dram, draught, glass, gulp, hooch, liquid, liquor, noggin, plonk, potion, refreshment, sip, slug, snifter, snort, spirits, stiffener, suck, swallow, swig, taste, the bottle, tipple, tot.

drink in absorb, assimilate, attend to, be absorbed by, ingest, soak up.

drink to pledge (the health of), salute, toast.

drinker *n* alcoholic, bibber, boozer, carouser, dipso, dipsomaniac, drunk, drunkard, guzzler, inebriate, lush, soak, sot, souse, sponge, tippler, toper, wino. *antonyms* abstainer, teetotaller.

drip *v* dribble, drizzle, drop, exude, filter, plop, splash, sprinkle, trickle, weep.

n dribble, dripping, drop, leak, milk-sop, ninny, softy, trickle, weakling, weed, wet.

drive *v* actuate, bear, coerce, compel, constrain, dash, dig, direct, force, goad, guide, hammer, handle, harass, herd, hurl, impel, manage, motivate, motor, oblige, operate, overburden, overwork, plunge, press, prod, propel, push, ram, ride, rush, send, sink, spur, stab, steer, task, tax, thrust, travel, urge.

n action, advance, ambition, appeal, campaign, crusade, determination, effort, energy, enterprise, excursion, get-up-and-go, hurl, initiative, jaunt, journey, motivation, outing, pressure, push, ride, run, spin, surge, trip, turn, vigour, vim, zip.

drive at aim, allude to, get at, imply, indicate, insinuate, intend, intimate, mean, refer to, signify, suggest.

drive up the wall annoy, dement, derange, drive round the bend, exasperate, infuriate, irritate, madden.

drivel *n* blathering, bunkum, eyewash, gibberish, gobbledegook, guff, jive, mumbo-jumbo, nonsense, twaddle, waffle.

driving *adj* compelling, dynamic, energetic, forceful, forthright, galvanic, heavy, sweeping, vigorous, violent.

droll *adj* amusing, clownish, comic, comical, diverting, eccentric, entertaining, farcical, funny, humorous, jocular, laughable, ludicrous, quaint, ridiculous, waggish, whimsical, witty.

drone *v* buzz, chant, drawl, hum, intone, purr, thrum, vibrate, whirr.

n buzz, chant, hum, murmuring, purr, thrum, vibration, whirr, whirring.

drool *v* dote, dribble, drivel, enthuse, fondle, gloat, gush, rave, salivate, slaver, slobber, water at the mouth.

droop *v* bend, dangle, decline, despond, diminish, drop, fade, faint, fall down, falter, flag, hang (down), languish, lose heart, sag, sink, slouch, slump, stoop, wilt, wither. *antonyms* rise, straighten.

drop *n* abyss, bead, bubble, chasm, cut, dab, dash, decline, declivity, decrease, descent, deterioration, downturn, drip, droplet, fall, falling-off, glob, globule, lowering, mouthful, nip, pearl, pinch, plunge, precipice, reduction, shot, sip, slope, slump, spot, taste, tear, tot, trace, trickle.

v abandon, cease, chuck, decline, depress, descend, desert, diminish, discontinue, disown, dive, dribble, drip, droop, fall, forsake, give up, jilt, kick, leave, lower, plummet, plunge, quit, reject, relinquish, remit, renounce, repudiate, sink, stop, terminate, throw over, trickle, tumble. *antonyms* mount, rise.

drop off catnap, decline, decrease, deliver, depreciate, diminish, doze, drowse, dwindle, fall off, have forty winks, leave, lessen, nod, nod off, set down, slacken, snooze. *antonym* increase.

drop out abandon, back out, cry off, forsake, leave, quit, renegue, stop, withdraw.

drop-out *n* Bohemian, dissenter, hippie, non-conformist, rebel, renegade.

droppings *n* dung, excrement, excreta, faeces, guano, manure, ordure, spraint, stools.

dross *n* crust, debris, dregs, impurity, lees, refuse, remains, rubbish, scum, trash, waste.

drought *n* aridity, dearth, deficiency, dehydration, desiccation, drouth, dryness, insufficiency, lack, need, scarcity, shortage, want.

drove *n* collection, company, crowd, drift, flock, gathering, herd, horde, mob, multitude, swarm, throng.

drown *v* deaden, deluge, drench, engulf, extinguish, flood, go under, immerse, inundate, muffle, obliterate, overcome, overpower, overwhelm, silence, sink, stifle, submerge, swallow up, swamp, wipe out.

drowsy *adj* comatose, dazed, dopey, dozy, dreamy, drugged, heavy, lethargic, nodding, restful, sleepy, somnolent, soothing, soporific, tired, torpid. *antonyms* alert, awake.

drubbing *n* beating, clobbering, defeat, flogging, hammering, licking, pounding, pummelling, thrashing, trouncing, walloping, whipping, whitewash.

drudge *n* dogsbody, factotum, galley-slave, hack, lackey, menial, scullion, servant, skivvy, slave, toiler, worker.
v beaver, grind, labour, plod, plug away, slave, toil, work. *antonyms* idle, laze.

drudgery *n* chore, donkey-work, grind, labour, skivvying, slavery, slog, sweat, sweated labour, toil.

drug *n* depressant, dope, medicament, medication, medicine, Mickey, Mickey Finn, narcotic, opiate, poison, potion, remedy, stimulant.
v anaesthetise, deaden, dope, dose, drench, knock out, load, medicate, numb, poison, stupefy, treat.

drug-addict *n* acid head, acidfreak, dope-fiend, head, hop-head, junkie, tripper.

drugged *adj* comatose, doped, dopey, high, looped, spaced out, stoned, stupefied, tripping, zonked.

drum *v* beat, pulsate, rap, reverberate, tap, tattoo, throb, thrum.
drum into drive home, hammer, harp on, instil, reiterate.
drum up attract, canvass, collect, gather, obtain, petition, round up, solicit.

drunk *adj* a peg too low, a sheet (three sheets) in the wind, bevvied, blind, blotto, bottled, canned, cockeyed, corked, drunken, fuddled, half-seas-over, inebriated, intoxicated, legless, liquored, lit up, loaded, lushy, maudlin, merry, mortal, muddled, obfuscated, paralytic, pickled, pie-eyed, pissed, plastered, shickered, sloshed, smashed, soaked, soused, sozzled, stewed, stoned, stotious, tanked up, tiddly, tight, tipsy, up the pole, well-oiled, wet. *antonym* sober.
n boozer, drunkard, inebriate, lush, soak, sot, toper, wino.

drunkard *n* alcoholic, carouser, dipsomaniac, drinker, drunk, lush, soak, sot, souse, sponge, tippler, toper, wino.

drunken *adj* bacchanalian, bibulous, boozing, boozy, crapulent, crapulous, debauched, Dionysiac, dissipated, drunk, intoxicated, orgiastic, riotous, saturnalian, sodden, spongy, tippling, toping, under the influence. *antonym* sober.

dry *adj* arid, barren, boring, cutting, cynical, deadpan, dehydrated, desiccated, dreary, dried up, droll, droughty, drouthy, dull, juiceless, keen, low-key, moistureless, monotonous, parched, plain, sapless, sarcastic, sharp, sly, tedious, thirsty, tiresome, uninteresting, waterless, withered. *antonyms* interesting, sweet, wet.
v dehumidify, dehydrate, desiccate, drain, harden, parch, sear, shrivel, welt, wilt, wither, wizen. *antonyms* soak, wet.

dual *adj* binary, combined, coupled, double, duplex, duplicate, matched, paired, twin, twofold.

dub *v* bestow, call, christen, confer, denominate, designate, entitle, knight, label, name, nickname, style, tag, term.

dubious *adj* ambiguous, debatable, doubtful, equivocal, fishy, hesitant, iffy, indefinite, indeterminate, obscure, problematical, questionable, sceptical, shady, speculative, suspect, suspicious, uncertain, unclear, unconvinced, undecided, undependable, unreliable, unsettled, unsure, untrustworthy, wavering. *antonyms* certain, reliable, trustworthy.

duck[1] *v* avoid, bend, bob, bow, crouch, dodge, drop, escape, evade, lower, shirk, shun, sidestep, squat, stoop.

duck[2] *v* dip, dive, dook, douse, dunk, immerse, plunge, souse, submerge, wet.

duct *n* blood, canal, channel, conduit, funnel, passage, pipe, tube, vessel.

ductile *adj* amenable, biddable, compliant, docile, extensible, flexible, malleable, manageable, manipul(at)able, plastic, pliable, pliant, tractable, yielding. *antonyms* intractable, refractory.

dud *n* bum steer, failure, flop, lemon, stumer, wash-out.
adj broken, bust, duff, failed, inoperative, kaput, valueless, worthless.

due *adj* adequate, ample, appropriate, becoming, deserved, enough, expected, fit, fitting, in arrears, just, justified, mature, merited, obligatory, outstanding, owed, owing, payable, plenty of, proper, requisite, returnable, right, rightful, scheduled, sufficient, suitable, unpaid, well-earned.

n birthright, come-uppance, deserts, merits, prerogative, privilege, right(s).

adv dead, direct, directly, exactly, precisely, straight.

duffer *n* blunderer, bonehead, booby, bungler, clod, clot, dolt, lummox, oaf.

dull *adj* apathetic, blank, blunt, blunted, boring, callous, cloudy, commonplace, corny, dead, dense, depressed, dim, dimwitted, dismal, doltish, drab, dreary, dry, dulled, edgeless, empty, faded, featureless, feeble, flat, gloomy, heavy, humdrum, inactive, indifferent, indistinct, insensible, insensitive, insipid, lack-lustre, leaden, lifeless, listless, monotonous, mopish, muffled, murky, muted, opaque, overcast, passionless, pedestrian, plain, prosaic, run-of-the-mill, slack, sleepy, slow, sluggish, sombre, stodgy, stolid, stultifying, stupid, subdued, sullen, sunless, tame, tedious, thick, tiresome, toneless, torpid, turbid, uneventful, unexciting, unfunny, ungifted, unimaginative, unintelligent, uninteresting, unresponsive, unsharpened, unsympathetic, untalented, vacuous, vapid. *antonyms* alert, bright, clear, exciting, sharp.

v allay, alleviate, assuage, blunt, cloud, dampen, darken, deject, depress, dim, discourage, dishearten, dispirit, fade, lessen, mitigate, moderate, muffle, obscure, palliate, paralyse, relieve, sadden, soften, stain, stupefy, subdue, sully, tarnish. *antonyms* brighten, sharpen, stimulate.

dullard *n* blockhead, bonehead, chump, clod, clot, dimwit, dolt, dope, dummy, dunce, dunderhead, idiot, ignoramus, imbecile, moron, nitwit, numskull, oaf, simpleton. *antonym* brain.

dullness *n* dreariness, dryness, emptiness, flatness, monotony, plainness, slowness, sluggishness, stolidity, stupidity, tedium, torpor, vacuity, vapidity. *antonyms* brightness, clarity, excitement, interest, sharpness.

duly *adv* accordingly, appropriately, befittingly, correctly, decorously, deservedly, fitly, fittingly, properly, punctually, rightfully, suitably, sure enough.

dumb *adj* dense, dimwitted, dull, foolish, inarticulate, mum, mute, silent, soundless, speechless, stupid, thick, tongue-tied, unintelligent, voiceless, wordless. *antonym* intelligent.

dum(b)founded *adj* amazed, astonished, astounded, bewildered, bowled over, breathless, confounded, confused, dumb, flabbergasted, floored, knocked sideways, nonplussed, overcome, overwhelmed, paralysed, speechless, staggered, startled, stunned, taken aback, thrown, thunderstruck.

dummy *n* blockhead, copy, counterfeit, dimwit, dolt, dullard, dunce, duplicate, figure, fool, form, imitation, lay-figure, manikin, mannequin, model, numskull, pacifier, sham, simpleton, substitute, teat.

adj artificial, bogus, dry, fake, false, imitation, mock, phoney, practice, sham, simulated, trial.

dump *v* deposit, discharge, dispose of, ditch, drop, empty out, get rid of, jettison, let fall, offload, park, scrap, throw away, throw down, tip, unload.

n coup, hole, hovel, joint, junk-yard, mess, midden, pigsty, rubbish-heap, rubbish-tip, shack, shanty, slum, tip.

dumpy *adj* chubby, chunky, plump, podgy, pudgy, roly-poly, short, squat, stout, stubby, tubby. *antonyms* rangy, tall.

dunce *n* ass, blockhead, bonehead, dimwit, dolt, donkey, duffer, dullard, dunderhead, goose, half-wit, ignoramus, loon, moron, nincompoop, numskull, simpleton. *antonyms* brain, intellectual.

dung *n* excrement, faeces, guano, manure, ordure, spraint.

dupe *n* fall guy, gull, instrument, mug, pawn, pigeon, puppet, push-over, sap, simpleton, soft mark, stooge, sucker, tool, victim.

v bamboozle, beguile, cheat, con, cozen, deceive, defraud, delude, gammon, grift, gudgeon, gull, hoax, hoodwink, humbug, outwit, pigeon, rip off, swindle, trick.

duplicate *adj* corresponding, identical, matched, matching, twin, twofold.

n carbon copy, copy, facsimile, match, photocopy, Photostat®, replica, reproduction, Xerox®.

v clone, copy, ditto, double, echo, geminate, photocopy, Photostat®, repeat, replicate, reproduce, Xerox®.

duplication *n* clone, cloning, copy(ing), photocopy(ing), repetition, replication, reproduction.

duplicity *n* artifice, chicanery, deceit, deception, dishonesty, dissimulation, double-dealing, falsehood, fraud, guile, hypocrisy, mendacity, perfidy, treachery.

durability *n* constancy, durableness, endurance, imperishability, lastingness longevity, permanence, persistence, stability, strength. **antonyms** fragility, impermanence, weakness.

durable *adj* abiding, constant, dependable, enduring, fast, firm, fixed, hard-wearing, lasting, long-lasting, permanent, persistent, reliable, resistant, sound, stable, strong, sturdy, substantial, tough, unfading. **antonyms** fragile, impermanent, perishable, weak.

duration *n* continuance, continuation, extent, fullness, length, period, perpetuation, span, spell, stretch, term-time. **antonym** shortening.

duress *n* bullying, captivity, coercion, compulsion, confinement, constraint, force, hardship, imprisonment, incarceration, pressure, restraint, threat.

dusk *n* crepuscule, dark, darkness, evening, eventide, gloaming, gloom, murk, nightfall, obscurity, shade, shadowiness, sundown, sunset, twilight. **antonyms** brightness, dawn.

dusky *adj* cloudy, crepuscular, dark, dark-hued, darkish, dim, gloomy, murky, obscure, overcast, sable, shadowy, shady, sooty, swarthy, tenebr(i)ous, twilight, twilit, veiled. **antonyms** bright, light, white.

dust-up *n* argument, argy-bargy, brawl, brush, commotion, conflict, disagreement, disturbance, encounter, fight, fracas, punch-up, quarrel, scrap, scuffle, set-to, skirmish, tussle.

dutiful *adj* acquiescent, complaisant, compliant, conscientious, deferential, devoted, docile, duteous, filial, obedient, punctilious, regardful, respectful, reverential, submissive.

duty *n* allegiance, assignment, business, calling, charge, chore, customs, debt, deference, devoir, due, engagement, excise, function, job, levy, loyalty, mission, obedience, obligation, office, onus, province, respect, responsibility, reverence, role, service, tariff, task, tax, toll, work.

dwarf *n* elf, gnome, goblin, Lilliputian, man(n)ikin, midget, pygmy, Tom Thumb.
adj baby, bonsai, diminutive, dwarfed, dwarfish, Lilliputian, mini, miniature, petite, pint-size(d), pocket, small, tiny, undersized.
v check, dim, diminish, dominate, lower, minimise, overshadow, retard, stunt.

dwell *v* abide, bide, hang out, inhabit, live, lodge, people, populate, quarter, remain, reside, rest, settle, sojourn, stay, stop.
dwell on elaborate, emphasise, expatiate, harp on, harp on about, linger over, mull over. **antonym** pass over.

dwelling *n* abode, domicile, dwelling-house, establishment, habitation, home, house, lodge, lodging, quarters, residence.

dwindle *v* abate, contract, decay, decline, decrease, die, die out, diminish, disappear, ebb, fade, fall, lessen, peter out, pine, shrink, shrivel, sink, subside, tail off, taper off, vanish, wane, waste away, weaken, wither. **antonym** increase.

dye *n* colorant, colour, colouring, grain, pigment, stain, tinge, tint.
v colour, grain, imbue, pigment, stain, tincture, tinge, tint.

dyed-in-the-wool *adj* card-carrying, complete, confirmed, deep-rooted, die-hard, entrenched, established, fixed, hard-core, hardened, inflexible, inveterate, long-standing, settled, unchangeable, uncompromising, unshakable. **antonym** superficial.

dying *adj* at death's door, declining, disappearing, ebbing, expiring, fading, failing, final, going, in extremis, moribund, mortal, not long for this world, obsolescent, passing, perishing, sinking, vanishing. **antonyms** coming, reviving.

dynamic *adj* active, driving, electric, energetic, forceful, go-ahead, go-getting, high-powered, lively, powerful, self-starting, spirited, vigorous, vital, zippy. **antonyms** apathetic, inactive, slow.

dynamism *n* drive, energy, enterprise, forcefulness, get-up-and-go, go, initiative, liveliness, pep, pizzazz, push, vigour, vim, zap, zip. **antonyms** apathy, inactivity, slowness.

dynasty *n* ascendancy, authority, dominion, empire, government, house, regime, rule, sovereignty, succession, sway.

dyspeptic *adj* bad-tempered, crabbed, crabby, crotchety, gloomy, grouchy, peevish, short-tempered, snappish, testy, touchy.

E

each *adv* apiece, individually, per capita, per head, per person, respectively, separately, singly.

eager *adj* agog, anxious, ardent, avid, desirous, earnest, enthusiastic, fervent, fervid, greedy, gung-ho, hot, hungry, impatient, intent, keen, longing, raring, unshrinking, vehement, yearning, zealous. **antonyms** apathetic, unenthusiastic.

eagerly *adv* ardently, avidly, earnestly, enthusiastically, fain, fervently, greedily, intently, keenly, zealously. **antonyms** apathetically, listlessly.

eagerness *n* ardour, avidity, earnestness, enthusiasm, fervency, fervour, greediness, heartiness, hunger, impatience, impetuosity, intentness, keenness, longing, thirst, vehemence, yearning, zeal. **antonyms** apathy, disinterest.

ear *n* ability, appreciation, attention, consideration, discrimination, hearing, heed, notice, perception, regard, sensitivity, skill, taste.

early *adj* advanced, forward, prehistoric, premature, primeval, primitive, primordial, undeveloped, untimely, young.
adv ahead of time, beforehand, betimes, in advance, in good time, prematurely, too soon. **antonym** late.

earmark *v* allocate, designate, keep back, label, put aside, reserve, set aside, tag.

earn *v* acquire, attain, bring in, collect, deserve, draw, gain, get, gross, make, merit, obtain, procure, rate, realise, reap, receive, warrant, win. **antonyms** lose, spend.

earnest *adj* ardent, close, constant, determined, devoted, eager, enthusiastic, fervent, fervid, firm, fixed, grave, heartfelt, impassioned, intent, keen, passionate, purposeful, resolute, resolved, serious, sincere, solemn, stable, staid, steady, thoughtful, urgent, vehement, warm, zealous. **antonyms** apathetic, flippant, unenthusiastic.
n assurance, deposit, determination, down payment, guarantee, pledge, promise, resolution, security, seriousness, sincerity, token, truth.

earnestly *adv* eagerly, fervently, firmly, intently, keenly, resolutely, seriously, sincerely, warmly, zealously. **antonyms** flippantly, listlessly.

earnings *n* emoluments, gain, income, pay, proceeds, profits, receipts, remuneration, return, revenue, reward, salary, stipend, takings, wages. **antonyms** expenses, outgoings.

earthly *adj* base, carnal, conceivable, feasible, fleshly, gross, human, imaginable, likely, low, material, materialistic, mortal, physical, possible, practical, profane, secular, sensual, slight, slightest, sordid, temporal, terrestrial, worldly. **antonyms** heavenly, spiritual.

earthy *adj* bawdy, blue, coarse, crude, down-to-earth, homely, indecorous, lusty, natural, raunchy, ribald, robust, rough, simple, uninhibited, unrefined, unsophisticated, vulgar. **antonyms** cultured, refined.

ease *n* affluence, aplomb, calmness, comfort, composure, content, contentment, deftness, dexterity, easiness, effortlessness, enjoyment, facility, flexibility, freedom, happiness, informality, insouciance, leisure, liberty, naturalness, nonchalance, peace, peace of mind, poise, quiet, quietude, readiness, relaxation, repose, rest, restfulness, serenity, simplicity, solace, tranquillity. **antonyms** difficulty, discomfort.
v abate, aid, allay, alleviate, appease, assist, assuage, calm, comfort, edge, expedite, facilitate, forward, further, guide, inch, lessen, lighten, manoeuvre, mitigate, moderate, mollify, pacify, palliate, quiet, relax, relent, relieve, simplify, slacken, slide, slip, smooth, solace, soothe, speed up, squeeze, steer, still, tranquillise. **antonyms** hinder, retard, torment.

ease off abate, decrease, die away, die down, moderate, relent, slacken, subside, wane. **antonym** increase.

easily[1] *adv* comfortably, effortlessly, readily, simply, smoothly, standing on one's head, with one arm tied behind one's back. **antonym** laboriously.

easily[2] *adv* absolutely, by far, certainly, clearly, definitely, doubtlessly, far and away, indisputably, indubitably, plainly, probably, simply, surely, undeniably, undoubtedly, unequivocally, unquestionably, well.

easy *adj* a doddle, a piece of

cake, a pushover, accommodating, affable, amenable, biddable, calm, carefree, casual, child's play, clear, comfortable, compliant, contented, cushy, docile, easy-going, effortless, facile, flexible, friendly, gentle, graceful, gracious, gullible, idiot-proof, indulgent, informal, leisurely, lenient, liberal, light, manageable, mild, moderate, natural, no bother, open, painless, peaceful, permissive, pleasant, pliant, quiet, relaxed, satisfied, serene, simple, smooth, soft, straightforward, submissive, suggestible, susceptible, temperate, tolerant, tractable, tranquil, trusting, unaffected, unceremonious, uncomplicated, unconstrained, undemanding, undisturbed, unexacting, unforced, unhurried, unlaboured, unpretentious, untroubled, unworried, user-friendly, well-to-do, yielding. **antonyms** demanding, difficult, fast, impossible, intolerant.

easy-going *adj* amenable, calm, carefree, casual, complacent, downbeat, easy, easy-osy, even-tempered, flexible, happy-go-lucky, indulgent, laid-back, lenient, liberal, mild, moderate, nonchalant, permissive, placid, relaxed, serene, tolerant, unconcerned, uncritical, undemanding, unhurried, unworried. **antonyms** fussy, intolerant.

eat *v* banquet, break bread, chew, chop, consume, corrode, crumble, decay, devour, dine, dissolve, erode, feed, ingest, knock back, munch, pig, rot, scoff, swallow, wear away.

eat one's words abjure, recant, rescind, retract, take back, unsay.

ebb *v* abate, decay, decline, decrease, degenerate, deteriorate, diminish, drop, dwindle, fade away, fall away, fall back, flag, flow back, go out, lessen, peter out, recede, retire, retreat, shrink, sink, slacken, subside, wane, weaken, withdraw. **antonyms** increase, rise.

n decay, decline, decrease, degeneration, deterioration, diminution, drop, dwindling, ebb tide, flagging, lessening, low tide, low water, regression, retreat, shrinkage, sinking, slackening, subsidence, wane, waning, weakening, withdrawal. **antonyms** flow, increase, rising.

ebullient *adj* boiling, breezy, bright, bubbling, buoyant, chirpy, effervescent, effusive, elated, enthusiastic, excited, exhilarated, exuberant, foaming, frothing, frothy, gushing, irrepressible, seething, vivacious, zestful. **antonyms** apathetic, dull, lifeless.

eccentric *adj* aberrant, abnormal, anomalous, bizarre, capricious, dotty, erratic, fey, freakish, fruity, idiosyncratic, irregular, nuts, nutty, odd, offbeat, outlandish, peculiar, queer, quirky, screwball, screwy, singular, strange, uncommon, unconventional, way-out, weird, whimsical. **antonyms** normal, sane.

n case, character, crank, freak, fruit-cake, nonconformist, nut, nutter, oddball, oddity, queer fish, screwball, weirdo.

ecclesiastic(al) *adj* church, churchly, churchy, clerical, divine, holy, pastoral, priestly, religious, spiritual.

echelon *n* degree, grade, level, place, position, rank, status, step, tier.

echo *v* ape, copy, imitate, mimic, mirror, parallel, parrot, recall, reflect, reiterate, repeat, reproduce, resemble, resound, reverberate, ring, second.

n allusion, answer, copy, evocation, hint, image, imitation, memory, mirror image, parallel, reflection, reiteration, reminder, repetition, reproduction, reverberation, suggestion, sympathy, trace.

éclat *n* acclaim, acclamation, applause, approval, brilliance, celebrity, display, distinction, fame, glory, lustre, ostentation, plaudits, pomp, renown, show, showmanship, splendour, success. **antonyms** disapproval, dullness.

eclectic *adj* all-embracing, broad, catholic, comprehensive, diverse, diversified, general, heterogeneous, liberal, many-sided, multifarious, varied, wide-ranging. **antonyms** narrow, one-sided.

eclipse *v* blot out, cloud, darken, dim, dwarf, exceed, excel, extinguish, obscure, outdo, outshine, overshadow, shroud, surpass, transcend, veil.

n darkening, decline, diminution, dimming, extinction, failure, fall, loss, obscuration, overshadowing, shading.

economic *adj* budgetary, business, cheap, commercial, cost-effective, economical, economy-size, fair, financial, fiscal, inexpensive, low, low-priced, modest, monetary, money-making, productive, profitable, profit-making, reasonable, remunerative, solvent, trade, viable. **antonyms** expensive, uneconomic.

economical *adj* careful, cheap,

cost-effective, economic, economising, efficient, fair, frugal, inexpensive, labour-saving, low, low-priced, modest, prudent, reasonable, saving, scrimping, sparing, thrifty, time-saving. *antonyms* expensive, uneconomical.

economise *v* cut back, cut corners, retrench, save, scrimp, tighten one's belt. *antonym* squander.

economy *n* frugality, frugalness, parsimony, providence, prudence, restraint, retrenchment, saving, scrimping, sparingness, thrift, thriftiness. *antonym* improvidence.

ecstasy *n* bliss, delight, elation, enthusiasm, euphoria, exaltation, fervour, frenzy, joy, rapture, ravishment, rhapsody, seventh heaven, sublimation, trance, transport. *antonym* torment.

ecstatic *adj* blissful, delirious, elated, enraptured, enthusiastic, entranced, euphoric, exultant, fervent, frenzied, joyful, joyous, on cloud nine, over the moon, overjoyed, rapturous, rhapsodic, transported. *antonym* downcast.

edge *n* acuteness, advantage, animation, ascendancy, bite, border, bound, boundary, brim, brink, contour, dominance, effectiveness, force, fringe, incisiveness, interest, keenness, lead, limit, line, lip, margin, outline, perimeter, periphery, point, pungency, rim, sharpness, side, sting, superiority, threshold, upper hand, urgency, verge, zest.
v bind, border, creep, ease, fringe, gravitate, hem, hone, inch, rim, shape, sharpen, sidle, steal, strop, trim, verge, whet, work, worm.

edgy *adj* anxious, ill at ease, irascible, irritable, keyed-up, nervous, on edge, prickly, restive, tense, testy, touchy. *antonym* calm.

edict *n* act, command, decree, dictate, dictum, enactment, fiat, injunction, law, mandate, manifesto, order, ordinance, proclamation, pronouncement, pronunciamento, regulation, rescript, ruling, statute, ukase.

edifice *n* building, construction, erection, structure.

edify *v* educate, elevate, enlighten, guide, improve, inform, instruct, school, teach, train, tutor.

edit *v* adapt, annotate, assemble, blue-pencil, bowdlerise, censor, check, compose, condense, correct, emend, polish, rearrange, redact, reorder, rephrase, revise, rewrite, select.

edition *n* copy, exemplar, impression, issue, number, printing, programme, version, volume.

educate *v* civilise, coach, cultivate, develop, discipline, drill, edify, exercise, improve, indoctrinate, inform, instruct, learn, mature, rear, school, teach, train, tutor.

educated *adj* civilised, coached, cultivated, cultured, enlightened, experienced, informed, instructed, knowledgeable, learned, lettered, literary, polished, refined, schooled, sophisticated, taught, trained, tutored, well-bred. *antonyms* uncultured, uneducated.

education *n* breeding, civilisation, coaching, cultivation, culture, development, discipline, drilling, edification, enlightenment, erudition, guidance, improvement, indoctrination, instruction, knowledge, scholarship, schooling, teaching, training, tuition, tutelage, tutoring.

educational *adj* cultural, didactic, edifying, educative, enlightening, improving, informative, instructive, scholastic. *antonym* uninformative.

eerie *adj* awesome, chilling, creepy, fearful, frightening, ghastly, ghostly, mysterious, scary, spectral, spine-chilling, spooky, strange, uncanny, unearthly, unnatural, weird. *antonyms* natural, ordinary.

efface *v* annihilate, blank out, blot out, blue-pencil, cancel, cross out, delete, destroy, dim, eliminate, eradicate, erase, excise, expunge, extirpate, humble, lower, obliterate, raze, remove, rub out, wipe out, withdraw.

effect *n* action, aftermath, clout, conclusion, consequence, drift, éclat, effectiveness, efficacy, efficiency, enforcement, essence, event, execution, fact, force, fruit, impact, implementation, import, impression, influence, issue, meaning, operation, outcome, power, purport, purpose, reality, result, sense, significance, strength, tenor, upshot, use, validity, vigour, weight, work.
v accomplish, achieve, actuate, cause, complete, consummate, create, effectuate, execute, fulfil, initiate, make, perform, produce.

effective *adj* able, active, adequate, capable, cogent, compelling, competent, convincing, current, effectual, efficacious, efficient, emphatic, energetic, forceful, forcible, implemental, impressive, moving, operative, persuasive, potent, powerful, productive, real, serviceable, striking, telling, useful. **antonyms** ineffective, useless.

effects *n* belongings, chattels, gear, goods, movables, paraphernalia, possessions, property, things, trappings.

effectual *adj* authoritative, binding, capable, effective, efficacious, efficient, forcible, influential, lawful, legal, licit, operative, perficient, potent, powerful, productive, serviceable, sound, successful, telling, useful, valid. **antonyms** ineffective, useless.

effeminate *adj* delicate, epicene, feminine, pansy, poofy, sissy, soft, tender, unmanly, weak, womanish, womanlike. **antonym** manly.

effervesce *v* boil, bubble, ferment, fizz, foam, froth, sparkle.

effervescent *adj* animated, bubbling, bubbly, buoyant, carbonated, ebullient, enthusiastic, excited, exhilarated, exuberant, fermenting, fizzing, fizzy, foaming, frothing, frothy, gay, irrepressible, lively, merry, sparkling, vital, vivacious, zingy. **antonyms** apathetic, dull, flat.

effete *adj* barren, corrupt, debased, debilitated, decadent, decayed, decrepit, degenerate, dissipated, drained, enervated, enfeebled, exhausted, feeble, fruitless, incapable, ineffectual, infertile, overrefined, played out, spent, spoiled, sterile, tired out, unfruitful, unproductive, used up, wasted, weak, worn out. **antonym** vigorous.

efficacious *adj* active, adequate, capable, competent, effective, effectual, efficient, energetic, operative, potent, powerful, productive, serviceable, strong, successful, sufficient, useful. **antonyms** ineffective, useless.

efficacy *n* ability, capability, competence, effect, effectiveness, efficaciousness, efficiency, energy, force, influence, potency, power, strength, success, use, virtue. **antonyms** ineffectiveness, uselessness.

efficiency *n* ability, adeptness, capability, competence, competency, economy, effectiveness, efficacy, mastery, power, productivity, proficiency, readiness, skilfulness, skill.

efficient *adj* able, adept, businesslike, capable, competent, economic, effective, effectual, powerful, productive, proficient, ready, skilful, streamlined, well-conducted, well-ordered, well-organised, well-regulated, workmanlike.

effigy *n* carving, dummy, figure, guy, icon, idol, image, likeness, mumbo-jumbo, picture, portrait, representation, statue.

effluent *n* discharge, effluence, emission, exhalation, outflow, pollutant, pollution, sewage, waste.

effort *n* accomplishment, achievement, application, attempt, creation, deed, endeavour, energy, essay, exertion, feat, force, go, job, labour, pains, power, product, production, shot, stab, strain, stress, stretch, striving, struggle, toil, travail, trouble, try, work.

effortless *adj* easy, facile, painless, simple, smooth, uncomplicated, undemanding, unlaboured. **antonym** difficult.

effrontery *n* arrogance, assurance, audacity, boldness, brashness, brass (neck), brazenness, cheek, cheekiness, disrespect, face, front, gall, impertinence, impudence, incivility, insolence, neck, nerve, presumption, rudeness, shamelessness, temerity.

effusion *n* discharge, effluence, efflux, emission, gush, outflow, outpouring, shedding, stream, voidance.

effusive *adj* demonstrative, ebullient, enthusiastic, expansive, extravagant, exuberant, gushing, gushy, lavish, overflowing, profuse, talkative, unreserved, unrestrained, voluble, wordy. **antonyms** quiet, restrained.

egg on coax, encourage, exhort, goad, incite, prick, prod, prompt, push, spur, stimulate, urge. **antonym** discourage.

egotism *n* bigheadedness, conceitedness, egocentricity, egoism, egomania, narcissism, self-admiration, self-centredness, self-conceit, self-esteem, self-importance, self-love, self-praise, self-pride, superiority, vainglory, vanity. **antonym** humility.

egotist *n* bighead, boaster, braggart, egoist, egomaniac, swaggerer.

egotistic *adj* bigheaded, boasting, bragging, conceited, egocentric, egoistic, egoistical, egotistical, narcissistic, opinionated, self-centred, self-important, superior, swollen-headed, vain, vainglorious. **antonym** humble.

egregious *adj* arrant, flagrant, glaring, grievous, gross, heinous, infamous, insufferable, intolerable, monstrous, notorious, outrageous, rank, scandalous, shocking. **antonym** slight.

eject *v* banish, belch, boot out, bounce, deport, discharge, disgorge, dislodge, dismiss, dispossess, drive out, emit, evacuate, evict, exile, expel, fire, kick out, oust, remove, sack, spew, spout, throw out, turn out, unhouse, vomit.

ejection *n* banishment, deportation, discharge, disgorgement, dislodgement, dismissal, dispossession, evacuation, eviction, exile, expulsion, firing, ousting, removal, sacking, the boot, the sack.

eke out add to, economise on, increase, make (something) stretch, stretch, supplement.

elaborate *adj* careful, complex, complicated, decorated, detailed, exact, extravagant, fancy, fussy, Heath-Robinson, intricate, involved, laboured, minute, ornamental, ornate, ostentatious, painstaking, precise, showy, skilful, studied, thorough. *antonyms* plain, simple.
v amplify, complicate, decorate, detail, develop, devise, embellish, enhance, enlarge, expand, expatiate, explain, flesh out, garnish, improve, ornament, polish, refine. *antonyms* précis, simplify.

élan *n* animation, brio, dash, esprit, flair, flourish, impetuosity, liveliness, oomph, panache, pizzazz, spirit, style, verve, vigour, vivacity, zest. *antonyms* apathy, lifelessness.

elastic *adj* accommodating, adaptable, adjustable, bouncy, buoyant, complaisant, compliant, distensible, ductile, flexible, irrepressible, plastic, pliable, pliant, resilient, rubbery, springy, stretchable, stretchy, supple, tolerant, variable, yielding. *antonym* rigid.

elasticity *n* adaptability, adjustability, bounce, buoyancy, complaisance, compliance, compliancy, ductility, flexibility, give, irrepressibility, plasticity, pliability, pliancy, resilience, rubberiness, springiness, stretch, stretchiness, suppleness, tolerance, variability. *antonym* rigidity.

elated *adj* animated, blissful, cheered, delighted, ecstatic, euphoric, excited, exhilarated, exultant, gleeful, joyful, joyous, jubilant, on the high ropes, over the moon, overjoyed, pleased, proud, roused. *antonym* downcast.

elation *n* bliss, delight, ecstasy, euphoria, exaltation, exhilaration, exultation, glee, high spirits, joy, joyfulness, joyousness, jubilation, rapture, transports of delight. *antonym* depression.

elbow *v* bulldoze, bump, crowd, hustle, jostle, knock, nudge, plough, push, shoulder, shove.

elderly *adj* aged, aging, hoary, old, senile. *antonyms* young, youthful.

elect *v* adopt, appoint, choose, designate, determine, opt for, pick, prefer, select, vote.
adj choice, chosen, designate, designated, elite, hand-picked, picked, preferred, presumptive, prospective, select, selected, to be.

election *n* appointment, ballot-box, choice, choosing, decision, determination, judgement, preference, selection, vote, voting.

electric *adj* charged, dynamic, electrifying, exciting, rousing, stimulating, stirring, tense, thrilling. *antonyms* tedious, unexciting.

electrify *v* amaze, animate, astonish, astound, excite, fire, galvanise, invigorate, jolt, rouse, shock, stagger, startle, stimulate, stir, stun, thrill. *antonym* bore.

elegance *n* beauty, chic, courtliness, dignity, discernment, distinction, exquisiteness, gentility, grace, gracefulness, grandeur, luxury, polish, politeness, propriety, refinement, style, sumptuousness, taste. *antonym* inelegance.

elegant *adj* à la mode, appropriate, apt, artistic, beautiful, chic, choice, clever, comely, courtly, cultivated, debonair, delicate, effective, exquisite, fashionable, fine, genteel, graceful, handsome, ingenious, luxurious, modish, neat, nice, polished, refined, simple, smart, smooth, stylish, sumptuous, tasteful. *antonym* inelegant.

elegy *n* coronach, dirge, keen, lament, plaint, requiem, threnode, threnody.

element *n* basis, component, constituent, domain, environment, factor, feature, field, fragment, habitat, hint, ingredient, medium, member, milieu, part, piece, section, sphere, subdivision, trace, unit.

elementary *adj* basic, clear, easy, elemental, facile, fundamental, initial, introductory, original, plain, primary, rudimentary, simple, straightforward, uncomplicated. *antonyms* advanced, complex.

elevate *v* advance, aggrandise, animate, augment, boost, brighten, buoy up, cheer, elate, exalt, excite, exhilarate, hearten, heighten, hoist, increase intensify, lift, magnify, prefer, promote, raise, rouse, sublimate, swell, upgrade, uplift, upraise. **antonyms** lessen, lower.

elevated *adj* animated, cheerful, cheery, dignified, elated, exalted, excited, exhilarated, grand, high, high-flown, high-minded, inflated, lofty, noble, overjoyed, raised, sublime, tipsy. **antonyms** base, informal, lowly.

elevation *n* acclivity, advancement, aggrandisement, altitude, eminence, exaltation, exaltedness, grandeur, height, hill, hillock, loftiness, mountain, nobility, preferment, promotion, rise, sublimation, sublimity, upgrading, uplift. **antonyms** baseness, informality.

elfin *adj* arch, charming, delicate, elfish, elflike, elvish, frolicsome, impish, mischievous, petite, playful, puckish, small, sprightly.

elicit *v* cause, derive, draw out, educe, evoke, evolve, exact, extort, extract, fish, mole out, obtain, wrest, wring.

eligible *adj* acceptable, appropriate, available, desirable, fit, proper, qualified, suitable, suited, worthy. **antonym** ineligible.

eliminate *v* annihilate, bump off, cut out, delete, dispense with, dispose of, disregard, do away with, drop, eject, eradicate, exclude, expel, expunge, exterminate, extinguish, get rid of, ignore, kill, knock out, liquidate, murder, omit, reject, remove, rub out, slay, stamp out, take out, terminate, waste. **antonym** accept.

elite *n* aristocracy, best, cream, crème de la crème, elect, establishment, gentry, high society, meritocracy, nobility, pick. *adj* aristocratic, best, choice, crack, exclusive, first-class, noble, pick, selected, top, top-class, upper-class. **antonyms** ordinary, run-of-the-mill.

elliptical *adj* abstruse, ambiguous, concentrated, concise, condensed, cryptic, incomprehensible, obscure, recondite, unfathomable. **antonym** clear.

elocution *n* articulation, declamation, delivery, diction, enunciation, oratory, pronunciation, rhetoric, speech, speechmaking, utterance.

elongated *adj* extended, lengthened, long, prolonged, protracted, stretched.

elope *v* abscond, bolt, decamp, disappear, do a bunk, escape, leave, run away, run off, slip away, steal away.

eloquence *n* expression, expressiveness, fluency, forcefulness, oratory, persuasiveness, rhetoric. **antonym** inarticulateness.

eloquent *adj* articulate, expressive, fluent, forceful, graceful, honeyed, meaningful, moving, persuasive, plausible, revealing, silver-tongued, stirring, suggestive, telling, vivid, vocal, voluble, well-expressed. **antonyms** inarticulate, tongue-tied.

elucidate *v* annotate, clarify, explain, expound, gloss, illuminate, illustrate, interpret, spell out, unfold. **antonyms** confuse, obscure.

elude *v* avoid, baffle, beat, circumvent, confound, dodge, duck, escape, evade, flee, foil, frustrate, outrun, puzzle, shirk, shun, stump, thwart.

elusive *adj* ambiguous, baffling, deceitful, deceptive, equivocal, evasive, fallacious, fleeting, fraudulent, fugitive, illusory, indefinable, intangible, misleading, puzzling, shifty, slippery, subtle, transient, transitory, tricky, unanalysable.

emaciated *adj* atrophied, attenuate, attenuated, cadaverous, gaunt, haggard, lank, lean, meagre, pinched, scrawny, skeletal, thin, wasted. **antonyms** plump, well-fed.

emanate *v* arise, come, derive, discharge, emerge, emit, exhale, flow, give off, give out, issue, originate, proceed, radiate, send out, spring, stem.

emanation *n* arising, derivation, discharge, effluence, effluent, effusion, emergence, emission, exhalation, flow, generation, origination, proceeding, procession, radiation.

emancipate *v* deliver, discharge, enfranchise, free, liberate, manumit, release, set free, unbind, unchain, unfetter, unshackle. **antonym** enslave.

emancipation *n* deliverance, discharge, enfranchisement, freedom, liberation, liberty, manumission, release, unbinding, unchaining. **antonym** enslavement.

emasculate *v* castrate, cripple, debilitate, enervate, geld, impoverish, neuter, soften, spay, weaken. **antonyms** boost, vitalise.

embargo *n* ban, bar, barrier, blockage, check, hindrance, impediment, interdict, interdiction, prohibition, proscription, restraint, restriction, seizure, stoppage. *v* ban, bar, block, check, impede, interdict, prohibit, proscribe, restrict, seize, stop. *antonym* allow.

embark v board ship, emplane, entrain, take ship. *antonym* disembark.

embark on begin, broach, commence, engage, enter, initiate, launch, start, undertake. *antonym* finish.

embarrass v abash, chagrin, confuse, discomfit, discomfort, disconcert, distress, fluster, mortify, shame, show up.

embarrassed adj abashed, constrained, discomfited, disconcerted, mortified, shamed, shown up, uncomfortable. *antonym* unembarrassed.

embarrassing adj awkward, compromising, discomfiting, disconcerting, distressing, humiliating, mortifying, sensitive, shameful, shaming, touchy, tricky, uncomfortable.

embarrassment n awkwardness, bashfulness, bind, chagrin, confusion, constraint, difficulty, discomfiture, discomfort, distress, excess, humiliation, mess, mortification, overabundance, pickle, predicament, scrape, self-consciousness, shame, superfluity, surfeit, surplus.

embed v fix, imbed, implant, insert, plant, root, set, sink.

embellish v adorn, beautify, bedeck, deck, decorate, dress up, elaborate, embroider, enhance, enrich, exaggerate, festoon, garnish, gild, grace, ornament, trim, varnish. *antonyms* denude, simplify.

embellishment n adornment, decoration, elaboration, embroidery, enhancement, enrichment, exaggeration, garnish, gilding, ornament, ornamentation, trimming.

embezzle v abstract, appropriate, filch, misapply, misappropriate, misuse, pilfer, pinch, purloin, steal.

embezzlement n abstraction, appropriation, filching, fraud, larceny, misapplication, misappropriation, misuse, pilfering, purloining, stealing, theft, thieving.

embittered adj bitter, disaffected, disillusioned, sour, soured. *antonym* pacified.

emblem n badge, crest, device, figure, image, insignia, mark, representation, sign, symbol, token, type.

embodiment n collection, combination, concentration, consolidation, example, exemplar, exemplification, expression, incarnation, inclusion, incorporation, integration, manifestation, organisation, personification, realisation, representation, symbol, type.

embody v collect, combine, comprehend, comprise, concentrate, consolidate, contain, exemplify, express, include, incorporate, integrate, manifest, organise, personify, realise, represent, stand for, symbolise, typify.

embolden v animate, cheer, encourage, enhearten, fire, hearten, inflame, inspire, invigorate, nerve, reassure, rouse, stimulate, stir, strengthen, vitalise. *antonym* dishearten.

embrace v accept, canoodle, clasp, comprehend, comprise, contain, cover, cuddle, encircle, enclose, encompass, enfold, enlace, espouse, grab, grasp, hold, hug, include, incorporate, involve, neck, receive, seize, snog, squeeze, subsume, take up, welcome.
n clasp, clinch, cuddle, hug, squeeze.

embroglio *see* **imbroglio**.

embroidery n fancywork, needle-point, needlework, sewing, tapestry, tatting.

embroil v confound, confuse, distract, disturb, enmesh, ensnare, entangle, implicate, incriminate, involve, mire, mix up, muddle, perplex, trouble.

embryonic adj beginning, early, germinal, immature, inchoate, incipient, primary, rudimentary, seminal, underdeveloped. *antonyms* advanced, developed.

emend v alter, amend, correct, edit, improve, rectify, redact, revise, rewrite.

emendation n alteration, amendment, correction, editing, improvement, rectification, redaction, revision.

emerge v appear, arise, crop up, develop, emanate, issue, materialise, proceed, rise, surface, transpire, turn up. *antonyms* disappear, fade.

emergence n advent, apparition, appearance, arrival, coming, dawn, development, disclosure, emanation, emersion, issue, materialisation, rise. *antonyms* decline, disappearance.

emergency n crisis, crunch, danger, difficulty, exigency, extremity, necessity, pass, pinch, plight, predicament, quandary, scrape, strait.
adj alternative, back-up, extra, fall-back, reserve, spare, substitute.

emergent adj budding, coming, developing, emerging, independent, rising. *antonyms* declining, disappearing.

emigration n departure, exodus, journey, migration, removal.

eminence *n* celebrity, dignity, distinction, elevation, esteem, fame, greatness, height, hill, hillock, illustriousness, importance, knob, knoll, notability, note, peak, pre-eminence, prestige, prominence, rank, renown, reputation, repute, ridge, rise, summit, superiority.

eminent *adj* august, celebrated, conspicuous, distinguished, elevated, esteemed, exalted, famous, grand, great, high, high-ranking, illustrious, important, notable, noted, noteworthy, outstanding, paramount, pre-eminent, prestigious, prominent, renowned, reputable, respected, revered, signal, superior, well-known. **antonyms** unimportant, unknown.

emissary *n* agent, ambassador, courier, delegate, deputy, envoy, herald, messenger, plenipotentiary, representative, scout, spy.

emission *n* diffusion, discharge, ejaculation, ejection, emanation, exhalation, issue, radiation, release, shedding, transmission, utterance, vent, venting.

emit *v* diffuse, discharge, eject, emanate, exhale, exude, give off, give out, issue, radiate, shed, vent. **antonym** absorb.

emollient *adj* assuaging, balsamic, mitigative, mollifying, softening, soothing.
n balm, cream, lenitive, liniment, lotion, moisturiser, oil, ointment, poultice, salve, unguent.

emolument *n* allowance, benefit, compensation, earnings, fee, gain, hire, honorarium, pay, payment, profits, recompense, remuneration, return, reward, salary, stipend, wages.

emotion *n* affect, agitation, ardour, excitement, feeling, fervour, passion, perturbation, reaction, sensation, sentiment, vehemence, warmth.

emotional *adj* affecting, ardent, demonstrative, emotive, enthusiastic, excitable, exciting, feeling, fervent, fervid, fiery, heart-warming, heated, hot-blooded, impassioned, moved, moving, overcharged, passionate, pathetic, poignant, responsive, roused, sensitive, sentimental, stirred, stirring, susceptible, tear-jerking, temperamental, tempestuous, tender, thrilling, touching, volcanic, warm, zealous. **antonyms** calm, cold, detached, emotionless, unemotional.

emotionless *adj* blank, cold, cold-blooded, cool, detached, distant, frigid, glacial, impassive, imperturbable, indifferent, phlegmatic, remote, toneless, undemonstrative, unemotional, unfeeling. **antonym** emotional.

emotive *adj* affecting, ardent, controversial, delicate, emotional, enthusiastic, exciting, fervent, fervid, fiery, heart-warming, heated, impassioned, inflammatory, moving, passionate, pathetic, poignant, roused, sensitive, sentimental, stirred, stirring, tear-jerking, thrilling, touching, touchy, zealous.

emphasis *n* accent, accentuation, attention, force, import, importance, impressiveness, insistence, intensity, mark, moment, positiveness, power, pre-eminence, priority, prominence, significance, strength, stress, underscoring, urgency, weight.

emphasise *v* accent, accentuate, dwell on, feature, highlight, insist on, intensify, play up, point up, press home, punctuate, spotlight, strengthen, stress, underline, underscore, weight. **antonyms** depreciate, play down, understate.

emphatic *adj* absolute, categorical, certain, decided, definite, direct, distinct, earnest, energetic, forceful, forcible, graphic, important, impressive, insistent, marked, momentous, positive, powerful, pronounced, punctuated, resounding, significant, striking, strong, telling, trenchant, unequivocal, unmistakable, vigorous, vivid. **antonyms** quiet, understated, unemphatic.

empire *n* authority, bailiwick, command, commonwealth, control, domain, dominion, government, imperium, jurisdiction, kingdom, power, realm, rule, sovereignty, supremacy, sway, territory.

employ *v* apply, bring to bear, commission, engage, enlist, exercise, exert, fill, hire, occupy, retain, spend, take on, take up, use, utilise.
n employment, hire, pay, service.

employment *n* application, avocation, business, calling, craft, employ, engagement, enlistment, errand, exercise, exertion, hire, job, line, métier, occupation, profession, pursuit, service, trade, use, utilisation, vocation, work. **antonym** unemployment.

empower *v* accredit, allow, authorise, commission, delegate, enable, enfranchise, entitle, license, permit, qualify, sanction, warrant.

emptiness *n* aimlessness, banality, bareness, barrenness, blankness, desertedness, desire, desolation, destitution, frivolity, futility, hollowness, hunger, idleness, inanity, ineffectiveness, insincerity, insubstantiality, meaninglessness, purposelessness, senselessness, silliness, triviality, unreality, vacancy, vacuity, vacuousness, vacuum, vainness, vanity, void, waste, worthlessness. *antonym* fullness.

empty *adj* absent, aimless, banal, bare, blank, clear, deserted, desolate, destitute, expressionless, famished, frivolous, fruitless, futile, hollow, hungry, idle, inane, ineffective, insincere, insubstantial, meaningless, purposeless, ravenous, senseless, silly, starving, superficial, trivial, unfed, unfilled, unfrequented, unfurnished, uninhabited, unintelligent, unoccupied, unreal, unsatisfactory, unsubstantial, untenanted, vacant, vacuous, vain, valueless, void, waste, worthless. *antonyms* filled, full, replete.
v clear, consume, deplete, discharge, drain, dump, evacuate, exhaust, gut, lade, pour out, unburden, unload, vacate, void. *antonym* fill.

empty-headed *adj* batty, brainless, dizzy, dotty, flighty, frivolous, giddy, hare-brained, inane, scatter-brained, scatty, silly, skittish, vacuous.

emulate *v* challenge, compete with, contend with, copy, echo, follow, imitate, match, mimic, rival, vie with.

emulation *n* challenge, competition, contention, contest, copying, echoing, envy, following, imitation, jealousy, matching, mimicry, rivalry, strife.

en masse all at once, all together, as a group, as a whole, as one, en bloc, ensemble, in a body, together, wholesale.

enable *v* accredit, allow, authorise, commission, empower, equip, facilitate, fit, license, permit, prepare, qualify, sanction, warrant. *antonyms* inhibit, prevent.

enact *v* act (out), authorise, command, decree, depict, establish, impersonate, legislate, ordain, order, pass, perform, personate, play, portray, proclaim, ratify, represent, sanction. *antonym* repeal.

enactment *n* acting, authorisation, command, commandment, decree, depiction, dictate, edict, impersonation, law, legislation, order, ordinance, performance, personation, play-acting, playing, portrayal, proclamation, ratification, regulation, representation, statute. *antonym* repeal.

enamoured *adj* besotted, bewitched, captivated, charmed, enchanted, enraptured, entranced, fascinated, fond, infatuated, smitten, taken.

encapsulate *v* abridge, capture, compress, condense, digest, epitomise, exemplify, incapsulate, précis, represent, sum up, summarise, typify.

enchant *v* becharm, beguile, bewitch, captivate, charm, delight, enamour, enrapture, enravish, enthral, fascinate, hypnotise, mesmerise, spellbind. *antonyms* bore, disenchant.

enchanting *adj* alluring, appealing, attractive, bewitching, captivating, charming, delightful, endearing, entrancing, fascinating, lovely, mesmerising, pleasant, ravishing, winsome, wonderful. *antonyms* boring, repellent.

enchantment *n* allure, allurement, beguilement, bliss, charm, conjuration, delight, fascination, glamour, hypnotism, incantation, magic, mesmerism, necromancy, rapture, sorcery, spell, transport, witchcraft, wizardry. *antonym* disenchantment.

encircle *v* circle, circumscribe, compass, enclose, encompass, enfold, enlace, envelop, gird, girdle, hem in, ring, surround.

enclose *v* bound, circumscribe, compass, comprehend, confine, contain, cover, embosom, embrace, encase, encircle, encompass, fence, hedge, hem in, hold, inclose, include, incorporate, insert, pen, shut in, wall in, wrap.

enclosed *adj* bound, caged, cocooned, confined, contained, encased, encircled, encompassed, immured, imprisoned, included, surrounded. *antonyms* open, unenclosed.

enclosure *n* arena, cloister, compound, corral, court, encasement, fold, paddock, pen, pinfold, pound, ring, stockade, sty.

encompass *v* admit, bring about, cause, circle, circumscribe, comprehend, comprise, contain, contrive, cover, devise, effect, embody, embrace, encircle, enclose, envelop, girdle, hem in, hold, include, incorporate, involve, manage, ring, subsume, surround.

encounter *v* chance upon, clash with, combat, come upon, confront, contend, cross swords with, engage, experience, face, fight, grapple with, happen on, meet, run across, run into, strive, struggle.

n action, battle, brush, clash, collision, combat, conflict, confrontation, contest, dispute, engagement, fight, meeting, run-in, set-to, skirmish.

encourage *v* abet, advance, advocate, aid, animate, boost, buoy up, cheer, comfort, console, egg on, embolden, embrace, favour, forward, foster, further, hearten, help, incite, inspire, inspirit, promote, rally, reassure, rouse, second, spirit, spur, stimulate, strengthen, succour, support, urge. **antonyms** depress, discourage, dissuade.

encouragement *n* advocacy, aid, boost, cheer, come-on, consolation, favour, help, incentive, incitement, inspiration, promotion, reassurance, stimulation, stimulus, succour, support, urging. **antonyms** disapproval, discouragement.

encouraging *adj* auspicious, bright, cheerful, cheering, comforting, heartening, hopeful, incentive, promising, reassuring, rosy, satisfactory, stimulating, uplifting. **antonym** discouraging.

encroach *v* appropriate, arrogate, impinge, infringe, intrude, invade, make inroads, muscle in, obtrude, overstep, trespass, usurp.

encroachment *n* appropriation, arrogation, impingement, incursion, infringement, inroad, intrusion, invasion, obtrusion, trespass, usurpation, violation.

encumber *v* burden, clog, cramp, embarrass, hamper, handicap, hinder, impede, incommode, inconvenience, lumber, obstruct, oppress, overload, retard, saddle, slow down, trammel, weigh down.

encumbrance *n* burden, clog, cumbrance, difficulty, drag, embarrassment, handicap, hindrance, impediment, inconvenience, liability, load, lumber, millstone, obstacle, obstruction, onus. **antonym** aid.

encyclopaedic *adj* all-embracing, all-encompassing, all-inclusive, broad, compendious, complete, comprehensive, exhaustive, thorough, universal, vast, wide-ranging. **antonyms** incomplete, narrow.

end *n* aim, annihilation, aspiration, attainment, bit, bound, boundary, butt, cessation, close, closure, completion, conclusion, consequence, consummation, culmination, curtain,

death, demise, dénouement, design, destruction, dissolution, doom, downfall, drift, edge, ending, expiration, expiry, extent, extermination, extinction, extreme, extremity, finale, finish, fragment, goal, intent, intention, issue, left-over, limit, object, objective, outcome, part, pay-off, piece, point, portion, purpose, reason, remainder, remnant, resolution, responsibility, result, ruin, ruination, scrap, share, side, stop, stub, termination, terminus, tip, upshot. **antonyms** beginning, opening, start.

v abate, abolish, annihilate, cease, close, complete, conclude, culminate, destroy, dissolve, expire, exterminate, extinguish, fetch up, finish, resolve, ruin, stop, terminate, wind up. **antonyms** begin, start.

endanger *v* compromise, expose, hazard, imperil, jeopardise, risk, threaten. **antonyms** protect, shelter, shield.

endearing *adj* adorable, attractive, captivating, charming, delightful, enchanting, engaging, lovable, sweet, winning, winsome.

endearment *n* affection, attachment, diminutive, fondness, love, pet-name, sweet nothing.

endeavour *n* aim, attempt, crack, effort, enterprise, essay, go, nisus, shot, stab, trial, try, undertaking, venture.

v aim, aspire, attempt, essay, labour, strive, struggle, take pains, try, undertake, venture.

ending *n* cessation, climax, close, completion, conclusion, consummation, culmination, dénouement, end, epilogue, finale, finish, resolution, termination. **antonyms** beginning, start.

endless *adj* boundless, ceaseless, constant, continual, continuous, eternal, everlasting, immortal, incessant, infinite, interminable, interminate, limitless, measureless, monotonous, overlong, perpetual, termless, unbounded, unbroken, undivided, undying, unending, uninterrupted, unlimited, whole.

endorse *v* adopt, advocate, affirm, approve, authorise, back, champion, confirm, countenance, countersign, favour, indorse, ratify, recommend, sanction, sign, subscribe to, superscribe, support, sustain, undersign, vouch for, warrant. **antonyms** denounce, disapprove.

endorsement *n* advocacy, affirmation,

approbation, approval, authorisation, backing, championship, commendation, comment, confirmation, corroboration, countersignature, favour, fiat, indorsement, OK, qualification, ratification, recommendation, sanction, seal of approval, signature, superscription, support, testimonial, warrant. *antonyms* denouncement, disapproval.

endow *v* award, bequeath, bestow, confer, donate, endue, enrich, favour, finance, fund, furnish, give, grant, invest, leave, make over, present, provide, settle on, supply, will. *antonym* divest.

endowment *n* ability, aptitude, attribute, award, benefaction, bequest, bestowal, boon, capability, capacity, donation, dowry, faculty, flair, fund, genius, gift, grant, income, largesse, legacy, power, presentation, property, provision, qualification, quality, revenue, talent.

endurance *n* bearing, continuation, continuity, durability, fortitude, immutability, longevity, patience, permanence, perseverance, persistence, pertinacity, resignation, resolution, stability, stamina, staying power, strength, submission, sufferance, sustainment, sustenance, tenacity, toleration.

endure *v* abear, abide, allow, bear, brave, brook, continue, cope with, countenance, digest, experience, go through, hold, last, live, permit, persist, prevail, put up with, remain, stand, stay, stick, stomach, submit to, suffer, support, survive, sustain, swallow, tolerate, undergo, weather, withstand. *antonyms* cease, end.

enduring *adj* abiding, continuing, durable, eternal, firm, immortal, imperishable, lasting, living, long-lasting, perennial, permanent, persistent, persisting, prevailing, remaining, steadfast, steady, surviving, unfaltering, unwavering. *antonyms* changeable, fleeting.

enemy *n* adversary, antagonist, competitor, foe, opponent, opposer, rival, the opposition. *antonyms* ally, friend.

energetic *adj* active, animated, brisk, dynamic, forceful, forcible, high-powered, indefatigable, lively, pithy, potent, powerful, spirited, strenuous, strong, throughgoing, tireless, vigorous, zippy. *antonyms* idle, inactive, lazy, sluggish.

energise *v* activate, animate, electrify, enliven, galvanise, inspirit, invigorate, liven, motivate, pep up, quicken, stimulate, vitalise, vivify. *antonym* daunt.

energy *n* activity, animation, ardour, brio, drive, efficiency, élan, exertion, fire, force, forcefulness, get-up-and-go, intensity, inworking, juice, life, liveliness, pluck, power, spirit, stamina, steam, strength, strenuousness, verve, vigour, vim, vitality, vivacity, vroom, zeal, zest, zip. *antonyms* inertia, lethargy, weakness.

enervate *v* debilitate, deplete, devitalise, enfeeble, exhaust, fatigue, incapacitate, paralyse, prostrate, sap, tire, unman, unnerve, weaken, wear out. *antonyms* activate, energise.

enervated *adj* debilitated, depleted, devitalised, done in, effete, enfeebled, exhausted, fatigued, feeble, incapacitated, limp, paralysed, prostrate, prostrated, run-down, sapped, spent, tired, undermined, unmanned, unnerved, washed out, weak, weakened, worn out. *antonyms* active, energetic.

enfeeble *v* debilitate, deplete, devitalise, diminish, enervate, exhaust, fatigue, geld, reduce, sap, undermine, unhinge, unnerve, weaken, wear out. *antonym* strengthen.

enfold *v* clasp, embrace, encircle, enclose, encompass, envelop, fold, hold, hug, shroud, swathe, wrap (up).

enforce *v* administer, apply, carry out, coerce, compel, constrain, discharge, exact, execute, implement, impose, insist on, oblige, prosecute, reinforce, require, urge.

enforced *adj* binding, compelled, compulsory, constrained, dictated, imposed, involuntary, necessary, ordained, prescribed, required, unavoidable.

enforcement *n* administration, application, coercion, compulsion, constraint, execution, implementation, imposition, insistence, obligation, pressure, prosecution, requirement.

enfranchise *v* affranchise, emancipate, free, liberate, manumit, release. *antonym* disenfranchise.

engage *v* absorb, activate, affiance, agree, allure, apply, appoint, arrest, assail, attach, attack, attract, betroth, bind, book, busy, captivate, catch, charm, charter, combat, commission, commit, contract, covenant, draw, embark, employ, enamour, enchant, encounter, energise, engross, enlist, enrol, enter, fascinate, fit, fix, gain, grip, guarantee, hire, interact, interconnect, interlock, involve, join, lease, meet, mesh, obligate, oblige, occupy, operate, partake, participate, pledge, practise, prearrange, preoccupy, promise, rent, reserve, retain, secure, take on, tie up, undertake, vouch, vow, win. **antonyms** discharge, disengage, dismiss.

engaged *adj* absorbed, affianced, betrothed, busy, committed, employed, engrossed, immersed, involved, occupied, pledged, preoccupied, promised, spoken for, tied up, unavailable.

engagement *n* action, appointment, arrangement, assurance, battle, betrothal, bond, combat, commission, commitment, compact, conflict, confrontation, contest, contract, date, employment, encounter, fight, gig, job, meeting, oath, obligation, pact, pledge, post, promise, situation, stint, troth, undertaking, vow, word, work. **antonym** disengagement.

engaging *adj* agreeable, appealing, attractive, beguiling, captivating, charming, enchanting, fascinating, fetching, lik(e)able, lovable, pleasant, pleasing, prepossessing, winning, winsome. **antonyms** boring, loathsome.

engender *v* beget, breed, bring about, cause, create, encourage, excite, father, foment, generate, give rise to, hatch, incite, induce, instigate, lead to, make, nurture, occasion, precipitate, procreate, produce, propagate, provoke, sire, spawn.

engine *n* agency, agent, apparatus, appliance, contraption, contrivance, device, dynamo, implement, instrument, machine, means, mechanism, motor, tool, turbine, weapon.

engineer *n* architect, contriver, designer, deviser, driver, inventor, operator, originator, planner.
v cause, concoct, contrive, control, create, devise, effect, encompass, machinate, manage, manipulate, manoeuvre, mastermind, originate, plan, plot, scheme, wangle.

engrave *v* blaze, carve, chase, chisel, cut, embed, enchase, etch, fix, grave, impress, imprint, ingrain, inscribe, lodge, mark, print.

engrossed *adj* absorbed, captivated, caught up, enthralled, fascinated, fixated, gripped, immersed, intent, intrigued, lost, preoccupied, rapt, riveted, taken. **antonyms** bored, disinterested.

engulf *v* absorb, bury, consume, deluge, drown, encompass, engross, envelop, flood, immerse, inundate, overrun, overwhelm, plunge, submerge, swallow up, swamp.

enhance *v* amplify, augment, boost, complement, deodorise, elevate, embellish, escalate, exalt, heighten, improve, increase, intensify, lift, magnify, raise, reinforce, strengthen, swell. **antonyms** decrease, minimise.

enigma *n* brain-teaser, conundrum, mystery, poser, problem, puzzle, riddle.

enigmatic *adj* ambiguous, cryptic, doubtful, equivocal, impenetrable, incomprehensible, indecipherable, inexplicable, inscrutable, mysterious, obscure, perplexing, puzzling, recondite, riddling, strange, uncertain, unfathomable, unintelligible. **antonyms** simple, straightforward.

enjoin *v* advise, ban, bar,· bid, call upon, charge, command, comply, counsel, demand, direct, disallow, forbid, instruct, interdict, obey, order, preclude, prescribe, prohibit, proscribe, require, restrain, urge, warn.

enjoy *v* appreciate, delight in, dig, experience, have, like, own, possess, rejoice in, relish, revel in, savour, take pleasure in, use. **antonyms** abhor, detest.

enjoy oneself have a ball, have a good time, have fun, make merry, party.

enjoyable *adj* agreeable, amusing, delectable, delicious, delightful, entertaining, fun, good, gratifying, pleasant, pleasing, pleasurable, satisfying. **antonyms** disagreeable, unpleasant.

enjoyment *n* advantage, amusement, benefit, comfort, delectation, delight, diversion, ease, entertainment, exercise, fun, gaiety, gladness, gratification, gusto, happiness, indulgence, jollity, joy, ownership, pleasure, possession, recreation, relish, satisfaction, use, zest. **antonyms** displeasure, dissatisfaction.

enlarge *v* add to, amplify, augment, blow up, broaden, develop, diffuse, dilate, distend, elaborate, elongate, expand, expatiate, extend, greaten, grow, heighten, increase, inflate, lengthen, magnify, multiply, stretch, swell, wax, widen. **antonyms** decrease, diminish, shrink.

enlargement *n* amplification, augmentation, blow-up, dilation, distension, expansion, extension, growth, increase, increment, intumescence, magnification, oedema, protuberation, supplementation, swelling. *antonyms* contraction, decrease.

enlighten *v* advise, apprise, civilise, counsel, edify, educate, illuminate, indoctrinate, inform, instruct, teach. *antonyms* confuse, puzzle.

enlightened *adj* aware, broad-minded, civilised, conversant, cultivated, educated, informed, knowledgeable, liberal, literate, open-minded, reasonable, refined, sophisticated, wise. *antonyms* confused, ignorant.

enlightenment *n* awareness, broad-mindedness, civilisation, comprehension, cultivation, edification, education, erudition, information, insight, instruction, knowledge, learning, literacy, open-mindedness, refinement, sophistication, teaching, understanding, wisdom. *antonyms* confusion, ignorance.

enlist *v* conscript, employ, engage, enrol, enter, gather, join (up), muster, obtain, procure, recruit, register, secure, sign up, volunteer.

enliven *v* animate, brighten, buoy up, cheer (up), excite, exhilarate, fire, gladden, hearten, inspire, inspirit, invigorate, juice up, kindle, liven (up), pep up, perk up, quicken, rouse, spark, stimulate, vitalise, vivify, wake up. *antonym* subdue.

enmity *n* acrimony, animosity, animus, antagonism, antipathy, aversion, bad blood, bitterness, feud, hate, hatred, hostility, ill-will, invidiousness, malevolence, malice, malignity, rancour, spite, venom. *antonyms* amity, friendship.

ennoble *v* aggrandise, dignify, elevate, enhance, exalt, glorify, honour, magnify, nobilitate, raise.

enormity *n* abomination, atrociousness, atrocity, crime, depravity, disgrace, evil, evilness, heinousness, horror, iniquity, monstrosity, monstrousness, nefariousness, outrage, outrageousness, turpitude, viciousness, vileness, villainy, wickedness. *antonyms* triviality, unimportance.

enormous *adj* abominable, astronomic(al), atrocious, colossal, depraved, disgraceful, evil, excessive, gargantuan, gigantic, gross, heinous, herculean, huge, hulking, immense, jumbo, leviathan, mammoth, massive, monstrous, mountainous, nefarious, odious, outrageous, prodigious, titanic,

tremendous, vast, vicious, vile, villainous, wicked. *antonyms* small, tiny.

enough *adj* abundant, adequate, ample, plenty, sufficient.
n abundance, adequacy, plenitude, plenty, repletion, sufficiency.
adv abundantly, adequately, amply, aplenty, fairly, moderately, passably, reasonably, satisfactorily, sufficiently, tolerably.

enquire, inquire *v* ask, examine, explore, inspect, investigate, probe, query, question, quiz, scrutinise, search.

enquiry, inquiry *n* examination, exploration, inquest, inspection, investigation, probe, query, quest, question, research, scrutiny, search, study, survey.

enrage *v* aggravate, anger, exasperate, incense, incite, inflame, infuriate, irritate, madden, make someone's hackles rise, provoke. *antonyms* calm, placate, soothe.

enraged *adj* aggravated, angered, angry, exasperated, fizzing, fuming, furious, incensed, inflamed, infuriated, irate, irritated, livid, mad, raging, storming, wild. *antonym* calm.

enrich *v* adorn, aggrandise, ameliorate, augment, cultivate, decorate, develop, embellish, endow, enhance, fortify, grace, improve, ornament, prosper, refine, supplement. *antonym* impoverish.

enrol *v* accept, admit, chronicle, empanel, engage, enlist, enregister, inscribe, join up, list, matriculate, note, record, recruit, register, sign on, sign up, take on. *antonyms* leave, reject.

enrolment *n* acceptance, admission, engagement, enlistment, matriculation, recruitment, register, registration.

ensconce *v* entrench, establish, install, locate, lodge, nestle, place, protect, put, screen, settle, shelter, shield.

ensemble *n* aggregate, assemblage, band, case, chorus, collection, company, corps de ballet, costume, entirety, get-up, group, outfit, rig-out, set, suit, sum, total, totality, troupe, whole.

enshrine *v* cherish, consecrate, dedicate, embalm, exalt, hallow, idolise, preserve, revere, sanctify, treasure.

enslave *v* bind, conquer, dominate, enthrall, overcome, subject, subjugate, yoke. *antonyms* emancipate, free.

enslavement *n* bondage, captivity, duress, enthralment, oppression, repression, serfdom, servitude, slavery, subjection, subjugation, vassalage. **antonym** emancipation.

ensnare v catch, embroil, enmesh, entangle, net, snare, snarl, trap.

ensue v arise, attend, befall, derive, eventuate, flow, follow, happen, issue, proceed, result, stem, succeed, turn out, turn up. **antonym** precede.

ensure v certify, clinch, confirm, effect, guarantee, guard, insure, protect, safeguard, secure, warrant.

entail v cause, demand, encompass, give rise to, impose, involve, lead to, necessitate, occasion, predetermine, require, result in.

entangle v bewilder, catch, complicate, compromise, confuse, embroil, enlace, enmesh, ensnare, entrap, foul, implicate, involve, jumble, knot, mat, mix up, muddle, perplex, puzzle, ravel, snag, snare, snarl, tangle, trammel, trap, twist. **antonym** disentangle.

enter v arrive, begin, board, commence, embark upon, enlist, enrol, inscribe, insert, introduce, join, list, log, note, offer, participate, participate in, penetrate, pierce, present, proffer, record, register, set about, set down, sign up, start, submit, take down, take up, tender. **antonyms** delete, issue, leave.

enterprise n activity, adventure, adventurousness, alertness, audacity, boldness, business, company, concern, daring, dash, drive, eagerness, effort, endeavour, energy, enthusiasm, establishment, firm, get-up-and-go, gumption, imagination, initiative, operation, plan, programme, project, push, readiness, resource, resourcefulness, spirit, undertaking, venture, vigour, zeal. **antonyms** apathy, inertia.

enterprising adj active, adventurous, alert, ambitious, aspiring, audacious, bold, daring, dashing, eager, energetic, enthusiastic, go-ahead, imaginative, intrepid, keen, ready, resourceful, self-reliant, spirited, stirring, up-and-coming, venturesome, vigorous, zealous. **antonyms** lethargic, unadventurous.

entertain v accommodate, accourt, amuse, charm, cheer, cherish, conceive, consider, contemplate, countenance, delight, divert, foster, harbour, hold, imagine, lodge, maintain, occupy, please, ponder, put up, regale, support, treat. **antonyms** bore, reject.

entertaining adj amusing, charming, cheering, delightful, diverting, droll, fun, funny, humorous, interesting, pleasant, pleasing, pleasurable, witty. **antonym** boring.

entertainment n amusement, cheer, distraction, diversion, enjoyment, extravaganza, fun, pastime, play, pleasure, recreation, satisfaction, show, spectacle, sport, table, treat.

enthral(l) v beguile, captivate, charm, enchant, enrapture, entrance, fascinate, grip, hypnotise, intrigue, mesmerise, rivet, spellbind, thrill. **antonyms** bore, weary.

enthralling adj beguiling, captivating, charming, compelling, compulsive, enchanting, entrancing, fascinating, gripping, hypnotising, intriguing, mesmeric, mesmerising, riveting, spellbinding, thrilling. **antonym** boring.

enthuse v absorb, drool, effervesce, emote, excite, gush, impassion, inflame, involve, possess, wax lyrical.

enthusiasm n ardour, avidity, craze, devotion, eagerness, earnestness, excitement, fad, fervour, frenzy, interest, keenness, mania, oomph, passion, rage, relish, spirit, vehemence, warmth, zeal, zest. **antonym** apathy.

enthusiast n addict, admirer, aficionado, buff, bug, devotee, eager beaver, fan, fanatic, fiend, follower, freak, lover, supporter, zealot. **antonym** detractor.

enthusiastic adj ardent, avid, devoted, eager, earnest, ebullient, excited, exuberant, fervent, fervid, forceful, gung-ho, hearty, keen, keen as mustard, lively, passionate, spirited, unstinting, vehement, vigorous, warm, whole-hearted, zealous. **antonyms** apathetic, reluctant, unenthusiastic.

entice v allure, attract, beguile, blandish, cajole, coax, decoy, draw, induce, inveigle, lead on, lure, persuade, prevail on, seduce, sweet-talk, tempt, wheedle.

enticement n allurement, attraction, bait, beguilement, blandishments, cajolery, coaxing, come-on, decoy, inducement, inveiglement, lure, persuasion, seduction, sweet-talk, temptation.

entire adj absolute, all-in, complete, continuous, full, intact, integrated, outright, perfect, sound, thorough, total, unabridged, unbroken, uncut, undamaged, undiminished, undivided, unified, unmarked, unmarred, unmitigated, unreserved, unrestricted, whole. **antonyms** impaired, incomplete, partial.

entirely *adv* absolutely, altogether, completely, every inch, exclusively, fully, hook line and sinker, in toto, lock stock and barrel, only, perfectly, solely, thoroughly, totally, unreservedly, utterly, wholly, without exception, without reservation. *antonym* partially.

entitle *v* accredit, allow, authorise, call, christen, denominate, designate, dub, empower, enable, enfranchise, label, license, name, permit, style, term, title, warrant.

entity *n* being, body, creature, essence, existence, individual, object, organism, presence, quantity, quiddity, quintessence, substance, thing.

entourage *n* associates, attendants, companions, company, cortège, coterie, court, escort, followers, following, retinue, staff, suite, train.

entrance[1] *n* access, admission, admittance, appearance, arrival, atrium, avenue, beginning, commencement, debut, door, doorway, entry, gate, ingress, initiation, inlet, introduction, opening, outset, passage, portal, start. *antonyms* departure, exit.

entrance[2] *v* bewitch, captivate, charm, delight, enchant, enrapture, enthrall, fascinate, gladden, hypnotise, magnetise, mesmerise, spellbind, transport. *antonyms* bore, repel.

entrant *n* beginner, candidate, competitor, contender, contestant, convert, entry, initiate, newcomer, novice, participant, player.

entrap *v* allure, beguile, capture, catch, decoy, embroil, enmesh, ensnare, entangle, entice, implicate, inveigle, involve, lure, net, seduce, snare, trap, trick.

entreat *v* appeal to, ask, beg, beseech, conjure, crave, enjoin, exhort, implore, importune, invoke, petition, plead with, pray, request, sue, supplicate.

entreaty *n* appeal, entreatment, exhortation, importunity, invocation, petition, plea, prayer, request, solicitation, suing, suit, supplication.

entrenched *adj* deep-rooted, deep-seated, firm, fixed, implanted, inbred, indelible, ineradicable, ingrained, rooted, set, unshakable, well-established.

entrust *v* assign, authorise, charge, commend, commit, confide, consign, delegate, deliver, depute, invest, trust, turn over.

entry[1] *n* access, admission, admittance, appearance, avenue, door, doorway, entering, entrance, gate, ingress, initiation, inlet, introduction, opening, passage, passageway, portal, threshold. *antonym* exit.

entry[2] *n* account, attempt, bulletin, candidate, competitor, contestant, effort, entrant, item, jotting, listing, memo, memorandum, minute, note, participant, player, record, registration, statement, submission.

entwine *v* braid, embrace, encircle, enlace, entwist, interlace, interlink, intertwine, interweave, knit, plait, splice, surround, thatch, twine, twist, weave, wind. *antonym* unravel.

enumerate *v* calculate, cite, count, detail, itemise, list, mention, name, number, quote, recapitulate, recite, reckon, recount, rehearse, relate, specify, spell out, tell.

enunciate *v* articulate, broadcast, declare, proclaim, promulgate, pronounce, propound, publish, say, sound, speak, state, utter, vocalise, voice.

envelop *v* blanket, cloak, conceal, cover, embrace, encase, encircle, enclose, encompass, enfold, engulf, enshroud, enwrap, hide, obscure, sheathe, shroud, surround, swaddle, swathe, veil, wrap.

envelope *n* case, casing, coating, cover, covering, jacket, sheath, shell, skin, wrapper, wrapping.

enviable *adj* advantageous, blessed, covetable, desirable, excellent, favoured, fine, fortunate, good, lucky, privileged. *antonym* unenviable.

envious *adj* begrudging, covetous, dissatisfied, green, green with envy, green-eyed, grudging, jaundiced, jealous, malcontent, malicious, resentful, spiteful.

environment *n* ambience, atmosphere, background, conditions, context, domain, element, entourage, habitat, locale, medium, milieu, scene, setting, situation, surroundings, territory.

environs *n* district, locality, neighbourhood, outskirts, precincts, suburbs, surround(ing)s, vicinity.

envisage *v* anticipate, conceive of, conceptualise, contemplate, fancy, foresee, imagine, picture, preconceive, predict, see, visualise.

envoy *n* agent, ambassador, courier, delegate, deputy, diplomat, emissary, intermediary, legate, messenger, minister, plenipotentiary, representative.

envy *n* covetousness, cupidity, dissatisfaction, enviousness, grudge, hatred, ill-will, jealousy, malice, malignity, resentfulness, resentment, spite.

v begrudge, covet, crave, grudge, resent.

ephemeral *adj* brief, evanescent, fleeting, flitting, impermanent, momentary, passing, short, short-lived, temporary, transient, transitory. *antonyms* enduring, lasting, perpetual.

epic *adj* colossal, elevated, exalted, grand, grandiloquent, great, heroic, Homeric, huge, imposing, impressive, lofty, majestic, sublime, vast. *antonym* ordinary.

epidemic *adj* general, pandemic, prevailing, prevalent, rampant, rife, sweeping, wide-ranging, widespread.

n growth, outbreak, pandemic, plague, rash, spread, upsurge, wave.

epigram *n* aphorism, apophthegm, bon mot, gnome, quip, witticism.

epilogue *n* afterword, coda, conclusion, postscript. *antonyms* foreword, preface, prologue.

episode *n* adventure, affaire, business, chapter, circumstance, event, experience, happening, incident, instalment, matter, occasion, occurrence, part, passage, scene, section.

episodic *adj* digressive, disconnected, disjointed, intermittent, irregular, occasional, picaresque, spasmodic, sporadic.

epistle *n* communication, letter, line, message, missive, note.

epithet *n* appellation, denomination, description, designation, name, nickname, so(u)briquet, tag, title.

epitome *n* abbreviation, abridgement, abstract, archetype, compendium, compression, condensation, contraction, digest, embodiment, essence, exemplar, personification, précis, quintessence, reduction, representation, résumé, summary, syllabus, synopsis, type.

epitomise *v* abbreviate, abridge, abstract, compress, condense, contract, curtail, cut, embody, encapsulate, exemplify, illustrate, incarnate, personify, précis, reduce, represent, shorten, summarise, symbolise, typify. *antonyms* elaborate, expand.

equable *adj* agreeable, calm, composed, consistent, constant, easy-going, even, even-tempered, imperturbable, level-headed, phlegmatic, placid, regular, serene, smooth, stable, steady, temperate, tranquil, unchanging, unexcitable, unflappable, uniform, unruffled, unvarying, unworrying. *antonyms* excitable, variable.

equal *adj* able, adequate, alike, balanced, capable, commensurate, competent, corresponding, egalitarian, equable, equivalent, even, even-handed, evenly-balanced, evenly-matched, evenly-proportioned, fair, fifty-fifty, fit, identical, impartial, just, level-pegging, like, matched, proportionate, ready, regular, sufficient, suitable, symmetrical, tantamount, the same, unbiased, uniform, unvarying, up to. *antonyms* different, inequitable, unequal.

n brother, coequal, counterpart, equivalent, fellow, match, mate, parallel, peer, rival, twin.

v balance, correspond to, equalise, equate, even, level, match, parallel, rival, square with, tally with.

equalise *v* balance, compensate, draw level, equal, equate, even up, level, match, regularise, smooth, square, standardise.

equality *n* balance, coequality, correspondence, egalitarianism, equitability, equivalence, evenness, fairness, identity, likeness, par, parity, proportion, sameness, similarity, uniformity. *antonym* inequality.

equanimity *n* aplomb, calm, calmness, composure, coolness, equability, imperturbability, level-headedness, peace, phlegm, placidity, poise, presence of mind, self-possession, serenity, steadiness, tranquillity. *antonyms* alarm, anxiety, discomposure.

equate *v* agree, balance, compare, correspond to, correspond with, equalise, juxtapose, liken, match, offset, pair, parallel, square, tally.

equation *n* agreement, balancing, bracketing, comparison, correspondence, equalisation, equality, equating, equivalence, juxtaposition, likeness, match, pairing, parallel.

equilibrium *n* balance, calm, calmness, collectedness, composure, cool, coolness, counterpoise, equanimity, equipoise, evenness, poise, rest, self-possession, serenity, stability, steadiness, symmetry. *antonym* imbalance.

equip *v* arm, array, attire, deck out, dress, endow, fit out, fit up, furnish, kit out, outfit, prepare, provide, rig, stock, supply.

equipment *n* accessories, accoutrements, apparatus, baggage, furnishings, furniture, gear, impedimenta,

implements, material, muniments, outfit,
paraphernalia, rig-out, stuff, supplies,
tackle, things, tools.

equitable *adj* disinterested,
dispassionate, due, ethical, even-handed,
fair, fair-and-square, honest, impartial,
just, legitimate, objective, proper,
proportionate, reasonable, right, rightful,
square, unbiased, unprejudiced.
antonyms inequitable, unfair.

equity *n* disinterestedness, equality,
equitableness, even-handedness, fair
play, fair-mindedness, fairness, honesty,
impartiality, integrity, justice, justness,
objectivity, reasonableness, rectitude,
righteousness, uprightness. *antonym*
inequity.

equivalence *n* agreement, alikeness,
conformity, correspondence, equality,
evenness, identity, interchangeability,
interchangeableness, likeness, match,
parallel, parity, sameness, similarity,
substitutability, synonymy. *antonyms*
dissimilarity, inequality.

equivalent *adj* alike, commensurate,
comparable, convertible, correlative,
correspondent, corresponding, equal,
even, homologous, interchangeable,
same, similar, substitutable, synonymous, tantamount, twin. *antonyms*
dissimilar, unlike.
n correlative, correspondent, counterpart, equal, homologue, homotype,
match, opposite number, parallel, peer,
twin.

equivocal *adj* ambiguous, ambivalent,
confusing, doubtful, dubious, evasive,
indefinite, indeterminate, misleading,
oblique, obscure, questionable,
suspicious, uncertain, vague. *antonyms*
clear, unequivocal.

equivocate *v* dodge, evade, fence,
fudge, hedge, mislead, parry, prevaricate,
pussyfoot, quibble, shift, shuffle,
sidestep, weasel.

equivocation *n* ambiguity, confusion,
double talk, doubtfulness, evasion,
hedging, prevarication, quibbling,
shifting, shuffling, sophistry, waffle,
weasel-words. *antonym* directness.

era *n* aeon, age, century, cycle, date,
day, days, epoch, generation, period,
stage, time.

eradicable *adj* destroyable, destructible,
effaceable, eliminable, erasable, ex-
terminable, extinguishable, removable.
antonyms ineradicable, permanent.

eradicate *v* abolish, annihilate, destroy,
efface, eliminate, erase, expunge,
exterminate, extinguish, extirpate, get
rid of, obliterate, rase, remove, root
out, stamp out, suppress, unroot, uproot,
weed out.

eradication *n* abolition, annihilation,
destruction, effacement, elimination,
erasure, expunction, extermination,
extinction, extirpation, obliteration,
removal, riddance, suppression.

erase *v* blot out, cancel, cleanse, delete,
efface, eliminate, eradicate, expunge, get
rid of, obliterate, remove, rub out.

erect *adj* elevated, engorged, firm,
hard, perpendicular, pricked, raised,
rigid, standing, stiff, straight, taut,
tense, tumescent, upright, upstanding,
vertical. *antonyms* limp, relaxed.
v assemble, build, constitute, construct,
create, elevate, establish, fabricate, form,
found, initiate, institute, lift, mount,
organise, pitch, put up, raise, rear, set up.

erection *n* assembly, building,
construction, creation, edifice, elevation,
establishment, fabrication, manufacture,
pile, raising, rigidity, stiffness, structure,
tumescence.

ergo *adv* accordingly, consequently, for
this reason, hence, in consequence, so,
then, therefore, this being the case, thus.

erode *v* abrade, consume,
corrade, denude, destroy, deteriorate,
disintegrate, eat away, grind down, spoil,
wear away, wear down.

erosion *n* abrasion, attrition,
consumption, corrasion, denudation,
destruction, deterioration, diminish-
ment, disintegration, fragmentation,
undermining.

erotic *adj* amatory, amorous,
aphrodisiac, carnal, concupiscent,
erotogenic, erotogenous, libidinous,
lustful, page-three, rousing, seductive,
sensual, sexy, stimulating, suggestive,
titillating, venereal, voluptuous.

err *v* blunder, deviate, fail, go
astray, lapse, misapprehend, misbehave,
miscalculate, misjudge, mistake,
misunderstand, offend, sin, slip up, stray,
stumble, transgress, trespass, trip up,
wander.

errand *n* assignment, charge,
commission, duty, job, message,
mission, task.

errant *adj* aberrant, deviant, erring,
itinerant, journeying, loose, nomadic,
offending, peripatetic, rambling,
roaming, roving, sinful, sinning, stray,
straying, vagrant, wandering, wayward,
wrong.

erratic *adj* aberrant, abnormal, capricious, changeable, desultory, directionless, eccentric, fitful, fluctuating, inconsistent, inconstant, irregular, meandering, planetary, shifting, unpredictable, unreliable, unstable, variable, wandering, wayward. **antonyms** consistent, reliable, stable, straight.

erroneous *adj* amiss, fallacious, false, faulty, flawed, illogical, inaccurate, incorrect, inexact, invalid, mistaken, specious, spurious, unfounded, unsound, untrue, wrong. **antonym** correct.

error *n* barbarism, bloomer, blunder, boob, delinquency, delusion, deviation, erratum, fallacy, fault, faux pas, flaw, howler, ignorance, illusion, inaccuracy, inexactitude, lapse, literal, malapropism, misapprehension, miscalculation, misconception, misdeed, misprint, mistake, misunderstanding, offence, omission, oversight, overslip, sin, slip, slip-up, solecism, transgression, trespass, wrong, wrongdoing.

erstwhile *adj* bygone, ex, former, late, old, once, one-time, past, previous, sometime.

erudite *adj* academic, cultivated, cultured, educated, highbrow, knowledgeable, learned, lettered, literate, profound, recondite, scholarly, scholastic, well-educated, well-read, wise. **antonym** unlettered.

erupt *v* belch, break, break out, burst, discharge, eruct, eructate, explode, flare, gush, rift, spew, spout, vent, vomit.

eruption *n* discharge, ejection, eructation, explosion, inflammation, outbreak, outburst, rash, sally, venting.

escalate *v* accelerate, amplify, ascend, climb, enlarge, expand, extend, grow, heighten, increase, intensify, magnify, mount, raise, rise, spiral, step up. **antonym** diminish.

escapade *n* adventure, antic, caper, doing, exploit, fling, lark, prank, romp, scrape, spree, stunt, trick.

escape *v* abscond, avoid, baffle, bolt, break free, break loose, break off, break out, circumvent, decamp, discharge, do a bunk, dodge, drain, duck, elude, emanate, evade, flee, flit, flow, fly, foil, get away, gush, issue, leak, ooze, pass, pour forth, scarper, seep, shake off, shun, skedaddle, skip, slip, slip away, spurt, take it on the run, take to one's heels, trickle, vamoose.
n avoidance, bolt, break, break-out, circumvention, decampment, discharge, distraction, diversion, drain, effluence, effluent, elusion, emanation, emission, escapism, evasion, flight, flit, getaway, gush, jail-break, leak, leakage, out, outflow, outlet, outpour, pastime, recreation, relaxation, relief, safety-valve, seepage, spurt, vent.

escape route bolthole, egress, escape road, exit, loophole, out, outlet, secret passage, vent.

eschew *v* abandon, abjure, abstain from, avoid, disdain, forgo, forswear, give up, keep clear of, refrain from, renounce, repudiate, shun, spurn, swear off. **antonym** embrace.

escort *n* aide, attendant, beau, bodyguard, chaperon, companion, company, convoy, cortège, entourage, gigolo, guard, guardian, guide, partner, pilot, procession, protection, protector, retinue, safeguard, squire, suite, train.
v accompany, chaperon, chum, conduct, convoy, guard, guide, lead, partner, protect, shepherd, squire, usher.

esoteric *adj* abstruse, arcane, cabbalistic, confidential, cryptic, hermetic, hidden, inner, inscrutable, inside, mysterious, mystic, mystical, obscure, occult, private, recondite, secret. **antonyms** familiar, popular.

especial *adj* chief, conspicuous, distinguished, eminent, exceptional, exclusive, express, extraordinary, individual, marked, notable, noteworthy, outstanding, particular, peculiar, personal, pre-eminent, principal, private, proper, remarkable, signal, singular, special, specific, striking, uncommon, unique, unusual.

especially *adv* chiefly, conspicuously, eminently, exceedingly, exceptionally, exclusively, expressly, extraordinarily, mainly, markedly, notably, noticeably, outstandingly, particularly, passing, peculiarly, pre-eminently, principally, remarkably, signally, singularly, specially, specifically, strikingly, supremely, uncommonly, uniquely, unusually, very.

espionage *n* counter-intelligence, infiltration, intelligence, investigation, probing, reconnaissance, spying, surveillance, undercover operations.

espouse *v* adopt, advocate, affiance, back, befriend, betroth, champion, choose, defend, embrace, maintain, marry, opt for, patronise, support, take up, wed.

espy v behold, descry, detect, discern, discover, distinguish, glimpse, make out, notice, observe, perceive, see, sight, spot, spy.

essay[1] n article, assignment, commentary, composition, critique, discourse, dissertation, paper, piece, review, thesis, tract, treatise.

essay[2] n attempt, bash, bid, crack, effort, endeavour, experiment, go, shot, stab, struggle, test, trial, try, undertaking, venture, whack, whirl.

v attempt, endeavour, go for, have a bash, have a crack, have a go, have a stab, strain, strive, struggle, tackle, take on, test, try, undertake.

essence n attributes, being, centre, character, characteristics, concentrate, core, crux, decoction, distillate, elixir, entity, extract, fragrance, heart, kernel, life, lifeblood, marrow, meaning, nature, perfume, pith, principle, properties, qualities, quality, quintessence, scent, significance, soul, spirit, spirits, substance, tincture, virtuality.

essential[1] adj absolute, basic, cardinal, characteristic, complete, constituent, constitutional, crucial, definitive, elemental, elementary, formal, fundamental, ideal, important, indispensable, inherent, innate, intrinsic, key, main, must, necessary, needed, perfect, principal, quintessential, required, requisite, typical, vital. **antonym** inessential.

n basic, fundamental, must, necessary, necessity, prerequisite, principle, qualification, quality, requirement, requisite, rudiment, sine qua non. **antonym** inessential.

essential[2] adj concentrated, decocted, distilled, extracted, pure, purified, refined, volatile.

establish v affirm, attest to, authenticate, authorise, base, certify, confirm, constitute, corroborate, create, decree, demonstrate, enact, ensconce, entrench, fix, form, found, ground, implant, inaugurate, install, institute, introduce, invent, lodge, ordain, organise, plant, prove, ratify, root, sanction, seat, secure, set up, settle, show, start, station, substantiate, validate, verify.

established adj accepted, attested, confirmed, conventional, ensconced, entrenched, experienced, fixed, proved, proven, respected, routed, secure, settled, stated, steadfast, traditional. **antonyms** impermanent, unreliable.

establishment n abode, building, business, company, concern, construction, corporation, creation, domicile, dwelling, edifice, enactment, enterprise, erection, factory, firm, formation, foundation, founding, home, house, household, inauguration, inception, installation, institute, institution, introduction, invention, office, ordination, organisation, outfit, plant, quarters, residence, ruling class, set-up, structure, system, the powers that be, the system.

estate n area, assets, belongings, caste, class, condition, demesne, domain, effects, fortune, goods, grade, holdings, lands, lot, manor, order, period, place, position, possessions, property, quality, ranch, rank, situation, standing, state, station, status, wealth.

esteem v account, adjudge, admire, believe, calculate, cherish, consider, count, deem, estimate, hold, honour, include, judge, like, love, prize, rate, reckon, regard, regard highly, respect, revere, reverence, think, treasure, value, venerate, view.

n account, admiration, consideration, count, credit, estimation, good opinion, honour, judgement, love, reckoning, regard, respect, reverence, veneration.

estimable adj admirable, commendable, considerable, distinguished, egregious, esteemed, excellent, good, honourable, laudable, meritorious, notable, noteworthy, praiseworthy, reputable, respectable, respected, valuable, valued, worthy. **antonyms** despicable, insignificant.

estimate v appraise, approximate, assess, believe, calculate, compute, conjecture, consider, count, evaluate, gauge, guess, judge, number, opine, rank, rate, reckon, surmise, think, value.

n appraisal, approximation, assessment, belief, computation, conceit, conception, conjecture, estimation, evaluation, guess, guesstimate, judgement, opinion, reckoning, surmise, valuation.

estimation n account, admiration, appraisal, appreciation, assessment, belief, calculation, computation, conception, consideration, credit, esteem, estimate, evaluation, good opinion, honour, judgement, opinion, rating, reckoning, regard, respect, reverence, veneration, view.

estrange v alienate, antagonise,

disaffect, disunite, divide, drive a wedge between, drive apart, part, put a barrier between, separate, set at variance, sever, sunder, withdraw, withhold. *antonyms* ally, attract, bind, unite.

tch *v* bite, burn, carve, corrode, cut, dig, engrave, furrow, grave, groove, hatch, impress, imprint, incise, ingrain, inscribe, stamp.

ternal *adj* abiding, ceaseless, changeless, constant, deathless, durable, endless, enduring, eterne, everlasting, immortal, immutable, imperishable, incessant, indestructible, infinite, interminable, lasting, limitless, never-ending, perennial, permanent, perpetual, timeless, unceasing, unchanging, undying, unending, unremitting. *antonyms* changeable, ephemeral, temporary.

ternally *adv* ceaselessly, constantly, endlessly, everlastingly, immutably, incessantly, indestructibly, interminably, lastingly, never-endingly, perennially, permanently, perpetually, unendingly. *antonyms* briefly, temporarily.

ternity *n* aeon, afterlife, age, ages, endlessness, everlasting, everlastingness, heaven, hereafter, immortality, immutability, infinitude, infinity, next world, paradise, perpetuity, timelessness, world to come.

thereal *adj* aerial, airy, celestial, dainty, delicate, diaphanous, elemental, essential, exquisite, fairy, fine, gossamer, heavenly, impalpable, insubstantial, intangible, light, rarefied, rectified, refined, spiritual, subtle, tenuous, unearthly, unworldly. *antonyms* earthly, solid.

thical *adj* commendable, conscientious, correct, decent, fair, fitting, good, honest, honourable, just, meet, moral, noble, principled, proper, right, righteous, seemly, upright, virtuous. *antonym* unethical.

thics *n* code, conscience, equity, mind philosophy, moral philosophy, moral values, morality, principles, probity, propriety, rule, rules, seemliness, standards.

thnic *adj* aboriginal, ancestral, cultural, folk, historic, indigenous, national, native, racial, traditional, tribal.

thos *n* attitude, beliefs, character, code, disposition, ethic, manners, morality, principles, rationale, spirit, standards, tenor.

tiquette *n* ceremony, civility, code, convention, conventionalities, correctness, courtesy, customs, decency, decorum, formalities, manners, politeness, politesse, propriety, protocol, rules, seemliness, usage, use.

etymology *n* derivation, descent, lexicology, origin, pedigree, source, word history, word-lore.

eulogise *v* acclaim, adulate, applaud, approve, celebrate, commend, compliment, congratulate, cry up, exalt, extol, flatter, glorify, honour, laud, magnify, praise. *antonym* condemn.

eulogy *n* acclaim, acclamation, accolade, applause, commendation, compliment, exaltation, glorification, laud, plaudit, praise, tribute. *antonym* condemnation.

euphemism *n* evasion, fig-leaf, genteelism, polite term, politeness, substitution, understatement.

euphony *n* consonance, harmoniousness, harmony, melliflu-ousness, mellowness, melodiousness, melody, music, musicality, tunefulness. *antonym* cacophony.

euphoria *n* bliss, buoyancy, cheerfulness, cloud nine, ecstasy, elation, enthusiasm, exaltation, exhilaration, exultation, glee, high, high spirits, intoxication, joy, joyousness, jubilation, rapture, transport. *antonym* depression.

euphoric *adj* blissful, buoyant, cheerful, ecstatic, elated, enraptured, enthusiastic, exhilarated, exultant, exulted, gleeful, happy, high, intoxicated, joyful, joyous, jubilant, rapturous. *antonym* depressed.

evacuate *v* abandon, clear, clear out, decamp, depart, desert, forsake, leave, quit, relinquish, remove, retire from, vacate, withdraw.

evacuation *n* abandonment, clearance, departure, desertion, exodus, quitting, relinquishment, removal, retiral, retreat, vacation, withdrawal.

evade *v* avert, avoid, balk, blink, chicken out of, circumvent, cop out, decline, dodge, duck, elude, equivocate, escape, fence, fend off, fudge, give the runaround, parry, prevaricate, quibble, scrimshank, shirk, shun, sidestep, skive, steer clear of, temporise. *antonym* face.

evaluate *v* appraise, assay, assess, calculate, compute, estimate, gauge, judge, rank, rate, reckon, size up, value, weigh.

evaluation *n* appraisal, assessment, calculation, computation, estimate, estimation, judgement, opinion, rating, reckoning, valuation.

evanescent *adj* brief, changing, disappearing, ephemeral, fading, fleeting, fugitive, impermanent, insubstantial, momentary, passing, perishable, short-lived, temporary, transient, transitory, unstable, vanishing. *antonym* permanent.

evaporate *v* condense, dehydrate, dematerialise, desiccate, disappear, dispel, disperse, dissipate, dissolve, distil, dry, evanesce, exhale, fade, melt (away), vanish, vaporise.

evaporation *n* condensation, dehydration, dematerialisation, desiccation, disappearance, dispelling, dispersal, dissipation, dissolution, distillation, drying, evanescence, fading, melting, vanishing, vaporisation.

evasion *n* artifice, avoidance, circumvention, cop-out, cunning, dodge, elusion, equivocation, escape, euphemism, evasiveness, excuse, fudging, obfuscation, obliqueness, pretext, prevarication, put-off, ruse, shift, shirking, shuffling, sophism, sophistry, subterfuge, trickery, weasel-words. *antonyms* directness, frankness.

evasive *adj* ambiguous, cag(e)y, cunning, deceitful, deceptive, devious, disingenuous, dissembling, elusive, equivocating, indirect, misleading, oblique, prevaricating, secretive, shifty, shuffling, slippery, tricky, unforthcoming, vacillating. *antonyms* direct, frank.

eve *n* brink, edge, evening, moment, point, threshold, verge, vigil.

even *adj* abreast, alongside, balanced, calm, commensurate, comparable, composed, constant, cool, disinterested, dispassionate, drawn, equable, equal, equalised, equanimous, equitable, even-tempered, fair, fair and square, fifty-fifty, flat, fluent, flush, horizontal, identical, impartial, impassive, imperturbable, just, level, level-pegging, like, matching, metrical, monotonous, neck and neck, on a par, parallel, peaceful, placid, plane, plumb, proportionate, quits, regular, rhythmical, serene, side by side, similar, smooth, square, stable, steady, straight, symmetrical, tied, tranquil, true, unbiased, unbroken, undisturbed, unexcitable, unexcited, uniform, uninterrupted, unprejudiced, unruffled, unvarying, unwavering, well-balanced. *antonyms* unequal, uneven.

adv all the more, also, although, as well, at all, directly, exactly, hardly, including just, much, scarcely, so much as, still, yet *v* align, balance, equal, equalise, flatten, flush, level, match, regularise, regulate, smooth, square, stabilise, steady, straighten.

even so all the same, despite that however, however that may be, in spite of that, nevertheless, nonetheless notwithstanding that, still, yet.

even-handed *adj* balanced, disinterested, dispassionate, equitable, fair, fair and square, impartial, just, neutral, non-discriminatory, reasonable, square, unbiased, unprejudiced, without fear or favour. *antonym* inequitable.

evening *n* crepuscule, dusk, eve, even, eventide, gloaming, nightfall, sundown, sunset, twilight, vesper.

evenness *n* alikeness, balance, calmness, commensurateness, comparability, composure, constancy, coolness, equability, equality, equanimity, flatness, fluency, identicalness, impassivity, imperturbability, levelness, monotony, peacableness, placidity, proportion, regularity, rhythmicality, serenity, similarity, smoothness, stability, steadiness, straightness, symmetry, tranquillity, trueness, uniformity. *antonyms* inequality, unevenness.

event *n* adventure, affair, bout, business, case, circumstance, competition, conclusion, consequence, contest, effect, end, engagement, episode, eventuality, experience, fact, game, happening, incident, issue, match, matter, milestone, occasion, occurrence, outcome, possibility, result, termination, tournament, upshot.

even-tempered *adj* calm, composed, cool, cool-headed, equable, impassive, imperturbable, level-headed, peaceable, peaceful, placid, serene, stable, steady, tranquil, unexcitable, unfussed, unruffled. *antonym* excitable.

eventful *adj* active, busy, consequential, critical, crucial, decisive, exciting, fateful, full, historic, important, interesting, lively, memorable, momentous, notable, noteworthy, portentous, remarkable, significant, unforgettable. *antonyms* dull, ordinary, uneventful.

eventual *adj* concluding, consequent, ensuing, final, future, impending, last, later, overall, planned, projected, prospective, resulting, subsequent, ultimate.

eventuality *n* case, chance,

circumstance, contingency, crisis, emergency, event, happening, happenstance, likelihood, mishap, outcome, possibility, probability.

ventually *adv* after all, at last, at length, finally, in one's own good time, sooner or later, subsequently, ultimately.

ver *adv* always, at all, at all times, at any time, ceaselessly, constantly, continually, endlessly, eternally, everlastingly, evermore, for ever, in any case, in any circumstances, incessantly, on any account, perpetually, unceasingly, unendingly.

verlasting *adj* abiding, boring, ceaseless, changeless, constant, continual, continuous, deathless, durable, endless, enduring, eternal, immortal, imperishable, incessant, indestructible, infinite, interminable, lasting, monotonous, never-ending, permanent, perpetual, relentless, tedious, timeless, unceasing, unchanging, undying, unfading, uninterrupted, unremitting. **antonyms** temporary, transient.

vermore *adv* always, eternally, ever, ever after, for ever, for ever and a day, for ever and ever, henceforth, hereafter, till doomsday, to the end of time, unceasingly.

verybody *n* all and sundry, each one, everyone, one and all, the whole world.

veryday *adj* accustomed, banal, boring, common, common-or-garden, commonplace, conventional, customary, daily, dull, familiar, frequent, habitual, informal, monotonous, mundane, normal, ordinary, plain, prosaic, quotidian, regular, routine, run-of-the-mill, simple, stock, unexceptional, unimaginative, usual, wonted, workaday. **antonyms** exceptional, special.

veryone *n* all and sundry, each one, every man-jack, every mother's son, everybody, one and all, the whole world.

verything *n* all, lock stock and barrel, the aggregate, the entirety, the lot, the sum, the total, the whole caboodle, the whole lot, the whole shoot, the whole shooting-match.

verywhere *adv* all along the line, all around, all over, far and near, far and wide, high and low, left right and centre, omnipresent, passim.

vict *v* boot out, cast out, chuck out, dislodge, dispossess, eject, expel, expropriate, give the bum's rush, kick out, oust, put out, remove, show the door, turf out.

eviction *n* clearance, dislodgement, dispossession, ejection, expropriation, expulsion, removal, the bum's rush.

evidence *n* affirmation, attestation, betrayal, confirmation, corroboration, data, declaration, demonstration, deposition, documentation, grounds, hint, indication, manifestation, mark, pledge, proof, sign, substantiation, suggestion, testimony, token, voucher, witness.
v affirm, attest, betray, confirm, demonstrate, denote, display, establish, evince, exhibit, indicate, manifest, prove, reveal, show, signify, testify to, witness.

evident *adj* apparent, clear, clearcut, confessed, conspicuous, detectable, discernible, distinct, incontestable, incontrovertible, indisputable, manifest, noticeable, obvious, ostensible, palpable, patent, perceptible, plain, tangible, undeniable, unmistakable, visible. **antonym** uncertain.

evidently *adv* apparently, clearly, distinctly, doubtless, doubtlessly, incontestably, incontrovertibly, indisputably, indubitably, manifestly, obviously, ostensibly, outwardly, patently, plainly, seemingly, undoubtedly, unmistakably, unquestionably.

evil *adj* adverse, bad, baleful, baneful, base, blackguardly, blackhearted, calamitous, catastrophic, corrupt, cruel, deadly, deleterious, depraved, destructive, detrimental, devilish, dire, disastrous, foul, ghastly, grim, harmful, heinous, hurtful, immoral, inauspicious, inimical, iniquitous, injurious, malefactory, malevolent, malicious, malignant, mephitic, mischievous, miscreant, nefarious, noxious, offensive, painful, perfidious, pernicious, poisonous, putrid, reprobate, ruinous, sinful, sorrowful, ugly, unfortunate, unlucky, unpleasant, unspeakable, vicious, vile, villainous, wicked, woeful, wrong.
n adversity, affliction, amiss, badness, bane, baseness, blow, calamity, catastrophe, corruption, curse, depravity, disaster, distress, foulness, harm, heinousness, hurt, ill, immorality, impiety, improbity, iniquity, injury, malignity, mischief, misery, misfortune, pain, perfidy, ruin, sin, sinfulness, sorrow, suffering, turpitude, ulcer, vice, viciousness, villainy, wickedness, woe, wrong, wrong-doing.

evil spirit bogey, demon, devil, fiend,

ghost, goblin, gremlin, hobgoblin, imp, incubus, nightmare, succubus, troll.

evince v attest, betoken, betray, confess, declare, demonstrate, display, establish, evidence, exhibit, express, indicate, manifest, reveal, show, signify. **antonyms** conceal, suppress.

evoke v activate, actuate, arouse, awaken, call, call forth, call up, conjure up, educe, elicit, excite, induce, invoke, produce, provoke, raise, recall, rekindle, stimulate, stir, summon, summon up. **antonyms** quell, suppress.

evolution n Darwinism, derivation, descent, development, expansion, growth, increase, maturation, progress, progression, ripening, unfolding, unrolling.

evolve v derive, descend, develop, disclose, elaborate, emerge, enlarge, expand, grow, increase, mature, progress, result, unravel.

exacerbate v aggravate, deepen, embitter, enrage, exaggerate, exasperate, excite, heighten, increase, inflame, infuriate, intensify, irritate, provoke, sharpen, vex, worsen. **antonym** soothe.

exact adj accurate, blow-by-blow, careful, close, correct, definite, detailed, explicit, express, factual, faithful, faultless, finical, finicky, flawless, identical, letter-perfect, literal, methodical, meticulous, nice, orderly, painstaking, particular, perfectionist, precise, punctilious, right, rigorous, scrupulous, severe, specific, square, strict, true, unambiguous, unequivocal, unerring, veracious, very, word-perfect. **antonym** inexact.

v bleed, claim, command, compel, demand, extort, extract, force, impose, insist on, milk, require, requisition, squeeze, wrest, wring.

exacting adj arduous, demanding, difficult, exigent, hard, harsh, imperious, laborious, oppressive, painstaking, rigid, rigorous, severe, stern, strict, stringent, taxing, tough, trying, tyrannical, unsparing, uphill. **antonyms** easy, tolerant.

exactitude n accuracy, authenticity, care, carefulness, clarity, conscientiousness, correctness, detail, exactness, faithfulness, faultlessness, fidelity, meticulousness, nicety, orderliness, painstakingness, perfectionism, preciseness, precision, promptitude, promptness, punctilio, punctuality, regularity, rigorousness, rigour, scrupulousness,

strictness, thoroughness, truth, veracity. **antonyms** carelessness, inaccuracy.

exactly adv absolutely, accurately, bang, carefully, correctly, dead, definitely, explicitly, expressly, faithfully, faultlessly, just, literally, methodically, particularly, plumb, precisely, punctiliously, quite, rigorously, scrupulously, severely, specifically, strictly, to the letter, truly, truthfully, unambiguously, unequivocally, unerringly, veraciously, verbatim.

interj absolutely, agreed, certainly, indeed, just so, of course, precisely, quite, right, true.

exactness n accuracy, authenticity, carefulness, correctness, detail, exactitude, faithfulness, faultlessness, fidelity, meticulousness, nicety, orderliness, painstakingness, perfectionism, preciseness, precision, promptitude, regularity, rigorousness, rigour, scrupulousness, strictness, truth, veracity, verity. **antonyms** carelessness, inaccuracy.

exaggerate v amplify, bounce, caricature, distend, embellish, embroider, emphasise, enlarge, exalt, hyperbolise, inflate, magnify, overdo, overdraw, overemphasise, overestimate, oversell, overstate, pile it on. **antonyms** belittle, understate.

exaggeration n amplification, burlesque, caricature, embellishment, emphasis, enlargement, exaltation, excess, extravagance, hyperbole, inflation, magnification, overemphasis, overestimation, overstatement, parody, pretension, pretentiousness. **antonyms** meiosis, understatement.

exalt v acclaim, advance, aggrandise, animate, applaud, arouse, bless, crown, deify, delight, dignify, elate, electrify, elevate, enliven, ennoble, enthrone, excite, exhilarate, extol, fire, glorify, heighten, honour, idolise, inspire, inspirit, laud, magnify, praise, promote, raise, revere, reverence, stimulate, sublimise, thrill, upgrade, uplift, venerate, worship. **antonym** debase.

exaltation n acclaim, adoration, adulation, advancement, aggrandisement, animation, apotheosis, applause, blessing, bliss, canonisation, deification, delight, dignification, dignity, ecstasy, elation, elevation, eminence, ennoblement, enthusiasm, excitement, exhilaration, extolment, exultation, glorification, glory, grandeur, homage, honour, idealisation, idolisation, inspiration, joy, joyfulness, joyousness, jubilation, laudation, lionisation, loftiness, magnification, plaudits, praise, prestige, promotion, rapture, reverence, rise, stimulation, transport, tribute, upgrading, uplift, veneration, worship. *antonym* debasement.

exalted *adj* animated, august, blissful, dignified, ecstatic, elate, elated, elevated, eminent, enhanced, enlivened, enthusiastic, exaggerated, excessive, excited, exhilarated, exultant, glorified, glorious, grand, happy, high, high-minded, high-ranking, honoured, ideal, idealised, in high spirits, in seventh heaven, inflated, inspired, inspirited, intellectual, joyful, joyous, jubilant, lofty, lordly, noble, overblown, prestigious, pretentious, princely, rapturous, stately, stimulated, sublime, superior, transcendent, transported, uplifted, uplifting. *antonym* debased.

examination *n* analysis, appraisal, assay, audit, check, check-up, critique, cross-examination, cross-questioning, exam, exploration, inquiry, inquisition, inspection, interrogation, investigation, observation, once-over, perusal, probe, questioning, quiz, research, review, scan, scrutiny, search, sift, study, survey, test, trial, viva.

examine *v* analyse, appraise, assay, audit, case, check (out), consider, cross-examine, cross-question, explore, eyeball, grill, inquire, inspect, interrogate, investigate, peruse, ponder, pore over, probe, question, quiz, review, scan, scrutinise, sift, study, survey, sus out, test, vet, weigh.

example *n* archetype, case, case in point, caution, citation, exemplar, exemplification, exemplum, ideal, illustration, instance, lesson, mirror, model, occurrence, paradigm, paragon, parallel, pattern, precedent, prototype, sample, specimen, standard, type, warning.

exasperate *v* aggravate, anger, annoy, bug, enrage, exacerbate, excite, gall, get, get in someone's hair, get on someone's nerves, get on someone's wick, get to, goad, incense, inflame, infuriate, irk, irritate, madden, needle, nettle, peeve, pique, plague, provoke, rankle, rile, rouse, vex. *antonyms* calm, soothe.

exasperated *adj* aggravated, angered, angry, annoyed, at the end of one's tether, bored, bugged, fed up, galled, goaded, incensed, indignant, infuriated, irked, irritated, maddened, needled, nettled, peeved, piqued, provoked, riled, vexed.

exasperating *adj* aggravating, annoying, boring, bothersome, disagreeable, galling, infuriating, irksome, irritating, maddening, pernicious, pesky, provoking, troublesome, vexatious, vexing.

exasperation *n* aggravation, anger, annoyance, arousal, discontent, disgust, displeasure, dissatisfaction, enragement, exacerbation, fury, gall, indignation, inflammation, ire, irritation, passion, pique, provocation, rage, resentment, vexation, wrath. *antonym* calmness.

excavate *v* burrow, cut, delve, dig, dig out, dig up, disinter, drive, exhume, gouge, hollow, mine, quarry, sap, scoop, trench, tunnel, uncover, undermine, unearth.

excavation *n* burrow, cavity, cut, cutting, dig, diggings, ditch, dugout, hole, hollow, mine, pit, quarry, sap, sapping, shaft, trench, trough, undermining.

exceed *v* beat, better, cap, contravene, eclipse, excel, outdistance, outdo, outrun, outshine, outstrip, overdo, overstep, overtake, pass, surmount, surpass, take liberties with, top, transcend, transgress.

exceeding *adj* amazing, astonishing, enormous, exceptional, excessive, extraordinary, great, huge, outstanding, pre-eminent, superior, superlative, surpassing, transcendent, unequalled, unprecedented, unusual, vast.

exceedingly *adv* amazingly, astonishingly, enormously, especially, exceeding, exceptionally, excessively, extraordinarily, extremely, greatly, highly, hugely, inordinately, passing, superlatively, surpassingly, unprecedentedly, unusually, vastly, very.

excel *v* beat, better, cap, eclipse, exceed, outclass, outdo, outperform, outrank, outrival, outshine, outstrip, overshadow, pass, predominate, shine, stand out, surmount, surpass, top, transcend, trump.

excellence *n* distinction, eminence, fineness, goodness, greatness, merit, perfection, pre-eminence, purity, quality, superiority, supremacy, transcendence, virtue, worth. *antonym* inferiority.

excellent *adj* A1, admirable, boss, brave, bully, capital, champion, choice, commendable, corking, crack, cracking, distinguished, estimable, exemplary, exquisite, fine, first-class, first-rate, good, great, hot stuff, laudable, meritorious, nonpareil, notable, noted, noteworthy, outstanding, peerless, prime, remarkable, ripping, select, splendid, sterling, stunning, superb, superior, superlative, surpassing, tiptop, top-notch, topping, unequalled, unexceptionable, wonderful, worthy. **antonym** inferior.

except *prep* apart from, bar, barring, besides, but, except for, excepting, excluding, exclusive of, leaving out, less, minus, not counting, omitting, other than, save, saving.
v ban, bar, debar, disallow, eliminate, exclude, leave out, omit, pass over, reject, rule out.

exception *n* abnormality, anomaly, curiosity, debarment, departure, deviation, eccentricity, excepting, exclusion, exemption, freak, inconsistency, irregularity, oddity, omission, peculiarity, prodigy, quirk, rarity, rejection, special case.

exceptional *adj* aberrant, abnormal, anomalous, atypical, curious, deviant, eccentric, excellent, extraordinary, freakish, inconsistent, irregular, marvellous, notable, noteworthy, odd, outstanding, peculiar, phenomenal, prodigious, quirky, rare, remarkable, singular, special, strange, superior, superlative, uncommon, unconventional, unequalled, unexpected, unusual. **antonyms** mediocre, unexceptional.

excess *n* debauchery, dissipation, dissoluteness, excesses, exorbitance, extravagance, glut, gluttony, immoderateness, intemperance, left-over, libertinism, licentiousness, overabundance, overdose, overflow, overindulgence, overkill, overload, plethora, prodigality, remainder, superabundance, superfluity, surfeit, surplus, unrestraint. **antonym** dearth.
adj additional, extra, left-over, redundant, remaining, residual, spare, superfluous, supernumerary, surplus.

excessive *adj* disproportionate, exaggerated, exorbitant, extravagant, extreme, fanatical, immoderate, inordinate, intemperate, needless, overdone, overmuch, prodigal, profligate, steep, stiff, superfluous, unasked-for, uncalled-for, unconscionable, undue, unnecessary, unneeded, unreasonable. **antonym** insufficient.

exchange *v* bandy, bargain, barter, change, commute, convert, interchange, reciprocate, replace, substitute, swap switch, toss about, trade, truck.
n bargain, barter, brush, chat commerce, conversation, converse conversion, dealing, interchange intercourse, market, quid pro quo reciprocity, replacement, substitution swap, switch, tit for tat, trade, traffic truck.

excitable *adj* edgy, emotional, explosive, feisty, fiery, hasty, highly-strung, hot-headed, hot-tempered inflammable, irascible, mercurial nervous, nervy, passionate, quick-tempered, restive, restless, sensitive susceptible, temperamental, unstable violent, volatile. **antonyms** calm, impassive.

excite *v* activate, actuate, aerate, affect, agitate, animate, arouse, awaken discompose, disturb, elate, electrify, elicit, engender, evoke, fire, foment galvanise, generate, ignite, impress, incite, induce, inflame, initiate, inspire instigate, kindle, motivate, move, provoke, quicken, rouse, stimulate, stir up, suscitate, sway, thrill, titillate, touch, turn on, upset, waken, warm, whet. **antonyms** bore, quell.

excited *adj* aflame, agitated, animated, aroused, awakened, breathless, corybantic, discomposed, disturbed, eager, elated, enthused, enthusiastic, feverish, flurried, flustered, fluttered, frantic, frenzied, high, impassioned, moved, nervous, overwrought, restive, restless, roused, ruffled, stimulated, stirred, thrilled, titillated, upset, wild, worked up, wrought-up. **antonyms** apathetic, bored.

excitement *n* action, activity, ado, adventure, agitation, animation, brouha-ha, clamour, commotion, deliriousness, delirium, discomposure, eagerness, elation, enthusiasm, excitation, ferment, fever, flurry, furore, fuss, heat, hubbub, hue and cry, hurly-burly, kerfuffle, kicks, passion, perturbation, restlessness, stimulation, stimulus, tew, thrill, titillation, tumult, unrest, urge. **antonyms** apathy, calm.

exciting *adj* cliff-hanging, electrifying, encouraging, enthralling, exhilarating, impressive, inspiring, intoxicating, moving, nail-biting, promising, provocative, rousing, sensational, stimulating, stirring, striking, suspenseful, swashbuckling, thrilling, titillating. **antonyms** boring, unexciting.

exclaim v blurt, call, cry, declare, ejaculate, interject, proclaim, shout, utter, vociferate.

exclude v ban, bar, blackball, blacklist, bounce, boycott, debar, disallow, eject, eliminate, embargo, evict, except, excommunicate, expel, forbid, ignore, include out, interdict, keep out, leave out, omit, ostracise, oust, preclude, prohibit, proscribe, refuse, reject, remove, repudiate, rule out, shut out, veto. **antonyms** admit, allow, include.

exclusion n ban, bar, boycott, debarment, ejection, elimination, embargo, eviction, exception, expulsion, interdict, non-admission, omission, ostracisation, preclusion, prohibition, proscription, refusal, rejection, removal, repudiation, veto. **antonyms** admittance, allowance, inclusion.

exclusive adj absolute, arrogant, chic, choice, clannish, classy, cliquey, cliquish, closed, complete, confined, discriminative, elegant, entire, esoteric, fashionable, full, limited, luxurious, monopolistic, narrow, only, peculiar, posh, private, restricted, restrictive, select, selective, selfish, single, snobbish, sole, total, undivided, unique, unshared, whole.

exclusive of barring, debarring, except, except for, excepting, excluding, omitting, ruling out. **antonym** inclusive of.

excrescence n appendage, bump, excrement, growth, knob, lump, misgrowth, outgrowth, process, projection, prominence, protrusion, protuberance, swelling, tumour, wart.

excrete v crap, defecate, discharge, egest, eject, eliminate, evacuate, expel, exude, secrete, shit, urinate, void.

excretion n crap, defecation, discharge, droppings, dung, ejection, elimination, evacuation, excrement, excreta, expulsion, ordure, perspiration, shit(e), stool, urination, voidance.

excruciating adj acute, agonising, atrocious, bitter, burning, exquisite, extreme, harrowing, insufferable, intense, intolerable, painful, piercing, racking, savage, searing, severe, sharp, tormenting, torturing, torturous, unbearable, unendurable.

exculpate v absolve, acquit, clear, deliver, discharge, disculpate, excuse, exonerate, forgive, free, justify, let off, pardon, release, vindicate. **antonyms** blame, condemn.

exculpation n absolution, acquittal, clearance, discharge, excuse, exoneration, expurgation, freedom, justification, pardon, release, vindication. **antonym** condemnation.

excursion n airing, breather, day trip, detour, deviation, digression, episode, expedition, jaunt, journey, outing, ramble, ride, tour, trip, walk, wandering.

excusable adj allowable, defensible, explainable, explicable, forgivable, ignorable, justifiable, minor, pardonable, permissible, slight, understandable, venial, vindicable, warrantable. **antonym** blameworthy.

excuse v absolve, acquit, apologise for, condone, defend, discharge, exculpate, exempt, exonerate, explain, extenuate, forgive, free, ignore, indulge, justify, let off, liberate, mitigate, overlook, palliate, pardon, release, relieve, sanction, spare, tolerate, vindicate, warrant, wink at.
n alibi, apology, cop-out, defence, disguise, evasion, exculpation, exoneration, expedient, explanation, extenuation, grounds, justification, makeshift, mitigation, mockery, palliation, parody, plea, pretence, pretext, put-off, reason, semblance, shift, substitute, subterfuge, travesty, vindication.

execrable adj abhorrent, abominable, accursed, appalling, atrocious, damnable, deplorable, despicable, detestable, disgusting, foul, hateful, heinous, horrible, loathsome, nauseous, obnoxious, odious, offensive, repulsive, revolting, shocking, sickening, vile. **antonyms** admirable, estimable.

execrate v abhor, abominate, blast, condemn, curse, damn, denounce, denunciate, deplore, despise, detest, excoriate, fulminate, hate, imprecate, inveigh against, loathe, revile, vilify. **antonyms** commend, praise.

execute v accomplish, achieve, administer, complete, consummate, deliver, discharge, dispatch, do, effect, effectuate, enact, enforce, expedite, finish, fulfil, implement, perform, prosecute, realise, render, seal, serve, sign, validate.

execution n accomplishment, achievement, administration, completion, consummation, delivery, discharge, dispatch, effect, effectuation, enactment, enforcement, implementation, manner, mode, operation, performance, prosecution, realisation, rendering, rendition, style, technique, warrant, writ.

executive *n* administration, administrator, controller, director, directorate, directors, government, hierarchy, leadership, management, manager, official, organiser.
adj administrative, controlling, decision-making, directing, directorial, governing, guiding, leading, managerial, organisational, organising, regulating, supervisory.

exemplary *adj* admirable, cautionary, commendable, correct, estimable, excellent, faultless, flawless, good, honourable, ideal, laudable, meritorious, model, monitory, perfect, praiseworthy, punctilious, sterling, unerring, unexceptionable, warning, worthy. *antonyms* imperfect, unworthy.

exemplify *v* demonstrate, depict, display, embody, epitomise, evidence, example, exhibit, illustrate, instance, manifest, represent, show, typify.

exempt *v* absolve, discharge, dismiss, except, excuse, exonerate, free, let off, liberate, make an exception of, release, relieve, spare.
adj absolved, clear, discharged, excepted, excluded, excused, favoured, free, immune, liberated, released, spared. *antonym* liable.

exemption *n* absolution, discharge, dispensation, exception, exclusion, exoneration, freedom, immunity, indulgence, privilege, release. *antonym* liability.

exercise *v* afflict, agitate, annoy, apply, burden, discharge, discipline, distress, disturb, drill, employ, enjoy, exert, habituate, inure, occupy, operate, pain, perturb, practise, preoccupy, train, trouble, try, upset, use, utilise, vex, wield, work out, worry.
n accomplishment, action, activity, aerobics, application, assignment, daily dozen, discharge, discipline, drill, drilling, effort, employment, enjoyment, exertion, fulfilment, implementation, labour, lesson, operation, physical jerks, practice, problem, schooling, school-work, task, toil, training, use, utilisation, war-game, work, work-out.

exert *v* apply, bring to bear, employ, exercise, expend, use, utilise, wield.

exert oneself apply oneself, concentrate, endeavour, labour, strain, strive, struggle, sweat, take pains, toil, work.

exertion *n* action, application, assiduity, attempt, diligence, effort, employment, endeavour, exercise, industry, labour, operation, pains, perseverance, sedulousness, strain, stretch, struggle, toil, travail, trial, use, utilisation, work. *antonyms* idleness, rest.

exhalation *n* air, breath, discharge, emission, evaporation, exhaust, expiration, flow, fog, fume, fumes, mist, respiration, smoke, vapour, vapours. *antonym* inhalation.

exhale *v* breathe (out), discharge, eject, emanate, emit, evaporate, expel, expire, give off, issue, respire, steam. *antonym* inhale.

exhaust *v* bankrupt, beggar, bugger, consume, cripple, debilitate, deplete, disable, dissipate, drain, dry, empty, enervate, enfeeble, expend, fatigue, finish, impoverish, overtax, overtire, overwork, prostrate, run through, sap, spend, squander, strain, tax, tire (out), use up, void, waste, weaken, wear out, weary. *antonym* refresh.
n discharge, emanation, emission, exhalation, fumes.

exhausted *adj* all in, bare, beat, buggered, burned out, clapped-out, consumed, crippled, dead, dead tired, dead-beat, debilitated, depleted, disabled, dissipated, dog-tired, done, done in, drained, dry, effete, empty, enervated, enfeebled, expended, fatigued, finished, gone, jaded, jiggered, knackered, out for the count, pooped, prostrated, sapped, spent, squandered, tired out, used up, void, washed-out, washed-up, wasted, weak, weary, whacked, worn out, zonked. *antonyms* conserved, fresh, vigorous.

exhausting *adj* arduous, backbreaking, crippling, debilitating, difficult, draining, enervating, fatiguing, formidable, gruelling, hard, knackering, laborious, punishing, sapping, severe, strenuous, taxing, testing, tiring, vigorous. *antonym* refreshing.

exhaustion *n* consumption, debilitation, depletion, effeteness, emptying, enervation, fatigue, feebleness, jet-lag, lassitude, prostration, tiredness, weariness. *antonym* freshness.

exhaustive *adj* all-embracing, all-inclusive, all-out, complete, comprehensive, definitive, detailed, encyclopaedic, expansive, extensive, far-reaching, full, full-scale, in-depth, intensive, sweeping, thorough, thoroughgoing, total. *antonym* incomplete.

exhibit *v* air, demonstrate, disclose,

display, evidence, evince, expose, express, flaunt, indicate, manifest, offer, parade, present, reveal, show, showcase, sport. **antonym** hide.

n display, exhibition, illustration, model, show.

exhibition *n* airing, array, demonstration, display, exhibit, expo, exposition, fair, manifestation, performance, presentation, representation, show, showcase, showing, spectacle.

exhilarate *v* animate, cheer, delight, elate, energise, enhearten, enliven, exalt, excite, gladden, hearten, invigorate, lift, stimulate, thrill, vitalise. **antonyms** bore, discourage.

exhilarating *adj* breathtaking, cheering, enlivening, exalting, exciting, gladdening, invigorating, mind-blowing, stimulating, thrilling, vitalising. **antonyms** boring, discouraging.

exhilaration *n* animation, ardour, cheerfulness, dash, delight, élan, elation, exaltation, excitement, gaiety, gladness, glee, gleefulness, gusto, high spirits, hilarity, joy, joyfulness, liveliness, mirth, sprightliness, vivacity, zeal. **antonyms** boredom, discouragement.

exhort *v* admonish, advise, beseech, bid, call upon, caution, counsel, encourage, enjoin, entreat, goad, implore, incite, inflame, inspire, instigate, persuade, press, spur, urge, warn.

exhortation *n* admonition, advice, beseeching, bidding, caution, counsel, encouragement, enjoinder, entreaty, goading, incitement, lecture, persuasion, sermon, urging, warning.

exigency *n* acuteness, bind, constraint, crisis, crunch, demand, difficulty, distress, emergency, exigence, extremity, fix, hardship, imperativeness, jam, necessity, need, pass, pickle, pinch, plight, predicament, pressure, quandary, requirement, scrape, stew, strait, stress, urgency.

exigent *adj* acute, arduous, constraining, critical, crucial, demanding, difficult, exacting, exhausting, hard, harsh, imperative, importunate, insistent, necessary, needful, pressing, rigorous, severe, stiff, strict, stringent, taxing, tough, urgent. **antonym** mild.

exile *n* banishment, deportation, deportee, émigré, expatriate, expatriation, expulsion, ostracism, outcast, proscription, refugee, separation.

v banish, deport, drive out, expatriate, expel, ostracise, oust, proscribe.

exist *v* abide, be, be available, be extant, breathe, continue, endure, happen, have one's being, last, live, obtain, occur, prevail, remain, stand, subsist, survive.

existence *n* actuality, animation, being, breath, continuance, continuation, creation, creature, duration, endurance, entity, life, reality, subsistence, survival, the world, thing. **antonym** non-existence.

existent *adj* abiding, actual, around, current, enduring, existing, extant, living, obtaining, present, prevailing, real, remaining, standing, surviving. **antonym** non-existent.

exit *n* adieu, aperture, departure, door, doorway, egress, evacuation, exodus, farewell, gate, going, leave-taking, outlet, retirement, retreat, vent, way out, withdrawal. **antonym** entrance.

v arrive, depart, enter, issue, leave, retire, retreat, take one's leave, withdraw.

exodus *n* departure, evacuation, exit, flight, leaving, long march, migration, retirement, retreat, withdrawal.

exonerate *v* absolve, acquit, clear, discharge, disculpate, dismiss, except, exculpate, excuse, exempt, free, justify, let off, liberate, pardon, release, relieve, vindicate. **antonym** incriminate.

exoneration *n* absolution, acquittal, amnesty, deliverance, discharge, dismissal, exception, exculpation, exemption, freeing, immunity, indemnity, justification, liberation, pardon, release, relief, vindication. **antonym** incrimination.

exorbitance *n* excess, excessiveness, extravagance, immoderateness, immoderation, inordinateness, monstrousness, preposterousness, unreasonableness. **antonyms** fairness, reasonableness.

exorbitant *adj* enormous, excessive, extortionate, extravagant, extreme, immoderate, inordinate, monstrous, outrageous, preposterous, unconscionable, undue, unreasonable, unwarranted. **antonyms** fair, reasonable.

exotic *adj* alien, bizarre, colourful, curious, different, external, extraneous, extraordinary, fascinating, foreign, foreign-looking, glamorous, imported, introduced, mysterious, naturalised, outlandish, peculiar, strange, striking, unfamiliar, unusual. **antonym** ordinary.

expand *v* amplify, augment, bloat, blow up, branch out, broaden, develop, diffuse, dilate, distend, diversify, elaborate, embellish, enlarge, expatiate, expound, extend, fatten, fill out, flesh out, grow, heighten, increase, inflate, lengthen, magnify, multiply, open, outspread, prolong, protract, snowball, spread, stretch, swell, thicken, unfold, unfurl, unravel, unroll, wax, widen. **antonyms** contract, précis.

expanded *adj* bloated, blown out, blown up, dilated, distended, enlarged, increased, inflated, puffed out, swollen.

expanse *n* area, breadth, extent, field, plain, range, space, stretch, sweep, tract, vastness.

expansion *n* amplification, augmentation, development, diffusion, dilation, distension, diversification, enlargement, expanse, extension, growth, increase, inflation, magnification, multiplication, spread, swelling, unfolding, unfurling. **antonym** contraction.

expansive *adj* affable, all-embracing, broad, communicative, comprehensive, dilating, distending, easy, effusive, elastic, expanding, expatiatory, extendable, extensive, far-reaching, free, friendly, garrulous, genial, inclusive, loquacious, open, outgoing, sociable, stretching, stretchy, swelling, talkative, thorough, unreserved, voluminous, warm, wide, wide-ranging, widespread. **antonyms** cold, reserved.

expect *v* anticipate, assume, await, bank on, bargain for, believe, calculate, conjecture, contemplate, count on, demand, envisage, forecast, foresee, hope for, imagine, insist on, look for, look forward to, predict, presume, project, reckon, rely on, require, suppose, surmise, think, trust, want, wish.

expectancy *n* anticipation, assumption, belief, conjecture, curiosity, eagerness, expectation, hope, likelihood, outlook, prediction, presumption, probability, prospect, supposition, surmise, suspense, waiting.

expectant *adj* agog, anticipating, anxious, apprehensive, awaiting, curious, eager, expecting, hopeful, in suspense, pregnant, ready, watchful.

expectation *n* anticipation, apprehension, assumption, assurance, belief, calculation, chance, confidence, conjecture, demand, eagerness, expectancy, fear, forecast, hope, insistence, likelihood, optimism, outlook, possibility, prediction, presumption, probability, projection, promise, prospect, reliance, requirement, supposition, surmise, suspense, trust, want, wish.

expecting *adj* expectant, in the club, in the family way, pregnant, with child.

expedience *n* advantage, advantageousness, advisability, appropriateness, aptness, benefit, convenience, desirability, effectiveness, expediency, fitness, gainfulness, helpfulness, judiciousness, practicality, pragmatism, profitability, profitableness, properness, propriety, prudence, suitability, usefulness, utilitarianism, utility.

expedient *adj* advantageous, advisable, appropriate, beneficial, convenient, desirable, effective, fit, helpful, judicious, meet, opportune, politic, practical, pragmatic, profitable, proper, prudent, serviceable, suitable, useful, utilitarian, worthwhile. **antonym** inexpedient.

n contrivance, device, dodge, makeshift, manoeuvre, means, measure, method, resort, resource, ruse, scheme, shift, stop-gap, stratagem, substitute.

expedite *v* accelerate, advance, aid, assist, dispatch, facilitate, forward, further, hasten, hurry, precipitate, press, promote, quicken, rush, speed. **antonym** delay.

expedition[1] *n* company, crusade, enterprise, excursion, exploration, explorers, hike, journey, mission, pilgrimage, quest, raid, ramble, safari, sail, team, tour, travellers, trek, trip, undertaking, voyage, voyagers.

expedition[2] *n* alacrity, briskness, celerity, dispatch, expeditiousness, haste, hurry, immediacy, promptness, quickness, rapidity, readiness, speed, swiftness. **antonym** delay.

expeditious *adj* active, alert, brisk, diligent, efficient, fast, hasty, immediate, instant, meteoric, prompt, quick, rapid, ready, speedy, swift. **antonym** slow.

expel *v* ban, banish, bar, belch, blackball, cast out, disbar, discharge, dislodge, dismiss, drive out, drum out, eject, evict, exclude, exile, expatriate, oust, proscribe, remove, send packing, spew, throw out, turf out. **antonym** admit.

expend *v* consume, disburse, dissipate, employ, exhaust, fork out, pay, shell out, spend, use, use up. **antonym** save.

expendable *adj* dispensable, disposable, inessential, non-essential, replaceable, unimportant, unnecessary. **antonyms** indispensable, necessary.

expenditure *n* application, charge,

consumption, cost, expense, outgoings, outlay, output, payment, spending. **antonyms** profit, savings.

expense *n* charge, consumption, cost, damage, expenditure, loss, outlay, output, payment, sacrifice, spending, toll, use.

expenses *n* costs, incidentals, outgoings, outlay, overheads.

expensive *adj* costly, dear, excessive, exorbitant, extortionate, extravagant, high-priced, lavish, overpriced, rich, steep, stiff. **antonyms** cheap, inexpensive.

experience *n* adventure, affair, assay, contact, doing, encounter, episode, event, evidence, exposure, familiarity, happening, incident, involvement, know-how, knowledge, observation, occurrence, ordeal, participation, practice, proof, taste, test, training, trial, understanding. **antonym** inexperience. *v* apprehend, behold, empathise, encounter, endure, face, feel, have, know, meet, observe, perceive, sample, sense, suffer, sustain, taste, try, undergo.

experienced *adj* accomplished, adept, capable, competent, expert, familiar, knowing, knowledgeable, master, mature, practised, professional, qualified, schooled, seasoned, skilful, sophisticated, streetwise, tested, trained, travailed, travelled, tried, veteran, well-versed, wise, worldly, worldly-wise. **antonym** inexperienced.

experiment *n* assay, attempt, examination, experimentation, investigation, procedure, proof, research, test, trial, trial and error, trial run, venture. *v* assay, examine, investigate, research, sample, test, try, verify.

experimental *adj* empiric(al), exploratory, pilot, preliminary, probationary, provisional, speculative, tentative, test, trial, trial-and-error.

expert *n* ace, adept, authority, boffin, connoisseur, dab hand, maestro, master, pastmaster, pro, professional, specialist, virtuoso, wizard. *adj* able, adept, adroit, apt, clever, crack, deft, dexterous, experienced, handy, knowledgeable, master, masterly, practised, professional, proficient, qualified, skilful, skilled, trained, virtuoso. **antonym** novice.

expertise *n* adroitness, aptness, cleverness, command, deftness, dexterity, facility, judgement, knack, know-how, knowledge, masterliness, mastery, proficiency, skilfulness, skill, virtuosity. **antonym** inexpertness.

expertness *n* ableness, adroitness, aptness, command, deftness, dexterity, expertise, facility, finesse, judgement, know-how, knowledge, masterliness, mastery, proficiency, savoir-faire, skilfulness, skill. **antonym** inexpertness.

expire *v* cease, close, conclude, decease, depart, die, discontinue, emit, end, exhale, finish, lapse, perish, run out, stop, terminate. **antonyms** begin, continue.

expiry *n* cease, cessation, close, conclusion, death, decease, demise, departure, end, expiration, finish, termination. **antonyms** beginning, continuation.

explain *v* account for, clarify, clear up, construe, decipher, decode, define, demonstrate, describe, disclose, elucidate, excuse, explicate, expound, gloss, illustrate, interpret, justify, resolve, simplify, solve, spell out, teach, translate, unfold, unravel, untangle. **antonyms** obfuscate, obscure.

explanation *n* account, answer, cause, clarification, definition, demonstration, description, elucidation, excuse, exegesis, explication, exposition, gloss, illustration, interpretation, justification, legend, meaning, mitigation, motive, reason, resolution, sense, significance, solution, vindication.

explanatory *adj* demonstrative, descriptive, elucidative, elucidatory, exegetic, exegetical, expository, illuminative, illustrative, interpretive, justifying.

explicable *adj* accountable, definable, determinable, explainable, intelligible, interpretable, justifiable, resolvable, solvable, understandable.

explicit *adj* absolute, accurate, categorical, certain, clear, declared, definite, detailed, direct, distinct, exact, express, frank, open, outspoken, patent, plain, positive, precise, specific, stated, straightforward, unambiguous, unequivocal, unqualified, unreserved. **antonyms** inexplicit, vague.

explode *v* blow up, burst, debunk, detonate, discharge, discredit, disprove, erupt, go off, invalidate, rebut, refute, repudiate, set off, shatter, shiver. **antonym** prove.

exploit *n* accomplishment, achievement, adventure, attainment, deed, feat, stunt. *v* abuse, bleed, capitalise on, cash in on, fleece, impose on, make capital out of, manipulate, milk, misuse, profit by, rip off, skin, soak, take advantage of, turn to account, use, utilise.

exploration *n* analysis, examination, expedition, inquiry, inquisition, inspection, investigation, probe, reconnaissance, research, safari, scrutiny, search, study, survey, tour, travel, trip, voyage.

exploratory *adj* experimental, fact-finding, investigative, pilot, probing, searching, tentative, trial.

explore *v* case, examine, inspect, investigate, probe, prospect, reconnoitre, research, scout, scrutinise, search, survey, tour, travel, traverse.

explosion *n* bang, blast, burst, clap, crack, debunking, detonation, discharge, discrediting, eruption, fit, outbreak, outburst, refutation, report.

explosive *adj* charged, dangerous, fiery, hazardous, overwrought, perilous, stormy, tense, touchy, ugly, unstable, vehement, violent, volatile, volcanic. **antonym** calm.
n cordite, dynamite, gelignite, gunpowder, jelly, nitroglycerine, TNT.

exponent *n* advocate, backer, champion, commentator, defender, demonstrator, elucidator, example, exemplar, expounder, illustration, illustrator, indication, interpreter, model, performer, player, presenter, promoter, propagandist, proponent, representative, sample, specimen, spokesman, spokeswoman, supporter, type, upholder.

expose *v* air, betray, bring to light, denounce, detect, disclose, display, divulge, endanger, exhibit, hazard, imperil, jeopardise, manifest, present, reveal, risk, show, uncover, unearth, unmask, unveil, wash one's dirty linen in public. **antonym** cover.

expose to acquaint with, bring into contact with, familiarise with, introduce to, lay open to, subject to. **antonym** protect.

exposed *adj* bare, exhibited, laid bare, liable, on display, on show, on view, open, prey to, revealed, shown, susceptible, unconcealed, uncovered, unprotected, unsheltered, unveiled, vulnerable. **antonyms** covered, sheltered.

exposure *n* acquaintance, airing, aspect, betrayal, cold, contact, danger, denunciation, detection, disclosure, discovery, display, divulgence,

divulging, exhibition, experience, exposé, familiarity, frontage, hazard, introduction, jeopardy, knowledge, lack of shelter, location, manifestation, outlook, position, presentation, publicity, revelation, risk, setting, showing, uncovering, unmasking, unveiling, view, vulnerability.

expound *v* describe, elucidate, explain, explicate, illustrate, interpet, preach, sermonise, set forth, spell out, unfold.

express *v* articulate, assert, asseverate, communicate, conceive, convey, couch, declare, denote, depict, designate, disclose, divulge, embody, enunciate, evince, exhibit, extract, force out, formulate, formulise, indicate, intimate, manifest, phrase, pronounce, put, put across, represent, reveal, say, show, signify, speak, stand for, state, symbolise, tell, testify, utter, verbalise, voice, word.
adj accurate, categorical, certain, clear, clear-cut, definite, direct, distinct, especial, exact, explicit, fast, high-speed, manifest, non-stop, outright, particular, plain, pointed, precise, quick, rapid, singular, special, speedy, stated, swift, unambiguous, unqualified. **antonym** vague.

expression *n* air, announcement, appearance, aspect, assertion, asseveration, communication, countenance, declaration, delivery, demonstration, diction, embodiment, emphasis, enunciation, execution, exhibition, face, idiom, indication, intonation, language, locution, look, manifestation, mention, phrase, phraseology, phrasing, pronouncement, reflex, remark, representation, set phrase, show, sign, speaking, speech, statement, style, symbol, term, token, turn of phrase, utterance, verbalisation, verbalism, voicing, word, wording.

expressionless *adj* blank, deadpan, dull, empty, glassy, impassive, inscrutable, poker-faced, straight-faced, vacuous, wooden. **antonym** expressive.

expressive *adj* allusive, demonstrative, eloquent, emphatic, energetic, forcible, indicative, informative, lively, meaningful, mobile, moving, poignant, pointed, representative, revealing, significant, striking, strong, suggestive, sympathetic, telling, thoughtful, vivid. **antonyms** expressionless, poker-faced.

expressly *adv* absolutely, categorically, clearly, decidedly, definitely, distinctly, especially, exactly, explicitly, intentionally, manifestly, on purpose, outright, particularly, plainly, pointedly, positively, precisely, purposely, specially, specifically, unambiguously, unequivocally.

expulsion *n* banishment, debarment, discharge, dislodging, dismissal, ejection, eviction, exclusion, exile, expatriation, proscription, removal.

expunge *v* abolish, annihilate, annul, blot out, cancel, delete, destroy, efface, eradicate, erase, exterminate, extinguish, extirpate, obliterate, raze, remove, wipe out.

expurgate *v* blue-pencil, bowdlerise, censor, clean up, cut, emend, purge, purify, sanitise.

exquisite *adj* acute, admirable, attractive, beautiful, charming, choice, comely, consummate, cultivated, dainty, delicate, delicious, discerning, discriminating, elegant, excellent, excruciating, fastidious, fine, flawless, impeccable, incomparable, intense, keen, lovely, matchless, meticulous, outstanding, peerless, perfect, piercing, pleasing, poignant, polished, precious, rare, refined, select, selective, sensitive, sharp, splendid, striking, superb, superlative. **antonyms** flawed, imperfect, poor, ugly.

extant *adj* alive, existent, existing, in existence, living, remaining, subsistent, subsisting, surviving. **antonyms** dead, extinct, non-existent.

extemporary *adj* ad-lib, expedient, extemporaneous, extempore, free, impromptu, improvised, made-up, makeshift, offhand, off-the-cuff, on-the-spot, spontaneous, temporary, unplanned, unpremeditated, unprepared, unrehearsed. **antonym** planned.

extemporise *v* ad-lib, improvise, make up, play by ear.

extend *v* advance, amplify, attain, augment, bestow, broaden, confer, continue, develop, dilate, drag out, draw out, elongate, enhance, enlarge, expand, give, grant, hold out, impart, increase, last, lengthen, offer, present, proffer, prolong, protract, pull out, reach, spin out, spread, stretch, supplement, take, uncoil, unfold, unfurl, unroll, widen, yield. **antonym** shorten.

extension *n* addition, adjunct, amplification, annexe, appendage, appendix, augmentation, branch, broadening, continuation, delay, development, distension, elongation, enhancement, enlargement, expansion, extent, increase, lengthening, postponement, prolongation, protraction, spread, stretching, supplement, widening, wing.

extensive *adj* all-inclusive, broad, capacious, commodious, comprehensive, expanded, expansive, extended, far-flung, far-reaching, general, great, huge, large, large-scale, lengthy, long, pervasive, prevalent, protracted, roomy, spacious, sweeping, thorough, thoroughgoing, universal, unrestricted, vast, voluminous, wholesale, wide, widespread. **antonyms** narrow, restricted.

extent *n* amount, amplitude, area, bounds, breadth, bulk, compass, degree, dimension(s), duration, expanse, expansion, length, magnitude, measure, play, proportions, quantity, range, reach, scope, size, sphere, spread, stretch, sweep, term, time, volume, width.

extenuate *v* decrease, diminish, excuse, lessen, minimise, mitigate, moderate, modify, palliate, qualify, reduce, soften, temper, weaken.

extenuating *adj* justifying, mitigating, moderating, palliative, qualifying.

exterior *n* appearance, aspect, coating, covering, externals, façade, face, finish, outside, shell, skin, surface. **antonym** interior.
adj alien, exotic, external, extraneous, foreign, outer, outermost, outside, outward, peripheral, superficial, surface, surrounding. **antonym** interior.

exterminate *v* abolish, annihilate, destroy, eliminate, eradicate, extirpate, massacre, wipe out.

external *adj* alien, apparent, exotic, exterior, extramural, extraneous, foreign, independent, outer, outermost, outside, outward, superficial, surface, visible. **antonym** internal.

extinct *adj* abolished, dead, defunct, ended, exterminated, extinguished, gone, inactive, lost, obsolete, out, quenched, terminated, vanished, void. **antonyms** extant, living.

extinction *n* abolition, annihilation, death, destruction, eradication, extermination, extirpation, obliteration, oblivion, quietus.

extinguish *v* abolish, annihilate, destroy, douse, dout, eliminate, end, eradicate, erase, expunge, exterminate, extirpate, kill, obscure, put out, quench, remove, slake, smother, snuff out, stifle, suppress.

extirpate v abolish, annihilate, cut out, destroy, eliminate, eradicate, erase, expunge, exterminate, extinguish, remove, root out, uproot, wipe out.

extol v acclaim, applaud, celebrate, commend, eulogise, exalt, glorify, laud, magnify, praise. *antonyms* blame, denigrate.

extortion n blackmail, coercion, compulsion, demand, exaction, exorbitance, expensiveness, force, milking, oppression, overcharging, rapacity.

extortionate adj blood-sucking, exacting, excessive, exorbitant, extravagant, grasping, hard, harsh, immoderate, inflated, inordinate, oppressive, outrageous, preposterous, rapacious, rigorous, severe, sky-high, unreasonable, usurious. *antonym* reasonable.

extra adj accessory, added, additional, ancillary, auxiliary, excess, extraneous, for good measure, fresh, further, inessential, leftover, more, needless, new, other, redundant, reserve, spare, superfluous, supernumerary, supplemental, supplementary, surplus, unnecessary, unneeded, unused. *antonym* integral.
n accessory, addition, adjunct, affix, appendage, attachment, bonus, complement, extension, supernumerary, supplement.
adv especially, exceptionally, extraordinarily, extremely, particularly, remarkably, uncommonly, unusually.

extract v abstract, choose, cite, cull, decoct, deduce, derive, develop, distil, draw, draw out, educe, elicit, evoke, evolve, exact, express, gather, get, glean, obtain, quote, reap, remove, select, uproot, withdraw, wrest, wring. *antonym* insert.
n abstract, citation, clip, clipping, concentrate, cutting, decoction, decocture, distillate, distillation, essence, excerpt, juice, passage, quotation, selection.

extraction n ancestry, birth, blood, derivation, descent, distillation, drawing, educt, extirpation, family, lineage, origin, parentage, pedigree, pulling, race, removal, separation, stock, withdrawal. *antonym* insertion.

extraneous adj accidental, additional, alien, exotic, exterior, external, extra, foreign, immaterial, inadmissible, inapplicable, inappropriate, incidental, inessential, irrelevant, needless, non-essential, peripheral, redundant, strange, superfluous, supplementary, tangential, unconnected, unessential, unnecessary, unrelated. *antonym* integral.

extraordinary adj amazing, bizarre, curious, exceptional, fantastic, marvellous, notable, noteworthy, odd, outstanding, particular, peculiar, phenomenal, rare, remarkable, significant, singular, special, strange, striking, surprising, uncommon, unfamiliar, unheard-of, unimaginable, unique, unprecedented, unusual, weird, wonderful. *antonyms* commonplace, ordinary.

extravagance n absurdity, dissipation, exaggeration, excess, exorbitance, folly, hyperbole, immoderation, improvidence, lavishness, outrageousness, overspending, preposterousness, prodigality, profligacy, profusion, recklessness, squandering, unreasonableness, unrestraint, unthrift, unthriftiness, waste, wastefulness, wildness. *antonyms* moderation, thrift.

extravagant adj absurd, costly, exaggerated, excessive, exorbitant, expensive, extortionate, fanciful, fancy, fantastic, flamboyant, flashy, foolish, garish, gaudy, grandiose, immoderate, improvident, imprudent, inordinate, lavish, ornate, ostentatious, outrageous, outré, overpriced, preposterous, pretentious, prodigal, profligate, reckless, showy, spendthrift, steep, thriftless, unreasonable, unrestrained, wasteful, wild. *antonyms* moderate, thrifty.

extravert see **extrovert**.

extreme adj acute, deep-dyed, dire, downright, Draconian, drastic, egregious, exaggerated, exceptional, excessive, exquisite, extraordinary, extravagant, fanatical, faraway, far-off, farthest, final, great, greatest, harsh, high, highest, immoderate, inordinate, intemperate, intense, last, maximum, out-and-out, outermost, outrageous, radical, red-hot, remarkable, remotest, rigid, severe, sheer, stern, strict, supreme, terminal, ultimate, ultra, unbending, uncommon, uncompromising, unconventional, unreasonable, unusual, utmost, utter, worst, zealous. *antonyms* mild, moderate.
n acme, apex, apogee, boundary, climax, consummation, depth, edge, end, excess, extremity, height, limit,

maximum, minimum, nadir, peak, pinnacle, pole, termination, top, ultimate, utmost, zenith.

extremely *adv* acutely, awfully, exceedingly, exceptionally, excessively, extraordinarily, greatly, highly, inordinately, intensely, markedly, passing, quite, severely, terribly, too, ultra, uncommonly, unusually, utterly, very.

extremity *n* acme, acuteness, adversity, apex, apogee, border, bound, boundary, brim, brink, climax, consummation, crisis, crunch, depth, disaster, edge, emergency, end, excess, exigency, extreme, foot, frontier, hand, hardship, height, limit, margin, maximum, minimum, nadir, peak, pinnacle, plight, pole, rim, setback, terminal, termination, terminus, tip, top, trouble, ultimate, utmost, verge, zenith.

extricate *v* clear, deliver, disentangle, free, liberate, release, relieve, remove, rescue, withdraw. *antonym* involve.

extrovert *adj* amiable, amicable, extravert, exuberant, friendly, hail-fellow-well-met, hearty, outgoing, social. *antonym* introvert.
n life and soul of the party, mixer, socialiser. *antonyms* introvert, loner.

exuberant *adj* abundant, animated, baroque, buoyant, cheerful, copious, eager, ebullient, effervescent, effusive, elated, energetic, enthusiastic, exaggerated, excessive, excited, exhilarated, fulsome, high-spirited, lavish, lively, lush, luxuriant, overdone, overflowing, plenteous, plentiful, prodigal, profuse, rambunctious, rank, rich, sparkling, spirited, sprightly, superabundant, superfluous, teeming,

vigorous, vivacious, zestful. *antonyms* apathetic, lifeless, scant.

exude *v* bleed, discharge, display, emanate, emit, excrete, exhibit, flow out, issue, leak, manifest, ooze, perspire, radiate, secrete, seep, show, sweat, trickle, weep, well.

exult *v* boast, brag, celebrate, crow, delight, gloat, glory, jubilate, rejoice, relish, revel, taunt, triumph.

exultant *adj* cock-a-hoop, delighted, elated, exulting, gleeful, joyful, joyous, jubilant, over the moon, overjoyed, rejoicing, revelling, transporting, triumphant. *antonym* depressed.

exultation *n* boasting, bragging, celebration, crowing, delight, elation, glee, gloating, glory, glorying, joy, joyfulness, joyousness, jubilation, merriness, rejoicing, revelling, transport, triumph. *antonym* depression.

eye *n* appreciation, belief, discernment, discrimination, eyeball, judgement, mind, opinion, optic, peeper, perception, recognition, taste, viewpoint.
v contemplate, examine, eye up, gaze at, glance at, inspect, leer at, look at, make eyes at, observe, ogle, peruse, regard, scan, scrutinise, stare at, study, survey, view, watch.

eye-catching *adj* arresting, attractive, beautiful, captivating, gorgeous, imposing, impressive, showy, spectacular, striking, stunning. *antonyms* plain, unattractive.

eyeful *n* beauty, dazzler, knockout, show, sight, sight for sore eyes, spectacle, stunner, view, vision.

eyesore *n* atrocity, blemish, blight, blot, disfigurement, disgrace, horror, mess, monstrosity, sight, ugliness.

F

fabled *adj* fabulous, famed, famous, feigned, fictional, legendary, mythical, renowned, storied. *antonym* unknown.

fabric *n* cloth, constitution, construction, foundations, framework, infrastructure, make-up, material, organisation, structure, stuff, textile, texture, web.

fabricate *v* assemble, build, coin, concoct, construct, create, devise, erect, fake, falsify, fashion, feign, forge, form, frame, invent, make, manufacture, shape, trump up.

fabulous *adj* amazing, apocryphal, astounding, breathtaking, fabled, false, fantastic, feigned, fictitious, imaginary, immense, inconceivable, incredible, invented, legendary, marvellous, mythical, phenomenal, renowned, spectacular, superb, unbelievable, unreal, wonderful. *antonyms* moderate, real, small.

façade *n* appearance, cloak, cover, disguise, exterior, face, front, frontage, guise, mask, pretence, semblance, show, veil, veneer.

face *n* air, appearance, aspect, assurance, audacity, authority, boldness, brass neck, cheek, confidence, countenance, cover, dial, dignity, disguise, display, effrontery, expression, exterior, façade, facet, favour, features, front, frown, gall, grimace, honour, image, impudence, kisser, lineaments, look, mask, mug, nerve, outside, phizog, physiognomy, pout, prestige, presumption, pretence, reputation, sauce, scowl, self-respect, semblance, show, side, smirk, standing, status, surface, visage.
v clad, coat, confront, cope with, cover, deal with, defy, dress, encounter, experience, finish, front, give on to, level, line, meet, oppose, overlay, overlook, sheathe, surface, tackle, veneer.

face to face confronting, eye to eye, eyeball to eyeball, in confrontation, opposite.

face up to accept, acknowledge, come to terms with, confront, cope with, deal with, meet head-on, recognise, square up to, stand up to.

facet *n* angle, aspect, characteristic, face, feature, part, phase, plane, point, side, slant, surface.

facetious *adj* amusing, comical, droll, flippant, frivolous, funny, humorous, jesting, jocular, merry, playful, pleasant, tongue-in-cheek, waggish, witty.

facile *adj* adept, adroit, complaisant, cursory, dexterous, easy, effortless, fluent, glib, hasty, light, plausible, proficient, quick, ready, shallow, simple, skilful, slick, smooth, superficial, uncomplicated, yielding. *antonyms* clumsy, implausible, profound.

facilitate *v* assist, ease, expedite, forward, further, grease, help, promote, speed up.

facility *n* ability, adeptness, adroitness, bent, dexterity, ease, efficiency, effortlessness, expertness, fluency, gift, knack, proficiency, quickness, readiness, skilfulness, skill, smoothness, talent, turn.

facsimile *n* carbon, carbon copy, copy, duplicate, image, photocopy, Photostat®, print, replica, reproduction, transcript, Xerox®.

fact *n* act, actuality, certainty, circumstance, datum, deed, detail, event, fait accompli, feature, gospel, happening, incident, item, occurrence, particular, point, reality, specific, truth.

faction[1] *n* band, bloc, cabal, cadre, camp, caucus, clique, coalition, combination, confederacy, contingent, coterie, crowd, division, gang, group, junta, lobby, minority, party, pressure group, ring, section, sector, set, splinter group, troop.

faction[2] *n* conflict, disagreement, discord, disharmony, dissension, disunity, division, divisiveness, fighting, friction, infighting, quarrelling, rebellion, sedition, strife, tumult, turbulence. *antonyms* agreement, peace.

factious *adj* conflicting, contentious, disputatious, dissident, divisive, insurrectionary, mutinous, partisan, quarrelling, quarrelsome, rebellious, refractory, rival, sectarian, seditious, troublemaking, tumultuous, turbulent, warring. *antonyms* calm, co-operative.

factitious *adj* affected, artificial, assumed, contrived, counterfeit, engineered, fabricated, fake, false, imitation, insincere, made-up, manufactured, mock, phoney, put-on, sham, simulated, spurious, supposititious, synthetic, unnatural, unreal. *antonym* genuine.

factor *n* agent, aspect, cause,

circumstance, component, consideration, deputy, determinant, element, estate manager, influence, item, joker, middleman, parameter, part, point, reeve, steward, thing, unknown quantity.

facts *n* data, details, gen, info, information, story, the low-down, the score.

factual *adj* accurate, authentic, circumstantial, close, correct, credible, detailed, exact, faithful, genuine, literal, objective, precise, real, straight, sure, true, unadorned, unbiased, veritable. **antonym** false.

faculty *n* ability, adroitness, aptitude, bent, brain-power, capability, capacity, cleverness, dexterity, facility, gift, knack, power, propensity, readiness, skill, talent, turn.

fad *n* affectation, craze, cult, fancy, fashion, mania, mode, trend, vogue, whim.

fade *v* blanch, bleach, blench, decline, die, dim, diminish, disappear, discolour, disperse, dissolve, droop, dull, dwindle, ebb, etiolate, evanesce, fail, fall, flag, languish, pale, perish, shrivel, vanish, wane, wilt, wither, yellow.

faded *adj* bleached, dim, discoloured, dull, etiolated, indistinct, lustreless, pale, passé, past one's best, washed-out. **antonym** bright.

faeces *n* dregs, droppings, dung, excrement, excreta, ordure, sediment, stools.

fag *n* bind, bore, bother, chore, drag, inconvenience, irritation, nuisance, pest.

fagged *adj* all in, beat, exhausted, fatigued, jaded, jiggered, knackered, on one's last legs, wasted, weary, worn out, zonked. **antonym** refreshed.

fail *v* abandon, cease, come to grief, conk out, crack up, crash, cut out, decline, desert, die, disappoint, droop, dwindle, fade, fall, flop, flunk, fold, forget, forsake, founder, fudge, give out, give up, go bankrupt, go bust, go to the wall, go under, languish, lay an egg, let down, miscarry, misfire, miss, neglect, omit, peter out, plough, sink, smash, underachieve, underperform, wane, weaken. **antonyms** gain, improve, prosper, succeed.

failing *n* blemish, blind spot, decay, decline, defect, deficiency, deterioration, drawback, error, failure, fault, flaw, foible, frailty, imperfection, lapse, miscarriage, misfortune, peccadillo, shortcoming, weakness. **antonyms** advantage, strength.

adj collapsing, decaying, declining, deteriorating, drooping, dwindling, dying, flagging, languishing, moribund, waning, weak, weakening. **antonyms** thriving, vigorous.

prep in default of, in the absence of, lacking, wanting, without.

failure *n* abortion, also-ran, bankruptcy, breakdown, bummer, collapse, crash, cropper, damp squib, dead duck, decay, decline, default, defeat, deficiency, dereliction, deterioration, disappointment, downfall, dud, failing, fiasco, flop, folding, frustration, goner, incompetent, insolvency, loser, loss, miscarriage, neglect, negligence, no-hoper, non-performance, omission, remissness, ruin, shortcoming, slip-up, stoppage, turkey, unsuccess, wash-out, wreck. **antonym** success.

faint *adj* bleached, delicate, dim, distant, dizzy, drooping, dull, enervated, exhausted, faded, faltering, fatigued, feeble, feint, giddy, hazy, hushed, ill-defined, indistinct, languid, lethargic, light, light-headed, low, muffled, muted, muzzy, remote, slight, soft, subdued, thin, unenthusiastic, vague, vertiginous, weak, whispered, woozy. **antonyms** clear, strong.

v black out, collapse, droop, drop, flag, flake out, keel over, pass out, swoon.

n blackout, collapse, swoon, unconsciousness.

faint-hearted *adj* diffident, faint-heart, half-hearted, hen-hearted, irresolute, lily-livered, spiritless, timid, timorous, weak. **antonym** courageous.

fair *adj* adequate, all right, average, beauteous, beautiful, bonny, bright, clean, clear, clement, cloudless, comely, decent, disinterested, dispassionate, dry, equal, equitable, even-handed, favourable, fine, handsome, honest, honourable, impartial, just, lawful, legitimate, lovely, mediocre, middling, moderate, not bad, objective, OK, on the level, passable, pretty, proper, reasonable, respectable, satisfactory, so-so, square, sunny, sunshiny, tolerable, trustworthy, unbiased, unclouded, unprejudiced, upright, well-favoured. **antonyms** cloudy, inclement, poor, unfair.

fairly *adv* absolutely, adequately, deservedly, equitably, fully, honestly, impartially, justly, moderately, objectively, plainly, positively, pretty, properly, quite, rather, really, reasonably, somewhat, tolerably, unbiasedly, veritably. **antonym** unfairly.

fairy *n* brownie, elf, fay, fée, hobgoblin, leprechaun, pixie, Robin Goodfellow, sprite.

fairy tale cock-and-bull story, fabrication, fairy story, fantasy, fiction, folk-tale, invention, lie, myth, romance, tall story, untruth.

faith *n* allegiance, assurance, belief, church, communion, confidence, constancy, conviction, credence, credit, creed, denomination, dependence, dogma, faithfulness, fealty, fidelity, honesty, honour, loyalty, persuasion, pledge, promise, reliance, religion, sincerity, trust, truth, truthfulness, vow, word, word of honour. **antonyms** mistrust, treachery, unfaithfulness.

faithful *adj* accurate, attached, card-carrying, close, constant, convinced, dependable, devoted, exact, just, loyal, precise, reliable, staunch, steadfast, strict, true, true-blue, true-hearted, trusty, truthful, unswerving, unwavering. **antonyms** disloyal, inaccurate, treacherous.

n adherents, believers, brethren, communicants, congregation, followers, supporters.

faithless *adj* adulterous, delusive, disloyal, doubting, false, false-hearted, fickle, inconstant, perfidious, traitorous, treacherous, unbelieving, unfaithful, unreliable, untrue, untrustworthy, untruthful. **antonyms** believing, faithful.

fake *v* affect, assume, copy, counterfeit, fabricate, feign, forge, pretend, put on, sham, simulate.

n charlatan, copy, forgery, fraud, hoax, imitant, imitation, impostor, mountebank, phoney, reproduction, sham, simulation.

adj affected, artificial, assumed, bastard, bogus, counterfeit, ersatz, false, forged, hyped up, imitation, mock, phoney, pinchbeck, pretended, pseudo, reproduction, sham, simulated, spurious. **antonym** genuine.

fall *v* abate, backslide, become, befall, capitulate, cascade, chance, collapse, come about, come to pass, crash, decline, decrease, depreciate, descend, die, diminish, dive, drop, drop down, dwindle, ebb, err, fall away, fall off, fall out, flag, give in, give up, give way, go astray, go down, happen, incline, keel over, lapse, lessen, measure one's length,

meet one's end, nose-dive, occur, offend, perish, pitch, plummet, plunge, push, resign, settle, sin, sink, slope, slump, stumble, subside, succumb, surrender, take place, topple, transgress, trespass, trip, trip over, tumble, yield, yield to temptation. **antonym** rise.

n capitulation, collapse, cropper, cut, death, decline, declivity, decrease, defeat, degradation, descent, destruction, diminution, dip, dive, downfall, downgrade, drop, dwindling, failure, incline, lapse, lessening, lowering, nose-dive, overthrow, plummet, plunge, reduction, resignation, ruin, sin, slant, slip, slope, slump, spill, surrender, transgression, tumble, voluntary. **antonym** rise.

fall apart break, crumble, decay, decompose, disband, disintegrate, disperse, dissolve, rot, shatter.

fall asleep doze off, drop off, nod off.

fall back on have recourse to, look to, resort to, turn to, use.

fall for accept, be taken in by, swallow.

fall guy dupe, patsy, scapegoat, victim.

fall in cave in, collapse, come down, crumble, give way, sink.

fall in with accept, acquiesce, agree with, assent, comply, concur with, co-operate with, go along with, meet, support.

fall off decelerate, decline, decrease, deteriorate, drop, slacken, slow, slump, wane, worsen.

fall on assail, assault, attack, descend on, lay into, pounce on, snatch.

fall out[1] altercate, argue, bicker, clash, differ, disagree, fight, quarrel, squabble. **antonym** agree.

fall out[2] befall, chance, happen, occur, result, take place.

fall through collapse, come to nothing, fail, fizzle out, founder, miscarry. **antonym** succeed.

fall to apply oneself, begin, commence, get stuck in, set about, start.

fallacious *adj* deceptive, delusive, delusory, erroneous, false, fictitious, illogical, illusory, incorrect, misleading, mistaken, spurious, untrue, wrong. **antonyms** correct, true.

fallacy *n* deceit, deception, deceptiveness, delusion, error, falsehood, faultiness, flaw, illusion, inconsistency, misapprehension, misconception, mistake, sophism, sophistry, untruth. **antonym** truth.

fallible *adj* errant, erring, frail, human,

ignorant, imperfect, mortal, uncertain, weak. **antonym** infallible.

false *adj* artificial, bastard, bogus, concocted, counterfeit, deceitful, deceiving, deceptive, delusive, dishonest, dishonourable, disloyal, double-dealing, double-faced, duplicitous, erroneous, ersatz, faithless, fake, fallacious, false-hearted, faulty, feigned, fictitious, forged, fraudulent, hypocritical, illusive, imitation, improper, inaccurate, incorrect, inexact, invalid, lying, mendacious, misleading, mistaken, mock, perfidious, pretended, pseudo, sham, simulated, spurious, synthetic, treacherous, treasonable, trumped-up, truthless, two-faced, unfaithful, unfounded, unreal, unreliable, unsound, untrue, untrustworthy, untruthful, wrong. **antonyms** honest, reliable, true.

falsehood *n* deceit, deception, dishonesty, dissimulation, fable, fabrication, fib, fiction, inexactitude, lie, mendacity, perjury, prevarication, story, untruth, untruthfulness. **antonyms** truth, truthfulness.

falsification *n* adulteration, alteration, change, deceit, dissimulation, distortion, forgery, misrepresentation, perversion, tampering.

falsify *v* adulterate, alter, belie, cook, counterfeit, distort, doctor, fake, forge, garble, misrepresent, pervert, sophisticate, take liberties with, tamper with.

falter *v* break, fail, flag, flinch, halt, hem and haw, hesitate, shake, stammer, stumble, stutter, totter, tremble, vacillate, waver.

faltering *adj* broken, failing, flagging, hesitant, irresolute, stammering, stumbling, tentative, timid, uncertain, unsteady, weak. **antonyms** firm, strong.

fame *n* celebrity, credit, eminence, esteem, glory, honour, illustriousness, kudos, name, prominence, renown, reputation, repute, stardom.

famed *adj* acclaimed, celebrated, famous, noted, recognised, renowned, well-known, widely-known. **antonym** unknown.

familiar *adj* abreast, accustomed, acquainted, amicable, au fait, aware, bold, chummy, close, common, common-or-garden, confidential, conscious, conventional, conversant, cordial, customary, disrespectful, domestic, easy, everyday, forward, free, free-and-easy, frequent, friendly, household,

impudent, informal, intimate, intrusive, knowledgeable, mundane, near, open, ordinary, overfree, presuming, presumptuous, private, recognisable, relaxed, repeated, routine, stock, unceremonious, unconstrained, unreserved, versed, well-known. **antonyms** formal, reserved, unfamiliar, unversed.

familiarity *n* acquaintance, awareness, boldness, cheek, closeness, conversance, disrespect, ease, experience, fellowship, forwardness, freedom, friendliness, grasp, impertinence, impudence, informality, intimacy, liberties, liberty, licence, naturalness, openness, presumption, sociability, unceremoniousness, understanding. **antonyms** formality, reservation, unfamiliarity.

family *n* ancestors, ancestry, birth, blood, brood, children, clan, class, classification, descendants, descent, dynasty, extraction, folk, forebears, forefathers, genealogy, genre, group, house, household, issue, kin, kind, kindred, kinsmen, kith and kin, line, lineage, network, offspring, parentage, pedigree, people, progeny, race, relations, relatives, strain, subdivision, system, tribe.

family tree ancestry, extraction, genealogy, line, lineage, pedigree.

famous *adj* acclaimed, celebrated, conspicuous, distinguished, eminent, excellent, famed, glorious, great, honoured, illustrious, legendary, lionised, notable, noted, prominent, remarkable, renowned, signal, well-known. **antonym** unknown.

fan¹ *v* aggravate, agitate, air-condition, air-cool, arouse, blow, cool, enkindle, excite, impassion, increase, provoke, refresh, rouse, stimulate, stir up, ventilate, whip up, winnow, work up.

fan² *n* adherent, admirer, aficionado, buff, devotee, enthusiast, fiend, follower, freak, groupie, lover, supporter, zealot.

fanatic *n* activist, addict, bigot, devotee, enthusiast, extremist, fiend, freak, militant, visionary, zealot.

fanatical *adj* bigoted, burning, enthusiastic, extreme, fervent, fervid, frenzied, immoderate, mad, obsessive, overenthusiastic, passionate, rabid, visionary, wild, zealous. **antonyms** moderate, unenthusiastic.

fanaticism *n* bigotry, dedication, devotion, enthusiasm, extremism, fervidness, fervour, immoderacy, immoderateness, immoderation, infatuation, madness, monomania, obsessiveness, overenthusiasm, singlemindedness, zeal. **antonym** moderation.

fanciful *adj* capricious, curious, extravagant, fabulous, fairy-tale, fantastic, ideal, imaginary, imaginative, metaphysical, mythical, poetic, romantic, unreal, vaporous, visionary, whimsical, wild. **antonym** ordinary.

fancy *v* be attracted to, believe, conceive, conjecture, crave, desire, dream of, favour, go for, guess, hanker after, have an eye for, imagine, infer, like, long for, lust after, picture, prefer, reckon, relish, suppose, surmise, take a liking to, take to, think, think likely, whim, wish for, yearn for, yen for. **antonym** dislike.

n caprice, chim(a)era, conception, daydream, delusion, desire, dream, fantasy, fondness, hankering, humour, idea, image, imagination, impression, impulse, inclination, liking, nightmare, notion, partiality, penchant, phantasm, predilection, preference, relish, thought, urge, vapour, vision, whim. **antonyms** dislike, fact, reality.

adj baroque, capricious, decorated, decorative, delusive, elaborate, elegant, embellished, extravagant, fanciful, fantastic, far-fetched, illusory, ornamented, ornate, rococo, whimsical. **antonym** plain.

fantasise *v* build castles in the air, daydream, dream, hallucinate, imagine, invent, live in a dream, romance.

fantastic *adj* absurd, ambitious, capricious, chimerical, comical, eccentric, enormous, excellent, exotic, extravagant, extreme, fanciful, far-fetched, first-rate, freakish, grandiose, great, grotesque, illusory, imaginative, implausible, incredible, irrational, ludicrous, mad, marvellous, odd, out of this world, outlandish, overwhelming, peculiar, phantasmagorical, preposterous, quaint, queer, ridiculous, sensational, severe, strange, superb, tremendous, unlikely, unreal, unrealistic, visionary, weird, whimsical, wild, wonderful. **antonyms** ordinary, plain, poor.

fantasy *n* apparition, caprice, creativity, daydream, delusion, dream, fancy, fantasia, flight of fancy, hallucination, illusion, imagination, invention, mirage, nightmare, originality, phantasy, pipedream, reverie, vision, whims(e)y. **antonym** reality.

far *adv* a good way, a long way, afar, considerably, decidedly, deep, extremely, greatly, incomparably, miles, much. **antonym** near.

adj distant, faraway, far-flung, far-off, far-removed, further, god-forsaken, long, opposite, other, outlying, out-of-the-way, remote, removed. **antonyms** close, nearby.

far and wide all about, broadly, everywhere, extensively, far and near, widely, worldwide.

faraway *adj* absent, absent-minded, abstracted, distant, dreamy, far, far-flung, far-off, lost, outlying, remote. **antonyms** alert, nearby.

farce *n* absurdity, buffoonery, burlesque, comedy, commedia dell'arte, exode, joke, low comedy, mockery, nonsense, parody, ridiculousness, satire, sham, slapstick, travesty.

farcical *adj* absurd, amusing, comic, derisory, diverting, droll, facetious, funny, laughable, ludicrous, nonsensical, preposterous, ridiculous, silly, slapstick, stupid. **antonym** sensible.

fare[1] *n* charge, cost, fee, passage, passenger, pick-up, price, traveller.

fare[2] *v* be, do, get along, get on, go, go on, happen, make out, manage, proceed, prosper, turn out.

farewell *n* adieu, departure, goodbye, leave-taking, parting, send-off, valediction. **antonym** hello.

adj final, parting, valedictory.

interj aloha, bye-bye, cheers, ciao, good-bye.

far-fetched *adj* crazy, doubtful, dubious, fantastic, forced, implausible, improbable, incredible, preposterous, strained, unbelievable, unconvincing, unlikely, unnatural, unrealistic. **antonym** plausible.

farrago *n* dog's breakfast, hash, hotchpotch, jumble, medley, mélange, miscellany, mishmash, mixture, potpourri.

far-reaching *adj* broad, consequential, extensive, important, momentous, pervasive, significant, sweeping, widespread. **antonym** insignificant.

far-sighted *adj* acute, canny, cautious, circumspect, discerning, far-seeing, judicious, prescient, provident, prudent, sage, shrewd, wise. **antonyms** imprudent, unwise.

fascinate *v* absorb, allure, beguile, bewitch, captivate, charm, delight, enchant, engross, enrapture, enravish, enthrall, entrance, hypnotise, infatuate, intrigue, mesmerise, rivet, spellbind, transfix. *antonym* bore.

fascinated *adj* absorbed, beguiled, bewitched, captivated, charmed, engrossed, enthralled, entranced, hooked, hypnotised, infatuated, mesmerised, smitten, spellbound. *antonyms* bored, uninterested.

fascinating *adj* alluring, bewitching, captivating, charming, compelling, delightful, enchanting, engaging, engrossing, enticing, gripping, interesting, intriguing, irresistible, mesmerising, ravishing, riveting, seductive. *antonyms* boring, uninteresting.

fascination *n* allure, attraction, charm, enchantment, glamour, interest, lure, magic, magnetism, pull, sorcery, spell. *antonym* boredom.

fascism *n* absolutism, authoritarianism, autocracy, dictatorship, Hitlerism, totalitarianism.

fashion *n* appearance, attitude, configuration, convention, craze, cult, custom, cut, demeanour, description, fad, figure, form, guise, haute couture, high society, jet set, kind, latest, line, look, make, manner, method, mode, model, mould, pattern, shape, sort, style, trend, type, usage, vogue, way.
v accommodate, adapt, adjust, alter, construct, contrive, create, design, fit, forge, form, make, manufacture, mould, shape, suit, tailor, work.

fashionable *adj* all the rage, chic, chichi, contemporary, cult, current, customary, funky, in, in vogue, latest, modern, modish, popular, prevailing, smart, snazzy, stylish, swagger, trendsetting, trendy, up-to-date, up-to-the-minute, usual, with it. *antonym* unfashionable.

fast¹ *adj* accelerated, brisk, fleet, flying, hasty, hurried, mercurial, nippy, quick, rapid, spanking, speedy, swift, winged. *antonym* slow.
adv apace, hastily, hell for leather, hurriedly, like a flash, like a shot, posthaste, presto, quickly, rapidly, speedily, swiftly. *antonym* slowly.

fast² *adj* close, constant, fastened, firm, fixed, fortified, immovable, impregnable, lasting, loyal, permanent, secure, sound, staunch, steadfast, tight, unflinching, unwavering. *antonyms* impermanent, loose.
adv close, deeply, firmly, fixedly, near, rigidly, securely, soundly, sound(ly),

tightly, unflinchingly. *antonym* loosely.

fast³ *adj* dissipated, dissolute, extravagant, immoral, intemperate, licentious, loose, profligate, promiscuous, rakish, reckless, self-indulgent, wanton, whorish, wild. *antonyms* chaste, moral.

fasten *v* affix, aim, anchor, attach, belay, bend, bind, bolt, chain, clamp, concentrate, connect, direct, fix, focus, grip, join, lace, link, lock, nail, rivet, secure, spar, tie, unite. *antonym* unfasten.

fasten together interlink, interlock, join, link, unite. *antonyms* unfasten, untie.

fastened *adj* anchored, attached, bolted, chained, clamped, closed, fixed, joined, knotted, linked, locked, nailed, sealed, secured, shut, tied.

fastidious *adj* choosy, critical, difficult, discriminating, finicky, fussy, meticulous, particular, pernickety, picky, precise, punctilious, squeamish. *antonym* undemanding.

fat *adj* affluent, beefy, blowzy, corpulent, elephantine, fatty, fertile, fleshed, fleshy, flourishing, fruitful, greasy, gross, heavy, lucrative, lush, obese, oily, oleaginous, overweight, paunchy, plump, podgy, portly, pot-bellied, productive, profitable, prosperous, pudgy, remunerative, rich, roly-poly, rotund, round, solid, stout, thriving, tubbish, tubby, well-upholstered. *antonyms* thin, unproductive.
n blubber, cellulite, corpulence, fatness, flab, obesity, overweight, paunch, pot (belly).

fatal *adj* baleful, baneful, calamitous, catastrophic, deadly, destructive, disastrous, final, incurable, killing, lethal, malignant, mortal, pernicious, ruinous, terminal, vital. *antonym* harmless.

fatality *n* casualty, deadliness, death, disaster, lethalness, loss, mortality, unavoidability.

fate *n* chance, cup, death, destiny, destruction, divine will, doom, downfall, end, fortune, future, horoscope, issue, kismet, lot, nemesis, outcome, portion, predestination, predestiny, providence, ruin, stars, upshot.

fated *adj* destined, doomed, ineluctable, inescapable, inevitable, predestined, pre-elected, preordained, sure, unavoidable, written. *antonym* avoidable.

fateful *adj* critical, crucial, deadly, decisive, destructive, disastrous, fatal, important, lethal, momentous, ominous, portentous, ruinous, significant. *antonym* unimportant.

fathead *n* ass, booby, dimwit, dolt, dope, dumb-cluck, dumbo, dunderhead, fool, goose, idiot, imbecile, jackass, nincompoop, nitwit, numskull, twerp, twit.

father *n* ancestor, architect, author, begetter, confessor, creator, dad, daddy, elder, forebear, forefather, founder, governor, inventor, leader, maker, old boy, old man, originator, pa, papa, pappy, parent, pastor, pater, paterfamilias, patriarch, patron, pop, pops, predecessor, priest, prime mover, procreator, senator, sire.
v beget, conceive, create, dream up, engender, establish, found, get, institute, invent, originate, procreate, produce, sire.

fatherly *adj* affectionate, avuncular, benevolent, benign, indulgent, kind, kindly, paternal, patriarchal, protective, supportive, tender. *antonyms* cold, harsh, unkind.

fathom *v* comprehend, deduce, divine, estimate, gauge, get to the bottom of, grasp, interpret, measure, penetrate, plumb, plummet, probe, see, sound, understand, work out.

fatigue *v* do in, drain, exhaust, fag, jade, knacker, overtire, shatter, tire, weaken, wear out, weary, whack. *antonym* refresh.
n debility, decay, degeneration, failure, heaviness, languor, lethargy, listlessness, overtiredness, tiredness. *antonyms* energy, freshness.

fatigued *adj* all in, beat, bushed, dead-beat, exhausted, fagged, jaded, jiggered, knackered, overtired, tired, tired out, wasted, weary, whacked, zonked. *antonym* refreshed.

fatness *n* bulk, bulkiness, corpulence, flab, flesh, fleshiness, girth, grossness, heaviness, obesity, overweight, podginess, portliness, rotundity, size, stoutness, tubbiness, weight.

fatten *v* bloat, broaden, build up, coarsen, cram, distend, expand, feed, feed up, fertilise, nourish, overfeed, spread, stuff, swell, thicken, thrive.

fatuous *adj* absurd, asinine, brainless, daft, dense, dull, foolish, idiotic, imbecile, inane, ludicrous, lunatic, mindless, moronic, puerile, silly, stupid, vacuous, weak-minded, witless. *antonym* sensible.

fault *n* blemish, blunder, boob, booboo, culpability, defect, deficiency, delinquency, demerit, dislocation, drawback, error, failing, flaw, frailty, goof, imperfection, inaccuracy, indiscretion, infirmity, lack, lapse, liability, misconduct, misdeed, mistake, negligence, offence, omission, oversight, peccadillo, responsibility, shortcoming, sin, slip, slip-up, snag, solecism, transgression, trespass, weakness, wrong. *antonyms* advantage, strength.
v blame, call to account, censure, criticise, find fault with, impugn, pick at, pick holes in. *antonym* praise.

fault-finding *n* carping, finger-pointing, grumbling, hair-splitting, nagging, niggling, nit-picking. *antonym* praise.
adj captious, carping, censorious, critical, grumbling, hypercritical, nagging, querulous. *antonym* complimentary.

faultless *adj* accurate, blameless, classic, correct, exemplary, faithful, flawless, foolproof, guiltless, immaculate, impeccable, innocent, irreproachable, model, perfect, pure, sinless, spotless, stainless, unblemished, unspotted, unsullied, untainted, word-perfect. *antonym* imperfect.

faulty *adj* bad, blemished, broken, damaged, defective, erroneous, fallacious, flawed, illogical, impaired, imperfect, imprecise, inaccurate, incorrect, invalid, malfunctioning, out of order, specious, unsound, weak, wrong.

faux pas blunder, boob, booboo, clanger, gaffe, goof, impropriety, indiscretion, solecism.

favour *n* acceptance, approbation, approval, backing, badge, benefit, bias, boon, championship, courtesy, decoration, esteem, favouritism, friendliness, gift, good turn, goodwill, grace, indulgence, keepsake, kindness, knot, love-token, memento, partiality, patronage, present, regard, rosette, service, smile, souvenir, support, token. *antonym* disfavour.
v abet, accommodate, advance, advocate, aid, approve, assist, back, befriend, champion, choose, commend, countenance, ease, encourage, esteem, extenuate, facilitate, fancy, have in one's good books, help, indulge, like, oblige, opt for, pamper, patronise, prefer, promote, resemble, spare, spoil,

succour, support, take after, take kindly to, value. *antonyms* disfavour, hinder, thwart.

favourable *adj* advantageous, affirmative, agreeable, amicable, appropriate, approving, auspicious, beneficial, benign, convenient, encouraging, enthusiastic, fair, fit, friendly, good, helpful, hopeful, kind, opportune, positive, promising, propitious, reassuring, suitable, sympathetic, timely, understanding, welcoming, well-disposed, well-minded, white. *antonym* unfavourable.

favourite *adj* best-loved, choice, dearest, esteemed, favoured, pet, preferred. *antonyms* hated, unfavourite.
n beloved, blue-eyed boy, choice, darling, dear, idol, pet, pick, preference, teacher's pet, the apple of one's eye. *antonym* pet hate.

favouritism *n* bias, injustice, jobs for the boys, nepotism, old school tie, one-sidedness, partiality, partisanship, preference, preferential treatment. *antonym* impartiality.

fawn *v* bootlick, bow and scrape, court, crawl, creep, curry favour, dance attendance, flatter, grovel, ingratiate oneself, kneel, kowtow, pay court, smarm, toady.

fawning *adj* abject, bootlicking, crawling, cringing, deferential, flattering, grovelling, knee-crooking, obsequious, servile, slavish, sycophantic, toadying, toadyish, unctuous. *antonyms* cold, proud.

fear *n* agitation, alarm, anxiety, apprehension, apprehensiveness, awe, bogey, bugbear, concern, consternation, cravenness, danger, dismay, disquietude, distress, doubt, dread, foreboding(s), fright, funk, horror, likelihood, misgiving(s), nightmare, panic, phobia, qualms, reverence, risk, solicitude, spectre, suspicion, terror, timidity, tremors, trepidation, unease, uneasiness, veneration, wonder, worry. *antonyms* courage, fortitude.
v anticipate, apprehend, dread, expect, foresee, respect, reverence, shudder at, suspect, take fright, tremble, venerate, worry.

fearful[1] *adj* afraid, alarmed, anxious, apprehensive, diffident, faint-hearted, frightened, hesitant, intimidated, jittery, jumpy, nervous, nervy, panicky, pusillanimous, scared, shrinking, tense, timid, timorous, uneasy. *antonym* courageous.

fearful[2] *adj* appalling, atrocious, awful, dire, distressing, dreadful, fearsome, frightful, ghastly, grievous, grim, gruesome, hair-raising, hideous, horrendous, horrible, horrific, monstrous, shocking, terrible, unspeakable. *antonym* delightful.

fearless *adj* aweless, bold, brave, confident, courageous, daring, dauntless, doughty, gallant, game, gutsy, heroic, indomitable, intrepid, lion-hearted, plucky, unabashed, unafraid, unapprehensive, unblenching, unblinking, undaunted, unflinching, valiant, valorous. *antonyms* afraid, timid.

fearsome *adj* alarming, appalling, awe-inspiring, awesome, awful, daunting, dismaying, formidable, frightening, frightful, hair-raising, horrendous, horrible, horrific, horrifying, menacing, terrible, unnerving. *antonym* delightful.

feasible *adj* achievable, attainable, likely, possible, practicable, practical, realisable, reasonable, viable, workable. *antonym* impossible.

feast *n* banquet, barbecue, beanfeast, beano, binge, blow-out, carousal, carouse, celebration, delight, dinner, enjoyment, entertainment, festival, fête, gala day, gratification, holiday, holy day, jollification, junket, pleasure, repast, revels, saint's day, spread, treat.
v delight, eat one's fill, entertain, gladden, gorge, gratify, indulge, overindulge, regale, rejoice, stuff, stuff one's face, thrill, treat, wine and dine.

feat *n* accomplishment, achievement, act, attainment, deed, exploit, performance.

feature *n* article, aspect, attraction, attribute, character, characteristic, column, comment, draw, facet, factor, hallmark, highlight, innovation, item, mark, peculiarity, piece, point, property, quality, report, special, speciality, specialty, story, trait.
v accentuate, emphasise, headline, highlight, play up, present, promote, push, recommend, show, spotlight, star.

feckless *adj* aimless, feeble, futile, gormless, hopeless, incompetent, ineffectual, irresponsible, shiftless, useless, weak, worthless. *antonyms* efficient, sensible.

fed up annoyed, blue, bored, brassed

off, browned off, cheesed off, depressed, discontented, dismal, dissatisfied, down, gloomy, glum, scunnered, sick and tired, tired, weary. **antonym** contented.

federate *v* amalgamate, associate, combine, confederate, integrate, join together, league, syndicate, unify, unite. **antonyms** disunite, separate.

federation *n* alliance, amalgamation, association, coalition, combination, confederation, entente, league, syndicate, union.

fee *n* account, bill, charge, compensation, emolument, hire, honorarium, pay, payment, recompense, remuneration, retainer, reward, terms, toll.

feeble *adj* debilitated, delicate, doddering, effete, enervated, enfeebled, exhausted, failing, faint, flat, flimsy, forceless, frail, inadequate, incompetent, indecisive, ineffective, ineffectual, inefficient, insignificant, insufficient, lame, languid, paltry, poor, powerless, puny, sickly, silly, slight, tame, thin, unconvincing, vacillating, weak, weakened, weakly. **antonyms** strong, worthy.

feeble-minded *adj* cretinous, deficient, dim-witted, dull, dumb, half-witted, idiotic, imbecilic, irresolute, lacking, moronic, retarded, simple, slow on the uptake, slow-witted, soft in the head, stupid, two bricks short of a load, vacant, weak-minded. **antonyms** bright, intelligent.

feed *v* augment, bolster, cater for, dine, eat, encourage, fare, foster, fuel, graze, nourish, nurture, pasture, provide for, provision, strengthen, subsist, supply, sustain.

n banquet, feast, fodder, food, forage, meal, nosh, pasture, provender, repast, silage, spread, tuck-in, victuals.

feed in inject, input, key in, supply.

feed on consume, devour, eat, exist on, live on, partake of.

feel *v* appear, believe, caress, consider, deem, empathise, endure, enjoy, experience, explore, finger, fondle, fumble, go through, grope, handle, have, have a hunch, hold, intuit, judge, know, manipulate, maul, notice, observe, paw, perceive, reckon, resemble, seem, sense, sound, stroke, suffer, take to heart, test, think, touch, try, undergo.

n bent, feeling, finish, gift, impression, knack, quality, sense, surface, texture, touch, vibes.

feel for be sorry for, bleed for, commiserate (with), compassionate, empathise with, pity, sympathise with.

feel like desire, fancy, want.

feeling *n* affection, air, ambience, appreciation, apprehension, ardour, atmosphere, aura, compassion, concern, consciousness, emotion, empathy, feel, fervour, fondness, heat, hunch, idea, impression, inclination, inkling, instinct, intensity, mood, notion, opinion, passion, perception, pity, point of view, presentiment, quality, sensation, sense, sensibility, sensitivity, sentiment, sentimentality, suspicion, sympathy, touch, understanding, vibes, vibrations, view, warmth.

feign *v* act, affect, assume, counterfeit, devise, dissemble, dissimulate, fabricate, fake, forge, imitate, invent, make a show of, pretend, put on, sham, simulate.

feigned *adj* affected, artificial, assumed, counterfeit, fabricated, fake, false, imitation, insincere, personated, pretend, pretended, pseudo, sham, simulated, spurious. **antonyms** genuine, sincere.

feint *n* artifice, blind, bluff, deception, distraction, dodge, dummy, expedient, manoeuvre, mock-assault, play, pretence, ruse, stratagem, subterfuge, wile.

felicitous *adj* apposite, appropriate, apropos, apt, delightful, fitting, happy, inspired, neat, opportune, propitious, prosperous, suitable, timely, well-chosen, well-timed, well-turned. **antonyms** inappropriate, inept.

fell[1] *v* cut down, demolish, flatten, floor, hew down, lay level, level, prostrate, raze, strike down.

fell[2] *adj* baneful, barbarous, bloody, cruel, deadly, destructive, fatal, ferocious, fierce, grim, implacable, inhuman, malevolent, malicious, malign, malignant, merciless, mortal, nefarious, noxious, pernicious, pitiless, relentless, ruinous, ruthless, sanguinary, savage, vicious. **antonyms** benign, gentle, kind.

fellow[1] *n* bloke, boy, buffer, bugger, cat, chap, character, codger, cove, customer, dog, fucker, guy, individual, Johnny, joker, man, person, punter.

fellow[2] *n* associate, brother, colleague, companion, comrade, counterpart, double, equal, fellow-member, friend, like, match, mate, member, partner, peer, twin.

adj associate, associated, co-, like, related, similar.

fellowship *n* amity, association, brotherhood, camaraderie, club, communion, companionability, companionship, endowment, familiarity, fraternisation, fraternity, guild, intercourse, intimacy, kindliness, league, order, sisterhood, sociability, society, sodality.

eminine *adj* delicate, effeminate, gentle, girlish, graceful, ladylike, modest, petticoat, sissy, soft, tender, unmanly, unmasculine, weak, womanish, womanly. *antonym* masculine.

emininity *n* delicacy, effeminacy, feminineness, gentleness, girlishness, sissiness, softness, unmanliness, womanhood, womanishness, womanliness. *antonym* masculinity.

emme fatale charmer, enchantress, seductress, siren, temptress, vamp.

ence[1] *n* barricade, barrier, defence, guard, hedge, paling, palisade, railings, rampart, shield, stockade, wall, windbreak.

v bound, circumscribe, confine, coop, defend, encircle, enclose, fortify, guard, hedge, pen, protect, restrict, secure, separate, surround.

ence[2] *v* beat about the bush, dodge, equivocate, evade, hedge, parry, prevaricate, pussyfoot, quibble, shift, stonewall.

end for look after, maintain, provide for, support, sustain.

end off avert, beat off, defend, deflect, hold at bay, keep off, parry, repel, repulse, resist, shut out, stave off, ward off.

erment *v* agitate, boil, brew, bubble, concoct, effervesce, excite, fester, foam, foment, froth, heat, incite, inflame, leaven, provoke, rise, rouse, seethe, smoulder, stir up, work, work up.

n agitation, brouhaha, commotion, disruption, excitement, fever, frenzy, furore, glow, heat, hubbub, imbroglio, stew, stir, tumult, turbulence, turmoil, unrest, uproar, yeast. *antonym* calm.

erocious *adj* barbaric, barbarous, bloodthirsty, bloody, brutal, brutish, cruel, fearsome, fiendish, fierce, homicidal, inhuman, merciless, murderous, pitiless, predatory, rapacious, ravening, relentless, ruthless, sadistic, sanguinary, savage, truculent, vicious, violent, wild. *antonyms* gentle, mild.

erocity *n* barbarity, bloodthirstiness, brutality, cruelty, ferociousness, fiendishness, fierceness, inhumanity, murderousness, rapacity, ruthlessness, sadism, savageness, savagery, viciousness, wildness. *antonyms* gentleness, mildness.

ferret out dig up, disclose, discover, disinter, drive out, elicit, extract, find, hunt down, nose out, root out, run to earth, smell out, sniff out, sus out, trace, track down, unearth, worm out.

ferry *v* carry, chauffeur, convey, drive, move, remove, run, shift, ship, shuttle, taxi, transport.

fertile *adj* abundant, fat, fecund, flowering, fructiferous, fruit-bearing, fruitful, generative, lush, luxuriant, plenteous, plentiful, potent, productive, prolific, rich, teeming, virile, yielding. *antonyms* arid, barren.

fertilise *v* compost, dress, enrich, fecundate, feed, fructify, impregnate, inseminate, manure, mulch, pollinate, top-dress.

fertility *n* abundance, fatness, fecundity, fruitfulness, lushness, luxuriance, plenteousness, potency, productiveness, richness, virility. *antonyms* aridity, barrenness.

fervent *adj* animated, ardent, devout, eager, earnest, emotional, energetic, enthusiastic, excited, fervid, fiery, full-blooded, heartfelt, impassioned, intense, passionate, spirited, vehement, vigorous, warm, whole-hearted, zealous.

fervour *n* animation, ardour, eagerness, earnestness, energy, enthusiasm, excitement, intensity, passion, spirit, vehemence, verve, vigour, warmth, zeal. *antonym* apathy.

fester *v* chafe, decay, discharge, gall, gather, irk, maturate, putrefy, rankle, smoulder, suppurate, ulcerate. *antonyms* dissipate, heal.

festival *n* anniversary, carnival, celebration, commemoration, entertainment, feast, festa, festivities, fête, field day, fiesta, gala, holiday, holy day, jubilee, merrymaking, saint's day, treat.

festive *adj* carnival, celebratory, cheery, Christmassy, convivial, cordial, gala, gay, gleeful, happy, hearty, holiday, jolly, jovial, joyful, joyous, jubilant, merry, mirthful, rollicking, sportive, uproarious. *antonyms* gloomy, sober, sombre.

festivity *n* amusement, conviviality, enjoyment, feasting, fun, gaiety, jollification, jollity, joviality, joyfulness, merriment, merrymaking, mirth, pleasure, revelry, sport.

festoon *v* adorn, array, bedeck, deck,

decorate, drape, garland, garnish, hang, swathe, wreath.

fetch v be good for, bring, bring in, carry, conduct, convey, deliver, draw, earn, elicit, escort, evoke, get, go for, lead, make, obtain, produce, realise, retrieve, sell for, transport, uplift, utter, yield.

fetch up arrive, come, come to a halt, end up, finish, finish up, halt, land, reach, stop, turn up.

fetching *adj* alluring, attractive, beguiling, captivating, charming, cute, disarming, enchanting, enticing, fascinating, pretty, sweet, taking, winning, winsome. **antonym** repellent.

fête n bazaar, carnival, fair, festival, gala, garden party, sale of work.
v banquet, bring out the red carpet for, entertain, honour, lionise, make much of, regale, treat, welcome, wine and dine.

fetid *adj* corrupt, disgusting, filthy, foul, malodorous, nauseating, noxious, odorous, offensive, rancid, rank, reeking, sickly, smelly, stinking. **antonym** fragrant.

fetish n amulet, charm, cult object, fixation, idée fixe, idol, image, ju-ju, mania, obsession, talisman, thing, totem.

fetter v bind, chain, confine, curb, encumber, hamper, hamshackle, hamstring, hobble, manacle, pinion, restrain, restrict, shackle, tie (up), trammel, truss. **antonym** free.

feud n animosity, antagonism, argument, bad blood, bickering, bitterness, conflict, contention, disagreement, discord, dispute, dissension, enmity, estrangement, faction, feuding, grudge, hostility, ill will, quarrel, rivalry, row, strife, variance, vendetta. **antonyms** agreement, peace.
v altercate, argue, be at odds, bicker, brawl, clash, contend, dispute, duel, fight, quarrel, row, squabble, war, wrangle. **antonym** agree.

fever n agitation, delirium, ecstasy, excitement, ferment, fervour, feverishness, flush, frenzy, heat, intensity, passion, restlessness, temperature, turmoil, unrest.

feverish *adj* agitated, anxious, burning, distracted, eager, excited, fanatical, febrile, fevered, flurried, flushed, flustered, frantic, frenetic, frenzied, hasty, hectic, hot, hurried, impatient, inflamed, nervous, obsessive, overwrought, restless. **antonyms** calm, cool.

few *adj* few and far between, hard to come by, in short supply, inadequate, inconsiderable, infrequent, insufficient, meagre, negligible, rare, scant, scanty, scarce, scattered, sparse, sporadic, thin, uncommon.
pron a couple, handful, not many, oddments, one or two, scarcely any, scattering, small number, small quantity, some, sprinkling.

fiasco n bummer, calamity, catastrophe, collapse, cropper, damp squib, débâcle, disaster, failure, flop, mess, rout, ruin, turkey, wash-out. **antonym** success.

fiat n authorisation, command, decree, dictate, dictum, diktat, directive, edict, injunction, mandate, OK, order, ordinance, permission, precept, prescript, proclamation, sanction, warrant.

fib n concoction, evasion, falsehood, fantasy, fiction, invention, lie, misrepresentation, prevarication, story, tale, untruth, white lie, whopper, yarn.
v dissemble, evade, fabricate, falsify, fantasise, invent, lie, prevaricate, sidestep.

fibre n backbone, calibre, character, courage, determination, essence, filament, grit, guts, nature, nerve, pile, pluck, quality, resolution, sinew, spirit, stamina, stapie, strand, strength, substance, temperament, tenacity, tendril, texture, thread, toughness.

fickle *adj* capricious, changeable, disloyal, dizzy, erratic, faithless, fitful, flighty, fluctuating, inconstant, irresolute, mercurial, mutable, quicksilver, treacherous, unfaithful, unpredictable, unreliable, unstable, unsteady, vacillating, variable, volatile. **antonym** constant.

fiction n cock-and-bull story, concoction, fable, fabrication, falsehood, fancy, fantasy, fib, figment, imagination, improvisation, invention, legend, lie, myth, novel, parable, romance, story, story-telling, tale, tall story, untruth, whopper, yarn. **antonym** truth.

fictional *adj* fabulous, imaginary, invented, legendary, made-up, mythical, non-existent, unreal. **antonyms** real, true.

fictitious *adj* aprocryphal, artificial, assumed, bogus, counterfeit, fabricated, false, fanciful, feigned, fictive, fraudulent, imaginary, imagined, improvised, invented, made-up, make-believe, mythical, non-existent, spurious, supposed, suppositional, unreal, untrue. *antonyms* genuine, real.

iddle *v* cheat, cook, cook the books, diddle, fidget, finger, fix, gerrymander, interfere, juggle, manoeuvre, mess around, play, racketeer, swindle, tamper, tinker, toy, trifle, wangle.
n chicanery, con, fix, fraud, monkey-business, racket, rip-off, sharp practice, swindle, trickery, wangle.

idelity *n* accuracy, adherence, allegiance, authenticity, closeness, constancy, correspondence, dedication, dependability, devotedness, devotion, dutifulness, exactitude, exactness, faith, faithfulness, incorruptibility, integrity, loyalty, preciseness, precision, reliability, scrupulousness, staunchness, steadfastness, true-heartedness, trustworthiness. *antonyms* inaccuracy, inconstancy, treachery.

dget *v* bustle, chafe, fiddle, fidge, fret, jerk, jiggle, jitter, jump, mess about, play around, squirm, toy, twitch, worry.
n agitation, anxiety, creeps, discomposure, edginess, fidgetiness, fidgets, heebie-jeebies, jitteriness, jitters, jumpiness, nerves, nerviness, nervousness, restlessness, shakes, twitchiness, unease, uneasiness, willies.

dgety *adj* agitated, frisky, impatient, jerky, jittery, jumpy, nervous, nervy, on edge, restive, restless, skittish, twitchy, uneasy. *antonym* still.

ield[1] *n* arena, battlefield, battleground, grassland, green, lawn, lea, meadow, paddock, pasture, pitch, playing-field, theatre.

ield[2] *n* applicants, candidates, competition, competitors, contenders, contestants, entrants, opponents, opposition, possibilities, runners.

ield[3] *n* area, bailiwick, ball park, bounds, confines, department, discipline, domain, environment, forte, limits, line, métier, period, province, range, scope, speciality, specialty, territory.

ield[4] *v* answer, catch, cope with, deal with, deflect, handle, parry, pick up, receive, retrieve, return, stop.

iend *n* addict, aficionado, barbarian, beast, brute, degenerate, demon, devil, devotee, enthusiast, evil spirit, fanatic, freak, ghoul, goblin, hobgoblin, incubus, maniac, monster, nut, ogre, Satan, savage, succubus.

iendish *adj* accursed, atrocious, baleful, black-hearted, cruel, damnable, devilish, diabolic, diabolical, hellish, impious, implacable, infernal, inhuman, maleficent, malevolent, malicious, malign, malignant, mischievous, monstrous, nefarious, satanic, savage, ungodly, unspeakable, vicious, vile, wicked.

fierce *adj* baleful, barbarous, blustery, boisterous, brutal, cruel, cut-throat, dangerous, fearsome, fell, ferocious, fiery, frightening, furious, grim, howling, intense, keen, menacing, merciless, murderous, passionate, powerful, raging, relentless, savage, stern, stormy, strong, tempestuous, threatening, truculent, tumultuous, uncontrollable, unrelenting, untamed, vicious, violent, wild. *antonyms* calm, gentle, kind.

fiercely *adv* ardently, bitterly, fanatically, ferociously, furiously, implacably, intensely, keenly, menacingly, mercilessly, murderously, passionately, relentlessly, savagely, sternly, tempestuously, tigerishly, tooth and nail, viciously, violently, wildly, zealously. *antonyms* gently, kindly.

fiery *adj* ablaze, afire, aflame, aglow, ardent, blazing, burning, excitable, febrile, fervent, fervid, fevered, feverish, fierce, flaming, flushed, glowing, heated, hot, hot-headed, impatient, impetuous, impulsive, inflamed, irascible, irritable, passionate, peppery, precipitate, red-hot, sultry, torrid, truculent, violent, volcanic. *antonyms* cold, impassive.

fight *v* altercate, argue, assault, battle, bear arms against, bicker, box, brawl, clash, close, combat, conduct, conflict, contend, contest. cross swords, defy, dispute, do battle, engage, exchange blows, fence, feud, grapple, joust, lock horns, measure strength, measure swords, mell, mix it, oppose, prosecute, quarrel, resist, scrap, scuffle, skirmish, spar, squabble, stand up to, strive, struggle, take the field, tilt, tussle, wage, wage war, war, withstand, wrangle, wrestle.
n action, affray, altercation, argument, barney, battle, belligerence, bicker, bout, brawl, brush, clash, combat, conflict, contest, courage, dispute, dissension, dogfight, duel, encounter, engagement, fisticuffs, fracas, fray, free-for-all, gameness, hostilities, joust, mêlée, mettle, militancy, pluck, quarrel, resilience, resistance, riot, row, ruck, rumble, scrap, scuffle, set-to, skirmish, spirit, strength, struggle, tenacity, tussle, war.

fight back[1] defend oneself, give as good as one gets, put up a fight, reply, resist, retaliate, retort.

fight back[2] bottle up, contain, control, curb, hold back, hold in check, repress, resist, restrain, suppress.

fight off beat off, hold off, keep at bay, put to flight, rebuff, repel, repress, repulse, resist, rout, stave off, ward off.

fight shy of avoid, disdain, eschew, give a wide berth, keep at arm's length, shun, spurn, steer clear of.

fighter *n* adventurer, antagonist, battler, boxer, brave, bruiser, champion, combatant, contender, contestant, fighting man, gladiator, man-at-arms, mercenary, militant, prize-fighter, pugilist, soldier, soldier of fortune, swordsman, trouper, warrior, wrestler.

fighting *adj* aggressive, argumentative, bellicose, belligerent, combative, contentious, fierce, hawkish, martial, militant, militaristic, pugnacious, quarrelsome, sabre-rattling, warfaring, warlike.
n battle, bloodshed, boxing, brawling, clash, combat, conflict, encounter, engagement, fisticuffs, fray, hostilities, mêlée, quarrelling, scuffle, scuffling, struggle, war, warfare, wrangling, wrestling.

figment *n* concoction, creation, deception, delusion, fable, fabrication, falsehood, fancy, fiction, illusion, improvisation, invention, mare's nest, production, work.

figurative *adj* allegorical, analogous, descriptive, embellished, emblematic, fanciful, florid, flowery, metaphorical, ornate, parabolic, pictorial, picturesque, poetical, representative, symbolic. **antonym** literal.

figure *n* amount, body, build, celebrity, character, chassis, cipher, configuration, conformation, cost, depiction, design, device, diagram, digit, dignitary, drawing, embellishment, emblem, form, frame, illustration, image, leader, motif, notability, notable, number, numeral, outline, pattern, personage, personality, physique, presence, price, proportions, representation, shadow, shape, sign, silhouette, sketch, somebody, sum, symbol, torso, total, trope, value.
v act, add, appear, believe, calculate, compute, count, estimate, feature, guess, judge, opine, reckon, sum, surmise, tally, think, tot up, work out.

figure of speech conceit, figure image, imagery, rhetorical device, turn o phrase.

figure out calculate, comprehend compute, decipher, explain, fathom make out, puzzle out, reason out, reckon resolve, see, understand, work out.

figurehead *n* bust, carving, cipher, fron man, image, leader, mouthpiece, name nominal head, puppet, straw man, titula head, token.

filch *v* abstract, borrow, crib embezzle, fake, finger, half-inch, lift misappropriate, nick, palm, pilfer, pinch plagiarise, purloin, rip off, snaffle, snitch steal, swipe, take, thieve.

file[1] *v* abrade, burnish, furbish, grate hone, pare, plane, polish, rasp, refine rub (down), sand, scour, scrape, shape shave, smooth, trim, whet.

file[2] *n* binder, cabinet, case, date documents, dossier, folder, information portfolio, record.
v capture, document, enter, memorise pigeonhole, process, record, register store.

file[3] *n* column, cortège, line, list procession, queue, row, stream, string trail, train.
v defile, march, parade, stream, trail troop.

filial *adj* affectionate, daughterly devoted, dutiful, fond, loving, loyal respectful, sonlike, sonly. **antonyms** disloyal, unfilial.

fill *v* assign, block, bung, charge clog, close, congest, cork, cram, crowd discharge, drench, engage, englut engorge, execute, fulfil, furnish, glut gorge, hold, imbue, impregnate, inflate load, occupy, overspread, pack, perform permeate, pervade, plug, replenish, sate satiate, satisfy, saturate, seal, soak, stock stop, stuff, suffuse, supply, surfeit, swell take up. **antonyms** clear, empty.
n abundance, ample, enough, plenty sufficiency, sufficient.

fill in acquaint, act for, advise, answer apprise, brief, bring up to date complete, deputise, fill out, inform, pu wise, replace, represent, stand in, sub substitute, understudy.

filling *n* contents, filler, grouting innards, inside, insides, padding, rubble stuffing, wadding.
adj ample, big, bulky, generous, heavy large, nutritious, satisfying, solid, square substantial, sustaining, tidy. **antonym** insubstantial.

illip *n* boost, flick, goad, impetus, incentive, prod, push, shove, spice, spur, stimulus, zest. **antonym** damper.

ilm¹ *n* bloom, blur, cloud, coat, coating, covering, dusting, gauze, glaze, haze, haziness, layer, membrane, mist, screen, scum, sheet, skin, tissue, veil, web.
v blear, blur, cloud, dull, glaze, haze, mist, screen, veil.

ilm² *n* documentary, epic, feature film, flick, motion picture, movie, oldie, picture, short, video.
v photograph, shoot, take, video, videotape.

ilmy *adj* cobwebby, delicate, diaphanous, fine, flimsy, fragile, gauzy, gossamer, insubstantial, light, see-through, sheer, shimmering, thin, translucent, transparent. **antonym** opaque.

ilter *v* clarify, dribble, escape, exude, filtrate, leach, leak, ooze, penetrate, percolate, purify, refine, screen, seep, sieve, sift, strain, transpire, transude, trickle, well.
n colander, gauze, membrane, mesh, riddle, sieve, sifter, strainer.

ilth *n* bilge, carrion, coarseness, contamination, corruption, crud, defilement, dirt, dirty-mindedness, dung, excrement, excreta, faeces, filthiness, foulness, garbage, grime, grossness, gunge, impurity, indecency, muck, nastiness, obscenity, ordure, pollution, pornography, putrefaction, refuse, scatology, sewage, slime, sludge, smut, smuttiness, soil, sordidness, squalor, uncleanness, vileness, vulgarity. **antonyms** cleanliness, decency, purity.

ilthy *adj* base, bawdy, black, blackened, blue, coarse, contemptible, corrupt, depraved, despicable, dirty, dirty-minded, foul, foul-mouthed, grimy, gross, grubby, impure, indecent, lavatorial, lewd, licentious, low, mean, miry, mucky, muddy, nasty, nasty-minded, obscene, offensive, polluted, pornographic, putrid, scatological, scurrilous, slimy, smoky, smutty, sooty, sordid, squalid, suggestive, swinish, unclean, unwashed, vicious, vile, vulgar. **antonyms** clean, decent, inoffensive, pure.

inal *adj* absolute, clinching, closing, concluding, conclusive, decided, decisive, definite, definitive, determinate, dying, eleventh-hour, end, eventual, finished, incontrovertible, irrefutable, irrevocable, last, last-minute, latest, settled, terminal, terminating, ultimate, undeniable.

finale *n* climax, close, conclusion, crescendo, crowning glory, culmination, curtain, dénouement, epilogue, final curtain, last act, supreme moment.

finalise *v* agree, clinch, complete, conclude, decide, dispose of, finish, get signed and sealed, get taped, resolve, round off, seal, settle, sew up, tie up, work out, wrap up.

finality *n* certitude, conclusiveness, conviction, decidedness, decisiveness, definiteness, firmness, inevitability, irreversibility, irrevocability, resolution, unavoidability.

finally *adv* absolutely, at last, at length, completely, conclusively, convincingly, decisively, definitely, eventually, for ever, for good, for good and all, in conclusion, in the end, inescapably, inexorably, irreversibly, irrevocably, lastly, once and for all, permanently, ultimately.

finance *n* accounting, accounts, banking, business, commerce, economics, investment, money, money management, stock market, trade.
v back, bail out, bankroll, capitalise, float, fund, guarantee, pay for, set up, subsidise, support, underwrite.

finances *n* affairs, assets, bank account, bread, budget, capital, cash, coffers, funds, income, liquidity, money, purse, resources, revenue, wealth, wherewithal.

find *v* achieve, acquire, ascertain, attain, bring, catch, chance on, come across, consider, contribute, cough up, descry, detect, discover, earn, encounter, espy, experience, expose, ferret out, furnish, gain, get, hit on, judge, learn, light on, locate, meet, note, notice, observe, obtain, perceive, procure, provide, reach, realise, recognise, recover, rediscover, regain, remark, repossess, retrieve, spot, stumble on, supply, think, track down, turn up, uncover, unearth, win.
n acquisition, asset, bargain, catch, coup, discovery, good buy.

find fault bitch, carp, cavil, censure, complain, criticise, depreciate, disparage, gripe, hypercriticise, kvetch, nag, niggle, nitpick, pick holes, pull to pieces, quarrel with, quibble, reprove, take to task, ultracrepidate. **antonym** praise.

find out ascertain, catch, detect, dig up, disclose, discover, establish, expose, learn, note, observe, perceive, realise, reveal, rumble, show up, sus out, tumble to, uncover, unmask.

finding *n* award, breakthrough, conclusion, decision, decree, discovery, evidence, find, judgement, pronouncement, recommendation, verdict.

fine[1] *adj* abstruse, acceptable, acute, admirable, agreeable, all right, attractive, balmy, beautiful, bonny, brave, bright, brilliant, choice, clear, clement, cloudless, convenient, critical, cutting, dandy, delicate, diaphanous, discriminating, dry, elegant, elusive, excellent, exceptional, expensive, exquisite, fair, fastidious, fine-drawn, first-class, first-rate, flimsy, fragile, gauzy, good, good-looking, gorgeous, gossamer, great, hair-splitting, handsome, honed, hunky, hunky-dory, impressive, intelligent, keen, light, lovely, magnificent, masterly, minute, nice, OK, ornate, outstanding, pleasant, polished, powdery, precise, pure, quick, rare, refined, robust, satisfactory, select, sensitive, sharp, sheer, showy, skilful, skilled, slender, small, smart, solid, splendid, sterling, strong, sturdy, stylish, sublime, subtle, suitable, sunny, superior, supreme, tasteful, tenuous, thin, ticketyboo, unalloyed, virtuoso, well-favoured, wiredrawn.

fine[2] *v* mulct, penalise, punish, sting.
n damages, forfeit, mulct, penalty, punishment.

finery *n* decorations, frippery, gear, glad rags, jewellery, ornaments, showiness, splendour, Sunday best, trappings.

finesse *n* address, adeptness, adroitness, artfulness, artifice, cleverness, deftness, delicacy, diplomacy, discretion, elegance, expertise, gracefulness, know-how, neatness, polish, quickness, refinement, savoir-faire, skill, sophistication, subtlety, tact.
v bluff, evade, manipulate, manoeuvre, trick.

finger *v* caress, feel, fiddle with, fondle, handle, manipulate, maul, meddle with, palpate, paw, play about with, stroke, touch, toy with.

finicky *adj* choosy, critical, delicate, difficult, fastidious, fussy, meticulous, nit-picking, particular, pernickety, scrupulous, squeamish, tricky. **antonyms** easy, easy-going.

finish *v* accomplish, achieve, annihilate, buff, burnish, cease, close, coat, complete, conclude, consume, consummate, culminate, deal with,

defeat, destroy, devour, discharge, dispatch, dispose of, do, drain, drink, eat, elaborate, empty, encompass, end, execute, exhaust, expend, exterminate, face, finalise, fulfil, get rid of, gild, hone, kill, lacquer, overcome, overpower, overthrow, perfect, polish, put an end to, put the last hand to, refine, round off, rout, ruin, settle, smooth, smooth off, sophisticate, spend, stain, stop, terminate, texture, use (up), veneer, wax, wind up, zap.
n annihilation, appearance, bankruptcy, cessation, close, closing, completion, conclusion, coup de grâce, culmination, cultivation, culture, curtain, curtains, death, defeat, dénouement, elaboration, end, end of the road, ending, finale, gloss, grain, liquidation, lustre, perfection, polish, refinement, ruin, shine, smoothness, sophistication, surface, termination, texture, wind-up.

finished *adj* accomplished, bankrupt, clapped-out, consummate, cultivated, defeated, done, done for, doomed, drained, elegant, empty, exhausted, expert, faultless, flawless, impeccable, jiggered, lost, masterly, overpast, perfected, played out, polished, professional, proficient, refined, ruined, skilled, smooth, sophisticated, spent, through, urbane, virtuoso, washed up, wrecked, zonked. **antonyms** coarse, crude, undone, unfinished.

finite *adj* bounded, calculable, circumscribed, definable, delimited, demarcated, fixed, limited, measurable, restricted, terminable. **antonym** infinite.

fire *n* animation, ardour, barrage, blaze, bombardment, bonfire, brio, broadside, burning, cannonade, combustion, conflagration, dash, eagerness, earnestness, élan, enthusiasm, excitement, feeling, fervour, fierceness, flak, flames, force, fusillade, hail, heat, impetuosity, inferno, intensity, life, light, lustre, passion, radiance, salvo, scintillation, shelling, sniping, sparkle, spirit, splendour, verve, vigour, virtuosity, vivacity, volley, warmth, zeal.
v activate, animate, arouse, boot out, cashier, depose, detonate, discharge, dismiss, eject, electrify, enkindle, enliven, excite, explode, galvanise, give marching orders, give the bum's rush, hurl, ignite, impassion, incite, inflame, inspire, inspirit, kindle, launch, let off, light, loose, put a match to, quicken,

rouse, sack, send off, set alight, set fire to, set off, set on fire, shell, shoot, show the door, stimulate, stir, touch off, trigger off, whet.

fireworks n explosions, firecrackers, hysterics, illuminations, pyrotechnics, rage, rockets, rows, sparks, storm, temper, trouble, uproar.

firm¹ adj abiding, adamant, anchored, balanced, braced, cast-iron, cemented, changeless, committed, compact, compressed, concentrated, congealed, constant, convinced, crisp, definite, dense, dependable, determined, dogged, durable, embedded, enduring, established, fast, fastened, fixed, grounded, hard, hardened, immovable, impregnable, indurate, inelastic, inflexible, iron-hearted, jelled, jellified, motionless, obdurate, reliable, resolute, resolved, rigid, robust, secure, secured, set, settled, solid, solidified, stable, stationary, staunch, steadfast, steady, stiff, strict, strong, sturdy, substantial, sure, taut, tight, true, unalterable, unassailable, unbending, unchanging, undeviating, unfaltering, unflinching, unmoved, unmoving, unshakable, unshakeable, unshaken, unshifting, unswerving, unwavering, unyielding. **antonyms** infirm, soft, unsound.

firm² n association, business, company, concern, conglomerate, corporation, enterprise, establishment, house, institution, organisation, outfit, partnership, set-up, syndicate.

firmly adv compactly, decisively, definitely, determinedly, doggedly, enduringly, immovably, inflexibly, motionlessly, resolutely, robustly, securely, solidly, squarely, stably, staunchly, steadfastly, steadily, strictly, strongly, sturdily, surely, tightly, unalterably, unchangeably, unflinchingly, unshakeably, unwaveringly. **antonyms** hesitantly, uncertainly, unsoundly.

firmness n changelessness, compactness, constancy, conviction, density, dependability, determination, doggedness, durability, fixedness, fixity, hardness, immovability, impregnability, indomitability, inelasticity, inflexibility, obduracy, reliability, resistance, resolution, resolve, rigidity, solidity, soundness, stability, staunchness, steadfastness, steadiness, stiffness, strength, strength of will, strictness, sureness, tautness, tension, tightness,

will, will-power. **antonyms** infirmity, uncertainty, unsoundness.

first adj basic, cardinal, chief, earliest, eldest, elementary, embryonic, foremost, fundamental, head, highest, initial, introductory, key, leading, maiden, main, oldest, opening, original, paramount, predominant, pre-eminent, premier, primal, primary, prime, primeval, primitive, primordial, principal, prior, rudimentary, ruling, senior, sovereign, uppermost.
adv at the outset, before all else, beforehand, early on, firstly, in preference, in the beginning, initially, originally, primarily, rather, sooner, to begin with, to start with.

first name baptismal name, Christian name, forename, given name.

firsthand adj direct, immediate, personal, straight from the horse's mouth. **antonyms** hearsay, indirect.

first-rate adj A1, admirable, crack, élite, excellent, exceptional, exclusive, fine, first-class, leading, matchless, outstanding, peerless, prime, second-to-none, splendid, superb, superior, superlative, tiptop, top, top-notch, tops. **antonym** inferior.

fiscal adj budgetary, economic, financial, monetary, money, treasury.

fish v angle, cast, delve, elicit, hint, hunt, invite, seek, solicit, trawl, troll.

fish out come up with, dredge up, extract, extricate, find, haul up, produce.

fish out of water freak, misfit, nonconformist, rogue, square peg in a round hole. **antonym** conformist.

fishy adj doubtful, dubious, fish-like, funny, glassy, implausible, improbable, irregular, odd, queer, questionable, rummy, shady, suspect, suspicious, unlikely. **antonyms** honest, legitimate.

fissure n breach, break, chasm, chink, cleavage, cleft, crack, cranny, crevasse, crevice, fault, fracture, gap, gash, grike, hole, interstice, opening, rent, rift, rupture, slit, split, vein.

fit¹ adj able, able-bodied, adapted, adequate, apposite, appropriate, apt, becoming, blooming, capable, commensurate, competent, convenient, correct, deserving, due, eligible, equipped, expedient, fit as a fiddle, fitted, fitting, hale, hale and hearty, healthy, in fine fettle, in good form, in good nick, in good shape, in good trim, in the pink, meet, prepared, proper, qualified, ready, right, robust, satisfactory, seemly, sound, strapping, strong, sturdy, suitable, suited, trained, trim, well, well-suited, worthy. **antonym** unfit.

v accommodate, accord, adapt, adjust, agree, alter, arrange, assimilate, belong, change, concur, conform, correspond, dispose, dovetail, fashion, figure, follow, go, harmonise, interlock, join, match, meet, modify, place, position, reconcile, shape, suit, tally.

fit out accommodate, arm, equip, kit out, outfit, prepare, provide, rig out, supply.

fit² *n* access, attack, bout, burst, caprice, convulsion, eruption, explosion, fancy, humour, mood, outbreak, outburst, paroxysm, seizure, spasm, spell, storm, surge, whim.

fitful *adj* broken, desultory, disturbed, erratic, fluctuating, haphazard, intermittent, irregular, occasional, spasmodic, sporadic, uneven, unstable, unsteady, variable. **antonyms** regular, steady.

fitness *n* adaptation, adequacy, applicability, appropriateness, aptness, competence, condition, eligibility, haleness, health, healthiness, pertinence, preparedness, propriety, qualifications, readiness, robustness, seemliness, strength, suitability, vigour. **antonym** unfitness.

fitted *adj* adapted, appointed, armed, built-in, equipped, fit, furnished, kitted, outfitted, permanent, prepared, provided, qualified, rigged out, right, suitable, supplied, tailor-made. **antonym** unfitted.

fitting *adj* apposite, appropriate, apt, becoming, correct, decent, decorous, deserved, desirable, harmonious, meet, merited, proper, right, seasonable, seemly, suitable. **antonym** unsuitable.
n accessory, attachment, component, connection, fitment, fixture, part, piece, unit.

fix¹ *v* adjust, agree on, anchor, appoint, arrange, arrive at, attach, bind, cement, conclude, confirm, congeal, connect, consolidate, correct, couple, decide, define, determine, direct, embed, establish, fasten, fiddle, finalise, firm, focus, freeze, glue, harden, implant, influence, install, limit, link, locate, make, manipulate, manoeuvre, mend, nail, name, ordain, pin, place, plant, point, position, prearrange, preordain, produce, regulate, repair, resolve, restore, rivet, root, seal, seat, secure,

see to, set, settle, solidify, sort, sort out, specify, stabilise, stick, stiffen, straighten, swing, thicken, tidy, tie.
n corner, difficulty, dilemma, embarrassment, hole, jam, mess, muddle, pickle, plight, predicament, quagmire, quandary, scrape, spot.

fix up accommodate, agree on, arrange (for), bring about, equip, fix, furnish, lay on, organise, plan, produce, provide, settle, sort out, supply.

fix² *n* dose, hit, injection, score, shot, slug.

fixation *n* complex, compulsion, fetish, hang-up, idée fixe, infatuation, mania, monomania, obsession, preoccupation, thing.

fixed *adj* agreed, anchored, arranged, attached, decided, definite, determinate, entrenched, established, fast, fiddled, firm, framed, immovable, inflexible, ingrained, intent, invariable, lasting, level, manipulated, packed, permanent, planned, put-up, radicate, resolute, resolved, rigged, rigid, rooted, secure, set, settled, standing, steadfast, steady, sure, unalterable, unbending, unblinking, unchanging, undeviating, unflinching, unvarying, unwavering, unyielding. **antonyms** alterable, variable.

fizz *v* bubble, effervesce, fizzle, froth, fume, hiss, sizzle, sparkle, spit, sputter.

fizzle out abort, collapse, come to nothing, die away, die down, disappear, dissipate, evaporate, fail, fall through, fold, peter out, stop, subside, taper off.

fizzy *adj* aerated, bubbling, bubbly, carbonated, effervescent, frothy, gassy, sparkling.

flabbergasted *adj* amazed, astonished, astounded, bowled over, confounded, dazed, disconcerted, dumbfounded, nonplussed, overcome, overwhelmed, speechless, staggered, stunned, stupefied.

flabbiness *n* bloatedness, fat, flab, flaccidity, flesh, fleshiness, heaviness, laxness, limpness, looseness, overweight, pendulousness, plumpness, slackness. **antonyms** firmness, leanness, strength.

flabby *adj* baggy, drooping, feckless, feeble, flaccid, fleshy, floppy, hanging, impotent, ineffective, ineffectual, inert, lax, limp, loose, nerveless, pendulous, plump, sagging, slack, sloppy, spineless, toneless, unfit, weak, yielding. **antonyms** firm, lean, strong.

flaccid *adj* drooping, flabby, floppy

inert, lax, limp, loose, nerveless, relaxed, sagging, slack, soft, toneless, weak. **antonym** firm.

ag¹ v abate, decline, degenerate, deteriorate, die, diminish, droop, dwindle, ebb, fade, fail, faint, fall (off), falter, flop, languish, lessen, peter out, sag, sink, slow, slump, subside, succumb, taper off, tire, wane, weaken, weary, wilt. **antonym** revive.

ag² n banner, colours, ensign, gonfalon, jack, Jolly Roger, pennant, standard, streamer, vane.

v docket, hail, indicate, label, mark, motion, note, salute, signal, tab, tag, warn, wave.

agellation n beating, castigation, chastisement, flaying, flogging, lashing, scourging, thrashing, whipping.

agging adj declining, decreasing, deteriorating, diminishing, drooping, dwindling, ebbing, fading, failing, faltering, lessening, sagging, sinking, slowing, subsiding, tiring, waning, weakening, wilting. **antonyms** returning, reviving.

agrant adj arrant, atrocious, audacious, barefaced, blatant, bold, brazen, conspicuous, crying, egregious, enormous, flaunting, glaring, heinous, immodest, infamous, notorious, open, ostentatious, outrageous, overt, rank, scandalous, shameless, unashamed, undisguised. **antonyms** covert, secret.

air n ability, accomplishment, acumen, aptitude, chic, dash, discernment, elegance, facility, faculty, feel, genius, gift, knack, mastery, nose, panache, skill, style, stylishness, talent, taste. **antonym** ineptitude.

ak n abuse, aspersions, bad press, brickbats, censure, complaints, condemnation, criticism, disapprobation, disapproval, disparagement, fault-finding, hostility, invective, opposition, stick, strictures.

ake n chip, disc, lamina, layer, paring, peeling, scale, shaving, sliver, wafer.

v blister, chip, exfoliate, peel, scale.

amboyance n brilliance, colour, dash, élan, extravagance, glamour, ostentation, panache, pizzazz, showiness, style, theatricality. **antonyms** diffidence, restraint.

amboyant adj brilliant, colourful, dashing, dazzling, elaborate, exciting, extravagant, flashy, florid, gaudy, glamorous, jaunty, ornate, ostentatious, rich, showy, striking, stylish,

swashbuckling, theatrical. **antonyms** modest, restrained.

flame v beam, blaze, burn, flare, flash, glare, glow, radiate, shine.

n affection, ardour, beau, blaze, brightness, enthusiasm, fervency, fervour, fire, heart-throb, intensity, keenness, light, lover, passion, radiance, sweetheart, warmth, zeal.

flaming adj ablaze, afire, alight, angry, ardent, aroused, blazing, brilliant, burning, fervid, fiery, frenzied, glowing, hot, impassioned, intense, raging, red, red-hot, scintillating, smouldering, vehement, vivid.

flammable adj combustible, combustive, ignitable, inflammable. **antonyms** fire-resistant, flameproof, incombustible, non-flammable, non-inflammable.

flank n edge, flitch, ham, haunch, hip, loin, quarter, side, thigh, wing.

v accompany, border, bound, confine, edge, fringe, line, screen, skirt, wall.

flap v agitate, beat, dither, flacker, flaff, flaffer, flail, flutter, fuss, panic, shake, swing, swish, thrash, thresh, vibrate, wag, wave.

n agitation, commotion, dither, fluster, flutter, fuss, kerfuffle, pother, state, stew, sweat, tizzy, twitter.

flare v blaze, burn (up), burst, dazzle, erupt, explode, flame, flash, flicker, flutter, glare, waver.

n bell-bottom, blaze, broadening, burst, dazzle, flame, flash, flicker, glare, splay, widening.

flare out broaden, splay, spread out, widen.

flare up blaze, blow one's top, erupt, explode, fly off the handle, lose one's cool.

flash v blaze, bolt, brandish, dart, dash, display, exhibit, expose, flare, flaunt, flicker, flourish, fly, glare, gleam, glint, glisten, glitter, light, race, scintillate, shimmer, shoot, show, sparkle, speed, sprint, streak, sweep, twinkle, whistle.

n blaze, burst, dazzle, demonstration, display, flare, flicker, gleam, hint, instant, jiff, jiffy, manifestation, moment, outburst, ray, scintillation, second, shaft, shake, shimmer, show, sign, spark, sparkle, split second, streak, touch, trice, twinkle, twinkling.

flashy adj bold, brassy, cheap, flamboyant, flash, garish, gaudy, glamorous, glittery, glitzy, jazzy, loud, meretricious, obtrusive, ostentatious, raffish, rakish, ritzy, showy, snazzy,

tacky, tasteless, tawdry, tinselly, vulgar.
antonyms plain, simple, tasteful.

flat¹ *adj* even, horizontal, level, levelled, low, outstretched, planar, plane, prone, prostrate, reclining, recumbent, smooth, supine, unbroken, uniform.
n lowland, marsh, morass, moss, mud flat, plain, shallow, strand, swamp.

flat out all out, at full speed, at full tilt, at top speed, double-quick, for all one is worth, hell for leather, posthaste.

flat² *adj* bored, boring, burst, collapsed, dead, deflated, depressed, dull, empty, flavourless, insipid, lacklustre, lifeless, monotonous, pointless, prosaic, punctured, spiritless, stale, tedious, uninteresting, unpalatable, vapid, watery, weak.

flat³ *adj* absolute, categorical, direct, downright, explicit, final, fixed, out-and-out, peremptory, plain, point-blank, positive, straight, total, uncompromising, unconditional, unequivocal, unqualified. *antonym* equivocal.
adv absolutely, categorically, completely, entirely, exactly, point-blank, precisely, totally, utterly.

flat⁴ *n* apartment, bed-sit, bed-sitter, maison(n)ette, pad, penthouse, pied-à-terre, rooms, tenement.

flatly *adv* absolutely, categorically, completely, peremptorily, point-blank, positively, uncompromisingly, unconditionally, unhesitatingly.

flatten *v* compress, crush, demolish, even out, fell, floor, iron out, knock down, level, overwhelm, plaster, raze, roll, slight, smooth, squash, subdue, trample.

flatter *v* adulate, become, blandish, blarney, butter up, cajole, claw, compliment, court, enhance, fawn, flannel, humour, inveigle, laud, play up to, praise, set off, show to advantage, soap, soft-soap, soothe, suit, sweet-talk, sycophantise, wheedle. *antonym* criticise.

flattering *adj* adulatory, becoming, complimentary, effusive, enhancing, favourable, fawning, gratifying, honeyed, honey-tongued, ingratiating, kind, laudatory, obsequious, servile, smooth-spoken, smooth-tongued, sugared, sugary, sycophantic, unctuous.
antonyms candid, uncompromising, unflattering.

flattery *n* adulation, backscratching, blandishment, blarney, bootlicking, butter, cajolery, fawning, flannel,

ingratiation, obsequiousness, servility, soap, soft soap, sugar, sweet talk, sycophancy, toadyism, unctuousness.
antonym criticism.

flaunt *v* air, boast, brandish, dangle, display, disport, exhibit, flash, flourish, parade, show off, sport, vaunt.

flavour *n* aroma, aspect, character, essence, extract, feel, feeling, flavouring, hint, odour, piquancy, property, quality, relish, savour, savouriness, seasoning, smack, soupçon, stamp, style, suggestion, tang, taste, tastiness, tinge, tone, touch, zest, zing.
v contaminate, ginger up, imbue, infuse, lace, leaven, season, spice, taint.

flaw *n* blemish, breach, break, cleft, crack, craze, crevice, defect, disfigurement, failing, fallacy, fault, fissure, fracture, imperfection, lapse, macula, mark, mistake, rent, rift, shortcoming, slip, speck, split, spot, tear, weakness, wreath.

flawed *adj* blemished, broken, chipped, cracked, damaged, defective, disfigured, erroneous, faulty, imperfect, marked, marred, spoilt, unsound, vicious, vitiated. *antonyms* flawless, perfect.

flawless *adj* faultless, immaculate, impeccable, intact, irreproachable, perfect, sound, spotless, stainless, unblemished, unbroken, undamaged, unsullied, whole. *antonyms* flawed, imperfect.

flay *v* castigate, excoriate, execrate, flog, lambast, pull to pieces, revile, scourge, skin, skin alive, tear a strip off, upbraid.

flea-bitten *adj* crawling, decrepit, dingy, fly-blown, frowsty, grotty, grubby, infested, insalubrious, lousy, mangy, mean, moth-eaten, mucky, run-down, scabby, scruffy, sleazy, slummy, sordid, squalid, tatty, unhealthy, unhygienic. *antonym* salubrious.

fleck *v* dapple, dot, dust, mark, mottle, speckle, spot, stipple, streak, variegate.
n dot, macula, mark, point, speck, speckle, spot, streak.

flee *v* abscond, avoid, beat a hasty retreat, bolt, bunk (off), cut and run, decamp, depart, escape, fly, get away, leave, make off, make oneself scarce, scarper, scram, shun, skedaddle, split, take flight, take off, take to one's heels, vamoose, vanish, withdraw. *antonyms* stand, stay.

fleece *v* bilk, bleed, cheat, clip, con, defraud, diddle, mulct, overcharge, plunder, rifle, rip off, rob, rook, shear, skin, soak, squeeze, steal, sting, swindle.

leet *adj* expeditious, fast, flying, light-footed, mercurial, meteoric, nimble, quick, rapid, speedy, swift, winged. **antonym** slow.

leeting *adj* brief, disappearing, ephemeral, evanescent, flitting, flying, fugitive, impermanent, momentary, passing, short, short-lived, temporary, transient, transitory, vanishing. **antonym** lasting.

lesh *n* animality, beef, blood, body, brawn, carnality, corporeality, dead-meat, family, fat, fatness, flesh and blood, food, human nature, kin, kindred, kinsfolk, kith and kin, matter, meat, physicality, pulp, relations, relatives, sensuality, substance, tissue.

leshly *adj* animal, bestial, bodily, brutish, carnal, corporal, corporeal, earthly, earthy, erotic, human, lustful, material, physical, secular, sensual, terrestrial, wordly. **antonym** spiritual.

leshy *adj* ample, beefy, brawny, chubby, chunky, corpulent, fat, flabby, hefty, meaty, obese, overweight, paunchy, plump, podgy, portly, rotund, stout, tubby, well-padded. **antonym** thin.

lex *v* angle, bend, bow, contract, crook, curve, double up, ply, tighten. **antonyms** extend, straighten.

lexibility *n* adaptability, adjustability, agreeability, amenability, bendability, complaisance, elasticity, flexion, give, pliability, pliancy, resilience, spring, springiness, suppleness. **antonym** inflexibility.

lexible *adj* accommodating, adaptable, adjustable, agreeable, amenable, bendable, biddable, complaisant, compliant, docile, double-jointed, ductile, elastic, gentle, limber, lissome, lithe, loose-limbed, manageable, mobile, mouldable, open, plastic, pliable, pliant, responsive, springy, stretchy, supple, tensile, tractable, variable, whippy, willowy, yielding. **antonym** inflexible.

lick *v* bat, click, dab, fillip, flap, flicker, flip, flirt, hit, jab, peck, rap, strike, tap, touch, whip.
n click, fillip, flap, flip, flutter, jab, peck, rap, tap, touch.

flick through flip, glance, scan, skim, skip, thumb.

licker *v* flare, flash, flutter, glimmer, quiver, scintillate, shimmer, sparkle, twinkle, vibrate, waver.

n atom, breath, drop, flare, flash, gleam, glimmer, glint, indication, inkling, iota, scintillation, spark, trace, vestige.

flight[1] *n* aeronautics, air transport, air travel, aviation, cloud, echelon, flock, flying, formation, journey, mounting, soaring, squadron, swarm, trip, unit, voyage, wing, winging.

flight[2] *n* breakaway, departure, escape, exit, exodus, fleeing, getaway, retreat, running away.

flighty *adj* bird-brained, bubble-headed, capricious, changeable, dizzy, fickle, frivolous, giddy, hare-brained, impetuous, impulsive, inconstant, irresponsible, light-headed, mercurial, rattle-brained, rattle-headed, scatterbrained, silly, skittish, thoughtless, unbalanced, unstable, unsteady, volatile, wild. **antonym** steady.

flimsy *adj* cardboard, chiffon, cobweb-by, delicate, diaphanous, ethereal, feeble, fragile, frail, frivolous, gauzy, gossamer, implausible, inadequate, insubstantial, light, makeshift, meagre, poor, rickety, shaky, shallow, sheer, slight, superficial, thin, transparent, trivial, unconvincing, unsatisfactory, unsubstantial, vaporous, weak. **antonym** sturdy.

flinch *v* baulk, blench, cower, cringe, draw back, duck, flee, quail, quake, recoil, retreat, shake, shirk, shiver, shrink, shudder, shy away, start, swerve, tremble, wince, withdraw.

fling *v* bung, cant, cast, catapult, chuck, heave, hurl, jerk, let fly, lob, pitch, precipitate, propel, send, shoot, shy, sling, slug, throw, toss.
n attempt, bash, binge, cast, crack, gamble, go, heave, indulgence, lob, pitch, shot, spree, stab, throw, toss, trial, try, turn, venture, whirl.

flip *v* cast, fillip, flap, flick, jerk, pitch, snap, spin, throw, toss, turn, twirl, twist.
n bob, fillip, flap, flick, jerk, toss, turn, twirl, twist.

flippant *adj* brash, cheeky, cocky, disrespectful, flip, frivolous, glib, impertinent, impudent, irreverent, nonchalant, offhand, pert, rude, saucy, superficial. **antonym** earnest.

flirt *v* chat up, coquet, dally, ogle, philander, tease.
n coquet(te), heart-breaker, hussy, philanderer, tease, trifler, wanton.

flirt with consider, dabble in, entertain, make up to, play with, toy with, trifle with, try.

flirtation *n* affair, amorousness,

amour, chatting up, coquetry, dalliance, dallying, intrigue, philandering, sport, teasing, toying, trifling.

flirtatious *adj* amorous, arch, come-hither, come-on, coquettish, coy, flirty, loose, promiscuous, provocative, sportive, teasing, wanton.

flit *v* beat, bob, dance, dart, elapse, flash, fleet, flutter, fly, pass, skim, slip, speed, whisk, wing.

float *v* bob, drift, glide, hang, hover, initiate, launch, poise, promote, ride, sail, set up, slide, swim, waft. **antonym** sink.

floating *adj* afloat, bobbing, buoyant, buoyed up, fluctuating, free, migratory, movable, ocean-going, sailing, swimming, unattached, uncommitted, unfixed, unsinkable, variable, wandering, water-borne.

flock *v* bunch, cluster, collect, congregate, converge, crowd, gather, gravitate, group, herd, huddle, mass, swarm, throng, troop.

n assembly, bevy, collection, colony, company, congregation, convoy, crowd, drove, flight, gaggle, gathering, group, herd, horde, host, mass, multitude, pack, shoal, swarm, throng.

flog *v* beat, birch, breech, chastise, drive, drub, flagellate, flay, hide, lash, overexert, overtax, overwork, punish, push, scourge, strain, swish, tax, thrash, trounce, welt, whack, whip, whop.

flood *v* bog down, brim, choke, deluge, drench, drown, engulf, fill, flow, glut, gush, immerse, inundate, overflow, oversupply, overwhelm, pour, rush, saturate, soak, submerge, surge, swamp, swarm, sweep.

n abundance, bore, cataclysm, débâcle, deluge, downpour, flash flood, flow, glut, inundation, multitude, outpouring, overflow, plethora, profusion, rush, spate, stream, superfluity, tide, torrent. **antonyms** dearth, drought, trickle.

floor *n* base, basis, deck, landing, level, stage, storey, tier.

v baffle, beat, bewilder, confound, conquer, defeat, discomfit, disconcert, down, dumbfound, frustrate, nonplus, overthrow, overwhelm, perplex, prostrate, puzzle, stump, stun, throw, trounce, worst.

flop *v* bomb, close, collapse, dangle, droop, drop, fail, fall, fall flat, flap, flump, fold, founder, hang, misfire, plump, sag, slump, topple, tumble.

n balls-up, cock-up, debacle, disaster,

failure, fiasco, loser, non-starter, turkey, wash-out.

floppy *adj* baggy, dangling, droopy, flabby, flaccid, flapping, flappy, flopping, hanging, limp, loose, pendulous, sagging, soft. **antonym** firm.

florid *adj* baroque, blowzy, bombastic, busy, elaborate, embellished, euphuistic, figurative, flamboyant, flourishy, flowery, flushed, fussy, grandiloquent, high-coloured, high-falutin(g), high-flown, ornate, overelaborate, purple, red, rococo, rubicund, ruddy. **antonyms** pale, plain.

flounce *v* bob, bounce, fling, jerk, spring, stamp, storm, throw, toss, twist.

flounder *v* blunder, bungle, falter, flail, fumble, grope, muddle, plunge, stagger, struggle, stumble, thrash, toss, tumble, wallop, wallow, welter.

flourish[1] *v* advance, bloom, blossom, boom, burgeon, develop, do well, flower, get on, grow, increase, mushroom, progress, prosper, succeed, thrive, wax. **antonyms** fail, languish.

flourish[2] *v* brandish, display, flaunt, flutter, parade, shake, sweep, swing, swish, twirl, vaunt, wag, wave, wield.

n arabesque, brandishing, ceremony, dash, decoration, display, élan, embellishment, fanfare, ornament, ornamentation, panache, parade, pizzazz, plume, shaking, show, sweep, twirling, wave.

flourishing *adj* blooming, booming, burgeoning, developing, going strong, in the pink, lush, luxuriant, mushrooming, progressing, prospering, rampant, rank, riotous, successful, thriving. **antonyms** failing, languishing.

flout *v* affront, contemn, defy, deride, disregard, insult, jeer at, mock, outrage, reject, ridicule, scoff at, scorn, spurn, taunt. **antonym** respect.

flow *v* arise, bubble, cascade, circulate, course, deluge, derive, distil, drift, emanate, emerge, flood, glide, gush, inundate, issue, move, originate, overflow, pour, proceed, result, ripple, roll, run, rush, slide, slip, spew, spill, spring, spurt, squirt, stream, surge, sweep, swirl, teem, well, whirl.

n abundance, cascade, course, current, deluge, drift, effluence, effusion, emanation, flood, flux, gush, outflow, outpouring, plenty, plethora, spate, spurt, stream, succession, tide, train, wash.

flower *n* best, bloom, blossom, choice,

cream, crème de la crème, efflorescence,
élite, floret, freshness, height, pick,
prime, vigour.
v blossom, blow, burgeon, effloresce,
flourish, mature, open, unfold.
flowering *adj* blooming, bloomy,
blossoming, efflorescent, florescent.
n blooming, blossoming, burgeoning,
development, florescence, flourishing,
maturing.
flowery *adj* affected, baroque, elaborate,
embellished, euphuistic, fancy,
figurative, floral, florid, high-flown,
ornate, overelaborate, overwrought,
rhetorical. **antonym** plain.
flowing *adj* abounding, brimming,
cascading, continuous, easy, facile,
falling, flooded, fluent, full,
gushing, overrun, prolific, rich,
rolling, rushing, smooth, streaming,
surging, sweeping, teeming, unbroken,
uninterrupted, voluble. **antonyms**
hesitant, interrupted.
fluctuate *v* alter, alternate, change,
ebb and flow, float, hesitate, oscillate,
pendulate, rise and fall, seesaw, shift,
shuffle, sway, swing, undulate, vacillate,
vary, veer, waver.
fluctuating *adj* capricious, changeable,
fickle, fluctuant, irresolute, mutable,
oscillating, oscillatory, rising and falling,
swaying, swinging, unstable, unsteady,
vacillating, variable, wavering.
antonym stable.
fluctuation *n* alternation, ambivalence,
capriciousness, change, ficklessness,
inconstancy, instability, irresolution,
oscillation, shift, swing, unsteadiness,
vacillation, variability, variableness,
variation, wavering.
fluency *n* articulateness, assurance,
command, control, ease, eloquence,
facility, glibness, readiness, slickness,
smoothness, volubility. **antonym**
incoherence.
fluent *adj* articulate, easy, effortless,
eloquent, facile, flowing, fluid, glib,
mellifluous, natural, ready, smooth,
smooth-talking, voluble, well-versed.
antonym tongue-tied.
fluff *n* down, dust, dustball, floss, fuzz,
nap, oose, pile.
v balls up, botch, bungle, cock up,
fumble, mess up, muddle, muff, screw
up, spoil. **antonym** bring off.
fluid *adj* adaptable, adjustable,
aqueous, changeable, easy, elegant,
flexible, floating, flowing, fluctuating,
fluent, graceful, inconstant, indefinite,

liquefied, liquid, melted, mercurial,
mobile, molten, mutable, protean,
running, runny, shifting, sinuous,
smooth, unstable, watery. **antonyms**
solid, stable.
n humour, juice, liquid, liquor, sanies,
sap, solution.
fluke *n* accident, blessing, break, chance,
coincidence, fortuity, freak, lucky break,
quirk, serendipity, stroke, windfall.
flummox *v* baffle, bamboozle, befuddle,
bewilder, confound, confuse, defeat, fox,
mystify, nonplus, perplex, puzzle, stump,
stymie.
flummoxed *adj* at a loss, at sea, baffled,
befuddled, bewildered, confounded,
confused, foxed, mystified, nonplussed,
perplexed, puzzled, stumped, stymied.
flurry *n* ado, agitation, burst, bustle,
commotion, disturbance, excitement,
ferment, flap, flaw, fluster, flutter, furore,
fuss, gust, hubbub, hurry, kerfuffle,
outbreak, pother, spell, spurt, squall, stir,
to-do, tumult, upset, whirl.
v abash, agitate, bewilder,
bother, bustle, confuse, disconcert,
discountenance, disturb, fluster, flutter,
fuss, hassle, hurry, hustle, perturb, rattle,
ruffle, unsettle, upset.
flush¹ *v* blush, burn, colour, crimson,
flame, glow, go red, redden, rouge,
suffuse. **antonym** pale.
n bloom, blush, colour, freshness, glow,
redness, rosiness, vigour.
flush² *v* cleanse, douche, drench, eject,
empty, evacuate, expel, hose, rinse,
swab, syringe, wash.
adj abundant, affluent, full, generous,
lavish, liberal, moneyed, overflowing,
prodigal, prosperous, rich, rolling,
wealthy, well-heeled, well-off, well-
supplied, well-to-do.
flush³ *adj* even, flat, level, plane, smooth,
square, true.
flush⁴ *v* discover, disturb, drive out, force
out, rouse, run to earth, start, uncover.
flushed *adj* ablaze, aflame, aglow,
animated, aroused, blowzy, blushing,
burning, crimson, elated, embarrassed,
enthused, excited, exhilarated, exultant,
febrile, feverish, glowing, hectic, high,
hot, inspired, intoxicated, red, rosy,
rubicund, ruddy, sanguine, scarlet,
thrilled. **antonym** pale.
fluster *v* abash, agitate, bother,
bustle, confound, confuse, disconcert,
discountenance, disturb, embarrass,
excite, faze, flurry, hassle, heat, hurry,
perturb, pother, pudder, rattle, ruffle,

unnerve, unsettle, upset. *antonym* calm.

n agitation, bustle, commotion, discomposure, distraction, disturbance, dither, embarrassment, faze, flap, flurry, flutter, furore, kerfuffle, perturbation, ruffle, state, tizzy, turmoil. *antonym* calm.

flutter *v* agitate, bat, beat, dance, discompose, flap, flicker, flit, flitter, fluctuate, hover, palpitate, quiver, ripple, ruffle, shiver, toss, tremble, vibrate, volitate, wave, waver.

n agitation, commotion, confusion, discomposure, dither, excitement, flurry, fluster, nervousness, palpitation, perturbation, quiver, quivering, shiver, shudder, state, tremble, tremor, tumult, twitching, upset, vibration, volitation.

fluttering *adj* beating, dancing, flapping, flickering, flitting, hovering, palpitating, quivering, tossing, trembling, volitant, waving.

flux *n* alteration, change, chaos, development, flow, fluctuation, fluidity, instability, modification, motion, movement, mutability, mutation, stir, transition, unrest. *antonym* stability.

fly¹ *v* abscond, aviate, avoid, bolt, career, clear out, dart, dash, decamp, disappear, display, elapse, escape, flap, flee, flit, float, flutter, get away, glide, hare, hasten, hasten away, hedge-hop, hightail it, hoist, hover, hurry, light out, mount, operate, pass, pilot, race, raise, retreat, roll by, run, run for it, rush, sail, scamper, scarper, scoot, shoot, show, shun, skim, soar, speed, sprint, take flight, take off, take to one's heels, take wing, tear, vamoose, volitate, wave, whisk, whiz, wing, zoom.

fly at assail, assault, attack, fall upon, go for, have at, light into, pitch into, rush at.

fly in the face of affront, defy, disobey, flout, insult, oppose.

fly² *adj* alert, artful, astute, canny, careful, cunning, knowing, nobody's fool, on the ball, prudent, sagacious, sharp, shrewd, smart, wide-awake.

fly-by-night *adj* brief, cowboy, discreditable, disreputable, dubious, ephemeral, here today gone tomorrow, impermanent, irresponsible, questionable, shady, short-lived, unreliable, untrustworthy. *antonym* reliable.

flying *adj* airborne, brief, express, fast, flapping, fleet, fleeting, floating, fluttering, fugitive, gliding, hasty, hovering, hurried, mercurial, mobile, rapid, rushed, short-lived, soaring, speedy, streaming, transitory, vanishing, waving, wind-borne, winged, winging.

foam *n* bubbles, effervescence, foaminess, froth, frothiness, head, lather, scum, spume, suds, surf.

v boil, bubble, effervesce, fizz, froth, lather, spume.

fob off appease, deceive, dump, foist, get rid of, give a sop to, impose, inflict, palm off, pass off, placate, put off, stall, unload.

focus *n* axis, centre, centre of attraction, core, crux, focal point, headquarters, heart, hinge, hub, kernel, linchpin, nucleus, pivot, target.

v aim, centre, concentrate, concentre, converge, direct, fix, home in, join, meet, rivet, spotlight, zero in, zoom in.

foe *n* adversary, antagonist, enemy, opponent, rival. *antonym* friend.

fog *n* bewilderment, blanket, blindness, confusion, daze, gloom, haze, miasma, mist, muddle, murk, murkiness, obscurity, pea-souper, perplexity, puzzlement, smog, stupor, trance, vagueness.

v befuddle, bewilder, blanket, blind, cloud, confuse, darken, daze, dim, dull, mist, muddle, obfuscate, obscure, perplex, shroud, steam up, stupefy.

foggy *adj* befuddled, bewildered, blurred, blurry, clouded, cloudy, confused, dark, dazed, dim, grey, hazy, indistinct, misty, muddled, murky, muzzy, nebulous, obscure, shadowy, smoggy, stupefied, stupid, unclear, vague, vaporous. *antonym* clear.

foible *n* defect, eccentricity, failing, fault, habit, idiosyncrasy, imperfection, infirmity, oddity, peculiarity, quirk, shortcoming, strangeness, weakness.

foil¹ *v* baffle, balk, check, checkmate, circumvent, counter, defeat, disappoint, elude, frustrate, nullify, obstruct, outsmart, outwit, spike (someone's) guns, stop, stump, thwart. *antonym* abet.

foil² *n* antithesis, background, balance, complement, contrast, relief, setting.

foist *v* fob off, force, get rid of, impose, insert, insinuate, interpolate, introduce, palm off, pass off, thrust, unload, wish on.

fold *v* bend, clasp, close, collapse, crash, crease, crimp, crumple, dog-ear, double, embrace, enclose, enfold, entwine, envelop, fail, fake, gather, go bust, hug, intertwine, overlap, pleat, ply, shut down, tuck, wrap, wrap up.

n bend, crease, crimp, furrow, layer, overlap, pleat, ply, turn, wrinkle.

folk *n* clan, family, kin, kindred, kinfolk, kinsmen, nation, people, race, society, tribe.

adj ancestral, ethnic, indigenous, national, native, traditional, tribal.

follow *v* accompany, accord, act according to, appreciate, arise, attend, catch, catch on, chase, come after, come next, comply, comprehend, conform, cultivate, dangle, develop, dog, emanate, ensue, escort, fathom, get, get the picture, grasp, haunt, heed, hound, hunt, imitate, keep abreast of, live up to, mind, note, obey, observe, pursue, realise, regard, result, second, see, shadow, stalk, succeed, supersede, supervene, supplant, support, tag along, tail, track, trail, twig, understand, watch. **antonyms** desert, precede.

follow through complete, conclude, consummate, continue, finish, fulfil, implement, pursue, see through.

follow up check out, consolidate, continue, investigate, pursue, reinforce, substantiate.

follower *n* acolyte, adherent, admirer, aficionado, apostle, attendant, backer, believer, buff, cohort, companion, devotee, disciple, emulator, fan, fancier, freak, hanger-on, helper, henchman, imitator, lackey, minion, partisan, pupil, representative, retainer, running dog, servitor, sidekick, supporter, votary, worshipper. **antonyms** leader, opponent.

following *adj* coming, consecutive, consequent, consequential, ensuing, later, next, resulting, sequent, subsequent, succeeding, successive.

n audience, backing, circle, clientèle, coterie, entourage, fans, followers, patronage, public, retinue, suite, support, supporters, train.

folly *n* absurdity, craziness, daftness, fatuity, foolishness, idiocy, illogicality, imbecility, imprudence, indiscretion, insanity, irrationality, irresponsibility, lunacy, madness, nonsense, preposterousness, rashness, recklessness, senselessness, silliness, stupidity, unreason, unwisdom. **antonym** prudence.

foment *v* activate, agitate, arouse, brew, encourage, excite, foster, goad, incite, instigate, kindle, promote, prompt,

provoke, quicken, raise, rouse, spur, stimulate, stir up, whip up, work up. **antonym** quell.

fond *adj* absurd, adoring, affectionate, amorous, caring, credulous, deluded, devoted, doting, empty, foolish, indiscreet, indulgent, loving, naive, over-optimistic, sanguine, tender, vain, warm. **antonyms** hostile, realistic.

fond of addicted to, attached to, enamoured of, hooked on, keen on, partial to, predisposed towards, stuck on, sweet on.

fondle *v* caress, coddle, cuddle, pat, pet, stroke.

fondly *adv* absurdly, adoringly, affectionately, credulously, dearly, foolishly, indulgently, lovingly, naïvely, over-optimistically, sanguinely, stupidly, tenderly, vainly.

fondness *n* affection, attachment, devotion, enthusiasm, fancy, inclination, kindness, leaning, liking, love, partiality, penchant, predilection, preference, soft spot, susceptibility, taste, tenderness, weakness. **antonym** aversion.

food *n* aliment, ambrosia, board, bread, cheer, chow, comestibles, cooking, cuisine, diet, eatables, eats, edibles, fare, feed, fodder, foodstuffs, forage, grub, larder, meat, menu, nosh, nourishment, nutriment, nutrition, provender, provisions, rations, refreshment, scoff, scran, stores, subsistence, sustenance, table, tack, tuck, tucker, viands, victuals, vittles.

fool *n* ass, berk, bird-brain, blockhead, bonehead, buffoon, burk, butt, Charlie, chump, clot, clown, cluck, comic, coxcomb, cuckoo, daftie, dimwit, dolt, dope, drongo, dumb-bell, dumb-cluck, dumbo, dunce, dunderhead, dupe, easy mark, fall guy, fathead, git, goon, goop, goose, greenhorn, gudgeon, gull, halfwit, harlequin, idiot, ignoramus, illiterate, imbecile, jackass, jerk, jester, loon, moron, mug, nerd, nig-nog, nincompoop, ninny, nit, nitwit, numskull, nurd, pillock, pot-head, prat, prick, sap, saphead, schlep, schmuck, silly, silly-billy, simpleton, soft, soft-head, softie, softy, stooge, stupe, stupid, sucker, thicko, turnip, twerp, twit, wally, wooden-head, zombie.

v act the fool, act up, bamboozle, be silly, beguile, bluff, cavort, cheat, clown, con, cozen, cut capers, deceive, delude, diddle, dupe, feign, fiddle, frolic, gull, have on, hoax, hoodwink, horse around, jest, joke, kid, lark, meddle, mess, mess about, mislead, monkey, play, play the fool, play the goat, play up, pretend, put one over on, string, string along, swindle, take in, tamper, tease, toy, trick, trifle.

fool about dawdle, idle, kill time, lark, lark about, mess about, play about, trifle.

foolhardy *adj* adventurous, bold, dare-devil, hot-headed, ill-advised, ill-considered, impetuous, imprudent, incautious, irresponsible, madcap, precipitate, rash, reckless, unheeding, unwary. *antonym* cautious.

foolish *adj* absurd, brainless, crazy, daft, doltish, dotish, dunderheaded, fatuous, glaikit, gudgeon, half-baked, half-witted, hare-brained, idiotic, idle-headed, ill-advised, ill-considered, ill-judged, imbecile, imprudent, incautious, indiscreet, inept, injudicious, insipient, lean-witted, ludicrous, mad, moronic, nonsensical, potty, ridiculous, senseless, short-sighted, silly, simple, simple-minded, sottish, stupid, unintelligent, unreasonable, unwise, weak, wet, witless. *antonym* wise.

foolproof *adj* certain, fail-safe, guaranteed, idiot-proof, infallible, safe, sure-fire, unassailable, unbreakable. *antonym* unreliable.

footing *n* base, basis, condition, conditions, establishment, foot-hold, foundation, grade, ground, groundwork, installation, position, purchase, rank, relations, relationship, settlement, standing, state, status, terms.

foppish *adj* affected, dandified, dandyish, dapper, dressy, la-di-da, natty, overdressed, preening, spruce, vain. *antonym* unkempt.

for dear life desperately, energetically, for all one is worth, intensely, strenuously, urgently, vigorously, with might and main.

for fun facetiously, for kicks, for thrills, in jest, jokingly, light-heartedly, mischievously, playfully, roguishly, sportively, teasingly, tongue in cheek.

for good finally, for ever, irreparably, irreversibly, irrevocably, once and for all, permanently, sine die.

for good measure as a bonus, as an extra, besides, gratis, in addition, into the bargain, to boot.

for love for nothing, for pleasure, free of charge, freely, gratis, voluntarily.

for love or money by any means, ever, for anything, on any condition, under any circumstances.

for the most part chiefly, commonly, generally, in the main, largely, mainly, mostly, on the whole, principally, usually.

for the present for a while, for now, for the moment, for the time being, in the interim, in the meantime, pro tem, pro tempore, provisionally, temporarily.

for the time being for now, for the moment, for the present, in the meantime, meantime, meanwhile, pro tem, pro tempore, temporarily.

forage *v* cast about, explore, hunt, plunder, raid, ransack, rummage, scavenge, scour, scrounge, search, seek.

forbear *v* abstain, avoid, cease, decline, desist, eschew, hesitate, hold, hold back, keep from, omit, pause, refrain, restrain oneself, stay, stop, withhold.

forbearance *n* abstinence, avoidance, clemency, endurance, indulgence, leniency, long-suffering, mildness, moderation, patience, refraining, resignation, restraint, self-control, sufferance, temperance, toleration. *antonym* intolerance.

forbearing *adj* clement, easy, forgiving, indulgent, lenient, long-suffering, merciful, mild, moderate, patient, restrained, self-controlled, tolerant. *antonyms* intolerant, merciless.

forbid *v* ban, block, debar, deny, disallow, exclude, hinder, inhibit, interdict, outlaw, preclude, prevent, prohibit, proscribe, refuse, rule out, veto. *antonym* allow.

forbidden *adj* banned, barred, debarred, disallowed, out of bounds, outlawed, prohibited, proscribed, taboo, vetoed.

forbidding *adj* abhorrent, awesome, daunting, formidable, frightening, gaunt, grim, hostile, inhospitable, menacing, off-putting, ominous, repellent, repulsive, sinister, stern, threatening, unapproachable, unfriendly. *antonyms* approachable, congenial.

force¹ *n* aggression, arm-twisting, beef, big stick, bite, coercion, cogency, compulsion, constraint, drive, duress, dynamism, effect, effectiveness, emphasis, energy, enforcement, fierceness, forcefulness, impact, impetus, impulse, incentive, influence, intensity, life, might, momentum, motivation, muscle, persistence, persuasiveness, potency, power, pressure, punch, shock, steam, stimulus, strength, stress, validity, vehemence, vigour, violence, vitality, weight.

v bulldoze, coerce, compel, constrain, drag, drive, exact, extort, impel, impose, lean on, make, necessitate, obligate, oblige, press, press-gang, pressure, pressurise, prise, propel, push, strong-arm, thrust, urge, wrench, wrest, wring.

force² *n* army, battalion, body, corps, detachment, detail, division, host, legion, patrol, phalanx, regiment, squad, squadron, troop, unit.

forced *adj* affected, artificial, compulsory, contrived, enforced, false, feigned, insincere, involuntary, laboured, mandatory, obligatory, stiff, stilted, strained, synthetic, unnatural, unspontaneous, wooden. **antonyms** spontaneous, voluntary.

forceful *adj* cogent, compelling, convincing, domineering, drastic, dynamic, effective, emphatic, energetic, persuasive, pithy, potent, powerful, strong, telling, urgent, vigorous, weighty. **antonym** feeble.

forcible *adj* active, aggressive, coercive, cogent, compelling, compulsory, drastic, effective, efficient, energetic, forceful, impressive, mighty, pithy, potent, powerful, strong, telling, urgent, vehement, violent, weighty. **antonym** feeble.

forebear *n* ancestor, antecedent, father, forefather, forerunner, predecessor. **antonym** descendant.

forebode *v* augur, betoken, foreshadow, foretell, forewarn, import, indicate, omen, portend, predict, presage, prognosticate, promise, signify, warn.

foreboding *n* anticipation, anxiety, apprehension, apprehensiveness, augury, boding, chill, dread, fear, foreshadowing, intuition, misgiving, omen, portent, prediction, premonition, presage, presentiment, prognostication, sign, token, warning, worry.

forecast *v* augur, bode, calculate, conjecture, divine, estimate, expect, foresee, foretell, plan, predict, prognosticate, prophesy.
n augury, conjecture, foresight, forethought, guess, guesstimate, outlook, planning, prediction, prognosis, projection, prophecy.

forefront *n* avant-garde, centre, firing line, fore, foreground, front, front line, lead, prominence, spearhead, vanguard. **antonym** rear.

forego *see* **forgo**.

foreground *n* centre, fore, forefront, front, limelight, prominence. **antonym** background.

foreign *adj* alien, borrowed, distant, exotic, external, extraneous, imported, irrelevant, outlandish, outside, overseas, remote, strange, uncharacteristic, unfamiliar, unknown, unnative, unrelated. **antonym** native.

foreman *n* charge-hand, gaffer, overseer, steward, supervisor.

foremost *adj* cardinal, central, chief, first, front, headmost, highest, inaugural, initial, leading, main, paramount, pre-eminent, primary, prime, principal, salient, supreme, uppermost.

forerunner *n* ancestor, announcer, antecedent, envoy, forebear, harbinger, herald, indication, omen, portent, precursor, predecessor, premonition, prognostic, prototype, sign, token. **antonyms** aftermath, result.

foresee *v* anticipate, augur, divine, envisage, expect, forebode, forecast, foretell, predict, prognosticate, prophesy.

foreshadow *v* anticipate, augur, betoken, bode, forebode, imply, import, indicate, omen, portend, predict, prefigure, presage, promise, prophesy, signal.

foresight *n* anticipation, care, caution, circumspection, far-sightedness, forethought, perspicacity, precaution, preparedness, prescience, prevision, providence, provision, prudence, readiness, vision. **antonym** improvidence.

forestall *v* anticipate, avert, balk, circumvent, frustrate, head off, hinder, intercept, obstruct, obviate, parry, preclude, pre-empt, prevent, thwart, ward off. **antonyms** encourage, facilitate.

foretaste *n* example, indication, prelude, preview, sample, specimen, trailer, warning, whiff.

foretell *v* augur, bode, forebode, forecast, foreshadow, forewarn, portend, predict, presage, prognosticate, prophesy, signify.

forethought *n* anticipation, circumspection, far-sightedness, foresight, precaution, preparation, providence, provision, prudence. **antonym** improvidence.

foretold *adj* forecast, predicted, prophesied, written. **antonym** unforeseen.

forever *adv* always, ceaselessly, constantly, continually, endlessly, eternally, everlastingly, evermore, for all time, for good and all, for keeps, in perpetuity, incessantly, interminably, permanently, perpetually, persistently, till the cows come home, till the end of time, unremittingly, world without end.

forewarn v admonish, advise, alert, apprise, caution, dissuade, tip off.

foreword n introduction, preamble, preface, preliminary, prologue. **antonyms** epilogue, postscript.

forfeit n damages, fine, loss, mulct, penalisation, penalty, surrender.
v abandon, forgo, give up, lose, relinquish, renounce, sacrifice, surrender.

forge[1] v beat out, cast, coin, construct, contrive, copy, counterfeit, create, devise, fabricate, fake, falsify, fashion, feign, form, frame, hammer out, imitate, invent, make, mould, shape, simulate, work.

forge[2] v advance, gain ground, improve, make great strides, make headway, press on, proceed, progress, push on.

forgery n coining, counterfeit, counterfeiting, dud, fake, falsification, fraud, fraudulence, imitation, phoney, sham, stumer. **antonym** original.

forget v consign to oblivion, discount, dismiss, disregard, fail, ignore, lose sight of, neglect, omit, overlook, think no more of, unlearn. **antonym** remember.

forgetful adj absent-minded, amnesiac, careless, dreamy, heedless, inattentive, lax, neglectful, negligent, oblivious, unmindful, unretentive. **antonyms** attentive, heedful.

forgivable adj excusable, innocent, minor, pardonable, petty, slight, trifling, venial. **antonym** unforgivable.

forgive v absolve, acquit, condone, exculpate, excuse, exonerate, let off, overlook, pardon, remit, shrive. **antonym** censure.

forgiveness n absolution, acquittal, amnesty, exculpation, exoneration, mercy, pardon, remission, shrift, shriving. **antonyms** blame, censure.

forgiving adj clement, compassionate, forbearing, humane, indulgent, lenient, magnanimous, merciful, mild, remissive, soft-hearted, sparing, tolerant. **antonym** censorious.

forgo, forego v abandon, abjure, abstain from, cede, do without, eschew, forfeit, give up, pass up, refrain from, relinquish, renounce, resign, sacrifice, surrender, waive, yield. **antonyms** claim, indulge in, insist on.

forgotten adj blotted out, buried, bygone, disregarded, ignored, irrecoverable, irretrievable, lost, neglected, obliterated, omitted, out of mind, overlooked, past, past recall, past recollection, unrecalled, unremembered, unretrieved. **antonym** remembered.

fork v bifurcate, branch, branch off, diverge, divide, part, ramify, separate, split.
n bifurcation, branching, divergence, division, intersection, junction, separation, split.

forlorn adj abandoned, abject, cheerless, comfortless, deserted, desolate, desperate, destitute, disconsolate, forgotten, forsaken, friendless, helpless, homeless, hopeless, lonely, lost, miserable, pathetic, piteous, pitiable, pitiful, unhappy, woebegone, woeful, wretched. **antonym** hopeful.

form v accumulate, acquire, appear, arrange, assemble, bring up, build, combine, compose, comprise, concoct, constitute, construct, contract, contrive, create, crystallise, cultivate, design, develop, devise, discipline, dispose, draw up, educate, establish, evolve, fabricate, fashion, forge, formulate, found, frame, group, grow, hatch, instruct, invent, make, make up, manufacture, materialise, model, mould, organise, pattern, plan, produce, put together, rear, rise, school, serve as, settle, shape, take shape, teach, train.
n anatomy, appearance, application, arrangement, behaviour, being, body, build, cast, ceremony, character, class, condition, conduct, configuration, construction, convention, custom, cut, description, design, document, etiquette, fashion, fettle, figure, fitness, formality, format, formation, frame, framework, genre, grade, guise, harmony, health, kind, manifestation, manner, manners, method, mode, model, mould, nature, nick, order, orderliness, organisation, outline, paper, pattern, person, physique, plan, practice, procedure, proportion, protocol, questionnaire, rank, ritual, rule, schedule, semblance, shape, sheet, silhouette, sort, species, spirits, stamp, structure, style, symmetry, system, trim, type, variety, way.

formal adj academic, aloof, approved, ceremonial, ceremonious, conventional, correct, exact, explicit, express, fixed, full-dress, impersonal, lawful, legal, methodical, nominal, official, precise, prescribed, prim, punctilious, recognised, regular, reserved, rigid, ritualistic, set, solemn, starch, starched, starchy, stiff, stiff-necked, stilted, strict, unbending. **antonym** informal.

formality *n* ceremoniousness, ceremony, convention, correctness, custom, decorum, etiquette, form, formalism, gesture, matter of form, politeness, politesse, procedure, propriety, protocol, red tape, rite, ritual. **antonym** informality.

format *n* appearance, arrangement, configuration, construction, dimensions, form, lay-out, look, make-up, pattern, plan, shape, structure, style, type.

formation *n* accumulation, appearance, arrangement, compilation, composition, configuration, constitution, construction, creation, crystallisation, design, development, disposition, emergence, establishment, evolution, fabrication, figure, format, forming, generation, genesis, grouping, manufacture, organisation, pattern, production, rank, shaping, structure.

formative *adj* controlling, determinative, determining, developmental, dominant, guiding, impressionable, influential, malleable, mouldable, moulding, pliant, sensitive, shaping, susceptible. **antonym** destructive.

former *adj* above, aforementioned, aforesaid, ancient, antecedent, anterior, bygone, departed, earlier, erstwhile, ex-, first mentioned, late, long ago, of yore, old, old-time, one-time, past, preceding, previous, prior, sometime. **antonyms** current, future, later, present, prospective, subsequent.

formerly *adv* already, at one time, before, earlier, erstwhile, heretofore, hitherto, lately, once, previously. **antonyms** currently, later, now, presently, subsequently.

formidable *adj* alarming, appalling, arduous, awesome, challenging, colossal, dangerous, daunting, difficult, dismaying, dreadful, enormous, fearful, frightening, frightful, great, horrible, huge, impressive, indomitable, intimidating, leviathan, mammoth, menacing, mighty, onerous, overwhelming, powerful, redoubtable, shocking, staggering, terrific, terrifying, threatening, toilsome, tremendous. **antonyms** easy, genial.

formless *adj* chaotic, confused, disorganised, incoherent, indefinite, indeterminate, indigest, nebulous, shapeless, unformed, unshaped, vague. **antonyms** definite, orderly.

formula *n* blueprint, code, form, formulary, method, modus operandi, password, precept, prescription, principle, procedure, recipe, rite, ritual, rubric, rule, rule of thumb, way, wording.

formulate *v* block out, codify, create, define, detail, develop, devise, evolve, express, form, frame, invent, originate, particularise, plan, specify, systematise, work out.

forsake *v* abandon, abdicate, cast off, desert, discard, disown, forgo, forswear, give up, jettison, jilt, leave, leave in the lurch, quit, reject, relinquish, renounce, repudiate, surrender, throw over, turn one's back on, vacate, yield. **antonyms** resume, revert to.

forsaken *adj* abandoned, cast off, deserted, desolate, destitute, discarded, disowned, forlorn, friendless, ignored, isolated, jilted, left in the lurch, lonely, lovelorn, marooned, outcast, rejected, shunned, solitary.

forswear *v* abandon, abjure, deny, disavow, disclaim, disown, drop, forgo, forsake, give up, lie, perjure oneself, recant, reject, renegue, renounce, repudiate, retract, swear off. **antonym** revert to.

fort *n* acropolis, camp, castle, citadel, fastness, fortification, fortress, garrison, station, stronghold, tower.

forte *n* aptitude, bent, gift, métier, skill, speciality, strength, strong point, talent. **antonyms** inadequacy, weak point.

forthcoming[1] *adj* accessible, approaching, at hand, available, coming, expected, future, imminent, impending, obtainable, projected, prospective, ready.

forthcoming[2] *adj* chatty, communicative, conversational, expansive, frank, free, informative, loquacious, open, sociable, talkative, unreserved. **antonyms** bygone, distant, lacking, reserved.

forthright *adj* above-board, blunt, bold, candid, direct, frank, open, outspoken, plain-speaking, plain-spoken, straightforward, straight-from-the-shoulder, trenchant, unequivocal. **antonyms** devious, tactful.

forthwith *adv* at once, directly, immediately, instantly, posthaste, pronto, quickly, right away, straightaway, tout de suite, without delay.

fortification *n* bastion, bulwark,

buttressing, castle, citadel, defence, earthwork, embattlement, entrenchment, fastness, fort, fortress, keep, munition, outwork, protection, rampart, reinforcement, stockade, strengthening, stronghold.

fortify *v* boost, brace, bulwark, buttress, cheer, confirm, embattle, embolden, encourage, entrench, garrison, hearten, invigorate, lace, load, mix, munify, protect, reassure, reinforce, secure, shore up, spike, steel, stiffen, strengthen, support, sustain. **antonyms** dilute, weaken.

fortitude *n* backbone, bottle, braveness, bravery, courage, dauntlessness, determination, endurance, fearlessness, firmness, grit, guts, hardihood, indomitability, intrepidity, long-suffering, patience, perseverance, pluck, resoluteness, resolution, staying power, stout-heartedness, strength, strength of mind, valour. **antonyms** cowardice, weakness.

fortress *n* castle, citadel, fastness, fortification, stronghold.

fortuitous *adj* accidental, arbitrary, casual, chance, coincidental, contingent, felicitous, fluky, fortunate, happy, incidental, lucky, providential, random, serendipitous, unexpected, unforeseen, unintentional, unplanned. **antonym** intentional.

fortunate *adj* advantageous, auspicious, blessed, bright, convenient, encouraging, favourable, favoured, felicitous, fortuitous, golden, happy, helpful, lucky, opportune, profitable, promising, propitious, prosperous, providential, rosy, serendipitous, successful, timely, well-off, well-timed. **antonym** unfortunate.

fortunately *adv* happily, luckily, providentially. **antonym** unfortunately.

fortune[1] *n* affluence, assets, bomb, bundle, estate, income, king's ransom, means, mint, opulence, packet, pile, possessions, property, prosperity, riches, treasure, wealth.

fortune[2] *n* accident, adventures, chance, circumstances, contingency, cup, destiny, doom, expectation, experience, fate, fortuity, hap, happenstance, hazard, history, kismet, life, lot, luck, portion, providence, star, success, weird.

forward[1] *adj* advance, advanced, early, enterprising, first, fore, foremost, forward-looking, front, go-ahead, head, leading, onward, precocious,

premature, progressive, well-advanced, well-developed. **antonym** retrograde.

adv ahead, forth, forwards, into view, on, onward, out, outward, to light, to the fore, to the surface. **antonym** backward

v accelerate, advance, aid, assist, back, dispatch, encourage, expedite, facilitate, favour, foster, freight, further, hasten, help, hurry, post, promote, route, send, send on, ship, speed, support, transmit. **antonyms** impede, obstruct.

forward[2] *adj* assertive, assuming, audacious, bare-faced, bold, brash, brass-necked, brazen, cheeky, confident, familiar, fresh, impertinent, impudent, overweening, pert, presuming, presumptuous, pushy. **antonym** diffident.

forward-looking *adj* avant-garde, dynamic, enlightened, enterprising, far-sighted, go-ahead, go-getting, innovative, liberal, modern, progressive, reforming. **antonyms** conservative, retrograde.

forwardness *n* assurance, audacity, boldness, brashness, brazenness, cheek, cheekiness, impertinence, impudence, overconfidence, pertness, presumption, presumptuousness. **antonyms** reserve, retiring.

fossilised *adj* anachronistic, antediluvian, antiquated, archaic, dead, extinct, inflexible, obsolete, old-fashioned, old-fog(e)yish, ossified, out of date, outmoded, passé, petrified, prehistoric, stony, superannuated. **antonym** up-to-date.

foster *v* accommodate, bring up, care for, cherish, cultivate, encourage, entertain, feed, foment, harbour, make much of, nourish, nurse, nurture, promote, raise, rear, stimulate, support, sustain, take care of. **antonyms** discourage, neglect.

foul *adj* abhorrent, abominable, abusive, bad, base, blasphemous, blue, blustery, coarse, contaminated, crooked, despicable, detestable, dirty, disagreeable, disfigured, disgraceful, disgusting, dishonest, dishonourable, entangled, fetid, filthy, foggy, foul-mouthed, fraudulent, gross, hateful, heinous, impure, indecent, inequitable, infamous, iniquitous, lewd, loathsome, low, malodorous, murky, nasty, nauseating, nefarious, notorious, obscene, offensive, polluted, profane, putrid, rainy, rank, repulsive, revolting, rotten, rough, scandalous, scatological, scurrilous, shady, shameful, smutty squalid, stinking, stormy, sullied, tainted, unclean, underhand, unfair, unfavourable, unjust, unsportsmanlike, untidy, vicious, vile, vulgar, wet, wicked, wild. *antonyms* clean, fair, pure, worthy.

v besmirch, block, catch, choke, clog, contaminate, defile, dirty, ensnare, entangle, foul up, jam, pollute, smear, snarl, soil, stain, sully, taint, twist. *antonyms* clean, clear, disentangle.

foul play chicanery, corruption, crime, deception, dirty work, double-dealing, duplicity, fraud, funny business, jiggery-pokery, perfidy, sharp practice, skulduggery, treachery, villainy. *antonyms* fair play, justice.

foul-mouthed *adj* abusive, blasphemous, coarse, obscene, offensive, profane.

found *v* base, bottom, build, constitute, construct, create, endow, erect, establish, fix, ground, inaugurate, initiate, institute, organise, originate, plant, raise, rest, root, set up, settle, start, sustain.

foundation *n* base, basis, bedrock, bottom, endowment, establishment, fond, footing, ground, groundwork, inauguration, institution, organisation, setting up, settlement, substance, substratum, substructure, underpinning.

founder[1] *n* architect, author, beginner, benefactor, builder, constructor, designer, endower, establisher, father, generator, initiator, institutor, inventor, maker, organiser, originator, patriarch.

founder[2] *v* abort, break down, collapse, come to grief, come to nothing, fail, fall, fall through, go lame, lurch, miscarry, misfire, sink, sprawl, stagger, stick, stumble, submerge, subside, trip.

foxy *adj* artful, astute, canny, crafty, cunning, devious, fly, guileful, knowing, sharp, shrewd, sly, tricky, vulpine, wily. *antonyms* naïve, open.

fracas *n* affray, aggro, barney, brawl, disturbance, fight, free-for-all, mêlée, quarrel, riot, row, ruckus, ruction, rumpus, scrimmage, scuffle, trouble, uproar.

fractious *adj* awkward, captious, crabbed, crabby, cross, crotchety, fretful, grouchy, irritable, peevish, petulant, quarrelsome, querulous, recalcitrant, refractory, testy, touchy, unruly. *antonyms* complaisant, placid.

fracture *n* breach, break, cleft, crack, fissure, gap, opening, rent, rift, rupture, schism, scission, split.

v break, crack, rupture, splinter, split. *antonym* join.

fragile *adj* breakable, brittle, dainty, delicate, feeble, fine, flimsy, frail, infirm, insubstantial, slight, weak. *antonyms* durable, robust, tough.

fragility *n* breakableness, brittleness, delicacy, feebleness, frailty, infirmity, weakness. *antonyms* durability, robustness, strength.

fragment *n* bit, chip, fraction, fritter, morceau, morsel, part, particle, piece, portion, remnant, scrap, shard, sheave, shiver, shred, sliver.

v break, break up, come apart, come to pieces, crumble, disintegrate, disunite, divide, fractionalise, fritter, shatter, shiver, splinter, split, split up. *antonyms* hold together, join.

fragmentary *adj* bitty, broken, disconnected, discrete, disjointed, incoherent, incomplete, partial, piecemeal, scattered, scrappy, separate, sketchy, unsystematic. *antonym* complete.

fragrance *n* aroma, balm, balminess, bouquet, fragrancy, odour, perfume, redolence, scent, smell.

fragrant *adj* aromatic, balmy, balsamy, odorous, perfumed, redolent, sweet, sweet-scented, sweet-smelling. *antonyms* smelly, unscented.

frail *adj* breakable, brittle, decrepit, delicate, feeble, flimsy, fragile, infirm, insubstantial, puny, slight, tender, unsound, vulnerable, weak. *antonyms* firm, robust, strong, tough.

frailty *n* blemish, defect, deficiency, failing, fallibility, fault, feebleness, flaw, foible, frailness, imperfection, infirmity, peccadillo, puniness, shortcoming, susceptibility, vice, weakness. *antonyms* firmness, robustness, strength, toughness.

frame *v* assemble, block out, build, case, compose, conceive, concoct, constitute, construct, contrive, cook up, devise, draft, draw up, enclose, fabricate, fashion, forge, form, formulate, hatch, institute, invent, make, manufacture, map out, model, mould, mount, plan, put together, redact, set up, shape, sketch, surround, trap, victimise.

n anatomy, body, bodyshell, bodywork, build, carcass, casing, chassis, construction, fabric, flake, form, framework, mount, mounting, physique, scaffolding, scheme, setting, shell, skeleton, structure, system.

frame of mind attitude, disposition,

fettle, humour, mood, morale, outlook, spirit, state, temper, vein.

frame-up *n* fabrication, fit-up, fix, put-up job, trap, trumped-up charge.

framework *n* bare bones, core, fabric, foundation, frame, gantry, groundwork, plan, schema, shell, skeleton, structure.

franchise *n* authorisation, charter, concession, exemption, freedom, immunity, liberty, prerogative, privilege, right, suffrage, vote.

frank *adj* artless, blunt, candid, direct, downright, forthright, free, honest, ingenuous, open, outright, outspoken, plain, plain-spoken, simple-hearted, sincere, straight, straightforward, transparent, truthful, unconcealed, undisguised, unreserved, unrestricted. **antonyms** evasive, insincere.

frankly *adv* bluntly, candidly, directly, freely, honestly, in truth, openly, plainly, straight, to be frank, to be honest, unreservedly, without reserve. **antonyms** evasively, insincerely.

frankness *n* bluntness, candour, forthrightness, ingenuousness, openness, outspokenness, plain speaking, truthfulness, unreserve.

frantic *adj* berserk, beside oneself, desperate, distracted, distraught, fraught, frenetic, frenzied, furious, hairless, hectic, mad, overwrought, raging, raving, wild. **antonym** calm.

fraternise *v* affiliate, associate, concur, consort, cooperate, forgather, hobnob, mingle, mix, socialise, sympathise, unite. **antonyms** ignore, shun.

fraternity *n* association, brotherhood, camaraderie, circle, clan, club, companionship, company, comradeship, confraternity, confrèrie, fellowship, guild, kinship, league, set, society, union.

fraud[1] *n* artifice, cheat, chicane, chicanery, deceit, deception, double-dealing, duplicity, fake, forgery, guile, hoax, humbug, sham, sharp practice, spuriousness, swindling, swiz, swizzle, take-in, treachery, trickery.

fraud[2] *n* bluffer, charlatan, cheat, counterfeit, double-dealer, hoaxer, impostor, malingerer, mountebank, phoney, pretender, pseud, quack, swindler.

fraudulent *adj* bogus, counterfeit, crafty, criminal, crooked, deceitful, deceptive, dishonest, double-dealing, duplicitous, false, phoney, sham, specious, spurious, swindling, treacherous. **antonyms** genuine, honest.

fraught *adj* abounding, accompanied, agitated, anxious, attended, bristling, charged, difficult, distracted, distressed, distressing, emotive, filled, full, heavy, hotching, laden, replete, stuffed, tense, tricky, troublesome, trying, uptight, worrisome. **antonyms** calm, untroublesome.

fray *n* affray, bagarre, barney, battle, brawl, broil, clash, combat, conflict, disturbance, dust-up, fight, free-for-all, mêlée, quarrel, riot, row, ruckus, ruction, rumble, rumpus, scuffle, set-to.

freak[1] *n* aberration, abnormality, abortion, anomaly, caprice, fad, fancy, folly, grotesque, humour, irregularity, malformation, misgrowth, monster, monstrosity, mutant, oddity, queer fish, quirk, turn, twist, vagary, weirdo, whim, whimsy.
adj aberrant, abnormal, atypical, bizarre, capricious, erratic, exceptional, fluky, fortuitous, odd, queer, surprise, unaccountable, unexpected, unforeseen, unparalleled, unpredictable, unpredicted, unusual. **antonyms** common, expected.

freak[2] *n* addict, aficionado, buff, devotee, enthusiast, fan, fanatic, fiend, monomaniac, nut.

freakish *adj* aberrant, abnormal, arbitrary, bizarre, capricious, changeable, erratic, fanciful, fantastic, fitful, freakful, freaky, grotesque, malformed, monstrous, odd, outlandish, strange, unconventional, unpredictable, unusual, wayward, weird, whimsical. **antonym** ordinary.

free *adj* able, allowed, at large, at leisure, at liberty, autarchic, autonomous, available, bounteous, bountiful, buckshee, casual, charitable, clear, complimentary, cost-free, democratic, disengaged, eager, easy, emancipated, empty, extra, familiar, footloose, forward, frank, free and easy, free of charge, generous, gratis, hospitable, idle, independent, informal, laid-back, lavish, lax, leisured, liberal, liberated, loose, munificent, natural, off the hook, on the house, on the loose, open, open-handed, permitted, prodigal, relaxed, self-governing, self-ruling, solute, sovereign, spare, spontaneous, unattached, unbidden, unbowed, unceremonious, uncommitted, unconstrained, unencumbered, unengaged, unfettered, unforced, unhampered, unhindered, unimpeded, uninhabited, uninhibited, unobstructed, unoccupied, unregimented, unregulated, unrestrained, unrestricted, unsparing, unstinting, untrammelled, unused, vacant, willing, without charge. **antonyms** attached, confined, costly, formal, mean, niggardly, restricted, tied.

adv abundantly, copiously, for free, for love, for nothing, freely, gratis, idly, loosely, without charge. **antonym** meanly.

v absolve, affranchise, clear, declassify, decolonise, decontrol, deliver, discharge, disengage, disentangle, emancipate, exempt, extricate, let go, liberate, loose, manumit, ransom, release, relieve, rescue, rid, set free, turn loose, unbind, unburden, uncage, unchain, undo, unfetter, unhand, unleash, unlock, unloose, unstick, untie. **antonyms** confine, enslave, imprison.

free hand authority, carte-blanche, discretion, freedom, latitude, liberty, permission, power, scope.

free of devoid of, exempt from, immune to, innocent of, lacking, not liable to, safe from, sans, unaffected by, unencumbered by, untouched by, without.

freedom *n* abandon, ability, autonomy, boldness, brazenness, candour, carte-blanche, deliverance, directness, discretion, disrespect, ease, elbow-room, emancipation, exemption, facility, familiarity, flexibility, forwardness, frankness, free rein, home rule, immunity, impertinence, impunity, independence, informality, ingenuousness, lack of restraint or reserve, latitude, laxity, leeway, liberty, licence, manumission, openness, opportunity, overfamiliarity, play, power, presumption, privilege, range, release, scope, self-government, unconstraint. **antonyms** confinement, reserve, restriction.

freely *adv* abundantly, amply, bountifully, candidly, cleanly, copiously, easily, extravagantly, frankly, generously, lavishly, liberally, loosely, of one's own accord, open-handedly, openly, plainly, readily, smoothly, spontaneously, unchallenged, unreservedly, unstintingly, voluntarily, willingly. **antonyms** evasively, meanly, roughly, under duress.

free-will *n* autarky, autonomy, election, freedom, independence, liberty, self-determination, self-sufficiency, spontaneity, volition.

freeze *v* benumb, chill, congeal, fix, glaciate, harden, hold, ice, ice over, inhibit, peg, rigidify, shelve, solidify, stiffen, stop, suspend.

n abeyance, discontinuation, embargo, freeze-up, frost, halt, interruption, moratorium, postponement, shut-down, standstill, stay, stoppage, suspension.

freezing *adj* arctic, biting, bitter, chill, chilled, chilly, cutting, frosty, glacial, icy, numbing, penetrating, polar, raw, Siberian, wintry. **antonyms** hot, warm.

freight *n* bulk, burden, cargo, carriage, charge, consignment, contents, conveyance, fee, goods, haul, lading, load, merchandise, pay-load, shipment, tonnage, transportation.

frenetic *adj* demented, distraught, excited, fanatical, frantic, frenzied, hyperactive, insane, mad, maniacal, obsessive, overwrought, unbalanced, wild. **antonyms** calm, placid.

frenzied *adj* agitated, convulsive, distracted, distraught, excited, feverish, frantic, frenetic, furious, hysterical, mad, maniacal, rabid, uncontrolled, wild. **antonyms** calm, placid.

frenzy *n* aberration, agitation, bout, burst, convulsion, delirium, derangement, distraction, fit, fury, hysteria, insanity, lunacy, madness, mania, outburst, paroxysm, passion, rage, seizure, spasm, transport, turmoil. **antonyms** calm, placidness.

frequency *n* constancy, frequence, frequentness, oftenness, periodicity, prevalence, recurrence, repetition. **antonym** infrequency.

frequent[1] *adj* common, commonplace, constant, continual, customary, everyday, familiar, habitual, incessant, numerous, persistent, recurrent, recurring, regular, reiterated, repeated, usual. **antonym** infrequent.

frequent[2] *v* associate with, attend, crowd, hang about, hang out at, haunt, patronise, visit.

frequently *adv* commonly, continually, customarily, habitually, many a time, many times, much, oft, often, oftentimes, over and over, persistently, repeatedly. **antonyms** infrequently, seldom.

fresh *adj* added, additional, alert, artless, auxiliary, blooming, bold, bouncing, bracing, brazen, bright, brisk, callow, cheeky, chipper, clean, clear, cool, crisp, crude, dewy, different, disrespectful, energetic, extra, fair, familiar, flip, forward, further, glowing, green, hardy, healthy, impudent, inexperienced, innovative, insolent, inventive, invigorated, invigorating, keen, latest, lively, modern, modernistic, more, natural, new, novel, original, other, pert, presumptuous, pure, raw, recent, refreshed, refreshing, renewed, rested, restored, revived, rosy, ruddy, saucy, spanking, sparkling, sprightly, spry, stiff, supplementary, sweet, unblown, unconventional, uncultivated, undimmed, unhackneyed, unjaded, unjaundiced, unpolluted, unspoilt, unusual, unwearied, up-to-date, verdant, vernal, vigorous, vital, vivid, warm, wholesome, young, youthful. *antonyms* experienced, faded, old hat, polite, stale, tired.

freshen *v* air, enliven, liven, purify, refresh, reinvigorate, restore, resuscitate, revitalise, spruce up, tart up, titivate, ventilate. *antonym* tire.

freshness *n* bloom, brightness, cleanness, clearness, dewiness, glow, newness, novelty, originality, shine, sparkle, vigour, wholesomeness. *antonyms* staleness, tiredness.

fret *v* abrade, agitate, agonise, annoy, bother, brood, chafe, chagrin, corrode, distress, disturb, eat into, erode, fray, gall, goad, grieve, harass, irk, irritate, nag, nettle, peeve, pique, provoke, rankle, rile, ripple, rub, ruffle, torment, trouble, vex, wear, wear away, worry. *antonym* calm.

fretful *adj* cantankerous, captious, complaining, cross, crotchety, edgy, fractious, irritable, peevish, petulant, querulous, short-tempered, snappish, snappy, splenetic, testy, touchy, uneasy. *antonym* calm.

friction *n* abrasion, animosity, antagonism, attrition, bad blood, bad feeling, bickering, chafing, conflict, contention, disagreement, discontent, discord, disharmony, dispute, dissension, erosion, fretting, grating, hostility, ill-feeling, incompatibility, irritation, opposition, quarrelling, rasping, resentment, resistance, rivalry, rubbing, scraping, wearing away, wrangling.

friend *n* adherent, advocate, ally, alter ego, associate, backer, benefactor, boon companion, bosom friend, buddy, china, chum, cobber, companion, comrade, confidant, crony, familiar, gossip, intimate, mate, pal, partisan, partner, patron, playmate, side-kick, soul mate, supporter, well-wisher. *antonym* enemy.

friendless *adj* abandoned, alienated, alone, deserted, estranged, forlorn, forsaken, isolated, lonely, lonely-heart, lonesome, ostracised, shunned, solitary, unattached, unloved.

friendly *adj* affable, affectionate, amiable, amicable, approachable, attached, attentive, auspicious, beneficial, benevolent, benign, chummy, close, clubby, companionable, comradely, conciliatory, confiding, convivial, cordial, familiar, favourable, fond, fraternal, genial, good, helpful, intimate, kind, kindly, maty, neighbourly, outgoing, palsy-walsy, peaceable, propitious, receptive, sociable, sympathetic, thick, welcoming, well-disposed. *antonyms* cold, unsociable.

friendship *n* affection, affinity, alliance, amity, attachment, benevolence, closeness, concord, familiarity, fellowship, fondness, friendliness, goodwill, harmony, intimacy, love, neighbourliness, rapport, regard. *antonym* enmity.

fright *n* alarm, apprehension, consternation, dismay, dread, eyesore, fear, funk, horror, mess, monstrosity, panic, quaking, scare, scarecrow, shock, sight, spectacle, sweat, terror, the shivers, trepidation.

frighten *v* affray, alarm, appal, cow, daunt, dismay, intimidate, petrify, scare, scare stiff, shock, spook, startle, terrify, terrorise, unman, unnerve. *antonyms* calm, reassure.

frightened *adj* afraid, alarmed, cowed, dismayed, frozen, panicky, petrified, scared, scared stiff, startled, terrified, terrorised, terror-stricken, unnerved, windy. *antonyms* calm, courageous.

frightening *adj* alarming, appalling, bloodcurdling, daunting, dismaying, dreadful, fearful, fearsome, hair-raising, horrifying, intimidating, menacing, scary, shocking, spine-chilling, spooky, terrifying, traumatic, unnerving. *antonym* reassuring.

frightful *adj* alarming, appalling, awful, dire, disagreeable, dread, dreadful, fearful, fearsome, ghastly, great, grim, grisly, gruesome, harrowing, hideous, horrendous, horrible, horrid, insufferable, macabre, petrifying, shocking, terrible, terrific, terrifying, traumatic, unnerving, unpleasant, unspeakable. *antonyms* agreeable, pleasant.

frigid *adj* aloof, arctic, austere,

chill, chilly, cold, cold-hearted, cool, forbidding, formal, frosty, frozen, glacial, icy, lifeless, passionless, passive, repellent, rigid, stand-offish, stiff, unanimated, unapproachable, unbending, unfeeling, unloving, unresponsive, wintry. **antonyms** responsive, warm.

ill *n* flounce, gathering, ruche, ruching, ruff, ruffle, trimming, tuck, valance.

ills *n* accessories, additions, affectation, decoration, embellishment, extras, fanciness, finery, frilliness, frippery, mannerisms, nonsense, ornamentation, ostentation, tomfoolery, trimmings.

illy *adj* fancy, flouncy, lacy, ornate, ruched, ruffled. **antonyms** plain, unadorned.

inge *n* borderline, edge, limits, march, marches, margin, outskirts, perimeter, periphery.
adj alternative, unconventional, unofficial, unorthodox.
v border, edge, enclose, fimbriate, skirt, surround, trim.

isk[1] *v* bounce, caper, cavort, dance, frolic, gambol, hop, jump, leap, pirouette, play, prance, rollick, romp, skip, sport, trip.

isk[2] *v* check, inspect, search, shake down.

isky *adj* bouncy, buckish, coltish, frolicsome, gamesome, high-spirited, kittenish, lively, playful, rollicking, romping, skittish, spirited, sportive. **antonym** quiet.

itter *v* blow, dissipate, idle, misspend, run through, squander, waste.

ivolity *n* childishness, flightiness, flippancy, folly, frivolousness, fun, gaiety, giddiness, jest, levity, light-heartedness, lightness, nonsense, puerility, shallowness, silliness, skittishness, superficiality, triviality. **antonym** seriousness.

ivolous *adj* bubble-headed, childish, dizzy, empty-headed, extravagant, facetious, flighty, flippant, foolish, giddy, idle, ill-considered, impractical, jocular, juvenile, light, light-minded, petty, pointless, puerile, shallow, silly, skittish, superficial, trifling, trivial, unimportant, unserious, vacuous, vain. **antonym** serious.

rizzy *adj* crimped, crisp, curled, curly, frizzed, wiry. **antonym** straight.

rolic *v* caper, cavort, cut capers, frisk, gambol, lark, make merry, play, rollick, romp, skylark, sport, wanton.

n amusement, antic, drollery, escapade, fun, gaiety, gambol, game, high jinks, lark, merriment, prank, razzle-dazzle, revel, rig, romp, skylarking, sport, spree.

from hand to mouth dangerously, from day to day, improvidently, in poverty, insecurely, necessitously, on the breadline, precariously, uncertainly.

from time to time at times, every now and then, every so often, intermittently, now and then, occasionally, on occasion, once in a while, sometimes, spasmodically, sporadically. **antonym** constantly.

front *n* air, anterior, appearance, aspect, bearing, beginning, countenance, cover, cover-up, demeanour, disguise, expression, exterior, façade, face, facing, fore, forefront, foreground, front line, frontage, head, lead, manner, mask, obverse, pretence, pretext, show, top, van, vanguard. **antonym** back.
adj anterior, first, fore, foremost, head, lead, leading. **antonyms** back, last, least, posterior.
v confront, face, look over, meet, oppose, overlook.

frontier *n* borderland, borderline, bound, boundary, confines, edge, limit, march, marches, perimeter, verge.

frosty *adj* chilly, cold, discouraging, frigid, frozen, hoar, ice-capped, icicled, icy, off-putting, stand-offish, stiff, unfriendly, unwelcoming, wintry. **antonym** warm.

froth *n* bubbles, effervescence, foam, frivolity, head, lather, scum, spume, suds, triviality.
v bubble, effervesce, ferment, fizz, foam, lather.

frothy *adj* bubbling, bubbly, empty, foaming, foamy, frilly, frivolous, insubstantial, light, slight, sudsy, trifling, trivial, vain. **antonym** flat.

frown *v* glare, glower, grimace, lower, scowl.
n dirty look, glare, glower, grimace, scowl.

frown on deprecate, disapprove of, discountenance, discourage, dislike, look askance at, object to, take a dim view of. **antonym** approve of.

frowzy *adj* blowzy, dirty, dishevelled, draggle-tailed, frumpy, messy, slatternly, sloppy, slovenly, sluttish, ungroomed, unkempt, untidy, unwashed. **antonym** well-groomed.

frozen *adj* arctic, chilled, fixed,

frigid, frosted, icebound, ice-cold, ice-covered, icy, in abeyance, numb, pegged, petrified, rigid, rooted, shelved, solidified, stiff, stock-still, stopped, suspended, turned to stone. **antonym** warm.

frugal adj abstemious, careful, cheese-paring, economical, meagre, niggardly, parsimonious, penny-wise, provident, prudent, saving, sparing, spartan, thrifty, ungenerous. **antonym** wasteful.

frugality n carefulness, conservation, economising, economy, frugalness, good management, providence, prudence, thrift, thriftiness. **antonym** wastefulness.

fruit n advantage, benefit, consequence, crop, effect, harvest, outcome, produce, product, profit, result, return, reward, yield.

fruitful adj abundant, advantageous, beneficial, copious, effective, fecund, fertile, flush, fructiferous, gainful, plenteous, plentiful, productive, profitable, profuse, prolific, rewarding, rich, spawning, successful, teeming, useful, well-spent, worthwhile. **antonyms** barren, fruitless.

fruition n accomplishment, actualisation, attainment, completion, consummation, enjoyment, fulfilment, materialisation, maturation, maturity, perfection, realisation, ripeness, success. **antonym** failure.

fruitless adj abortive, barren, futile, hopeless, idle, ineffectual, pointless, profitless, unavailing, unproductive, unprofitable, unsuccessful, useless, vain. **antonyms** fruitful, successful.

fruity adj bawdy, blue, full, indecent, indelicate, juicy, mellow, racy, resonant, rich, ripe, risqué, salacious, saucy, sexy, smutty, spicy, suggestive, titillating, vulgar. **antonyms** decent, light.

frustrate v baffle, balk, block, bugger, check, circumvent, confront, counter, countermine, crab, defeat, depress, disappoint, discourage, dishearten, foil, forestall, inhibit, neutralise, nullify, scotch, spike, stymie, thwart. **antonyms** fulfil, further, promote.

frustrated adj disappointed, discontented, discouraged, disheartened, embittered, foiled, irked, resentful, scunnered, thwarted. **antonym** fulfilled.

frustration n annoyance, balking, circumvention, contravention, curbing, disappointment, dissatisfaction, failure, foiling, irritation, non-fulfilment, non-success, obstruction, resentment, thwarting, vexation. **antonym** fulfilment, furthering, promoting.

fuddled adj bemused, confused, drunk, groggy, hazy, inebriated, intoxicated, muddled, mused, muzzy, sozzled, stupefied, tipsy, woozy. **antonym** clear, sober.

fudge v avoid, cook, dodge, equivocate, evade, fake, falsify, fiddle, fix, hedge, misrepresent, shuffle, stall.

fuel n ammunition, encouragement, food, incitement, material, means, nourishment, provocation.
v charge, encourage, fan, feed, fire, incite, inflame, nourish, stoke, up, sustain. **antonyms** damp down, discourage.

fugitive n deserter, escapee, refugee, runagate, runaway.
adj brief, elusive, ephemeral, evanescent, fleeing, fleeting, flitting, flying, intangible, momentary, passing, short, short-lived, temporary, transient, transitory, unstable. **antonym** permanent.

fulfil v accomplish, achieve, answer, carry out, complete, comply with, conclude, conform to, consummate, discharge, effect, effectuate, execute, fill, finish, implement, keep, meet, obey, observe, perfect, perform, realise, satisfy. **antonyms** break, defect, fail, frustrate.

fulfilment n accomplishment, achievement, attainment, bringing about, carrying out, completion, consummation, crowning, discharge, discharging, effecting, effectuation, end, implementation, observance, perfection, performance, realisation, success. **antonyms** failure, frustration.

full adj abundant, adequate, all inclusive, ample, baggy, brimming, broad, buxom, capacious, chock-a-block, chock-full, clear, complete, comprehensive, copious, crammed, crowded, curvaceous, deep, detailed, distinct, entire, exhaustive, extensive, filled, generous, gorged, intact, jammed, large, loaded, loud, maximum, occupied, packed, plenary, plenteous, plentiful, plump, replete, resonant, rich, rounded, sated, satiated, satisfied, saturated, stocked, sufficient, taken, thorough, unabbreviated, unabridged, uncut, unedited, unexpurgated, voluminous, voluptuous. **antonyms** empty, incomplete.

full-grown *adj* adult, developed, full-blown, full-scale, grown-up, marriageable, mature, nubile, of age, ripe. *antonyms* undeveloped, young.

fullness *n* abundance, adequateness, ampleness, broadness, clearness, completeness, comprehensiveness, copiousness, curvaceousness, dilation, distension, enlargement, entirety, extensiveness, fill, glut, loudness, plenitude, plenty, profusion, repletion, resonance, richness, roundness, satiety, saturation, strength, sufficiency, swelling, totality, tumescence, vastness, voluptuousness, wealth, wholeness. *antonyms* emptiness, incompleteness.

full-scale *adj* all-encompassing, all-out, comprehensive, exhaustive, extensive, full-dress, in-depth, intensive, major, proper, sweeping, thorough, thorough-going, wide-ranging. *antonym* partial.

fully *adv* absolutely, abundantly, adequately, altogether, amply, completely, comprehensively, enough, entirely, every inch, from first to last, heart and soul, in all respects, intimately, perfectly, plentifully, positively, quite, satisfactorily, sufficiently, thoroughly, totally, utterly, wholly, without reserve. *antonym* partly.

fully-fledged *adj* experienced, full-blown, graduate, mature, professional, proficient, qualified, senior, trained. *antonym* inexperienced.

fulminate *v* criticise, curse, denounce, detonate, fume, inveigh, protest, rage, rail, thunder, vituperate. *antonym* praise.

fulsome *adj* adulatory, cloying, effusive, excessive, extravagant, fawning, gross, immoderate, ingratiating, inordinate, insincere, nauseating, nauseous, offensive, overdone, sickening, smarmy, sycophantic, unctuous. *antonym* sincere.

fumble *v* botch, bumble, bungle, faff, flail, flounder, fluff, footer, grope, misfield, mishandle, mismanage, muff, scrabble, spoil.

fume *v* boil, chafe, fizz, get steamed up, give off, rage, rant, rave, reek, seethe, smoke, smoulder, storm.

fuming *adj* angry, boiling, enraged, fizzing, incensed, raging, roused, seething, spitting, steamed up. *antonym* calm.

fun *n* amusement, buffoonery, cheer, clowning, distraction, diversion, enjoyment, entertainment, foolery, frolic, gaiety, game, high jinks, horseplay, jesting, jocularity, joking, jollification, jollity, joy, merriment, merrymaking, mirth, nonsense, play, playfulness, pleasure, recreation, romp, skylarking, sport, teasing, tomfoolery, treat, whoopee.

function¹ *n* activity, business, capacity, charge, concern, duty, employment, exercise, faculty, job, mission, occupation, office, operation, part, post, province, purpose, raison d'être, responsibility, role, situation, task.
v act, be in running order, behave, do duty, go, officiate, operate, perform, run, serve, work.

function² *n* affair, dinner, do, gathering, junket, luncheon, party, reception, shindig.

functional *adj* hard-wearing, operational, operative, plain, practical, serviceable, useful, utilitarian, utility, working. *antonyms* effective, inoperative, ornate, useless.

functionary *n* bureaucrat, dignitary, employee, office-bearer, office-holder, officer, official.

functionless *adj* aimless, decorative, futile, hollow, idle, inactive, inert, irrelevant, needless, otiose, pointless, redundant, superfluous, useless. *antonym* useful.

fund *n* cache, capital, endowment, foundation, hoard, kitty, mine, pool, repository, reserve, reservoir, source, stack, stock, store, storehouse, supply, treasury, well.
v back, capitalise, endow, finance, float, promote, stake, subsidise, support, underwrite.

fundamental *adj* axiomatic, basic, cardinal, central, constitutional, crucial, elementary, essential, first, important, indispensable, integral, intrinsic, key, keynote, necessary, organic, primal, primary, prime, principal, rudimentary, underlying, vital. *antonym* advanced.
n axiom, basic, cornerstone, essential, first principle, keystone, law, principle, rudiment, rule, sine qua non.

fundamentally *adv* at bottom, at heart, basically, essentially, intrinsically, primarily, radically.

fundamentals *n* basics, brass tacks, business, nitty-gritty, practicalities.

funds *n* backing, bread, capital, cash, dough, finance, hard cash, money, ready money, resources, savings, spondulicks, the ready, the wherewithal.

funereal *adj* dark, deathlike, depressing, dismal, dreary, gloomy, grave, lamenting, lugubrious, mournful, sad, sepulchral, solemn, sombre, woeful. *antonyms* happy, lively.

funnel *v* channel, conduct, convey, direct, filter, move, pass, pour, siphon, transfer.

funny *adj* a card, a scream, absurd, amusing, comic, comical, curious, diverting, droll, dubious, entertaining, facetious, farcical, funny ha-ha, funny peculiar, hilarious, humorous, jocular, jolly, killing, laughable, ludicrous, mysterious, odd, peculiar, perplexing, puzzling, queer, remarkable, rib-tickling, rich, ridiculous, riotous, risible, side-splitting, silly, slapstick, strange, suspicious, unusual, weird, witty. *antonyms* sad, solemn, unamusing, unfunny.

furious *adj* agitated, angry, boiling, boisterous, enraged, fierce, fizzing, frantic, frenzied, fuming, impetuous, incensed, infuriated, intense, livid, mad, maddened, raging, savage, stormy, tempestuous, tumultuous, turbulent, up in arms, vehement, violent, waxy, wild, wrathful, wroth. *antonyms* calm, pleased.

furnish *v* afford, appoint, bestow, decorate, endow, equip, fit out, fit up, give, grant, offer, outfit, present, provide, provision, reveal, rig, stake, stock, store, suit, supply. *antonym* divest.

furniture *n* appliances, appointments, chattels, effects, equipment, fittings, furnishings, goods, household goods, movables, possessions, things.

furore *n* commotion, craze, disturbance, enthusiasm, excitement, flap, frenzy, fury, fuss, hullabaloo, mania, outburst, outcry, rage, stir, to-do, tumult, uproar. *antonym* calm.

furrow *n* chamfer, channel, corrugation, crease, crow's-foot, flute, fluting, groove, hollow, line, rut, seam, trench, vallecula, wrinkle.
v corrugate, crease, draw together, flute, knit, seam, wrinkle.

further *adj* additional, distant, extra, far, fresh, more, new, opposite, other, supplementary.
v accelerate, advance, aid, assist, champion, contribute to, ease, encourage, expedite, facilitate, forward, foster, hasten, help, patronise, plug, promote, push, speed, succour. *antonyms* frustrate, stop.

furtherance *n* advancement, advancing, advocacy, backing, boosting, carrying-out, championship, promoting, promotion, prosecution, pursuit.

furthermore *adv* additionally, also, as well, besides, further, in addition, into the bargain, likewise, moreover, not to mention, to boot, too, what's more.

furthest *adj* extreme, farthest, furthermost, most distant, outermost, outmost, remotest, ultimate, uttermost. *antonym* nearest.

furtive *adj* back-door, backstairs, clandestine, cloaked, conspiratorial, covert, hidden, secret, secretive, skulking, slinking, sly, sneaking, sneaky, stealthy, surreptitious, underhand. *antonym* open.

fury *n* anger, desperation, ferocity, fierceness, force, frenzy, impetuosity, intensity, ire, madness, passion, power, rage, savagery, severity, tempestuousness, turbulence, vehemence, violence, wax, wrath. *antonym* calm.

fuse *v* agglutinate, amalgamate, blend, coalesce, combine, commingle, federate, integrate, intermingle, intermix, join, meld, melt, merge, solder, unite, weld.

fusion *n* alloy, amalgam, amalgamation, blend, blending, coalescence, commingling, commixture, federation, integration, liquefaction, liquefying, melting, merger, merging, mixture, synthesis, union, uniting, welding.

fuss *n* ado, agitation, bother, bustle, coil, commotion, confusion, difficulty, display, doodah, excitement, fidget, flap, flurry, fluster, flutter, furore, hassle, hoo-ha, hurry, kerfuffle, objection, palaver, pother, row, squabble, stew, stir, to-do, trouble, unrest, upset, worry. *antonym* calm.
v bustle, chafe, complain, emote, fidget, flap, fret, fume, niggle, pother, take pains, worry.

fussy *adj* busy, choosy, cluttered, difficult, discriminating, exacting, faddish, faddy, fastidious, finicky, hard to please, niggling, nit-picking, old womanish, old-maidish, overdecorated, overelaborate, overparticular, particular, pernickety, picky, squeamish. *antonyms* plain, uncritical, undemanding.

fusty *adj* airless, antediluvian, antiquated, archaic, close, damp, dank, frowsty, ill-smelling, malodorous, mildewed, mildewy, mouldering, mouldy, musty, old-fashioned, old-fog(e)yish, outdated, out-of-date, passé, rank, stale, stuffy, unventilated. **antonyms** airy, chic, up-to-date.

futile *adj* abortive, barren, empty, forlorn, fruitless, hollow, idle, ineffectual, otiose, pointless, profitless, sterile, trifling, trivial, unavailing, unimportant, unproductive, unprofitable, unsuccessful, useless, vain, valueless, worthless. **antonyms** fruitful, profitable.

futility *n* aimlessness, emptiness, fruitlessness, hollowness, idleness, ineffectiveness, pointlessness, triviality, unimportance, uselessness, vanity. **antonyms** fruitfulness, profitability.

future *n* expectation, hereafter, outlook, prospects. **antonym** past.
adj approaching, coming, designate, destined, eventual, expected, fated, forthcoming, impending, in the offing, later, prospective, rising, subsequent, to be, to come, ultimate, unborn. **antonym** past.

fuzzy *adj* bleary, blurred, blurry, distorted, downy, faint, fluffy, frizzy, hazy, ill-defined, indistinct, muffled, shadowy, unclear, unfocused, vague, woolly. **antonyms** base, distinct.

G

gab *v* babble, blabber, blether, buzz, chatter, drivel, gossip, jabber, jaw, prattle, talk, tattle, yabber, yak, yatter.
n blab, blarney, blethering, blethers, chat, chatter, chitchat, conversation, drivel, gossip, palaver, prattle, prattling, small talk, tête-à-tête, tittle-tattle, tongue-wagging, yabber, yackety-yak, yak, yatter.

gabble *v* babble, blab, blabber, blether, cackle, chatter, gaggle, gibber, gush, jabber, prattle, rattle, splutter, spout, sputter, yabber, yatter.
n babble, blabber, blethering, cackling, chatter, drivel, gibberish, jargon, nonsense, prattle, twaddle, waffle, yabber, yatter.

gadget *n* appliance, contraption, contrivance, device, gimmick, gismo, gizmo, invention, novelty, thing, thingumajig, tool.

gaffe *n* bloomer, blunder, boob, booboo, brick, clanger, faux pas, goof, howler, indiscretion, mistake, slip, solecism.

gaffer *n* boss, foreman, overseer, superintendent, supervisor.

gag *v* choke, choke up, curb, disgorge, gasp, heave, muffle, muzzle, puke, quiet, retch, silence, spew, stifle, still, stop up, suppress, throttle, throw up, vomit.

gaiety *n* animation, blitheness, brightness, brilliance, celebration, cheerfulness, colour, colourfulness, conviviality, effervescence, elation, exhilaration, festivity, fun, gaudiness, glee, glitter, good humour, high spirits, hilarity, joie de vivre, jollification, jollity, joviality, joyousness, light-heartedness, liveliness, merriment, merrymaking, mirth, revelry, revels, show, showiness, sparkle, sprightliness, vivacity. **antonyms** drabness, dreariness, sadness.

gaily *adv* blithely, brightly, brilliantly, cheerfully, colourfully, fancily, flamboyantly, flashily, gaudily, gleefully, happily, joyfully, joyously, light-heartedly, merrily, showily. **antonyms** dully, sadly.

gain *v* achieve, acquire, advance, arrive at, attain, avail, bag, bring in, capture, clear, collect, come to, earn, enlist, gather, get, get to, glean, harvest, improve, increase, make, net, obtain, pick up, procure, produce, profit, progress, reach, realise, reap, secure, win, win over, yield. **antonym** lose.
n accretion, achievement, acquisition, advance, advancement, advantage, attainment, benefit, dividend, earnings, emolument, growth, headway, improvement, income, increase, increment, proceeds, produce, profit, progress, return, rise, winnings, yield. **antonym** loss, losses.

gain on approach, catch up, catch up with, close with, come up with, encroach on, leave behind, level with, narrow the gap, outdistance, overtake, widen the gap.

gain time delay, drag one's feet, procrastinate, stall, temporise.

gainful *adj* advantageous, beneficial, feracious, fructuous, fruitful, lucrative, moneymaking, paying, productive, profitable, remunerative, rewarding, useful, worthwhile. **antonym** useless.

gains *n* booty, earnings, fruits, gainings, pickings, prize, proceeds, profits, revenue, takings, winnings. **antonym** losses.

gainsay *v* contradict, contravene, controvert, deny, disaffirm, disagree with, dispute. **antonym** agree.

gait *n* bearing, carriage, manner, pace, step, stride, tread, walk.

gall¹ *n* acrimony, animosity, animus, antipathy, assurance, bad blood, bile, bitterness, brass, brass neck, brazenness, cheek, effrontery, enmity, hostility, impertinence, impudence, insolence, malevolence, malice, neck, nerve, presumption, presumptuousness, rancour, sauciness, sourness, spite, spleen, venom. **antonyms** friendliness, modesty, reserve.

gall² *v* abrade, aggravate, annoy, bother, chafe, exasperate, excoriate, get, get to, graze, harass, hurt, irk, irritate, nag, nettle, peeve, pester, plague, provoke, rankle, rile, rub raw, ruffle, scrape, skin, vex.

gallant *adj* attentive, august, bold, brave, chivalrous, courageous, courteous, courtly, daring, dashing, dauntless, dignified, doughty, elegant, fearless, game, gentlemanly, glorious, gracious, grand, heroic, high-spirited, honourable, imposing, indomitable, intrepid, lion-hearted, lofty, magnanimous, magnificent, manful, manly, noble, plucky, polite, splendid, stately, valiant. **antonyms** cowardly, craven, ungentlemanly.

n admirer, adventurer, beau, blade, boyfriend, cavalier, champion, dandy, daredevil, escort, fop, hero, knight, ladies' man, lady-killer, lover, suitor, wooer.

galling *adj* aggravating, annoying, bitter, bothersome, exasperating, harassing, humiliating, infuriating, irksome, irritating, nettling, plaguing, provoking, rankling, vexatious, vexing. **antonym** pleasing.

gallop *v* bolt, career, dart, dash, fly, gal(l)umph, hasten, hurry, lope, race, run, rush, scud, shoot, speed, sprint, tear, zoom.

galore *adv* aplenty, everywhere, heaps of, in abundance, in numbers, in profusion, lots of, millions of, stacks of, to spare, tons of. **antonym** scarce.

galvanise *v* animate, arouse, awaken, electrify, excite, fire, inspire, invigorate, jolt, move, prod, provoke, quicken, shock, spur, startle, stimulate, stir, thrill, vitalise, wake. **antonym** retard.

gambit *n* artifice, device, manoeuvre, move, ploy, stratagem, trick, wile.

gamble *v* back, bet, chance, game, have a flutter, hazard, play, punt, risk, speculate, stake, stick one's neck out, take a chance, try one's luck, venture, wager.
n bet, chance, flutter, leap in the dark, lottery, punt, risk, speculation, uncertainty, venture, wager.

gambol *v* bounce, bound, caper, cavort, cut a caper, frisk, frolic, hop, jump, prance, rollick, skip.
n antic, bound, caper, frisk, frolic, hop, jump, prance, skip, spring.

game¹ *n* adventure, amusement, business, competition, contest, design, device, distraction, diversion, enterprise, entertainment, event, frolic, fun, jest, joke, lark, line, match, meeting, merriment, merry-making, occupation, pastime, plan, play, plot, ploy, proceeding, recreation, romp, round, scheme, sport, stratagem, strategy, tactic, tournament, trick, undertaking.

game² *adj* bold, brave, courageous, dauntless, disposed, dogged, eager, fearless, gallant, heroic, inclined, interested, intrepid, persevering, persistent, plucky, prepared, ready, resolute, spirited, spunky, unflinching,

valiant, willing. **antonyms** cowardly, unwilling.

gamut *n* area, catalogue, compass, field, gamme, range, scale, scope, series, spectrum, sweep.

gang *n* band, circle, clique, club, company, core, coterie, crew, crowd, group, herd, horde, lot, mob, pack, party, ring, set, shift, squad, team, troupe.

gangling *adj* angular, awkward, bony, gangly, gauche, gawky, lanky, loose-jointed, rangy, raw-boned, skinny, spindly, tall, ungainly.

gangster *n* bandit, brigand, crook, desperado, heavy, hood, hoodlum, mobster, racketeer, robber, rough, ruffian, thug, tough.

gaol *see* jail.

gap *n* blank, breach, break, chink, cleft, crack, cranny, crevice, difference, disagreement, discontinuity, disparity, divergence, divide, hiatus, hole, inconsistency, interlude, intermission, interruption, interspace, interstice, interval, lacuna, lull, opening, pause, recess, rent, rift, space, vacuity, void.

gape *v* crack, gawk, gawp, goggle, open, split, stare, wonder, yawn.

gaping *adj* broad, cavernous, great, open, vast, wide, yawning. **antonym** tiny.

garb *n* apparel, appearance, array, aspect, attire, clothes, clothing, costume, covering, cut, dress, fashion, garment, gear, guise, habit, look, mode, outfit, robes, style, uniform, wear.
v apparel, array, attire, clothe, cover, dress, rig out, robe.

garbage *n* bits and pieces, debris, detritus, dross, filth, junk, litter, muck, odds and ends, offal, refuse, rubbish, scourings, scraps, slops, sweepings, swill, trash, waste.

garble *v* confuse, corrupt, distort, doctor, edit, falsify, jumble, misinterpret, misquote, misreport, misrepresent, mistranslate, mix up, muddle, mutilate, pervert, slant, tamper with, twist. **antonym** decipher.

gargantuan *adj* big, colossal, elephantine, enormous, giant, gigantic, huge, immense, large, leviathan, mammoth, massive, monstrous, monumental, mountainous, prodigious, titanic, towering, tremendous, vast. **antonym** small.

garish *adj* brassy, cheap, flash, flashy, flaunting, flaunty, gaudy, glaring, glittering, glitzy, loud, showy, tasteless, tawdry, vulgar. *antonyms* modest, plain, quiet.

garments *n* apparel, array, attire, clothes, clothing, costume, dress, duds, garb, gear, get-up, habit, outfit, robes, togs, uniform, wear.

garner *v* accumulate, amass, assemble, collect, cull, deposit, gather, hoard, husband, lay up, put by, reserve, save, stockpile, store, stow away, treasure. *antonym* dissipate.

garnish *v* adorn, beautify, bedeck, deck, decorate, embellish, enhance, furnish, grace, ornament, set off, trim. *antonym* divest.

n adornment, decoration, embellishment, enhancement, garniture, ornament, ornamentation, relish, trim, trimming.

garrison *n* armed force, barracks, base, camp, command, detachment, encampment, fort, fortification, fortress, post, station, stronghold, troops, unit.

v assign, defend, furnish, guard, man, mount, occupy, place, position, post, protect, station.

garrulity *n* babble, babbling, chatter, chattering, chattiness, diffuseness, effusiveness, gabbiness, garrulousness, gassing, gift of the gab, glibness, long-windedness, loquaciousness, loquacity, prattle, talkativeness, verbosity, volubility, windiness, wordiness. *antonyms* taciturnity, terseness.

garrulous *adj* babbling, chattering, chatty, diffuse, effusive, gabby, glib, gossiping, gushing, long-winded, loquacious, mouthy, prattling, talkative, verbose, voluble, windy, wordy, yabbering. *antonyms* taciturn, terse.

gash *v* cleave, cut, gouge, incise, lacerate, nick, notch, rend, score, slash, slit, split, tear, wound.

n cleft, cut, gouge, incision, laceration, nick, notch, rent, score, slash, slit, split, tear, wound.

gasp *v* blow, breathe, choke, ejaculate, gulp, pant, puff, utter.

n blow, breath, ejaculation, exclamation, gulp, pant, puff.

gather *v* accumulate, amass, assemble, assume, build, clasp, collect, conclude, congregate, convene, crop, cull, deduce, deepen, draw, embrace, enfold, enlarge, expand, flock, fold, foregather, garner, glean, group, grow, harvest, heap, hear, heighten, hoard, hold, hug, increase, infer, intensify, learn, make, marshal, mass, muster, pick, pile up, pleat, pluck, pucker, rake up, reap, rise, round up,

ruche, ruffle, select, shirr, stockpile, surmise, swell, thicken, tuck, understand, wax. *antonyms* dissipate, scatter.

gathering *n* accumulation, acquisition, aggregate, assemblage, assembly, collection, company, concentration, conclave, concourse, congregation, congress, convention, convocation, crowd, flock, gain, get-together, group, heap, hoard, jamboree, knot, mass, meeting, muster, party, pile, procurement, rally, round-up, rout, stock, stockpile, throng, turn-out. *antonym* scattering.

gauche *adj* awkward, clumsy, gawky, graceless, ignorant, ill-bred, ill-mannered, inelegant, inept, insensitive, maladroit, tactless, uncultured, ungainly, ungraceful, unpolished, unsophisticated. *antonym* graceful.

gaudy *adj* bright, brilliant, chintzy, flash, flashy, florid, garish, gay, glaring, glitzy, loud, ostentatious, showy, tasteless, tawdry, tinsel(ly), vulgar. *antonyms* drab, plain, quiet.

gauge[1] *v* adjudge, adjust, appraise, ascertain, assess, calculate, check, compute, count, determine, estimate, evaluate, figure, guess, judge, measure, rate, reckon, value, weigh.

n basis, criterion, example, exemplar, guide, guideline, indicator, measure, meter, micrometer, model, pattern, rule, sample, standard, test, touchstone, yardstick.

gauge[2] *n* bore, calibre, capacity, degree, depth, extent, height, magnitude, measure, scope, size, span, thickness, width.

gaunt *adj* angular, attenuated, bare, bleak, bony, cadaverous, desolate, dismal, dreary, emaciated, forbidding, forlorn, grim, haggard, harsh, hollow-eyed, lank, lean, meagre, pinched, scraggy, scrawny, skeletal, skinny, spare, thin, wasted. *antonyms* hale, plump.

gauzy *adj* delicate, diaphanous, filmy, flimsy, gossamer, insubstantial, light, see-through, sheer, thin, transparent, unsubstantial. *antonyms* heavy, thick.

gawk *v* gape, gaup, gaze, goggle, look, ogle, stare.

gawky *adj* awkward, clownish, clumsy, gangling, gauche, loutish, lumbering, lumpish, oafish, uncouth, ungainly, ungraceful. *antonym* graceful.

gay[1] *adj* animated, blithe, bright, brilliant, carefree, cavalier, cheerful, colourful, convivial, debonair, festive, flamboyant, flashy, fresh, frivolous, frolicsome, fun-loving, garish, gaudy, glad, gleeful, happy, hilarious, insouciant, jolly, jovial, joyful, joyous, light-hearted, lively, merry, playful, pleasure-seeking, rich, rollicking, showy, sparkling, sportive, sunny, vivacious, vivid, waggish. **antonyms** gloomy, sad.

gay² *adj* bent, dikey, homosexual, lesbian, queer. **antonyms** heterosexual, straight.

n dike, homo, homosexual, lesbian, poof, queer, sapphist. **antonym** heterosexual.

gaze *v* contemplate, gape, gaup, gawp, look, ogle, regard, stare, view, watch.

n gaup, gawp, look, stare.

gear *n* accessories, accoutrements, apparatus, apparel, armour, array, attire, baggage, belongings, business, clothes, clothing, costume, doings, dress, effects, equipment, garb, garments, gearing, get-up, habit, instruments, kit, luggage, machinery, matter, mechanism, outfit, paraphernalia, possessions, rigging, rig-out, stuff, supplies, tackle, things, togs, tools, trappings, wear, works.

v adapt, adjust, equip, fit, harness, rig, suit, tailor.

gel *see* **jell**.

gelatinous *adj* congealed, gluey, glutinous, gooey, gummy, jellied, jellified, jelly, jelly-like, mucilaginous, rubbery, sticky, viscid, viscous.

gem *n* angel, brick, flower, honey, jewel, masterpiece, pearl, pick, pièce de résistance, precious stone, prize, stone, treasure.

genealogy *n* ancestry, background, blood-line, derivation, descent, extraction, family, family tree, line, lineage, pedigree, stock, strain.

general *adj* accepted, accustomed, across-the-board, all-inclusive, approximate, blanket, broad, catholic, collective, common, comprehensive, conventional, customary, ecumenical, encyclop(a)edic, everyday, extensive, generic, habitual, ill-defined, imprecise, inaccurate, indefinite, indiscriminate, inexact, loose, miscellaneous, normal, ordinary, panoramic, popular, prevailing, prevalent, public, regular, sweeping, total, typical, universal, unspecific, usual, vague, widespread. **antonyms** limited, novel, particular.

n chief, c-in-c, commander, commander in chief, leader, marshal, officer.

generally *adv* approximately, as a rule, broadly, by and large, characteristically, chiefly, commonly, conventionally, customarily, extensively, for the most part, habitually, in the main, largely, mainly, mostly, normally, on average, on the whole, ordinarily, popularly, predominantly, principally, publicly, regularly, typically, universally, usually, widely. **antonym** rarely.

generate *v* beget, breed, bring about, cause, create, engender, father, form, give rise to, initiate, make, originate, procreate, produce, propagate, spawn, whip up. **antonym** prevent.

generation *n* age, age group, breed, breeding, creation, crop, day, days, epoch, era, formation, generating, genesis, origination, period, procreation, production, propagation, reproduction, time, times.

generic *adj* all-inclusive, blanket, collective, common, comprehensive, general, inclusive, sweeping, universal, wide. **antonym** particular.

generosity *n* beneficence, benevolence, big-heartedness, bounteousness, bounty, charity, goodness, high-mindedness, kindness, large-heartedness, liberality, magnanimity, munificence, nobleness, open-handedness, soft-heartedness, unselfishness, unsparingness. **antonyms** meanness, selfishness.

generous *adj* abundant, ample, beneficent, benevolent, big-hearted, bounteous, bountiful, charitable, copious, disinterested, free, full, good, high-minded, hospitable, kind, lavish, liberal, lofty, magnanimous, munificent, noble, open-handed, overflowing, plentiful, princely, rich, soft-boiled, soft-hearted, ungrudging, unreproachful, unresentful, unselfish, unsparing, unstinted, unstinting. **antonyms** mean, selfish.

genesis *n* beginning, birth, commencement, creation, dawn, engendering, formation, foundation, founding, generation, inception, initiation, origin, outset, propagation, root, source, start. **antonym** end.

genial *adj* affable, agreeable, amiable, cheerful, cheery, congenial, convivial, cordial, easy-going, expansive, friendly, glad, good-natured, happy, hearty, jolly, jovial, joyous, kind, kindly, merry, pleasant, sunny, warm, warm-hearted. **antonym** cold.

geniality *n* affability, agreeableness, amiability, cheerfulness, cheeriness, congenialness, conviviality, cordiality, friendliness, gladness, good nature, happiness, heartiness, jollity, joviality, kindliness, kindness, mirth, openness, pleasantness, sunniness, warm-heartedness, warmth. *antonym* coldness.

genitals *n* fanny, genitalia, private parts, privates, pudenda, pudendum, pussy, quim.

genius[1] *n* adept, brain, expert, intellect, maestro, master, master-hand, mastermind, pastmaster, virtuoso.

genius[2] *n* ability, aptitude, bent, brightness, brilliance, capacity, endowment, faculty, flair, gift, inclination, intellect, knack, propensity, talent, turn.

genre *n* brand, category, character, class, fashion, genus, group, kind, race, school, sort, species, strain, style, type, variety.

genteel *adj* aristocratic, civil, courteous, courtly, cultivated, cultured, elegant, fashionable, formal, gentlemanly, graceful, ladylike, mannerly, polished, polite, refined, respectable, stylish, urbane, well-bred, well-mannered. *antonyms* crude, rough, unpolished.

gentility *n* aristocracy, blue blood, breeding, civility, courtesy, courtliness, cultivation, culture, decorum, elegance, elite, etiquette, formality, gentlefolk, gentry, good family, high birth, mannerliness, manners, nobility, nobles, polish, politeness, propriety, rank, refinement, respectability, upper class. *antonyms* crudeness, discourteousness, roughness.

gentle *adj* amiable, aristocratic, balmy, benign, biddable, bland, broken, calm, clement, compassionate, courteous, cultured, docile, easy, elegant, genteel, gentlemanlike, gentlemanly, gradual, high-born, humane, imperceptible, kind, kindly, ladylike, lamb-like, lenient, light, low, maidenly, manageable, meek, merciful, mild, moderate, muted, noble, pacific, peaceful, placid, polished, polite, quiet, refined, serene, slight, slow, smooth, soft, soothing, sweet, sweet-tempered, tame, temperate, tender, tractable, tranquil, untroubled, upper-class, well-born, well-bred. *antonyms* crude, rough, unkind, unpolished.

gentlemanly *adj* civil, civilised, courteous, cultivated, gallant, genteel, gentlemanlike, gentlewomanly, honourable, mannerly, noble, obliging, polished, polite, refined, reputable, suave, urbane, well-bred, well-mannered. *antonyms* impolite, rough.

gentry *n* aristocracy, elite, gentility, gentlefolk, nobility, nobles, quality, upper class.

genuine *adj* actual, artless, authentic, bona fide, candid, earnest, frank, heartfelt, honest, kosher, legitimate, natural, original, pukka, pure, real, sincere, sound, sterling, sure-enough, true, unadulterate(d), unaffected, unalloyed, unfeigned, veritable. *antonyms* artificial, insincere.

genus *n* breed, category, class, division, genre, group, kind, order, race, set, sort, species, type.

germ *n* bacterium, beginning, bud, bug, cause, egg, embryo, microbe, micro-organism, nucleus, origin, root, rudiment, seed, source, spark, spore, sprout, virus, zyme.

germane *adj* akin, allied, applicable, apposite, appropriate, apropos, apt, cognate, connected, fitting, kin, kindred, material, pertinent, proper, related, relevant, suitable. *antonym* irrelevant.

germinal *adj* developing, embryonic, preliminary, rudimentary, seminal, undeveloped.

germinate *v* bud, develop, generate, grow, originate, root, shoot, sprout, swell.

gestation *n* conception, development, drafting, evolution, incubation, maturation, planning, pregnancy, ripening.

gesticulate *v* gesture, indicate, motion, point, sign, signal, wave.

gesture *n* act, action, gesticulation, indication, motion, sign, signal, wave. *v* gesticulate, indicate, motion, point, sign, signal, wave.

get *v* achieve, acquire, affect, annoy, arouse, arrange, arrest, arrive, attain, baffle, bag, become, bother, bring, bug, capture, catch, coax, collar, come, come by, come down with, communicate with, comprehend, confound, contact, contract, contrive, convince, earn, excite, fathom, fetch, fix, follow, gain, glean, grab, grow, hear, impress, induce, influence, inherit, irk, irritate, make, make it, manage, move, mystify, net, nonplus, notice, obtain, perceive, perplex, persuade, pick up, prevail upon, procure, puzzle, reach, realise, reap, receive, secure, see, seize, stimulate, stir, stump, succeed, sway, take, touch, trap, turn, twig, understand, upset, vex, wangle, wax, win. *antonyms* lose, misunderstand, pacify.

get a move on get cracking, get going, go to it, hurry (up), jump to it, make haste, shake a leg, speed up, step on it. *antonym* slow down.

get across bring home to, communicate, convey, cross, ford, impart, negotiate, put over, transmit, traverse.

get ahead advance, flourish, get there, go places, make good, make it, progress, prosper, succeed, thrive. *antonyms* fail, fall behind.

get along cope, develop, fare, get by, get on, harmonise, hit it off, make out, manage, progress, shift, survive. *antonym* argue.

get at acquire, annoy, attack, attain, blame, bribe, buy off, corrupt, criticise, find fault with, hint, imply, influence, intend, irritate, make fun of, mean, mock, nag, pervert, pick on, poke fun at, suborn, suggest, tamper with, taunt. *antonym* praise.

get away break out, decamp, depart, disappear, escape, flee, get out, leave, run away.

get back get even, get one's own back (on), recoup, recover, regain, repossess, retaliate, retrieve, return, revenge oneself (on), revert, revisit.

get by contrive, cope, exist, fare, get along, make both ends meet, manage, negotiate, pass muster, shift, subsist, survive.

get down alight, depress, descend, disembark, dishearten, dismount, dispirit, lower, sadden. *antonyms* board, encourage.

get even even the score, get one's own back, pay back, reciprocate, repay, requite, revenge oneself, settle the score.

get in alight, appear, arrive, collect, come, embark, enter, gather in, include, insert, interpose, land, mount, penetrate, take. *antonym* get out.

get off alight, depart, descend, detach, disembark, dismount, escape, exit, learn, leave, remove, shed, swot up. *antonyms* arrive, board, put on.

get on advance, agree, ascend, board, climb, concur, cope, embark, fare, get along, hit it off, make out, manage, mount, proceed, progress, prosper, succeed. *antonyms* alight, argue.

get out alight, break out, clear out, decamp, deliver, escape, evacuate, extricate oneself, flee, flit, free oneself, leave, produce, publish, quit, scarper, vacate, withdraw. *antonym* board.

get out of avoid, dodge, escape, evade, shirk, skive.

get over communicate, convey, cross, defeat, explain, ford, get the better of, impart, master, overcome, pass, put across, recover from, shake off, surmount, survive, traverse.

get ready arrange, fix up, get psyched up, gird one's loins, prepare, psych oneself up, ready, rehearse, set out.

get rid of dispense with, dispose of, do away with, dump, eject, eliminate, expel, jettison, remove, rid oneself of, shake off, unload. *antonyms* accumulate, acquire.

get round bypass, cajole, circumvent, coax, convert, edge, evade, outmanoeuvre, persuade, prevail upon, skirt, talk over, talk round, wheedle.

get the better of beat, defeat, outdo, outfox, outsmart, outwit, surpass.

get the message catch on, comprehend, get it, get the point, see, take the hint, twig, understand. *antonym* misunderstand.

get there advance, arrive, go places, make good, make it, prosper, succeed.

get together accumulate, assemble, collaborate, collect, congregate, convene, converge, gather, join, meet, muster, rally, unite.

get under one's skin annoy, get, get to, infuriate, irk, irritate, needle, nettle. *antonym* pacify.

get up arise, arrange, ascend, climb, fix up, increase, learn, memorise, mount, organise, rise, scale, stand.

ghastly *adj* ashen, cadaverous, deathlike, deathly, dreadful, frightful, ghostly, grim, grisly, gruesome, hideous, horrendous, horrible, horrid, loathsome, lurid, pale, pallid, repellent, shocking, spectral, terrible, terrifying, wan. *antonym* delightful.

ghost *n* apparition, astral body, glimmer, hint, jumby, larva, phantasm, phantom, possibility, semblance, shade, shadow, simulacrum, soul, spectre, spirit, spook, suggestion, trace, umbra, visitant.

ghostly *adj* eerie, faint, ghostlike, illusory, insubstantial, phantasmal, phantom, spectral, spooky, supernatural, uncanny, unearthly, weird, wraith-like.

ghoulish *adj* grisly, gruesome, macabre, morbid, revolting, sick, unhealthy, unwholesome.

giant *n* colossus, Goliath, Hercules, leviathan, monster, titan.
adj colossal, elephantine, enormous, gargantuan, gigantesque, gigantic, huge, immense, jumble, king-size, large, leviathan, mammoth, monstrous, prodigious, titanic, vast.

gibberish *n* babble, balderdash, drivel, gobbledegook, jabber, jargon, mumbo-jumbo, nonsense, prattle, twaddle. *antonym* sense.

gibe *see* **jibe**.

giddy *adj* capricious, careless, changeable, dizzy, dizzying, erratic, faint, fickle, flighty, frivolous, heedless, impulsive, inconstant, irresolute, irresponsible, light-headed, reckless, reeling, scatterbrained, scatty, silly, thoughtless, unbalanced, unstable, unsteady, vacillating, vertiginous, volatile, wild. *antonyms* sensible, sober.

gift *n* ability, aptitude, attribute, benefaction, benificence, bent, bequest, bonus, boon, bounty, cadeau, capability, capacity, contribution, dolly, donary, donation, endowment, faculty, flair, freebie, genius, grant, gratuity, knack, largess(e), legacy, manna, offering, power, present, sop, talent, turn.

gifted *adj* able, accomplished, ace, adroit, bright, brilliant, capable, clever, expert, ingenious, intelligent, masterly, skilful, skilled, talented. *antonym* dull.

gigantic *adj* colossal, elephantine, enormous, gargantuan, giant, herculean, huge, immense, leviathan, mammoth, monstrous, prodigious, stupendous, titanic, tremendous, vast. *antonym* small.

giggle *v* chortle, chuckle, laugh, snigger, tee-hee, titter.
n chortle, chuckle, laugh, snigger, tee-hee, titter.

gild *v* adorn, array, beautify, bedeck, brighten, coat, deck, dress up, embellish, embroider, enhance, enrich, festoon, garnish, grace, ornament, paint, trim.

gimmick *n* angle, attraction, contrivance, device, dodge, gadget, gambit, gizmo, manoeuvre, ploy, scheme, stratagem, stunt, trick.

gingerly *adv* carefully, cautiously, charily, circumspectly, daintily, delicately, fastidiously, gently, hesitantly, reluctantly, squeamishly, suspiciously, timidly, warily. *antonyms* carelessly, roughly.

gipsy *see* **gypsy**.

gird *v* belt, bind, blockade, brace, encircle, enclose, encompass, enfold, environ, fortify, girdle, hem in, pen, prepare, ready, ring, steel, surround.

girdle *n* band, belt, cincture, corset, cummerbund, fillet, sash, waistband.
v bind, bound, encircle, enclose, encompass, environ, gird, gird round, go round, hem, ring, surround.

girl *n* bird, chick, chicken, chit, colleen, damsel, daughter, demoiselle, filly, flapper, flibbertigibbet, floosie, fluff, fräulein, gal, girlfriend, gouge, lass, lassie, maid, maiden, miss, moppet, peach, piece, sheila, sweetheart, wench.

gist *n* core, direction, drift, essence, force, idea, import, marrow, matter, meaning, nub, pith, point, quintessence, sense, significance, substance.

give *v* accord, administer, admit, allow, announce, award, bend, bestow, break, cause, cede, collapse, commit, communicate, concede, confer, consign, contribute, deliver, demonstrate, devote, display, do, donate, emit, engender, entrust, evidence, fall, furnish, grant, hand, hand over, impart, indicate, issue, lead, lend, make, make over, manifest, notify, occasion, offer, pay, perform, permit, present, produce, proffer, pronounce, provide, publish, recede, relinquish, render, retire, set forth, show, sink, state, supply, surrender, transmit, utter, vouchsafe, yield. *antonyms* hold out, take, withstand.

give away betray, disclose, divulge, expose, grass, inform on, leak, let out, let slip, rat, reveal, uncover.

give in capitulate, collapse, comply, concede, crack, give way, quit, submit, surrender, yield. *antonym* hold out.

give off discharge, emit, exhale, exude, outpour, pour out, produce, release, send out, throw out, vent.

give on to lead to, open on to, overlook.

give out announce, broadcast, communicate, discharge, disseminate, emit, exhale, exude, give off, impart, notify, outpour, pour out, produce, publish, release, send out, transmit, utter, vent. *antonym* take in.

give rise to breed, bring about, bring on, cause, effect, engender, generate, produce, provoke, result in.

give up abandon, capitulate, cease, cede, cut out, desist, despair, forswear, hand over, leave off, quit, relinquish, renounce, resign, stop, surrender, throw in the towel, waive. *antonym* hold out.

give way accede, acquiesce, back down, bend, break (down), cave in, cede, collapse, concede, crack, crumple, fall, give ground, give place, sink, submit, subside, withdraw, yield. **antonyms** hold out, withstand.

given *adj* addicted, admitted, agreed, apt, bestowed, disposed, granted, inclined, liable, likely, prone, specified.

glacial *adj* antagonistic, arctic, biting, bitter, chill, chilly, cold, freezing, frigid, frosty, frozen, hostile, icy, inimical, piercing, polar, raw, Siberian, stiff, unfriendly, wintry. **antonym** warm.

glad *adj* animated, blithe, bright, cheerful, cheering, cheery, chuffed, contented, delighted, delightful, felicitous, gay, gleeful, gratified, gratifying, happy, jovial, joyful, joyous, merry, over the moon, overjoyed, pleasant, pleased, pleasing, willing. **antonym** sad.

gladden *v* brighten, cheer, delight, elate, enliven, exhilarate, gratify, hearten, please, rejoice. **antonym** sadden.

gladly *adv* blithely, cheerfully, fain, freely, gaily, gleefully, happily, jovially, joyfully, joyously, merrily, readily, willingly, with good grace, with pleasure. **antonyms** sadly, unwillingly.

glamorous *adj* alluring, attractive, beautiful, bewitching, captivating, charming, classy, dazzling, elegant, enchanting, entrancing, exciting, exotic, fascinating, glittering, glossy, gorgeous, lovely, prestigious, smart. **antonyms** boring, drab, plain.

glamour *n* allure, appeal, attraction, beauty, bewitchment, charm, enchantment, fascination, magic, magnetism, prestige, ravishment.

glance[1] *v* browse, dip, flip, gaze, glimpse, leaf, look, peek, peep, riffle, scan, skim, thumb, touch on, view.
n allusion, dekko, gander, glimpse, look, mention, once over, peek, peep, reference, squint, view.

glance[2] *v* bounce, brush, cannon, flash, gleam, glimmer, glint, glisten, glister, glitter, graze, rebound, reflect, ricochet, shimmer, shine, skim, twinkle.

glare *v* blaze, dazzle, flame, flare, frown, glower, look daggers, lower, scowl, shine.
n black look, blaze, brilliance, dazzle, dirty look, flame, flare, flashiness, floridness, frown, gaudiness, glow, glower, light, look, loudness, lower, scowl, showiness, stare, tawdriness.

glaring *adj* audacious, blatant, blazing, bright, conspicuous, dazzling, dreadful, egregious, flagrant, flashy, florid, garish, glowing, gross, horrendous, loud, manifest, obvious, open, outrageous, outstanding, overt, patent, rank, terrible, unconcealed, visible. **antonyms** dull, hidden, minor.

glass *n* beaker, crystal, goblet, lens, looking-glass, magnifying glass, pane, schooner, tumbler, window.

glassy *adj* blank, clear, cold, dazed, dull, empty, expressionless, fixed, glasslike, glazed, glazy, glossy, icy, lifeless, shiny, slick, slippery, smooth, transparent, vacant, vitreous.

glaze *v* burnish, coat, crystallise, enamel, furbish, gloss, lacquer, polish, varnish.
n coat, enamel, finish, gloss, lacquer, lustre, polish, shine, varnish.

gleam *n* beam, brightness, brilliance, flash, flicker, glimmer, glint, gloss, glow, hint, inkling, lustre, ray, sheen, shimmer, sparkle, splendour, suggestion, trace.
v flare, flash, glance, glimmer, glint, glisten, glister, glitter, glow, scintillate, shimmer, shine, sparkle.

gleaming *adj* ablaze, bright, brilliant, burnished, glistening, glowing, lustrous, polished, shining. **antonym** dull.

glean *v* accumulate, amass, collect, cull, find out, garner, gather, harvest, learn, pick (up), reap, select.

glee *n* cheerfulness, delight, elation, exhilaration, exuberance, exultation, fun, gaiety, gladness, gratification, hilarity, jocularity, jollity, joviality, joy, joyfulness, joyousness, liveliness, merriment, mirth, pleasure, sprightliness, triumph, verve.

glib *adj* artful, easy, facile, fast-talking, fluent, garrulous, insincere, plausible, quick, ready, slick, slippery, smooth, smooth-tongued, suave, talkative, voluble. **antonyms** implausible, tongue-tied.

glide *v* coast, drift, float, flow, fly, roll, run, sail, skate, skim, slide, slip, soar.

glimmer *v* blink, flicker, gleam, glint, glisten, glitter, glow, shimmer, shine, sparkle, twinkle.
n blink, flicker, gleam, glimmering, glint, glow, grain, hint, inkling, ray, shimmer, sparkle, suggestion, trace, twinkle.

glimpse *n* glance, look, peek, peep, sight, sighting, squint.
v descry, espy, sight, spot, spy, view.

glint v flash, gleam, glimmer, glitter, reflect, shine, sparkle, twinkle.
 n flash, gleam, glimmer, glimmering, glitter, shine, sparkle, twinkle, twinkling.
glisten v flash, glance, glare, gleam, glimmer, glint, glister, glitter, scintillate, shimmer, shine, sparkle, twinkle.
glitter v flare, flash, glare, gleam, glimmer, glint, glisten, scintillate, shimmer, shine, spangle, sparkle, twinkle.
 n beam, brightness, brilliance, display, flash, gaudiness, glamour, glare, gleam, lustre, pageantry, radiance, scintillation, sheen, shimmer, shine, show, showiness, sparkle, splendour, tinsel.
gloat v crow, exult, glory, rejoice, relish, revel in, rub it in, triumph, vaunt.
global adj all-encompassing, all-inclusive, all-out, comprehensive, encylopaedic, exhaustive, general, globular, international, pandemic, planetary, spherical, thorough, total, unbounded, universal, unlimited, world, world-wide. **antonyms** limited, parochial.
gloom n blackness, blues, cloud, cloudiness, damp, dark, darkness, dejection, depression, desolation, despair, despondency, dimness, downheartedness, dullness, dusk, duskiness, gloominess, glumness, low spirits, melancholy, misery, murk, murkiness, obscurity, sadness, shade, shadow, sorrow, twilight, unhappiness, woe. **antonym** brightness.
gloomy adj bad, black, blue, cheerless, comfortless, crepuscular, crestfallen, dark, dejected, depressing, despondent, dim, disheartening, dismal, dispirited, dispiriting, down, down in the dumps, down in the mouth, down-beat, downcast, downhearted, dreary, dreich, dull, dusky, gloomful, glum, joyless, long-faced, low-spirited, melancholy, mirk(y), miserable, moody, morose, murk(y), obscure, overcast, pessimistic, sad, saddening, sepulchral, shadowy, sombre, sullen, tenebrous. **antonym** bright.
glorify v adore, adorn, aggrandise, augment, beatify, bless, canonise, celebrate, deify, dignify, elevate, enhance, ennoble, enshrine, eulogise, exalt, extol, honour, hymn, idolise, illuminate, immortalise, laud, lift up, magnify, panegyrise, praise, raise, revere, sanctify, venerate, worship. **antonyms** denounce, vilify.

glorious adj beautiful, bright, brilliant, celebrated, dazzling, delightful, distinguished, divine, drunk, effulgent, elated, elevated, eminent, enjoyable, excellent, famed, famous, fine, gorgeous, grand, great, heavenly, honoured, illustrious, intoxicated, magnificent, majestic, marvellous, noble, noted, pleasurable, radiant, renowned, resplendent, shining, splendid, sublime, superb, tipsy, triumphant, wonderful. **antonyms** dreadful, inglorious, plain, unknown.
glory n adoration, beauty, benediction, blessing, brightness, brilliance, celebrity, dignity, distinction, effulgence, eminence, exaltation, fame, gorgeousness, grandeur, gratitude, greatness, heaven, homage, honour, illustriousness, immortality, kudos, laudation, lustre, magnificence, majesty, nobility, pageantry, pomp, praise, prestige, radiance, renown, resplendence, richness, splendour, sublimity, thanksgiving, triumph, veneration, worship. **antonyms** blame, restraint.
 v boast, crow, delight, exult, gloat, pride oneself, rejoice, relish, revel, triumph.
gloss[1] n appearance, brightness, brilliance, burnish, façade, front, gleam, lustre, mask, polish, semblance, sheen, shine, show, surface, varnish, veneer, window-dressing.
gloss over camouflage, conceal, disguise, explain away, gild, glaze over, hide, mask, smooth over, veil, whitewash.
gloss[2] n annotation, comment, commentary, elucidation, explanation, footnote, interpretation, note, translation.
 v annotate, comment, construe, elucidate, explain, interpret, translate.
glossary n dictionary, lexicon, phrase-book, vocabulary, word-book, word-list.
glossy adj bright, brilliant, burnished, enamelled, glacé, glassy, glazed, lustrous, polished, sheeny, shining, shiny, silken, silky, sleek, smooth. **antonym** mat(t).
glow n ardour, bloom, blush, brightness, brilliance, burning, effulgence, enthusiasm, excitement, fervour, flush, gleam, glimmer, incandescence, intensity, lambency, light, luminosity, passion, phosphorescence, radiance, reddening, redness, rosiness, splendour, vividness, warmth.
 v blush, brighten, burn, colour, fill.

flush, gleam, glimmer, glowing, radiate, redden, shine, smoulder, thrill, tingle.

glower v frown, glare, look daggers, lower, scowl.

n black look, dirty look, frown, glare, look, lower, scowl, stare.

glowing adj adulatory, aglow, beaming, bright, complimentary, ecstatic, enthusiastic, eulogistic, flaming, flushed, gleamy, laudatory, luminous, rave, red, rhapsodic, rich, ruddy, suffused, vibrant, vivid, warm. **antonyms** dull, restrained.

glue n adhesive, cement, gum, mucilage, paste, size.

v affix, agglutinate, cement, fix, gum, paste, seal, stick.

gluey adj adhesive, glutinous, gummy, sticky, viscid, viscous.

glum adj crabbed, crestfallen, dejected, doleful, down, gloomy, gruff, grumpy, low, moody, morose, pessimistic, saturnine, sour, sulky, sullen, surly. **antonyms** ecstatic, happy.

glut n excess, overabundance, oversupply, plethora, saturation, superabundance, superfluity, surfeit, surplus. **antonyms** lack, scarcity.

v choke, clog, cram, deluge, fill, flood, gorge, inundate, overfeed, overload, oversupply, saturate, stuff.

glutinous adj adhesive, cohesive, gluey, gummy, mucilaginous, ropy, sticky, viscid, viscous.

glutton n cormorant, free-liver, gannet, guzzler, hog, pig.

gluttonous adj gluttonish, gormandising, greedy, gutsy, insatiable, piggish, rapacious, ravenous, voracious. **antonyms** abstemious, ascetic.

gnarled adj contorted, distorted, gnarly, knotted, knotty, knurled, leathery, rough, rugged, twisted, weather-beaten, wrinkled.

gnaw v bite, chew, consume, devour, distress, eat, erode, fret, harry, haunt, munch, nag, nibble, niggle, plague, prey, trouble, wear, worry.

go v accord, advance, agree, avail, beat it, blend, chime, complement, concur, conduce, connect, contribute, correspond, decamp, decease, depart, develop, die, disappear, elapse, eventuate, expire, extend, fare, fit, flow, function, happen, harmonise, incline, journey, lapse, lead, lead to, leave, make for, match, mosey, move, naff off, nip, operate, pass, pass away, perform, perish,

proceed, progress, rate, reach, repair, result, retreat, roll, run, sally, scram, serve, shift, shove off, slip, sod off, span, spread, stretch, suit, take one's leave, tend, travel, trot, vanish, wag, walk, wend, withdraw, work.

n animation, attempt, bid, crack, drive, dynamism, effort, energy, essay, force, get-up-and-go, life, oomph, pep, shot, spirit, stab, try, turn, verve, vigour, vim, vitality, vivacity, whack, whirl, zest.

go about address, approach, begin, circulate, get abroad, journey, set about, tackle, travel, undertake, wander.

go ahead advance, begin, continue, march on, move, proceed, progress.

go at argue, attack, blame, criticise, impugn, set about, turn on.

go away bugger off, decamp, depart, disappear, eff off, exit, fuck off, get lost, hop it, imshi, leave, piss off, recede, retreat, scat, scram, vanish, withdraw.

go back backslide, desert, forsake, renege, repudiate, retract, retreat, return, revert.

go by adopt, elapse, flow, follow, heed, observe, pass, proceed, trust.

go down collapse, decline, decrease, degenerate, deteriorate, drop, fail, fall, founder, go under, lose, set, sink, submerge, submit, succumb.

go far advance, blaze a trail, do well, progress, succeed.

go for admire, assail, assault, attack, be into, choose, clutch at, dig, enjoy, fall on, favour, fetch, hold with, like, lunge at, obtain, prefer, reach, seek, set about.

go ill with destroy, endanger, harm, imperil, injure, jeopardise, put at hazard, put at risk, ruin.

go in for adopt, embrace, engage in, enter, enter for, espouse, follow, participate in, practise, pursue, take part in, take up, undertake.

go into analyse, begin, check out, consider, delve into, develop, discuss, dissect, enquire into, enter, examine, investigate, make a study of, participate in, probe, pursue, review, scrutinise, study, sus out, undertake.

go mad go bonkers, go crazy, go nuts, take leave of one's senses.

go missing be nowhere to be found, disappear, get lost, vanish.

go off abscond, blow up, decamp, depart, deteriorate, detonate, dislike, explode, fire, happen, leave, occur, part, proceed, quit, rot, turn, vamoose, vanish.

go on behave, blether, chatter, continue, endure, happen, last, last out, occur, persist, prattle, proceed, ramble on, stay, waffle, witter.

go out depart, die out, exit, expire, fade out, leave, obsolesce.

go over detail, examine, inspect, list, overname, peruse, read, recall, recapitulate, rehearse, reiterate, review, revise, scan, skim, study.

go through bear, brave, check, consume, endure, examine, exhaust, experience, explore, face, hunt, investigate, look, rehearse, search, squander, suffer, tolerate, undergo, use, withstand.

go to bed bed down, go to sleep, hit the hay, hit the sack, kip, kip down, retire, turn in.

go together accord, agree, fit, harmonise, match.

go to pieces break down, capitulate, collapse, crack up, crumble, crumple, disintegrate, fall apart, lose control, lose one's head.

go to seed decay, decline, degenerate, deteriorate, go downhill, go to pot, go to waste.

go to the dogs be ruined, degenerate, deteriorate, fail, go down the drain, go to pot, go to rack and ruin.

go under close down, collapse, default, die, drown, fail, fold, founder, go down, sink, submerge, succumb.

go with accompany, agree, blend, complement, concur, correspond, court, date, fit, go steady, harmonise, match, suit.

go wrong boob, break, break down, come to grief, come to nothing, come unstuck, conk out, cut out, err, fail, fall through, flop, go astray, go off the rails, go on the blink, lapse, malfunction, miscarry, misfire, sin, slip up.

goad *n* fillip, impetus, incentive, incitement, irritation, jab, motivation, poke, pressure, prod, push, spur, stimulation, stimulus, thrust, urge.

v annoy, arouse, badger, chivvy, drive, egg on, exasperate, exhort, harass, hassle, hector, hound, impel, incite, infuriate, instigate, irritate, lash, madden, nag, needle, persecute, prick, prod, prompt, propel, push, spur, stimulate, sting, urge, vex, worry.

go-ahead *n* agreement, assent, authorisation, clearance, consent, green light, leave, OK, permission, sanction. *antonyms* ban, embargo, moratorium, veto.

adj ambitious, avant-garde, enterprising, go-getting, pioneering, progressive. *antonyms* sluggish, unenterprising.

goal *n* aim, ambition, aspiration, design, destination, destiny, end, grail, intention, limit, mark, object, objective, purpose, target.

gobble *v* bolt, consume, cram, devour, gorge, gulp, guzzle, hog, put away, shovel, stuff, swallow, wire into, wolf.

go-between *n* agent, broker, contact, dealer, informer, intermediary, liaison, mediator, medium, messenger, middleman.

goblin *n* bogey, demon, fiend, gremlin, hobgoblin, imp, red-cap, spirit, sprite.

God, god *n* Allah, avatar, Brahma, deity, divinity, genius, Godhead, Holy One, idol, Jah, Jehovah, Jove, Lord, Lord God, numen, power, Providence, spirit, the Almighty, the Creator, Yahweh.

god-forsaken *adj* abandoned, backward, bleak, deserted, desolate, dismal, dreary, forlorn, gloomy, isolated, lonely, miserable, neglected, remote, unfrequented, wretched. *antonym* congenial.

godless *adj* atheistic, depraved, evil, heathen, impious, irreligious, irreverent, pagan, profane, sacrilegious, ungodly, unholy, unprincipled, unrighteous, wicked. *antonyms* godly, pious.

godly *adj* blameless, devout, god-fearing, good, holy, innocent, pious, pure, religious, righteous, saintly, virtuous. *antonyms* godless, impious.

godsend *n* blessing, boon, fluke, lucky break, manna, miracle, stroke of luck, windfall. *antonyms* blow, bolt from the blue, bombshell, setback.

going-over *n* analysis, beating, castigation, chastisement, check, check-up, chiding, doing, dressing-down, drubbing, examination, inspection, investigation, lecture, probe, rebuke, reprimand, review, row, scolding, scrutiny, study, survey, thrashing, thumping, treatment, trouncing, whipping.

golden *adj* advantageous, aureate, auric, auspicious, best, blissful, blond(e), bright, brilliant, delightful, excellent, fair, favourable, favoured, flaxen, flourishing, glorious, happy, invaluable, joyful, lustrous, opportune, precious, priceless, promising, propitious, prosperous, resplendent, rich, rosy, shining, successful, timely, valuable, yellow.

gone *adj* absent, astray, away, broken, bygone, closed, concluded, consumed, dead, deceased, defunct, departed, disappeared, done, elapsed, ended, extinct, finished, kaput, lacking, lost, missed, missing, over, over and done with, past, pregnant, spent, used, vanished, wanting.

goo *n* crud, grease, grime, gunge, gunk, matter, mire, muck, mud, ooze, scum, slime, sludge, slush, stickiness.

good *adj* able, acceptable, accomplished, adept, adequate, admirable, adroit, advantageous, agreeable, altruistic, amiable, ample, appropriate, approved, approving, auspicious, authentic, balmy, beneficent, beneficial, benevolent, benign, bona fide, bright, brotherly, buoyant, calm, capable, capital, charitable, cheerful, choice, clear, clever, cloudless, commendable, competent, complete, congenial, considerate, convenient, convivial, correct, decorous, dependable, deserving, dexterous, dutiful, eatable, efficient, enjoyable, entire, estimable, ethical, excellent, exemplary, expert, extensive, fair, favourable, fine, first-class, first-rate, fit, fitting, friendly, full, genuine, gracious, gratifying, great, happy, healthy, helpful, honest, honourable, humane, kind, kindly, large, legitimate, long, loyal, mannerly, merciful, meritorious, mild, moral, nice, noble, nourishing, nutritious, obedient, obliging, opportune, orderly, pious, pleasant, pleasing, pleasurable, polite, positive, praiseworthy, precious, presentable, professional, proficient, profitable, proper, propitious, rattling, real, reliable, right, righteous, safe, salubrious, salutary, satisfactory, satisfying, seemly, serviceable, sizeable, skilful, skilled, solid, sound, special, splendid, substantial, sufficient, suitable, sunny, super, superior, sustaining, talented, tested, thorough, tranquil, true, trustworthy, uncorrupted, untainted, upright, useful, valid, valuable, virtuous, well-behaved, well-disposed, well-mannered, whole, wholesome, worthwhile, worthy.

n advantage, avail, behalf, benefit, boon, convenience, excellence, gain, goodness, interest, merit, morality, probity, profit, rectitude, right, righteousness, service, uprightness, use, usefulness, virtue, weal, welfare, well-being, worth, worthiness.

good health *interj* cheers, kia-ora, prosit, salud, salute, slàinte, your health.
n haleness, hardiness, health, healthiness, heartiness, lustiness, robustness, soundness, strength, vigour, vitality. **antonyms** ill health, invalidism.

good-bye *n, interj* adieu, adiós, arrivederci, au revoir, auf Wiedersehen, chin-chin, ciao, farewell, leave-taking, parting, valediction, valedictory.

good-for-nothing *n* black sheep, bum, drone, idler, layabout, lazy-bones, loafer, ne'er-do-well, profligate, rapscallion, reprobate, waster, wastrel. **antonyms** achiever, success, winner.
adj do-nothing, feckless, idle, indolent, irresponsible, no-good, profligate, reprobate, slothful, useless, worthless. **antonyms** conscientious, successful.

good-humoured *adj* affable, amiable, approachable, blithe, cheerful, congenial, expansive, genial, good-tempered, happy, jovial, pleasant.

good-looking *adj* attractive, beautiful, bonny, comely, easy on the eye, fair, handsome, personable, presentable, pretty, well-favoured, well-proportioned. **antonyms** plain, ugly.

good-natured *adj* agreeable, amenable, approachable, benevolent, broad-minded, friendly, gentle, good-hearted, helpful, kind, kind-hearted, kindly, neighbourly, open-minded, sympathetic, tolerant, warm-hearted. **antonym** ill-natured.

goodness *n* advantage, altruism, beneficence, benefit, benevolence, excellence, fairness, friendliness, generosity, goodwill, graciousness, honesty, honour, humaneness, humanity, integrity, justness, kindliness, kindness, mercy, merit, morality, nourishment, nutrition, piety, probity, quality, rectitude, righteousness, salubriousness, superiority, unselfishness, uprightness, value, virtue, wholesomeness, worth. **antonyms** badness, inferiority, wickedness.

goods *n* bags and baggage, belongings, chattels, commodities, effects, furnishings, furniture, gear, merchandise, movables, paraphernalia, possessions, property, stock, stuff, wares.

goodwill *n* altruism, amity, benevolence, compassion, favour, friendliness, friendship, generosity, heartiness, kindliness, loving-kindness, sincerity, sympathy, zeal. *antonym* ill-will.

goody-goody *adj* pious, priggish, sanctimonious, self-righteous.

gooey *adj* gluey, glutinous, gummy, gungy, maudlin, mawkish, mucilaginous, sentimental, slushy, soft, sticky, syrupy, tacky, thick, viscid, viscous.

gooseflesh *n* creeps, formication, goose bumps, goose-pimples, heebie-jeebies, horripilation, horrors, shivers, shudders.

gore[1] *n* blood, bloodiness, bloodshed, butchery, carnage, slaughter.

gore[2] *v* impale, penetrate, pierce, rend, spear, spit, stab, stick, transfix, wound.

gorge[1] *n* abyss, canyon, chasm, cleft, fissure, gap, gulch, gully, pass, ravine.

gorge[2] *v* bolt, cram, devour, feed, fill, fill one's face, glut, gluttonise, gobble, gormandise, gulp, guzzle, hog, make a pig of oneself, overeat, stuff, surfeit, swallow, wolf. *antonym* abstain.

gorgeous *adj* attractive, beautiful, bright, brilliant, dazzling, delightful, elegant, enjoyable, exquisite, fine, flamboyant, glamorous, glittering, glorious, good, good-looking, grand, lovely, luxuriant, luxurious, magnificent, opulent, pleasing, ravishing, resplendent, rich, showy, splendid, splendiferous, stunning, sumptuous, superb. *antonyms* dull, plain, seedy.

gory *adj* blood-soaked, bloodstained, bloodthirsty, bloody, brutal, murderous, sanguinary, sanguineous, savage.

gospel *n* certainty, credo, creed, doctrine, fact, message, news, revelation, teaching, testament, tidings, truth, verity.

gossamer *adj* airy, cobwebby, delicate, diaphanous, fine, flimsy, gauzy, insubstantial, light, sheer, shimmering, silky, thin, translucent, transparent. *antonyms* heavy, opaque, thick.

gossip[1] *n* blether, bush telegraph, chinwag, chitchat, clash, clash-ma-clavers, hearsay, idle talk, jaw, newsmongering, prattle, report, rumour, scandal, schmooze, small talk, tittle-tattle, yackety-yak.

gossip[2] *n* babbler, blether, busybody, chatterbox, chatterer, gossip-monger, newsmonger, nosy parker, prattler, rumourer, scandalmonger, tattler, telltale, whisperer.

v blether, bruit, chat, clash, gabble, jaw, prattle, rumour, tattle, whisper.

gouge *v* chisel, claw, cut, dig, extract, force, gash, grave, groove, hack, hollow, incise, scoop, score, scratch, slash.

n cut, furrow, gash, groove, hack, hollow, incision, notch, scoop, score, scratch, slash, trench.

govern *v* administer, allay, bridle, check, command, conduct, contain, control, curb, decide, determine, direct, guide, influence, inhibit, lead, manage, master, order, oversee, pilot, preside, quell, regulate, reign, restrain, rule, steer, subdue, superintend, supervise, sway, tame, underlie.

governing *adj* commanding, dominant, guiding, leading, overriding, predominant, prevailing, reigning, ruling, supreme, uppermost.

government *n* administration, authority, charge, command, conduct, control, direction, dominion, Establishment, executive, governance, guidance, law, management, ministry, powers-that-be, régime, regulation, restraint, rule, sovereignty, state, supervision, surveillance, sway.

governor *n* administrator, alderman, boss, chief, commander, commissioner, controller, director, executive, head, leader, manager, overseer, ruler, superintendent, supervisor.

grab *v* affect, annex, appropriate, bag, capture, catch, catch hold of, clutch, collar, commandeer, grasp, grip, impress, latch on to, nab, pluck, seize, snap up, snatch, strike, usurp.

grace *n* attractiveness, beauty, benefaction, beneficence, benevolence, breeding, charity, charm, clemency, comeliness, compassion, consideration, courtesy, cultivation, decency, decorum, deftness, ease, elegance, eloquence, etiquette, favour, finesse, fluency, forgiveness, generosity, goodness, goodwill, gracefulness, graciousness, indulgence, kindliness, kindness, leniency, love, loveliness, mannerliness, manners, mercifulness, mercy, merit, pardon, pleasantness, poise, polish, propriety, refinement, reprieve, shapeliness, tact, tastefulness, unction, virtue.

v adorn, beautify, bedeck, deck, decorate, dignify, distinguish, dress, elevate, embellish, enhance, enrich, favour, garnish, glorify, honour, ornament, prettify, set off, trim. *antonyms* deface, detract from, spoil.

graceful *adj* agile, balletic, beautiful, becoming, charming, comely, deft, easy, elegant, facile, fine, flowing, fluid, gainly, natural, pleasing, pliant, slender, smooth, suave, supple, tasteful, willowy. *antonym* graceless.

graceless *adj* awkward, barbarous, boorish, brazen, clumsy, coarse, crude, forced, gauche, gawky, ill-mannered, improper, incorrigible, indecorous, inelegant, inept, loutish, reprobate, rough, rude, shameless, uncouth, ungainly, ungraceful, unmannerly, unsophisticated, untutored, vulgar. *antonym* graceful.

gracious *adj* accommodating, affable, affluent, amenable, amiable, beneficent, benevolent, benign, charitable, chivalrous, civil, compassionate, complaisant, considerate, cordial, courteous, courtly, elegant, friendly, grand, hospitable, indulgent, kind, kindly, lenient, loving, luxurious, merciful, mild, obliging, pleasant, pleasing, polite, refined, sweet, well-mannered. *antonym* ungracious.

gradation *n* arrangement, array, classification, degree, depth, grade, grading, grouping, level, mark, measurement, notch, ordering, place, point, position, progress, progression, rank, sequence, series, shading, sorting, stage, step, succession.

grade *n* bank, brand, category, class, condition, dan, degree, echelon, gradation, group, level, mark, notch, order, place, position, quality, rank, rise, rung, size, stage, station, step.
v arrange, blend, brand, categorise, class, classify, docket, evaluate, group, label, mark, order, pigeonhole, range, rank, rate, shade, size, sort, type, value.

gradual *adj* cautious, deliberate, even, gentle, graduated, leisurely, measured, moderate, piecemeal, progressive, regular, slow, steady, step-by-step, successive, unhurried. *antonyms* precipitate, sudden.

gradually *adv* bit by bit, by degrees, cautiously, drop by drop, evenly, gently, gingerly, imperceptibly, inch by inch, little by little, moderately, piece by piece, piecemeal, progressively, slowly, steadily, step by step, unhurriedly.

graduate *v* arrange, calibrate, classify, grade, group, make the grade, mark off, measure out, order, pass, proportion, qualify, range, rank, regulate, sort.

grain *n* atom, bit, cereals, corn, crumb, fibre, fragment, granule, grist, grits, iota, jot, kernel, marking, mite, modicum, molecule, morsel, mote, nap, ounce, particle, pattern, piece, scintilla, scrap, seed, smidgeon, spark, speck, surface, suspicion, texture, trace, weave, whit.

grand *adj* A1, admirable, affluent, ambitious, august, chief, dignified, elevated, eminent, exalted, excellent, fine, first-class, first-rate, glorious, gracious, grandiose, great, haughty, head, highest, illustrious, imperious, imposing, impressive, large, leading, lofty, lordly, luxurious, magnificent, main, majestic, marvellous, monumental, noble, opulent, ostentatious, outstanding, palatial, pre-eminent, pretentious, princely, principal, regal, senior, smashing, splendid, stately, striking, sublime, sumptuous, super, superb, supreme, wonderful.

grandeur *n* augustness, dignity, graciousness, greatness, imperiousness, importance, loftiness, magnificence, majesty, nobility, pomp, splendour, state, stateliness, sublimity. *antonyms* humbleness, lowliness, simplicity.

grandiloquent *adj* bombastic, euphuistic, flowery, high-flown, high-sounding, inflated, magniloquent, orotund, pompous, pretentious, rhetorical, swollen, turgid. *antonyms* plain, restrained, simple.

grandiose *adj* affected, ambitious, bombastic, euphuistic, extravagant, flamboyant, grand, high-flown, imposing, impressive, lofty, magnificent, majestic, monumental, ostentatious, pompous, ponderous, pretentious, showy, stately, weighty. *antonym* unpretentious.

grant *v* accede to, accord, acknowledge, admit, agree to, allocate, allot, allow, apportion, assign, award, bestow, cede, concede, confer, consent to, deign, dispense, donate, give, impart, permit, present, provide, transfer, transmit, vouchsafe, yield. *antonyms* deny, refuse.
n accord, admission, allocation, allotment, allowance, annuity, award, benefaction, bequest, bounty, bursary, concession, donation, endowment, gift, honorarium, present, scholarship, subsidy, subvention.

granule *n* atom, bead, crumb, fragment, grain, iota, jot, molecule, particle, pellet, scrap, seed, speck.

graphic *adj* blow-by-blow, clear, cogent, descriptive, detailed, diagrammatic, drawn, explicit, expressive, forcible, illustrative, lively, lucid, pictorial, picturesque, representational, seen, specific, striking, telling, visible, visual, vivid. **antonyms** impressionistic, vague.

grapple v attack, battle, catch, clash, clasp, clinch, close, clutch, combat, come to grips, confront, contend, cope, deal with, encounter, engage, face, fasten, fight, grab, grasp, grip, gripe, hold, hug, lay hold, make fast, seize, snatch, struggle, tackle, tussle, wrestle. **antonyms** avoid, evade.

grasp v catch, catch on, clasp, clinch, clutch, comprehend, follow, get, grab, grapple, grip, gripe, hold, hold, lay hold of, realise, savvy, see, seize, snatch, twig, understand.

n acquaintance, apprehension, awareness, capacity, clasp, clutches, compass, competence, comprehension, control, embrace, expertness, extent, familiarity, grip, hold, holt, intimacy, ken, knowledge, mastery, perception, possession, power, range, reach, realisation, scope, sway, sweep, tenure, understanding.

grasping adj acquisitive, avaricious, close-fisted, covetous, greedy, mean, mercenary, miserly, niggardly, parsimonious, penny-pinching, rapacious, selfish, stingy, tight-fisted, usurious. **antonym** generous.

grate v aggravate, annoy, chafe, exasperate, fret, gall, get on one's nerves, granulate, grind, irk, irritate, jar, mince, nettle, peeve, pulverise, rankle, rasp, rub, scrape, scratch, set one's teeth on edge, shred, vex.

grateful adj appreciative, aware, beholden, indebted, mindful, obligated, obliged, sensible, thankful. **antonym** ungrateful.

gratification n contentment, delight, elation, enjoyment, fruition, fulfilment, glee, indulgence, joy, jubilation, kicks, pleasure, recompense, relish, reward, satisfaction, thrill, triumph. **antonym** frustration.

gratify v appease, cater to, content, delight, favour, fulfil, gladden, humour, indulge, pander to, please, pleasure, recompense, requite, satisfy, thrill. **antonyms** frustrate, thwart.

grating adj annoying, cacophonous, disagreeable, discordant, displeasing, grinding, harsh, irksome, irritating, jarring, rasping, raucous, scraping, squeaky, strident, unharmonious, unmelodious, unpleasant, vexatious. **antonyms** harmonious, pleasing.

gratitude n acknowledgement, appreciation, awareness, gratefulness, indebtedness, mindfulness, obligation, recognition, thankfulness, thanks. **antonym** ingratitude.

gratuitous adj assumed, baseless, buckshee, causeless, complimentary, free, gratis, groundless, irrelevant, needless, spontaneous, superfluous, unasked-for, uncalled-for, undeserved, unearned, unfounded, unjustified, unmerited, unnecessary, unpaid, unprovoked, unrewarded, unsolicited, unwarranted, voluntary, wanton. **antonyms** justified, reasonable.

grave[1] n barrow, burial-place, crypt, mausoleum, pit, sepulchre, tomb, vault.

grave[2] adj acute, Catonian, critical, crucial, dangerous, depressing, dignified, disquieting, dour, dull, earnest, exigent, gloomy, grim, grim-faced, hazardous, heavy, important, leaden, long-faced, momentous, muted, perilous, ponderous, preoccupied, pressing, quiet, reserved, restrained, sad, sage, saturnine, sedate, serious, severe, significant, sober, solemn, sombre, staid, subdued, thoughtful, threatening, unsmiling, urgent, vital, weighty. **antonyms** cheerful, light, slight, trivial.

gravitate v descend, drop, fall, head for, incline, lean, move, precipitate, settle, sink, tend.

gravity n acuteness, consequence, demureness, dignity, earnestness, exigency, gloom, gravitas, grimness, hazardousness, importance, magnitude, moment, momentousness, perilousness, ponderousness, reserve, restraint, sedateness, seriousness, severity, significance, sobriety, solemnity, sombreness, thoughtfulness, urgency, weightiness. **antonyms** gaiety, levity, triviality.

graze v abrade, brush, chafe, gride, rub, scart, score, scrape, scratch, shave, skim, skin, touch.

n abrasion, score, scrape, scratch.

greasy adj fatty, fawning, glib, grovelling, ingratiating, oily, oleaginous, sebaceous, slick, slimy, slippery, smarmy, smeary, smooth, sycophantic, tallowy, toadying, unctuous, waxy.

great adj able, ace, active, adept, admirable, adroit, august, big, bulky, capital, celebrated, chief, colossal, consequential, considerable, crack, critical, crucial, decided, devoted, dignified, distinguished, eminent, enormous, enthusiastic, exalted, excellent, excessive, expert, extended, extensive, extravagant, extreme, fab, fabulous, famed, famous, fantastic, fine, finished, first-rate, generous, gigantic, glorious, good, grand, grave, great-hearted, grievous, heavy, heroic, high, high-minded, huge, idealistic, illustrious, immense, important, impressive, inordinate, invaluable, jake, keen, large, leading, lengthy, lofty, long, magnanimous, main, major, mammoth, manifold, marked, marvellous, massive, masterly, momentous, multitudinous, munificent, noble, notable, noteworthy, noticeable, outstanding, paramount, ponderous, precious, pre-eminent, priceless, primary, princely, principal, prodigious, proficient, prolific, prolonged, prominent, pronounced, protracted, remarkable, renowned, senior, serious, significant, skilful, skilled, strong, stupendous, sublime, superb, superior, superlative, swingeing, talented, terrific, tremendous, valuable, vast, virtuoso, voluminous, weighty, wonderful, zealous. *antonyms* insignificant, pusillanimous, small, unimportant.

greatly *adv* abundantly, considerably, enormously, exceedingly, extremely, highly, hugely, immensely, impressively, markedly, mightily, much, notably, noticeably, powerfully, remarkably, significantly, substantially, tremendously, vastly.

greatness *n* amplitude, bulk, celebrity, dignity, distinction, eminence, excellence, fame, force, generosity, genius, glory, grandeur, gravity, heaviness, heroism, high-mindedness, hugeness, idealism, illustriousness, immensity, import, importance, intensity, largeness, length, loftiness, lustre, magnanimity, magnitude, majesty, mass, moment, momentousness, nobility, nobleness, note, potency, power, prodigiousness, renown, seriousness, significance, size, stateliness, strength, sublimity, superbness, urgency, vastness, weight. *antonyms* insignificance, pettiness, pusillanimity, smallness.

greed *n* acquisitiveness, anxiety, avidity, covetousness, craving, desire, eagerness, gluttony, gormandising, greediness, hunger, insatiability, itchy palm, longing, ravenousness, selfishness, voraciousness, voracity. *antonym* abstemiousness.

greedy *adj* acquisitive, anxious, avaricious, avid, covetous, craving, curious, eager, gluttonish, gluttonous, gormandising, grasping, gutsy, hungry, impatient, itchy-palmed, money-grubbing, rapacious, ravenous, selfish, voracious. *antonym* abstemious.

green *adj* blooming, budding, callow, covetous, credulous, emerald, envious, flourishing, fresh, glaucous, grassy, grudging, gullible, ignorant, ill, immature, inexperienced, inexpert, ingenuous, innocent, jealous, leafy, naive, nauseous, new, pale, pliable, raw, recent, resentful, sick, starry-eyed, supple, tender, unhealthy, unpractised, unripe, unseasoned, unsophisticated, untrained, untried, unversed, verdant, wan, wet behind the ears, young.

greet *v* accost, acknowledge, address, compliment, hail, hallo, halloo, meet, receive, salute, wave to, welcome. *antonym* ignore.

greeting *n* acknowledgement, address, aloha, hail, reception, salaam, salutation, salute, the time of day, welcome.

greetings *n* best wishes, civilities, compliments, formalities, good wishes, love, regards, respects, salutations.

gregarious *adj* affable, chummy, companionable, convivial, cordial, extrovert, friendly, outgoing, pally, sociable, social, warm. *antonym* unsociable.

grey *adj* aged, ancient, anonymous, ashen, bloodless, characterless, cheerless, cloudy, colourless, dark, depressing, dim, dismal, drab, dreary, dull, elderly, experienced, glaucous, gloomy, grizzled, hoary, indistinct, leaden, mature, murky, neutral, old, overcast, pale, pallid, sunless, uncertain, unclear, unidentifiable, wan.

grief *n* ache, affliction, agony, anguish, bereavement, blow, burden, dejection, desolation, distress, dole, grievance, heartache, heartbreak, lamentation, misery, mournfulness, mourning, pain, regret, remorse, sadness, sorrow, suffering, tragedy, trial, tribulation, trouble, woe. *antonym* happiness.

grief-stricken *adj* afflicted, agonised, broken, broken-hearted, crushed, desolate, despairing, devastated, disconsolate, distracted, grieving, heartbroken, inconsolable, mourning, overcome, overwhelmed, sad, sorrowful, sorrowing, stricken, unhappy, woebegone, wretched. *antonym* overjoyed.

grievance *n* affliction, beef, charge, complaint, damage, distress, grief, gripe, grouse, hardship, injury, injustice, moan, peeve, resentment, sorrow, trial, tribulation, trouble, unhappiness, wrong.

grieve *v* ache, afflict, agonise, bemoan, bewail, complain, crush, cut to the quick, deplore, distress, disturb, eat one's heart out, hurt, injure, lament, mourn, pain, regret, rue, sadden, sorrow, suffer, upset, wail, weep, wound.

grievous *adj* appalling, atrocious, calamitous, damaging, deplorable, devastating, distressing, dreadful, flagrant, glaring, grave, harmful, heart-rending, heavy, heinous, hurtful, injurious, intolerable, lamentable, monstrous, mournful, offensive, oppressive, outrageous, overwhelming, painful, pitiful, plightful, severe, shameful, shocking, sorrowful, tragic, unbearable, wounding.

grim *adj* cruel, doom-laden, dour, fearsome, ferocious, fierce, forbidding, formidable, frightening, frightful, ghastly, grisly, gruesome, harsh, hideous, horrible, horrid, implacable, merciless, morose, relentless, repellent, resolute, ruthless, severe, shocking, sinister, stern, sullen, surly, terrible, unpleasant, unrelenting, unwelcome, unyielding.
antonyms benign, congenial, pleasant.

grimace *n* face, frown, mouth, pout, scowl, smirk, sneer.
v fleer, frown, girn, make a face, mouth, pout, scowl, smirk, sneer.

grimy *adj* besmirched, contaminated, dirty, filthy, foul, grubby, murky, smudgy, smutty, soiled, sooty, squalid.
antonyms clean, pure.

grind *v* abrade, crush, drudge, file, gnash, granulate, grate, grit, kibble, labour, mill, polish, pound, powder, pulverise, sand, scrape, sharpen, slave, smooth, sweat, swot, toil, whet.
n chore, drudgery, exertion, labour, round, routine, slavery, sweat, task, toil.

grind down afflict, crush, harass, harry, hound, oppress, persecute, plague, trouble, tyrannise.

grip *n* acquaintance, clasp, clutches, comprehension, control, domination, embrace, grasp, hold, influence, keeping, mastery, perception, possession, power, purchase, sway, tenure, understanding.
v absorb, catch, clasp, clutch, compel, divert, engross, enthrall, entrance, fascinate, grasp, hold, involve, latch on to, mesmerise, rivet, seize, spellbind, thrill, vice.

gripe *v* beef, bellyache, bitch, carp, complain, groan, grouch, grouse, grumble, moan, nag, whine, whinge.
n ache, aching, affliction, beef, colic, collywobbles, complaint, cramps, distress, grievance, groan, grouch, grouse, grumble, moan, objection, pain, pang, pinching, spasm, stomach-ache, twinge.

gripping *adj* absorbing, compelling, compulsive, diverting, engrossing, enthralling, entrancing, exciting, fascinating, riveting, spellbinding, suspenseful, thrilling, unputdownable.

grisly *adj* abominable, appalling, awful, dreadful, frightful, ghastly, grim, gruesome, hair-raising, hideous, horrible, horrid, macabre, shocking, sickening, terrible, terrifying, weird.
antonym delightful.

grit *n* backbone, bottle, bravery, courage, determination, doggedness, fortitude, guts, mettle, nerve, perseverance, pluck, resolution, spine, spirit, spunk, stamina, staying power, tenacity, toughness.

gritty *adj* abrasive, brave, courageous, determined, dogged, game, grainy, granular, gravelly, hardy, pebbly, plucky, resolute, rough, sandy, shingly, spirited, spunky, steadfast, tenacious, tough.
antonyms fine, smooth, spineless.

groan *n* complaint, cry, moan, objection, outcry, protest, sigh, wail. ***antonym*** cheer.
v complain, cry, lament, moan, object, protest, sigh, wail. ***antonym*** cheer.

groggy *adj* confused, dazed, dizzy, dopey, faint, fuddled, muzzy, punch-drunk, reeling, shaky, stunned, stupefied, unsteady, weak, wobbly, woozy.
antonym lucid.

groom *v* brush, clean, coach, dress, drill, educate, neaten, nurture, preen, prepare, prime, ready, school, smarten, spruce up, tart up, tend, tidy, titivate, train, turn out, tutor.

groove *n* canal, chamfer, channel, chase, cut, cutting, flute, furrow, gutter, hollow, indentation, rebate, rut, score, trench.
antonym ridge.

grope *v* cast about, feel, feel about, feel up, finger, fish, flounder, fumble, goose, grabble, probe, scrabble, search.

gross[1] *adj* apparent, arrant, bawdy, bestial, big, blatant, blue, boorish, broad, brutish, bulky, callous, coarse, colossal, corpulent, crass, crude, cumbersome, dense, downright, dull, earthy, egregious, fat, flagrant, foul, glaring, great, grievous, heavy, heinous, huge, hulking, ignorant, immense, imperceptive, improper, impure, indecent, indelicate, insensitive, large, lewd, low, manifest, massive, obese, obscene, obtuse, obvious, offensive, outrageous, outright, overweight, plain, rank, ribald, rude, sensual, serious, shameful, shameless, sheer, shocking, slow, sluggish, smutty, tasteless, thick, uncivil, uncouth, uncultured, undiscriminating, undisguised, unfeeling, unmitigated, unseemly, unsophisticated, unwieldy, utter, vulgar. **antonyms** delicate, fine, seemly, slight.

gross² n aggregate, bulk, entirety, sum, total, totality, whole.

adj aggregate, all-inclusive, complete, entire, inclusive, total, whole.

v accumulate, aggregate, bring, earn, make, rake in, take, total.

grotesque adj absurd, bizarre, deformed, distorted, extravagant, fanciful, fantastic, freakish, gruesome, hideous, incongruous, laughable, ludicrous, macabre, malformed, misshapen, monstrous, odd, outlandish, preposterous, ridiculous, strange, ugly, unnatural, unsightly, weird.

grouch v beef, bellyache, carp, complain, find fault, gripe, grouse, grumble, moan, whine, whinge. **antonym** acquiesce.

n complaint, crab, fault-finder, grievance, gripe, grouse, grumble, moan, objection, whine, whinge.

grouchy adj bad-tempered, cantankerous, captious, complaining, cross, crotchety, discontented, dissatisfied, grumbling, grumpy, ill-tempered, irascible, irritable, mutinous, peevish, petulant, querulous, sulky, surly, testy, truculent. **antonym** contented.

ground n arena, background, ball-park, bottom, clay, clod, deck, dirt, dry land, dust, earth, field, foundation, land, loam, mould, park, pitch, sod, soil, stadium, surface, terra firma, terrain, turf.

v acquaint with, base, build up, coach, drill, establish, familiarise with, fix, found, inform, initiate, instruct, introduce, prepare, set, settle, teach, train, tutor.

groundless adj absurd, baseless, chimerical, empty, false, gratuitous, idle, illusory, imaginary, irrational, unauthorised, uncalled-for, unfounded, unjustified, unproven, unprovoked, unreasonable, unsubstantiated, unsupported, unwarranted. **antonyms** justified, reasonable.

grounds¹ n acres, area, country, district, domain, estate, fields, gardens, habitat, holding, land, park, property, realm, surroundings, terrain, territory, tract.

grounds² n account, argument, base, basis, call, cause, excuse, factor, foundation, inducement, justification, motive, occasion, premise, pretext, principle, rationale, reason, score, vindication.

groundwork n base, basis, cornerstone, essentials, footing, foundation, fundamentals, homework, preliminaries, preparation, research, spadework.

group n accumulation, aggregation, assemblage, association, band, batch, bracket, bunch, category, circle, class, classification, clique, clump, cluster, clutch, cohort, collection, collective, combination, company, conclave, conglomeration, congregation, constellation, coterie, crowd, detachment, faction, formation, front, gang, gathering, genus, grouping, knot, lot, nexus, organisation, pack, parti, party, pop-group, set, shower, species, squad, squadron, team, troop.

v arrange, assemble, associate, assort, band, bracket, categorise, class, classify, cluster, collect, congregate, deploy, dispose, fraternise, gather, get together, link, marshal, mass, order, organise, range, sort.

grouse v beef, belly-ache, carp, complain, find fault, fret, gripe, grouch, grumble, moan, mutter, whine, whinge. **antonym** acquiesce.

n belly-ache, complaint, grievance, gripe, grouch, grumble, moan, murmur, mutter, objection, whine, whinge.

grovel v backscratch, bootlick, cower, crawl, creep, cringe, defer, demean oneself, fawn, flatter, kowtow, sycophantise, toady.

grovelling adj backscratching, bootlicking, fawning, flattering, ingratiating, obsequious, sycophantic, wormy. **antonyms** outspoken, straightforward.

grow v advance, arise, augment, become, branch out, breed, broaden, burgeon, cultivate, develop, diversify, enlarge, evolve, expand, extend, farm, flourish, flower, germinate, get, heighten, improve, increase, issue, mature, multiply, originate, produce, progress, proliferate, propagate, prosper, raise, ripen, rise, shoot, spread, spring, sprout, stem, stretch, succeed, swell, thicken, thrive, turn, wax, widen. **antonyms** decrease, fail, halt.

growing *adj* blossoming, broadening, burgeoning, deepening, developing, enlarging, escalating, expanding, extending, flourishing, heightening, increasing, lengthening, maturing, mounting, multiplying, proliferating, rising, spreading, swelling, thickening, thriving, waxing, widening. **antonyms** decreasing, failing, stagnant, static, waning.

growl *v* snap, snarl, yap.

growth *n* advance, advancement, aggrandisement, augmentation, broadening, change, crop, cultivation, development, diversification, enlargement, evolution, excrement, excrescence, expansion, extension, flowering, gall, germination, growing, heightening, improvement, increase, lump, maturation, multiplication, outgrowth, produce, production, progress, proliferation, prosperity, protuberance, ripening, rise, shooting, sprouting, stretching, success, swelling, thickening, transformation, tumour, vegetation, waxing, widening. **antonyms** decrease, failure, stagnation, stoppage.

grub[1] *v* burrow, delve, dig, explore, ferret, forage, grout, hunt, investigate, nose, probe, pull up, root, rummage, scour, uproot.
n caterpillar, chrysalis, larva, maggot, pupa, worm.

grub[2] *n* chow, eats, edibles, fodder, food, nosh, provisions, rations, scoff.

grubby *adj* crummy, dirty, filthy, flyblown, frowzy, grimy, manky, mean, messy, mucky, scruffy, seedy, shabby, slovenly, smutty, soiled, sordid, squalid, unkempt, untidy, unwashed. **antonyms** clean, smart.

grudge *n* animosity, animus, antagonism, antipathy, aversion, bitterness, dislike, enmity, envy, grievance, hard feelings, hate, ill-will, jealousy, malevolence, malice, pique, rancour, resentment, spite. **antonyms** favour, regard.
v begrudge, covet, dislike, envy, mind, object to, regret, repine, resent, stint, take exception to. **antonyms** applaud, approve.

grudging *adj* cautious, guarded, half-hearted, hesitant, reluctant, secret, unenthusiastic, unwilling.

gruelling *adj* arduous, backbreaking, brutal, crushing, demanding, difficult, exhausting, fatiguing, fierce, grinding, hard, hard-going, harsh, laborious, punishing, severe, stern, stiff, strenuous, taxing, tiring, tough, trying, uphill, wearing, wearying. **antonym** easy.

gruesome *adj* abominable, awful, chilling, fearful, fearsome, ghastly, grim, grisly, grooly, hideous, horrible, horrid, horrific, horrifying, loathsome, macabre, monstrous, repellent, repugnant, repulsive, shocking, sick, spine-chilling, terrible, weird. **antonyms** charming, congenial.

gruff *adj* abrupt, bad-tempered, bearish, blunt, brusque, churlish, crabbed, croaking, crusty, curt, discourteous, gravelly, grouchy, grumpy, guttural, harsh, hoarse, husky, ill-humoured, ill-natured, impolite, low, rasping, rough, rude, sour, sullen, surly, throaty, uncivil, ungracious, unmannerly. **antonyms** clear, courteous, sweet.

grumble *v* beef, bellyache, bitch, bleat, carp, chunter, complain, croak, find fault, gripe, grouch, grouse, growl, gurgle, moan, murmur, mutter, nark, repine, roar, rumble, whine. **antonym** acquiesce.
n beef, bleat, complaint, grievance, gripe, grouch, grouse, growl, gurgle, moan, murmur, muttering, objection, roar, rumble, whinge.

grumpy *adj* bad-tempered, cantankerous, churlish, crabbed, cross, crotchety, discontented, grouchy, grumbling, ill-tempered, irritable, mutinous, peevish, petulant, querulous, sulky, sullen, surly, testy, truculent. **antonyms** civil, contented.

guarantee *n* assurance, attestation, bond, certainty, collateral, covenant, earnest, endorsement, insurance, oath, pledge, promise, security, surety, testimonial, undertaking, voucher, warranty, word, word of honour.
v answer for, assure, avouch, certify, ensure, insure, maintain, make certain, make sure of, pledge, promise, protect, secure, swear, underwrite, vouch for, warrant.

guard *v* be on the watch, beware, conserve, cover, defend, escort, keep, look out, mind, oversee, patrol, police, preserve, protect, safeguard, save, screen, secure, shelter, shield, supervise, tend, ward, watch.
n attention, barrier, buffer, bulwark, bumper, care, caution, convoy,

custodian, defence, defender, escort, guarantee, heed, lookout, minder, pad, patrol, picket, precaution, protection, protector, rampart, safeguard, screen, security, sentinel, sentry, shield, vigilance, wall, warder, wariness, watch, watchfulness, watchman.

guarded *adj* cagey, careful, cautious, circumspect, discreet, disingenuous, non-committal, prudent, reserved, restrained, reticent, secretive, suspicious, uncommunicative, unforthcoming, wary, watchful. **antonyms** frank, whole-hearted.

guardian *n* attendant, carer, champion, conservator, curator, custodian, defender, depositary, depository, escort, guard, keeper, minder, preserver, protector, trustee, warden, warder.

guess *v* assume, believe, conjecture, dare say, deem, divine, estimate, fancy, fathom, feel, guesstimate, hazard, hypothesise, imagine, intuit, judge, opine, penetrate, predict, reckon, solve, speculate, suppose, surmise, suspect, think, work out.

n assumption, belief, conjecture, fancy, feeling, guesstimate, hypothesis, intuition, judgement, notion, opinion, prediction, reckoning, shot (in the dark), speculation, supposition, surmise, suspicion, theory.

guesswork *n* assumption, conjecture, estimation, intuition, presumption, presupposition, reckoning, speculation, supposition, surmise, suspicion, theory.

guidance *n* advice, aegis, auspices, clues, conduct, control, counsel, counselling, direction, government, guidelines, help, illumination, indications, instruction, leadership, management, pointers, recommendation, regulation, steering, teaching.

guide *v* accompany, advise, attend, command, conduct, control, convoy, counsel, direct, educate, escort, govern, handle, head, influence, instruct, lead, manage, manoeuvre, oversee, pilot, point, regulate, rule, shape, shepherd, steer, superintend, supervise, sway, teach, train, usher.

n ABC, adviser, attendant, beacon, catalogue, chaperon, clue, companion, conductor, controller, counsellor, courier, criterion, director, directory, escort, example, exemplar, guide-book, guideline, handbook, index, indication, informant, inspiration, instructions, key, landmark, leader, lodestar, manual,

mark, marker, master, mentor, model, pilot, pointer, sign, signal, signpost, standard, steersman, teacher, usher.

guiding *adj* advisory, consultant, consultative, consultatory, consulting, controlling, counselling, directorial, directory, formative, governing, influential, instructional, instructive, managing, monitoring, piloting, shepherding, steering, supervisory, tutorial.

guild *n* association, brotherhood, chapel, club, company, corporation, fellowship, fraternity, incorporation, league, lodge, order, organisation, society, union.

guile *n* art, artfulness, artifice, cleverness, craftiness, cunning, deceit, deception, deviousness, duplicity, gamesmanship, slyness, treachery, trickery, trickiness, wiliness. **antonyms** artlessness, guilelessness.

guileful *adj* artful, clever, crafty, cunning, deceitful, devious, disingenuous, duplicitous, sly, sneaky, treacherous, tricky, underhand, wily. **antonyms** artless, guileless.

guileless *adj* artless, candid, direct, frank, genuine, honest, ingenuous, innocent, naïve, natural, open, simple, sincere, straightforward, transparent, trusting, truthful, unreserved, unworldly. **antonyms** artful, guileful.

guilt *n* blame, blameworthiness, compunction, conscience, contrition, criminality, culpability, delinquency, disgrace, dishonour, guiltiness, guilty conscience, infamy, iniquity, regret, remorse, responsibility, self-condemnation, self-reproach, self-reproof, shame, sinfulness, stigma, wickedness, wrong. **antonyms** innocence, shamelessness.

guiltless *adj* blameless, clean, clear, immaculate, impeccable, inculpable, innocent, irreproachable, pure, sinless, spotless, unimpeachable, unspotted, unsullied, untainted, untarnished. **antonyms** guilty, tainted.

guilty *adj* ashamed, blamable, blame-worthy, compunctious, conscience-stricken, contrite, convicted, criminal, culpable, delinquent, errant, erring, evil, felonious, guilt-ridden, hangdog, illicit, iniquitous, nefarious, offending, penitent, regretful, remorseful, repentant, reprehensible, responsible, rueful, shamefaced, sheepish, sinful, sorry, wicked, wrong. **antonyms** guiltless, innocent.

guise *n* air, appearance, aspect,

behaviour, custom, demeanour, disguise, dress, façade, face, fashion, features, form, front, likeness, manner, mask, mode, pretence, semblance, shape, show.

gulf *n* abyss, basin, bay, breach, chasm, cleft, gap, gorge, opening, rent, rift, separation, split, void.

gullibility *n* credulity, innocence, naïvety, simplicity, trustfulness. *antonym* astuteness.

gullible *adj* born yesterday, credulous, foolish, green, innocent, naïve, trusting, unsuspecting. *antonym* astute.

gulp *v* bolt, choke, devour, gasp, gobble, guzzle, knock back, quaff, stifle, stuff, swallow, swig, swill, wolf. *antonyms* nibble, sip.
n draught, mouthful, slug, swallow, swig.

gum *n* adhesive, cement, glue, goo, mucilage, paste, resin, sap.
v affix, block, cement, clog, fix, glue, paste, seal, stick.

gummy *adj* adhesive, gluey, gooey, sticky, tacky, viscid, viscous.

gumption *n* ability, acumen, acuteness, astuteness, cleverness, common sense, discernment, enterprise, initiative, mother wit, nous, resourcefulness, sagacity, savvy, shrewdness, spirit, wit(s). *antonym* foolishness.

gunman *n* assassin, bandit, desperado, gangster, gunslinger, hatchet man, hit man, killer, mobster, murderer, shootist, sniper, terrorist, thug.

gurgle *v* babble, bubble, burble, guggle, lap, murmur, plash, purl, ripple, splash.
n babble, guggle, murmur, purl, ripple.

guru *n* authority, instructor, leader, luminary, master, mentor, pundit, sage, Svengali, swami, teacher, tutor.

gush *v* babble, burst, cascade, chatter, drivel, effuse, enthuse, flood, flow, fountain, jabber, jet, pour, run, rush, spout, spurt, stream, yatter.
n babble, burst, cascade, chatter, effusion, flood, flow, jet, outburst, outflow, rush, spout, spurt, stream, tide, torrent.

gushing *adj* cloying, effusive, emotional, excessive, gushy, mawkish, over-enthusiastic, saccharine, sentimental, sickly. *antonyms* restrained, sincere.

gust *n* blast, blow, breeze, burst, flaught, flaw, flurry, gale, puff, rush, squall, williwaw.
v blast, blow, bluster, breeze, puff, squall.

gusto *n* appetite, appreciation, brio, delight, élan, enjoyment, enthusiasm, exhilaration, exuberance, fervour, liking, pleasure, relish, savour, verve, zeal, zest. *antonyms* apathy, distaste.

gut *v* clean, clean out, despoil, disembowel, empty, pillage, plunder, ransack, ravage, rifle, sack, strip.
adj basic, deep-seated, emotional, heartfelt, innate, instinctive, intuitive, involuntary, natural, spontaneous, strong, unthinking.

gutless *adj* abject, chicken, chicken-hearted, chicken-livered, cowardly, craven, faint-hearted, feeble, irresolute, lily-livered, spineless, submissive, timid, weak. *antonym* courageous.

guts *n* audacity, backbone, belly, boldness, bottle, bowels, courage, daring, endurance, entrails, forcefulness, grit, innards, insides, intestines, mettle, nerve, paunch, pluck, spirit, spunk, stamina, staying power, stomach, tenacity, toughness, viscera. *antonym* spinelessness.

gutsy *adj* bold, brave, courageous, determined, gallant, game, indomitable, mettlesome, passionate, plucky, resolute, spirited, staunch. *antonyms* quiet, timid.

guy *n* bloke, buffer, cat, chap, codger, cove, customer, fellow, individual, lad, man, person, punter, youth.

guzzle *v* bolt, carouse, cram, devour, gobble, stuff, wolf.

gypsy, gipsy *n* Bohemian, nomad, rambler, roamer, Romany, rover, tink, tinker, traveller, vagabond, vagrant, wanderer.

H

habit *n* addiction, bent, convention, custom, dependence, disposition, fixation, frame of mind, inclination, make-up, manner, mannerism, mode, nature, obsession, practice, proclivity, propensity, quirk, routine, rule, second nature, tendency, usage, vice, way, weakness, wont.

habitat *n* abode, domain, element, environment, home, locality, surroundings, terrain, territory.

habitation *n* abode, domicile, dwelling, dwelling-place, home, house, living quarters, lodging, quarters, residence.

habitual *adj* accustomed, chronic, common, confirmed, constant, customary, established, familiar, fixed, frequent, hardened, ingrained, inveterate, natural, normal, ordinary, persistent, recurrent, regular, routine, standard, traditional, usual, wonted. **antonym** occasional.

habituate *v* acclimatise, accustom, break in, condition, discipline, familiarise, harden, inure, school, season, tame, train.

hack¹ *v* bark, chop, cough, cut, gash, haggle, hew, kick, lacerate, mangle, mutilate, notch, rasp, slash.
n bark, chop, cough, cut, gash, notch, rasp, slash.

hack² *adj* banal, hackneyed, mediocre, pedestrian, poor, stereotyped, tired, undistinguished, uninspired, unoriginal.
n journalist, paper-stainer, penny-a-liner, scribbler.

hackneyed *adj* banal, clichéd, common, commonplace, corny, hack, overworked, pedestrian, played-out, run-of-the-mill, second-hand, stale, stereotyped, stock, time-worn, tired, trite, unoriginal, worn-out. **antonyms** arresting, new.

hag *n* battle-axe, crone, fury, harpy, harridan, ogress, shrew, termagant, virago, vixen, witch.

haggard *adj* cadaverous, careworn, drawn, emaciated, gaunt, ghastly, hollow-eyed, pinched, shrunken, thin, wan, wasted, wrinkled. **antonym** hale.

haggle *v* bargain, barter, bicker, chaffer, dicker, dispute, quarrel, squabble, wrangle.

hail¹ *n* barrage, bombardment, rain, shower, storm, torrent, volley.
v assail, barrage, batter, bombard, pelt, rain, shower, storm, volley.

hail² *v* acclaim, accost, acknowledge, address, applaud, call, cheer, exalt, flag down, glorify, greet, halloo, honour, salute, shout, signal to, wave, welcome.
n call, cry, halloo, holla, shout.

hair-raising *adj* alarming, blood-curdling, breathtaking, creepy, eerie, exciting, frightening, ghastly, ghostly, horrifying, petrifying, scary, shocking, spine-chilling, startling, terrifying, thrilling. **antonym** calming.

hair-splitting *adj* captious, carping, fault-finding, fine, finicky, nice, niggling, nit-picking, overnice, over-refined, quibbling, subtle, word-splitting. **antonym** unfussy.

hairy *adj* bearded, bushy, dangerous, dicey, difficult, fleecy, furry, hazardous, hirsute, perilous, risky, scaring, shaggy, stubbly, tricky, woolly. **antonyms** bald, clean-shaven.

halcyon *adj* balmy, calm, carefree, flourishing, gentle, golden, happy, mild, pacific, peaceful, placid, prosperous, quiet, serene, still, tranquil, undisturbed. **antonym** stormy.

hale *adj* able-bodied, athletic, blooming, fit, flourishing, healthy, hearty, in fine fettle, in the pink, robust, sound, strong, vigorous, well, youthful. **antonym** ill.

half *n* division, fifty per cent, fraction, half-back, half-share, hemisphere, portion, section, segment, term.
adj divided, halved, incomplete, limited, moderate, part, partial, semi-. **antonym** whole.
adv barely, imperfectly, in part, inadequately, incompletely, partially, partly, slightly. **antonym** completely.

half-baked *adj* brainless, crazy, foolish, harebrained, ill-conceived, ill-judged, impractical, senseless, short-sighted, silly, stupid, unplanned. **antonym** sensible.

half-hearted *adj* apathetic, cool, indifferent, lackadaisical, lacklustre, listless, lukewarm, neutral, passive, perfunctory, uninterested. **antonym** enthusiastic.

halfway *adv* barely, imperfectly, in the middle, incompletely, midway, moderately, nearly, partially, partly, rather, slightly. **antonym** completely.
adj central, equidistant, incomplete,

intermediate, mid, middle, midway, partial, part-way. **antonym** complete.

half-wit n cretin, dimwit, dolt, dunce, dunderhead, fool, idiot, imbecile, moron, nitwit, nut, simpleton. **antonym** brain.

half-witted adj barmy, batty, crazy, cretinous, dull, dull-witted, feeble-minded, foolish, idiotic, moronic, nuts, nutty, silly, simple, simple-minded, stupid, two bricks short of a load. **antonym** clever.

hallmark n authentication, badge, brand-name, device, emblem, endorsement, indication, mark, seal, sign, stamp, symbol, trademark.

hallo see **hello**.

hallowed adj age-old, beatified, blessed, consecrated, dedicated, established, holy, honoured, inviolable, revered, sacred, sacrosanct, sanctified.

hallucinate v daydream, fantasise, freak out, imagine, trip.

hallucination n apparition, delusion, dream, fantasy, figment, illusion, mirage, phantasmagoria, pink elephants, vision.

halo n aura, aureole, gloriole, glory, nimbus, radiance.

halt v arrest, block, break off, call it a day, cease, check, curb, desist, draw up, end, impede, obstruct, pack it in, quit, rest, stem, stop, terminate, wait. **antonyms** assist, continue, start.
n arrest, break, close, end, impasse, interruption, pause, stand, standstill, stop, stoppage, termination, way point. **antonyms** continuation, start.

halting adj awkward, broken, faltering, hesitant, imperfect, laboured, stammering, stumbling, stuttering, uncertain. **antonym** fluent.

halve v bisect, cut down, divide, go Dutch, lessen, reduce, share, split.

hammer v bang, beat, clobber, defeat, din, drive, drive home, drub, drum, grind, hit, impress upon, instruct, knock, make, malleate, pan, repeat, shape, slate, thrash, trounce, worst.

hammer out accomplish, bring about, complete, contrive, fashion, finish, negotiate, produce, settle, sort out, thrash out.

hamper v bind, cramp, curb, curtail, distort, embarrass, encumber, entangle, fetter, frustrate, hamstring, handicap, hinder, hobble, hold up, impede, interfere with, obstruct, pinch, prevent, restrain, restrict, shackle, slow down, tangle, thwart, trammel. **antonyms** aid, expedite.

hamstrung adj balked, crippled, disabled, foiled, frustrated, handicapped, helpless, incapacitated, paralysed, stymied.

hand n ability, agency, aid, applause, art, artistry, assistance, clap, direction, fist, handwriting, help, influence, mitt, ovation, palm, part, participation, paw, penmanship, script, share, skill, support.
v aid, assist, conduct, convey, deliver, give, guide, help, lead, offer, pass, present, provide, transmit, yield.

hand down bequeath, give, grant, pass on, transfer, will.

hand in glove allied, in cahoots, in collusion, in league, intimate.

hand out deal out, dish out, dispense, disseminate, distribute, give out, mete, share out.

hand over deliver, donate, fork out, present, release, relinquish, surrender, turn over, yield. **antonym** retain.

handful n few, scattering, smattering, sprinkling. **antonym** lot.

handicap n barrier, block, defect, disability, disadvantage, drawback, encumbrance, hindrance, impairment, impediment, limitation, millstone, obstacle, odds, penalty, restriction, short-coming, stumbling-block. **antonyms** assistance, benefit.
v burden, disadvantage, encumber, hamper, hamstring, hinder, impede, limit, restrict, retard. **antonyms** assist, further.

handle n ear, grip, haft, heft, hilt, knob, lug, stock.
v administer, carry, conduct, control, cope with, deal in, deal with, direct, discourse, discuss, feel, finger, fondle, grasp, guide, hold, manage, manipulate, manoeuvre, market, maul, operate, paw, pick up, poke, sell, steer, stock, supervise, touch, trade, traffic in, treat, use, wield.

handling n administration, approach, conduct, direction, discussion, management, manipulation, operation, running, transaction, treatment.

hand-out[1] n alms, charity, dole, freebie, issue, share, share-out.

hand-out[2] n bulletin, circular, free sample, leaflet, literature, press release, statement.

hand-picked adj choice, chosen, elect, elite, picked, screened, select, selected.

hands n authority, care, charge, command, control, custody, disposal, guardianship, guidance, jurisdiction, keeping, possession, power, supervision, tutelage.

hands down easily, effortlessly, with ease. *antonym* with difficulty.

handsome *adj* abundant, admirable, ample, attractive, becoming, bountiful, comely, considerable, elegant, fine, generous, good-looking, graceful, gracious, large, liberal, magnanimous, majestic, personable, plentiful, seemly, sizeable, stately, well-favoured, well-looking, well-proportioned, well-set-up. *antonyms* mean, stingy, ugly.

handy *adj* accessible, adept, adroit, at hand, available, clever, close, convenient, deft, dexterous, expert, helpful, manageable, near, nearby, neat, nimble, practical, proficient, ready, serviceable, skilful, skilled, useful. *antonyms* clumsy, inconvenient, unwieldy.

hang *v* adhere, attach, bow, cling, cover, dangle, deck, decorate, depend, drape, drift, droop, drop, execute, fasten, fix, float, furnish, hold, hover, incline, lean, loll, lower, remain, rest, sag, stick, string up, suspend, swing, trail, weep.

hang about/around associate with, dally, frequent, haunt, linger, loiter, resort, roam, tarry, waste time.

hang back demur, hesitate, hold back, recoil, shy away.

hang fire delay, hang back, hold back, hold on, procrastinate, stall, stick, stop, vacillate, wait. *antonym* press on.

hang on carry on, cling, clutch, continue, depend on, endure, grasp, grip, hang fire, hang in there, hinge, hold fast, hold on, hold out, hold the line, persevere, persist, remain, rest, stop, turn on, wait. *antonym* give up.

hang over impend, loom, menace, threaten.

hangdog *adj* abject, browbeaten, cowed, cringing, defeated, downcast, furtive, guilty, miserable, shamefaced, sneaking, wretched. *antonym* bold.

hanger-on *n* camp follower, dependant, follower, freeloader, lackey, leech, minion, parasite, sponger, sycophant, toady.

hanging *adj* dangling, drooping, flapping, flopping, floppy, loose, pendent, pendulous, suspended, swinging, unattached, undecided, unresolved, unsettled, unsupported.

hang-up *n* block, difficulty, idée fixe,

inhibition, mental block, obsession, preoccupation, problem, thing.

hanker for/after covet, crave, desire, hunger for, itch for, long for, lust after, pine for, thirst for, want, wish, yearn for, yen for. *antonym* dislike.

hankering *n* craving, desire, hunger, itch, longing, pining, thirst, urge, wish, yearning, yen. *antonym* dislike.

hanky-panky *n* cheating, chicanery, deception, devilry, dishonesty, funny business, jiggery-pokery, machinations, mischief, monkey business, nonsense, shenanigans, subterfuge, trickery, tricks. *antonym* openness.

haphazard *adj* accidental, aimless, arbitrary, careless, casual, chance, disorderly, disorganised, flukey, hit-or-miss, indiscriminate, random, slapdash, slipshod, unmethodical, unsystematic. *antonyms* deliberate, planned.

hapless *adj* cursed, ill-fated, jinxed, luckless, miserable, star-crossed, unfortunate, unhappy, unlucky, wretched. *antonym* lucky.

happen *v* appear, arise, befall, chance, come about, crop up, develop, ensue, eventuate, fall out, follow, materialise, occur, result, supervene, take place, transpire, turn out.

happen on chance on, come on, discover, find, hit on, light on, stumble on.

happening *n* accident, adventure, affair, case, chance, circumstance, episode, event, experience, incident, occasion, occurrence, phenomenon, proceeding, scene.

happily *adv* agreeably, appropriately, aptly, auspiciously, blithely, by chance, cheerfully, contentedly, delightedly, enthusiastically, favourably, felicitously, fittingly, fortunately, freely, gaily, gladly, gleefully, gracefully, heartily, joyfully, joyously, luckily, merrily, opportunely, propitiously, providentially, seasonably, successfully, willingly. *antonym* unhappily.

happiness *n* bliss, cheer, cheerfulness, cheeriness, chirpiness, contentment, delight, ecstasy, elation, enjoyment, exuberance, felicity, gaiety, gladness, high spirits, joy, joyfulness, jubilation, light-heartedness, merriment, pleasure, satisfaction, well-being. *antonym* unhappiness.

happy *adj* advantageous, appropriate, apt, auspicious, befitting, blessed, blissful, blithe, chance, cheerful, content, contented, convenient, delighted, ecstatic, elated, enviable, favourable, felicitous, fit, fitting, fortunate, glad, gratified, idyllic, jolly, joyful, joyous, jubilant, lucky, merry, opportune, over the moon, overjoyed, pleased, promising, propitious, satisfactory, seasonable, starry-eyed, successful, sunny, thrilled, timely, well-timed. *antonym* unhappy.

happy-go-lucky *adj* blithe, carefree, casual, cheerful, devil-may-care, easy-going, heedless, improvident, irresponsible, light-hearted, nonchalant, reckless, unconcerned, untroubled, unworried. *antonyms* anxious, wary.

harangue *n* address, declamation, diatribe, discourse, exhortation, homily, lecture, oration, sermon, speech, spiel, tirade.
v address, declaim, exhort, hold forth, lecture, orate, preach, rant, sermonise, spout.

harass *v* annoy, badger, bait, beleaguer, bother, chivvy, distress, disturb, exasperate, exhaust, fatigue, harry, hassle, hound, perplex, persecute, pester, plague, tease, tire, torment, trash, trouble, vex, wear out, weary, worry. *antonym* assist.

harassed *adj* careworn, distraught, distressed, harried, hassled, hounded, pestered, plagued, pressured, pressurised, strained, stressed, tormented, troubled, vexed, worried. *antonym* carefree.

harassment *n* aggravation, annoyance, badgering, bedevilment, bother, distress, hassle, irritation, molestation, nuisance, persecution, pestering, pressuring, torment, trouble, vexation. *antonym* assistance.

harbinger *n* herald, indication, messenger, omen, portent, precursor, presage, sign, warning.

harbour *n* anchorage, asylum, destination, haven, marina, port, refuge, sanctuary, sanctum, security, shelter.
v believe, cherish, cling to, conceal, entertain, foster, hide, hold, imagine, lodge, maintain, nurse, nurture, protect, retain, secrete, shelter, shield.

hard *adj* acrimonious, actual, alcoholic, angry, antagonistic, arduous, backbreaking, baffling, bare, bitter, burdensome, calamitous, callous, cast-iron, cold, compact, complex, complicated, cruel, crusty, dark, definite, dense, difficult, disagreeable, disastrous, distressing, driving, exacting, exhausting, fatiguing,

fierce, firm, flinty, forceful, formidable, grievous, grim, habit-forming, hard-hearted, harsh, heavy, Herculean, hostile, impenetrable, implacable, indisputable, inflexible, intolerable, intricate, involved, knotty, laborious, obdurate, painful, perplexing, pitiless, plain, powerful, puzzling, rancorous, resentful, rigid, rigorous, ruthless, severe, shrewd, solid, stern, stiff, stony, strenuous, strict, strong, stubborn, tangled, thorny, toilsome, tough, undeniable, unfathomable, unfeeling, ungentle, unjust, unkind, unpleasant, unrelenting, unsparing, unsympathetic, unvarnished, unyielding, uphill, verified, violent, wearying. *antonyms* harmless, kind, mild, non-alcoholic, pleasant, pleasing, soft, yielding.
adv agonisingly, assiduously, badly, bitterly, close, completely, determinedly, diligently, distressingly, doggedly, earnestly, energetically, fiercely, forcefully, forcibly, fully, hardly, harshly, heavily, industriously, intensely, intently, keenly, laboriously, near, painfully, persistently, powerfully, rancorously, reluctantly, resentfully, roughly, severely, sharply, slowly, sorely, steadily, strenuously, strongly, uneasily, untiringly, vigorously, violently, with difficulty. *antonyms* gently, mildly, moderately, unenthusiastically.

hard and fast binding, fixed, immutable, incontrovertible, inflexible, invariable, rigid, set, strict, stringent, unalterable, unchangeable, unchanging. *antonym* flexible.

hard up bankrupt, broke, bust, cleaned out, destitute, impecunious, impoverished, in the red, penniless, penurious, poor, short, skint, strapped for cash. *antonym* rich.

hard-bitten *adj* callous, case-hardened, cynical, down-to-earth, hard-boiled, hard-headed, hard-nosed, matter-of-fact, practical, realistic, ruthless, shrewd, tough, unsentimental. *antonym* callow.

hard-core *adj* blatant, dedicated, die-hard, dyed-in-the-wool, explicit, extreme, intransigent, obstinate, rigid, staunch, steadfast. *antonym* moderate.

harden *v* accustom, bake, brace, brutalise, buttress, cake, case-harden, concrete, fortify, freeze, gird, habituate, indurate, inure, nerve, reinforce, sclerose, season, set, solidify, steel, stiffen, strengthen, toughen, train. *antonym* soften.

ardened *adj* accustomed, chronic, fixed, habitual, habituated, incorrigible, inured, inveterate, irredeemable, obdurate, reprobate, seasoned, set, shameless, toughened, unfeeling. *antonyms* callow, soft.

ard-headed *adj* astute, clear-thinking, cool, hard-boiled, level-headed, practical, pragmatic, realistic, sensible, shrewd, tough, unsentimental. *antonym* unrealistic.

ard-hearted *adj* callous, cold, cruel, hard, heartless, indifferent, inhuman, insensitive, intolerant, iron-hearted, marble-breasted, merciless, pitiless, stony, uncaring, uncompassionate, unfeeling, unkind, unsympathetic. *antonyms* kind, merciful.

ard-hitting *adj* condemnatory, critical, forceful, no-holds-barred, strongly-worded, tough, unsparing, vigorous. *antonym* mild.

ardiness *n* boldness, courage, fortitude, intrepidity, resilience, resolution, robustness, ruggedness, sturdiness, toughness, valour. *antonym* timidity.

ardline *adj* definite, extreme, immoderate, inflexible, intransigent, militant, tough, uncompromising, undeviating, unyielding. *antonym* moderate.

ardly *adv* barely, by no means, faintly, harshly, infrequently, just, no way, not at all, not quite, only, only just, roughly, scarcely, severely, with difficulty. *antonyms* easily, very.

ardness *n* coldness, difficulty, firmness, harshness, inhumanity, insensitivity, laboriousness, pitilessness, rigidity, severity, solidity, steel, sternness, toughness. *antonyms* ease, mildness, softness.

ard-pressed *adj* hard-pushed, harassed, harried, pushed, under pressure, up against it, with one's back to the wall. *antonym* untroubled.

ardship *n* adversity, affliction, austerity, burden, calamity, destitution, difficulty, fatigue, grievance, labour, misery, misfortune, need, oppression, persecution, privation, strait, suffering, toil, torment, trial, tribulation, trouble, want. *antonym* ease.

ard-wearing *adj* durable, resilient, rugged, stout, strong, sturdy, tough. *antonym* delicate.

ard-working *adj* assiduous, busy, conscientious, diligent, energetic, indefatigable, industrious, sedulous, workaholic, zealous. *antonym* lazy.

hardy *adj* audacious, bold, brave, brazen, courageous, daring, firm, fit, foolhardy, hale, headstrong, healthy, hearty, heroic, impudent, intrepid, lusty, manly, plucky, rash, reckless, resolute, robust, rugged, sound, spartan, stalwart, stout, stout-hearted, strong, sturdy, tough, valiant, vigorous. *antonyms* unhealthy, weak.

hare-brained *adj* asinine, careless, daft, empty-headed, flighty, foolish, giddy, half-baked, harum-scarum, headlong, heedless, inane, mindless, rash, reckless, scatter-brained, scatty, unstable, unsteady, wild. *antonym* sensible.

hark *v* attend, give ear, hear, hearken, listen, mark, note, notice, pay attention, pay heed.

hark back go back, recall, recollect, regress, remember, revert.

harlot *n* call-girl, fallen woman, hussy, loose woman, Paphian, pro, prostitute, scrubber, street-walker, strumpet, tart, tramp, whore.

harm *n* abuse, damage, detriment, disservice, evil, hurt, ill, immorality, iniquity, injury, loss, mischief, misfortune, scathe, sin, sinfulness, vice, wickedness, wrong. *antonyms* benefit, service.

v abuse, blemish, damage, hurt, ill-treat, ill-use, impair, injure, mar, molest, ruin, scathe, spoil, wound. *antonyms* benefit, improve.

harmful *adj* baleful, baneful, damaging, deleterious, destructive, detrimental, disadvantageous, evil, hurtful, injurious, noxious, pernicious. *antonym* harmless.

harmless *adj* gentle, innocent, innocuous, inoffensive, non-toxic, safe, unobjectionable. *antonym* harmful.

harmonious *adj* according, agreeable, amicable, compatible, concordant, congenial, congruous, consonant, co-ordinated, cordial, correspondent, dulcet, euphonic, euphonious, eurhythmic, friendly, harmonic, harmonising, matching, mellifluous, melodious, musical, sweet-sounding, sympathetic, symphonious, tuneful. *antonym* inharmonious.

harmonise *v* accommodate, accord, adapt, agree, arrange, attune, blend, chime, cohere, compose, co-ordinate, correspond, match, reconcile, suit, tally, tone. *antonym* clash.

harmony *n* accord, agreement,

amicability, amity, balance, chime, compatibility, concord, conformity, congruity, consensus, consistency, consonance, co-operation, co-ordination, correspondence, correspondency, euphony, fitness, friendship, goodwill, likemindedness, melodiousness, melody, parallelism, peace, rapport, suitability, symmetry, sympathy, tune, tunefulness, unanimity, understanding, unity. **antonym** discord.

harp on (about) dwell on, labour, press, reiterate, renew, repeat.

harridan *n* battle-axe, dragon, fury, gorgon, harpy, hell-cat, nag, scold, shrew, tartar, termagant, virago, vixen, witch.

harried *adj* agitated, anxious, beset, bothered, distressed, hagridden, harassed, hard-pressed, hassled, plagued, pressured, pressurised, ravaged, tormented, troubled, worried. **antonym** untroubled.

harrow *v* agonise, daunt, dismay, distress, harass, lacerate, perturb, rack, rend, tear, torment, torture, vex, wound, wring. **antonyms** assuage, hearten.

harrowing *adj* agonising, alarming, chilling, distressing, disturbing, excruciating, frightening, heart-rending, nerve-racking, soaring, terrifying, tormenting, traumatic. **antonyms** calming, heartening.

harry *v* annoy, badger, bedevil, chivvy, disturb, fret, harass, hassle, maraud, molest, persecute, pester, plague, tease, torment, trouble, vex, worry. **antonyms** aid, calm.

harsh *adj* abrasive, abusive, austere, bitter, bleak, brutal, coarse, comfortless, croaking, crude, cruel, discordant, dissonant, dour, Draconian, glaring, grating, grim, guttural, hard, jarring, pitiless, punitive, rasping, raucous, relentless, rough, ruthless, severe, sharp, Spartan, stark, stern, strident, stringent, unfeeling, ungentle, unkind, unmelodious, unpleasant, unrelenting. **antonyms** mild, smooth, soft.

harshness *n* abrasiveness, acerbity, acrimony, asperity, bitterness, brutality, churlishness, coarseness, crudity, hardness, ill-temper, rigour, roughness, severity, sourness, starkness, sternness, strictness. **antonyms** mildness, softness.

harum-scarum *adj* careless, erratic, flighty, giddy, haphazard, hare-brained, hasty, ill-considered, impetuous, imprudent, irresponsible, precipitate, rash, reckless, scatter-brained, scatty, wild. **antonym** sensible.

hash[1] *n* botch, confusion, cow's arse, fuck-up, hotchpotch, jumble, mess, mishmash, mix-up, muddle, shambles.

hash[2] *see* **hashish**.

hashish *n* cannabis, dope, ganja, grass, hash, hemp, marijuana, pot.

hassle *n* altercation, argument, bickering, bother, difficulty, disagreement, dispute, fight, inconvenience, nuisance, problem, quarrel, squabble, struggle, trial, trouble, tussle, upset, wrangle. **antonyms** agreement, peace.
v annoy, badger, bother, bug, chivvy, harass, harry, hound, pester. **antonyms** assist, calm.

haste *n* alacrity, briskness, bustle, celerity, dispatch, expedition, fleetness, hastiness, hurry, hustle, impetuosity, nimbleness, precipitation, promptitude, quickness, rapidity, rapidness, rashness, recklessness, rush, speed, swiftness, urgency, velocity. **antonyms** care, deliberation, slowness.

hasten *v* accelerate, advance, bolt, dash, dispatch, expedite, fly, gallop, goad, haste, hightail it, hurry, make haste, precipitate, press, quicken, race, run, rush, scurry, scuttle, speed, speed up, sprint, step on it, step up, tear, trot, urge. **antonym** dawdle.

hastily *adv* apace, chop-chop, doublequick, fast, heedlessly, hurriedly, impetuously, impulsively, posthaste, precipitately, promptly, quickly, rapidly, rashly, recklessly, speedily, straightaway. **antonyms** carefully, deliberately, slowly.

hasty *adj* brief, brisk, brusque, cursory, eager, excited, expeditious, fast, fiery, fleet, fleeting, foolhardy, headlong, heedless, hot-headed, hot tempered, hurried, impatient, impetuous, impulsive, indiscreet, irascible, irritable, passing, passionate, perfunctory, precipitant, precipitate, prompt, quick tempered, rapid, rash, reckless, rushed, short, snappy, speedy, superficial, swift, thoughtless, urgent. **antonyms** careful, deliberate, placid, slow.

hatch *v* breed, brood, conceive, concoct, contrive, cook up, design, develop, devise, dream up, incubate, originate, plan, plot, project, scheme, think up.

hate *v* abhor, abominate, despise, detest, dislike, execrate, loathe, spite. **antonym** like.

n abhorrence, abomination, animosity, animus, antagonism, antipathy, aversion, detestation, dislike, enmity, execration, hatred, hostility, loathing, odium. *antonym* like.

hateful *adj* abhorrent, abominable, damnable, despicable, detestable, disgusting, execrable, forbidding, foul, heinous, horrible, loathsome, obnoxious, odious, offensive, repellent, repugnant, repulsive, revolting, vile. *antonym* pleasing.

hatred *n* abomination, animosity, animus, antagonism, antipathy, aversion, detestation, dislike, enmity, execration, hate, ill-will, misanthropy, odium, repugnance, revulsion. *antonym* like.

haughty *adj* arrogant, assuming, conceited, contemptuous, disdainful, high, high and mighty, hoity-toity, imperious, lofty, overweening, proud, scornful, snobbish, snooty, stiff-necked, stuck-up, supercilious, superior, uppish. *antonyms* friendly, humble.

haul *v* carry, cart, convey, drag, draw, heave, hump, lug, move, pull, tow, trail, transport, tug.
n booty, catch, drag, find, gain, harvest, heave, loot, pull, spoils, swag, takings, tug, yield.

haunt *v* beset, frequent, obsess, plague, possess, prey on, recur, repair, resort, torment, trouble, visit, walk.
n den, gathering-place, hangout, howf(f), meeting place, rendezvous, resort, stamping ground.

haunted *adj* cursed, eerie, ghostly, hag-ridden, jinxed, obsessed, plagued, possessed, preoccupied, spooky, tormented, troubled, worried.

haunting *adj* disturbing, eerie, evocative, indelible, memorable, nostalgic, persistent, poignant, recurrent, recurring, unforgettable. *antonym* unmemorable.

have *v* accept, acquire, allow, bear, beget, cheat, comprehend, comprise, consider, contain, deceive, deliver, dupe, embody, endure, enjoy, entertain, experience, feel, fool, gain, get, give birth to, hold, include, keep, obtain, occupy, outwit, own, permit, possess, procure, produce, put up with, receive, retain, secure, suffer, sustain, swindle, take, tolerate, trick, undergo.

have done with be through with, cease, desist, finish with, give up, stop, throw over, wash one's hands of.

have to be compelled, be forced, be obliged, be required, have got to, must, ought, should.

haven *n* anchorage, asylum, harbour, port, refuge, retreat, sanctuary, sanctum, shelter.

havoc *n* carnage, chaos, confusion, damage, depopulation, desolation, despoliation, destruction, devastation, disorder, disruption, mayhem, rack and ruin, ravages, ruin, shambles, slaughter, waste, wreck.

hawk *v* bark, cry, market, offer, peddle, sell, tout, vend.

hawker *n* barrow-boy, cheap-jack, coster, costermonger, crier, huckster, pedlar, vendor.

haywire *adj* amiss, chaotic, confused, crazy, disarranged, disordered, disorganised, erratic, kaput, mad, shambolic, tangled, topsy-turvy, wild. *antonyms* correct, in order.

hazard *n* accident, chance, coincidence, danger, death-trap, endangerment, fluke, imperilment, jeopardy, luck, mischance, misfortune, mishap, peril, risk, threat. *antonym* safety.
v advance, attempt, chance, conjecture, dare, endanger, expose, gamble, imperil, jeopardise, offer, presume, proffer, risk, speculate, stake, submit, suggest, suppose, threaten, venture, volunteer.

hazardous *adj* chancy, dangerous, dicey, difficult, fraught, hairy, haphazard, insecure, perilous, precarious, risky, thorny, ticklish, uncertain, unpredictable, unsafe. *antonyms* safe, secure.

haze *n* cloud, dimness, film, fog, mist, obscurity, smog, smokiness, steam, unclearness, vapour.

hazy *adj* blurry, clouded, cloudy, dim, dull, faint, foggy, fuzzy, ill-defined, indefinite, indistinct, loose, milky, misty, muddled, muzzy, nebulous, obscure, overcast, smoky, uncertain, unclear, vague, veiled. *antonyms* clear, definite.

head *n* ability, apex, aptitude, bean, beginning, bonce, boss, brain, brains, branch, capacity, cape, captain, caput, category, chief, chieftain, chump, class, climax, commander, commencement, conclusion, conk, cop, cranium, crest, crisis, crown, culmination, department, director, division, end, faculty, flair, fore, forefront, front, godfather, head teacher, heading, headland, headmaster, headmistress, height, intellect, intelligence, knowledge box, leader, loaf, manager, master, mastermind, mentality, mind, nab, napper, nob, noddle, nut, origin, pate, peak, pitch, point, principal, promontory, rise, section, skull, source, start, subject, summit, superintendent, supervisor, talent, thought, tip, top, topic, topknot, turning-point, understanding, upperworks, van, vanguard, vertex. **antonyms** foot, subordinate, tail.

adj arch, chief, dominant, first, foremost, front, highest, leading, main, pre-eminent, premier, prime, principal, supreme, top, topmost.

v aim, cap, command, control, crown, direct, govern, guide, lead, make a beeline, make for, manage, oversee, point, precede, rule, run, steer, superintend, supervise, top, turn.

head for aim for, direct towards, gravitate towards, make for, point to, steer for, turn for, zero in on.

head off avert, deflect, distract, divert, fend off, forestall, intercept, interpose, intervene, parry, prevent, stop, ward off.

head over heels completely, intensely, recklessly, thoroughly, uncontrollably, utterly, whole-heartedly, wildly.

heading *n* caption, category, class, descriptor, division, headline, lemma, name, rubric, section, title.

headlong *adj* breakneck, dangerous, hasty, head-first, head-on, hell-for-leather, impetuous, impulsive, inconsiderate, precipitate, reckless, thoughtless.

adv hastily, head first, head-on, heedlessly, hell for leather, helter-skelter, hurriedly, lickety-split, pell-mell, precipitately, rashly, thoughtlessly, wildly.

headstrong *adj* bull-headed, contrary, foolhardy, fractious, heedless, imprudent, impulsive, intractable, mulish, obstinate, perverse, pig-headed, rash, reckless, self-willed, stubborn, ungovernable, unruly, wilful. **antonyms** biddable, docile, obedient.

heady *adj* exciting, exhilarating, hasty, impetuous, impulsive, inconsiderate, inebriant, intoxicating, overpowering, potent, precipitate, rash, reckless, spirituous, stimulating, strong, thoughtless, thrilling.

heal *v* alleviate, ameliorate, compose, conciliate, cure, harmonise, mend, patch up, reconcile, regenerate, remedy, restore, salve, settle, soothe, treat.

healing *adj* assuaging, comforting, curative, emollient, gentle, medicinal, mild, palliative, remedial, restorative, restoring, soothing, styptic, therapeutic.

health *n* condition, constitution, fettle, fitness, form, good condition, haleness, heal, healthiness, robustness, salubrity, shape, soundness, state, strength, tone, vigour, welfare, well-being. **antonyms** disease, infirmity.

healthy *adj* active, beneficial, blooming, bracing, fine, fit, flourishing, good, hale (and hearty), hardy, healthful, health-giving, hearty, hygienic, in fine feather, in fine fettle, in fine form, in good condition, in good shape, in the pink, invigorating, nourishing, nutritious, physically fit, robust, salubrious, salutary, sound, strong, sturdy, vigorous, well, wholesome. **antonyms** diseased, ill, infirm, sick, unhealthy.

heap *n* accumulation, aggregation, clamp, cock, collection, hoard, lot, mass, mound, mountain, pile, ruck, stack, stockpile, store.

v accumulate, amass, assign, augment, bank, bestow, build, burden, collect, confer, gather, hoard, increase, lavish, load, mound, pile, shower, stack, stockpile, store.

heaps *n* a lot, abundance, great deal, lashings, load(s), lots, mass, millions, mint, ocean(s), oodles, plenty, pot(s), quantities, scores, stack(s), tons.

hear *v* acknowledge, ascertain, attend, catch, discover, eavesdrop, examine, find, gather, hark, hearken, heed, investigate, judge, learn, listen, overhear, pick up, understand.

heart *n* affection, benevolence, boldness, bravery, centre, character, compassion, concern, core, courage, crux, disposition, emotion, essence, feeling, fortitude, guts, hub, humanity, inclination, kernel, love, marrow, mettle, middle, mind, nature, nerve, nerve centre, nub, nucleus, pith, pity, pluck, purpose, quintessence, resolution, root, sentiment, soul, spirit, spunk, sympathy, temperament, tenderness, ticker, understanding, will.

heart and soul absolutely, completely, devotedly, eagerly, entirely, gladly, heartily, unreservedly, whole-heartedly.

heartache *n* affliction, agony, anguish, bitterness, dejection, despair, despondency, distress, grief, heartbreak, heart-sickness, pain, remorse, sorrow, suffering, torment, torture.

heartbreaking *adj* agonising, bitter, desolating, disappointing, distressing, grievous, harrowing, heart-rending, pitiful, poignant, sad, tragic. **antonyms** heartening, heartwarming, joyful.

heartbroken *adj* broken-hearted, crestfallen, crushed, dejected, desolate, despondent, disappointed, disconsolate, disheartened, dispirited, down, downcast, grieved, heart-sick, miserable, woebegone. *antonyms* delighted, elated.

hearten *v* animate, assure, buck up, buoy up, cheer, comfort, console, embolden, encourage, gladden, incite, inspire, inspirit, pep up, reassure, revivify, rouse, stimulate. *antonym* dishearten.

heart-felt *adj* ardent, cordial, deep, devoted, devout, earnest, fervent, genuine, hearty, honest, impassioned, profound, sincere, unfeigned, warm, whole-hearted. *antonyms* false, insincere.

heartily *adv* absolutely, completely, cordially, deeply, eagerly, earnestly, enthusiastically, feelingly, genuinely, gladly, profoundly, resolutely, sincerely, thoroughly, totally, unfeignedly, very, vigorously, warmly, zealously.

heartless *adj* brutal, callous, cold, cold-hearted, cold-hearted, cruel, hard, hard-hearted, harsh, inhuman, merciless, pitiless, stern, uncaring, unfeeling, unkind. *antonyms* considerate, kind, merciful, sympathetic.

heart-rending *adj* affecting, distressing, harrowing, heartbreaking, moving, pathetic, piteous, pitiful, poignant, sad, tear-jerking, tragic.

heartwarming *adj* affecting, cheering, encouraging, gladsome, gratifying, heartening, moving, pleasing, rewarding, satisfying, touching, warming. *antonym* heart-breaking.

hearty *adj* active, affable, ample, ardent, cordial, doughty, eager, earnest, ebullient, effusive, energetic, enthusiastic, exuberant, filling, friendly, generous, genial, genuine, hale, hardy, healthy, heartfelt, honest, jovial, nourishing, real, robust, sincere, sizeable, solid, sound, square, stalwart, strong, substantial, true, unfeigned, unreserved, vigorous, warm, well, whole-hearted. *antonyms* cold, emotionless.

heat *n* agitation, ardour, earnestness, excitement, fervour, fever, fieriness, fury, impetuosity, incandescence, intensity, passion, sizzle, sultriness, swelter, vehemence, violence, warmness, warmth, zeal. *antonyms* cold(ness), coolness.
v animate, excite, flush, glow, impassion, inflame, inspirit, reheat, rouse, stimulate, stir, toast, warm up. *antonyms* chill, cool.

heated *adj* acrimonious, angry, bitter, excited, fierce, fiery, frenzied, furious, impassioned, intense, passionate, raging, stormy, tempestuous, vehement, violent. *antonym* dispassionate.

heathen *n* barbarian, infidel, pagan, philistine, savage, unbeliever. *antonym* believer.
adj barbaric, godless, heathenish, infidel, irreligious, pagan, philistine, savage, uncivilised, unenlightened. *antonyms* Christian, godly.

heave *v* billow, breathe, cast, chuck, drag, elevate, exhale, expand, fling, gag, groan, haul, heft, hitch, hoist, hurl, let fly, lever, lift, palpitate, pant, pitch, puff, pull, raise, retch, rise, send, sigh, sling, sob, spew, surge, swell, throb, throw, throw up, toss, tug, vomit.

heaven *n* bliss, ecstasy, Elysian fields, Elysium, enchantment, ether, firmament, happiness, happy hunting-ground(s), hereafter, next world, nirvana, paradise, rapture, sky, transport, utopia, Valhalla, Zion. *antonym* hell.

heavenly *adj* alluring, ambrosial, angelic, beatific, beautiful, blessed, blissful, celestial, delightful, divine, entrancing, exquisite, extra-terrestrial, glorious, godlike, holy, immortal, lovely, rapturous, ravishing, seraphic, sublime, superhuman, supernal, supernatural, wonderful. *antonym* hellish.

heavens *n* ether, firmament, sky, the blue, the wild blue yonder.

heavily *adv* awkwardly, closely, clumsily, compactly, completely, considerably, copiously, decisively, deep, deeply, dejectedly, densely, dully, excessively, fast, frequently, gloomily, hard, heftily, laboriously, painfully, ponderously, profoundly, roundly, sluggishly, solidly, sound, soundly, thick, thickly, thoroughly, to excess, utterly, weightily, woodenly. *antonym* lightly.

heavy *adj* abundant, apathetic, boisterous, bulky, burdened, burden-some, complex, considerable, copious, crestfallen, deep, dejected, depressed, despondent, difficult, disconsolate, downcast, drowsy, dull, encumbered, excessive, gloomy, grave, grieving, grievous, hard, harsh, hefty, inactive, indolent, inert, intolerable, laborious, laden, large, leaden, listless, loaded, lumping, lumpish, massive, melancholy, onerous, oppressed, oppressive, ponderous, portly, profound, profuse, rough, sad, serious, severe, slow, sluggish, solemn, sorrowful, stodgy, stormy, stupid, tedious, tempestuous, torpid, turbulent, vexatious, violent, wearisome, weighted, weighty, wild, wooden. **antonyms** airy, insignificant, light.

heavy-handed *adj* autocratic, awkward, bungling, clumsy, domineering, graceless, ham-fisted, harsh, inconsiderate, inept, inexpert, insensitive, oppressive, overbearing, tactless, thoughtless, unsubtle.

heavy-hearted *adj* crushed, depressed, despondent, discouraged, disheartened, downcast, downhearted, forlorn, glum, melancholy, miserable, morose, mournful, sad, sorrowful. **antonym** light-hearted.

heckle *v* bait, barrack, catcall, disrupt, gibe, interrupt, jeer, pester, shout down, taunt.

hectic *adj* animated, boisterous, chaotic, excited, fast, fevered, feverish, flurrying, flustering, frantic, frenetic, frenzied, furious, heated, rapid, riotous, rumbustious, tumultuous, turbulent, wild. **antonym** leisurely.

hector *v* badger, bluster, boast, browbeat, bully, chivvy, harass, intimidate, menace, nag, provoke, threaten, worry.

hedge *v* block, circumscribe, confine, cover, dodge, duck, equivocate, fortify, guard, hem in, hinder, insure, obstruct, protect, quibble, restrict, safeguard, shield, sidestep, stall, temporise, waffle.

hedonism *n* epicurism, gratification, luxuriousness, pleasure-seeking, self-indulgence, sensualism, sensuality, voluptuousness. **antonym** asceticism.

hedonistic *adj* epicurean, luxurious, pleasure-seeking, self-indulgent, voluptuous. **antonyms** ascetic, austere.

heed *n* attention, care, caution, consideration, ear, heedfulness, mind, note, notice, regard, respect, thought, watchfulness. **antonyms** inattention, indifference, unconcern.
v attend, consider, follow, listen, mark, mind, note, obey, observe, regard, take notice of. **antonyms** disregard, ignore.

heedful *adj* attentive, careful, cautious, chary, circumspect, mindful, observant, prudent, regardful, vigilant, wary, watchful. **antonym** heedless.

heedless *adj* careless, foolhardy,

imprudent, inattentive, incautious, incurious, neglectful, negligent, oblivious, precipitate, rash, reckless, thoughtless, uncaring, unconcerned, unheedful, unmindful, unobservant, unthinking. **antonym** heedful.

heel *n* blackguard, bounder, cad, crust, end, remainder, rotter, rump, scoundrel, spur, stub, stump, swine.

hefty *adj* ample, awkward, beefy, big, brawny, bulky, burly, colossal, cumbersome, forceful, heavy, hulking, husky, large, massive, muscular, ponderous, powerful, robust, solid, strapping, strong, substantial, thumping, tremendous, unwieldy, vigorous, weighty. **antonyms** slight, small.

height *n* acme, altitude, apex, apogee, ceiling, climax, crest, crown, culmination, degree, dignity, elevation, eminence, exaltation, extremity, grandeur, highness, hill, limit, loftiness, maximum, mountain, peak, pinnacle, prominence, stature, summit, tallness, top, ultimate, utmost, uttermost, vertex, zenith. **antonym** depth.

heighten *v* add to, aggrandise, aggravate, amplify, augment, elevate, enhance, ennoble, exalt, greaten, improve, increase, intensify, magnify, raise, sharpen, strengthen, uplift. **antonyms** decrease, diminish.

heinous *adj* abhorrent, abominable, atrocious, awful, evil, execrable, flagrant, grave, hateful, hideous, infamous, iniquitous, monstrous, nefarious, odious, outrageous, revolting, shocking, unspeakable, vicious, villainous.

hell *n* abyss, affliction, agony, anguish, Hades, hellfire, infernal regions, inferno, lower regions, misery, nether world, nightmare, ordeal, suffering, torment, trial, underworld, wretchedness. **antonym** heaven.

hell-bent *adj* bent, determined, dogged, fixed, inflexible, intent, intransigent, obdurate, resolved, set, settled, tenacious, unhesitating, unwavering.

hellish *adj* abominable, accursed, atrocious, barbarous, cruel, damnable, damned, demoniacal, detestable, devilish, diabolical, execrable, fiendish, infernal, inhuman, monstrous, nefarious, Stygian, sulphurous, vicious, wicked. **antonym** heavenly.

hello, hallo *interj* chin-chin, ciao, hail, hi, hiya, how-do-you-do, howdy, what cheer, wotcher. **antonym** good-bye.

helm *n* command, control, direction,

driving seat, leadership, reins, rudder, rule, saddle, tiller, wheel.

help v abet, abstain, aid, alleviate, ameliorate, assist, avoid, back, befriend, control, co-operate, cure, ease, facilitate, forbear, improve, keep from, lend a hand, mitigate, prevent, promote, rally round, refrain from, relieve, remedy, resist, restore, save, second, serve, stand by, succour, support, withstand. **antonym** hinder.

n adjuvant, advice, aid, aidance, assistance, avail, benefit, co-operation, guidance, leg up, service, support, use, utility. **antonym** hindrance.

helper n adjutant, aide, aider, ally, assistant, attendant, auxiliary, collaborator, colleague, deputy, helpmate, mate, partner, right-hand man, second, subsidiary, supporter.

helpful adj accommodating, adjuvant, advantageous, beneficent, beneficial, benevolent, caring, considerate, constructive, co-operative, favourable, fortunate, friendly, kind, neighbourly, practical, productive, profitable, serviceable, supportive, sympathetic, timely, useful. **antonyms** futile, useless, worthless.

helping n amount, dollop, piece, plateful, portion, ration, serving, share.

helpless adj abandoned, aidless, defenceless, dependent, destitute, disabled, exposed, feeble, forlorn, friendless, impotent, incapable, incompetent, infirm, paralysed, powerless, unfit, unprotected, vulnerable, weak. **antonyms** competent, enterprising, independent, resourceful, strong.

helter-skelter adv carelessly, confusedly, hastily, headlong, hurriedly, impulsively, pell-mell, rashly, recklessly, wildly.

adj anyhow, confused, disordered, disorganised, haphazard, higgledy-piggledy, hit-or-miss, jumbled, muddled, random, topsy-turvy, unsystematic.

hem n border, edge, fringe, margin, skirt, trimming.

v beset, border, circumscribe, confine, edge, enclose, engird, environ, gird, hedge, restrict, skirt, surround.

hence adv accordingly, ergo, therefore, thus.

henceforth adv hence, henceforward, hereafter, hereinafter.

henchman n aide, associate, attendant, bodyguard, cohort, crony, follower, heavy, minder, minion, right-hand

man, running dog, satellite, sidekick, subordinate, supporter.

henpecked adj browbeaten, bullied, cringing, dominated, intimidated, meek, subject, subjugated, timid. **antonym** dominant.

herald n courier, crier, forerunner, harbinger, indication, messenger, omen, precursor, sign, signal, token.

v advertise, announce, broadcast, forebode, harbinger, indicate, pave the way, portend, precede, presage, proclaim, prognosticate, promise, publicise, publish, show, trumpet, usher in.

herculean adj arduous, athletic, brawny, colossal, daunting, demanding, difficult, enormous, exacting, exhausting, formidable, gigantic, great, gruelling, hard, heavy, huge, husky, laborious, large, mammoth, massive, mighty, muscular, onerous, powerful, prodigious, rugged, sinewy, stalwart, strapping, strenuous, strong, sturdy, titanic, toilsome, tough, tremendous.

herd n assemblage, collection, crowd, crush, drove, flock, horde, mass, mob, multitude, populace, press, rabble, riff-raff, swarm, the hoi polloi, the masses, the plebs, throng.

v assemble, associate, collect, congregate, drive, flock, force, gather, goad, guard, guide, huddle, lead, muster, protect, rally, shepherd, spur, watch.

hereafter adv eventually, hence, henceforth, henceforward, in future, later.

n after-life, Elysian fields, happy hunting-ground, heaven, life after death, next world.

hereditary adj ancestral, bequeathed, congenital, family, genetic, handed down, inborn, inbred, inheritable, inherited, traditional, transmissible, transmittable, transmitted, willed.

heresy n dissidence, error, free-thinking, heterodoxy, iconoclasm, impiety, unorthodoxy. **antonym** orthodoxy.

heretic n dissenter, dissident, free-thinker, nonconformist, renegade, separatist. **antonym** conformist.

heritage n bequest, birthright, deserts, due, endowment, estate, history, inheritance, legacy, lot, past, patrimony, portion, record, share, tradition.

hero n celebrity, champion, conqueror, exemplar, goody, heart-throb, idol, paragon, protagonist, star, superstar, victor.

heroic adj bold, brave, classic,

classical, courageous, daring, dauntless, doughty, elevated, epic, exaggerated, extravagant, fearless, gallant, game, grand, grandiose, gritty, high-flown, Homeric, inflated, intrepid, legendary, lion-hearted, mythological, spunky, stout-hearted, undaunted, valiant. **antonyms** cowardly, pusillanimous, timid.

heroism *n* boldness, bravery, courage, courageousness, daring, derring-do, fearlessness, fortitude, gallantry, grit, intrepidity, prowess, spirit, valour. **antonyms** cowardice, pusillaniminity, timidity.

hero-worship *n* admiration, adoration, adulation, deification, idolisation, veneration.

hesitant *adj* diffident, dilatory, doubtful, half-hearted, halting, hesitating, irresolute, reluctant, sceptical, shy, swithering, timid, uncertain, unsure, vacillating, wavering. **antonyms** resolute, staunch.

hesitate *v* balk, be reluctant, be uncertain, be unwilling, delay, demur, dither, doubt, falter, fumble, halt, haver, pause, scruple, shillyshally, shrink from, stammer, stumble, stutter, swither, think twice, vacillate, wait, waver.

hesitation *n* delay, demurral, doubt, faltering, fumbling, indecision, irresolution, misgiving(s), qualm(s), reluctance, scruple(s), second thought(s), stammering, stumbling, stuttering, swithering, uncertainty, unwillingness, vacillation. **antonyms** alacrity, assurance, eagerness.

heterogeneous *adj* assorted, catholic, contrary, contrasted, different, disparate, dissimilar, divergent, diverse, diversified, incongruous, miscellaneous, mixed, motley, multiform, opposed, unlike, unrelated, varied. **antonym** homogeneous.

hew *v* axe, carve, chop, cut, fashion, fell, form, hack, lop, make, model, sculpt, sculpture, sever, shape, smooth, split.

heyday *n* bloom, boom time, florescence, floruit, flower, flowering, golden age, pink, prime, salad days, vigour.

hiatus *n* aperture, breach, break, chasm, discontinuance, discontinuity, gap, interruption, interval, lacuna, lapse, opening, rift, space.

hidden *adj* abstruse, clandestine, close, concealed, covered, covert, cryptic, dark, hermetic, latent, mysterious, mystic,

mystical, obscure, occult, recondite, secret, shrouded, ulterior, unapparent, unseen, veiled. **antonyms** open, showing.

hide *v* abscond, bury, cache, camouflage, cloak, conceal, cover, disguise, earth, eclipse, ensconce, go to ground, go underground, hole up, keep dark, lie low, mask, obscure, occult, screen, secrete, shadow, shelter, shroud, stash, suppress, take cover, veil, withhold. **antonyms** display, reveal, show.

hide-away *n* cloister, haven, hideout, hiding-place, nest, refuge, retreat, sanctuary.

hidebound *adj* conventional, entrenched, narrow, narrow-minded, rigid, set, set in one's ways, strait-laced, ultra-conservative, unprogressive. **antonyms** liberal, unconventional.

hideous *adj* abominable, appalling, awful, detestable, disgusting, dreadful, frightful, ghastly, grim, grisly, grotesque, gruesome, horrendous, horrible, horrid, loathsome, macabre, monstrous, odious, repulsive, revolting, shocking, sickening, terrible, terrifying, ugly, unsightly. **antonym** beautiful.

hideout *n* den, hide-away, hiding-place, hole, lair, retreat, shelter.

hiding *n* beating, caning, drubbing, flogging, hammering, lathering, leathering, licking, spanking, tanning, thrashing, walloping, whipping.

hiding-place *n* den, haven, hide-away, hideout, hole, lair, priest hole, refuge, retreat, sanctuary, stash.

higgledy-piggledy *adv* any old how, anyhow, confusedly, haphazardly, helter-skelter, indiscriminately, pell-mell, topsy-turvy.
adj confused, disorderly, disorganised, haphazard, indiscriminate, jumbled, muddled, topsy-turvy.

high *adj* acute, alto, arch, arrogant, boastful, boisterous, bouncy, bragging, capital, cheerful, chief, consequential, costly, dear, delirious, distinguished, domineering, elated, elevated, eminent, euphoric, exalted, excessive, excited, exhilarated, exorbitant, expensive, extraordinary, extravagant, extreme, exuberant, freaked out, gamy, grand, grave, great, haughty, high-pitched, important, inebriated, influential, intensified, intoxicated, joyful, lavish, leading, light-hearted, lofty, lordly, luxurious, merry, niffy, ostentatious, overbearing, penetrating, piercing, piping, pongy, powerful, prominent, proud, rich, ruling, serious, sharp, shrill, significant, soaring, soprano, spaced out, steep, stiff, stoned, strident, strong, superior, tainted, tall, towering, treble, tripping, tumultuous, turbulent, tyrannical, vainglorious, whiffy. *antonyms* deep, low, lowly, short.

n apex, apogee, delirium, ecstasy, euphoria, height, intoxication, level, peak, record, summit, top, trip, zenith. *antonyms* low, nadir.

high and dry abandoned, bereft, destitute, helpless, marooned, stranded.

high and mighty arrogant, conceited, disdainful, haughty, imperious, overbearing, overweening, self-important, snobbish, stuck-up, superior.

high society aristocracy, beautiful people, crème de la crème, élite, gentry, jet set, nobility, upper crust. *antonym* hoi polloi.

high spirits boisterousness, bounce, buoyancy, exhilaration, exuberance, good cheer, hilarity, joie de vivre, liveliness, sparkle, vivacity.

high-born *adj* aristocratic, blue-blooded, gentle, noble, patrician, pedigreed, thoroughbred, well-born, well-connected.

highbrow *adj* bookish, brainy, cultivated, cultured, deep, intellectual, serious, sophisticated. *antonym* lowbrow.

high-class *adj* A1, choice, classy, de luxe, elite, exclusive, first-rate, high-quality, posh, quality, select, superior, tiptop, tops, U, upper-class. *antonyms* mediocre, ordinary.

high-flown *adj* elaborate, elevated, exaggerated, extravagant, florid, grandiose, high-falutin(g), inflated, la(h)-di-da(h), lofty, magniloquent, overblown, pretentious, turgid.

high-handed *adj* arbitrary, autocratic, bossy, despotic, dictatorial, domineering, imperious, oppressive, overbearing, peremptory, self-willed, tyrannical, wilful.

highlight *n* best, climax, cream, feature, focal point, focus, high point, high spot, peak, zenith.

v accent, accentuate, emphasise, feature, focus on, illuminate, play up, point up, set off, show up, spotlight, stress, underline.

highly *adv* appreciatively, approvingly, considerably, decidedly, eminently, enthusiastically, exceptionally, extraordinarily, extremely, favourably, greatly, immensely, supremely, tremendously, vastly, very, warmly, well.

highly-strung *adj* edgy, excitable, irascible, irritable, jittery, nervous, nervy, neurotic, restless, sensitive, skittish, stressed, taut, temperamental, tense. *antonyms* calm, relaxed.

high-minded *adj* elevated, ethical, fair, good, honourable, idealistic, lofty, magnanimous, moral, noble, principled, pure, righteous, scrupulous, upright, virtuous, worthy. *antonyms* immoral, unscrupulous.

high-powered *adj* aggressive, driving, dynamic, effective, energetic, enterprising, forceful, go-ahead, go-getting, industrious, vigorous.

high-quality *adj* blue-chip, choice, classy, de luxe, gilt-edged, quality, select, superior, tiptop, top-class.

high-sounding *adj* affected, artificial, bombastic, extravagant, flamboyant, florid, grandiloquent, grandiose, high-flown, magniloquent, orotund, ostentatious, overblown, pompous, ponderous, pretentious, stilted, strained.

high-spirited *adj* animated, boisterous, bold, bouncy, daring, dashing, ebullient, effervescent, energetic, exuberant, frolicsome, lively, mettlesome, peppy, sparkling, spirited, spunky, vibrant, vital, vivacious. *antonyms* downcast, glum.

hike *v* back-pack, footslog, hoof it, leg it, plod, ramble, tramp, treck, trudge, walk. *n* march, plod, ramble, tramp, trek, trudge, walk.

hilarious *adj* amusing, comical, convivial, entertaining, funny, gay, happy, humorous, hysterical, jolly, jovial, joyful, joyous, killing, merry, mirthful, noisy, rollicking, side-splitting, uproarious. *antonyms* grave, serious.

hilarity *n* amusement, boister-ousness, cheerfulness, conviviality, entertainment, exhilaration, exuberance, frivolity, gaiety, glee, high spirits, jollification, jollity, joviality, joyousness, laughter, levity, merriment, mirth, uproariousness. *antonyms* gravity, seriousness.

hill *n* acclivity, brae, butte, climb, down, drift, elevation, eminence, fell, gradient, heap, height, hillock, hilltop, hummock, incline, knoll, kop, law, mound, mount, pile, prominence, rise, slope, stack, tor.

hinder *v* arrest, check, counteract,

debar, delay, deter, encumber, frustrate, hamper, hamstring, handicap, hold back, hold up, impede, interrupt, obstruct, oppose, prevent, retard, slow down, stop, stymie, thwart, trammel. *antonyms* aid, assist, help.

hindrance *n* bar, barrier, check, deterrent, difficulty, drag, drawback, encumbrance, handicap, hitch, impediment, interruption, limitation, obstacle, obstruction, pull-back, restraint, restriction, snag, stoppage, stumbling-block, trammel. *antonyms* aid, assistance, help.

hinge *v* be contingent, centre, depend, hang, pivot, rest, revolve around, turn.

hint *n* advice, allusion, breath, clue, dash, help, implication, indication, inkling, innuendo, insinuation, intimation, mention, pointer, reminder, scintilla, sign, signal, soupçon, speck, suggestion, suspicion, taste, tinge, tip, tip-off, touch, trace, undertone, whiff, whisper, wrinkle.

v allude, imply, indicate, inkle, innuendo, insinuate, intimate, mention, prompt, subindicate, suggest, tip off.

hire *v* appoint, book, charter, commission, employ, engage, lease, let, rent, reserve, retain, sign up, take on. *antonyms* dismiss, fire.

n charge, cost, fare, fee, price, rent, rental, toll.

hire-purchase *n* easy terms, never-never.

hiss *n* boo, buzz, catcall, contempt, derision, hissing, hoot, jeer, mockery, raspberry, sibilation, whistle.

v boo, catcall, condemn, damn, decry, deride, hoot, jeer, mock, rasp, revile, ridicule, shrill, sibilate, wheeze, whirr, whiss, whistle, whiz.

historic *adj* celebrated, consequential, epoch-making, extraordinary, famed, famous, momentous, notable, outstanding, red-letter, remarkable, renowned, significant.

historical *adj* actual, archival, attested, authentic, documented, factual, real, traditional, verifiable.

history *n* account, annals, antecedents, antiquity, autobiography, biography, chronicle, chronology, days of old, days of yore, genealogy, memoirs, narration, narrative, olden days, recapitulation, recital, record, relation, saga, story, tale, the past.

histrionic *adj* affected, artificial, bogus, dramatic, forced, ham, insincere,

melodramatic, ranting, sensational, theatrical, unnatural.

histrionics *n* dramatics, overacting, performance, ranting and raving, scene, staginess, tantrums, temperament, theatricality.

hit *v* accomplish, achieve, affect, arrive at, attain, bang, bash, batter, beat, belt, bump, clip, clobber, clock, clonk, clout, collide with, crown, cuff, damage, devastate, flog, gain, impinge on, influence, knock, lob, move, overwhelm, prop, punch, reach, secure, slap, slog, slosh, slug, smack, smash, smite, sock, strike, swat, thump, touch, volley, wallop, whack, wham, whap, w(h)op, wipe.

n blow, bump, clash, clout, collision, cuff, impact, knock, sell-out, sensation, shot, slap, slog, slosh, smack, smash, sock, stroke, success, swipe, triumph, venue, wallop, winner.

hit back recalcitrate, reciprocate, retaliate.

hit on arrive at, chance on, contrive, discover, guess, invent, light on, realise, stumble on.

hit out assail, attack, castigate, condemn, criticise, denounce, inveigh, lash, lay about one, rail.

hitch *v* attach, connect, couple, fasten, harness, heave, hike (up), hitch-hike, hoi(c)k, hoist, jerk, join, pull, tether, thumb a lift, tie, tug, unite, yank, yoke. *antonyms* unfasten, unhitch.

n catch, check, delay, difficulty, drawback, hiccup, hindrance, hold-up, impediment, mishap, problem, snag, stick, stoppage, trouble.

hitherto *adv* beforehand, heretofore, previously, so far, thus far, till now, until now, up to now.

hit-or-miss *adj* aimless, apathetic, casual, cursory, disorganised, haphazard, indiscriminate, lackadaisical, perfunctory, random, undirected, uneven.

hoard *n* accumulation, cache, fund, heap, mass, pile, profusion, reserve, reservoir, stockpile, store, supply, treasure-trove.

v accumulate, amass, cache, coffer, collect, deposit, garner, gather, hive, lay up, put by, reposit, save, stash away, stockpile, store, treasure. *antonyms* spend, squander, use.

hoarse *adj* croaky, grating, gravelly, growling, gruff, guttural, harsh, husky, rasping, raspy, raucous, rough, throaty. *antonyms* clear, smooth.

hoax *n* cheat, con, deception, fast one, fraud, grift, hum, joke, josh, leg-pull, practical joke, prank, put-on, ruse, spoof, string, swindle, trick.
v bamboozle, bluff, con, deceive, delude, dupe, fool, gull, have on, hoodwink, lead on, pull someone's leg, spoof, string, stuff, swindle, take for a ride, trick.

hobble *v* dodder, falter, fetter, hamshackle, hamstring, limp, restrict, shackle, shamble, shuffle, stagger, stumble, tie, totter.

hobnob *v* associate, consort, fraternise, hang about, keep company, mingle, mix, pal around, socialise.

hocus-pocus *n* artifice, cheat, chicanery, conjuring, deceit, deception, delusion, gibberish, gobbledegook, humbug, jargon, mumbo-jumbo, nonsense, trickery.

hogwash *n* balderdash, bilge, bunk, bunkum, claptrap, drivel, eyewash, hooey, nonsense, piffle, rot, rubbish, tosh, trash, tripe, twaddle.

hoi polloi *n* citizenry, commonalty, riff-raff, the common people, the great unwashed, the herd, the masses, the plebs, the populace, the proles, the proletariat, the rabble, the third estate.
antonyms aristocracy, élite, nobility.

hoist *v* elevate, erect, heave, jack up, lift, raise, rear, uplift, upraise.

hoity-toity *adj* arrogant, conceited, haughty, high and mighty, lofty, overweening, pompous, proud, snobbish, snooty, stuck-up, supercilious, toffee-nosed, uppish, uppity.

hold *v* accommodate, account, adhere, apply, arrest, assemble, assume, be in force, be the case, bear, believe, bond, brace, call, carry, carry on, celebrate, check, clasp, cleave, clinch, cling, clip, clutch, comprise, conduct, confine, consider, contain, continue, convene, cradle, curb, deem, delay, detain, embrace, endure, enfold, entertain, esteem, exist, grasp, grip, have, hold good, imprison, judge, keep, last, maintain, occupy, operate, own, persevere, persist, possess, preside over, presume, prop, reckon, regard, remain, remain true, remain valid, resist, restrain, retain, run, seat, shoulder, solemnise, stand up, stay, stick, stop, summon, support, suspend, sustain, take, think, view, wear.
n authority, clasp, clout, clutch, control, dominance, dominion, foothold, footing, grasp, grip, holt, influence, leverage, mastery, prop, pull, purchase, stay, support, sway, vantage.

hold back check, control, curb, desist, forbear, inhibit, refuse, repress, restrain, retain, stifle, suppress, withhold.
antonym release.

hold forth declaim, discourse, go on, harangue, lecture, orate, preach, sermonise, speak, speechify, spiel, spout.

hold off avoid, defer, delay, fend off, keep off, postpone, put off, rebuff, refrain, repel, repulse, stave off, wait.

hold out continue, endure, extend, give, hang on, last, offer, persevere, persist, present, proffer, stand fast.

hold over adjourn, defer, delay, postpone, put off, shelve, suspend.

hold up brace, delay, detain, display, endure, exhibit, hinder, impede, last, lift, present, raise, retard, show, slow, stop, survive, sustain, waylay, wear.

hold water bear scrutiny, convince, make sense, pass the test, ring true, wash, work.

hold with accept, agree to, approve of, countenance, go along with, subscribe to, support.

holder *n* bearer, case, container, cover, cradle, custodian, housing, incumbent, keeper, occupant, owner, possessor, proprietor, purchaser, receptacle, rest, sheath, stand.

hold-up¹ *n* bottle-neck, delay, difficulty, gridlock, hitch, obstruction, setback, snag, stoppage, (traffic) jam, trouble, wait.

hold-up² *n* heist, robbery, stick-up.

hole *n* aperture, breach, break, burrow, cave, cavern, cavity, chamber, crack, defect, den, depression, dilemma, dimple, discrepancy, dive, dump, earth, error, excavation, eyelet, fallacy, fault, fissure, fix, flaw, gap, hollow, hovel, imbroglio, inconsistency, jam, joint, lair, loophole, mess, nest, opening, orifice, outlet, perforation, pit, pocket, pore, predicament, puncture, quandary, rent, retreat, scoop, scrape, shaft, shelter, slum, split, spot, tangle, tear, tight spot.

holiday *n* anniversary, break, celebration, exeat, feast, festival, festivity, fête, furlough, gala, hols, leave, recess, respite, rest, sabbatical, saint's day, time off, vacation.

holier-than-thou *adj* complacent, goody-goody, pious, sanctimonious, self-approving, self-righteous, self-

satisfied, smug, unctuous. *antonyms* humble, meek.

holiness *n* blessedness, devoutness, divinity, godliness, piety, purity, religiousness, righteousness, sacredness, saintliness, sanctimoniousness, sanctity, self-righteousness, spirituality, unctuousness, virtuousness. *antonyms* impiety, wickedness.

holler *n, v* bawl, bellow, call, cheer, clamour, cry, hail, halloo, howl, hurrah, roar, shout, shriek, whoop, yell, yelp, yowl.

hollow *adj* artificial, cavernous, concave, coreless, cynical, deaf, deceitful, deceptive, deep, deep-set, depressed, dished, dull, empty, expressionless, faithless, false, flat, fleeting, flimsy, fruitless, futile, gaunt, hungry, hypocritical, indented, insincere, lantern-jawed, low, meaningless, muffled, muted, pointless, pyrrhic, ravenous, reverberant, rumbling, sepulchral, specious, starved, sunken, toneless, treacherous, unavailing, unfilled, unreal, unreliable, unsound, useless, vacant, vain, void, weak, worthless.
n basin, bottom, bowl, cave, cavern, cavity, channel, concave, concavity, coomb, crater, cup, dale, dell, den, dent, depression, dimple, dingle, dint, dish, excavation, glen, groove, hole, indentation, pit, trough, vacuity, valley, well.
v burrow, channel, dent, dig, dint, dish, excavate, furrow, gouge, groove, indent, pit, scoop.

holocaust *n* annihilation, carnage, conflagration, destruction, devastation, extermination, extinction, flames, genocide, inferno, mass murder, massacre, pogrom, slaughter.

holy *adj* blessed, consecrated, dedicated, devout, divine, evangelical, evangelistic, faithful, god-fearing, godly, good, hallowed, pietistic, pious, pure, religious, righteous, sacred, sacrosanct, saintly, sanctified, sanctimonious, spiritual, sublime, unctuous, venerable, venerated, virtuous. *antonyms* impious, unsanctified, wicked.

homage *n* acknowledgement, admiration, adoration, adulation, allegiance, awe, deference, devotion, duty, esteem, faithfulness, fidelity, honour, loyalty, obeisance, praise, recognition, regard, respect, reverence, service, tribute, veneration, worship.

home *n* abode, asylum, birthplace, clinic, domicile, dwelling, dwelling-place, element, environment, family, fireside, habitat, habitation, haunt, hearth, home ground, home town, homestead, hospice, hospital, house, household, institution, native heath, nest, nursing-home, old people's home, pad, pied-à-terre, range, residence, roof, stamping-ground, territory.
adj candid, central, direct, domestic, familiar, family, household, incisive, inland, internal, intimate, local, national, native, penetrating, plain, pointed, unanswerable, uncomfortable, wounding.

homeless *adj* abandoned, destitute, disinherited, displaced, dispossessed, down-and-out, exiled, forlorn, forsaken, houseless, itinerant, outcast, unsettled, vagabond, wandering.
n derelicts, dossers, down-and-outs, nomads, squatters, tramps, travellers, vagrants.

homely *adj* comfortable, comfy, congenial, cosy, domestic, easy, everyday, familiar, folksy, friendly, homelike, homespun, hom(e)y, informal, intimate, modest, natural, ordinary, plain, relaxed, simple, snug, unaffected, unassuming, unpretentious, unsophisticated, welcoming. *antonyms* formal, unfamiliar.

homespun *adj* amateurish, artless, coarse, crude, folksy, homely, home-made, inelegant, plain, rough, rude, rustic, unpolished, unrefined, unsophisticated. *antonym* sophisticated.

homicide *n* assassination, bloodshed, killing, manslaughter, murder, slaying.

homogeneous *adj* akin, alike, analogous, cognate, comparable, consistent, consonant, harmonious, identical, indiscrete, kindred, of a piece, similar, uniform, unvarying. *antonym* different.

homologous *adj* analogous, comparable, correspondent, corresponding, equivalent, like, matching, parallel, related, similar. *antonyms* different, dissimilar.

homosexual *n* dike, dyke, fag, fairy, fruit, homophile, invert, les, lesbian, lez, nancy, pederast, poof, pooftah, puff, queen, queer, rent-boy, sapphist. *antonyms* heterosexual, straight.
adj bent, camp, dikey, dykey, fruity, gay, lesbian, pederastic, poofy, queer,

sapphic. **antonyms** heterosexual, straight.

honest *adj* above-board, authentic, bona fide, candid, chaste, conscientious, decent, direct, equitable, ethical, fair, fair and square, forthright, frank, genuine, high-minded, honourable, humble, impartial, ingenuous, just, law-abiding, legitimate, objective, on the level, open, outright, outspoken, plain, proper, real, reliable, reputable, respectable, scrupulous, seemly, simple, sincere, square, straight, straightforward, true, trustworthy, trusty, truthful, undisguised, unequivocal, unfeigned, upright, veracious, virtuous, well-gotten, well-won, white. **antonyms** covert, devious, dishonest, dishonourable.

honestly *adv* by fair means, candidly, cleanly, conscientiously, directly, dispassionately, equitably, ethically, fairly, frankly, honourably, in all sincerity, in good faith, justly, lawfully, legally, legitimately, objectively, on the level, openly, outright, plainly, really, scrupulously, sincerely, straight, straight out, truly, truthfully, undisguisedly, unreservedly, uprightly, verily. **antonyms** dishonestly, dishonourably.

honesty *n* artlessness, bluntness, candour, equity, even-handedness, explicitness, fairness, faithfulness, fidelity, frankness, genuineness, honour, incorruptibility, integrity, justness, morality, objectivity, openness, outspokenness, plain-heartedness, plainness, plain-speaking, probity, rectitude, reputability, scrupulousness, sincerity, squareness, straightforwardness, straightness, trustworthiness, truthfulness, uprightness, veracity, verity, virtue. **antonyms** deviousness, dishonesty.

honorary *adj* complimentary, ex officio, formal, honorific, in name only, nominal, titular, unofficial, unpaid. **antonyms** gainful, paid, salaried, waged.

honour *n* acclaim, accolade, acknowledgement, admiration, adoration, chastity, commendation, compliment, credit, decency, deference, dignity, distinction, duty, elevation, esteem, fairness, favour, good name, goodness, homage, honesty, honourableness, innocence, integrity, kudos, laudation, laurels, loyalty, modesty, morality, pleasure, praise, principles, privilege, probity, purity, rank, recognition, rectitude, regard, renown, reputation, repute, respect, reverence, righteousness, self-respect, tribute, trust, trustworthiness, uprightness, veneration, virginity, virtue, worship. **antonyms** disgrace, dishonour, obloquy.
v accept, acclaim, acknowledge, admire, adore, applaud, appreciate, carry out, cash, celebrate, clear, commemorate, commend, compliment, credit, crown, decorate, dignify, discharge, esteem, exalt, execute, fulfil, glorify, hallow, homage, keep, laud, laureate, lionise, observe, pass, pay, pay homage, perform, praise, prize, remember, respect, revere, reverence, take, value, venerate, worship. **antonyms** betray, debase, disgrace, dishonour.

honourable *adj* creditable, distinguished, eminent, equitable, estimable, ethical, fair, great, high-minded, honest, illustrious, irreproachable, just, meritorious, moral, noble, prestigious, principled, proper, renowned, reputable, respectable, respected, right, righteous, sincere, straight, true, trustworthy, trusty, unexceptionable, upright, upstanding, venerable, virtuous, worthful, worthy. **antonyms** dishonest, dishonourable, unworthy.

honours *n* awards, crowns, decorations, dignities, distinctions, laurels, prizes, rewards, titles, trophies. **antonyms** aspersions, indignities.

hoodwink *v* bamboozle, cheat, con, cozen, deceive, delude, dupe, fool, gull, have on, hoax, impose, mislead, rook, swindle, take in, trick.

hook *v* bag, catch, clasp, collar, enmesh, ensnare, entangle, entrap, fasten, fix, grab, hasp, hitch, nab, secure, snare, trap.

hooked *adj* addicted, aquiline, barbed, beaked, beaky, bent, curled, curved, devoted, enamoured, obsessed, uncinate.

hooligan *n* bovver boy, delinquent, droog, hood, hoodlum, lout, mobster, rough, roughneck, rowdy, ruffian, thug, tough, vandal, yob, yobbo.

hoot *n* beep, boo, call, catcall, cry, hiss, howl, jeer, laugh, raspberry, scream, shout, shriek, toot, whistle, whoop, yell.
v beep, boo, catcall, condemn, cry, decry, deride, explode, hiss, howl down, jeer, ridicule, scream, shout, shriek, toot, whistle, whoop, yell, yell at.

hop *v* bound, caper, dance, fly, frisk, hobble, jump, leap, limp, nip, prance, skip, spring, vault.

hope *n* ambition, anticipation, aspiration, assumption, assurance, belief, confidence, conviction, desire, dream, expectancy, expectation, faith, hopefulness, longing, optimism, promise, prospect, wish. *antonyms* apathy, despair, pessimism.

v anticipate, aspire, assume, await, believe, contemplate, desire, expect, foresee, long, reckon on, rely, trust, wish. *antonym* despair.

hopeful *adj* assured, auspicious, bright, bullish, buoyant, cheerful, confident, encouraging, expectant, favourable, heartening, optimistic, promising, propitious, reassuring, rosy, sanguine. *antonyms* despairing, discouraging, pessimistic.

hopefully *adv* all being well, bullishly, conceivably, confidently, eagerly, expectedly, feasibly, optimistically, probably, sanguinely, with a bit of luck.

hopeless *adj* defeatist, dejected, demoralised, despairing, desperate, despondent, disconsolate, downhearted, foolish, forlorn, futile, helpless, impossible, impracticable, inadequate, incompetent, incorrigible, incurable, ineffectual, irredeemable, irremediable, irreparable, irreversible, lost, madcap, no-win, past cure, pessimistic, pointless, poor, reckless, unachievable, unattainable, useless, vain, woebegone, worthless, wretched. *antonyms* curable, hopeful, optimistic.

horde *n* band, bevy, crew, crowd, drove, flock, gang, herd, host, mob, multitude, pack, swarm, throng, troop.

horny *adj* ardent, lascivious, lecherous, libidinous, lubricious, lustful, randy, ruttish. *antonyms* cold, frigid.

horrible *adj* abhorrent, abominable, appalling, atrocious, awful, beastly, bloodcurdling, cruel, disagreeable, dreadful, fearful, fearsome, frightful, ghastly, grim, grisly, gruesome, heinous, hideous, horrid, horrific, loathsome, macabre, nasty, repulsive, revolting, shameful, shocking, terrible, terrifying, unkind, unpleasant, weird. *antonyms* agreeable, pleasant.

horrid *adj* abominable, alarming, appalling, awful, beastly, bloodcurdling, cruel, despicable, disagreeable, disgusting, dreadful, formidable, frightening, hair-raising, harrowing, hateful, hideous, horrible, horrific, mean, nasty, odious, offensive, repulsive, revolting, shocking, terrible, terrifying, unkind, unpleasant. *antonyms* agreeable, lovely, pleasant.

horrific *adj* appalling, awful, dreadful, frightening, frightful, ghastly, grim, grisly, hair-raising, harrowing, horrendous, horrifying, scaring, shocking, spine-chilling, terrifying.

horrify *v* abash, alarm, appal, disgust, dismay, frighten, harrow, intimidate, outrage, petrify, scandalise, scare, shock, sicken, startle, terrify, unnerve. *antonyms* delight, gratify, please.

horror *n* abhorrence, abomination, alarm, antipathy, apprehension, aversion, awe, awfulness, consternation, detestation, disgust, dismay, dread, fear, fright, frightfulness, ghastliness, gooseflesh, goose-pimples, grimness, hatred, hideousness, horripilation, loathing, outrage, panic, repugnance, revulsion, shock, terror.

horseplay *n* buffoonery, capers, clowning, fooling, fooling around, fun and games, high jinks, pranks, romping, rough-and-tumble, rough-housing, rough-stuff, rumpus, skylarking.

hospitable *adj* accessible, amenable, amicable, approachable, congenial, convivial, cordial, friendly, generous, genial, gracious, kind, sociable, welcoming. *antonyms* hostile, inhospitable.

hospitality *n* cheer, congeniality, conviviality, cordiality, friendliness, generosity, graciousness, open-handedness, sociability, warmth, welcome. *antonyms* hostility, inhospitality.

host¹ *n* anchor-man, announcer, compère, emcee, innkeeper, landlord, link man, master of ceremonies, MC, presenter, proprietor.

v compère, introduce, present.

host² *n* army, array, band, company, drove, horde, legion, multitude, myriad, pack, swarm, throng.

hostile *adj* adverse, alien, antagonistic, anti, antipathetic, bellicose, belligerent, contrary, ill-disposed, inhospitable, inimical, malevolent, opposed, opposite, rancorous, unfriendly, ungenial, unkind, unsympathetic, unwelcoming, warlike. *antonyms* friendly, sympathetic.

hostility *n* abhorrence, animosity, animus, antagonism, antipathy, aversion, detestation, disaffection, dislike, enmity, estrangement, hate, hatred, ill-will, malevolence, malice, opposition, resentment, unfriendliness. *antonyms* friendliness, sympathy.

hot *adj* acrid, animated, approved, ardent, biting, blistering, boiling, burning, clever, close, dangerous, eager, excellent, excited, exciting, favoured, fervent, fevered, feverish, fierce, fiery, flaming, fresh, heated, hotheaded, impetuous, impulsive, in demand, in vogue, incandescent, inflamed, intense, irascible, latest, lustful, near, new, passionate, peppery, piping, piquant, popular, pungent, quick, raging, recent, risky, roasting, scalding, scorching, searing, sensual, sharp, sizzling, skilful, sought-after, spicy, steaming, stormy, strong, sultry, sweltering, torrid, touchy, tropical, vehement, violent, voluptuous, warm, zealous. *antonyms* calm, cold, mild, moderate.

hot air balderdash, blether, bluster, bombast, bosh, bullshit, bunk, bunkum, claptrap, emptiness, foam, froth, gas, guff, nonsense, vapour, verbiage, wind, words. *antonym* wisdom.

hotbed *n* breeding-ground, den, hive, nest.

hot-blooded *adj* ardent, bold, eager, excitable, fervent, fiery, heated, high-spirited, impetuous, impulsive, lustful, lusty, passionate, precipitate, rash, sensual, spirited, temperamental, warm-blooded, wild. *antonyms* cool, dispassionate.

hotchpotch *n* collection, confusion, conglomeration, hash, jumble, medley, mélange, mess, miscellany, mishmash, mix, mixture, olio, pot-pourri.

hotfoot *adv* at top speed, hastily, helter-skelter, hurriedly, in haste, pell-mell, posthaste, quickly, rapidly, speedily, without delay. *antonyms* dilatorily, slowly.

hotheaded *adj* daredevil, fiery, foolhardy, hasty, headstrong, hot-tempered, impetuous, impulsive, intemperate, madcap, over-eager, precipitate, quick-tempered, rash, reckless, unruly, volatile. *antonyms* calm, cool.

hound *v* badger, chase, chivvy, drive, goad, harass, harry, hunt (down), impel, importune, persecute, pester, prod, provoke, pursue.

house *n* abode, ancestry, blood, building, business, clan, company, concern, domicile, dwelling, dynasty, edifice, establishment, family, family tree, firm, habitation, home, homestead, hostelry, hotel, household, inn, kindred, line, lineage, lodgings, maison, maison(n)ette, ménage, organisation, outfit, parliament, partnership, pied-à-terre, public house, race, residence, roof, stem, tavern, tribe.
v accommodate, bed, billet, board, contain, cover, domicile, domiciliate, harbour, hold, keep, lodge, place, protect, put up, quarter, sheathe, shelter, store, take in.

household *adj* common, domestic, domiciliary, established, everyday, familiar, family, home, ordinary, plain, well-known.

house-trained *adj* domesticated, house-broken, tame, tamed, well-mannered. *antonym* unsocial.

housing *n* accommodation, case, casing, container, cover, covering, dwellings, enclosure, habitation, holder, homes, houses, living quarters, protection, roof, sheath, shelter.

hovel *n* bothy, but-and-ben, cabin, cot, croft, den, dump, hole, hut, hutch, shack, shanty, shed.

hover *v* alternate, dally, dither, drift, falter, flap, float, fluctuate, flutter, fly, hang, hang about, hesitate, impend, linger, loom, menace, oscillate, pause, poise, seesaw, threaten, vacillate, waver.

however *conj* anyhow, but, even so, in spite of that, nevertheless, nonetheless, notwithstanding, still, though, yet.

howl *n* bay, bellow, clamour, cry, groan, holler, hoot, outcry, roar, scream, shriek, wail, yell, yelp, yowl.
v bellow, cry, holler, hoot, lament, quest, roar, scream, shout, shriek, wail, waul, weep, yell, yelp.

howler *n* bloomer, blunder, clanger, error, gaffe, malapropism, mistake, solecism.

hub *n* axis, centre, core, focal point, focus, heart, linchpin, middle, nave, nerve centre, pivot.

hubbub *n* ado, agitation, babel, bedlam, chaos, clamour, confusion, din, disorder, disturbance, hue and cry, hullabaloo, hurly-burly, kerfuffle, noise, palaver, pandemonium, racket, riot, ruckus, ruction, rumpus, tumult, turbulence, uproar, upset. *antonym* calm.

huddle *n* clump, clutch, confab, conference, confusion, crowd, discussion, disorder, heap, jumble, mass, meeting, mess, muddle.
v cluster, conglomerate, congregate, converge, crouch, crowd, cuddle, curl up, flock, gather, hunch, nestle, press, ruck, snuggle, throng. *antonym* disperse.

hue *n* aspect, cast, character, colour, complexion, dye, light, nuance, shade, tincture, tinge, tint, tone.

hue and cry ado, clamour, furore, howls, hullabaloo, outcry, ruction, rumpus, uproar.

huff *n* anger, bad mood, mood, passion, pet, pique, sulks, tiff.

huffy *adj* angry, crabbed, cross, crotchety, crusty, disgruntled, grumpy, hoity-toity, huffish, irritable, miffed, miffy, moody, moping, morose, offended, peevish, pettish, petulant, querulous, resentful, shirty, short, snappy, sulky, surly, testy, touchy, waspish. *antonyms* cheery, happy.

hug *v* cherish, clasp, cling to, cuddle, embrace, enclose, enfold, follow, grip, hold, lock, nurse, retain, skirt, squeeze.
n clasp, clinch, cuddle, embrace, squeeze.

huge *adj* bulky, colossal, enormous, extensive, gargantuan, giant, gigantesque, gigantic, great, gross, immense, jumbo, large, leviathan, mammoth, massive, monumental, mountainous, prodigious, stupendous, swingeing, thundering, titanic, tremendous, unwieldy, vast, walloping, whacking. *antonyms* dainty, tiny.

hulking *adj* awkward, bulky, cloddish, clodhopping, clumsy, cumbersome, gross, hulky, loutish, lumbering, massive, oafish, overgrown, ponderous, ungainly, unwieldy. *antonyms* delicate, small.

hullabaloo *n* agitation, babel, bedlam, chaos, clamour, commotion, confusion, din, disturbance, furore, fuss, hubbub, hue and cry, hurly-burly, kerfuffle, noise, outcry, pandemonium, panic, racket, ruckus, ruction, rumpus, to-do, tumult, turmoil, uproar.

hum *v* bustle, buzz, croon, drone, lilt, move, mumble, murmur, pulsate, pulse, purr, sing, stir, throb, thrum, vibrate, whirr, zoom.
n bustle, busyness, buzz, drone, mumble, murmur, noise, pulsation, pulse, purr, purring, singing, stir, throb, thrum, vibration, whirr.

human *adj* anthropoid, approachable, compassionate, considerate, fallible, fleshly, forgivable, humane, kind, kindly, man-like, mortal, natural, reasonable, susceptible, understandable, understanding, vulnerable. *antonym* inhuman.
n body, child, creature, human being,

individual, living soul, man, mortal, person, soul, woman.

humane *adj* beneficent, benevolent, benign, charitable, civilising, clement, compassionate, forbearing, forgiving, gentle, good, good-natured, human, humanising, kind, kind-hearted, kindly, lenient, loving, magnanimous, merciful, mild, sympathetic, tender, understanding. *antonym* inhumane.

humanitarian *adj* altruistic, beneficent, benevolent, charitable, compassionate, humane, philanthropic, public-spirited.
n altruist, benefactor, do-gooder, Good Samaritan, philanthropist. *antonyms* egoist, self-seeker.

humanity *n* altruism, benevolence, brotherly love, charity, compassion, everyman, fellow-feeling, flesh, generosity, gentleness, goodwill, human nature, human race, humankind, humaneness, kind-heartedness, kindness, loving-kindness, man, mankind, men, mercy, mortality, people, philanthropy, sympathy, tenderness, tolerance, understanding. *antonym* inhumanity.

humble *adj* common, commonplace, courteous, deferential, demiss, docile, homespun, humdrum, insignificant, low, low-born, lowly, mean, meek, modest, obedient, obliging, obscure, obsequious, ordinary, plebeian, polite, poor, respectful, self-effacing, servile, simple, submissive, subservient, supplicatory, unassertive, unassuming, undistinguished, unimportant, unpretentious. *antonyms* assertive, important, pretentious, proud.
v abase, abash, break, bring down, bring low, chagrin, chasten, confound, crush, debase, deflate, degrade, demean, discomfit, discredit, disgrace, humiliate, lower, mortify, reduce, shame, sink, subdue, take down a peg. *antonyms* exalt, raise.

humbly *adv* deferentially, diffidently, docilely, heepishly, meekly, modestly, obsequiously, respectfully, servilely, simply, submissively, subserviently, unassumingly, unpretentiously. *antonyms* confidently, defiantly.

humbug *n* baloney, bluff, bullshit, bunk, bunkum, cheat, claptrap, con, deceit, deception, dodge, eyewash, feint, fraud, fudge, gaff, hoax, hollowness, hype, hypocrisy, nonsense, phoney, pretence, quackery, rubbish, sham, shenanigans, swindle, trick, trickery.
v bamboozle, beguile, cajole, cheat,

cozen, deceive, delude, dupe, fool, gull, hoax, hoodwink, impose, mislead, swindle, trick.

humdrum *adj* boring, commonplace, dreary, droning, dull, everyday, humble, monotonous, mundane, ordinary, repetitious, routine, tedious, tiresome, uneventful, uninteresting, unvaried, wearisome. **antonyms** exceptional, unusual.

humid *adj* clammy, damp, dank, moist, muggy, soggy, steamy, sticky, sultry, vaporous, watery, wet. **antonym** dry.

humidity *n* clamminess, damp, dampness, dankness, dew, humidness, moistness, moisture, mugginess, sogginess, steaminess, wetness. **antonym** dryness.

humiliate *v* abase, abash, bring low, chagrin, chasten, confound, crush, debase, deflate, degrade, discomfit, discredit, disgrace, embarrass, humble, mortify, shame, subdue, undignify. **antonyms** boost, dignify, exalt, vindicate.

humiliating *adj* chastening, crushing, deflating, degrading, discomfiting, disgraceful, disgracing, embarrassing, humbling, ignominious, mortifying, shaming, snubbing. **antonyms** gratifying, triumphant.

humiliation *n* abasement, affront, chagrin, deflation, degradation, discomfiture, discrediting, disgrace, dishonour, embarrassment, humbling, ignominy, indignity, mortification, put-down, rebuff, resignation, shame, snub. **antonyms** gratification, triumph.

humility *n* deference, diffidence, lowliness, meekness, modesty, obedience, resignation, self-abasement, servility, submissiveness, unassertiveness, unpretentiousness. **antonym** pride.

humorous *adj* absurd, amusing, comic, comical, entertaining, facetious, farcical, funny, hilarious, humoristic, jocular, laughable, ludicrous, merry, playful, pleasant, satirical, side-splitting, waggish, whimsical, wisecracking, witty, zany. **antonym** humourless.

humour *n* amusement, banter, bias, caprice, comedy, disposition, facetiousness, fancy, farce, frame of mind, fun, funniness, gags, jesting, jests, jocularity, jokes, joking, ludicrousness, melancholy, mood, pleasantries, propensity, quirk, raillery, repartee, spirits, temper, temperament, vagary, vein, whim, wisecracks, wit, witticisms, wittiness.

v accommodate, appease, coax, comply with, cosset, favour, flatter, go along with, gratify, indulge, mollify, pamper, spoil. **antonym** thwart.

humourless *adj* austere, boring, crass, dour, dry, dull, glum, heavy-going, mirthless, morose, obtuse, po-faced, self-important, tedious, unamused, unamusing, unfunny, unwitty. **antonyms** humorous, witty.

hump *n* bulge, bump, excrescence, hunch, knob, lump, mound, projection, prominence, protrusion, protuberance, swelling.

v arch, carry, curve, heave, hoist, hunch, lift, lug, shoulder, yomp.

hunch *n* feeling, guess, guesswork, idea, impression, inkling, intuition, premonition, presentiment, suspicion.

v arch, bend, crouch, curl up, curve, draw in, huddle, hump, shrug, squat, stoop, tense.

hunger *n* appetite, craving, desire, emptiness, famine, greediness, hungriness, itch, lust, rapacity, ravenousness, starvation, voracity, yearning, yen. **antonyms** appeasement, satisfaction.

v ache, crave, desire, hanker, itch, long, lust, pine, starve, thirst, want, wish, yearn.

hungry *adj* aching, avid, covetous, craving, desirous, eager, empty, famished, greedy, hollow, keen, lean, longing, peckish, ravenous, starved, starving, underfed, undernourished, voracious, yearning. **antonyms** replete, satisfied.

hunk *n* block, chunk, clod, dod, dollop, gobbet, lump, mass, piece, slab, wedge, wodge.

hunt *v* chase, chevy, course, dog, ferret, forage, gun for, hound, investigate, look for, pursue, rummage, scour, search, seek, stalk, track, trail.

n chase, chevy, hue and cry, hunting, investigation, pursuit, quest, search.

hunted *adj* careworn, desperate, distraught, gaunt, haggard, hag-ridden, harassed, harried, henpecked, persecuted, stricken, terror-stricken, tormented, worn, worried. **antonym** serene.

hurdle *n* barricade, barrier, complication, difficulty, fence, handicap, hedge, hindrance, impediment, jump, obstacle, obstruction, problem, snag, stumbling-block, wall.

hurl *v* cast, catapult, chuck, dash, fire, fling, heave, launch, let fly, pitch, project, propel, send, shy, sling, throw, toss.

hurly-burly *n* agitation, bedlam, bustle, chaos, commotion, confusion, disorder, distraction, frenzy, furore, hassle, hubbub, hustle, tumult, turbulence, turmoil, upheaval.

hurried *adj* breakneck, brief, careless, cursory, hasty, headlong, hectic, passing, perfunctory, precipitate, quick, rushed, shallow, short, slapdash, speedy, superficial, swift, unthorough. *antonym* leisurely.

hurry *v* accelerate, belt, bustle, dash, dispatch, expedite, fly, get a move on, goad, hasten, hightail it, hustle, jump to it, look lively, move, quicken, rush, scoot, scurry, scuttle, shake a leg, shift, speed up, step on it, step on the gas, urge. *antonyms* dally, delay.
n bustle, celerity, commotion, dispatch, expedition, flurry, haste, precipitation, promptitude, quickness, rush, scurry, speed, sweat, urgency. *antonyms* calm, leisureliness.

hurt *v* abuse, ache, afflict, aggrieve, annoy, bruise, burn, damage, disable, distress, grieve, harm, impair, injure, maim, mar, pain, sadden, smart, spoil, sting, throb, tingle, torture, upset, wound.
n abuse, bruise, damage, detriment, disadvantage, discomfort, distress, harm, injury, lesion, loss, mischief, pain, pang, sore, soreness, suffering, wound, wrong.
adj aggrieved, annoyed, bruised, crushed, cut, damaged, displeased, grazed, harmed, huffed, injured, maimed, miffed, offended, pained, piqued, rueful, sad, saddened, scarred, scraped, scratched, wounded.

hurtful *adj* catty, cruel, cutting, damaging, derogatory, destructive, detrimental, disadvantageous, distressing, harmful, humiliating, injurious, maleficent, malicious, malignant, mean, mischievous, nasty, pernicious, pointed, prejudicial, scathing, spiteful, unkind, upsetting, vicious, wounding. *antonyms* helpful, kind.

hurtle *v* bowl, charge, chase, crash, dash, fly, plunge, race, rattle, rush, scoot, scramble, shoot, speed, spin, spurt, tear.

hush *v* calm, compose, mollify, mute, muzzle, quieten, settle, shush, silence, soothe, still. *antonyms* disturb, rouse.
n calm, calmness, peace, peacefulness, quiet, quietness, repose, serenity, silence,

still, stillness, tranquillity. *antonyms* clamour, uproar.
interj belt up, hold your tongue, leave it out, not another word, pipe down, quiet, say no more, shush, shut up, ssh, stow it, wheesht, whisht.

hush up conceal, cover up, gag, keep dark, muzzle, smother, soft-pedal, squash, stifle, suppress. *antonym* publicise.

hush-hush *adj* classified, confidential, restricted, secret, top-secret, under wraps, unpublished. *antonyms* open, public.

huskiness *n* croakiness, dryness, gruffness, gutturalness, harshness, hoarseness, roughness, throatiness. *antonym* clarity.

husky[1] *adj* croaking, croaky, gruff, guttural, harsh, hoarse, low, rasping, raucous, rough, throaty.

husky[2] *adj* beefy, brawny, burly, hefty, muscular, powerful, rugged, stocky, strapping, strong, sturdy, thickset, tough.

hussy *n* baggage, broad, floozy, minx, piece, scrubber, slut, strumpet, tart, temptress, tramp, trollop, vamp, wanton, wench.

hustle *v* bustle, crowd, elbow, force, frog-march, haste, hasten, hurry, impel, jostle, pressgang, pressure, push, rush, shove, thrust.

hut *n* booth, bothy, cabin, caboose, crib, den, hovel, lean-to, shack, shanty, shed, shelter.

hybrid *n* amalgam, combination, composite, compound, conglomerate, cross, crossbreed, half-blood, half-breed, heterogeny, mixture, mongrel, pastiche.
adj bastard, combined, composite, compound, cross, heterogeneous, hybridous, hyphenated, mixed, mongrel, mule, patchwork. *antonyms* pure, pure-bred.

hygiene *n* cleanliness, purity, salubriousness, sanitation, sterility, wholesomeness. *antonyms* filth, insanitariness.

hygienic *adj* clean, cleanly, disinfected, germ-free, healthy, pure, salubrious, sanitary, sterile, wholesome. *antonym* unhygenic.

hype *n* advertisement, advertising, ballyhoo, build-up, deception, fuss, kidology, plugging, publicity, racket, razzmatazz, trumpet-blowing.

hyperbole *n* enlargement, exaggeration, excess, extravagance, magnification, overkill, overplay, overstatement. **antonyms** meiosis, understatement.

ypercritical *adj* captious, carping, censorious, fault-finding, finicky, fussy, hair-splitting, niggling, nit-picking, over-particular, pedantic, pernickety, quibbling, strict. **antonyms** tolerant, uncritical.

ypnotic *adj* compelling, dazzling, fascinating, irresistible, magnetic, mesmeric, mesmerising, narcotic, opiate, sleep-inducing, somniferous, soothing, soporific, spellbinding.

ypnotise *v* bewitch, captivate, dazzle, entrance, fascinate, magnetise, mesmerise, spellbind, stupefy.

adj hypochondriacal, neurotic, valetudinarian.

ypocrisy *n* deceit, deceitfulness, deception, dissembling, double-talk, duplicity, insincerity, lip-service, phoneyness, pretence, sanctimoniousness, self-righteousness, speciousness, two-facedness. **antonyms** humility, sincerity.

ypocritical *adj* deceitful, deceptive, dissembling, duplicitous, false, fraudulent, hollow, insincere, phoney, sanctimonious, self-pious, self-righteous, specious, spurious, two-faced. **antonyms** genuine, humble, sincere.

hypothesis *n* assumption, conjecture, guess, premise, premiss, presumption, proposition, starting-point, supposition, theory, thesis.

hypothetical *adj* academic, assumed, conjectural, imaginary, postulated, proposed, putative, speculative, supposed, suppositional, theoretical. **antonyms** actual, real.

hysteria *n* agitation, frenzy, hysterics, instability, madness, neurosis, panic. **antonyms** calm, composure, reason.

hysterical *adj* berserk, comical, crazed, distracted, distraught, falling about, farcical, frantic, frenzied, hairless, hilarious, mad, neurotic, overwrought, priceless, raving, side-splitting, uncontrollable, uproarious. **antonyms** calm, composed.

hysterics *n* drama, dramatics, histrionics, melodrama, (screaming) habdabs.

ice *n* chill, chilliness, coldness, distance, formality, frigidity, frost, frostiness, ice-cream, iciness, icing, reserve, stiffness.
v freeze, frost, glaciate, glaze.

ice-cold *adj* arctic, biting, bitter, chilled to the bone, freezing, frigid, frozen, frozen to the marrow, glacial, icy, icy cold, raw, refrigerated.

iced *adj* frappé(e), frosted, glazed.

icon *n* figure, idol, ikon, image, portrait, representation, symbol.

iconoclasm *n* criticism, demythologisation, denunciation, disabusing, dissent, dissidence, heresy, irreverence, opposition, questioning, radicalism, scepticism, subversion, undeceiving. **antonyms** credulity, trustfulness.

iconoclast *n* critic, denouncer, denunciator, dissenter, dissident, heretic, image-breaker, opponent, questioner, radical, rebel, sceptic, unbeliever. **antonyms** believer, devotee.

iconclastic *adj* critical, denunciatory, dissentient, dissident, heretical, impious, innovative, irreverent, questioning, radical, rebellious, sceptical, subversive. **antonyms** trustful, uncritical, unquestioning.

icy *adj* aloof, arctic, biting, bitter, chill, chilling, chilly, cold, distant, forbidding, formal, freezing, frigid, frost-bound, frosty, frozen over, glacial, glassy, hoar, hostile, ice-cold, indifferent, raw, reserved, slippery, slippy, steely, stiff, stony, unfriendly.

idea *n* abstraction, aim, approximation, archetype, belief, clue, conceit, concept, conception, conceptualisation, conclusion, conjecture, construct, conviction, design, doctrine, end, essence, estimate, fancy, form, guess, guesstimate, hint, hypothesis, idée fixe, image, import, impression, inkling, intention, interpretation, intimation, judgement, meaning, monomania, notion, object, opinion, pattern, perception, plan, purpose, reason, recommendation, scheme, sense, significance, solution, suggestion, surmise, suspicion, teaching, theory, thought, type, understanding, view, viewpoint, vision.

ideal *n* archetype, criterion, dreamboat, epitome, example, exemplar, image, last word, model, paradigm, paragon, pattern, perfection, principle, prototype, standard, type.
adj abstract, archetypal, best, classic, complete, conceptual, consummate, fanciful, highest, hypothetical, imaginary, impractical, model, optimal, optimum, perfect, quintessential, supreme, theoretical, transcendent, transcendental, unattainable, unreal, Utopian, visionary.

idealisation *n* apotheosis, ennoblement, exaltation, glorification, romanticisation, romanticising, worship.

idealise *v* apotheosise, deify, ennoble, exalt, glorify, romanticise, worship. **antonyms** caricature, travesty.

idealism *n* impracticality, perfectionism, romanticism, utopianism. **antonyms** pragmatism, realism.

idealist *n* dreamer, perfectionist, romantic, romanticist, utopian, visionary. **antonyms** pragmatist, realist.

idealistic *adj* impracticable, impractical, optimistic, perfectionist, quixotic, romantic, starry-eyed, unrealistic, utopian, visionary. **antonyms** pragmatic, realistic.

idée fixe complex, fixation, fixed idea, hang-up, monomania, obsession.

identical *adj* alike, clonal, coincident, corresponding, duplicate, equal, equivalent, indistinguishable, interchangeable, like, matching, same, self-same, synonymous, twin. **antonym** different.

identifiable *adj* ascertainable, detectable, discernible, distinguishable, known, noticeable, perceptible, recognisable, unmistakable. **antonyms** indefinable, unfamiliar, unidentifiable, unknown.

identification *n* association, cataloguing, classifying, connection, credentials, detection, diagnosis, documents, empathy, fellow-feeling, ID, involvement, labelling, naming, papers, pinpointing, rapport, recognition, relating, relationship, sympathy.

identify *v* catalogue, classify, detect, diagnose, distinguish, finger, know, label, make out, name, pick out, pinpoint, place, recognise, single out, specify, spot, tag.

identify with ally with, associate with, connect with, empathise with, equate with, feel for, relate to, respond to.

identity *n* accord, coincidence,

correspondence, empathy, existence, individuality, oneness, particularity, personality, rapport, sameness, self, selfhood, singularity, unanimity, uniqueness, unity.

ideology *n* belief(s), convictions, creed, doctrine(s), dogma, ethic, faith, ideas, philosophy, principles, speculation, tenets, world view.

idiocy *n* asininity, cretinism, dementia, fatuity, fatuousness, folly, foolishness, imbecility, inanity, insanity, irrationality, lunacy, mental deficiency, senselessness, silliness, stupidity, tomfoolery. **antonyms** sanity, wisdom.

idiom *n* colloquialism, expression, idiolect, jargon, language, locution, parlance, phrase, regionalism, set phrase, style, talk, turn of phrase, usage, vernacular.

idiomatic *adj* colloquial, correct, dialectal, grammatical, idiolectal, idiolectic, native, vernacular. **antonym** unidiomatic.

idiosyncrasy *n* characteristic, eccentricity, feature, freak, habit, mannerism, oddity, oddness, peculiarity, quirk, singularity, trait.

idiosyncratic *adj* characteristic, distinctive, eccentric, individual, individualistic, inimitable, odd, peculiar, quirky, typical. **antonyms** common, general.

idiot *n* ass, bampot, blockhead, crazy, cretin, cuckoo, dimwit, dolt, dumbbell, dummy, dunderhead, fat-head, featherbrain, fool, half-wit, imbecile, klutz, knuckle-head, mental defective, moron, nig-nog, nincompoop, nitwit, noodle, pillock, saphead, schlep, schmuck, simpleton, thick, thickhead, thicko.

idiotic *adj* asinine, crazy, cretinous, daft, dumb, fat-headed, fatuous, foolhardy, foolish, hair-brained, half-witted, harebrained, imbecile, imbecilic, inane, insane, knuckleheaded, loony, lunatic, moronic, nutty, screwy, senseless, simple, stupid, tomfool, unintelligent. **antonyms** sane, sensible.

idle *adj* abortive, dead, dormant, dronish, empty, foolish, frivolous, fruitless, futile, good-for-nothing, groundless, inactive, indolent, ineffective, ineffectual, inoperative, jobless, lackadaisical, lazy, mothballed, otiose, pointless, purposeless, redundant, shiftless, slothful, sluggish, stationary, superficial, torpid, trivial, unavailing, unemployed, unproductive, unsuccessful, unused, useless, vain, work-shy, worthless. **antonyms** active, effective, purposeful. *v* coast, dally, dawdle, drift, fool, fritter, kill time, lallygag, laze, loiter, lounge, potter, rest on one's laurels, shirk, skive, slack, take it easy, tick over, vegetate, waste, while. **antonyms** act, work.

idleness *n* ease, inaction, inactivity, indolence, inertia, inoccupation, laziness, lazing, leisure, loafing, pottering, shiftlessness, skiving, sloth, slothfulness, sluggishness, torpor, vegetating. **antonyms** activity, employment.

idler *n* clock-watcher, dawdler, dodger, good-for-nothing, laggard, layabout, lazybones, loafer, lotus-eater, lounger, malingerer, shirker, skiver, slacker, sloth, slouch, sluggard, waster, wastrel.

idling *adj* dawdling, drifting, loafing, pottering, resting, resting on one's oars, shirking, skiving, taking it easy, ticking over.

idol *n* beloved, darling, deity, favourite, god, graven image, hero, icon, image, pet, pin-up, superstar.

idolatrous *adj* adoring, adulatory, idolising, idol-worshipping, reverential, uncritical, worshipful.

idolatry *n* adoration, adulation, deification, exaltation, glorification, hero-worship, idolising, idolism, mammetry. **antonym** vilification.

idolise *v* admire, adore, apotheosise, deify, dote on, exalt, glorify, hero-worship, iconise, lionise, love, revere, reverence, venerate, worship. **antonym** vilify.

idyllic *adj* arcadian, charming, delightful, halcyon, happy, heavenly, idealised, innocent, pastoral, peaceful, picturesque, rustic, unspoiled. **antonym** disagreeable.

ignite *v* burn, catch fire, combust, conflagrate, fire, flare up, inflame, kindle, light, set alight, set fire to, spark off, touch off. **antonym** quench.

ignoble *adj* abject, base, base-born, common, contemptible, cowardly, craven, dastardly, degenerate, degraded, despicable, disgraceful, dishonourable, heinous, humble, infamous, low, low-born, lowly, mean, petty, plebeian, shabby, shameless, unworthy, vile, vulgar, worthless, wretched. **antonyms** honourable, noble.

ignominious *adj* abject, crushing, degrading, despicable, discreditable, disgraceful, dishonourable, disreputable, humiliating, indecorous, inglorious, mortifying, scandalous, shameful, sorry, undignified. *antonyms* honourable, triumphant.

ignominy *n* contempt, degradation, discredit, disgrace, dishonour, disrepute, humiliation, indignity, infamy, mortification, obloquy, odium, opprobrium, reproach, scandal, shame, stigma. *antonyms* credit, honour.

ignoramus *n* ass, blockhead, bonehead, dolt, donkey, duffer, dullard, dunce, fool, illiterate, know-nothing, lowbrow, num(b)skull, simpleton. *antonyms* high-brow, intellectual, scholar.

ignorance *n* denseness, greenness, illiteracy, illiterateness, inexperience, innocence, naïvety, unawareness, unconsciousness, unfamiliarity. *antonyms* knowledge, wisdom.

ignorant *adj* as thick as two short planks, blind, bookless, clueless, dense, green, gross, half-baked, ill-informed, illiterate, ill-versed, inexperienced, innocent, innumerate, insensitive, know-nothing, naïve, oblivious, pig-ignorant, stupid, thick, unacquainted, unaware, unconscious, uncultivated, uneducated, unenlightened, uninformed, uninitiated, uninstructed, unknowing, unlearned, unlettered, unread, unscholarly, unschooled, untaught, untrained, untutored, unwitting. *antonyms* knowlegeable, wise.

ignore *v* blink, cold-shoulder, cut, disregard, neglect, omit, overlook, pass over, pay no attention to, reject, send to Coventry, set aside, shut one's eyes to, slight, take no notice of, turn a blind eye to, turn a deaf ear to, turn one's back on. *antonym* note.

ilk *n* brand, breed, cast cut, character, class, description, kidney, kind, make, sort, stamp, style, type, variety.

ill¹ *adj* ailing, dicky, diseased, frail, funny, indisposed, infirm, laid up, off-colour, on the sick list, out of sorts, peelie-wally, poorly, queasy, queer, seedy, sick, under the weather, unhealthy, unwell, valetudinarian. *antonym* well.
n affliction, ailment, complaint, disease, disorder, illness, indisposition, infection, infirmity, malady, malaise, sickness.

ill² *adj* acrimonious, adverse, antagonistic, bad, cantankerous, cross, damaging, deleterious, detrimental, difficult, disturbing, evil, foul, harmful, harsh, hateful, hostile, hurtful, inauspicious,

incorrect, inimical, iniquitous, injurious malevolent, malicious, ominou reprehensible, ruinous, sinister, sulle surly, threatening, unfavourable, unfo tunate, unfriendly, unhealthy, unkin unlucky, unpromising, unpropitiou unwholesome, vile, wicked, wrong. *antonyms* beneficial, fortunate, goo kind.
n abuse, affliction, badness, cruelt damage, depravity, destruction, ev harm, hurt, ill-usage, injury, malic mischief, misery, misfortune, pai sorrow, suffering, trial, tribulatio trouble, unpleasantness, wickednes woe. *antonym* benefit.
adv amiss, badly, by no means, har hardly, inauspiciously, insufficiently poorly, scantily, scarcely, unfavourabl unluckily, wrongfully. *antonym* well.

ill at ease anxious, awkward, dis quieted, disturbed, edgy, embarrasse fidgety, hesitant, like a cat o hot bricks, nervous, on edge, o tenderhooks, restless, self-consciou strange, tense, uncomfortable, uneas unrelaxed, unsettled, unsure, worried. *antonym* at ease.

ill-advised *adj* daft, foolhardy foolish, hasty, hazardous, ill-considere ill-judged, imprudent, inappropriate incautious, indiscreet, injudiciou misguided, overhasty, rash, reckles short-sighted, thoughtless, unseemly unwise, wrong-headed. *antonym* sensible.

ill-assorted *adj* discordant, incom patible, incongruous, inharmoniou misallied, mismatched, unsuited. *antonym* harmonious.

ill-considered *adj* careless, foolish hasty, heedless, ill-advised, ill-judged improvident, imprudent, injudiciou overhasty, precipitate, rash, unwise. *antonym* sensible.

ill-defined *adj* blurred, blurry, dim fuzzy, hazy, imprecise, indefinite indistinct, nebulous, shadowy, unclea vague, woolly. *antonym* clear.

ill-disposed *adj* against, antagonistic anti, antipathetic, averse, hostile inimical, opposed, unco-operative, un friendly, unsympathetic, unwelcoming. *antonym* well-disposed.

illegal *adj* actionable, banned, black market, contraband, criminal, felonious forbidden, illicit, outlawed, pirate, pro hibited, unauthorised, unconstitutiona under-the-counter, unlawful, unlicensed wrongful, wrongous.

legality n crime, criminality, felony, illegitimacy, illicitness, lawlessness, unconstitutionality, unlawfulness, wrong, wrongfulness, wrongness.

legible adj faint, hieroglyphic, indecipherable, indistinct, obscure, scrawled, undecipherable, unreadable.

legitimate adj bastard, born on the wrong side of the blanket, born out of wedlock, fatherless, illegal, illicit, illogical, improper, incorrect, invalid, misbegotten, natural, spurious, unauthorised, unconstitutional, unfathered, unjustifiable, unjustified, unlawful, unsanctioned, unsound, unwarrantable, unwarranted.

ll-fated adj blighted, doomed, forlorn, hapless, ill-omened, ill-starred, luckless, star-crossed, unfortunate, unhappy, unlucky. **antonym** lucky.

ll-favoured adj hideous, repulsive, ugly, unattractive, unlovely, unprepossessing, unsightly. **antonym** beautiful.

ll-feeling n animosity, animus, antagonism, bad blood, bitterness, disgruntlement, dissatisfaction, dudgeon, enmity, frustration, grudge, hardfeelings, hostility, ill-will, odium, offence, rancour, resentment, sourness, spite. **antonyms** friendship, goodwill.

ll-humour n acrimony, crabbiness, disagreeableness, distemper, grumpiness, irascibility, moroseness, petulance, spleen, sulkiness. **antonym** amiability.

ll-humoured adj acrimonious, badtempered, cantankerous, crabbed, crabby, cross, crossgrained, disagreeable, grumpy, huffy, impatient, irascible, irritable, moody, morose, peevish, petulant, sharp, snappish, snappy, sulky, sullen, tart, testy, waspish. **antonym** amiable.

lliberal adj bigoted, close-fisted, hidebound, intolerant, mean1, miserly, narrow-minded, niggardly, parsimonious, petty, prejudiced, reactionary, small-minded, sordid, stingy, tight, tightfisted, uncharitable, ungenerous. **antonym** liberal.

llicit adj black, black-market, bootleg, clandestine, contraband, criminal, felonious, forbidden, furtive, guilty, illegal, illegitimate, ill-gotten, immoral, improper, inadmissible, prohibited, unauthorised, unlawful, unlicensed, unsanctioned, wrong. **antonyms** legal, licit.

llliterate adj ignorant, uncultured, uneducated, unlettered, untaught, untutored. **antonym** literate.

ill-judged adj daft, foolhardy, foolish, hasty, ill-advised, ill-considered, imprudent, incautious, indiscreet, injudicious, misguided, overhasty, rash, reckless, short-sighted, unwise, wrongheaded. **antonym** sensible.

ill-mannered adj badly-behaved, boorish, churlish, coarse, crude, discourteous, ill-behaved, ill-bred, impolite, insensitive, insolent, loutish, rude, uncivil, uncouth, ungallant, unmannerly. **antonym** polite.

ill-natured adj bad-tempered, churlish, crabbed, cross, cross-grained, disagreeable, disobliging, malevolent, malicious, malignant, mean, nasty, perverse, petulant, spiteful, sulky, sullen, surly, unfriendly, unkind, unpleasant, vicious, vindictive. **antonym** good-natured.

illness n affliction, ailment, attack, complaint, disability, disease, disorder, distemper, ill-health, indisposition, infirmity, lurgy, malady, malaise, sickness. **antonym** health.

illogical adj absurd, fallacious, faulty, illegitimate, inconclusive, inconsistent, incorrect, invalid, Irish, irrational, meaningless, senseless, sophistical, specious, spurious, unreasonable, unscientific, unsound. **antonym** logical.

ill-tempered adj bad-tempered, cross, curt, grumpy, ill-humoured, ill-natured, impatient, irascible, irritable, sharp, spiteful, testy, tetchy, touchy, vicious. **antonym** good-tempered.

ill-timed adj awkward, inappropriate, inconvenient, inept, inopportune, tactless, unseasonable, untimely, unwelcome. **antonym** well-timed.

illuminate v adorn, brighten, clarify, clear up, decorate, edify, elucidate, enlighten, explain, illumine, illustrate, instruct, irradiate, light, light up, ornament. **antonyms** darken, deface, divest.

illuminating adj edifying, enlightening, explanatory, helpful, informative, instructive, revealing, revelatory. **antonym** unhelpful.

illumination n adornment, awareness, beam, brightening, brightness, clarification, decoration, edification, enlightenment, insight, inspiration, instruction, light, lighting, lights, ornamentation, perception, radiance, ray, revelation, splendour, understanding. **antonym** darkness.

illusion *n* apparition, chimera, daydream, deception, delusion, error, fallacy, fancy, fantasy, figment, hallucination, mirage, misapprehension, misconception, phantasm, semblance, will-o'-the-wisp. **antonym** reality.

illusory *adj* apparent, beguiling, deceitful, deceptive, deluding, delusive, fallacious, false, hallucinatory, illusive, misleading, mistaken, seeming, sham, unreal, unsubstantial, untrue, vain. **antonym** real.

illustrate *v* adorn, clarify, decorate, demonstrate, depict, draw, elucidate, emphasise, exemplify, exhibit, explain, illuminate, instance, interpret, ornament, picture, show, sketch.

illustration *n* adornment, analogy, case, case in point, clarification, decoration, delineation, demonstration, drawing, elucidation, example, exemplification, explanation, figure, graphic, halftone, instance, interpretation, photograph, picture, plate, representation, sketch, specimen.

illustrative *adj* delineative, descriptive, diagrammatic, explanatory, explicatory, graphic, illustrational, interpretive, pictorial, representative, sample, specimen, typical.

illustrious *adj* brilliant, celebrated, distinguished, eminent, exalted, excellent, famed, famous, glorious, great, magnificent, noble, notable, noted, outstanding, prominent, remarkable, renowned, resplendent, signal, splendid. **antonyms** inglorious, shameful.

ill-will *n* acrimony, animosity, animus, antagonism, antipathy, aversion, bad blood, dislike, enmity, envy, grudge, hard feelings, hatred, hostility, malevolence, malice, odium, rancour, resentment, spite, unfriendliness, venom. **antonyms** friendship, good-will.

image *n* appearance, conceit, concept, conception, counterpart, dead ringer, double, effigies, effigy, facsimile, figure, icon, idea, idol, impression, likeness, perception, picture, portrait, reflection, replica, representation, semblance, similitude, spit, spitting image, statue.

imaginable *adj* believable, comprehensible, conceivable, credible, likely, plausible, possible, predictable, supposable, thinkable, visualisable. **antonym** unimaginable.

imaginary *adj* assumed, chimerical, dreamlike, fancied, fanciful, fictional, fictitious, hallucinatory, hypothetic ideal, illusive, illusory, imagine insubstantial, invented, legendar made-up, mythological, non-exister phantasmal, shadowy, supposed, unrea unsubstantial, visionary. **antonym** rea

imagination *n* chimera, conceptio creativity, enterprise, fancy, idea, idea ity, illusion, image, imaginativenes ingenuity, innovativeness, insight, insp ration, invention, inventiveness, notio originality, resourcefulness, suppositio unreality, vision, wit, wittiness. **antonyms** reality, unimaginativeness.

imaginative *adj* clever, creativ dreamy, enterprising, fanciful, fantasti fertile, ingenious, innovative, inspire inventive, original, resourceful, visio ary, vivid. **antonym** unimaginative.

imagine *v* apprehend, assume, believ conceive, conceptualise, conjectur conjure up, create, deduce, deem, devis dream up, envisage, envision, fanc fantasise, frame, gather, guess, ideat infer, invent, judge, picture, plan, projec realise, scheme, suppose, surmis suspect, take it, think, think of, think u visualise.

imbalance *n* bias, disparit disproportion, imparity, inequalit lopsidedness, partiality, top-heavines unequalness, unevenness, unfairness. **antonym** parity.

imbecile *n* blockhead, bungler, clow cretin, dolt, fool, half-wit, idiot, moro thickhead.
adj asinine, doltish, fatuous, feeble minded, foolish, idiotic, imbecili inane, ludicrous, moronic, senile, simpl stupid, thick, witless. **antonym** intelligent, sensible.

imbibe *v* absorb, acquire, assimilate consume, drink, drink in, gain, gathe gulp, ingest, knock back, lap up, quaf receive, sink, sip, soak in, soak u swallow, swig, take in.

imbroglio, embroglio *n* confusio difficulty, dilemma, entanglemen involvement, mess, muddle, quandar scrape, tangle.

imbue *v* bathe, colour, dye, fil impregnate, inculcate, infuse, ingrai instil, moisten, permeate, pervad saturate, stain, steep, suffuse, tinge, tint

imitate *v* affect, ape, caricature clone, copy, counterfeit, do, duplicate echo, emulate, follow, follow sui forge, impersonate, mimic, mirro mock, monkey, parody, parrot, repea reproduce, send up, simulate, spoof, take off.

imitation *n* copy, counterfeit, counterfeiting, duplication, echoing, fake, forgery, impersonation, impression, likeness, mimesis, mimicry, mockery, parody, reflection, replica, reproduction, resemblance, sham, simulation, substitution, take-off, travesty.

adj artificial, dummy, ersatz, man-made, mock, phoney, pinchbeck, pseudo, repro, reproduction, sham, simulated, synthetic. **antonym** genuine.

imitative *adj* copied, copycat, copying, derivative, echoic, mimetic, mimicking, mock, onomatopoeic, parodistic, parrot-like, plagiarised, pseudo, put-on, second-hand, simulated, unoriginal.

immaculate *adj* blameless, clean, faultless, flawless, guiltless, impeccable, incorrupt, innocent, neat, perfect, pure, scrupulous, sinless, spick-and-span, spotless, spruce, stainless, trim, unblemished, uncontaminated, undefiled, unexceptionable, unpolluted, unsullied, untainted, untarnished, virtuous. **antonyms** contaminated, spoiled.

immaterial *adj* airy, disembodied, ethereal, extraneous, ghostly, inapposite, inconsequential, inconsiderable, incorporeal, inessential, insignificant, insubstantial, irrelevant, minor, spiritual, trifling, trivial, unimportant, unnecessary, unsubstantial. **antonyms** important, material, solid.

immature *adj* adolescent, babyish, callow, childish, crude, green, immatured, imperfect, inexperienced, infantile, juvenile, premature, puerile, raw, under-age, undeveloped, unfinished, unfledged, unformed, unripe, unseasonable, untimely, young. **antonym** mature.

immaturity *n* babyishness, callowness, childishness, crudeness, crudity, greenness, imperfection, inexperience, juvenility, prematureness, prematurity, puerility, rawness, unripeness.

immeasurable *adj* bottomless, boundless, endless, illimitable, immense, immensurable, incalculable, inestimable, inexhaustible, infinite, limitless, measureless, unbounded, unfathomable, unlimited, unmeasureable, vast. **antonym** limited.

immediacy *n* directness, imminence, instancy, instantaneity, promptness, simultaneity, spontaneity, swiftness.

antonym remoteness.

immediate *adj* actual, adjacent, close, contiguous, current, direct, existing, extant, instant, instantaneous, near, nearest, neighbouring, next, on hand, present, pressing, primary, prompt, proximate, recent, unhesitating, up-to-date, urgent. **antonym** distant.

immediately *adv* at once, closely, directly, forthwith, instantly, lickety-split, nearly, now, off the top of one's head, on the instant, posthaste, promptly, pronto, right away, soonest, straight away, straight off, unhesitatingly, without delay. **antonyms** eventually, never.

immemorial *adj* age-old, ancestral, ancient, archaic, fixed, hoary, long-standing, time-honoured, traditional. **antonym** recent.

immense *adj* colossal, elephantine, enormous, extensive, giant, gigantic, great, herculean, huge, illimitable, immeasurable, infinite, interminable, jumbo, large, limitless, mammoth, massive, monstrous, monumental, prodigious, rounceval, stupendous, titanic, tremendous, vast. **antonym** minute.

immensity *n* bulk, enormousness, expanse, extent, greatness, hugeness, infinity, magnitude, massiveness, scope, size, sweep, vastness. **antonym** minuteness.

immerse *v* bathe, dip, douse, duck, dunk, plunge, sink, submerge, submerse.

immersed *adj* absorbed, buried, busy, consumed, deep, engrossed, involved, occupied, preoccupied, rapt, sunk, taken up, wrapped up.

immigrate *v* come in, migrate, move in, remove, resettle, settle. **antonym** emigrate.

imminent *adj* afoot, approaching, at hand, brewing, close, coming, forthcoming, gathering, impending, in the air, in the offing, looming, menacing, near, nigh, overhanging, threatening. **antonym** far-off.

immobile *adj* at a standstill, at rest, expressionless, fixed, frozen, immobilised, immovable, motionless, rigid, riveted, rooted, solid, stable, static, stationary, stiff, still, stock-still, stolid, unexpressive, unmoving. **antonyms** mobile, moving.

immobilise *v* cripple, disable, fix, freeze, halt, paralyse, stop, transfix.

immoderate *adj* egregious, enormous,

exaggerated, excessive, exorbitant, extravagant, extreme, hubristic, inordinate, intemperate, over the top, profligate, steep, uncalled-for, unconscionable, uncontrolled, undue, unjustified, unreasonable, unrestrained, unwarranted, wanton.

immoderation n excess, exorbitance, extravagance, intemperance, overindulgence, prodigality, unreason, unrestraint.

immodest adj bawdy, bold, brassnecked, brazen, coarse, depraved, forward, fresh, gross, immoral, improper, impudent, impure, indecent, indecorous, indelicate, lewd, obscene, pushy, revealing, risqué, shameless, titillating, unblushing, unchaste, unmaidenly. **antonym** modest.

immodesty n audacity, bawdiness, boldness, brass, coarseness, forwardness, gall, impudence, impurity, indecorousness, indecorum, indelicacy, lewdness, obscenity, shamelessness, temerity. **antonym** modesty.

immoral adj abandoned, bad, corrupt, debauched, degenerate, depraved, dishonest, dissolute, evil, foul, impure, indecent, iniquitous, lecherous, lewd, licentious, nefarious, obscene, pornographic, profligate, reprobate, sinful, unchaste, unethical, unprincipled, unrighteous, unscrupulous, vicious, vile, wanton, wicked, wrong. **antonym** moral.

immorality n badness, corruption, debauchery, depravity, dissoluteness, evil, iniquity, libertinage, licence, licentiousness, profligacy, sin, turpitude, vice, wickedness, wrong. **antonym** morality.

immortal adj abiding, ambrosial, constant, deathless, endless, enduring, eternal, everlasting, imperishable, incorruptible, indestructable, lasting, perennial, perpetual, sempiternal, timeless, undying, unfading, unforgettable. **antonym** mortal.

n deity, divinity, genius, god, goddess, great, hero, Olympian.

immortalise v apotheosise, celebrate, commemorate, deify, enshrine, eternalise, eternise, exalt, glorify, hallow, memorialise, perpetuate, solemnise.

immortality n athanasy, celebrity, deathlessness, deification, endlessness, eternity, everlasting life, fame, glorification, gloriousness, glory, greatness, incorruptibility, indestructibility, perpetuity, renown, timelessness. **antonym** mortality.

immovable adj adamant, constant, determined, entrenched, fast, firm, fixed, immutable, impassive, inflexible, jammed, marble-constant, moveless, obdurate, obstinate, resolute, rooted, secure, set, stable, stationary, steadfast, stony, stuck, unbudgeable, unchangeable, unimpressionable, unmovable, unshakable, unshaken, unwavering, unyielding. **antonym** movable.

immune adj clear, exempt, free, insusceptible, insusceptive, invulnerable, proof, protected, resistant, safe, unaffected, unsusceptible. **antonym** susceptible.

immunity n amnesty, charter, exemption, exoneration, franchise, freedom, immunisation, indemnity, insusceptibility, invulnerability, liberty, licence, mithridatism, prerogative, privilege, protection, release, resistance, right. **antonym** susceptibility.

immutable adj abiding, changeless, constant, enduring, fixed, inflexible, invariable, lasting, permanent, perpetual, sacrosanct, solid, stable, steadfast, unalterable, unchangeable. **antonym** mutable.

imp n brat, demon, devil, flibbertigibbet, gamin, minx, prankster, rascal, rogue, scamp, sprite, trickster, urchin.

impact n aftermath, bang, blow, brunt, bump, burden, collision, concussion, consequences, contact, crash, effect, force, impression, influence, jolt, knock, knock-on effect, meaning, power, repercussions, shock, significance, smash, stroke, thrust, thump, weight.

v clash, collide, crash, crush, fix, hit, press together, strike, wedge.

impair v blunt, craze, damage, debilitate, decrease, deteriorate, devalue, diminish, enervate, enfeeble, harm, hinder, injure, lessen, mar, reduce, spoil, undermine, vitiate, weaken, worsen. **antonym** enhance.

impaired adj damaged, defective, faulty, flawed, imperfect, poor, unsound, vicious, vitiated. **antonym** enhanced.

impale v ga(u)nch, lance, perforate, pierce, puncture, run through, skewer, spear, spike, spit, stick, transfix.

impalpable adj airy, delicate, disembodied, elusive, fine, imperceptible, inapprehensible, incorporeal, indistinct, insubstantial, intangible, shadowy, tenuous, thin, unsubstantial. **antonym** palpable.

impart v accord, afford, bestow, communicate, confer, contribute, convey, disclose, discover, divulge, give, grant, hand over, lend, make known, offer, pass on, relate, reveal, tell, yield.

impartial adj detached, disinterested, dispassionate, equal, equitable, even-handed, fair, just, neutral, non-discriminating, non-partisan, objective, open-minded, uncommitted, unbiased, unprejudiced. **antonym** biased.

impartiality n detachment, disinterest, disinterestedness, equality, equity, even-handedness, fairness, neutrality, non-partisanship, objectivity, open-mindedness, unbiasedness. **antonym** bias.

impassable adj blocked, closed, impenetrable, obstructed, pathless, trackless, unnavigable, unpassable. **antonym** passable.

impasse n blind alley, cul-de-sac, dead end, deadlock, halt, stalemate, stand-off, standstill.

impassioned adj animated, ardent, blazing, enthusiastic, excited, fervent, fervid, fiery, furious, glowing, heated, inflamed, inspired, intense, passionate, rousing, spirited, stirring, vehement, vigorous, violent, vivid, warm. **antonyms** apathetic, mild.

impassive adj apathetic, callous, calm, composed, cool, dispassionate, emotionless, expressionless, immobile, impassible, imperturbable, indifferent, inscrutable, insensible, insusceptible, laid back, phlegmatic, poker-faced, reserved, serene, stoical, stolid, unconcerned, unemotional, unexcitable, unfeeling, unimpressible, unmoved, unruffled. **antonyms** moved, responsive, warm.

impatience n agitation, anxiety, avidity, avidness, eagerness, edginess, haste, hastiness, heat, impetuosity, intolerance, irritability, irritableness, nervousness, rashness, restiveness, restlessness, shortness, snappishness, testiness, uneasiness, vehemence. **antonym** patience.

impatient adj abrupt, brusque, chafing, champing at the bit, curt, demanding, eager, edgy, fretful, hasty, headlong, impetuous, intolerant, irritable, precipitate, quick-tempered, restless, snappy, testy, vehement, violent. **antonym** patient.

impeach v accuse, arraign, blame, cast doubt on, censure, challenge, charge, denounce, disparage, grass on, impugn, indict, peach on, question, tax.

impeccable adj blameless, exact, exquisite, flawless, immaculate, incorrupt, innocent, irreproachable, perfect, precise, pure, scrupulous, sinless, squeaky-clean, stainless, unblemished, unerring, unimpeachable. **antonym** flawed.

impecunious adj broke, cleaned out, destitute, impoverished, indigent, insolvent, penniless, penurious, poor, poverty-stricken, skint, stony. **antonym** rich.

impede v bar, block, brake, check, clog, curb, delay, disrupt, hamper, hinder, hobble, hold up, let, obstruct, restrain, retard, slow, stop, thwart, trammel. **antonym** aid.

impediment n bar, barrier, block, burr, check, clog, curb, defect, difficulty, encumbrance, hindrance, obstacle, obstruction, snag, stammer, stumbling-block, stutter. **antonym** aid.

impel v actuate, chivvy, compel, constrain, drive, excite, force, goad, incite, induce, influence, inspire, instigate, motivate, move, oblige, poke, power, prod, prompt, propel, push, spur, stimulate, urge. **antonym** dissuade.

impending adj approaching, brewing, close, collecting, coming, forthcoming, gathering, hovering, imminent, in store, looming, menacing, near, nearing, threatening. **antonym** remote.

impenetrable adj arcane, baffling, cabbalistic, cryptic, dark, dense, enigmatic(al), fathomless, hermetic, hidden, impassable, impermeable, impervious, incomprehensible, indiscernible, inexplicable, inscrutable, inviolable, mysterious, obscure, solid, thick, unfathomable, unintelligible, unpiercable. **antonyms** imtelligible, penetrable.

impenitent adj defiant, hardened, incorrigible, obdurate, remorseless, unabashed, unashamed, uncontrite, unreformed, unregenerate, unremorseful, unrepentant. **antonym** penitent.

imperative adj authoritative, autocratic, bossy, commanding, compulsory, crucial, dictatorial, domineering, essential, exigent, high-handed, imperious, indispensable, insistent, lordly, magisterial, obligatory, peremptory, pressing, tyrannical, tyrannous, urgent, vital. *antonyms* humble, optional.

imperceptible *adj* faint, fine, gradual, impalpable, inappreciable, inaudible, inconsensequential, indiscernible, indistinguishable, infinitesimal, insensible, invisible, microscopic, minute, shadowy, slight, small, subtle, tiny, undetectable, unnoticeable. *antonym* perceptible.

imperceptibly *adv* inappreciably, indiscernibly, insensibly, invisibly, little by little, slowly, subtly, unnoticeably, unobtrusively, unseen.

imperfect *adj* abortive, broken, damaged, defective, deficient, faulty, flawed, impaired, incomplete, inexact, limited, partial, patchy, rudimentary, unfinished, unideal.

imperfection *n* blemish, blot, blotch, crack, defect, deficiency, dent, failing, fallibility, fault, flaw, foible, frailty, glitch, inadequacy, incompleteness, insufficiency, peccadillo, shortcoming, stain, taint, weakness. *antonym* asset.

imperial *adj* august, exalted, grand, great, imperious, kingly, lofty, magnificent, majestic, noble, princely, queenly, regal, royal, sovereign, superior, supreme.

imperialism *n* acquisitiveness, colonialism, empire-building, expansionism.

imperil *v* compromise, endanger, expose, hazard, jeopardise, risk, threaten.

imperious *adj* arrogant, authoritarian, autocratic, bossy, commanding, demanding, despotic, dictatorial, domineering, exacting, haughty, high-and-mighty, high-handed, imperative, lordly, magisterial, overbearing, overweening, peremptory, tyrannical, tyrannous. *antonym* humble.

impermanent *adj* brief, elusive, ephemeral, evanescent, fleeting, fly-by-night, flying, fugacious, fugitive, inconstant, momentary, mortal, passing, perishable, short-lived, temporary, transient, transitory, unfixed, unsettled, unstable. *antonym* permanent.

impermeable *adj* damp-proof, hermetic, impassable, impenetrable, impervious, non-porous, resistant, waterproof, water-repellent, water-resistant. *antonym* permeable.

impersonal *adj* aloof, bureaucratic, businesslike, cold, detached, dispassionate, faceless, formal, frosty, glassy, inhuman, neutral, official, remote, unfriendly, unsympathetic. *antonym* friendly.

impersonate *v* act, ape, caricature, do, imitate, masquerade as, mimic, mock, parody, pose as, take off.

impertinence *n* assurance, audacity, backchat, boldness, brass, brazenness, cheek, discourtesy, disrespect, effrontery, forwardness, impoliteness, impudence, incivility, insolence, nerve, pertness, politeness, presumption, rudeness, sauce, sauciness.

impertinent *adj* bold, brattish, brazen, bumptious, cheeky, discourteous, disrespectful, forward, fresh, ill-mannered, impolite, impudent, insolent, interfering, pert, presumptuous, rude, saucy, uncivil, unmannerly. *antonym* polite.

imperturbable *adj* calm, collected, complacent, composed, cool, equanimous, impassible, optimistic, sanguine, sedate, self-possessed, stoical, tranquil, unexcitable, unflappable. *antonyms* jittery, touchy.

impervious *adj* closed, damp-proof, hermetic, immune, impassable, impenetrable, impermeable, invulnerable, resistant, sealed, unaffected, unmoved, unreceptive, unswayable, untouched. *antonyms* pervious, responsive.

impetuosity *n* dash, élan, haste, hastiness, impetuousness, impulsiveness, precipitancy, precipitateness, rashness, vehemence, violence. *antonym* circumspection.

impetuous *adj* ardent, bull-headed, eager, furious, hasty, headlong, impassioned, impulsive, overhasty, passionate, precipitate, rash, spontaneous, tearaway, unplanned, unpremeditated, unreflecting, unrestrained, unthinking. *antonym* circumspect.

impetus *n* drive, energy, force, goad, impulse, impulsion, incentive, momentum, motivation, motive, power, push, spur, stimulus.

impiety *n* blasphemy, godlessness, hubris, iniquity, irreligion, irreverence, profanity, sacrilege, sacrilegiousness, sinfulness, ungodliness, unholiness, unrighteousness, wickedness. *antonym* piety.

impinge *v* affect, clash, collide, dash, encroach, enter, hit, influence, infringe, intrude, invade, obtrude, strike, touch, touch on, trespass, violate.

impious *adj* blasphemous, godless, hubristic, iniquitous, irreligious, irreverent, profane, sacrilegious, sinful, ungodly, unholy, unrighteous, wicked. *antonym* pious.

impish *adj* arch, devilish, elfin, frolicsome, mischievous, naughty, puckish, rascally, roguish, sportive, tricksome, waggish, wanton, wicked.

implacable *adj* cruel, immovable, inappeasable, inexorable, inflexible, intractable, intransigent, irreconcilable, merciless, pitiless, rancorous, relentless, remorseless, ruthless, unappeasable, unbending, uncompromising, unforgiving, unrelenting, unyielding. **antonym** placable.

implant *v* embed, fix, graft, inculcate, infix, infuse, inoculate, inseminate, insert, inset, instil, place, plant, root, sow.

implausible *adj* dubious, far-fetched, flimsy, improbable, incredible, suspect, thin, transparent, unbelievable, unconvincing, unlikely, unreasonable, weak. **antonym** plausible.

implement *n* agent, apparatus, appliance, device, gadget, gimmick, gismo, instrument, tool, utensil.
v accomplish, bring about, carry out, complete, discharge, do, effect, enforce, execute, fulfil, perfect, perform, realise.

implementation *n* accomplishment, carrying out, completion, discharge, effecting, enforcement, execution, fulfilling, fulfilment, performance, performing, realisation.

implicate *v* associate, compromise, connect, embroil, entangle, include, incriminate, inculpate, involve, throw suspicion on. **antonyms** absolve, exonerate.

implication *n* association, assumption, conclusion, connection, entanglement, hint, incrimination, inference, innuendo, insinuation, involvement, meaning, overtone, presupposition, ramification, repercusssion, significance, signification, suggestion, undertone.

implicit *adj* absolute, constant, contained, entire, firm, fixed, full, implied, inherent, latent, presupposed, steadfast, tacit, total, undeclared, understood, unhesitating, unqualified, unquestioning, unreserved, unshakable, unshaken, unspoken, wholehearted. **antonym** explicit.

implicitly *adv* absolutely, by implication, completely, firmly, unconditionally, unhesitatingly, unquestioningly, unreservedly, utterly. **antonym** explicitly.

implied *adj* assumed, hinted, implicit, indirect, inherent, insinuated, suggested, tacit, undeclared, understood,

unexpressed, unspoken, unstated. **antonym** stated.

implore *v* ask, beg, beseech, crave, entreat, importune, plead, pray, solicit, supplicate.

imply *v* betoken, connote, denote, entail, evidence, hint, import, indicate, insinuate, intimate, involve, mean, point to, presuppose, require, signify, suggest. **antonym** state.

impolite *adj* abrupt, bad-mannered, boorish, churlish, clumsy, coarse, cross, discourteous, disrespectful, gauche, ill-bred, ill-mannered, indecorous, indelicate, inept, insolent, loutish, rough, rude, uncivil, uncourteous, ungallant, ungentlemanly, ungracious, unladylike, unmannerly, unrefined. **antonym** polite.

impoliteness *n* abruptness, bad manners, boorishness, churlishness, clumsiness, coarseness, crassness, discourtesy, disrespect, gaucherie, incivility, indelicacy, ineptitude, insolence, rudeness, unmannerliness. **antonym** politeness.

impolitic *adj* daft, foolish, ill-advised, ill-judged, imprudent, indiscreet, inexpedient, injudicious, maladroit, misguided, rash, undiplomatic, unwise. **antonym** politic.

import *n* bearing, consequence, drift, essence, gist, implication, importance, intention, magnitude, meaning, message, moment, nub, purport, sense, significance, substance, thrust, weight.
v betoken, bring in, imply, indicate, introduce, mean, purport, signify.

importance *n* concern, concernment, consequence, consideration, distinction, eminence, esteem, gravitas, import, influence, interest, mark, moment, momentousness, pith, pre-eminence, prestige, prominence, significance, signification, standing, status, substance, usefulness, value, weight, worth. **antonym** unimportance.

important *adj* basic, earthshaking, earthshattering, eminent, essential, far-reaching, foremost, grave, heavy, high-level, high-ranking, influential, key, keynote, large, leading, material, meaningful, momentous, notable, noteworthy, on the map, outstanding, powerful, pre-eminent, primary, prominent, relevant, salient, seminal, serious, signal, significant, substantial, urgent, valuable, valued, weighty. **antonym** unimportant.

importune *v* badger, beset, besiege, dun, earwig, entreat, flagitate, harass, hound, pester, plague, plead with, press, solicit, urge.

impose¹ *v* appoint, burden, charge (with), decree, dictate, encumber, enforce, enjoin, establish, exact, fix, inflict, institute, introduce, lay, levy, ordain, place, prescribe, promulgate, put, saddle, set.

impose² *v* butt in, encroach, foist, force oneself, interpose, intrude, obtrude, presume, take liberties, trespass.

impose on abuse, deceive, exploit, fool, hoodwink, mislead, play on, take advantage of, trick, use.

imposing *adj* august, commanding, dignified, distinguished, effective, grand, grandiose, impressive, majestic, pompous, stately, striking. *antonyms* modest, unimposing.

imposition¹ *n* application, decree, exaction, infliction, introduction, levying, promulgation.

imposition² *n* burden, charge, cheek, constraint, deception, duty, encroachment, intrusion, levy, liberty, lines, presumption, punishment, task, tax.

impossibility *n* hopelessness, impracticability, inability, inconceivability, unattainableness, unobtainableness, untenability, unviability. *antonym* possibility.

impossible *adj* absurd, hopeless, impracticable, inadmissible, inconceivable, insoluble, intolerable, ludicrous, outrageous, preposterous, unacceptable, unachievable, unattainable, ungovernable, unobtainable, unreasonable, untenable, unthinkable, unviable, unworkable. *antonym* possible.

impostor *n* charlatan, cheat, con man, deceiver, fake, fraud, grifter, hypocrite, impersonator, mountebank, phoney, pretender, quack, rogue, sham, swindler, trickster.

impotence *n* disability, enervation, feebleness, frailty, helplessness, inability, inadequacy, incapacity, incompetence, ineffectiveness, inefficacy, inefficiency, infirmity, paralysis, powerlessness, resourcelessness, uselessness, weakness. *antonym* strength.

impotent *adj* disabled, enervated, feeble, frail, helpless, impuissant, inadequate, incapable, incapacitated, incompetent, ineffective, infirm, paralysed, powerless, resourceless, unable, unmanned, weak. *antonyms* potent, strong.

impoverish *v* bankrupt, beggar, break, denude, deplete, diminish, drain, exhaust, reduce, ruin, weaken. *antonym* enrich.

impoverished *adj* arid, bankrupt, barren, decayed, denuded, depleted, destitute, distressed, drained, empty, exhausted, impecunious, in reduced circumstances, indigent, necessitous, needy, on the rocks, penurious, poor, poorly off, reduced, skint, spent, straitened. *antonym* rich.

impracticability *n* futility, hopelessness, impossibility, impracticality, infeasibility, unsuitableness, unviability, unworkability, uselessness. *antonym* practicability.

impracticable *adj* awkward, doctrinaire, impossible, impractical, inapplicable, inconvenient, infeasible, unachievable, unattainable, unfeasible, unpractical, unserviceable, unsuitable, unworkable, useless, visionary. *antonym* practicable.

impractical *adj* academic, idealistic, impossible, impracticable, inoperable, ivory-tower, non-viable, romantic, starry-eyed, unbusinesslike, unrealistic, unserviceable, unworkable, visionary, wild. *antonym* practical.

impracticality *n* hopelessness, idealism, impossibility, infeasibility, romanticism, unworkability, unworkableness. *antonym* practicality.

imprecation *n* abuse, blasphemy, curse, denunciation, execration, malediction, profanity, vilification, vituperation.

imprecise *adj* ambiguous, careless, equivocal, estimated, fluctuating, hazy, ill-defined, inaccurate, indefinite, indeterminate, inexact, inexplicit, loose, rough, sloppy, unprecise, unscholarly, unscientific, vague, woolly. *antonym* precise.

impregnable *adj* fast, fortified, immovable, impenetrable, impugnable, indestructible, invincible, invulnerable, secure, solid, strong, unassailable, unbeatable, unconquerable. *antonym* vulnerable.

impregnate *v* fertilise, fill, imbrue, imbue, infuse, inseminate, percolate, permeate, pervade, saturate, soak, steep, suffuse.

impress *v* affect, emboss, emphasise, engrave, excite, fix, grab, imprint, inculcate, indent, influence, inspire, instil, make one's mark, mark, move, namedrop, print, slay, stamp, stand out, stir, strike, sway, touch, wow.

impressed *adj* affected, excited, grabbed, imprinted, indented, influenced, marked, moved, stamped, stirred, struck, taken, touched, turned on. *antonym* unimpressed.

impression[1] *n* awareness, belief, concept, consciousness, conviction, effect, fancy, feeling, hunch, idea, impact, influence, memory, notion, opinion, reaction, recollection, sense, suspicion, sway.

impression[2] *n* dent, edition, hollow, impress, imprint, imprinting, incuse, indentation, issue, mark, outline, pressure, printing, stamp, stamping.

impressionable *adj* gullible, ingenuous, naïve, open, receptive, responsive, sensitive, suggestible, susceptible, vulnerable.

impressive *adj* affecting, effective, exciting, forcible, imposing, moving, powerful, stirring, striking, touching. *antonym* unimpressive.

imprint *n* badge, brand mark, impression, indentation, logo, mark, print, sign, stamp.
v brand, engrave, etch, fix, impress, mark, print, stamp.

imprison *v* cage, confine, constrain, detain, encage, enchain, immure, incarcerate, intern, jail, lock up, put away, send down. *antonym* free.

imprisoned *adj* behind bars, caged, captive, confined, doing bird, doing time, immured, incarcerated, jailed, locked up, put away, sent down. *antonym* free.

imprisonment *n* bird, confinement, custody, detention, durance, duress(e), enchainment, incarceration, internment, porridge. *antonym* freedom.

improbability *n* doubt, doubtfulness, dubiety, dubiousness, far-fetchedness, implausibility, uncertainty, unlikelihood, unlikeliness. *antonym* probability.

improbable *adj* doubtful, dubious, fanciful, far-fetched, implausible, preposterous, questionable, tall, unbelievable, uncertain, unconvincing, unlikely, weak. *antonym* probable.

impromptu *adj* ad-lib, extemporaneous, extempore, extemporised, improvised, off the cuff, offhand, spontaneous, unpremeditated, unprepared, unrehearsed, unscripted, unstudied. *antonyms* planned, rehearsed.

adv ad lib, extempore, off the cuff, off the top of one's head, on the spur of the moment, spontaneously.
n extemporisation, improvisation, voluntary.

improper *adj* abnormal, erroneous, false, illegitimate, ill-timed, impolite, inaccurate, inadmissible, inapplicable, inapposite, inappropriate, inapt, incongruous, incorrect, indecent, indecorous, indelicate, infelicitous, inopportune, irregular, off-colour, out of place, risqué, smutty, suggestive, unbecoming, uncalled-for, unfit, unfitting, unmaidenly, unparliamentary, unprintable, unquotable, unrepeatable, unseasonable, unseemly, unsuitable, unsuited, untoward, unwarranted, vulgar, wrong. *antonym* proper.

impropriety *n* bad taste, blunder, faux pas, gaffe, gaucherie, immodesty, incongruity, indecency, indecorousness, indecorum, lapse, mistake, slip, solecism, unseemliness, unsuitability, vulgarity. *antonym* propriety.

improve *v* advance, ameliorate, amend, augment, better, correct, culture, develop, enhance, gentrify, help, increase, look up, mend, mend one's ways, perk up, pick up, polish, progress, rally, recover, rectify, recuperate, reform, rise, touch up, turn over a new leaf, turn the corner, up, upgrade. *antonyms* decline, diminish.

improvement *n* advance, advancement, amelioration, amendment, augmentation, bettering, betterment, correction, development, enhancement, furtherance, gain, gentrification, increase, progress, rally, recovery, rectification, reformation, rise, upswing. *antonyms* decline, retrogression.

improvident *adj* careless, feckless, heedless, imprudent, negligent, prodigal, profligate, reckless, shiftless, spendthrift, thoughtless, thriftless, underprepared, uneconomical, unprepared, unthrifty, wasteful. *antonym* thrifty.

improvisation *n* ad-lib, ad-libbing, expedient, extemporising, impromptu, invention, makeshift, spontaneity, vamp.

improvise *v* ad-lib, coin, concoct, contrive, devise, extemporise, invent, noodle, play it by ear, throw together, vamp.

improvised *adj* ad-lib, extemporaneous, extempore, extemporised, improvisational, makeshift, off-the-cuff, spontaneous, unprepared, unrehearsed.

antonym rehearsed.

imprudent *adj* careless, foolhardy, foolish, hasty, heedless, ill-advised, ill-considered, ill-judged, impolitic, improvident, incautious, inconsiderate, indiscreet, injudicious, irresponsible, overhasty, rash, reckless, short-sighted, temerarious, unthinking, unwise. *antonym* prudent.

impudence *n* assurance, audacity, backchat, boldness, brass neck, brazenness, cheek, chutzpah, effrontery, face, impertinence, impudicity, insolence, lip, neck, nerve, pertness, presumption, presumptuousness, rudeness, sauciness, shamelessness. *antonym* politeness.

impudent *adj* audacious, bold, bold-faced, brazen, brazen-faced, cheeky, cocky, forward, fresh, immodest, impertinent, insolent, pert, presumptuous, rude, saucy, shameless. *antonym* polite.

impugn *v* assail, attack, call in question, challenge, criticise, dispute, oppose, question, resist, revile, traduce, vilify, vituperate. *antonym* praise.

impulse *n* caprice, catalyst, desire, drive, feeling, force, impetus, incitement, inclination, influence, instinct, momentum, motive, movement, notion, passion, pressure, push, resolve, stimulus, surge, thrust, urge, whim, wish.

impulsive *adj* hasty, headlong, impetuous, instinctive, intuitive, passionate, precipitant, precipitate, quick, rash, reckless, spontaneous, unconsidered, unpredictable, unpremeditated. *antonym* cautious.

impunity *n* amnesty, dispensation, exemption, freedom, immunity, liberty, licence, permission, security. *antonym* liability.

impure *adj* adulterated, alloyed, carnal, coarse, contaminated, corrupt, debased, defiled, dirty, filthy, foul, gross, immodest, immoral, indecent, indelicate, infected, lascivious, lewd, licentious, lustful, mixed, obscene, polluted, prurient, salacious, smutty, sullied, tainted, turbid, unchaste, unclean, unrefined, unwholesome, vicious, vitiated. *antonyms* chaste, pure.

impurity *n* adulteration, carnality, coarseness, contaminant, contamination, corruption, dirt, dirtiness, dross, filth, foreign body, foreign matter, foulness, grime, grossness, immodesty, immorality, indecency, infection, lasciviousness, lewdness, licentiousness,

mark, mixture, obscenity, pollutant, pollution, prurience, salaciousness, scum, smuttiness, spot, stain, taint, turbidity, turbidness, unchastity, uncleanness, vulgarity. *antonyms* chasteness, purity.

imputation *n* accusation, arrogation, ascription, aspersion, attribution, blame, censure, charge, insinuation, reproach, slander, slur, suggestion.

impute *v* accredit, ascribe, assign, attribute, charge, credit, put down to, refer.

in a state agitated, anxious, distressed, disturbed, flustered, hassled, het up, in a stew, in a tizzy, panic-stricken, ruffled, steamed up, troubled, upset, worked up, worried. *antonym* calm.

in a word briefly, concisely, in a nutshell, in short, succinctly, to be brief, to put it briefly, to sum up. *antonym* at length.

in abeyance dormant, hanging fire, on ice, pending, shelved, suspended.

in addition additionally, also, as well, besides, further, furthermore, into the bargain, moreover, over and above, to boot, too.

in advance ahead, beforehand, earlier, in front, in the forefront, in the lead, previously, sooner. *antonyms* behind, later.

in camera behind closed doors, huggermugger, in private, in secret, privately, secretly, sub rosa. *antonym* openly.

in confidence in private, privately, secretly, sub rosa.

in conflict at daggers drawn, at loggerheads, at odds, at variance, at war, disagreeing, disunited, in disagreement, opposed. *antonyms* at peace, in agreement.

in depth comprehensively, exhaustively, extensively, in detail, intensively, thoroughly. *antonyms* broadly, superficially.

in detail comprehensively, exhaustively, in depth, in particular, inside out, item by item, particularly, point by point, thoroughly. *antonyms* broadly, superficially.

in difficulties in a hole, in dire straits, in the shit, up shit creek, up the creek.

in effect actually, effectively, essentially, for practical purposes, in actuality, in fact, in reality, in the end, in truth, really, to all intents and purposes, virtually, when all is said and done.

in fact actually, in point of fact, in reality, in truth, indeed, really, truly.

in favour of all for, backing, for, on the side of, pro, supporting, to the advantage of. *antonym* against.

in force binding, current, effective, in crowds, in droves, in flocks, in hordes, in large numbers, in operation, in strength, on the statute book, operative, valid, working. *antonym* inoperative.

in front ahead, before, first, in advance, leading, preceding, to the fore. *antonym* behind.

in full completely, entirely, in its entirety, in total, in toto, unabridged, uncut, wholly. *antonyms* partially, partly.

in good part cheerfully, cordially, good-naturedly, laughingly, well. *antonyms* angrily, touchily.

in hiding concealed, doggo, hidden.

in keeping appropriate, befitting, fit, fitting, harmonious, in harmony, of a piece, suitable. *antonym* inappropriate.

in kind in like manner, similarly, tit for tat.

in league allied, collaborating, conniving, conspiring, hand in glove, in cahoots, in collusion. *antonym* at odds.

in love besotted, charmed, doting, enamoured, enraptured, hooked, infatuated, smitten.

in motion functioning, going, in progress, moving, on the go, operational, running, sailing, travelling, under way. *antonym* stationary.

in order acceptable, all right, allowed, appropriate, arranged, called for, correct, done, fitting, in sequence, neat, OK, orderly, permitted, right, shipshape, suitable, tidy. *antonyms* disallowed, out of order.

in order to intending to, so that, to, with a view to, with the intention of, with the purpose of.

in part a little, in some measure, part way, partially, partly, slightly, somewhat, to a certain extent, to some degree. *antonym* wholly.

in particular distinctly, especially, exactly, expressly, in detail, particularly, specifically.

in pieces broken, burst, damaged, disintegrated, in bits, in smithereens, kaput, piecemeal, ruined, shattered, smashed.

in place of as a replacement for, as a substitute for, as an alternative to, in exchange for, in lieu of, instead of.

in private behind closed doors, hugger-mugger, in camera, in confidence, in secret, privately, secretly, sub rosa. *antonym* openly.

in progress going on, happening, occurring, proceeding, under way.

in public for all to see, in full view, in open view, in the open, openly, publicly. *antonyms* in camera, in secret.

in secret hugger-mugger, in confidence, inwardly, on the q.t., on the quiet, sub rosa. *antonym* openly.

in spite of despite, notwithstanding.

in the interest(s) of for the sake of, on behalf of, on the part of, to the advantage of, to the benefit of.

in the light of bearing/keeping in mind, because of, considering, in view of, taking into account.

in the making budding, coming, developing, emergent, growing, nascent, potential, up and coming.

in the middle of among, busy with, during, engaged in, in the midst of, in the process of, occupied with, surrounded by, while.

in the midst of among, during, in the middle of, in the thick of, surrounded by.

in the money affluent, flush, loaded, opulent, prosperous, rich, rolling in it, wealthy, well-heeled, well-off, well-to-do. *antonym* poor.

in the mood disposed, in the right frame of mind, inclined, interested, keen, minded, of a mind, willing.

in the offing at hand, close at hand, coming up, imminent, in sight, on the horizon, on the way. *antonym* far off.

in the red bankrupt, in arrears, in debt, insolvent, on the rocks, overdrawn. *antonym* in credit.

in the wrong at fault, blameworthy, guilty, in error, mistaken, to blame. *antonym* in the right.

in toto as a whole, completely, entirely, in its entirety, in total, totally, unabridged, uncut, wholly.

in two minds dithering, hesitant, hesitating, shilly-shallying, swithering, uncertain, undecided, unsure, vacillating, wavering. *antonym* certain.

in vain fruitlessly, ineffectually, to no avail, unsuccessfully, uselessly, vainly. *antonym* successfully.

inability *n* disability, disqualification, handicap, impotence, inadequacy, incapability, incapacity, incompetence, ineptitude, ineptness, powerlessness, weakness.

inaccessible *adj* impassible, isolated, remote, solitary, unapproachable, unattainable, unfrequented, unget-at-able, unreachable.

inaccuracy *n* blunder, boob, careless-ness, defect, erratum, erroneousness, error, fault, faultiness, howler, imprecision, incorrectness, inexactness, looseness, miscalculation, mistake, slip, unreliability. *antonym* accuracy.

inaccurate *adj* careless, defective, discrepant, erroneous, faulty, imprecise, in error, incorrect, inexact, loose, mistaken, out, unfaithful, unreliable, unrepresentative, unsound, wide of the mark, wild, wrong.

inaction *n* dormancy, idleness, immobility, inactivity, inertia, rest, stagnation, stasis, torpidity, torpor. *antonym* activeness.

inactive *adj* abeyant, dormant, dull, idle, immobile, indolent, inert, inoperative, jobless, kicking one's heels, latent, lazy, lethargic, low-key, mothballed, out of service, out of work, passive, quiet, sed-entary, sleepy, slothful, slow, sluggish, somnolent, stagnant, stagnating, torpid, unemployed, unoccupied, unused.

inactivity *n* abeyance, dilatoriness, dormancy, dullness, heaviness, hiber-nation, idleness, immobility, inaction, indolence, inertia, inertness, languor, lassitude, laziness, lethargy, passivity, quiescence, sloth, sluggishness, stagnation, stasis, torpor, unemployment, vegetation. *antonym* activeness.

inadequacy *n* dearth, defect, defec-tiveness, deficiency, failing, faultiness, imperfection, inability, inadequateness, inaptness, incapacity, incompetence, incompetency, incompleteness, ineffec-tiveness, ineffectuality, ineffectualness, inefficacy, inefficiency, insufficiency, lack, meagreness, paucity, poverty, scantiness, shortage, shortcoming, skimpiness, unfitness, unsuitableness, want, weakness.

inadequate *adj* defective, deficient, faulty, imperfect, inapt, incapa-ble, incommensurate, incompetent, incomplete, ineffective, ineffectual, inefficacious, inefficient, insubstantial, insufficient, leaving a little/a lot/much to be desired, meagre, niggardly, scanty, short, sketchy, skimpy, sparse, unequal, unfitted, unqualified, wanting.

inadequately *adv* badly, carelessly, imperfectly, insufficiently, meagrely, poorly, scantily, sketchily, skimpily, sparsely, thinly.

inadmissible *adj* disallowed,

immaterial, improper, inappropriate, incompetent, irrelevant, prohibited, unacceptable, unallowable, unqualified.

inadvertent *adj* accidental, careless, chance, heedless, inattentive, negligent, thoughtless, unguarded, unheeding, unintended, unintentional, unplanned, unpremeditated, unthinking, unwitting. *antonym* deliberate.

inadvertently *adv* accidentally, by accident, by mistake, carelessly, heedlessly, involuntarily, mistakenly, negligently, remissly, thoughtlessly, un-guardedly, unintentionally, unthinkingly, unwittingly. *antonym* deliberately.

inadvisable *adj* daft, foolish, ill-advised, ill-judged, impolitic, imprudent, incautious, indiscreet, inexpedient, injudicious, misguided, unwise. *antonym* advisable.

inalienable *adj* absolute, entailed, imprescriptible, infrangible, inherent, inviolable, non-negotiable, non-transferable, permanent, sacrosanct, unassailable, unremovable, untransfer-able. *antonym* impermanent.

inane *adj* asinine, daft, drippy, empty, fatuous, foolish, frivolous, futile, idiotic, imbecilic, mindless, nutty, puerile, senseless, silly, stupid, trifling, unintelligent, vacuous, vain, vapid, worthless. *antonym* sensible.

inanimate *adj* dead, dormant, dull, extinct, heavy, inactive, inert, inorganic, insensate, insentient, leaden, lifeless, listless, slow, spiritless, stagnant, torpid. *antonyms* alive, animate, lively, living.

inapplicable *adj* inapposite, inappro-priate, inapt, inconsequent, irrelevant, unrelated, unsuitable, unsuited.

inappropriate *adj* disproportionate, ill-fitted, ill-suited, ill-timed, improper, incongruous, infelicitous, out of place, tactless, tasteless, unbecoming, unbefitting, unfit, unfitting, unseemly, unsuitable, untimely.

inapt *adj* awkward, clumsy, crass, dull, gauche, ill-fitted, ill-suited, ill-timed, inapposite, inappropriate, incompetent, inept, inexpert, infelicitous, inopportune, slow, stupid, tactless, unapt, unfortunate, unhappy, unsuitable, unsuited.

inaptitude *n* awkwardness, clumsiness, crassness, inaptness, incompetence, inopportuneness, tactlessness, unfitness, unreadiness, unsuitableness.

inarticulate *adj* blurred, dumb, faltering, halting, hesitant, incoherent, incomprehensible, indistinct, muffled, mumbled, silent, speechless, tongue-tied, unclear, unintelligible.

inattention n absence of mind, absent-mindedness, carelessness, daydreaming, disregard, forgetfulness, heedlessness, inadvertence, inattentiveness, neglect, preoccupation, wool-gathering. **antonym** attentiveness.

inattentive adj absent-minded, careless, deaf, distracted, dreaming, dreamy, heedless, inadvertent, neglectful, negligent, preoccupied, regardless, remiss, unheeding, unmindful, unobservant, vague.

inaudible adj faint, imperceptible, indistinct, low, muffled, mumbled, mumbling, muted, noiseless, out of earshot, silent.

inaugural adj consecratory, dedicatory, first, initial, introductory, launching, maiden, opening.

inaugurate v begin, christen, commence, commission, consecrate, dedicate, enthrone, induct, initiate, install, instate, institute, introduce, invest, kick off, launch, open, ordain, originate, set up, start, start off, usher in.

inauguration n consecration, enthronement, induction, initiation, installation, installing, institution, investiture, launch, launching, opening, setting up.

inauspicious adj bad, black, discouraging, ill-boding, ill-omened, ominous, threatening, unfavourable, unfortunate, unlucky, unpromising, unpropitious, untoward.

inborn adj congenital, hereditary, inbred, ingenerate, ingrained, inherent, inherited, innate, instinctive, intuitive, native, natural. **antonym** learned.

inbred adj constitutional, ingenerate, ingrained, inherent, innate, native, natural. **antonym** learned.

incalculable adj boundless, countless, enormous, immense, incomputable, inestimable, infinite, innumerable, limitless, measureless, numberless, uncountable, unforeseeable, unlimited, unmeasureable, unpredictable, untold, vast. **antonym** limited.

incapable adj disqualified, drunk, feeble, helpless, impotent, inadequate, incompetent, ineffective, ineffectual, inept, insufficient, powerless, tipsy, unable, unfit, unfitted, unqualified, weak.

incapacitate v cripple, disable, disqualify, hamstring, immobilise, lay up, paralyse, prostrate, put out of action, scupper, unfit. **antonyms** facilitate, set up.

incapacitated adj disqualified, drunk, hamstrung, immobilised, indisposed, laid up, out of action, prostrate, scuppered, tipsy, unfit, unwell. **antonym** operative.

incapacity n disability, disqualification, feebleness, impotence, inability, inadequacy, incapability, incompetency, ineffectiveness, powerlessness, unfitness, weakness. **antonym** capability.

incapsulate see **encapsulate**.

incarcerate v cage, commit, confine, coop up, detain, encage, gaol, immure, impound, imprison, intern, jail, lock up, put away, restrain, restrict, send down, wall in. **antonym** free.

incarceration n bondage, captivity, confinement, custody, detention, imprisonment, internment, jail, restraint, restriction. **antonym** freedom.

incarnation n avatar, embodiment, exemplification, impersonation, manifestation, personification, type.

incautious adj careless, hasty, heedless, illadvised, ill-judged, improvident, imprudent, impulsive, inconsiderate, indiscreet, injudicious, negligent, overhasty, precipitate, rash, reckless, thoughtless, unchary, unguarded, unthinking, unwary. **antonym** cautious.

incense v anger, enrage, exasperate, excite, inflame, infuriate, irritate, madden, make one see red, make one's blood boil, make one's hackles rise, provoke, raise one's hackles, rile. **antonym** calm.

incensed adj angry, enraged, exasperated, fuming, furious, indignant, infuriated, irate, mad, maddened, on the warpath, steamed up, up in arms, wrathful. **antonym** calm.

incentive n bait, carrot, cause, consideration, encouragement, enticement, impetus, impulse, inducement, lure, motivation, motive, reason, reward, spur, stimulant, stimulus. **antonym** disincentive.

inception n beginning, birth, commencement, dawn, inauguration, initiation, installation, kick-off, origin, outset, rise, start. **antonym** end.

incessant adj ceaseless, constant, continual, continuous, endless, eternal, everlasting, interminable, never-ending, non-stop, perpetual, persistent, relentless, unbroken, unceasing, unending, unrelenting, unremitting. *antonym* intermittent.

incidence *n* amount, commonness, degree, extent, frequency, occurrence, prevalence, range, rate.

incident *n* adventure, affair, brush, circumstance, clash, commotion, confrontation, contretemps, disturbance, episode, event, fight, happening, mishap, occasion, occurrence, scene, skirmish.

incidental *adj* accidental, accompanying, ancillary, attendant, casual, chance, concomitant, contingent, contributory, fortuitous, incident, inconsequential, inessential, irrelevant, minor, nonessential, occasional, odd, random, related, secondary, subordinate, subsidiary. *antonym* essential.

incidentally *adv* accidentally, by chance, by the by(e), by the way, casually, digressively, fortuitously, in passing, parenthetically.

incinerate *v* burn, char, cremate, reduce to ashes.

incipient *adj* beginning, commencing, developing, embryonic, inceptive, inchoate, nascent, originating, rudimentary, starting. *antonym* developed.

incisive *adj* acid, acute, astute, biting, caustic, cutting, keen, mordant, penetrating, perceptive, perspicacious, piercing, sarcastic, sardonic, satirical, severe, sharp, tart, trenchant. *antonym* woolly.

incisiveness *n* acidity, astuteness, keenness, penetration, perspicacity, pungency, sarcasm, sharpness, tartness, trenchancy. *antonym* woolliness.

incite *v* abet, animate, drive, egg on, encourage, excite, foment, goad, impel, inflame, instigate, prompt, provoke, put up to, rouse, set on, solicit, spur, stimulate, stir up, urge, whip up. *antonym* restrain.

incitement *n* abetment, agitation, encouragement, goad, hortation, impetus, impulse, inducement, instigation, motivation, motive, prompting, provocation, spur, stimulus. *antonyms* check, discouragement.

inciting *adj* exciting, incendiary, inflammatory, provocative, rabble-rousing. *antonym* calming.

incivility *n* bad manners, boorishness, coarseness, discourteousness, discourtesy, disrespect, ill-breeding, impoliteness, inurbanity, roughness, rudeness, unmannerliness, vulgarity. *antonym* civility.

inclement *adj* bitter, boisterous, callous, cruel, draconian, foul, harsh, intemperate, merciless, pitiless, rigorous, rough, severe, stormy, tempestuous, tyrannical, unfeeling, ungenial, unmerciful. *antonym* clement.

inclination[1] *n* affection, aptitude, bent, bias, desire, disposition, fancy, fondness, leaning, liking, month's mind, partiality, penchant, predilection, predisposition, prejudice, proclivity, proneness, propensity, stomach, taste, tendency, turn, turn of mind, velleity, wish. *antonym* disinclination.

inclination[2] *n* angle, bend, bending, bow, bowing, deviation, gradient, incline, leaning, nod, pitch, slant, slope, tilt.

incline[1] *v* affect, bias, dispose, influence, nod, persuade, predispose, prejudice, stoop, sway.

incline[2] *v* bend, bevel, bow, cant, deviate, diverge, lean, slant, slope, tend, tilt, tip, veer.
n acclivity, ascent, brae, declivity, descent, dip, grade, gradient, hill, ramp, rise, slope.

inclined *adj* apt, bent, disposed, given, liable, likely, minded, oblique, of a mind, predisposed, prone, sloping, tilted, willing. *antonym* flat.

inclose *see* **enclose**.

include *v* add, allow for, comprehend, comprise, connote, contain, cover, embody, embrace, enclose, encompass, incorporate, involve, number among, rope in, subsume, take in, take into account. *antonyms* exclude, ignore.

inclusion *n* addition, incorporation, insertion, involvement. *antonym* exclusion.

inclusive *adj* across-the-board, all in, all-embracing, blanket, catch-all, compendious, comprehensive, full, general, overall, sweeping, umbrella. *antonyms* exclusive, narrow.

incognito *adj* disguised, in disguise, masked, unknown, unrecognisable, unrecognised, veiled. *antonyms* open, undisguised.

incoherent *adj* confused, disconnected, disjointed, dislocated, disordered, inarticulate, inconsequent, inconsistent, jumbled, loose, muddled, rambling, stammering, stuttering, unconnected, unco-ordinated, unintelligible, unjointed, wandering, wild.

incombustible *adj* fireproof, fire-resistant, flameproof, flame-resistant, non-flammable, non-inflammable.

income *n* earnings, gains, interest, means, pay, proceeds, profits, receipts, returns, revenue, salary, takings, wages, yield. **antonym** expenses.

incoming *adj* accruing, approaching, arriving, coming, ensuing, entering, homeward, landing, new, next, returning, succeeding. **antonym** outgoing.

incommensurate *adj* disproportionate, excessive, extravagant, extreme, inadequate, inequitable, inordinate, insufficient, unequal. **antonym** appropriate.

incommunicable *adj* indescribable, ineffable, inexpressible, unimpartable, unspeakable, unutterable. **antonym** expressible.

incomparable *adj* brilliant, inimitable, matchless, paramount, peerless, superb, superlative, supreme, unequalled, unmatched, unparalleled, unrivalled. **antonyms** poor, run-of-the-mill.

incomparably *adv* brilliantly, by far, eminently, far and away, immeasurably, superbly, superlatively. **antonyms** poorly, slightly.

incompatibility *n* antagonism, clash, conflict, difference, discrepancy, disparateness, disparity, incongruity, inconsistency, irreconcilability, mismatch, uncongeniality.

incompatible *adj* antagonistic, antipathetic, clashing, conflicting, contradictory, discordant, discrepant, disparate, ill-assorted, incongruous, inconsistent, inconsonant, inharmonious, irreconcilable, mismatched, uncongenial, unsuitable, unsuited.

incompetence *n* bungling, inability, inadequacy, incapability, incapacity, incompetency, ineffectiveness, ineffectuality, ineffectualness, inefficiency, ineptitude, ineptness, insufficiency, stupidity, unfitness, uselessness.

incompetent *adj* bungling, floundering, incapable, incapacitated, ineffective, ineffectual, inept, inexpert, insufficient, stupid, unable, unfit, unfitted, unskilful, useless.

incomplete *adj* broken, defective, deficient, fragmentary, imperfect, insufficient, lacking, part, partial, short, unaccomplished, undeveloped, undone, unexecuted, unfinished, wanting.

incomprehensible *adj* above one's head, arcane, baffling, beyond one's comprehension, beyond one's grasp, double-Dutch, enigmatic, impenetrable, inapprehensible, inconceivable, inscrutable, mysterious, obscure, opaque, perplexing, puzzling, unfathomable, unimaginable, unintelligible, unthinkable.

inconceivable *adj* implausible, incogitable, incredible, mind-boggling, out of the question, staggering, unbelievable, unheard-of, unimaginable, unknowable, unthinkable.

inconclusive *adj* ambiguous, indecisive, indeterminate, open, uncertain, unconvincing, undecided, unsatisfying, unsettled, vague.

incongruity *n* conflict, discrepancy, disparity, dissociability, inappropriateness, inaptness, incompatibility, inconsistency, inharmoniousness, unsuitability. **antonyms** consistency, harmoniousness.

incongruous *adj* absurd, conflicting, contradictory, contrary, disconsonant, discordant, dissociable, extraneous, improper, inappropriate, inapt, incoherent, incompatible, inconsistent, out of keeping, out of place, unbecoming, unsuitable, unsuited. **antonyms** consistent, harmonious.

inconsequential *adj* illogical, immaterial, inconsequent, inconsiderable, insignificant, minor, negligible, paltry, petty, trifling, trivial, unimportant. **antonym** important.

inconsiderable *adj* exiguous, inconsequential, insignificant, light, minor, negligible, petty, piddling, piffling, slight, small, small-time, trifling, trivial, unimportant, unnoticeable.

inconsiderate *adj* careless, imprudent, indelicate, insensitive, intolerant, rash, rude, self-centred, selfish, tactless, thoughtless, unconcerned, ungracious, unkind, unthinking.

inconsistency *n* changeableness, contrariety, disagreement, discrepancy, disparity, divergence, fickleness, incompatibility, incongruity, inconsonance, inconstancy, instability, paradox, unpredictability, unreliability, unsteadiness, variance.

inconsistent *adj* at odds, at variance, capricious, changeable, conflicting, contradictory, contrary, discordant, discrepant, erratic, fickle, incoherent, incompatible, incongruous, inconstant, irreconcilable, irregular, unpredictable, unstable, unsteady, variable, varying.

inconsistently *adv* contradictorily, differently, eccentrically, erratically, illogically, inequably, randomly, unequally, unfairly, unpredictably, variably.

inconsolable *adj* brokenhearted, desolate, desolated, despairing, devastated, disconsolate, heartbroken, wretched.

inconspicuous *adj* camouflaged, hidden, insignificant, low-key, modest, muted, ordinary, plain, quiet, retiring, unassuming, unnoticeable, unobtrusive, unostentatious.

inconstant *adj* capricious, chameleon(ic), changeable, erratic, fickle, fluctuating, inconsistent, irresolute, mercurial, mutable, uncertain, undependable, unreliable, unsettled, unstable, unsteady, vacillating, variable, varying, volatile, wavering, wayward.

incontestable *adj* certain, clear, evident, incontrovertible, indisputable, indubitable, irrefutable, obvious, self-evident, sure, undeniable, unquestionable. **antonym** uncertain.

incontinent *adj* debauched, dissipated, dissolute, enuretic, lascivious, lecherous, lewd, licentious, loose, lustful, profligate, promiscuous, unbridled, unchaste, unchecked, uncontrollable, uncontrolled, ungovernable, ungoverned, unrestrained, wanton.

incontrovertible *adj* certain, clear, established, evident, incontestable, indisputable, indubitable, irrefutable, positive, self-evident, sure, undeniable, unquestionable, unshakable. **antonym** uncertain.

inconvenience *n* annoyance, awkwardness, bother, cumbersomeness, difficulty, disadvantage, disruption, disturbance, drawback, fuss, hindrance, nuisance, trouble, uneasiness, unhandiness, unsuitableness, untimeliness, unwieldiness, upset, vexation.

v bother, disaccommodate, discommode, disrupt, disturb, irk, put out, put to trouble, trouble, upset.

inconvenient *adj* annoying, awkward, bothersome, cumbersome, difficult, disadvantageous, disturbing, embarrassing, inopportune, tiresome, troublesome, unhandy, unmanageable, unseasonable, unsocial, unsuitable, untimely, untoward, unwieldy, vexatious.

incorporate *v* absorb, amalgamate, assimilate, blend, coalesce, combine, consolidate, embody, fuse, incarnate, include, integrate, merge, mix, subsume, unite. **antonyms** separate, split off.

incorporation *n* absorption, amalgamation, assimilation, association, blend, coalescence, company, federation, fusion, inclusion, integration, merger, society, unification, unifying. **antonyms** separation, splitting off.

incorrect *adj* erroneous, false, faulty, flawed, illegitimate, imprecise, improper, inaccurate, inappropriate, inexact, mistaken, out, specious, ungrammatical, unidiomatic, unsuitable, untrue, wrong.

incorrectness *n* erroneousness, error, fallacy, falseness, faultiness, illegitimacy, impreciseness, imprecision, impropriety, inaccuracy, inexactness, speciousness, ungrammaticalness, unsoundness, unsuitability, wrongness. **antonym** correctness.

incorrigible *adj* hardened, hopeless, impenitent, incurable, intractable, inveterate, irreclaimable, irredeemable, irreformable, unreformable, unreformed, unteachable. **antonym** reformable.

incorruptibility *n* honesty, honour, integrity, justness, nobility, probity, uprightness, virtue.

incorruptible *adj* everlasting, honest, honourable, imperishable, incorrupt, just, straight, trustworthy, unbribable, undecaying, upright.

increase *v* add to, advance, aggrandise, amplify, augment, boost, build up, develop, dilate, eke, eke out, enhance, enlarge, escalate, expand, extend, greaten, grow, heighten, inflate, intensify, magnify, mount, multiply, proliferate, prolong, pullulate, raise, snowball, soar, spread, step up, strengthen, swell, wax. **antonym** decrease.

n addition, augmentation, boost, development, enlargement, escalation, expansion, extension, gain, growth, increment, intensification, proliferation, rise, step-up, surge, upsurge, upsurgence, upturn. **antonym** decrease.

increasing *adj* advancing, broadening, developing, expanding, growing, intensifying, mounting, rising, rocketing, sprouting, waxing, widening. **antonym** decreasing.

incredible *adj* absurd, amazing, astonishing, astounding, extraordinary, fabulous, far-fetched, great, implausible, impossible, improbable, inconceivable, inspired, marvellous, preposterous, prodigious, superb, superhuman, unbelievable, unimaginable, unthinkable, wonderful. **antonyms** believable, run-of-the-mill.

incredulity *n* disbelief, distrust, doubt, doubting, incredulousness, scepticism, unbelief.

incredulous *adj* disbelieving, distrustful, doubtful, doubting, dubious, mistrustful, sceptical, suspicious, unbelieving, uncertain, unconvinced.

increment *n* addition, advancement, augmentation, enlargement, expansion, extension, gain, growth, increase, step up, supplement. **antonym** decrease.

incriminate *v* accuse, arraign, blame, charge, impeach, implicate, inculpate, indict, involve, point the finger at, recriminate, stigmatise. **antonym** exonerate.

inculcate *v* drill into, drum into, engrain, hammer into, implant, impress, indoctrinate, infuse, instil, teach.

inculpate *v* accuse, blame, censure, charge, connect, drag into, impeach, implicate, incriminate, involve, recriminate. **antonym** exonerate.

incumbent *adj* binding, compulsory, mandatory, necessary, obligatory, prescribed, up to.

incur *v* arouse, bring upon, contract, draw, earn, expose oneself to, gain, induce, meet with, provoke, run up, suffer.

incurable *adj* dyed-in-the-wool, fatal, hopeless, incorrigible, inoperable, inveterate, irrecoverable, irremediable, terminal, untreatable.

incurious *adj* apathetic, careless, inattentive, indifferent, unconcerned, uncurious, unenquiring, uninquiring, uninquisitive, uninterested, unreflective.

incursion *n* attack, foray, infiltration, inroads, invasion, irruption, penetration, raid.

indebted *adj* beholden, grateful, in debt, obligated, obliged, thankful.

indecency *n* bawdiness, coarseness, crudity, foulness, grossness, immodesty, impropriety, impurity, indecorum, indelicacy, lewdness, licentiousness, obscenity, outrageousness, pornography, smut, smuttiness, unseemliness, vileness, vulgarity. **antonym** modesty.

indecent *adj* blue, coarse, crude, dirty, filthy, foul, gross, immodest, improper, impure, indecorous, indelicate, lewd, licentious, near the knuckle, offensive, outrageous, pornographic, salacious, scatological, smutty, tasteless, unbecoming, uncomely, unseemly, vile, vulgar. **antonym** modest.

indecipherable *adj* illegible, indistinct,

indistinguishable, unclear, unintelligible, unreadable. **antonym** readable.

indecision *n* ambivalence, doubt, hesitancy, hesitation, indecisiveness, irresoluteness, irresolution, shilly-shallying, swither, uncertainty, vacillation, wavering. **antonym** decisiveness.

indecisive *adj* doubtful, faltering, hesitating, hung, in two minds, inconclusive, indefinite, indeterminate, irresolute, pussyfooting, swithering, tentative, uncertain, unclear, undecided, undetermined, unsure, vacillating, wavering.

indecorous *adj* boorish, churlish, coarse, crude, ill-bred, immodest, impolite, improper, indecent, rough, rude, tasteless, uncivil, uncouth, undignified, unmannerly, unseemly, untoward, vulgar.

indeed *adv* actually, certainly, doubtlessly, forsooth, positively, really, strictly, to be sure, truly, undeniably, undoubtedly, verily, veritably.

indefatigable *adj* assiduous, diligent, dogged, inexhaustible, patient, persevering, pertinacious, relentless, sedulous, tireless, undying, unfailing, unflagging, unremitting, unresting, untiring, unwearying. **antonyms** flagging, slothful.

indefensible *adj* faulty, inexcusable, insupportable, unforgivable, unjustifiable, unjustified, unpardonable, untenable, unwarrantable, wrong.

indefinable *adj* dim, hazy, impalpable, indescribable, indistinct, inexpressible, nameless, obscure, subtle, unclear, unrealised, vague.

indefinite *adj* ambiguous, confused, doubtful, equivocal, evasive, general, ill-defined, imprecise, indeterminate, indistinct, inexact, loose, obscure, uncertain, unclear, undecided, undefined, undetermined, unfixed, unfocus(s)ed, unformed, unformulated, unknown, unlimited, unresolved, unsettled, vague. **antonyms** clear, limited.

indefinitely *adv* ad infinitum, continually, endlessly, eternally, for ever, for life, sine die, time without end, world without end.

indelible *adj* enduring, indestructible, ineffaceable, ineradicable, inerasable, inexpungible, inextirpable, ingrained, lasting, permanent, unerasable. **antonyms** erasable, impermanent.

indelicacy *n* bad taste, coarseness,

crudity, grossness, immodesty, impropriety, indecency, obscenity, offensiveness, rudeness, smuttiness, suggestiveness, tastelessness, vulgarity.

indelicate *adj* blue, coarse, crude, embarrassing, gross, immodest, improper, indecent, indecorous, low, obscene, off-colour, offensive, risqué, rude, suggestive, tasteless, unbecoming, unmaidenly, unseemly, untoward, vulgar, warm.

indemnify *v* compensate, endorse, exempt, free, guarantee, insure, pay, protect, reimburse, remunerate, repair, repay, requite, satisfy, secure, underwrite.

indemnity *n* amnesty, compensation, exemption, guarantee, immunity, impunity, insurance, privilege, protection, redress, reimbursement, remuneration, reparation, requital, restitution, satisfaction, security.

indent *v* cut, dent, dint, mark, nick, notch, pink, scallop, serrate.

indentation *n* bash, cut, dent, depression, dimple, dint, dip, hollow, nick, notch, pit.

independence *n* autarchy, autarky, autonomy, decolonisation, freedom, home rule, individualism, liberty, manumission, self-determination, self-government, self-reliance, self-rule, self-sufficiency, separation, sovereignty, unconventionality. **antonym** conventionality.

independent *adj* absolute, autarchical, autonomous, bold, decontrolled, free, individualistic, liberated, non-aligned, one's own man, self-contained, self-determining, self-governing, self-reliant, self-sufficient, self-supporting, separate, separated, sovereign, unaided, unbiased, unconnected, unconstrained, uncontrolled, unconventional, unrelated. **antonyms** conventional, timid.

independently *adv* alone, autonomously, by oneself, individually, on one's own, on one's tod, separately, solo, unaided. **antonym** together.

indescribable *adj* incommunicable, indefinable, ineffable, inexpressible, phraseless, unutterable.

indestructible *adj* abiding, durable, enduring, eternal, everlasting, immortal, imperishable, incorruptible, indissoluble, infrangible, lasting, permanent, unbreakable, unfading. **antonyms** breakable, mortal.

indeterminate *adj* imprecise,

inconclusive, indefinite, inexact, open-ended, uncertain, undecided, undefined, undetermined, unfixed, unspecified, unstated, unstipulated, vague. **antonyms** exact, limited.

index *n* clue, guide, hand, indication, indicator, mark, needle, pointer, sign, symptom, table, token.

indicate *v* add up to, betoken, denote, designate, display, evince, express, imply, manifest, mark, point out, point to, read, record, register, reveal, show, signify, specify, suggest, telegraph, tip.

indicated *adj* advisable, called-for, desirable, necessary, needed, recommended, required, suggested.

indication *n* clue, evidence, explanation, forewarning, hint, index, inkling, intimation, manifestation, mark, note, omen, portent, prognostic, sign, signal, signpost, suggestion, symptom, warning.

indicative *adj* denotative, exhibitive, indicatory, significant, suggestive, symptomatic.

indicator *n* display, gauge, guide, index, mark, marker, meter, pointer, sign, signal, signpost, symbol.

indict *v* accuse, arraign, charge, criminate, impeach, incriminate, prosecute, recriminate, summon, summons, tax. **antonym** exonerate.

indictment *n* accusation, allegation, charge, crimination, impeachment, incrimination, prosecution, recrimination, summons. **antonym** exoneration.

indifference *n* aloofness, apathy, callousness, coldness, coolness, detachment, disinterestedness, dispassion, disregard, equity, heedlessness, impartiality, inattention, insignificance, irrelevance, negligence, neutrality, objectivity, unconcern, unimportance. **antonyms** bias, interest.

indifferent *adj* aloof, apathetic, average, callous, careless, cold, cool, detached, disinterested, dispassionate, distant, equitable, fair, heedless, immaterial, impartial, impervious, inattentive, incurious, insignificant, mediocre, middling, moderate, neutral, non-aligned, objective, ordinary, passable, perfunctory, regardless, so-so, unbiased, uncaring, unconcerned, undistinguished, unenquiring, unenthusiastic, unexcited, unimportant, unimpressed, uninspired, uninterested, uninvolved, unmoved, unprejudiced, unresponsive, unsympathetic. **antonyms** biased, interested.

indigence *n* deprivation, destitution, distress, necessity, need, penury, poverty, privation, want. **antonym** affluence.

indigenous *adj* aboriginal, home-grown, indigene, local, native, original. **antonym** foreign.

indigent *adj* destitute, impecunious, impoverished, in want, necessitous, needy, penniless, penurious, poor, poverty-stricken, straitened. **antonym** affluent.

indignant *adj* angry, annoyed, disgruntled, exasperated, fuming, furious, heated, huffy, incensed, irate, livid, mad, marked, miffed, peeved, provoked, resentful, riled, scornful, sore, wroth. **antonym** pleased.

indignation *n* anger, exasperation, fury, ire, pique, rage, resentment, scorn, umbrage, wrath. **antonym** pleasure.

indignity *n* abuse, affront, contempt, disgrace, dishonour, disrespect, humiliation, incivility, injury, insult, obloquy, opprobrium, outrage, reproach, slight, snub. **antonym** honour.

indirect *adj* ancillary, backhanded, circuitous, circumlocutory, collateral, contingent, crooked, devious, incidental, meandering, mediate, oblique, periphrastic, rambling, roundabout, secondary, slanted, subsidiary, tortuous, unintended, wandering, winding, zigzag.

indirectly *adv* circumlocutorily, deviously, hintingly, oblique-ly, periphrastically, roundaboutedly, roundaboutly, second-hand.

indiscernible *adj* hidden, impalpable, imperceptible, indistinct, indistinguish-able, invisible, minuscule, minute, tiny, unapparent, undiscernible. **antonym** clear.

indiscreet *adj* careless, foolish, hasty, heedless, ill-advised, ill-considered, ill-judged, impolitic, imprudent, incautious, injudicious, naïve, rash, reckless, tactless, temerarious, undiplomatic, unthinking, unwise.

indiscretion *n* boob, error, faux pas, folly, foolishness, gaffe, imprudence, mistake, rashness, recklessness, slip, slip of the tongue, tactlessness, temerity.

indiscriminate *adj* aimless, careless, chaotic, confused, desultory, general, haphazard, higgledy-piggledy, hit or miss, jumbled, mingled, miscellaneous, mixed, mongrel, motley, promiscuous, random, sweeping, uncritical, undifferentiated, undiscrimi-nating, undistinguishable, unmethodical, unparticular, unselective, unsystematic, wholesale. **antonyms** deliberate, selective.

indiscriminately *adv* carelessly, haphazardly, in the mass, randomly, unsystematically, wholesale, without fear or favour. **antonyms** deliberately, selectively.

indispensable *adj* basic, crucial, essential, imperative, key, necessary, needed, needful, required, requisite, vital. **antonym** unnecessary.

indisposed[1] *adj* ailing, ill, laid up, poorly, sick, sickly, under the weather, unwell. **antonym** well.

indisposed[2] *adj* averse, disinclined, loath, not of a mind (to), not willing, reluctant, unwilling. **antonym** inclined.

indisposition[1] *n* ailment, illness, sickness. **antonym** health.

indisposition[2] *n* aversion, disincli-nation, dislike, distaste, hesitancy, reluctance, unwillingness. **antonym** inclination.

indissoluble *adj* abiding, binding, enduring, eternal, fixed, imperishable, incorruptible, indestructible, inseparable, inviolable, lasting, permanent, solid, unbreakable. **antonym** impermanent.

indistinct *adj* ambiguous, bleary, blurred, confused, dim, distant, doubtful, faint, fuzzy, hazy, ill-defined, indefinite, indeterminate, indiscernible, indistinguishable, misty, muffled, mumbled, obscure, shadowy, slurred, unclear, undefined, unintelligible, vague.

indistinguishable *adj* alike, identical, interchangeable, same, tantamount, twin. **antonym** unlike.

individual *n* being, bloke, body, chap, character, creature, fellow, mortal, party, person, personage, punter, soul.
adj characteristic, discrete, distinct, distinctive, exclusive, identical, idiosyncratic, own, particular, peculiar, personal, personalised, proper, respective, separate, several, single, singular, special, specific, unique.

individualism *n* anarchism, egocentricity, egoism, free-thinking, free-thought, independence, libertarianism, originality, self-direction, self-interest, self-reliance. **antonym** conventionality.

individualist *n* anarchist, free-thinker, independent, libertarian, lone wolf, loner, maverick, nonconformist, original. **antonym** conventionalist.

individualistic *adj* anarchistic, characteristic, distinctive, egocentric, egoistic, iconoclastic, idiosyncratic, independent, individual, libertarian, non-conformist, original, particular, self-reliant, special, typical, unconventional, unique. *antonym* conventionalistic.

individuality *n* character, discreteness, distinction, distinctiveness, originality, peculiarity, personality, separateness, singularity, uniqueness. *antonym* sameness.

indoctrinate *v* brainwash, drill, ground, imbue, initiate, instruct, school, teach, train.

indolence *n* heaviness, idleness, inactivity, inertia, inertness, languidness, languor, laziness, lethargy, shirking, slacking, sloth, sluggishness, torpidity, torpor. *antonyms* activeness, enthusiasm, industriousness.

indolent *adj* idle, inactive, inert, lackadaisical, languid, lazy, lethargic, listless, lumpish, slack, slothful, slow, sluggard, sluggish, torpid. *antonyms* active, enthusiastic, industrious.

indomitable *adj* bold, intrepid, invincible, resolute, staunch, steadfast, unbeatable, unconquerable, undaunted, unflinching, untameable, unyielding. *antonyms* compliant, timid.

indubitable *adj* certain, evident, incontestable, incontrovertible, indisputable, irrebuttable, irrefutable, obvious, sure, unanswerable, unarguable, undeniable, undoubtable, undoubted, unquestionable, veritable. *antonym* arguable.

induce *v* actuate, bring about, cause, convince, draw, effect, encourage, engender, generate, get, give rise to, impel, incite, influence, instigate, lead to, move, occasion, persuade, press, prevail upon, produce, prompt, talk into.

inducement *n* attraction, bait, carrot, cause, come-on, consideration, encouragement, impulse, incentive, incitement, influence, lure, motive, reason, reward, spur, stimulus. *antonym* disincentive.

induction *n* conclusion, consecration, deduction, enthronement, generalisation, inauguration, inference, initiation, installation, institution, introduction, investiture, ordination.

indulge *v* baby, coddle, cosset, favour, foster, give in to, go along with, gratify, humour, mollycoddle, pamper, pander to, pet, regale, satiate, satisfy, spoil, treat (oneself), yield to.

indulge in give free rein to, give oneself up to, give way to, luxuriate in, revel in, wallow in.

indulgence *n* appeasement, courtesy, excess, extravagance, favour, forbearance, good will, gratification, immoderateness, immoderation, intemperance, intemperateness, kindness, leniency, luxury, pampering, partiality, patience, permissiveness, privilege, prodigality, profligacy, profligateness, satiation, satisfaction, self-gratification, self-indulgence, spoiling, tolerance, treat, understanding. *antonyms* moderation, strictness.

indulgent *adj* complaisant, compliant, easy-going, favourable, fond, forbearing, gentle, gratifying, intemperate, kind, kindly, lenient, liberal, mild, permissive, prodigal, self-indulgent, tender, tolerant, understanding. *antonyms* moderate, strict.

industrialist *n* baron, boss, capitalist, captain of industry, financier, magnate, manufacturer, producer, tycoon.

industrious *adj* active, assiduous, busy, conscientious, diligent, energetic, hard-working, laborious, persevering, persistent, productive, purposeful, sedulous, steady, tireless, zealous. *antonym* indolent.

industriously *adv* assiduously, conscientiously, diligently, doggedly, hard, perseveringly, sedulously, steadily, with one's nose to the grindstone. *antonym* indolently.

industry *n* activity, application, assiduity, business, commerce, determination, diligence, effort, labour, manufacturing, perseverance, persistence, production, tirelessness, toil, trade, vigour, zeal. *antonym* indolence.

inebriated *adj* befuddled, blind drunk, blotto, drunk, glorious, half seas over, half-cut, half-drunk, incapable, intoxicated, legless, merry, paralytic, pie-eyed, plastered, sloshed, smashed, sozzled, stoned, stotious, three sheets in the wind, tight, tipsy, under the influence. *antonym* sober.

ineffective, ineffectual *adj* abortive, barren, feeble, fruitless, futile, idle, impotent, inadequate, incompetent, ineffective, ineffectual, inefficacious, inefficient, inept, lame, powerless, unavailing, unproductive, useless, vain, void, weak, worthless.

inefficiency *n* carelessness, disorganisation, incompetence, muddle, negligence, slackness, sloppiness, waste, wastefulness.

inefficient *adj* incompetent, inept, inexpert, money-wasting, negligent, slipshod, sloppy, time-wasting, unworkmanlike, wasteful.

inelegant *adj* awkward, barbarous, clumsy, coarse, crass, crude, gauche, graceless, indelicate, laboured, rough, uncourtly, uncouth, uncultivated, ungainly, ungraceful, unpolished, unrefined, unsophisticated.

ineligible *adj* disqualified, improper, inappropriate, incompetent, objectionable, unacceptable, undesirable, unequipped, unfit, unfitted, unqualified, unsuitable, unworthy.

inept *adj* absurd, awkward, bungling, cackhanded, clumsy, fatuous, futile, gauche, improper, inappropriate, inapt, incompetent, inexpert, infelicitous, irrelevant, meaningless, ridiculous, unfit, unhandy, unskilful, unworkmanlike. *antonyms* adroit, apt.

ineptitude *n* absurdity, clumsiness, crassness, fatuity, futility, gaucheness, gaucherie, inappropriateness, incapacity, incompetence, ineptness, inexpertness, irrelevance, pointlessness, stupidity, unfitness, unhandiness, uselessness. *antonyms* aptitude, skill.

inequality *n* bias, difference, disparity, disproportion, dissimilarity, diversity, imparity, inadequacy, irregularity, preferentiality, prejudice, unequalness, unevenness.

inequitable *adj* biased, discriminatory, one-sided, partial, partisan, preferential, prejudiced, unequal, unfair, unjust, wrongful.

inert *adj* apathetic, dead, dormant, dull, idle, immobile, inactive, inanimate, indolent, insensible, lazy, leaden, lifeless, motionless, nerveless, numb, passive, quiescent, senseless, slack, sleepy, slothful, sluggish, somnolent, static, still, torpid, unmoving, unreacting, unresponsive. *antonyms* alive, animated.

inertia *n* apathy, deadness, drowsiness, dullness, idleness, immobility, inactivity, indolence, insensibility, languor, lassitude, laziness, lethargy, listlessness, nervelessness, numbness, passivity, sleepiness, sloth, sluggishness, somnolence, stillness, stupor, torpor, unresponsiveness. *antonyms* activity, liveliness.

inescapable *adj* certain, destined, fated, ineluctable, inevitable, inexorable, irrevocable, sure, unalterable, unavoidable, unpreventable.

inessential *adj* accidental, dispensable, expendable, extraneous, extrinsic, irrelevant, needless, non-essential, optional, redundant, secondary, spare, superfluous, surplus, unasked-for, uncalled-for, unessential, unimportant, unnecessary.
n accessory, appendage, expendable, extra, extravagance, luxury, non-essential, superfluity, trimming.

inestimable *adj* immeasurable, immense, incalculable, incomputable, infinite, invaluable, measureless, precious, priceless, prodigious, uncountable, unfathomable, unlimited, untold, vast. *antonym* insignificant.

inevitable *adj* assured, automatic, certain, compulsory, decreed, destined, fated, fixed, ineluctable, inescapable, inexorable, irrevocable, mandatory, necessary, obligatory, ordained, settled, sure, unalterable, unavertable, unavoidable, unpreventable. *antonyms* alterable, avoidable, uncertain.

inevitably *adv* automatically, certainly, incontestably, ineluctably, inescapably, necessarily, of necessity, perforce, surely, unavoidably.

inexact *adj* erroneous, fuzzy, imprecise, inaccurate, incorrect, indefinite, indeterminate, indistinct, lax, loose, muddled, woolly.

inexactitude *n* blunder, error, impreciseness, imprecision, inaccuracy, incorrectness, indefiniteness, inexactness, laxness, looseness, misalculation, mistake, woolliness.

inexcusable *adj* blameworthy, indefensible, inexpiable, intolerable, outrageous, reprehensible, shameful, unacceptable, unforgivable, unjustifiable, unpardonable, unwarrantable. *antonym* venial.

inexorable *adj* adamant, cruel, hard, harsh, immovable, implacable, ineluctable, inescapable, inflexible, intransigent, irreconcilable, irresistible, irrevocable, merciless, obdurate, pitiless, relentless, remorseless, severe, unalterable, unappeasable, unavertable, unbending, uncompromising, unrelenting, unyielding. *antonyms* flexible, lenient, yielding.

inexpedient *adj* detrimental, disadvantageous, foolish, ill-advised, ill-chosen, ill-judged, impolitic, impractical, imprudent, inadvisable, inappropriate, indiscreet, injudicious, misguided, senseless, unadvisable, undesirable, undiplomatic, unfavourable, unsuitable, unwise, wrong.

inexpensive *adj* bargain, budget, cheap, economical, low-cost, low-priced, modest, reasonable, uncostly.

inexperience *n* callowness, greenness, ignorance, inexpertness, innocence, naïvety, newness, rawness, strangeness, unexpertness, unfamiliarity, unsophistication.

inexperienced *adj* amateur, callow, fresh, green, immature, inexpert, innocent, nescient, new, raw, unaccustomed, unacquainted, unbearded, unfamiliar, unpractical, unpractised, unschooled, unseasoned, unskilled, unsophisticated, untrained, untravelled, untried, unused, unversed.

inexpert *adj* amateurish, awkward, blundering, bungling, clumsy, hammy, incompetent, inept, unpractised, unprofessional, unskilful, unskilled, untaught, untrained, untutored, unworkmanlike. **antonym** expert.

inexplicable *adj* baffling, enigmatic, impenetrable, incomprehensible, incredible, inscrutable, insoluble, intractable, miraculous, mysterious, mystifying, puzzling, strange, unaccountable, unexplainable, unfathomable, unintelligible, unsolvable.

inexplicably *adv* bafflingly, incomprehensibly, incredibly, miraculously, mysteriously, mystifyingly, puzzlingly, strangely, unaccountably, unexplainably.

inexpressible *adj* incommunicable, indefinable, indescribable, ineffable, nameless, undescribable, unsayable, unspeakable, untellable, unutterable.

inexpressive *adj* bland, blank, deadpan, emotionless, empty, expressionless, immobile, impassive, inanimate, inscrutable, lifeless, poker-faced, stolid, stony, unexpressive, vacant.

inextricably *adv* indissolubly, indistinguishably, inseparably, intricately, irresolubly, irretrievably, irreversibly.

infallibility *n* accuracy, dependability, faultlessness, impeccability, inevitability, irrefutability, irreproachability, perfection, reliability, safety, supremacy, sureness, trustworthiness, unerringness. **antonym** fallibility.

infallible *adj* accurate, certain, dependable, fail-safe, faultless, foolproof, impeccable, irreproachable, perfect, reliable, sound, sure, sure-fire, trustworthy, unbeatable, unerring, unfailing, unfaltering, unfaulty, unimpeachable. **antonym** fallible.

infamous *adj* abhorrent, abominable, atrocious, base, dastardly, despicable, detestable, discreditable, disgraceful, dishonourable, disreputable, egregious, execrable, hateful, heinous, ignoble, ignominious, ill-famed, iniquitous, loathsome, monstrous, nefarious, notorious, odious, opprobrious, outrageous, scandalous, scurvy, shameful, shocking, vile, villainous, wicked. **antonym** glorious.

infamy *n* atrocity, baseness, crime, dastardliness, depravity, discredit, disgrace, dishonour, disrepute, enormity, ignominy, improbity, notoriety, obloquy, odium, opprobrium, outrageousness, scandal, shame, stigma, turpitude, villainy, wickedness. **antonym** glory.

infancy *n* babyhood, beginnings, birth, childhood, commencement, cradle, dawn, embryonic stage, emergence, genesis, inception, origins, outset, start, youth. **antonym** adulthood.

infant *n* babe, babe in arms, baby, bairn, bambino, child, nipper, nurseling, suckling, tiny, toddler, tot, wean. **antonym** adult.
adj baby, childish, dawning, developing, early, emergent, growing, immature, inchoate, incipient, initial, juvenile, nascent, newborn, rudimentary, unfledged, unformed, young, youthful. **antonym** adult.

infantile *adj* adolescent, babyish, childish, immature, juvenile, puerile, tender, undeveloped, young, youthful. **antonyms** adult, mature.

infatuated *adj* befooled, beguiled, besotted, bewitched, captivated, crazy, deluded, enamoured, enraptured, fascinated, fixated, hypnotised, mad, mesmerised, obsessed, possessed, ravished, smitten, spellbound. **antonyms** disenchanted, indifferent.

infatuation *n* crush, fascination, fixation, folly, fondness, madness, mania, obsession, passion, possession. **antonyms** disenchantment, indifference.

infect *v* affect, blight, contaminate, corrupt, defile, enthuse, influence, inject, inspire, pervert, poison, pollute, taint, touch, vitiate.

infection *n* contagion, contamination, corruption, defilement, disease, epidemic, illness, inflammation, influence, miasma, pestilence, poison, pollution, taint, virus.

infectious *adj* catching, communicable, contagious, contaminating, corrupting, deadly, defiling, epidemic, infective, miasmic, miasmous, pestilential, poisoning, poisonous, polluting, spreading, transmissible, transmittable, venemous, virulent, vitiating.

infelicitous *adj* gauche, ill-timed, inappropriate, inopportune, tactless, unapt, unfortunate, unhappy, unsuitable, untimely.

infelicity *n* despair, gaucheness, inappositeness, inappropriateness, inaptness, incongruity, inopportuneness, misery, misfortune, sadness, sorrow, tactlessness, unfortunateness, unhappiness, unsuitability, untimeliness, woe, wretchedness, wrongness. **antonyms** aptness, happiness.

infer *v* assume, conclude, conjecture, construe, deduce, derive, extract, extrapolate, gather, presume, surmise, understand.

inference *n* assumption, conclusion, conjecture, consequence, construction, corollary, deduction, extrapolation, interpretation, presumption, reading, surmise.

inferior *adj* bad, crummy, grotty, humble, imperfect, indifferent, junior, lesser, low, lower, low-grade, mean, mediocre, menial, minor, poor, poorer, schlock, secondary, second-class, second-rate, shoddy, slipshod, slovenly, subordinate, subsidiary, substandard, under, underneath, undistinguished, unsatisfactory, unworthy, worse. **antonym** superior.
n junior, menial, minion, subordinate, underling, vassal. **antonym** superior.

inferiority *n* badness, baseness, deficiency, humbleness, imperfection, inadequacy, insignificance, lowliness, meanness, mediocrity, shoddiness, slovenliness, subordination, subservience, unimportance, unworthiness, worthlessness. **antonym** superiority.

infernal *adj* accursed, damnable, damned, demonic, devilish, diabolical, fiendish, Hadean, hellish, malevolent, malicious, satanic, Stygian, underworld. **antonym** heavenly.

infertile *adj* arid, barren, dried-up, effete, infecund, non-productive, parched, sterile, unbearing, unfruitful, unproductive.

infertility *n* aridity, aridness, barrenness, effeteness, infecundity, sterility, unfruitfulness, unproductiveness.

infest *v* beset, flood, infiltrate, invade, overrun, overspread, penetrate, permeate, pervade, ravage, swarm, throng.

infidel *n* atheist, disbeliever, freethinker, heathen, heretic, iconoclast, irreligionist, pagan, sceptic, unbeliever. **antonym** believer.

infidelity *n* adultery, bad faith, betrayal, cheating, disbelief, disloyalty, duplicity, faithlessness, false-heartedness, falseness, iconoclasm, irreligion, perfidy, scepticism, traitorhood, traitorousness, treachery, unbelief, unfaithfulness.

infiltrate *v* creep into, filter, infilter, insinuate, interpenetrate, intrude, penetrate, percolate, permeate, pervade, sift.

infinite *adj* absolute, bottomless, boundless, countless, enormous, eternal, everlasting, fathomless, illimitable, immeasurable, immense, incomputable, inestimable, interminable, limitless, measureless, never-ending, numberless, perpetual, stupendous, total, unbounded, uncountable, uncounted, unfathomable, untold, vast, wide. **antonym** finite.

infirm *adj* ailing, crippled, debilitated, decrepit, dicky, doddering, doddery, enfeebled, failing, faltering, feeble, frail, hesitant, indecisive, insecure, irresolute, lame, poorly, sickly, unreliable, wavering, weak, wobbly. **antonyms** healthy, strong.

infirmity *n* ailment, complaint, debility, decrepitude, defect, deficiency, dickiness, disease, disorder, failing, fault, feebleness, foible, frailty, ill health, illness, imperfection, instability, malady, sickliness, sickness, vulnerability, weakness. **antonyms** health, strength.

inflame *v* aggravate, agitate, anger, arouse, dynamise, embitter, enkindle, enrage, exacerbate, exasperate, excite, fan, fire, foment, fuel, galvanise, heat, ignite, impassion, incense, increase, infatuate, infuriate, intensify, intoxicate, kindle, madden, provoke, rile, rouse, stimulate, worsen. **antonyms** cool, quench.

inflamed *adj* angry, chafing, enraged, excited, festering, fevered, heated, hot, impassioned, incensed, infected, poisoned, red, septic, sore, swollen.

inflammable *adj* burnable, combustible, flammable, incendiary, irascible, short-tempered, volatile. **antonyms** flame-proof, incombustible, non-flammable, non-inflammable.

inflammation *n* abscess, burning, heat, infection, painfulness, rash, redness, sore, soreness, tenderness.

inflammatory *adj* anarchic, explosive, fiery, incendiary, incitative, inflaming, instigative, insurgent, intemperate, provocative, rabble-rousing, rabid, riotous, seditious. **antonyms** calming, pacific.

inflate *v* aerate, aggrandise, amplify, balloon, bloat, blow out, blow up, bombast, boost, dilate, distend, enlarge, escalate, exaggerate, expand, increase, puff out, puff up, pump up, swell. **antonym** deflate.

inflated *adj* ballooned, bloated, blown up, bombastic, dilated, distended, euphuistic, exaggerated, flatulent, grandiloquent, magniloquent, ostentatious, overblown, pompous, puffed out, swollen, turgid. **antonym** deflated.

inflexibility *n* fixity, hardness, immovability, immutability, immutableness, inelasticity, intractability, intransigence, obduracy, obstinacy, rigidity, steeliness, stiffness, stringency, stubbornness, unsuppleness.

inflexible *adj* adamant, dyed-in-the-wool, entrenched, fast, firm, fixed, hard, hardened, immovable, immutable, implacable, inelastic, inexorable, intractable, intransigent, iron, non-flexible, obdurate, obstinate, relentless, resolute, rigid, rigorous, set, steadfast, steely, stiff, strict, stringent, stubborn, taut, unaccommodating, unadaptable, unbending, unchangeable, uncompromising, unpliable, unpliant, unsupple, unyielding.

inflict *v* administer, afflict, apply, burden, deal, deliver, enforce, exact, force, impose, lay, levy, mete, perpetrate, visit, wreak.

infliction *n* administration, affliction, burden, castigation, chastisement, exaction, imposition, nemesis, penalty, perpetration, punishment, retribution, trouble, visitation, worry.

influence *n* agency, ascendancy, authority, bias, charisma, clout, connections, control, credit, direction, domination, drag, effect, éminence grise, good offices, guidance, hold, importance, leverage, magnetism, mastery, power, pressure, prestige, pull, reach, rule, scope, spell, standing, strength, string-pulling, sway, teaching, training, weight, wire-pulling.

v affect, alter, arouse, bias, change, control, direct, dispose, dominate, edge, guide, head, impel, impress, incite, incline, induce, instigate, manipulate, manoeuvre, modify, motivate, move, persuade, point, predispose, prompt, pull, pull strings, rouse, sway, teach, train, weigh with.

influential *adj* ascendant, authoritative, charismatic, cogent, compelling, controlling, dominant, dominating, effective, efficacious, forcible, guiding, important, instrumental, leading, momentous, moving, persuasive, potent, powerful, significant, strong, telling, weighty, well-placed. **antonym** ineffectual.

influx *n* access, accession, arrival, consignment, convergence, flood, flow, incursion, inundation, invasion, rush.

inform *v* acquaint, advise, apprise, brief, clue up, communicate, enlighten, fill in, illuminate, impart, instruct, intimate, leak, notify, teach, tell, tip off, wise up.

inform on accuse, betray, blab, blow the whistle, denounce, denunciate, grass, incriminate, inculpate, nark, rat, sing, snitch, squeal, tell on, whistle.

informal *adj* approachable, casual, colloquial, congenial, cosy, easy, familiar, free, homely, irregular, natural, relaxed, relaxing, simple, unbuttoned, unceremonious, unconstrained, unofficial, unorthodox, unpretentious, unsolemn.

informality *n* approachability, casualness, congeniality, cosiness, ease, familiarity, freedom, homeliness, irregularity, naturalness, relaxation, simplicity, unceremoniousness, unpretentiousness. **antonym** formality.

informally *adj* casually, colloquially, confidentially, cosily, easily, en famille, familiarly, freely, on the quiet, privately, simply, unceremoniously, unofficially. **antonym** formally.

information *n* advices, blurb, briefing, bulletin, bumf, clues, communiqué, data, databank, database, dope, dossier, enlightenment, facts, gen, illumination, info, input, instruction, intelligence, knowledge, low-down, message, news, notice, report, tidings, word.

informative *adj* communicative, constructive, edifying, educational, enlightening, forthcoming, illuminating, informatory, instructive, newsy, revealing, revelatory, useful, valuable.

informed *adj* abreast, acquainted, apprised, au fait, authoritative, briefed clued up, conversant, enlightened, erudite, expert, familiar, filled in, genned up, hep, in the know, knowledgeable, learned, posted, primed, scholarly, trained, up to date, versed, well-informed, well-read, well-researched. *antonyms* ignorant, unaware.

informer *n* betrayer, canary, denouncer, denunciator, fink, grass, Judas, nark, singer, sneak, snitch(er), snout, squeak, squealer, stool pigeon, stoolie, supergrass, whistle-blower.

infrequent *adj* exceptional, intermittent, occasional, rare, scanty, sparse, spasmodic, sporadic, uncommon, unusual.

infringe *v* break, contravene, defy, disobey, encroach, flout, ignore, infract, intrude, invade, overstep, transgress, trespass, violate.

infringement *n* breach, contravention, defiance, encroachment, evasion, infraction, intrusion, invasion, non-compliance, non-observance, transgression, trespass, violation.

infuriate *v* anger, antagonise, bug, enrage, exasperate, incense, irritate, madden, provoke, put someone's back up, rile, rouse, vex. *antonyms* calm, mollify.

infuriated *adj* agitated, angry, beside oneself, enraged, exasperated, flaming, furious, heated, incensed, irate, irritated, maddened, provoked, roused, vexed, violent, wild. *antonyms* calm, gratified, pleased.

infuriating *adj* aggravating, annoying, exasperating, frustrating, galling, intolerable, irritating, maddening, mortifying, pesky, provoking, thwarting, unbearable, vexatious. *antonyms* agreeable, pleasing.

infuse *v* breathe into, brew, draw, imbue, impart to, implant, inculcate, inject, inspire, instil, introduce, leach, macerate, saturate, soak, steep.

infusion *n* brew, implantation, inculcation, infusing, instillation, soaking, steeping.

ingenious *adj* adroit, bright, brilliant, clever, crafty, creative, cunning, daedal, deft, dexterous, imaginative, innovative, intricate, inventive, masterly, original, pretty, ready, resourceful, shrewd, skilful, sly, subtle. *antonyms* clumsy, unimaginative.

ingenuity *n* adroitness, cleverness, cunning, deftness, faculty, flair, genius, gift, ingeniousness, innovativeness, invention, inventiveness, knack,

originality, resourcefulness, sharpness, shrewdness, skill, slyness, turn. *antonyms* clumsiness, dullness.

ingenuous *adj* artless, candid, childlike, frank, guileless, honest, innocent, naïf, naïve, open, plain, simple, sincere, trustful, trusting, unreserved, unsophisticated, unstudied. *antonyms* artful, sly.

inglorious *adj* discreditable, disgraceful, dishonourable, disreputable, humiliating, ignoble, ignominious, infamous, mortifying, obscure, shameful, unheroic, unhonoured, unknown, unsuccessful, unsung. *antonym* glorious.

ingrained *adj* constitutional, deep-rooted, deep-seated, entrenched, fixed, fundamental, hereditary, immovable, inborn, inbred, inbuilt, indelible, ineradicable, infixed, inherent, intrinsic, inveterate, permanent, rooted. *antonym* superficial.

ingratiate *v* blandish, crawl, fawn, flatter, get in with, grovel, insinuate, suck up, toady, worm.

ingratiating *adj* bland, bootlicking, crawling, fawning, flattering, obsequious, servile, smooth-tongued, suave, sycophantic, time-serving, toadying, unctuous.

inhabit *v* abide, bide, dwell, habit, live, lodge, make one's home, occupy, people, populate, possess, reside, settle, settle in, stay, take up one's abode, tenant.

inhale *v* breathe in, draw, draw in, inspire, respire, suck in, toke, whiff.

inharmonious *adj* antipathetic, atonal, cacophonous, clashing, conflicting, discordant, dissonant, grating, harsh, incompatible, inconsonant, jangling, jarring, raucous, strident, tuneless, unharmonious, unmelodious, unmusical, untuneful. *antonym* harmonious.

inherent *adj* basic, characteristic, congenital, connate, essential, fundamental, hereditary, immanent, inborn, inbred, inbuilt, ingrained, inherited, innate, instinctive, intrinsic, native, natural.

inherit *v* accede to, assume, be bequeathed, be left, come in for, come into, fall heir to, receive, succeed to.

inheritance *n* accession, bequest, birthright, descent, heredity, heritage, legacy, patrimony, succession.

inhibit *v* arrest, bar, bridle, check, constrain, cramp, curb, debar, discourage, forbid, frustrate, hinder, hold, impede, interfere with, obstruct, prevent, prohibit, repress, restrain, stanch, stem, stop, suppress, thwart.

inhibited *adj* bashful, constrained, diffident, frustrated, guarded, repressed, reserved, reticent, self-conscious, shamefaced, shy, strained, subdued, tense, uptight, withdrawn.

inhibition *n* bar, check, constraint, embargo, hang-up, hindrance, impediment, interdict, interference, obstacle, obstruction, prohibition, repression, reserve, restraint, restriction, reticence, self-consciousness, shyness, suppression. **antonym** freedom.

inhospitable *adj* antisocial, bare, barren, bleak, cold, cool, desolate, forbidding, hostile, inimical, intolerant, sterile, unaccommodating, uncivil, uncongenial, unfavourable, unfriendly, ungenerous, uninhabitable, unkind, unneighbourly, unreceptive, unsociable, unwelcoming, xenophobic. **antonym** favourable.

inhuman *adj* animal, barbaric, barbarous, bestial, brutal, brutish, callous, cold-blooded, cruel, diabolical, fiendish, heartless, inhumane, insensate, merciless, pitiless, remorseless, ruthless, savage, sublime, unfeeling, vicious.

inhumane *adj* brutal, callous, cold-hearted, cruel, heartless, inhuman, insensitive, pitiless, uncaring, uncompassionate, unfeeling, unkind, unsympathetic.

inhumanity *n* atrocity, barbarism, barbarity, brutality, brutishness, callousness, cold-bloodedness, cold-heartedness, cruelty, hard-heartedness, heartlessness, pitilessness, ruthlessness, sadism, unkindness, viciousness. **antonym** humanity.

inimical *adj* adverse, antagonistic, antipathetic, contrary, destructive, disaffected, harmful, hostile, hurtful, ill-disposed, inhospitable, injurious, intolerant, noxious, opposed, pernicious, repugnant, unfavourable, unfriendly, unwelcoming. **antonyms** favourable, friendly, sympathetic.

inimitable *adj* consummate, distinctive, exceptional, incomparable, matchless, peerless, sublime, superlative, supreme, unequalled, unexampled, unique, unmatched, unparalleled, unrivalled, unsurpassable, unsurpassed.

iniquitous *adj* abominable, accursed, atrocious, awful, base, criminal, dreadful, evil, heinous, immoral, infamous, nefarious, reprehensible, reprobate, sinful, unjust, unrighteous, vicious, wicked. **antonym** virtuous.

iniquity *n* abomination, baseness, crime, enormity, evil, evil-doing, heinousness, impiety, infamy, injustice, misdeed, offence, sin, sinfulness, ungodliness, unrighteousness, vice, viciousness, wickedness, wrong, wrong-doing. **antonym** virtue.

initial *adj* beginning, commencing, early, embryonic, first, formative, inaugural, inchoate, incipient, infant, introductory, opening, original, primary. **antonym** final.

initially *adv* at first, at the beginning, at the outset, at the start, first, first of all, firstly, in the beginning, originally, to begin with, to start with. **antonym** finally.

initiate *v* activate, actuate, begin, cause, coach, commence, inaugurate, indoctrinate, induce, induct, instate, institute, instruct, introduce, invest, launch, open, originate, prompt, start, stimulate, teach, train.

initiation *n* admission, commencement, début, enrolment, entrance, entry, inauguration, inception, induction, installation, instatement, instruction, introduction, investiture, reception, rite of passage.

initiative *n* advantage, ambition, drive, dynamism, energy, enterprise, forcefulness, get-up-and-go, innovativeness, inventiveness, lead, move, originality, prompting, push, recommendation, resource, resourcefulness, suggestion.

inject *v* add, bring, fix, hit, infuse, inoculate, insert, instil, interject, introduce, jab, mainline, pop, shoot, shoot up, skin-pop, vaccinate.

injection *n* dose, fix, hit, infusion, inoculation, insertion, interjection, introduction, jab, mainlining, popping, shot, skin-popping, vaccination, vaccine.

injudicious *adj* foolish, hasty, ill-advised, ill-judged, ill-timed, impolitic, imprudent, inadvisable, incautious, inconsiderate, indiscreet, inexpedient, misguided, rash, stupid, unthinking, unwise, wrong-headed. **antonym** judicious.

injure *v* abuse, aggrieve, blemish, blight, break, cripple, damage, deface, disable, disfigure, disserve, harm, hurt, ill-treat, impair, maim, maltreat, mar, ruin, scathe, spoil, tarnish, undermine, vandalise, vitiate, weaken, wound, wrong.

injured *adj* abused, aggrieved, blemished, broken, cut to the quick, defamed, disabled, disgruntled, displeased, grieved, hurt, ill-treated, insulted, lamed, long-suffering, maligned, maltreated, misused, offended, pained, put out, stung, tarnished, undermined, unhappy, upset, vilified, weakened, wounded, wronged.

injurious *adj* adverse, bad, baneful, calumnious, corrupting, damaging, deleterious, destructive, detrimental, disadvantageous, harmful, hurtful, iniquitous, insulting, libellous, mischievous, noxious, pernicious, prejudicial, ruinous, slanderous, unconducive, unhealthy, unjust, wrongful. **antonyms** beneficial, favourable.

injury *n* abuse, annoyance, damage, damnification, detriment, disservice, evil, grievance, harm, hurt, ill, impairment, injustice, insult, lesion, loss, mischief, prejudice, ruin, trauma, vexation, wound, wrong.

injustice *n* bias, discrimination, disparity, favouritism, imposition, inequality, inequitableness, inequity, iniquity, one-sidedness, oppression, partiality, partisanship, prejudice, unevenness, unfairness, unjustness, unlawfulness, unreason, wrong. **antonym** justice.

inkling *n* allusion, clue, conception, earthly, faintest, foggiest, glimmering, hint, idea, indication, intimation, notion, pointer, sign, suggestion, suspicion, umbrage, whisper.

innards *n* entrails, guts, insides, intestines, organs, umbles, viscera.

innate *adj* basic, congenital, constitutional, essential, fundamental, immanent, inborn, inbred, ingenerate, ingrained, inherent, inherited, instinctive, intrinsic, intuitive, native, natural.

inner *adj* central, concealed, emotional, esoteric, essential, hidden, inside, interior, internal, intimate, inward, mental, middle, personal, private, psychological, secret, spiritual. **antonyms** outer, patent.

innocence *n* artlessness, blamelessness, chastity, credulousness, freshness, greenness, guilelessness, guiltlessness, gullibility, harmlessness, honesty, ignorance, incorruptibility, incorruption, inexperience, ingenuousness, innocuousness, inoffensiveness, irreproachability, naïvety, naturalness, purity, righteousness, simplicity, sinlessness, stainlessness, trustfulness, unawareness, unfamiliarity, unimpeachability, unsophistication, unworldliness, virginity, virtue. **antonyms** experience, guilt, knowledge.

innocent *adj* Arcadian, artless, benign, blameless, canny, chaste, childlike, clear, credulous, dewy-eyed, faultless, frank, fresh, green, guileless, guiltless, gullible, harmless, honest, immaculate, impeccable, incorrupt, ingenuous, innocuous, inoffensive, intact, irreproachable, naïve, natural, nescient, open, pristine, pure, righteous, simple, sinless, spotless, stainless, trustful, trusting, unblemished, uncontaminated, unimpeachable, unobjectionable, unoffending, unsullied, unsuspicious, untainted, untouched, unworldly, virginal, well-intentioned, well-meaning, well-meant. **antonyms** experienced, guilty, knowing.
n babe, babe in arms, beginner, child, greenhorn, infant, neophyte. **antonyms** connoisseur, expert.

innocently *adv* artlessly, blamelessly, credulously, harmlessly, ingenuously, innocuously, inoffensively, like a lamb to the slaughter, simply, trustfully, trustingly, unoffendingly, unsuspiciously.

innocuous *adj* bland, harmless, innocent, inoffensive, non-irritant, safe, unimpeachable, unobjectionable. **antonym** harmful.

innovation *n* alteration, change, departure, introduction, modernisation, modernism, neologism, newness, novelty, progress, reform, variation.

innovative *adj* adventurous, bold, daring, enterprising, fresh, go-ahead, groundbreaking, imaginative, inventive, modernising, new, on the move, original, progressive, reforming, resourceful, revolutionary. **antonyms** conservative, unimaginative.

innuendo *n* aspersion, hint, implication, insinuation, intimation, overtone, slant, slur, suggestion, whisper.

innumerable *adj* countless, incalculable, incomputable, infinite, many, multitudinous, myriad, numberless, numerous, uncountable, uncounted, unnumbered, untold.

inoffensive *adj* gentle, harmless, humble, innocent, innocuous, mild, mousy, non-provocative, peaceable, quiet, retiring, unassertive, unobjectionable, unobtrusive, unoffending. **antonym** malicious.

inoperative *adj* broken, broken-down,

defective, idle, ineffective, ineffectual, invalid, non-active, non-functioning, out of action, out of commission, out of order, out of service, unserviceable, unused, unworkable, useless.

inopportune *adj* clumsy, ill-chosen, ill-timed, inappropriate, inauspicious, inconvenient, infelicitous, mistimed, tactless, unfortunate, unpropitious, unseasonable, unsuitable, untimely.

inordinate *adj* disproportionate, excessive, exorbitant, extravagant, immoderate, intemperate, overweening, preposterous, prohibitive, unconscionable, undue, unreasonable, unrestrained, unwarranted. *antonyms* moderate, reasonable.

inquietude *n* agitation, anxiety, apprehension, discomposure, disquiet, disquietude, jumpiness, nervousness, perturbation, restlessness, solicitude, unease, uneasiness, worry. *antonym* composure.

inquire *v* ask, delve, enquire, examine, explore, inspect, interrogate, investigate, look into, probe, query, question, scrutinise, search.

inquiring *adj* analytical, curious, doubtful, eager, inquisitive, interested, interrogatory, investigative, investigatory, nosy, outward-looking, probing, prying, questioning, searching, wondering. *antonym* incurious.

inquiry *n* enquiry, examination, exploration, inquest, interrogation, investigation, probe, query, question, research, scrutiny, search, study, survey, witch-hunt.

inquisition *n* cross-examination, cross-questioning, examination, grilling, inquest, inquiry, interrogation, investigation, questioning, quizzing, third degree, witch-hunt.

inquisitive *adj* curious, eager, inquiring, intrusive, investigative, meddlesome, nosy, peeping, peering, probing, prying, questing, questioning, snooping, snoopy. *antonym* incurious.

insane *adj* barmy, batty, bizarre, bonkers, cracked, crackers, crazed, cuckoo, daft, delirious, demented, deranged, distracted, disturbed, fatuous, foolish, idiotic, impractical, irrational, irresponsible, loony, loopy, lunatic, mad, manic, mental, mentally ill, non compos mentis, nuts, nutty, preposterous, psychotic, queer, schizoid, schizophrenic, screwy, senseless, stupid, touched, unbalanced, unhinged.

insanitary *adj* contaminated, dirty,

disease-ridden, feculent, filthy, foul, impure, infected, infested, insalubrious, insalutary, noxious, polluted, unclean, unhealthful, unhealthy, unhygienic, unsanitary.

insanity *n* aberration, alienation, brainstorm, craziness, delirium, dementia, derangement, folly, frenzy, lunacy, madness, mania, mental illness, neurosis, preposterousness, psychoneurosis, psychosis, senselessness, stupidity.

insatiable *adj* gluttonous, greedy, immoderate, incontrollable, inordinate, insatiate, intemperate, persistent, rapacious, ravenous, uncurbable, unquenchable, unsatisfiable, voracious. *antonym* moderate.

inscrutable *adj* baffling, blank, cryptic, dead-pan, deep, enigmatic, esoteric, expressionless, hidden, impassive, impenetrable, incomprehensible, inexplicable, mysterious, poker-faced, sphinx-like, undiscoverable, unexplainable, unfathomable, unintelligible, unknowable, unsearchable. *antonyms* clear, comprehensible, expressive.

insecure *adj* afraid, anxious, apprehensive, dangerous, defenceless, diffident, exposed, expugnable, flimsy, frail, hazardous, insubstantial, loose, nervous, perilous, precarious, rickety, rocky, shaky, uncertain, unconfident, uneasy, unguarded, unprotected, unsafe, unshielded, unsound, unstable, unsteady, unsure, vulnerable, weak, wobbly, worried. *antonyms* confident, safe.

insecurity *n* anxiety, apprehension, danger, defencelessness, diffidence, dubiety, fear, flimsiness, frailness, hazard, instability, nervousness, peril, precariousness, ricketiness, risk, shakiness, uncertainty, uneasiness, unsafeness, unsafety, unsteadiness, unsureness, vulnerability, weakness, worry. *antonyms* confidence, safety.

insensibility *n* apathy, callousness, coma, crassness, deafness, dullness, indifference, inertness, insensitivity, lethargy, nervelessness, numbness, oblivion, thoughtlessness, torpor, unawareness, unconsciousness. *antonym* consciousness.

insensible *adj* anaesthetised, apathetic, blind, callous, cataleptic, cold, deaf, dull, hard-hearted, impassive, impercipient, impervious, indifferent, inert, insensate, marble, nerveless, numb, numbed, oblivious, senseless, stupid, torpid, unaffected, unaware, unconscious, unfeeling, unmindful, unmoved, unnoticing, unobservant, unresponsive, unsusceptible, untouched. **antonym** conscious.

insensitive *adj* blunted, callous, crass, dead, hardened, immune, impenetrable, imperceptive, impercipient, impervious, indifferent, insusceptible, obtuse, proof, resistant, tactless, thick-skinned, tough, unaffected, uncaring, unconcerned, unfeeling, unimpressionable, unmoved, unreactive, unresponsive, unsusceptible.

insensitivity *n* bluntness, callousness, crassness, hard-headedness, impenetrability, imperceptiveness, imperviousness, indifference, obtuseness, tactlessness, unconcern, unresponsiveness.

inseparable *adj* bosom, close, conjoined, devoted, impartible, inalienable, indissociable, indissoluble, indivisible, inextricable, inseverable, intimate, undividable.

insert *v* embed, enter, implant, infix, inset, intercalate, interject, interlaminate, interlard, interleave, interline, interpolate, interpose, introduce, intromit, let in, place, pop in, put, put in, set, stick in.
n ad, advertisement, enclosure, graft, gusset, implant, insertion, inset, notice.

insertion *n* addition, entry, implant, inclusion, insert, inset, intercalation, interpolation, introduction, intromission, intrusion, supplement.

insides *n* belly, bowels, entrails, gut, guts, innards, organs, stomach, viscera, vitals.

insidious *adj* artful, crafty, crooked, cunning, deceitful, deceptive, designing, devious, disingenuous, duplicitous, furtive, guileful, intriguing, Machiavellian, slick, sly, smooth, sneaking, stealthy, subtle, surreptitious, treacherous, tricky, wily.

insight *n* acumen, acuteness, apprehension, awareness, comprehension, discernment, grasp, ingenuity, intelligence, intuition, intuitiveness, judgement, knowledge, observation, penetration, perception, percipience, perspicacity, sensitivity, shrewdness, understanding, vision, wisdom.

insightful *adj* acute, astute, discerning, intelligent, knowledgeable, observant, penetrating, perceptive, percipient, perspicacious, prudent, sagacious, sage, shrewd, understanding, wise. **antonym** superficial.

insignificance *n* immateriality, inconsequence, inconsequentiality, insubstantiality, irrelevance, meaninglessness, meanness, negligibility, paltriness, pettiness, triviality, unimportance, worthlessness.

insignificant *adj* dinky, flimsy, humble, immaterial, inappreciable, inconsequential, inconsiderable, insubstantial, irrelevant, meagre, meaningless, minor, negligible, nondescript, nonessential, paltry, petty, piddling, scanty, scrub, tiny, trifling, trivial, unimportant, unsubstantial.

insincere *adj* artificial, deceitful, deceptive, devious, dishonest, disingenuous, dissembling, dissimulating, double-dealing, duplicitous, evasive, faithless, false, hollow, hypocritical, lying, mendacious, perfidious, phoney, pretended, synthetic, two-faced, unfaithful, ungenuine, untrue, untruthful.

insincerity *n* artificiality, cant, deceitfulness, deviousness, dishonesty, disingenuousness, dissembling, dissimulation, duplicity, evasiveness, faithlessness, falseness, falsity, hollowness, hypocrisy, lip service, mendacity, perfidy, phoniness, pretence, untruthfulness.

insinuate *v* allude, get at, hint, imply, indicate, innuendo, intimate, suggest.
insinuate oneself curry favour, get in with, ingratiate, sidle, work, worm, wriggle.

insinuation *n* allusion, aspersion, hint, implication, infiltration, ingratiating, innuendo, intimation, introduction, slant, slur, suggestion.

insipid *adj* anaemic, banal, bland, characterless, colourless, dilute, drab, dry, dull, flat, flavourless, lifeless, limp, monotonous, pointless, prosaic, prosy, savourless, spiritless, stale, tame, tasteless, trite, unappetising, unimaginative, uninteresting, unsavoury, vapid, watery, weak, wearish, weedy, wishy-washy. **antonyms** appetising, piquant, punchy, tasty.

insist *v* assert, asseverate, aver, claim, contend, demand, dwell on, emphasise, harp on, hold, maintain, persist, reiterate, repeat, request, require, stand firm, stress, swear, urge, vow.

insistence *n* advice, assertion, averment, certainty, contention, demand, determination, emphasis, encouragement, entreaty, exhortation, firmness, importunity, instance, persistence, persuasion, pressing, reiteration, solicitations, stress, urgency, urging.

insistent *adj* demanding, dogged, emphatic, exigent, forceful, importunate, incessant, peremptory, persevering, persistent, pressing, relentless, tenacious, unrelenting, unremitting, urgent.

insolence *n* abuse, arrogance, assurance, audacity, backchat, boldness, cheek, cheekiness, chutzpah, contemptuousness, defiance, disrespect, effrontery, forwardness, gall, gum, impertinence, impudence, incivility, insubordination, lip, offensiveness, pertness, presumption, presumptuousness, rudeness, sauce, sauciness. **antonyms** politeness, respect.

insolent *adj* abusive, arrogant, bold, brazen, cheeky, contemptuous, defiant, disrespectful, forward, fresh, impertinent, impudent, insubordinate, insulting, pert, presumptuous, rude, saucy, uncivil. **antonyms** polite, respectful.

insoluble *adj* baffling, impenetrable, indecipherable, inexplicable, inextricable, intractable, mysterious, mystifying, obscure, perplexing, unaccountable, unexplainable, unfathomable, unsolvable. **antonym** explicable.

insolvent *adj* bankrupt, broke, bust, defaulting, destitute, failed, flat broke, in queer street, on the rocks, ruined.

inspect *v* audit, check, examine, give the once-over, investigate, look over, oversee, peruse, reconnoitre, scan, scrutinise, search, study, superintend, supervise, survey, vet, visit.

inspection *n* audit, autopsy, check, check-up, examination, investigation, once-over, post-mortem, reconnaissance, review, scan, scrutiny, search, superintendence, supervision, surveillance, survey, visitation.

inspiration *n* arousal, awakening, brainstorm, brain-wave, creativity, elevation, encouragement, enthusiasm, exaltation, genius, illumination, influence, insight, muse, Muse, revelation, spur, stimulation, stimulus.

inspire *v* activate, animate, arouse, encourage, enkindle, enliven, enthuse, excite, fill, galvanise, hearten, imbue, influence, infuse, inhale, inspirit, instil, motivate, produce, quicken, spark off, spur, stimulate, stir, trigger.

inspired *adj* afflated, aroused, brilliant, dazzling, elated, enthralling, enthused, enthusiastic, exalted,

exciting, exhilarated, fired, galvanised impressive, invigorated, memorable outstanding, possessed, reanimated stimulated, superlative, thrilled, thrilling uplifted, wonderful. **antonyms** dull uninspired.

inspiring *adj* affecting, emboldening encouraging, exciting, exhilarating heartening, inspiriting, invigorating moving, rousing, stimulating, stirring uplifting. **antonyms** dull, uninspiring.

inspirit *v* animate, cheer, embolden encourage, enliven, exhilarate, fire galvanise, gladden, hearten, incite inspire, invigorate, move, nerve quicken, refresh, reinvigorate, rouse stimulate.

instability *n* capriciousness changeableness, fickleness, fitfulness flimsiness, fluctuation, fluidity, frailty imbalance, impermanence, inconstancy insecurity, insolidity, irresolution lability, mutability, oscillation precariousness, restlessness, shakiness transience, uncertainty, undependableness, unpredictability, unreliability unsafeness, unsoundness, unsteadiness vacillation, variability, volatility wavering, weakness.

instal(l) *v* consecrate, ensconce establish, fix, inaugurate, induct, instate institute, introduce, invest, lay, locate lodge, ordain, place, plant, position, put set, set up, settle, site, situate, station.

instance *n* case, case in point citation, example, illustration, occasion occurrence, precedent, sample, situation time.
v adduce, cite, mention, name, point to quote, refer to, specify.

instant *n* flash, jiffy, juncture, minute mo, moment, occasion, point, second shake, split second, tick, time, trice twinkling, two shakes.
adj convenience, direct, fast immediate, instantaneous, on-the-spot precooked, prompt, quick, rapid ready-mixed, split-second, unhesitating urgent.

instantaneous *adj* direct, immediate instant, on-the-spot, prompt, rapid unhesitating. **antonym** eventual.

instantaneously *adv* at once, directly forthwith, immediately, instantly, on the spot, promptly, rapidly, straight away there and then, unhesitatingly. **antonym** eventually.

instantly *adv* at once, directly forthwith, immediately, instantaneously now, on the spot, pronto, right away, straight away, there and then, without delay. **antonym** eventually.

instead *adv* alternatively, as a substitute, as an alternative, in lieu, in preference, preferably, rather.

instead of in default of, in lieu of, in place of, in preference to, on behalf of, rather than.

instigate *v* actuate, cause, encourage, excite, foment, generate, impel, incite, influence, initiate, inspire, kindle, move, persuade, prompt, provoke, rouse, set on, spur, start, stimulate, stir up, urge, whip up.

instigation *n* behest, bidding, encouragement, incentive, incitement, initiative, insistence, instance, prompting, urging.

instil *v* din into, engender, imbue, implant, impress, inculcate, infix, infuse, inject, insinuate, introduce.

instinct *n* ability, aptitude, faculty, feel, feeling, flair, gift, gut feeling, gut reaction, id, impulse, intuition, knack, nose, predisposition, proclivity, sixth sense, talent, tendency, urge.

instinctive *adj* automatic, gut, immediate, impulsive, inborn, inherent, innate, instinctual, intuitional, intuitive, involuntary, mechanical, native, natural, reflex, spontaneous, unlearned, unpremeditated, unthinking, visceral. **antonyms** conscious, deliberate, voluntary.

instinctively *adv* automatically, intuitively, involuntarily, mechanically, naturally, spontaneously, unthinkingly, without thinking. **antonyms** consciously, deliberately, voluntarily.

institute[1] *v* appoint, begin, commence, constitute, create, enact, establish, fix, found, inaugurate, induct, initiate, install, introduce, invest, launch, open, ordain, organise, originate, pioneer, set up, settle, start. **antonyms** abolish, cancel, discontinue.

institute[2] *n* custom, decree, doctrine, dogma, edict, law, maxim, precedent, precept, principle, regulation, rescript, rule, tenet.

institution[1] *n* constitution, creation, enactment, establishment, formation, foundation, founding, inception, initiation, installation, introduction, investiture, organisation, protectory.

institution[2] *n* convention, custom, law, practice, ritual, rule, tradition, usage.

institutional *adj* accepted, bureaucratic, cheerless, clinical, cold, conventional, customary, drab, dreary, dull, established, establishment, forbidding, formal, impersonal, monotonous, orthodox, regimented, ritualistic, routine, set, societal, uniform, unwelcoming. **antonyms** individualistic, unconventional.

instruct *v* acquaint, advise, apprise, bid, brief, catechise, charge, coach, command, counsel, direct, discipline, drill, educate, enjoin, enlighten, ground, guide, inform, mandate, notify, order, school, teach, tell, train, tutor.

instruction *n* apprenticeship, briefing, coaching, command, direction, directive, discipline, drilling, education, enlightenment, grounding, guidance, information, injunction, lesson(s), mandate, order, preparation, ruling, schooling, teaching, training, tuition, tutelage.

instructive *adj* cautionary, didactic, edifying, educational, educative, educatory, enlightening, helpful, illuminating, improving, informative, instructional, revealing, useful. **antonym** unenlightening.

instructor *n* adviser, coach, demonstrator, exponent, guide, guru, master, mentor, preceptor, teacher, trainer, tutor.

instrument *n* agency, agent, apparatus, appliance, channel, contraption, contrivance, device, dupe, factor, force, gadget, implement, means, mechanism, medium, organ, pawn, puppet, tool, utensil, vehicle, way.

instrumental *adj* active, assisting, auxiliary, conducive, contributive, contributory, helpful, helping, implemental, influential, involved, subsidiary, useful. **antonyms** obstructive, unhelpful.

insubordinate *adj* defiant, disobedient, disorderly, fractious, impertinent, impudent, insurgent, mutinous, rebellious, recalcitrant, refractory, riotous, rude, seditious, turbulent, undisciplined, ungovernable, unruly. **antonyms** docile, obedient.

insubordination *n* defiance, disobedience, impertinence, impudence, indiscipline, insurrection, mutiny, rebellion, recalcitrance, revolt, riotousness, rudeness, sedition, ungovernability. **antonyms** docility, obedience.

insubstantial *adj* chimerical, ephemeral, false, fanciful, feeble, flimsy, frail, idle, illusory, imaginary, immaterial, incorporeal, poor, slight, tenuous, thin, unreal, vaporous, weak, windy. **antonyms** real, strong.

insufferable *adj* detestable, dreadful, hateful, impossible, insupportable, intolerable, loathesome, outrageous, unbearable, unendurable, unspeakable. **antonyms** pleasant, tolerable.

insufficiency *n* dearth, deficiency, inadequacy, inadequateness, lack, need, paucity, poverty, scantiness, scarcity, shortage, sparsity, want. **antonym** excess.

insufficient *adj* deficient, inadequate, incapable, incommensurate, lacking, scanty, scarce, short, sparse, wanting. **antonym** excessive.

insular *adj* blinkered, circumscribed, closed, contracted, cut off, detached, illiberal, inward-looking, isolated, limited, narrow, narrow-minded, parish-pump, parochial, petty, prejudiced, provincial, xenophobic. **antonym** cosmopolitan.

insult *v* abuse, affront, call names, fling/throw mud at, give offence to, injure, libel, miscall, offend, outrage, revile, slag, slander, slight, snub, vilify. **antonyms** compliment, honour.
n abuse, affront, aspersion, indignity, insolence, libel, offence, outrage, rudeness, slander, slap in the face, slight, snub. **antonyms** compliment, honour.

insulting *adj* abusive, affronting, contemptuous, degrading, disparaging, insolent, libellous, offensive, rude, scurrilous, slanderous, slighting. **antonyms** complimentary, respectful.

insuperable *adj* formidable, impassable, insurmountable, invincible, overwhelming, unconquerable. **antonym** surmountable.

insupportable *adj* detestable, dreadful, hateful, indefensible, insufferable, intolerable, invalid, loathesome, unbearable, unendurable, unjustifiable, untenable. **antonym** bearable.

insurgent *n* insurrectionist, mutineer, partisan, rebel, resister, revolter, revolutionist, revolutionary, rioter.
adj disobedient, insubordinate, insurrectionary, mutinous, partisan, rebellious, revolting, revolutionary, riotous, seditious.

insurmountable *adj* hopeless, impassable, impossible, insuperable, invincible, overwhelming, unclimable, unconquerable, unscalable.

insurrection *n* coup, insurgence, insurgency, mutiny, putsch, rebellion, revolt, revolution, riot, rising, sedition, uprising.

intact *adj* all in one piece, complete, entire, inviolate, perfect, sound, together, unbroken, undamaged, undefiled, unharmed, unhurt, unimpaired, uninjured, unscathed, untouched, unviolated, virgin, whole. **antonyms** broken, damaged, harmed.

intangible *adj* airy, bodiless, dim, elusive, ethereal, evanescent, impalpable, imperceptible, incorporeal, indefinite, insubstantial, invisible, shadowy, unreal, unsubstantial, vague. **antonym** real.

integral *adj* basic, complete, component, constituent, elemental, entire, essential, full, fundamental, indispensable, intact, intrinsic, necessary, requisite, undivided, unitary, whole. **antonyms** accessory, partial.

integrate *v* accommodate, amalgamate, assimilate, blend, coalesce, combine, commingle, desegregate, fuse, harmonise, incorporate, intermix, join, knit, merge, mesh, mix, unite. **antonym** separate.

integrated *adj* cohesive, concordant, connected, desegregated, harmonious, interrelated, part and parcel, unified, unsegregated, unseparated. **antonym** unintegrated.

integration *n* amalgamation, assimilation, blending, combining, commingling, desegregation, fusing, harmony, incorporation, mixing, unification. **antonym** separation.

integrity *n* candour, coherence, cohesion, completeness, entireness, goodness, honesty, honour, incorruptibility, principle, probity, purity, rectitude, righteousness, soundness, unity, uprightness, virtue, wholeness. **antonyms** dishonesty, incompleteness, unreliability.

intellect *n* brain, brain power, brains, egghead, genius, highbrow, intellectual, intelligence, judgement, mind, nous, reason, sense, thinker, understanding. **antonym** dunce.

intellectual *adj* bookish, cerebral, deep-browed, highbrow, intelligent, mental, rational, scholarly, studious, thoughtful. **antonym** low-brow.
n academic, egghead, highbrow mastermind, thinker. **antonym** low-brow.

intelligence *n* acumen, advice alertness, aptitude, brain power brains, brightness, capacity, cleverness, comprehension, discernment, disclosure, facts, findings, gen, grey matter, information, intellect, knowledge, lowdown, mind, news, notice, notification, nous, penetration, perception, quickness, reason, report, rumour, tidings, tipoff, understanding, word. **antonym** foolishness.

intelligent *adj* acute, alert, apt, brainy, bright, clever, deep-browed, discerning, enlightened, instructed, knowing, penetrating, perspicacious, quick, quickwitted, rational, sharp, smart, thinking, well-informed.

intelligibility *n* clarity, clearness, comprehensibility, distinctness, explicitness, lucidity, lucidness, plainness, precision, simplicity. **antonym** unintelligibility.

intelligible *adj* clear, comprehensible, decipherable, distinct, fathomable, lucid, open, penetrable, plain, understandable. **antonym** unintelligible.

intemperance *n* crapulence, drunkenness, excess, extravagance, immoderation, inebriation, insobriety, intoxication, licence, overindulgence, self-indulgence.

intemperate *adj* drunken, excessive, extravagant, extreme, immoderate, incontinent, inordinate, intoxicated, licentious, over the top, passionate, prodigal, profligate, self-indulgent, severe, tempestuous, unbridled, uncontrollable, ungovernable, unrestrained, violent, wild.

intend *v* aim, consign, contemplate, design, destine, determine, earmark, have a mind, mark out, mean, meditate, plan, project, propose, purpose, scheme, set apart.

intended *adj* betrothed, deliberate, designate, designated, destined, future, intentional, planned, proposed, prospective. **antonym** accidental.
n betrothed, fiancé, fiancée, husband-to-be, wife-to-be.

intense *adj* acute, agonising, ardent, burning, close, concentrated, consuming, eager, earnest, energetic, fanatical, fervent, fervid, fierce, forceful, forcible, great, harsh, heightened, impassioned, intensive, keen, passionate, powerful, profound, severe, strained, strong, vehement. **antonyms** apathetic, mild.

intensely *adv* ardently, deeply, extremely, fervently, fiercely, greatly, passionately, profoundly, strongly, very. **antonym** mildly.

intensify *v* add to, aggravate, boost, concentrate, deepen, emphasise, enhance, escalate, exacerbate, fire, fuel, heighten, hot up, increase, magnify, quicken, redouble, reinforce, sharpen, step up, strengthen, whet, whip up. **antonyms** damp down, die down.

intensity *n* accent, ardour, concentration, depth, earnestness, emotion, energy, excess, extremity, fanaticism, fervency, fervour, fierceness, fire, force, intenseness, keenness, passion, potency, power, severity, strain, strength, tension, vehemence, vigour, voltage.

intensive *adj* all-out, comprehensive, concentrated, demanding, detailed, exhaustive, in detail, in-depth, thorough, thoroughgoing. **antonym** superficial.

intent *adj* absorbed, alert, attentive, bent, committed, concentrated, concentrating, determined, eager, earnest, engrossed, fixed, hell-bent, industrious, intense, mindful, occupied, piercing, preoccupied, rapt, resolute, resolved, set, steadfast, steady, watchful, wrapped up. **antonyms** absent-minded, distracted.
n aim, design, end, goal, intention, meaning, object, objective, plan, purpose.

intention *n* aim, concept, design, end, end in view, goal, idea, intent, meaning, object, objective, plan, point, purpose, scope, target, view.

intentional *adj* calculated, deliberate, designed, intended, meant, planned, prearranged, preconcerted, premeditated, purposed, studied, wilful. **antonym** accidental.

intentionally *adv* by design, deliberately, designedly, meaningly, on purpose, wilfully, with malice aforethought. **antonym** accidentally.

intently *adv* attentively, carefully, closely, fixedly, hard, keenly, searchingly, staringly, steadily, watchfully. **antonym** absent-mindedly.

intercede *v* advocate, arbitrate, interpose, intervene, mediate, plead, speak.

intercept *v* arrest, block, catch, check, cut off, deflect, delay, frustrate, head off, impede, interrupt, obstruct, retard, seize, stop, take, thwart.

intercession *n* advocacy, agency, beseeching, entreaty, good offices, intervention, mediation, plea, pleading, prayer, solicitation, supplication.

interchange *n* alternation, crossfire,

exchange, interplay, intersection, junction, reciprocation, trading.

interchangeable *adj* commutable, equal, equivalent, exchangeable, identical, reciprocal, similar, standard, synonymous, the same, transposable. *antonym* different.

interdict *v* ban, bar, debar, disallow, forbid, outlaw, preclude, prevent, prohibit, proscribe, rule out, veto. *antonym* allow.

n ban, disallowance, injunction, interdiction, prohibition, proscription, taboo, veto. *antonym* permission.

interest *n* activity, advantage, affair, affection, attention, attentiveness, attraction, authority, benefit, business, care, claim, commitment, concern, consequence, curiosity, diversion, finger, gain, good, hobby, importance, influence, investment, involvement, matter, moment, note, notice, participation, pastime, portion, preoccupation, profit, pursuit, regard, relaxation, relevance, right, share, significance, stake, study, suspicion, sympathy, weight. *antonyms* boredom, irrelevance.

v affect, amuse, attract, concern, divert, engage, engross, fascinate, intrigue, involve, move, touch, warm. *antonym* bore.

interested *adj* affected, attentive, attracted, biased, concerned, curious, drawn, engrossed, fascinated, implicated, intent, involved, keen, partisan, predisposed, prejudiced, responsive, stimulated. *antonyms* apathetic, indifferent, unaffected.

interesting *adj* absorbing, amusing, appealing, attractive, compelling, curious, engaging, engrossing, entertaining, gripping, intriguing, provocative, stimulating, thought-provoking, unusual, viewable, visitable. *antonym* boring.

interfere *v* block, butt in, clash, collide, conflict, cramp, frustrate, hamper, handicap, hinder, impede, inhibit, interlope, intermeddle, interpose, intervene, intrude, meddle, obstruct, poke one's nose in, stick one's oar in, tamper, trammel. *antonyms* assist, forbear.

interference *n* clashing, collision, conflict, impedance, intervention, intrusion, meddlesomeness, meddling, mush, obstruction, opposition, paternalism, prying, statics. *antonyms* assistance, forbearance.

interim *adj* acting, caretaker, improvised, intervening, makeshift, permanent, pro tem, provisional, stand-in, stop-gap, temporary.

n interregnum, interval, meantime, meanwhile.

interior *adj* central, domestic, hidden, home, inland, inly, inner, inside, internal, intimate, inward, mental, personal, private, remote, secret, spiritual, up-country. *antonyms* exterior, external.

n bowels, centre, core, heart, heartland, hinterland, inside, up-country.

interject *v* call, cry, exclaim, interpolate, interpose, interrupt, introduce, shout.

interlace *v* braid, cross, enlace, entwine, interlock, intermix, intersperse, intertwine, interweave, knit, plait, twine.

interlink *v* clasp together, interconnect, intergrow, interlock, intertwine, interweave, knit, link, link together, lock together, mesh. *antonym* separate.

interlude *n* break, breathing-space, breathing-time, delay, episode, halt, hiatus, intermission, interval, pause, respite, rest, spell, stop, stoppage, wait.

intermediary *n* agent, broker, entrepreneur, go-between, in-between, mediator, middleman.

intermediate *adj* halfway, in-between, intermediary, interposed, intervening, mean, medial, median, mid, middle, midway, transitional. *antonym* extreme.

interminable *adj* boundless, ceaseless, dragging, endless, everlasting, immeasurable, infinite, limitless, long, long-drawn-out, long-winded, never-ending, perpetual, prolix, protracted, unbounded, unlimited, wearisome. *antonym* limited.

intermingle *v* amalgamate, blend, combine, commingle, fuse, interlace, intermix, interweave, merge, mix, mix together, mix up. *antonym* separate.

intermission *n* break, breather, breathing-space, cessation, entr'acte, interlude, interruption, interval, let-up, lull, pause, recess, remission, respite, rest, stop, stoppage, suspense, suspension.

intermittent *adj* broken, discontinuous, fitful, irregular, occasional, periodic, periodical, punctuated, recurrent, recurring, remittent, spasmodic, sporadic, stop-go. *antonym* continuous.

intern *v* confine, detain, hold, imprison, jail. *antonym* free.

internal *adj* domestic, in-house, inner,

inside, interior, intimate, inward, private, subjective. *antonym* external.

international *adj* cosmopolitan, general, global, intercontinental, interterritorial, universal, worldwide. *antonym* parochial.

internecine *adj* bloody, civil, deadly, destructive, exterminating, exterminatory, family, fatal, internal, mortal, murderous, ruinous.

interplay *n* exchange, give-and-take, interaction, interchange, meshing, reciprocation, reciprocity.

interpolate *v* add, insert, intercalate, interject, introduce.

interpose *v* come between, insert, intercede, interfere, interject, interrupt, intervene, introduce, intrude, mediate, offer, place between, step in, thrust in. *antonym* forbear.

interpret *v* adapt, clarify, construe, decipher, decode, define, elucidate, explain, explicate, expound, paraphrase, read, render, solve, take, throw light on, translate, understand, unfold.

interpretation *n* analysis, clarification, diagnosis, elucidation, exegesis, explanation, explication, exposition, meaning, performance, portrayal, reading, rendering, rendition, sense, signification, translation, understanding, version.

interrogate *v* ask, cross-examine, cross-question, debrief, enquire, examine, give (someone) the third degree, grill, inquire, investigate, pump, question, quiz.

interrogation *n* cross-examination, cross-questioning, enquiry, examination, grilling, inquiry, inquisition, probing, questioning, third degree.

interrogative *adj* curious, inquiring, inquisitional, inquisitive, inquisitorial, interrogatory, questioning, quizzical.

interrupt *v* barge in, break, break in, break off, butt in, check, cut, cut off, cut short, delay, disconnect, discontinue, disjoin, disturb, disunite, divide, heckle, hinder, hold up, interfere, interject, intrude, obstruct, punctuate, separate, sever, stay, stop, suspend. *antonym* forbear.

interrupted *adj* broken, cut off, disconnected, discontinuous, disturbed, incomplete, intermittent, uneven, unfinished. *antonyms* complete, continuous.

interruption *n* break, cessation, disconnection, discontinuance, disruption, dissolution, disturbance, disuniting, division, halt, hiatus, hindrance, hitch, impediment, intrusion, obstacle, obstruction, pause, separation, severance, stop, stoppage, suspension.

intersperse *v* dot, interlard, intermix, pepper, scatter, sprinkle.

interval *n* break, delay, distance, entr'acte, gap, hiatus, interim, interlude, intermission, interspace, interstice, meantime, meanwhile, opening, pause, period, playtime, rest, season, space, spell, term, time, wait.

intervene *v* arbitrate, befall, ensue, happen, intercede, interfere, interpose oneself, interrupt, intrude, involve, mediate, occur, step in, succeed, supervene, take a hand.

interview *n* audience, conference, consultation, dialogue, enquiry, evaluation, inquisition, meeting, oral, oral examination, press conference, talk, viva.
v examine, interrogate, question.

interwoven *adj* blended, connected, entwined, interconnected, interlaced, interlocked, intermingled, knit.

intestines *n* bowels, chitterlings, entrails, guts, innards, insides, offal, umbles, viscera.

intimacy *n* closeness, coitus, confidence, confidentiality, copulating, copulation, familiarity, fornication, fraternisation, friendship, intercourse, sexual intercourse, understanding.

intimate[1] *v* allude, announce, communicate, declare, hint, impart, imply, indicate, insinuate, state, suggest, tell.

intimate[2] *adj* as thick as thieves, bosom, cherished, close, confidential, cosy, dear, deep, deep-seated, detailed, exhaustive, friendly, informal, innermost, internal, near, palsy-walsy, penetrating, personal, private, privy, profound, secret, warm. *antonyms* cold, distant, unfriendly.
n associate, bosom buddy, buddy, china, chum, comrade, confidant, confidante, crony, familiar, friend, mate, mucker, pal. *antonym* stranger.

intimately *adv* affectionately, closely, confidentially, confidingly, exhaustively, familiarly, fully, in detail, inside out, personally, tenderly, thoroughly, warmly. *antonyms* coldly, distantly.

intimation *n* allusion, announcement, communication, declaration, hint, indication, inkling, insinuation, notice, reminder, statement, suggestion, warning.

intimidate v alarm, appal, browbeat, bulldoze, bully, coerce, cow, daunt, dishearten, dismay, dispirit, frighten, lean on, overawe, psych out, put the frighteners on, scare, subdue, terrify, terrorise, threaten. *antonym* persuade.

intimidation n arm-twisting, browbeating, bullying, coercion, fear, menaces, pressure, terror, terrorisation, terrorising, threats. *antonym* persuasion.

intolerable adj beyond the pale, excruciating, impossible, insufferable, insupportable, painful, unbearable, unendurable.

intolerance n bigotry, chauvinism, discrimination, dogmatism, fanaticism, illiberality, impatience, jingoism, narrow-mindedness, narrowness, prejudice, racialism, racism, xenophobia.

intolerant adj bigoted, chauvinistic, dictatorial, dogmatic, fanatical, illiberal, impatient, narrow, narrow-minded, opinionated, opinioned, persecuting, prejudiced, racialist, racist, small-minded, uncharitable.

intoxicated adj blotto, canned, cut, dizzy, drunk, drunken, elated, enraptured, euphoric, excited, exhilarated, fuddled, glorious, half seas over, high, incapable, inebriated, legless, lit up, looped, pickled, pissed, plastered, sent, sloshed, smashed, sozzled, stewed, stiff, stoned, stotious, three sheets in the wind, tight, tipsy, under the influence. *antonym* sober.

intractable adj awkward, bull-headed, cantankerous, contrary, difficult, fractious, haggard, headstrong, incurable, insoluble, intransigent, obdurate, obstinate, perverse, pig-headed, refractory, self-willed, stubborn, unamenable, unbending, unco-operative, undisciplined, ungovernable, unmanageable, unruly, unyielding, wayward, wild, wilful. *antonym* amenable.

intransigent adj hardline, immovable, intractable, irreconcilable, obdurate, obstinate, stubborn, tenacious, tough, unamenable, unbending, unbudgeable, uncompromising, unpersuadable, unyielding, uppity. *antonym* amenable.

intrepid adj audacious, bold, brave, courageous, daring, dashing, dauntless, doughty, fearless, gallant, game, gutsy, heroic, lion-hearted, nerveless, plucky, resolute, stalwart, stout-hearted, unafraid, undashed, undaunted, unflinching, valiant. *antonyms* cowardly, timid.

intricacy n complexity, complication, convolutions, elaborateness, entanglement, intricateness, involution, involvement, knottiness, obscurity. *antonym* simplicity.

intricate adj complex, complicated, convoluted, difficult, elaborate, entangled, fancy, involved, knotty, labyrinthine, perplexing, sophisticated, tangled, tortuous. *antonym* simple.

intrigue[1] v attract, charm, fascinate, interest, puzzle, rivet, tantalise, tickle one's fancy, titillate. *antonym* bore.

intrigue[2] n affair, amour, cabal, chicanery, collusion, conspiracy, double-dealing, intimacy, liaison, machination(s), manipulation, manoeuvre, plot, romance, ruse, scheme, sharp practice, stratagem, string-pulling, trickery, wheeler-dealing, wile, wire-pulling.
v connive, conspire, machinate, manoeuvre, plot, scheme.

intriguing adj beguiling, compelling, diverting, exciting, fascinating, interesting, puzzling, tantalising, titillating. *antonyms* boring, uninteresting.

intrinsic adj basic, basically, built-in, central, congenital, constitutional, constitutionally, elemental, essential, essentially, fundamental, fundamentally, genuine, inborn, inbred, inherent, intrinsically, inward, native, natural, underlying. *antonym* extrinsic.

introduce v acquaint, add, advance, air, announce, begin, bring in, bring up, broach, commence, conduct, establish, familiarise, found, inaugurate, inject, insert, institute, interpolate, interpose, launch, lead in, lead into, moot, offer, open, organise, pioneer, preface, present, propose, put forward, put in, recommend, set forth, start, submit, suggest, throw in, ventilate. *antonym* take away.

introduction n addition, baptism, commencement, debut, establishment, foreword, inauguration, induction, initiation, insertion, institution, interpolation, intro, launch, lead-in, opening, overture, pioneering, preamble, preface, preliminaries, prelude, presentation, prologue. *antonym* withdrawal.

introductory adj early, elementary, first, inaugural, initial, initiatory, opening, precursory, prefatory, preliminary, preparatory, starting.

introspection n brooding, heart-searching, introversion, self-analysis, self-examination, self-observation, soul-searching.

introspective *adj* brooding, contemplative, introverted, inward-looking, meditative, pensive, ruminative, subjective, thoughtful. *antonym* outward-looking.

introverted *adj* indrawn, introspective, inward-looking, self-centred, self-contained, withdrawn. *antonym* extroverted.

intrude *v* aggress, butt in, encroach, infringe, interfere, interrupt, meddle, obtrude, trespass, violate. *antonyms* stand back, withdraw.

intrusive *adj* disturbing, forward, impertinent, importunate, interfering, invasive, meddlesome, nosy, obtrusive, officious, presumptuous, pushy, uncalled-for, unwanted, unwelcome. *antonyms* unintrusive, welcome.

intuition *n* discernment, feeling, gut feeling, hunch, insight, instinct, perception, presentiment, sixth sense. *antonym* reasoning.

intuitive *adj* innate, instinctive, instinctual, involuntary, spontaneous, unreflecting, untaught. *antonym* reasoned.

inundate *v* bury, deluge, drown, engulf, fill, flood, glut, immerse, overflow, overrun, overwhelm, submerge, swamp.

inure *v* accustom, desensitise, familiarise, flesh, habituate, harden, strengthen, temper, toughen, train.

invade *v* assail, assault, attack, burst in, come upon, descend upon, encroach, enter, fall upon, infest, infringe, occupy, overrun, overspread, penetrate, pervade, raid, rush into, seize, swarm over, violate. *antonym* withdraw.

invalid[1] *adj* ailing, bedridden, disabled, feeble, frail, ill, infirm, poorly, sick, sickly, valetudinarian, valetudinary, weak. *antonym* healthy.
n case, convalescent, patient, sufferer, valetudinarian, valetudinary.

invalid[2] *adj* baseless, fallacious, false, ill-founded, illogical, incorrect, inoperative, irrational, null, null and void, unfounded, unscientific, unsound, untrue, void, worthless. *antonym* valid.

invalidate *v* abrogate, annul, cancel, nullify, overrule, overthrow, quash, rescind, undermine, undo, vitiate, weaken. *antonym* validate.

invalidity *n* fallaciousness, fallacy, falsity, illogicality, inconsistency, incorrectness, invalidness, irrationality, sophism, speciousness, unsoundness, voidness.

invaluable *adj* costly, exquisite, inestimable, precious, priceless, valuable. *antonym* worthless.

invariable *adj* changeless, consistent, constant, fixed, immutable, inflexible, permanent, regular, rigid, set, static, unalterable, unchangeable, unchanging, unfailing, uniform, unvarying, unwavering.

invariably *adv* always, consistently, customarily, habitually, inevitably, perpetually, regularly, unfailingly, without exception, without fail.

invasion *n* aggression, assault, attack, breach, encroachment, foray, incursion, infiltration, infraction, infringement, inroad, intrusion, offensive, onslaught, raid, seizure, usurpation, violation. *antonym* withdrawal.

invective *n* abuse, berating, castigation, censure, denunciation, diatribe, obloquy, reproach, revilement, sarcasm, scolding, tirade, tongue-lashing, vilification, vituperation. *antonym* praise.

inveigh *v* berate, blame, castigate, censure, condemn, denounce, expostulate, fulminate, lambast, rail, recriminate, reproach, scold, sound off, tongue-lash, upbraid, vituperate. *antonym* praise.

inveigle *v* allure, bamboozle, beguile, cajole, coax, con, decoy, ensnare, entice, entrap, lead on, lure, manipulate, manoeuvre, persuade, seduce, sweet-talk, wheedle, wile. *antonym* force.

invent *v* coin, conceive, concoct, contrive, cook up, create, design, devise, discover, dream up, fabricate, formulate, frame, imagine, improvise, make up, originate, think up, trump up.

invention *n* brainchild, coinage, contraption, contrivance, creation, creativeness, creativity, deceit, design, development, device, discovery, fabrication, fake, falsehood, fantasy, fib, fiction, figment of (someone's) imagination, forgery, gadget, genius, imagination, ingenuity, inspiration, inventiveness, lie, originality, resourcefulness, sham, story, tall story, untruth, yarn. *antonym* truth.

inventive *adj* creative, fertile, gifted, imaginative, ingenious, innovative, inspired, original, resourceful. *antonym* uninventive.

inventory *n* account, catalogue, equipment, file, list, listing, record, register, roll, roster, schedule, stock.

inverse *adj* contrary, converse, inverted, opposite, reverse, reversed, transposed, upside down.

inversion *n* antipode, antithesis, contraposition, contrariety, contrary, opposite, reversal, transposal, transposition.

invert *v* capsize, introvert, inverse, overturn, reverse, transpose, turn turtle, turn upside down, upset, upturn. **antonym** right.

invest *v* adopt, advance, authorise, charge, consecrate, devote, empower, endow, endue, enthrone, establish, inaugurate, induct, install, lay out, license, ordain, provide, put in, sanction, sink, spend, supply, vest. **antonym** divest.

investigate *v* consider, enquire into, examine, explore, go into, inspect, look into, probe, scrutinise, search, see how the land lies, sift, study, suss out.

investigation *n* analysis, enquiry, examination, exploration, fact finding, hearing, inquest, inquiry, inspection, probe, research, review, scrutiny, search, study, survey, witch-hunt.

inveterate *adj* chronic, confirmed, deep-rooted, deep-seated, diehard, dyed-in-the-wool, entrenched, established, habitual, hard-core, hardened, incorrigible, incurable, ineradicable, ingrained, irreformable, long-standing, obstinate. **antonym** impermanent.

invidious *adj* discriminating, discriminatory, hateful, objectionable, obnoxious, odious, offensive, repugnant, slighting, undesirable. **antonym** desirable.

invigorate *v* animate, brace, buck up, energise, enliven, exhilarate, fortify, freshen, galvanise, harden, inspirit, liven up, pep up, perk up, quicken, refresh, rejuvenate, revitalise, stimulate, strengthen, vitalise, vivify. **antonyms** dishearten, weary.

invigorating *adj* bracing, energising, exhilarating, fresh, generous, healthful, inspiriting, refreshing, rejuvenating, rejuvenative, restorative, salubrious, stimulating, tonic, uplifting, vivifying. **antonyms** disheartening, wearying.

invincible *adj* impenetrable, impregnable, indestructible, indomitable, inseparable, insuperable, invulnerable, irreducible, unassailable, unbeatable, unconquerable, unreducible, unsurmountable, unyielding. **antonym** beatable.

inviolable *adj* hallowed, holy, inalienable, sacred, sacrosanct, unalterable. **antonym** violable.

inviolate *adj* entire, intact, pure, sacred, stainless, unbroken, undefiled, undisturbed, unhurt, uninjured, unpolluted, unprofaned, unstained, unsullied, untouched, virgin, whole. **antonym** sullied.

invisible *adj* concealed, disguised, hidden, imperceptible, inappreciable, inconspicuous, indetectable, indiscernible, infinitesimal, microscopic, out of sight, unperceivable, unseeable, unseen. **antonym** visible.

invitation *n* allurement, asking, begging, bidding, call, challenge, come-on, coquetry, enticement, exhortation, glad eye, incitement, inducement, invite, overture, provocation, request, solicitation, summons, supplication, temptation.

invite *v* allure, ask, ask for, attract, beckon, beg, bid, bring on, call, court, draw, encourage, entice, lead, provoke, request, seek, solicit, summon, tempt, welcome. **antonyms** force, order.

inviting *adj* alluring, appealing, appetising, attractive, beguiling, captivating, delightful, engaging, enticing, fascinating, intriguing, magnetic, mouthwatering, pleasing, seductive, tantalising, tempting, warm, welcoming, winning. **antonym** uninviting.

invoke *v* adjure, appeal to, apply, base on, beg, beseech, call upon, conjure, conjure up, entreat, implement, implore, initiate, petition, pray, put into effect, refer to, resort to, solicit, supplicate, use.

involuntary *adj* automatic, compulsory, conditioned, forced, instinctive, instinctual, obligatory, reflex, reluctant, spontaneous, unconscious, uncontrolled, unintentional, unthinking, unwilled, unwilling. **antonym** voluntary.

involve *v* absorb, affect, associate, bind, commit, comprehend, comprise, compromise, concern, connect, contain, cover, draw in, embrace, engage, engross, entail, grip, hold, implicate, imply, include, incorporate, incriminate, inculpate, mean, mix up, necessitate, number among, preoccupy, presuppose, require, rivet, take in, touch.

involved *adj* caught up/in, complex, complicated, concerned, confusing, convoluted, difficult, elaborate, implicated, in on, intricate, knotty, labyrinthine, mixed up in/with, occupied, participating, sophisticated, tangled, tortuous. *antonyms* simple, uninvolved.

involvement *n* association, commitment, complexity, complication, concern, connection, dedication, difficulty, embarrassment, entanglement, imbroglio, implication, interest, intricacy, participation, problem, ramification, responsibility.

inward *adj* confidential, entering, hidden, incoming, inner, innermost, inside, interior, internal, penetrating, personal, private, privy, secret. *antonyms* external, outward.

inwardly *adv* at heart, deep down, inly, inside, privately, secretly, to oneself, within. *antonyms* externally, outwardly.

iota *n* atom, bit, drop, grain, hint, jot, mite, particle, scintilla, scrap, smidgeon, soupçon, speck, trace, whit.

irascible *adj* bad-tempered, cantankerous, crabbed, crabby, cross, hasty, hot-tempered, ill-natured, ill-tempered, irritable, narky, peppery, petulant, prickly, quick-tempered, short-tempered, testy, touchy, volcanic. *antonym* placid.

irate *adj* angered, angry, annoyed, enraged, exasperated, fuming, furious, gusty, incensed, indignant, infuriated, irritated, livid, mad, piqued, provoked, riled, up in arms, worked up, wroth. *antonym* calm.

ire *n* anger, annoyance, displeasure, exasperation, fury, indignation, passion, rage, wrath. *antonym* calmness.

iridescent *adj* glittering, opalescent, pearly, polychromatic, prismatic, rainbow, rainbow-coloured, rainbow-like, shimmering, shot.

irk *v* aggravate, annoy, bug, disgust, distress, gall, get, get to, irritate, miff, nettle, peeve, provoke, put out, rile, rub up the wrong way, ruffle, vex, weary. *antonym* please.

irksome *adj* aggravating, annoying, boring, bothersome, burdensome, disagreeable, exasperating, infuriating, irritating, tedious, tiresome, troublesome, trying, vexatious, vexing, wearisome. *antonym* pleasing.

iron *adj* adamant, cruel, fast-binding, fixed, grating, hard, harsh, heavy, immovable, implacable, indomitable, inflexible, insensitive, obdurate, rigid, robust, steel, steely, strong, tough, unbending, unyielding. *antonyms* pliable, weak.

iron out clear up, deal with, eliminate, eradicate, erase, expedite, fix, get rid of, harmonise, put right, reconcile, resolve, settle, smooth over, solve, sort out, straighten out.

ironic *adj* contemptuous, derisive, incongruous, ironical, mocking, paradoxical, sarcastic, sardonic, satirical, scoffing, scornful, sneering, wry.

irony *n* contrariness, incongruity, mockery, paradox, sarcasm, satire.

irradiate *v* brighten, enlighten, expose, illuminate, illumine, light up, lighten, radiate, shine on.

irrational *adj* aberrant, absurd, brainless, crazy, demented, foolish, illogical, injudicious, insane, mindless, muddle-headed, nonsensical, preposterous, raving, senseless, silly, unreasonable, unreasoning, unsound, unstable, unthinking, unwise, wild.

irrationality *n* absurdity, brainlessness, illogicality, insanity, lunacy, madness, preposterousness, senselessness, unreason, unreasonableness, unsoundness.

irreconcilable *adj* clashing, conflicting, hardline, implacable, incompatible, incongruous, inconsistent, inexorable, inflexible, intransigent, opposed, unappeasable, uncompromising, unreconcilable.

irrecoverable *adj* irreclaimable, irredeemable, irremediable, irreparable, irretrievable, lost, unrecoverable, unsalvageable, unsavable.

irrefutable *adj* certain, impregnable, incontestable, incontrovertible, indisputable, indubitable, invincible, irrebuttable, irresistible, sure, unanswerable, unassailable, undeniable, unquestionable. *antonym* refutable.

irregular *adj* abnormal, anomalous, asymmetrical, broken, bumpy, capricious, craggy, crooked, disconnected, disorderly, eccentric, erratic, exceptional, extraordinary, extravagant, fitful, fluctuating, fragmentary, haphazard, immoderate, improper, inappropriate, inordinate, intermittent, jagged, lopsided, lumpy, occasional, odd, patchy, peculiar, pitted, queer, quirky, ragged, random, rough, serrated, shifting, snatchy, spasmodic, sporadic, uncertain, unconventional, unequal, uneven, unofficial, unorthodox, unsteady, unsuitable, unsymmetrical, unsystematic, unusual, variable, wavering. *antonyms* conventional, regular, smooth.

irregularity *n* aberration, abnormality, anomaly, asymmetry, breach, bumpiness, confusion, crookedness, desultoriness, deviation, difformity, disorderliness, disorganisation, eccentricity, freak, haphazardness, heterodoxy, jaggedness, lop-sidedness, lumpiness, malfunction, malpractice, oddity, patchiness, peculiarity, raggedness, randomness, roughness, singularity, uncertainty, unconventionality, unevenness, unorthodoxy, unsteadiness. *antonyms* conventionality, regularity, smoothness.

irregularly *adv* anyhow, by fits and starts, disconnectedly, eccentrically, erratically, fitfully, haphazardly, intermittently, jerkily, now and again, occasionally, off and on, spasmodically, unevenly, unmethodically.

irrelevance *n* inappositeness, inappropriateness, inaptness, inconsequence, irrelevancy, unimportance.

irrelevant *adj* extraneous, immaterial, impertinent, inapplicable, inapposite, inappropriate, inapt, inconsequent, inessential, peripheral, tangential, unapt, unconnected, unnecessary, unrelated.

irreligious *adj* agnostic, atheistic, blasphemous, free-thinking, godless, heathen, heathenish, iconoclastic, impious, irreverent, pagan, profane, rationalistic, sacrilegious, sceptical, sinful, unbelieving, undevout, ungodly, unholy, unreligious, unrighteous, wicked. *antonym* pious.

irreparable *adj* incurable, irreclaimable, irrecoverable, irremediable, irretrievable, irreversible, unrepairable. *antonyms* recoverable, remediable.

irreplaceable *adj* essential, indispensable, inimitable, invaluable, matchless, peerless, priceless, sublime, unique, unmatched, vital.

irrepressible *adj* boisterous, bubbling over, buoyant, ebullient, effervescent, inextinguishable, insuppressible, resilient, uncontainable, uncontrollable, ungovernable, uninhibited, unmanageable, unquenchable, unrestrainable, unstoppable. *antonyms* depressed, depressive, despondent, resistible.

irresistible *adj* alluring, beckoning, beguiling, charming, compelling, enchanting, fascinating, imperative, ineluctable, inescapable, inevitable,

inexorable, overmastering, overpowering, overwhelming, potent, pressing, ravishing, resistless, seductive, tempting, unavoidable, uncontrollable, urgent. *antonym* avoidable.

irresolute *adj* dithering, doubtful, faint-hearted, fluctuating, half-hearted, hesitant, hesitating, indecisive, infirm, shifting, shilly-shallying, swithering, tentative, undecided, undetermined, unsettled, unstable, unsteady, vacillating, variable, wavering, weak.

irresolution *n* dithering, faint-heartedness, fluctuation, half-heartedness, hesitancy, hesitation, inconsistency, inconstancy, indecisiveness, infirmity, infirmness, shifting, shilly-shallying, tentativeness, uncertainty, unsteadiness, vacillation, wavering.

irresponsible *adj* carefree, careless, feather-brained, feckless, flibbertigibbit, flighty, foot-loose, giddy, harebrained, harum-scarum, heedless, ill-considered, immature, light-hearted, madcap, negligent, rash, reckless, scatter-brained, shiftless, thoughtless, undependable, unreliable, untrustworthy, wild.

irretrievable *adj* damned, hopeless, irrecoverable, irredeemable, irremediable, irreparable, irreversible, irrevocable, lost, unrecallable, unrecoverable, unsalvageable. *antonyms* recoverable, reversible.

irreverence *n* blasphemy, cheek, cheekiness, derision, discourtesy, disrespect, disrespectfulness, flippancy, godlessness, impertinence, impiety, impudence, levity, mockery, profanity, sauce. *antonym* reverence.

irreverent *adj* blasphemous, cheeky, contemptuous, derisive, discourteous, disrespectful, flip, flippant, godless, iconoclastic, impertinent, impious, impudent, mocking, profane, rude, sacrilegious, saucy, tongue-in-cheek. *antonym* reverent.

irreversible *adj* final, hopeless, incurable, irremediable, irreparable, irretrievable, irrevocable, lasting, lost, permanent, remediless, unalterable. *antonyms* curable, remediable.

irrevocable *adj* changeless, fated, fixed, hopeless, immutable, inexorable, invariable, irremediable, irrepealable, irretrievable, irreversible, predestined, predetermined, settled, unalterable, unchangeable. *antonyms* alterable, flexible, mutable, reversible.

irritability *n* edge, edginess, fractiousness, fretfulness, ill-humour, ill-temper, impatience, irascibility, peevishness, petulance, prickliness, testiness, tetchiness, touchiness. *antonyms* cheerfulness, complacence, good humour.

irritable *adj* bad-tempered, cantankerous, captious, crabbed, crabby, cross, crotchety, crusty, edgy, feisty, fractious, fretful, hasty, ill-humoured, ill-tempered, impatient, irascible, narky, nettlesome, peevish, petulant, prickly, querulous, short, short-tempered, snappish, snappy, snarling, sore, tense, testy, te(t)chy, thin-skinned, touchy. *antonyms* cheerful, complacent.

irritate *v* aggravate, anger, annoy, bedevil, bother, bug, chafe, enrage, exacerbate, exasperate, faze, fret, get on one's nerves, get to, gravel, harass, incense, inflame, infuriate, intensify, irk, needle, nettle, offend, pain, peeve, pester, pique, provoke, put out, rankle, rile, rouse, rub, ruffle, vex. *antonyms* gratify, mollify, placate, please.

irritated *adj* angry, annoyed, bothered, cross, discomposed, displeased, edgy, exasperated, fazed, flappable, flustered, harassed, impatient, irked, irritable, nettled, peeved, piqued, put out, ratty, riled, roused, ruffled, uptight, vexed. *antonyms* composed, gratified, pleased.

irritating *adj* abrasive, aggravating, annoying, bothersome, displeasing, disturbing, galling, infuriating, irksome, maddening, nagging, pesky, provoking, thorny, troublesome, trying, upsetting, vexatious, vexing, worrisome. *antonyms* pleasant, pleasing.

isolate *v* abstract, cut off, detach, disconnect, divorce, exclude, identify, insulate, keep apart, ostracise, pinpoint, quarantine, remove, seclude, segregate, separate, sequester, set apart. *antonyms* assimilate, incorporate.

isolated *adj* abnormal, anomalous, atypical, backwoods, deserted, detached, dissociated, exceptional, freak, godforsaken, hermitical, hidden, incommunicado, insular, lonely, monastic, outlying, out-of-the-way, reclusive, remote, retired, secluded, single, solitary, special, sporadic, unfrequented, unique, unrelated, untrodden, untypical, unusual, unvisited. *antonyms* populous, typical.

isolation *n* aloofness, detachment, disconnection, dissociation, exile, insularity, insulation, loneliness, quarantine, reclusion, remoteness, retirement, seclusion, segregation, self-sufficiency, separation, solitariness, solitude, withdrawal.

issue[1] *n* affair, argument, concern, controversy, crux, debate, matter, point, problem, question, subject, topic.

issue[2] *n* announcement, broadcast, circulation, copy, delivery, dispersal, dissemination, distribution, edition, emanation, flow, granting, handout, impression, instalment, issuance, issuing, number, printing, promulgation, propagation, publication, release, supply, supplying, vent.
v announce, broadcast, circulate, deal out, deliver, distribute, emit, give out, mint, produce, promulgate, publicise, publish, put out, release, supply.

issue[3] *n* conclusion, consequence, culmination, effect, end, finale, outcome, pay-off, product, result, termination, upshot.
v arise, burst forth, emanate, emerge, flow, leak, originate, proceed, rise, spring, stem.

issue[4] *n* brood, children, descendants, heirs, offspring, progeny, seed, young.

itching *adj* aching, avid, burning, dying, eager, greedy, hankering, impatient, inquisitive, itch, longing, raring, spoiling.

item *n* account, article, aspect, bulletin, component, consideration, detail, element, entry, factor, feature, ingredient, matter, minute, note, notice, object, paragraph, particular, piece, point, report, thing.

itemise *v* count, detail, document, enumerate, instance, inventory, list, mention, number, overname, particularise, record, specify, tabulate.

itinerant *adj* drifting, journeying, migratory, nomadic, peripatetic, rambling, roaming, rootless, roving, travelling, vagabond, vagrant, wandering, wayfaring. *antonyms* settled, stationary.
n gypsy, hobo, nomad, peripatetic, pilgrim, Romany, tinker, toe-rag, tramp, traveller, vagabond, vagrant, wanderer, wayfarer.

itinerary *n* circuit, course, journey, line, plan, programme, route, schedule, tour.

J

jab v dig, elbow, jag, lunge, nudge, poke, prod, punch, push, shove, stab, tap, thrust.

jaded adj blunted, bored, cloyed, dulled, effete, exhausted, fagged, fatigued, played-out, satiated, spent, surfeited, tired, tired out, weary. **antonyms** fresh, refreshed.

jagged adj barbed, broken, craggy, indented, irregular, notched, pointed, ragged, ridged, rough, saw-edged, serrated, snagged, snaggy, spiked, spiky, toothed, uneven. **antonym** smooth.

jail, gaol n borstal, brig, can, cells, clink, cooler, coop, custody, guardhouse, house of correction, inside, jailhouse, jug, lock-up, nick, pen, penitentiary, pokey, porridge, prison, reformatory, slammer, stir.
v confine, detain, immure, impound, imprison, incarcerate, intern, lock up, send down.

jam[1] v block, clog, compact, confine, congest, cram, crowd, crush, force, obstruct, pack, press, ram, sandwich, squash, squeeze, stall, stick, stuff, throng, thrust, vice, wedge.
n bottle-neck, concourse, crowd, crush, gridlock, herd, horde, mass, mob, multitude, pack, press, swarm, throng, traffic jam.

jam[2] n bind, difficulty, dilemma, fix, hitch, hole, hot water, imbroglio, impasse, pickle, plight, predicament, quandary, scrape, spot, straits, tangle, tight corner, trouble.

jamboree n carnival, celebration, convention, festival, festivity, fête, field day, frolic, gathering, get-together, jubilee, junket, merriment, party, potlatch, rally, revelry, shindig, spree.

jangle v chime, clank, clash, clatter, jar, jingle, rattle, upset, vibrate.
n cacophony, clang, clangour, clash, din, dissonance, jar, racket, rattle, reverberation, stridence, stridency. **antonyms** euphony, harmony.

jar[1] n amphora, can, carafe, container, crock, ewer, flagon, jug, mug, pitcher, pot, receptacle, urn, vase, vessel.

jar[2] v agitate, annoy, clash, convulse, disagree, discompose, disturb, grate, grind, interfere, irk, irritate, jangle, jolt, nettle, offend, quarrel, rasp, rattle, rock, shake, upset, vibrate.
n clash, disagreement, discord, dissonance, grating, irritation, jangle, jolt, quarrel, rasping, wrangling.

jargon n argot, balderdash, bunkum, cant, dialect, double-Dutch, drivel, gabble, gibberish, gobbledegook, gobbledygook, idiom, jive, lingo, mumbo-jumbo, nonsense, parlance, patois, slang, tongue, twaddle, vernacular.

jarring adj cacophonous, discordant, dissonant, disturbing, grating, irritating, jangling, jolting, rasping, strident, upsetting.

jaundiced adj biased, bitter, cynical, disbelieving, distorted, distrustful, envious, hostile, jaded, jealous, misanthropic, partial, pessimistic, preconceived, prejudiced, resentful, sceptical, suspicious. **antonyms** fresh, naïve, optimistic.

jaunty adj airy, breezy, buoyant, carefree, cheeky, chipper, dapper, debonair, gay, high-spirited, lively, perky, self-confident, showy, smart, sparkish, sprightly, spruce, trim. **antonyms** anxious, depressed, dowdy, seedy.

jazzy adj animated, bold, fancy, flashy, gaudy, goey, lively, smart, snazzy, spirited, stylish, swinging, vivacious, wild, zestful. **antonyms** conservative, prosaic, square.

jealous adj anxious, apprehensive, attentive, careful, covetous, desirous, envious, green, green-eyed, grudging, invidious, mistrustful, possessive, proprietorial, protective, resentful, rival, suspicious, zealous.

jealousy n covetousness, distrust, envy, grudge, heart-burning, ill-will, mistrust, possessiveness, resentment, spite, suspicion.

jeer v banter, barrack, chaff, contemn, deride, explode, flout, gibe, heckle, hector, knock, mock, rail, razz, ridicule, scoff, sneer, taunt, twit.
n abuse, aspersion, catcall, chaff, derision, dig, gibe, hiss, hoot, mockery, raillery, raspberry, ridicule, scoff, sneer, taunt, thrust.

jell, gel v coagulate, congeal, crystallise, finalise, form, gelatinise, harden, jelly, materialise, set, solidify, take form, take shape, thicken. **antonym** disintegrate.

jeopardise v chance, endanger, expose, gamble, hazard, imperil, menace, risk, stake, threaten, venture. **antonyms** protect, safeguard.

jeopardy n danger, endangerment, exposure, hazard, imperilment, insecurity, liability, peril, plight, precariousness, risk, venture, vulnerability. **antonyms** safety, security.

jerk¹ n bounce, jog, jolt, lurch, pluck, pull, shrug, throw, thrust, tug, tweak, twitch, wrench, yank.

v bounce, flirt, jog, jolt, jounce, lurch, peck, pluck, pull, shrug, throw, thrust, tug, tweak, twitch, wrench, yank.

jerk² n bum, clod, clot, clown, creep, dimwit, dolt, dope, fool, halfwit, idiot, klutz, ninny, prick, schlep, schmuck, twit.

jerky adj bouncy, bumpy, convulsive, disconnected, fitful, incoherent, jolting, jumpy, rough, shaky, spasmodic, tremulous, twitchy, uncontrolled, uncoordinated. **antonym** smooth.

jest n banter, clowning, crack, foolery, fooling, fun, gag, hoax, jape, joke, josh, kidding, leg-pull, pleasantry, prank, quip, sally, sport, trick, trifling, waggery, wisecrack, witticism.

v banter, chaff, clown, deride, fool, gibe, jeer, joke, josh, kid, mock, quip, scoff, tease, trifle.

jet n atomiser, flow, fountain, gush, issue, nose, nozzle, rose, rush, spout, spray, sprayer, spring, sprinkler, spurt, squirt, stream, surge.

jettison v abandon, chuck, discard, ditch, dump, eject, expel, heave, offload, scrap, unload. **antonyms** load, take on.

jewel n charm, find, flower, gaud, gem, gemstone, humdinger, locket, masterpiece, ornament, paragon, pearl, precious stone, pride, prize, rarity, rock, sparkler, stone, treasure, wonder.

Jezebel n Delilah, femme fatale, harlot, hussy, jade, man-eater, scarlet woman, seductress, temptress, vamp, wanton, whore, witch.

jibe, gibe v deride, flout, jeer, mock, rail, ridicule, scoff, scorn, sneer, taunt, twit.

n barb, crack, derision, dig, fling, jeer, mockery, poke, quip, raillery, ridicule, sarcasm, scoff, slant, sneer, taunt, thrust.

jiffy n flash, instant, minute, moment, no time, sec, second, split second, tick, trice, twinkling, two shakes, two ticks, whiff. **antonym** age.

jig v bob, bobble, bounce, caper, hop, jerk, jiggle, jounce, jump, prance, shake, skip, twitch, wiggle, wobble.

jiggle v agitate, bounce, fidget, jerk, jig, jog, joggle, shake, shift, shimmy, twitch, waggle, wiggle, wobble.

jilt v abandon, betray, brush off, chuck, deceive, desert, discard, ditch, drop, forsake, reject, repudiate, spurn, throw over. **antonym** cleave to.

jingle v chime, chink, clatter, clink, jangle, rattle, ring, tink, tinkle, tintinnabulate.

n clang, clangour, clink, rattle, reverberation, ringing, tink, tinkle, tintinnabulation.

jingoism n chauvinism, flag-waving, imperialism, insularity, nationalism, parochialism, patriotism, xenophobia.

jinx n black magic, charm, curse, evil eye, gremlin, hex, hoodoo, plague, spell, voodoo.

v bedevil, bewitch, curse, doom, hex, hoodoo, plague.

jitters n anxiety, fidgets, habdabs, heebie-jeebies, nerves, nervousness, tenseness, the creeps, the shakes, the shivers, the willies.

jittery adj agitated, anxious, edgy, fidgety, flustered, jumpy, nervous, panicky, perturbed, quaking, quivering, shaky, shivery, trembling, uneasy. **antonyms** calm, composed, confident.

job n activity, affair, allotment, assignment, batch, business, calling, capacity, career, charge, chore, commission, concern, consignment, contract, contribution, craft, duty, employment, enterprise, errand, function, livelihood, lot, message, métier, mission, occupation, office, output, part, piece, place, portion, position, post, proceeding, product, profession, project, province, pursuit, responsibility, role, share, situation, stint, task, trade, undertaking, venture, vocation, work.

jockey v cajole, coax, ease, edge, engineer, induce, inveigle, manage, manipulate, manoeuvre, negotiate, wheedle.

jocular adj amusing, arch, blithe, comical, droll, entertaining, facetious, funny, humorous, jesting, joking, jolly, jovial, merry, playful, roguish, sportive, teasing, waggish, whimsical, witty. **antonym** serious.

jocularity n absurdity, comicality, drollery, facetiousness, fooling, gaiety, hilarity, humour, jesting, jolliness, joviality, laughter, merriment, playfulness, pleasantry, roguishness, sport, sportiveness, teasing, waggery, waggishness, whimsicality, whimsy, wit.

jog v activate, arouse, bounce, jar, jerk, joggle, jolt, jostle, jounce, nudge, poke, prod, prompt, push, remind, rock, shake, shove, stimulate, stir.

n jerk, jiggle, jolt, nudge, poke, prod, push, reminder, shake, shove.

joie de vivre blitheness, bounce, buoyancy, cheerfulness, ebullience, enjoyment, enthusiasm, gaiety, get-up-and-go, gusto, joy, joyfulness, merriment, mirth, pleasure, relish, zest. **antonym** depression.

join v abut, accompany, add, adhere, adjoin, affiliate, amalgamate, annex, append, associate, attach, border, border on, butt, cement, coincide, combine, conglutinate, conjoin, conjugate, connect, couple, dock, enlist, enrol, enter, fasten, knit, link, march with, marry, meet, merge, reach, sign up, splice, team, tie, touch, unite, verge on, yoke. **antonyms** leave, separate.

join in chip in, contribute, co-operate, help, lend a hand, muck in, partake, participate, pitch in.

join up enlist, enroll, enter, sign up, take the king's shilling.

joint n articulation, connection, hinge, intersection, junction, juncture, knot, nexus, node, seam, union.

adj adjunct, amalgamated, collective, combined, communal, concerted, consolidated, co-operative, co-ordinated, joined, mutual, shared, united.

v articulate, carve, connect, couple, cut up, dismember, dissect, divide, fasten, fit, geniculate, join, segment, sever, unite.

joke n buffoon, butt, clown, frolic, fun, funny, gag, guy, hoot, jape, jest, lark, laughing-stock, play, pun, quip, quirk, sally, simpleton, sport, target, whimsy, wisecrack, witticism, yarn, yell.

v banter, chaff, clown, deride, fool, frolic, gambol, jest, kid, laugh, mock, quip, ridicule, spoof, taunt, tease, wisecrack.

joker n buffoon, card, character, clown, comedian, comic, droll, humorist, jester, joculator, jokesmith, kidder, prankster, sport, trickster, wag, wit.

jolly adj blithe, carefree, cheerful, cheery, convivial, exuberant, festive, frisky, funny, gay, gladsome, happy, hearty, hilarious, jaunty, jovial, joyful, joyous, jubilant, merry, mirthful, playful, sportive, sprightly, sunny. **antonym** sad.

jolt v astonish, bounce, bump, discompose, disconcert, dismay, disturb, jar, jerk, jog, jostle, jounce, knock, nonplus, perturb, push, shake, shock, shove, stagger, startle, stun, surprise, upset.

n blow, bolt from the blue, bombshell, bump, hit, impact, jar, jerk, jog, jump, lurch, quiver, reversal, setback, shake, shock, start, surprise, thunderbolt.

jostle v bump, butt, crowd, elbow, force, hustle, jog, joggle, jolt, press, push, rough up, scramble, shake, shoulder, shove, squeeze, throng, thrust.

jot n atom, bit, detail, fraction, glimmer, grain, hint, iota, mite, morsel, particle, scintilla, scrap, smidgen, speck, tittle, trace, trifle, whit.

jot down enter, list, note, record, register, scribble, take down, write down.

journalism n copy-writing, correspondence, feature-writing, Fleet Street, gossip-writing, Grub Street, news, press, reportage, reporting, writing.

journalist n broadcaster, chronicler, columnist, commentator, contributor, correspondent, diarist, feature-writer, hack, journo, newshound, newsman, newspaperman, news-writer, periodicalist, pressman, reporter, scribe, stringer, sub, subeditor.

journey n career, course, excursion, expedition, itinerary, jaunt, odyssey, outing, passage, pilgrimage, progress, ramble, route, safari, tour, travel, trek, trip, voyage, wanderings.

v fare, fly, gallivant, go, jaunt, proceed, ramble, range, roam, rove, safari, tour, tramp, travel, traverse, trek, voyage, wander, wend.

jovial adj affable, airy, animated, blithe, buoyant, cheery, convivial, cordial, ebullient, expansive, gay, glad, happy, hilarious, jaunty, jolly, jubilant, merry, mirthful. **antonyms** morose, sad, saturnine.

joviality n affability, buoyancy, cheerfulness, cheeriness, ebullience, fun, gaiety, gladness, glee, happiness, hilarity, jollity, merriment, mirth. **antonyms** moroseness, sadness.

joy n blessedness, bliss, charm, delight, ecstasy, elation, exaltation, exultation, felicity, festivity, gaiety, gem, gladness, gladsomeness, glee, gratification happiness, hilarity, jewel, joyance, joyfulness, joyousness, pleasure, pride, prize, rapture, ravishment, satisfaction, transport, treasure, treat, triumph, wonder. *antonyms* mourning, sorrow.

joyful *adj* blithe, delighted, ecstatic, elated, enraptured, glad, gratified, happy, jolly, jovial, jubilant, light-hearted, merry, pleased, rapturous, satisfied, transported, triumphant. *antonyms* mournful, sorrowful.

joyless *adj* bleak, cheerless, dejected, depressed, despondent, discouraged, discouraging, dismal, dispirited, doleful, dour, downcast, dreary, forlorn, gloomy, glum, grim, miserable, sad, sombre, sunless, unhappy. *antonym* joyful.

joyous *adj* cheerful, ecstatic, festive, frabjous, glad, gleeful, happy, joyful, jubilant, merry, rapturous. *antonym* sad.

jubilant *adj* celebratory, delighted, elated, enraptured, euphoric, excited, exuberant, exultant, flushed, glad, gratified, joyous, over the moon, overjoyed, rejoicing, thrilled, triumphal, triumphant. *antonyms* defeated, depressed.

jubilation *n* celebration, ecstasy, elation, euphoria, excitement, exultation, festivity, jollification, joy, triumph. *antonyms* depression, lamentation.

Judas *n* betrayer, deceiver, quisling, renegade, traitor, turncoat.

judge *n* adjudicator, arbiter, arbitrator, assessor, authority, connoisseur, critic, evaluator, expert, justice, Law Lord, magistrate, mediator, moderator, pundit, referee, umpire, wig.
v adjudge, adjudicate, appraise, appreciate, arbitrate, ascertain, assess, conclude, condemn, consider, criticise, decide, decree, determine, discern, distinguish, doom, esteem, estimate, evaluate, examine, find, gauge, mediate, opine, rate, reckon, referee, review, rule, sentence, sit, try, umpire, value.

judgement *n* acumen, appraisal, arbitration, assessment, assize, award, belief, common sense, conclusion, conviction, damnation, decision, decree, decreet, deduction, determination, diagnosis, discernment, discretion, discrimination, doom, enlightenment, estimate, expertise, fate, finding, intelligence, mediation, misfortune, opinion, order, penetration, perceptiveness, percipience, perspicacity, prudence, punishment, result, retribution, ruling, sagacity,

sense, sentence, shrewdness, taste, understanding, valuation, verdict, view, virtuosity, wisdom.

judicious *adj* acute, astute, canny, careful, cautious, circumspect, considered, diplomatic, discerning, discreet, discriminating, enlightened, expedient, informed, percipient, perspicacious, politic, prescient, prudent, rational, reasonable, sagacious, sage, sensible, shrewd, skilful, sober, sound, thoughtful, wary, well-advised, well-judged, well-judging, wise. *antonym* injudicious.

jug *n* amphora, carafe, churn, container, crock, ewer, flagon, jar, pitcher, urn, vessel.

juggle *v* alter, change, cook, disguise, doctor, fake, falsify, fix, manipulate, manoeuvre, misrepresent, modify, rig, tamper with.

juicy *adj* colourful, interesting, lush, moist, naughty, provocative, racy, risqué, salacious, sappy, sensational, spicy, succulent, suggestive, vivid, watery. *antonym* dry.

jumble *v* confuse, disarrange, disarray, disorder, disorganise, mix, mix up, muddle, shuffle, tangle, tumble. *antonym* order.
n agglomeration, chaos, clutter, collection, confusion, conglomeration, disarrangement, disarray, disorder, hotch-potch, medley, mess, miscellany, mishmash, mixture, mix-up, muddle, pot-pourri, salad.

jumbled *adj* chaotic, confused, disarrayed, disordered, disorganised, miscellaneous, mixed-up, muddled, shuffled, tangled, tumbled, unsorted, untidy. *antonym* orderly.

jump[1] *v* bounce, bound, caper, clear, dance, frisk, frolic, gambol, hop, hurdle, jig, leap, pounce, prance, skip, spring, vault.
n bounce, bound, capriole, dance, frisk, frolic, hop, leap, pounce, prance, saltation, skip, spring, vault.

jump[2] *v* avoid, bypass, digress, disregard, evade, ignore, leave out, miss, omit, overshoot, pass over, skip, switch.
n breach, break, gap, hiatus, interruption, interval, lacuna, lapse, omission, saltation, switch.

jump[3] *v* advance, appreciate, ascend, boost, escalate, gain, hike, increase, mount, rise, spiral, surge.
n advance, ascent, augmentation,

boost, escalation, increase, increment, mounting, rise, upsurge, upturn.

jump⁴ *v* flinch, jerk, jump out of one's skin, leap in the air, quail, recoil, resile, shrink, start, wince.

n jar, jerk, jolt, lurch, quiver, shiver, shock, spasm, start, swerve, twitch, wrench.

jumpy *adj* agitated, anxious, apprehensive, discomposed, edgy, fidgety, jittery, nervous, nervy, restive, restless, shaky, tense, tremulous, uneasy. **antonyms** calm, composed.

junction *n* abutment, combination, confluence, conjunction, connection, coupling, intersection, interstice, join, joining, joint, linking, meeting-point, nexus, seam, union.

junior *adj* inferior, lesser, lower, minor, secondary, subordinate, subsidiary, younger. **antonym** senior.

junk *n* clutter, debris, detritus, dregs, garbage, litter, oddments, refuse, rubbish, rummage, scrap, trash, waste, wreckage.

jurisdiction *n* area, authority, bailiwick, bounds, cognisance, command, control, domination, dominion, field, influence, power, prerogative, province, range, reach, rule, scope, sovereignty, sphere, sway, zone.

just *adj* accurate, apposite, appropriate, apt, blameless, conscientious, correct, decent, deserved, disinterested, due, equitable, even-handed, exact, fair, fair-minded, faithful, fitting, good, honest, honourable, impartial, impeccable, irreproachable, justified, lawful, legitimate, merited, normal, precise, proper, pure, reasonable, regular, right, righteous, rightful, sound, suitable, true, unbiased, unimpeachable, unprejudiced, upright, virtuous, well-deserved. **antonym** unjust.

justice *n* amends, appositeness, appropriateness, compensation, correction, equitableness, equity, fairness, honesty, impartiality, integrity, justifiableness,

justness, law, legality, legitimacy, penalty, propriety, reasonableness, recompense, redress, reparation, requital, right, rightfulness, rightness, satisfaction. **antonym** injustice.

justifiable *adj* acceptable, allowable, defensible, excusable, explainable, explicable, fit, forgivable, justified, lawful, legitimate, maintainable, pardonable, proper, reasonable, right, sound, tenable, understandable, valid, vindicable, warrantable, warranted, well-founded. **antonyms** culpable, illicit, unjustifiable.

justification *n* absolution, apology, approval, authorisation, basis, defence, exculpation, excuse, exoneration, explanation, extenuation, foundation, grounds, mitigation, palliation, plea, rationalisation, reason, substance, vindication, warrant.

justify *v* absolve, acquit, condone, confirm, defend, establish, exculpate, excuse, exonerate, explain, forgive, legalise, legitimise, maintain, pardon, substantiate, support, sustain, uphold, validate, vindicate, warrant.

justly *adv* accurately, conscientiously, correctly, duly, equally, equitably, even-handedly, fairly, honestly, impartially, lawfully, legitimately, objectively, properly, rightfully, rightly.

jut *v* beetle, bulge, extend, impend, overhang, poke, project, protrude, stick out. **antonym** recede.

juvenile *n* adolescent, boy, child, girl, halfling, infant, kid, minor, young person, youngster, youth. **antonym** adult.

adj adolescent, babyish, boyish, callow, childish, girlish, immature, impressionable, inexperienced, infantile, puerile, tender, undeveloped, unsophisticated, young, youthful. **antonym** mature.

juxtaposition *n* adjacency, closeness, contact, contiguity, immediacy, nearness, propinquity, proximity, vicinity. **antonyms** dissociation, separation.

K

kaput *adj* broken, conked out, dead, defunct, destroyed, extinct, finished, phut, ruined, smashed, undone, wrecked.

keel over black out, capsize, collapse, crumple, drop, faint, fall, founder, go out like a light, overturn, pass out, stagger, swoon, topple over, upset.

keen *adj* acid, acute, anxious, ardent, assiduous, astute, avid, biting, brilliant, canny, caustic, clever, cutting, devoted, diligent, discerning, discriminating, eager, earnest, ebullient, edged, enthusiastic, fervid, fierce, fond, forthright, impassioned, incisive, industrious, intense, intent, mordant, penetrating, perceptive, perspicacious, piercing, pointed, pungent, quick, razorlike, sagacious, sardonic, satirical, scathing, sedulous, sensitive, sharp, shrewd, shrill, tart, trenchant, wise, zealous. **antonyms** apathetic, blunt, dull.

keenness *n* acerbity, anxiety, ardour, assiduity, astuteness, avidity, avidness, canniness, cleverness, diligence, discernment, eagerness, earnestness, ebullience, enthusiasm, fervour, forthrightness, harshness, impatience, incisiveness, industriousness, industry, insight, intensity, intentness, mordancy, passion, penetration, pungency, rigour, sagacity, sedulity, sensitivity, severity, sharpness, shrewdness, sternness, trenchancy, virulence, wisdom, zeal, zest. **antonyms** apathy, bluntness, dullness.

keep¹ *v* accumulate, amass, carry, collect, conserve, control, deal in, deposit, furnish, garner, hang on to, heap, hold, hold on to, maintain, pile, place, possess, preserve, retain, stack, stock, store.

keep an eye on guard, keep tabs on, keep under surveillance, look after, look to, monitor, observe, regard, scrutinise, supervise, survey, watch.

keep at be steadfast, beaver away at, carry on, complete, continue, drudge, endure, finish, grind, labour, last, maintain, persevere, persist, plug away at, remain, slave, slog at, stay, stick at, toil. **antonyms** abandon, neglect.

keep on carry on, continue, endure, hold on, keep at it, last, maintain, persevere,

persist, prolong, remain, retain, soldier on, stay, stay the course.

keep on at badger, chivvy, dun, go on at, harass, harry, importune, nag, pester, plague, pursue.

keep one's distance avoid, be aloof, give a wide berth, keep at arm's length, keep oneself to oneself, shun, withdraw.

keep secret conceal, dissemble, hide, keep back, keep dark, keep under one's hat, keep under wraps, suppress, wash one's dirty linen at home. **antonym** reveal.

keep track of follow, grasp, keep up with, monitor, oversee, plot, record, trace, track, understand, watch.

keep up be on a par with, compete, contend, continue, emulate, equal, keep pace, maintain, match, pace, persevere, preserve, rival, support, sustain, vie.

keep² *v* be responsible for, board, care for, defend, feed, foster, guard, have charge of, have custody of, look after, maintain, manage, mind, nourish, nurture, operate, protect, provide for, provision, safeguard, shelter, shield, subsidise, support, sustain, tend, watch, watch over.
n board, food, livelihood, living, maintenance, means, nourishment, subsistence, support, upkeep.

keep³ *v* arrest, block, check, constrain, control, curb, delay, detain, deter, hamper, hamstring, hinder, hold, hold back, hold up, impede, inhibit, interfere with, keep back, limit, obstruct, prevent, restrain, retard, shackle, stall, trammel, withhold.

keep back censor, check, conceal, constrain, control, curb, delay, hide, hold back, hush up, impede, limit, prohibit, quell, ration, reserve, restrain, restrict, retain, retard, stifle, stop, suppress, withhold.

keep in bottle up, conceal, confine, control, detain, hide, inhibit, keep back, quell, restrain, retain, stifle, stop up, suppress. **antonyms** declare, release.

keep⁴ *v* adhere to, celebrate, commemorate, comply with, fulfil, hold, honour, keep faith with, keep up, maintain, obey, observe, perform, perpetuate, recognise, respect, ritualise, solemnise.

keeping *n* accord, accordance,

aegis, agreement, auspices, balance, care, charge, compliance, conformity, congruity, consistency, correspondence, custody, guardianship, harmony, keep, maintenance, obedience, observance, patronage, possession, proportion, protection, safe-keeping, supervision, surveillance, trust, tutelage, ward.

keg *n* barrel, butt, cask, drum, firkin, hogshead, round, tun, vat.

ken *n* acquaintance, appreciation, awareness, cognisance, compass, comprehension, field, grasp, knowledge, notice, perception, range, reach, realisation, scope, sight, understanding, view, vision.

kernel *n* core, essence, germ, gist, grain, heart, marrow, nitty-gritty, nub, pith, seed, substance.

key *n* answer, clue, code, cue, explanation, glossary, guide, index, indicator, interpretation, lead, means, pointer, secret, sign, solution, table, translation.
adj basic, cardinal, central, chief, core, crucial, decisive, essential, fundamental, important, leading, main, major, pivotal, principal, salient.

keynote *n* accent, centre, core, emphasis, essence, flavour, flavour of the month, gist, heart, kernel, marrow, motif, pith, stress, substance, theme.

keystone *n* base, basis, core, cornerstone, crux, foundation, fundamental, ground, linchpin, mainspring, motive, principle, root, source, spring.

kick *v* abandon, boot, break, desist from, drop, foot, give up, leave off, leave out, punt, quit, spurn, stop, toe.
n bite, buzz, dash, élan, enjoyment, excitement, feeling, force, fun, gratification, gusto, intensity, panache, pep, pizzazz, pleasure, power, punch, pungency, relish, snap, sparkle, stimulation, strength, tang, thrill, verve, vitality, zest, zing, zip.

kick off begin, break the ice, commence, get under way, inaugurate, initiate, introduce, open, open the proceedings, set the ball rolling, start.

kick out chuck out, discharge, dismiss, eject, evict, expel, get rid of, give the bum's rush, oust, reject, remove, sack, throw out, toss out.

kick-off *n* beginning, bully-off, commencement, face-off, inception, introduction, opening, outset, start, word go.

kid¹ *n* babe, baby, bairn, bambino, boy, child, girl, halfling, infant, juvenile, kiddy, lad, nipper, shaver, stripling, teenager, tot, wean, whippersnapper, youngster, youth.

kid² *v* bamboozle, beguile, con, cozen, delude, dupe, fool, gull, have on, hoax, hoodwink, humbug, jest, joke, josh, mock, pretend, pull someone's leg, put one over on, rag, ridicule, tease, trick.

kidnap *v* abduct, capture, hijack, remove, seize, skyjack, snatch, steal.

kill *v* abolish, annihilate, assassinate, beguile, bump off, butcher, cancel, cease, deaden, defeat, destroy, dispatch, do away with, do in, do to death, eliminate, eradicate, execute, exterminate, extinguish, extirpate, fill, finish off, halt, knock off, knock on the head, liquidate, mar, martyr, massacre, murder, neutralise, nip in the bud, nullify, obliterate, occupy, pass, pip, put to death, quash, quell, rub out, ruin, scotch, slaughter, slay, smite, smother, spoil, stifle, still, stop, suppress, top, veto, vitiate, while away, zap.
n climax, coup de grâce, death, death-blow, dispatch, end, finish, mop-up, shoot-out.

killer *n* assassin, butcher, cut-throat, destroyer, executioner, exterminator, gunman, hatchet man, hit-man, liquidator, murderer, ripper, shootist, slaughterer, slayer, triggerman.

killing *n* assassination, bloodshed, carnage, elimination, execution, extermination, fatality, fratricide, homicide, infanticide, liquidation, manslaughter, massacre, matricide, murder, patricide, pogrom, slaughter, slaying.
adj deadly, death-dealing, deathly, debilitating, enervating, exhausting, fatal, fatiguing, final, lethal, lethiferous, mortal, murderous, punishing, tiring, vital.

kin *n* affinity, blood, clan, connection, connections, cousins, extraction, family, flesh and blood, kindred, kinsfolk, kinship, kinsmen, kith, lineage, people, relations, relationship, relatives, stock, tribe.
adj akin, allied, close, cognate, connected, consanguine, consanguineous, interconnected, kindred, linked, near, related, similar, twin.

kind¹ *n* brand, breed, category, character, class, description, essence, family, genus, habit, ilk, kidney, manner, mould, nature, persuasion, race, set, sort, species, stamp, style, temperament, type, variety.

kind² *adj* accommodating, affectionate, altruistic, amiable, amicable, avuncular, beneficent, benevolent, benign, boon, bounteous, bountiful, charitable, clement, compassionate, congenial, considerate, cordial, courteous, diplomatic, friendly, generous, gentle, giving, good, gracious, hospitable, humane, indulgent, kind-hearted, kindly, lenient, loving, mild, neighbourly, obliging, philanthropic, propitious, soft-boiled, soft-hearted, sweet, sympathetic, tactful, tender-hearted, thoughtful, understanding. *antonyms* cruel, inconsiderate, unhelpful.

kind-hearted *adj* altruistic, amicable, benign, big-hearted, compassionate, considerate, generous, good-hearted, good-natured, gracious, helpful, humane, humanitarian, kind, kindly, obliging, philanthropic, sympathetic, tender-hearted, warm, warm-hearted. *antonym* ill-natured.

kindle *v* activate, actuate, agitate, animate, arouse, awaken, exasperate, excite, fan, fire, foment, ignite, incite, induce, inflame, initiate, inspire, inspirit, light, provoke, rouse, set alight, sharpen, stimulate, stir, thrill.

kindly *adj* beneficent, benevolent, benign, charitable, comforting, compassionate, cordial, favourable, generous, genial, gentle, giving, good-natured, hearty, helpful, indulgent, kind, mild, patient, pleasant, polite, sympathetic, tender, warm.
adv agreeably, charitably, comfortingly, considerately, cordially, generously, gently, graciously, indulgently, patiently, politely, tenderly, thoughtfully. *antonyms* cruel, inconsiderate, uncharitable, unpleasant.

kindness *n* affection, aid, altruism, amiability, assistance, benefaction, beneficence, benevolence, bounty, charity, chivalry, clemency, compassion, cordiality, courtesy, favour, forbearance, friendliness, gallantry, generosity, gentleness, good will, goodness, grace, help, hospitality, humaneness, humanity, indulgence, kindliness, liberality, loving-kindness, magnanimity, mildness, munificence, obligingness, patience, philanthropy, service, tenderness, tolerance, understanding. *antonyms* cruelty, illiberality, inhumanity.

king *n* boss, chief, chieftain, doyen, emperor, kingpin, leading light, luminary, majesty, monarch, overlord, paramount, patriarch, potentate, prince, ruler, sovereign, supremo.

kingdom *n* area, commonwealth, country, division, domain, dominion, dynasty, empire, field, land, monarchy, nation, palatinate, principality, province, realm, reign, royalty, sovereignty, sphere, state, territory, tract.

kink *n* bend, coil, complication, corkscrew, crick, crimp, defect, dent, difficulty, entanglement, flaw, hitch, imperfection, indentation, knot, loop, tangle, twist, wrinkle.
v bend, coil, crimp, curl, tangle, twist, wrinkle.

kinky¹ *adj* coiled, crimped, crumpled, curled, curly, frizzy, tangled, twisted, wrinkled.

kinky² *adj* bizarre, degenerate, depraved, deviant, eccentric, freakish, idiosyncratic, licentious, odd, outlandish, peculiar, perverted, queer, quirky, strange, unconventional, unnatural, warped, weird.

kinship *n* affinity, alliance, association, bearing, community, conformity, connection, consanguinity, correspondence, kin, relation, relationship, similarity.

kismet *n* destiny, doom, fate, fortune, lot, portion, predestiny, providence.

kiss¹ *v* canoodle, neck, peck, smooch, snog.
n peck, smack, smacker, snog.

kiss² *v* brush, caress, fan, glance, graze, lick, scrape, touch.

kit *n* accoutrements, apparatus, baggage, effects, equipage, equipment, gear, implements, instruments, luggage, muniments, outfit, paraphernalia, provisions, rig, rig-out, set, supplies, tackle, tools, trappings, traps, utensils.

kit out arm, deck out, dress, equip, fit out, fix up, furnish, habilitate, outfit, prepare, supply.

knack *n* ability, adroitness, aptitude, bent, capacity, dexterity, expertise, expertness, facility, faculty, flair, forte, genius, gift, handiness, hang, ingenuity, propensity, quickness, skilfulness, skill, talent, trick, trick of the trade, turn.

knave *n* bastard, blackguard, blighter, bounder, dastard, rapscallion, rascal, reprobate, rogue, rotter, scallywag, scamp, scoundrel, stinker, swine, varlet, villain.

knead *v* form, knuckle, manipulate, massage, mould, ply, press, rub, shape, squeeze, work.

knickers *n* bloomers, breeks, briefs,

drawers, knickerbockers, panties, pants, smalls, underwear.

knick-knack *n* bagatelle, bauble, bric-à-brac, gadget, plaything, pretty, toy, trifle, trinket.

knife *n* blade, carver, cutter, dagger, flick-knife, jack-knife, machete, pen-knife, pocket-knife, skean, skene, skene-dhu, switchblade.

v cut, impale, lacerate, pierce, rip, slash, stab, wound.

knight *n* cavalier, champion, chevalier, gallant, horseman, knight-at-arms, knight-errant, man-at-arms, soldier, warrior.

knightly *adj* bold, chivalrous, courageous, courtly, dauntless, gallant, gracious, heroic, honourable, intrepid, noble, soldierly, valiant, valorous. *antonyms* cowardly, ignoble, ungallant.

knit *v* ally, bind, connect, crease, crotchet, fasten, furrow, heal, interlace, intertwine, join, knot, link, loop, mend, secure, tie, unite, weave, wrinkle.

knob *n* boss, bump, door-handle, knot, knurl, lump, projection, protrusion, protuberance, stud, swell, swelling, tuber, tumour.

knock[1] *v* buffet, clap, cuff, ding, hit, knobble, punch, rap, slap, smack, smite, strike, thump, thwack.

n blow, box, chap, clip, clout, cuff, hammering, rap, slap, smack, thump.

knock about[1] associate, go around, loaf, ramble, range, roam, rove, saunter, traipse, travel, wander.

knock about[2] abuse, bash, batter, beat up, biff, bruise, buffet, damage, hit, hurt, manhandle, maul, mistreat.

knock down batter, clout, demolish, destroy, fell, floor, level, pound, raze, smash, wallop, wreck.

knock off[1] cease, clock off, clock out, complete, conclude, finish, pack (it) in, stop, terminate.

knock off[2] deduct, filch, nick, pilfer, pinch, purloin, rob, steal, take away, thieve.

knock off[3] assassinate, bump off, do away with, do in, kill, liquidate, murder, rub out, slay, waste.

knock up achieve, build, construct, erect, make. *antonym* demolish.

knock[2] *v* abuse, belittle, carp, cavil, censure, condemn, criticise, deprecate, disparage, find fault, lambaste, run down, slam, vilify.

n blame, censure, condemnation, criticism, defeat, failure, rebuff,

rejection, reversal, setback, stricture. *antonyms* boost, praise.

knockout *n* bestseller, coup de grâce, hit, kayo, KO, sensation, smash, smash-hit, stunner, success, triumph, winner. *antonyms* flop, loser.

knoll *n* barrow, hill, hillock, hummock, mound.

knot *v* bind, entangle, entwine, knit, loop, secure, tangle, tether, tie, weave.

n aggregation, bond, bow, braid, bunch, burl, clump, cluster, collection, connection, gnarl, hitch, joint, knarl, ligature, loop, mass, pile, rosette, tie, tuft.

knotty *adj* baffling, complex, complicated, difficult, gnarled, hard, intricate, knotted, mystifying, nodular, perplexing, problematical, puzzling, rough, rugged, thorny, tricky, troublesome.

know *v* apprehend, comprehend, discern, distinguish, experience, fathom, identify, intuit, ken, learn, make out, notice, perceive, realise, recognise, see, tell, undergo, understand.

know-all *n* clever-clogs, smart Alec, smarty-pants.

know-how *n* ability, adroitness, aptitude, capability, dexterity, experience, expertise, faculty, flair, gumption, ingenuity, knack, knowledge, proficiency, savoir-faire, savvy, skill, talent.

knowing *adj* acute, astute, aware, clever, competent, conscious, cunning, discerning, eloquent, experienced, expert, expressive, intelligent, meaningful, perceptive, qualified, sagacious, shrewd, significant, skilful, well-informed. *antonyms* ignorant, obtuse.

knowingly *adv* consciously, deliberately, designedly, intentionally, on purpose, purposely, studiedly, wilfully, wittingly.

knowledge *n* ability, acquaintance, acquaintanceship, apprehension, book-learning, cognisance, cognition, comprehension, consciousness, discernment, education, enlightenment, erudition, familiarity, grasp, information, instruction, intelligence, intimacy, judgement, know-how, learning, notice, recognition, scholarship, schooling, science, tuition, understanding, wisdom. *antonym* ignorance.

knowledgeable *adj* acquainted, au fait, aware, book-learned, bright, cognisant, conscious, conversant, educated, erudite, experienced, familiar, in the know, intelligent, learned, lettered, scholarly, well-informed. *antonym* ignorant.

known *adj* acknowledged, admitted, avowed, celebrated, commonplace, confessed, familiar, famous, manifest, noted, obvious, patent, plain, published, recognised, well-known.

knuckle under accede, acquiesce, capitulate, defer, give in, give way, submit, succumb, surrender, yield.

kowtow *v* bow, cringe, defer, fawn, flatter, genuflect, grovel, kneel, pander, suck up, toady.

kudos *n* acclaim, applause, distinction, esteem, fame, glory, honour, laudation, laurels, plaudits, praise, prestige, regard, renown, repute.

L

label *n* badge, brand, categorisation, characterisation, classification, company, description, docket, epithet, mark, marker, sticker, tag, tally, ticket, trademark.
v brand, call, categorise, characterise, class, classify, define, describe, designate, dub, identify, mark, name, stamp, tag.

laborious *adj* arduous, assiduous, backbreaking, burdensome, difficult, diligent, fatiguing, forced, hard, hard-working, heavy, herculean, indefatigable, industrious, laboured, onerous, painstaking, persevering, ponderous, sedulous, strained, strenuous, tireless, tiresome, toilsome, tough, unflagging, uphill, wearing, wearisome. *antonyms* easy, effortless, relaxing, simple.

labour¹ *n* chore, donkey-work, drudgery, effort, employees, exertion, grind, hands, industry, job, labourers, pains, slog, sweat, task, toil, undertaking, work, workers, workforce, workmen. *antonyms* ease, leisure, relaxation, rest.
v drudge, endeavour, grind, heave, pitch, plod, roll, slave, strive, struggle, suffer, sweat, toil, travail, work. *antonyms* idle, laze, loaf, lounge.

labour² *v* dwell on, elaborate, overdo, overemphasise, overstress, strain.

laboured *adj* affected, awkward, complicated, contrived, difficult, forced, heavy, overdone, overwrought, ponderous, stiff, stilted, strained, studied, unnatural. *antonyms* easy, natural.

labyrinth *n* circumvolution, coil, complexity, complication, convolution, entanglement, intricacy, jungle, maze, perplexity, puzzle, riddle, tangle, windings.

labyrinthine *adj* complex, confused, convoluted, intricate, involved, knotty, mazy, perplexing, puzzling, tangled, tortuous, winding. *antonyms* simple, straightforward.

lace *v* attach, bind, close, do up, fasten, intertwine, interweave, string, thread, tie.

lacerate *v* afflict, claw, cut, distress, gash, harrow, jag, maim, mangle, rend, rip, slash, torment, torture, wound.

laceration *n* cut, gash, injury, mutilation, rent, rip, slash, tear, wound.

lachrymose *adj* crying, dolorous, mournful, sad, sobbing, tearful, teary, weeping, weepy, woeful. *antonyms* happy, laughing.

lack *n* absence, dearth, deficiency, deprivation, destitution, emptiness, insufficiency, need, privation, scantiness, scarcity, shortage, shortcoming, shortness, vacancy, void, want. *antonyms* abundance, profusion.
v miss, need, require, want.

lackadaisical *adj* abstracted, apathetic, dreamy, dull, half-hearted, idle, indifferent, indolent, inert, languid, languorous, lazy, lethargic, limp, listless, spiritless. *antonyms* active, dynamic, energetic, vigorous.

lackey *n* attendant, creature, fawner, flatterer, flunky, footman, gofer, hanger-on, manservant, menial, minion, parasite, pawn, servitor, sycophant, toady, valet, yes-man.

lacking *adj* defective, deficient, flawed, impaired, inadequate, minus, missing, needing, short of, wanting, without.

lacklustre *adj* boring, dim, drab, dry, dull, flat, leaden, lifeless, lustreless, mundane, muted, prosaic, sombre, spiritless, unimaginative, uninspired, vapid. *antonyms* brilliant, polished.

laconic *adj* brief, close-mouthed, compact, concise, crisp, curt, pithy, sententious, short, succinct, taciturn, terse. *antonyms* garrulous, verbose, wordy.

lad *n* boy, bucko, chap, fellow, guy, halfling, juvenile, kid, laddie, nipper, schoolboy, shaver, stripling, youngster, youth.

laden *adj* burdened, charged, chock-a-block, chock-full, encumbered, fraught, full, hampered, jammed, loaded, oppressed, packed, stuffed, taxed, weighed down, weighted. *antonym* empty.

la-di-da *adj* affected, conceited, foppish, high-falutin(g), mannered, mincing, over-refined, posh, precious, pretentious, put-on, snobbish, snooty, stuck-up, toffee-nosed.

ladylike *adj* courtly, cultured, decorous, elegant, genteel, matronly, modest, polite, proper, queenly, refined, respectable, well-bred.

lag *v* dawdle, delay, hang back, idle,

linger, loiter, mosey, saunter, shuffle, straggle, tarry, trail. **antonym** lead.

laid up bedridden, disabled, housebound, ill, immobilised, incapacitated, injured, on the sick list, out of action, sick.

laid-back *adj* at ease, calm, casual, cool, easy-going, free and easy, passionless, relaxed, unflappable, unhurried, untroubled, unworried. **antonyms** tense, uptight.

lair *n* burrow, den, earth, hideout, hole, nest, refuge, retreat, roost, sanctuary, stronghold.

lam *v* batter, beat, clout, hit, knock, lambaste, leather, pelt, pound, pummel, strike, thrash, thump.

lambaste *v* beat, berate, bludgeon, castigate, censure, cudgel, drub, flay, flog, leather, rebuke, reprimand, roast, scold, strike, thrash, upbraid, whip.

lambent *adj* brilliant, dancing, flickering, fluttering, gleaming, glistening, glowing, incandescent, licking, light, luminous, lustrous, radiant, refulgent, shimmering, sparkling, touching, twinkling.

lame *adj* crippled, defective, disabled, disappointing, feeble, flimsy, game, half-baked, halt, handicapped, hobbling, inadequate, insufficient, limping, poor, thin, unconvincing, unsatisfactory, weak. *v* cripple, damage, disable, hamstring, hobble, hurt, incapacitate, injure, maim, wing.

lament *v* bemoan, bewail, complain, deplore, grieve, keen, mourn, regret, sorrow, wail, weep. **antonyms** celebrate, rejoice.
n complaint, coronach, dirge, elegy, lamentation, moan, moaning, monody, plaint, requiem, threnody, wail, wailing.

lamentable *adj* deplorable, disappointing, distressing, grievous, inadequate, insufficient, low, meagre, mean, miserable, mournful, pitiful, poor, regrettable, sorrowful, tragic, unfortunate, unsatisfactory, woeful, wretched.

lamentation *n* deploration, dirge, grief, grieving, lament, moan, mourning, plaint, sobbing, sorrow, wailing, weeping. **antonyms** celebration, rejoicing.

laminate *v* coat, cover, exfoliate, face, flake, foliate, layer, plate, separate, split, stratify, veneer.

lampoon *n* burlesque, caricature, mickey-take, parody, satire, send-up, skit, spoof, take-off.
v burlesque, caricature, make fun of, mock, parody, ridicule, satirise, send up, spoof, take off, take the mickey out of.

land[1] *n* country, countryside, dirt, district, earth, estate, farmland, fatherland, ground, grounds, loam, motherland, nation, property, province, real estate, region, soil, terra firma, territory, tract.
v alight, arrive, berth, bring, carry, cause, come to rest, debark, deposit, disembark, dock, drop, end up, plant, touch down, turn up, wind up.

land[2] *v* achieve, acquire, capture, gain, get, net, obtain, secure, win.

landmark *n* beacon, boundary, cairn, feature, milestone, monument, signpost, turning-point, watershed.

landscape *n* aspect, countryside, outlook, panorama, prospect, scene, scenery, view, vista.

landslide *n* avalanche, earthfall, landslip, rock-fall.
adj decisive, emphatic, overwhelming, runaway.

lane *n* alley(way), avenue, byroad, byway, driveway, footpath, footway, loan, passage(way), path(way), towpath, way, wynd.

language *n* argot, cant, conversation, dialect, diction, discourse, expression, idiolect, idiom, interchange, jargon, lingo, lingua franca, parlance, patois, phraseology, phrasing, speech, style, talk, terminology, tongue, utterance, vernacular, vocabulary, wording.

languid *adj* debilitated, drooping, dull, enervated, faint, feeble, heavy, inactive, indifferent, inert, lackadaisical, languorous, lazy, lethargic, limp, listless, pining, sickly, slow, sluggish, spiritless, torpid, unenthusiastic, uninterested, weak, weary. **antonyms** alert, lively, vivacious.

languish *v* brood, decline, desire, despond, droop, fade, fail, faint, flag, grieve, hanker, hunger, long, mope, pine, repine, rot, sicken, sigh, sink, sorrow, suffer, sulk, want, waste, waste away, weaken, wilt, wither, yearn. **antonym** flourish.

languishing *adj* brooding, declining, deteriorating, dreamy, drooping, droopy, fading, failing, flagging, longing, lovelorn, lovesick, melancholic, moping, nostalgic, pensive, pining, sickening, sinking, soulful, sulking, tender, wasting away, weak, weakening, wilting, wistful,

withering, woebegone, yearning.
antonyms flourishing, thriving.

languor *n* apathy, calm, debility, dreaminess, drowsiness, enervation, faintness, fatigue, feebleness, frailty, heaviness, hush, indolence, inertia, lassitude, laziness, lethargy, listlessness, lull, oppressiveness, relaxation, silence, sleepiness, sloth, stillness, torpor, weakness, weariness. **antonyms** alacrity, gusto.

lank *adj* attenuated, drooping, dull, emaciated, flabby, flaccid, gaunt, lanky, lean, lifeless, limp, long, lustreless, rawboned, scraggy, scrawny, skinny, slender, slim, spare, straggling, thin. **antonym** burly.

lanky *adj* angular, bony, gangling, gangly, gaunt, loose-jointed, rangy, rawboned, scraggy, scrawny, spare, tall, thin, twiggy, weedy. **antonyms** short, squat.

lap¹ *v* drink, lick, sip, sup, tongue.

lap² *v* gurgle, plash, purl, ripple, slap, slosh, splash, swish, wash.

lap³ *n* ambit, circle, circuit, course, distance, loop, orbit, round, tour.
v cover, encase, enfold, envelop, fold, surround, swaddle, swathe, turn, twist, wrap.

lapse *n* aberration, backsliding, break, decline, descent, deterioration, drop, error, failing, fall, fault, gap, indiscretion, intermission, interruption, interval, lull, mistake, negligence, omission, oversight, passage, pause, relapse, slip.
v backslide, decline, degenerate, deteriorate, drop, end, expire, fail, fall, run out, sink, slide, slip, stop, terminate, worsen.

lapsed *adj* discontinued, ended, expired, finished, invalid, obsolete, out of date, outdated, outworn, run out, unrenewed.

large *adj* abundant, ample, big, broad, bulky, capacious, colossal, comprehensive, considerable, copious, enormous, extensive, full, generous, giant, gigantic, goodly, grand, grandiose, great, huge, immense, jumbo, king-sized, liberal, mammoth, man-sized, massive, monumental, outsize, plentiful, roomy, sizeable, spacious, spanking, substantial, sweeping, swingeing, tidy, vast, wide. **antonyms** diminutive, little, slight, small, tiny.

largely *adv* abundantly, by and large, chiefly, considerably, extensively, generally, greatly, highly, mainly, mostly, predominantly, primarily, principally, widely.

largeness *n* bigness, breadth, broadness, bulk, bulkiness, dimension, enormity, enormousness, expanse, extent, greatness, heaviness, heftiness, height, immensity, magnitude, mass, massiveness, measure, mightiness, obesity, prodigiousness, size, vastness, wideness, width. **antonym** smallness.

large-scale *adj* broad, country-wide, epic, expansive, extensive, far-reaching, global, nationwide, sweeping, vast, wholesale, wide, wide-ranging. **antonym** minor.

largess(e) *n* aid, allowance, alms, benefaction, bequest, bounty, charity, donation, endowment, generosity, gift, grant, handout, liberality, munificence, open-handedness, philanthropy, present. **antonym** meanness.

lark *n* antic, caper, escapade, fling, frolic, fun, gambol, game, jape, mischief, prank, revel, rollick, romp, skylark.
v caper, cavort, frolic, gambol, play, rollick, romp, skylark, sport.

lascivious *adj* bawdy, blue, coarse, crude, dirty, horny, indecent, lecherous, lewd, libidinous, licentious, lustful, obscene, offensive, pornographic, prurient, randy, ribald, salacious, scurrilous, sensual, smutty, suggestive, unchaste, voluptuous, vulgar, wanton.

lash¹ *n* blow, cat, cat-o'-nine-tails, hit, stripe, stroke, swipe, whip.
v attack, beat, belabour, berate, birch, buffet, castigate, censure, chastise, criticise, dash, drum, flagellate, flay, flog, hammer, hit, horsewhip, knock, lace, lam, lambaste, lampoon, pound, ridicule, satirise, scold, scourge, smack, strike, tear into, thrash, upbraid, welt, whip.

lash² *v* affix, bind, fasten, join, make fast, rope, secure, strap, tether, tie.

lass *n* bird, chick, colleen, damsel, girl, lassie, maid, maiden, miss.

lassitude *n* apathy, drowsiness, dullness, enervation, exhaustion, fatigue, heaviness, languor, lethargy, listlessness, sluggishness, tiredness, torpor, weariness. **antonyms** energy, vigour.

last¹ *adj* aftermost, closing, concluding, conclusive, definitive, extreme, final, furthest, hindmost, latest, rearmost, remotest, terminal, ultimate, utmost. **antonyms** first, initial.
adv after, behind, finally, ultimately. **antonyms** first, firstly.

n close, completion, conclusion, curtain, end, ending, finale, finish, termination. **antonyms** beginning, start.

last word¹ final decision, final say, ultimatum.

last word² best, cream, crème de la crème, latest, perfection, pick, quintessence, rage, ultimate, vogue.

last² *v* abide, carry on, continue, endure, hold on, hold out, keep (on), persist, remain, stand up, stay, survive, wear.

last-ditch *adj* all-out, desperate, eleventh-hour, final, frantic, heroic, last-gasp, straining, struggling.

lasting *adj* abiding, continuing, deep-rooted, durable, enduring, immutable, indelible, indestructible, lifelong, long-standing, long-term, perennial, permanent, perpetual, unceasing, unchanging, undying, unending. **antonyms** ephemeral, fleeting, short-lived.

lastly *adv* finally, in conclusion, in the end, to sum up, ultimately. **antonym** firstly.

latch *n* bar, bolt, catch, fastening, hasp, hook, lock, sneck.

latch on to apprehend, attach oneself to, comprehend, twig, understand.

late¹ *adj* behind, behind-hand, belated, delayed, dilatory, last-minute, overdue, slow, tardy, unpunctual. **antonyms** early, punctual.
adv behind-hand, belatedly, dilatorily, formerly, recently, slowly, tardily, unpunctually. **antonyms** early, punctually.

late² *adj* dead, deceased, defunct, departed, ex-, former, old, past, preceding, previous.

lately *adv* formerly, heretofore, latterly, recently.

lateness *n* belatedness, delay, dilatoriness, retardation, tardiness, unpunctuality. **antonym** earliness.

latent *adj* concealed, dormant, hidden, inherent, invisible, lurking, potential, secret, underlying, undeveloped, unexpressed, unrealised, unseen, veiled. **antonyms** active, live, patent.

later *adv* after, afterwards, next, sequentially, subsequently, successively, thereafter. **antonym** earlier.

lateral *adj* edgeways, flanking, marginal, oblique, side, sideward, sideways. **antonym** central.

latest *adj* current, fashionable, in, modern, newest, now, ultimate, up-

to-date, up-to-the-minute, with it. **antonym** earliest.

lather¹ *n* bubbles, foam, froth, shampoo, soap, soap-suds, suds.
v foam, froth, shampoo, soap, whip up.

lather² *n* agitation, dither, fever, flap, fluster, flutter, fuss, pother, state, stew, sweat, tizzy, twitter.

lather³ *v* beat, cane, drub, flog, lambaste, lash, leather, strike, thrash, whip.

latitude *n* breadth, clearance, compass, elbow-room, extent, field, freedom, indulgence, laxity, leeway, liberty, licence, play, range, reach, room, scope, space, span, spread, sweep, width.

latter *adj* closing, concluding, ensuing, last, last-mentioned, later, latest, modern, recent, second, succeeding, successive. **antonym** former.

latterly *adv* hitherto, lately, of late, recently. **antonym** formerly.

laud *v* acclaim, applaud, approve, celebrate, extol, glorify, hail, honour, magnify, praise. **antonyms** blame, condemn, curse, damn.

laudable *adj* admirable, commendable, creditable, estimable, excellent, exemplary, meritorious, of note, praiseworthy, sterling, worthy. **antonyms** damnable, execrable.

laudation *n* acclaim, acclamation, accolade, adulation, blessing, celebrity, commendation, devotion, eulogy, extolment, glorification, glory, homage, kudos, paean, praise, reverence, tribute, veneration. **antonyms** condemnation, criticism.

laudatory *adj* acclamatory, adulatory, approbatory, approving, celebratory, commendatory, complimentary, eulogistic, glorifying. **antonym** damning.

laugh *v* chortle, chuckle, crease up, fall about, giggle, guffaw, snicker, snigger, split one's sides, te(e)hee, titter. **antonym** cry.
n belly-laugh, card, case, chortle, chuckle, clown, comedian, comic, entertainer, giggle, guffaw, hoot, humorist, joke, lark, scream, snicker, snigger, te(e)hee, titter, wag, wit.

laugh at belittle, deride, jeer, lampoon, make fun of, mock, ridicule, scoff at, scorn, take the mickey out of, taunt.

laugh off belittle, brush aside, dismiss, disregard, ignore, make little of, minimise, pooh-pooh, shrug off.

laughable *adj* absurd, amusing, comical, derisive, derisory, diverting, droll, farcical, funny, hilarious, humorous, laughworthy, ludicrous, mirthful, mockable, nonsensical, preposterous, ridiculous. *antonyms* impressive, serious, solemn.

laughing *adj* cackling, cheerful, cheery, chortling, chuckling, giggling, gleeful, guffawing, happy, jolly, jovial, merry, mirthful, snickering, sniggering, tittering.

laughter *n* amusement, chortling, chuckling, convulsions, giggling, glee, guffawing, hilarity, laughing, merriment, mirth, tittering.

launch *v* begin, cast, commence, discharge, dispatch, embark on, establish, fire, float, found, inaugurate, initiate, instigate, introduce, open, project, propel, send off, set in motion, start, throw.

lavatory *n* bathroom, bog, can, cloakroom, convenience, Gents, john, Ladies, latrine, lav, loo, powder-room, privy, public convenience, smallest room, toilet, urinal, washroom, water-closet, WC.

lavish *adj* abundant, bountiful, copious, exaggerated, excessive, extravagant, exuberant, free, generous, gorgeous, immoderate, improvident, intemperate, liberal, lush, luxuriant, munificent, open-handed, opulent, plentiful, princely, prodigal, profuse, prolific, sumptuous, thriftless, unlimited, unreasonable, unrestrained, unstinting, wasteful, wild. *antonyms* economical, frugal, parsimonious, scanty, sparing, thrifty.

v bestow, deluge, dissipate, expend, heap, pour, shower, spend, squander, waste.

law *n* act, axiom, canon, charter, code, command, commandment, constitution, covenant, criterion, decree, edict, enactment, formula, institute, jurisprudence, order, ordinance, precept, principle, regulation, rule, standard, statute. *antonym* chance.

law-abiding *adj* compliant, decent, dutiful, good, honest, honourable, lawful, obedient, orderly, peaceable, peaceful, upright. *antonym* lawless.

lawful *adj* allowable, authorised, constitutional, kosher, legal, legalised, legitimate, permissible, proper, rightful, valid, warranted. *antonyms* illegal, illicit, lawless, unlawful.

lawless *adj* anarchic(al), chaotic, disorderly, felonious, insubordinate, insurgent, mutinous, rebellious, reckless, riotous, seditious, unbridled,

ungoverned, unrestrained, unruly, wild. *antonym* lawful.

lawlessness *n* anarchy, chaos, disorder, insurgency, mobocracy, mob-rule, piracy, racketeering. *antonym* order.

lawsuit *n* action, argument, case, cause, contest, dispute, litigation, proceedings, process, prosecution, suit, trial.

lax *adj* broad, careless, casual, derelict, easy-going, flabby, flaccid, general, imprecise, inaccurate, indefinite, inexact, lenient, loose, neglectful, negligent, overindulgent, remiss, shapeless, slack, slipshod, soft, vague, wide, wide-open, yielding. *antonyms* rigid, strict, stringent.

laxness *n* carelessness, freedom, heedlessness, imprecision, indifference, indulgence, laissez-faire, latitude, laxity, leniency, looseness, neglect, negligence, nonchalance, permissiveness, slackness, sloppiness, slovenliness, softness, tolerance. *antonyms* severity, strictness.

lay¹ *v* advance, allay, alleviate, allocate, allot, appease, apply, arrange, ascribe, assess, assign, assuage, attribute, bet, burden, calm, charge, concoct, contrive, deposit, design, devise, dispose, encumber, establish, gamble, hatch, hazard, impose, impute, leave, locate, lodge, offer, organise, place, plan, plant, plot, posit, position, prepare, present, put, quiet, relieve, risk, saddle, set, set down, set out, settle, soothe, spread, stake, still, submit, suppress, tax, wager, work out.

lay aside abandon, cast aside, discard, dismiss, pigeon-hole, postpone, put aside, put off, reject, shelve, store.

lay bare disclose, divulge, exhibit, exhume, explain, expose, reveal, show, uncover, unveil.

lay down affirm, assert, assume, discard, drop, establish, formulate, give, give up, ordain, postulate, prescribe, relinquish, state, stipulate, surrender, yield.

lay down the law crack down, dictate, dogmatise, emphasise, pontificate, read the riot act, rule the roost.

lay hands on acquire, assault, attack, beat up, bless, clasp, clutch, confirm, consecrate, discover, find, get, get hold of, grab, grasp, grip, lay hold of, lay into, ordain, seize, set on, unearth.

lay in accumulate, amass, build up, collect, gather, glean, hoard, stock up, stockpile, store (up).

lay into assail, attack, belabour, berate,

chastise, lambaste, let fly at, pitch into, set about, slam, tear into, turn on.

lay it on butter up, exaggerate, flatter, overdo it, overpraise, soft-soap, sweet-talk.

lay off axe, cease, desist, discharge, dismiss, drop, give it a rest, give over, give up, leave alone, leave off, let go, let up, make redundant, oust, pay off, quit, stop, withhold.

lay on contribute, furnish, give, provide, set up, supply.

lay out arrange, demolish, design, disburse, display, exhibit, expend, fell, flatten, fork out, give, invest, knock out, pay, plan, set out, shell out, spend, spread out.

lay up accumulate, amass, garner, hive, hoard, hospitalise, incapacitate, keep, preserve, put away, save, squirrel away, store up, treasure.

lay waste desolate, despoil, destroy, devastate, pillage, ravage, raze, ruin, sack, spoil, vandalise.

lay[2] *adj* amateur, inexpert, laic, laical, non-professional, non-specialist, secular.

layabout *n* good-for-nothing, idler, laggard, loafer, lounger, ne'er-do-well, shirker, skiver, slug-a-bed, waster.

layer *n* bed, blanket, coat, coating, cover, covering, film, folium, lamina, mantle, plate, ply, row, seam, sheet, stratum, table, thickness, tier, touch.

laze *v* idle, lie around, loaf, loll, lounge, sit around.

laziness *n* dilatoriness, idleness, inactivity, indolence, slackness, sloth, slothfulness, slowness, sluggishness, tardiness. *antonym* industriousness.

lazy *adj* dormant, drowsy, idle, inactive, indolent, inert, languid, languorous, lethargic, remiss, shiftless, slack, sleepy, slobby, slothful, slow, slow-moving, sluggish, somnolent, torpid, work-shy. *antonyms* active, diligent, energetic, industrious.

lazy-bones *n* idler, laggard, loafer, lounger, shirker, skiver, sleepy-head, slouch, slug-a-bed, sluggard.

lead *v* antecede, cause, command, conduct, direct, dispose, draw, escort, exceed, excel, experience, govern, guide, have, head, incline, induce, influence, live, manage, outdo, outstrip, pass, persuade, pilot, precede, preside over, prevail, prompt, spend, steer, supervise, surpass, undergo, usher. *antonym* follow.

n advance, advantage, clue, direction, edge, example, first place, guidance, guide, hint, indication, leadership, margin, model, precedence, primacy, principal, priority, protagonist, starring role, start, suggestion, supremacy, tip, title role, trace, vanguard.

adj chief, first, foremost, head, leading, main, premier, primary, prime, principal, star.

lead off begin, commence, get going, inaugurate, initiate, kick off, open, start, start off, start out, start the ball rolling.

lead on beguile, deceive, draw on, entice, hoax, inveigle, lure, persuade, seduce, string along, tempt, trick.

lead to bring about, bring on, cause, conduce, contribute to, produce, result in, tend towards.

lead up to approach, intimate, introduce, make advances, make overtures, overture, pave the way, prepare (the way) for.

leaden *adj* ashen, burdensome, crushing, cumbersome, dingy, dismal, dreary, dull, gloomy, grey, greyish, heavy, humdrum, inert, laboured, lacklustre, languid, lead, lifeless, listless, lowering, lustreless, onerous, oppressive, overcast, plodding, sluggish, sombre, spiritless, stiff, stilted, wooden.

leader *n* boss, captain, chief, chieftain, commander, conductor, counsellor, director, doyen, figurehead, flagship, guide, head, principal, ringleader, ruler, skipper, superior, supremo. *antonym* follower.

leadership *n* administration, authority, command, control, direction, directorship, domination, guidance, influence, initiative, management, pre-eminence, premiership, running, superintendency, supremacy, sway.

leading *adj* chief, dominant, first, foremost, governing, greatest, highest, main, number one, outstanding, paramount, pre-eminent, primary, principal, ruling, superior, supreme. *antonym* subordinate.

league *n* alliance, association, band, cartel, category, coalition, combination, combine, compact, confederacy, confederation, consortium, federation, fellowship, fraternity, group, guild, level, partnership, sorority, syndicate, union.

v ally, amalgamate, associate, band, collaborate, combine, confederate, consort, join forces, unite.

leak *n* aperture, chink, crack, crevice, disclosure, divulgence, drip, fissure, hole, leakage, leaking, oozing, opening, percolation, perforation, puncture, seepage.

v discharge, disclose, divulge, drip, escape, exude, give away, let slip, let the cat out of the bag, make known, make public, ooze, pass, pass on, percolate, reveal, seep, spill, spill the beans, tell, trickle, weep.

lean[1] *v* bend, confide, count on, depend, favour, incline, list, prefer, prop, recline, rely, repose, rest, slant, slope, tend, tilt, tip, trust.

lean on force, persuade, pressurise, put pressure on.

lean[2] *adj* angular, bare, barren, bony, emaciated, gaunt, inadequate, infertile, lank, meagre, pitiful, poor, rangy, scanty, scragged, scraggy, scrawny, skinny, slender, slim, slink(y), spare, sparse, thin, unfruitful, unproductive, wiry. **antonyms** fat, fleshy.

leaning *n* aptitude, bent, bias, disposition, inclination, liking, partiality, penchant, predilection, proclivity, propensity, susceptibility, taste, tendency, velleity.

leap *v* advance, bounce, bound, caper, capriole, cavort, clear, curvet, escalate, frisk, gambol, hasten, hop, hurry, increase, jump, jump (over), reach, rocket, rush, skip, soar, spring, surge, vault. **antonyms** drop, fall, sink.

n bound, caper, escalation, frisk, hop, increase, jump, rise, skip, spring, surge, upsurge, upswing, vault.

learn *v* acquire, ascertain, assimilate, attain, detect, determine, discern, discover, find out, gather, get off pat, grasp, hear, imbibe, learn by heart, master, memorise, pick up, see, understand.

learned *adj* academic, adept, cultured, erudite, experienced, expert, highbrow, intellectual, lettered, literate, proficient, sage, scholarly, skilled, versed, well-informed, well-read, wise. **antonyms** ignorant, illiterate, uneducated.

learner *n* apprentice, beginner, disciple, neophyte, novice, pupil, scholar, student, trainee.

learning *n* attainments, culture, edification, education, enlightenment, erudition, information, knowledge, letters, literature, lore, research, scholarship, schooling, study, tuition, wisdom.

lease *v* charter, farm out, hire, let, loan, rent, sublet.

leash *n* check, control, curb, discipline, hold, lead, rein, restraint, tether.

least *adj* fewest, last, lowest, meanest, merest, minimum, minutest, poorest, slightest, smallest, tiniest. **antonym** most.

leave[1] *v* abandon, allot, assign, bequeath, cause, cease, cede, commit, consign, decamp, depart, deposit, desert, desist, disappear, do a bunk, drop, entrust, exit, flit, forget, forsake, generate, give over, give up, go, go away, hand down, leave behind, move, produce, pull out, quit, refer, refrain, relinquish, renounce, retire, set out, stop, surrender, take off, transmit, will, withdraw. **antonym** arrive.

leave off abstain, break off, cease, desist, discontinue, end, give over, halt, knock off, lay off, quit, refrain, stop, terminate.

leave out bar, cast aside, count out, cut (out), disregard, eliminate, except, exclude, ignore, neglect, omit, overlook, pass over, reject.

leave[2] *n* allowance, authorisation, concession, consent, dispensation, freedom, furlough, holiday, indulgence, liberty, permission, sabbatical, sanction, time off, vacation. **antonyms** refusal, rejection.

lecherous *adj* carnal, goatish, lascivious, lewd, libidinous, licentious, lubricous, lustful, prurient, randy, raunchy, salacious, unchaste, wanton, womanising.

lechery *n* carnality, debauchery, goatishness, lasciviousness, lecherousness, leching, lewdness, libertinism, libidinousness, licentiousness, lubricity, lust, lustfulness, profligacy, prurience, rakishness, randiness, raunchiness, salaciousness, sensuality, wantonness, womanising.

lecture *n* address, castigation, censure, chiding, discourse, disquisition, dressing-down, going-over, harangue, instruction, lesson, rebuke, reprimand, reproof, scolding, speech, talk, talking-to, telling-off.

v address, admonish, berate, carpet, castigate, censure, chide, discourse, expound, harangue, hold forth, rate, reprimand, reprove, scold, speak, talk, teach, tell off.

leech *n* bloodsucker, freeloader, hanger-on, parasite, sponger, sycophant, usurer.

leer *v* eye, gloat, goggle, grin, ogle, smirk, squint, stare, wink.

n grin, ogle, smirk, squint, stare, wink.

leeway *n* elbow-room, latitude, play, room, scope, space.

left *adj* communist, left-hand, leftist, left-wing, liberal, port, progressive, radical, red, sinistral, socialist. *antonym* right.

left-overs *n* dregs, fag-end, leavings, oddments, odds and ends, refuse, remainder, remains, remnants, residue, scraps, surplus, sweepings.

leg *n* brace, gam, lap, limb, member, part, pin, portion, prop, section, segment, shank, stage, stretch, stump, support, upright.

legacy *n* bequest, birthright, devise, endowment, estate, gift, heirloom, heritage, inheritance, patrimony.

legal *adj* above-board, allowable, allowed, authorised, constitutional, forensic, judicial, juridical, lawful, legalised, legitimate, permissible, proper, rightful, sanctioned, valid, warrantable. *antonym* illegal.

legalise *v* allow, approve, authorise, legitimise, license, permit, sanction, validate, warrant.

legality *n* admissibleness, constitutionality, lawfulness, legitimacy, permissibility, rightfulness, validity. *antonym* illegality.

legation *n* commission, consulate, delegation, deputation, embassy, ministry, mission, representation.

legend *n* caption, celebrity, fable, fiction, folk-tale, household name, inscription, key, luminary, marvel, motto, myth, narrative, phenomenon, prodigy, saga, spectacle, story, tale, tradition, wonder.

legendary *adj* apocryphal, celebrated, fabled, fabulous, famed, famous, fanciful, fictional, fictitious, illustrious, immortal, mythical, renowned, romantic, storied, story-book, traditional, unhistoric(al), well-known.

legible *adj* clear, decipherable, discernible, distinct, intelligible, neat, readable. *antonym* illegible.

legion *n* army, battalion, brigade, cohort, company, division, drove, force, horde, host, mass, multitude, myriad, number, regiment, swarm, throng, troop.
adj countless, illimitable, innumerable, multitudinous, myriad, numberless, numerous.

legislate *v* authorise, constitute, constitutionalise, enact, establish, ordain, prescribe.

legislation *n* act, authorisation, bill, charter, constitutionalisation, enactment, law, law-making, measure, prescription, regulation, ruling, statute.

legitimate *adj* acknowledged, admissible, authentic, authorised, correct, genuine, just, justifiable, kosher, lawful, legal, logical, proper, real, reasonable, rightful, sanctioned, sensible, statutory, true, true-born, valid, warranted, well-founded. *antonym* illegitimate.
v authorise, charter, entitle, legalise, legitimise, license, permit, sanction.

legitimise *v* authorise, charter, entitle, legalise, license, permit, sanction.

leisure *n* breather, ease, freedom, holiday, let-up, liberty, opportunity, pause, quiet, recreation, relaxation, respite, rest, retirement, spare time, time off, vacation. *antonyms* toil, work.

leisurely *adj* carefree, comfortable, deliberate, easy, gentle, indolent, laid-back, lazy, lingering, loose, relaxed, restful, slow, tranquil, unhasty, unhurried. *antonyms* hectic, hurried, rushed.

lend *v* add, advance, afford, bestow, confer, contribute, furnish, give, grant, impart, lease, loan, present, provide, supply. *antonym* borrow.

lend a hand aid, assist, do one's bit, give a helping hand, help, help out, pitch in.

lend an ear give ear, hearken, heed, listen, pay attention, take notice.

length *n* distance, duration, elongation, extensiveness, extent, lengthiness, longitude, measure, period, piece, portion, protractedness, reach, section, segment, space, span, stretch, tediousness, term.

lengthen *v* continue, draw out, eke, eke out, elongate, expand, extend, increase, pad out, prolong, prolongate, protract, spin out, stretch. *antonym* shorten.

lengthy *adj* diffuse, drawn-out, extended, interminable, lengthened, long, long-drawn-out, long-winded, loquacious, marathon, overlong, prolix, prolonged, protracted, rambling, tedious, verbose, voluble. *antonym* short.

leniency *n* clemency, compassion, forbearance, gentleness, indulgence, lenience, lenity, mercy, mildness, moderation, permissiveness, soft-heartedness, softness, tenderness, tolerance. *antonym* severity.

lenient *adj* clement, compassionate, easy-going, forbearing, forgiving, gentle, indulgent, kind, merciful, mild, soft, soft-hearted, sparing, tender, tolerant. **antonym** severe.

lesbian n butch, dike, gay, homosexual, les, sapphist.

adj butch, dikey, gay, homosexual, sapphic.

lesion n abrasion, bruise, contusion, cut, gash, hurt, impairment, injury, scrape, scratch, sore, trauma, wound.

lessen v abate, abridge, contract, curtail, deaden, decrease, degrade, die down, diminish, dwindle, ease, erode, fail, flag, impair, lighten, lower, minimise, moderate, narrow, reduce, shrink, slack, slow down, weaken. **antonym** increase.

lessening n abatement, contraction, curtailment, deadening, decline, decrease, diminution, dwindling, ebbing, erosion, failure, flagging, let-up, minimisation, moderation, petering out, reduction, shrinkage, slackening, waning, weakening. **antonym** increase.

lesser adj inferior, lower, minor, secondary, slighter, smaller, subordinate. **antonym** greater.

lesson n admonition, assignment, censure, chiding, class, coaching, deterrent, drill, example, exemplar, exercise, homework, instruction, lecture, message, model, moral, period, practice, precept, punishment, reading, rebuke, recitation, reprimand, reproof, schooling, scolding, task, teaching, tutorial, tutoring, warning.

let[1] v agree to, allow, authorise, cause, charter, consent to, empower, enable, entitle, give leave, give permission, give the go-ahead, give the green light, grant, hire, lease, make, OK, permit, rent, sanction, tolerate. **antonym** forbid.

let down abandon, betray, desert, disappoint, disenchant, disillusion, dissatisfy, fail, fall short. **antonym** satisfy.

let go free, liberate, manumit, release, set free, unhand. **antonyms** catch, imprison.

let in accept, admit, include, incorporate, receive, take in, welcome. **antonym** bar.

let off absolve, acquit, detonate, discharge, dispense, emit, excuse, exempt, exonerate, explode, exude, fire, forgive, give off, ignore, leak, pardon, release, spare. **antonym** punish.

let on act, admit, counterfeit, disclose, dissemble, dissimulate, divulge, feign, give away, leak, let out, make believe, make known, make out, pretend, profess, reveal, say, simulate. **antonym** keep mum.

let out betray, discharge, disclose, emit, free, give, give vent to, leak, let fall, let go, let slip, liberate, make known, produce, release, reveal, utter. **antonym** keep in.

let slip blab, blurt out, come out with, disclose, divulge, give away, leak, let out, let the cat out of the bag, reveal. **antonym** keep mum.

let up abate, cease, decrease, diminish, ease, ease up, end, halt, moderate, slacken, stop, subside. **antonym** continue.

let[2] n check, constraint, hindrance, impediment, interference, obstacle, obstruction, prohibition, restraint, restriction. **antonym** assistance.

let-down n anticlimax, betrayal, blow, desertion, disappointment, disillusionment, frustration, set-back, wash-out. **antonym** satisfaction.

lethal adj baleful, dangerous, deadly, deathly, destructive, devastating, fatal, mortal, murderous, noxious, pernicious, poisonous, virulent. **antonym** harmless.

lethargic adj apathetic, comatose, debilitated, drowsy, dull, enervated, heavy, inactive, indifferent, inert, languid, lazy, listless, sleepy, slothful, slow, sluggish, somnolent, stupefied, torpid. **antonym** lively.

lethargy n apathy, drowsiness, dullness, inaction, indifference, inertia, languor, lassitude, listlessness, sleepiness, sloth, slowness, sluggishness, stupor, torpor. **antonym** liveliness.

letter n acknowledgement, answer, billet, chit, communication, dispatch, epistle, line, message, missive, note, reply.

lettered adj accomplished, cultivated, cultured, educated, erudite, highbrow, informed, knowledgeable, learned, literary, literate, scholarly, studied, versed, well-educated, well-read. **antonym** ignorant.

let-up n abatement, break, breather, cessation, interval, lessening, lull, pause, recess, remission, respite, slackening. **antonym** continuation.

level[1] adj abreast, aligned, balanced, calm, commensurate, comparable, consistent, equable, equal, equivalent, even, even-tempered, flat, flush, horizontal, neck and neck, on a par, plain, proportionate, smooth, stable, steady uniform. *antonyms* behind, uneven, unstable.

v aim, bulldoze, demolish, destroy, devastate, direct, equalise, even out, flatten, flush, focus, knock down, lay low, plane, point, pull down, raze, smooth, tear down, wreck.

n altitude, bed, class, degree, echelon, elevation, floor, grade, height, horizontal, layer, plain, plane, position, rank, stage, standard, standing, status, storey, stratum, zone.

level[2] *v* admit, avow, come clean, confess, divulge, open up, tell. *antonym* prevaricate.

level-headed *adj* balanced, calm, collected, commonsensical, composed, cool, dependable, even-tempered, reasonable, sane, self-possessed, sensible, steady, together, unflappable.

leverage *n* advantage, ascendancy, authority, clout, force, influence, pull, purchase, rank, strength, weight.

leviathan *n* colossus, giant, hulk, mammoth, monster, Titan, whale.

levity *n* buoyancy, facetiousness, fickleness, flightiness, flippancy, frivolity, giddiness, irreverence, light-heartedness, silliness, skittishness, triviality. *antonyms* seriousness, sobriety.

levy *v* assemble, call, call up, charge, collect, conscript, demand, exact, gather, impose, mobilise, muster, press, raise, summon, tax.

n assessment, collection, contribution, duty, exaction, excise, fee, gathering, imposition, impost, subscription, tariff, tax, toll.

lewd *adj* bawdy, blue, dirty, harlot, impure, indecent, lascivious, libidinous, licentious, loose, lubricious, lustful, obscene, pornographic, profligate, salacious, smutty, unchaste, vile, vulgar, wanton, wicked. *antonyms* chaste, polite.

lewdness *n* bawdiness, carnality, crudity, debauchery, depravity, impurity, indecency, lasciviousness, lechery, licentiousness, lubricity, lustfulness, obscenity, pornography, profligacy, randiness, salaciousness, smut, smuttiness, unchastity, vulgarity, wantonness. *antonyms* chasteness, politeness.

lexicon *n* dictionary, encyclopaedia, glossary, phrase-book, vocabulary, word-book, word-list.

liability *n* accountability, albatross, answerability, arrears, burden, culpability, debit, debt, disadvantage, drag, drawback, duty, encumbrance, handicap, hindrance, impediment, inconvenience, indebtedness, likeliness, millstone, minus, nuisance, obligation, onus, responsibility. *antonyms* asset(s), unaccountability.

liable *adj* accountable, amenable, answerable, apt, bound, chargeable, disposed, exposed, inclined, likely, obligated, open, predisposed, prone, responsible, subject, susceptible, tending, vulnerable. *antonyms* unaccountable, unlikely.

liaison *n* affair, amour, communication, conjunction, connection, contact, entanglement, interchange, intermediary, intrigue, link, love affair, romance, union.

libel *n* aspersion, calumny, defamation, denigration, obloquy, slander, slur, smear, vilification, vituperation. *antonym* praise.

v blacken, calumniate, defame, derogate, malign, revile, slander, slur, smear, traduce, vilify, vituperate. *antonym* praise.

libellous *adj* calumniatory, calumnious, defamatory, defaming, derogatory, false, injurious, malicious, maligning, scurrilous, slanderous, traducing, untrue, vilifying, vituperative. *antonyms* laudative, praising.

liberal *adj* abundant, advanced, altruistic, ample, beneficent, bounteous, bountiful, broad, broad-minded, catholic, charitable, copious, enlightened, flexible, free, free-handed, general, generous, handsome, high-minded, humanistic, humanitarian, indulgent, inexact, kind, large-hearted, latitudinarian, lavish, lenient, libertarian, loose, magnanimous, munificent, open-handed, open-hearted, permissive, plentiful, profuse, progressive, radical, reformist, rich, tolerant, unbiased, unbigoted, unprejudiced, unstinting. *antonyms* conservative, illiberal, mean, narrow-minded.

liberalism *n* free-thinking, humanitarianism, latitudinarianism, libertarianism, progressivism, radicalism. *antonyms* conservatism, narrow-mindedness.

liberality *n* altruism, beneficence, benevolence, bounty, breadth, broad-mindedness, candour, catholicity, charity, free-handedness, generosity, impartiality, kindness, large-heartedness, largess(e), latitude, liberalism, libertarianism, magnanimity, munificence, open-handedness, open-mindedness, permissiveness, philanthropy, progressivism, tolerance, toleration. **antonyms** illiberality, meanness.

liberate v affranchise, deliver, discharge, emancipate, free, let go, let loose, let out, manumit, ransom, redeem, release, rescue, set free, uncage, unchain, unfetter, unpen, unshackle. **antonyms** enslave, imprison, restrict.

liberation n deliverance, emancipation, freedom, freeing, liberating, liberty, manumission, ransoming, redemption, release, uncaging, unchaining, unfettering, unpenning, unshackling. **antonyms** enslavement, imprisonment, restriction.

liberties n audacity, disrespect, familiarity, forwardness, impertinence, impropriety, impudence, insolence, misuse, overfamiliarity, presumption, presumptuousness. **antonyms** politeness, respect.

liberty n authorisation, autonomy, carte blanche, dispensation, emancipation, exemption, franchise, free rein, freedom, immunity, independence, latitude, leave, liberation, licence, permission, prerogative, privilege, release, right, sanction, self-determination, sovereignty. **antonyms** imprisonment, restriction, slavery.

libidinous adj carnal, debauched, impure, incontinent, lascivious, lecherous, lewd, loose, lustful, prurient, randy, ruttish, salacious, sensual, unchaste, wanton, wicked. **antonyms** modest, temperate.

licence n authorisation, authority, carte blanche, certificate, charter, dispensation, entitlement, exemption, freedom, immunity, independence, latitude, leave, liberty, permission, permit, privilege, right, self-determination, warrant. **antonyms** banning, dependence, restriction.

license v accredit, allow, authorise, certificate, certify, commission, empower, entitle, permit, sanction, warrant. **antonym** ban.

licentious adj abandoned, debauched, disorderly, dissolute, immoral, impure, lascivious, lax, lewd, libertine, libidinous, lubricious, lustful, profligate, promiscuous, sensual, uncontrollable, uncontrolled, uncurbed, unruly, wanton.

licentiousness n abandon, debauchery,

dissipation, dissoluteness, lechery, lewdness, libertinism, libidinousness, lubriciousness, lubricity, lust, lustfulness, profligacy, promiscuity, prurience, salaciousness, salacity, wantonness. **antonyms** modesty, temperance.

lick¹ v brush, dart, flick, lap, play over, smear, taste, tongue, touch, wash.

n bit, brush, dab, hint, little, sample, smidgeon, speck, spot, stroke, taste, touch.

lick one's lips anticipate, drool over, enjoy, relish, savour.

lick² v beat, best, defeat, excel, flog, outdo, outstrip, overcome, rout, skelp, slap, smack, spank, strike, surpass, thrash, top, trounce, vanquish, wallop.

licking n beating, defeat, drubbing, flogging, hiding, skelping, smacking, spanking, tanning, thrashing, trouncing, whipping.

lie¹ v dissimulate, equivocate, fabricate, falsify, fib, forswear oneself, invent, misrepresent, perjure.

n deceit, fabrication, falsehood, falsification, falsity, fib, fiction, flam, invention, inveracity, mendacity, untruth, white lie, whopper. **antonym** truth.

lie² v be, belong, couch, dwell, exist, extend, inhere, laze, loll, lounge, recline, remain, repose, rest, slump, sprawl, stretch out.

lie in wait for ambush, waylay.

lie low go to earth, hide, hide away, hide out, hole up, keep a low profile, lie doggo, lurk, skulk, take cover.

life n activity, animation, autobiography, behaviour, being, biography, breath, brio, career, conduct, confessions, continuance, course, creatures, duration, energy, entity, essence, existence, fauna, flora and fauna, get-up-and-go, go, growth, heart, high spirits, history, life story, life-blood, life-style, lifetime, liveliness, memoirs, oomph, organisms, sentience, soul, span, sparkle, spirit, story, the world, this mortal coil, time, verve, viability, vigour, vital flame, vital spark, vitality, vivacity, way of life, wildlife, zest.

lifeless adj bare, barren, cold, colourless, comatose, dead, deceased, defunct, dull, empty, extinct, flat, heavy, hollow, inanimate, inert, insensate, insipid, lacklustre, lethargic, listless, nerveless, out cold, out for the count, passive, pointless, slow, sluggish, spent, spiritless, static, sterile, stiff, torpid, unconscious, uninhabited, unproductive, waste, wooden. *antonyms* alive, lively.

lifelike *adj* authentic, exact, expressive, faithful, graphic, natural, photographic, pictorial, real, realistic, true, true-to-life, undistorted, vivid. *antonyms* inexact, unnatural.

lifelong *adj* abiding, constant, deep-rooted, deep-seated, enduring, entrenched, inveterate, lasting, lifetime, long-lasting, long-standing, perennial, permanent, persistent. *antonyms* impermanent, temporary.

lift *v* advance, ameliorate, annul, appropriate, arrest, ascend, boost, buoy up, climb, collar, copy, countermand, crib, dignify, disappear, disperse, dissipate, draw up, elevate, end, enhance, exalt, half-inch, heft, hoist, improve, mount, nab, nick, pick up, pilfer, pinch, pirate, plagiarise, pocket, promote, purloin, raise, rear, relax, remove, rescind, revoke, rise, steal, stop, take, terminate, thieve, up, upgrade, uplift, upraise, vanish. *antonyms* drop, fall, impose, lower.
n boost, encouragement, fillip, pick-me-up, reassurance, shot in the arm, spur, uplift. *antonym* discouragement.

light¹ *n* beacon, blaze, brightness, brilliance, bulb, candle, cockcrow, dawn, day, daybreak, daylight, daytime, effulgence, flame, flare, flash, glare, gleam, glim, glint, glow, illumination, incandescence, lambency, lamp, lantern, lighter, lighthouse, luminescence, luminosity, lustre, match, morn, morning, phosphorescence, radiance, ray, refulgence, scintillation, shine, sparkle, star, sunrise, sunshine, taper, torch, window. *antonym* darkness.
v animate, beacon, brighten, cheer, fire, floodlight, ignite, illuminate, illumine, inflame, irradiate, kindle, light up, lighten, put on, set alight, set fire to, switch on, turn on. *antonyms* darken, extinguish.
adj bleached, blond, bright, brilliant, faded, faint, fair, glowing, illuminated, lucent, luminous, lustrous, pale, pastel, shining, sunny, well-lit. *antonym* dark.

light² *n* angle, approach, aspect, attitude, awareness, clue, comprehension, context, elucidation, enlightenment, example, exemplar, explanation, hint, illustration, information, insight, interpretation, knowledge, model, paragon, point of view, slant, understanding, viewpoint.

light³ *adj* agile, airy, amusing, animated, blithe, buoyant, carefree, cheerful, cheery, crumbly, delicate, delirious, digestible, diverting, dizzy, easy, effortless, entertaining, facile, faint, fickle, flimsy, frivolous, funny, gay, gentle, giddy, graceful, humorous, idle, imponderous, inconsequential, inconsiderable, indistinct, insignificant, insubstantial, light-footed, light-headed, light-hearted, lightweight, lithe, lively, loose, manageable, merry, mild, minute, moderate, modest, nimble, pleasing, porous, portable, reeling, restricted, sandy, scanty, simple, slight, small, soft, spongy, sprightly, sunny, superficial, thin, tiny, trifling, trivial, unchaste, undemanding, underweight, unexacting, unheeding, unsteady, unsubstantial, untaxing, volatile, wanton, weak, witty, worthless. *antonyms* clumsy, harsh, heavy, important, sad, severe, sober, solid, stiff.

light on chance on, come across, discover, encounter, find, happen upon, hit on, spot, stumble on.

lighten¹ *v* beacon, brighten, illuminate, illumine, light up, shine. *antonym* darken.

lighten² *v* alleviate, ameliorate, assuage, brighten, buoy up, cheer, disburden, disencumber, ease, elate, encourage, facilitate, gladden, hearten, inspire, inspirit, lessen, lift, mitigate, perk up, reduce, relieve, revive, unload, uplift. *antonyms* burden, depress, oppress.

light-footed *adj* active, agile, buoyant, graceful, lithe, nimble, sprightly, spry, swift, tripping, winged. *antonyms* clumsy, slow.

light-headed *adj* bird-brained, delirious, dizzy, faint, feather-brained, fickle, flighty, flippant, foolish, frivolous, giddy, hazy, inane, shallow, silly, superficial, thoughtless, trifling, unsteady, vacuous, vertiginous, woozy. *antonym* sober.

light-hearted *adj* blithe, blithesome, bright, carefree, cheerful, effervescent, elated, frolicsome, gay, glad, gleeful, happy-go-lucky, jolly, jovial, joyful, joyous, light-spirited, merry, perky, playful, sunny, untroubled, upbeat. *antonym* sad.

lightly *adv* airily, breezily, carelessly, delicately, easily, effortlessly, facilely, faintly, flippantly, frivolously, gaily, gently, gingerly, heedlessly, indifferently, moderately, readily, simply, slightingly, slightly, softly, sparingly, sparsely, thinly, thoughtlessly, timidly, wantonly. **antonyms** heavily, soberly.

lightness n agility, airiness, animation, blitheness, buoyancy, cheerfulness, cheeriness, crumbliness, delicacy, delicateness, facileness, faintness, fickleness, flimsiness, frivolity, gaiety, grace, idleness, inconsequentiality, indistinctness, insignificance, levity, light-heartedness, litheness, liveliness, mildness, minuteness, moderation, nimbleness, porosity, porousness, sandiness, scantiness, slightness, triviality, wantonness. **antonyms** clumsiness, harshness, heaviness, importance, sadness, severity, sobriety, solidness, stiffness.

lightweight adj inconsequential, insignificant, negligible, paltry, petty, slight, trifling, trivial, unimportant, worthless. **antonyms** important, major.

like¹ adj akin, alike, allied, analogous, approximating, cognate, corresponding, equivalent, homologous, identical, parallel, related, relating, resembling, same, similar. **antonym** unlike.

n counterpart, equal, fellow, match, opposite number, parallel, peer, twin.

prep in the same manner as, on the lines of, similar to.

like² v admire, adore, appreciate, approve, care to, cherish, choose, choose to, delight in, desire, dig, enjoy, esteem, fancy, feel inclined, go a bundle on, go for, hold dear, love, prefer, prize, relish, revel in, select, take a shine to, take kindly to, take to, want, wish. **antonym** dislike.

n cup of tea, favourite, liking, love, partiality, penchant, predilection, preference. **antonym** dislike.

likeable adj agreeable, amiable, appealing, attractive, charming, congenial, engaging, friendly, genial, loveable, nice, pleasant, pleasing, sympathetic, winning. **antonym** disagreeable.

likelihood n chance, liability, likeliness, possibility, probability, prospect, reasonableness, verisimilitude. **antonym** unlikeliness.

likely adj acceptable, agreeable, anticipated, appropriate, apt, befitting, believable, bright, credible, disposed, expected, fair, favourite, feasible, fit, foreseeable, hopeful, inclined, liable, odds-on, on the cards, plausible, pleasing, possible, predictable, probable,

promising, prone, proper, qualified, reasonable, suitable, tending, up-and-coming, verisimilar. **antonyms** unlikely, unsuitable.

adv doubtlessly, in all probability, like as not, like enough, no doubt, odds on, presumably, probably, very like.

like-minded adj agreeing, compatible, harmonious, in accord, in agreement, in harmony, in rapport, of one mind, of the same mind, unanimous. **antonym** disagreeing.

liken v associate, compare, equate, juxtapose, link, match, parallel, relate, set beside.

likeness n affinity, appearance, copy, correspondence, counterpart, delineation, depiction, effigy, facsimile, form, guise, image, model, photograph, picture, portrait, replica, representation, reproduction, resemblance, semblance, similarity, similitude, study. **antonym** unlikeness.

likewise adv also, besides, by the same token, eke, further, furthermore, in addition, moreover, similarly, too. **antonym** contrariwise.

liking n affection, affinity, appreciation, attraction, bent, bias, desire, favour, fondness, inclination, love, partiality, penchant, predilection, preference, proneness, propensity, satisfaction, soft spot, taste, tendency, weakness. **antonym** dislike.

lily-white adj chaste, incorrupt, innocent, irreproachable, milk-white, pure, spotless, uncorrupt, uncorrupted, unsullied, untainted, untarnished, virgin, virtuous. **antonym** corrupt.

limb n appendage, arm, bough, branch, extension, extremity, fork, leg, member, offshoot, part, projection, spur, wing.

limber adj agile, elastic, flexible, flexile, graceful, lissom, lithe, loose-jointed, loose-limbed, plastic, pliable, pliant, supple. **antonym** stiff.

limber up exercise, loosen up, prepare, warm up, work out. **antonym** stiffen up.

limelight n attention, big time, celebrity, fame, prominence, public notice, publicity, recognition, renown, stardom, the public eye, the spotlight.

limit n bitter end, border, bound, boundary, brim, brink, ceiling, check, compass, confines, curb, cut-off point, deadline, edge, end, extent, frontier, limitation, maximum, obstruction, perimeter, periphery, precinct, restraint, restriction, rim, saturation point, termination, terminus, threshold, ultimate, utmost, verge.

v bound, check, circumscribe, condition, confine, constrain, curb, delimit, delimitate, demarcate, fix, hem in, hinder, ration, restrain, restrict, specify. *antonyms* extend, free.

limitation *n* block, check, condition, constraint, control, curb, delimitation, demarcation, disadvantage, drawback, impediment, obstruction, qualification, reservation, restraint, restriction, snag. *antonyms* asset, extension, furtherance.

limited *adj* bounded, checked, circumscribed, confined, constrained, controlled, cramped, curbed, defined, determinate, finite, fixed, hampered, hemmed in, inadequate, insufficient, minimal, narrow, restricted, short, unsatisfactory. *antonym* limitless.

limitless *adj* boundless, countless, endless, illimitable, illimited, immeasurable, immense, incalculable, inexhaustible, infinite, measureless, never-ending, numberless, unbounded, undefined, unending, unlimited, untold, vast. *antonym* limited.

limp¹ *v* dot, falter, halt, hobble, hop, shamble, shuffle.

limp² *adj* debilitated, drooping, enervated, exhausted, flabby, flaccid, flexible, flexile, floppy, lethargic, loose, pooped, relaxed, slack, soft, spent, tired, toneless, weak, worn out. *antonym* strong.

limpid *adj* bright, clear, comprehensible, crystal-clear, crystalline, glassy, intelligible, lucid, pure, still, translucent, transparent. *antonyms* muddy, ripply, turbid, unintelligible.

line¹ *n* band, bar, border, borderline, boundary, cable, chain, channel, column, configuration, contour, cord, crease, crow's foot, dash, demarcation, disposition, edge, features, figure, filament, file, firing line, formation, front, front line, frontier, furrow, groove, limit, mark, outline, position, procession, profile, queue, rank, rope, rule, score, scratch, sequence, series, silhouette, strand, streak, string, stroke, tail, thread, trail, trenches, underline, wire, wrinkle.

v border, bound, crease, cut, draw, edge, fringe, furrow, hatch, inscribe, mark, rank, rim, rule, score, skirt, verge.

line up align, arrange, array, assemble, dispose, engage, fall in, form ranks, hire, lay on, marshal, obtain, order, organise, prepare, procure, produce, queue up, range, regiment, secure, straighten.

line² *n* activity, approach, area, avenue, axis, belief, business, calling, course, course of action, department, direction, employment, field, forte, ideology, interest, job, method, occupation, path, policy, position, practice, procedure, profession, province, pursuit, route, scheme, specialisation, specialism, speciality, specialty, system, track, trade, trajectory, vocation.

line³ *n* ancestry, breed, family, lineage, pedigree, race, stock, strain, succession.

lineage *n* ancestors, ancestry, birth, breed, descendants, descent, extraction, family, forebears, forefathers, genealogy, heredity, house, line, offspring, pedigree, progeny, race, stock, succession.

line-up *n* arrangement, array, bill, cast, queue, row, selection, team.

linger *v* abide, continue, dally, dawdle, delay, dilly-dally, endure, hang around, hang on, hold out, idle, lag, last out, loiter, persist, procrastinate, remain, stay, stop, survive, tarry, wait. *antonyms* leave, rush.

lingerie *n* frillies, smalls, under-clothes, underclothing, undergarments, unmentionables.

lingering *adj* dragging, long-drawn-out, persistent, prolonged, protracted, remaining, slow. *antonym* quick.

lingo *n* argot, cant, dialect, idiom, jargon, language, parlance, patois, atter, speech, talk, terminology, tongue, vernacular, vocabulary.

link *n* association, attachment, bond, communication, component, connection, constituent, division, element, joint, knot, liaison, member, part, piece, relationship, tie, tie-up, union.

v associate, attach, bind, bracket, concatenate, connect, couple, fasten, identify, join, relate, tie, unite, yoke. *antonyms* separate, unfasten.

link up ally, amalgamate, connect, dock, hook up, join, join forces, merge, team up, unify. *antonym* separate.

link-up *n* alliance, amalgamation, association, connection, merger, tie-in, union. *antonym* separation.

lion-hearted *adj* bold, brave, courageous, daring, dauntless, gallant, heroic, intrepid, resolute, stalwart, stout-hearted, valiant. *antonym* cowardly.

lionise *v* acclaim, adulate, aggrandise, celebrate, eulogise, exalt, fête, glorify, hero-worship, honour, idolise, magnify, praise, sing the praises of. *antonym* vilify.

lip¹ *n* border, brim, brink, edge, margin, rim, verge.

lip² *n* backchat, cheek, effrontery, impertinence, impudence, insolence, rudeness, sauce. *antonym* politeness.

liquid *n* drink, fluid, juice, liquor, lotion, potation, sap, solution.
adj aqueous, clear, convertible, flowing, fluid, liquefied, melted, molten, negotiable, running, runny, serous, shining, smooth, soft, thawed, translucent, transparent, watery, wet. *antonyms* harsh, solid.

liquidate *v* abolish, annihilate, annul, assassinate, bump off, cancel, cash, clear, destroy, discharge, dispatch, dissolve, do away with, do in, eliminate, exterminate, finish off, honour, kill, massacre, murder, pay, pay off, realise, remove, rub out, sell off, sell up, settle, silence, square, terminate, wipe out.

liquor *n* alcohol, booze, drink, fire-water, grog, hard stuff, hooch, intoxicant, juice, jungle juice, potation, rotgut, spirits, strong drink.

lissom(e) *adj* agile, flexible, graceful, light, limber, lithe, lithesome, loose-jointed, loose-limbed, nimble, pliable, pliant, supple, willowy. *antonym* stiff.

list¹ *n* catalogue, directory, enumeration, file, index, inventory, invoice, leet, listing, litany, record, register, roll, schedule, series, syllabus, table, tabulation, tally.
v alphabeticise, bill, book, catalogue, enrol, enter, enumerate, file, index, itemise, note, record, register, schedule, set down, tabulate, write down.

list² *v* cant, careen, heel, heel over, incline, lean, slope, tilt, tip.
n cant, leaning, slant, slope, tilt.

listen *v* attend, get a load of, give ear, give heed to, hang on (someone's) words, hang on (someone's) lips, hark, hear, hearken, heed, keep one's ears open, lend an ear, mind, obey, observe, pay attention, pin back one's ears, prick up one's ears, take notice.

listless *adj* apathetic, bored, depressed, enervated, heavy, impassive, inattentive, indifferent, indolent, inert, languid, languishing, lethargic, lifeless, limp, mopish, sluggish, spiritless, torpid, uninterested, vacant. *antonym* lively.

listlessness *n* apathy, enervation, inattention, indifference, indolence, languidness, languor, lethargy, lifelessness, sloth, sluggishness, spiritlessness, torpor. *antonym* liveliness.

litany *n* account, catalogue, enumeration, list, petition, prayer, recital, recitation, refrain, repetition, supplication, tale.

literacy *n* ability, articulacy, articulateness, cultivation, culture, education, erudition, intelligence, knowledge, learning, proficiency, scholarship. *antonym* illiteracy.

literal *adj* accurate, actual, boring, close, colourless, down-to-earth, dull, exact, factual, faithful, genuine, matter-of-fact, plain, prosaic, prosy, real, simple, strict, true, unexaggerated, unimaginative, uninspired, unvarnished, verbatim, word-for-word. *antonym* loose.

literally *adv* actually, closely, exactly, faithfully, literatim, plainly, precisely, really, simply, strictly, to the letter, truly, verbatim, word for word. *antonym* loosely.

literary *adj* bookish, cultivated, cultured, erudite, formal, learned, lettered, literate, refined, scholarly, well-read. *antonym* illiterate.

lithe *adj* double-jointed, flexible, flexile, limber, lissom(e), lithesome, loose-jointed, loose-limbed, pliable, pliant, supple. *antonym* stiff.

litigation *n* action, case, contention, lawsuit, process, prosecution, suit.

litter¹ *n* clutter, confusion, debris, disarray, disorder, fragments, jumble, mess, muck, refuse, rubbish, scatter, shreds, untidiness.
v bestrew, clutter, derange, disarrange, disorder, mess up, scatter, strew. *antonym* tidy.

litter² *n* brood, family, offspring, progeny, young.

little *adj* babyish, base, brief, diminutive, dwarf, elfin, fleeting, hasty, immature, inconsiderable, infant, infinitesimal, insignificant, insufficient, junior, Lilliputian, meagre, mean, microscopic, miniature, minor, minute, negligible, paltry, passing, petite, petty, pint-size(d), pygmy, scant, short, short-lived, skimpy, slender, small, sparse, tiny, transient, trifling, trivial, undeveloped, unimportant, wee, young. *antonyms* important, large, long.
adv barely, hardly, infrequently, rarely, scarcely, seldom. *antonyms* frequently, greatly.
n bit, dab, dash, drib, fragment, hint, modicum, particle, pinch, snippet, speck,

spot, taste, touch, trace, trifle. *antonym* lot.

little by little bit by bit, by degrees, gradually, imperceptibly, piecemeal, progressively, slowly, step by step. *antonyms* all at one go, quickly.

liturgy *n* celebration, ceremony, form, formula, office, rite, ritual, sacrament, service, usage, worship.

live¹ *v* abide, breathe, continue, draw breath, dwell, earn a living, endure, exist, fare, feed, get along, hang out, inhabit, last, lead, lodge, make ends meet, pass, persist, prevail, remain, reside, settle, stay, subsist, survive. *antonyms* cease, die.

live it up celebrate, go on the spree, have a ball, make merry, make whoopee, paint the town red, revel.

live² *adj* active, alert, alight, alive, animate, blazing, breathing, brisk, burning, connected, controversial, current, dynamic, earnest, energetic, existent, glowing, hot, ignited, lively, living, pertinent, pressing, prevalent, relevant, sentient, smouldering, topical, unsettled, vigorous, vital, vivid, wide-awake. *antonyms* apathetic, dead, out.

liveable *adj* acceptable, adequate, bearable, comfortable, endurable, habitable, inhabitable, possible, satisfactory, sufferable, supportable, tolerable, worthwhile. *antonyms* unbearable, uninhabitable.

liveable with bearable, companionable, compatible, congenial, harmonious, passable, sociable, tolerable. *antonyms* impossible, unbearable.

livelihood *n* employment, income, job, living, maintenance, means, occupation, subsistence, support, sustenance, work.

liveliness *n* activity, animation, boisterousness, brio, briskness, dynamism, energy, gaiety, quickness, smartness, spirit, sprightliness, vitality, vivacity. *antonyms* apathy, inactivity.

lively *adj* active, agile, alert, animated, astir, blithe, breezy, bright, brisk, bustling, busy, buxom, buzzing, cheerful, chipper, chirpy, colourful, crowded, energetic, eventful, exciting, forceful, frisky, frolicsome, gay, invigorating, keen, merry, moving, nimble, perky, quick, racy, refreshing, skittish, sparkling, spirited, sprightly, spry, stimulating, stirring, swinging, vigorous, vivacious, vivid, zippy. *antonyms* apathetic, inactive, moribund.

liven up animate, brighten, buck up, energise, enliven, hot up, invigorate, pep up, perk up, put life into, rouse, stir, stir up, vitalise, vivify. *antonyms* deaden, dishearten.

liverish *adj* crabbed, crabby, crotchety, crusty, disagreeable, grumpy, ill-humoured, irascible, irritable, peevish, snappy, splenetic, testy, tetchy. *antonyms* calm, easy-going.

live-wire ball of fire, dynamo, life and soul of the party. *antonym* wet blanket.

livid *adj* angry, beside oneself, boiling, enraged, exasperated, fuming, furious, incensed, indignant, infuriated, irate, mad, outraged. *antonym* calm.

living *adj* active, alive, animated, breathing, existing, live, lively, strong, vigorous, vital. *antonyms* dead, sluggish.
n being, benefice, existence, income, job, life, livelihood, maintenance, occupation, profession, property, subsistence, support, sustenance, way of life, work.

load *n* affliction, albatross, burden, cargo, consignment, encumbrance, freight, goods, lading, millstone, onus, oppression, pressure, shipment, trouble, weight, worry.
v adulterate, burden, charge, cram, doctor, drug, encumber, fill, fortify, freight, hamper, heap, lade, oppress, overburden, pack, pile, prime, saddle with, stack, stuff, trouble, weigh down, weight, worry.

loaded *adj* affluent, biased, burdened, charged, distorted, drugged, drunk, flush, freighted, full, high, inebriated, insidious, intoxicated, laden, moneyed, prejudicial, primed, rich, rolling, tight, tipsy, tricky, under the influence, wealthy, weighted, well-heeled, well-off, well-to-do. *antonyms* poor, sober, straightforward, unloaded.

loads *n* a million, dozens, heaps, hordes, hundreds, lots, millions, scores, thousands, tons.

loaf *v* idle, laze, lie around, loiter, loll, lounge around, moon, stand about, take it easy. *antonym* toil.

loafer *n* bum, idler, layabout, lazybones, lounge-lizard, lounger, ne'er-do-well, shirker, skiver, sluggard, time-waster. *antonym* worker.

loan *n* accommodation, advance, allowance, credit, loan-word, mortgage, touch.

v accommodate, advance, allow, credit, lend, let out, oblige. **antonym** borrow.

lo(a)th *adj* against, averse, backward, counter, disinclined, grudging, hesitant, indisposed, opposed, reluctant, resisting, unwilling. **antonym** willing.

loathe *v* abhor, abominate, despise, detest, dislike, execrate, hate. **antonym** like.

loathing *n* abhorrence, abomination, antipathy, aversion, detestation, disgust, dislike, execration, hatred, horror, nausea, odium, repugnance, repulsion, revulsion. **antonym** liking.

loathsome *adj* abhorrent, abominable, detestable, disgusting, execrable, hateful, horrible, loathful, nasty, nauseating, obnoxious, odious, offensive, repellent, repugnant, repulsive, revolting, vile. **antonym** likeable.

lob *v* chuck, fling, heave, launch, lift, loft, pitch, shy, throw, toss.

lobby[1] *v* call for, campaign for, demand, influence, persuade, press for, pressure, promote, pull strings, push for, solicit, urge.

n ginger group, pressure group.

lobby[2] *n* anteroom, corridor, entrance hall, foyer, hall, hallway, passage, passageway, porch, vestibule, waiting-room.

local *adj* community, confined, district, limited, narrow, neighbourhood, parish, parochial, provincial, regional, restricted, small-town, vernacular, vicinal. **antonym** far-away.

locale *n* area, locality, location, locus, place, position, scene, setting, site, spot, venue, zone.

localise *v* ascribe, assign, circumscribe, concentrate, confine, contain, delimit, delimitate, limit, narrow down, pinpoint, restrain, restrict, specify, zero in on.

locality *n* area, district, locale, location, neck of the woods, neighbourhood, place, position, region, scene, setting, site, spot, vicinity, zone.

locate *v* detect, discover, establish, find, fix, identify, lay one's hands on, pinpoint, place, put, run to earth, seat, set, settle, situate, track down, unearth.

location *n* bearings, locale, locus, place, point, position, site, situation, spot, venue, whereabouts.

lock *n* bolt, clasp, fastening, padlock, sneck.

v bolt, clasp, clench, close, clutch, disengage, embrace, encircle, enclose,

engage, entangle, entwine, fasten, grapple, grasp, hug, join, latch, link, mesh, press, seal, secure, shut, sneck, unite, unlock.

lock out ban, bar, debar, exclude, keep out, ostracise, refuse admittance to, shut out.

lock up cage, close up, confine, detain, imprison, incarcerate, jail, pen, secure, shut, shut in, shut up. **antonym** free.

lodge *n* abode, assemblage, association, branch, cabin, chalet, chapter, club, cottage, den, gatehouse, group, haunt, house, hunting-lodge, hut, lair, meeting-place, retreat, shelter, society.

v accommodate, billet, board, deposit, dig, entertain, file, get stuck, harbour, imbed, implant, lay, place, put, put on record, put up, quarter, register, room, set, shelter, sojourn, stay, stick, stop, submit.

lodgings *n* abode, accommodation, apartments, billet, boarding, digs, dwelling, pad, quarters, residence, rooms, shelter.

lofty *adj* arrogant, condescending, dignified, disdainful, distinguished, elevated, esteemed, exalted, grand, haughty, high, high and mighty, illustrious, imperial, imposing, lordly, majestic, noble, patronising, proud, raised, renowned, sky-high, snooty, soaring, stately, sublime, supercilious, superior, tall, toffee-nosed, towering. **antonyms** humble, low(ly), modest.

log *n* account, chart, daybook, diary, journal, listing, logbook, record, tally.

v book, chart, note, record, register, report, tally, write down, write in, write up.

logical *adj* clear, cogent, coherent, consistent, deducible, judicious, necessary, obvious, pertinent, plausible, rational, reasonable, relevant, sensible, sound, valid, well-founded, well-grounded, well-organised, wise. **antonyms** illogical, irrational.

logistics *n* co-ordination, engineering, management, masterminding, orchestration, organisation, planning, plans, strategy.

loiter *v* dally, dawdle, delay, dilly-dally, hang about, idle, lag, linger, loaf, loll, saunter, skulk, stroll.

loll *v* dangle, droop, drop, flap, flop, hang, lean, loaf, lounge, recline, relax, sag, slouch, slump, sprawl.

lone *adj* deserted, isolated, lonesome, one, only, separate, separated, single, sole, solitary, unaccompanied, unattached, unattended. *antonym* accompanied.

loneliness *n* aloneness, desolation, forlornness, friendlessness, isolation, lonesomeness, seclusion, solitariness, solitude.

lonely *adj* abandoned, alone, apart, companionless, destitute, estranged, forlorn, forsaken, friendless, isolated, lonely-heart, lonesome, outcast, out-of-the-way, remote, secluded, sequestered, solitary, unfrequented, uninhabited, untrodden.

long *adj* dragging, elongated, expanded, expansive, extended, extensive, far-reaching, interminable, lengthy, lingering, long-drawn-out, marathon, prolonged, protracted, slow, spread out, stretched, sustained, tardy. *antonyms* abbreviated, brief, fleeting, short.

long for covet, crave, desire, dream of, hanker for, hunger after, itch for, lust after, pine, thirst for, want, wish, yearn for, yen for.

long-drawn-out *adj* interminable, lengthy, long-winded, marathon, over-extended, overlong, prolix, prolonged, protracted, spun out, tedious. *antonyms* brief, curtailed.

longing *n* ambition, aspiration, coveting, craving, desire, hankering, hungering, itch, thirst, urge, wish, yearning, yen.
adj anxious, ardent, avid, craving, desirous, eager, hungry, languishing, pining, wishful, wistful, yearning.

long-lasting *adj* abiding, continuing, enduring, entrenched, established, evergreen, imperishable, lifelong, long-lived, long-standing, permanent, prolonged, protracted, unchanging, unfading. *antonyms* ephemeral, short-lived, transient.

long-lived *adj* durable, enduring, lasting, long-lasting, long-standing. *antonyms* brief, ephemeral, short-lived.

long-standing *adj* abiding, enduring, established, fixed, hallowed, long-established, long-lasting, long-lived, time-honoured, traditional.

long-winded *adj* circumlocutory, diffuse, discursive, garrulous, lengthy, long-drawn-out, overlong, prolix, prolonged, rambling, repetitious, tedious, verbose, voluble, wordy. *antonyms* brief, compact, curt, terse.

look *v* appear, behold, consider, contemplate, display, evidence, examine, exhibit, eye, gape, gawk, gawp, gaze, get a load of, glance, goggle, inspect, observe, ogle, peep, regard, scan, scrutinise, see, seem, show, stare, study, survey, take a butcher's, take a gander, take a shufti, view, watch.
n air, appearance, aspect, bearing, butcher's, cast, complexion, countenance, decko, demeanour, effect, examination, expression, eyeful, eye-glance, face, fashion, gander, gaze, glance, glimpse, guise, inspection, look-see, manner, observation, once-over, peek, review, semblance, shufti, sight, squint, survey, view.

look after attend to, care for, chaperon, guard, keep an eye on, mind, nurse, protect, supervise, take care of, take charge of, tend, watch. *antonym* neglect.

look down on contemn, despise, disdain, hold in contempt, look down one's nose at, misprise, pooh-pooh, scorn, sneer at, spurn, turn one's nose up at. *antonyms* approve, esteem.

look for forage for, hunt, hunt for, hunt out, quest, search for, seek.

look forward to anticipate, await, count on, envisage, envision, expect, hope for, long for, look for, wait for.

look into check out, delve into, enquire about, examine, explore, fathom, follow up, go into, inspect, investigate, look over, plumb, probe, research, scrutinise, study.

look like resemble, take after.

look out be careful, beware, keep an eye out, keep one's eyes peeled, keep one's eyes skinned, pay attention, watch out.

look out on face, front, front on, give on (to), overlook.

look over cast an eye over, check, examine, flick through, give the once-over, inspect, look through, monitor, peruse, scan, view.

look to/for anticipate, await, count on, expect, hope for, reckon on, rely on.

look up[1] call on, drop by, drop in on, find, hunt for, look in on, pay a visit to, research, search for, seek out, stop by, track down, visit.

look up[2] ameliorate, come on, get better, improve, perk up, pick up, progress, shape up.

look up to admire, esteem, have a high opinion of, honour, respect, revere.

look-alike *n* clone, dead ringer, doppel-gänger, double, living image, replica, ringer, spit, spitting image, twin.

loom *v* appear, bulk, dominate, emerge,

hang over, hover, impend, materialise, menace, mount, overhang, overshadow, overtop, rise, soar, take shape, threaten, tower.

loop *n* arc, bend, circle, coil, convolution, curl, curve, hoop, kink, loophole, noose, ring, spiral, turn, twirl, twist, whorl.

v bend, braid, circle, coil, connect, curl, curve round, encircle, fold, gird, join, knot, roll, spiral, turn, twist.

loophole *n* aperture, avoidance, escape, evasion, excuse, get-out, let-out, opening, plea, pretence, pretext, slot, subterfuge.

loose[1] *adj* baggy, diffuse, disconnected, disordered, easy, floating, free, hanging, ill-defined, imprecise, inaccurate, indefinite, indistinct, inexact, insecure, loosened, movable, rambling, random, relaxed, released, shaky, slack, slackened, sloppy, unattached, unbound, unconfined, unfastened, unfettered, unrestricted, unsecured, untied, vague, wobbly. **antonyms** close, compact, precise, strict, taut, tense, tight.

v absolve, detach, disconnect, disengage, ease, free, let go, liberate, loosen, release, set free, slacken, unbind, unbrace, unclasp, uncouple, undo, unfasten, unhand, unleash, unlock, unloose, unmoor, unpen, untie.

antonyms bind, fasten, fix, secure.

loose[2] *adj* abandoned, careless, debauched, disreputable, dissipated, dissolute, fast, heedless, immoral, imprudent, lax, lewd, libertine, licentious, negligent, profligate, promiscuous, rash, thoughtless, unchaste, unmindful, wanton. **antonyms** strict, stringent, tight.

loosen *v* deliver, detach, free, let go, let out, liberate, release, eparate, set free, slacken, unbind, undo, unfasten, unloose, unloosen, unstick, untie. **antonym** tighten.

loosen up ease up, go easy, lessen, let up, mitigate, moderate, relax, soften, unbend, weaken.

loot *n* booty, cache, goods, haul, plunder, prize, riches, spoils, swag.

v despoil, pillage, plunder, raid, ransack, ravage, rifle, rob, sack.

lop *v* chop, clip, crop, curtail, cut, detach, dock, hack, prune, sever, shorten, trim, truncate.

lop-sided *adj* askew, asymmetrical, awry, cockeyed, crooked, disproportionate, ill-balanced, off balance, one-sided, out of true, squint, tilting, unbalanced,

unequal, uneven, warped. **antonyms** balanced, straight, symmetrical.

loquacious *adj* babbling, blathering, chattering, chatty, gabby, garrulous, gassy, gossipy, talkative, voluble, wordy. **antonyms** succinct, taciturn, terse.

lord *n* baron, commander, count, duke, earl, governor, king, leader, liege, master, monarch, noble, nobleman, overlord, peer, potentate, prince, ruler, sovereign, superior, viscount.

lord it over act big, boss around, domineer, oppress, order around, pull rank, put on airs, repress, swagger, tyrannise.

lordly *adj* aristocratic, arrogant, authoritarian, condescending, despotic, dictatorial, dignified, disdainful, domineering, exalted, gracious, grand, haughty, high and mighty, high-handed, hoity-toity, imperial, imperious, lofty, majestic, masterful, noble, overbearing, patronising, princely, proud, regal, stately, stuck-up, supercilious, swanky, toffee-nosed, tyrannical. **antonyms** humble, low(ly), mean.

lose *v* capitulate, come a cropper, come to grief, consume, default, deplete, displace, dissipate, dodge, drain, drop, duck, elude, escape, evade, exhaust, expend, fail, fall short, forfeit, forget, get the worst of, give (someone) the slip, leave behind, lose out on, misfile, mislay, misplace, miss, misspend, outdistance, outrun, outstrip, overtake, pass, pass up, shake off, slip away, squander, stray from, suffer defeat, take a licking, throw off, use up, wander from, waste, yield. **antonyms** gain, make, win.

loser *n* also-ran, bum, bum steer, dud, failure, flop, lemon, no-hoper, runner-up, sucker, underdog, wash-out. **antonym** winner.

loss *n* bereavement, cost, damage, debit, debt, defeat, deficiency, deficit, depletion, deprivation, destruction, detriment, disadvantage, disappearance, failure, forfeiture, harm, hurt, impairment, injury, losing, losings, misfortune, privation, ruin, shrinkage, squandering, waste, write-off. **antonyms** benefit, gain.

lost *adj* abandoned, abolished, absent, absorbed, abstracted, adrift, annihilated, astray, baffled, bewildered, confused, consumed, corrupt, damned, demolished, depraved, destroyed, devastated, disappeared, disoriented, dissipated, dissolute, distracted, dreamy, engrossed, entranced, eradicated, exterminated, fallen, forfeited, frittered away, irreclaimable, licentious, misapplied, misdirected, mislaid, misplaced, missed, missing, misspent, misused, mystified, obliterated, off-course, off-track, perished, perplexed, preoccupied, profligate, puzzled, rapt, ruined, spellbound, squandered, strayed, unrecoverable, untraceable, vanished, wanton, wasted, wayward, wiped out, wrecked. **antonym** found.

lot n accident, allowance, assortment, batch, chance, collection, consignment, crowd, cut, destiny, doom, fate, fortune, group, hazard, parcel, part, percentage, piece, plight, portion, quantity, quota, ration, set, share, weird.

loth *see* **loath**.

loud adj blaring, blatant, boisterous, booming, brash, brassy, brazen, clamorous, coarse, crass, crude, deafening, ear-piercing, ear-splitting, flamboyant, flashy, garish, gaudy, glaring, high-sounding, loud-mouthed, lurid, noisy, offensive, ostentatious, piercing, raucous, resounding, rowdy, showy, sonorous, stentorian, strident, strong, tasteless, tawdry, thundering, tumultuous, turbulent, vehement, vocal, vociferous, vulgar. **antonyms** low, quiet, soft.

loudly adv clamorously, deafeningly, fortissimo, noisily, resoundingly, shrilly, stridently, strongly, uproariously, vehemently, vigorously, vocally, vociferously. **antonyms** quietly, softly.

loud-voiced adj full-throated, penetrating, piercing, roaring, sonorous, stentorian. **antonyms** quiet, soft.

lounge v dawdle, idle, kill time, laze, lie about, lie back, loaf, loiter, loll, potter, recline, relax, slump, sprawl, take it easy, waste time.

lour, lower v be brewing, blacken, cloud over, darken, frown, give a dirty look, glare, glower, impend, look daggers, loom, menace, scowl, threaten.

louring, lowering adj black, brooding, dark, darkening, forbidding, foreboding, gloomy, glowering, grey, grim, heavy, impending, menacing, ominous, overcast, scowling, sullen, surly, threatening.

lousy adj awful, bad, base, contemptible, crap, despicable, dirty, hateful, inferior, lice-infested, lice-ridden, low, mean, miserable, no good, poor, rotten, second-

rate, shoddy, slovenly, terrible, trashy, vicious, vile. **antonyms** excellent, superb.

lout n boor, churl, clod, dolt, hick, hobbledehoy, lager lout, oaf, yahoo, yob, yobbo.

loutish adj boorish, churlish, coarse, gross, ill-bred, ill-mannered, oafish, rough, uncouth, unmannerly, yobbish.

lovable adj adorable, amiable, attractive, captivating, charming, cuddly, delightful, enchanting, endearing, engaging, fetching, likable, lovely, pleasing, sweet, taking, winning, winsome. **antonym** hateful.

love v adore, adulate, appreciate, cherish, delight in, desire, dote on, enjoy, fancy, hold dear, idolise, like, prize, relish, savour, take pleasure in, think the world of, treasure, want, worship. **antonyms** detest, hate, loathe.

n adoration, adulation, affection, amity, amorosity, amorousness, ardour, attachment, delight, devotion, enjoyment, fondness, friendship, inclination, infatuation, liking, partiality, passion, rapture, regard, relish, soft spot, taste, tenderness, warmth, weakness. **antonyms** detestation, hate, loathing.

love-affair n affair, intrigue, liaison, love, passion, relationship, romance.

lovely adj admirable, adorable, agreeable, amiable, attractive, beautiful, captivating, charming, comely, delightful, enchanting, engaging, enjoyable, exquisite, graceful, gratifying, handsome, idyllic, nice, pleasant, pleasing, pretty, sweet, taking, winning. **antonyms** hideous, ugly, unlovely.

loving adj affectionate, amorous, ardent, cordial, dear, demonstrative, devoted, doting, fond, friendly, kind, passionate, solicitous, tender, warm, warm-hearted.

low adj abject, base, base-born, blue, brassed off, browned off, cheap, coarse, common, contemptible, crude, dastardly, debilitated, deep, deficient, degraded, dejected, depleted, depraved, depressed, despicable, despondent, disgraceful, disheartened, dishonourable, disreputable, down, down in the dumps, downcast, dying, economical, exhausted, fed up, feeble, forlorn, frail, gloomy, glum, gross, humble, hushed, ignoble, ill, ill-bred, inadequate, inexpensive, inferior, insignificant, low-born, low-grade, lowly, low-lying, meagre, mean, mediocre, meek, menial, miserable, moderate, modest, morose, muffled, muted, nasty, obscene, obscure, paltry, plain, plebeian, poor, prostrate, puny, quiet, reasonable, reduced, rough, rude, sad, scant, scurvy, second-rate, servile, shallow, shoddy, short, simple, sinking, small, soft, sordid, sparse, squat, stricken, stunted, subdued, substandard, sunken, trifling, unbecoming, undignified, unhappy, unpretentious, unrefined, unworthy, vile, vulgar, weak, whispered, worthless. *antonyms* elevated, high, lofty, noble.

low-down *n* dope, gen, info, information, inside story, intelligence, news.

lower[1] *adj* inferior, insignificant, junior, lesser, low-level, lowly, minor, secondary, second-class, smaller, subordinate, subservient, under, unimportant.

v abase, abate, belittle, condescend, curtail, cut, debase, decrease, degrade, deign, demean, demolish, depress, devalue, diminish, discredit, disgrace, downgrade, drop, fall, humble, humiliate, lessen, let down, minimise, moderate, prune, raze, reduce, sink, slash, soften, stoop, submerge, take down, tone down. *antonyms* elevate, increase, raise, rise.

lower[2] *see* **lour**.

lowering *see* **louring**.

low-grade *adj* bad, cheap-jack, inferior, poor, second-class, second-rate, substandard, third-rate. *antonyms* good, quality.

low-key *adj* downbeat, low-pitched, muffled, muted, quiet, restrained, slight, soft, subdued, understated.

lowly *adj* average, common, docile, dutiful, homespun, humble, ignoble, inferior, low-born, mean, mean-born, meek, mild, modest, obscure, ordinary, plain, plebeian, poor, proletarian, simple, submissive, subordinate, unassuming, unexalted, unpretentious. *antonyms* lofty, noble.

low-spirited *adj* apathetic, blue, brassed off, browned off, dejected, depressed, despondent, down, down in the dumps, down-hearted, fed up, gloomy, glum, heavy-hearted, low, miserable, moody, pissed off, sad, unhappy. *antonyms* cheerful, high-spirited.

loyal *adj* attached, constant, dependable, devoted, dutiful, faithful, honest, patriotic, sincere, staunch, steadfast, true, true-blue, true-hearted, trustworthy, trusty, unswerving, unwavering. *antonyms* disloyal, traitorous.

loyalty *n* allegiance, constancy, dependability, devotion, faithfulness, fidelity, honesty, patriotism, reliability, sincerity, staunchness, steadfastness, true-heartedness, trueness, trustiness, trustworthiness. *antonyms* disloyalty, treachery.

lucid *adj* beaming, bright, brilliant, clear, clear-cut, clear-headed, compos mentis, comprehensible, crystalline, diaphanous, distinct, effulgent, evident, explicit, glassy, gleaming, intelligible, limpid, luminous, obvious, plain, pure, radiant, rational, reasonable, resplendent, sane, sensible, shining, sober, sound, translucent, transparent. *antonyms* dark, murky, unclear.

luck *n* accident, blessing, break, chance, destiny, fate, fluke, fortuity, fortune, godsend, good fortune, hap, happenstance, hazard, jam, prosperity, serendipity, stroke, success, windfall. *antonym* misfortune.

luckily *adv* fortuitously, fortunately, haply, happily, opportunely, propitiously, providentially. *antonym* unfortunately.

luckless *adj* calamitous, catastrophic, cursed, disastrous, doomed, fey, hapless, hopeless, ill-fated, ill-starred, jinxed, star-crossed, unfortunate, unhappy, unlucky, unpropitious, unsuccessful. *antonym* lucky.

lucky *adj* advantageous, adventitious, auspicious, blessed, charmed, favoured, fluk(e)y, fortuitous, fortunate, jammy, opportune, propitious, prosperous, providential, serendipitous, successful, timely. *antonyms* luckless, unlucky.

ludicrous *adj* absurd, amusing, burlesque, comic, comical, crazy, droll, farcical, funny, incongruous, laughable, nonsensical, odd, outlandish, preposterous, ridiculous, silly, zany.

lug *v* carry, drag, haul, heave, hump, humph, pull, tote, tow, yank.

lugubrious *adj* dismal, doleful, dreary, funereal, gloomy, glum, melancholy, morose, mournful, sad, sepulchral, serious, sombre, sorrowful, woebegone, woeful. *antonyms* cheerful, jovial, merry.

lull *v* abate, allay, calm, cease, compose, decrease, diminish, dwindle, ease off, hush, let up, lullaby, moderate, pacify, quell, quiet, quieten down, sedate, slacken, soothe, still, subdue, subside, tranquillise, wane. *antonym* agitate.

n calm, calmness, hush, let-up, pause,

peace, quiet, respite, silence, stillness, tranquillity. *antonym* agitation.

lumber[1] *v* burden, charge, encumber, hamper, impose, land, load, saddle.

lumber[2] *v* clump, galumph, plod, shamble, shuffle, stump, trudge, trundle, waddle.

lumbering *adj* awkward, blundering, bumbling, clumsy, heavy, heavy-footed, hulking, lubberly, lumpish, massive, overgrown, ponderous, ungainly, unwieldy. *antonyms* agile, nimble.

luminary *n* celeb, celebrity, dignitary, leader, leading light, lion, notable, personage, star, superstar, VIP, worthy.

luminous *adj* bright, brilliant, dayglow, glowing, illuminated, lighted, lit, luminescent, lustrous, radiant, resplendent, shining, vivid.

lump[1] *n* ball, bulge, bump, bunch, cake, chuck, chump, chunk, clod, cluster, cyst, dab, dod, gob, gobbet, group, growth, hunch, hunk, mass, nugget, piece, protrusion, protuberance, spot, swelling, tumour, wedge, wodge.
v coalesce, collect, combine, consolidate, group, mass, unite.

lump[2] *v* bear (with), brook, endure, put up with, stand, stomach, suffer, swallow, take, tolerate.

lumpy *adj* bumpy, bunched, cloggy, clotted, curdled, grainy, granular, knobbly, nodular. *antonyms* even, smooth.

lunacy *n* aberration, absurdity, craziness, dementia, derangement, folly, foolhardiness, foolishness, idiocy, imbecility, insanity, madness, mania, psychosis, senselessness, stupidity, tomfoolery. *antonym* sanity.

lunatic *n* loony, madman, maniac, nut, nutcase, nutter, psychopath.
adj barmy, bonkers, crazy, daft, demented, deranged, insane, irrational, mad, maniacal, moon-struck, nuts, psychotic, unhinged. *antonyms* sane, sensible.

lunge *v* bound, charge, dash, dive, fall upon, grab (at), hit (at), leap, pitch into, plunge, pounce, set upon, strike (at), thrust.
n charge, pass, pounce, spring, swing, swipe, thrust.

lurch *v* heave, lean, list, pitch, reel, rock, roll, stagger, stumble, sway, tilt, totter.

lure *v* allure, attract, beckon, decoy, draw, ensnare, entice, inveigle, invite, lead on, seduce, tempt.
n allurement, attraction, bait,

carrot, come-on, decoy, enticement, inducement, magnet, siren, song, temptation, train.

lurid *adj* bloody, disgusting, exaggerated, fiery, flaming, ghastly, glaring, glowering, gory, graphic, grim, grisly, gruesome, intense, livid, loud, macabre, melodramatic, revolting, sanguine, savage, sensational, shocking, startling, unrestrained, violent, vivid.

lurk *v* crouch, hide, hide out, lie in wait, lie low, prowl, skulk, slink, sneak, snoop.

luscious *adj* appetising, delectable, delicious, honeyed, juicy, luxuriant, luxurious, mouth-watering, palatable, rich, savoury, scrumptious, succulent, sweet, tasty, yummy. *antonym* austere.

lush *adj* abundant, dense, elaborate, extravagant, flourishing, grand, green, juicy, lavish, luxuriant, luxurious, opulent, ornate, overgrown, palatial, plush, prolific, ripe, ritzy, succulent, sumptuous, superabundant, teeming, tender, verdant.

lust *n* appetite, avidity, carnality, covetousness, craving, desire, greed, lasciviousness, lechery, lewdness, libido, licentiousness, longing, passion, prurience, randiness, salaciousness, sensuality, thirst, wantonness.

lust after crave, desire, have the hots for, hunger for, need, slaver over, thirst for, want, yearn for, yen for.

lustful *adj* carnal, craving, goatish, hankering, horny, lascivious, lecherous, lewd, libidinous, licentious, passionate, prurient, randy, raunchy, ruttish, sensual, unchaste, wanton.

lustre *n* brightness, brilliance, burnish, dazzle, distinction, effulgence, fame, gleam, glint, glitter, glory, gloss, glow, gorm, honour, illustriousness, lambency, luminousness, prestige, radiance, renown, resplendence, sheen, shimmer, shine, sparkle.

lustrous *adj* bright, burnished, dazzling, gleaming, glistening, glittering, glossy, glowing, lambent, luminous, radiant, shimmering, shining, shiny, sparkling. *antonyms* dull, lacklustre, matt.

luxuriance *n* abundance, copiousness, denseness, excess, exuberance, fertility, lavishness, lushness, profusion, richness, sumptuousness.

luxuriant *adj* abundant, ample, copious, dense, elaborate, excessive, extravagant, exuberant, fancy, fertile, flamboyant, florid, lavish, lush, opulent, ornate, overflowing, plenteous, plentiful, prodigal, productive, profuse, prolific, rich, sumptuous, superabundant, teeming, thriving. **antonyms** barren, infertile.

luxuriate *v* abound, bask, bloom, burgeon, delight, enjoy, flourish, grow, have a ball, indulge, live the life of Riley, prosper, relish, revel, thrive, wallow.

luxurious *adj* comfortable, costly, deluxe, epicurean, expensive, hedonistic, lavish, magnificent, opulent, pampered, plush, rich, ritzy, self-indulgent, sensual, splendid, sumptuous, voluptuous, well-appointed. **antonyms** ascetic, austere, economical, frugal, scant(y), spartan.

luxury *n* affluence, bliss, comfort, delight, enjoyment, extra, extravagance, indulgence, milk and honey, non-essential, opulence, pleasure, richness, satisfaction, splendour, sumptuousness, treat, voluptuousness, well-being. **antonym** essential.

lying *adj* deceitful, dishonest, dissembling, double-dealing, duplicitous, false, guileful, mendacious, perfidious, treacherous, two-faced, untruthful. **antonyms** honest, truthful. *n* deceit, dishonesty, dissimulation, double-dealing, duplicity, fabrication, falsity, fibbing, guile, mendacity, perjury, prevarication, untruthfulness. **antonyms** honesty, truthfulness.

M

macabre *adj* cadaverous, deathlike, deathly, dreadful, eerie, frightening, frightful, ghastly, ghostly, ghoulish, grim, grisly, gruesome, hideous, horrible, horrid, morbid, sick, weird.

Machiavellian *adj* amoral, artful, astute, calculating, crafty, cunning, cynical, deceitful, designing, double-dealing, guileful, intriguing, opportunist, perfidious, scheming, shrewd, sly, underhand, unscrupulous, wily.

machination *n* artifice, cabal, conspiracy, design, device, dodge, finagling, intrigue, manoeuvre, plot, ploy, ruse, scheme, shenanigans, stratagem, trick.

machine *n* agency, agent, apparatus, appliance, automaton, contraption, contrivance, device, engine, gadget, gizmo, instrument, machinery, mechanism, organisation, party, puppet, robot, set-up, structure, system, tool, zombi(e).

machinery *n* agency, apparatus, channels, equipment, gear, instruments, kit, machine, mechanism, organisation, procedure, structure, system, tackle, tools, works.

mad *adj* abandoned, aberrant, absurd, agitated, angry, ardent, avid, bananas, barmy, bats, batty, berserk, boisterous, bonkers, crackers, crazed, crazy, cuckoo, daft, delirious, demented, deranged, devoted, distracted, dotty, ebullient, enamoured, energetic, enraged, enthu-siastic, exasperated, excited, fanatical, fond, foolhardy, foolish, frantic, frenetic, frenzied, fuming, furious, have bats in the belfry, hooked, impassioned, imprudent, incensed, infatuated, infuriated, insane, irate, irrational, irritated, keen, livid, loony, loopy, ludicrous, lunatic, madcap, mental, moon-struck, non compos mentis, nonsensical, nuts, nutty, off one's chump, off one's head, off one's nut, off one's rocker, off one's trolley, out of one's mind, possessed, preposterous, psychotic, rabid, raging, raving, resentful, riotous, round the bend, round the twist, screwball, screwy, senseless, unbalanced, uncontrolled, unhinged, unreasonable, unrestrained, unsafe, unsound, unstable, up the pole, wild, wrathful, zealous. **antonyms** lucid, rational, sane.

madcap *adj* bird-brained, crazy, foolhardy, hare-brained, heedless, hot-headed, ill-advised, imprudent, impulsive, lively, rash, reckless, silly, thoughtless, wild.

madden *v* annoy, craze, dement, derange, enrage, exasperate, incense, inflame, infuriate, irritate, provoke, unhinge, upset, vex. **antonyms** calm, pacify, please.

made-up *adj* fabricated, fairy-tale, false, fictional, imaginary, invented, make-believe, mythical, specious, trumped-up, unreal, untrue.

madhouse *n* asylum, bedlam, chaos, disarray, disorder, funny farm, loony bin, nut-house, pandemonium, turmoil, uproar.

madly *adv* absurdly, crazily, deliriously, dementedly, desperately, devotedly, distractedly, energetically, exceedingly, excessively, excitedly, extremely, fanatically, foolishly, frantically, frenziedly, furiously, hastily, hurriedly, hysterically, insanely, intensely, irrationally, like mad, ludicrously, nonsensically, passionately, quickly, rabidly, rapidly, recklessly, senselessly, speedily, to distraction, unreasonably, violently, wildly.

madman *n* loony, lunatic, maniac, mental case, nut, nutcase, nutter, psycho, psychopath, psychotic, schizo, screwball.

madness *n* abandon, aberration, absurdity, agitation, anger, ardour, craze, craziness, daftness, delusion, dementia, derangement, distraction, enthusiasm, exasperation, excitement, fanaticism, folly, fondness, foolhardiness, foolishness, frenzy, fury, infatuation, insanity, intoxication, ire, keenness, lunacy, mania, monomania, nonsense, passion, preposterousness, psychosis, rage, raving, riot, unrestraint, uproar, wildness, wrath, zeal. **antonym** sanity.

maelstrom *n* bedlam, chaos, confusion, disorder, mess, pandemonium, tumult, turmoil, uproar, vortex, whirlpool.

magic *n* black art, charm, conjuring, diablerie, enchantment, fascination, glamour, hocus-pocus, hoodoo, illusion, jiggery-pokery, jugglery, legerdemain, magnetism, necromancy, occultism, prestidigitation, sleight of hand, sorcery, spell, trickery, voodoo, witchcraft, wizardry.

adj bewitching, charismatic, charming, enchanting, entrancing, fascinating, magical, magnetic, marvellous, miraculous, sorcerous, spellbinding.

magician *n* conjurer, conjuror, enchanter, enchantress, genius, illusionist, maestro, mage, magus, marvel, miracle-worker, necromancer, prestidigitator, sorcerer, spellbinder, virtuoso, warlock, witch, witch-doctor, wizard.

magisterial *adj* arrogant, assertive, authoritarian, authoritative, bossy, commanding, despotic, dictatorial, domineering, high-handed, imperious, lordly, masterful, overbearing, peremptory.

magnanimity *n* beneficence, big-heartedness, bountifulness, charitableness, charity, generosity, high-mindedness, largess(e), liberality, munificence, nobility, open-handedness, selflessness, unselfishness. *antonym* meanness.

magnanimous *adj* altruistic, beneficent, big, big-hearted, bountiful, charitable, free, generous, great-hearted, handsome, high-minded, kind, kindly, large-minded, liberal, munificent, noble, open-handed, philanthropic, selfless, ungrudging, unselfish, unstinting. *antonyms* mean, paltry, petty.

magnate *n* aristocrat, baron, big cheese, big noise, big shot, big wheel, bigwig, captain of industry, chief, fat cat, grandee, leader, magnifico, merchant, mogul, noble, notable, personage, plutocrat, prince, tycoon, VIP.

magnetic *adj* absorbing, alluring, attractive, captivating, charismatic, charming, enchanting, engrossing, entrancing, fascinating, gripping, hypnotic, irresistible, mesmerising, seductive. *antonyms* repellent, repugnant, repulsive.

magnetism *n* allure, appeal, attraction, attractiveness, charisma, charm, draw, drawing power, enchantment, fascination, grip, hypnotism, lure, magic, mesmerism, power, pull, seductiveness, spell.

magnification *n* aggrandisement, amplification, augmentation, blow-up, boost, build-up, deepening, dilation, enhancement, enlargement, exaggeration, expansion, extolment, heightening, increase, inflation, intensification, lionisation. *antonyms* diminution, reduction.

magnificence *n* brilliance, glory, gorgeousness, grandeur, grandiosity, impressiveness, luxuriousness, luxury, majesty, nobility, opulence, pomp, resplendence, splendour, stateliness, sublimity, sumptuousness. *antonyms* modesty, plainness, simplicity.

magnificent *adj* august, brilliant, elegant, elevated, exalted, excellent, fine, glorious, gorgeous, grand, grandiose, imposing, impressive, lavish, luxurious, majestic, noble, opulent, outstanding, plush, posh, princely, regal, resplendent, rich, ritzy, splendid, stately, sublime, sumptuous, superb, superior, transcendent. *antonyms* humble, modest, plain, simple.

magnify *v* aggrandise, aggravate, amplify, augment, blow up, boost, build up, deepen, dilate, dramatise, enhance, enlarge, exaggerate, expand, greaten, heighten, increase, inflate, intensify, lionise, overdo, overemphasise, overestimate, overplay, overrate, overstate, praise. *antonyms* belittle, play down.

magniloquent *adj* bombastic, declamatory, elevated, euphuistic, exalted, grandiloquent, high-flown, high-sounding, lofty, overblown, pompous, pretentious, rhetorical, sonorous, stilted, turgid. *antonyms* simple, straightforward.

magnitude *n* amount, amplitude, bigness, brightness, bulk, capacity, consequence, dimensions, eminence, enormousness, expanse, extent, grandeur, greatness, hugeness, immensity, importance, intensity, largeness, mass, measure, moment, note, proportions, quantity, significance, size, space, strength, vastness, volume, weight. *antonym* smallness.

maiden *n* damsel, demoiselle, girl, lass, lassie, maid, miss, nymph, virgin, wench.

adj chaste, female, first, fresh, inaugural, initial, initiatory, intact, introductory, new, pure, unbroached, uncaptured, undefiled, unmarried, unpolluted, untapped, untried, unused, unwed, virgin, virginal. *antonyms* defiled, deflowered, unchaste.

maim *v* cripple, disable, hack, hamstring, hurt, impair, incapacitate, injure, lame, mutilate, savage, wound. *antonyms* heal, repair.

main *adj* absolute, brute, capital, cardinal, central, chief, critical, crucial, direct, downright, entire, essential, extensive, first, foremost, general, great, head, leading, mere, necessary, outstanding, paramount, particular, predominant, pre-eminent, premier, primary, prime, principal, pure, sheer, special, staple, supreme, undisguised, utmost, utter, vital. *antonyms* minor, unimportant.

n effort, force, might, potency, power, strength, vigour. *antonym* weakness.

mainly *adv* above all, as a rule, chiefly, especially, for the most part, generally, in general, in the main, largely, mostly, on the whole, overall, predominantly, primarily, principally, substantially, usually.

mainspring *n* cause, driving force, fountainhead, generator, impulse, incentive, inspiration, motivation, motive, origin, prime mover, source.

mainstay *n* anchor, backbone, bulwark, buttress, linchpin, pillar, prop, support.

mainstream *adj* accepted, average, conventional, established, general, normal, orthodox, received, regular, standard. *antonyms* heterodox, peripheral.

maintain *v* advocate, affirm, allege, argue, assert, asseverate, aver, avow, back, care for, carry on, champion, claim, conserve, contend, continue, declare, defend, fight for, finance, hold, insist, justify, keep, keep up, look after, make good, nurture, observe, perpetuate, plead for, practise, preserve, profess, prolong, provide, retain, stand by, state, supply, support, sustain, take care of, uphold, vindicate. *antonyms* deny, neglect, oppose.

maintenance *n* alimony, allowance, care, conservation, continuance, continuation, defence, food, keep, keeping, livelihood, living, nurture, perpetuation, preservation, prolongation, protection, provision, repairs, retainment, subsistence, supply, support, sustainment, sustenance, upkeep. *antonym* neglect.

majestic *adj* august, awesome, dignified, distinguished, elevated, exalted, grand, grandiose, imperial, imperious, imposing, impressive, kingly, lofty, magisterial, magnificent, monumental, noble, pompous, princely, queenly, regal, royal, splendid, stately, sublime, superb. *antonyms* unimportant, unimpressive.

majesty *n* augustness, awesomeness, dignity, exaltedness, glory, grandeur,

impressiveness, kingliness, loftiness, magnificence, majesticness, nobility, pomp, queenliness, regalness, resplendence, royalty, splendour, state, stateliness, sublimity. *antonyms* unimportance, unimpressiveness.

major *adj* better, bigger, chief, critical, crucial, elder, grave, great, greater, higher, important, key, keynote, larger, leading, main, most, notable, older, outstanding, pre-eminent, radical, senior, serious, significant, superior, supreme, uppermost, vital, weighty. *antonym* minor.

majority *n* adulthood, bulk, manhood, mass, maturity, plurality, preponderance, seniority, superiority, the many, womanhood, years of discretion. *antonyms* childhood, minority.

make *v* accomplish, acquire, act, add up to, amount to, appoint, arrive at, assemble, assign, attain, beget, bring about, build, calculate, carry out, catch, cause, clear, coerce, compel, compose, conclude, constitute, constrain, construct, contract, contribute, convert, create, designate, do, dragoon, draw up, drive, earn, effect, elect, embody, enact, engage in, engender, establish, estimate, execute, fabricate, fashion, fix, flow, force, forge, form, frame, gain, gauge, generate, get, give rise to, impel, induce, install, invest, judge, lead to, manufacture, meet, mould, net, nominate, oblige, obtain, occasion, ordain, originate, pass, perform, practise, press, pressurise, prevail upon, proceed, produce, prosecute, put together, reach, reckon, render, require, secure, shape, suppose, synthesise, take in, tend, think, turn, win. *antonyms* dismantle, lose, persuade.

n brand, build, character, composition, constitution, construction, cut, designation, disposition, form, formation, humour, kind, make-up, manner, manufacture, mark, model, nature, shape, sort, stamp, structure, style, temper, temperament, texture, type, variety.

make believe act, dream, enact, fantasise, feign, imagine, play, play-act, pretend.

make do cope, get along, get by, improvise, make out, manage, muddle through, scrape by, survive.

make eyes at flirt, give (someone) the come-on, leer at, make sheep's eyes at, ogle.

make for aim for, conduce to, contribute

to, facilitate, favour, forward, further, head for, promote.

make fun of deride, lampoon, laugh at, make sport of, mock, parody, poke fun at, queer, quiz, rag, rib, ridicule, roast, rot, satirise, scoff at, send up, sneer at, take off, taunt. *antonym* praise.

make inroads into consume, eat away, eat into, eat up, encroach upon, get on with, make progress with, progress with. *antonym* add to.

make it arrive, come through, get on, prosper, pull through, reach, succeed, survive. *antonym* fail.

make love canoodle, copulate, cuddle, embrace, enjoy, fuck, go to bed, neck, pet, romance, screw, smooch.

make merry carouse, celebrate, feast, frolic, make whoopee, paint the town red, revel, whoop it up.

make no difference be six and half a dozen, count for nothing, cut no ice.

make off abscond, beat a hasty retreat, bolt, clear off, cut and run, decamp, depart, flee, fly, leave, make away, run away, run for it, run off, take to one's heels.

make off with abduct, appropriate, carry off, filch, kidnap, knock off, nab, nick, pilfer, pinch, purloin, run away, run off with, steal, swipe, walk off with. *antonym* bring.

make one's mark get on, make good, make it, make the big-time, prosper, succeed. *antonym* fail.

make out assert, claim, complete, comprehend, decipher, demonstrate, describe, descry, detect, discern, discover, distinguish, draw up, espy, fare, fathom, fill in, fill out, follow, get on, grasp, imply, infer, inscribe, let on, make as if, manage, perceive, pretend, prosper, prove, realise, recognise, represent, see, show, succeed, survive, thrive, understand, work out, write, write out. *antonym* fail.

make sense of apprehend, comprehend, fathom, figure out, grasp, make head or tail of, make much of, make out, understand.

make tracks beat it, dash, dash off, depart, disappear, go, hit the road, hurry, leave, make off, scram, set out, split, take off.

make up¹ arrange, coin, collect, complement, complete, compose, comprise, concoct, constitute, construct, cook up, create, devise, dream up, fabricate, feign, fill, form, formulate, frame, hatch, invent, meet, originate, parcel, put together, repair, supplement, supply, trump up, write.

make up² bury the hatchet, call it quits, come to terms, forgive and forget, make peace, mend one's fences, settle, settle differences, shake hands.

make up for atone for, balance, compensate, expiate, make amends for, offset, recompense, redeem, redress, requite.

make up one's mind choose, decide, determine, resolve, settle. *antonym* waver.

make up to butter up, chat up, court, curry favour with, fawn on, flirt with, make overtures to, toady to, woo.

make-believe *n* charade, dream, fantasy, imagination, play-acting, pretence, role-play, unreality. *antonym* reality.
adj dream, fantasised, fantasy, feigned, imaginary, imagined, made-up, mock, pretend, pretended, sham, simulated, unreal. *antonym* real.

maker *n* architect, author, builder, constructor, contriver, creator, director, fabricator, manufacturer, producer. *antonym* dismantler.

makeshift *adj* band-aid, expedient, improvised, make-do, provisional, rough and ready, stop-gap, substitute, temporary. *antonyms* finished, permanent.
n band-aid, expedient, fig-leaf, shift, stop-gap, substitute.

make-up *n* arrangement, assembly, build, cast, character, complexion, composition, configuration, constitution, construction, disposition, figure, form, format, formation, make, nature, organisation, stamp, structure, style, temper, temperament.

makings *n* beginnings, capability, capacity, earnings, income, ingredients, materials, possibilities, potential, potentiality, proceeds, profits, promise, qualities, returns, revenue, takings.

malady *n* affliction, ailment, breakdown, complaint, disease, disorder, illness, indisposition, infirmity, malaise, sickness. *antonym* health.

malaise *n* angst, anguish, anxiety, depression, discomfort, disquiet, distemper, doldrums, future shock, illness, indisposition, lassitude, melancholy, sickness, unease, uneasiness, weakness. *antonyms* happiness, well-being.

malcontent *adj* belly-aching,

disaffected, discontented, disgruntled, dissatisfied, dissentious, factious, ill-disposed, morose, rebellious, resentful, restive, unhappy, unsatisfied. *antonym* contented.

n agitator, belly-acher, complainer, grouch, grouser, grumbler, mischief-maker, moaner, rebel, troublemaker.

male *adj* bull, cock, dog, manlike, manly, masculine, virile. *antonym* female.

n boy, bull, cock, daddy, dog, father, man. *antonym* female.

malediction *n* curse, damnation, damning, denunciation, execration, imprecation. *antonyms* blessing, praise.

malefactor *n* convict, criminal, crook, culprit, delinquent, evil-doer, felon, law-breaker, miscreant, offender, outlaw, transgressor, villain, wrong-doer.

malevolence *n* bitterness, hate, hatred, hostility, ill-will, malice, maliciousness, malignance, malignancy, malignity, rancour, spite, spitefulness, vengefulness, venom, viciousness, vindictiveness. *antonym* benevolence.

malevolent *adj* baleful, bitter, despiteful, evil-minded, hostile, ill-natured, malicious, malign, malignant, pernicious, rancorous, spiteful, vengeful, venomous, vicious, vindictive. *antonym* benevolent.

malformation *n* crookedness, deformity, distortion, irregularity, misshape, misshapenness, warp, warpedness, warping.

malformed *adj* abnormal, bent, contorted, crooked, deformed, distorted, imperfect, irregular, misshapen, twisted, warped. *antonym* perfect.

malfunction *n* breakdown, defect, failure, fault, flaw, glitch.

v break down, fail, go wrong, misbehave.

malice *n* animosity, animus, bad blood, bitterness, enmity, hate, hatred, ill-will, malevolence, maliciousness, malignity, rancour, spite, spitefulness, spleen, vengefulness, venom, viciousness, vindictiveness. *antonym* kindness.

malicious *adj* baleful, bitchy, bitter, catty, despiteful, evil-minded, hateful, ill-natured, injurious, malevolent, malignant, mischievous, pernicious, rancorous, resentful, sham, spiteful, vengeful, venomous, vicious. *antonyms* kind, thoughtful.

malign *adj* bad, baleful, baneful, deleterious, destructive, evil, harmful,

hostile, hurtful, injurious, malevolent, malignant, noxious, pernicious, venomous, vicious, wicked. *antonym* benign.

v abuse, badmouth, blacken the name of, calumniate, defame, denigrate, derogate, disparage, harm, injure, libel, revile, run down, slander, smear, traduce, vilify. *antonym* praise.

malignant *adj* baleful, bitter, cancerous, cankered, dangerous, deadly, destructive, devilish, evil, fatal, harmful, hostile, hurtful, inimical, injurious, irremediable, malevolent, malicious, malign, pernicious, spiteful, uncontrollable, venomous, vicious, viperish, viperous, virulent. *antonyms* harmless, kind.

malignity *n* animosity, animus, bad blood, balefulness, bitterness, deadliness, destructiveness, gall, harmfulness, hate, hatred, hostility, hurtfulness, ill-will, malevolence, malice, maliciousness, perniciousness, rancour, spite, vengefulness, venom, viciousness, vindictiveness, virulence, wickedness. *antonyms* harmlessness, kindness.

malinger *v* dodge, loaf, shirk, skive, slack, swing the lead. *antonym* toil.

malingerer *n* dodger, lead-swinger, loafer, shirker, skiver, slacker. *antonym* toiler.

malleable *adj* adaptable, biddable, compliant, ductile, governable, impressionable, manageable, plastic, pliable, pliant, soft, tractable, tractile, workable. *antonyms* intractable, unworkable.

malodorous *adj* evil-smelling, fetid, foul-smelling, nauseating, niffy, offensive, putrid, rank, reeking, smelly, stinking. *antonym* sweet-smelling.

malpractice *n* abuse, dereliction, malversation, misbehaviour, misconduct, misdeed, mismanagement, negligence, offence, transgression.

mammoth *adj* colossal, enormous, formidable, gargantuan, giant, gigantic, herculean, huge, immense, leviathan, massive, mighty, monumental, mountainous, prodigious, stupendous, titanic, vast. *antonym* small.

man *n* adult, attendant, beau, bloke, body, boyfriend, cat, chap, employee, fellow, follower, gentleman, guy, hand, hireling, hombre, human, human being, husband, individual, lover, male, manservant, partner, person, retainer, servant, soldier, spouse, subject, subordinate, valet, vassal, worker, workman.

v crew, fill, garrison, occupy, operate, people, staff, take charge of.

manacle *v* bind, chain, check, clap in irons, confine, constrain, curb, fetter, hamper, hamstring, handcuff, inhibit, put in chains, restrain, shackle, trammel. **antonym** unshackle.

manage *v* accomplish, administer, arrange, bring about, bring off, carry on, command, concert, conduct, contrive, control, cope, cope with, deal with, direct, dominate, effect, engineer, fare, get along, get by, get on, govern, guide, handle, influence, make do, make out, manipulate, muddle through, operate, oversee, pilot, ply, preside over, rule, run, shift, solicit, stage-manage, steer, succeed, superintend, supervise, survive, train, use, wield. **antonym** fail.

manageable *adj* amenable, biddable, compliant, controllable, convenient, docile, easy, governable, handy, submissive, tamable, tractable, wieldable, wieldy. **antonym** unmanageable.

management *n* administration, board, bosses, care, charge, command, conduct, control, direction, directorate, directors, employers, executive, executives, governance, government, governors, guidance, handling, managers, manipulation, operation, oversight, rule, running, stewardry, superintendence, supervision, supervisors.

manager *n* administrator, boss, conductor, controller, director, executive, gaffer, governor, head, organiser, overseer, proprietor, steward, superintendent, supervisor.

mandate *n* authorisation, authority, bidding, charge, command, commission, decree, directive, edict, fiat, injunction, instruction, order, precept, right, sanction, warrant.

mandatory *adj* binding, compulsory, imperative, necessary, obligatory, required, requisite. **antonym** optional.

manful *adj* bold, brave, courageous, daring, determined, gallant, hardy, heroic, indomitable, intrepid, lion-hearted, manly, noble, noble-minded, powerful, resolute, stalwart, stout, stout-hearted, strong, unflinching, valiant, vigorous. **antonyms** half-hearted, timid.

mangle *v* butcher, crush, cut, deform, destroy, disfigure, distort, hack, lacerate, maim, mar, maul, mutilate, rend, ruin, spoil, tear, twist, wreck.

mangy *adj* dirty, grotty, mean, moth-eaten, ratty, scabby, scruffy, seedy, shabby, shoddy, squalid, tatty. **antonyms** clean, neat, spruce.

manhandle *v* carry, haul, heave, hump, knock about, lift, maltreat, manoeuvre, maul, mishandle, mistreat, misuse, paw, pull, push, rough up, shove, tug.

manhood *n* adulthood, bravery, courage, determination, firmness, fortitude, hardihood, machismo, manfulness, manliness, masculinity, maturity, mettle, resolution, spirit, strength, valour, virility. **antonym** timidity.

mania *n* aberration, compulsion, craving, craze, craziness, delirium, dementia, derangement, desire, disorder, enthusiasm, fad, fetish, fixation, frenzy, infatuation, insanity, itch, lunacy, madness, obsession, partiality, passion, preoccupation, rage, thing.

maniac *n* enthusiast, fan, fanatic, fiend, freak, fruit-cake, loony, lunatic, madman, madwoman, nutcase, nutter, psycho, psychopath.

manic *adj* berserk, crazed, crazy, demented, deranged, frenzied, insane, lunatic, mad, maniacal, psychotic, raving, screwy, unbalanced, unhinged, wild. **antonym** sane.

manifest *adj* apparent, clear, conspicuous, distinct, evident, glaring, noticeable, obvious, open, palpable, patent, plain, unconcealed, undeniable, unmistakable, visible. **antonym** unclear.

v demonstrate, display, establish, evidence, evince, exhibit, expose, illustrate, prove, reveal, set forth, show. **antonym** hide.

manifestation *n* appearance, demonstration, disclosure, display, exhibition, exposure, expression, indication, instance, mark, mass-meeting, materialisation, procession, reflex, revelation, show, sign, sit-in, symptom, token.

manifold *adj* abundant, assorted, copious, diverse, diversified, kaleidoscopic, many, multifarious, multifold, multiple, multiplex, multiplied, multitudinous, numerous, varied, various. **antonym** simple.

manipulate *v* conduct, control, cook, direct, employ, engineer, gerrymander, guide, handle, influence, juggle with, manoeuvre, negotiate, operate, ply, shuffle, steer, use, wield, work.

mankind *n* Everyman, fellow-men, Homo sapiens, human race, humanity, humankind, man, people.

manliness *n* boldness, bravery, courage, fearlessness, firmness, hardihood, heroism, independence, intrepidity, machismo, manfulness, manhood, masculinity, mettle, resolution, stalwartness, stout-heartedness, valour, vigour, virility. **antonyms** timidity, unmanliness.

manly *adj* bold, brave, courageous, daring, dauntless, fearless, gallant, hardy, heroic, macho, male, manful, masculine, muscular, noble, powerful, resolute, robust, stalwart, stout-hearted, strapping, strong, sturdy, valiant, vigorous, virile. **antonyms** timid, unmanly.

man-made *adj* artificial, ersatz, imitation, manufactured, simulated, synthetic. **antonym** natural.

manner *n* address, air, appearance, approach, aspect, bearing, behaviour, brand, breed, category, character, comportment, conduct, custom, demeanour, deportment, description, fashion, form, genre, habit, kind, line, look, means, method, mien, mode, nature, practice, presence, procedure, process, routine, sort, style, tack, tenor, tone, type, usage, variety, way, wise, wont.

mannered *adj* affected, artificial, euphuistic, posed, precious, pretentious, pseudo, put-on, stilted. **antonym** natural.

mannerism *n* characteristic, feature, foible, habit, idiosyncrasy, peculiarity, quirk, stiltedness, trait, trick.

mannerly *adj* civil, civilised, courteous, decorous, deferential, formal, genteel, gentlemanly, gracious, ladylike, polished, polite, refined, respectful, well-behaved, well-bred, well-mannered. **antonym** unmannerly.

manners *n* bearing, behaviour, breeding, carriage, ceremony, comportment, conduct, courtesy, decorum, demeanour, deportment, etiquette, formalities, mores, polish, politeness, politesse, proprieties, protocol, p's and q's, refinement, social graces. **antonyms** impoliteness, indecorousness.

manoeuvre *n* action, artifice, device, dodge, exercise, gambit, intrigue, machination, move, movement, operation, plan, plot, ploy, ruse, scheme, stratagem, subterfuge, tactic, trick.

v contrive, deploy, devise, direct, drive, engineer, exercise, guide, handle, intrigue, jockey, machinate, manage, manipulate, move, navigate, negotiate, pilot, plan, plot, pull strings, scheme, steer, wangle.

mansion *n* abode, big house, castle, château, dwelling, habitation, hall, home, house, manor, manor-house, residence, schloss, seat, villa.

mantle *n* blanket, canopy, cape, cloak, cloud, cover, covering, curtain, envelope, hood, screen, shawl, shroud, veil, wrap.

manual[1] *n* bible, companion, guide, guide-book, handbook, instructions, primer.

manual[2] *adj* hand, hand-operated, human, physical.

manufacture *v* assemble, build, churn out, compose, concoct, construct, cook up, create, devise, fabricate, forge, form, hatch, invent, make, make up, mass-produce, mould, process, produce, shape, think up, trump up, turn out.

n assembly, construction, creation, fabrication, facture, formation, making, mass-production, production.

many *adj* abundant, copious, countless, divers, frequent, innumerable, manifold, multifarious, multifold, multitudinous, myriad, n, numerous, profuse, sundry, umpteen, varied, various. **antonym** few.

mar *v* blemish, blight, blot, damage, deface, detract from, disfigure, foul up, harm, hurt, impair, injure, maim, mangle, mutilate, pollute, ruin, scar, spoil, stain, sully, taint, tarnish, temper, vitiate, wreck. **antonym** enhance.

march *v* file, flounce, goose-step, pace, parade, slog, stalk, stride, strut, stump, tramp, tread, walk.

n advance, career, demo, demonstration, development, evolution, footslog, gait, hike, pace, parade, passage, procession, progress, progression, step, stride, tramp, trek, walk.

margin *n* allowance, border, bound, boundary, brim, brink, compass, confine, edge, extra, latitude, leeway, limit, marge, perimeter, periphery, play, rim, room, scope, side, skirt, space, surplus, verge. **antonyms** centre, core.

marginal *adj* bordering, borderline, doubtful, infinitesimal, insignificant, low, minimal, minor, negligible, peripheral, slight, small. **antonyms** central, core.

marijuana n bhang, cannabis, dope, ganja, grass, hash, hashish, hemp, keif, mary jane, pot, tea, weed.

marine adj maritime, nautical, naval, ocean-going, oceanic, salt-water, sea, seafaring, sea-going.

marital adj conjugal, connubial, married, matrimonial, nuptial, wedded.

mark n aim, badge, blaze, blemish, blot, blotch, brand, bruise, character, characteristic, consequence, criterion, dent, device, dignity, distinction, earmark, emblem, eminence, end, evidence, fame, feature, fingermark, footmark, footprint, goal, hallmark, importance, impression, incision, index, indication, influence, label, level, line, marque, measure, nick, norm, notability, note, noteworthiness, notice, object, objective, pock, prestige, print, proof, purpose, quality, regard, scar, scratch, seal, sign, smudge, splotch, spot, stain, stamp, standard, standing, streak, symbol, symptom, target, token, trace, track, trail, vestige, yardstick.
v appraise, assess, attend, betoken, blemish, blot, blotch, brand, bruise, characterise, colour-code, correct, denote, dent, distinguish, evaluate, evince, exemplify, grade, hearken, heed, identify, illustrate, impress, imprint, label, list, listen, mind, nick, note, notice, observe, print, regard, remark, scar, scratch, show, smudge, splotch, stain, stamp, streak, take to heart, traumatise, watch.

marked adj apparent, clear, considerable, conspicuous, decided, distinct, doomed, emphatic, evident, glaring, indicated, manifest, notable, noted, noticeable, obvious, outstanding, patent, prominent, pronounced, remarkable, salient, signal, striking, strong, suspected, watched. **antonyms** slight, unnoticeable.

maroon v abandon, cast away, desert, isolate, leave, put ashore, strand. **antonym** rescue.

marriage n alliance, amalgamation, association, confederation, coupling, espousal, link, match, matrimony, merger, nuptials, union, wedding, wedlock. **antonym** divorce.

married adj conjugal, connubial, hitched, joined, marital, matrimonial, nuptial, spliced, united, wed, wedded, yoked. **antonyms** divorced, single.

marrow n core, cream, essence, gist, heart, kernel, nub, pith, quick, quintessence, soul, spirit, stuff, substance.

marry v ally, bond, espouse, get hitched, get spliced, join, jump the broomstick, knit, link, match, merge, splice, tie, tie the knot, unify, unite, wed, yoke. **antonyms** divorce, separate.

marshal v align, arrange, array, assemble, collect, conduct, convoy, deploy, dispose, draw up, escort, gather, group, guide, lead, line up, muster, order, organise, rank, shepherd, take, usher.

marvel n genius, miracle, phenomenon, portent, prodigy, sensation, spectacle, whiz, wonder.
v gape, gaze, goggle, wonder.

marvellous adj amazing, astonishing, astounding, beyond belief, breathtaking, excellent, extraordinary, fabulous, fantastic, glorious, great, hell of a, implausible, improbable, incredible, magnificent, miraculous, phenomenal, prodigious, remarkable, sensational, singular, smashing, spectacular, splendid, stupendous, super, superb, surprising, terrific, unbelievable, unlikely, wonderful, wondrous. **antonyms** ordinary, plausible, run-of-the-mill.

masculine adj bold, brave, butch, gallant, hardy, macho, male, manlike, manly, mannish, muscular, powerful, red-blooded, resolute, robust, stout-hearted, strapping, strong, tomboyish, vigorous, virile. **antonym** feminine.

masculinity n butchness, maleness, manhood, manliness, mannishness, potency, sexuality, tomboyishness, virility. **antonym** femininity.

mash v beat, champ, crush, grind, pound, pulverise, pummel, smash.

mask n blind, camouflage, cloak, concealment, cover, cover-up, disguise, façade, false face, front, guise, pretence, screen, semblance, show, veil, veneer, visor.
v camouflage, cloak, conceal, cover, disguise, hide, obscure, screen, shield, veil. **antonym** uncover.

masked adj camouflaged, cloaked, concealed, covered, disguised, screened, shielded, shrouded, visored. **antonyms** uncovered, unshielded.

masquerade n cloak, costume, costume ball, counterfeit, cover, cover-up, deception, disguise, dissimulation, fancy dress party, front, guise, mask, masked ball, masque, mummery, pose, pretence, put-on, revel, screen, subterfuge.

v disguise, dissemble, dissimulate, impersonate, mask, pass oneself off, play, pose, pretend, profess.

mass¹ *n* accumulation, aggregate, aggregation, assemblage, band, batch, block, body, bulk, bunch, chunk, collection, combination, concretion, conglomeration, crowd, dimension, entirety, extensity, group, heap, horde, host, hunk, lion's share, load, lot, lump, magnitude, majority, mob, number, piece, pile, preponderance, quantity, size, stack, sum, sum total, throng, totality, troop, welter, whole.

adj across-the-board, blanket, comprehensive, extensive, general, indiscriminate, large-scale, pandemic, popular, sweeping, wholesale, widespread. *antonym* limited.

v assemble, cluster, collect, congregate, crowd, for(e)gather, gather, muster, rally. *antonym* separate.

mass² *n* communion, eucharist, holy communion, Lord's Supper, Lord's Table.

massacre *n* annihilation, blood bath, butchery, carnage, decimation, extermination, holocaust, killing, murder, slaughter.

v annihilate, butcher, decimate, exterminate, kill, mow down, murder, slaughter, slay, wipe out.

massive *adj* big, bulky, colossal, enormous, extensive, gargantuan, gigantic, great, heavy, hefty, huge, hulking, immense, imposing, impressive, jumbo, mammoth, monster, monstrous, monumental, ponderous, solid, substantial, titanic, vast, weighty, whacking, whopping. *antonyms* slight, small.

master *n* ace, adept, boss, captain, chief, commander, controller, dab hand, director, doyen, employer, expert, genius, governor, guide, guru, head, instructor, lord, maestro, manager, overlord, overseer, owner, past master, principal, pro, ruler, skipper, superintendent, teacher, tutor, virtuoso, wizard. *antonyms* amateur, learner, pupil, servant, slave.

adj ace, adept, chief, controlling, crack, expert, foremost, grand, great, leading, main, masterly, predominant, prime, principal, proficient, skilful, skilled. *antonyms* copy, subordinate, unskilled.

v acquire, bridle, check, command, conquer, control, curb, defeat, direct, dominate, get the hang of, govern,

grasp, learn, manage, overcome, quash, quell, regulate, rule, subdue, subjugate, suppress, tame, triumph over, vanquish.

masterful *adj* adept, adroit, arrogant, authoritative, autocratic, bossy, clever, consummate, crack, deft, despotic, dexterous, dictatorial, domineering, excellent, expert, exquisite, fine, finished, first-rate, high-handed, imperious, magisterial, masterly, overbearing, overweening, peremptory, powerful, professional, self-willed, skilful, skilled, superior, superlative, supreme, tyrannical. *antonyms* clumsy, humble, unskilful.

masterly *adj* adept, adroit, clever, consummate, crack, dexterous, excellent, expert, exquisite, fine, finished, first-rate, magistral, masterful, skilful, skilled, superb, superior, superlative, supreme. *antonyms* clumsy, poor, unskilled.

mastermind *v* conceive, design, devise, direct, dream up, forge, hatch, manage, organise, originate, plan.

n architect, authority, brain(s), creator, director, engineer, genius, intellect, manager, organiser, originator, planner, prime mover, virtuoso.

mastery *n* ability, acquirement, advantage, ascendancy, attainment, authority, cleverness, command, comprehension, conquest, control, conversancy, deftness, dexterity, domination, dominion, expertise, familiarity, finesse, grasp, know-how, knowledge, pre-eminence, proficiency, prowess, rule, skill, superiority, supremacy, sway, triumph, understanding, upper hand, victory, virtuosity, whip-hand. *antonyms* clumsiness, unfamiliarity.

masturbate *v* frig, jerk off, play with oneself, toss off, wank.

match¹ *n* bout, competition, contest, game, main, test, trial, venue.

v compete, contend, oppose, pit against, rival, vie.

match² *n* affiliation, alliance, combination, companion, complement, copy, counterpart, couple, dead ringer, double, duet, duplicate, equal, equivalent, fellow, like, look-alike, marriage, mate, pair, pairing, parallel, partnership, peer, replica, ringer, rival, spit, spitting image, tally, twin, union.

v accompany, accord, adapt, agree, ally, blend, combine, compare, co-ordinate, correspond, couple, emulate, equal, fit, gee, go together, go with, harmonise, join, link, marry, mate, measure up to, pair, relate, rival, suit, tally, team, tone with, unite, yoke. **antonyms** clash, separate.

matching *adj* analogous, comparable, co-ordinating, corresponding, double, duplicate, equal, equivalent, identical, like, parallel, same, similar, toning, twin. **antonyms** clashing, different.

matchless *adj* consummate, excellent, exquisite, incomparable, inimitable, peerless, perfect, superlative, supreme, unequalled, unique, unmatched, unparalleled, unrivalled, unsurpassed. **antonyms** commonplace, poor.

mate *n* assistant, associate, better half, buddy, china, chum, colleague, companion, comrade, confidant(e), co-worker, crony, double, fellow, fellow-worker, friend, gossip, helper, helpmate, husband, match, pal, partner, side-kick, spouse, subordinate, twin, wife.
v breed, copulate, couple, join, marry, match, pair, wed, yoke.

material *n* body, cloth, constituents, data, element, evidence, fabric, facts, information, literature, matter, notes, stuff, substance, textile, work.
adj applicable, apposite, bodily, central, concrete, consequential, corporeal, essential, fleshly, germane, grave, important, indispensable, key, meaningful, momentous, non-spiritual, palpable, pertinent, physical, relevant, serious, significant, substantial, tangible, vital, weighty, worldly. **antonyms** ethereal, immaterial.

materialise *v* appear, arise, happen, occur, take shape, turn up. **antonym** disappear.

materially *adv* basically, considerably, essentially, fundamentally, gravely, greatly, much, palpably, physically, seriously, significantly, substantially, tangibly. **antonym** insignificantly.

matrimonial *adj* conjugal, connubial, marital, marriage, married, nuptial, wedded, wedding.

matted *adj* knotted, tangled, tangly, tousled, uncombed. **antonyms** tidy, untangled.

matter *n* affair, amount, argument, body, business, complication, concern, consequence, context, difficulty, distress, episode, event, import, importance, incident, issue, material, moment, note, occurrence, problem, proceeding, purport, quantity, question, sense, significance, situation, stuff, subject, substance, sum, text, thesis,

thing, topic, transaction, trouble, upset, weight, worry. **antonym** insignificance.
v count, make a difference, mean something, signify.

matter-of-fact *adj* deadpan, direct, down-to-earth, dry, dull, emotionless, flat, lifeless, literal, mundane, plain, prosaic, sober, unembellished, unimaginative, unsentimental, unvarnished. **antonym** emotional.

mature *adj* adult, complete, due, fit, full-blown, full-grown, fully fledged, grown, grown-up, matured, mellow, nubile, perfect, perfected, prepared, ready, ripe, ripened, seasoned, well-thought-out. **antonym** immature.
v age, bloom, come of age, develop, fall due, grow up, maturate, mellow, perfect, ripen, season.

maturity *n* adulthood, completion, experience, fullness, majority, manhood, maturation, nubility, perfection, readiness, ripeness, wisdom, womanhood. **antonym** immaturity.

maudlin *adj* drunk, emotional, fuddled, half-drunk, lachrymose, mawkish, mushy, sentimental, sickly, slushy, soppy, tearful, tipsy, weepy. **antonym** matter-of-fact.

maul *v* abuse, batter, beat, beat up, claw, ill-treat, knock about, lacerate, maltreat, mangle, manhandle, molest, paw, pummel, rough up, thrash.

mawkish *adj* emotional, feeble, gushy, insipid, maudlin, mushy, nauseous, schmaltzy, sentimental, sickly, slushy, soppy. **antonyms** matter-of-fact, pleasant.

maxim *n* adage, aphorism, apophthegm, axiom, byword, epigram, gnome, motto, precept, proverb, rule, saying, sentence.

maximum *adj* biggest, greatest, highest, largest, maximal, most, paramount, supreme, topmost, utmost. **antonym** minimum.
n apogee, ceiling, crest, extremity, height, most, peak, pinnacle, summit, top (point), upper limit, utmost, zenith. **antonym** mimimum.

meagre *adj* barren, bony, deficient, emaciated, gaunt, hungry, inadequate, insubstantial, lank, lean, little, negligible, paltry, penurious, poor, puny, scanty, scraggy, scrawny, scrimpy, short, skimpy, skinny, slender, slight, small, spare, sparse, starved, thin, underfed, weak. **antonym** substantial.

meal *n* banquet, barbecue, beanfeast, beano, blow-out, breakfast, brunch, collation, dinner, feast, lunch, luncheon, nosh, nosh-up, picnic, repast, scoff, snack, spread, supper, tea, tiffin(g), tuck-in.

mean¹ *adj* abject, bad-tempered, base, base-born, beggarly, callous, cheese-paring, churlish, close, close-fisted, close-handed, common, contemptible, degraded, despicable, disagreeable, disgraceful, dishonourable, down-at-heel, excellent, fast-handed, good, great, hard-hearted, hostile, humble, ignoble, illiberal, inconsiderable, inferior, insignificant, low, low-born, lowly, malicious, malignant, mean-spirited, menial, mercenary, mingy, miserable, miserly, modest, narrow-minded, nasty, near, niggardly, obscure, one-horse, ordinary, paltry, parsimonious, penny-pinching, penurious, petty, plebeian, poor, proletarian, rude, run-down, scrub, scurvy, seedy, selfish, servile, shabby, shameful, skilful, slink, small-minded, sordid, sour, squalid, stingy, tawdry, tight, tight-fisted, undistinguished, unfriendly, ungenerous, ungiving, unpleasant, vicious, vile, vulgar, wretched. *antonyms* generous, kind, noble, superior.

mean² *v* aim, aspire, augur, betoken, cause, connote, contemplate, convey, denote, design, desire, destine, drive at, engender, entail, express, fate, foreshadow, foretell, get at, give rise to, herald, hint, imply, indicate, insinuate, intend, involve, lead to, make, match, necessitate, omen, plan, portend, predestine, preordain, presage, produce, promise, propose, purport, purpose, represent, result in, say, set out, signify, spell, stand for, suggest, suit, symbolise, want, wish.

mean³ *adj* average, half-way, intermediate, medial, median, medium, middle, middling, moderate, normal, standard. *antonym* extreme.
n average, balance, compromise, golden mean, happy medium, middle, middle course, middle way, mid-point, norm. *antonym* extreme.

meandering *adj* circuitous, convoluted, indirect, roundabout, serpentine, sinuous, snaking, tortuous, twisting, wandering, winding. *antonym* straight.

meaning *n* aim, connotation, construction, denotation, design, drift, end, explanation, force, gist, goal, idea, implication, import, intention, interpretation, matter, message, object,

plan, point, purpose, sense, significance, signification, substance, thrust, trend, upshot, validity, value, worth.

meaningful *adj* eloquent, expressive, important, material, pointed, pregnant, purposeful, relevant, serious, significant, speaking, suggestive, useful, valid, warning, worthwhile.

meaningless *adj* absurd, aimless, empty, expressionless, futile, hollow, inane, inconsequential, insignificant, insubstantial, nonsense, nonsensical, pointless, purposeless, senseless, trifling, trivial, useless, vain, valueless, worthless. *antonym* meaningful.

means *n* ability, affluence, agency, avenue, capacity, capital, channel, course, estate, expedient, fortune, funds, income, instrument, machinery, measure, medium, method, money, process, property, resources, riches, substance, way, wealth, wherewithal.

meantime, meanwhile *advs* at the same time, concurrently, for now, for the moment, in the interim, in the interval, in the meantime, in the meanwhile, simultaneously.

measly *adj* beggarly, contemptible, meagre, mean, mingy, miserable, miserly, niggardly, paltry, pathetic, petty, piddling, pitiful, poor, puny, scanty, skimpy, stingy, trivial, ungenerous.

measurable *adj* appreciable, assessable, computable, determinable, fathomable, gaugeable, material, perceptible, quantifiable, quantitative, significant. *antonym* measureless.

measure *n* act, action, allotment, allowance, amount, amplitude, beat, bill, bounds, cadence, capacity, control, course, criterion, deed, degree, enactment, example, expedient, extent, foot, gauge, law, limit, limitation, magnitude, manoeuvre, means, method, metre, model, moderation, norm, portion, procedure, proceeding, proportion, quantity, quota, range, ration, reach, resolution, restraint, rhythm, rule, scale, scope, share, size, standard, statute, step, system, test, touchstone, verse, yardstick.
v appraise, assess, calculate, calibrate, choose, compute, determine, estimate, evaluate, fathom, gauge, judge, mark out, measure off, measure out, plumb, quantify, rate, size, sound, step, survey, value, weigh.

measure off circumscribe, delimit, demarcate, determine, fix, lay down, lay off, limit, mark out, measure (out), pace out.

measure out allot, apportion, assign, deal out, dispense, distribute, divide, dole out, hand out, issue, measure (off), mete out, parcel out, pour out, proportion, share out.

measure up do, fill/fit the bill, make the grade, pass muster, shape up, suffice.

measure up to compare with, equal, match, meet, rival, touch.

measured *adj* calculated, considered, constant, deliberate, dignified, even, exact, gauged, grave, leisurely, metronomic, modulated, planned, precise, predetermined, premeditated, quantified, reasoned, regular, regulated, sedate, slow, sober, solemn, standard, stately, steady, studied, unhurried, uniform, verified, well-thought-out.

measureless *adj* bottomless, boundless, endless, immeasurable, immense, incalculable, inestimable, infinite, innumerable, limitless, unbounded, vast. **antonym** measurable.

measurement *n* amount, amplitude, appraisal, appreciation, area, assessment, calculation, calibration, capacity, computation, depth, dimension, estimation, evaluation, extent, gauging, height, judgement, length, magnitude, size, survey, valuation, volume, weight, width.

meat¹ *n* aliment, cheer, chow, eats, fare, flesh, food, grub, nourishment, nutriment, provender, provisions, rations, subsistence, sustenance, victuals.

meat² *n* core, crux, essence, fundamentals, gist, heart, kernel, marrow, nub, nucleus, pith, point, substance.

meaty *adj* beefy, brawny, burly, fleshy, hearty, heavy, husky, interesting, matterful, meaningful, muscular, nourishing, pithy, profound, rich, significant, solid, strapping, sturdy, substantial.

mechanical *adj* automated, automatic, cold, cursory, dead, dull, emotionless, habitual, impersonal, instinctive, involuntary, lack-lustre, lifeless, machine-driven, machine-like, matter-of-fact, perfunctory, routine, spiritless, unanimated, unconscious, unfeeling, unthinking.

mechanism *n* action, agency, apparatus, appliance, components, contrivance, device, execution, functioning, gadgetry, gears, instrument, machine, machinery,

means, medium, method, motor, operation, performance, procedure, process, structure, system, technique, tool, workings, works.

medal *n* award, decoration, gong, honour, medallion, prize, reward, trophy.

meddle *v* interfere, interlope, interpose, intervene, intrude, pry, put one's oar in, tamper.

meddlesome *adj* interfering, intruding, intrusive, meddling, mischievous, prying.

mediate *v* arbitrate, conciliate, intercede, interpose, intervene, moderate, negotiate, reconcile, referee, resolve, settle, step in, umpire.

mediation *n* arbitration, conciliation, good offices, intercession, interposition, intervention, negotiation, parley, reconciliation.

medicinal *adj* curative, healing, medical, remedial, restorative, therapeutic.

mediocre *adj* amateurish, average, commonplace, indifferent, inferior, insignificant, mean, medium, middling, ordinary, passable, pedestrian, run-of-the-mill, second-rate, so-so, undistinguished, unexceptional, uninspired. **antonyms** excellent, exceptional, extraordinary.

mediocrity *n* amateurishness, indifference, inferiority, insignificance, lightweight, ordinariness, poorness, unimportance.

meditate *v* cerebrate, cogitate, consider, contemplate, deliberate, devise, excogitate, mull over, muse, ponder, reflect, ruminate, speculate, study, think, think over.

meditation *n* cerebration, cogitation, concentration, contemplation, excogitation, musing, pondering, reflection, reverie, ruminating, rumination, speculation, study, thought.

meditative *adj* cogitative, contemplative, deliberative, museful, pensive, reflective, ruminative, studious, thoughtful.

medium¹ *adj* average, fair, intermediate, mean, medial, median, mediocre, middle, middling, midway, standard.
n average, centre, compromise, golden mean, happy medium, mean, middle, middle ground, midpoint, way.

medium² *n* agency, avenue, base, channel, excipient, form, instrument, instrumentality, means, organ, vehicle, way.

medium³ *n* ambience, atmosphere, circumstances, conditions, element, environment, habitat, influences, milieu, setting, surroundings.

medley *n* assortment, collection, confusion, conglomeration, hodge-podge, hotchpotch, jumble, mélange, miscellany, mishmash, mixture, patchwork, pot-pourri.

meek *adj* acquiescent, compliant, deferential, docile, forbearing, gentle, humble, long-suffering, mild, modest, patient, peaceful, resigned, slavish, soft, spineless, spiritless, subdued, submissive, tame, timid, unambitious, unassuming, unpretentious, unresisting, weak, yielding. **antonyms** arrogant, rebellious.

meekness *n* acquiescence, compliance, deference, docility, forbearance, gentleness, humbleness, humility, long-suffering, lowliness, mildness, modesty, patience, peacefulness, resignation, self-abasement, self-disparagement, self-effacement, softness, spinelessness, spiritlessness, submission, submissiveness, tameness, timidity, weakness. **antonym** arrogance.

meet *v* abut, adjoin, answer, assemble, bear, bump into, chance on, collect, come across, come together, comply, confront, congregate, connect, contact, convene, converge, cross, discharge, encounter, endure, equal, experience, face, find, forgather, fulfil, gather, go through, gratify, handle, happen on, intersect, join, link up, match, measure up to, muster, perform, rally, run across, run into, satisfy, suffer, touch, undergo, unite.

meeting *n* abutment, assembly, assignation, audience, company, conclave, concourse, conference, confluence, confrontation, congregation, conjunction, consult, convention, convergence, convocation, crossing, encounter, engagement, forum, gathering, get-together, intersection, introduction, junction, meet, moot, rally, rendezvous, reunion, session, synod, tryst, union.

meeting-point *n* confluence, convergence, convergency, crossroads, interface, intersection, junction.

melancholy *adj* blue, dejected, depressed, despondent, disconsolate, dismal, dispirited, doleful, down, down in the dumps, down in the mouth, downcast, down-hearted, gloomy, glum, heavy-hearted, joyless, low, low-spirited, lugubrious, melancholic, miserable, moody, mournful, pensive, sad, sombre, sorrowful, unhappy, woebegone, woeful. **antonyms** cheerful, gay, happy, joyful.

n blues, dejection, depression, despondency, dole, dolour, gloom, gloominess, glumness, low spirits, pensiveness, sadness, sorrow, unhappiness, woe. **antonym** exhilaration.

mélange *n* assortment, confusion, hash, hodge-podge, hotch-potch, jumble, medley, miscellany, mishmash, mix, mixed bag, mixture, pot-pourri.

mêlée *n* affray, battle royal, brawl, broil, dogfight, fight, fracas, fray, free-for-all, ruckus, ruction, rumpus, scrimmage, scrum, scuffle, set-to, tussle.

mellifluous *adj* dulcet, euphonious, honeyed, mellow, silvery, smooth, soft, soothing, sweet, sweet-sounding, tuneful. **antonyms** discordant, grating, harsh.

mellow *adj* cheerful, cordial, delicate, dulcet, elevated, expansive, full, full-flavoured, genial, happy, jolly, jovial, juicy, mature, mellifluous, melodious, merry, perfect, placid, relaxed, rich, ripe, rounded, serene, smooth, soft, sweet, tipsy, tranquil, well-matured. **antonyms** immature, unripe.

v improve, mature, perfect, ripen, season, soften, sweeten, temper.

melodious *adj* concordant, dulcet, euphonious, harmonious, melodic, musical, silvery, sonorous, sweet-sounding, tuneful. **antonyms** discordant, grating, harsh.

melodramatic *adj* exaggerated, hammy, histrionic, overdone, overdramatic, overemotional, overwrought, sensational, stagy, theatrical.

melt *v* diffuse, disarm, dissolve, flux, fuse, liquefy, mollify, relax, soften, thaw, touch, uncongeal, unfreeze. **antonyms** freeze, harden, solidify.

melt away dematerialise, disappear, disperse, dissolve, evanesce, evaporate, fade, vanish.

member *n* appendage, arm, associate, component, constituent, element, extremity, fellow, initiate, leg, limb, organ, part, portion, representative.

membership *n* adherence, allegiance, associates, body, enrolment, fellows, fellowship, members, participation.

memorable *adj* catchy, celebrated, distinguished, extraordinary, famous, historic, illustrious, important,

impressive, marvellous, momentous, notable, noteworthy, outstanding, remarkable, signal, significant, striking, unforgettable. *antonym* forgettable.

memorial *n* cairn, cromlech, dolmen, mausoleum, memento, menhir, monument, plaque, record, remembrance, souvenir, stone.
adj celebratory, commemorative, monumental.

memorise *v* learn, learn by heart, learn by rote, learn off, mug up, swot up. *antonym* forget.

memory *n* bank, celebrity, commemoration, database, fame, glory, honour, memorial, name, recall, recollection, remembrance, reminiscence, renown, reputation, repute, retention, store. *antonym* forgetfulness.

menace *v* browbeat, bully, cow, frighten, impend, intimidate, loom, lour (lower), terrorise, threaten.
n annoyance, danger, hazard, intimidation, jeopardy, nuisance, peril, pest, plague, scare, terror, threat, troublemaker, warning.

menacing *adj* dangerous, frightening, impending, intimidating, intimidatory, looming, louring (lowering), minatory, ominous, portentous, threatening.

mend *v* ameliorate, amend, better, cobble, convalesce, correct, cure, darn, fix, heal, improve, patch, recover, rectify, recuperate, refit, reform, remedy, renew, renovate, repair, restore, retouch, revise, solder. *antonyms* break, destroy, deteriorate.

mendacious *adj* deceitful, deceptive, dishonest, duplicitous, fallacious, false, fraudulent, insincere, lying, perfidious, perjured, untrue, untruthful. *antonyms* honest, truthful.

mendacity *n* deceit, deceitfulness, dishonesty, distortion, duplicity, falsehood, falsification, fraudulence, insincerity, lie, lying, mendaciousness, misrepresentation, perfidy, perjury, untruth, untruthfulness. *antonyms* honesty, truthfulness.

menial *adj* abject, attending, base, boring, degrading, demeaning, dull, fawning, grovelling, humble, humdrum, ignoble, ignominious, low, lowly, mean, obsequious, routine, servile, slavish, subservient, sycophantic, unskilled, vile.
n attendant, creature, dog's-body, domestic, drudge, flunky, labourer, lackey, serf, servant, skivvy, slave, underling.

mental[1] *adj* abstract, cerebral, cognitive, conceptual, intellectual, rational, theoretical. *antonym* physical.

mental[2] *adj* crazy, deranged, disturbed, insane, loony, loopy, lunatic, mad, psychiatric, psychotic, unbalanced, unstable. *antonyms* balanced, sane.

mentality *n* attitude, brains, capacity, character, comprehension, disposition, endowment, faculty, frame of mind, intellect, IQ, make-up, mind, outlook, personality, psychology, rationality, understanding, wit.

mentally *adv* emotionally, intellectually, inwardly, psychologically, rationally, subjectively, temperamentally.

mention *v* acknowledge, adduce, advise, allude to, apprise, bring up, broach, cite, communicate, declare, disclose, divulge, hint at, impart, intimate, make known, name, point out, recount, refer to, report, reveal, speak of, state, tell, touch on.
n acknowledgement, allusion, announcement, citation, indication, notification, observation, recognition, reference, remark, tribute.

mercenary *adj* acquisitive, avaricious, bought, covetous, grasping, greedy, hired, materialistic, meretricious, money-grubbing, paid, sordid, venal.

merciful *adj* beneficent, clement, compassionate, forbearing, forgiving, generous, gracious, humane, humanitarian, kind, lenient, liberal, mild, pitying, soft, sparing, sympathetic, tender-hearted. *antonyms* cruel, merciless.

merciless *adj* barbarous, callous, cruel, hard, hard-hearted, harsh, heartless, implacable, inexorable, inhuman, inhumane, pitiless, relentless, remorseless, ruthless, severe, unappeasable, unforgiving, unmerciful, unpitying, unsparing. *antonym* merciful.

mercurial *adj* active, capricious, changeable, erratic, fickle, flighty, gay, impetuous, impulsive, inconstant, irrepressible, light-hearted, lively, mobile, spirited, sprightly, temperamental, unpredictable, unstable, variable, volatile. *antonym* saturnine.

mercy *n* benevolence, blessing, boon, charity, clemency, compassion, favour, forbearance, forgiveness, godsend, grace, humanitarianism, kindness, leniency, pity, quarter, relief. *antonyms* cruelty, revenge.

mere *adj* absolute, bare, common, complete, entire, paltry, petty, plain, pure, pure and simple, sheer, simple, stark, unadulterated, unmitigated, unmixed, utter, very.

merge v amalgamate, blend, coalesce, combine, confederate, consolidate, converge, fuse, incorporate, intermix, join, meet, meld, melt into, mingle, mix, unite.

merger n amalgamation, coalescence, coalition, combination, confederation, consolidation, fusion, incorporation, union.

merit n advantage, asset, claim, credit, desert, due, excellence, good, goodness, integrity, justification, quality, right, strong point, talent, value, virtue, worth, worthiness. **antonyms** demerit, fault.

v deserve, earn, incur, justify, rate, warrant.

merited adj appropriate, condign, deserved, due, earned, entitled, fitting, just, justified, rightful, warranted, worthy. **antonyms** inappropriate, unjustified.

meritorious adj admirable, commendable, creditable, deserving, estimable, excellent, exemplary, good, honourable, laudable, praiseworthy, right, righteous, virtuous, worthful, worthy. **antonym** unworthy.

merriment n amusement, conviviality, elation, exhilaration, festivity, frolic, fun, gaiety, glee, hilarity, jocularity, jollity, joviality, laughter, levity, liveliness, merry-making, mirth, revelry, sport, waggery. **antonyms** gloom, gravity, sadness, seriousness.

merry adj amusing, blithe, boon, carefree, cheerful, chirpy, comic, comical, convivial, elevated, facetious, festive, frolicsome, fun-loving, funny, gay, glad, gleeful, happy, heartsome, hilarious, humorous, jocular, jolly, joyful, joyous, light-hearted, mellow, mirthful, rollicking, saturnalian, sportful, sportive, squiffy, tiddly, tipsy, vivacious. **antonyms** gloomy, glum, grave, melancholy, serious, sober, sombre.

merrymaking n carousal, carouse, carousing, celebration, conviviality, festivity, fun, gaiety, jollification, merriment, party, rejoicings, revel, revelry.

mesh n entanglement, lattice, net, netting, network, plexus, reticulation, snare, tangle, tracery, trap, web.

v catch, combine, come together, connect, co-ordinate, dovetail, engage, enmesh, entangle, fit, harmonise, inmesh, interlock, knit.

mesmerise v captivate, enthral, entrance, fascinate, grip, hypnotise, magnetise, spellbind, stupefy.

mess n bollocks, botch, chaos, clutter, cock-up, confusion, difficulty, dilemma, dirtiness, disarray, disorder, disorganisation, fix, hash, imbroglio, jam, jumble, litter, mishmash, mix-up, muddle, perplexity, pickle, plight, predicament, shambles, shemozzle, stew, turmoil, untidiness, yuck. **antonyms** order, tidiness.

v befoul, besmirch, clutter, dirty, disarrange, disarray, dishevel, foul, litter, pollute, tousle. **antonyms** order, tidy.

mess about amuse oneself, arse about, dabble, fiddle, interfere, meddle, mess around, muck about, play, play about, play around, potter, tamper, tinker, toy, trifle.

mess up botch, bungle, disrupt, jumble, make a hash of, muck up, muddle, spoil, tangle.

mess with fiddle with, interfere, meddle with, play with, tamper with, tangle with, tinker with.

message n bulletin, cable, commission, communication, communiqué, dispatch, errand, fax, idea, import, intimation, job, letter, meaning, memorandum, mission, missive, moral, note, notice, point, purport, send, task, Telemessage®, telex, theme, tidings, word.

messenger n agent, ambassador, bearer, carrier, courier, delivery boy, emissary, envoy, errand-boy, go-between, harbinger, herald, mercury, runner.

messy adj chaotic, cluttered, confused, dirty, dishevelled, disordered, disorganised, grubby, grungy, littered, muddled, shambolic, sloppy, slovenly, unkempt, untidy, yucky. **antonyms** neat, ordered, tidy.

metamorphose v alter, change, convert, modify, mutate, remake, remodel, reshape, transfigure, transform, translate, transmogrify, transmute, transubstantiate.

metamorphosis n alteration, change, change-over, conversion, modification, mutation, rebirth, transfiguration, transformation, translation, transmogrification, transmutation, transubstantiation.

metaphysical adj abstract, abstruse, basic, deep, esoteric, essential, eternal, fundamental, high-flown, ideal, immaterial, impalpable, incorporeal, insubstantial, intangible, intellectual, oversubtle, philosophical, profound, recondite, speculative, spiritual, supernatural, theoretical, transcendental, universal, unreal, unsubstantial.

mete out administer, allot, apportion, assign, deal out, dispense, distribute, divide out, dole out, hand out, measure out, parcel out, portion, ration out, share out.

meteoric adj brief, brilliant, dazzling, fast, instantaneous, momentary, overnight, rapid, spectacular, speedy, sudden, swift.

method n approach, arrangement, course, design, fashion, form, manner, mode, modus operandi, order, orderliness, organisation, pattern, plan, planning, practice, procedure, process, programme, purpose, regularity, routine, rule, scheme, structure, style, system, technique, way.

methodical adj business-like, deliberate, disciplined, efficient, meticulous, neat, ordered, orderly, organised, painstaking, planned, precise, punctilious, regular, scrupulous, structured, systematic, tidy. **antonyms** confused, desultory, irregular.

meticulous adj accurate, detailed, exact, fastidious, fussy, nice, painstaking, particular, perfectionist, precise, punctilious, scrupulous, strict, thorough. **antonyms** careless, slapdash.

métier n calling, craft, field, forte, line, occupation, profession, pursuit, speciality, specialty, sphere, trade, vocation.

mettle n ardour, boldness, bottle, bravery, calibre, character, courage, daring, disposition, fire, fortitude, gallantry, gameness, ginger, grit, guts, heart, indomitability, life, make-up, nature, nerve, pith, pluck, quality, resolution, resolve, spirit, spunk, stamp, temper, temperament, valour, vigour.

miasmal adj fetid, foul, insalubrious, malodorous, noxious, polluted, putrid, reeking, smelly, stinking, unwholesome.

microscopic adj imperceptible, indiscernible, infinitesimal, invisible, minuscule, minute, negligible, tiny. **antonyms** huge, vast.

middle adj central, halfway, inner, inside, intermediate, intervening, mean, medial, median, mediate, medium, mid, middle-bracket.
n centre, focus, golden mean, halfway

mark, halfway point, happy medium, heart, inside, mean, middle way, midpoint, midriff, midsection, midst, thick, waist. **antonyms** beginning, border, edge, end, extreme.

middleman n broker, distributor, go-between, intermediary, negotiator, retailer.

middling adj adequate, average, fair, indifferent, mean, median, mediocre, medium, moderate, modest, OK, ordinary, passable, run-of-the-mill, so-so, tolerable, unexceptional, unremarkable.

miffed adj aggrieved, annoyed, chagrined, disgruntled, displeased, hurt, in a huff, irked, irritated, narked, nettled, offended, piqued, put out, resentful, upset, vexed. **antonyms** chuffed, delighted, pleased.

might n ability, capability, capacity, clout, efficacy, efficiency, energy, force, heftiness, muscularity, potency, power, powerfulness, prowess, strength, sway, valour, vigour.

mightily adv decidedly, energetically, exceedingly, extremely, forcefully, greatly, highly, hugely, intensely, lustily, manfully, much, powerfully, strenuously, strongly, very, very much, vigorously.

mighty adj bulky, colossal, doughty, enormous, forceful, gigantic, grand, great, hardy, hefty, huge, immense, indomitable, large, manful, massive, monumental, muscular, potent, powerful, prodigious, robust, stalwart, stout, strapping, strenuous, strong, stupendous, sturdy, titanic, towering, tremendous, vast, vigorous. **antonyms** frail, weak.

migrate v drift, emigrate, journey, move, roam, rove, shift, travel, trek, voyage, wander.

mild adj amiable, balmy, bland, calm, clement, compassionate, docile, easy, easy-going, equable, forbearing, forgiving, gentle, indulgent, kind, lenient, meek, mellow, merciful, moderate, pacific, passive, peaceable, placid, pleasant, serene, smooth, soft, temperate, tender, tranquil, warm. **antonyms** fierce, harsh, stormy, strong, violent.

mildness n blandness, calmness, clemency, docility, forbearance, gentleness, indulgence, kindness, leniency, lenity, meekness, mellowness, moderation, passivity, placidity, smoothness, softness, temperateness, tenderness, tractability, tranquillity, warmth. *antonyms* ferocity, harshness, strength, violence.

milieu *n* arena, background, element, environment, locale, location, medium, scene, setting, sphere, surroundings.

militant *adj* active, aggressive, assertive, belligerent, combating, combative, contending, embattled, fighting, hawkish, pugnacious, vigorous, warring. *n* activist, aggressor, belligerent, combatant, fighter, partisan, struggler, warrior.

militate against contend, count against, counter, counteract, oppose, resist, tell against, weigh against.

militate for advance, aid, back, further, help, promote, speak for.

milk *v* bleed, drain, draw off, exploit, express, extract, impose on, press, pump, siphon, squeeze, tap, use, wring.

milk-and-water *adj* bland, feeble, innocuous, insipid, tasteless, vapid, weak, wishy-washy.

mill[1] *v* crush, granulate, grate, grind, pound, powder, press, pulverise, roll.

mill[2] *n* factory, foundry, plant, shop, works.

mill[3] *v* crowd, scurry, seethe, swarm, throng, wander.

millstone *n* affliction, burden, drag, encumbrance, load, weight.

mimic *v* ape, caricature, echo, imitate, impersonate, look like, mirror, parody, parrot, resemble, simulate, take off. *n* caricaturist, copy, copy-cat, imitator, impersonator, impressionist, parrot. *adj* echoic, fake, imitation, imitative, make-believe, mimetic, mock, pseudo, sham, simulated.

mimicry *n* apery, burlesque, caricature, copying, imitating, imitation, impersonation, impression, mimesis, mimicking, mockery, parody, parrotry, take-off.

mince[1] *v* chop, crumble, cut, dice, grind, hash.

mince[2] *v* diminish, euphemise, extenuate, hold back, moderate, palliate, play down, soften, spare, suppress, tone down, weaken.

mince[3] *v* attitudinise, ponce, pose, posture, simper.

mincing *adj* affected, dainty, effeminate, foppish, nice, poncy, precious, pretentious, ripperty-tipperty, sissy.

mind[1] *n* attention, attitude, belief, bent, brains, concentration, desire,

disposition, fancy, feeling, genius, grey matter, head, imagination, inclination, inner, intellect, intellectual, intelligence, intention, judgement, leaning, marbles, memory, mentality, notion, opinion, outlook, point of view, psyche, purpose, rationality, reason, recollection, remembrance, sanity, sense, senses, sensorium, sensory, sentiment, spirit, tendency, thinker, thinking, thoughts, understanding, urge, view, will, wish, wits.

mind's eye contemplation, head, imagination, memory, mind, recollection, remembrance.

mind[2] *v* care, demur, disapprove, dislike, object, resent, take offence.

mind[3] *v* adhere to, attend, attend to, be careful, be on one's guard, comply with, ensure, follow, guard, have charge of, heed, keep an eye on, listen to, look after, make certain, mark, note, notice, obey, observe, pay attention, pay heed to, regard, respect, take care, take care of, take heed, tend, watch.

mind out be careful, be on one's guard, beware, keep one's eyes open, look out, pay attention, take care, watch, watch out.

mindful *adj* alert, alive (to), attentive, aware, careful, chary, cognisant, compliant, conscious, heedful, obedient, regardful, remindful, respectful, sensible, thoughtful, wary, watchful. *antonyms* heedless, inattentive, mindless.

mindless *adj* asinine, automatic, brainless, brutish, careless, foolish, forgetful, gratuitous, heedless, idiotic, illogical, imbecilic, inattentive, irrational, mechanical, moronic, neglectful, negligent, oblivious, obtuse, stupid, thoughtless, unintelligent, unmindful, unreasoning, unthinking, witless. *antonyms* intelligent, mindful, thoughtful.

mine *n* abundance, coalfield, colliery, deposit, excavation, fund, hoard, lode, pit, reserve, sap, shaft, source, stock, store, supply, treasury, trench, tunnel, wealth. *v* delve, dig for, dig up, excavate, extract, quarry, remove, subvert, tunnel, undermine, unearth, weaken.

mingle *v* alloy, associate, blend, circulate, coalesce, combine, compound, hobnob, intermingle, intermix, interweave, join, marry, merge, mix, rub shoulders, socialise, unite.

miniature *adj* baby, diminutive, dwarf, Lilliputian, little, midget, mini, minuscule, minute, pint-size(d), pocket, pocket-sized, pygmy, reduced, scaled-down, small, tiny, toy, wee. *antonym* giant.

minimal *adj* least, littlest, minimum, minuscule, minute, nominal, slightest, smallest, token.

minimise *v* abbreviate, attenuate, belittle, curtail, decrease, decry, dedramatise, de-emphasise, deprecate, depreciate, diminish, discount, disparage, make light of, make little of, play down, reduce, shrink, underestimate, underrate. *antonym* maximise.

minimum *n* bottom, least, lowest point, nadir, slightest. *antonym* maximum.
adj least, littlest, lowest, minimal, slightest, smallest, tiniest, weeniest, weest. *antonym* maximum.

minion *n* arse-licker, backscratcher, bootlicker, creature, dependant, flatterer, flunky, follower, hanger-on, heeler, henchman, hireling, lackey, lickspittle, parasite, pet, sycophant, toady, underling, yes-man.

minister *n* administrator, agent, aide, ambassador, assistant, churchman, clergyman, cleric, delegate, diplomat, divine, ecclesiastic, envoy, executive, office-holder, official, parson, pastor, plenipotentiary, preacher, priest, servant, subordinate, underling, vicar.
v accommodate, administer, attend, cater to, nurse, pander to, serve, take care of, tend.

ministration *n* aid, assistance, care, favour, help, patronage, relief, service, succour, supervision, support.

minor *adj* inconsequential, inconsiderable, inferior, insignificant, junior, lesser, light, negligible, paltry, petty, piddling, secondary, second-class, slight, small, smaller, subordinate, trifling, trivial, unclassified, unimportant, younger. *antonym* major.

mint *v* cast, coin, construct, devise, fabricate, fashion, forge, invent, make, make up, manufacture, produce, punch, stamp, strike.
adj brand-new, excellent, first-class, fresh, immaculate, perfect, unblemished, undamaged, untarnished.
n bomb, bundle, fortune, heap, million, packet, pile, stack.

minuscule *adj* diminutive, fine, infinitesimal, itsy-bitsy, Lilliputian, little, microscopic, miniature, minute, teensy-weensy, teeny, tiny. *antonym* gigantic, huge.

minute[1] *n* flash, instant, jiff, jiffy, mo, moment, sec, second, shake, tick, trice.

minute[2] *adj* close, critical, detailed, diminutive, exact, exhaustive, fine, inconsiderable, infinitesimal, itsy-bitsy, Lilliputian, little, meticulous, microscopic, miniature, minuscule, negligible, painstaking, paltry, petty, piddling, precise, punctilious, puny, slender, slight, small, tiny, trifling, trivial, unimportant. *antonym* gigantic, huge, immense.

minutely *adv* closely, critically, exactly, exhaustively, in detail, meticulously, painstakingly, precisely, scrupulously, systematically, with a fine-tooth comb.

minutiae *n* details, niceties, particulars, subtleties, trifles, trivialities.

minx *n* baggage, coquette, flirt, harpy, harridan, hoyden, hussy, jade, tomboy, wanton.

miraculous *adj* amazing, astonishing, astounding, extraordinary, incredible, inexplicable, magical, marvellous, otherworldly, phenomenal, prodigious, stupendous, superhuman, supernatural, unaccountable, unbelievable, wonderful, wondrous. *antonyms* natural, normal.

mire *n* bog, difficulties, dirt, marsh, morass, muck, mud, ooze, quagmire, slime, swamp, trouble.

mirror *n* copy, double, glass, hand-glass, image, likeness, looking glass, reflection, reflector, replica, representation, spitting image, twin.
v copy, depict, echo, emulate, follow, imitate, mimic, reflect, represent, show.

mirth *n* amusement, cheerfulness, festivity, frolic, fun, gaiety, gladness, glee, hilarity, jocularity, jollity, joviality, joyousness, laughter, levity, merriment, merrymaking, pleasure, rejoicing, revelry, sport. *antonyms* gloom, glumness, melancholy.

misadventure *n* accident, calamity, cataclysm, catastrophe, debacle, disaster, failure, ill fortune, ill luck, mischance, misfortune, mishap, reverse, setback, tragedy.

misanthropic *adj* antisocial, cynical, egoistic, surly, unfriendly, unsociable, unsympathetic. *antonym* philanthropic.

misanthropy *n* antisociality, cynicism, egoism, unsociableness. *antonym* philanthropy.

misapply *v* abuse, exploit, misappropriate, misemploy, misuse, pervert.

misapprehend *v* get the wrong idea, miscomprehend, misconceive, misconstrue, misinterpret, misread, mistake, misunderstand.

misapprehension *n* delusion, error, fallacy, misacceptation, misconception, misconstruction, misinterpretation, misreading, mistake, misunderstanding.

misappropriate *v* abuse, defalcate, embezzle, misapply, misspend, misuse, pervert, pocket, steal, swindle.

misappropriation *n* defalcation, embezzlement, misapplication, misuse, pocketing, stealing, theft.

misbegotten *adj* abortive, dishonest, disreputable, hare-brained, ill-advised, ill-conceived, ill-gotten, illicit, monstrous, poorly thought-out, purloined, shady, stolen, unlawful.

misbehave *v* act up, carry on, get up to mischief, mess about, muck about, offend, transgress, trespass. *antonym* behave.

misbehaviour *n* disobedience, impropriety, incivility, indiscipline, insubordination, mayhem, misconduct, misdeeds, misdemeanour, monkey business, naughtiness, rudeness, shenanigans.

miscalculate *v* blunder, boob, err, get wrong, misjudge, overestimate, overrate, overvalue, slip up, underestimate, underrate, undervalue.

miscarriage *n* abortion, botch, breakdown, casualty, disappointment, error, failure, misadventure, mischance, misfire, mishap, mismanagement, perversion, thwarting, undoing. *antonym* success.

miscarry *v* abort, bite the dust, come to grief, come to nothing, fail, fall through, flounder, misfire, warp. *antonym* succeed.

miscellaneous *adj* assorted, confused, diverse, diversified, heterogeneous, indiscriminate, jumbled, manifold, many, mingled, mixed, motley, multifarious, multiform, sundry, varied, various.

miscellany *n* anthology, assortment, collection, diversity, hash, hotch-potch, jumble, medley, mélange, mixed bag, mixture, pot-pourri, variety.

mischief *n* bane, damage, detriment, devilment, disruption, evil, harm, hurt, impishness, injury, misbehaviour, misfortune, monkey business, naughtiness, pranks, roguery, roguishness, shenanigans, trouble, waywardness.

mischievous *adj* arch, bad, damaging, deleterious, destructive, detrimental, elfish, evil, exasperating, frolicsome, harmful, hurtful, impish, injurious, malicious, malignant, naughty, pernicious, playful, puckish, rascally, roguish, sinful, spiteful, sportive, teasing, tricksy, troublesome, vexatious, vicious, wayward, wicked. *antonyms* good, well-behaved.

misconceive *v* misapprehend, misconstrue, misinterpret, misjudge, misread, mistake, misunderstand.

misconception *n* delusion, error, fallacy, misapprehension, misconstruction, misreading, misunderstanding, the wrong end of the stick.

misconduct *n* delinquency, dereliction, hanky-panky, immorality, impropriety, malpractice, misbehaviour, misdemeanour, mismanagement, naughtiness, rudeness, transgression, wrong-doing.

misconstrue *v* misapprehend, misconceive, misinterpret, misjudge, misread, misreckon, mistake, mistranslate, misunderstand, take the wrong way.

miscreant *n* blackguard, caitiff, criminal, dastard, evil-doer, knave, malefactor, mischief-maker, profligate, rascal, reprobate, rogue, scallywag, scamp, scoundrel, sinner, trouble-maker, varlet, villain, wretch, wrong-doer. *antonym* worthy.

misdeed *n* crime, delinquency, error, fault, felony, misconduct, misdemeanour, offence, peccadillo, sin, transgression, trespass, villainy, wrong.

misdemeanour *n* fault, indiscretion, infringement, lapse, misbehaviour, misconduct, misdeed, offence, peccadillo, transgression, trespass.

miser *n* cheapskate, meanie, money-grubber, niggard, penny-pincher, pinchfist, pinchpenny, save-all, Scrooge, skinflint, tightwad. *antonym* spendthrift.

miserable *adj* abject, anguished, bad, broken-hearted, caitiff, cheerless, contemptible, crestfallen, crushed, dejected, deplorable, depressed, depressive, desolate, despicable, despondent, destitute, detestable, disconsolate, disgraceful, dismal, distressed, doleful, dolorous, down, downcast, dreary, forlorn, gloomy, glum, grief-stricken, hapless, heartbroken, ignominious, impoverished, indigent, joyless, lachrymose, lamentable, low, luckless, lugubrious, meagre, mean, melancholic, melancholy, miz, mournful, needy, niggardly, paltry, pathetic, penniless, piteous, pitiable, pitiful, poor, sad, scanty, scurvy, shabby, shameful, sordid, sorrowful, sorrowing, sorry, squalid, star-crossed, stricken, tearful, unhappy, vile, woebegone, worthless, wretched. *antonyms* cheerful, comfortable, generous, honourable, noble.

miserly *adj* avaricious, beggarly, cheese-paring, close, close-fisted, close-handed, covetous, gare, grasping, grudging, illiberal, mean, mercenary, mingy, money-grubbing, near, niggardly, parsimonious, penny-pinching, penurious, sparing, stingy, thrifty, tight-fisted, ungenerous. *antonyms* generous, lavish, prodigal, spendthrift.

misery[1] *n* abjectness, adversity, affliction, agony, anguish, bane, bitter pill, blow, burden, calamity, catastrophe, cross, curse, depression, desolation, despair, destitution, disaster, discomfort, distress, dole, dolour, extremity, gloom, grief, hardship, heartache, heartbreak, humiliation, living death, melancholia, melancholy, misfortune, miz, mortification, need, oppression, ordeal, penury, poverty, privation, sadness, sorrow, squalor, suffering, torment, torture, trial, tribulation, trouble, unhappiness, want, woe, wretchedness.

misery[2] *n* grouch, killjoy, moaner, moper, pessimist, prophet of doom, ray of sunshine, sourpuss, spoil-sport, wet blanket, whiner, whinger. *antonym* sport.

misfire *v* abort, bomb, come a cropper, come to grief, fail, fall flat, fall short, fall through, fizzle out, flop, founder, go phut, go wrong, miscarry. *antonym* succeed.

misfit *n* drop-out, eccentric, fish out of water, individualist, lone wolf, loner, maverick, nonconformist, odd man out, oddball, rogue, square peg in a round hole, weirdo. *antonym* conformist.

misfortune *n* accident, adversity, affliction, bad luck, blow, calamity, catastrophe, disaster, failure, grief, hardship, harm, ill-luck, infelicity, loss, misadventure, mischance, misery, mishap, reverse, setback, sorrow, tragedy, trial, tribulation, trouble, woe. *antonyms* luck, success.

misgiving *n* anxiety, apprehension,

backward glance, compunction, distrus doubt, dubiety, fear, hesitatio misdoubt, niggle, presentiment, qualr reservation, scruple, second thought suspicion, uncertainty, unease, worry *antonym* confidence.

misguided *adj* deluded, erroneou foolish, ill-advised, ill-considere ill-judged, imprudent, incautiou injudicious, misconceived, misle misplaced, mistaken, rash, unreasonabl unsuitable, unwarranted, unwise *antonym* sensible.

mishandle *v* balls up, bollocks, botcl bungle, fumble, make a balls of, make hash of, make a mess of, make a pig's e of, mess up, misjudge, mismanage, muf screw up. *antonyms* cope, manage.

mishap *n* accident, adversity, balls-u calamity, disaster, hiccup, ill-fortun ill-luck, misadventure, mischanc misfortune, misventure, setback.

mishmash *n* conglomeration, hasl hotchpotch, jumble, medley, mes muddle, pot-pourri, salad.

misinform *v* bluff, deceive, give a bui steer, hoodwink, lead up the garden pat misdirect, misguide, mislead, mistel take for a ride.

misinformation *n* baloney, bluff, bui steer, disinformation, dope, eyewasl guff, lies, misdirection, misleadin nonsense.

misinterpret *v* distort, garble, get th wrong end of the stick, misapprehen misconceive, misconstruct, misconstru misjudge, misread, misrepresen mistake, misunderstand, pervert, warj wrest.

misjudge *v* miscalculate, miscoun misestimate, misinterpret, misprisi mistake, overestimate, overrat underestimate, underrate, undervalue.

mislay *v* lose, lose sight of, misplac miss.

mislead *v* beguile, bluff, deceiv delude, fool, give a bum steer, hoodwinl lead up the garden path, misadvise misdirect, misguide, misinform, pull th wool over someone's eyes, take for ride, take in.

misleading *adj* ambiguous, biase confusing, deceitful, deceptive, delusiv delusory, disingenuous, distorte equivocatory, evasive, fallaciou false, loaded, mendacious, sophistica specious, spurious, tricky, unreliable *antonyms* authentic, authoritativ informative, plain, unequivocal.

mismanage v balls up, bollocks, botch, bungle, fluff, foul up, louse up, make a hash of, make a mess of, maladminister, mangle, mess up, misconduct, misdirect, misgovern, mishandle, misjudge, misrule, misspend, muff, screw up, squander, waste.

mismatched adj antipathetic, clashing, discordant, disparate, ill-assorted, incompatible, incongruous, irregular, misallied, mismated, unmatching, unreconcilable, unsuited. **antonyms** compatible, matching.

misplace v lose, misapply, misassign, misfile, mislay, miss.

misprint n erratum, error, literal, mistake, typo.

misprise v belittle, depreciate, disparage, hold cheap, look down on, mistake, misunderstand, slight, underestimate, underrate, undervalue. **antonyms** appreciate, understand.

misrepresent v belie, bend, disguise, distort, exaggerate, falsify, garble, minimise, miscolour, misconstrue, misinterpret, misquote, misstate, pervert, slant, twist.

misrule n anarchy, chaos, confusion, disorder, disorganisation, indiscipline, lawlessness, maladministration, mismanagement, riot, tumult, turbulence, turmoil, unreason.

miss¹ v avoid, bypass, circumvent, escape, evade, fail, forego, jump, lack, leave out, let go, let slip, lose, miscarry, mistake, obviate, omit, overlook, pass over, pass up, sidestep, skip, slip, trip.
n blunder, error, failure, fault, fiasco, flop, lack, lacuna, loss, mistake, need, omission, oversight, want.

miss out bypass, dispense with, disregard, ignore, jump, leave out, omit, pass over, skip.

miss² v grieve for, lack, lament, long for, mourn, need, pine for, regret, sorrow for, want, wish, yearn for.

misshapen adj contorted, crippled, crooked, deformed, distorted, grotesque, ill-made, ill-proportioned, malformed, monstrous, twisted, ugly, ungainly, unshapely, unsightly, warped, wry. **antonyms** regular, shapely.

missile n arrow, ball, bomb, dart, grenade, projectile, rocket, shell, shot, torpedo, weapon.

missing adj absent, astray, disappeared, gone, lacking, lost, minus, mislaid, misplaced, strayed, unaccounted-for, wanting. **antonyms** found, present.

mission n aim, assignment, business, calling, campaign, charge, commission, crusade, delegation, deputation, duty, embassy, errand, goal, job, legation, mandate, ministry, object, office, operation, purpose, pursuit, quest, raison d'être, remit, task, task force, trust, undertaking, vocation, work.

missive n bulletin, communication, communiqué, dispatch, epistle, letter, line, memo, memorandum, message, note, report.

misspent adj dissipated, frittered away, idle, idled away, misapplied, misused, prodigal, profitless, squandered, thrown away, unprofitable, wasted. **antonym** profitable.

misstate v distort, falsify, garble, misquote, misrelate, misremember, misreport, misrepresent, mistell, pervert, twist.

mist n brume, cloud, condensation, dew, dimness, drizzle, exhalation, film, fog, haze, mizzle, smog, spray, steam, vapour, veil.
v bedim, befog, blur, cloud, dim, film, fog, glaze, obscure, steam up, veil. **antonym** clear.

mistake n aberration, bloomer, blunder, boob, booboo, clanger, clinker, erratum, error, fallacy, false move, fault, faux pas, folly, gaffe, goof, howler, inaccuracy, indiscretion, inexactitude, lapse, lapsus, literal, malapropism, misapprehension, miscalculation, misconception, misjudgement, misprint, mispronunciation, misreading, misspelling, misunderstanding, oversight, slip, slip-up, solecism, tactlessness, trespass.
v blunder, confound, confuse, err, get the wrong end of the stick, goof, misapprehend, miscalculate, misconceive, misconstrue, misinterpret, misjudge, misobserve, misprise, misrate, misread, misreckon, misunderstand, slip up.

mistaken adj deceived, deluded, erroneous, fallacious, false, faulty, ill-judged, inaccurate, inappropriate, inauthentic, incorrect, inexact, misguided, misinformed, misinstructed, mislead, misprised, off base, off beam, unfair, unfounded, unjust, unsound, untrue, wide of the mark, wrong. **antonyms** correct, justified.

mistakenly adv by mistake, erroneously, fallaciously, falsely, inaccurately, inappropriately, incorrectly, misguidedly, unfairly, unjustly, wrongly. *antonyms* appropriately, correctly, fairly, justly.

mistimed *adj* ill-timed, inconvenient, infelicitous, inopportune, tactless, unfortunate, unseasonable, unsynchronised, untimely. *antonym* opportune.

mistreat *v* abuse, batter, brutalise, bully, harm, hurt, ill-treat, ill-use, injure, knock about, manhandle, maul, mishandle, misuse, molest, rough up. *antonym* pamper.

mistreatment *n* abuse, battering, brutalisation, bullying, cruelty, harm, ill-treatment, ill-usage, ill-use, injury, manhandling, mauling, mishandling, misuse, molestation, unkindness. *antonyms* cosseting, pampering.

mistress *n* châtelaine, concubine, courtesan, doxy, fancy woman, girlfriend, kept woman, lady, lady-love, lover, owner, paramour, proprietress, woman.

mistrust *n* apprehension, caution, chariness, distrust, doubt, dubiety, fear, hesitancy, misgiving, reservations, scepticism, suspicion, uncertainty, wariness. *antonym* trust.
v be wary of, beware, disbelieve, distrust, doubt, fear, fight shy of, look askance at, question, suspect. *antonym* trust.

mistrustful *adj* apprehensive, cautious, chary, cynical, distrustful, doubtful, dubious, fearful, hesitant, leery, sceptical, shy, suspicious, uncertain, wary. *antonym* trustful.

misty *adj* bleary, blurred, blurry, cloudy, dark, dim, faint, foggy, fuzzy, gauzy, hazy, indistinct, murky, nebulous, obscure, opaque, smoky, translucent, unclear, vague, veiled. *antonyms* bright, clear.

misunderstand *v* get the wrong end of the stick, get wrong, misapprehend, miscomprehend, misconceive, misconstrue, misesteem, mishear, misinterpret, misjudge, misprise, misread, miss the point, mistake, take up wrong(ly). *antonyms* grasp, understand.

misunderstanding *n* argument, clash, conflict, difference, difficulty, disagreement, discord, disharmony, dispute, dissension, error, misacceptation, misapprehension, misconception, misconstruction, misinterpretation, misjudgement, misreading, mistake, mix-up, quarrel, rift, rupture, squabble, variance. *antonyms* agreement, reconciliation.

misunderstood *adj* ill-judged,

misappreciated, misconstrued, mishea. misinterpreted, misjudged, misprise misread, misrepresented, mistake unappreciated, unrecognised.

misuse *n* abuse, barbarism, corruptic desecration, dissipation, distortic exploitation, harm, ill-treatment, i usage, injury, malappropriatic malapropism, manhandling, misapplic tion, misappropriation, misemploymer mistreatment, misusage, perversic profanation, prostitution, solecis squandering, waste.
v abuse, brutalise, corrupt, desecra dissipate, distort, exploit, harm, ill-tre ill-use, injure, malappropriate, ma handle, maul, misapply, misappropria misemploy, mistreat, molest, overloa overtax, pervert, profane, prostitu squander, strain, waste, wrong.

mite *n* atom, grain, iota, jot, modicut morsel, ounce, scrap, smidgen, spar trace, whit.

mitigate *v* abate, allay, allevia appease, assuage, attemper, blunt, cal check, decrease, diminish, dull, eas extenuate, lessen, lighten, modera modify, mollify, pacify, palliate, placa quiet, reduce, remit, slake, softe soothe, still, subdue, temper, to down, weaken. *antonyms* aggrava exacerbate, increase.

mitigating *adj* exculpator extenuating, justificatory, justifyin lenitive, mitigative, mitigator modifying, palliating, palliativ qualifying, vindicating.

mitigation *n* abatement, allayin alleviation, appeasement, assuagemer decrease, diminution, extenuatic lessening, moderation, mollificatic palliation, qualification, reductic relief, remission, tempering. *antonyr* aggravation, exacerbation, increase.

mix *v* alloy, amalgamate, associat blend, coalesce, combine, comming compound, consort, cross, fold i fraternise, fuse, hobnob, homogenis incorporate, intermingle, intermi interweave, join, jumble, merge, ming shuffle, socialise, synthesise, unite *antonym* separate.
n alloy, amalgam, assortment, blen combination, composite, compoun conglomerate, fusion, medle mishmash, mixture, synthesis.

mix in admix, blend, imming immix, incorporate, infiltrate, infus inject, interject, interlard, interming interpolate, intersperse, introduce, merge. **antonyms** extract, isolate.

mix up bewilder, blend, combine, complicate, confound, confuse, disturb, embroil, entangle, fluster, garble, implicate, involve, jumble, mix, muddle, perplex, puzzle, scramble, snarl up, upset.

mixed *adj* alloyed, amalgamated, ambivalent, assorted, blended, combined, composite, compound, cosmopolitan, crossbred, diverse, diversified, ecumenical, equivocal, fused, heterogeneous, hybrid, incorporated, indecisive, integrated, interbred, interdenominational, international, joint, mingled, miscellaneous, mongrel, motley, polyglot, uncertain, united, unsegregated, varied.

mixed up bewildered, chaotic, complicated, confused, disordered, disoriented, distracted, distraught, disturbed, maladjusted, muddled, perplexed, puzzled, upset.

mixing *n* amalgamation, association, blending, coalescence, combination, fraternisation, fusion, hybridisation, interbreeding, intercourse, interflow, intermingling, miscegenation, socialising, synthesis, union. **antonym** separation.

mixture *n* alloy, amalgam, amalgamation, association, assortment, blend, brew, coalescence, combination, combine, composite, compost, compound, concoction, conglomeration, cross, fusion, half-breed, hotchpotch, hybrid, jumble, medley, mélange, miscegenation, miscellany, mix, mixed bag, mongrel, pot-pourri, salad, synthesis, union, variety.

mix-up *n* balls-up, chaos, complication, confusion, disorder, foul-up, jumble, mess, mistake, misunderstanding, muddle, nonsense, snarl-up, tangle.

moan *n* beef, belly-ache, bitch, complaint, gripe, groan, grouch, grouse, grumble, howl, keen, lament, lamentation, sigh, snivel, sob, sough, wail, whimper, whine, whinge.
v beef, belly-ache, bemoan, bewail, bitch, carp, complain, deplore, grieve, gripe, groan, grouch, grouse, grumble, howl, keen, lament, mourn, sigh, snivel, sob, sough, wail, weep, whimper, whine, whinge, wuther. **antonym** rejoice.

mob *n* assemblage, bevy, body, class, collection, common herd, commonalty, company, crew, crowd, drove, flock,

gang, gathering, great unwashed, group, herd, hoi polloi, horde, host, lot, mass, masses, mobile, multitude, pack, plebs, populace, rabble, riff-raff, scum, set, swarm, throng, tribe, troop.
v besiege, charge, cram, crowd, crowd round, descend on, fill, jam, jostle, overrun, pack, pester, set upon, surround, swarm round. **antonym** shun.

mobile *adj* active, agile, ambulatory, animated, changeable, changing, energetic, ever-changing, expressive, flexible, fluid, itinerant, lively, locomotive, mercurial, migrant, movable, moving, nimble, peripatetic, portable, roaming, roving, supple, travelling, wandering. **antonym** immobile.

mobilise *v* activate, animate, assemble, call up, enlist, galvanise, levy, marshal, muster, organise, prepare, rally, ready, shift, stir, summon.

mock *v* ape, burlesque, caricature, chaff, cheat, counterfeit, debunk, defeat, defy, deride, disappoint, disparage, dupe, elude, explode, fleer, flout, foil, frustrate, guy, imitate, insult, jeer, lampoon, laugh at, laugh in (someone's) face, laugh to scorn, make fun of, make sport of, mimic, parody, parrot, poke fun at, queer, ridicule, satirise, scoff, scorn, send up, sneer, take the mickey, taunt, tease, thwart, travesty, twit. **antonyms** flatter, praise.
adj artificial, bogus, counterfeit, dummy, ersatz, fake, faked, false, feigned, forged, fraudulent, imitation, phoney, pinchbeck, pretended, pseudo, sham, simulated, spurious, synthetic.

mockery *n* apology, burlesque, caricature, contempt, derision, disappointment, disdain, disrespect, farce, imitation, insults, invective, irrision, jeering, joke, lampoon, lampoonery, let-down, mickey-taking, mimesis, mimicry, misrepresentation, parody, pretence, ridicule, sarcasm, satire, scoffing, scorn, send-up, sham, spoof, take-off, travesty, wisecracks.

mocking *adj* contemptuous, cynical, derisive, derisory, disdainful, disrespectful, impudent, insulting, irreverent, sarcastic, sardonic, satiric, satirical, scoffing, scornful, snide, taunting. **antonym** laudatory.

mode *n* approach, condition, convention, course, craze, custom, fad, fashion, form, latest thing, look, manner, method, plan, practice, procedure, process, quality, rage, rule, state, style, system, technique, trend, vein, vogue, way.

model *n* archetype, configuration, copy, criterion, design, draft, dummy, embodiment, epitome, example, exemplar, facsimile, form, gauge, ideal, image, imitation, kind, loadstar, manikin, mannequin, mark, miniature, mock-up, mode, mould, original, paradigm, paragon, pattern, personification, plan, praxis, prototype, replica, representation, sitter, sketch, standard, style, subject, template, touchstone, type, variety, version, yardstick.

adj archetypal, complete, consummate, dummy, exemplary, facsimile, ideal, illustrative, imitation, miniature, par excellence, paradigmatic, perfect, prototypical, representative, standard, typical.

v base, carve, cast, create, design, display, fashion, form, make, mould, pattern, plan, sculpt, shape, show off, sport, wear, work.

moderate *adj* abstemious, average, calm, centrist, continent, controlled, cool, deliberate, disciplined, equable, fair, fairish, frugal, gentle, indifferent, judicious, limited, mediocre, medium, middle-of-the-road, middling, mild, modest, non-extreme, ordinary, passable, peaceable, quiet, rational, reasonable, restrained, sensible, sober, so-so, steady, temperate, unexceptional, well-regulated.

v abate, allay, alleviate, appease, assuage, blunt, calm, chasten, check, control, curb, cushion, decrease, diminish, dwindle, ease, lessen, mitigate, modify, modulate, pacify, palliate, play down, quiet, regulate, repress, restrain, slake, soften, soft-pedal, subdue, subside, tame, temper, tone down.

moderately *adv* fairly, frugally, gently, in moderation, modestly, passably, pretty, quite, rather, reasonably, slightly, soberly, somewhat, sparingly, to a certain degree, to a certain extent, to some extent, tolerably, unpretentiously, within limits, within measure, within reason. *antonym* immoderately.

moderation *n* abatement, abstemiousness, alleviation, calmness, caution, centrism, chastity, composure, continence, control, coolness, decrease, diminution, discipline, discretion, easing, equanimity, extenuation, fairness, golden mean, judiciousness, justice, justness, let-up, mildness, mitigation, moderateness, modification, modulation, palliation, reasonableness, reduction, restraint, self-control, sobriety, temperance. *antonyms* increase, intemperance.

modern *adj* advanced, avant-garde, contemporary, current, emancipated, fashionable, fresh, go-ahead, innovative, inventive, late, latest, mod, modernistic, new, newfangled, novel, present, present-day, progressive, recent, stylish, trendy, twentieth-century, up-to-date, up-to-the-minute, with-it. *antonyms* antiquated, old.

modernise *v* do up, improve, modify, neoterise, progress, redesign, reform, refresh, refurbish, regenerate, rejuvenate, remake, remodel, renew, renovate, revamp, streamline, tart up, transform, update. *antonym* regress.

modernity *n* contemporaneity, currency, fashionableness, freshness, innovation, innovativeness, newness, novelty, originality, recentness. *antonyms* antiquatedness, antiquity.

modest *adj* bashful, blushing, chaste, chastened, coy, demure, diffident, discreet, fair, humble, limited, maidenly, meek, middling, moderate, ordinary, proper, quiet, reserved, reticent, retiring, seemly, self-conscious, self-effacing, shamefaced, shy, simple, small, timid, unassuming, unexceptional, unpresuming, unpresumptuous, unpretending, unpretentious. *antonyms* conceited, immodest, pretentious, vain.

modesty *n* bashfulness, coyness, decency, demureness, diffidence, discreetness, humbleness, humility, meekness, propriety, quietness, reserve, reticence, seemliness, self-effacement, shamefacedness, shyness, simplicity, timidity, unobtrusiveness, unpretentiousness. *antonyms* conceit, immodesty, vanity.

modicum *n* atom, bit, crumb, dash, drop, fragment, grain, hint, inch, iota, little, mite, ounce, particle, pinch, scrap, shred, speck, suggestion, tinge, touch, trace.

modification *n* adjustment, alteration, change, limitation, moderation, modulation, mutation, qualification, refinement, reformation, restriction, revision, tempering, variation.

modify *v* abate, adapt, adjust, allay, alter, change, convert, improve, lessen, limit, lower, moderate, modulate, qualify, recast, redesign, redo, reduce, refashion reform, remodel, reorganise, reshape, restrain, restrict, revise, rework, soften, temper, tone down, transform, vary.

modulate v adjust, alter, attune, balance, harmonise, inflect, lower, moderate, regulate, soften, tone, tune, vary. **antonyms** increase, raise.

mogul n baron, big cheese, big gun, big noise, big shot, big wheel, bigwig, grandee, magnate, Mr Big, notable, personage, potentate, supremo, top dog, tycoon, VIP. **antonym** nobody.

moist adj clammy, damp, dampish, dank, dewy, dripping, drizzly, humid, marshy, muggy, rainy, soggy, swampy, tearful, vaporous, watery, wet, wettish. **antonyms** arid, dry.

moisten v damp, dampen, humidify, imbue, irrigate, lick, moisturise, slake, soak, water, wet. **antonym** dry.

moisture n damp, dampness, dankness, dew, humidity, liquid, mugginess, perspiration, sweat, tears, vapour, water, wateriness, wet, wetness. **antonym** dryness.

molest v abuse, accost, afflict, annoy, assail, attack, badger, beset, bother, bug, disturb, harass, harm, harry, hassle, hector, hound, hurt, ill-treat, injure, irritate, manhandle, mistreat, persecute, pester, plague, tease, torment, trouble, upset, vex, worry.

mollify v abate, allay, appease, assuage, blunt, calm, compose, conciliate, cushion, ease, lessen, lull, mellow, mitigate, moderate, modify, pacify, placate, propitiate, quell, quiet, relax, relieve, soften, soothe, sweeten, temper. **antonyms** aggravate, anger.

mollycoddle v baby, coddle, cosset, indulge, mother, overprotect, pamper, pander to, pet, ruin, spoil, spoon-feed. **antonyms** ill-treat, neglect.

moment[1] n flash, hour, instant, jiff, jiffy, juncture, less than no time, minute, mo, point, second, shake, split second, stage, tick, time, trice, twink, twinkling.

moment[2] n concern, consequence, gravity, import, importance, interest, note, seriousness, significance, substance, value, weight, weightiness, worth. **antonym** insignificance.

momentarily adv briefly, fleetingly, for a moment, for a second, for an instant, temporarily.

momentary adj brief, elusive, ephemeral, evanescent, fleeting, flying, hasty, momentaneous, passing, quick, short, short-lived, temporary, transient, transitory. **antonyms** lasting, permanent.

momentous adj apocalyptic, consequential, critical, crucial, decisive, earth-shaking, epoch-making, eventful, fateful, grave, historic, important, major, pivotal, serious, significant, tremendous, vital, weighty. **antonym** insignificant.

momentum n drive, energy, force, impact, impetus, impulse, incentive, power, propulsion, push, speed, stimulus, strength, thrust, urge, velocity.

monastery n abbey, Charterhouse, Chartreuse, cloister, convent, friary, nunnery, priory.

monastic adj ascetic, austere, celibate, cloistered, contemplative, hermitical, monasterial, monkish, recluse, reclusive, secluded, withdrawn. **antonyms** gregarious, materialistic, worldly.

money n akkas, akkers, banco, banknotes, bankroll, brass, bread, capital, cash, chips, coin, currency, dibbs, dibs, dough, filthy lucre, funds, gelt, gold, gravy, hard cash, hard money, legal tender, lolly, loot, moolah, readies, ready money, riches, shekels, silver, specie, spondulix (spondulicks), sugar, the ready, the wherewithal, wealth.

moneyed, monied adj affluent, comfortable, flush, loaded, opulent, prosperous, rich, rolling, stinking, wealthy, well-heeled, well-off, well-to-do. **antonym** impoverished.

mongrel n cross, crossbreed, half-breed, hybrid, mutt.
adj bastard, crossbred, half-breed, hybrid, mixed, mongrelly, nondescript. **antonyms** pedigree, pure-bred.

monitor n adviser, detector, guide, invigilator, overseer, prefect, recorder, scanner, screen, supervisor, watchdog.
v check, detect, follow, keep an eye on, keep track of, keep under surveillance, note, observe, oversee, plot, record, scan, supervise, survey, trace, track, watch.

monkey n ass, butt, devil, dupe, fool, imp, jackanapes, laughing-stock, mug, rapscallion, rascal, rogue, scallywag, scamp.
v fiddle, fidget, fool, interfere, meddle, mess, play, potter, tamper, tinker, trifle.

monkey business carry-on, chicanery, clowning, dishonesty, foolery, hanky-panky, jiggery-pokery, mischief, monkey tricks, pranks, shenanigans, skulduggery, tomfoolery, trickery. **antonyms** honesty, probity.

monolithic *adj* colossal, faceless, giant, gigantic, huge, immobile, immovable, inflexible, intractable, massive, monumental, rigid, solid, vast.

monologue *n* harangue, homily, lecture, oration, sermon, soliloquy, speech, spiel. *antonyms* conversation, dialogue, discussion.

monomania *n* bee in one's bonnet, fanaticism, fetish, fixation, hobby-horse, idée fixe, mania, neurosis, obsession, ruling passion, thing.

monopolise *v* appropriate, control, corner, dominate, hog, occupy, take over, take up, tie up. *antonym* share.

monopoly *n* ascendancy, control, corner, domination, exclusive right, sole right.

monotonous *adj* boring, colourless, droning, dull, flat, humdrum, plodding, prosaic, repetitious, repetitive, routine, samey, soul-destroying, tedious, tiresome, toneless, unchanging, uneventful, uniform, uninflected, unvaried, unvarying, wearisome. *antonyms* colourful, lively, varied.

monotony *n* boredom, colourlessness, dullness, flatness, humdrumness, monotonousness, prosaicness, repetitiousness, repetitiveness, routine, routineness, sameness, tediousness, tedium, tiresomeness, uneventfulness, uniformity, wearisomeness. *antonyms* colour, liveliness.

monster *n* barbarian, beast, bogeyman, brute, centaur, chimera, colossus, demon, devil, fiend, freak, giant, harpy, hellhound, kraken, leviathan, mammoth, miscreation, monstrosity, mutant, ogre, ogress, prodigy, savage, titan, villain. *adj* colossal, enormous, gargantuan, giant, gigantic, huge, immense, jumbo, mammoth, massive, monstrous, prodigious, stupendous, titanic, tremendous, vast. *antonym* minute.

monstrosity *n* abnormality, abortion, atrocity, dreadfulness, enormity, evil, eyesore, freak, frightfulness, heinousness, hellishness, hideousness, horror, loathsomeness, miscreation, monster, mutant, obscenity, ogre, prodigy.

monstrous *adj* abhorrent, abnormal, atrocious, colossal, criminal, cruel, deformed, devilish, diabolical, disgraceful, dreadful, egregious, elephantine, enormous, evil, fiendish, foul, freakish, frightful, gargantuan, giant, gigantic, great, grotesque, gruesome, heinous, hellish, hideous, horrend[o], horrible, horrific, horrifying, hu[lking], hulking, immense, infamous, inhum[an], intolerable, loathsome, malform[ed], mammoth, massive, miscrea[nt], misshapen, monster, obscene, odi[ous], outrageous, prodigious, sata[nic], scandalous, shocking, stupend[ous], terrible, titanic, towering, tremend[ous], unnatural, vast, vicious, villain[ous], wicked.

monument *n* ancient monum[ent], antiquity, barrow, cairn, cenotaph, c[om]memoration, cross, dolmen, eviden[ce], gravestone, headstone, mausole[um], memento, memorial, obelisk, pil[lar], prehistoric monument, record, re[membrance], remembrance, reminder, shrine, sta[tue], testament, token, tombstone, witness.

monumental *adj* abiding, a[we-inspiring], inspiring, awesome, catastrop[hic], classic, colossal, commemorat[ive], conspicuous, cyclopean, dura[ble], egregious, enduring, enormous, epo[ch-making], making, gigantic, great, histo[ric], horrible, huge, immense, immor[tal], important, imposing, impress[ive], indefensible, lasting, magnifice[nt], majestic, massive, memorable, me[mo]rial, monolithic, notable, outstand[ing], overwhelming, prodigious, significa[nt], staggering, statuary, stupendous, terri[ble], tremendous, vast, whopping. *antony[ms]* insignificant, unimportant.

mood *n* blues, caprice, depress[ion], disposition, doldrums, dumps, fit, fra[me] of mind, grumps, humour, melanch[oly], pique, spirit, state of mind, sulk, temp[er], tenor, the sulks, vein, whim.

moody *adj* angry, broody, cantanker[ous], capricious, cast-down, changea[ble], crabbed, crabby, cranky, cro[ss], crotchety, crusty, dejected, depress[ed], dismal, doleful, dour, downcast, erra[tic], faddish, fickle, fitful, flighty, gloor[my], glum, huffish, huffy, ill-humour[ed], impulsive, inconstant, introspecti[ve], introvert, irascible, irritable, lugubrio[us], melancholy, mercurial, miserable, mo[rose], morose, peevish, pensive, petula[nt], piqued, sad, saturnine, short-temper[ed], splenetic, sulky, sullen, temperamen[tal], testy, touchy, unpredictable, unsocia[ble], unstable, unsteady, volatile, waspis[h]. *antonyms* cheerful, equable.

moon *v* brood, daydream, drea[m], fantasise, idle, languish, loaf, mope, pi[ne], potter.

moonshine *n* baloney, blether, bo[sh],

bullshit, bunk, bunkum, claptrap, crap, eyewash, gas, guff, hogwash, hot air, nonsense, piffle, rot, rubbish, stuff, tommyrot, tosh, tripe, twaddle. **antonym** sense.

moot *v* advance, argue, bring up, broach, debate, discuss, introduce, pose, propose, propound, put forward, submit, suggest, ventilate.
adj academic, arguable, contestable, controversial, crucial, debatable, disputable, disputed, doubtful, insoluble, knotty, open, open to debate, problematic, questionable, undecided, undetermined, unresolvable, unresolved, unsettled, vexed.

moot point controversial issue, difficulty, knot, poser, problem, question mark, stumbling-block, vexed question.

mop *n* head of hair, mane, mass, mat, shock, sponge, squeegee, swab, tangle, thatch.
v absorb, clean, soak, sponge, swab, wash, wipe.

mop up absorb, clean up, eliminate, finish off, neutralise, round up, secure, soak up, sponge, swab, take care of, tidy up, wash, wipe.

mope *v* agonise, brood, despair, droop, fret, grieve, idle, languish, moon, pine, sulk.
n depressive, grouch, grump, introvert, killjoy, melancholic, misery, moaner, moper, pessimist.

moral *adj* blameless, chaste, clean-living, decent, equitable, ethical, good, high-minded, honest, honourable, incorruptible, innocent, just, meritorious, moralistic, noble, principled, proper, pure, responsible, right, righteous, square, straight, temperate, upright, upstanding, virtuous. **antonym** immoral.
n adage, aphorism, apophthegm, dictum, epigram, gnome, lesson, maxim, meaning, message, motto, point, precept, proverb, saying, significance, teaching.

moralise *v* discourse, edify, lecture, pontificate, preach, sermonise.

morality *n* chastity, conduct, decency, equity, ethicality, ethicalness, ethics, ethos, goodness, habits, honesty, ideals, integrity, justice, manners, morals, philosophy, principle, principles, probity, propriety, rationale, rectitude, righteousness, standards, tightness, uprightness, virtue. **antonym** immorality.

morals *n* behaviour, conduct, equity,

ethics, ethos, habits, ideals, integrity, manners, morality, principles, probity, propriety, rectitude, scruples, standards.

morass *n* bog, can of worms, chaos, clutter, confusion, jam, jumble, marsh, marshland, mess, mire, mix-up, muddle, quagmire, quicksand, slough, swamp, tangle.

moratorium *n* ban, delay, embargo, freeze, halt, postponement, respite, standstill, stay, stoppage, suspension. **antonyms** go-ahead, green light.

morbid *adj* ailing, brooding, corrupt, deadly, diseased, dreadful, ghastly, ghoulish, gloomy, grim, grisly, gruesome, hideous, horrid, infected, lugubrious, macabre, malignant, melancholy, neurotic, pathological, pessimistic, putrid, sick, sickly, sombre, unhealthy, unsound, unwholesome, vicious.

mordant *adj* acerbic, acid, acidic, acrimonious, astringent, biting, bitter, caustic, corrosive, cutting, edged, harsh, incisive, pungent, sarcastic, scathing, sharp, stinging, trenchant, venomous, vicious, waspish, wounding. **antonyms** gentle, sparing.

more *adj* added, additional, alternative, extra, fresh, further, increased, new, other, renewed, repeated, spare, supplementary.
adv again, better, further, longer.

moreover *adv* additionally, also, as well, besides, further, furthermore, in addition, into the bargain, likewise, may I add, more, more to the point, to boot, too, what is more.

moribund *adj* at a standstill, collapsing, crumbling, declining, doomed, dwindling, dying, ebbing, fading, failing, in extremis, obsolescent, on one's last legs, on the way out, senile, stagnant, stagnating, waning, wasting away, weak, with one foot in the grave. **antonyms** alive, flourishing, lively, nascent.

morning *n* am, break of day, cock-crow, dawn, daybreak, daylight, first thing, forenoon, morn, sunrise, sun-up.

moron *n* ass, blockhead, bonehead, clot, cretin, daftie, dimwit, dolt, dope, dumbbell, dummy, dunce, dunderhead, fool, halfwit, idiot, imbecile, klutz, mental defective, muttonhead, numskull, schmuck, simpleton, thickhead, vegetable, zombie.

moronic *adj* asinine, brainless, cretinous, daft, defective, dimwitted, doltish, dopey, foolish, gormless, halfwitted, idiotic, imbecilic, lacking, mindless, retarded, simple, simple-minded, stupid, subnormal, thick, unintelligent.

morose *adj* blue, cheerless, crabbed, crabby, cross, crusty, depressed, dour, down, gloomy, glum, grim, grouchy, gruff, grum, huffy, humourless, ill-humoured, ill-natured, ill-tempered, low, melancholy, misanthropic, moody, mournful, perverse, pessimistic, saturnine, sour, stern, sulky, sullen, surly, taciturn, testy, unsociable. **antonyms** cheerful, communicative.

morsel *n* atom, bit, bite, crumb, fraction, fragment, grain, modicum, mouthful, nibble, part, piece, scrap, segment, slice, smidgen, snack, soupçon, taste, titbit.

mortal *adj* agonising, awful, bodily, corporeal, deadly, deathful, dire, earthly, enormous, ephemeral, extreme, fatal, fleshly, grave, great, human, imperma-nent, implacable, intense, irreconcilable, lethal, passing, perishable, relentless, remorseless, severe, sworn, temporal, terrible, transient, unrelenting, worldly. **antonym** immortal.

n being, body, creature, earthling, human, human being, individual, man, person, woman. **antonyms** god, immortal.

mortality *n* bloodshed, carnage, death, destruction, ephemerality, fatality, humanity, humans, impermanence, killing, mankind, mortals, perishability, temporality, transience, transitoriness. **antonym** immortality.

mortified *adj* abashed, affronted, annoyed, ashamed, chagrined, chastened, confounded, crushed, dead, decayed, deflated, discomfited, displeased, embarrassed, gangrenous, humbled, humiliated, put out, put to shame, putrefied, putrid, rotted, rotten, shamed, vexed. **antonyms** elated, jubilant.

mortify *v* abase, abash, affront, annoy, chagrin, chasten, confound, conquer, control, corrupt, crush, deflate, deny, die, disappoint, discipline, discomfit, embarrass, fester, gangrene, humble, humiliate, macerate, put to shame, putrefy, shame, subdue, vex.

mostly *adv* as a rule, characteristically, chiefly, commonly, customarily, for the most part, generally, largely, mainly, normally, on the whole, particularly, predominantly, primarily, principally, typically, usually.

mote *n* atom, grain, iota, jot, mite, particle, speck, spot, trace.

moth-eaten *adj* ancient, antiquated, archaic, dated, decayed, decrepit, dilapidated, mangy, moribund, mouldy, musty, obsolete, old-fashioned, outdated, outworn, ragged, seedy, shabby, stale, tattered, threadbare, worn-out. **antonyms** fresh, new.

mother *v* baby, bear, care for, cherish, cosset, foster, fuss over, indulge, nurse, nurture, overprotect, pamper, produce, protect, raise, rear, spoil, tend. **antonym** neglect.

motherly *adj* affectionate, caring, comforting, fond, gentle, indulgent, kind, kindly, loving, maternal, protective, solicitous, tender, warm. **antonym** indifferent, neglectful, uncaring.

motion *n* action, change, dynamics, flow, flux, gesture, inclination, kinetics, locomotion, mechanics, mobility, move, movement, node, passage, passing, progress, proposal, proposition, recommendation, sign, signal, submission, suggestion, transit, travel, wave.

v beckon, direct, gesture, nod, sign, signal, usher, wave.

motionless *adj* at a standstill, at rest, calm, fixed, frozen, halted, immobile, inanimate, inert, lifeless, moveless, paralysed, resting, rigid, stagnant, standing, static, stationary, still, stock-still, transfixed, unmoved, unmoving. **antonym** active.

motivate *v* actuate, arouse, bring, cause, draw, drive, encourage, impel, incite, induce, inspire, inspirit, instigate, kindle, lead, move, persuade, prompt, propel, provoke, push, spur, stimulate, stir, trigger, urge. **antonyms** deter, prevent.

motivation *n* ambition, desire, drive, hunger, impulse, incentive, incitement, inducement, inspiration, instigation, interest, momentum, motive, persuasion, provocation, push, reason, spur, stimulus, urge, wish. **antonym** discouragement, prevention.

motive *n* cause, consideration, design, desire, encouragement, ground(s), impulse, incentive, incitement, inducement, influence, inspiration, intention, mainspring, motivation, object, occasion, purpose, rationale, reason, spur, stimulus, thinking, urge. **antonyms** deterrent, discouragement, disincentive.

adj activating, actuating, driving,

impelling, initiating, motivating, moving, operative, prompting, propellent. **antonyms** deterrent, inhibitory, preventive.

motley *adj* assorted, chequered, disparate, dissimilar, diverse, diversified, haphazard, heterogeneous, ill-assorted, mingled, miscellaneous, mixed, multicoloured, particoloured, patchwork, unlike, varied, variegated. **antonyms** homogeneous, uniform.

mottled *adj* blotchy, brindled, chequered, dappled, flecked, freckled, marbled, piebald, pied, skewbald, speckled, spotted, stippled, streaked, tabby, variegated, veined, watered. **antonyms** plain, uniform.

motto *n* adage, apophthegm, byword, catchword, cry, dictum, epigraph, formula, gnome, golden rule, maxim, precept, proverb, rule, saw, saying, sentence, slogan, watchword.

mould *n* arrangement, brand, build, calibre, cast, character, configuration, construction, cut, design, die, fashion, form, format, frame, framework, ilk, kidney, kind, line, make, matrix, model, nature, pattern, quality, shape, sort, stamp, structure, style, template, type.
v affect, carve, cast, construct, control, create, design, direct, fashion, fit, forge, form, hew, influence, make, model, sculpt, sculpture, shape, stamp, work.

moulder *v* corrupt, crumble, decay, decompose, disintegrate, perish, rot, turn to dust, waste.

mouldy *adj* bad, blighted, corrupt, decaying, fusty, mildewed, musty, putrid, rotten, rotting, spoiled, stale. **antonyms** fresh, wholesome.

mound *n* bank, barrow, bulwark, drift, dune, earthwork, elevation, embankment, heap, hill, hillock, hummock, knoll, motte, pile, rampart, ridge, rise, stack, tuffet, tumulus, tussock.

mount *v* accumulate, arise, ascend, bestride, build, clamber up, climb, climb on, climb up on, copulate, cover, deliver, display, emplace, enchase, escalade, escalate, exhibit, fit, frame, get astride, get on, get up, get up on, go up, grow, horse, increase, install, intensify, jump on, launch, lift, multiply, pile up, place, position, prepare, produce, put in place, put on, ready, ride, rise, rocket, scale, set, set in motion, set off, set up, soar, stage, straddle, swell, tower, tread.
n backing, base, fixture, frame, horse,

mounting, pedestal, podium, setting, stand, steed, support.

mountain *n* abundance, alp, backlog, ben, berg, elevation, eminence, fell, heap, height, mass, massif, mound, mount, Munro, peak, pile, reserve, stack, ton.

mountainous *adj* alpine, daunting, enormous, formidable, gigantic, great, gross, high, highland, hilly, huge, hulking, immense, mammoth, mighty, monumental, ponderous, prodigious, rocky, rugged, soaring, steep, towering, unwieldy, upland. **antonyms** easy, flat, small.

mountebank *n* charlatan, cheat, con man, fake, fraud, huckster, impostor, phoney, pretender, quack, rogue, swindler, trickster.

mourn *v* bemoan, bewail, deplore, grieve, keen, lament, miss, regret, rue, sorrow, wail, weep. **antonyms** bless, rejoice.

mournful *adj* broken-hearted, cast-down, cheerless, dejected, deplorable, depressed, desolate, disconsolate, dismal, distressing, doleful, dolorous, downcast, funereal, gloomy, grief-stricken, grieving, heartbroken, heavy, heavy-hearted, joyless, lachrymose, lamentable, long-faced, lugubrious, melancholy, miserable, painful, piteous, plaintive, plangent, rueful, sad, sombre, sorrowful, stricken, tragic, unhappy, woeful, woesome. **antonyms** cheerful, joyful.

mourning *n* bereavement, black, desolation, grief, grieving, keening, lamentation, sackcloth and ashes, sadness, sorrow, wailing, weeds, weeping, widow's weeds, woe. **antonym** rejoicing.

mous(e)y *adj* brownish, characterless, colourless, diffident, drab, dull, indeterminate, ineffectual, mouse-like, plain, quiet, self-effacing, shy, timid, timorous, unassertive, unforthcoming, uninteresting, withdrawn. **antonyms** assertive, bright, extrovert, irrepressible.

mouth¹ *n* aperture, cake-hole, cavity, chops, crevice, door, entrance, estuary, gateway, gob, inlet, jaws, kisser, lips, mandibles, maw, moue, opening, orifice, outlet, portal, potato-trap, pout, rattle-trap, scowl, threshold, trap, vent.
v articulate, declaim, elegise, enunciate, form, pronounce, shape, spout, utter, whisper.

mouth² *n* backchat, boasting, bragging, cheek, effrontery, gas, hot air,

mouthful *n* bit, bite, drop, forkful, gob, gobbet, gulp, morsel, sample, sip, slug, spoonful, sup, swallow, taste, titbit.

mouthpiece *n* agent, delegate, journal, organ, propagandist, representative, spokesman, spokeswoman.

movable *adj* adjustable, alterable, changeable, detachable, flexible, mobile, portable, transferable, transportable. *antonyms* fixed, immovable.

move *v* activate, actuate, adjust, advance, advise, advocate, affect, agitate, budge, carry, cause, change, cover the ground, decamp, depart, disturb, drift, drive, ease, edge, excite, flit, get, give rise to, go, go away, gravitate, impel, impress, incite, induce, influence, inspire, instigate, jiggle, lead, leave, make strides, march, migrate, motivate, move house, operate, persuade, proceed, progress, prompt, propel, propose, pull, push, put forward, quit, recommend, relocate, remove, rouse, run, set going, shift, shove, start, stimulate, stir, submit, suggest, switch, take, touch, transfer, transport, transpose, turn, urge, walk.
n act, action, deed, dodge, draught, flit, flitting, go, manoeuvre, measure, migration, motion, movement, ploy, relocation, removal, ruse, shift, step, stratagem, stroke, tack, tactic, transfer, turn.

movement *n* act, action, activity, advance, agitation, beat, cadence, campaign, change, crusade, current, development, displacement, division, drift, drive, evolution, exercise, faction, flow, front, gesture, ground swell, group, grouping, machinery, manoeuvre, measure, mechanism, metre, motion, move, moving, operation, organisation, pace, part, party, passage, progress, progression, rhythm, section, shift, steps, stir, stirring, swing, tempo, tendency, transfer, trend, workings, works.

movies *n* cinema, film, films, flicks, pictures, silver screen.

moving *adj* affecting, ambulatory, arousing, dynamic, emotional, emotive, exciting, impelling, impressive, inspirational, inspiring, mobile, motivating, movable, pathetic, persuasive, poignant, portable, propelling, running, stimulating, stimulative, stirring, touching, unfixed. *antonyms* fixed, stationary, unemotional.

mow *v* clip, crop, cut, scythe, shear, trim.

mow down butcher, cut down, cut to pieces, decimate, massacre, shoot down, slaughter.

much *adv* considerably, copiously, decidedly, exceedingly, frequently, greatly, often.
adj a lot of, abundant, ample, considerable, copious, great, plenteous, plenty of, siz(e)able, substantial.
n heaps, lashings, loads, lots, oodles, plenty. *antonym* little.

muck *n* dirt, droppings, dung, faeces, filth, gunge, gunk, manure, mire, mud, ooze, scum, sewage, slime, sludge.

muck up botch, bungle, make a mess of, make a muck of, mess up, muff, ruin, screw up, spoil, waste.

mucky *adj* begrimed, bespattered, dirty, filthy, grimy, messy, miry, mud-caked, muddy, oozy, soiled, sticky. *antonym* clean.

muddle *v* befuddle, bewilder, confound, confuse, daze, disarrange, disorder, disorganise, disorient(ate), fuddle, jumble, make a mess of, mess, mix up, perplex, scramble, spoil, stupefy, tangle.
n bollocks, chaos, clutter, cock-up, confusion, daze, disarray, disorder, disorganisation, jumble, mess, mix-up, perplexity, plight, predicament, snarl-up, tangle.

muddle through cope, get along, get by, make it, manage, muddle along, scrape by.

muddled *adj* at sea, befuddled, bewildered, chaotic, confused, dazed, disarrayed, disordered, disorganised, disorient(at)ed, higgledy-piggledy, incoherent, jumbled, loose, messy, mixed-up, muddle-headed, perplexed, puzzle-headed, scrambled, stupefied, tangled, unclear, vague, woolly.

muddy *adj* bespattered, blurred, boggy, clarty, cloudy, confused, dingy, dirty, dull, foul, fuzzy, grimy, hazy, impure, indistinct, marshy, miry, mucky, mud-caked, muddled, opaque, sloppy, soiled, swampy, turbid, unclear, vague, woolly. *antonyms* clean, clear.
v bedaub, begrime, besmirch, bespatter, cloud, dirty, smear, soil. *antonym* clean.

muff *v* botch, bungle, fluff, mess up, mishit, mismanage, miss, spoil.

muffle *v* cloak, conceal, cover, damp down, dampen, deaden, disguise, dull, envelop, gag, hood, hush, mask, mute, muzzle, quieten, shroud, silence, soften, stifle, suppress, swaddle, swathe, wrap up. *antonym* amplify.

mug[1] *n* beaker, cup, flagon, jug, pot, tankard, toby jug.

mug[2] *n* chump, fool, gull, innocent, muggins, sap, saphead, simpleton, soft touch, sucker.

mug[3] *n* clock, countenance, dial, face, features, mush, phiz(og), puss, visage.

mug up bone up, cram, get up, study, swot.

mug[4] *v* attack, bash, batter, beat up, jump (on), rob, roll, set upon, steal from, waylay.

muggy *adj* clammy, close, damp, humid, moist, oppressive, sticky, stuffy, sultry, sweltering. *antonym* dry.

mulish *adj* bull-headed, defiant, difficult, headstrong, inflexible, intractable, intransigent, obstinate, perverse, pig-headed, recalcitrant, refractory, self-willed, stiff-necked, stubborn, unreasonable, wilful, wrong-headed.

mull *v* chew, consider, contemplate, deliberate, examine, meditate, muse on, ponder, reflect on, review, ruminate, study, think about, think over, weigh up.

multifarious *adj* different, diverse, diversified, legion, manifold, many, miscellaneous, multiform, multiple, multiplex, multitudinous, numerous, sundry, varied, variegated.

multiple *adj* collective, manifold, many, multifarious, multiplex, multitudinous, numerous, several, sundry, various.

multiplicity *n* abundance, array, diversity, heaps, host, loads, lot, lots, manifoldness, mass, myriad, number, numerousness, oodles, piles, profusion, scores, stacks, tons, variety.

multiply *v* accumulate, augment, boost, breed, build up, expand, extend, increase, intensify, proliferate, propagate, reproduce, spread. *antonyms* decrease, lessen.

multitude *n* army, assemblage, assembly, collection, commonalty, congregation, crowd, herd, hive, hoi polloi, horde, host, legion, lot, lots, mass, mob, myriad, people, populace, proletariat, public, rabble, sea, swarm, throng. *antonyms* handful, scattering.

multitudinous *adj* abounding, abundant, considerable, copious, countless, great, infinite, innumerable, legion, manifold, many, myriad, numerous, profuse, swarming, teeming, umpteen.

mum *adj* close-lipped, close-mouthed, dumb, mute, quiet, reticent, secretive,

silent, tight-lipped, uncommunicative, unforthcoming.

mumbo-jumbo *n* cant, chant, claptrap, conjuration, double talk, gibberish, gobbledegook, hocus-pocus, humbug, incantation, jargon, magic, mummery, nonsense, rite, ritual, spell, superstition.

munch *v* champ, chew, chomp, crunch, eat, masticate, scrunch.

mundane *adj* banal, commonplace, day-to-day, earthly, everyday, fleshly, human, humdrum, material, mortal, ordinary, prosaic, routine, secular, temporal, terrestrial, workaday, worldly. *antonyms* cosmic, extraordinary, supernatural.

munificent *adj* beneficent, benevolent, big-hearted, bounteous, bountiful, free-handed, generous, hospitable, lavish, liberal, magnanimous, open-handed, philanthropic, princely, rich, unstinting. *antonym* mean.

murder *n* agony, assassination, bloodshed, butchery, carnage, danger, difficulty, fractricide, hell, homicide, infanticide, killing, manslaughter, massacre, misery, ordeal, patricide, slaying, trial, trouble.

v abuse, assassinate, bump off, butcher, destroy, dispatch, do in, drub, eliminate, hammer, hit, kill, mangle, mar, massacre, misuse, rub out, ruin, slaughter, slay, spoil, thrash, waste.

murderous *adj* ardous, barbarous, bloodthirsty, bloody, brutal, cruel, cutthroat, dangerous, deadly, death-dealing, destructive, devastating, difficult, exhausting, fatal, fell, ferocious, harrowing, hellish, internecine, killing, lethal, sanguinary, sapping, savage, slaughterous, strenuous, unpleasant, withering.

murky *adj* cloudy, dark, dim, dismal, dreary, dull, dusky, enigmatic, foggy, gloomy, grey, misty, mysterious, obscure, overcast, veiled. *antonyms* bright, clear.

murmur *n* babble, burble, buzz, buzzing, complaint, drone, grumble, humming, moan, mumble, muttering, purl, purling, purr, rumble, undertone, whisper, whispering.

v babble, burble, burr, buzz, drone, gurgle, hum, mumble, mutter, purl, purr, rumble.

murmuring *adj* buzzing, droning, mumbling, murmurous, muttering, purring, rumbling, whispering.

n buzz(ing), drone, mumble, mumbling,

murmuration, muttering, purr(ing), rumble, rumbling, whisper(ing).

muscle *n* brawn, clout, force, forcefulness, might, potency, power, sinew, stamina, strength, sturdiness, tendon, weight.

muscle in butt in, elbow one's way in, force one's way in, impose oneself, jostle, push in, shove, strongarm.

muscular *adj* athletic, beefy, brawny, hefty, husky, powerful, powerfully-built, robust, sinewy, stalwart, strapping, strong, sturdy, vigorous, wiry. **antonyms** delicate, feeble, flabby, puny, weak.

muse *v* brood, chew, cogitate, consider, contemplate, deliberate, dream, meditate, mull over, ponder, reflect, review, ruminate, speculate, think, think over, weigh.

mush *n* corn, dough, hogwash, mash, mawkishness, pap, paste, pulp, schmaltz, sentimentality, slush, swill.

mushroom *v* boom, burgeon, expand, flourish, grow, increase, luxuriate, proliferate, shoot up, spread, spring up, sprout.

mushy *adj* doughy, maudlin, mawkish, pappy, pulpy, saccharine, schmaltzy, sentimental, sloppy, slushy, soft, squashy, squelchy, squidgy, sugary, syrupy, weepy, wet.

musing *n* absent-mindedness, abstraction, cerebration, cogitation, contemplation, daydreaming, dreaming, introspection, meditation, reflection, reverie, rumination, thinking, wool-gathering.

must *n* basic, duty, essential, fundamental, imperative, necessity, obligation, prerequisite, provision, requirement, requisite, sine qua non, stipulation.

muster *v* assemble, call together, call up, collect, come together, congregate, convene, convoke, enrol, gather, group, marshal, mass, meet, mobilise, rally, round up, summon, throng.
n assemblage, assembly, collection, congregation, convention, convocation, gathering, mass, meeting, mobilisation, rally, round-up, throng.

musty *adj* airless, ancient, antiquated, banal, clichéd, dank, decayed, dull, frowsty, fusty, hackneyed, hoary, mildewed, mildewy, moth-eaten, mouldy, obsolete, old, old-fashioned, smelly, stale, stuffy, threadbare, trite, worn-out.

mutable *adj* adaptable, alterable, changeable, changing, fickle, flexible, inconsistent, inconstant, interchangeable, irresolute, uncertain, undependable, unreliable, unsettled, unstable, unsteady, vacillating, variable, volatile, wavering. **antonyms** constant, invariable, permanent.

mutation *n* alteration, change, deviant, deviation, evolution, metamorphosis, modification, mutant, transfiguration, transformation, variation.

mute *adj* dumb, mum, noiseless, silent, speechless, unexpressed, unpronounced, unspeaking, unspoken, voiceless, wordless. **antonyms** articulate, vocal, voluble.
v dampen, deaden, lower, moderate, muffle, silence, soften, soft-pedal, subdue, tone down.

muted *adj* dampened, dull, faint, low-key, muffled, quiet, soft, stifled, suppressed.

mutilate *v* adulterate, amputate, bowdlerise, butcher, censor, cut, cut to pieces, cut up, damage, disable, disfigure, dismember, distort, expurgate, hack, hamble, injure, lacerate, lame, maim, mangle, mar, spoil.

mutinous *adj* bolshie, bolshy, disobedient, insubordinate, insurgent, rebellious, recusant, refractory, revolutionary, riotous, seditious, subversive, turbulent, ungovernable, unmanageable, unruly. **antonyms** compliant, dutiful, obedient.

mutiny *n* defiance, disobedience, insubordination, insurrection, putsch, rebellion, resistance, revolt, revolution, riot, rising, strike, uprising.
v disobey, protest, rebel, resist, revolt, rise up, strike.

mutt *n* cur, dog, dolt, drongo, dunderhead, fool, idiot, ignoramus, imbecile, mongrel, moron, sap, saphead, thickhead.

mutter *v* chunter, complain, grouch, grouse, grumble, mumble, murmur, rumble.

mutual *adj* common, communal, complementary, exchanged, interchangeable, interchanged, joint, reciprocal, reciprocated, requited, returned, shared.

muzzle *v* censor, choke, curb, gag, mute, restrain, silence, stifle, suppress.

muzzy *adj* addled, befuddled, bewildered, blurred, confused, dazed, hazy, muddled, mused, tipsy. **antonym** clear.

myriad *adj* boundless, countless, immeasurable, incalculable, innumerable, limitless, multitudinous, untold.
n army, flood, horde, host, millions, mountain, multitude, scores, sea, swarm, thousands, throng.

mysterious *adj* abstruse, arcane, baffling, concealed, covert, cryptic, curious, dark, enigmatic, furtive, hidden, impenetrable, incomprehensible, inexplicable, inscrutable, insoluble, mystical, mystifying, obscure, perplexing, puzzling, recondite, secret, secretive, strange, uncanny, unfathomable, unsearchable, veiled, weird. **antonyms** comprehensible, frank, straightforward.

mystical *adj* abstruse, arcane, cryptic, enigmatical, esoteric, hidden, inscrutable, metaphysical, mysterious, mystic, occult, otherworldly, paranormal, supernatural, transcendental.

mystify *v* baffle, bamboozle, beat, bewilder, confound, confuse, escape, perplex, puzzle, stump.

mystique *n* appeal, awe, charisma, charm, fascination, glamour, magic, spell.

myth *n* allegory, delusion, fable, fairy tale, fancy, fantasy, fiction, figment, illusion, legend, old wives' tale, parable, saga, story, superstition, tradition.

mythical *adj* fabled, fabricated, fabulous, fairy-tale, fanciful, fantasy, fictitious, imaginary, invented, legendary, made-up, make-believe, mythological, non-existent, pretended, unhistoric(al), unreal. **antonyms** actual, historical, real, true.

mythological *adj* fabulous, folkloric, legendary, mythical, traditional.

mythology *n* folklore, folk-tales, legend, lore, myths, tales, tradition(s).

N

nab *v* apprehend, arrest, capture, catch, collar, grab, nail, nick, seize, snatch.

nadir *n* all-time low, bottom, depths, low point, lowest point, minimum, rock bottom, zero. **antonyms** acme, apex, peak, zenith.

nag *v* annoy, badger, berate, chivvy, goad, harass, harry, henpeck, irritate, pain, pester, plague, scold, torment, upbraid, vex.

n harpy, harridan, scold, shrew, tartar, termagant, virago.

nagging *adj* continuous, distressing, irritating, painful, persistent, scolding, shrewish, tormenting, upsetting, worrying.

nail *v* apprehend, attach, beat, capture, catch, clinch, collar, fasten, fix, hammer, join, nab, nick, pin, secure, seize, tack.

naïve *adj* artless, callow, candid, childlike, confiding, credulous, dewy-eyed, facile, frank, green, guileless, gullible, ingenuous, innocent, natural, open, simple, simplistic, small-town, trusting, unaffected, uncritical, unpretentious, unsophisticated, unsuspecting, unsuspicious, unworldly, wide-eyed.

antonyms experienced, sophisticated.

naïvety *n* artlessness, callowness, candour, credulity, frankness, guilelessness, gullibility, inexperience, ingenuousness, innocence, naturalness, openness, simplicity. **antonyms** experience, sophistication.

naked *adj* bare, blatant, defenceless, denuded, disrobed, divested, evident, exposed, helpless, in the altogether, in the buff, insecure, manifest, mother-naked, nude, open, overt, patent, plain, simple, stark, starkers, stark-naked, stripped, unadorned, unarmed, unclothed, unconcealed, uncovered, undisguised, undraped, undressed, unexaggerated, unguarded, unmistakable, unprotected, unqualified, unvarnished, vulnerable.

antonyms clothed, concealed, covered.

name *n* appellation, character, credit, denomination, designation, distinction, eminence, epithet, esteem, fame, handle, honour, moni(c)ker, nickname, note, praise, renown, reputation, repute, soubriquet, stage name, term, title, to-name.

v appoint, baptise, call, choose, christen, cite, classify, commission, denominate, designate, dub, entitle, identify, label, mention, nominate, select, specify, style, term, title.

named *adj* appointed, baptised, called, chosen, christened, cited, classified, commissioned, denominated, designated, dubbed, entitled, identified, known as, labelled, mentioned, nominated, picked, selected, singled out, specified, styled, termed. **antonym** nameless.

nameless *adj* abominable, anonymous, dreadful, fearsome, horrendous, horrible, incognito, indescribable, ineffable, inexpressible, innominate, obscure, terrible, undesignated, undistinguished, unheard-of, unknown, unmentionable, unnamed, unspeakable, unsung, untitled, unutterable. **antonym** named.

namely *adv* ie, specifically, that is, that is to say, to wit, videlicet, viz.

nap[1] *v* catnap, doze, drop off, drowse, kip, nod, nod off, rest, sleep, snooze.

n catnap, forty winks, kip, rest, shuteye, siesta, sleep.

nap[2] *n* down, downiness, fibre, fuzz, grain, pile, shag, weave.

narcissistic *adj* conceited, egocentric, egomaniacal, ego(t)istic, self-centred, self-loving, vain.

nark *v* annoy, bother, bug, exasperate, gall, get, irk, irritate, miff, nettle, peeve, pip, pique, provoke, rile.

narrate *v* chronicle, describe, detail, recite, recount, rehearse, relate, repeat, report, set forth, state, tell, unfold.

narrow *adj* attenuated, avaricious, biased, bigoted, circumscribed, close, confined, constricted, contracted, cramped, dogmatic, exclusive, fine, illiberal, incapacious, intolerant, limited, meagre, mean, mercenary, narrow-minded, near, niggardly, partial, pinched, prejudiced, reactionary, restricted, scanty, select, short-head, simplistic, slender, slim, small-minded, spare, straitened, tapering, thin, tight, ungenerous. **antonyms** broad, liberal, tolerant, wide.

v circumscribe, constrict, diminish, limit, reduce, simplify, straiten, tighten. **antonyms** broaden, increase, loosen, widen.

narrowing *n* attenuation, compression, constipation, constriction, contraction, curtailment, emaciation, reduction, tapering, thinning. **antonyms** broadening, widening.

narrowly *adv* barely, by a hair's breadth, by a whisker, carefully, closely, just, only just, painstakingly, precisely, scarcely, scrutinisingly, strictly.

narrow-minded *adj* biased, bigoted, blinkered, conservative, hidebound, illiberal, insular, intolerant, mean, opinionated, parochial, petty, prejudiced, provincial, reactionary, short-sighted, small-minded, strait-laced. **antonym** broad-minded.

narrowness *n* attenuation, closeness, constriction, crowdedness, exclusiveness, insularity, limitation, meagreness, narrow-mindedness, nearness, parochialism, restrictedness, slenderness, thinness, tightness. **antonyms** breadth, width.

nascent *adj* advancing, budding, developing, embryonic, evolving, growing, incipient, rising, young. **antonym** dying.

nastiness *n* defilement, dirtiness, disagreeableness, filth, filthiness, foulness, impurity, indecency, licentiousness, malice, meanness, obscenity, offensiveness, pollution, porn, pornography, ribaldry, smuttiness, spitefulness, squalor, uncleanliness, unpleasantness, unsavouriness, waspishness.

nasty *adj* abusive, annoying, bad, bad-tempered, base, beastly, critical, dangerous, despicable, dirty, disagreeable, disgusting, distasteful, filthy, foul, gross, horrible, impure, indecent, lascivious, lewd, licentious, loathsome, low-down, malicious, malodorous, mean, nauseating, noisome, objectionable, obnoxious, obscene, odious, offensive, painful, polluted, pornographic, repellent, repugnant, ribald, serious, severe, sickening, smutty, spiteful, unappetising, unpleasant, unsavoury, vicious, vile, waspish. **antonyms** agreeable, clean, decent, pleasant.

nation *n* citizenry, commonwealth, community, country, people, population, race, realm, society, state, tribe.

national *adj* civil, countrywide, domestic, general, governmental, internal, nationwide, public, social, state, widespread.

nationalistic *adj* chauvinistic, ethnocentrist, jingoistic, loyal, patriotic, xenophobic.

native *adj* aboriginal, congenital, domestic, endemic, genuine, hereditary, home, home-born, home-bred, home-grown, home-made, inborn, inbred, indigenous, ingrained, inherent, inherited, innate, instinctive, intrinsic, inveterate, local, mother, natal, natural, original, real, vernacular.
n aborigine, citizen, countryman, inhabitant, national, resident. **antonyms** foreigner, outsider, stranger.

natter *v* blether, chatter, confabulate, gab, gabble, gossip, jabber, jaw, prate, prattle, talk.
n blether, chat, chinwag, chitchat, confab, confabulation, conversation, gab, gabble, gossip, jabber, jaw, prattle, talk.

natty *adj* chic, dapper, elegant, fashionable, neat, ritzy, smart, snazzy, spruce, stylish, swanky, trim.

natural *adj* artless, candid, characteristic, common, congenital, constitutional, essential, everyday, frank, genuine, inborn, indigenous, ingenuous, inherent, innate, instinctive, intuitive, legitimate, logical, native, normal, open, ordinary, organic, plain, pure, real, regular, simple, spontaneous, typical, unaffected, unbleached, unforced, unlaboured, unlearned, unmixed, unpolished, unpretentious, unrefined, unsophisticated, unstudied, untaught, usual, whole. **antonyms** abnormal, affected, alien, artificial, pretended, unnatural.

naturalistic *adj* graphic, lifelike, natural, photographic, realistic, real-life, representational, true-to-life.

naturally *adj* absolutely, artlessly, as a matter of course, candidly, certainly, customarily, frankly, genuinely, informally, normally, of course, plainly, simply, spontaneously, typically, unaffectedly, unpretentiously.

naturalness *n* artlessness, candidness, frankness, genuineness, informality, ingenuousness, openness, plainness, pureness, purity, realism, simpleness, simplicity, spontaneity, spontaneousness, unaffectedness, unpretentiousness, wholeness.

nature *n* attributes, category, character, complexion, constitution, cosmos, creation, description, disposition, earth, environment, essence, features, humour, kind, make-up, mood, outlook, quality, sort, species, style, temper, temperament, traits, type, universe, variety, world.

naughty *adj* annoying, bad, bawdy, blue, disobedient, exasperating, fractious, impish, improper, lewd, misbehaved, mischievous, obscene, off-colour, perverse, playful, refractory, remiss, reprehensible, ribald, risqué, roguish, sinful, smutty, teasing, vulgar, wayward, wicked, worthless. *antonyms* good, polite, well-behaved.

nausea *n* abhorrence, aversion, biliousness, disgust, loathing, motion sickness, queasiness, repugnance, retching, revulsion, sickness, squeamishness, vomiting.

nauseate *v* disgust, horrify, offend, repel, repulse, revolt, sicken, turn one's stomach.

nauseating *adj* abhorrent, detestable, disgusting, distasteful, fulsome, loathsome, nauseous, offensive, repugnant, repulsive, revolting, sickening.

navigate *v* cross, cruise, direct, drive, guide, handle, helm, journey, manoeuvre, pilot, plan, plot, sail, skipper, steer, voyage.

near *adj* accessible, adjacent, adjoining, akin, allied, alongside, approaching, at close quarters, attached, beside, bordering, close, connected, contiguous, dear, familiar, forthcoming, handy, imminent, impending, in the offing, intimate, looming, near-at-hand, nearby, neighbouring, next, nigh, on the cards, proximal, related, touching. *antonyms* distant, far, remote.

near thing close shave, narrow escape, nasty moment, near miss.

nearby *adj* accessible, adjacent, adjoining, convenient, handy, near, neighbouring. *antonym* faraway.
adv at close quarters, close at hand, near, not far away, within reach.

nearly *adv* about, all but, almost, approaching, approximately, as good as, closely, just about, not quite, practically, pretty much, pretty well, roughly, virtually, well-nigh.

nearness *n* accessibility, availability, chumminess, closeness, contiguity, dearness, familiarity, handiness, immediacy, imminence, intimacy, juxtaposition, propinquity, proximity, vicinity.

neat *adj* accurate, adept, adroit, agile, apt, clean-cut, clever, dainty, deft, dexterous, dinky, efficient, effortless, elegant, expert, fastidious, genty, graceful, handy, methodical, nice, nimble, orderly, practised, precise, pure, shipshape, skilful, smart, spick-and-span, spruce, straight, stylish, systematic, tiddley, tidy, trim, uncluttered, undiluted, unmixed, well-judged. *antonyms* disordered, disorderly, messy, untidy.

neaten *v* arrange, clean up, groom, put to rights, smarten, straighten, tidy, trim.

neatly *adv* accurately, adeptly, adroitly, agilely, aptly, cleverly, daintily, deftly, dexterously, efficiently, effortlessly, elegantly, expertly, fastidiously, featly, gracefully, handily, methodically, nicely, nimbly, precisely, skilfully, smartly, sprucely, stylishly, systematically, tidily. *antonyms* inelegantly, inexpertly, unskilfully, untidily.

nebulous *adj* cloudy, confused, dim, fuzzy, hazy, imprecise, indefinite, indeterminate, indistinct, misty, murky, obscure, shadowy, shapeless, uncertain, unclear, unformed, unspecific, vague. *antonym* clear.

necessarily *adv* accordingly, automatically, axiomatically, by definition, certainly, compulsorily, consequently, incontrovertibly, ineluctably, inescapably, inevitably, inexorably, naturally, of course, of necessity, perforce, therefore, thus.

necessary *adj* certain, compulsory, de rigueur, essential, fated, imperative, indispensable, ineluctable, inescapable, inevitable, inexorable, mandatory, must, needed, needful, obligatory, required, requisite, unavoidable, vital. *antonyms* inessential, unimportant, unnecessary.

necessitate *v* call for, coerce, compel, constrain, demand, entail, force, impel, involve, oblige, require.

necessity *n* compulsion, demand, destiny, destitution, essential, exigency, extremity, fate, fundamental, indigence, indispensability, inevitability, inexorableness, necessary, need, needfulness, obligation, penury, poverty, prerequisite, privation, requirement, requisite, sine qua non, want.

need *v* call for, crave, demand, lack, miss, necessitate, require, want.
n demand, deprivation, destitution, distress, emergency, essential, exigency, extremity, impecuniousness, inadequacy, indigence, insufficiency, lack, longing, necessity, neediness, obligation, paucity, penury, poverty, privation, requirement, requisite, shortage, urgency, want, wish. *antonym* sufficiency.

needed *adj* called for, compulsory,

desired, essential, lacking, necessary, obligatory, required, requisite, wanted. **antonyms** unnecessary, unneeded.

needful *adj* essential, indispensable, necessary, needed, needy, required, requisite, stipulated, vital. **antonyms** excess, needless, superfluous.

needle *v* aggravate, annoy, bait, goad, harass, irk, irritate, nag, nettle, pester, prick, prod, provoke, rile, ruffle, spur, sting, taunt, torment.

needless *adj* causeless, dispensable, excessive, expendable, gratuitous, groundless, inessential, non-essential, pointless, purposeless, redundant, superfluous, uncalled-for, unessential, unnecessary, unwanted, useless. **antonyms** necessary, needful.

needy *adj* deprived, destitute, disadvantaged, impecunious, impoverished, indigent, penniless, penurious, poor, poverty-stricken, underprivileged. **antonyms** affluent, wealthy, well-off.

nefarious *adj* abominable, atrocious, base, criminal, depraved, detestable, dreadful, evil, execrable, foul, heinous, horrible, infamous, infernal, iniquitous, monstrous, odious, opprobrious, satanic, shameful, sinful, unholy, vicious, vile, villainous, wicked. **antonym** exemplary.

negate *v* abrogate, annul, cancel, contradict, countermand, deny, disallow, disprove, gainsay, invalidate, neutralise, nullify, oppose, quash, refute, repeal, rescind, retract, reverse, revoke, void, wipe out. **antonym** affirm.

negation *n* antithesis, cancellation, contradiction, contrary, converse, counterpart, denial, disavowal, disclaimer, inverse, neutralisation, nullification, opposite, rejection, renunciation, repeal, reverse, veto. **antonym** affirmation.

negative *adj* annulling, antagonistic, apathetic, below zero, colourless, contradictory, contrary, counteractive, cynical, denying, dissenting, gloomy, invalidating, jaundiced, neutralising, nullifying, opposing, pessimistic, refusing, rejecting, unco-operative, unenthusiastic, uninterested, unwilling, weak. **antonyms** optimistic, positive.
n contradiction, denial, opposite, refusal.

neglect *v* contemn, disdain, disprovide, disregard, forget, ignore, leave alone, let slide, omit, overlook, pass by, rebuff, scorn, shirk, skimp, slight, spurn.

antonyms cherish, nurture, treasure.
n carelessness, default, dereliction, disdain, disregard, disrespect, failure, forgetfulness, heedlessness, inattention, indifference, laxity, laxness, neglectfulness, negligence, oversight, slackness, slight, slovenliness, unconcern.

neglected *adj* abandoned, derelict, disregarded, overgrown, unappreciated, uncared-for, uncultivated, underestimated, undervalued, unmaintained, untended, untilled, unweeded. **antonyms** cherished, treasured.

neglectful *adj* careless, disregardful, forgetful, heedless, inattentive, indifferent, lax, negligent, oblivious, remiss, thoughtless, uncaring, unmindful. **antonyms** attentive, careful.

negligence *n* carelessness, default, dereliction, disregard, failure, forgetfulness, heedlessness, inadvertence, inattention, inattentiveness, indifference, laxity, laxness, neglect, neglectfulness, omission, oversight, remissness, shortcoming, slackness, slight, stupidity, thoughtlessness. **antonyms** attentiveness, care, regard.

negligent *adj* careless, cursory, forgetful, inattentive, indifferent, lax, neglectful, nonchalant, offhand, regardless, remiss, slack, thoughtless, uncareful, uncaring, unmindful, unthinking. **antonyms** attentive, careful, heedful, scrupulous.

negligible *adj* imperceptible, inconsequential, insignificant, minor, minute, petty, small, trifling, trivial, unimportant. **antonym** significant.

negotiate *v* adjudicate, arbitrate, arrange, bargain, clear, conciliate, confer, consult, contract, cross, deal, debate, discuss, get past, handle, manage, mediate, parley, pass, settle, surmount, transact, traverse, treat, work out.

neighbourhood *n* community, confines, district, environs, locale, locality, precincts, proximity, quarter, region, surroundings, vicinity.

neighbouring *adj* abutting, adjacent, adjoining, bordering, connecting, contiguous, near, nearby, nearest, next, surrounding. **antonyms** distant, faraway, remote.

neighbourly *adj* amiable, chummy, civil, companionable, considerate, friendly, genial, helpful, hospitable, kind, obliging, sociable, social, solicitous, well-disposed.

nerve *n* audacity, boldness, bottle,

brass, bravery, brazenness, cheek, chutzpah, coolness, courage, daring, determination, effrontery, endurance, energy, fearlessness, firmness, force, fortitude, gall, gameness, grit, guts, impertinence, impudence, insolence, intrepidity, mettle, might, pluck, resolution, sauce, spirit, spunk, steadfastness, temerity, vigour, will. **antonyms** cowardice, weakness.

v bolster, brace, embolden, encourage, fortify, hearten, invigorate, steel, strengthen. **antonym** unnerve.

nerve-racking *adj* annoying, difficult, disquieting, distressing, frightening, harassing, harrowing, maddening, stressful, tense, trying, worrisome, worrying.

nervous *adj* agitated, anxious, apprehensive, edgy, excitable, fearful, fidgety, flustered, hesitant, highly-strung, high-strung, hysterical, jittery, jumpy, nervy, neurotic, on edge, shaky, tense, timid, timorous, twitchy, uneasy, uptight, weak, windy, worried. **antonyms** bold, calm, confident, cool, relaxed.

nervousness *n* agitation, anxiety, disquiet, excitability, fluster, (h)abdabs, heebie-jeebies, perturbation, tension, timidity, touchiness, tremulousness, willies, worry. **antonyms** calmness, coolness.

nestle *v* cuddle, curl up, ensconce, huddle, nuzzle, snuggle.

net *n* drag, lattice, mesh, netting, network, open-work, reticulum, tracery, web.

v apprehend, bag, capture, catch, enmesh, ensnare, entangle, nab, trap.

nettle *v* annoy, chafe, exasperate, fret, goad, harass, incense, irritate, needle, pique, provoke, ruffle, sting, tease, vex.

nettled *adj* aggrieved, angry, annoyed, chafed, cross, exasperated, galled, goaded, harassed, huffy, incensed, irritable, irritated, miffed, needled, peeved, peevish, piqued, provoked, riled, ruffled, stung, vexed.

network *n* arrangement, channels, circuitry, complex, convolution, grid, grill, interconnections, labyrinth, maze, mesh, meshwork, net, nexus, organisation, plexus, reticulation, structure, system, tracks, web.

neurotic *adj* abnormal, anxious, compulsive, deviant, disordered, distraught, disturbed, maladjusted, manic, morbid, nervous, obsessive,

overwrought, unhealthy, unstable, wearisome. **antonyms** normal, stable.

neutral *adj* colourless, disinterested, dispassionate, dull, even-handed, expressionless, impartial, indeterminate, indifferent, indistinct, indistinguishable, intermediate, non-aligned, non-committal, nondescript, non-partisan, unbia(s)sed, uncommitted, undecided, undefined, uninvolved, unprejudiced. **antonyms** biased, prejudiced.

neutralise *v* cancel, counteract, counterbalance, counterpoise, frustrate, invalidate, negate, nullify, offset, undo.

neutrality *n* detachment, disinterest, disinterestedness, impartiality, impartialness, non-alignment, non-intervention, non-involvement, unbiasedness.

never *adv* at no time, not at all, not on your life, not on your Nellie, on no account, under no circumstances, when pigs fly. **antonym** always.

never-ending *adj* boundless, ceaseless, constant, continual, continuous, eternal, everlasting, incessant, interminable, non-stop, permanent, perpetual, persistent, relentless, unbroken, unceasing, unchanging, uninterrupted, unremitting. **antonyms** fleeting, transitory.

nevertheless *adv* anyhow, anyway, but, even so, however, nonetheless, notwithstanding, regardless, still, yet.

new *adj* added, advanced, altered, changed, contemporary, current, different, extra, fresh, improved, latest, modern, modernised, modernistic, more, newborn, newfangled, novel, original, recent, redesigned, renewed, restored, supplementary, topical, trendy, ultra modern, unfamiliar, unknown, unused, unusual, up-to-date, up-to-the-minute, virgin. **antonyms** hackneyed, old, outdated, out-of-date, usual.

newcomer *n* alien, arrival, arriviste, beginner, colonist, foreigner, immigrant, incomer, Johnny-come-lately, novice, outsider, parvenu, settler, stranger.

newfangled *adj* contemporary, fashionable, futuristic, gimmicky, modern, modernistic, new, novel, recent, trendy. **antonym** old-fashioned.

newly *adv* afresh, anew, freshly, just, lately, latterly, recently.

newness *n* freshness, innovation, novelty, oddity, originality, recency, strangeness, unfamiliarity, uniqueness, unusualness. **antonyms** oldness, ordinariness.

news *n* account, advice, bulletin

communiqué, disclosure, dispatch, expose, gen, gossip, hearsay, information, intelligence, latest, leak, release, report, revelation, rumour, scandal, statement, story, tidings, update, word.

next *adj* adjacent, adjoining, closest, consequent, ensuing, following, later, nearest, neighbouring, sequential, subsequent, succeeding. *antonyms* preceding, previous.

adv afterwards, later, subsequently, then, thereafter.

nibble *n* bit, bite, crumb, morsel, peck, piece, snack, soupçon, taste, titbit.

v bite, eat, gnaw, munch, nip, nosh, peck, pickle.

nice *adj* accurate, agreeable, amiable, attractive, careful, charming, commendable, courteous, critical, cultured, dainty, delicate, delightful, discriminating, exact, exacting, fastidious, fine, friendly, genteel, good, kind, lik(e)able, meticulous, neat, particular, pleasant, pleasurable, polite, precise, prepossessing, punctilious, purist, refined, respectable, rigorous, scrupulous, strict, subtle, tidy, trim, virtuous, well-bred, well-mannered. *antonyms* careless, disagreeable, haphazard, nasty, unpleasant.

nicely *adv* acceptably, accurately, agreeable, amiably, attractively, carefully, charmingly, commendably, courteously, critically, daintily, delicately, delightfully, discriminatingly, elegantly, exactingly, exactly, fastidiously, finely, genteelly, kindly, lik(e)ably, meticulously, neatly, pleasantly, pleasingly, pleasurably, politely, precisely, prepossessingly, respectably, rigorously, scrupulously, strictly, subtly, tidily, trimly, virtuously, well. *antonyms* carelessly, disagreeably, haphazardly, nastily, unpleasantly.

niceness *n* accuracy, agreeableness, amiability, attractiveness, care, carefulness, charm, courtesy, daintiness, delicacy, delightfulness, discrimination, exactitude, exactness, fastidiousness, fineness, friendliness, gentility, goodness, kindness, lik(e)ableness, meticulousness, neatness, pleasantness, pleasurableness, politeness, preciseness, precision, punctiliousness, purism, refinement, respectability, rigorousness, rigour, scrupulousness, strictness, subtleness, subtlety, tidiness, trimness, virtue. *antonyms* carelessness, disagreeableness, haphazardness, nastiness,

unpleasantness.

niche[1] *n* alcove, corner, cubby-hole, hollow, nook, opening, recess.

niche[2] *n* calling, métier, place, position, slot, vocation.

nick[1] *n* chip, cut, damage, dent, indent, indentation, mark, notch, scar, score, scratch, snick.

v chip, cut, damage, dent, indent, mark, notch, scar, score, scratch, snick.

nick[2] *v* finger, knock off, pilfer, pinch, snitch, steal.

nifty *adj* adroit, agile, apt, chic, clever, deft, enjoyable, excellent, neat, nippy, pleasing, quick, sharp, smart, spruce, stylish.

niggardly *adj* avaricious, beggarly, cheese-paring, close, covetous, frugal, grudging, hard-fisted, inadequate, insufficient, meagre, mean, mercenary, miserable, miserly, near, paltry, parsimonious, penurious, scanty, skimpy, small, sparing, stinging, stingy, tight-fisted, ungenerous, ungiving, wretched. *antonyms* bountiful, generous.

nightfall *n* dusk, eve, evening, eventide, gloaming, sundown, sunset, twilight, vespers. *antonyms* dawn, sunrise.

nightmarish *adj* agonising, alarming, creepy, disturbing, dreadful, fell, frightening, harrowing, horrible, horrific, scaring, terrifying, unreal.

nihilist *n* agitator, agnostic, anarchist, atheist, cynic, disbeliever, extremist, negativist, pessimist, revolutionary, sceptic.

nimble *adj* active, agile, alert, brisk, deft, dexterous, light-foot(ed), lissom(e), lively, nippy, proficient, prompt, quick, quick-witted, ready, smart, sprightly, spry, swift. *antonyms* awkward, clumsy.

nimbleness *n* adroitness, agility, alacrity, alertness, deftness, dexterity, finesse, grace, lightness, niftiness, nippiness, skill, smartness, sprightliness, spryness.

nimbly *adv* actively, acutely, agilely, alertly, briskly, deftly, dexterously, easily, fast, fleetly, proficiently, promptly, quickly, quick-wittedly, readily, sharply, smartly, snappily, speedily, spryly, swiftly. *antonyms* awkwardly, clumsily.

nincompoop *n* blockhead, dimwit, dolt, dunce, fool, idiot, ignoramus, ninny, nitwit, noodle, numskull, sap, saphead, simpleton.

nip[1] *v* bite, catch, check, clip, compress,

grip, nibble, pinch, snag, snap, snip, squeeze, tweak, twitch.

nip² *n* dram, draught, drop, finger, mouthful, portion, shot, sip, slug, snifter, soupçon, sup, swallow, taste.

nippy¹ *adj* astringent, biting, chilly, nipping, pungent, sharp, stinging.

nippy² *adj* active, agile, fast, nimble, quick, speedy, sprightly, spry. *antonym* slow.

nirvana *n* bliss, ecstasy, exaltation, joy, paradise, peace, serenity, tranquillity.

nit-picking *adj* captious, carping, finicky, fussy, hair-splitting, pedantic, quibbling.

nitwit *n* dimwit, drongo, dummy, fool, half-wit, nincompoop, ninny, numskull, simpleton.

no doubt admittedly, assuredly, certainly, doubtless, doubtlessly, presumably, probably, surely, unquestionably.

nob *n* aristocrat, big shot, bigwig, fat cat, personage, toff, VIP.

nobble *v* bribe, disable, filch, get at, grab, hamper, handicap, incapacitate, influence, injure, intimidate, knock off, nick, outwit, pilfer, pinch, purloin, snitch, steal, swipe, take, weaken.

nobility *n* aristocracy, dignity, elite, eminence, excellence, generosity, gentry, grandeur, greatness, high society, honour, illustriousness, incorruptibility, integrity, loftiness, lords, magnanimity, magnificence, majesty, nobleness, nobles, patricians, peerage, stateliness, sublimity, superiority, uprightness, virtue, worthiness. *antonyms* baseness, proletariat.

noble *n* aristocrat, baron, lord, nobleman, patrician, peer. *antonyms* pleb, prole.
adj aristocratic, august, blue-blooded, dignified, distinguished, elevated, eminent, excellent, generous, gentle, grand, great, high-born, honourable, honoured, imposing, impressive, lofty, lordly, magnanimous, magnificent, majestic, patrician, splendid, stately, titled, upright, virtuous, worthy. *antonyms* base, ignoble, low-born.

nobody *n* also-ran, cipher, lightweight, man of straw, menial, minnow, nonentity, no-one, nothing. *antonym* somebody.

nod *v* acknowledge, agree, assent, beckon, bob, bow, concur, dip, doze, droop, drowse, duck, gesture, indicate, nap, salute, sign, signal, sleep, slip up, slump.

n acknowledgement, beck, cue, gesture, greeting, indication, salute, sign, signal.

noise *n* babble, ballyhoo, blare, clamour, clash, clatter, coil, commotion, cry, din, fracas, hubbub, outcry, pandemonium, racket, row, sound, talk, tumult, uproar. *antonyms* quiet, silence.
v advertise, announce, circulate, gossip, publicise, repeat, report, rumour.

noisy *adj* boisterous, cacophonous, chattering, clamorous, clangorous, deafening, ear-piercing, ear-splitting, loud, piercing, plangent, rackety, riotous, strident, tumultuous, turbulent, uproarious, vocal, vociferous. *antonyms* peaceful, quiet, silent.

nomadic *adj* drifting, gypsy, itinerant, migrant, migratory, peripatetic, roaming, roving, travelling, unsettled, vagrant, wandering.

nominal *adj* figurehead, formal, inconsiderable, insignificant, minimal, ostensible, pretended, professed, puppet, purported, self-styled, small, so-called, supposed, symbolic, theoretical, titular, token, trifling, trivial. *antonyms* actual, genuine, real, true.

nominate *v* appoint, assign, choose, commission, designate, elect, elevate, empower, mention, name, present, propose, put up, recommend, select, submit, suggest, term.

nomination *n* appointment, choice, designation, election, proposal, recommendation, selection, submission, suggestion.

non compos mentis crazy, deranged, insane, mentally ill, of unsound mind, unbalanced, unhinged. *antonyms* sane, stable.

non-aligned *adj* impartial, independent, neutral, uncommitted, undecided.

nonchalance *n* aplomb, calm, composure, cool, equanimity, imperturbability, indifference, self-possession, unconcern. *antonyms* anxiousness, worriedness.

nonchalant *adj* apathetic, blasé, calm, careless, casual, collected, cool, detached, dispassionate, impassive, indifferent, offhand, unconcerned, unemotional, unperturbed. *antonyms* anxious, careful, concerned, worried.

non-committal *adj* ambiguous, careful, cautious, circumspect, discreet, equivocal, evasive, guarded, indefinite, neutral, politic, reserved, tactful, tentative, unrevealing, vague, wary.

nonconformist *n* deviant, dissenter,

dissentient, eccentric, heretic, iconoclast, individualist, maverick, oddball, protester, radical, rebel. **antonym** conformist.

nondescript *adj* commonplace, dull, featureless, indeterminate, mousy, ordinary, plain, unclassified, undistinctive, undistinguished, unexceptional, uninspiring, uninteresting, unmemorable, unremarkable, vague.

none *pron* nil, nobody, no-one, not any, not one, zero, zilch.

non-essential *adj* dispensable, excessive, expendable, extraneous, extrinsic(al), inessential, peripheral, superfluous, supplementary, unimportant, unnecessary. **antonym** essential.

none-the-less *adv* even so, however, nevertheless, notwithstanding, yet.

non-existent *adj* chimerical, fancied, fictional, hallucinatory, hypothetical, illusory, imaginary, imagined, immaterial, incorporeal, insubstantial, legendary, mythical, null, unreal. **antonyms** actual, existing, real.

non-flammable *adj* fire-proof, fire-resistant, flame-resistant, incombustible, uninflammable. **antonyms** flammable, inflammable.

non-partisan *adj* detached, dispassionate, even-handed, impartial, independent, neutral, objective, unbiased, unprejudiced. **antonym** partisan.

nonplus *v* astonish, astound, baffle, bewilder, confound, confuse, discomfit, disconcert, discountenance, dismay, dumbfound, embarrass, flabbergast, flummox, mystify, perplex, puzzle, stump, stun, take aback.

nonsense *n* absurdity, balderdash, balls, baloney, bilge, bollocks, bombast, bosh, bull, bullshit, bunk, bunkum, claptrap, cobblers, codswallop, crap, double-Dutch, drivel, fiddlesticks, folly, foolishness, fudge, gibberish, gobbledygook, guff, hogwash, hooey, inanity, jest, ludicrousness, moonshine, piffle, pulp, ridiculousness, rot, rubbish, senselessness, silliness, stuff, stupidity, tommy-rot, tosh, trash, twaddle, waffle. **antonym** sense.

nonsensical *adj* absurd, crazy, daft, fatuous, foolish, inane, incomprehensible, irrational, ludicrous, meaningless, ridiculous, senseless, silly. **antonyms** logical, sensible.

non-stop *adj* ceaseless, constant, continuous, direct, endless, incessant, interminable, never-ending, on-going, relentless, round-the-clock, steady, unbroken, unceasing, unending, unfaltering, uninterrupted, unrelenting, unremitting. **antonyms** intermittent, occasional.

adv ceaselessly, constantly, continuously, directly, endlessly, incessantly, interminably, relentlessly, round-the-clock, steadily, unbrokenly, unceasingly, unendingly, unfalteringly, uninterruptedly, unrelentingly, unremittingly. **antonyms** intermittently, occasionally.

nook *n* alcove, cavity, corner, cranny, crevice, cubby-hole, hide-out, inglenook, nest, niche, opening, recess, retreat, shelter.

norm *n* average, bench-mark, canon, criterion, mean, measure, model, pattern, reference, rule, standard, type, yardstick.

normal *adj* accustomed, acknowledged, average, common, common-or-garden, conventional, habitual, mainstream, natural, ordinary, par for the course, popular, rational, reasonable, regular, routine, run-of-the-mill, sane, standard, straight, typical, usual, well-adjusted. **antonyms** abnormal, irregular, odd, peculiar.

normality *n* adjustment, balance, commonness, conventionality, naturalness, ordinariness, popularity, rationality, reason, regularity, routine, routineness, sanity, typicality, usualness. **antonyms** abnormality, irregularity, oddity, peculiarity.

normally *adv* as a rule, characteristically, commonly, habitually, ordinarily, regularly, straight, typically, usually. **antonym** abnormally.

nose *n* beak, bill, conk, hooter, neb, proboscis, schnozzle, snitch, snout.

v detect, inquire, interfere, intrude, meddle, nudge, nuzzle, pry, push, scent, search, shove, smell, sniff, snoop.

nos(e)y *adj* curious, eavesdropping, inquisitive, interfering, intermeddling, intrusive, meddlesome, officious, prying, snooping.

nostalgic *adj* emotional, homesick, longing, maudlin, regretful, romantic, sentimental, wistful.

nosy *see* **nosey**.

not bad all right, average, fair, fair to middling, moderate, OK, passable, reasonable, respectable, satisfactory, so-so, tolerable.

notability *n* celebrity, dignitary, distinction, eminence, esteem, fame, luminary, magnate, notable, personage, renown, somebody, VIP, worthy. *antonym* nonentity.

notable *adj* celebrated, conspicuous, distinguished, eminent, evident, extraordinary, famous, impressive, manifest, marked, memorable, noteworthy, noticeable, notorious, outstanding, overt, pre-eminent, pronounced, rare, remarkable, renowned, signal, striking, uncommon, unusual, well-known. *antonyms* commonplace, ordinary, usual.

n celebrity, dignitary, luminary, notability, personage, somebody, VIP, worthy. *antonyms* nobody, nonentity.

notch *n* cleft, cut, degree, grade, incision, indentation, level, mark, nick, score, snip, step.

v cut, indent, mark, nick, scallop, score, scratch.

notch up achieve, gain, make, record, register, score.

note *n* annotation, celebrity, character, comment, communication, consequence, distinction, eminence, epistle, fame, heed, indication, jotting, letter, line, mark, memo, memorandum, message, minute, notice, observation, prestige, record, regard, remark, reminder, renown, reputation, signal, symbol, token.

v denote, designate, detect, enter, indicate, mark, mention, notice, observe, perceive, record, register, remark, see, witness.

noted *adj* acclaimed, celebrated, conspicuous, distinguished, eminent, famous, great, illustrious, notable, notorious, prominent, recognised, renowned, respected, well-known.

noteworthy *adj* exceptional, extraordinary, important, notable, on the map, outstanding, remarkable, significant, unusual, visitable. *antonyms* commonplace, ordinary, unexceptional, usual.

nothing *n* bagatelle, cipher, damn all, emptiness, naught, nix, nobody, nonentity, non-existence, nothingness, nought, nullity, sweet Fanny Adams, (sweet) fuck all, trifle, void, zero. *antonyms* everything, something.

notice *v* descry, detect, discern, distinguish, espy, heed, mark, mind, note, observe, perceive, remark, see, spot. *antonyms* ignore, overlook.

n advertisement, advice, announcement, attention, bill, comment, communication, consideration, criticism, heed, instruction, intelligence, intimation, news, note, notification, observation, order, poster, regard, respect, review, sign, warning.

noticeable *adj* appreciable, clear, conspicuous, distinct, dramatic, evident, manifest, measurable, observable, obvious, perceptible, plain, significant, striking, unmistakable. *antonym* hidden, insignificant, obscure.

notification *n* advice, alert, announcement, declaration, disclosure, information, intelligence, message, notice, publication, revelation, statement, telling, warning.

notify *v* acquaint, advise, alert, announce, apprise, declare, disclose, inform, publish, reveal, tell, warn.

notion *n* belief, caprice, concept, conception, construct, desire, fancy, idea, image, impression, impulse, inclination, inkling, judgement, knowledge, opinion, sentiment, understanding, view, whim, wish.

notional *adj* abstract, conceptual, fanciful, hypothetical, imaginary, speculative, theoretical, unfounded, unreal, visionary. *antonym* real.

notoriety *n* dishonour, disrepute, infamy, opprobrium, scandal.

notorious *adj* arrant, blatant, dishonourable, disreputable, egregious, flagrant, glaring, infamous, obvious, open, opprobrious, overt, patent, scandalous, undisputed.

notoriously *adv* arrantly, blatantly, dishonourably, disreputably, egregiously, flagrantly, glaringly, infamously, notably, obviously, openly, opprobriously, overtly, particularly, patently, scandalously, spectacularly.

notwithstanding *adv* although, despite, however, nevertheless, nonetheless, though, yet.

nourish *v* attend, cherish, comfort, cultivate, encourage, feed, foster, furnish, harbour, maintain, nurse, nurture, promote, supply, support, sustain, tend.

novel *adj* different, fresh, imaginative, innovative, new, original, rare, singular, strange, surprising, uncommon, unconventional, unfamiliar, unusual. *antonyms* familiar, ordinary.

novelty *n* bagatelle, bauble, curiosity, freshness, gadget, gimmick, innovation, knick-knack, memento, newness, oddity, originality, peculiarity, souvenir, strangeness, surprise, trifle, trinket, unfamiliarity, uniqueness.

novice *n* amateur, apprentice, beginner, convert, cub, learner, neophyte, newcomer, pupil. *antonyms* doyen, expert, professional.

now *adv* at once, at present, directly, immediately, instanter, instantly, next, nowadays, presently, promptly, straightaway, these days.

now and then at times, desultorily, from time to time, infrequently, intermittently, now and again, occasionally, on and off, on occasion, once in a while, periodically, sometimes, spasmodically, sporadically.

nowadays *adv* any more, as things are, at the moment, now, these days, today.

noxious *adj* baneful, corrupting, deadly, deleterious, destructive, detrimental, foul, harmful, hurtful, injurious, insalubrious, pernicious, poisonous, unhealthy, unwholesome. *antonyms* innocuous, wholesome.

nuance *n* degree, distinction, gradation, hint, nicety, overtone, refinement, shade, soupçon, subtlety, suggestion, suspicion, tinge, touch, trace.

nub *n* centre, core, crux, essence, gist, heart, kernel, nitty-gritty, nucleus, pith, point.

nucleus *n* basis, centre, core, crux, focus, heart, kernel, nub, pivot.

nude *adj* bare, disrobed, exposed, in one's birthday suit, in the altogether, in the buff, naked, starkers, stark-naked, stripped, unattired, unclad, unclothed, uncovered, undressed, without a stitch. *antonyms* clothed, covered, dressed.

nudge *v, n* bump, dig, jog, poke, prod, prompt, push, shove, touch.

nuisance *n* annoyance, bore, bother, drag, drawback, inconvenience, infliction, irritation, offence, pain, pest, plague, problem, trouble, vexation.

nullify *v* abate, abolish, abrogate, annul, cancel, counteract, invalidate, negate, neutralise, quash, repeal, rescind, revoke, undermine, veto, vitiate, void. *antonym* validate.

numb *adj* dead, deadened, frozen, immobilised, insensate, insensible, insensitive, paralysed, stunned, stupefied, torpid, unfeeling. *antonym* sensitive.
v anaesthetise, deaden, dull, freeze, immobilise, paralyse, stun, stupefy. *antonym* sensitise.

number *n* aggregate, amount, character, collection, company, count, crowd, digit, figure, folio, horde, index, integer, many, multitude, numeral, quantity, several, sum, throng, total, unit.
v account, add, apportion, calculate, compute, count, enumerate, include, inventory, reckon, tell, total.

numberless *adj* countless, endless, infinite, innumerable, multitudinous, myriad, uncounted, unnumbered, untold.

numerous *adj* abundant, copious, divers, many, multitudinous, myriad, plentiful, profuse, several, sundry. *antonyms* few, scanty.

numerousness *n* abundance, copiousness, manifoldness, multiplicity, multitudinousness, plentifulness, plurality, profusion. *antonyms* scantiness, scarcity.

numskull *n* blockhead, bonehead, buffoon, clot, dimwit, dolt, dope, drongo, dullard, dummy, dunce, dunderhead, fathead, fool, sap, saphead, simpleton, thickhead, twit.

nuptial *adj* bridal, conjugal, connubial, marital, matrimonial, wedded, wedding.

nurse *v* breast-feed, care for, cherish, cultivate, encourage, feed, foster, harbour, keep, nourish, nurture, preserve, promote, succour, suckle, support, sustain, tend, treat, wet-nurse.

nurture *n* care, cultivation, development, diet, discipline, education, food, instruction, nourishment, rearing, training, upbringing.
v bring up, care for, cultivate, develop, discipline, educate, feed, instruct, nourish, nurse, rear, school, support, sustain, tend, train.

nut *n* brain, crackpot, crank, eccentric, head, head-banger, loony, lunatic, madman, maniac, mind, nutcase, nutter, psychopath, reason, senses.

nutritious *adj* beneficial, good, health-giving, invigorating, nourishing, nutritive, strengthening, substantial, wholesome. *antonyms* bad, unwholesome.

nuts *adj* bananas, batty, crazy, demented, deranged, eccentric, insane, irrational, loony, loopy, mad, nutty, psychopathic, unbalanced, unhinged. *antonym* sane.

nuts and bolts basics, bits and pieces, components, details, essentials, fundamentals, nitty-gritty, practicalities.

nuzzle *v* burrow, cuddle, fondle, nestle, nudge, pet, snuggle.

O

oaf *n* baboon, blockhead, bonehead, brute, clod, dolt, dullard, dummy, dunce, fool, gawk, goon, gorilla, half-wit, hick, hobbledehoy, hulk, idiot, imbecile, lout, lummox, moron, nincompoop, oik, sap, schlemiel, schlep, simpleton, yob.

oafish *adj* blockish, boneheaded, boorish, brutish, crass, dense, dim, dimwitted, doltish, dull, dumb, heavy, loutish, lubberly, lumbering, moronic, obtuse, schleppy, stupid, thick.

oasis *n* enclave, haven, island, refuge, resting-place, retreat, sanctuary, sanctum, watering-hole.

oath *n* affirmation, assurance, avowal, blasphemy, bond, curse, cuss, expletive, imprecation, malediction, pledge, plight, profanity, promise, swear-word, vow, word, word of honour.

obdurate *adj* adamant, callous, dogged, firm, fixed, flinty, hard, hard-hearted, harsh, immovable, implacable, inexorable, inflexible, intransigent, iron, mulish, obstinate, perverse, pig-headed, relentless, stiff-necked, stony, stubborn, unbending, unfeeling, unrelenting, unshakable, unyielding. **antonyms** submissive, tender.

obedience *n* accordance, acquiescence, agreement, allegiance, amenableness, compliance, conformability, deference, docility, dutifulness, duty, passivity, respect, reverence, submission, submissiveness, subservience, tractability. **antonym** disobedience.

obedient *adj* acquiescent, amenable, biddable, compliant, deferential, docile, duteous, dutiful, law-abiding, passive, regardful, respectful, submissive, subservient, tractable, unquestioning, unresisting, well-trained, yielding. **antonyms** disobedient, rebellious, refractory, unruly, wilful.

obese *adj* bulky, corpulent, fat, fleshy, gross, heavy, outsize, overweight, paunchy, plump, podgy, ponderous, portly, pursy, roly-poly, rotund, stout, tubby. **antonyms** skinny, slender, thin.

obey *v* abide by, act upon, adhere to, be ruled by, bow to, carry out, comply, conform, defer (to), discharge, embrace, execute, follow, fulfil, give in, give way, heed, implement, keep, knuckle under, mind, observe, perform, respond, serve, submit, surrender, take orders from, toe the line, yield. **antonym** disobey.

object¹ *n* aim, article, body, butt, design, end, entity, fact, focus, goal, idea, intent, intention, item, motive, objective, phenomenon, point, purpose, raison d'être, reality, reason, recipient, target, thing, victim, visible.

object² *v* argue, complain, demur, dissent, expostulate, oppose, protest, rebut, refuse, repudiate, take exception. **antonyms** accede, acquiesce, agree, assent.

objection *n* cavil, censure, challenge, complaint, counter-argument, demur, doubt, exception, niggle, opposition, protest, remonstrance, scruple. **antonyms** agreement, assent.

objectionable *adj* abhorrent, antisocial, deplorable, despicable, detestable, disagreeable, dislik(e)able, displeasing, distasteful, exceptionable, indecorous, insufferable, intolerable, loathsome, noxious, obnoxious, offensive, regrettable, repugnant, unacceptable, undesirable, unpleasant, unseemly. **antonyms** acceptable, pleasant, welcome.

objective *adj* calm, detached, disinterested, dispassionate, equitable, even-handed, fair, impartial, impersonal, judicial, just, open-minded, sensible, sober, unbiased, uncoloured, unemotional, unimpassioned, uninvolved, unprejudiced. **antonyms** biased, subjective.
n aim, ambition, aspiration, design, destination, end, goal, intention, mark, object, prize, purpose, target.

objectivity *n* detachment, disinterest, disinterestedness, dispassion, equitableness, even-handedness, impartiality, impersonality, open mind, open-mindedness. **antonyms** bias, subjectivity.

obligation *n* accountability, accountableness, agreement, bond, burden, charge, commitment, compulsion, contract, debt, duty, engagement, indebtedness, liability, must, obstriction, onus, promise, requirement, responsibility, stipulation, trust, understanding. **antonyms** choice, discretion.

obligatory *adj* binding, bounden, coercive, compulsory, de rigueur, enforced, essential, imperative, mandatory,

oblige *v* accommodate, assist, benefit, bind, coerce, compel, constrain, do a favour, favour, force, gratify, help, impel, indulge, make, necessitate, obligate, please, require, serve.

obliged *adj* appreciative, beholden, bound, compelled, constrained, forced, grateful, gratified, in debt (to), indebted, obligated, required, thankful, under an obligation, under compulsion.

obliging *adj* accommodating, agreeable, amiable, civil, complaisant, considerate, co-operative, courteous, eager, friendly, good-natured, helpful, kind, polite, willing. *antonyms* inconsiderate, unhelpful, unkind.

oblique *adj* angled, aslant, at an angle, back-handed, circuitous, circumlocutory, evasive, inclined, indirect, roundabout, sidelong, skew, slanted, slanting, sloped, sloping, tilted, transverse.

obliquely *adv* askance, askant, aslant, aslope, at an angle, circuitously, diagonally, evasively, in a roundabout way, indirectly, not in so many words, slantwise.

obliterate *v* annihilate, blot out, cancel, delete, destroy, efface, eradicate, erase, expunge, extirpate, rub out, vaporise, wipe out.

obliteration *n* annihilation, blotting out, deletion, effacement, elimination, eradication, erasure, expunction, extirpation.

oblivion *n* blackness, coma, darkness, disregard, eclipse, extinction, forgetfulness, insensibility, limbo, neglect, nothingness, obliviousness, obscurity, stupor, unawareness, unconsciousness, void. *antonyms* awareness, consciousness.

oblivious *adj* blind, careless, comatose, deaf, forgetful, heedless, ignorant, inattentive, insensible, neglectful, negligent, regardless, unaware, unconcerned, unconscious, unmindful, unobservant. *antonyms* aware, conscious.

obnoxious *adj* abhorrent, abominable, detestable, disagreeable, disgusting, foul, fulsome, hateful, horrid, insufferable, loathsome, nasty, nauseating, objectionable, odious, offensive, repellent, reprehensible, repugnant, repulsive, revolting, sickening, unpleasant. *antonyms* agreeable, lik(e)able, pleasant.

obscene *adj* atrocious, barrack-room, bawdy, blue, coarse, dirty, disgusting, evil, filthy, foul, gross, heinous, immodest, immoral, improper, impure, indecent, lewd, licentious, loathsome, loose, offensive, outrageous, pornographic, prurient, ribald, salacious, scurrilous, shameless, shocking, sickening, smutty, suggestive, unchaste, unwholesome, vile, wicked. *antonyms* clean, decent, decorous.

obscenity *n* abomination, affront, atrocity, bawdiness, blight, blueness, coarseness, dirtiness, evil, expletive, filthiness, foulness, four-letter word, grossness, immodesty, impropriety, impurity, indecency, indelicacy, lewdness, licentiousness, offence, outrage, pornography, profanity, prurience, salacity, scurrility, smut, smuttiness, suggestiveness, swear-word, vileness, vulgarism.

obscure *adj* abstruse, ambiguous, arcane, blurred, caliginous, clear as mud, clouded, cloudy, concealed, confusing, cryptic, deep, dim, doubtful, dusky, enigmatic, esoteric, faint, gloomy, hazy, hermetic, hidden, humble, incomprehensible, inconspicuous, indefinite, indistinct, little-known, lowly, minor, misty, murky, mysterious, nameless, obfuscated, occult, opaque, out-of-the-way, recondite, remote, shadowy, shady, sombre, tenebr(i)ous, twilight, unclear, undistinguished, unheard-of, unknown, unlit, unnoted, unobvious, unseen, unsung, vague, veiled. *antonyms* clear, definite, explicit, famous, lucid.
v bedim, befog, block out, blur, cloak, cloud, conceal, cover, darken, dim, disguise, dull, eclipse, hide, mask, muddy, obfuscate, overshadow, screen, shade, shadow, shroud, veil. *antonyms* clarify, illuminate.

obscurity *n* abstruseness, ambiguity, darkness, dimness, dusk, duskiness, fogginess, gloom, haze, haziness, impenetrability, incomprehensibility, inconspicuousness, indistinctness, insignificance, lowliness, mirk, mirkiness, murk, murkiness, mysticism, namelessness, reconditeness, shadowiness, shadows, vagueness. *antonyms* clarity, fame, lucidity.

obsequious *adj* cringing, deferential, fawning, flattering, grovelling, ingratiating, knee-crooking, menial, oily, servile, slavish, slimy, smarmy, submissive, subservient, sycophantic, toadying, unctuous. *antonym* assertive.

observance *n* adherence, attention, celebration, ceremonial, ceremony, compliance, custom, discharge, fashion, form, formality, fulfilment, heeding, honouring, notice, obedience, observation, orthodoxy, performance, practice, rite, ritual, service, tradition.

observant *adj* alert, attentive, eagle-eyed, eagle-sighted, heedful, mindful, perceptive, percipient, quick, sharp-eyed, vigilant, watchful, wide-awake. *antonyms* inattentive, unobservant.

observation *n* annotation, attention, cognition, comment, consideration, discernment, examination, experience, finding, information, inspection, knowledge, monitoring, note, notice, opinion, perception, pronouncement, reading, reflection, remark, review, scrutiny, study, surveillance, thought, utterance, watching.

observe *v* abide by, adhere to, celebrate, commemorate, comment, comply, conform to, contemplate, declare, detect, discern, discover, espy, follow, fulfil, heed, honour, keep, keep an eye on, keep tabs on, mention, mind, monitor, note, notice, obey, opine, perceive, perform, regard, remark, remember, respect, say, scrutinise, see, solemnise, spot, state, study, survey, view, watch, witness. *antonyms* break, miss, overlook, violate.

obsess *v* bedevil, consume, dominate, engross, grip, haunt, hold, monopolise, nag, plague, possess, preoccupy, prey on, rule, torment.

obsessed *adj* bedevilled, beset, dominated, gripped, hag-ridden, haunted, hounded, hung up on, immersed in, in the grip of, infatuated, plagued, preoccupied. *antonyms* detached, indifferent, unconcerned.

obsession *n* bee in one's bonnet, complex, enthusiasm, fetish, fixation, hang-up, idée fixe, infatuation, mania, monomania, phobia, preoccupation, ruling passion, thing.

obsessive *adj* besetting, compulsive, consuming, fixed, gripping, haunting, maddening, nagging, tormenting, unforgettable.

obsolescent *adj* ag(e)ing, declining, disappearing, dying out, fading, moribund, on the decline, on the wane, on the way out, past its prime, waning.

obsolete *adj* anachronistic, ancient, antediluvian, antiquated, antique, archaic, bygone, dated, dead, démodé, discarded, disused, extinct, musty, old, old hat, old-fashioned, out, out of date, outmoded, outworn, passé, superannuated. *antonyms* contemporary, current, modern, new, up-to-date.

obstacle *n* bar, barrier, catch, check, difficulty, drawback, hindrance, hitch, hurdle, impediment, interference, interruption, obstruction, snag, stop, stumbling-block. *antonyms* advantage, help.

obstinacy *n* doggedness, firmness, inflexibility, intransigence, mulishness, obduracy, perseverance, persistence, pertinacity, perversity, pig-headedness, resoluteness, stubbornness, tenacity, wilfulness, wrong-headedness. *antonyms* co-operativeness, flexibility, submissiveness.

obstinate *adj* bull-headed, bullish, determined, dogged, firm, headstrong, immovable, inflexible, intractable, intransigent, mulish, obdurate, opinionated, persistent, pertinacious, perverse, pig-headed, recalcitrant, refractory, restive, rusty, self-willed, steadfast, stomachful, strong-minded, stubborn, sturdy, tenacious, unadvisable, unyielding, uppity, wilful, wrong-headed. *antonyms* co-operative, flexible, pliant, submissive.

obstreperous *adj* boisterous, clamorous, disorderly, intractable, loud, noisy, out of hand, rackety, rambunctious, rampaging, raucous, refractory, restive, riotous, rip-roaring, roistering, roisterous, rough, rowdy, stroppy, tempestuous, tumultuous, turbulent, uncontrolled, undisciplined, unmanageable, unruly, uproarious, vociferous, wild. *antonyms* calm, disciplined, quiet.

obstruct *v* arrest, bar, barricade, block, check, choke, clog, crab, cumber, curb, cut off, frustrate, hamper, hamstring, hide, hinder, hold up, impede, inhibit, interfere with, interrupt, mask, obscure, occlude, prevent, restrict, retard, shield, shut off, slow down, stall, stonewall, stop, stuff, thwart, trammel. *antonym* help.

obstruction *n* bar, barricade, barrier, blockage, check, difficulty, filibuster, hindrance, impediment, snag, stop, stoppage, trammel, traverse. *antonym* help.

obstructive *adj* awkward, blocking, delaying, difficult, hindering, inhibiting, restrictive, stalling, unaccommodating, unco-operative, unhelpful. ***antonym*** helpful.

obtain[1] *v* achieve, acquire, attain, come by, compass, earn, gain, get, procure, secure.

obtain[2] *v* be in force, be prevalent, be the case, exist, hold, prevail, reign, rule, stand.

obtainable *adj* accessible, achievable, at hand, attainable, available, on call, on tap, procurable, ready, realisable, to be had.

obtrusive *adj* blatant, forward, importunate, interfering, intrusive, manifest, meddling, nosy, noticeable, obvious, officious, prominent, protruding, protuberant, prying, pushy. ***antonym*** unobtrusive.

obtuse *adj* blunt, boneheaded, dense, dopey, dull, dull-witted, dumb, imperceptive, inattentive, insensitive, retarded, rounded, slow, stolid, stupid, thick, thick-skinned, uncomprehending, unintelligent. ***antonyms*** bright, sharp.

obviate *v* avert, counter, counteract, preclude, prevent, remove.

obvious *adj* apparent, clear, conspicuous, discernible, distinct, evident, glaring, indisputable, manifest, noticeable, open, open-and-shut, overt, palpable, patent, perceptible, plain, prominent, pronounced, recognisable, self-evident, self-explanatory, straightforward, transparent, unconcealed, undeniable, undisguised, unmistakable, unsubtle, visible. ***antonyms*** obscure, unclear.

obviously *adv* certainly, clearly, distinctly, evidently, manifestly, of course, palpably, patently, plainly, undeniably, unmistakably, unquestionably, visibly, without doubt.

occasion *n* affair, call, case, cause, celebration, chance, convenience, event, excuse, experience, ground(s), incident, inducement, influence, instance, justification, moment, motive, occurrence, opening, opportunity, prompting, provocation, reason, time.
v bring about, bring on, cause, create, effect, elicit, engender, evoke, generate, give rise to, induce, influence, inspire, lead to, make, originate, persuade, produce, prompt, provoke.

occasional *adj* casual, desultory, fitful, incidental, infrequent, intermittent, irregular, odd, periodic, rare, scattered, sporadic, uncommon. ***antonym*** frequent.

occasionally *adv* at intervals, at times, every so often, from time to time, infrequently, irregularly, now and again, now and then, off and on, on and off, on occasion, once in a while, periodically, sometimes, sporadically. ***antonym*** frequently.

occult *adj* abstruse, arcane, concealed, esoteric, faint, hidden, impenetrable, invisible, magical, mysterious, mystic, mystical, mystifying, obscure, recondite, secret, supernatural, unknown, unrevealed, veiled.
v conceal, cover (up), enshroud, hide, mask, obscure, screen, shroud, veil. ***antonym*** reveal.

occultism *n* black magic, diabolism, magic, mysticism, sorcery, spiritualism, supernaturalism, the black arts, witchcraft.

occupation *n* absorption, activity, business, calling, craft, employment, job, line, post, profession, pursuit, trade, vocation, way of life, work.

occupied *adj* absorbed, busy, employed, engaged, engrossed, full, hard at it, in use, inhabited, lived-in, peopled, settled, taken, tenanted, tied up, unavailable, working.

occupy *v* absorb, amuse, beguile, busy, capture, conquer, cover, divert, dwell in, employ, engage, engross, ensconce oneself in, entertain, establish oneself in, fill, garrison, hold, immerse, inhabit, interest, invade, involve, keep, keep busy, live in, monopolise, overrun, own, permeate, pervade, possess, preoccupy, reside in, seize, stay in, take over, take possession of, take up, tenant, tie up, use, utilise.

occur *v* appear, arise, be found, be met with, be present, befall, betide, chance, come about, come off, come to pass, crop up, develop, eventuate, exist, happen, intervene, manifest itself, materialise, obtain, result, show itself, take place, transpire, turn up.

occur to come to mind, come to one, cross one's mind, dawn on, enter one's head, present itself, spring to mind, strike one, suggest itself.

occurrence *n* action, adventure, affair, appearance, case, circumstance, development, episode, event, existence, happening, incident, instance, manifestation, materialisation, proceeding, transaction.

odd[1] *adj* abnormal, atypical, bizarre, curious, deviant, different, eccentric, exceptional, extraordinary, fantastic, freak, freakish, freaky, funny, irregular, kinky, outlandish, peculiar, quaint, queer, rare, remarkable, singular, strange, uncanny, uncommon, unconventional, unexplained, unusual, weird, whimsical. **antonym** normal.

odd² *adj* auxiliary, casual, fragmentary, ill-matched, incidental, irregular, left-over, lone, miscellaneous, occasional, periodic, random, remaining, seasonal, single, solitary, spare, sundry, surplus, uneven, unmatched, unpaired, varied, various.

oddity *n* abnormality, anomaly, bizarreness, character, crank, curiosity, eccentricity, extraordinariness, freak, freakishness, idiosyncrasy, incongruity, irregularity, maverick, misfit, oddball, oddness, outlandishness, peculiarity, phenomenon, queerness, quirk, rarity, screwball, singularity, strangeness, unconventionality, unnaturalness, weirdo.

oddment *n* bit, end, fragment, leftover, offcut, patch, remnant, scrap, shred, sliver, snippet.

odds *n* advantage, balance, chances, difference, discrepancy, disparity, dissimilarity, distinction, edge, lead, likelihood, probability, superiority.

odds and ends bits, bits and pieces, debris, flotsam and jetsam, junk, leavings, litter, oddments, odds and sods, remnants, rubbish, scraps, tatt.

odious *adj* abhorrent, abominable, annoying, detestable, disgusting, execrable, foul, hateful, heinous, horrible, horrid, insufferable, loathsome, obnoxious, offensive, repellent, repugnant, repulsive, revolting, unpleasant, vile. **antonym** pleasant.

odium *n* abhorrence, animosity, antipathy, censure, condemnation, contempt, detestation, disapprobation, disapproval, discredit, disfavour, disgrace, dishonour, dislike, disrepute, execration, hatred, infamy, obloquy, opprobrium, reprobation, shame.

odorous *adj* aromatic, balmy, fragrant, odoriferous, perfumed, pungent, redolent, scented, sweet-smelling. **antonym** odourless.

odour *n* air, aroma, atmosphere, aura, bouquet, breath, emanation, essence, exhalation, flavour, fragrance, perfume, quality, redolence, scent, smell, spirit, stench, stink.

of course certainly, definitely, doubtlessly, indubitably, naturally, no doubt, obviously, undoubtedly.

off *adj* abnormal, absent, bad, below par, cancelled, decomposed, disappointing, disheartening, displeasing, finished, gone, high, inoperative, mouldy, poor, postponed, quiet, rancid, rotten, slack, sour, substandard, turned, unavailable, unsatisfactory, wrong.
adv apart, aside, at a distance, away, elsewhere, out.

off and on fitfully, from time to time, intermittently, now and again, now and then, occasionally, on and off, once in a while, periodically, sometimes, sporadically.

off guard napping, unprepared, unready, unwary, with one's defences down, with one's pants down.

off the cuff ad lib, extempore, impromptu, improvised, offhand, spontaneous, spontaneously, unofficially, unprepared, unrehearsed, unscripted.

off the hook acquitted, cleared, exonerated, in the clear, scot free, vindicated.

off the record confidential, confidentially, private, privately, sub rosa, unofficial, unofficially. **antonym** officially.

off-colour *adj* faded, ill, indecent, indisposed, off form, out of sorts, pasty-faced, peaky, peelie-wally, poorly, queasy, sick, under the weather, unwell.

off-duty *adj* at leisure, at liberty, free, not at work, off, off work, on holiday.

offence *n* affront, anger, annoyance, crime, delinquency, displeasure, fault, hard feelings, harm, huff, hurt, indignation, indignity, infraction, infringement, injury, injustice, insult, ire, lapse, misdeed, misdemeanour, needle, outrage, peccadillo, pique, put-down, resentment, sin, slight, snub, transgression, trespass, umbrage, violation, wrath, wrong, wrong-doing.

offend *v* affront, annoy, disgruntle, disgust, displease, fret, gall, hurt, insult, irritate, miff, nauseate, outrage, pain, pique, provoke, repel, repulse, rile, sicken, slight, snub, transgress, turn off, upset, vex, violate, wound, wrong. **antonym** please.

offended *adj* affronted, disgruntled, disgusted, displeased, huffy, in a huff, miffed, outraged, pained, piqued, put out, resentful, smarting, stung, upset, wounded. **antonym** pleased.

offensive *adj* abominable, abusive,

aggressive, annoying, attacking, detestable, disagreeable, discourteous, disgusting, displeasing, disrespectful, embarrassing, grisly, impertinent, insolent, insulting, intolerable, invading, irritating, loathsome, nasty, nauseating, objectionable, obnoxious, odious, rank, repellent, repugnant, revolting, rude, sickening, uncivil, unmannerly, unpalatable, unpleasant, unsavoury, vile. *antonyms* defensive, pleasing.

n attack, drive, onslaught, push, raid, sortie, thrust.

offer *v* advance, afford, bid, extend, furnish, give, hold out, make available, move, present, proffer, propose, propound, provide, put forth, put forward, show, submit, suggest, tender, volunteer.

n approach, attempt, bid, endeavour, essay, overture, presentation, proposal, proposition, submission, suggestion, tender.

offhand *adj* abrupt, aloof, brusque, careless, casual, cavalier, curt, glib, informal, offhanded, perfunctory, take-it-or-leave-it, unappreciative, uncaring, unceremonious, unconcerned, uninterested. *antonyms* calculated, planned.

adv at once, extempore, immediately, off the cuff, off the top of one's head, straightaway.

office *n* appointment, business, capacity, charge, commission, duty, employment, function, obligation, occupation, place, post, responsibility, role, room, service, situation, station, trust, work.

offices *n* advocacy, aegis, aid, auspices, backing, back-up, favour, help, intercession, intervention, mediation, patronage, recommendation, referral, support, word.

official *adj* accredited, approved, authentic, authenticated, authorised, authoritative, bona fide, certified, formal, legitimate, licensed, proper, sanctioned. *antonym* unofficial.

n agent, bureaucrat, executive, functionary, mandarin, officer, representative.

officiate *v* adjudicate, chair, conduct, emcee, manage, oversee, preside, referee, serve, superintend, umpire.

officious *adj* bustling, dictatorial, forward, impertinent, inquisitive, interfering, intrusive, meddlesome, meddling, mischievous, obtrusive, opinionated, over-zealous, pushy, self-important.

off-key *adj* discordant, dissonant, inappropriate, indecent, inharmonious, jarring, out of keeping, out of tune, unsuitable.

offload *v* deposit, disburden, discharge, drop, dump, get rid of, jettison, shift, transfer, unburden, unload, unship.

off-putting *adj* daunting, demoralising, discomfiting, disconcerting, discouraging, disheartening, dismaying, dispiriting, disturbing, formidable, frustrating, intimidating, unnerving, unsettling, upsetting.

offset *v* balance out, cancel out, compare, compensate for, counteract, counterbalance, counterpoise, juxtapose, make up for, neutralise.

offspring *n* brood, child, children, creation, descendant, descendants, family, heir, heirs, issue, kids, litter, progeny, result, seed, spawn, successor, successors, young. *antonym* parent(s).

often *adv* again and again, frequently, generally, habitually, many a time, much, oft, over and over, regularly, repeatedly, time after time, time and again. *antonym* seldom.

ogle *v* eye, eye up, leer, look, make eyes at, stare.

oily *adj* fatty, flattering, glib, greasy, obsequious, oiled, oleaginous, plausible, sebaceous, servile, slippery, smarmy, smeary, smooth, swimming, unctuous.

okay *adj* acceptable, accurate, adequate, all right, approved, convenient, correct, fair, fine, good, in order, not bad, OK, passable, permitted, reasonable, right as rain, satisfactory, tolerable.

n agreement, approbation, approval, assent, authorisation, consent, endorsement, go-ahead, green light, OK, permission, sanction, say-so, seal of approval, support.

v accredit, agree to, approve, authorise, consent to, endorse, give the go-ahead to, give the green light to, OK, pass, rubber-stamp, sanction, validate.

interj agreed, all right, fine, OK, right, very good, very well, yes.

old *adj* aged, age-old, ancient, antediluvian, antiquated, antique, archaic, bygone, cast-off, crumbling, dated, decayed, decrepit, done, earlier, early, elderly, erstwhile, ex-, experienced, familiar, former, grey, grey-haired, grizzled, hackneyed, hardened, hoary, immemorial, long-established, long-standing, mature, obsolete, of old, of yore, olden, old-fashioned, one-time, original, out of date, outdated, outmoded, over the hill, passé, patriarchal, practised, prehistoric, previous, prim(a)eval, primitive, primordial, remote, senescent, senile, skilled, stale, superannuated, time-honoured, time-worn, traditional, unfashionable, unoriginal, venerable, versed, veteran, vintage, worn-out. **antonym** young.

old age advancing years, age, agedness, dotage, second childhood, senescence, senility, twilight of one's life. **antonym** youth.

old-fashioned adj ancient, antiquated, archaic, behind the times, corny, dated, dead, fog(e)yish, fusty, musty, neanderthal, obsolescent, obsolete, old hat, old-fog(e)yish, old-time, out of date, outdated, outmoded, passé, past, square, superannuated, unfashionable. **antonyms** contemporary, modern, up-to-date.

omen n augury, auspice, boding, foreboding, foretoken, indication, portent, premonition, presage, prognostication, sign, straw in the wind, warning, writing on the wall.

ominous adj baleful, bodeful, dark, fateful, inauspicious, menacing, minatory, portentous, premonitory, sinister, threatening, unpromising, unpropitious. **antonym** auspicious.

omission n avoidance, default, ellipsis, exclusion, failure, forgetfulness, gap, lack, neglect, oversight. **antonyms** addition, inclusion.

omit v disregard, drop, edit out, eliminate, exclude, fail, forget, give something a miss, leave out, leave undone, let slide, miss out, neglect, overlook, pass over, skip. **antonyms** add, include.

omnipotent adj all-powerful, almighty, plenipotent, supreme. **antonym** impotent.

omnipresent adj pervasive, ubiquitous, universal.

omniscient adj all-knowing, all-seeing, pansophic.

on and off discontinuously, fitfully, from time to time, intermittently, now and again, now and then, off and on, on occasion, periodically, sometimes, spasmodically, sporadically.

on duty at work, busy, engaged, working. **antonym** off.

on edge apprehensive, eager, edgy, excited, fidgety, ill at ease, impatient, irritable, keyed up, nervous, on tenterhooks, tense, touchy, uptight. **antonym** relaxed.

on fire ablaze, aflame, alight, ardent, blazing, burning, eager, enthusiastic, excited, fiery, fired, flaming, ignited, in flames, inspired, kindled, passionate.

on guard alert, cautious, chary, circumspect, on the alert, on the lookout, prepared, ready, vigilant, wary, watchful, wide awake.

on one's last legs at death's door, dying, exhausted, fading fast, failing, moribund, with one foot in the grave, worn out.

on one's own alone, by oneself, independently, isolated, off one's own bat, on one's tod, singly, unaccompanied, unaided, unassisted.

on purpose deliberately, designedly, intentionally, knowingly, premeditatedly, purposely, wilfully, wittingly. **antonym** accidentally.

on the ball alert, attentive, aware, in touch, informed, on one's toes, quick, wide awake.

on the dot exactly, on time, precisely, promptly, punctually, spot on, to the minute.

on the fence between two stools, dithering, irresolute, uncertain, uncommitted, undecided, unsure, vacillating.

on the increase accelerating, escalating, expanding, growing, increasing, multiplying, proliferating, rising, spreading. **antonym** on the wane.

on the level above board, candid, fair, frank, genuine, honest, open, sincere, square, straight, straightforward, up front.

on the mend convalescent, convalescing, healing, improving, recovering, recuperating, reviving.

on the move active, advancing, astir, moving, on the go, progressing, stirring, succeeding.

on the rampage amok, berserk, frenzied, in a frenzy, rampageous(ly), rampant(ly), riotous(ly), violent(ly), wild(ly).

on the scrap-heap discarded, ditched, dumped, forgotten, jettisoned, redundant, rejected, written off.

on the sly clandestinely, covertly, furtively, on the q.t., privately, secretly, surreptitiously, underhandedly. **antonym** openly.

on the spur of the moment capriciously, impetuously, impromptu, impulsively, on impulse, on the spot, thoughtlessly, unpremeditatedly, unthinkingly.

on the wane declining, degenerating, deteriorating, dropping, dwindling, ebbing, fading, lessening, moribund, obsolescent, on its last legs, on the decline, on the way out, subsiding, tapering off, weakening, withering. *antonym* on the increase.

on the whole all in all, all things considered, as a rule, by and large, for the most part, generally, generally speaking, in general, in the main, mostly, predominantly.

on thin ice at risk, in jeopardy, insecure, open to attack, precarious, unsafe, vulnerable.

on top of the world ecstatic, elated, exhilarated, exultant, happy, on cloud nine, over the moon, overjoyed, thrilled.

once *adv* at one time, formerly, heretofore, in the old days, in the past, in times gone by, in times past, long ago, once upon a time, previously.

once (and) for all conclusively, decisively, definitively, finally, for good, for the last time, permanently, positively.

once in a blue moon hardly ever, infrequently, rarely, seldom.

oncoming *adj* advancing, approaching, forthcoming, gathering, imminent, impending, looming, onrushing, upcoming.

one *adj* alike, compatible, complete, entire, equal, harmonious, identical, like-minded, united, whole.

onerous *adj* backbreaking, burdensome, crushing, demanding, difficult, exacting, exhausting, exigent, formidable, grave, hard, heavy, herculean, laborious, oppressive, responsible, taxing, troublesome, weighty. *antonyms* easy, light.

one-sided *adj* asymmetrical, biased, coloured, discriminatory, inequitable, lopsided, partial, partisan, prejudiced, unequal, unfair, unilateral, unjust. *antonym* impartial.

one-time *adj* erstwhile, ex-, former, late, previous, sometime.

ongoing *adj* advancing, continuing, continuous, current, developing, evolving, growing, in progress, lasting, progressing, successful, unfinished, unfolding.

only *adv* at most, barely, exclusively, just, merely, purely, simply, solely.

adj exclusive, individual, lone, single, sole, solitary, unique.

onrush *n* career, cascade, charge, flood, flow, onset, onslaught, push, rush, stampede, stream, surge.

onset *n* assault, attack, beginning, charge, commencement, inception, kick-off, onrush, onslaught, outbreak, outset, start. *antonyms* end, finish.

onslaught *n* assault, attack, barrage, blitz, bombardment, charge, offensive, onrush, onset.

onus *n* burden, duty, encumbrance, liability, load, obligation, responsibility, task.

onward(s) *adv* ahead, beyond, forth, forward, frontward(s), in front, on. *antonym* backward(s).

oodles *n* abundance, bags, heaps, lashings, loads, lots, masses, tons. *antonym* scarcity.

oomph *n* animation, bounce, energy, enthusiasm, exuberance, get-up-and-go, pep, pizzazz, sex-appeal, sparkle, vigour, vitality, vivacity, zing.

ooze *v* bleed, discharge, drain, dribble, drip, drop, emit, escape, exude, filter, leach, leak, overflow with, percolate, seep, strain, sweat, transude, weep.

opaque *adj* abstruse, baffling, clouded, cloudy, cryptic, difficult, dim, dull, enigmatic, filmy, hazy, impenetrable, incomprehensible, inexplicable, lustreless, muddied, muddy, murky, obfuscated, obscure, turbid, unclear, unfathomable, unintelligible. *antonym* transparent.

open *adj* above-board, accessible, agape, airy, ajar, apparent, arguable, artless, available, avowed, bare, barefaced, blatant, bounteous, bountiful, candid, clear, conspicuous, debatable, disinterested, downright, evident, expanded, exposed, extended, extensive, fair, flagrant, frank, free, fretted, gaping, general, generous, guileless, holey, honest, honeycombed, impartial, ingenuous, innocent, lacy, liberal, lidless, loose, manifest, moot, munificent, natural, navigable, noticeable, objective, obvious, overt, passable, plain, porous, public, receptive, revealed, rolling, sincere, spacious, spongy, spread out, sweeping, transparent, unbarred, unbiased, unclosed, uncluttered, uncommitted, unconcealed, unconditional, uncovered, uncrowded, undecided, undefended, undisguised, unenclosed, unengaged, unfastened, unfenced, unfolded, unfortified, unfurled, unlidded, unlocked, unobstructed, unoccupied, unprejudiced, unprotected, unqualified, unreserved, unresolved, unrestricted, unroofed, unsealed, unsettled, unsheltered, unwalled, upfront, vacant, visible, wide, wide-open, yawning. *antonyms* closed, shut.

v begin, clear, come apart, commence, crack, disclose, divulge, exhibit, explain, expose, inaugurate, initiate, launch, lay bare, pour out, rupture, separate, set in motion, show, split, spread (out), start, throw wide, unbar, unbare, unblock, unclose, uncork, uncover, undo, unfasten, unfold, unfurl, unlatch, unlid, unlock, unroll, unseal, unshutter. *antonyms* close, shut.

open to accessible, disposed, exposed, liable, susceptible, vulnerable.

open-handed *adj* bountiful, free, generous, lavish, liberal, munificent, unstinting. *antonym* tight-fisted.

opening *n* aperture, beginning, birth, breach, break, chance, chasm, chink, cleft, commencement, crack, dawn, fissure, gap, hole, inauguration, inception, initiation, interstice, kick-off, launch, launching, occasion, onset, opportunity, orifice, outset, perforation, place, rent, rupture, slot, space, split, start, vacancy, vent, vista. *antonyms* closing, closure.

adj beginning, commencing, early, first, inaugural, inceptive, initial, initiatory, introductory, maiden, primary. *antonym* closing.

openly *adv* blatantly, brazenly, candidly, face to face, flagrantly, forthrightly, frankly, glaringly, in full view, in public, overtly, plainly, publicly, shamelessly, unabashedly, unashamedly, unhesitatingly, unreservedly, wantonly. *antonyms* secretly, slyly.

open-minded *adj* broad, broad-minded, catholic, dispassionate, enlightened, free, impartial, latitudinarian, liberal, objective, reasonable, receptive, tolerant, unbiased, unprejudiced. *antonyms* bigoted, intolerant, prejudiced.

operate *v* act, function, go, handle, manage, manoeuvre, perform, run, serve, use, utilise, work.

operation *n* action, activity, affair, agency, assault, business, campaign, course, deal, effect, effort, employment, enterprise, exercise, force, influence, instrumentality, manipulation, manoeuvre, motion, movement, performance, procedure, proceeding, process, surgery, transaction, undertaking, use, utilisation, working.

operative *adj* active, crucial, current, effective, efficient, engaged, functional, functioning, important, in action, in force, in operation, indicative, influential, key, operational, relevant, serviceable, significant, standing, workable. *antonym* inoperative.

opine *v* believe, conceive, conclude, conjecture, declare, guess, judge, presume, say, suggest, suppose, surmise, suspect, think, venture, volunteer.

opinion *n* assessment, belief, conception, conjecture, conventional wisdom, estimation, feeling, idea, impression, judgement, mind, notion, perception, persuasion, point of view, sentiment, stance, tenet, theory, view, voice, vox pop, vox populi.

opinionated *adj* adamant, biased, bigoted, bull-headed, cocksure, dictatorial, doctrinaire, dogmatic, inflexible, obdurate, obstinate, overbearing, partisan, pig-headed, prejudiced, self-assertive, single-minded, stubborn, uncompromising, wilful. *antonym* open-minded.

opponent *n* adversary, antagonist, challenger, competitor, contestant, disputant, dissentient, dissident, enemy, foe, objector, opposer, opposition, rival. *antonyms* ally, proponent.

opportune *adj* advantageous, appropriate, apt, auspicious, convenient, favourable, felicitous, fit, fitting, fortunate, good, happy, lucky, pertinent, proper, propitious, seasonable, suitable, timely, well-timed. *antonym* inopportune.

opportunity *n* break, chance, convenience, hour, moment, occasion, opening, scope, shot, time, turn.

oppose *v* bar, beard, breast, check, combat, compare, confront, contradict, contrary, contrast, contravene, controvert, counter, counterattack, counterbalance, defy, face, fight, fly in the face of, gainsay, hinder, obstruct, pit against, play off, prevent, resist, stand up to, take a stand against, take issue with, thwart, withstand. *antonyms* favour, support.

opposed *adj* against, agin, antagonistic, anti, antipathetic, antithetical, clashing, conflicting, contrary, contrasted, dissentient, hostile, in opposition, incompatible, inimical, opposing, opposite. *antonym* in favour.

opposing *adj* antagonistic, antipathetic, clashing, combatant, conflicting, contentious, contrary, disputatious, enemy, hostile, incompatible, irreconcilable, opposed, opposite, oppugnant, rival, warring.

opposite *adj* adverse, antagonistic, antipodean, antithetical, conflicting, contradictory, contrary, contrasted, corresponding, different, differing, diverse, facing, fronting, hostile, inconsistent, inimical, irreconcilable, opposed, reverse, unlike. *antonym* same.

opposition *n* antagonism, antagonist, clash, competition, contraposition, contrariety, counteraction, disapproval, foe, hostility, obstruction, obstructiveness, opponent, other side, polarity, prevention, resistance, rival, unfriendliness. *antonyms* co-operation, support.

oppress *v* abuse, afflict, burden, crush, depress, dispirit, harass, harry, lie hard on, lie heavy on, maltreat, overpower, overwhelm, persecute, sadden, subdue, subjugate, suppress, torment, trample, tyrannise, vex, weigh heavy.

oppressed *adj* abused, browbeaten, burdened, disadvantaged, downtrodden, enslaved, harassed, henpecked, misused, persecuted, slave, subject, subjugated, troubled, tyrannised, underprivileged. *antonym* free.

oppression *n* abuse, brutality, calamity, cruelty, hardship, harshness, injury, injustice, jackboot, misery, persecution, severity, subjection, suffering, tyranny.

oppressive *adj* airless, brutal, burdensome, close, cruel, despotic, grinding, harsh, heavy, inhuman, intolerable, muggy, onerous, overbearing, overpowering, overwhelming, repressive, severe, stifling, stuffy, suffocating, sultry, torrid, tyrannical, unendurable, unjust. *antonym* gentle.

opprobrious *adj* abusive, calumnious, contemptuous, damaging, defamatory, derogatory, insolent, insulting, invective, offensive, scandalous, scurrilous, vitriolic, vituperative.

opprobrium *n* calumny, censure, debasement, degradation, discredit, disfavour, disgrace, dishonour, disrepute, ignominy, infamy, obloquy, odium, reproach, scurrility, shame, slur, stigma.

opt *v* choose, decide (on), elect, go for, plump for, prefer, select, single out.

optimistic *adj* assured, bright, bullish, buoyant, cheerful, confident, encouraged, expectant, heartened, hopeful, positive, sanguine, upbeat. *antonym* pessimistic.

optimum *adj* A1, best, choicest, highest, ideal, optimal, peak, perfect, superlative, top. *antonym* worst.
n best, peak, zenith.

option *n* alternative, choice, election, possibility, preference, selection.

optional *adj* discretionary, elective, extra, open, possible, unforced, voluntary. *antonym* compulsory.

opulence *n* abundance, affluence, copiousness, cornucopia, easy street, fortune, fullness, lavishness, luxuriance, luxury, plenty, profusion, prosperity, riches, richness, sumptuousness, superabundance, wealth. *antonyms* penury, poverty.

opulent *adj* abundant, affluent, copious, lavish, luxuriant, luxurious, moneyed, plentiful, profuse, prolific, prosperous, rich, sumptuous, superabundant, wealthy, well-heeled, well-off, well-to-do. *antonyms* penurious, poor.

oracle *n* adviser, answer, augur, augury, authority, divination, guru, high priest, mastermind, mentor, prediction, prognostication, prophecy, prophet, pundit, revelation, sage, seer, soothsayer, vision, wizard.

oration *n* address, declamation, discourse, harangue, homily, lecture, sermon, speech, spiel.

oratory *n* declamation, diction, elocution, eloquence, grandiloquence, public speaking, rhetoric, speech, speechifying, speech-making.

orbit *n* ambit, circle, compass, course, cycle, domain, ellipse, influence, path, range, reach, revolution, rotation, scope, sphere, sphere of influence, sweep, track, trajectory.
v circle, circumnavigate, encircle, revolve.

orchestrate *v* arrange, compose, concert, co-ordinate, fix, integrate, organise, prepare, present, score, stage-manage.

ordain *v* anoint, appoint, call, consecrate, decree, destine, dictate, elect, enact, enjoin, fate, fix, foredoom, foreordain, frock, instruct, intend, invest, lay down, legislate, nominate, order, predestine, predetermine, prescribe, pronounce, require, rule, set, will.

ordeal *n* affliction, agony, anguish,

nightmare, pain, persecution, suffering, test, torture, trial, tribulation(s), trouble(s).

order[1] *n* application, arrangement, array, behest, booking, calm, categorisation, chit, classification, command, commission, control, cosmos, decree, dictate, diktat, direction, directive, discipline, disposal, disposition, grouping, harmony, injunction, instruction, law, law and order, layout, line, line-up, mandate, method, neatness, ordering, orderliness, ordinance, organisation, pattern, peace, placement, plan, precept, progression, propriety, quiet, regularity, regulation, request, requisition, reservation, rule, sequence, series, stipulation, structure, succession, symmetry, system, tidiness, tranquillity. **antonym** disorder.

v adjure, adjust, align, arrange, authorise, bid, book, catalogue, charge, class, classify, command, conduct, control, decree, direct, dispose, enact, engage, enjoin, group, instruct, lay out, manage, marshal, neaten, ordain, organise, prescribe, put to rights, regulate, request, require, reserve, sort out, systematise, tabulate, tidy. **antonym** disorder.

order[2] *n* association, breed, brotherhood, cast, caste, class, community, company, degree, family, fraternity, genre, genus, grade, guild, hierarchy, ilk, kind, league, lodge, organisation, pecking order, phylum, position, rank, sect, sisterhood, society, sort, species, status, subclass, tribe, type, union.

orderly *adj* businesslike, controlled, decorous, disciplined, in order, law-abiding, methodical, neat, non-violent, peaceable, quiet, regular, restrained, ruly, scientific, shipshape, systematic, systematised, tidy, trim, well-behaved, well-organised, well-regulated. **antonym** disorderly.

ordinarily *adv* as a rule, commonly, conventionally, customarily, familiarly, generally, habitually, in general, normally, usually.

ordinary *adj* accustomed, average, common, common-or-garden, commonplace, conventional, customary, established, everyday, fair, familiar, habitual, homespun, household, humble, humdrum, inconsequential, indifferent, inferior, mean, mediocre, modest, normal, pedestrian, plain, prevailing, prosaic, quotidian, regular, routine, run-of-the-mill, settled, simple, standard, stock, typical, undistinguished, unexceptional, unmemorable, unpretentious, unremarkable, usual, wonted, workaday. **antonyms** extraordinary, special, unusual.

organ *n* agency, channel, device, element, forum, implement, instrument, journal, means, medium, member, mouthpiece, newspaper, paper, periodical, process, publication, structure, tool, unit, vehicle, voice.

organisation *n* arrangement, assembling, assembly, association, body, business, chemistry, combine, company, composition, concern, confederation, configuration, conformation, consortium, constitution, construction, co-ordination, corporation, design, disposal, federation, firm, format, formation, formulation, framework, group, grouping, institution, league, make-up, management, method, methodology, organism, outfit, pattern, plan, planning, regulation, running, standardisation, structure, structuring, syndicate, system, unity, whole. **antonym** disorganisation.

organise *v* arrange, catalogue, classify, codify, constitute, construct, co-ordinate, dispose, establish, form, frame, group, marshal, pigeonhole, regiment, run, see to, set up, shape, structure, systematise, tabulate. **antonym** disorganise.

organism *n* animal, being, body, cell, creature, entity, living thing, structure.

orgy *n* bacchanal, bacchanalia, binge, bout, carousal, debauch, excess, indulgence, love-in, overindulgence, revel, revelry, saturnalia, splurge, spree, surfeit.

orient *v* acclimatise, accommodate, adapt, adjust, align, familiarise, get one's bearings, habituate, orientate.

orientation *n* acclimatisation, adaptation, adjustment, assimilation, attunement, bearings, co-ordination, direction, familiarisation, introduction, location, position, sense of direction, settling in.

orifice *n* aperture, cleft, hole, inlet, mouth, opening, perforation, pore, rent, slit, vent.

origin *n* ancestry, base, basis, beginning, beginnings, birth, cause, commencement, creation, dawning, derivation, descent, emergence, etymology, etymon, extraction, family, font, foundation, fountain, fountainhead, genesis, heritage, inauguration, inception, launch, lineage, occasion origination, outset, parentage, paternity, pedigree, provenance, root, roots, source, spring, start, stock, well-spring. *antonyms* end, termination.

original *adj* aboriginal, archetypal, authentic, commencing, creative, earliest, early, embryonic, fertile, first, first-hand, fresh, genuine, imaginative, infant, ingenious, initial, innovative, introductory, inventive, master, new, novel, opening, primal, primary, primitive, primordial, prototypical, resourceful, rudimentary, seminal, starting, unborrowed, unconventional, unhackneyed, unprecedented, unusual. *antonym* unoriginal.

n archetype, case, character, cure, eccentric, master, model, nonconformist, oddity, paradigm, pattern, prototype, queer fish, standard, type, weirdo.

originality *n* boldness, cleverness, creative spirit, creativeness, creativity, daring, eccentricity, freshness, imagination, imaginativeness, individuality, ingenuity, innovation, innovativeness, inventiveness, newness, novelty, resourcefulness, singularity, unconventionality, unorthodoxy.

originally *adv* at first, at the outset, at the start, by birth, by derivation, first, in origin, in the beginning, initially.

originate *v* arise, be born, begin, come, commence, conceive, create, derive, develop, discover, emanate, emerge, establish, evolve, flow, form, formulate, generate, give birth to, inaugurate, initiate, institute, introduce, invent, issue, launch, pioneer, proceed, produce, result, rise, set up, spring, start, stem. *antonyms* end, terminate.

ornament *v* adorn, beautify, bespangle, brighten, deck, decorate, dress up, embellish, festoon, garnish, gild, grace, prettify, trim.

ornamental *adj* attractive, beautifying, decorative, embellishing, flashy, for show, showy.

ornate *adj* baroque, beautiful, busy, convoluted, decorated, elaborate, elegant, fancy, florid, flowery, fussy, ornamented, sumptuous. *antonyms* austere, plain.

orthodox *adj* accepted, approved, conformist, conventional, correct, customary, doctrinal, established, kosher, official, received, sound, traditional, true, usual, well-established. *antonym* unorthodox.

oscillate *v* fluctuate, seesaw, sway,

swing, vacillate, vary, vibrate, waver, yo-yo.

oscillation *n* fluctuation, instability, seesawing, swing, swinging, vacillation, variation, wavering.

ostensible *adj* alleged, apparent, avowed, exhibited, manifest, outward, plausible, presumed, pretended, professed, purported, put-on, seeming, so-called, specious, superficial, supposed.

ostensibly *adv* apparently, professedly, purportedly, reputedly, seemingly, supposedly.

ostentation *n* affectation, boasting, display, exhibitionism, flamboyance, flashiness, flaunting, flourish, pageantry, parade, pomp, pretension, pretentiousness, show, showiness, showing off, swank, tinsel, trappings, vaunting, window-dressing. *antonym* unpretentiousness.

ostentatious *adj* aggressive, boastful, conspicuous, extravagant, flamboyant, flash, flashy, garish, gaudy, loud, obtrusive, pretentious, self-advertising, showy, splashy, swanking, swanky, vain, vulgar. *antonyms* quiet, restrained.

ostracise *v* avoid, banish, bar, black, blackball, blacklist, boycott, cast out, cold-shoulder, cut, debar, exclude, excommunicate, exile, expatriate, expel, reject, segregate, send to Coventry, shun, snub. *antonyms* accept, receive, reinstate, welcome.

other *adj* added, additional, alternative, auxiliary, contrasting, different, differing, dissimilar, distinct, diverse, extra, fresh, further, more, new, remaining, separate, spare, supplementary, unrelated.

ounce *n* atom, crumb, drop, grain, iota, jot, modicum, morsel, particle, scrap, shred, speck, spot, trace, whit.

oust *v* depose, disinherit, dislodge, displace, dispossess, drive out, eject, evict, expel, overthrow, replace, supplant, throw out, topple, turn out, unseat, upstage. *antonyms* ensconce, install, reinstate, settle.

out¹ *adj* abroad, absent, away, disclosed, elsewhere, evident, exposed, gone, manifest, not at home, outside, public, revealed.

out of bounds banned, barred, disallowed, forbidden, off-limits, prohibited, taboo.

out of date antiquated, archaic, behind the times, dated, obsolete, old, old

hat, old-fashioned, outmoded, passé.
antonyms fashionable, modern, new.

out of doors alfresco, out, outdoors, outside. **antonym** indoors.

out of focus blurred, blurry, fuzzy, hazy, ill-defined, indistinct, muzzy. **antonyms** clear, sharp.

out of order broken, broken down, burst, conked out, haywire, in disrepair, inoperative, kaput, non-functional, on the blink, out of commission. **antonym** serviceable.

out of place disarranged, in disorder, inappropriate, tactless, topsy-turvy, unbecoming, unfitting, unseemly, unsuitable. **antonyms** appropriate.

out of sorts below par, depressed, down in the dumps, down in the mouth, fed up, gloomy, ill, moody, off-colour, peelie-wally, poorly, sick, under the weather. **antonyms** cheerful, well.

out of the blue all of a sudden, suddenly, unexpectedly. .

out of the wood(s) home and dry, in the clear, on dry land, out of danger, out of difficulty, safe, safe and sound, secure. **antonyms** insecure, vulnerable.

out of this world excellent, fabulous, fantastic, great, incredible, indescribable, marvellous, phenomenal, remarkable, superb, unbelievable, wonderful. **antonyms** mundane, ordinary.

out² *adj* antiquated, banned, blacked, dated, dead, disallowed, ended, excluded, exhausted, expired, extinguished, finished, forbidden, impossible, not on, old hat, old-fashioned, out of date, passé, square, taboo, unacceptable, unfashionable, used up. **antonyms** acceptable, fashionable, in.

out-and-out *adj* absolute, arrant, complete, consummate, downright, dyed-in-the-wool, inveterate, outright, perfect, thoroughgoing, total, uncompromising, unmitigated, unqualified, utter.

outbreak *n* burst, epidemic, eruption, explosion, flare-up, flash, outburst, upsurge.

outburst *n* access, attack, discharge, eruption, explosion, fit, fit of temper, flare-up, gale, gush, outbreak, outpouring, storm, surge, volley.

outcast *n* castaway, derelict, exile, leper, outsider, pariah, persona non grata, refugee, reject, reprobate, unperson, untouchable, vagabond, wretch. **antonyms** favourite, idol.

outclass *v* beat, eclipse, excel over,

leave standing, outdistance, outdo, outrank, outrival, outshine, outstrip, overshadow, put in the shade, surpass, top.

outcome *n* after-effect, aftermath, conclusion, consequence, effect, end, end result, harvest, issue, pay-off, result, upshot.

outcry *n* clamour, commotion, complaint, cry, exclamation, flap, howl, hue and cry, hullaballoo, noise, outburst, protest, row, scream, screech, uproar, vociferation, yell.

outdated *adj* antediluvian, antiquated, antique, archaic, behind the times, dated, obsolescent, obsolete, old-fashioned, out of date, out of style, outmoded, passé, square, unfashionable, unmodish. **antonyms** fashionable, modern, modish.

outdistance *v* leave behind, leave standing, outpace, outrun, outstrip, overhaul, overtake, pass, pull ahead of, shake off, surpass.

outdo *v* beat, best, eclipse, excel over, get the better of, outclass, outdistance, outfox, out-Herod, outmanoeuvre, outshine, outsmart, outstrip, outwit, overcome, surpass, top.

outdoor *adj* alfresco, open-air, out-of-door(s), outside. **antonym** indoor.

outer *adj* distant, exterior, external, further, outlying, outside, outward, peripheral, remote, superficial, surface. **antonyms** central, inner, proximal.

outfit¹ *n* accoutrements, clothes, costume, ensemble, equipment, garb, gear, get-up, kit, paraphernalia, rig, rig-out, suit, togs, trappings, turn-out.
v apparel, appoint, attire, equip, fit out, fit up, furnish, kit out, provision, stock, supply, turn out.

outfit² *n* business, clan, clique, company, corps, coterie, crew, firm, gang, group, organisation, set, set-up, squad, team, unit.

outgoing *adj* affable, approachable, chatty, communicative, cordial, demonstrative, departing, easy, ex-, expansive, extrovert, former, friendly, genial, gregarious, informal, last, open, past, retiring, sociable, sympathetic, unreserved, warm, withdrawing. **antonyms** incoming, introvert, new, unsociable.

outing *n* excursion, expedition, jaunt, picnic, pleasure trip, ramble, spin, trip.

outlandish *adj* alien, barbarous, bizarre, eccentric, exotic, extraordinary, fantastic, foreign, grotesque, odd, preposterous, queer, strange, unheard-of, weird. *antonyms* familiar, ordinary.

outlaw *v* ban, banish, bar, condemn, debar, disallow, embargo, exclude, excommunicate, forbid, illegalise, interdict, prohibit, proscribe, waive. *antonyms* allow, legalise.

outlet *n* avenue, channel, duct, egress, emissary, exit, market, opening, orifice, outfall, release, safety valve, vent, way out. *antonyms* entry, inlet.

outline *n* bare facts, contour, draft, drawing, figure, form, frame, framework, lay-out, plan, profile, recapitulation, résumé, rough, run-down, scenario, schema, shape, silhouette, skeleton, sketch, summary, synopsis, thumbnail sketch, tracing.
v adumbrate, delineate, draft, plan, recapitulate, rough out, sketch, summarise, trace.

outlive *v* come through, live through, outlast, survive, weather. *antonym* predecease.

outlook *n* angle, aspect, attitude, expectations, forecast, frame of mind, future, look-out, panorama, perspective, point of view, prognosis, prospect, scene, slant, standpoint, vantage-point, view, viewpoint, views, vista.

outlying *adj* distant, far-away, far-flung, far-off, further, outer, outlandish, peripheral, provincial, remote. *antonyms* central, inner.

outmoded *adj* anachronistic, antediluvian, antiquated, antique, archaic, behind the times, bygone, dated, fossilised, obsolescent, obsolete, olden, old-fashioned, out of date, outworn, passé, square, superannuated, superseded, unfashionable, unmodish, unusable. *antonyms* fashionable, fresh, modern, modish, new.

out-of-the-way *adj* abnormal, abstruse, curious, distant, exceptional, extraordinary, far-away, far-flung, far-off, inaccessible, isolated, little-known, lonely, obscure, odd, outlying, peculiar, remote, secluded, strange, uncommon, unfamiliar, unfrequented, unget-at-able, unusual.

outpace *v* beat, outdistance, outdo, outrun, outstrip, overhaul, overtake, pass, surpass.

output *n* achievement, manufacture, print-out, product, production, productivity, read-out, yield. *antonyms* input, outlay.

outrage *n* hurt, abuse, affront, anger, atrocity, barbarism, crime, desecration, disgrace, enormity, evil, fury, horror, indignation, indignity, inhumanity, injury, insult, offence, profanation, ravishing, resentment, scandal, shock, violation, violence, wrath.
v abuse, affront, astound, defile, desecrate, disgust, incense, infuriate, injure, insult, madden, make someone's blood boil, offend, ravage, ravish, repel, scandalise, shock, violate.

outrageous *adj* abominable, atrocious, barbaric, beastly, disgraceful, egregious, excessive, exorbitant, extortionate, extravagant, flagrant, godless, heinous, horrible, immoderate, infamous, inhuman, iniquitous, inordinate, monstrous, nefarious, offensive, preposterous, scandalous, shocking, steep, turbulent, unconscionable, ungodly, unholy, unreasonable, unspeakable, villainous, violent, wicked. *antonyms* acceptable, irreproachable.

outright *adj* absolute, arrant, categorical, complete, consummate, definite, direct, downright, flat, out-and-out, perfect, point-blank, pure, straightforward, thorough, thoroughgoing, total, uncompromising, unconditional, undeniable, unequivocal, unmitigated, unqualified, utter, wholesale. *antonyms* ambiguous, indefinite, provisional.
adv absolutely, at once, cleanly, completely, directly, explicitly, immediately, instantaneously, instantly, on the spot, openly, positively, straight away, straightaway, straightforwardly, there and then, thoroughly, unhesitatingly, without restraint.

outrun *v* beat, exceed, excel, leave behind, lose, outdistance, outdo, outpace, outstrip, overhaul, overtake, pass, shake off, surpass.

outset *n* beginning, commencement, early days, forthgoing, inauguration, inception, kick-off, opening, start. *antonyms* conclusion, end, finish.

outshine *v* beat, best, dwarf, eclipse, excel, outclass, outdo, outrank, outstrip, overshadow, put in the shade, surpass, top, transcend, upstage.

outside[1] *adj* exterior, external, extramural, extraneous, extreme, outdoor, outer, outermost, outward, superficial, surface. *antonym* inside.
n cover, exterior, façade, face, front, skin, surface, topside. *antonym* inside.
prep outwith, without.

outside[2] *adj* distant, faint, infinitesimal,

marginal, minute, negligible, remote, slight, slim, small, unlikely. *antonyms* likely, real, substantial.

outsider *n* alien, foreigner, immigrant, incomer, interloper, intruder, misfit, newcomer, non-member, non-resident, observer, odd man out, outcast, outlander, settler, stranger. *antonyms* inhabitant, insider, local, member, native, resident, specialist.

outskirts *n* borders, boundary, edge, environs, fringes, margin, periphery, suburbia, suburbs, vicinity. *antonyms* centre, city-centre.

outsmart *v* beat, best, deceive, dupe, get the better of, outfox, outmanoeuvre, outperform, out-think, outwit.

outspoken *adj* abrupt, blunt, candid, direct, explicit, forthright, frank, free, open, plain-spoken, pointed, rude, sharp, trenchant, unceremonious, unequivocal, unreserved. *antonyms* diplomatic, tactful.

outspread *adj* expanded, extended, fanned out, flared, open, opened, outstretched, spread out, stretched, unfolded, unfurled, wide, wide-open.

outstanding¹ *adj* ace, arresting, celebrated, conspicuous, distinguished, egregious, eminent, excellent, exceptional, extraordinary, eye-catching, great, important, impressive, marked, memorable, notable, noteworthy, pre-eminent, prominent, remarkable, salient, signal, singular, special, striking, superior, superlative, surpassing. *antonyms* ordinary, unexceptional.

outstanding² *adj* due, left, ongoing, open, over, owing, payable, pending, remaining, uncollected, undone, unpaid, unresolved, unsettled.

outstrip *v* beat, best, better, eclipse, exceed, excel, gain on, leave behind, leave standing, outclass, outdistance, outdo, outpace, outperform, outrun, outshine, overhaul, overtake, pass, surpass, top.

outward *adj* alleged, apparent, avowed, evident, exterior, external, noticeable, observable, obvious, ostensible, outer, outside, professed, public, superficial, supposed, surface, visible. *antonyms* inner, private.

outwardly *adv* apparently, at first sight, evidently, externally, in appearance, officially, on the surface, ostensibly, seemingly, superficially, supposedly, to all appearances, to the eye. *antonyms* internally, inwardly, privately.

outweigh *v* cancel out, compensat for, eclipse, make up for, outbalance overcome, override, overrule predominate, preponderate, prevail ove take precedence over.

outwit *v* beat, best, better, circumven get the better of, outfox, outmanoeuvre outsmart, out-think.

outworn *adj* abandoned, antiquatec clichéd, defunct, discredited, disusec exhausted, hackneyed, moth-eater obsolete, out of date, outdatec outmoded, overused, rejected, stale superannuated, threadbare, tired, trite worn-out. *antonyms* fresh, new.

over¹ *adj* accomplished, bygone, closec completed, concluded, done with, endec finished, forgotten, gone, in the pasl past, settled, up.

over² *prep* above, exceeding, in charg of, in command of, in excess of, mor than, on, on top of, superior to, upon.
adv above, aloft, beyond, extra in addition, in excess, left, oι high, overhead, remaining, superfluous surplus, unclaimed, unused, unwanted.

over and above added to, along with as well as, besides, in addition to, lε alone, not to mention, on top of, plus together with.

over and over (again) ad infinitum, a nauseam, again and again, continually endlessly, frequently, often, repeatedly time and (time) again.

over the top a bit much, excessive histrionic, immoderate, inordinate overdone, too much, uncalled-for.

overabundance *n* excess, glut oversupply, plethora, profusion superabundance, superfluity, surfeit surplus, too much of a good thing. *antonyms* dearth, lack.

overact *v* emote, exaggerate, ham ham up, overdo, overplay. *antonym* underact, underplay.

overall *adj* all-embracing, all-inclusive all-over, blanket, broad, complete comprehensive, general, global inclusive, total, umbrella. *antonyms* narrow, short-term.
adv by and large, generally speaking, iι general, in the long term, on the whole.

overawe *v* abash, alarm, awe, browbeal cow, daunt, disconcert, dismay, frighten intimidate, petrify, scare, terrify unnerve. *antonym* reassure.

overbalance *v* capsize, fall over, keε over, lose (one's) balance, lose one' footing, overset, overturn, slip, tip ovei topple over, trip, tumble, turn turtle, upset.

overbearing *adj* arrogant, autocratic, bossy, cavalier, despotic, dictatorial, dogmatic, domineering, haughty, high and mighty, high-handed, imperious, lordly, magisterial, officious, oppressive, overweening, peremptory, pompous, supercilious, superior, tyrannical. *antonyms* modest, unassertive, unassuming.

overcast *adj* black, clouded, clouded over, cloudy, dark, darkened, dismal, dreary, dull, grey, hazy, leaden, lowering, murky, sombre, sunless, threatening. *antonyms* bright, clear, sunny.

overcome *v* beat, best, better, conquer, crush, defeat, lick, master, overpower, overthrow, overwhelm, prevail, rise above, subdue, subjugate, surmount, survive, triumph over, vanquish, weather, worst.
adj affected, beaten, bowled over, broken, defeated, exhausted, overpowered, overwhelmed, speechless, swept off one's feet.

over-confident *adj* arrogant, brash, cocksure, cocky, foolhardy, incautious, over-optimistic, overweening, presumptuous, rash, sanguine, temerarious, uppish. *antonyms* cautious, diffident.

overcrowded *adj* chock-a-block, chock-full, choked, congested, crammed full, hotching, jam-packed, overloaded, overpopulated, packed, packed out, seething, swarming. *antonyms* deserted, empty.

overdo *v* do to death, exaggerate, gild the lily, go to extremes, go too far, labour, lay it on thick, overact, overexert, overindulge, overplay, overreach, overstate, overtax, overuse, overwork. *antonyms* neglect, underuse.

overdone *adj* burnt, burnt to a cinder, charred, dried up, exaggerated, excessive, fulsome, histrionic, immoderate, inordinate, over the top, overcooked, overelaborate, overplayed, overstated, preposterous, spoiled, undue, unnecessary. *antonyms* raw, underdone, underplayed, understated.

overdue *adj* behind schedule, behindhand, belated, delayed, late, owing, slow, tardy. *antonym* early.

overemphasise *v* belabour, exaggerate, labour, overdramatise, overstress. *antonyms* belittle, minimise, underplay, understate.

overflow *v* brim over, bubble over, cover, deluge, discharge, drown, flood, inundate, pour over, shower, soak, spill, spray, submerge, surge, swamp, well over.
n flood, inundation, overabundance, overspill, spill, superfluity, surplus.

overflowing *adj* abounding, bountiful, brimful, copious, inundant, plenteous, plentiful, profuse, rife, superabundant, swarming, teeming, thronged. *antonyms* lacking, scarce.

overhanging *adj* beetling, jutting, projecting, protruding.

overhaul[1] *v* check, do up, examine, fix, inspect, mend, recondition, re-examine, repair, restore, service, survey.
n check, check-up, examination, going-over, inspection, reconditioning, repair, restoration, service.

overhaul[2] *v* gain on, outpace, outstrip, overtake, pass, pull ahead of.

overhead *adv* above, aloft, on high, up above, upward. *antonyms* below, underfoot.
adj aerial, elevated, overhanging, roof, upper. *antonyms* floor, ground, underground.

overheated *adj* agitated, excited, fiery, flaming, impassioned, inflamed, overexcited, overwrought, passionate, roused. *antonyms* calm, cool, dispassionate, impassive.

overindulge *v* binge, booze, debauch, gluttonise, gorge, gormandise, guzzle. *antonym* abstain.

overindulgence *n* binge, debauch, excess, immoderation, intemperance, overeating, surfeit. *antonyms* abstemiousness, abstention.

overjoyed *adj* delighted, delirious, ecstatic, elated, enraptured, euphoric, in raptures, joyful, jubilant, on cloud nine, over the moon, rapturous, thrilled, tickled pink, transported. *antonyms* disappointed, sad.

overlap *v* coincide, cover, flap over, overlay, overlie.

overload *v* burden, encumber, oppress, overburden, overcharge, overtax, saddle, strain, surcharge, tax, weigh down.

overlook[1] *v* condone, disregard, excuse, forget, forgive, ignore, let pass, let ride, miss, neglect, omit, pardon, pass, pass over, skip, slight, turn a blind eye to, wink at. *antonyms* note, notice, penalise, record, remember.

overlook[2] *v* command a view of, face, front on to, give upon, look on to.

overly *adv* exceedingly, excessively,

immoderately, inordinately, over, too, unduly, unreasonably. **antonyms** inadequately, insufficiently.

overpower v beat, best, conquer, crush, defeat, floor, immobilise, master, overcome, overthrow, overwhelm, quell, subdue, subjugate, vanquish.

overpowering adj compelling, convincing, extreme, forceful, insuppressible, invincible, irrefutable, irrepressible, irresistible, nauseating, oppressive, overwhelming, powerful, sickening, strong, suffocating, telling, unbearable, uncontrollable.

overrate v blow up, magnify, make too much of, overestimate, overpraise, overprize, oversell, overvalue. **antonym** underrate.

overriding adj cardinal, compelling, determining, dominant, essential, final, first, major, number one, overruling, paramount, pivotal, predominant, prevailing, primary, prime, prior, ruling, supreme, ultimate. **antonyms** insignificant, unimportant.

overrule v abrogate, annul, cancel, countermand, disallow, invalidate, outvote, override, overturn, recall, repeal, rescind, reverse, revoke, set aside, veto, vote down. **antonyms** allow, approve.

overrun v choke, infest, inundate, invade, occupy, overflow, overgrow, overspread, overwhelm, permeate, ravage, run riot, spread over, surge over, swamp, swarm over. **antonyms** desert, evacuate.

overshadow v adumbrate, becloud, bedim, blight, cloud, darken, dim, dominate, dwarf, eclipse, excel, mar, obfuscate, obscure, outshine, outweigh, protect, put in the shade, rise above, ruin, shelter, spoil, surpass, tower above, veil.

oversight n blunder, boob, carelessness, delinquency, error, fault, inattention, lapse, laxity, mistake, neglect, omission, slip, slip-up.

overt adj apparent, avowed, evident, manifest, observable, obvious, open, patent, plain, professed, public, unconcealed, undisguised, visible. **antonyms** covert, secret.

overtake v befall, catch up with, come upon, draw level with, engulf, happen, hit, outdistance, outdo, outstrip, overhaul, pass, pull ahead of, strike.

overthrow v abolish, beat, bring down, conquer, crush, defeat, demolish, depose, destroy, dethrone, displace, knock down, level, master, oust, overcome, overpower, overturn, overwhelm, raze, ruin, subdue, subjugate, subvert, topple, unseat, upset, vanquish. **antonyms** install, reinstate.

n confounding, defeat, deposition, destruction, dethronement, discomfiture, disestablishment, displacement, dispossession, downfall, end, fall, ousting, rout, ruin, subjugation, subversion, suppression, undoing, unseating.

overtone n association, connotation, feeling, flavour, hint, implication, innuendo, intimation, nuance, sense, slant, something, suggestion, undercurrent.

overturn v abolish, abrogate, annul, capsize, countermand, depose, destroy, invalidate, keel over, knock down, knock over, overbalance, overset, overthrow, quash, repeal, rescind, reverse, set aside, spill, tip over, topple, tumble, unsea, upend, upset, upturn.

overused adj clichéd, commonplace, hackneyed, platitudinous, stale, stereotyped, threadbare, tired, trite, unoriginal, worn. **antonyms** fresh, original.

overweight adj ample, bulky, chubby, chunky, corpulent, fat, flabby, fleshy, gross, heavy, hefty, huge, massive, obese, outsize, plump, podgy, portly, potbellied, stout, tubby, well-padded, wellupholstered. **antonyms** emaciated, skinny, thin, underweight.

overwhelm v bowl over, bury, confuse, crush, cut to pieces, defeat, deluge, destroy, devastate, engulf, floor, inundate, knock for six, massacre, overcome, overpower, overrun, prostrate, rout, snow under, stagger, submerge, swamp.

overwhelming adj breathtaking, crushing, devastating, insuppressible, invincible, irrepressible, irresistible, overpowering, shattering, stunning, towering, uncontrollable, vast. **antonyms** insignificant, negligible, resistible.

overwork v burden, burn the midnight oil, exhaust, exploit, fatigue, oppress, overburden, overload, overstrain, overtax, overuse, strain, sweat, tax, wear out, weary, work one's fingers to the bone.

overwrought adj agitated, beside oneself, distracted, emotional, excited, frantic, keyed up, on edge, overcharged, overexcited, overheated, overworked, stirred, strung up, tense, uptight, worked up, wound up. **antonyms** calm, cool, impassive.

owing *adj* due, in arrears, outstanding, overdue, owed, payable, unpaid, unsettled.

owing to as a result of, because of, on account of, thanks to.

own¹ *adj* idiosyncratic, individual, inimitable, particular, personal, private.

own² *v* acknowledge, admit, agree, allow, avow, concede, confess, disclose, enjoy, grant, have, hold, keep, possess, recognise, retain.

own up admit, come clean, confess, make a clean breast of it, spill the beans, tell the truth.

P

pace *n* celerity, clip, gait, lick, measure, momentum, motion, movement, progress, quickness, rapidity, rate, speed, step, stride, tempo, time, tread, velocity, walk.
v count, determine, march, mark out, measure, pad, patrol, pound, step, stride, tramp, tread, walk.

pacific *adj* appeasing, calm, complaisant, conciliatory, diplomatic, dovelike, dovish, equable, friendly, gentle, halcyon, mild, nonbelligerent, nonviolent, pacifist, peaceable, peaceful, peace-loving, peacemaking, placatory, placid, propitiatory, quiet, serene, smooth, still, tranquil, unruffled.
antonyms aggressive, belligerent, contentious, pugnacious.

pacify *v* allay, ameliorate, appease, assuage, calm, chasten, compose, conciliate, crush, humour, lull, moderate, mollify, placate, propitiate, put down, quell, quiet, repress, silence, smooth down, soften, soothe, still, subdue, tame, tranquillise. *antonyms* aggravate, anger.

pack *n* assemblage, back-pack, bale, band, boodle, bunch, bundle, burden, collection, company, crew, crowd, deck, drove, flock, gang, group, haversack, herd, kit, kitbag, knapsack, load, lot, mob, outfit, package, packet, parcel, rucksack, set, troop, truss.
v batch, bundle, burden, charge, compact, compress, cram, crowd, fill, jam, load, mob, package, packet, press, ram, store, stow, stuff, tamp, throng, thrust, wedge.

packed *adj* brim-full, chock-a-block, chock-full, congested, cram-full, crammed, crowded, filled, full, hotching, jammed, jam-packed, overflowing, overloaded, seething, swarming. *antonyms* deserted, empty.

pact *n* agreement, alliance, arrangement, bargain, bond, cartel, compact, concord, concordat, contract, convention, covenant, deal, entente, league, protocol, treaty, understanding. *antonyms* breach, disagreement, quarrel.

pad¹ *n* block, buffer, cushion, jotter, notepad, pillow, protection, stiffening, stuffing, tablet, wad, writing-pad.
v cushion, fill, line, pack, protect, shape, stuff, wrap.

pad out amplify, augment, bombast, elaborate, expand, fill out, flesh out, inflate, lengthen, protract, spin out, stretch.

pad² *n* apartment, flat, hang-out, home, penthouse, place, quarters, room, rooms.

pad³ *v* lope, move, run, step, tiptoe, tramp, tread, trudge, walk.

pagan *n* atheist, heathen, idolater, infidel, unbeliever. *antonym* believer.
adj atheistic, godless, heathen, heathenish, idolatrous, infidel, irreligious.

page *n* chapter, episode, epoch, era, event, folio, incident, leaf, period, phase, point, recto, sheet, side, stage, time, verso.

pageant *n* display, extravaganza, masque, parade, play, procession, representation, ritual, scene, show, spectacle, tableau.

pageantry *n* ceremony, display, drama, extravagance, glamour, glitter, grandeur, magnificence, melodrama, ostentation, parade, pomp, show, showiness, spectacle, splash, splendour, state, theatricality.

pain *n* ache, affliction, aggravation, agony, anguish, annoyance, bitterness, bore, bother, burden, cramp, discomfort, distress, dole, dolour, drag, grief, gyp, headache, heartache, heartbreak, hurt, irritation, misery, nuisance, pang, pest, smart, soreness, spasm, suffering, tenderness, throb, throe, torment, torture, tribulation, trouble, twinge, vexation, woe, wretchedness.
v afflict, aggrieve, agonise, annoy, chagrin, cut to the quick, disappoint, disquiet, distress, exasperate, gall, grieve, harass, hurt, irritate, nettle, rile, sadden, torment, torture, vex, worry, wound, wring. *antonyms* gratify, please.

pained *adj* aggrieved, chagrined, cut to the quick, cut up, disappointed, distressed, galled, grieved, hurt, injured, miffed, nettled, offended, reproachful, saddened, stung, upset, wounded. *antonyms* gratified, pleased.

painful *adj* aching, achy, afflictive, agonising, arduous, difficult, disagreeable, distasteful, distressing, doloriferous, dolorific, excruciating, grievous, hard, harrowing, laborious, lancinating, saddening, severe, smarting, sore, tedious, tender, troublesome, trying, unpleasant, vexatious. **antonyms** easy, painless.

painfully *adv* alarmingly, clearly, deplorably, distressingly, dreadfully, excessively, markedly, pitiably, pitifully, sadly, unfortunately, woefully, wretchedly.

painless *adj* downhill, easy, effortless, fast, pain-free, plain sailing, quick, simple, trouble-free, undemanding. **antonyms** difficult, painful.

painstaking *adj* assiduous, careful, conscientious, dedicated, devoted, diligent, earnest, exacting, hardworking, industrious, meticulous, perfectionist, persevering, punctilious, scrupulous, sedulous, strenuous, thorough, thoroughgoing. **antonyms** careless, negligent.

paint *n* colour, colouring, cosmetics, distemper, dye, emulsion, enamel, glaze, greasepaint, lacquer, lake, make-up, maquillage, oils, pigment, primer, stain, tint, undercoat, warpaint, wash, water-colour, whitewash.

v apply, coat, colour, cover, daub, decorate, delineate, depict, describe, distemper, evoke, glaze, lacquer, limn, picture, portray, recount, render, represent.

pair *n* brace, combination, couple, doublet, doubleton, duad, duo, dyad, match, span, twins, two of a kind, twosome, yoke.

v bracket, couple, join, link, marry, match, match up, mate, pair off, put together, splice, team, twin, wed, yoke. **antonyms** dissever, sever.

pal *n* amigo, buddy, china, chum, companion, comrade, confidant(e), crony, friend, gossip, intimate, mate, partner, side-kick, soul mate. **antonym** enemy.

palatable *adj* acceptable, agreeable, appetising, attractive, enjoyable, fair, pleasant, sapid, satisfactory, savoury, tasty, toothsome. **antonyms** unacceptable, unpleasant.

palate *n* appetite, appreciation, enjoyment, gout, gusto, heart, liking, relish, stomach, taste, zest.

palatial *adj* de luxe, grand, grandiose, illustrious, imposing, luxurious, magnificent, majestic, opulent, plush, posh, regal, spacious, splendid, stately, sumptuous, swanky. **antonyms** cramped, poky.

palaver *n* activity, babble, blather, blether, business, bustle, carry-on, chatter, colloquy, confab, conference, confusion, discussion, fuss, fuss about nothing, get-together, hubbub, natter, parley, performance, pow-wow, prattle, procedure, rigmarole, session, song and dance, to-do, tongue-wagging, yak.

v blab, blather, blether, chatter, confab, confer, discuss, gabble, jabber, jaw, natter, parley, powwow, prattle, tattle, yak.

pale *adj* anaemic, ashen, ashy, bleached, bloodless, chalky, colourless, dim, etiolated, faded, faint, feeble, inadequate, light, lily-livered, pallid, pasty, poor, sallow, thin, wan, washed-out, waxy, weak, whey-faced, white, white-livered, whitish. **antonym** ruddy.

v blanch, decrease, dim, diminish, dull, etiolate, fade, lessen, whiten. **antonyms** blush, colour.

pall[1] *n* check, cloud, cold water, damp, damper, dismay, gloom, mantle, melancholy, shadow, shroud, veil.

pall[2] *v* bore, cloy, glut, jade, lose savour, satiate, sicken, surfeit, tire, weary.

palliate *v* abate, allay, alleviate, assuage, cloak, conceal, cover, diminish, ease, excuse, extenuate, lessen, lighten, minimise, mitigate, moderate, mollify, relieve, soften, soothe, temper.

palliative *adj* alleviative, anodyne, assuasive, calmative, calming, lenitive, mitigative, mitigatory, mollifying, sedative, soothing. **antonym** irritant.

pallid *adj* anaemic, ashen, ashy, bloodless, cadaverous, colourless, doughy, etiolated, insipid, lifeless, pale, pasty, pasty-faced, peelie-wally, sallow, spiritless, sterile, tame, tired, uninspired, vapid, wan, waxen, waxy, whey-faced, whitish. **antonyms** high-complexioned, ruddy, vigorous.

pally *adj* affectionate, chummy, close, familiar, friendly, intimate, palsy, palsy-walsy, thick. **antonym** unfriendly.

palm *v* appropriate, conceal, grab, half-inch, nick, sneak, snitch.

palm off fob off, foist, foist off, impose, offload, pass off, thrust, unload.

palpable *adj* apparent, blatant, clear, concrete, conspicuous, evident, manifest, material, obvious, open, overt, patent, plain, real, solid, substantial, tangible, touchable, unmistakable, visible. **antonyms** elusive, impalpable, imperceptible, intangible.

palpitate *v* beat, flutter, pitapat, pitter-patter, pound, pulsate, pulse, quiver, shiver, throb, thump, tremble, vibrate.

paltry *adj* base, beggarly, contemptible, derisory, despicable, inconsiderable, insignificant, low, meagre, mean, minor, miserable, negligible, petty, piddling, piffling, pitiful, poor, puny, rubbishy, slight, small, sorry, tinpot, trifling, trivial, two-bit, twopenny-halfpenny, unimportant, worthless, wretched. *antonyms* significant, substantial.

pamper *v* baby, coddle, cosset, fondle, gratify, humour, indulge, mollycoddle, mother, overindulge, pet, spoil. *antonyms* ill-treat, neglect.

pan¹ *n* casserole, container, pancheon, pot, saucepan, skillet, stewpot, vessel, wok.

v censure, criticise, flay, hammer, knock, pick to pieces, pull to pieces, roast, rubbish, slam, slate. *antonym* praise.

pan out come to an end, culminate, eventuate, happen, result, turn out, work out, yield.

pan² *v* circle, follow, move, scan, sweep, swing, track, traverse, turn.

panache *n* brio, dash, élan, enthusiasm, flair, flamboyance, flourish, grand manner, ostentation, pizzazz, spirit, style, swagger, theatricality, verve, vigour, zest.

pandemonium *n* babel, bedlam, chaos, clamour, commotion, confusion, din, disorder, frenzy, hubbub, hue and cry, hullaballoo, racket, ruckus, ruction, rumpus, to-do, tumult, turbulence, turmoil, uproar. *antonyms* calm, order, peace.

pander *v* cater to, furnish, gratify, indulge, pamper, please, provide, purvey, satisfy.

pang *n* ache, agony, anguish, crick, discomfort, distress, gripe, pain, prick, spasm, stab, sting, stitch, throe, twinge, twitch, wrench.

panic *n* agitation, alarm, consternation, dismay, fear, fright, hassle, horror, hysteria, scare, terror, tizzy, to-do. *antonyms* assurance, confidence.

v alarm, get one's knickers in a twist, go to pieces, lose one's cool, lose one's nerve, overreact, put the wind up, scare, startle, terrify, unnerve. *antonyms* reassure, relax.

panic-stricken *adj* aghast, agitated, alarmed, appalled, fearful, frenzied, frightened, horrified, horror-stricken, hysterical, in a cold sweat, panicky,

perturbed, petrified, scared, scared stiff, startled, stunned, stupefied, terrified, terror-stricken, unnerved. *antonyms* confident, laid-back, relaxed.

panorama *n* bird's-eye view, overview, perspective, prospect, scene, scenery, spectacle, survey, view, vision, vista.

panoramic *adj* bird's-eye, comprehensive, extensive, far-reaching, general, inclusive, overall, scenic, sweeping, universal, wide, widespread. *antonym* limited.

pansy *n* fag, faggot, homo, homosexual, Jessie, namby-pamby, nancy, nancy-boy, poof, poofter, queen, queer.

pant *v* ache, blow, breathe, covet, crave, desire, gasp, hanker, heave, huff, hunger, long, palpitate, pine, puff, sigh, thirst, throb, want, wheeze, yearn, yen.

pants *n* briefs, drawers, knickers, panties, shorts, slacks, trunks, underpants, Y-fronts.

paper *n* analysis, archive, article, assignment, authorisation, certificate, composition, credential, critique, daily, diary, dissertation, document, dossier, essay, examination, file, gazette, instrument, journal, letter, monograph, news, newspaper, notepaper, organ, rag, record, report, script, stationery, study, thesis, treatise.

par *n* average, balance, equal footing, equality, equilibrium, equivalence, level, mean, median, norm, parity, similarity, standard, usual.

parade *n* array, cavalcade, ceremony, column, display, exhibition, flaunting, march, motorcade, ostentation, pageant, procession, promenade, review, show, spectacle, train, vaunting.

v air, brandish, defile, display, exhibit, flaunt, make a show of, march, peacock, process, show, show off, strut, swagger, vaunt.

paradise *n* bliss, City of God, delight, Eden, Elysian fields, Elysium, felicity, Garden of Eden, heaven, heavenly kingdom, Olympus, Promised Land, seventh heaven, utopia, Valhalla, Zion. *antonyms* Hades, hell.

paradox *n* absurdity, ambiguity, anomaly, contradiction, enigma, equivocation, incongruity, inconsistency, mystery, oddity, puzzle, riddle.

paradoxical *adj* absurd, ambiguous, baffling, conflicting, confounding, contradictory, enigmatic, equivocal, illogical, impossible, improbable, incongruous, inconsistent, puzzling, self-contradictory.

paragon *n* apotheosis, archetype, crème de la crème, criterion, epitome, exemplar, ideal, jewel, masterpiece, model, non(e)such, paradigm, pattern, prototype, quintessence, standard, the bee's knees.

parallel *adj* akin, aligned, alongside, analogous, co-extensive, collateral, correspondent, corresponding, equidistant, homologous, like, matching, resembling, similar, uniform. *antonyms* divergent, separate.

n analogue, analogy, comparison, corollary, correlation, correspondence, counterpart, duplicate, equal, equivalent, homologue, likeness, match, parallelism, resemblance, similarity, twin.

v agree, compare, conform, correlate, correspond, duplicate, emulate, equal, match. *antonyms* diverge, separate.

paralyse *v* anaesthetise, arrest, benumb, clamp down on, cripple, debilitate, disable, freeze, halt, immobilise, incapacitate, lame, numb, petrify, stun, stupefy, transfix.

paralysis *n* arrest, break-down, halt, immobility, palsy, shut-down, stagnation, standstill, stoppage, torpor.

paralytic[1] *adj* crippled, disabled, immobile, immobilised, incapacitated, lame, numb, palsied, paralysed.

paralytic[2] *adj* canned, drunk, inebriated, intoxicated, legless, pie-eyed, pissed, plastered, sloshed, smashed, stewed, stoned, stotious, three sheets in the wind. *antonym* (stone-cold) sober.

parameter *n* boundary, constant, criterion, framework, guideline, indication, limit, limitation, restriction, specification, variable.

paramount *adj* capital, cardinal, chief, dominant, eminent, first, foremost, highest, main, outstanding, predominant, pre-eminent, premier, primary, prime, principal, superior, supreme, topmost, top-rank. *antonyms* inferior, last, lowest.

paraphernalia *n* accessories, accoutrements, apparatus, appurtenances, baggage, belongings, bits and pieces, clobber, clutter, effects, equipment, gear, material, odds and ends, stuff, tackle, things, trappings.

paraphrase *n* gloss, interpretation, recapitulation, rehash, rendering, rendition, rephrasing, restatement, rewording, translation, version.

v gloss, interpret, recapitulate, rehash,

render, rephrase, restate, reword, translate.

parasite *n* bloodsucker, cadger, freeloader, hanger-on, leech, scrounger, sponge, sponger.

parcel *n* band, batch, bunch, bundle, carton, collection, company, crew, crowd, gang, group, lot, pack, package, packet, plot, portion, property, quantity, set, tract.

v bundle, collect, pack, package, tie up, wrap.

parched *adj* arid, dehydrated, dried up, drouthy, dry, scorched, shrivelled, thirsty, waterless, withered.

pardon *v* absolve, acquit, amnesty, condone, emancipate, exculpate, excuse, exonerate, forgive, free, let off, liberate, overlook, release, remit, reprieve, respite, vindicate.

n absolution, acquittal, allowance, amnesty, compassion, condonation, discharge, excuse, exoneration, forgiveness, grace, humanity, indulgence, mercy, release, remission, reprieval, reprieve.

pardonable *adj* allowable, condonable, dispensable, excusable, forgivable, justifiable, minor, permissible, remissible, understandable, venial, warrantable. *antonym* inexcusable.

pare *v* clip, crop, cut, cut back, decrease, diminish, dock, lop, peel, prune, reduce, shave, shear, skin, trim.

parent *n* architect, author, begetter, cause, creator, father, forerunner, guardian, mother, origin, originator, procreator, prototype, root, sire, source.

parentage *n* affiliation, ancestry, birth, derivation, descent, extraction, family, line, lineage, origin, paternity, pedigree, race, source, stock.

parenthetic *adj* bracketed, extraneous, extrinsic, in parenthesis, incidental, inserted, interposed, intervening, parenthetical, qualifying. *antonyms* basic, original.

pariah *n* black sheep, castaway, exile, leper, outcast, outlaw, undesirable, untouchable.

parish *n* brethren, church, churchgoers, community, congregation, district, flock, fold, parishioners.

parity *n* affinity, agreement, analogy, conformity, congruence, congruity, consistency, consonance, correspondence, equality, equivalence, likeness, par, parallelism, resemblance, sameness, semblance, similarity, similitude, uniformity, unity.

parlance n argot, cant, diction, idiom, jargon, language, lingo, phraseology, speech, talk, tongue.

parley n confab, conference, council, deliberation, dialogue, discussion, get-together, meeting, negotiation, powwow, talk(s), tête-à-tête.

v confabulate, confer, consult, deliberate, discuss, get together, negotiate, powwow, speak, talk.

parochial adj blinkered, confined, incestuous, insular, inward-looking, limited, narrow, narrow-minded, parish-pump, petty, provincial, restricted, small-minded.

parody n burlesque, caricature, imitation, lampoon, mimicry, satire, send-up, skit, spoof, take-off.

v burlesque, caricature, lampoon, mimic, satirise, send up, spoof, take off, travesty.

parrot v ape, copy, echo, imitate, mimic, rehearse, reiterate, repeat.

parrot-fashion adv automatically, by rote, mechanically, mindlessly, unthinkingly.

parry v avert, avoid, block, circumvent, deflect, divert, dodge, duck, evade, fence, fend off, field, forestall, obviate, rebuff, repel, repulse, shun, sidestep, stave off, ward off.

parsimonious adj cheese-paring, close, close-fisted, close-handed, frugal, grasping, mean, mingy, miserable, miserly, money-grubbing, niggardly, penny-pinching, penny-wise, penurious, saving, scrimpy, sparing, stingy, stinting, tight-fisted. **antonyms** generous, liberal, open-handed.

parsimony n frugality, meanness, minginess, niggardliness, penny-pinching, stinginess, tight-fistedness. **antonyms** generosity, liberality.

parson n churchman, clergyman, cleric, divine, ecclesiastic, incumbent, man of God, minister, padre, pastor, preacher, priest, rector, reverend, vicar.

part n area, behalf, bit, branch, business, capacity, cause, character, charge, clause, complement, component, concern, constituent, department, district, division, duty, element, faction, factor, fraction, fragment, function, heft, ingredient, interest, involvement, limb, lines, lot, member, module, neck of the woods, neighbourhood, office, organ, particle, partwork, party, piece, place, portion, quarter, region, responsibility, role, scrap, section, sector, segment, share, side, slice, task, territory, tip of the iceberg, unit, vicinity, work.

v break, break up, cleave, come apart, depart, detach, disband, disconnect, disjoin, dismantle, disperse, disunite, divide, go, go away, leave, part company, quit, rend, scatter, separate, sever, split, split up, take leave, tear, withdraw.

part with abandon, cede, discard, forgo, give up, jettison, let go of, relinquish, renounce, sacrifice, surrender, yield.

partake v be involved, engage, enter, participate, share, take part.

partake of consume, drink, eat, evince, evoke, have, manifest, receive, share, show, suggest, take.

partial[1] adj fragmentary, imperfect, incomplete, inexhaustive, limited, part, uncompleted, unfinished. **antonyms** complete, exhaustive, total.

partial[2] adj affected, biased, coloured, discriminatory, ex parte, influenced, interested, one-sided, partisan, predisposed, prejudiced, tendentious, unfair, unjust. **antonyms** disinterested, fair, unbiased.

partial to crazy about, daft about, fond of, keen on, mad about, taken with.

partiality n affinity, bias, discrimination, favouritism, fondness, inclination, liking, love, partisanship, penchant, predilection, predisposition, preference, prejudice, proclivity, propensity, soft spot, taste, weakness. **antonyms** dislike, justice.

partially adv fractionally, in part, incompletely, partly, somewhat.

participate v be involved, co-operate, engage, enter, join, muck in, partake, perform, share, take part.

participation n a piece of the action, assistance, contribution, co-operation, involvement, mucking in, partaking, partnership, sharing.

particle n atom, bit, corn, crumb, drop, electron, grain, iota, jot, mite, molecule, morsel, mote, neutron, piece, proton, scrap, shred, sliver, smidgen, speck, tittle, whit.

particular[1] adj blow-by-blow, circumstantial, detailed, distinct, especial, exact, exceptional, express, itemised, marked, minute, notable, noteworthy, painstaking, peculiar, precise, remarkable, selective, several, singular, special, specific, thorough, uncommon, unique, unusual, very. **antonym** general.

n circumstance, detail, fact, feature,

item, point, specific, specification.

particular² *adj* choosy, critical, dainty, demanding, discriminating, exacting, fastidious, finicky, fussy, meticulous, nice, overnice, pernickety, picky. *antonym* casual.

particularity *n* accuracy, carefulness, characteristic, choosiness, circumstance, detail, distinctiveness, fact, fastidiousness, feature, fussiness, idiosyncrasy, individuality, instance, item, mannerism, meticulousness, peculiarity, point, precision, property, quirk, singularity, thoroughness, trait, uniqueness.

particularly *adv* decidedly, distinctly, especially, exceptionally, explicitly, expressly, extraordinarily, in particular, markedly, notably, noticeably, outstandingly, peculiarly, remarkably, singularly, specifically, surprisingly, uncommonly, unusually.

parting *n* adieu, breaking, departure, detachment, disjunction, disunion, divergence, division, farewell, going, goodbye, leave-taking, partition, rift, rupture, separation, severance, split, valediction. *antonyms* convergence, meeting.
adj closing, concluding, deathbed, departing, dying, farewell, final, last, valedictory. *antonyms* arriving, first.

partisan *n* adherent, champion, devotee, disciple, follower, guerrilla, stalwart, supporter, upholder.
adj biased, discriminatory, factional, guerrilla, interested, one-sided, partial, predisposed, prejudiced, resistance, sectarian, tendentious, underground.

partition¹ *n* allocation, allotment, apportionment, distribution, dividing, division, part, portion, rationing out, section, segregation, separation, severance, share, splitting.
v allocate, allot, apportion, assign, divide, parcel out, portion, section, segment, separate, share, split up, subdivide.

partition² *n* barrier, diaphragm, membrane, screen, traverse, wall.
v bar, divide, fence off, screen, separate, wall off.

partly *adv* halfway, in part, incompletely, moderately, partially, relatively, slightly, somewhat, to a certain degree, to a certain extent, up to a point. *antonyms* completely, in toto, totally.

partner *n* accomplice, ally, associate, bedfellow, collaborator, colleague, companion, comrade, confederate, consort, co-partner, helper, helpmate, husband, mate, participant, side-kick, spouse, team-mate, wife.

partnership *n* affiliation, alliance, association, brotherhood, combination, combine, companionship, company, conglomerate, connection, co-operation, co-operative, co-partnership, corporation, fellowship, firm, fraternity, interest, participation, sharing, society, syndicate, union.

party¹ *n* assembly, bash, beanfeast, beano, ceilidh, celebration, do, entertainment, -fest, festivity, function, gathering, get-together, housewarming, hurricane, jollification, knees-up, rave-up, reception, shindig, social, soirée, thrash.

party² *n* alliance, association, band, body, bunch, cabal, caucus, clique, coalition, combination, company, confederacy, contingent, contractor, coterie, crew, defendant, detachment, faction, gang, gathering, group, grouping, individual, junto, league, litigant, participant, person, plaintiff, set, side, squad, team, unit.

pass¹ *v* accept, adopt, answer, approve, authorise, beat, befall, beguile, blow over, cease, come up, come up to scratch, convey, declare, decree, defecate, deliver, depart, develop, devote, die, die away, disappear, discharge, disregard, dissolve, do, dwindle, ebb, elapse, eliminate, employ, empty, enact, end, establish, evacuate, evaporate, exceed, excel, exchange, excrete, expel, experience, expire, express, fade, fall out, fill, flow, get through, give, go, go beyond, go by, go past, graduate, hand, happen, ignore, impersonate, lapse, leave, legislate, melt away, miss, move, neglect, occupy, occur, omit, ordain, outdistance, outdo, outstrip, overlook, overtake, pass muster, proceed, pronounce, qualify, ratify, roll, run, sanction, send, serve as, skip, spend, succeed, suffer, suffice, suit, surmount, surpass, take place, terminate, throw, transcend, transfer, transmit, undergo, utter, validate, vanish, void, waft, wane, while away.

pass away croak, decease, die, expire, give up the ghost, kick the bucket, pass on, pass over, peg out, snuff it.

pass by disregard, forget, ignore, leave, miss, neglect, omit, overlook, pass over.

pass muster be adequate, be up to

scratch, fill/fit the bill, make the grade, measure up, qualify.

pass off come to an end, counterfeit, die away, disappear, dismiss, disregard, emit, evaporate, fade out, fake, feign, give off, go off, happen, ignore, occur, palm off, pass by, send forth, take place, turn out, utter, vanish, vaporise, wink at.

pass out[1] black out, die, drop, faint, flake out, keel over, lose consciousness, swoon.

pass out[2] deal out, dispense, distribute, dole out, give out, hand out, share out.

pass over ignore, neglect, omit, overlook.

pass[2] *n* advances, approach, authorisation, chit, condition, feint, identification, jab, juncture, laissez-passer, licence, lunge, overture, passport, permission, permit, play, plight, predicament, proposition, safe-conduct, situation, stage, state, state of affairs, straits, swing, thrust, ticket, warrant.

passable *adj* acceptable, adequate, admissible, all right, allowable, average, clear, fair, mediocre, middling, moderate, navigable, OK, open, ordinary, presentable, so-so, tolerable, traversable, unblocked, unexceptional, unobstructed.

passably *adv* after a fashion, fairly, moderately, rather, reasonably, relatively, somewhat, tolerably.

passage *n* acceptance, access, advance, allowance, authorisation, avenue, change, channel, citation, clause, close, communication, conduit, conversion, corridor, course, crossing, doorway, drift, duct, enactment, entrance, entrance hall, establishment, excerpt, exit, extract, flow, freedom, gallery, hall, hallway, journey, lane, legalisation, legislation, lobby, motion, movement, opening, orifice, paragraph, part, passageway, passing, path, permission, piece, portion, progress, progression, quotation, ratification, reading, right, road, route, safe-conduct, section, sentence, text, thorough, thoroughfare, tour, transit, transition, trek, trip, vent, verse, vestibule, visa, vista, voyage, warrant, way.

passé *adj* antiquated, dated, obsolete, old hat, old-fashioned, out, outdated, outmoded, out-of-date, outworn, past one's best, unfashionable. **antonyms** fashionable, in.

passing *adj* brief, casual, cursory, ephemeral, evanescent, fleeting, fly-by-night, glancing, hasty, impermanent, momentary, quick, shallow, shirt, short, short-lived, slight, superficial, temporary, transient, transitory. **antonyms** long-lasting, permanent.

n death, decease, demise, end, expiration, finish, loss, quietus, termination.

passion *n* adoration, affection, anger, animation, ardour, attachment, avidity, bug, chafe, craving, craze, dander, desire, eagerness, emotion, enthusiasm, excitement, fancy, fascination, feeling, fervour, fire, fit, flare-up, fondness, frenzy, fury, heat, idol, indignation, infatuation, intensity, ire, itch, joy, keenness, love, lust, mania, monomania, obsession, outburst, rage, rapture, resentment, spirit, storm, transport, vehemence, verve, vivacity, warmth, wrath, zeal, zest. **antonyms** calm, coolness, self-possession.

passionate *adj* amorous, animated, ardent, aroused, desirous, eager, emotional, enthusiastic, erotic, excitable, excited, fervent, fervid, fierce, fiery, frenzied, heartfelt, heated, hot, hot-headed, hot-tempered, impassioned, impetuous, impulsive, incensed, inflamed, inspirited, intense, irascible, irate, irritable, loving, lustful, peppery, quick-tempered, sensual, sexy, stormy, strong, sultry, tempestuous, torrid, vehement, violent, wanton, warm, wild, zealous. **antonyms** frigid, laid-back, phlegmatic.

passionless *adj* apathetic, callous, calm, cold, cold-blooded, cold-hearted, detached, dispassionate, emotionless, frigid, frosty, icy, impartial, impassive, indifferent, insensible, neutral, restrained, uncaring, unemotional, unfeeling, uninvolved, unloving, unresponsive, withdrawn. **antonyms** caring, sensitive, sympathetic.

passive *adj* acquiescent, compliant, docile, enduring, impassive, inactive, indifferent, indolent, inert, lifeless, long suffering, non-participating, non-violent, patient, quiescent, receptive, resigned, submissive, unaffected, unassertive, uninvolved, unresisting. **antonyms** active, involved, lively.

past *adj* accomplished, ancient, bygone, completed, defunct, done, early, elapsed, ended, erstwhile, extinct, finished, foregone, forgotten, former, gone, gone by, late, long-ago, no more, olden, over, over and done with, preceding, previous, prior, recent, spent, vanished.

n antiquity, auld lang syne, background, days of yore, experience, former times, good old days, history, life, old times, olden days, track record, yesteryear.

past one's best not what one was, over the hill.

paste *n* adhesive, cement, dough, glue, gum, mastic, mucilage, putty.

v beat, cement, fasten, fix, glue, gum, hammer, stick, thrash, thump, whitewash.

pastel *adj* delicate, faint, gentle, light, muted, pale, soft, soft-hued, subdued.

pastime *n* activity, amusement, avocation, distraction, diversion, entertainment, game, hobby, play, recreation, relaxation, sport. *antonyms* business, employment, occupation, vocation, work.

pastmaster *n* ace, adept, artist, dab hand, expert, old hand, virtuoso, wizard. *antonym* incompetent.

pastor *n* canon, churchman, clergyman, cleric, ecclesiastic, minister, parson, priest, rector, vicar.

pastoral *adj* agrarian, Arcadian, bucolic, clerical, countrified, country, ecclesiastical, idyllic, ministerial, priestly, rural, rustic, simple. *antonym* urban.

pasty *adj* anaemic, doughy, gluey, glutinous, mucilaginous, pale, pallid, pasty-faced, peelie-wally, sallow, sickly, starchy, sticky, unhealthy, viscous, wan, waxy, whey-faced. *antonyms* healthy, rubicund.

pat *v* caress, clap, dab, fondle, pet, rub, slap, stroke, tap, touch.

n cake, caress, clap, dab, lump, piece, portion, slap, stroke, tap, touch.

adv exactly, faultlessly, flawlessly, fluently, glibly, just right, off pat, opportunely, perfectly, plumb, precisely, relevantly, seasonably. *antonyms* imprecisely, wrongly.

adj apposite, appropriate, apt, automatic, easy, facile, felicitous, fitting, glib, happy, neat, pertinent, ready, relevant, right, simplistic, slick, smooth, spot-on, suitable, to the point, well-chosen. *antonyms* irrelevant, unsuitable.

patch *n* area, bit, ground, land, lot, parcel, piece, plot, scrap, shred, spot, stretch, tract.

v botch, cover, fix, mend, reinforce, repair, sew up, stitch, vamp.

patchy *adj* bitty, erratic, fitful, in-congruous, inconsistent, inharmonious, irregular, random, sketchy, spotty, uneven, variable, varying. *antonyms* consistent, even, regular, uniform.

patent *adj* apparent, blatant, clear, clear-cut, conspicuous, downright, evident, explicit, flagrant, glaring, indisputable, manifest, obvious, open, ostensible, overt, palpable, transparent, uncon-cealed, unequivocal, unmistakable. *antonyms* hidden, opaque.

n certificate, copyright, invention, licence, privilege, registered trademark.

path *n* avenue, course, direction, footpath, footway, gate, passage, pathway, procedure, ridgeway, road, route, towpath, track, trail, walk, walkway, way.

pathetic *adj* affecting, contemptible, crummy, deplorable, dismal-looking, distressing, feeble, heartbreaking, heart-rending, inadequate, lamentable, meagre, melting, miserable, moving, paltry, petty, piteous, pitiable, pitiful, plaintive, poign-ant, poor, puny, rubbishy, sad, sorry, tender, touching, trashy, uninteresting, useless, woebegone, woeful, worthless. *antonyms* admirable, cheerful.

patience *n* calmness, composure, constancy, cool, diligence, endurance, equanimity, forbearance, fortitude, long-suffering, perseverance, persistence, resignation, restraint, self-control, serenity, stoicism, submission, suffer-ance, tolerable, toleration. *antonyms* impatience, intolerance.

patient *adj* accommodating, calm, composed, enduring, even-tempered, forbearing, forgiving, indulgent, lenient, long-suffering, mild, persevering, persistent, philosophical, quiet, resigned, restrained, self-controlled, self-possessed, serene, stoical, submissive, tolerant, uncomplaining, understanding, untiring. *antonyms* impatient, intolerant.

patois *n* argot, cant, dialect, jargon, lingo, lingua franca, patter, slang, vernacular.

patrician *adj* aristocratic, blue-blooded, gentle, high-born, high-class, lordly, noble, thoroughbred, well-born. *antonyms* common, humble.

patriotic *adj* chauvinistic, flag-waving, jingoistic, loyal, nationalistic.

patron *n* advocate, backer, benefactor, buyer, champion, client, customer, defender, frequenter, friend, guardian, habitué, helper, partisan, philanthropist, protector, regular, shopper, sponsor, subscriber, supporter, sympathiser.

patronage *n* aegis, aid, assistance, backing, benefaction, business, championship, clientèle, commerce, custom, encouragement, help, participation, promotion, sponsorship, subscription, support, sustenance, trade, trading, traffic.

patronise *v* assist, back, befriend, encourage, foster, frequent, fund, habituate, help, humour, maintain, promote, shop at, sponsor, support, talk down to.

patronising *adj* condescending, contemptuous, disdaining, gracious, haughty, high-handed, imperious, lofty, overbearing, snobbish, stooping, supercilious, superior, toffee-nosed. **antonym** humble.

patter[1] *v* beat, pat, pelt, pitapat, pitter-patter, rat-a-rat, scurry, scuttle, skip, spatter, tap, tiptoe, trip.

patter[2] *n* argot, cant, chatter, gabble, glib talk, jabber, jargon, line, lingo, monologue, patois, pitch, prattle, slang, spiel, vernacular, yak.

pattern *n* archetype, arrangement, criterion, decoration, design, device, diagram, examplar, example, figuration, figure, guide, instructions, kind, method, model, motif, norm, order, orderliness, original, ornament, ornamentation, paradigm, plan, prototype, sample, sequence, shape, sort, specimen, standard, stencil, style, system, template, type, variety.

v copy, decorate, design, emulate, follow, form, imitate, match, model, mould, order, shape, stencil, style, trim.

paucity *n* dearth, deficiency, exiguousness, fewness, insufficiency, lack, meagreness, paltriness, poverty, rarity, scantiness, scarcity, shortage, slenderness, slightness, smallness, sparseness, sparsity, want. **antonym** abundance.

pause *v* break, cease, cut, delay, desist, discontinue, halt, hesitate, interrupt, rest, take a break, take a breather, take five, wait, waver.

n abatement, break, breather, caesura, cessation, delay, discontinuance, dwell, gap, halt, hesitation, interlude, intermission, interruption, interval, let-up, lull, respite, rest, slackening, stay, stoppage, suspension, wait.

pay *v* ante, benefit, bestow, bring in, clear, compensate, cough up, disburse, discharge, extend, foot, get eve with, give, grant, honour, indemnify liquidate, meet, offer, proffer, profit, punish present, produce, proffer, profit, punish reciprocate, recompense, reimburse remit, remunerate, render, repay, requit return, reward, serve, settle, square square up, yield.

n allowance, compensation consideration, earnings, emolument fee, hire, honorarium, income payment, recompense, reimbursemen remuneration, reward, salary, stipen takings, wages.

pay back avenge, chasten, g even with, get one's own back punish, reciprocate, recompense, refun reimburse, repay, retaliate, return, settl up, settle with, square.

pay for answer for, atone, compensat face the music, get one's deserts, mak amends, suffer.

pay off clear, discharge, dismiss, fir lay off, liquidate, sack, satisfy, settl square, succeed, work.

pay out cough up, disburse, dish ou expend, fork out, hand over, lay ou render, shell out, spend.

payable *adj* due, in arrears, matur obligatory, outstanding, owed, owin receivable, unpaid.

payment *n* advance, ante, consideratio defrayal, deposit, discharge, fee, hir instalment, outlay, paying, portio premium, remittance, remuneratio reward, settlement, sub, wage.

pay-off *n* climax, conclusio consequence, crunch, culmination, da of reckoning, dénouement, judgemen moment of truth, outcome, punch line, reimbursement, result, retributio reward, settlement, upshot.

peace *n* accord, agreement, amity armistice, calm, calmness, cease fire, composure, conciliation, concor contentment, harmony, hush, pacifi cation, pax, peacefulness, placidit quiet, quietude, relaxation, repose, res serenity, silence, stillness, tranquillit treaty, truce. **antonyms** disagreemen disturbance, war.

peaceable *adj* amiable, amicabl compatible, conciliatory, dovish, eas going, friendly, gentle, inoffensive, mil non-belligerent, pacific, peaceful, peace loving, placid, unwarlike. **antonym** belligerent, offensive.

peaceful *adj* amicable, at peac becalmed, calm, conciliatory, friendl gentle, halcyon, harmonious, non-violent, pacific, peaceable, peace-loving, placatory, placid, quiet, restful, serene, still, tranquil, unagitated, undisturbed, unruffled, untroubled, unwarlike. *antonyms* disturbed, noisy, troubled.

peak *n* acme, apex, apogee, brow, climax, crest, crown, culmination, high point, maximum, pinnacle, point, summit, tip, top, zenith. *antonyms* nadir, trough.
v climax, come to a head, culminate, spire, tower.

peaky *adj* drooping, emaciated, ill, off-colour, pale, peelie-wally, pinched, poorly, sick, sickly, under the weather, unwell, wan, washed-out, wilting. *antonyms* healthy, in the pink.

peal *n* blast, carillon, chime, clamour, clang, clangour, clap, clash, crash, resounding, reverberation, ring, ringing, roar, rumble, sound, tintinnabulation.
v chime, clash, crack, crash, resonate, resound, reverberate, ring, roar, roll, rumble, sound, tintinnabulate, toll, vibrate.

peasant *n* bumpkin, countryman, provincial, rustic, yokel. *antonym* sophisticate.

peccadillo *n* boob, error, fault, indiscretion, infraction, lapse, misdeed, misdemeanour, slip, slip-up.

peculiar¹ *adj* abnormal, bizarre, curious, eccentric, exceptional, extraordinary, far-out, freakish, funky, funny, odd, offbeat, out-of-the-way, quaint, queer, singular, strange, uncommon, unconventional, unusual, way-out, weird. *antonyms* normal, ordinary.

peculiar² *adj* appropriate, characteristic, discriminative, distinct, distinctive, distinguishing, endemic, idiosyncratic, individual, local, particular, personal, private, quintessential, restricted, special, specific, unique. *antonyms* general, uncharacteristic.

peculiarity *n* abnormality, attribute, bizarreness, characteristic, distinctiveness, eccentricity, exception, feature, foible, freakishness, idiosyncrasy, mannerism, mark, oddity, particularity, property, quality, queerness, quirk, singularity, speciality, trait, whimsicality.

pedagogy *n* instruction, teaching, training, tuition, tutelage.

pedantic *adj* abstruse, didactic, formal, fussy, hair-splitting, nit-picking, particular, perfectionist, pompous, precise, punctilious, sententious.

antonyms casual, imprecise, informal.

peddle *v* flog, hawk, huckster, market, push, retail, sell, tout, trade, trifle, vend.

pedestrian *adj* banal, boring, commonplace, dull, flat, humdrum, indifferent, mediocre, mundane, ordinary, plodding, prosaic, run-of-the-mill, stodgy, tolerable, unimaginative, uninspired, uninteresting. *antonyms* bright, brilliant, exciting, imaginative.

pedigree *n* ancestry, blood, breed, derivation, descent, dynasty, extraction, family, family tree, genealogy, heritage, line, lineage, parentage, race, stock, succession.

pedlar *n* boxwallah, chapman, cheap-jack, colporteur, hawker, huckster, seller, street-trader, vendor.

peek *v* glance, keek, look, peep, peer, spy.
n blink, dekko, gander, glance, glimpse, keek, look, look-see, peep, shufti.

peel *v* decorticate, denude, flake (off), pare, scale, skin, strip (off), undress.
n epicarp, exocarp, integument, peeling, rind, skin, zest.

peep *v* blink, emerge, glimpse, issue, keek, peek, peer.
n blink, dekko, gander, glim, glimpse, keek, look, look-see, peek, shufti.

peer¹ *v* appear, blink, emerge, examine, gaze, inspect, peep, scan, scrutinise, snoop, spy, squint.

peer² *n* counterpart, equal, equivalent, fellow, like, match.

peerless *adj* beyond compare, excellent, incomparable, matchless, outstanding, paramount, second to none, superlative, supreme, unbeatable, unequalled, unexcelled, unique, unmatched, unparalleled, unrivalled, unsurpassed.

peeved *adj* annoyed, exasperated, galled, irked, irritated, miffed, narked, nettled, pipped, piqued, put out, riled, sore, upset, vexed.

peevish *adj* acrimonious, cantankerous, captious, childish, churlish, crabbed, cross, crotchety, crusty, fractious, fretful, grumpy, ill-natured, ill-tempered, irritable, miffy, perverse, petulant, querulous, ratty, short-tempered, snappy, splenetic, sulky, sullen, surly, testy, touchy, waspish. *antonym* good-tempered.

peg *v* attach, control, fasten, fix, freeze, insert, join, limit, mark, pierce, score, secure, set, stabilise.

pejorative *adj* bad, belittling, condemnatory, damning, debasing, deprecatory, depreciatory, derogatory, detractive, detractory, disparaging, negative, slighting, uncomplimentary, unflattering, unpleasant. *antonyms* complimentary, laudatory.

pell-mell *adv* feverishly, full tilt, hastily, heedlessly, helter-skelter, hurriedly, hurry-scurry, impetuously, posthaste, precipitously, rashly, recklessly.
adj chaotic, confused, disordered, disorganised, haphazard, indiscriminate, scrambled, tumultuous.

pelt *v* assail, batter, beat, belabour, belt, bombard, bucket, career, cast, charge, dash, hit, hurl, hurry, pepper, pour, pummel, rain cats and dogs, rush, shoot, shower, sling, speed, strafe, strike, tear, teem, thrash, throw, wallop, whiz.

pen[1] *v* author, compose, draft, jot down, scribble, write.

pen name alias, nom de plume, pseudonym.

pen[2] *n* cage, coop, crib, enclosure, fold, hutch, stall, sty.
v cage, confine, coop, corral, enclose, fence, hedge, hem in, hurdle, shut up.

penalise *v* correct, disadvantage, discipline, handicap, mulct, punish. *antonym* reward.

penalty *n* disadvantage, fine, forfeit, forfeiture, handicap, mulct, price, punishment, retribution. *antonym* reward.

penance *n* atonement, mortification, penalty, placation, propitiation, punishment, reparation, sackcloth and ashes.

penchant *n* affinity, bent, bias, disposition, fondness, inclination, leaning, liking, partiality, predilection, predisposition, preference, proclivity, proneness, propensity, soft spot, taste, tendency, turn. *antonym* dislike.

pending *adj* awaiting, forthcoming, hanging, imminent, impending, in the balance, in the offing, on the back burner, undecided, undetermined, unfinished, unsettled. *antonyms* finished, settled.

pendulous *adj* dangling, drooping, droopy, hanging, pendent, sagging, suspended, swaying, swinging.

penetrable *adj* accessible, clear, comprehensible, explicable, fathomable, intelligible, open, passable, permeable, pervious, porous, understandable. *antonym* impenetrable.

penetrate *v* affect, bore, come across, come home, comprehend, decipher, diffuse, discern, enter, fathom, get through to, get to the bottom of, grasp,

impress, infiltrate, perforate, permeate, pervade, pierce, prick, probe, seep, sink, stab, strike, suffuse, touch, understand, unravel.

penetrating *adj* acute, astute, biting, carrying, critical, discerning, discriminating, harsh, incisive, intelligent, intrusive, keen, observant, penetrative, perceptive, percipient, perspicacious, pervasive, piercing, profound, pungent, quick, sagacious, searching, sharp, sharp-witted, shrewd, shrill, stinging, strong. *antonyms* gentle, obtuse, soft.

penetration *n* acumen, acuteness, astuteness, discernment, entrance, entry, incision, inroad, insight, interpenetration, invasion, keenness, perception, perforation, perspicacity, piercing, puncturing, sharpness, shrewdness, wit.

penis *n* cock, dick, John Thomas, knob, pecker, phallus, prick, rod, shaft, tool, winkle.

penitence *n* compunction, contrition, regret, regretfulness, remorse, repentance, rue, self-reproach, shame, sorrow.

penitent *adj* abject, apologetic, atoning, conscience-stricken, contrite, humble, in sackcloth and ashes, regretful, remorseful, repentant, rueful, sorrowful, sorry. *antonym* unrepentant.

penniless *adj* bankrupt, broke, cleaned out, destitute, flat broke, impecunious, impoverished, indigent, moneyless, necessitous, needy, on one's uppers, on the rocks, penurious, poor, poverty-stricken, ruined, skint, stoney-broke, strapped. *antonyms* rich, wealthy.

penny-pinching *adj* cheeseparing, close, frugal, mean, mingy, miserly, near, niggardly, parsimonious, scrimping, stingy, tight-fisted, ungenerous. *antonyms* generous, open-handed.

pensive *adj* absent-minded, absorbed, cogitative, contemplative, dreamy, grave, meditative, melancholy, musing, preoccupied, reflective, ruminative, serious, sober, solemn, thoughtful, wistful.

pent-up *adj* bottled-up, bridled, checked, constrained, curbed, inhibited, repressed, restrained, smothered, stifled, suppressed.

penurious *adj* beggarly, cheeseparing, close, close-fisted, deficient, destitute, flat broke, frugal, grudging, impecunious, impoverished, inadequate, indigent, meagre, mean, miserable, miserly, near, needy, niggardly, paltry, parsimonious, penniless, poor, poverty-stricken, scanty, skimping, stingy, tight-fisted, ungenerous. **antonyms** generous, wealthy.

penury n beggary, dearth, deficiency, destitution, indigence, lack, mendicancy, mendicity, need, paucity, pauperism, poverty, privation, scantiness, scarcity, shortage, sparseness, straitened circumstances, straits, want. **antonym** prosperity.

people n citizens, clan, commonalty, community, crowd, family, folk, general public, grass roots, hoi polloi, human beings, humanity, humans, inhabitants, mankind, masses, mob, mortals, multitude, nation, persons, plebs, populace, population, public, punters, rabble, race, rank and file, the herd, tribe. v colonise, inhabit, occupy, populate, settle.

pep n animation, energy, exuberance, get-up-and-go, gusto, high spirits, life, liveliness, pizzazz, spirit, verve, vigour, vim, vitality, vivacity, zip.

pep up animate, energise, enliven, excite, exhilarate, inspire, invigorate, jazz up, quicken, stimulate, vitalise, vivify.

peppery adj astringent, biting, caustic, choleric, fiery, grumpy, hot, hot-tempered, incisive, irascible, irritable, nippy, piquant, pungent, quick-tempered, sarcastic, sharp, snappish, spicy, stinging, testy, touchy, trenchant, waspish.

perceive v appreciate, apprehend, be aware of, behold, catch, comprehend, conclude, deduce, descry, discern, discover, distinguish, espy, feel, gather, get, grasp, intuit, know, learn, make out, note, observe, realise, recognise, remark, see, sense, spot, understand.

perceptible adj apparent, appreciable, clear, conspicuous, detectable, discernible, distinct, distinguishable, evident, noticeable, observable, obvious, palpable, perceivable, recognisable, salient, tangible, visible. **antonym** imperceptible.

perception n apprehension, awareness, conception, consciousness, discernment, feeling, grasp, idea, impression, insight, intellection, notion, observation, recognition, sensation, sense, taste, understanding, uptake.

perceptive adj able to see through a millstone, acute, alert, astute, aware, discerning, insightful, observant, penetrating, percipient, perspicacious, quick, responsive, sagacious, sapient, sensitive, sharp. **antonym** unobservant.

perch v alight, balance, drop, land, light, rest, roost, settle, sit on.

percipience n acuity, acuteness, alertness, astuteness, awareness, discernment, insight, intuition, judgement, penetration, perception, perspicacity, sagacity, sensitivity, understanding.

percipient adj alert, alive, astute, aware, discerning, discriminating, intelligent, judicious, knowing, penetrating, perceptive, perspicacious, quick-witted, sharp, wide-awake. **antonyms** obtuse, unaware.

percolate v drain, drip, exude, filter, filtrate, leach, leak, ooze, penetrate, permeate, pervade, seep, strain, transfuse.

perdition n condemnation, damnation, destruction, doom, downfall, hell, hellfire, ruin, ruination.

peremptory adj abrupt, absolute, arbitrary, assertive, authoritative, autocratic, binding, bossy, categorical, commanding, compelling, curt, decisive, dictatorial, dogmatic, domineering, final, high-handed, imperative, imperious, incontrovertible, intolerant, irrefutable, obligatory, overbearing, summary, undeniable.

perennial adj abiding, ceaseless, chronic, constant, continual, continuing, deathless, enduring, eternal, evergreen, everlasting, immortal, imperishable, incessant, inveterate, lasting, lifelong, never-ending, never-failing, permanent, perpetual, persistent, recurrent, unceasing, unchanging, undying, unfailing, uninterrupted.

perfect adj absolute, accomplished, accurate, adept, blameless, close, complete, completed, consummate, copybook, correct, entire, exact, excellent, experienced, expert, faithful, faultless, finished, flawless, full, ideal, immaculate, impeccable, irreproachable, masterly, model, polished, practised, precise, pure, right, sheer, skilful, skilled, splendid, spotless, spot-on, strict, sublime, superb, superlative, supreme, true, unadulterated, unalloyed, unblemished, unerring, unimpeachable, unmarred, unmitigated, untarnished, utter, whole. **antonyms** flawed, imperfect.

v accomplish, achieve, carry out, complete, consummate, effect, elaborate, finish, fulfil, perfectionate, perform, realise, refine.

perfection *n* accomplishment, achievement, acme, completeness, completion, consummation, crown, evolution, exactness, excellence, exquisiteness, flawlessness, fulfilment, ideal, integrity, maturity, paragon, perfectness, pinnacle, precision, purity, realisation, sublimity, superiority, wholeness. **antonyms** flaw, imperfection.

perfectly *adv* absolutely, admirably, altogether, completely, consummately, entirely, exquisitely, faultlessly, flawlessly, fully, ideally, impeccably, incomparably, irreproachably, quite, superbly, superlatively, supremely, thoroughly, to perfection, totally, unimpeachably, utterly, wholly, wonderfully. **antonyms** imperfectly, partially.

perfidious *adj* corrupt, deceitful, dishonest, disloyal, double-dealing, duplicitous, faithless, false, Machiavellian, traitorous, treacherous, treasonous, two-faced, unfaithful, untrustworthy. **antonyms** faithful, honest, loyal.

perfidy *n* betrayal, deceit, disloyalty, double-dealing, duplicity, faithlessness, falsity, infidelity, perfidiousness, traitorousness, treachery, treason. **antonyms** faithfulness, honesty, loyalty.

perforate *v* bore, drill, hole, honeycomb, penetrate, pierce, prick, punch, puncture, stab.

perform *v* accomplish, achieve, act, appear as, bring about, bring off, carry out, complete, depict, discharge, do, effect, enact, execute, fulfil, function, manage, observe, play, present, produce, pull off, put on, render, represent, satisfy, stage, transact, work.

performance *n* accomplishment, account, achievement, act, acting, action, appearance, behaviour, bother, business, carrying out, carry-on, completion, conduct, consummation, discharge, efficiency, execution, exhibition, exploit, feat, fulfilment, functioning, fuss, gig, implementation, interpretation, melodrama, operation, play, portrayal, practice, presentation, production, rendition, representation, rigmarole, running, show, to-do, work, working.

perfume *n* aroma, balm, balminess, bouquet, cologne, essence, fragrance, incense, odour, redolence, scent, smell, sweetness, toilet water.

perfunctory *adj* automatic, bri careless, cursory, heedless, hurrie inattentive, indifferent, mechanic negligent, offhand, routine, sketch slipshod, slovenly, stereotype superficial, wooden. **antcnym** cordia

perhaps *adv* conceivably, feasib happen, maybe, perchance, possibly, y never know.

peril *n* danger, exposure, haza insecurity, jeopardy, menace, pitf risk, threat, uncertainty, vulnerability **antonyms** safety, security.

perilous *adj* chancy, dangero desperate, dicey, difficult, dire, expose hairy, hazardous, menacing, parlo precarious, risky, threatening, unsa unsure, vulnerable. **antonyms** sa secure.

perimeter *n* ambit, border, borderlir boundary, bounds, circumferenc confines, edge, fringe, frontier, lim margin, periphery. **antonyms** cent heart, middle.

period *n* aeon, age, course, cyc date, days, end, epoch, era, generatic interval, season, space, span, spell, sta stint, stop, stretch, term, time, tu while, years.

periodic *adj* cyclic, cyclical, desulto infrequent, intermittent, occasion recurrent, regular, repeated, season spasmodic, sporadic.

peripatetic *adj* ambulatory, itinera journeying, migrant, mobile, nomad roaming, roving, travelling, vagabor wandering. **antonym** fixed.

peripheral *adj* borderline, exteri external, incidental, inessenti irrelevant, marginal, minor, out outermost, outlying, outside, perimetr secondary, superficial, surfac tangential, unimportant, unnecessar **antonyms** central, crucial.

periphery *n* ambit, border, bounda brim, brink, circuit, circumference, edg fringe, hem, margin, outskirts, perimet rim, skirt, verge. **antonyms** centre, nu

perish *v* collapse, croak, crumble, dec decline, decompose, decrease, d disappear, disintegrate, end, expire, fa moulder, pass away, rot, vanish, was wither.

perishable *adj* biodegradab corruptible, decomposable, destructib fast-decaying, fast-deteriorating, sho lived, unstable.

perjury *n* false oath, fal statement, false swearing, false witne falsification, forswearing, mendacity.

perk *n* benefit, bonus, bunce, dividend, extra, freebie, fringe benefit, perquisite, plus.

perk up brighten, buck up, cheer up, improve, liven up, look up, pep up, rally, recover, recuperate, revive, take heart, upturn.

perky *adj* animated, bouncy, bright, bubbly, buoyant, cheerful, cheery, effervescent, gay, jaunty, lively, peppy, spirited, sprightly, sunny, vivacious. **antonyms** cheerless, dull, gloomy.

permanence *n* constancy, continuance, continuity, deathlessness, dependability, durability, duration, endurance, finality, fixedness, fixity, immortality, imperishability, indestructibility, lastingness, longevity, perdurability, perpetuity, stability, survival. **antonym** impermanence.

permanent *adj* abiding, constant, durable, enduring, everlasting, fixed, immutable, imperishable, indestructible, ineffaceable, ineradicable, inerasable, invariable, lasting, long-lasting, perennial, perpetual, persistent, stable, standing, steadfast, unchanging, unfading. **antonyms** ephemeral, fleeting, temporary.

permanently *adv* always, ceaselessly, constantly, continually, endlessly, eternally, ever more, everlastingly, for keeps, forever, once and for all, unremittingly, unendingly. **antonym** temporarily.

permeable *adj* absorbent, passable, penetrable, pervious, porous, spongy. **antonyms** impermeable, watertight.

permeate *v* charge, fill, filter through, imbue, impenetrate, impregnate, infiltrate, interfuse, interpenetrate, pass through, penetrate, percolate, pervade, saturate, seep through, soak through.

permissible *adj* acceptable, admissible, all right, allowable, allowed, authorised, kosher, lawful, leal, legit, legitimate, OK, permitted, proper, sanctioned. **antonym** prohibited.

permission *n* allowance, approval, assent, authorisation, consent, dispensation, freedom, go-ahead, green light, leave, liberty, licence, permit, sanction, sufferance. **antonym** prohibition.

permissive *adj* acquiescent, complaisant, easy-going, forbearing, free, indulgent, latitudinarian, lax, lenient, liberal, open-minded, overindulgent, tolerant. **antonym** strict.

permit *v* admit, agree, allow, authorise, consent, empower, enable, endorse, endure, give leave, grant, let, warrant. **antonym** prohibit.
n authorisation, liberty, licence, pass, passport, permission, sanction, visa, warrant. **antonym** prohibition.

permutation *n* alteration, change, commutation, shift, transformation, transmutation, transposition, transubstantiation.

pernicious *adj* bad, baleful, baneful, damaging, dangerous, deadly, deleterious, destructive, detrimental, evil, fatal, harmful, hurtful, injurious, maleficent, malevolent, malicious, malign, malignant, noxious, offensive, pestilent, poisonous, ruinous, toxic, unhealthy, unwholesome, venomous, wicked. **antonym** innocuous.

pernickety *adj* careful, detailed, exacting, fastidious, fiddly, fine, finical, finicky, fussy, hair-splitting, nice, nit-picking, over-precise, painstaking, particular, punctilious, tricky.

perpetrate *v* carry out, commit, do, effect, enact, execute, inflict, perform, practise, wreak.

perpetual *adj* abiding, ceaseless, constant, continual, continuous, deathless, endless, enduring, eternal, everlasting, immortal, incessant, infinite, interminable, lasting, never-ending, never-failing, perennial, permanent, persistent, recurrent, repeated, unceasing, unchanging, undying, unending, unfailing, unflagging, uninterrupted, unremitting, unvarying. **antonyms** ephemeral, intermittent, transient.

perpetuate *v* commemorate, continue, eternalise, immortalise, keep alive, keep up, maintain, preserve, protract, sustain.

perplex *v* baffle, befuddle, beset, bewilder, complicate, confound, confuse, dumbfound, entangle, gravel, jumble, mix up, muddle, mystify, nonplus, pother, puzzle, stump, tangle, thicken, throw.

perplexed *adj* at a loss, baffled, bamboozled, bewildered, confounded, disconcerted, fuddled, muddled, mystified, puzzled, worried.

perplexing *adj* amazing, baffling, bewildering, complex, complicated, confusing, difficult, distractive, enigmatic, hard, inexplicable, intricate, involved, knotty, labyrinthine, mysterious, mystifying, paradoxical, puzzling, strange, taxing, thorny, unaccountable, vexatious, weird. *antonyms* easy, simple.

persecute *v* afflict, annoy, badger, bait, bother, castigate, crucify, distress, dragoon, harass, haze, hound, hunt, ill-treat, injure, martyr, molest, oppress, pester, pursue, tease, torment, torture, tyrannise, vex, victimise, worry. *antonyms* accommodate, humour, indulge, pamper.

persecution *n* abuse, baiting, bashing, castigation, discrimination, molestation, oppression, punishment, subjugation, suppression, torture, tyranny.

perseverance *n* assiduity, constancy, dedication, determination, diligence, doggedness, endurance, indefatigability, persistence, pertinacity, purposefulness, resolution, sedulity, stamina, steadfastness, tenacity.

persevere *v* adhere, carry on, continue, endure, go on, hang on, hold fast, hold on, keep going, persist, plug away, pursue, remain, soldier on, stand firm, stick at. *antonyms* desist, discontinue, give up, stop.

persist *v* abide, carry on, continue, endure, insist, keep at it, last, linger, perdure, persevere, remain, stand fast, stand firm. *antonyms* desist, stop.

persistence *n* assiduity, assiduousness, constancy, determination, diligence, doggedness, endurance, grit, inde-fatigableness, perseverance, pertinacity, pluck, resolution, sedulity, stamina, steadfastness, tenacity, tirelessness.

persistent *adj* assiduous, constant, continual, continuous, determined, dogged, endless, enduring, fixed, immovable, incessant, indefatigable, indomitable, interminable, never-ending, obdurate, obstinate, perpetual, persevering, pertinacious, relentless, repeated, resolute, steadfast, steady, stubborn, tenacious, tireless, unflagging, unrelenting, unremitting, zealous.

person *n* being, bod, body, cat, character, cookie, customer, human, human being, individual, living soul, party, soul, specimen, type.

persona *n* character, façade, face, front, image, mask, part, personality, public face, role.

personable *adj* affable, agreeable, amiable, attractive, charming, good-looking, handsome, lik(e)able, nice, outgoing, pleasant, pleasing, presentable, warm, winning. *antonyms* disagreeable, unattractive.

personage *n* big shot, celebrity, dignitary, luminary, name, notable, personality, public figure, somebody, VIP.

personal *adj* bodily, corporal, corporeal, derogatory, disparaging, exclusive, exterior, idiosyncratic, individual, inimitable, insulting, intimate, material, nasty, offensive, own, particular, peculiar, pejorative, physical, private, privy, slighting, special, tête-à-tête. *antonyms* general, public, universal.

personality *n* attraction, attractiveness, celebrity, character, charisma, charm, disposition, dynamism, humour, identity, individuality, lik(e)ableness, magnetism, make-up, nature, notable, personage, pleasantness, psyche, selfhood, selfness, star, temper, temperament, traits.

personally *adv* alone, idiosyncratically, independently, individually, privately, solely, specially, subjectively.

personification *n* embodiment, image, incarnation, likeness, manifestation, portrayal, recreation, representation, semblance.

personify *v* embody, epitomise, exemplify, express, image, incarnate, mirror, represent, symbolise, typify.

personnel *n* crew, employees, human resources, manpower, members, people, staff, workers, workforce.

perspective *n* angle, aspect, attitude, context, objectivity, outlook, overview, panorama, proportion, prospect, relation, scene, slant, view, vista.

perspicacious *adj* acute, alert, astute, aware, clear-eyed, clear-sighted, clever, discerning, far-sighted, keen, observant, penetrating, perceptive, percipient, sagacious, sharp, sharp-witted, shrewd. *antonyms* obtuse, unobservant.

perspicacity *n* acuity, acumen, acuteness, brains, cleverness, discernment, discrimination, insight, keenness, penetration, perceptiveness, percipience, perspicaciousness, perspicuity, sagaciousness, sagacity, sharpness, shrewdness, wit.

perspicuity *n* clarity, clearness, comprehensibility, comprehensibleness, distinctness, explicitness, intelligibility, limpidity, limpidness, lucidity, penetrability, plainness, precision, straightforwardness, transparency.

perspicuous *adj* apparent, clear, comprehensible, crystal-clear, distinct, explicit, intelligible, limpid, lucid, manifest, obvious, plain, self-evident, straightforward, transparent, unambiguous, understandable.

persuadable *adj* acquiescent, agreeable, amenable, compliant, flexible, impressionable, malleable, pliable, receptive, susceptive. *antonyms* firm, inflexible, stubborn.

persuade *v* actuate, advise, allure, bring round, cajole, coax, convert, convince, counsel, entice, fast-talk, impel, incite, induce, influence, inveigle, lead on, lean on, prevail upon, prompt, satisfy, sway, sweet-talk, talk into, urge, win over. *antonyms* discourage, dissuade.

persuasion *n* belief, blandishment, cajolery, camp, certitude, cogency, come-on, conversion, conviction, credo, creed, cult, denomination, enticement, exhortation, faction, faith, force, inducement, influence, inveiglement, opinion, party, persuasiveness, potency, power, pull, school (of thought), sect, side, sweet talk, tenet, views, wheedling.

persuasive *adj* cogent, compelling, convincing, credible, effective, eloquent, forceful, honeyed, impelling, impressive, inducing, influential, logical, moving, plausible, potent, sound, telling, touching, valid, weighty, winning.

pert *adj* bold, brash, brisk, cheeky, daring, flip, flippant, forward, fresh, gay, impertinent, impudent, insolent, jaunty, lively, nimble, perky, presumptuous, saucy, smart, spirited, sprightly. *antonyms* coy, shy.

pertain *v* appertain, apply, be appropriate, be part of, be relevant, bear on, befit, belong, come under, concern, refer, regard, relate.

pertinacious *adj* determined, dogged, headstrong, inflexible, intractable, mulish, obdurate, obstinate, persevering, persistent, perverse, purposeful, relentless, resolute, self-willed, strong-willed, stubborn, tenacious, uncompromising, unyielding, wilful.

pertinent *adj* analogous, applicable, apposite, appropriate, apt, befitting, fit, fitting, germane, material, pat, proper, relevant, suitable, to the point, to the purpose. *antonyms* inappropriate, irrelevant, unsuitable.

pertness *n* audacity, boldness, brashness, brass, brazenness, bumptiousness, cheek, cheekiness, chutzpah, cockiness, effrontery, forwardness, freshness, impertinence, impudence, insolence, presumption, rudeness, sauciness.

perturb *v* agitate, alarm, bother, confuse, disarrange, discompose, disconcert, discountenance, disorder, disquiet, disturb, fluster, muddle, ruffle, trouble, unsettle, upset, vex, worry. *antonyms* compose, reassure.

perturbed *adj* agitated, alarmed, anxious, discomposed, disconcerted, disturbed, dithery, fearful, flappable, flurried, flustered, nervous, restless, shaken, troubled, uncomfortable, uneasy, unsettled, upset, worried. *antonym* unperturbed.

perusal *n* browse, check, examination, inspection, look, read, run-through, scrutiny, study.

peruse *v* browse, check, examine, inspect, look through, pore over, read, scan, scrutinise, study, vet.

pervade *v* affect, charge, diffuse, extend, fill, imbue, infuse, overspread, penetrate, percolate, permeate, saturate, suffuse.

pervasive *adj* common, diffuse, extensive, general, immanent, inescapable, omnipresent, permeating, pervading, prevalent, rife, ubiquitous, universal, widespread.

perverse *adj* abnormal, balky, cantankerous, churlish, contradictory, contrary, crabbed, cross, delinquent, depraved, deviant, disobedient, dogged, fractious, headstrong, ill-natured, ill-tempered, improper, incorrect, intractable, intransigent, miscreant, mulish, obdurate, obstinate, peevish, petulant, pig-headed, rebellious, recalcitrant, refractory, spiteful, stroppy, stubborn, surly, thwart, troublesome, unhealthy, unmanageable, unreasonable, unyielding, uppity, wayward, wilful, wrong-headed, wry. *antonyms* normal, reasonable.

perversion *n* aberration, abnormality, anomaly, corruption, debauchery, depravity, deviance, deviancy, deviation, distortion, falsification, immorality, kinkiness, misapplication, misinterpretation, misrepresentation, misuse, twisting, unnaturalness, vice, vitiation, wickedness.

perversity *n* contradictoriness, contrariness, intransigence, obduracy, refractoriness, waywardness.

pervert *v* abuse, bend, corrupt, debase, debauch, degrade, deprave, distort, divert, falsify, garble, lead astray, misapply, misconstrue, misinterpret, misrepresent, misuse, subvert, twist, vitiate, warp.

perverted *adj* aberrant, abnormal,

corrupt, debased, debauched, depraved, deviant, distorted, evil, freakish, immoral, impaired, kinky, misguided, queer, sick, twisted, unhealthy, unnatural, vicious, vitiated, warped, wicked.

pessimism *n* cynicism, dejection, depression, despair, despondency, distrust, gloom, gloominess, glumness, hopelessness, melancholy. **antonym** optimism.

pessimist *n* cynic, defeatist, doom-merchant, gloom and doom merchant, killjoy, melancholic, wet blanket, worrier. **antonym** optimist.

pessimistic *adj* bleak, cynical, dark, defeatist, dejected, depressed, despairing, despondent, dismal, distrustful, downhearted, fatalistic, gloomy, glum, hopeless, melancholy, misanthropic, morose, resigned, sad, worried. **antonym** optimistic.

pest *n* annoyance, bane, blight, bore, bother, bug, canker, curse, irritation, nuisance, pain (in the neck), scourge, thorn in one's flesh, trial, vexation.

pester *v* annoy, badger, bedevil, bother, bug, chivvy, disturb, dog, drive round the bend, drive up the wall, fret, get at, harass, harry, hassle, hector, hound, irk, nag, pick on, plague, ride, torment, worry.

pestilent *adj* annoying, bothersome, catching, communicable, contagious, contaminated, corrupting, deleterious, destructive, detrimental, diseased, disease-ridden, evil, galling, harmful, infected, infectious, injurious, irksome, irritating, pernicious, plague-ridden, ruinous, tainted, tiresome, vexing, vicious.

pet *n* darling, doll, duck, favourite, idol, jewel, treasure.
adj cherished, dearest, favoured, favourite, particular, preferred, special.
v baby, canoodle, caress, coddle, cosset, cuddle, dote on, fondle, indulge, kiss, mollycoddle, neck, pamper, pat, smooch, snog, spoil, stroke.

peter out cease, dissolve, dwindle, ebb, evaporate, fade, fail, stop, taper off, wane.

petite *adj* bijou, dainty, delicate, dinky, elfin, little, slight, small. **antonyms** big, large.

petition *n* address, appeal, application, boon, entreaty, imploration, invocation, plea, prayer, request, solicitation, suit, supplication.

v appeal, ask, beg, beseech, bid, call upon, crave, entreat, implore, plead, pray, press, solicit, sue, supplicate, urge.

petrified *adj* aghast, appalled, benumbed, dazed, dumbfounded, fossilised, frozen, horrified, horror stricken, numb, ossified, scared stiff, shocked, speechless, stunned, stupefied, terrified, terror-stricken.

petrify *v* amaze, appal, astonish, astound, benumb, calcify, confound, dumbfound, fossilise, gorgonise, harden, horrify, immobilise, numb, paralyse, set, solidify, stun, stupefy, terrify, transfix, turn to stone.

petty *adj* cheap, contemptible, grudging, inconsiderable, inessential, inferior, insignificant, junior, lesser, little, lower, mean, measly, minor, negligible, one-horse, paltry, piddling, poking, poky, secondary, shabby, slight, small, small-minded, small-town, spiteful, stingy, subordinate, trifling, trivial, ungenerous, unimportant. **antonyms** generous, important, large-hearted, significant, vital.

petulance *n* bad temper, crabbedness, crabbiness, ill-humour, ill-temper, irritability, peevishness, pique, querulousness, spleen, sulkiness, sullenness, waspishness.

petulant *adj* bad-tempered, captious, crabbed, cross, crusty, fretful, ill-humoured, impatient, irascible, irritable, moody, peevish, perverse, querulous, snappish, sour, sulky, sullen, ungracious, waspish.

phantom *n* apparition, chimera, figment (of the imagination), ghost, hallucination, illusion, phantasm(a), shade, simulacrum, spectre, spirit, spook, vision.

phase *n* aspect, chapter, condition, development, juncture, period, point, position, season, spell, stage, state, step, time.

phase out close, deactivate, dispose of, ease off, eliminate, get rid of, remove, replace, run down, taper off, terminate, wind down, withdraw.

phenomenal *adj* amazing, exceptional, extraordinary, fantastic, marvellous, miraculous, outstanding, prodigious, remarkable, sensational, singular, stupendous, uncommon, unique, unparalleled, unusual, wondrous.

phenomenon *n* appearance, circumstance, curiosity, episode, event, fact, happening, incident, marvel, miracle, occurrence, prodigy, rarity, sensation, sight, spectacle, wonder.

philanderer n Casanova, Don Juan, flirt, gallant, ladies' man, lady-killer, libertine, Lothario, playboy, stud, womaniser.

philanthropic adj altruistic, beneficent, benevolent, bounteous, bountiful, charitable, gracious, humane, humanitarian, kind, kind-hearted, kindly, munificent, public-spirited. **antonym** misanthropic.

philanthropist n altruist, angel, benefactor, contributor, donor, giver, good fairy, humanitarian, patron. **antonyms** misanthrope, misanthropist.

philanthropy n altruism, beneficence, benevolence, bounty, brotherly love, charitableness, charity, generosity, humanitarianism, kind-heartedness, liberality, munificence, open-handedness, patronage, public-spiritedness, unselfishness.

Philistine adj boorish, crass, ignorant, tasteless, uncultivated, uncultured, uneducated, unlettered, unread, unrefined.

philosophical adj abstract, analytical, calm, collected, composed, cool, dispassionate, equanimous, erudite, impassive, imperturbable, learned, logical, metaphysical, patient, rational, resigned, sagacious, serene, stoical, theoretical, thoughtful, tranquil, unruffled, wise.

philosophy n aesthetics, attitude, beliefs, convictions, doctrine, epistemology, ideology, knowledge, logic, metaphysics, principle, rationale, rationalism, reason, reasoning, tenets, thinking, thought, values, viewpoint, wisdom, world-view.

phlegmatic adj apathetic, cold, dull, frigid, heavy, impassive, imperturbable, indifferent, lethargic, listless, matter-of-fact, nonchalant, placid, sluggish, stoical, stolid, unconcerned, undemonstrative, unemotional. **antonyms** demonstrative, passionate.

phobia n anxiety, aversion, detestation, dislike, distaste, dread, fear, hang-up, hatred, horror, loathing, neurosis, obsession, repulsion, revulsion, terror, thing. **antonyms** liking, love.

phoney adj affected, assumed, bogus, counterfeit, fake, false, forged, imitation, pseudo, put-on, quack, sham, spurious, trick. **antonyms** real, true.
n counterfeit, fake, faker, forgery, fraud, humbug, imposter, mountebank, pretender, pseud, quack, sham.

photograph n image, likeness, photo, picture, print, shot, slide, snap, snapshot, transparency.
v film, record, shoot, snap, take, video.

photographic adj accurate, cinematic, detailed, exact, faithful, filmic, graphic, lifelike, minute, natural, naturalistic, pictorial, precise, realistic, representational, retentive, visual, vivid.

phrase n construction, expression, idiom, locution, mention, motto, remark, saying, tag, utterance.
v couch, express, formulate, frame, present, pronounce, put, say, style, term, utter, voice, word.

phraseology n argot, cant, diction, expression, idiom, language, parlance, patois, phrase, phrasing, speech, style, syntax, wording.

physical adj actual, bodily, carnal, concrete, corporal, corporeal, earthly, fleshly, incarnate, material, mortal, natural, palpable, real, sensible, solid, substantial, tangible, visible. **antonyms** mental, spiritual.

pick v break into, break open, choose, collect, crack, cull, cut, decide on, elect, embrace, espouse, fix upon, foment, gather, harvest, incite, instigate, opt for, pluck, prise, provoke, pull, screen, select, settle on, sift out, single out, start. **antonym** reject.
n best, brightest and best, choice, choicest, choosing, cream, crème de la crème, decision, elect, élite, flower, option, preference, pride, prize, selection, tops.
pick at nibble, peck, play with, toy with.
pick off detach, drill, hit, kill, plug, remove, shoot, strike.
pick on badger, bait, blame, bully, carp at, criticise, find fault with, get at, nag, needle, quibble with, tease, torment.
pick out choose, cull, differentiate, discriminate, distinguish, hand-pick, notice, perceive, recognise, select, separate, single out, tell apart.
pick up acquire, apprehend, arrest, bust, buy, call for, collar, collect, come across, fetch, find, gain, gain ground, garner, gather, grasp, happen on, hoist, improve, learn, lift, master, mend, nab, nick, obtain, perk up, pinch, pull in, purchase, raise, rally, recover, recuperate, run in, score, snap up, uplift.
pickings n booty, bunce, earnings, gravy, loot, plunder, proceeds, profits, returns, rewards, spoils, take, yield.
pickle n bind, crisis, difficulty, dilemma,

exigency, fix, hot water, jam, pinch, predicament, quandary, scrape, spot, straits, tight spot.

pictorial *adj* diagrammatic, expressive, graphic, illustrated, representational, schematic, striking, vivid.

picture *n* account, archetype, carbon copy, copy, dead ringer, depiction, description, double, drawing, duplicate, effigy, embodiment, engraving, epitome, essence, film, flick, graphic, illustration, image, impression, likeness, living, image, lookalike, motion picture, movie, painting, personification, photograph, portrait, portrayal, print, re-creation, replica, report, representation, ringer, scene, similitude, sketch, spit, spitting image, twin.

v conceive of, depict, describe, draw, envisage, envision, illustrate, image, imagine, paint, photograph, portray, render, represent, see, show, sketch, visualise.

picturesque *adj* attractive, beautiful, charming, colourful, pretty, quaint, scenic, striking, vivid.

piece *n* allotment, article, bit, case, chunk, component, composition, constituent, creation, division, element, example, fraction, fragment, instance, item, length, morsel, mouthful, objet d'art, occurrence, offcut, part, piecemeal, portion, production, quantity, sample, scrap, section, segment, share, shred, slice, snippet, specimen, stroke, study, work, work of art.

piece together assemble, attach, compose, fit, fix, join, mend, patch, repair, restore, unite.

piecemeal *adv* at intervals, bit by bit, by degrees, fitfully, in dribs and drabs, intermittently, little by little, partially, slowly. *antonyms* completely, entirely, wholly.

adj discrete, fragmentary, intermittent, interrupted, partial, patchy, scattered, unsystematic. *antonyms* complete, entire, whole, wholesale.

pier *n* buttress, column, jetty, landing-place, promenade, quay, wharf.

pierce *v* affect, barb, bore, comprehend, discern, discover, drift, drill, enter, excite, fathom, grasp, hurt, impale, move, pain, penetrate, perforate, prick, probe, puncture, realise, rouse, run through, see, spike, stab, stick into, sting, stir, strike, thrill, thrust, touch, transfix, transpierce, understand, wound.

piercing *adj* acute, agonising, alert,

arctic, aware, biting, bitter, cold, ear-piercing, ear-splitting, excruciating exquisite, fierce, freezing, frosty, high pitched, intense, keen, loud, nipping nippy, numbing, painful, penetrating perceptive, perspicacious, powerful probing, quick-witted, racking, raw searching, severe, sharp, shattering shooting, shrewd, shrill, Siberian stabbing, wintry.

piety *n* devotion, devoutness dutifulness, duty, faith, godliness grace, holiness, piousness, religion religiosity, reverence, saintliness sanctity, veneration. *antonym* impiety.

piffle *n* balderdash, balls, bullshit, bunk bunkum, codswallop, drivel, guff, hooey nonsense, poppycock, rot, rubbish tommy-rot, tosh, trash, tripe, twaddle.

pig *n* animal, beast, boar, boor, brute glutton, greedy guts, grunter, guzzler hog, piggy, piglet, porker, slob, sloven sow, swine.

pigeonhole *v* catalogue, characterise classify, codify, compartmentalise defer, file, label, postpone, put off shelve, slot, sort, typecast.

pig-headed *adj* bull-headed, contrary cross-grained, dense, inflexible intractable, intransigent, mulish obstinate, perverse, self-willed, stiff-necked, stubborn, stupid, unyielding wilful, wrong-headed. *antonyms* flexible, tractable.

pile *n* accumulation, assemblage, assortment, bomb, building, collection edifice, erection, fortune, heap, hoard mass, mint, money, mound, mountain mow, packet, pot, stack, stockpile, structure, wealth.

v accumulate, amass, assemble, build up, charge, climb, collect, crowd, crush flock, flood, gather, heap, hoard, jam load up, mass, pack, rush, stack, store, stream.

piles *n* a great deal, a lot, loads, millions, oceans, oodles, quantities, stacks.

pilfer *v* appropriate, embezzle, filch finger, help oneself to, knock off, lift nick, pinch, purloin, rifle, rob, steal thieve.

pilgrimage *n* crusade, excursion, expedition, hadj, journey, mission, odyssey, tour, trip.

pillage *v* depredate, despoil, freeboot loot, maraud, plunder, raid, ransack ravage, raze, reive, rifle, rob, sack, spoil spoliate, strip, vandalise.

n booty, depredation, devastation,

harrying, loot, marauding, plunder, robbery, sack, seizure, spoils, spoliation.

pillar *n* bastion, column, leader, leading light, mainstay, mast, pier, post, prop, rock, shaft, stanchion, support, supporter, tower of strength, upholder, upright, worthy.

pillory *v* brand, cast a slur on, denounce, hold up to shame, lash, mock, pour scorn on, ridicule, show up, stigmatise.

pilot *n* airman, aviator, captain, conductor, coxswain, director, flier, guide, helmsman, leader, navigator.

v conduct, control, direct, drive, fly, guide, handle, lead, manage, navigate, operate, run, shepherd, steer.

adj experimental, model, test, trial.

pin *v* affix, attach, fasten, fix, hold down, hold fast, immobilise, join, nail, pinion, press, restrain, secure, tack.

n bolt, brooch, clip, fastener, nail, peg, rivet, screw, spike, spindle, tack, tie-pin.

pin down bind, compel, confine, constrain, designate, determine, fix, force, hold, hold down, home in on, identify, immobilise, locate, make, nail, nail down, name, pinpoint, press, pressurise, specify, tie down, zero in on.

pinch *v* afflict, apprehend, arrest, bust, chafe, check, collar, compress, confine, cramp, crush, distress, do, economise, filch, grasp, hurt, knap, knock off, lay, lift, nab, nick, nip, oppress, pain, pick up, pilfer, press, pull in, purloin, rob, run in, scrimp, skimp, snaffle, snatch, snitch, spare, squeeze, steal, stint, swipe, tweak.

n bit, crisis, dash, difficulty, emergency, exigency, hardship, jam, jot, mite, necessity, nip, oppression, pass, pickle, plight, predicament, pressure, soupçon, speck, squeeze, strait, stress, taste, tweak.

pine *v* ache, covet, crave, decay, decline, desire, droop, dwindle, fade, flag, hanker, hunger, languish, long, peak, sicken, sigh, sink, thirst, waste, weaken, wilt, wish, wither, yearn, yen.

pinnacle *n* acme, apex, apogee, cap, cone, crest, crown, eminence, height, needle, obelisk, peak, pyramid, spire, steeple, summit, top, turret, vertex, zenith.

pin-point *v* define, distinguish, home in on, identify, locate, place, spot, zero in on.

pint-size *adj* diminutive, dwarf, little, midget, miniature, pocket, pocket-sized, small, tiny, wee. **antonyms** giant, huge.

pioneer *n* coloniser, colonist, developer, explorer, founder, founding father, frontiersman, innovator, leader, settler, trail-blazer.

v blaze a trail, create, develop, discover, establish, found, initiate, instigate, institute, invent, launch, lead, open up, originate, prepare, start.

pious *adj* dedicated, devoted, devout, God-fearing, godly, good, goody-goody, holier-than-thou, holy, moral, pietistic, religiose, religious, reverent, righteous, saintly, sanctimonious, self-righteous, spiritual, unctuous, virtuous. **antonym** impious.

pipe *v* carry, channel, cheep, chirp, conduct, convey, funnel, peep, play, sing, siphon, sound, supply, tootle, transmit, trill, tweet, twitter, warble, whistle.

pipe-dream *n* castle in Spain, castle in the air, chimera, daydream, delusion, dream, fantasy, mirage, notion, reverie, romance, vagary.

piquancy *n* bite, colour, edge, excitement, flavour, ginger, interest, juice, kick, pep, pepperiness, pizzazz, punch, pungency, raciness, relish, sharpness, spice, spiciness, spirit, tang, vigour, vitality, zest, zip.

piquant *adj* biting, interesting, lively, peppery, poignant, provocative, pungent, racy, salty, savoury, scintillating, sharp, sparkling, spicy, spirited, stimulating, stinging, tangy, tart, zesty. **antonym** banal.

pique *n* annoyance, displeasure, grudge, huff, irritation, miff, offence, resentment, umbrage, vexation.

v affront, annoy, arouse, displease, excite, gall, galvanise, get, goad, incense, irk, irritate, kindle, miff, mortify, nettle, offend, peeve, provoke, put out, rile, rouse, spur, stimulate, sting, stir, vex, wound.

pit *n* abyss, cavity, chasm, crater, dent, depression, dimple, excavation, gulf, hole, hollow, indentation, pock-mark, pothole, trench.

pit against match, oppose, set against.

pitch *v* bung, cast, chuck, dive, drop, erect, fall headlong, fix, fling, flounder, heave, hurl, launch, lob, locate, lurch, peck, place, plant, plunge, raise, roll, set up, settle, sling, stagger, station, throw, topple, toss, tumble.

n angle, cant, degree, dip, gradient, ground, harmonic, height, incline, level, line, modulation, park, patter, playing-field, point, sales talk, slope, sound, spiel, sports field, steepness, summit, tilt, timbre, tone.

piteous *adj* affecting, deplorable, distressing, doleful, grievous, heart-breaking, heart-rending, lamentable, miserable, mournful, moving, pathetic, pitiable, pitiful, plaintive, poignant, sad, sorrowful, touching, woeful, wretched.

pitfall *n* catch, danger, difficulty, downfall, drawback, hazard, peril, snag, snare, stumbling-block, trap.

pith *n* consequence, core, crux, depth, essence, force, gist, heart, import, importance, kernel, marrow, matter, meat, moment, nub, point, power, quintessence, salient point, significance, strength, substance, value, weight.

pithy *adj* aphoristic, brief, cogent, compact, concise, epigrammatic, expressive, forceful, meaningful, pointed, short, succinct, telling, terse, trenchant. *antonyms* prolix, verbose, wordy.

pitiable *adj* contemptible, distressed, distressful, distressing, doleful, grievous, lamentable, miserable, mournful, pathetic, piteous, poor, sad, sorry, woeful, woesome, wretched.

pitiful *adj* abject, base, beggarly, contemptible, deplorable, despicable, distressing, grievous, heartbreaking, heart-rending, hopeless, inadequate, insignificant, lamentable, low, mean, miserable, paltry, pathetic, piteous, pitiable, sad, shabby, sorry, vile, woeful, worthless, wretched.

pitiless *adj* brutal, callous, cold-blooded, cold-hearted, cruel, flinty, hard-hearted, harsh, heartless, implacable, inexorable, inhuman, merciless, obdurate, relentless, ruthless, uncaring, unfeeling, unmerciful, unpitying, unsympathetic. *antonyms* compassionate, gentle, kind, merciful.

pitted *adj* blemished, dented, dinted, gouged, indented, marked, nicked, notched, pock-marked, pocky, potholed, riddled, rough, rutty, scarred, scratched.

pity *n* charity, clemency, commiseration, compassion, condolence, crime, crying shame, fellow-feeling, forbearance, kindness, mercy, misfortune, regret, shame, sin, sympathy, tenderness, understanding. *antonyms* cruelty, disdain, scorn.

v absolve, bleed for, commiserate with, feel for, forgive, grieve for, pardon, reprieve, sympathise with, weep for.

pivot *n* axis, axle, centre, focal point, fulcrum, heart, hinge, hub, kingpin, linchpin, spindle, swivel.

v depend, hang, hinge, lie, rely, revolve, rotate, spin, swing, swivel, turn, twirl.

pivotal *adj* axial, central, climactic, critical, crucial, decisive, determining, focal, vital.

placate *v* appease, assuage, calm, conciliate, humour, lull, mollify, pacify, propitiate, quiet, satisfy, soothe, win over. *antonyms* anger, enrage, incense, infuriate.

placatory *adj* appeasing, conciliatory, pacificatory, peace-making, propitiatory.

place *n* abode, accommodation, affair, apartment, appointment, area, berth, billet, charge, city, concern, district, domicile, duty, dwelling, employment, flat, function, grade, home, house, job, locale, locality, location, locus, manor, mansion, neighbourhood, pad, point, position, post, prerogative, property, quarter, rank, region, residence, responsibility, right, role, room, seat, site, situation, space, spot, station, status, stead, town, venue, vicinity, village, whereabouts.

v allocate, appoint, arrange, assign, associate, bung, charge, class, classify, commission, deposit, dispose, dump, entrust, establish, fix, give, grade, group, identify, install, know, lay, locate, order, plant, position, put, put one's finger on, rank, recognise, remember, rest, set, settle, situate, sort, stand, station, stick.

placement *n* appointment, arrangement, assignment, classification, deployment, disposition, distribution, employment, engagement, installation, locating, location, ordering, positioning, ranking, stationing.

placid *adj* calm, collected, composed, cool, equable, even, even-tempered, gentle, halcyon, imperturbable, level-headed, mild, peaceful, quiet, reposeful, restful, self-possessed, serene, still, tranquil, undisturbed, unexcitable, unmoved, unruffled, untroubled. *antonyms* agitated, jumpy.

plagiarise *v* appropriate, borrow, crib, infringe, lift, reproduce, steal, thieve.

plague *n* affliction, aggravation, annoyance, bane, blight, bother, calamity, cancer, contagion, curse, death, disease, epidemic, evil, infection, irritant, nuisance, pain, pandemic, pest, pestilence, problem, scourge, thorn in the flesh, torment, trial, vexation, visitation.

v afflict, annoy, badger, bedevil, bother, distress, disturb, fret, harass, harry, hassle, haunt, hound, molest, pain, persecute, pester, tease, torment, torture, trouble, vex.

plain *adj* apparent, artless, austere, bare, basic, blunt, candid, clear, clinical, common, commonplace, comprehensible, direct, discreet, distinct, downright, even, everyday, evident, flat, forthright, frank, frugal, guileless, home-bred, homely, homespun, honest, ill-favoured, ingenuous, legible, level, lowly, lucid, manifest, modest, muted, obvious, open, ordinary, outspoken, patent, plane, pure, restrained, self-coloured, severe, simple, sincere, smooth, spartan, stark, straightforward, transparent, ugly, unadorned, unaffected, unambiguous, unattractive, understandable, undistinguished, unelaborate, unembellished, unmistakable, unobstructed, unprepossessing, unpretentious, unvarnished, visible, whole-coloured, workaday. **antonyms** abstruse, attractive, elaborate, exaggerated, ostentatious, rich, striking, unclear.

plain-spoken *adj* blunt, candid, direct, downright, explicit, forthright, frank, honest, open, outright, outspoken, straightforward, truthful, unequivocal.

plaintive *adj* disconsolate, dismal, doleful, dolorous, grief-stricken, grievous, heart-rending, melancholy, mournful, pathetic, piteous, pitiful, rueful, sad, sorrowful, wistful, woebegone, woeful.

plan *n* blueprint, chart, contrivance, design, device, diagram, drawing, idea, illustration, layout, map, method, plot, procedure, programme, project, proposal, proposition, representation, scenario, schedule, scheme, sketch, strategy, suggestion, system.
v aim, arrange, concoct, conspire, contemplate, contrive, design, devise, draft, envisage, foreplan, foresee, formulate, frame, intend, invent, mean, organise, outline, plot, prepare, propose, purpose, represent, scheme.

plane *n* class, condition, degree, echelon, footing, level, position, rank, rung, stage, stratum.
adj even, flat, flush, horizontal, level, plain, planar, regular, smooth, uniform.

plangent *adj* clangorous, deep, loud, mournful, plaintive, resonant, resounding, reverberating, ringing, sonorous, vibrant.

plant¹ *n* bush, flower, herb, shrub, vegetable, weed.
v bury, establish, fix, found, imbed,

implant, inlay, insert, inset, institute, lodge, put in the ground, root, scatter, seed, set, set out, settle, sow, transplant.

plant² *n* apparatus, equipment, factory, foundry, gear, machinery, mill, shop, works, workshop, yard.

plaster *v* besmear, coat, cover, daub, overlay, smear, spread.

plastic *adj* compliant, docile, ductile, flexible, impressionable, malleable, manageable, mouldable, pliable, pliant, receptive, responsive, soft, supple, tractable. **antonyms** inflexible, rigid.

plasticity *n* flexibility, malleability, pliability, pliableness, pliancy, softness, suppleness, tractability. **antonyms** inflexibility, rigidity.

platitude *n* banality, bromide, chestnut, cliché, commonplace, inanity, stereotype, truism.

platitudinous *adj* banal, clichéd, commonplace, corny, dull, flat, hackneyed, overworked, set, stale, stereotyped, stock, tired, trite, truistic, vapid, well-worn.

platonic *adj* ideal, idealistic, incorporeal, intellectual, non-physical, spiritual.

plaudits *n* acclaim, acclamation, accolade, applause, approbation, approval, clapping, commendation, congratulations, hand, hurrahs, kudos, ovation, praise, standing ovation.

plausible *adj* believable, colourable, conceivable, convincing, credible, facile, fair-spoken, glib, likely, persuasive, possible, probable, reasonable, smooth, smooth-talking, smooth-tongued, specious, tenable, voluble. **antonyms** implausible, improbable, unlikely.

play *v* act, bet, caper, challenge, chance, compete, contend, execute, fiddle, fidget, flirt, fool around, frisk, frolic, gamble, gambol, hazard, impersonate, interfere, participate, perform, personate, portray, punt, represent, revel, risk, rival, romp, speculate, sport, string along, take, take on, take part, take the part of, trifle, vie with, wager. **antonym** work.
n action, activity, amusement, caper, comedy, diversion, doodle, drama, elbowroom, employment, entertainment, exercise, farce, foolery, frolic, fun, function, gambling, gambol, game, gaming, give, humour, jest, joking, lark, latitude, leeway, margin, masque, motion, movement, operation, pastime, performance, piece, prank, range, recreation, romp, room, scope, show,

space, sport, sweep, swing, teasing, tragedy, transaction, working.

play around dally, flirt, fool, mess around, philander, trifle, womanise.

play ball collaborate, co-operate, go along, play along, reciprocate, respond, show willing.

play down gloss over, make light of, make little of, minimise, soft-pedal, underplay, underrate, undervalue.

play for time delay, drag one's feet, filibuster, hang fire, hesitate, procrastinate, stall, temporise.

play havoc with confuse, demolish, destroy, devastate, disorganise, disrupt, mess up, ruin, wreck.

play on abuse, capitalise on, exploit, milk, misuse, profit by, take advantage of, trade on, turn to account, utilise.

play the fool act the (giddy) goat, clown around, fool around, horse around, mess about, monkey around, skylark.

play the game acquiesce, conform, keep in step, play by the rules, play fair, toe the line, yield.

play up accentuate, begin, bother, emphasise, exaggerate, fool, highlight, hurt, magnify, malfunction, overemphasise, pain, spotlight, start, stress, strike up, trouble.

play up to blandish, bootlick, butter up, fawn, flatter, ingratiate oneself, soft-soap, suck up to, toady.

playboy *n* debauchee, ladies' man, lady-killer, libertine, man about town, philanderer, rake, socialite, womaniser.

player *n* actor, actress, artist(e), competitor, contestant, cricketer, entertainer, footballer, instrumentalist, musician, participant, performer, sportsman, sportswoman, Thespian, trouper.

playful *adj* arch, cheerful, coquettish, coy, flirtatious, frisky, frolicsome, gamesome, gay, good-natured, humorous, impish, jesting, jokey, joking, joyous, kittenish, larkish, larky, lively, merry, mischievous, puckish, roguish, rollicking, spirited, sportive, sprightly, tongue-in-cheek, waggish. **antonyms** serious, stern.

plea *n* action, allegation, apology, appeal, begging, cause, claim, defence, entreaty, excuse, explanation, extenuation, imploration, intercession, invocation, justification, overture, petition, prayer, pretext, request, suit, supplication, vindication.

plead *v* adduce, allege, appeal, argue,

ask, assert, beg, beseech, crave, entreat, implore, importune, maintain, moot, petition, put forward, request, solicit, supplicate.

pleasant *adj* acceptable, affable, agreeable, amiable, amusing, charming, cheerful, cheery, congenial, cool, delectable, delightful, delightsome, engaging, enjoyable, fine, friendly, genial, good-humoured, gratifying, likeable, listenable, lovely, nice, pleasing, pleasurable, refreshing, satisfying, sunshiny, toothsome, welcome, winsome. **antonyms** distasteful, nasty, repugnant.

please *v* amuse, captivate, charm, cheer, choose, content, delight, desire, enchant, entertain, gladden, go for, gratify, humour, indulge, like, opt, prefer, rejoice, satisfy, see fit, suit, think fit, tickle, tickle pink, want, will, wish. **antonyms** anger, annoy, displease.

pleased *adj* chuffed, contented, delighted, elated, euphoric, glad, gratified, gruntled, happy, in high spirits, over the moon, satisfied, thrilled, tickled, tickled pink. **antonyms** annoyed, displeased.

pleasing *adj* acceptable, agreeable, amiable, amusing, attractive, charming, congenial, delightful, engaging, enjoyable, entertaining, good, gratifying, likable, nice, pleasurable, polite, satisfying, welcome, winning. **antonym** unpleasant.

pleasurable *adj* agreeable, amusing, congenial, delightful, diverting, enjoyable, entertaining, fun, good, gratifying, lovely, nice, pleasant, welcome. **antonyms** bad, disagreeable.

pleasure *n* amusement, bliss, choice, comfort, command, complacency, contentment, delectation, delight, desire, diversion, ease, enjoyment, gladness, gratification, happiness, inclination, joy, mind, option, preference, purpose, recreation, satisfaction, solace, will, wish. **antonyms** displeasure, pain, sorrow, trouble.

pleat *v* crease, crimp, flute, fold, gather, plait, pucker, tuck.

plebeian *adj* base, coarse, common, ignoble, low, low-born, lower-class, mean, non-U, peasant, proletarian, uncultivated, unrefined, vulgar, working-class. **antonyms** aristocratic, noble, patrician.

n common man, commoner, man in the street, peasant, pleb, prole, proletarian, worker. *antonyms* aristocrat, noble, patrician.

pledge *n* assurance, bail, bond, collateral, covenant, deposit, earnest, gage, guarantee, oath, pawn, promise, security, surety, toast, undertaking, vow, warrant, word, word of honour.

v bind, contract, engage, ensure, gage, guarantee, mortgage, plight, promise, secure, swear, undertake, vouch, vow.

plenary *adj* absolute, complete, entire, full, general, integral, open, sweeping, thorough, unconditional, unlimited, unqualified, unrestricted, whole.

plenitude *n* abundance, amplitude, bounty, completeness, copiousness, cornucopia, entireness, excess, fullness, plenteousness, plentifulness, plenty, plethora, profusion, repletion, wealth. *antonym* scarcity.

plenteous *adj* abounding, abundant, ample, bounteous, bountiful, bumper, copious, fertile, fruitful, generous, inexhaustible, infinite, lavish, liberal, luxuriant, overflowing, plentiful, productive, profuse, prolific. *antonym* scarce.

plentiful *adj* abounding, abundant, ample, bounteous, bountiful, bumper, complete, copious, fertile, fruitful, generous, inexhaustible, infinite, lavish, liberal, luxuriant, overflowing, plenteous, productive, profuse, prolific. *antonyms* rare, scanty, scarce.

plenty *n* abundance, affluence, copiousness, enough, fertility, fruitfulness, fund, heap(s), lots, luxury, mass, masses, milk and honey, mine, mountain(s), oodles, opulence, pile(s), plenitude, plenteousness, plentifulness, plethora, profusion, prosperity, quantities, quantity, stack(s), store, sufficiency, volume, wealth. *antonyms* lack, need, scarcity, want.

plethora *n* excess, glut, overabundance, profusion, superabundance, superfluity, surfeit, surplus.

pliability *n* adaptability, amenability, bendability, compliance, docility, ductility, elasticity, flexibility, impressionableness, malleability, mobility, plasticity, pliancy, suggestibility, susceptibility, tractableness. *antonyms* inflexibilty, rigidity.

pliable *adj* accommodating, adaptable, bendable, bendy, compliant, docile, ductile, flexible, impressionable, influenceable, limber, lithe, malleable, manageable, persuadable, plastic, pliant, receptive, responsive, suggestible, supple, susceptible, tractable, yielding. *antonyms* inflexible, rigid.

pliant *adj* adaptable, bendable, bendy, biddable, compliant, ductile, easily led, flexible, impressionable, influenceable, lithe, manageable, persuadable, plastic, pliable, supple, susceptible, tractable, yielding. *antonyms* inflexible, intractable.

plight *n* case, circumstances, condition, difficulty, dilemma, extremity, hole, jam, perplexity, pickle, predicament, quandary, scrape, situation, spot, state, straits, trouble.

plod *v* clump, drag, drudge, grind, grub, labour, lumber, peg, persevere, plough through, slog, soldier on, stomp, sweat, toil, tramp, tread, trudge.

plot *n* action, cabal, conspiracy, design, intrigue, machination(s), narrative, outline, plan, scenario, scheme, story, story line, stratagem, subject, theme, thread.

v brew, cabal, calculate, chart, collude, compass, compute, conceive, concoct, conspire, contrive, cook up, design, devise, draft, draw, hatch, imagine, intrigue, lay, locate, machinate, manoeuvre, map, mark, outline, plan, project, scheme.

ploy *n* artifice, contrivance, device, dodge, gambit, game, manoeuvre, move, ruse, scheme, stratagem, subterfuge, tactic, trick, wile.

pluck[1] *n* backbone, boldness, bottle, bravery, courage, determination, fortitude, gameness, grit, guts, hardihood, heart, intrepidity, mettle, nerve, resolution, spirit, spunk, tenacity.

pluck[2] *v* catch, clutch, collect, depilate, deplume, draw, evulse, gather, harvest, jerk, pick, plunk, pull, pull off, pull out, snatch, strum, thrum, tug, twang, tweak, yank.

plucky *adj* bold, brave, courageous, daring, doughty, game, gamy, gritty, gutsy, hardy, heroic, intrepid, mettlesome, spirited, spunky, tenacious, unflinching, valiant. *antonyms* feeble, weak.

plug *n* advert, advertisement, bung, cake, chew, cork, good word, hype, mention, pigtail, publicity, push, spigot, stopper, tampon, twist, wad.

v advertise, block, build up, bung, choke, close, cork, cover, drudge, fill, grind, hype, labour, mention, pack, peg away, plod, promote, publicise, push, seal, slog, stop, stop up, stopper, stuff, tamp, toil.

plumb *adv* bang, dead, exactly, perpendicularly, precisely, slap, spot-on, square, up and down, vertically.
v delve, explore, fathom, gauge, investigate, mark, measure, penetrate, probe, search, sound, unravel.

plummet *v* crash, descend, dive, drop, fall, hurtle, nose-dive, plunge, stoop, swoop, tumble. *antonym* soar.

plump[1] *adj* beefy, burly, buxom, chubby, corpulent, dumpy, fat, fleshy, full, matronly, obese, podgy, portly, roly-poly, rotund, round, stout, tubby, well-upholstered. *antonyms* skinny, thin.

plump[2] *v* collapse, descend, drop, dump, fall, flop, sink, slump.
adv abruptly, directly, straight.

plump for back, choose, favour, opt for, select, side with, support.

plumpness *n* chubbiness, corpulence, fatness, fleshiness, obesity, podginess, portliness, pudginess, rotundity, stoutness, tubbiness. *antonyms* skinniness, thinness.

plunder *v* depredate, despoil, devastate, loot, pillage, raid, ransack, ravage, rifle, rob, sack, spoil, spoliate, steal, strip.
n booty, despoilment, ill-gotten gains, loot, pickings, pillage, prey, prize, spoils, swag.

plunge *v* career, cast, charge, dash, demerge, descend, dip, dive, dive-bomb, dook, douse, drop, fall, go down, hurtle, immerse, jump, lurch, nose-dive, pitch, plummet, rush, sink, submerge, swoop, tear, throw, tumble.
n collapse, descent, dive, drop, fall, immersion, jump, submersion, swoop, tumble.

plurality *n* bulk, diversity, galaxy, majority, mass, most, multiplicity, multitudinousness, numerousness, preponderance, profusion, variety.

plus *n* advantage, asset, benefit, bonus, credit, extra, gain, good point, perk, surplus. *antonym* minus.

plush *adj* affluent, costly, de luxe, lavish, luxurious, luxury, opulent, palatial, rich, ritzy, sumptuous.

ply *v* assail, beseige, beset, bombard, carry on, employ, exercise, feed, follow, furnish, handle, harass, importune, manipulate, practise, press, provide, pursue, supply, swing, urge, utilise, wield, work at.

poach *v* appropriate, encroach, infringe, intrude, pilfer, plunder, rob, steal, trespass.

pocket *n* bag, compartment, envelope, hollow, pouch, receptacle, reticule, sack.
adj abridged, compact, concise, dwarf, little, mini, miniature, pint-size(d), portable, potted, small.
v appropriate, filch, help oneself to, lift, nick, pilfer, pinch, purloin, snaffle, steal, take.

podgy *adj* chubby, chunky, corpulent, dumpy, fat, fleshy, paunchy, plump, roly-poly, rotund, squat, stout, stubby, stumpy, tubby. *antonym* skinny.

poetic *adj* artistic, elegiac, flowing, graceful, lyric, lyrical, metrical, moving, rhythmical. *antonym* prosaic.

poignancy *n* bitterness, emotion, emotionalism, evocativeness, feeling, intensity, keenness, painfulness, pathos, piquancy, piteousness, plaintiveness, pungency, sadness, sentiment, sharpness, tenderness.

poignant *adj* acrid, acute, affecting, agonising, biting, bitter, caustic, distressing, heartbreaking, heart-rending, intense, keen, moving, painful, pathetic, penetrating, piercing, piquant, pointed, pungent, sad, sarcastic, severe, sharp, stinging, tender, touching, upsetting.

point[1] *n* aim, aspect, attribute, burden, characteristic, circumstance, condition, core, crux, degree, design, detail, dot, drift, end, essence, extent, facet, feature, full stop, gist, goal, import, instance, instant, intent, intention, item, juncture, location, mark, marrow, matter, meaning, moment, motive, nicety, nub, object, objective, particular, peculiarity, period, pith, place, position, property, proposition, purpose, quality, question, reason, respect, score, side, site, speck, spot, stage, station, stop, subject, tally, text, theme, thrust, time, trait, unit, use, usefulness, utility.
v aim, denote, designate, direct, draw attention to, hint, indicate, level, show, signal, signify, suggest, train.

point of view angle, approach, attitude, belief, judgement, opinion, orientation, outlook, perspective, position, slant, stance, standpoint, view, viewpoint.

point out allude to, bring up, call attention to, identify, indicate, mention, remind, reveal, show, specify.

point up accentuate, emphasise, headline, spotlight, stress, underline, underscore.

point[2] *n* apex, bill, cape, end,

foreland, head, headland, neb, ness, nib, promontory, prong, spike, spur, summit, tip, top.

oint-blank *adj* abrupt, blunt, categorical, direct, downright, explicit, express, forthright, plain, plain-spoken, straightforward, unreserved.
adv bluntly, brusquely, candidly, directly, explicitly, forthrightly, frankly, openly, plainly, straight, straightforwardly, unequivocally.

ointed *adj* accurate, acute, barbed, biting, cutting, edged, incisive, keen, penetrating, pertinent, sharp, telling, trenchant.

ointer *n* advice, caution, fingerpost, guide, hand, hint, indication, indicator, information, needle, recommendation, suggestion, tip, warning.

pointless *adj* absurd, aimless, bootless, fruitless, futile, inane, ineffectual, irrelevant, meaningless, nonsensical, profitless, senseless, silly, stupid, unavailing, unbeneficial, unproductive, unprofitable, useless, vague, vain, worthless. **antonyms** meaningful, profitable.

poise *n* aplomb, assurance, calmness, collectedness, composure, cool, coolness, dignity, elegance, equanimity, equilibrium, grace, presence, presence of mind, savoir-faire, self-possession, serenity.
v balance, float, hang, hold, hover, position, support, suspend.

poised *adj* calm, collected, composed, cool, dignified, expectant, graceful, nonchalant, prepared, ready, self-confident, self-possessed, serene, suave, unruffled, urbane, waiting.

poison *n* bane, blight, cancer, canker, contagion, contamination, corruption, malignancy, miasma, toxin, venom, virus.
v adulterate, contaminate, corrupt, defile, deprave, infect, kill, murder, pervert, pollute, subvert, taint, undermine, vitiate, warp.

poisonous *adj* baleful, baneful, corruptive, deadly, evil, fatal, lethal, malicious, mortal, noxious, pernicious, toxic, venomous, vicious, virulent.

poke *v* butt, butt in, dig, elbow, hit, interfere, intrude, jab. meddle, nose, nudge, peek, prod, pry, punch, push, shove, snoop, stab, stick, tamper, thrust.
n butt, dig, dunt, jab, nudge, prod, punch, shove, thrust.

poke fun at chaff, guy, jeer, make fun of, mock, parody, rag, rib, ridicule, send up, spoof, take the mickey, tease.

poky *adj* confined, cramped, crowded, incommodious, narrow, small, tight, tiny. **antonym** spacious.

pole¹ *n* bar, mast, post, rod, shaft, spar, staff, stake, standard, stick.

pole² *n* antipode, extremity, limit, terminus.

poles apart at opposite extremes, incompatible, irreconcilable, like chalk and cheese, like night and day, worlds apart.

polemic *n* argument, controversy, debate, dispute.
adj argumentative, contentious, controversial, disputatious, polemical.

police *n* boys in blue, constabulary, fuzz, gendarmerie, law, (the) Old Bill.
v check, control, defend, guard, keep a check on, keep guard over, keep in order, keep the peace, monitor, observe, oversee, patrol, protect, regulate, stand guard over, supervise, watch.

policeman *n* bluebottle, bobby, bogey, constable, cop, copper, flatfoot, fuzz, garda, gendarme, gumshoe, mountie, officer, peeler, pig, rozzer.

policy *n* action, approach, code, course, custom, discretion, good sense, guideline, line, plan, position, practice, procedure, programme, protocol, prudence, rule, sagacity, scheme, shrewdness, stance, stratagem, theory, wisdom.

polish *v* brighten, brush up, buff, burnish, clean, correct, cultivate, emend, emery, enhance, file, finish, furbish, improve, lustre, perfect, refine, rub, rub up, shine, shine up, slick, slicken, smooth, touch up, wax. **antonyms** dull, tarnish.
n breeding, brightness, brilliance, class, cultivation, elegance, expertise, finesse, finish, glaze, gloss, grace, lustre, perfectionism, politesse, proficiency, refinement, savoir-faire, sheen, smoothness, sophistication, sparkle, style, suavity, urbanity, varnish, veneer, wax. **antonyms** clumsiness, dullness, gaucherie.

polish off bolt, bump off, consume, devour, dispose of, down, eat, eliminate, finish, gobble, kill, liquidate, murder, put away, rub out, shift, stuff, wolf.

polished *adj* accomplished, adept, bright, burnished, civilised, courtly, cultivated, educated, elegant, expert, faultless, fine, finished, flawless, furbished, genteel, glassy, gleaming, glossy, graceful, gracious, impeccable, lustrous, masterly, outstanding, perfected, polite, professional, refined, sheeny, shining, skilful, slippery, smooth, sophisticated, suave, superlative, urbane, well-bred. **antonyms** clumsy, dull, gauche, inexpert, tarnished.

polite *adj* affable, attentive, civil, civilised, complaisant, considerate, cordial, courteous, courtly, cultured, deferential, diplomatic, discreet, elegant, genteel, gentlemanly, gracious, ladylike, mannerly, obliging, polished, refined, respectful, tactful, thoughtful, urbane, well-behaved, well-bred, well-mannered. **antonyms** impolite, uncultivated.

politeness *n* attention, civility, complaisance, considerateness, cordiality, courtesy, courtliness, cultivation, culture, deference, diplomacy, discretion, elegance, gentility, gentlemanliness, grace, graciousness, mannerliness, manners, polish, refinement, respect, respectfulness, tact, thoughtfulness. **antonym** impoliteness.

politic *adj* advantageous, advisable, artful, astute, canny, crafty, cunning, designing, diplomatic, discreet, expedient, ingenious, intriguing, judicious, Machiavellian, opportune, prudent, sagacious, sage, scheming, sensible, shrewd, sly, subtle, tactful, unscrupulous, wise. **antonym** impolitic.

pollute *v* adulterate, befoul, besmirch, canker, contaminate, corrupt, debase, debauch, defile, deprave, desecrate, dirty, dishonour, foul, infect, mar, poison, profane, soil, spoil, stain, sully, taint, violate, vitiate.

pollution *n* adulteration, befouling, contamination, corruption, defilement, desecration, dirtying, foulness, impurity, infection, profanation, stain, taint, uncleanness, violation, vitiation. **antonyms** purification, purity.

pomp *n* ceremonial, ceremoniousness, ceremony, display, éclat, flourish, formality, grandeur, grandiosity, magnificence, ostentation, pageant, pageantry, parade, pomposity, ritual, show, solemnity, splendour, state, vainglory. **antonyms** austerity, simplicity.

pomposity *n* affectation, airs, arrogance, bombast, euphuism, grandiloquence, grandiosity, loftiness, magniloquence, pompousness, pontificating, portentousness, preachiness,

presumption, pretension, pretentiousness, ranting, rhetoric, self-importance, stuffiness, turgidity, vainglory, vanity. **antonyms** economy, simplicity.

pompous *adj* affected, arrogant, bloated, bombastic, euphuistic, grandiloquent, grandiose, high-flown, imperious, inflated, magisterial, magniloquent, ostentatious, overbearing, overblown, pontifical, portentous, pretentious, ranting, self-important, stuffy, supercilious, turgid, vainglorious, windy. **antonyms** economical, modest, simple, unaffected, unassuming.

ponder *v* analyse, brood, cerebrate, cogitate, consider, contemplate, deliberate, examine, excogitate, give thought to, meditate, mull over, muse, puzzle over, reason, reflect, ruminate over, study, think, weigh.

ponderous *adj* awkward, bulky, clumsy, cumbersome, cumbrous, dreary, dull, elephantine, graceless, heavy, heavy-footed, heavy-handed, hefty, huge, humourless, laborious, laboured, lifeless, long-winded, lumbering, massive, pedantic, pedestrian, plodding, portentous, prolix, slow-moving, stilted, stodgy, stolid, tedious, unwieldy, verbose, weighty. **antonyms** delicate, light, simple.

pontifical *adj* apostolic, bloated, condescending, didactic, dogmatic, ecclesiastical, imperious, magisterial, overbearing, papal, pompous, portentous, preachy, pretentious, self-important, sermonising. **antonyms** reticent, unassuming.

pontificate *v* declaim, dogmatise, expound, harangue, hold forth, lay down the law, lecture, moralise, preach, pronounce, sermonise, sound off.

pooh-pooh *v* belittle, brush aside, deride, disdain, dismiss, disparage, disregard, make little of, minimise, play down, reject, ridicule, scoff, scorn, slight, sneer, sniff at, spurn, turn up one's nose at. **antonyms** consider, exaggerate, magnify, regard.

pool¹ *n* dub, lake, leisure pool, mere, pond, puddle, splash, stank, swimming bath, swimming pool, tarn, water-hole, watering-hole.

pool² *n* accumulation, bank, cartel, collective, combine, consortium, funds, group, jackpot, kitty, pot, purse, reserve, ring, stakes, syndicate, team, trust.
v amalgamate, chip in, combine,

contribute, merge, muck in, put together, share.

poor¹ *adj* badly off, bankrupt, beggared, beggarly, broke, deficient, destitute, distressed, embarrassed, exiguous, hard up, impecunious, impoverished, in reduced circumstances, inadequate, indigent, insufficient, lacking, meagre, miserable, moneyless, necessitious, needy, niggardly, on one's beam-ends, on one's uppers, on the rocks, pauperised, penniless, penurious, pinched, pitiable, poverty-stricken, reduced, scanty, skimpy, skint, slight, sparse, stony-broke, straitened, without means, without the wherewithal. *antonyms* affluent, opulent, rich, wealthy.

poor² *adj* bad, bare, barren, below par, depleted, exhausted, faulty, feeble, fruitless, grotty, humble, imperfect, impoverished, inferior, infertile, insignificant, low-grade, lowly, mean, mediocre, modest, paltry, pathetic, pitiful, plain, ropy, rotten, rubbishy, second-rate, shabby, shoddy, sorry, spiritless, sterile, substandard, third-rate, trivial, unfruitful, unimpressive, unproductive, unsatisfactory, valueless, weak, worthless. *antonym* superior.

poor³ *adj* accursed, cursed, forlorn, hapless, ill-fated, luckless, miserable, pathetic, pitiable, star-crossed, unfortunate, unhappy, unlucky, wretched. *antonym* lucky.

poorly *adv* badly, crudely, faultily, feebly, inadequately, incompetently, inexpertly, inferiorly, insufficiently, meanly, rottenly, shabbily, shoddily, unjustly, unsatisfactorily, unsuccessfully. *antonym* well.
adj ailing, below par, dicky, frail, groggy, ill, indisposed, off colour, out of sorts, rotten, seedy, shaky, sick, sickly, under the weather, unhealthy, unwell. *antonyms* healthy, robust, well.

pop *v* appear, bang, bulge, burst, call, come, crack, drop, drop in, explode, go, go bang, go off, go phut, insert, jump, nip, protrude, push, put, report, shove, slide, slip, snap, spring, step, stick, thrust, tuck, visit.
n bang, burst, crack, explosion, noise, report, snap.

poppycock *n* babble, balderdash, balls, baloney, bullshit, bunk, bunkum, drivel, eyewash, gibberish, gobbledegook, guff, hooey, nonsense, rot, rubbish, tommyrot, tosh, trash, twaddle. *antonym* sense.

populace *n* common herd, commonalty, crowd, general public, hoi polloi, inhabitants, masses, mob, multitude, people, plebs, proletariat, public, punters, rabble, rank and file, throng. *antonyms* aristocracy, élite, nobility.

popular *adj* accepted, approved, celebrated, common, conventional, current, democratic, demotic, famous, fashionable, favoured, favourite, fêted, general, hip, household, idolised, in, in demand, in favour, liked, lionised, modish, overpopular, overused, prevailing, prevalent, public, sought-after, standard, stock, trite, universal, vernacular, vulgar, well-liked, widespread. *antonyms* exclusive, unpopular, unusual.

popularise *v* debase, democratise, disseminate, familiarise, give currency to, propagate, simplify, spread, universalise, vulgarise. *antonym* discredit.

popularity *n* acceptance, acclaim, adoration, adulation, approbation, approval, celebrity, currency, esteem, fame, favour, glory, idolisation, kudos, lionisation, mass appeal, recognition, regard, renown, reputation, repute, vogue, worship. *antonym* unpopularity.

popularly *adv* commonly, conventionally, customarily, generally, in the vernacular, ordinarily, regularly, traditionally, universally, usually, vulgarly, widely.

populate *v* colonise, establish oneself in, habit, inhabit, live in, occupy, overrun, people, put down roots in, settle.

population *n* citizenry, citizens, community, folk, inhabitants, natives, occupants, people, populace, residents, society.

populous *adj* crawling, crowded, frequented, overpeopled, overpopulated, packed, swarming, teeming, thickly populated, thronged. *antonyms* deserted, unfrequented.

pore *v* brood, con, contemplate, devour, dwell on, examine, go over, peruse, ponder, read, scan, scrutinise, study.

pornographic *adj* bawdy, blue, coarse, dirty, filthy, girlie, gross, indecent, lewd, nudie, obscene, off-colour, offensive, porn, porno, prurient, risqué, salacious, smutty. *antonyms* innocent, inoffensive.

pornography *n* bawdiness, dirt, erotica, filth, grossness, indecency, obscenity, porn, porno, sexploitation, smut.

porous *adj* absorbent, absorptive, cellular, honeycombed, penetrable, permeable, pervious, pitted, sponge-like, spongy. *antonyms* impermeable, impervious.

portable *adj* compact, handy, light, lightweight, manageable, movable, portative, transportable. *antonyms* fixed, immovable.

portend *v* adumbrate, announce, augur, bespeak, betoken, bode, forebode, forecast, foreshadow, foretell, foretoken, forewarn, harbinger, herald, indicate, omen, point to, predict, presage, prognosticate, promise, signify, threaten, warn of.

portent *n* augury, foreboding, forecast, forerunner, foreshadowing, forewarning, harbinger, indication, omen, precursor, prefiguration, premonition, presage, presentiment, prognostic, prognostication, sign, signification, threat, warning.

portentous *adj* alarming, amazing, astounding, awe-inspiring, bloated, charged, consequential, crucial, earth-shaking, epoch-making, extraordinary, fateful, heavy, important, menacing, minatory, miraculous, momentous, ominous, phenomenal, pompous, ponderous, pontifical, pregnant, prodigious, remarkable, significant, sinister, solemn, threatening. *antonyms* insignificant, unimportant, unimpressive.

portion *n* allocation, allotment, allowance, assignment, bit, cup, destiny, division, fate, fortune, fraction, fragment, helping, kismet, lot, luck, measure, moiety, morsel, parcel, part, piece, quantity, quota, rake-off, ration, scrap, section, segment, serving, share, slice, something, tranche, whack.
v allocate, allot, apportion, assign, carve up, deal, distribute, divide, divvy up, dole, parcel, partion, partition, share out, slice up.

portliness *n* ampleness, beefiness, chubbiness, corpulence, dumpiness, fleshiness, fullness, heaviness, obesity, paunchiness, plumpness, rotundity, roundness, stoutness, tubbiness.

portly *adj* ample, beefy, bulky, chubby, corpulent, dumpy, fat, fleshy, full, heavy, large, obese, overweight, paunchy, plump, rotund, round, stout, tubby. *antonyms* slight, slim.

portrait *n* account, caricature, characterisation, depiction, description, icon, image, likeness, miniature, mug shot, painting, photograph, picture, portraiture, portrayal, profile, representation, sketch, vignette.

portray *v* act, capture, characterise, depict, describe, draw, emblazon, encapsulate, evoke, figure, illustrate, impersonate, paint, personify, picture, play, present, render, represent, sketch, suggest.

portrayal *n* characterisation, depiction, description, evocation, impersonation, interpretation, performance, picture, presentation, rendering, representation, sketch.

pose *v* advance, affect, arrange, assert, attitudinise, claim, feign, impersonate, masquerade, model, pass oneself off, place, posit, position, posture, present, pretend, profess to be, propound, put, put forward, put on an act, set, sham, sit, state, strike an attitude, submit.
n act, affectation, air, attitude, bearing, con, façade, front, mark, masquerade, position, posture, pretence, role, sham, stance, take-in.

poser *n* brain-teaser, chinese puzzle, conundrum, enigma, mystery, problem, puzzle, question, riddle, vexed question.

posh *adj* classy, de-luxe, elegant, exclusive, fashionable, grand, high-class, lavish, luxurious, luxury, opulent, plummy, ritzy, select, smart, stylish, sumptuous, swanky, swell, swish, up-market, upper-class. *antonyms* cheap, inferior.

posit *v* advance, assert, assume, pose, postulate, predicate, presume, propound, put forward, state, submit.

position *n* angle, area, arrangement, attitude, bearings, belief, berth, billet, capacity, character, circumstances, condition, deployment, disposition, duty, employment, function, grade, importance, job, level, locale, locality, location, niche, occupation, office, opinion, outlook, pass, perspective, pinch, place, placement, placing, plight, point, point of view, pose, positioning, post, posture, predicament, prestige, rank, reference, reputation, role, set, setting, site, situation, slant, slot, spot, stance, stand, standing, standpoint, state, station, stature, status, view, viewpoint, whereabouts.
v arrange, array, deploy, dispose, fix, lay out, locate, place, pose, put, range, set, settle, stand, stick.

positive *adj* absolute, actual, affirmative, arrant, assertive, assured, authoritative, beneficial, categorical, certain, clear, clear-cut, complete, conclusive, concrete, confident, constructive, consummate, convinced, decided, decisive, definite, direct, dogmatic, downright, effective, efficacious, emphatic, explicit, express, firm, forceful, forward-looking, helpful, hopeful, incontestable, incontrovertible, indisputable, irrefragable, irrefutable, open-and-shut, opinionated, optimistic, out-and-out, peremptory, perfect, practical, productive, progressive, promising, real, realistic, resolute, secure, self-evident, sheer, stubborn, sure, thorough, thoroughgoing, uncompromising, undeniable, unequivocal, unmistakable, unmitigated, unquestioning, useful, utter. *antonyms* indecisive, indefinite, negative, uncertain.

positively *adv* absolutely, assuredly, authoritatively, categorically, certainly, conclusively, constructively, decisively, definitely, dogmatically, emphatically, expressly, finally, firmly, incontestably, incontrovertibly, indisputably, surely, uncompromisingly, undeniably, unequivocally, unmistakably, unquestionably.

possess *v* acquire, be endowed with, control, dominate, enjoy, have, hold, obtain, occupy, own, possess oneself of, seize, take, take over, take possession of.

possessed *adj* bedevilled, berserk, besotted, bewitched, consumed, crazed, cursed, demented, dominated, enchanted, frenzied, hag-ridden, haunted, infatuated, maddened, mesmerised, obsessed, raving.

possession *n* colony, control, custody, dependency, dominion, enjoyment, hold, mandate, occupancy, occupation, ownership, proprietorship, protectorate, province, tenure, territory, title.

possessions *n* assets, belongings, chattels, effects, estate, goods, goods and chattels, junk, movables, paraphernalia, property, riches, stuff, things, traps, wealth, worldly wealth.

possessive *adj* acquisitive, clinging, covetous, dominating, domineering, grasping, jealous, overprotective, proprietorial, selfish. *antonyms* generous, sharing, unassertive.

possibilities *n* advantages, capabilities, expectations, potential, potentiality, promise, prospects, talent. *antonyms* disadvantages, liabilities.

possibility *n* achievability, chance, conceivability, feasibility, hazard, hope, liability, likelihood, odds, plausibility, potentiality, practicability, probability, prospect, realisability, risk, workableness. *antonym* impossibility.

possible *adj* accomplishable, achievable, alternative, attainable, available, conceivable, credible, doable, feasible, hopeful, hypothetical, imaginable, likely, on, potential, practicable, probable, promising, realisable, tenable, viable, workable. *antonym* impossible.

possibly *adv* at all, by any chance, by any means, God willing, happen, hopefully, in any way, maybe, perchance, perhaps, very like(ly).

post[1] *v* advertise, affix, announce, denounce, display, make known, placard, proclaim, promulgate, publicise, publish, report, stick up.

post[2] *n* appointment, assignment, beat, berth, billet, employment, incumbency, job, office, place, position, situation, station, vacancy.

v appoint, assign, establish, locate, move, place, position, put, second, send, shift, situate, station, transfer.

post[3] *n* collection, delivery, dispatch, mail, postal service, uplifting.

v acquaint, advise, apprise, brief, dispatch, fill in on, inform, keep posted, mail, notify, report to, send, transmit.

posterior *adj* after, back, behind, dorsal, ensuing, following, hind, hinder, later, latter, rear, rearward, subsequent, succeeding. *antonyms* anterior, front, previous.

n backside, behind, bottom, bum, buttocks, haunches, hinder end, hindquarters, rear, rump, seat, tail.

posterity *n* children, descendants, family, future, heirs, issue, offspring, progeny, seed, successors. *antonyms* ancestors, antiquity, forebears, past.

posthaste *adv* at once, directly, double-quick, full tilt, hastily, immediately, promptly, pronto, quickly, speedily, straightaway, swiftly, with all speed. *antonyms* eventually, gradually, slowly.

postmortem *n* analysis, autopsy, examination, review.

postpone *v* adjourn, defer, delay, freeze, hold over, put back, put off, put on ice, shelve, suspend, table. *antonyms* advance, forward.

postponed *adj* adjourned, deferred, frozen, in abeyance, on ice, shelved, suspended. *antonym* advanced.

postponement *n* adjournment, deferment, deferral, delay, freeze, moratorium, put-off, respite, stay, suspension.

postulate v advance, assume, hypothesise, lay down, posit, predicate, presuppose, propose, stipulate, suppose, take for granted, theorise.

posture n attitude, bearing, carriage, disposition, pose, position, set, stance.
v affect, attitudinise, ponce, pose, put on airs, show off, strike attitudes, strut.

pot n basin, beaker, bowl, coffee-pot, crock, crucible, flask, jar, pan, planter, receptacle, samovar, teapot, urn, vase, vessel.

potency n authority, capacity, cogency, control, effectiveness, efficaciousness, efficacy, energy, force, headiness, influence, kick, might, muscle, persuasiveness, potential, power, puissance, punch, strength, sway, vigour. **antonyms** impotence, weakness.

potent adj authoritative, cogent, commanding, compelling, convincing, dominant, dynamic, effective, efficacious, eloquent, forceful, formidable, heady, impressive, influential, intoxicating, mighty, moving, persuasive, powerful, puissant, pungent, strong, telling, vigorous, weighty. **antonyms** impotent, weak.

potential adj budding, concealed, conceivable, dormant, embryonic, future, hidden, imaginable, in embryo, in posse, inherent, latent, likely, possible, probable, promising, prospective, undeveloped, unrealised.
n ability, aptitude, capability, capacity, flair, possibility, potentiality, power, talent, the makings, what it takes, wherewithal.

potentiality n ability, aptitude, capability, capacity, likelihood, possibilities, potential, promise, prospect, virtuality.

potion n beverage, brew, concoction, cup, dose, draught, drink, elixir, medicine, mixture, philtre, potation, tonic.

pot-pourri n collection, combination, hotchpotch, jumble, medley, mélange, miscellany, mixture, motley, patchwork, salad.

potter v dabble, dodder, fiddle, fidget, footle, fritter, mess about, mooch, moon, tinker.

potty adj bananas, barmy, bonkers, crackers, crazy, daft, demented, dippy, dotty, eccentric, foolish, insignificant, nuts, nutty, petty, piddling, silly, soft, touched, trifling, trivial.

pounce v ambush, attack, dash at, dive

on, drop, fall upon, grab, jump, leap a lunge at, snatch, spring, strike, swoop.
n assault, attack, bound, dive, gra jump, leap, lunge, spring, swoop.

pound v bang, bash, baste, batte beat, belabour, bray, bruise, clobbe clomp, clump, comminute, crush, drun hammer, march, palpitate, pelt, powde pulsate, pulse, pulverise, pumme smash, stomp, strike, strum, thrasl throb, thrum, thud, thump, thunde tramp, triturate.

pour v bucket, cascade, course, crowc decant, effuse, emit, exude, flow, gush rain, rain cats and dogs, run, rush, shee spew, spill, spout, stream, swarm, teen throng, tumble.

pour out decant, discharge, disgorge embogue, emit, issue, lave, spew forth.

pout v glower, grimace, lower, mope pull a face, scowl, sulk. **antonym** grin, smile.
n glower, grimace, long face, scowl. **antonyms** grin, smile.

poverty n aridity, bareness, barrennes beggary, dearth, deficiency, depletion destitution, distress, exhaustior hardship, ill-being, impoverishment inadequacy, indigence, infertility insolvency, insufficiency, lack meagreness, necessitousness, necessity need, paucity, pauperism, pennilessness penury, poorness, privation, proletarian ism, scarcity, shortage, sterility, thinness unfruitfulness, want. **antonyms** affluence, fertility, fruitfulness, riches richness.

poverty-stricken adj bankrupt beggared, broke, destitute, distressed impecunious, impoverished, indigent necessitous, needy, on one's beam-ends, on one's uppers, penniless penurious, poor, skint, stony, stony-broke, strapped. **antonyms** affluent, rich.

powdery adj chalky, crumbling crumbly, dry, dusty, fine, grainy granular, loose, powder, pulverised sandy.

power n ability, ascendancy, autarchy, authorisation, authority, brawn, capability, capacity, clout, clutches, command, competence, competency, control, dominance, domination, dominion, efficiency, energy, faculty, force, forcefulness, hegemony, influence, intensity, juice, licence, mana, mastery, might, muscle, omnipotence, plenipotence, potency, potential, prerogative, privilege, right, rule, sovereignty, strength, supremacy, sway, teeth, vigour, virtue, voltage, vroom, warrant, weight.

powerful *adj* ascendant, authoritative, cogent, commanding, compelling, controlling, convincing, dominant, effective, effectual, energetic, forceful, forcible, impressive, influential, leading, masterful, mighty, muscular, omnipotent, persuasive, plutocratic, potent, pre-eminent, prevailing, robust, souped-up, sovereign, stalwart, strapping, strong, sturdy, supreme, telling, vigorous, weighty, winning. *antonyms* impotent, ineffective, weak.

powerfully *adv* cogently, convincingly, forcefully, forcibly, hard, impressively, mightily, persuasively, potently, strongly, tellingly, vigorously, with might and main.

powerless *adj* debilitated, defenceless, dependent, disabled, effete, feeble, frail, helpless, impotent, incapable, incapacitated, ineffective, ineffectual, inefficacious, inerm, infirm, nerveless, paralysed, prostrate, subject, tied, unarmed, vulnerable, weak, weak-headed. *antonyms* commanding, potent, powerful.

practicability *n* feasibility, handiness, operability, possibility, practicality, use, usefulness, utility, value, viability, workability, workableness. *antonym* impracticability.

practicable *adj* accomplishable, achievable, attainable, doable, effectible, feasible, negotiable, passable, performable, possible, viable, workable. *antonym* impracticable.

practical *adj* accomplished, active, applicative, applied, businesslike, commonsense, commonsensical, down-to-earth, efficient, empirical, everyday, expedient, experienced, experimental, factual, feasible, functional, hands-on, hard-headed, hard-nosed, material, matter-of-fact, mundane, nuts-and-bolts, ordinary, practicable, pragmatic, proficient, qualified, realistic, seasoned, sensible, serviceable, skilled, sound, trained, unsentimental, useful, utilitarian, workable, workaday, working. *antonym* impractical.

practicality *n* basics, common sense, experience, feasibility, nitty-gritty, nuts and bolts, practicability, practicalities, practicalness, practice, pragmatism, realism, sense, serviceability, soundness, usefulness, utility, workability.

practically[1] *adv* actually, all but, almost, essentially, fundamentally, in effect, in practice, in principle, just about, nearly, not quite, pretty nearly, pretty well, very nearly, virtually, well-nigh.

practically[2] *adv* clearly, from a commonsense angle, matter-of-factly, rationally, realistically, reasonably, sensibly, unsentimentally.

practice *n* action, application, business, career, clientèle, convention, custom, discipline, drill, dry run, dummy run, effect, exercise, experience, habit, ism, method, mode, modus operandi, operation, patronage, performance, policy, practic, practicalities, practicum, praxis, preparation, procedure, profession, rehearsal, repetition, routine, rule, run-through, study, system, tradition, training, usage, use, vocation, way, wont, work, work-out.

practise *v* apply, carry out, discipline, do, drill, enact, engage in, execute, exercise, follow, implement, live up to, observe, perfect, perform, ply, prepare, pursue, put into practice, rehearse, repeat, run through, study, train, undertake, warm up.

practised *adj* able, accomplished, consummate, experienced, expert, finished, highly-developed, knowing, knowledgeable, perfected, proficient, qualified, refined, seasoned, skilled, trained, versed, veteran, well-trained. *antonyms* inexpert, unpractised.

pragmatic *adj* businesslike, efficient, factual, hard-headed, opportunistic, practical, realistic, sensible, unidealistic, unsentimental, utilitarian. *antonyms* idealistic, romantic, unrealistic.

pragmatism *n* hard-headedness, humanism, opportunism, practicalism, practicality, realism, unidealism, utilitarianism. *antonyms* idealism, romanticism.

pragmatist *n* humanist, opportunist, practicalist, realist, utilitarian. *antonyms* idealist, romantic.

praise *n* acclaim, acclamation, accolade, acknowledgement, adoration, adulation, applause, approbation, approval, bouquet, cheering, commendation, compliment, compliments, congratulation, devotion, encomium, eulogy, extolment, flattery, glory, homage, honour, kudos, laud, laudation, ovation, plaudit, rave, recognition, testimonial, thanks, thanksgiving, tribute, worship. *antonyms* criticism, revilement.

v acclaim, acknowledge, admire, adore, applaud, approve, belaud, bless, celebrate, cheer, compliment, congratulate, cry up, eulogise, exalt, extol, flatter, give thanks to, glorify, hail, honour, laud, magnify, pay tribute to, promote, rave over, recognise, tout, wax lyrical, worship. *antonyms* criticise, revile.

praiseworthy *adj* admirable, commendable, creditable, deserving, estimable, excellent, exemplary, fine, honourable, laudable, meritorious, reputable, sterling, worthy. *antonyms* discreditable, dishonourable, ignoble.

praising *adj* adulatory, approbatory, approving, commendatory, complimentary, congratulatory, eulogistic, favourable, flattering, laudative, laudatory, plauditory, promotional, recommendatory, worshipful. *antonyms* condemnatory, critical.

prance *v* bound, caper, cavort, dance, frisk, frolic, gambol, jump, leap, parade, romp, show off, skip, spring, stalk, strut, swagger, swank, vault.

prank *n* antic, caper, escapade, frolic, jape, joke, lark, piece of mischief, practical joke, stunt, trick.

prattle *v* babble, blether, chat, chatter, clack, drivel, gabble, gossip, jabber, rattle, twitter, witter.
n blethers, chat, chatter, clack, drivel, foolishness, gab, gibberish, gossip, haverings, hot air, jaw, nonsense, prating, talk, tattle.

pray *v* adjure, ask, beg, beseech, call on, crave, entreat, implore, importune, invoke, obsecrate, petition, plead, press, request, solicit, sue, supplicate, urge.

prayer *n* appeal, collect, communion, devotion, entreaty, invocation, litany, petition, plea, request, solicitation, suit, supplication.

preach *v* address, admonish, advocate, ethicise, evangelise, harangue, lecture, moralise, orate, pontificate, sermonise.

preacher *n* clergyman, evangelist, minister, missionary, moraliser, parson, pontificater, pulpite(e)r, sermoniser.

preaching *n* doctrine, dogma, evangelism, exhortation, gospel, instruction, message, pontificating, precepts, sermonising, sermons, teaching.

preamble *n* foreword, introduction, lead-in, overture, preface, preliminaries, prelude, preparation, prologue. *antonyms* epilogue, postscript.

precarious *adj* chancy, dangerous, delicate, dicey, dodgy, doubtful, dubious, hairy, hazardous, iffy, insecure, perilous, problematic, risky, shaky, slippery, ticklish, tricky, uncertain, unpredictable, unreliable, unsafe, unsettled, unstable, unsteady, unsure, vulnerable. *antonyms* certain, safe, secure.

precaution *n* anticipation, backstop, buffer, care, caution, circumspection, foresight, forethought, insurance, preparation, prophylaxis, protection, providence, provision, prudence, safeguard, safety measure, security, surety, wariness.

precede *v* antecede, antedate, anticipate, come first, forerun, front, go before, head, herald, introduce, lead, preface, prefix, prelude, premise, take precedence. *antonym* follow.

precedence *n* antecedence, first place, lead, pre-eminence, preference, pride of place, primacy, priority, rank, seniority, superiority, supremacy.

precedent *n* antecedent, authority, citation, criterion, example, exemplar, guideline, instance, judgement, model, paradigm, past instance, pattern, prototype, ruling, standard, yardstick.

preceding *adj* above, aforementioned, aforesaid, antecedent, anterior, earlier, foregoing, former, past, precedent, precursive, previous, prior. *antonyms* following, later.

precept *n* axiom, behest, bidding, byword, canon, charge, command, commandment, convention, decree, dictum, direction, directive, guideline, injunction, institute, instruction, law, mandate, maxim, motto, order, ordinance, principle, regulation, rubric, rule, saying, sentence, statute.

precious *adj* adored, affected, artificial, arty-farty, beloved, cherished, chichi, choice, costly, darling, dear, dearest, expensive, exquisite, fastidious, favourite, fine, flowery, idolised, inestimable, invaluable, irreplaceable, loved, namby-pamby, overnice, over-refined, priceless, prized, rare, treasured, twee, valuable, valued.

precipitate *v* accelerate, advance, bring on, cause, discharge, drive, expedite, further, hasten, hurry, induce, occasion, press, quicken, speed, trigger.
adj abrupt, breakneck, brief, frantic, hasty, headlong, heedless, hot-headed, hurried, impatient, impetuous, impulsive, incautious, indiscreet,

madcap, pell-mell, plunging, precipitous, quick, rapid, rash, reckless, rushing, sudden, swift, unannounced, unexpected, violent. **antonym** cautious.

precipitous *adj* abrupt, dizzy, giddy, high, perpendicular, sheer, steep, vertiginous. **antonyms** gradual, sloping.

précis *n* abbreviation, abridgement, abstract, compendium, condensation, contraction, digest, encapsulation, epitome, outline, résumé, run-down, sketch, summary, synopsis, table.
v abbreviate, abridge, abstract, compress, condense, contract, digest, encapsulate, outline, shorten, sum up, summarise, synopsise. **antonyms** amplify, expand.

precise *adj* absolute, accurate, actual, authentic, blow-by-blow, careful, ceremonious, clear-cut, correct, definite, determinate, distinct, exact, explicit, express, factual, faithful, fastidious, finicky, fixed, formal, identical, literal, meticulous, minute, nice, particular, prim, punctilious, puritanical, rigid, scrupulous, specific, strict, succinct, unequivocal, verbatim, word-for-word. **antonym** imprecise.

precisely *adv* absolutely, accurately, bang, blow by blow, correctly, dead, distinctly, exactly, just, just so, literally, minutely, plumb, slap, smack, square, squarely, strictly, verbatim, word for word.

precision *n* accuracy, care, correctness, definiteness, detail, exactitude, exactness, explicitness, expressness, faithfulness, fastidiousness, fidelity, meticulousness, minuteness, neatness, niceness, nicety, particularity, preciseness, punctiliousness, rigour, scrupulosity, specificity. **antonym** imprecision.

preclude *v* avoid, check, debar, eliminate, exclude, forestall, hinder, inhibit, obviate, prevent, prohibit, restrain, rule out, stop. **antonyms** incur, involve.

precocious *adj* advanced, ahead, bright, clever, developed, fast, forward, gifted, mature, premature, quick, smart. **antonym** backward.

preconceive *v* anticipate, assume, conceive, conceptualise, envisage, imagine, picture, presume, presuppose, project, visualise.

preconception *n* anticipation, assumption, bias, conjecture, notion, predisposition, prejudice, prenotion, prepossession, presumption, presupposition.

precondition *n* essential, must, necessity, need, prerequisite, proviso, requirement, requisite, sine qua non, stipulation.

precursor *n* antecedent, forebear, forerunner, harbinger, herald, indication, messenger, originator, pathfinder, pioneer, predecessor, sign, trail-blazer, usher, vanguard, warning. **antonyms** after-effect, aftermath.

precursory *adj* antecedent, anterior, introductory, preambulatory, preceding, prefatory, preliminary, premonitory, preparatory, previous, prior, warning. **antonyms** following, resulting, subsequent.

predatory *adj* acquisitive, avaricious, carnivorous, covetous, despoiling, greedy, hunting, marauding, pillaging, plundering, predacious, predative, preying, rapacious, ravaging, ravening, thieving, voracious.

predecessor *n* ancestor, antecedent, forebear, forefather, forerunner, precursor. **antonyms** descendant, successor.

predestine *v* destine, doom, fate, foredoom, foreordain, intend, mean, predetermine, pre-elect, preordain.

predetermined *adj* agreed, cut and dried, decided beforehand, deliberate, fixed, foregone, foreordained, prearranged, preordained, preplanned, set, set up, settled.

predicament *n* can of worms, corner, crisis, dilemma, embarrassment, emergency, fix, hole, hot water, impasse, jam, mess, pickle, pinch, plight, quandary, scrape, situation, spot, state, trouble.

predicate *v* affirm, assert, aver, avouch, avow, base, build, contend, declare, establish, found, ground, maintain, posit, postulate, premise, proclaim, rest, state.

predict *v* augur, divine, forebode, forecast, foresay, foresee, foreshow, forespeak, foretell, portend, presage, prognosticate, project, prophesy, second-guess, soothsay.

predictable *adj* anticipated, calculable, certain, dependable, determinate, expected, finite, foregone, foreseeable, foreseen, imaginable, likely, presumable, probable, reliable, sure. **antonym** unpredictable.

prediction *n* augury, divination, forecast, fortune-telling, prognosis, prognostication, prophecy, second sight, soothsaying.

predilection n affection, affinity, bent, bias, enthusiasm, fancy, fondness, inclination, leaning, liking, love, partiality, penchant, predisposition, preference, proclivity, proneness, propensity, soft spot, taste, tendency, weakness. *antonyms* antipathy, disinclination.

predispose v affect, bias, dispose, head, incline, induce, influence, lead, lean, make, make liable, prejudice, prepare, prime, prompt, sway.

predisposed adj agreeable, amenable, biased, disposed, favourable, inclined, liable, minded, not unwilling, prejudiced, prepared, ready, subject, susceptible, well-disposed, willing.

predisposition n bent, bias, disposition, inclination, leaning, liability, likelihood, mind, penchant, potentiality, predilection, preference, prejudice, proclivity, proneness, propensity, susceptibility, tendency, vulnerability, willingness.

predominance n ascendancy, control, dominance, dominion, edge, hegemony, hold, influence, leadership, mastery, numbers, power, preponderance, prevalence, superiority, supremacy, sway, upper hand, weight. *antonyms* ineffectiveness, weakness.

predominant adj ascendant, capital, chief, controlling, dominant, forceful, important, influential, leading, main, paramount, potent, powerful, preponderant, prevailing, prevalent, primary, prime, principal, prominent, ruling, sovereign, strong, superior, supreme. *antonyms* ineffective, lesser, minor, weak.

predominate v dominate, obtain, outnumber, outweigh, override, overrule, overshadow, preponderate, prevail, reign, rule, tell, transcend.

pre-eminence n distinction, excellence, fame, incomparability, matchlessness, peerlessness, predominance, prestige, prominence, renown, repute, superiority, supremacy.

pre-eminent adj chief, consummate, distinguished, excellent, exceptional, foremost, incomparable, inimitable, leading, matchless, outstanding, paramount, passing, peerless, predominant, prominent, renowned, superior, superlative, supreme, surpassing, unequalled, unmatched, unrivalled, unsurpassed. *antonyms* undistinguished, unknown.

pre-eminently adv conspicuously, eminently, emphatically, especially, exceptionally, exclusively, incomparably, inimitably, matchlessly, notably, par excellence, particularly, peerlessly, signally, singularly, strikingly, superlatively, supremely, surpassingly.

pre-empt v acquire, anticipate, appropriate, arrogate, assume, bag, forestall, secure, seize, usurp.

preen v adorn, array, beautify, clean, deck, do up, doll up, dress up, fig out, groom, plume, prank, prettify, primp, slick, spruce up, tart up, titivate, trick out, trim.

preen (oneself) bask, congratulate, exult, gloat, pride.

preface n foreword, intro, introduction, preamble, preliminaries, prelims, prelude, prologue. *antonyms* afterthought, epilogue, postscript.

v begin, introduce, launch, lead up to, open, precede, prefix, prelude, premise, start. *antonyms* append, complete, finish.

prefatory adj antecedent, explanatory, introductory, opening, preambulatory, precursory, preliminary, preparatory. *antonyms* closing, final.

prefer v adopt, advocate, back, be partial to, choose, desire, elect, endorse, fancy, favour, go for, incline towards, like better, opt for, pick, plump for, recommend, select, single out, support, want, wish, would rather, would sooner. *antonym* reject.

preferable adj advantageous, advisable, best, better, choice, chosen, desirable, eligible, expedient, favoured, nicer, preferred, stronger, superior, worthier. *antonyms* ineligible, inferior, undesirable.

preferably adv first, for choice, for preference, rather, sooner.

preference¹ n choice, desire, election, fancy, favourite, first choice, inclination, liking, option, partiality, pick, predilection, selection, wish.

preference² n advantage, favour, favouritism, precedence, preferential treatment, priority, special consideration, special treatment.

preferential adj advantageous, better, biased, favourable, favoured, partial, partisan, prior, privileged, special, superior. *antonym* equal.

preferred adj approved, authorised, choice, chosen, desired, favoured, recommended, sanctioned, selected. *antonyms* rejected, undesirable.

pregnant[1] *adj* big, big-bellied, expectant, expecting, gravid, impregnated, in an interesting condition, in the club, in the family way, in the pudding club, preggers, teeming, with child.

pregnant[2] *adj* charged, eloquent, expressive, full, heavy, loaded, meaning, meaningful, ominous, pithy, pointed, significant, suggestive, telling, weighty.

prehistoric *adj* ancient, antediluvian, antiquated, archaic, earliest, early, hoary, obsolete, old, outmoded, out-of-date, primeval, primitive, primordial. *antonym* modern.

prejudge *v* anticipate, assume, forejudge, judge prematurely, predetermine, prejudicate, presume, presuppose.

prejudice[1] *n* bias, bigotry, chauvinism, discrimination, injustice, intolerance, narrow-mindedness, partiality, partisanship, preconception, prejudgement, racism, sexism, unfairness, warp. *antonyms* fairness, tolerance.
v bias, colour, condition, distort, incline, indoctrinate, influence, jaundice, load, poison, predispose, prepossess, slant, sway, warp, weight.

prejudice[2] *n* damage, detriment, disadvantage, harm, hurt, impairment, injury, loss, mischief, ruin, vitiation, wreck. *antonyms* advantage, benefit.
v damage, harm, hinder, hurt, impair, injure, mar, ruin, spoil, undermine, vitiate, wreck. *antonyms* advance, benefit, help.

prejudiced *adj* biased, bigoted, chauvinist, conditioned, discriminatory, distorted, ex parte, illiberal, influenced, intolerant, jaundiced, loaded, narrow-minded, one-sided, opinionated, partial, partisan, prepossessed, racist, sexist, subjective, unenlightened, unfair, warped, weighted. *antonyms* fair, tolerant.

prejudicial *adj* counter-productive, damaging, deleterious, detrimental, disadvantageous, harmful, hostile, hurtful, inimical, injurious, mischievous, noxious, pernicious, ruinous, undermining, unfavourable. *antonyms* advantageous, beneficial.

preliminaries *n* basics, beginning, first round, formalities, foundations, groundwork, initiation, introduction, opening, preamble, preface, prelims, prelude, preparation, rudiments, start.

preliminary *adj* earliest, early, embryonic, experimental, exploratory,

first, inaugural, initial, initiatory, introductory, opening, pilot, precursory, preparatory, primary, prior, qualifying, test, trial. *antonyms* closing, final.

prelude *n* beginning, commencement, curtain-raiser, foreword, introduction, intro, opener, overture, preamble, precursor, preface, preliminary, preparation, prologue, start, taster. *antonyms* aftermath, epilogue, postscript.

premature *adj* abortive, early, embryonic, forward, green, half-formed, hasty, ill-considered, ill-timed, immature, imperfect, impulsive, incomplete, inopportune, overhasty, precipitate, precocious, preterm, previous, rash, raw, undeveloped, unfledged, unripe, unseasonable, untimely. *antonyms* late, tardy.

premeditated *adj* aforethought, calculated, cold-blooded, conscious, considered, contrived, deliberate, intended, intentional, planned, plotted, prearranged, predetermined, preplanned, studied, wilful. *antonyms* spontaneous, unpremeditated.

premeditation *n* deliberateness, deliberation, design, determination, forethought, intention, malice aforethought, planning, plotting, prearrangement, predetermination, purpose, scheming. *antonyms* impulse, spontaneity.

premise *v* assert, assume, hypothesise, lay down, posit, postulate, predicate, presuppose, state, stipulate, take as true.
n argument, assertion, assumption, ground, hypothesis, postulation, predication, presupposition, proposition, statement, stipulation, supposition, thesis.

premonition *n* anxiety, apprehension, fear, feeling, foreboding, forewarning, hunch, idea, intuition, misgiving, niggle, omen, portent, presage, presentiment, sign, suspicion, unease, uneasiness, warning, worry.

preoccupation *n* absence of mind, absent-mindedness, absorption, abstraction, concern, daydreaming, distraction, engrossment, enthusiasm, fixation, hang-up, hobby-horse, idée fixe, immersion, inattention, inattentiveness, musing, oblivion, obliviousness, obsession, pensiveness, raptness, reverie, wool-gathering.

preoccupied *adj* absent-minded, absorbed, abstracted, daydreaming, distracted, distrait, engrossed, faraway, fixated, heedless, immersed, intent, oblivious, obsessed, pensive, rapt, taken up, unaware, visited, wrapped up.

preordain v destine, doom, fate, foreordain, prearrange, predestine, predetermine.

preparation n alertness, anticipation, arrangement, assignment, basics, development, expectation, foresight, foundation, groundwork, homework, imposition, lesson, measure, plan, precaution, preliminaries, prep, preparedness, provision, readiness, revision, rudiments, safeguard, schoolwork, study, task.

preparatory adj basic, elementary, fundamental, initial, introductory, opening, preliminary, preparative, primary, rudimentary.

preparatory to before, in advance of, in anticipation of, in expectation of, previous to, prior to.

prepare v adapt, adjust, anticipate, arrange, assemble, brace, brief, coach, compose, concoct, confect, construct, contrive, develop, devise, dispose, do one's homework, draft, draw up, dress, equip, fashion, fit, fit out, fix up, forearm, form, format, fortify, furnish, get up, gird, groom, instruct, limber up, make, make ready, outfit, plan, practise, predispose, prime, produce, provide, psych up, ready, rehearse, rig out, steel, strengthen, supply, train, trim, warm up.

prepare oneself brace oneself, fortify oneself, get psyched up, gird oneself, limber up, psych oneself up, ready oneself, steel oneself.

prepared adj able, arranged, briefed, disposed, expectant, fit, forearmed, inclined, minded, planned, predisposed, primed, psyched up, ready, set, waiting, well-rehearsed, willing, word-perfect. **antonyms** unprepared, unready.

preparedness n alertness, anticipation, expectancy, fitness, order, preparation, readiness. **antonym** unreadiness.

preponderance n ascendancy, bulk, dominance, domination, dominion, extensiveness, force, lion's share, majority, mass, power, predominance, prevalence, superiority, supremacy, sway, weight.

preponderant adj ascendant, controlling, dominant, extensive, foremost, greater, important, larger, overriding, overruling, paramount, predominant, prevailing, prevalent, significant, superior.

preponderate v dominate, outnumber, override, overrule, predominate, prevail, rule, tell, turn the balance, turn the scale, weigh with.

prepossessing adj alluring, amiable, appealing, attractive, beautiful, bewitching, captivating, charming, delightful, disarming, enchanting, engaging, fair, fascinating, fetching, good-looking, handsome, inviting, likable, lovable, magnetic, pleasing, striking, taking, winning, winsome. **antonyms** unattractive, unprepossessing.

prepossession n absorption, bias, engrossment, inclination, leaning, liking, partiality, predilection, predisposition, prejudice, preoccupation.

preposterous adj absurd, asinine, bizarre, crazy, derisory, excessive, exorbitant, extravagant, extreme, fatuous, foolish, imbecile, impossible, inane, incredible, insane, intolerable, irrational, laughable, ludicrous, monstrous, nonsensical, outrageous, ridiculous, risible, senseless, shocking, unbelievable, unconscionable, unreasonable, unthinkable. **antonym** reasonable.

prerogative n advantage, authority, birthright, carte blanche, choice, claim, due, exemption, immunity, liberty, licence, perquisite, privilege, right, sanction, title.

presage v adumbrate, augur, betoken, bode, divine, feel, forebode, forecast, foresee, foreshadow, foretell, foretoken, forewarn, intuit, omen, point to, portend, predict, previse, prognosticate, prophesy, sense, signify, soothsay, warn.

n apprehension, augury, auspice, bad vibes, feeling, foreboding, forecast, forewarning, harbinger, intimation, intuition, misgiving, omen, portent, prediction, premonition, presentiment, prognostication, prophecy, sign, warning.

prescient adj clairvoyant, discerning, divining, far-seeing, far-sighted, foresighted, perceptive, previsional, prophetic, psychic. **antonym** imperceptive.

prescribe v appoint, assign, command, decree, define, dictate, direct, enjoin, fix, impose, lay down, limit, ordain, order, require, rule, set, set bounds to, specify, stipulate.

prescribed adj assigned, decreed, formulary, laid down, ordained, set, specified, stipulated.

prescriptive *adj* authoritarian, customary, dictatorial, didactic, dogmatic, legislating, preceptive, prescribing, rigid.

presence *n* air, apparition, appearance, aspect, attendance, aura, bearing, carriage, closeness, companionship, company, comportment, demeanour, ease, existence, ghost, habitation, inhabitance, manifestation, nearness, neighbourhood, occupancy, personality, poise, propinquity, proximity, residence, self-assurance, shade, spectre, spirit, statuesqueness, vicinity. *antonym* absence.

presence of mind alertness, aplomb, calmness, composure, cool, coolness, gumption, imperturbability, level-headedness, nous, quickness, self-assurance, self-command, self-possession, wits. *antonyms* agitation, confusion.

present¹ *adj* at hand, attending, available, contemporary, current, existent, extant, here, immediate, instant, near, ready, there, to hand. *antonyms* absent, out-of-date, past.

present² *v* acquaint with, adduce, advance, award, bestow, confer, declare, demonstrate, display, donate, entrust, exhibit, expound, extend, furnish, give, grant, hand over, hold out, introduce, mount, offer, pose, produce, proffer, put on, raise, recount, relate, show, stage, state, submit, suggest, tender. *antonym* take.

n benefaction, boon, bounty, compliment, donation, endowment, favour, gift, grant, gratuity, offering, pressie, prezzie.

presentable *adj* acceptable, becoming, clean, decent, neat, passable, proper, respectable, satisfactory, suitable, tidy, tolerable. *antonyms* unpresentable, untidy.

presentation *n* appearance, arrangement, award, bestowal, conferral, delivery, demonstration, display, donation, exhibition, exposition, giving, introduction, investiture, offering, performance, production, rendition, representation, show, staging, submission.

present-day *adj* contemporary, current, existing, fashionable, living, modern, present, up-to-date. *antonyms* future, past.

presentiment *n* anticipation, apprehension, bad vibes, expectation, fear, feeling, foreboding, forecast, forethought, hunch, intuition, misgiving, premonition, presage.

presently *adv* anon, before long, by and by, directly, immediately, in a minute, shortly, soon.

preservation *n* conservation, defence, keeping, maintenance, perpetuation, protection, retention, safeguarding, safekeeping, safety, salvation, security, storage, support, upholding, upkeep. *antonyms* destruction, ruination.

preserve *v* care for, confect, conserve, continue, defend, embalm, entreasure, guard, keep, maintain, perpetuate, protect, retain, safeguard, save, secure, shelter, shield, store, sustain, uphold. *antonyms* destroy, ruin.

n area, confection, confiture, conserve, domain, field, game park, game reserve, jam, jelly, marmalade, realm, reservation, reserve, safari park, sanctuary, specialism, speciality, specialty, sphere, thing.

preside *v* administer, chair, conduct, control, direct, govern, head, lead, manage, officiate, run, supervise.

press¹ *v* afflict, assail, beg, beset, besiege, clasp, cluster, compel, compress, condense, constrain, crowd, crush, demand, depress, disquiet, dun, embrace, encircle, enfold, enforce, enjoin, entreat, exhort, finish, flatten, flock, force, force down, gather, harass, hasten, herd, hug, hurry, implore, importune, insist on, iron, jam, mangle, mash, mill, petition, plague, plead, pressurise, push, reduce, rush, seethe, smooth, squeeze, steam, stuff, sue, supplicate, surge, swarm, throng, torment, trouble, urge, vex, worry. *antonyms* expand, hang back, lighten, relieve.

press² *n* columnists, correspondents, Fleet Street, hacks, journalism, journalists, news media, newsmen, newspapers, papers, pressmen, reporters, writers.

pressed *adj* browbeaten, bullied, coerced, constrained, forced, harassed, hurried, pressured, pressurised, pushed, rushed, short. *antonyms* unhurried, well-off.

pressing *adj* burning, constraining, crowding, crucial, essential, exigent, high-priority, imperative, important, importunate, serious, thronging, urgent, vital. *antonyms* trivial, unimportant.

pressure *n* adversity, affliction, burden, coercion, compressing, compression,

compulsion, constraint, crushing, demands, difficulty, distress, exigency, force, hassle, heat, heaviness, hurry, influence, load, obligation, power, powerplay, press, pression, squeezing, strain, stress, sway, urgency, weight.
v browbeat, bulldoze, bully, coerce, compel, constrain, dragoon, drive, force, impel, induce, lean on, oblige, persuade, press, pressurise, squeeze.

pressurise *v* browbeat, bulldoze, bully, coerce, compel, constrain, dragoon, drive, force, impel, induce, lean on, oblige, persuade, press, pressure, squeeze.

prestige *n* authority, cachet, celebrity, clout, credit, distinction, eminence, esteem, fame, honour, importance, influence, kudos, pull, regard, renown, reputation, standing, stature, status, weight. *antonyms* humbleness, unimportance.

prestigious *adj* blue-chip, celebrated, eminent, esteemed, exalted, great, illustrious, important, imposing, impressive, influential, prominent, renowned, reputable, respected, up-market. *antonyms* humble, modest.

presumably *adv* apparently, as like as not, doubtless, doubtlessly, in all likelihood, in all probability, most likely, no doubt, probably, seemingly.

presume *v* assume, bank on, believe, conjecture, count on, dare, depend on, go so far, have the audacity, hypothesise, infer, make bold, make so bold, posit, postulate, presuppose, rely on, suppose, surmise, take for granted, take it, take the liberty, think, trust, undertake, venture.

presumption[1] *n* assurance, audacity, boldness, brass, brass neck, cheek, effrontery, forwardness, gall, impudence, insolence, neck, nerve, presumptuousness, temerity. *antonyms* humility, politeness.

presumption[2] *n* anticipation, assumption, basis, belief, chance, conjecture, grounds, guess, hypothesis, likelihood, opinion, plausibility, premiss, presupposition, probability, reason, supposition, surmise.

presumptive *adj* assumed, believable, believed, conceivable, credible, designate, expected, hypothetical, inferred, likely, plausible, possible, probable, prospective, reasonable, supposed, understood. *antonyms* known, unlikely.

presumptuous *adj* arrogant,

audacious, big-headed, bold, conceited, foolhardy, forward, impertinent, impudent, insolent, over-confident, over-familiar, overweening, presuming, pushy, rash, uppish. *antonym* modest.

presuppose *v* accept, assume, consider, imply, posit, postulate, premise, presume, suppose, take for granted.

presupposition *n* assumption, belief, hypothesis, preconception, premise, premiss, presumption, supposition, theory.

pretence *n* acting, affectation, aim, allegation, appearance, artifice, charade, claim, cloak, cover, deceit, deception, display, excuse, fabrication, façade, faking, falsehood, feigning, garb, guise, humbug, invention, make-believe, mask, masquerade, posing, posturing, pretentiousness, pretext, profession, purpose, ruse, semblance, sham, show, simulation, subterfuge, trickery, veil, veneer, wile. *antonyms* honesty, openness, reason.

pretend *v* act, affect, alge, allege, aspire, assume, claim, counterfeit, dissemble, dissimulate, fake, falsify, feign, go through the motions, imagine, impersonate, make believe, pass oneself off, profess, purport, put on, sham, simulate, suppose.

pretended *adj* alleged, avowed, bogus, counterfeit, fake, false, feigned, fictitious, imaginary, ostensible, phoney, pretend, professed, pseudo, purported, sham, so-called, specious, spurious, supposed, supposititious. *antonym* real.

pretension *n* affection, airs, aspiration, assertion, assumption, claim, conceit, demand, hypocrisy, ostentation, pomposity, pretence, pretentiousness, pretext, profession, self-importance, show, showiness, snobbery, snobbishness, vainglory, vanity. *antonyms* humility, modesty, simplicity, straightforwardness.

pretentious *adj* affected, ambitious, assuming, bombastic, conceited, exaggerated, extravagant, flaunting, grandiloquent, grandiose, highfalutin, high-flown, high-sounding, hollow, inflated, magniloquent, mannered, ostentatious, overambitious, overassuming, pompous, pseudish, pseudo, showy, snobbish, specious, uppish, vainglorious. *antonyms* humble, modest, simple, straightforward.

pretentiousness *n* attitudinising, flamboyance, floridness, floweriness, ostentation, posing, posturing, pretension, show, theatricality. **antonyms** humbleness, modesty, simplicity, straightforwardness.

pretext *n* appearance, cloak, cover, device, excuse, guise, mask, ploy, pretence, rationale, ruse, semblance, show, simulation, umbrage, veil.

prettify *v* adorn, beautify, deck, deck out, decorate, do up, doll up, embellish, garnish, gild, ornament, smarten up, tart up, titivate, trick out, trim. **antonyms** mar, uglify.

pretty *adj* appealing, attractive, beautiful, bijou, bonny, charming, comely, cute, dainty, delicate, elegant, fair, fine, good-looking, graceful, lovely, neat, nice, personable, pleasing, sightly, tasteful, trim. **antonyms** tasteless, ugly.
adv fairly, moderately, passably, quite, rather, reasonably, somewhat, tolerably.

prevail *v* abound, obtain, overcome, overrule, predominate, preponderate, reign, rule, succeed, triumph, win. **antonym** lose.

prevail upon bring round, convince, dispose, dissuade, incline, induce, influence, persuade, prompt, sway, talk into, talk out of, talk round, win over.

prevailing *adj* common, controlling, current, customary, dominant, established, fashionable, general, in style, in vogue, influential, main, mainstream, operative, ordinary, popular, predominating, preponderating, prepotent, prevalent, principal, ruling, set, usual, widespread. **antonyms** minor, uncommon.

prevalence *n* acceptance, ascendancy, commonness, currency, frequency, hold, mastery, omnipresence, pervasiveness, popularity, predominance, preponderance, primacy, profusion, regularity, rule, sway, ubiquity, universality. **antonym** uncommonness.

prevalent *adj* accepted, ascendant, common, commonplace, compelling, current, customary, dominant, epidemic, established, everyday, extensive, frequent, general, governing, habitual, popular, powerful, predominant, prevailing, rampant, rife, successful, superior, ubiquitous, universal, usual, victorious, widespread. **antonyms** subordinate, uncommon.

prevaricate *v* deceive, dodge, equivocate, evade, fib, hedge, lie, quibble, shift, shuffle, temporise.

prevarication *n* deceit, deception, equivocation, evasion, falsehood, falsification, fibbing, fib(s), half-truth, lie, misrepresentation, pretence, quibbling, untruth.

prevent *v* anticipate, avert, avoid, balk, bar, block, check, counteract, debar, defend against, foil, forestall, frustrate, hamper, head off, hinder, impede, inhibit, intercept, obstruct, obviate, preclude, restrain, stave off, stop, stymie, thwart, ward off. **antonyms** cause, foster, help.

prevention *n* anticipation, avoidance, bar, check, deterrence, elimination, forestalling, forethought, frustration, hindrance, impediment, interruption, obstacle, obstruction, obviation, precaution, preclusion, safeguard, stoppage, thwarting. **antonyms** causing, fostering, help.

preventive *adj* counteractive, deterrent, hampering, hindering, impeding, inhibitory, obstructive, precautionary, prevenient, preventative, prophylactic, protective, shielding. **antonyms** causative, fostering.
n block, deterrent, hindrance, impediment, neutraliser, obstacle, obstruction, prevention, prophylactic, protection, protective, remedy, safeguard, shield. **antonyms** cause, encouragement, incitement.

previous *adj* antecedent, anterior, arranged, earlier, erstwhile, ex-, foregoing, former, one-time, past, preceding, precipitate, premature, prior, sometime, untimely. **antonyms** later, timely.

previously *adv* before, beforehand, earlier, formerly, heretofore, hitherto, once. **antonym** later.

prey *n* booty, fall guy, game, kill, mark, mug, plunder, quarry, target, victim.
prey on blackmail, bleed, bully, burden, devour, distress, eat, eat away, exploit, feed on, gnaw at, haunt, hunt, intimidate, live off, moth-eat, oppress, seize, take advantage of, terrorise, trouble, victimise, waste, weigh down, weigh heavily, worry.

price *n* amount, assessment, bill, bounty, charge, consequences, cost, damage, estimate, expenditure, expense, fee, figure, levy, odds, outlay, payment, penalty, rate, reward, sacrifice, sum, toll, valuation, value, worth.
v assess, cost, estimate, evaluate, offer, put, rate, value.

priceless¹ *adj* beyond price, cherished,

costly, dear, expensive, incalculable, incomparable, inestimable, invaluable, irreplaceable, precious, prized, rare, rich, treasured, without price. **antonyms** cheap, run-of-the-mill.

priceless² *adj* a hoot, a scream, absurd, amusing, comic, droll, funny, hilarious, killing, rib-tickling, ridiculous, riotous, side-splitting.

pric(e)y *adj* costly, dear, excessive, exorbitant, expensive, extortionate, high-priced, over the odds, steep. **antonym** cheap.

prick *v* bite, bore, itch, jab, jag, pain, perforate, pierce, pink, point, prickle, punch, puncture, raise, rise, smart, stab, sting, thorn, tingle, touch, trouble.

n jag, pang, perforation, pinhole, prickle, puncture, smart, spasm, sting, twinge, wound.

prickle *v* itch, jab, nick, nip, prick, smart, sting, tingle.

prickly *adj* acanaceous, aculeate(d), barbed, brambly, bristly, cantankerous, complicated, crawling, difficult, echinate, edgy, fractious, grumpy, intricate, involved, irritable, itchy, jaggy, knotty, peevish, petulant, pricking, prickling, scratchy, sharp, short-tempered, smarting, spiny, stinging, tetchy, thorny, ticklish, tingling, touchy, tricky, troublesome, trying, waspish. **antonyms** easy-going, simple, smooth.

pricy *see* **pric(e)y**.

pride *n* arrogance, best, big-headedness, boast, choice, conceit, cream, delight, dignity, egotism, élite, flower, gem, glory, gratification, haughtiness, hauteur, high spirits, honour, hubris, jewel, joy, loftiness, magnificence, mettle, morgue, ostentation, pick, pleasure, presumption, pretension, pretensiousness, pride and joy, prize, satisfaction, self-esteem, self-importance, self-love, self-respect, smugness, snobbery, splendour, superciliousness, treasure, vainglory, vanity. **antonym** humility.

pride (oneself on) boast, brag, congratulate oneself, crow, exult, flatter oneself, glory, pat oneself on the back, plume, preen, revel, take pride, vaunt. **antonyms** belittle, humble.

priest *n* churchman, clergyman, cleric, curate, ecclesiast, ecclesiastic, father, father confessor, holy man, man of God, man of the cloth, minister, padre, vicar.

priggish *adj* goody-goody, holier-than-thou, narrow-minded, pedantic, prim,

prudish, puritanical, self-righteous, self satisfied, smug, starchy, stiff, stuffy. **antonyms** broad-minded, informal.

prim *adj* demure, fastidious, formal fussy, old-maidish, particular, po-faced precise, priggish, prissy, proper, prudish puritanical, school-marmish, sedate starchy, stiff, strait-laced. **antonyms** broad-minded, informal.

primacy *n* ascendancy, command dominance, dominion, leadership pre-eminence, seniority, sovereignty superiority, supremacy. **antonym** inferiority.

primal *adj* central, chief, earliest, first, fundamental, greatest, highest, initial, main, major, original, paramount primary, prime, primeval, primitive, primordial, principal. **antonyms** later, minor.

primarily *adv* at first, basically, chiefly, especially, essentially, fundamentally, generally, initially, mainly, mostly, originally, principally. **antonym** secondarily.

primary *adj* aboriginal, basic, beginning, best, capital, cardinal, chief, dominant, earliest, elemental, elementary, essential, first, first-formed, first-made, fundamental, greatest, highest, initial, introductory, leading, main, original, paramount, primal, prime, primeval, primitive, primordial, principal, radical, rudimentary, simple, top, ultimate, underlying. **antonym** secondary.

prime¹ *adj* basic, best, capital, chief, choice, earliest, excellent, first-class, first-rate, fundamental, highest, leading, main, original, predominant, pre-eminent, primary, principal, quality, ruling, select, selected, senior, superior, top, underlying. **antonyms** minor, second-rate.

n beginning, flowering, height, heyday, maturity, morning, opening, peak, perfection, spring, springtide, springtime, start, zenith.

prime² *v* brief, charge, clue up, coach, cram, fill, fill in, gen up, groom, inform, notify, post up, prepare, train.

primeval *adj* ancient, earliest, early, first, old, original, prehistoric, primal, primitive, primordial. **antonyms** developed, later, modern.

primitive *adj* aboriginal, barbarian, barbaric, crude, earliest, early, elementary, first, neanderthal, original, primal, primary, primeval, primordial, rough, rude, rudimentary, savage, simple, uncivilised, uncultivated, undeveloped, unrefined, unsophisticated, untrained, untutored. **antonyms** advanced, civilised, developed.

primordial *adj* basic, earliest, elemental, first, first-formed, first-made, fundamental, original, prehistoric, primal, primeval, primitive, radical. **antonyms** developed, later, modern.

princely *adj* august, bounteous, bountiful, dignified, generous, gracious, grand, imperial, imposing, lavish, liberal, lofty, magnanimous, magnificent, majestic, munificent, noble, open-handed, regal, rich, royal, sovereign, stately, sumptuous. **antonyms** humble, mean.

principal *adj* capital, cardinal, chief, controlling, dominant, essential, first, foremost, highest, key, leading, main, paramount, pre-eminent, primary, prime, strongest. **antonyms** least, lesser, minor.

principally *adv* above all, chiefly, especially, mainly, mostly, particularly, predominantly, primarily.

principle *n* assumption, attitude, axiom, belief, canon, code, conscience, credo, criterion, dictum, doctrine, dogma, duty, element, ethic, formula, fundamental, golden rule, honour, institute, integrity, law, maxim, moral, morality, morals, opinion, precept, probity, proposition, rectitude, rule, scruples, standard, tenet, truth, uprightness, verity. **antonyms** corruption, wickedness.

principled *adj* clear, clear-cut, conscientious, correct, decent, ethical, high-minded, honourable, just, logical, moral, rational, reasoned, righteous, right-minded, scrupulous, sensible, thought-out, upright, virtuous. **antonym** unprincipled.

print *v* engrave, impress, imprint, issue, mark, produce, publish, reproduce, run off, stamp, write.

prior *adj* aforementioned, antecedent, anterior, earlier, foregoing, former, preceding, pre-existent, previous. **antonym** later.

prior to before, earlier than, preceding, preparatory to, previous to. **antonym** after.

priority *n* precedence, pre-eminence, preference, prerogative, privilege, rank, right of way, seniority, superiority, supremacy, the lead. **antonyms** inferiority, subordinateness.

prise *see* **prize²**.

prison *n* borstal, cage, can, cell, clink, confinement, cooler, coop, dungeon, gaol, glasshouse, house of correction, imprisonment, jail, lock-up, penal institution, penitentiary, pokey, porridge, prison-house, prison-ship, slammer, stir.

prissy *adj* effeminate, fastidious, finicky, fussy, old-maidish, overnice, po-faced, precious, prim, prim and proper, prudish, school-marmish, starchy, strait-laced. **antonyms** broad-minded, informal.

privacy *n* clandestineness, concealment, confidentiality, isolation, quietness, quietude, seclusion, secrecy, separateness, solitude. **antonym** publicness.

private *adj* clandestine, closet, concealed, confidential, exclusive, home-felt, hush-hush, in camera, independent, individual, inside, intimate, inward, isolated, off the record, own, particular, personal, privy, reserved, retired, secluded, secret, separate, solitary, special, unofficial, withdrawn. **antonyms** open, public.

privation *n* affliction, austerity, destitution, distress, hardship, indigence, lack, loss, misery, necessary, need, neediness, penury, poverty, suffering, want. **antonyms** affluence, wealth.

privilege *n* advantage, benefit, birthright, claim, concession, due, entitlement, freedom, immunity, liberty, licence, prerogative, right, sanction, title. **antonym** disadvantage.

privileged *adj* advantaged, allowed, authorised, élite, empowered, entitled, exempt(ed), favoured, free, granted, honoured, indulged, licensed, permitted, powerful, ruling, sanctioned, special, vested. **antonyms** disadvantaged, under-privileged.

privy *n* bog, closet, John, latrine, lavatory, loo, toilet, water-closet.
adj confidential, hidden, hush-hush, intimate, off the record, personal, private, secret, top secret. **antonym** public.

privy to apprised of, aware of, cognisant of, in on, in the know, informed about, wise to. **antonym** unaware.

prize¹ *n* accolade, aim, ambition, award, conquest, desire, gain, goal, haul, honour, hope, jackpot, premium, purse, reward, stake(s), trophy, windfall, winnings.
adj award-winning, best, champion, excellent, first-rate, outstanding, top, top-notch, winning. **antonym** second-rate.
v appreciate, cherish, esteem, hold dear,

revere, reverence, set store by, treasure, value. **antonyms** despise, undervalue.

prize², **prise** v force, jemmy, lever, pry, winkle.

probability n assumption, chance, chances, expectation, liability, likelihood, likeliness, odds, presumption, prospect. **antonym** improbability.

probable adj apparent, credible, feasible, likely, odds-on, on the cards, plausible, possible, presumed, reasonable, seeming. **antonym** improbable.

probably adv as likely as not, doubtless, happen, in all likelihood, in all probability, likely, maybe, most likely, perhaps, possibly, presumably. **antonym** improbably.

probe v examine, explore, go into, investigate, look into, pierce, poke, prod, query, scrutinise, search, sift, sound, test, verify.
n detection, drill, examination, exploration, inquest, inquiry, investigation, research, scrutiny, study, test.

probity n equity, fairness, fidelity, goodness, honesty, honour, honourableness, integrity, justice, morality, rectitude, righteousness, sincerity, trustworthiness, truthfulness, uprightness, virtue, worth. **antonym** improbity.

problem n brain-teaser, complication, conundrum, difficulty, dilemma, disagreement, dispute, doubt, enigma, no laughing matter, poser, predicament, puzzle, quandary, question, riddle, trouble, vexed question.
adj delinquent, difficult, intractable, perverse, refractory, uncontrollable, unmanageable, unruly. **antonyms** manageable, well-behaved.

problematic adj chancy, debatable, doubtful, dubious, enigmatic, moot, problematical, puzzling, questionable, tricky, uncertain, unestablished, unsettled, unsure. **antonym** certain.

procedure n action, conduct, course, custom, form, formula, method, modus operandi, move, operation, performance, plan of action, policy, practice, process, routine, scheme, step, strategy, system, transaction.

proceed v advance, arise, carry on, come, continue, derive, emanate, ensue, flow, follow, go ahead, issue, move on, originate, press on, progress, result, set in motion, spring, start, stem. **antonyms** retreat, stop.

proceedings n account, action, affair, affairs, annals, archives, business, course of action, dealings, deeds, doings, event(s), matters, measures, minutes, moves, procedure, process, records, report, steps, transactions, undertaking.

proceeds n earnings, emoluments, gain, income, produce, products, profit, receipts, returns, revenue, takings, yield. **antonyms** losses, outlay.

process n action, advance, case, course, course of action, development, evolution, formation, growth, manner, means, measure, method, mode, movement, operation, performance, practice, procedure, proceeding, progress, progression, stage, step, suit, system, transaction, trial, unfolding.

procession n cavalcade, column, concatenation, cortège, course, cycle, file, march, motorcade, parade, run, sequence, series, string, succession, train.

proclaim v advertise, affirm, announce, blaze, blazon, circulate, declare, enounce, give out, herald, indicate, make known, profess, promulgate, publish, show, testify, trumpet.

proclamation n announcement, declaration, decree, edict, indiction, manifesto, notice, notification, promulgation, pronouncement, publication.

proclivity n bent, bias, disposition, facility, inclination, leaning, liability, liableness, penchant, predilection, predisposition, proneness, propensity, tendency, weakness. **antonym** disinclination.

procrastinate v adjourn, dally, defer, delay, dilly-dally, drag one's feet, gain time, play for time, postpone, prolong, protract, put off, retard, stall, temporise. **antonyms** advance, proceed.

procrastination n dallying, deferral, delaying, dilly-dallying, foot-dragging, stalling, temporising.

procreate v beget, breed, conceive, engender, father, generate, mother, produce, propagate, reproduce, sire, spawn.

procure v acquire, appropriate, bag, buy, come by, earn, effect, find, gain, get, induce, lay hands on, obtain, pander, pick up, pimp, purchase, secure, win. **antonym** lose.

prod v dig, drive, egg on, elbow, goad, impel, incite, jab, motivate, move, nudge, poke, prick, prog, prompt, propel, push, rouse, shove, spur, stimulate, urge.
n boost, cue, dig, elbow, jab, nudge,

poke, prog, prompt, push, reminder, shove, signal, stimulus.

prodigal *adj* bounteous, bountiful, copious, excessive, extravagant, exuberant, immoderate, improvident, intemperate, lavish, luxuriant, profligate, profuse, reckless, spendthrift, squandering, sumptuous, teeming, unsparing, unthrift, unthrifty, wanton, wasteful. *antonyms* modest, parsimonious, thrifty.

n big spender, profligate, spendall, spendthrift, squanderer, waster, wastrel.

prodigious *adj* abnormal, amazing, astounding, colossal, enormous, exceptional, extraordinary, fabulous, fantastic, giant, gigantic, huge, immeasurable, immense, impressive, inordinate, mammoth, marvellous, massive, miraculous, monstrous, monumental, phenomenal, remarkable, spectacular, staggering, startling, striking, stupendous, tremendous, unusual, vast, wonderful. *antonyms* commonplace, small, unremarkable.

produce *v* advance, afford, bear, beget, breed, bring forth, cause, compose, construct, create, deliver, demonstrate, develop, direct, effect, engender, exhibit, fabricate, factuate, furnish, generate, give, give rise to, invent, make, manufacture, mount, occasion, offer, originate, present, provoke, put forward, put on, render, result in, show, stage, supply, throw, yield. *antonyms* consume, result from.

product *n* artefact, commodity, concoction, consequence, creation, effect, fruit, goods, invention, issue, legacy, merchandise, offshoot, offspring, outcome, output, produce, production, result, returns, spin-off, upshot, work, yield. *antonym* cause.

production *n* assembly, construction, creation, direction, fabrication, formation, making, management, manufacture, manufacturing, origination, preparation, presentation, producing, staging. *antonym* consumption.

productive *adj* advantageous, beneficial, constructive, creative, dynamic, effective, energetic, fecund, fertile, fruitful, gainful, generative, gratifying, inventive, plentiful, producing, profitable, prolific, rewarding, rich, teeming, useful, valuable, vigorous, voluminous, worthwhile. *antonyms* fruitless, unproductive.

profane *adj* abusive, blasphemous, coarse, crude, disrespectful, filthy, forbidden, foul, godless, heathen, idolatrous, impious, impure, irreligious, irreverent, lay, obscene, pagan, sacrilegious, secular, sinful, temporal, unclean, unconsecrated, ungodly, unhallowed, unholy, uninitiated, unsanctified, vulgar, wicked, worldly. *antonyms* initiated, permitted, religious, sacred.

v abuse, contaminate, debase, defile, degrade, desecrate, misemploy, misuse, pervert, pollute, prostitute, violate, vitiate. *antonym* revere.

profanity *n* abuse, blasphemy, curse, cursing, execration, expletive, four-letter word, impiety, imprecation, irreverence, malediction, obscenity, profaneness, sacrilege, swearing, swear-word. *antonyms* politeness, reverence.

profess *v* acknowledge, admit, affirm, allege, announce, assert, asseverate, aver, avow, certify, claim, confess, confirm, declare, enunciate, fake, feign, maintain, make out, own, pretend, proclaim, propose, propound, purport, sham, state, vouch.

professed *adj* acknowledged, avowed, certified, confirmed, declared, ostensible, pretended, proclaimed, purported, self-acknowledged, self-confessed, self-styled, so-called, supposed, would-be.

profession *n* acknowledgement, affirmation, assertion, attestation, avowal, business, calling, career, claim, confession, declaration, employment, job, line (of work), manifesto, métier, occupation, office, position, sphere, statement, testimony, vocation, vow, walk of life.

professional *adj* adept, competent, crack, efficient, experienced, expert, finished, masterly, polished, practised, proficient, qualified, skilled, slick, trained, virtuoso, well-skilled. *antonyms* amateur, unprofessional.

n adept, authority, dab hand, expert, maestro, master, pastmaster, pro, proficient, specialist, virtuoso, wizard.

proffer *v* advance, extend, hand, hold out, offer, present, propose, propound, submit, suggest, tender, volunteer.

proficiency *n* ability, accomplishment, aptitude, competence, conversancy, dexterity, expertise, expertness, facility, finesse, knack, know-how, mastery, skilfulness, skill, talent, virtuosity. *antonyms* clumsiness, incompetence.

proficient *adj* able, accomplished, adept, apt, capable, clever, competent, conversant, efficient, experienced, expert, gifted, masterly, qualified, skilful, skilled, talented, trained, versed, virtuoso. **antonyms** clumsy, incompetent.

profile *n* analysis, biography, biopic, characterisation, chart, contour, diagram, drawing, examination, figure, form, graph, outline, portrait, review, shape, side view, silhouette, sketch, study, survey, table, thumbnail sketch, vignette.

profit *n* a fast buck, advancement, advantage, avail, benefit, bottom line, earnings, emoluments, fruit, gain, good, gravy, grist, interest, melon, percentage, proceeds, receipts, return, revenue, surplus, takings, use, value, velvet, winnings, yield. **antonym** loss.

v advance, advantage, aid, avail, benefit, better, contribute, gain, help, improve, line one's pockets, promote, serve, stand in good stead. **antonyms** harm, hinder.

profit by/from capitalise on, cash in on, exploit, learn from, put to good use, reap the benefit of, take advantage of, turn to account, turn to advantage, use, utilise. **antonym** lose by.

profitable *adj* advantageous, beneficial, commercial, cost-effective, fruitful, gainful, lucrative, money-making, paying, plummy, productive, remunerative, rewarding, serviceable, useful, utile, valuable, worthwhile. **antonym** unprofitable.

profitless *adj* fruitless, futile, gainless, idle, ineffective, ineffectual, pointless, thankless, unavailing, unproductive, unprofitable, unremunerative, useless, vain, worthless. **antonym** profitable.

profligacy *n* abandon, corruption, debauchery, degeneracy, depravity, dissipation, dissoluteness, excess, extravagance, immorality, improvidence, lavishness, laxity, libertinism, licentiousness, prodigality, promiscuity, recklessness, squandering, unrestraint, unthrift, unthriftiness, wantonness, waste, wastefulness. **antonyms** morality, parsimony, thrift, uprightness.

profligate *adj* abandoned, corrupt, debauched, degenerate, depraved, dissipated, dissolute, extravagant, immoderate, immoral, improvident, iniquitous, libertine, licentious, loose, prodigal, promiscuous, reckless, shameless, spendthrift, squandering, unprincipled, vicious, vitiated, wanton, wasteful, whorish, wicked, wild.

antonyms moral, parsimonious, thrifty, upright.

n debauchee, degenerate, libertine, prodigal, racketeer, rake, reprobate, spendthrift, squanderer, waster, wastrel.

profound *adj* abject, absolute, abstruse, abysmal, acute, awful, bottomless, cavernous, complete, consummate, deep, deep-seated, discerning, erudite, exhaustive, extensive, extreme, far-reaching, fathomless, great, heartfelt, heart-rending, hearty, intense, keen, learned, penetrating, philosophical, pronounced, recondite, sagacious, sage, serious, sincere, skilled, subtle, thoroughgoing, thoughtful, total, utter, weighty, wise, yawning. **antonyms** mild, shallow, slight.

profoundly *adv* abjectly, acutely, awfully, deeply, dreadfully, extremely, greatly, heartily, intensely, keenly, seriously, sincerely, thoroughly. **antonym** slightly.

profundity *n* abstruseness, acuity, acumen, depth, erudition, extremity, insight, intelligence, intensity, learning, penetration, perceptiveness, perspecuity, perspicacity, profoundness, sagacity, seriousness, severity, strength, wisdom. **antonym** shallowness.

profuse *adj* abundant, ample, bountiful, copious, excessive, extravagant, exuberant, fulsome, generous, immoderate, large-handed, lavish, liberal, luxuriant, open-handed, over the top, overflowing, plentiful, prodigal, prolific, teeming, unstinting. **antonyms** sparing, sparse.

profusion *n* abundance, bounty, copiousness, cornucopia, excess, extravagance, exuberance, glut, lavishness, luxuriance, multitude, plenitude, plethora, prodigality, quantity, riot, superabundance, superfluity, surplus, wealth. **antonyms** sparingness, sparsity.

progeny *n* breed, children, descendants, family, issue, lineage, offspring, posterity, race, seed, stock, young.

prognosis *n* diagnosis, expectation, forecast, outlook, prediction, prognostication, projection, prospect, speculation, surmise.

prognosticate *v* augur, betoken, divine, forebore, forecast, foreshadow, foretell, harbinger, herald, indicate, portend, predict, presage, prophesy, soothsay.

programme *n* agenda, broadcast, curriculum, design, line-up, list, listing, order of events, order of the day, performance, plan, plan of action, presentation, procedure, production, project, schedule, scheme, show, syllabus, transmission.

v arrange, bill, book, brainwash, design, engage, formulate, itemise, lay on, line up, list, map out, plan, prearrange, schedule, work out.

progress *n* advance, advancement, amelioration, betterment, breakthrough, circuit, continuation, course, development, gain, growth, headway, improvement, increase, journey, movement, passage, procession, progression, promotion, step forward, way. *antonyms* decline, deterioration.

v advance, ameliorate, better, blossom, come on, continue, develop, forge ahead, gain, gather momentum, grow, improve, increase, make headway, make strides, mature, proceed, prosper, travel. *antonyms* decline, deteriorate.

progression *n* advance, advancement, chain, concatenation, course, cycle, furtherance, gain, headway, order, progress, sequence, series, string, succession. *antonyms* decline, deterioration.

progressive *adj* accelerating, advanced, advancing, avant-garde, continuing, continuous, developing, dynamic, enlightened, enterprising, escalating, forward-looking, go-ahead, growing, increasing, intensifying, liberal, modern, ongoing, radical, reactionary, reformist, regressive, revolutionary, up-and-coming.

prohibit *v* ban, bar, constrain, debar, disallow, forbid, hamper, hinder, impede, interdict, obstruct, outlaw, preclude, prevent, proscribe, restrict, rule out, stop, veto. *antonym* permit.

prohibited *adj* banned, barred, disallowed, embargoed, forbidden, interdicted, off-limits, proscribed, taboo, vetoed. *antonym* permitted.

prohibition *n* ban, bar, constraint, disallowance, embargo, exclusion, injunction, interdict, interdiction, negation, obstruction, prevention, proscription, restruction, veto. *antonym* permission.

prohibitive *adj* excessive, exorbitant, extortionate, forbidding, impossible, preposterous, prohibiting, proscriptive, repressive, restraining, restrictive, sky-high, steep, suppressive. *antonyms* encouraging, reasonable.

project *n* activity, assignment, conception, design, enterprise, idea, job, occupation, plan, programme, proposal, purpose, scheme, task, undertaking, venture, work.

v beetle, bulge, calculate, cast, contemplate, contrive, design, devise, discharge, draft, estimate, exsert, extend, extrapolate, extrude, fling, forecast, frame, gauge, hurl, jut, launch, map out, outline, overhang, plan, predetermine, predict, propel, prophesy, propose, protrude, purpose, reckon, scheme, shoot, stand out, stick out, throw, transmit.

projection *n* blueprint, bulge, calculation, computation, diagram, eaves, estimate, estimation, extrapolation, forecast, jut, ledge, map, outline, overhang, plan, prediction, process, prominence, protrusion, protuberance, reckoning, representation, ridge, shelf, sill.

proletariat *n* common people, commonalty, commoners, great unwashed, herd, hoi polloi, lower classes, masses, mob, plebs, proles, rabble, working class.

proliferate *v* breed, burgeon, escalate, expand, exuberate, increase, multiply, mushroom, run riot, snowball. *antonym* dwindle.

proliferation *n* build-up, concentration, duplication, escalation, expansion, extension, increase, intensification, multiplication, mushrooming, snowballing, spread. *antonym* decrease.

prolific *adj* abounding, abundant, bountiful, copious, fecund, fertile, fertilising, fruitful, generative, luxuriant, productive, profuse, rank, reproductive, rich, teeming, voluminous. *antonyms* infertile, scarce.

prologue *n* foreword, introduction, preamble, preface, preliminary, prelude.

prolong *v* continue, delay, drag out, draw out, extend, lengthen, lengthen out, perpetuate, produce, protract, spin out, stretch. *antonym* shorten.

prominence[1] *n* bulge, bump, cliff, crag, crest, elevation, headland, height, hummock, hump, lump, mound, pinnacle, process, projection, promontory, protrusion, protuberance, rise, spur, swelling.

prominence[2] *n* celebrity, conspicuousness, distinction, eminence, fame, greatness, importance, markedness, name, notability, outstandingness, precedence, pre-eminence, prestige, rank, reputation, salience, standing, top billing, visibility, weight. *antonyms* inconspicuousness, unimportance.

prominent *adj* beetling, bulging, celebrated, chief, conspicuous, distinguished, eminent, eye-catching, famous, foremost, high-profile, important, jutting, leading, main, noted, noticeable, obtrusive, obvious, outstanding, popular, pre-eminent, projecting, pronounced, protruding, protrusive, protuberant, remarkable, renowned, respected, salient, standing out, striking, top, unmistakable, weighty, well-known. *antonyms* inconspicuous, unimportant.

promiscuity *n* abandon, amorality, debauchery, depravity, dissipation, immorality, laxity, laxness, lechery, libertinism, licentiousness, looseness, permissiveness, profligacy, promiscuousness, wantonness, whoring, whorishness. *antonym* chastity.

promiscuous *adj* abandoned, accidental, careless, casual, chaotic, confused, debauched, disordered, dissipated, dissolute, diverse, fast, haphazard, heterogeneous, ill-assorted, immoral, indiscriminate, intermingled, intermixed, jumbled, libertine, licentious, loose, mingled, miscellaneous, mixed, motley, of easy virtue, profligate, random, unbridled, unchaste, uncontrolled, undiscriminating, unselective, wanton, whorish, wild. *antonyms* chaste, controlled, selective.

promise *v* assure, augur, bespeak, betoken, bid fair, contract, denote, engage, guarantee, hint at, indicate, look like, pledge, plight, predict, presage, prophesy, stipulate, suggest, swear, take an oath, undertake, vouch, vow, warrant. *n* ability, aptitude, assurance, bond, capability, capacity, commitment, compact, covenant, engagement, flair, guarantee, oath, pledge, potential, talent, undertaking, vow, word, word of honour.

promised land land of milk and honey, paradise, Shangri-la, Zion.

promising *adj* able, auspicious, bright, encouraging, favourable, gifted, good, hopeful, likely, propitious, reassuring, rising, rosy, talented, up-and-coming. *antonym* unpromising.

promontory *n* cape, foreland, head, headland, hoe, mull, ness, peninsula, point, projection, ridge, spur.

promote *v* advance, advertise, advocate, aggrandise, aid, assist, back, blazon, boost, champion, contribute to, develop, dignify, elevate, encourage, endorse, espouse, exalt, forward, foster, further, help, honour, hype, kick upstairs, nurture, plug, popularise, prefer, publicise, push, raise, recommend, sell, sponsor, stimulate, support, trumpet, upgrade, urge. *antonyms* demote, disparage, obstruct.

promotion *n* advancement, advertising, advocacy, aggrandisement, backing, ballyhoo, boosting, campaign, cultivation, development, elevation, encouragement, ennoblement, espousal, exaltation, fanfare, furtherance, honour, hype, plugging, preferment, promo, propaganda, publicity, pushing, rise, support, trumpeting, upgrading. *antonyms* demotion, disparagement, obstruction.

prompt[1] *adj* alert, brisk, eager, early, efficient, expeditious, immediate, instant, instantaneous, on time, punctual, quick, rapid, ready, responsive, smart, speedy, swift, timely, unhesitating, willing. *antonym* slow.
adv exactly, on the dot, promptly, punctually, sharp, to the minute.

prompt[2] *v* advise, assist, call forth, cause, cue, elicit, evoke, give rise to, impel, incite, induce, inspire, instigate, motivate, move, occasion, prod, produce, provoke, remind, result in, spur, stimulate, urge. *antonym* dissuade.
n cue, help, hint, instigation, jog, jolt, prod, reminder, spur, stimulus.

promptly *adv* directly, forthwith, immediately, instantly, on time, posthaste, pronto, punctually, quickly, speedily, swiftly, unhesitatingly.

promulgate *v* advertise, announce, broadcast, circulate, communicate, declare, decree, disseminate, issue, notify, proclaim, promote, publicise, publish, spread.

prone[1] *adj* apt, bent, disposed, given, inclined, liable, likely, predisposed, propense, subject, susceptible, tending, vulnerable. *antonym* unlikely.

prone[2] *adj* face down, flat, full-length, horizontal, prostrate, recumbent, stretched. *antonym* upright.

proneness *n* aptness, bent, bias, disposition, inclination, leaning, liability, penchant, proclivity, propensity, susceptibility, tendency, weakness. *antonym* dislike.

pronounce *v* accent, affirm, announce, articulate, assert, breathe, declaim, declare, decree, deliver, enunciate, judge, proclaim, say, sound, speak, stress, utter, vocalise, voice.

pronounced *adj* broad, clear, conspicuous, decided, definite, distinct, evident, marked, noticeable, obvious, positive, striking, strong, unmistakable. **antonyms** unnoticeable, vague.

pronouncement *n* announcement, assertion, declaration, decree, dictum, edict, judgement, manifesto, notification, proclamation, promulgation, statement.

pronunciation *n* accent, accentuation, articulation, diction, elocution, enunciation, inflection, intonation, modulation, speech, stress.

proof *n* assay, attestation, authentication, certification, confirmation, corroboration, demonstration, documentation, evidence, examination, experiment, ordeal, scrutiny, substantiation, test, testimony, trial, verification, voucher.
adj impenetrable, impervious, proofed, rainproof, repellent, resistant, strong, tight, treated, waterproof, weatherproof, windproof. **antonyms** permeable, untreated.

prop *v* bolster, buttress, lean, maintain, rest, set, shore, stand, stay, strut, support, sustain, truss, underpin, uphold.
n brace, buttress, mainstay, stanchion, stay, strut, support, truss.

propagate *v* beget, breed, broadcast, circulate, diffuse, disseminate, engender, generate, increase, multiply, proclaim, procreate, produce, proliferate, promote, promulgate, publicise, publish, reproduce, spawn, spread, transmit.

propagation *n* breeding, circulation, communication, diffusion, dissemination, distribution, generation, increase, issuance, multiplication, procreation, proliferation, promotion, promulgation, reproduction, spawning, spread, spreading, transmission.

propel *v* drive, force, impel, launch, push, send, shoot, shove, start, thrust, waft. **antonyms** slow, stop.

propensity *n* aptness, bent, bias, disposition, foible, inclination, leaning, liability, penchant, predisposition, proclivity, proneness, readiness, susceptibility, tendency, weakness. **antonym** disinclination.

proper *adj* accepted, accurate, appropriate, apt, becoming, befitting, characteristic, conventional, correct, decent, decorous, established, exact, fit, fitting, formal, genteel, gentlemanly,

individual, kosher, ladylike, legitimate, mannerly, meet, orthodox, own, particular, peculiar, personal, polite, precise, prim, prissy, punctilious, refined, respectable, respective, right, sedate, seemly, special, specific, suitable, suited. **antonyms** common, general, improper.

property[1] *n* acres, assets, belongings, building(s), capital, chattels, effects, estate, freehold, goods, holding, holdings, house(s), land, means, possessions, real estate, realty, resources, riches, title, wealth.

property[2] *n* ability, affection, attribute, characteristic, feature, hallmark, idiosyncrasy, mark, peculiarity, quality, trait, virtue.

prophecy *n* augury, divination, forecast, foretelling, prediction, prognosis, prognostication, revelation, second-sight, soothsaying.

prophesy *v* augur, divine, forecast, foresee, foretell, forewarn, predict, presage, prognosticate, soothsay.

propinquity *n* adjacency, affiliation, affinity, blood, closeness, connection, consanguinity, contiguity, kinship, nearness, neighbourhood, proximity, relation, relationship, tie, vicinity. **antonym** remoteness.

propitiate *v* appease, conciliate, mollify, pacify, placate, reconcile, satisfy, soothe. **antonyms** anger, provoke.

propitious *adj* advantageous, auspicious, beneficial, benevolent, benign, bright, encouraging, favourable, fortunate, friendly, gracious, happy, kindly, lucky, opportune, promising, prosperous, reassuring, rosy, timely, well-disposed. **antonym** inauspicious.

proponent *n* advocate, apologist, backer, champion, defender, enthusiast, exponent, friend, partisan, patron, proposer, propounder, subscriber, supporter, upholder, vindicator. **antonym** opponent.

proportion *n* agreement, amount, balance, congruity, correspondence, cut, distribution, division, fraction, harmony, measure, part, percentage, quota, ratio, relationship, segment, share, symmetry. **antonyms** disproportion, imbalance.

proportional *adj* balanced, commensurate, comparable, compatible, consistent, correspondent, corresponding, equitable, even, fair, just, logistical, proportionate. **antonyms** disproportionate, unjust.

proportions *n* amplitude, breadth, bulk,

capacity, dimensions, expanse, extent, magnitude, measurements, range, scope, size, volume.

proposal *n* bid, design, draft, manifesto, motion, offer, outline, overture, plan, platform, presentation, programme, project, proposition, recommendation, scheme, sketch, suggestion, suit, tender, terms.

propose *v* advance, aim, bring up, design, enunciate, have in mind, intend, introduce, invite, lay before, mean, move, name, nominate, pay suit, plan, pop the question, present, proffer, propound, purpose, put forward, put up, recommend, scheme, submit, suggest, table, tender. *antonyms* oppose, withdraw.

proposition *n* manifesto, motion, plan, programme, project, proposal, recommendation, scheme, suggestion, tender.

v accost, solicit.

propound *v* advance, advocate, contend, enunciate, lay down, move, postulate, present, propose, put forward, set forth, submit, suggest. *antonym* oppose.

propriety *n* appropriateness, aptness, breeding, correctness, courtesy, decency, decorum, delicacy, etiquette, fitness, manners, modesty, politeness, protocol, rectitude, refinement, respectability, rightness, seemliness, suitableness. *antonym* impropriety.

propulsion *n* drive, impetus, impulse, impulsion, momentum, power, pressure, push, thrust.

prosaic *adj* banal, boring, commonplace, dry, dull, everyday, flat, hackneyed, humdrum, matter-of-fact, mundane, ordinary, pedestrian, routine, stale, tame, trite, unimaginative, uninspired, uninspiring, vapid, workaday. *antonyms* imaginative, interesting.

proscribe *v* ban, banish, bar, black, blackball, boycott, censure, condemn, damn, denounce, deport, doom, embargo, exclude, excommunicate, exile, expatriate, expel, forbid, interdict, ostracise, outlaw, prohibit, reject. *antonyms* admit, allow.

proscription *n* ban, banishment, bar, barring, boycott, censure, condemnation, damning, denunciation, deportation, ejection, embargo, eviction, exclusion, excommunication, exile, expatriation, expulsion, interdict, ostracism, outlawry, prohibition, rejection. *antonyms* admission, allowing.

prosecute *v* arraign, bring suit against, bring to trial, carry on, conduct, continue, direct, discharge, engage in, execute, follow through, indict, litigate, manage, perform, persevere, persist, practise, prefer charges, pursue, put on trial, see through, sue, summon, take to court, try, work at. *antonym* desist.

prospect *n* calculation, chance, contemplation, expectation, future, hope, landscape, likelihood, odds, opening, outlook, panorama, perspective, plan, possibility, presumption, probability, promise, proposition, scene, sight, spectacle, thought, view, vision, vista. *antonym* unlikelihood.

v explore, nose, quest, search, seek, survey.

prospective *adj* anticipated, approaching, awaited, coming, designate, designated, destined, eventual, expected, forthcoming, future, imminent, intended, likely, possible, potential, soon-to-be, to come, -to-be. *antonyms* agreed, current.

prosper *v* advance, bloom, boom, burgeon, fare well, flourish, flower, get on, grow rich, make good, progress, succeed, thrive, turn out well. *antonym* fail.

prosperity *n* affluence, boom, ease, fortune, good fortune, luxury, plenty, prosperousness, riches, success, the good life, wealth, well-being. *antonym* poverty.

prosperous *adj* affluent, blooming, booming, burgeoning, flourishing, fortunate, in the money, lucky, moneyed, opulent, palmy, profitable, rich, successful, thriving, wealthy, well-heeled, well-off, well-to-do. *antonym* poor.

prostitute *n* bawd, call-girl, courtesan, fallen woman, floosie, harlot, hooker, hustler, loose woman, pro, rent-boy, street-walker, strumpet, tart, trollop, wench, white slave, whore, woman of the town, working girl.

v cheapen, debase, degrade, demean, devalue, misapply, misuse, pervert, profane.

prostrate *adj* abject, brought to one's knees, crushed, defenceless, dejected, depressed, desolate, disarmed, done, drained, exhausted, fagged, fallen, flat, helpless, horizontal, impotent, inconsolable, knackered, kowtowing, overcome, overwhelmed, paralysed, pooped, powerless, prone, reduced, shattered, spent, worn out. *antonyms* elated, erect, hale, happy, strong, triumphant.

v crush, depress, disarm, drain, exhaust, fag out, fatigue, knacker, lay low, overcome, overthrow, overturn, overwhelm, paralyse, poop, reduce, ruin, sap, shatter, tire, wear out, weary. *antonyms* elate, exalt, strengthen.

prostrate oneself abase oneself, bend the knee, bow down, cringe, grovel, kneel, kowtow, submit. *antonym* exalt oneself.

protean *adj* changeable, ever-changing, inconstant, many-sided, mercurial, multiform, mutable, variable, volatile. *antonyms* stable, unchanging.

protect *v* care for, chaperon, convoy, cover, cover up for, defend, escort, guard, harbour, keep, look after, preserve, safeguard, save, screen, secure, shelter, shield, stand guard over, support, watch over. *antonyms* attack, threaten.

protection *n* aegis, armour, backstop, barrier, buffer, bulwark, care, charge, cover, custody, defence, guard, guardianship, guarding, preservation, protecting, refuge, safeguard, safekeeping, safety, screen, security, shelter, shield, umbrella, wardship. *antonyms* attack, threat.

protective *adj* careful, conservationist, covering, custodial, defensive, fatherly, insulating, jealous, maternal, motherly, paternal, possessive, safeguarding, sheltering, shielding, vigilant, warm, watchful. *antonyms* aggressive, threatening.

protest *n* complaint, declaration, demur, demurral, disapproval, dissent, formal complaint, objection, obtestation, outcry, protestation, remonstrance. *antonym* acceptance.

v affirm, argue, assert, asseverate, attest, avow, complain, contend, cry out, declare, demonstrate, demur, disagree, disapprove, expostulate, insist, maintain, object, oppose, profess, remonstrate, squawk, take exception, testify, vow. *antonym* accept.

protestation *n* affirmation, asseveration, assurance, avowal, complaint, declaration, disagreement, dissent, expostulation, oath, objection, outcry, pledge, profession, protest, remonstrance, remonstration, statement, vow.

protocol *n* conventions, courtesies, customs, decorum, etiquette, formalities, good form, manners, politesse,

procedure, propriety, p's and q's. *antonym* boorishness.

prototype *n* archetype, example, exemplar, mock-up, model, original, paradigm, pattern, precedent, standard, type.

protracted *adj* dragged out, drawn-out, extended, interminable, lengthy, long, long-drawn-out, overlong, prolix, prolonged, wearisome, wordy. *antonym* shortened.

protrude *v* bulge, come through, extend, extrude, jut out, obtrude, point, pop, project, protuberate, stand out, start, stick out, strout.

protruding *adj* astrut, jutting, prominent, protuberant, proud. *antonyms* flat, flush.

protrusion *n* bulge, bump, jut, lump, outgrowth, process, projection, protuberance, swelling.

protuberant *adj* beetling, bulbous, bulging, bunched, exsertive, gibbous, jutting, popping, prominent, protruding, proud, swelling, swollen. *antonym* flat.

proud *adj* appreciative, arrogant, august, boastful, conceited, content, contented, disdainful, distinguished, egotistical, eminent, exalted, glad, glorious, grand, gratified, gratifying, great, haughty, high and mighty, honoured, illustrious, imperious, imposing, lofty, lordly, magnificent, majestic, memorable, noble, overbearing, overweening, pleased, pleasing, presumptuous, projecting, raised, red-letter, rewarding, satisfied, satisfying, self-important, self-respecting, snobbish, snobby, snooty, splendid, stately, stuck-up, supercilious, toffee-nosed, vain. *antonym* humble.

prove *v* analyse, ascertain, assay, attest, authenticate, bear out, check, confirm, corroborate, demonstrate, determine, document, establish, evidence, evince, examine, experience, experiment, justify, show, substantiate, suffer, test, try, turn out, verify. *antonyms* discredit, disprove, falsify.

proven *adj* accepted, attested, authentic, certified, checked, confirmed, corroborated, definite, dependable, established, proved, reliable, tested, tried, trustworthy, undoubted, valid, verified.

provenance *n* birthplace, derivation, origin, source.

proverb *n* adage, aphorism, apophthegm, bromide, byword, dictum, gnome, maxim, precept, saying.

proverbial *adj* accepted, acknowledged, archetypal, axiomatic, conventional, current, customary, famed, famous, legendary, notorious, self-evident, time-honoured, traditional, typical, unquestioned, well-known.

provide *v* accommodate, add, afford, anticipate, arrange for, bring, cater, contribute, determine, equip, forearm, furnish, give, impart, lay down, lend, outfit, plan for, prepare for, present, produce, provision, render, require, serve, specify, state, stipulate, stock up, suit, supply, take measures, take precautions, yield. *antonyms* remove, take.

provide for endow, fend, keep, maintain, support, sustain. *antonyms* ignore, neglect.

providence *n* care, caution, destiny, discretion, divine intervention, far-sightedness, fate, foresight, forethought, fortune, God's will, kismet, perspicacity, predestination, predetermination, presence of mind, prudence. *antonym* improvidence.

provident *adj* canny, careful, cautious, discreet, economical, equipped, far-seeing, far-sighted, frugal, imaginative, long-sighted, prudent, sagacious, shrewd, thrifty, vigilant, wary, well-prepared, wise. *antonym* improvident.

providential *adj* convenient, fortuitous, fortunate, happy, heaven-sent, lucky, opportune, timely, welcome. *antonym* untimely.

providing *conj* as long as, contingent upon, given, on condition, on the assumption, on the understanding, provided, subject to, with the proviso.

province *n* area, bailiwick, business, capacity, charge, colony, concern, county, department, dependency, district, division, domain, duty, employment, field, function, line, orbit, part, pigeon, post, region, responsibility, role, section, sphere, territory, tract, zone.

provincial *adj* home-grown, homespun, insular, inward-looking, limited, local, narrow, narrow-minded, parish-pump, parochial, small-minded, small-town, uninformed, unsophisticated. *antonym* sophisticated.

provision *n* agreement, arrangement, catering, clause, condition, demand, equipping, fitting out, furnishing, plan, prearrangement, precaution, preparation, prerequisite, providing, proviso, purveying, requirement, specification,

stipulation, supplying, term. *antonyms* neglect, removal.

provisional *adj* conditional, contingent, interim, limited, pro tem, provisory, qualified, stop-gap, temporary, tentative, transitional. *antonyms* definite, fixed, permanent.

provisionally *adv* for the time being, interim, meanwhile, pro tem, pro tempore.

provisions *n* comestibles, eats, edibles, fare, food, foodstuffs, groceries, grub, provender, rations, stores, supplies, sustenance, victuals, vittles.

proviso *n* clause, condition, limitation, provision, qualification, requirement, reservation, restriction, rider, small print, stipulation.

provisory *adj* conditional, interim, provisional, qualified, temporary, tentative. *antonyms* definite, fixed, permanent.

provocation *n* affront, aggravation, annoyance, casus belli, cause, challenge, dare, grievance, grounds, incitement, indignity, inducement, injury, instigation, insult, justification, motivation, motive, offence, reason, red rag, stimulus, taunt, vexation.

provocative *adj* abusive, aggravating, alluring, annoying, arousing, challenging, disturbing, erotic, exciting, galling, goading, incensing, insulting, inviting, offensive, outrageous, provoking, seductive, sexy, stimulating, suggestive, tantalising, tempting. *antonyms* pacificatory, unprovocative.

provoke *v* affront, aggravate, anger, annoy, cause, chafe, elicit, enrage, evoke, exasperate, excite, fire, gall, generate, give rise to, incense, incite, induce, inflame, infuriate, inspire, instigate, insult, irk, irritate, kindle, madden, motivate, move, occasion, offend, pique, precipitate, produce, promote, prompt, put out, rile, rouse, stimulate, stir, vex. *antonyms* pacify, please, result.

provoking *adj* aggravating, annoying, exasperating, galling, infuriating, irking, irksome, irritating, maddening, obstructive, offensive, pesky, tiresome, vexatious, vexing. *antonyms* pacificatory, pleasing.

prowess *n* ability, accomplishment, adeptness, adroitness, aptitude, attainment, bravery, command, daring, dauntlessness, dexterity, doughtiness, excellence, expertise, expertness, facility, genius, heroism, mastery, skill, talent, valour. *antonyms* clumsiness, mediocrity.

prowl *v* creep, cruise, hunt, lurk, nose, patrol, range, roam, rove, scavenge, search, skulk, slink, sneak, snook, stalk, steal.

proximity *n* adjacency, closeness, contiguity, juxtaposition, nearness, neighbourhood, propinquity, proximation, vicinity. *antonym* remoteness.

prudence *n* care, caution, circumspection, common sense, discretion, economy, far-sightedness, foresight, forethought, frugality, good sense, heedfulness, judgement, judiciousness, planning, policy, precaution, preparedness, providence, sagacity, saving, thrift, vigilance, wariness, wisdom. *antonym* imprudence.

prudent *adj* canny, careful, cautious, circumspect, discerning, discreet, economical, far-sighted, frugal, judicious, politic, provident, sagacious, sage, sensible, shrewd, sparing, thrifty, vigilant, wary, well-advised, wise. *antonym* imprudent.

prudish *adj* demure, narrow-minded, old-maidish, overmodest, overnice, po-faced, priggish, prim, prissy, proper, puritanical, school-marmish, starchy, strait-laced, stuffy, ultra-virtuous, Victorian. *antonyms* easy-going, lax.

prurient *adj* desirous, dirty, erotic, indecent, lascivious, lecherous, lewd, libidinous, lustful, obscene, pornographic, salacious, smutty, voyeuristic. *antonym* decent.

pry *v* delve, dig, ferret, interfere, intrude, meddle, nose, peep, peer, poke, poke one's nose in, snoop. *antonym* mind one's own business.

prying *adj* curious, inquisitive, interfering, intrusive, meddlesome, meddling, nosy, peering, peery, snooping, snoopy, spying. *antonym* uninquisitive.

pseudo *adj* artificial, bogus, counterfeit, ersatz, fake, false, imitation, mock, phoney, pretended, sham, spurious, ungenuine. *antonym* genuine.

pseudonym *n* alias, assumed name, false name, incognito, monicker, nom de guerre, nom de plume, pen name, stage name.

psyche *n* anima, awareness, consciousness, individuality, intellect, intelligence, mind, personality, self, soul, spirit, subconscious, understanding.

psychological *adj* affective, cerebral, cognitive, emotional, imaginary, intellectual, mental, psychosomatic, subconscious, subjective, unconscious, unreal.

public *adj* accessible, acknowledged, circulating, civic, civil, common, communal, community, exposed, general, high-profile, important, known, national, notorious, obvious, open, overt, patent, plain, popular, prominent, published, recognised, social, state, universal, unrestricted, well-known, widespread. *antonym* private.
n audience, buyers, citizens, clientèle, commonalty, community, country, electorate, everyone, followers, following, masses, multitude, nation, patrons, people, populace, population, punters, society, supporters, voters.

publication *n* advertisement, airing, announcement, appearance, book, booklet, broadcasting, brochure, declaration, disclosure, dissemination, divulgation, handbill, issue, leaflet, magazine, newspaper, notification, pamphlet, periodical, proclamation, promulgation, publishing, reporting.

publicise *v* advertise, blazon, broadcast, hype, plug, promote, push, spotlight, spread about. *antonym* keep secret.

publicity *n* advertising, attention, ballyhoo, boost, build-up, hype, plug, press, promotion, public notice, splash. *antonym* secrecy.

publish *v* advertise, announce, bring out, broadcast, circulate, communicate, declare, diffuse, disclose, distribute, divulge, issue, leak, part, print, proclaim, produce, promulgate, publicise, reveal, spread, vent. *antonym* keep secret.

pucker *v* compress, contract, crease, crinkle, crumple, furrow, gather, purse, ruck, ruckle, ruffle, screw up, shrivel, tighten, wrinkle.
n crease, crinkle, crumple, fold, ruck, ruckle, wrinkle.

puerile *adj* babyish, childish, foolish, immature, inane, infantile, irresponsible, juvenile, naïve, petty, ridiculous, silly, trifling, trivial, weak. *antonym* mature.

puff *n* blast, breath, drag, draught, emanation, flurry, gust, pull, smoke, waft, whiff.
v bloat, blow, breathe, dilate, distend, drag, draw, exhale, expand, gasp, gulp, inflate, inhale, pant, pull, push, smoke, suck, swell, waft, wheeze, whiff, whiffle.

puffy *adj* bloated, distended, enlarged,

inflamed, inflated, puffed up, swollen. **antonym** flat.

pugnacious *adj* aggressive, antagonistic, argumentative, bare-knuckle, bellicose, belligerent, combative, contentious, disputatious, hostile, hot-tempered, irascible, petulant, quarrelsome. **antonym** easy-going.

puke *v* disgorge, heave, regurgitate, retch, spew, throw up, vomit.

pull *v* attract, cull, dislocate, drag, draw, draw out, entice, extract, gather, haul, jerk, lure, magnetise, pick, pluck, remove, rend, rip, sprain, strain, stretch, take out, tear, tow, track, trail, tug, tweak, uproot, weed, wrench, yank. **antonyms** deter, push, repel.

n advantage, allurement, attraction, clout, drag, drawing power, effort, exertion, force, forcefulness, influence, inhalation, jerk, leverage, lure, magnetism, muscle, power, seduction, tug, twitch, weight, yank. **antonyms** deterring, push, repelling.

pull a face frown, glower, grimace, knit one's brows, lower, pout, scowl, sulk.

pull a fast one on cheat, con, deceive, defraud, grift, hoodwink, put one over on, sting, swindle, take for a ride, trick.

pull apart attack, carp at, criticise, dismember, find fault, flay, knock, lay into, pan, part, pick holes in, pull to pieces, run down, separate, slam, slate. **antonym** praise.

pull down bulldoze, demolish, destroy, dismantle, knock down, raze, remove. **antonym** put up.

pull in arrest, arrive, attract, bring in, bust, clear, collar, come in, draw, draw in, draw up, earn, gain, gross, make, nab, nail, net, park, pinch, pocket, reach, run in, stop, take home. **antonyms** lose, pull away, repel.

pull off accomplish, achieve, bring off, carry out, manage, succeed, swing. **antonym** fail.

pull out abandon, depart, draw out, evacuate, leave, quit, retreat, withdraw. **antonym** join.

pull the wool over someone's eyes bamboozle, con, deceive, delude, dupe, fool, hoodwink, lead up the garden path, pull a fast one on, put one over on, snow, take in, trick.

pull through rally, recover, recuperate, survive, weather. **antonym** fail.

pull together collaborate, co-operate, team up, work together. **antonym** fight.

pull up admonish, brake, carpet, castigate, draw in, draw up, halt, lift, raise, rebuke, reprimand, reprove, stop, take to task, tell off, tick off, uproot.

pulsate *v* beat, drum, hammer, oscillate, palpitate, pound, pulse, quiver, throb, thud, thump, tick, vibrate.

pulverise *v* annihilate, crush, defeat, demolish, destroy, flatten, granulate, grind, hammer, mill, pestle, pound, smash, vanquish, wreck.

pummel *v* bang, batter, beat, hammer, knead, knock, nevel, pound, punch, strike, thump.

pump *v* cross-examine, debrief, drive, force, grill, inject, interrogate, pour, probe, push, question, quiz, send, supply.

pump out bail out, drain, draw off, empty, force out, siphon.

pump up blow up, dilate, distend, inflate, puff up.

punch¹ *v* bash, biff, bop, box, clout, hit, plug, pummel, slam, slug, smash, sock, strike, wallop.

n bash, biff, bite, blow, bop, clout, drive, effectiveness, force, forcefulness, hit, impact, jab, knock, knuckle sandwich, panache, pizzazz, plug, point, sock, thump, verve, vigour, wallop. **antonym** feebleness.

punch² *v* bore, cut, drill, perforate, pierce, pink, prick, puncture, stamp.

punch-up *n* argument, brawl, ding-dong, dust-up, fight, free-for-all, row, ruckus, scrap, set-to, shindy.

punctilious *adj* careful, ceremonious, conscientious, exact, finicky, formal, fussy, meticulous, nice, overnice, particular, precise, proper, scrupulous, strict. **antonyms** boorish, easy-going, informal.

punctual *adj* early, exact, in good time, on the dot, on time, precise, prompt, punctilious, strict, timely, up to time. **antonym** unpunctual.

punctually *adv* on the dot, on time, precisely, prompt, promptly, sharp. **antonym** unpunctually.

punctuate *v* accentuate, break, emphasise, interject, interrupt, intersperse, pepper, point, sprinkle.

puncture *n* break, cut, fissure, flat, flat tyre, hole, leak, nick, opening, perforation, rupture, slit.

v bore, cut, deflate, discourage, disillusion, flatten, humble, nick, penetrate, perforate, pierce, prick, rupture, take down a peg or two.

pungent *adj* acid, acrid, acrimonious, acute, aromatic, barbed, biting, bitter, caustic, cutting, fell, hot, incisive, keen, mordant, painful, penetrating, peppery, piercing, piquant, poignant, pointed, sarcastic, scathing, seasoned, sharp, sour, spicy, stinging, stringent, strong, tangy, tart, telling, trenchant. **antonyms** feeble, mild, tasteless.

punish v abuse, batter, beat, castigate, chasten, chastise, correct, crucify, discipline, flog, give a lesson to, give someone laldie, harm, hurt, injure, keelhaul, knee-cap, lash, manhandle, misuse, oppress, penalise, rough up, scourge, sort, strafe, trounce.

punishing adj arduous, backbreaking, burdensome, demanding, exhausting, fatiguing, grinding, gruelling, hard, strenuous, taxing, tiring, wearing. **antonym** easy.

punishment n abuse, beating, chastening, chastisement, comeuppance, correction, damnation, deserts, discipline, jankers, knee-capping, laldie, manhandling, medicine, pain, pay-off, penalty, penance, punition, retribution, sanction, torture, victimisation.

puny adj diminutive, dwarfish, feeble, frail, inconsequential, inferior, insignificant, little, meagre, minor, paltry, petty, piddling, sickly, stunted, tiny, trifling, trivial, underfed, undersized, undeveloped, weak, weakly, worthless. **antonyms** important, large, strong.

purchase v achieve, acquire, attain, buy, earn, gain, invest in, obtain, pay for, procure, ransom, realise, secure, win. **antonym** sell.

n acquisition, advantage, asset, buy, edge, foothold, footing, gain, grasp, grip, hold, influence, investment, lever, leverage, possession, property, support, toehold. **antonym** sale.

pure adj absolute, abstract, academic, antiseptic, authentic, blameless, chaste, clean, clear, disinfected, flawless, genuine, germ-free, guileless, highminded, honest, hygienic, immaculate, innocent, maidenly, modest, natural, neat, pasteurised, perfect, philosophical, real, refined, sanitary, sheer, simple, sincere, snow-white, speculative, spiritous, spotless, stainless, sterile, sterilised, straight, taintless, theoretical, thorough, true, unadulterate, unadulterated, unalloyed, unblemished, uncontaminated, uncorrupted, undefiled, unmingled, unmitigated, unmixed, unpolluted, unqualified, unsoiled,

unspoilt, unstained, unsullied, untainted, untarnished, upright, utter, virgin, virginal, virtuous, wholesome. **antonyms** adulterated, applied, defiled, immoral, impure, polluted, tainted.

purely adv absolutely, completely, entirely, exclusively, just, merely, only, plainly, sheerly, simply, solely, thoroughly, totally, utterly, wholly.

purge v absolve, clean out, cleanse, clear, dismiss, eject, eradicate, exonerate, expel, expiate, exterminate, extract, forgive, get rid of, kill, liquidate, oust, pardon, purify, remove, rid, root out, scour, wash, wipe out.

n aperient, catharsis, cathartic, ejection, elimination, emetic, enema, eradication, expulsion, extermination, laxative, liquidation, purgative, removal, witch hunt.

purification n absolution, catharsis, clarification, cleaning, cleansing, decontamination, deodorisation, disinfection, filtration, fumigation, purgation, redemption, refinement, sanctification, sanitisation. **antonyms** contamination, defilement, pollution.

purify v absolve, chasten, clarify, clean, cleanse, decontaminate, deodorise, disinfect, filter, fumigate, redeem, refine, sanctify, sanitise, sublimise, wash. **antonyms** contaminate, defile, pollute.

purifying adj cathartic, cleansing, purgative, purging, refining. **antonyms** contaminating, defiling, polluting.

purist adj austere, captious, fastidious, finicky, fussy, hypercritical, nitpicking, over-exact, over-fastidious, over-meticulous, over-particular, overprecise, pedantic, quibbling, strict, uncompromising. **antonyms** liberal, open-minded, tolerant.

puritan n disciplinarian, fanatic, killjoy, moralist, pietist, prude, spoil-sport, zealot. **antonyms** hedonist, libertarian. adj ascetic, austere, disciplinarian, hard-line, hide-bound, intolerant, moralistic, narrow, narrow-minded, prim, prudish, puritanical, selfdisciplined, severe, stern, strait-laced, strict, uncompromising. **antonyms** broad-minded, hedonistic, indulgent, liberal.

puritanism n abstemiousness, abstinence, asceticism, austerity, bigotry, fanaticism, narrow-mindedness, narrowness, priggishness, primness, propriety, prudishness, rigidity, rigorousness, self-denial, self-discipline, severity, sternness, stiffness, strictness, uncompromisingness, zealotry. *antonyms* broad-mindedness, hedonism, indulgence, liberality.

purity *n* blamelessness, chasteness, chastity, clarity, classicism, cleanliness, clearness, decency, faultlessness, fineness, genuineness, immaculateness, innocence, integrity, morality, piety, pureness, rectitude, refinement, sanctity, simplicity, sincerity, spotlessness, stainlessness, truth, untaintedness, uprightness, virginity, virtue, virtuousness, wholesomeness. *antonyms* immorality, impurity.

purloin *v* abstract, appropriate, filch, finger, half-inch, lift, nick, palm, pilfer, pinch, pocket, prig, remove, rob, snaffle, snitch, steal, swipe, take, thieve.

purport *v* allege, argue, assert, betoken, claim, convey, declare, denote, express, give out, imply, import, indicate, intend, maintain, mean, portend, pose as, pretend, proclaim, profess, seem, show, signify, suggest.

n bearing, direction, drift, gist, idea, implication, import, meaning, point, significance, spirit, substance, tendency, tenor, theme, thrust.

purpose *n* advantage, aim, ambition, aspiration, assiduity, avail, benefit, constancy, contemplation, decision, dedication, design, determination, devotion, drive, effect, end, firmness, function, gain, goal, good, hope, idea, ideal, intention, motive, object, objective, outcome, persistence, pertinacity, plan, point, principle, profit, project, rationale, reason, resolution, resolve, result, return, scheme, service, single-mindedness, steadfastness, target, tenacity, use, usefulness, utility, view, vision, will, wish, zeal.

v aim, aspire, contemplate, decide, design, desire, determine, intend, mean, meditate, plan, propose, resolve.

purposeful *adj* assiduous, decided, deliberate, determined, firm, fixed, motivated, persevering, persistent, pertinacious, positive, purposive, resolute, resolved, sedulous, settled, single-minded, steadfast, strong-willed, tenacious, unfaltering, unswerving. *antonym* purposeless.

purposeless *adj* aimless, empty, goalless, gratuitous, motiveless, needless, nonsensical, objectless, pointless, senseless, thoughtless, unasked-for, uncalled-for, unnecessary, useless,

vacuous, vain, wanton. *antonym* purposeful.

purposely *adv* by design, calculatedly, consciously, deliberately, designedly, expressly, intentionally, knowingly, o purpose, premeditatedly, specifically, wilfully, with malice aforethought. *antonyms* impulsively, spontaneously, unpremeditatedly.

purse *v* close, compress, contract, drav together, pucker, tighten, wrinkle.

pursue *v* accompany, adhere to, air at, aim for, aspire to, attend, bedevi beset, besiege, carry on, chase, chec out, conduct, continue, course, coun cultivate, desire, dog, engage in, follow follow up, go for, gun for, harass, harry haunt, hold to, hound, inquire into investigate, keep on, maintain, perform persecute, persevere in, persist in, plague practise, proceed, prosecute, purpose seek, set one's cap at, shadow, stalk strive for, tackle, tail, track, trail, try for wage, woo. *antonyms* eschew, shun.

pursuit[1] *n* chase, chevy, hounding hue and cry, hunt, hunting, inquiry investigation, quest, search, seeking stalking, tracking, trail, trailing.

pursuit[2] *n* activity, craft, hobby, interest line, occupation, pastime, pleasure, side line, speciality, vocation.

purvey *v* cater, communicate, deal ir disseminate, furnish, pass on, propagate provide, provision, publicise, publish put about, retail, sell, spread, stock supply, trade in, transmit.

push *v* advance, advertise, boost browbeat, bulldoze, bully, coerce constrain, depress, dragoon, drive edge, egg on, elbow, encourage expedite, force, hurry, hype, incite influence, inveigle, jockey, jog, joggle jostle, manhandle, manoeuvre, oblige peddle, persuade, plug, poke, press prod, promote, propagandise, propel publicise, ram, shoulder, shove, speed spur, squeeze, thrust, urge, wedge.

n advance, ambition, assault, attack butt, charge, determination, discharge dismissal, drive, dynamism, effort energy, enterprise, go, impetus, impulse initiative, jolt, knock, notice, nudge offensive, one's books, one's cards one's marching orders, onset, onslaught poke, pressure, prod, shove, the axe the boot, the bum's rush, the chop the sack, thrust, vigour, vim, vitality zip.

push off depart, go away, leave, mak

a move, make tracks, move, push along, shift, shove off.

ushed *adj* harassed, hard-pressed, hard-up, harried, hurried, in difficulties, pinched, pressed, rushed, short of, strapped, stretched, under pressure.

ushing *adj* aggressive, ambitious, assertive, bold, brash, bumptious, determined, driving, dynamic, enterprising, forceful, forward, go-ahead, high-powered, impertinent, intrusive, presumptuous, purposeful, pushy, resourceful, self-assertive, thrusting. *antonyms* conservative, diffident, unassertive, unassuming, unenterprising.

ush-over *n* child's play, cinch, doddle, dupe, easy mark, fall guy, gull, mug, picnic, piece of cake, sinecure, sitting duck, sitting target, soft touch, stooge, sucker, walk-over. *antonyms* challenge, labour.

ushy *adj* aggressive, ambitious, arrogant, assertive, assuming, bold, bossy, brash, bumptious, forceful, forward, loud, obtrusive, offensive, officious, over-confident, presumptuous, pushing, self-assertive. *antonyms* quiet, restrained, unassertive, unassuming.

usillanimous *adj* chicken, chicken-hearted, cowardly, craven, faint-hearted, fearful, feeble, gutless, lily-livered, mean-spirited, scared, spineless, timid, timorous, unassertive, unenterprising, weak, weak-kneed, yellow. *antonyms* ambitious, courageous, forceful, strong.

ussyfoot *v* beat about the bush, creep, equivocate, hedge, mess about, pad, prevaricate, prowl, sidestep, slink, steal, tiptoe.

ut *v* advance, apply, assign, bring, bring forward, cast, commit, condemn, consign, constrain, couch, deploy, deposit, dispose, drive, employ, enjoin, establish, express, fit, fix, fling, force, formulate, forward, frame, heave, hurl, impel, impose, induce, inflict, land, lay, levy, lob, make, oblige, offer, park, phrase, pitch, place, plonk, pose, position, post, present, propose, push, render, require, rest, send, set, set down, settle, situate, state, station, subject, submit, suggest, tender, throw, thrust, toss, utter, voice, word, write.

put across bring home to, communicate, convey, explain, express, get through to, put over, spell out.

put an end to abolish, annihilate, annul, cancel, check, destroy, discontinue, kibosh, knock on the head,

nullify, put a stop to, put paid to, put the kibosh on, put the lid on, put the mockers on, stem, stop, terminate.

put aside[1] deposit, hoard, keep, lay by, put by, reserve, retain, salt away, save, set aside, stash, stockpile, store, stow.

put aside[2] abandon, bury, discard, discount, dispense with, disregard, forget, ignore, set aside.

put away certify, commit, consume, eat, imprison, institutionalise, kill, put aside, remove, renounce, replace, repudiate, return, save, shift, store, tidy, wolf.

put back delay, postpone, replace, repulse, reschedule, return.

put down[1] enter, inscribe, log, note, record, register, report, state, transcribe, write down.

put down[2] abash, condemn, crush, defeat, deflate, degrade, destroy, dismiss, disparage, humble, humiliate, kill, mortify, put to sleep, quash, quell, reject, repress, shame, silence, slight, snub, suppress, take down a peg, topple.

put down[3] ascribe, assign, attribute, impute.

put forward advance, introduce, move, nominate, offer, present, press, proffer, propose, recommend, submit, suggest, table, tender.

put in enter, input, insert, key in.

put off abash, confuse, daunt, defer, delay, demoralise, deter, discomfit, disconcert, discourage, dishearten, dismay, dispirit, dissuade, distress, divert, nonplus, perturb, postpone, put out, rattle, reschedule, throw, unnerve, unsettle. *antonym* encourage.

put on add, affect, affix, apply, assume, attach, back, bet, deceive, do, don, dress, fake, feign, gain, impose, increase by, lay, make believe, mislead, mount, place, present, pretend, produce, sham, show, simulate, stage, stake, wager.

put one's finger on discover, find out, hit the nail on the head, hit upon, identify, indicate, isolate, locate, pin down, pinpoint, place, recall, remember.

put out affront, anger, announce, annoy, bother, broadcast, circulate, confound, discomfit, discompose, disconcert, discountenance, dislocate, dismiss, disturb, douse, embarrass, exasperate, exert, expel, extinguish, give out, harass, hurt, impose on, incommode, inconvenience, irk, irritate, issue, nettle, offend, perturb, produce, provoke, publish, quench, release, smother, trouble, upset, vex.

put the wind up agitate, alarm, daunt, discourage, frighten, panic, perturb, scare, sound the alarm, startle, unnerve. *antonym* reassure.

put through accomplish, achieve, bring off, conclude, effect, execute, finalise, manage.

put to shame disgrace, eclipse, humble, humiliate, outclass, outdo, outstrip, shame, show up, surpass.

put up accommodate, advance, assemble, board, build, construct, entertain, erect, fabricate, float, give, house, invest, lodge, nominate, offer, pay, pledge, present, propose, provide, put forward, quarter, raise, recommend, shelter, submit, supply.

put up to abet, encourage, goad, incite, instigate, prompt, urge. *antonyms* discourage, dissuade.

put up with abide, allow, bear, brook, endure, lump, stand, stand for, stomach, suffer, swallow, take, take lying down, tolerate. *antonyms* object to, protest against, reject.

put upon exploit, impose on, inconvenience, take a loan of, use.

putative *adj* alleged, assumed, conjectural, hypothetical, imputed, presumed, presumptive, reported, reputed, supposed, suppositional, supposititious.

put-down *n* affront, dig, disparagement, gibe, humiliation, insult, rebuff, sarcasm, slap in the face, slight, sneer, snub.

put-off *n* constraint, curb, damper, deterrent, discouragement, disincentive, hindrance, obstacle, restraint. *antonyms* encouragement, incentive.

putrefy *v* addle, corrupt, decay, decompose, deteriorate, fester, gangrene, go bad, mortify, mould, perish, rot, spoil, stink, taint.

putrescent *adj* decaying, decomposing, festering, perishing, putrefying, rotting, stinking.

putrid *adj* addled, bad, contaminated, corrupt, decayed, decomposed, fetid, foosty, foul, gangrenous, mouldy, off, putrefied, rancid, rank, reeking, rotten,

rotting, spoiled, stinking, tainted. *antonyms* fresh, wholesome.

put-upon *adj* abused, beset, exploited, harassed, harried, henpecked, ill-used, imposed on, inconvenienced, overworked, persecuted.

puzzle¹ *v* baffle, bamboozle, beat, bewilder, confound, confuse, fickle, floor, flummox, mystify, nonplus, perplex, pother, stump, worry.

n acrostic, anagram, brain-teaser, confusion, conundrum, crossword, difficulty, dilemma, enigma, jigsaw, knot, maze, mind-bender, mystery, paradox, poser, problem, quandary, question, riddle.

puzzle² *v* brood, cogitate, consider, deliberate, figure, meditate, mull over, muse, ponder, rack one's brains, reason, ruminate, study, think, wonder, worry.

puzzle out clear up, crack, decipher, decode, excogitate, figure out, reason out, resolve, see, solve, sort out, think out, unravel, unriddle, untangle, work out.

puzzled *adj* at a loss, at sea, baffled, bamboozled, beaten, bemused, bewildered, confounded, confused, disorientated, doubtful, flummoxed, in a haze, lost, mixed up, mystified, nonplussed, perplexed, stuck, stumped, stymied, uncertain. *antonyms* certain, clear.

puzzlement *n* astonishment, bafflement, bamboozlement, bewilderment, confusion, disorientation, doubt, doubtfulness, incertitude, mystification, perplexity, surprise, uncertainty, wonder. *antonyms* certainty, clarity, lucidity.

puzzling *adj* abstruse, ambiguous, baffling, bewildering, bizarre, cabalistic, circuitous, confusing, cryptic, curious, enigmatic, equivocal, impenetrable, inexplicable, intricate, involved, knotty, labyrinthine, mind-bending, mind-boggling, misleading, mysterious, mystical, mystifying, peculiar, perplexing, queer, riddling, Sphynx-like, strange, tangled, tortuous, unaccountable, unclear, unfathomable.

Q

quack *n* charlatan, cowboy, fake, fraud, impostor, masquerader, mountebank, phoney, pretender, pseud, sham, swindler, trickster, witch-doctor.
adj bogus, counterfeit, fake, false, fraudulent, phoney, pretended, sham, so-called, spurious, supposed, unqualified. **antonym** genuine.

quaff *v* booze, down, drain, drink, gulp, guzzle, imbibe, knock back, swallow, swig, swill, tipple, tope.

quail *v* back away, blench, cower, droop, faint, falter, flinch, quake, recoil, shake, shrink, shudder, shy away, tremble, wince.

quaint *adj* absurd, antiquated, antique, bizarre, charming, curious, droll, eccentric, fanciful, fantastic, freaky, funky, Heath-Robinson, ingenious, odd, old-fashioned, old-time, old-world, peculiar, picturesque, queer, rum, singular, strange, unconventional, unusual, weird, whimsical.

quake *v* convulse, heave, jolt, move, pulsate, quail, quiver, rock, shake, shiver, shudder, sway, throb, totter, tremble, vibrate, waver, wobble.

qualification[1] *n* ability, accomplishment, adequacy, aptitude, attribute, capability, capacity, certification, competence, eligibility, fitness, skill, suitability, suitableness, training.

qualification[2] *n* adaptation, adjustment, allowance, caveat, condition, criterion, exception, exemption, limitation, modification, objection, provision, proviso, reservation, restriction, stipulation.

qualified[1] *adj* able, accomplished, adept, adequate, capable, certificated, certified, competent, efficient, eligible, equipped, experienced, expert, fit, knowledgeable, licensed, practised, proficient, skilful, talented, trained. **antonym** unqualified.

qualified[2] *adj* bounded, cautious, circumscribed, conditional, confined, contingent, equivocal, guarded, limited, modified, provisional, reserved, restricted.

qualify[1] *v* authorise, capacitate, certificate, empower, endow, equip, fit, graduate, permit, prepare, sanction, shape, train. **antonym** unfit.

qualify[2] *v* abate, adapt, adjust, alleviate, assuage, categorise, characterise, circumscribe, classify, define, delimit, describe, designate, diminish, distinguish, ease, lessen, limit, mitigate, moderate, modify, modulate, reduce, regulate, restrain, restrict, soften, temper, vary, weaken.

quality *n* aspect, attribute, calibre, character, characteristic, class, complexion, condition, constitution, deal, description, distinction, essence, excellence, feature, fineness, grade, kidney, kind, make, mark, merit, nature, peculiarity, position, pre-eminence, property, rank, refinement, sort, standing, status, superiority, talent, timbre, tone, trait, value, water, worth.

qualm *n* anxiety, apprehension, compunction, disquiet, doubt, fear, hesitation, misgiving, pang, presentiment, regret, reluctance, remorse, scruple, twinge, uncertainty, unease, uneasiness, worry.

quandary *n* bewilderment, confusion, corner, difficulty, dilemma, doubt, embarrassment, entanglement, fix, hole, imbroglio, impasse, jam, mess, perplexity, plight, predicament, problem, puzzle, uncertainty.

quantity *n* aggregate, allotment, amount, breadth, bulk, capacity, content, dosage, expanse, extent, greatness, length, lot, magnitude, mass, measure, number, part, portion, proportion, quota, share, size, spread, strength, sum, total, volume, weight.

quarrel *n* affray, altercation, argument, barney, beef, bicker, brawl, breach, broil, clash, commotion, conflict, contention, controversy, debate, difference, disagreement, discord, disputation, dispute, dissension, dissidence, disturbance, dust-up, estrangement, feud, fight, fracas, fratch, fray, misunderstanding, row, rupture, schism, scrap, shouting match, slanging match, spat, split, squabble, strife, tiff, tumult, vendetta, wrangle. **antonyms** agreement, harmony.
v altercate, argue, be at loggerheads, be at variance, bicker, brawl, carp, clash, contend, differ, disagree, dispute, dissent, fall out, fight, find fault, object, pick holes, question, row, spar, spat, squabble, take exception, tiff, wrangle. **antonym** agree.

quarrelling *adj* at loggerheads, at odds, at variance, bickering, contending, discordant, dissentient, feuding, fighting, rowing, scrapping, squabbling, warring, wrangling. *antonyms* amicable, friendly.

quarrelsome *adj* antagonistic, argumentative, bellicose, belligerent, cantankerous, captious, combative, contentious, contrary, cross, disputatious, fractious, ill-tempered, irascible, irritable, peevish, perverse, petulant, pugnacious, querulous, stroppy, testy, truculent, turbulent, wranglesome. *antonyms* peaceable, placid.

quarter[1] *n* area, direction, district, division, locality, location, neighbourhood, part, place, point, position, province, quartier, region, section, sector, side, spot, station, territory, vicinity, zone.

quarter[2] *n* clemency, compassion, favour, forgiveness, grace, indulgence, leniency, mercy, pardon, pity.

quarters *n* abode, accommodation, apartment, barracks, billet, chambers, digs, domicile, dwelling, habitation, lodging, lodgings, post, residence, rooms, station.

quash *v* annul, cancel, crush, declare null and void, defeat, disannul, disenact, invalidate, nullify, overrule, overthrow, quell, repress, rescind, reverse, revoke, set aside, squash, subdue, suppress, void. *antonyms* confirm, justify, reinstate, vindicate.

quaver *v* break, crack, flicker, flutter, oscillate, pulsate, quake, quiver, shake, shudder, tremble, trill, twitter, vibrate, warble.

n break, quiver, shake, sob, throb, tremble, trembling, tremolo, tremor, trill, vibration, vibrato, warble.

queasy *adj* bilious, dizzy, faint, giddy, green, groggy, ill, indisposed, nauseated, off-colour, queer, sick, sickened, squeamish, unwell.

queen *n* beauty, belle, consort, diva, doyenne, empress, goddess, grande dame, idol, mistress, monarch, prima donna, princess, ruler, sovereign, star.

queenly *adj* dignified, gracious, grand, imperial, imperious, majestic, noble, regal, royal, sovereign, stately. *antonym* undignified.

queer *adj* aberrant, abnormal, absurd, anomalous, atypical, bizarre, cranky, crazy, curious, daft, demented, deranged, deviant, disquieting, dizzy, doubtful, droll, dubious, eccentric, eerie, erratic, exceptional, extraordinary, faint, fanciful, fantastic, fishy,

freakish, funny, giddy, grotesque, homosexual, idiosyncratic, ill, irrational, irregular, light-headed, mad, mysterious, odd, offbeat, outlandish, peculiar, preternatural, puzzling, quaint, queasy, questionable, reeling, remarkable, rum, screwy, shady, shifty, singular, strange, suspect, suspicious, touched, unaccountable, unbalanced, uncanny, uncommon, unconventional, uneasy, unhinged, unnatural, unorthodox, unusual, unwell, unwonted, weird. *antonyms* common, ordinary, straightforward, unexceptional, usual.

v botch, cheat, endanger, foil, frustrate, harm, impair, imperil, injure, jeopardise, mar, ruin, spoil, stymie, thwart, upset, wreck.

quell *v* allay, alleviate, appease, assuage, blunt, calm, compose, conquer, crush, deaden, defeat, dull, extinguish, hush, mitigate, moderate, mollify, overcome, overpower, pacify, put down, quash, quench, quiet, reduce, silence, soothe, squash, stifle, subdue, subjugate, suppress, vanquish.

quench *v* allay, appease, check, cool, crush, damp down, destroy, douse, end, extinguish, overcome, put out, quash, quell, sate, satisfy, silence, slake, smother, snuff out, stifle, suppress.

querulous *adj* cantankerous, captious, carping, cavilling, censorious, complaining, crabbed, critical, cross, crusty, discontented, dissatisfied, exacting, fault-finding, fretful, fussy, grouchy, grumbling, hypercritical, intolerant, irascible, irritable, peevish, perverse, petulant, plaintive, quarrelsome, sour, testy, thrawn, waspish, whingeing, whining. *antonyms* contented, equable, placid, uncomplaining.

query *v* ask, be sceptical of, call in question, challenge, disbelieve, dispute, distrust, doubt, enquire, mistrust, quarrel with, question, suspect. *antonym* accept.

n demand, doubt, hesitation, inquiry, misgiving, objection, problem, question, quibble, reservation, scepticism, suspicion, uncertainty.

quest *n* adventure, crusade, enterprise, expedition, exploration, hunt, inquiry, investigation, journey, mission, pilgrimage, pursuit, search, undertaking, venture, voyage.

question *v* ask, be sceptical of, challenge, controvert, cross-examine, debrief, disbelieve, dispute, distrust, doubt, enquire, examine, grill, impugn, interpellate, interrogate, interview, investigate, mistrust, oppose, probe, pump, quarrel with, query, quiz, suspect. *n* argument, confusion, contention, controversy, debate, difficulty, dispute, doubt, dubiety, examination, inquiry, interpellation, interrogation, investigation, issue, misgiving, motion, point, problem, proposal, proposition, query, quibble, subject, theme, topic, uncertainty.

uestionable *adj* arguable, borderline, controversial, debatable, disputable, doubtful, dubious, dubitable, equivocal, fishy, iffy, impugnable, moot, problematical, queer, shady, suspect, suspicious, uncertain, undetermined, unproven, unreliable, unsettled, vexed. *antonyms* certain, indisputable, straightforward.

ueue *n* file, line, line-up, order, procession, sequence, series, string, succession, tail, tail-back, train.

uibble *v* carp, cavil, chop logic, equivocate, prevaricate, shift, split hairs.

uibbling *adj* ambiguous, captious, carping, casuistic, critical, equivocating, evasive, hair-splitting, logic-chopping, niggling, nit-picking, overnice.

uick *adj* able, active, acute, adept, adroit, agile, alert, animated, apt, astute, awake, brief, bright, brisk, clever, cursory, deft, dexterous, discerning, energetic, expeditious, express, fast, fleet, flying, hasty, headlong, hurried, immediate, instant, instantaneous, intelligent, keen, lively, nifty, nimble, nippy, penetrating, perceptive, perfunctory, precipitate, prompt, quick-witted, rapid, ready, receptive, responsive, sharp, shrewd, skilful, smart, snappy, speedy, spirited, sprightly, spry, sudden, summary, swift, unhesitating, vivacious, wide-awake, winged. *antonyms* dull, slow.

uicken *v* accelerate, activate, advance, animate, arouse, dispatch, energise, enliven, excite, expedite, galvanise, hasten, hurry, impel, incite, inspire, invigorate, kindle, precipitate, reactivate, refresh, reinvigorate, resuscitate, revitalise, revive, revivify, rouse, sharpen, speed, stimulate, strengthen, vitalise, vivify. *antonyms* dull, retard.

uickly *adv* abruptly, at a rate of knots, at the double, before you can say Jack Robinson, briskly, by leaps and bounds, cursorily, expeditiously, express, fast,

hastily, hell for leather, hotfoot, hurriedly, immediately, instantaneously, instantly, lickety-split, like a bat out of hell, perfunctorily, posthaste, promptly, pronto, quick, rapidly, readily, soon, speedily, swiftly, unhesitatingly. *antonyms* slowly, tardily, thoroughly.

quickness *n* acuteness, agility, alertness, aptness, astuteness, briskness, deftness, dexterity, expedition, hastiness, immediacy, instantaneousness, intelligence, keenness, liveliness, nimbleness, penetration, precipitation, promptitude, promptness, quick-wittedness, rapidity, readiness, receptiveness, sharpness, shrewdness, speed, speediness, suddenness, summariness, swiftness, turn of speed. *antonyms* dullness, slowness, tardiness.

quick-tempered *adj* excitable, explosive, fiery, hot-tempered, impatient, impulsive, irascible, irritable, petulant, quarrelsome, shrewish, snappy, splenetic, temperamental, testy, touchy, volcanic, waspish. *antonyms* cool, dispassionate.

quick-witted *adj* acute, alert, astute, bright, clever, crafty, ingenious, intelligent, keen, nimble-witted, penetrating, perceptive, ready-witted, resourceful, sharp, shrewd, smart, wide-awake, witty. *antonyms* dull, slow, stupid.

quiescent *adj* asleep, calm, dormant, in abeyance, inactive, inert, latent, motionless, passive, peaceful, placid, quiet, reposeful, resting, serene, silent, sleeping, smooth, still, tranquil, undisturbed, untroubled. *antonym* active.

quiet *adj* calm, composed, conservative, contemplative, contented, docile, dumb, even-tempered, gentle, hushed, inaudible, isolated, lonely, low, low-pitched, meek, mild, modest, motionless, noiseless, pacific, passive, peaceable, peaceful, placid, plain, private, removed, reserved, restful, restrained, retired, retiring, secluded, secret, sedate, self-contained, serene, shtoom, shy, silent, simple, smooth, sober, soft, soundless, still, stilly, subdued, taciturn, thoughtful, tranquil, uncommunicative, undisturbed, uneventful, unexcitable, unexciting, unforthcoming, unfrequented, uninterrupted, unobtrusive, untroubled. *antonyms* busy, noisy, obtrusive. *n* calm, calmness, ease, hush, lull, peace, quiescence, quietness, quietude, repose, rest, serenity, silence, stillness, tranquillity. **antonyms** bustle, disturbance, noise.

quieten v abate, allay, alleviate, appease, assuage, blunt, calm, compose, deaden, diminish, dull, hush, lull, mitigate, mollify, muffle, mute, pacify, palliate, quell, quiet, reduce, silence, smooth, sober, soothe, stifle, still, stop, subdue, tranquillise. **antonyms** aggravate, discompose, disturb, exacerbate.

quietly adv calmly, composedly, confidentially, contentedly, demurely, diffidently, dispassionately, docilely, gently, humbly, inaudibly, meekly, mildly, modestly, mutely, noiselessly, obediently, patiently, peacefully, placidly, privately, secretly, serenely, silently, softly, soundlessly, surreptitiously, tranquilly, undemonstratively, unobtrusively, unostentatiously, unpretentiously. **antonyms** noisily, obtrusively.

quietness n calm, calmness, composure, dullness, hush, inactivity, inertia, lull, peace, placidity, quiescence, quiet, quietude, repose, serenity, silence, still, stillness, tranquillity, uneventfulness. **antonyms** activity, bustle, commotion, disturbance, noise, racket.

quietus n acquittance, coup de grâce, death, death-blow, death-stroke, decease, demise, discharge, dispatch, end, extinction, finishing stroke, quittance, silencing.

quintessential adj archetypical, complete, consummate, definitive, entire, essential, ideal, perfect, prototypical, ultimate.

quip n bon mot, crack, epigram, gag, gibe, jest, joke, mot, one-liner, pleasantry, retort, riposte, wisecrack, witticism.
v gag, gibe, jest, joke, quirk, retort, riposte, wisecrack.

quirk n aberration, caprice, characteristic, curiosity, eccentricity, fancy, fetish, foible, freak, habit, idiosyncrasy, mannerism, oddity, oddness, peculiarity, singularity, trait, turn, twist, vagary, warp, whim.

quisling n betrayer, collaborator, fi⬛ columnist, Judas, renegade, trait⬛ turncoat.

quit v abandon, abdicate, cea⬛ conclude, decamp, depart, dese⬛ disappear, discontinue, drop, end, ex⬛ forsake, give up, go, halt, leav⬛ relinquish, renege, renounce, repudia⬛ resign, retire, stop, surrender, suspen⬛ vamoose, vanish, withdraw.

quite adv absolutely, comparative⬛ completely, entirely, exactly, fair⬛ fully, moderately, perfectly, precise⬛ rather, relatively, somewhat, total⬛ utterly, wholly.

quits adj equal, even, level, square.

quiver v agitate, convulse, flick⬛ flutter, oscillate, palpitate, pulsa⬛ quake, quaver, shake, shiver, shudd⬛ tremble, vibrate, wobble.
n convulsion, flicker, flutt⬛ oscillation, palpitation, pulsation, shal⬛ shiver, shudder, spasm, throb, t⬛ tremble, tremor, vibration, wobble.

quixotic adj extravagant, fancif⬛ fantastical, idealistic, impetuo⬛ impracticable, impulsive, romant⬛ starry-eyed, unrealistic, unworld⬛ Utopian, visionary. **antonyms** har⬛ headed, practical, realistic.

quiz n examination, investigati⬛ questioning, questionnaire, test.
v ask, cross-examine, cross-questic⬛ debrief, examine, grill, interroga⬛ investigate, pump, question.

quota n allocation, allowan⬛ assignment, cut, part, percenta⬛ portion, proportion, ration, share, sli⬛ whack.

quotation[1] n citation, crib, cuttin⬛ excerpt, extract, gobbet, passage, pie⬛ quote, reference.

quotation[2] n charge, cost, estima⬛ figure, price, quote, rate, tender.

quote v adduce, attest, cite, detail, ech⬛ instance, name, parrot, recall, reci⬛ recollect, refer to, repeat, reprodu⬛ retell.

quoted adj above-mentioned, cite⬛ forementioned, instanced, referred ⬛ reported, reproduced, stated.

R

rabble *n* commonalty, commoners, crowd, herd, hoi polloi, horde, masses, mob, peasantry, plebs, populace, proles, proletariat, riffraff, scum, swarm, throng, trash. **antonyms** aristocracy, elite, nobility.

rabble-rouser *n* agitator, demagogue, firebrand, fomenter, mischief-maker, mob-orator, ringleader, troublemaker, tub-thumper.

rabid *adj* berserk, bigoted, crazed, extreme, fanatical, fervent, frantic, frenzied, furious, hydrophobic, hysterical, infuriated, intemperate, intolerant, irrational, mad, maniacal, narrow-minded, obsessive, overzealous, raging, unreasoning, violent, wild, zealous.

race¹ *n* chase, competition, contention, contest, dash, derby, marathon, pursuit, quest, regatta, rivalry, scramble, sprint, steeplechase.
v career, compete, contest, dart, dash, fly, gallop, hare, hasten, hurry, run, rush, speed, sprint, tear, zoom.

race² *n* ancestry, blood, breed, clan, descent, family, folk, house, issue, kin, kindred, line, lineage, nation, offspring, people, progeny, seed, stirps, stock, strain, tribe, type.

racial *adj* ancestral, ethnic, ethnological, folk, genealogical, genetic, inherited, national, tribal.

raciness *n* animation, bawdiness, boisterousness, breeziness, buoyancy, doubtfulness, dubiousness, dynamism, ebullience, energy, exhilaration, freshness, gaminess, indecency, indelicacy, jauntiness, lewdness, naughtiness, piquancy, pungency, relish, ribaldry, richness, salaciousness, sharpness, smuttiness, spiciness, suggestiveness, tanginess, tastiness, zest, zestfulness.

rack *v* afflict, agonise, convulse, crucify, distress, excruciate, harass, harrow, lacerate, oppress, pain, shake, strain, stress, stretch, tear, torment, torture, wrench, wrest, wring.

racket¹ *n* ballyhoo, clamour, clangour, commotion, din, disturbance, fuss, hubbub, hullabaloo, hurly-burly, kerfuffle, noise, outcry, pandemonium, row, shouting, tumult, uproar.

racket² *n* business, con, deception, dodge, fiddle, fraud, game, scheme, swindle, trick.

racy *adj* animated, bawdy, blue, boisterous, breezy, broad, buoyant, distinctive, doubtful, dubious, dynamic, ebullient, energetic, entertaining, enthusiastic, exciting, exhilarating, heady, immodest, indecent, indelicate, jaunty, lewd, lively, naughty, piquant, pungent, ribald, rich, risqué, salacious, sharp, smutty, sparkling, spicy, spirited, stimulating, strong, suggestive, tangy, tasty, vigorous, zestful. **antonyms** dull, ponderous.

radiance *n* brightness, brilliance, delight, effulgence, gaiety, glare, gleam, glitter, glow, happiness, incandescence, joy, lambency, light, luminosity, lustre, pleasure, rapture, refulgence, resplendence, shine, splendour, warmth.

radiant *adj* aglow, alight, beaming, beatific, blissful, bright, brilliant, delighted, ecstatic, effulgent, gleaming, glittering, glorious, glowing, happy, illuminated, incandescent, joyful, joyous, lambent, luminous, lustrous, rapturous, refulgent, resplendent, shining, sparkling, splendid, sunny. **antonym** dull.

radiate *v* branch, diffuse, disseminate, diverge, emanate, emit, gleam, glitter, issue, pour, scatter, shed, shine, spread, spread out.

radical *adj* basic, complete, comprehensive, constitutional, deep-seated, entire, essential, excessive, extreme, extremist, fanatical, far-reaching, fundamental, inherent, innate, intrinsic, native, natural, organic, primary, profound, revolutionary, rooted, severe, sweeping, thorough, thoroughgoing, total, violent. **antonym** superficial.
n extremist, fanatic, jacobin, left-winger, militant, reformer, reformist, revolutionary.

raffish *adj* bohemian, careless, casual, cheap, coarse, dashing, devil-may-care, disreputable, dissipated, dissolute, flamboyant, flashy, garish, gaudy, gross, improper, jaunty, loud, rakish, showy, sporty, tasteless, tawdry, trashy, uncouth, vulgar. **antonyms** decorous, proper, sedate, staid.

rag *v* badger, bait, chaff, jeer, mock, rib, ridicule, taunt, tease, torment.

ragbag *n* assemblage, confusion,

hotchpotch, jumble, medley, miscellany, mixture, pot-pourri, salad.

rage *n* agitation, anger, chafe, craze, enthusiasm, fad, fashion, frenzy, fury, ire, madness, mania, obsession, paddy, passion, style, tantrum, vehemence, violence, vogue, wrath.

v chafe, explode, fret, fulminate, fume, inveigh, ramp, rampage, rant, rave, seethe, storm, surge, thunder.

ragged *adj* broken, desultory, disorganised, down-at-heel, erratic, fragmented, frayed, irregular, jagged, moth-eaten, notched, patchy, rent, ripped, rough, rugged, scraggy, serrated, shabby, shaggy, tattered, tatty, threadbare, torn, uneven, unfinished, unkempt, worn-out.

raging *adj* enraged, fizzing, frenzied, fulminating, fuming, furious, incensed, infuriated, irate, mad, rabid, rampageous, raving, seething, wrathful.

raid *n* attack, break-in, bust, descent, foray, incursion, inroad, invasion, irruption, onset, onslaught, sally, seizure, sortie, strike, swoop.

v attack, bust, descend on, do, forage, foray, invade, loot, maraud, pillage, plunder, ransack, rifle, rush, sack.

rail *v* abuse, arraign, attack, castigate, censure, criticise, decry, denounce, fulminate, inveigh, jeer, mock, revile, ridicule, scoff, upbraid, vituperate, vociferate.

raillery *n* badinage, banter, chaff, invective, irony, jeering, jesting, joke, joking, kidding, mockery, pleasantry, ragging, repartee, ribbing, ridicule, satire, sport, teasing.

rain *n* cloudburst, deluge, downpour, drizzle, fall, flood, hail, mizzle, precipitation, raindrops, rainfall, rains, shower, squall, stream, torrent.

v bestow, bucket, deluge, deposit, drizzle, drop, expend, fall, heap, lavish, mizzle, pour, shower, spit, sprinkle, teem.

raise *v* abandon, activate, advance, aggrandise, aggravate, amplify, arouse, assemble, augment, awaken, boost, breed, broach, build, cause, collect, construct, create, cultivate, develop, discontinue, elate, elevate, emboss, end, engender, enhance, enlarge, erect, escalate, evoke, exaggerate, exalt, excite, foment, form, foster, gather, gentrify, get, grow, heave, heighten, hoist, incite, increase, inflate, instigate, intensify, introduce, kindle, levy, lift, loft, magnify,

mass, mobilise, moot, motivate, muster, nurture, obtain, occasion, originate, pose, prefer, produce, promote, propagate, provoke, rally, rear, recruit, reinforce, relinquish, remove, sky, start, strengthen, sublime, suggest, terminate, up, upgrade, uplift. **antonyms** debase, decrease, degrade, dismiss, lower, reduce, suppress.

rake¹ *v* accumulate, amass, bombard, collect, comb, drag, examine, gather, graze, harrow, haul in, hoe, hunt, make, pepper, ransack, remove, scan, scour, scrape, scratch, scrutinise, search, strafe, sweep.

rake² *n* debauchee, degenerate, dissolute, hedonist, lecher, libertine, loose-liver, playboy, pleasure-seeker, prodigal, profligate, sensualist, spendthrift, swinger, voluptuary. **antonyms** ascetic, puritan.

rakish *adj* abandoned, breezy, dapper, dashing, debauched, debonair, degenerate, depraved, devil-may-care, dissipated, dissolute, flamboyant, flashy, immoral, jaunty, lecherous, libertine, licentious, loose, natty, prodigal, profligate, raffish, sharp, sinful, smart, snazzy, sporty, stylish, wanton.

rally *v* assemble, bunch, cheer, cluster, collect, congregate, convene, embolden, encourage, gather, hearten, improve, marshal, mass, mobilise, muster, organise, pick up, rally round, reassemble, recover, recuperate, re-form, regroup, reorganise, revive, round up, summon, unite.

n assembly, comeback, concourse, conference, congregation, convention, convocation, gathering, improvement, jamboree, meeting, recovery, recuperation, regrouping, renewal, reorganisation, resurgence, reunion, revival, stand.

ram *v* beat, butt, cram, crash, crowd, dash, drive, drum, force, hammer, hit, impact, jam, pack, pound, slam, smash, strike, stuff, tamp, thrust.

ramble *v* amble, babble, chatter, digress, divagate, dodder, drift, expatiate, maunder, meander, perambulate, range, roam, rove, saunter, snake, straggle, stray, stroll, traipse, walk, wander, wind, zigzag.

n divagation, excursion, hike, perambulation, roaming, roving, saunter, stroll, tour, traipse, trip, walk.

rambling *adj* circuitous, desultory, diffuse, digressive, disconnected, discursive, disjointed, excursive, incoherent, irregular, long-drawn-out, long-winded, periphrastic, prolix, sprawling, spreading, straggling, trailing, wordy. **antonym** direct.

ramification *n* consequence, development, result, upshot.

rampage *v* rage, rant, rave, run amuck, run riot, run wild, rush, storm, tear.

n destruction, frenzy, furore, fury, rage, storm, tempest, tumult, uproar, violence.

rampant *adj* aggressive, dominant, epidemic, erect, excessive, exuberant, fierce, flagrant, luxuriant, outrageous, prevalent, prodigal, profuse, raging, rampaging, rank, rearing, rife, riotous, standing, unbridled, unchecked, uncontrollable, uncontrolled, ungovernable, unrestrained, upright, vehement, violent, wanton, widespread, wild.

ramshackle *adj* broken-down, crumbling, decrepit, derelict, dilapidated, flimsy, haywire, rickety, shaky, tottering, tumbledown, unsafe, unsteady. **antonyms** solid, stable.

rancid *adj* bad, fetid, foul, fusty, musty, off, putrid, rank, rotten, sour, stale, strong-smelling, tainted. **antonym** sweet.

rancorous *adj* acrimonious, bitter, hostile, implacable, malevolent, malignant, resentful, spiteful, splenetic, vengeful, venomous, vindictive, virulent.

rancour *n* acrimony, animosity, animus, antipathy, bitterness, enmity, grudge, hate, hatred, hostility, ill-feeling, ill-will, malevolence, malice, resentfulness, resentment, spite, spleen, venom, vindictiveness.

random *adj* accidental, adventitious, aimless, arbitrary, casual, chance, desultory, fortuitous, haphazard, incidental, indiscriminate, purposeless, scattershot, spot, stray, unfocused, unplanned, unpremeditated. **antonyms** deliberate, systematic.

randy *adj* amorous, aroused, goatish, horny, hot, lascivious, lecherous, lustful, raunchy, satyric, sexy, turned-on.

range *n* amplitude, area, assortment, band, bounds, chain, class, collection, compass, confines, distance, domain, extent, field, file, gamut, kind, latitude, limits, line, lot, orbit, order, parameters, province, radius, rank, reach, row, scale, scope, selection, sequence, series, sort, span, spectrum, sphere, string, sweep, tier, variety.

v aim, align, arrange, array, bracket, catalogue, categorise, class, classify, cruise, direct, dispose, explore, extend, file, fluctuate, go, grade, group, level, order, pigeonhole, point, ramble, rank, reach, roam, rove, run, straggle, stray, stretch, stroll, sweep, train, traverse, wander.

rangy *adj* gangling, lanky, leggy, long-legged, rawboned, skinny. **antonyms** compact, dumpy.

rank[1] *n* caste, class, classification, column, condition, degree, dignity, division, echelon, estate, file, formation, grade, group, level, line, nobility, order, position, quality, range, row, series, sort, standing, station, status, stratum, tier, type.

v align, arrange, array, class, classify, dispose, grade, locate, marshal, order, organise, place, position, range, sort.

rank[2] *adj* absolute, abundant, abusive, arrant, atrocious, bad, blatant, coarse, complete, crass, dense, disagreeable, disgusting, downright, egregious, excessive, extravagant, exuberant, fetid, filthy, flagrant, flourishing, foul, fusty, gamy, glaring, gross, indecent, lush, luxuriant, musty, nasty, noxious, obscene, off, offensive, out-and-out, outrageous, productive, profuse, pungent, putrid, rampant, rancid, repulsive, revolting, scurrilous, sheer, shocking, stale, stinking, strong-smelling, thorough, thoroughgoing, total, undisguised, unmitigated, utter, vigorous, vulgar. **antonyms** sparse, sweet.

rankle *v* anger, annoy, chafe, embitter, fester, gall, irk, irritate, nettle, peeve, rile.

ransack *v* comb, depredate, despoil, explore, gut, loot, maraud, pillage, plunder, raid, rake, ravage, rifle, rummage, sack, scour, search, strip.

ransom *n* deliverance, liberation, money, payment, pay-off, price, redemption, release, rescue.

v buy out, deliver, extricate, liberate, redeem, release, rescue.

rant *v* bellow, bluster, cry, declaim, mouth it, rave, roar, shout, spout, tub-thump, vociferate, yell.

n bluster, bombast, declamation, diatribe, harangue, rhetoric, storm, tirade, tub-thumping, vociferation.

rap *v* bark, castigate, censure, chat, confabulate, converse, crack, criticise, discourse, flirt, hit, knock, pan, reprimand, scold, strike, talk, tap.

n blame, blow, castigation,

censure, chat, chiding, clout, colloquy, confabulation, conversation, crack, dialogue, discourse, discussion, knock, punishment, rebuke, reprimand, responsibility, sentence, talk, tap.

rapacious *adj* avaricious, extortionate, grasping, greedy, insatiable, marauding, plundering, predatory, preying, ravenous, usurious, voracious.

rapid *adj* brisk, expeditious, express, fast, fleet, flying, hasty, headlong, hurried, precipitate, prompt, quick, speedy, swift. **antonyms** leisurely, slow, sluggish.

rapidity *n* alacrity, briskness, celerity, dispatch, expedition, expeditiousness, fleetness, haste, hurry, precipitateness, promptitude, promptness, quickness, rush, speed, speediness, swiftness, velocity. **antonym** slowness.

rapidly *adv* briskly, expeditiously, fast, hastily, hurriedly, lickety-split, precipitately, promptly, quickly, speedily, swiftly. **antonym** slowly.

rapport *n* affinity, bond, compatibility, empathy, harmony, link, relationship, sympathy, understanding.

rapt *adj* absorbed, beatific, bewitched, captivated, charmed, delighted, ecstatic, enchanted, engrossed, enraptured, enthralled, entranced, fascinated, gripped, held, intent, preoccupied, rapturous, spellbound, transported.

rapture *n* beatitude, bliss, delectation, delight, ecstasy, enthusiasm, entrancement, euphoria, exaltation, felicity, happiness, joy, rhapsody, spell, transport.

rapturous *adj* blissful, delighted, ecstatic, enthusiastic, entranced, euphoric, exalted, happy, joyful, joyous, overjoyed, rhapsodic, transported.

rare *adj* admirable, choice, curious, excellent, exceptional, exquisite, extreme, few, fine, great, incomparable, infrequent, invaluable, peerless, precious, priceless, rich, scarce, singular, sparse, sporadic, strange, superb, superlative, uncommon, unusual. **antonyms** abundant, common, usual.

rarefied *adj* clannish, cliquish, elevated, esoteric, exalted, exclusive, high, lofty, noble, occult, private, refined, select, spiritual, sublime.

rarely *adv* atypically, exceptionally, extraordinarily, finely, hardly, infrequently, little, notably, remarkably, seldom, singularly, uncommonly, unusually. **antonyms** frequently, often.

raring *adj* agog, athirst, avid, desperate, eager, enthusiastic, impatient, itching, keen, longing, ready, willing, yearning.

rarity *n* choiceness, curio, curiosity, excellence, exquisiteness, find, fineness, gem, incomparability, incomparableness, infrequency, object of virtu, one-off, pearl, peerlessness, preciousness, pricelessness, quality, richness, scarcity, shortage, singularity, sparseness, strangeness, treasure, uncommonness, unusualness, value, worth. **antonyms** commonness, commonplace.

rascal *n* blackguard, devil, disgrace, good-for-nothing, imp, knave, miscreant, ne'er-do-well, rake, ra(p)scallion, reprobate, rogue, scallywag, scamp, scoundrel, toe-rag, varmint, villain, wastrel, wretch.

rash[1] *adj* adventurous, audacious, brash, careless, foolhardy, harebrained, harum-scarum, hasty, headlong, headstrong, heedless, helter-skelter, hot-headed, ill-advised, ill-considered, impetuous, imprudent, impulsive, incautious, indiscreet, injudicious, insipient, madcap, precipitate, premature, reckless, slap-dash, temerarious, thoughtless, unguarded, unthinking, unwary, venturesome. **antonyms** calculating, careful, considered, wary.

rash[2] *n* epidemic, eruption, flood, hives, nettlerash, outbreak, plague, series, spate, succession, wave.

rashness *n* adventurousness, audacity, brashness, carelessness, foolhardiness, hastiness, heedlessness, incaution, incautiousness, indiscretion, precipitance, precipitation, precipitency, recklessness, temerity, thoughtlessness. **antonyms** carefulness, cautiousness.

rasp *n* croak, grating, grinding, harshness, hoarseness, scrape, scratch.
   v abrade, croak, file, grate, grind, irk, irritate, jar, rub, sand, scour, scrape.

rasping *adj* creaking, croaking, croaky, grating, gravelly, gruff, harsh, hoarse, husky, jarring, raspy, raucous, rough, scratchy.

rate *n* basis, charge, class, classification, cost, degree, dues, duty, fee, figure, gait, grade, hire, measure, pace, percentage, position, price, proportion, quality, rank, rating, ratio, reckoning, relation, scale, speed, standard, status, tariff, tax, tempo, time, toll, value, velocity, worth.
   v adjudge, admire, appraise, assess, class, classify, consider, count, deserve,

esteem, estimate, evaluate, figure, grade, judge, measure, measure up, merit, perform, rank, reckon, regard, respect, value, weigh.

rather *adv* a bit, fairly, instead, kinda, kind of, moderately, noticeably, preferably, pretty, quite, relatively, significantly, slightly, somewhat, sooner, sort of, very.

ratify *v* affirm, approve, authenticate, authorise, bind, certify, confirm, corroborate, endorse, establish, homologate, legalise, recognise, sanction, sign, uphold, validate. **antonyms** reject, repudiate.

rating *n* class, classification, degree, designation, estimate, evaluation, grade, grading, order, placing, position, rank, rate, sort, sorting, standing, status.

ratio *n* arrangement, balance, correlation, correspondence, equation, fraction, percentage, proportion, quotient, rate, relation, relationship.

ration *n* allocation, allotment, allowance, amount, dole, helping, measure, part, portion, provision, quota, share.
v allocate, allot, apportion, budget, conserve, control, deal, dispense, distribute, dole, issue, limit, mete, restrict, save, supply.

rational *adj* balanced, cerebral, cognitive, compos mentis, enlightened, intelligent, judicious, logical, lucid, normal, realistic, reasonable, reasoning, sagacious, sane, sensible, sound, thinking, well-founded, well-grounded, wise. **antonyms** crazy, illogical, irrational.

rationale *n* excuse, exposition, grounds, logic, motivation, philosophy, pretext, principle, raison d'être, reasons, theory.

rationalise *v* elucidate, excuse, extenuate, justify, reason out, reorganise, resolve, streamline, trim, vindicate.

rations *n* food, provender, provisions, stores, supplies.

rattle *v* bang, bounce, bump, clank, clatter, discomfit, discompose, disconcert, discountenance, disturb, faze, frighten, jangle, jiggle, jolt, jounce, perturb, scare, shake, upset, vibrate.

rattle off enumerate, itemise, list, recite, reel off, rehearse, repeat, run through.

rattle on blether, cackle, chatter, gab, gabble, jabber, prate, prattle, rabbit on, witter, ya(c)k.

ratty *adj* angry, annoyed, crabbed, cross, impatient, irritable, peeved, short, short-tempered, snappy, testy, touchy. **antonyms** calm, patient.

raucous *adj* grating, harsh, hoarse, husky, loud, noisy, rasping, rough, rusty, strident.

ravage *v* demolish, depredate, desolate, despoil, destroy, devastate, gut, lay waste, loot, pillage, plunder, ransack, raze, ruin, sack, shatter, spoil, wreck.
n damage, defilement, demolition, depredation, desecration, desolation, destruction, devastation, havoc, pillage, plunder, rapine, ruin, ruination, spoliation, waste, wreckage.

ravaged *adj* battle-torn, desolate, destroyed, devastated, ransacked, shattered, spoilt, war-torn, war-wasted, war-worn, wrecked. **antonym** unspoilt.

rave *v* babble, declaim, fulminate, fume, harangue, rage, ramble, rant, roar, splutter, storm, thunder.
adj ecstatic, enthusiastic, excellent, fantastic, favourable, laudatory, wonderful.

ravenous *adj* avaricious, covetous, devouring, famished, ferocious, gluttonous, grasping, greedy, insatiable, predatory, rapacious, starved, starving, voracious.

rave-up *n* bash, blow-out, carousal, celebration, debauch, do, orgy, party, shindig, thrash, wing-ding.

ravine *n* canyon, gap, gorge, gulch, gully, pass.

raving *adj* berserk, bonkers, crazed, crazy, delirious, frantic, frenzied, furious, hysterical, insane, irrational, mad, manic, rabid, raging, wild.

ravish *v* abuse, captivate, charm, deflower, delight, enchant, enrapture, entrance, fascinate, outrage, overjoy, rape, spellbind, transport, violate.

ravishing *adj* alluring, beautiful, bewitching, charming, dazzling, delightful, enchanting, entrancing, gorgeous, lovely, radiant, seductive, stunning.

raw *adj* abraded, bare, basic, biting, bitter, bleak, bloody, blunt, brutal, callow, candid, chafed, chill, chilly, coarse, cold, crude, damp, frank, freezing, fresh, grazed, green, harsh, ignorant, immature, inexperienced, naked, natural, new, open, organic, piercing, plain, realistic, rough, scraped, scratched, sensitive, skinned, sore, tender, unadorned, uncooked, undisciplined, undisguised, undressed, unfinished, unpleasant, unpractised, unprepared, unprocessed, unrefined, unripe, unseasoned, unskilled, untrained, untreated, untried, unvarnished, wet. *antonyms* cooked, experienced, refined.

ray *n* bar, beam, flash, flicker, gleam, glimmer, glint, hint, indication, scintilla, shaft, spark, stream, trace.

raze *v* bulldoze, delete, demolish, destroy, dismantle, efface, erase, expunge, extinguish, extirpate, flatten, level, obliterate, remove, ruin.

re *prep* about, apropos, concerning, regarding, respecting, touching, with reference to, with regard to.

reach *v* amount to, arrive at, attain, contact, drop, fall, get to, grasp, hand, land at, make, move, pass, rise, sink, stretch, strike, touch.
n ambit, capacity, command, compass, distance, extension, extent, grasp, influence, jurisdiction, latitude, mastery, power, range, scope, spread, stretch, sweep.

react *v* acknowledge, act, answer, behave, emote, function, operate, proceed, reply, respond, work.

reaction *n* acknowledgement, answer, backwash, compensation, conservatism, counteraction, counterbalance, counterbuff, counterpoise, counter-revolution, feedback, recoil, reply, response, swing-back.

reactionary *adj* blimpish, conservative, counter-revolutionary, obstructive, reactionist, rightist. *antonyms* progressive, radical, revolutionary.
n Colonel Blimp, conservative, counter-revolutionary, die-hard, obstructionist, reactionist, rightist, right-winger. *antonyms* progressive, radical, revolutionary.

read *v* announce, comprehend, construe, decipher, declaim, deliver, discover, display, indicate, interpret, peruse, pore over, recite, record, refer to, register, scan, see, show, speak, study, understand, utter.

readable *adj* clear, compelling, comprehensible, compulsive, decipherable, enjoyable, entertaining, enthralling, gripping, intelligible, interesting, legible, plain, pleasant, understandable, unputdownable. *antonyms* illegible, unreadable.

readily *adv* cheerfully, eagerly, easily, effortlessly, fain, freely, gladly, promptly, quickly, smoothly, speedily, unhesitatingly, voluntarily, willingly.

readiness *n* adroitness, alacrity, aptitude, aptness, dexterity, eagerness, ease, facility, fitness, gameness, handiness, inclination, keenness, maturity, preparation, preparedness, promptitude, promptness, quickness, rapidity, ripeness, skill, willingness.

reading *n* book-learning, conception, construction, edification, education, erudition, examination, grasp, homily, impression, inspection, interpretation, knowledge, learning, lecture, lesson, performance, perusal, recital, rendering, rendition, review, scholarship, scrutiny, sermon, study, treatment, understanding, version.

ready *adj* about, accessible, acute, adroit, agreeable, alert, apt, arranged, astute, available, bright, clever, close, completed, convenient, deft, dexterous, disposed, eager, expert, facile, fit, game, glad, handy, happy, inclined, intelligent, keen, liable, likely, minded, near, on call, on tap, organised, overflowing, perceptive, predisposed, prepared, present, primed, prompt, prone, quick, quick-witted, rapid, resourceful, ripe, set, sharp, skilful, smart, willing. *antonyms* unprepared, unready.
v alert, arrange, equip, order, organise, prepare, prime, set.

real *adj* absolute, actual, authentic, bona fide, certain, dinkum, essential, existent, factual, genuine, heartfelt, honest, intrinsic, legitimate, positive, right, rightful, sincere, substantial, substantive, sure-enough, tangible, thingy, true, unaffected, unfeigned, valid, veritable. *antonyms* imaginary, unreal.

realisation *n* accomplishment, achievement, actualisation, appreciation, apprehension, awareness, cognisance, completion, comprehension, conception, concretisation, consciousness, consummation, effectuation, fulfilment, grasp, imagination, perception, recognition, understanding.

realise *v* accomplish, achieve, acquire, actualise, appreciate, apprehend, catch on, clear, complete, comprehend, conceive, concretise, consummate, do, earn, effect, effectuate, fulfil, gain, get, grasp, imagine, implement, make, net, obtain, perform, produce, recognise, take in, twig, understand.

realistic *adj* authentic, businesslike, clear-sighted, common-sense, detached, down-to-earth, faithful, genuine, graphic, hard-headed, level-headed, lifelike, matter-of-fact, natural, naturalistic, objective, practical, pragmatic, rational, real, real-life, representational, sensible, sober, true, truthful, unromantic, unsentimental. **antonyms** fanciful, impractical, irrational.

reality *n* actuality, authenticity, certainty, corporeality, fact, factuality, genuineness, materiality, nitty-gritty, palpability, realism, tangibility, truth, validity, verisimilitude, verity.

really *adv* absolutely, actually, assuredly, categorically, certainly, essentially, genuinely, indeed, intrinsically, positively, surely, truly, undoubtedly, verily.

realm *n* area, bailiwick, branch, country, department, domain, dominion, empire, field, jurisdiction, kingdom, land, monarchy, orbit, principality, province, region, sphere, state, territory, world, zone.

reap *v* acquire, collect, crop, cut, derive, gain, garner, gather, get, harvest, mow, obtain, realise, secure, win.

rear[1] *n* back, backside, bottom, buttocks, croup, end, hindquarters, posterior, rearguard, rump, stern, tail. **antonym** front. *adj* aft, after, back, following, hind, hindmost, last. **antonym** front.

rear[2] *v* breed, build, construct, cultivate, educate, elevate, erect, fabricate, foster, grow, hoist, lift, loom, nurse, nurture, parent, raise, rise, soar, tower, train.

rearrange *v* adjust, alter, rejig, reorder, reposition, shift, vary.

reason *n* aim, apologia, apology, apprehension, argument, basis, bounds, brains, case, cause, common sense, comprehension, consideration, defence, design, end, excuse, explanation, exposition, goal, ground, grounds, gumption, impetus, incentive, inducement, intellect, intention, judgement, justification, limits, logic, mentality, mind, moderation, motive, nous, object, occasion, purpose, rationale, rationality, reasonableness, reasoning, sanity, sense, sensibleness, soundness, target, understanding, vindication, warrant, wisdom.
v conclude, deduce, infer, intellectualise, resolve, solve, think, work out.

reason with argue, debate, dispute, dissuade, expostulate, make representations, move, persuade, protest, remonstrate, talk, urge.

reasonable *adj* acceptable, advisable, arguable, average, believable, credible, equitable, fair, fit, honest, inexpensive, intelligent, judicious, just, justifiable, logical, moderate, modest, OK, passable, plausible, possible, practical, proper, rational, reasoned, right, sane, satisfactory, sensible, sober, sound, tenable, tolerable, viable, well-advised, well-thought-out, wise. **antonyms** crazy, extravagant, irrational, outrageous.

reasoned *adj* clear, judicious, logical, methodical, rational, sensible, sound, systematic, well-thought-out. **antonyms** illogical, unsystematic.

reasoning *n* analysis, argument, case, cogitation, deduction, explication, exposition, hypothesis, interpretation, logic, proof, reason, supposition, thinking, thought.

reassure *v* bolster, brace, comfort, encourage, hearten, inspirit, nerve, rally.

rebate *n* allowance, bonus, deduction, discount, reduction, refund, repayment.

rebel *v* defy, disobey, dissent, flinch, kick over the traces, mutiny, recoil, resist, revolt, rise up, run riot, shrink.
n dissenter, heretic, insurgent, insurrectionary, Jacobin, malcontent, mutineer, nonconformist, revolutionary, secessionist.
adj insubordinate, insurgent, insurrectionary, malcontent(ed), mutinous, rebellious, revolutionary.

rebellion *n* defiance, disobedience, dissent, heresy, insubordination, insurgence, insurgency, insurrection, intifada, mutiny, nonconformity, resistance, revolt, revolution, rising, sedition, uprising.

rebellious *adj* defiant, difficult, disaffected, disloyal, disobedient, disorderly, incorrigible, insubordinate, insurgent, insurrectionary, intractable, malcontent(ed), mutinous, obstinate, rebel, recalcitrant, refractory, resistant, revolutionary, seditious, turbulent, ungovernable, unmanageable, unruly. **antonyms** obedient, submissive.

rebirth *n* reactivation, reanimation, regeneration, reincarnation, rejuvenation, renaissance, renewal, restoration, resurgence, resurrection, revitalisation, revival.

rebound *v* backfire, boomerang, bounce, misfire, recoil, redound, resile, resound, return, ricochet.
n back-wash, bounce, reflection, repercussion, return, reverberation, ricochet.

rebuff v cold-shoulder, cut, decline, deny, discourage, put someone's nose out of joint, refuse, reject, repulse, resist, slight, snub, spurn, turn down.
n brush-off, check, cold shoulder, defeat, denial, discouragement, flea in one's ear, opposition, refusal, rejection, repulse, rubber, set-down, slight, snub.

rebuild v reassemble, reconstruct, re-edify, refashion, remake, remodel, renovate, restore. *antonyms* demolish, destroy.

rebuke v admonish, berate, blame, carpet, castigate, censure, chide, countercheck, keelhaul, lecture, lesson, rate, reprehend, reprimand, reproach, reprove, scold, slap down, tell off, tick off, trim, trounce, upbraid. *antonyms* compliment, praise.
n admonition, blame, castigation, censure, countercheck, dressing-down, lecture, reprimand, reproach, reproof, reproval, row, slap, telling-off, ticking-off, tongue-lashing. *antonyms* compliment, praise.

rebut v confute, defeat, discredit, disprove, explode, give the lie to, invalidate, negate, overturn, quash, refute.

rebuttal n confutation, defeat, disproof, invalidation, negation, overthrow, refutation.

recalcitrant adj contrary, defiant, disobedient, insubordinate, intractable, obstinate, refractory, stubborn, uncontrollable, unco-operative, ungovernable, unmanageable, unruly, unsubmissive, unwilling, wayward, wilful. *antonym* amenable.

recall v abjure, annul, cancel, cast one's mind back, countermand, evoke, mind, nullify, place, recognise, recollect, remember, repeal, rescind, retract, revoke, withdraw.
n abrogation, annulment, cancellation, memory, nullification, recollection, remembrance, repeal, rescission, retraction, revocation, withdrawal.

recant v abjure, abrogate, apostatise, deny, disavow, disclaim, disown, forswear, recall, renounce, repudiate, rescind, retract, revoke, unsay, withdraw.

recantation n abjuration, apostasy, denial, disavowal, disclaimer, disownment, renunciation, repudiation, retractation, retraction, revocation, withdrawal.

recapitulate v give a resumé, recap, recount, reiterate, repeat, restate, review, sum up, summarise.

recede v abate, decline, decrease, diminish, dwindle, ebb, fade, lessen, regress, retire, retreat, retrogress, return, shrink, sink, slacken, subside, wane, withdraw. *antonyms* advance, proceed.

receipt n acceptance, acknowledgement, counterfoil, delivery, receiving, reception, slip, stub, ticket, voucher.

receipts n gains, gate, income, proceeds, profits, return, take, takings.

receive v accept, accommodate, acquire, admit, apprehend, bear, collect, derive, encounter, entertain, experience, gather, get, greet, hear, meet, obtain, perceive, pick up, react to, respond to, suffer, sustain, take, undergo, welcome. *antonyms* donate, give.

recent adj contemporary, current, fresh, late, latter, latter-day, modern, new, novel, present-day, up-to-date, young. *antonyms* dated, old, out-of-date.

recently adv currently, lately, latterly, newly.

reception n acceptance, acknowledgement, admission, do, entertainment, function, greeting, levee, party, reaction, receipt, receiving, recognition, response, shindig, soirée, treatment, welcome.

receptive adj accessible, alert, amenable, approachable, bright, favourable, friendly, hospitable, interested, open, open-minded, perceptive, responsive, sensitive, suggestible, susceptible, sympathetic, welcoming.

recess n alcove, apse, bay, break, cavity, cessation, closure, corner, depression, embrasure, holiday, hollow, indentation, intermission, interval, niche, nook, oriel, respite, rest, vacation.

recession n decline, depression, downturn, slump, stagflation. *antonyms* boom, upturn.

reciprocal adj alternate, complementary, correlative, corresponding, equivalent, give-and-take, interchangeable, interdependent, mutual, shared.

reciprocate v alternate, barter, correspond, equal, exchange, interchange, match, reply, requite, respond, return, swap, trade.

recite v articulate, declaim, deliver, describe, detail, enumerate, itemise, narrate, orate, perform, recapitulate, recount, rehearse, relate, repeat, speak, tell.

reckless adj careless, daredevil, devil-may-care, foolhardy, harebrained, hasty, headlong, heedless, ill-advised, imprudent, inattentive, incautious, indiscreet, irresponsible, madcap, mindless, negligent, precipitate, rash, regardless, tearaway, thoughtless, wild. **antonyms** calculating, careful, cautious.

recklessness *n* carelessness, foolhardiness, heedlessness, imprudence, inattention, incaution, irresponsibility, madness, mindlessness, negligence, rashness, thoughtlessness. **antonym** carefulness.

reckon *v* account, add up, adjudge, appraise, assess, assume, believe, calculate, compute, conjecture, consider, count, deem, enumerate, esteem, estimate, evaluate, expect, fancy, gauge, guess, hold, imagine, judge, number, opine, rate, regard, suppose, surmise, tally, think, total.

reckon on bank, calculate, count, depend, figure on, hope for, rely, trust in.

reckon with anticipate, bargain for, consider, cope with, deal with, expect, face, foresee, handle, plan for, take into account, treat.

reckoning *n* account, adding, addition, bill, calculation, charge, computation, count, counting, doom, due, enumeration, estimate, judgement, retribution, score, settlement, summation, working.

reclaim *v* recapture, recover, redeem, reform, regain, regenerate, reinstate, rescue, restore, retrieve, salvage.

recline *v* couch, lean, lie, loll, lounge, repose, rest, sprawl, stretch out.

recluse *n* anchorite, ascetic, hermit, monk, solitary.

reclusive *adj* ascetic, cloistered, hermitical, isolated, monastic, recluse, retiring, secluded, sequestered, solitary, withdrawn.

recognise *v* accept, acknowledge, admit, allow, appreciate, approve, avow, concede, confess, grant, greet, honour, identify, know, notice, own, perceive, place, realise, recall, recollect, remember, respect, salute, see, spot, understand.

recognition *n* acceptance, acknowledgement, admission, allowance, appreciation, approval, avowal, awareness, cognisance, confession, detection, discovery, enlightenment, gratitude, greeting, honour, identification, notice, perception, realisation, recall, recollection, remembrance, respect, salute, understanding.

recoil *v* backfire, boomerang, falter, flinch, kick, misfire, quail, react, rebound, redound, shrink.

n backlash, kick, reaction, rebound, redound(ing), repercussion.

recollect *v* call up, cast one's mind back, mind, place, recall, remember, reminisce.

recollection *n* image, impression, memory, recall, remembrance, reminiscence, souvenir.

recommend *v* advance, advise, advocate, approve, commend, counsel, endorse, enjoin, exhort, plug, praise, propose, suggest, urge, vouch for. **antonyms** disapprove, veto.

recommendation *n* advice, advocacy, approbation, approval, blessing, commendation, counsel, endorsement, plug, praise, proposal, reference, sanction, suggestion, testimonial, urging. **antonyms** disapproval, veto.

recompense *v* compensate, indemnify, pay, redress, reimburse, remunerate, repay, requite, reward, satisfy.

n amends, compensation, damages, emolument, indemnification, indemnity, pay, payment, remuneration, reparation, repayment, requital, restitution, return, reward, satisfaction, wages.

reconcile *v* accept, accommodate, accord, adjust, appease, compose, conciliate, harmonise, pacify, placate, propitiate, rectify, resign, resolve, reunite, settle, square, submit, yield. **antonym** estrange.

reconciliation *n* accommodation, adjustment, agreement, appeasement, bridge-building, compromise, conciliation, détente, harmony, pacification, propitiation, rapprochement, reconcilement, rectification, reunion, settlement, understanding. **antonyms** estrangement, separation.

recondite *adj* abstruse, arcane, cabbalistic, complicated, concealed, dark, deep, difficult, esoteric, hidden, intricate, involved, mysterious, mystical, obscure, occult, profound, secret. **antonyms** simple, straightforward.

recondition *v* fix, overhaul, refurbish, remodel, renew, renovate, repair, restore, revamp, sort.

reconnaissance *n* examination, exploration, inspection, investigation, observation, patrol, probe, recce, reconnoitring, scan, scouting, scrutiny, survey.

reconnoitre *v* case, examine, explore, inspect, investigate, observe, patrol, probe, recce, scan, scout, scrutinise, spy out, survey.

reconsider *v* modify, reassess, re-examine, rethink, review, revise, think better of, think over, think twice.

reconstruct *v* reassemble, rebuild, recreate, re-establish, refashion, reform, reformulate, regenerate, remake, remodel, renovate, reorganise, restore.

record *n* account, album, annals, archives, background, career, chronicle, curriculum vitae, diary, disc, document, documentation, dossier, entry, EP, evidence, file, form, forty-five, gramophone record, history, journal, log, LP, memoir, memorandum, memorial, minute, performance, platter, recording, register, release, remembrance, report, single, talky, testimony, trace, tracing, track record, witness.
v chalk up, chronicle, contain, cut, diarise, document, enregister, enrol, enter, indicate, inscribe, log, minute, note, preserve, read, register, report, say, score, show, tape, tape-record, transcribe, video, video-tape, wax.

recount *v* communicate, delineate, depict, describe, detail, enumerate, narrate, portray, recite, rehearse, relate, repeat, report, tell.

recoup *v* compensate, indemnify, make good, recover, redeem, refund, regain, reimburse, remunerate, repay, requite, retrieve, satisfy.

recourse *n* access, alternative, appeal, choice, expedient, option, refuge, remedy, resort.

recover *v* convalesce, heal, improve, mend, pick up, pull through, rally, recapture, reclaim, recoup, recuperate, redeem, regain, repair, repossess, restore, retake, retrieve, revive. **antonyms** forfeit, lose, worsen.

recovery *n* amelioration, betterment, convalescence, healing, improvement, mending, rally, recapture, reclamation, recuperation, redemption, rehabilitation, repair, repossession, restoration, retrieval, revival, upturn. **antonyms** forfeit, loss, worsening.

recreation *n* amusement, distraction, diversion, enjoyment, entertainment, exercise, fun, games, hobby, leisure activity, pastime, play, pleasure, refreshment, relaxation, relief, sport.

recrimination *n* accusation, bickering, counter-attack, counterblast, countercharge, name-calling, quarrel, retaliation, retort, squabbling.

recruit *v* augment, draft, engage, enlist, enrol, gather, headhunt, impress, levy, mobilise, muster, obtain, procure, proselytise, raise, refresh, reinforce, renew, replenish, restore, strengthen, supply, trawl.
n apprentice, beginner, conscript, convert, draftee, greenhorn, helper, initiate, learner, novice, rookie, trainee.

rectify *v* adjust, amend, correct, distil, emend, fix, improve, mend, purify, redress, refine, reform, remedy, repair, right, separate, square, straighten.

rectitude *n* accuracy, correctness, decency, equity, exactness, goodness, honesty, honour, incorruptibility, integrity, irreproachability, justice, morality, precision, principle, probity, righteousness, rightness, scrupulousness, sinlessness, soundness, unimpeachability, uprightness, verity, virtue.

recumbent *adj* flat, horizontal, leaning, lounging, lying, prone, prostrate, reclining, resting, sprawling, supine. **antonyms** erect, upright.

recuperate *v* convalesce, get better, improve, mend, pick up, rally, recoup, recover, regain, revive. **antonym** worsen.

recur *v* persist, reappear, repeat, return.

recurrent *adj* continued, cyclical, frequent, habitual, haunting, periodic, recurring, regular, repeated, repetitive.

red *adj* bay, bloodshot, bloodstained, bloody, blooming, blushing, cardinal, carmine, carroty, cherry, chestnut, coral, crimson, damask, embarrassed, ensanguined, flame-coloured, flaming, florid, flushed, glowing, gory, healthy, inflamed, maroon, pink, reddish, rose, roseate, rosy, rubicund, rubied, ruby, ruby-red, ruddy, sanguine, scarlet, shamefaced, suffused, titian, vermilion, wine.

red-blooded *adj* hearty, lively, lusty, manly, robust, strong, vigorous, virile, vital.

redden *v* blush, colour, crimson, flush, suffuse.

redeem *v* absolve, acquit, atone for, cash (in), change, compensate for, defray, deliver, discharge, emancipate, exchange, extricate, free, fulfil, keep, liberate, make good, make up for, meet, offset, outweigh, perform, ransom, reclaim, recoup, recover, recuperate, redress, regain, rehabilitate, reinstate, repossess, repurchase, rescue, retrieve, salvage, satisfy, save, trade in.

redemption *n* amends, atonement,

compensation, deliverance, discharge, emancipation, exchange, expiation, fulfilment, liberation, performance, ransom, reclamation, recovery, rehabilitation, reinstatement, release, reparation, repossession, repurchase, rescue, retrieval, salvation, trade-in.

redolent *adj* aromatic, evocative, fragrant, odorous, perfumed, remindful, reminiscent, scented, suggestive, sweet-smelling.

redoubtable *adj* courageous, doughty, dreadful, fearful, fearsome, formidable, heroic, mighty, powerful, resolute, strong, terrible, valiant.

redound *v* accrue, conduce, contribute, effect, ensue, rebound, recoil, reflect, result, tend.

redress *v* adjust, amend, balance, correct, ease, expiate, mend, recompense, rectify, reform, regulate, relieve, remedy, repair, square.
n aid, amends, assistance, atonement, compensation, correction, cure, ease, expiation, help, indemnification, justice, payment, quittance, recompense, rectification, relief, remedy, reparation, requital, restitution, satisfaction. **antonyms** boost, fatten, increase.

reduce *v* abate, abridge, bankrupt, break, cheapen, conquer, contract, curtail, cut, debase, decimate, decrease, degrade, demote, deoxidise, depress, dilute, diminish, discount, downgrade, drive, force, humble, humiliate, impair, impoverish, lessen, lower, master, moderate, overpower, pauperise, rebate, ruin, scant, shorten, slake, slash, slenderise, slim, subdue, trim, truncate, vanquish, weaken. **antonyms** boost, fatten, increase, upgrade.

reduction *n* abbreviation, abridgement, abstraction, alleviation, attenuation, compression, condensation, constriction, contraction, curtailment, cut, cutback, decline, decrease, deduction, degradation, demotion, deoxidisation, depreciation, devaluation, diminution, discount, drop, easing, ellipsis, limitation, loss, miniature, mitigation, moderation, modification, muffling, muting, narrowing, rebate, refund, restriction, shortening, shrinkage, slackening, softening, subtraction, summarisation, summary, syncope. **antonyms** enlargement, improvement, increase.

redundancy *n* excess, pleonasm, prolixity, repetition, superfluity, surplus, tautology, uselessness, verbosity, wordiness.

redundant *adj* de trop, diffuse, excessive, extra, inessential, inordinate, padded, periphrastic, pleonastic, prolix, repetitious, supererogatory, superfluous, supernumerary, surplus, tautological, unemployed, unnecessary, unneeded, unwanted, verbose, wordy. **antonyms** concise, essential, necessary.

reek *v* exhale, fume, hum, pong, smell, smoke, stink.
n fume(s), malodour, odour, pong, smell, stench, stink.

reel *v* gyrate, lurch, pitch, revolve, rock, roll, spin, stagger, stumble, sway, swim, swirl, totter, twirl, waver, wheel, whirl, wobble.

refer *v* accredit, adduce, advert, allude, apply, ascribe, assign, attribute, belong, cite, commit, concern, consign, consult, credit, deliver, direct, go, guide, hint, impute, invoke, look up, mention, pertain, point, recommend, relate, send, speak of, submit, touch on, transfer, turn to.

reference *n* allusion, applicability, bearing, certification, character, citation, concern, connection, consideration, credentials, endorsement, illustration, instance, mention, note, quotation, recommendation, regard, relation, remark, respect, testimonial.

refine *v* chasten, civilise, clarify, cultivate, distil, elevate, exalt, filter, hone, improve, perfect, polish, process, purify, rarefy, spiritualise, sublimise, subtilise, temper.

refined *adj* civil, civilised, clarified, clean, courtly, cultivated, cultured, delicate, discerning, discriminating, distilled, elegant, exact, fastidious, filtered, fine, genteel, gentlemanly, gracious, ladylike, nice, polished, polite, precise, processed, punctilious, pure, purified, sensitive, sophisticated, sublime, subtle, urbane, well-bred, well-mannered. **antonyms** brutish, coarse, earthy, rude, vulgar.

refinement *n* breeding, chastity, civilisation, civility, clarification, cleansing, courtesy, courtliness, cultivation, culture, delicacy, discrimination, distillation, elegance, fastidiousness, filtering, fineness, finesse, finish, gentility, grace, graciousness, manners, nicety, nuance, polish, politeness, politesse, precision, processing, purification, rarefaction, rectification, sophistication, style, subtlety, taste, urbanity. **antonyms** coarseness, earthiness, vulgarity.

reflect v bespeak, cogitate, communicate, consider, contemplate, deliberate, demonstrate, display, echo, evince, exhibit, express, imitate, indicate, manifest, meditate, mirror, mull (over), muse, ponder, reproduce, return, reveal, ruminate, show, think, wonder.

reflection n censure, cerebration, cogitation, consideration, contemplation, counterpart, criticism, deliberation, derogation, echo, idea, image, impression, imputation, meditation, musing, observation, opinion, pondering, reflex, reproach, rumination, slur, study, thinking, thought, view.

reflective adj absorbed, cogitating, contemplative, deliberative, dreamy, meditative, pensive, pondering, reasoning, ruminative, thoughtful.

reform v ameliorate, amend, better, correct, emend, improve, mend, purge, rebuild, reclaim, reconstitute, reconstruct, rectify, regenerate, rehabilitate, remodel, renovate, reorganise, repair, restore, revamp, revolutionise.
n amelioration, amendment, betterment, correction, improvement, purge, rectification, rehabilitation, renovation, shake-out.

refractory adj balky, cantankerous, contentious, difficult, disobedient, disputatious, headstrong, intractable, mulish, obstinate, perverse, recalcitrant, resistant, restive, stubborn, uncontrollable, unco-operative, unmanageable, unruly, wilful. **antonyms** co-operative, malleable, obedient.

refrain v abstain, avoid, cease, desist, eschew, forbear, leave off, quit, renounce, stop, swear off.

refresh v brace, cheer, cool, energise, enliven, freshen, inspirit, jog, prod, prompt, reanimate, reinvigorate, rejuvenate, renew, renovate, repair, replenish, restore, revitalise, revive, revivify, stimulate. **antonyms** exhaust, tire.

refreshing adj bracing, cooling, different, energising, fresh, inspiriting, invigorating, new, novel, original, restorative, revivifying, stimulating, thirst-quenching. **antonyms** exhausting, tiring.

refuge n asylum, harbour, haven, hideaway, hideout, protection, resort, retreat, sanctuary, security, shelter.

refulgent adj beaming, bright, brilliant, gleaming, glistening, glittering, irradiant, lambent, lustrous, radiant, resplendent, shining.

refund v rebate, reimburse, repay, restore, return.
n rebate, reimbursement, repayment, return.

refurbish v mend, overhaul, recondition, re-equip, refit, remodel, renovate, repair, restore, revamp.

refusal n choice, consideration, defiance, denial, negation, no, opportunity, option, rebuff, rejection, repudiation. **antonym** acceptance.

refuse[1] v decline, deny, reject, repel, repudiate, spurn, withhold. **antonyms** accept, allow.

refuse[2] n chaff, dregs, dross, garbage, junk, landfill, leavings, lees, left-overs, litter, rubbish, scum, sediment, slops, sweepings, tailings, trash, waste.

refutation n confutation, disproof, negation, overthrow, rebuttal.

refute v confute, counter, discredit, disprove, give the lie to, negate, overthrow, rebut, silence.

regain v reattain, recapture, reclaim, recoup, recover, redeem, re-establish, repossess, retake, retrieve, return to.

regal adj kingly, magnificent, majestic, monarchic(al), noble, princely, proud, queenly, royal, sovereign, stately.

regale v amuse, captivate, delight, divert, entertain, fascinate, feast, gratify, ply, refresh, serve.

regard v account, adjudge, attend, behold, believe, concern, consider, deem, esteem, estimate, eye, heed, hold, imagine, interest, judge, mark, mind, note, notice, observe, pertain to, rate, relate to, remark, respect, scrutinise, see, suppose, think, treat, value, view, watch. **antonyms** despise, disregard.
n account, affection, aspect, attachment, attention, bearing, care, concern, connection, consideration, deference, detail, esteem, feature, gaze, glance, heed, honour, item, look, love, matter, mind, note, notice, particular, point, reference, relation, relevance, reputation, repute, respect, scrutiny, stare, store, sympathy, thought. **antonyms** contempt, disapproval, disregard.

regardful adj attentive, aware, canny, careful, circumspect, considerate, dutiful, heedful, mindful, observant, respectful, thoughtful, watchful. **antonyms** heedless, inattentive, regardless, unobservant.

egarding *prep* about, apropos, as regards, as to, concerning, in re, in respect of, in the matter of, on the subject of, re, respecting, touching, with reference to, with regard to.

egardless *adj* disregarding, heedless, inattentive, inconsiderate, indifferent, neglectful, negligent, nonchalant, rash, reckless, remiss, uncaring, unconcerned, unmindful. *antonyms* attentive, heedful, regardful.
adv anyhow, anyway, come what may, despite everything, in any case, nevertheless, no matter what, nonetheless, willy-nilly.

regenerate *v* change, inspirit, invigorate, reawaken, reconstitute, reconstruct, re-establish, refresh, reinvigorate, rejuvenate, renew, renovate, reproduce, restore, revive, revivify, uplift.

regeneration *n* reconstitution, reconstruction, re-establishment, reinvigoration, rejuvenation, renewal, renovation, reproduction, restoration.

regime *n* administration, command, control, establishment, government, leadership, management, reign, rule, system.

regimented *adj* controlled, co-ordinated, disciplined, methodical, ordered, organised, regulated, severe, standardised, stern, strict, systematic. *antonyms* disorganised, free, lax, loose.

region *n* area, clime, country, district, division, domain, expanse, field, land, locality, neighbourhood, part, place, province, quarter, range, realm, scope, section, sector, sphere, terrain, territory, tract, vicinity, world, zone.

register *n* almanac, annals, archives, catalogue, chronicle, diary, file, ledger, list, log, matricula, memorandum, record, roll, roster, schedule.
v bespeak, betray, catalogue, chronicle, display, enlist, enrol, enter, exhibit, express, indicate, inscribe, list, log, manifest, mark, note, read, record, reflect, reveal, say, score, show, sign on.

regress *v* backslide, degenerate, deteriorate, ebb, lapse, recede, relapse, retreat, retrocede, retrogress, return, revert, wane. *antonym* progress.

regret *v* bemoan, deplore, grieve, lament, miss, mourn, repent, rue, sorrow. *n* bitterness, compunction, contrition, disappointment, grief, lamentation, penitence, remorse, repentance, ruefulness, self-reproach, shame, sorrow.

regretful *adj* apologetic, ashamed, conscience-stricken, contrite, disappointed, mournful, penitent, remorseful, repentant, rueful, sad, sorrowful, sorry. *antonyms* impenitent, unashamed.

regrettable *adj* deplorable, disappointing, distressing, ill-advised, lamentable, pitiable, sad, shameful, sorry, unfortunate, unhappy, unlucky, woeful, wrong. *antonyms* fortunate, happy.

regular *adj* approved, balanced, bona fide, classic, common, commonplace, consistent, constant, conventional, correct, customary, daily, dependable, efficient, established, even, everyday, fixed, flat, formal, habitual, level, methodical, normal, official, ordered, orderly, ordinary, orthodox, periodic, prevailing, proper, rhythmic, routine, sanctioned, set, smooth, standard, standardised, stated, steady, straight, symmetrical, systematic, time-honoured, traditional, typical, uniform, unvarying, usual. *antonyms* irregular, sporadic, unconventional.

regulate *v* adjust, administer, arrange, balance, conduct, control, direct, fit, govern, guide, handle, manage, moderate, modulate, monitor, order, organise, oversee, regiment, rule, run, settle, square, superintend, supervise, systematise, tune.

regulation *n* adjustment, administration, arrangement, commandment, control, decree, dictate, direction, edict, governance, government, law, management, modulation, order, ordinance, precept, prodecure, regimentation, requirement, rule, statute, supervision, tuning.
adj accepted, customary, mandatory, normal, official, prescribed, required, standard, stock, usual.

rehabilitate *v* adjust, clear, convert, mend, normalise, rebuild, recondition, reconstitute, reconstruct, redeem, re-establish, reform, reinstate, reintegrate, reinvigorate, renew, renovate, restore, save.

rehash *n* rearrangement, rejig, rejigging, reshuffle, restatement, reworking, rewrite.
v alter, change, rearrange, refashion, rejig, reshuffle, restate, rework, rewrite.

rehearsal *n* account, catalogue, description, drill, dry-run, enumeration, list, narration, practice, preparation, reading, recital, recounting, relation, run-through, telling.

rehearse v act, delineate, depict, describe, detail, drill, enumerate, list, narrate, practise, prepare, ready, recite, recount, relate, repeat, review, run through, spell out, study, tell, train, trot out.

reign n ascendancy, command, control, dominion, empire, influence, monarchy, power, rule, sovereignty, supremacy, sway.

v administer, authority, command, govern, influence, kingship, obtain, predominate, prevail, rule.

reimburse v compensate, indemnify, recompense, refund, remunerate, repay, requite, restore, return, square up.

rein n brake, bridle, check, control, curb, harness, hold, overcheck, restraint, restriction.

v arrest, bridle, check, control, curb, halt, hold, hold back, limit, restrain, restrict, stop.

reinforce v augment, bolster, buttress, emphasise, fortify, harden, increase, prop, recruit, steel, stiffen, strengthen, stress, supplement, support, toughen, underline. **antonyms** undermine, weaken.

reinforcements n auxiliaries, back-up, reserves, support.

reinstate v reappoint, recall, re-establish, rehabilitate, reinstall, replace, restore, return.

reiterate v recapitulate, repeat, resay, restate, retell.

reject v condemn, decline, deny, despise, disallow, discard, eliminate, exclude, explode, jettison, jilt, rebuff, refuse, renounce, repel, repudiate, repulse, scrap, spike, spurn, veto. **antonyms** accept, select.

n cast-off, discard, failure, second.

rejection n brush-off, dear John letter, denial, dismissal, elimination, exclusion, rebuff, refusal, renunciation, repudiation, veto. **antonyms** acceptance, selection.

rejoice v celebrate, delight, exult, glory, joy, jubilate, revel, triumph.

rejoicing n celebration, cheer, delight, elation, exultation, festivity, gaiety, gladness, happiness, joy, jubilation, merrymaking, revelry, triumph.

rejoin v answer, quip, repartee, reply, respond, retort, riposte.

rejoinder n answer, come-back, counter, countercharge, counter-claim, quip, repartee, reply, response, retort, riposte.

rejuvenate v reanimate, recharge, refresh, regenerate, reinvigorate, rekindle, renew, restore, revitalise, revivify.

relapse v backslide, degenerate, deteriorate, fade, fail, lapse, regress, retrogress, revert, sicken, sink, weaken, worsen.

n backsliding, deterioration, lapse, recidivism, recurrence, regression, retrogression, reversion, setback, weakening, worsening.

relate v ally, appertain, apply, associate, chronicle, concern, connect, co-ordinate, correlate, couple, describe, detail, empathise, feel for, identify with, impart, join, link, narrate, pertain, present, recite, recount, refer, rehearse, report, sympathise, tell, understand.

related adj accompanying, affiliated, akin, allied, associated, cognate, concomitant, connected, consanguine, consanguineous, correlated, interconnected, joint, kin, kindred, linked. **antonyms** different, unconnected, unrelated.

relation n account, affiliation, affinity, application, bearing, bond, comparison, connection, consanguinity, correlation, description, interdependence, kin, kindred, kinship, kinsman, kinswoman, link, narration, narrative, pertinence, propinquity, recital, recountal, reference, regard, relationship, relative, report, sib, similarity, story, tale, tie-in.

relations n affairs, associations, clan, communications, connections, contact, dealings, doings, family, interaction, intercourse, kin, kindred, kinsmen, liaison, meetings, rapport, relationship, relatives, terms, tribe, truck.

relationship n affair, association, bond, communications, conjunction, connection, contract, correlation, dealings, exchange, intercourse, kinship, liaison, link, parallel, proportion, rapport, ratio, similarity, tie-up.

relative adj allied, applicable, apposite, appropriate, apropos, associated, comparative, connected, contingent, correlative, corresponding, dependent, germane, interrelated, pertinent, proportionate, reciprocal, related, relevant, respective.

n cognate, connection, kinsman, kinswoman, relation, sib.

relatively adv comparatively, fairly, quite, rather, somewhat.

relax v abate, diminish, disinhibit, ease, ebb, lessen, loosen, lower, mitigate, moderate, reduce, relieve, remit, rest, slacken, soften, tranquillise, unbend, unclench, unwind, weaken. *antonyms* intensify, tighten.

relaxation *n* abatement, amusement, détente, diminution, disinhibition, distraction, easing, emollition, enjoyment, entertainment, fun, leisure, lessening, let-up, moderation, pleasure, recreation, reduction, refreshment, rest, slackening, weakening. *antonyms* intensification, tension.

relaxed *adj* calm, carefree, casual, collected, composed, cool, downbeat, easy-going, even-tempered, happy-go-lucky, informal, laid-back, mellow, mild, nonchalant, placid, serene, together, tranquil, unhurried. *antonyms* edgy, nervous, stiff, tense, uptight.

relay *n* broadcast, communication, dispatch, message, programme, relief, shift, transmission, turn.
v broadcast, carry, communicate, rebroadcast, send, spread, supply, transmit.

release *v* absolve, acquit, break, circulate, declassify, deliver, discharge, disengage, disoblige, dispense, disseminate, distribute, drop, emancipate, exempt, excuse, exonerate, extricate, free, furlough, issue, launch, liberate, loose, manumit, present, publish, unbind, uncage, unchain, undo, unfasten, unfetter, unhand, unleash, unloose, unpen, unshackle, untie, unveil. *antonyms* check, detain.
n absolution, acquittal, acquittance, announcement, deliverance, delivery, discharge, dispensation, emancipation, exemption, exoneration, freedom, issue, let-off, liberation, liberty, manumission, offering, proclamation, publication, quittance, relief. *antonym* detention.

relegate *v* assign, banish, consign, delegate, demote, deport, dispatch, downgrade, eject, entrust, exile, expatriate, expel, refer, transfer. *antonym* promote.

relent *v* acquiesce, capitulate, drop, ease, fall, forbear, give in, melt, relax, slacken, slow, soften, unbend, weaken, yield.

relentless *adj* cruel, fierce, grim, hard, harsh, implacable, incessant, inexorable, inflexible, merciless, non-stop, persistent, pitiless, punishing, remorseless, ruthless, stern, sustained, unabated, unbroken, uncompromising, undeviating, unfaltering, unflagging, unforgiving, unrelenting, unrelieved, unremitting, unstoppable, unyielding. *antonyms* submissive, yielding.

relevant *adj* ad rem, admissible, applicable, apposite, appropriate, appurtenant, apt, congruous, fitting, germane, material, pertinent, proper, related, relative, significant, suitable, suited. *antonym* irrelevant.

reliable *adj* banker, certain, constant, copper-bottomed, dependable, faithful, honest, predictable, regular, responsible, safe, solid, sound, stable, staunch, sure, true, trustworthy, trusty, unfailing, upright, white. *antonyms* doubtful, suspect, unreliable, untrustworthy.

relief *n* abatement, aid, alleviation, assistance, assuagement, balm, break, breather, comfort, cure, deliverance, diversion, ease, easement, help, let-up, load off one's mind, mitigation, palliation, refreshment, relaxation, release, remedy, remission, respite, rest, solace, succour, support, sustenance.

relieve *v* abate, aid, alleviate, appease, assist, assuage, break, brighten, calm, comfort, console, cure, deliver, diminish, discharge, disembarrass, disencumber, dull, ease, exempt, free, help, interrupt, lighten, mitigate, mollify, palliate, relax, release, salve, slacken, soften, solace, soothe, spell, stand in for, substitute for, succour, support, sustain, take over from, take the place of, unburden, vary. *antonyms* aggravate, intensify.

religious *adj* church-going, conscientious, devotional, devout, divine, doctrinal, exact, faithful, fastidious, God-fearing, godly, holy, meticulous, pious, punctilious, pure, reverent, righteous, rigid, rigorous, sacred, scriptural, scrupulous, sectarian, spiritual, strict, theological, unerring, unswerving. *antonyms* irreligious, lax, ungodly.

relinquish *v* abandon, abdicate, cede, desert, discard, drop, forgo, forsake, hand over, leave, quit, release, renounce, repudiate, resign, surrender, vacate, waive, yield. *antonyms* keep, retain.

relish *v* appreciate, enjoy, fancy, lap up, like, prefer, revel in, savour, taste.
n appetiser, appetite, appreciation, condiment, enjoyment, fancy, flavour, fondness, gusto, liking, love, partiality, penchant, piquancy, predilection, sauce, savour, seasoning, smack, spice, stomach, tang, taste, trace, zest.

reluctance *n* aversion, backwardness, disinclination, dislike, distaste, hesitancy, indisposition, loathing, recalcitrance, repugnance, unwillingness. *antonyms* eagerness, willingness.

reluctant *adj* averse, backward, disinclined, grudging, hesitant, indisposed, loath, loth, recalcitrant, renitent, slow, unenthusiastic, unwilling. *antonyms* eager, willing.

rely *v* bank, bet, count, depend, lean, reckon, swear by, trust.

remain *v* abide, bide, cling, continue, delay, dwell, endure, last, linger, persist, prevail, rest, sojourn, stand, stay, survive, tarry, wait. *antonyms* depart, go, leave.

remainder *n* balance, dregs, excess, leavings, remnant, residuum, rest, surplus, trace, vestige(s).

remaining *adj* abiding, extant, lasting, left, lingering, outstanding, persisting, residual, surviving, unfinished, unspent, unused.

remains *n* ashes, balance, body, cadaver, carcass, corpse, crumbs, debris, dregs, fragments, leavings, left-overs, oddments, pieces, relics, remainder, remnants, residue, rest, scraps, traces, vestiges.

remark *v* comment, declare, espy, heed, mark, mention, note, notice, observe, perceive, reflect, regard, say, see, state. *n* acknowledgement, assertion, attention, comment, consideration, declaration, heed, mention, notice, observation, opinion, recognition, reflection, regard, say, statement, thought, utterance, word.

remarkable *adj* amazing, conspicuous, distinguished, exceptional, extraordinary, famous, impressive, miraculous, notable, noteworthy, odd, outstanding, phenomenal, pre-eminent, prominent, rare, signal, singular, strange, striking, surprising, uncommon, unusual, wonderful. *antonyms* average, commonplace, ordinary.

remedy *n* antidote, corrective, counteractive, countermeasure, cure, medicament, medicine, panacea, redress, relief, restorative, solution, specific, therapy, treatment.
v alleviate, ameliorate, assuage, control, correct, counteract, cure, ease, fix, heal, help, mitigate, palliate, put right, rectify, redress, reform, relieve, repair, restore, solve, soothe, treat.

remember *v* commemorate, place, recall, recognise, recollect, reminisce, retain, summon up, think back. *antonym* forget.

remembrance *n* commemoration, keepsake, memento, memorial, memory, mind, monument, recall, recognition, recollection, regard, relic, reminder, reminiscence, retrospect, souvenir, testimonial, thought, token.

remind *v* bring to mind, call to mind, call up, cue, hint, jog one's memory, prompt, put in mind, refresh one's memory.

reminder *n* aide-mémoire, cue, hint, memo, memorandum, nudge, prompt(ing), suggestion.

reminisce *v* hark back, look back, recall, recollect, remember, review, think back.

reminiscence *n* anecdote, memoir, memory, recall, recollection, reflection, remembrance, retrospection, review.

reminiscent *adj* evocative, nostalgic, redolent, remindful, similar, suggestive.

remiss *adj* careless, culpable, delinquent, dilatory, forgetful, heedless, inattentive, indifferent, lackadaisical, lax, neglectful, negligent, regardless, slack, slipshod, sloppy, slothful, slow, tardy, thoughtless, unmindful. *antonyms* careful, scrupulous.

remission *n* abatement, abeyance, absolution, acquittal, alleviation, amelioration, amnesty, decrease, diminution, discharge, ebb, excuse, exemption, exoneration, forgiveness, indulgence, lessening, let-up, lull, moderation, pardon, reduction, relaxation, release, relinquishment, reprieve, respite, slackening, suspension.

remit *v* abate, alleviate, cancel, decrease, defer, delay, desist, desist from, diminish, dispatch, dwindle, forbear, forward, halt, mail, mitigate, moderate, post, postpone, put back, reduce, relax, repeal, rescind, send, send back, shelve, sink, slacken, soften, stop, suspend, transfer, transmit, wane, weaken.
n authorisation, brief, guidelines, instructions, orders, responsibility, scope, terms of reference.

remnant *n* balance, bit, end, fragment, hangover, left-overs, piece, remainder, remains, residue, residuum, rest, rump, scrap, shred, survival, trace, vestige.

remonstrance *n* complaint, exception, expostulation, grievance, objection, petition, protest, protestation, reprimand, reproof.

remonstrate *v* argue, challenge, complain, dispute, dissent, expostulate, gripe, object, protest.

remorse *n* anguish, bad conscience, compassion, compunction, contrition, grief, guilt, penitence, pity, regret, repentance, ruefulness, ruth, self-reproach, shame, sorrow.

remorseful *adj* apologetic, ashamed, chastened, compunctious, conscience-stricken, contrite, guilt-ridden, guilty, penitent, regretful, repentant, rueful, sad, sorrowful, sorry. **antonyms** impenitent, remorseless.

remorseless *adj* callous, cruel, hard, hard-hearted, harsh, implacable, inexorable, inhumane, merciless, pitiless, relentless, ruthless, savage, stern, undeviating, unforgiving, unmerciful, unrelenting, unremitting, unstoppable. **antonyms** remorseful, sorry.

remote *adj* abstracted, alien, aloof, backwoods, cold, detached, distant, doubtful, dubious, extraneous, extrinsic, faint, far, faraway, far-off, foreign, god-forsaken, immaterial, implausible, inaccessible, inconsiderable, indifferent, introspective, introverted, irrelevant, isolated, lonely, meagre, negligible, outlying, out-of-the-way, outside, poor, removed, reserved, secluded, slender, slight, slim, small, standoffish, unconnected, uninterested, uninvolved, unlikely, unrelated, withdrawn. **antonyms** adjacent, close, nearby, significant.

removal *n* abstraction, departure, dislodgement, dismissal, displacement, dispossession, ejection, elimination, eradication, erasure, expulsion, expunction, extraction, flitting, move, purge, purging, relocation, riddance, stripping, subtraction, transfer, uprooting, withdrawal.

remove *v* abolish, abstract, amputate, assassinate, delete, depart, depose, detach, dethrone, discharge, dislodge, dismiss, displace, doff, efface, eject, eliminate, erase, execute, expunge, extract, flit, kill, liquidate, move, murder, oust, purge, quit, relegate, relocate, shave, shear, shed, shift, sideline, strike, subduct, transfer, transmigrate, transport, unseat, vacate, withdraw.

remunerate *v* compensate, fee, indemnify, pay, recompense, redress, reimburse, repay, requite, reward.

remuneration *n* compensation, earnings, emolument, fee, income, indemnity, pay, payment, profit, recompense, reimbursement, remittance, reparation, repayment, retainer, return, reward, salary, stipend, wages.

remunerative *adj* fruitful, gainful, lucrative, moneymaking, paying, profitable, rewarding, rich, worthwhile.

renaissance *n* awakening, new birth, new dawn, reappearance, reawakening, rebirth, re-emergence, regeneration, rejuvenation, renascence, renewal, restoration, resurgence, resurrection, revival.

rend *v* afflict, anguish, break, burst, cleave, crack, dissever, distress, disturb, disunite, divide, fracture, hurt, lacerate, pain, pierce, pull, rip, rive, rupture, separate, sever, shatter, smash, splinter, split, stab, sunder, tear, torment, wound, wrench, wring.

render *v* act, cede, clarify, construe, contribute, deliver, depict, display, do, evince, exchange, exhibit, explain, furnish, give, give back, give up, hand over, interpret, leave, make, make up, manifest, melt, pay, perform, play, portray, present, provide, put, relinquish, repay, represent, reproduce, restate, restore, return, show, show forth, submit, supply, surrender, swap, tender, trade, transcribe, translate, yield.

rendezvous *n* appointment, assignation, date, engagement, haunt, meeting, meeting-place, resort, tryst, venue.
 v assemble, collect, convene, converge, gather, meet, muster, rally.

rendition *n* arrangement, construction, delivery, depiction, execution, explanation, interpretation, performance, portrayal, presentation, reading, rendering, transcription, translation, version.

renew *v* extend, mend, modernise, overhaul, prolong, reaffirm, recommence, recreate, re-establish, refashion, refit, refresh, refurbish, regenerate, rejuvenate, remodel, renovate, reopen, repair, repeat, replace, replenish, restate, restock, restore, resume, revitalise, transform.

renewal *n* kiss of life, recommencement, reconditioning, reconstitution, reconstruction, recreation, recruit, recruital, refurbishment, reinvigoration, reiteration, rejuvenation, renovation, repair, replenishment, resumption, resurrection, resuscitation, revitalisation, revivification.

renounce *v* abandon, abdicate, abjure, abnegate, decline, deny, discard, disclaim, disown, disprofess, eschew, forgo, forsake, forswear, put away, quit, recant, reject, relinquish, repudiate, resign, spurn.

renovate *v* do up, furbish, improve, modernise, overhaul, recondition, reconstitute, recreate, refit, reform, refurbish, rehabilitate, remodel, renew, repair, restore, revamp.

renovation *n* face-lift, improvement, modernisation, reconditioning, refit, refurbishment, renewal, repair, restoration.

renown *n* acclaim, celebrity, distinction, eminence, fame, glory, honour, illustriousness, kudos, lustre, mark, note, reputation, repute, stardom. **antonyms** anonymity, obscurity.

renowned *adj* acclaimed, celebrated, distinguished, eminent, esteemed, famed, famous, illustrious, notable, noted, pre-eminent, supereminent, well-known. **antonyms** anonymous, obscure.

rent *n* fee, gale, hire, lease, payment, rental, tariff.
v charter, hire, lease, let, sublet, take.

renunciation *n* abandonment, abdication, abjuration, abnegation, abstention, denial, disavowal, disclaimer, eschewal, forgoing, forswearing, recantation, rejection, relinquishment, repudiation, resignation, spurning, surrender, waiver.

repair *v* debug, fix, heal, mend, patch up, recover, rectify, redress, renew, renovate, restore, retrieve, square.
n adjustment, condition, darn, fettle, form, improvement, mend, nick, overhaul, patch, restoration, shape, state.

reparation *n* amends, atonement, compensation, damages, indemnity, propitiation, recompense, redress, renewal, repair, requital, restitution, satisfaction, solatium.

repartee *n* badinage, banter, jesting, pleasantry, raillery, riposte, wit, witticism, wittiness, wordplay.

repay *v* avenge, compensate, get even with, make restitution, reciprocate, recompense, refund, reimburse, remunerate, requite, restore, retaliate, return, revenge, reward, settle the score, square.

repayment *n* amends, avengement, compensation, rebate, reciprocation, recompense, redress, refund, reimbursement, remuneration, reparation, requital, restitution, retaliation, retribution, revenge, reward, vengeance.

repeal *v* abolish, abrogate, annul, cancel, countermand, invalidate, nullify, quash, recall, rescind, reverse, revoke, set aside, void, withdraw. **antonyms** enact, establish.
n abolition, abrogation, annulment, cancellation, invalidation, nullification, quashing, rescinding, rescission,

reversal, revocation, withdrawal. **antonyms** enactment, establishment.

repeat *v* duplicate, echo, quote, rebroadcast, recapitulate, recite, re-do, rehearse, reiterate, relate, renew, replay, reproduce, rerun, reshow, restate, retell.
n duplicate, echo, rebroadcast, recapitulation, reiteration, repetition, replay, reproduction, rerun, reshowing.

repeatedly *adv* again and again, frequently, often, ofttimes, over and over, recurrently, time after time, time and (time) again.

repel *v* check, confront, decline, disadvantage, disgust, fight, hold off, nauseate, offend, oppose, parry, rebuff, refuse, reject, repulse, resist, revolt, sicken, ward off. **antonym** attract.

repellent *adj* abhorrent, abominable, discouraging, disgusting, distasteful, hateful, horrid, loathsome, nauseating, noxious, obnoxious, odious, offensive, off-putting, rebarbative, repugnant, repulsive, revolting, sickening. **antonym** attractive.

repent *n* atone, bewail, deplore, lament, regret, relent, rue, sorrow.

repentance *n* compunction, contrition, grief, guilt, penitence, regret, remorse, self-reproach, sorrow.

repentant *adj* apologetic, ashamed, chastened, compunctious, contrite, penitent, regretful, remorseful, rueful, sorry. **antonym** unrepentant.

repercussion *n* aftermath, backlash, backwash, consequence, echo, rebound, recoil, result, reverberation, side effect.

repetitious *adj* long-winded, pleonastic, prolix, redundant, tautological, tedious, verbose, windy, wordy.

repetitive *adj* boring, dull, interminable, mechanical, monotonous, recurrent, samey, tedious, unchanging, unvaried.

repine *v* beef, brood, complain, fret, grieve, grouse, grumble, lament, languish, moan, mope, murmur, sulk.

replace *v* deputise, follow, make good, oust, re-establish, reinstate, restore, substitute, succeed, supersede, supplant, supply.

replacement *n* double, fill-in, proxy, replacer, stand-in, substitute, successor, surrogate, understudy.

replenish *v* fill, furnish, provide, recharge, recruit, refill, reload, renew, replace, restock, restore, stock, supply, top up.

replete *adj* abounding, brimming, charged, chock-a-block, chock-full, crammed, filled, full, full up, glutted, gorged, jammed, jam-packed, sated, satiated, stuffed, teeming, well-provided, well-stocked.

repletion n completeness, fullness, glut, overfullness, plethora, satiation, satiety, superabundance, superfluity.

replica n clone, copy, duplicate, facsimile, imitation, model, reproduction.

replicate v ape, clone, copy, duplicate, follow, mimic, recreate, reduplicate, repeat, reproduce.

reply v acknowledge, answer, counter, echo, react, reciprocate, rejoin, repartee, respond, retaliate, retort, return, riposte.
n acknowledgement, answer, comeback, counter, echo, reaction, reciprocation, rejoinder, repartee, response, retaliation, retort, return, riposte.

report n account, announcement, article, bang, blast, boom, bruit, character, communication, communiqué, crack, crash, declaration, description, detail, detonation, discharge, dispatch, esteem, explosion, fame, gossip, hearsay, information, message, narrative, news, noise, note, paper, piece, recital, record, regard, relation, reputation, repute, reverberation, rumour, sound, statement, story, summary, tale, talk, tidings, version, word, write-up.
v air, announce, appear, arrive, broadcast, circulate, come, communicate, cover, declare, describe, detail, document, mention, narrate, note, notify, proclaim, publish, recite, record, recount, relate, relay, state, tell.

repose n aplomb, calm, calmness, composure, dignity, ease, equanimity, inactivity, peace, poise, quiet, quietness, quietude, relaxation, respite, rest, restfulness, self-possession, serenity, sleep, slumber, stillness, tranquillity. **antonyms** activity, strain, stress.
v laze, recline, relax, rest, sleep, slumber.

reprehensible adj bad, blamable, blameworthy, censurable, condemnable, culpable, delinquent, discreditable, disgraceful, errant, erring, ignoble, objectionable, opprobrious, remiss, shameful, unworthy. **antonyms** creditable, good, praiseworthy.

represent v act, appear as, be, betoken, delineate, denote, depict, describe, designate, embody, enact, epitomise, equal, evoke, exemplify, exhibit, express, illustrate, mean, outline, perform, personify, picture, portray, produce, render, reproduce, show, sketch, stage, symbolise, typify.

representation n account, argument, committee, delegates, delegation, delineation, depiction, description, embassy, exhibition, explanation, exposition, expostulation, icon, idol, illustration, image, likeness, model, narrative, performance, petition, picture, play, portrait, portrayal, production, relation, remonstrance, resemblance, show, sight, sketch, spectacle, statue.

representative n agent, archetype, commissioner, councillor, delegate, depute, deputy, embodiment, epitome, exemplar, member, MP, personification, proxy, rep, salesman, spokesman, spokesperson, spokeswoman, traveller, type.
adj archetypal, characteristic, chosen, delegated, elected, elective, emblematic, evocative, exemplary, illustrative, normal, symbolic, typical, usual. **antonyms** atypical, unrepresentative.

repress v bottle up, chasten, check, control, crush, curb, hamper, hinder, impede, inhibit, master, muffle, overcome, overpower, quash, quell, reprime, restrain, silence, smother, stifle, subdue, subjugate, suppress, swallow.

repression n authoritarianism, censorship, coercion, constraint, control, denial, despotism, domination, gagging, inhibition, restraint, subjugation, suffocation, suppression, tyranny.

repressive adj absolute, authoritarian, autocratic, coercive, despotic, dictatorial, harsh, iron-handed, oppressive, severe, tough, tyrannical.

reprieve v abate, allay, alleviate, mitigate, palliate, pardon, redeem, relieve, rescue, respite.
n abatement, abeyance, alleviation, amnesty, deferment, let-up, mitigation, palliation, pardon, postponement, redemption, relief, remission, rescue, respite, suspension.

reprimand n admonition, blame, bollocking, castigation, censure, dressing-down, lecture, rebuke, reprehension, reproach, reproof, row, talking-to, telling-off, ticking-off, tongue-lashing.
v admonish, bawl out, blame, bollock, bounce, castigate, censure, check, chide, keelhaul, lecture, lesson, rebuke, reprehend, reproach, reprove, scold, tongue-lash, upbraid.

reproach v abuse, blame, censure, chide, condemn, criticise, defame, discredit, disparage, dispraise, rebuke, reprehend, reprimand, reprove, scold, upbraid.
n abuse, blame, blemish, censure, condemnation, contempt, disapproval, discredit, disgrace, dishonour, disrepute, ignominy, indignity, obloquy, odium, opprobrium, reproof, scorn, shame, slight, stain, stigma, upbraiding.

reproachful adj abusive, admonitory, aggrieved, castigatory, censorious, condemnatory, contemptuous, critical, disappointed, disapproving, fault-finding, opprobrious, reproving, scolding, upbraiding. **antonym** complimentary.

reprobate adj abandoned, bad, base, condemnatory, corrupt, damned, degenerate, depraved, dissolute, hardened, immoral, incorrigible, profligate, shameless, sinful, unprincipled, vile, wicked. **antonym** upright.
n blackguard, degenerate, evildoer, knave, miscreant, ne'er-do-well, outcast, pariah, profligate, rake, rascal, rogue, scamp, scoundrel, sinner, villain, wastrel, wretch, wrongdoer.

reproduce v ape, breed, copy, duplicate, echo, emulate, facsimile, generate, imitate, match, mirror, multiply, parallel, parrot, print, procreate, proliferate, propagate, recreate, regurgitate, repeat, replicate, represent, simulate, spawn, transcribe.

reproduction n breeding, copy, duplicate, facsimile, generation, imitation, increase, multiplication, picture, print, procreation, proliferation, propagation, replica. **antonym** original.

reproof n admonition, blame, castigation, censure, chiding, condemnation, criticism, dressing-down, rebuke, reprehension, reprimand, reproach, reproval, reproving, scolding, ticking-off, tongue-lashing, upbraiding. **antonym** praise.

reprove v abuse, admonish, berate, blame, censure, check, chide, condemn, rate, rebuke, reprehend, reprimand, scold, upbraid. **antonym** praise.

repudiate v abandon, abjure, cast off, deny, desert, disaffirm, disavow, discard, disclaim, disown, disprofess, divorce, forsake, reject, renounce, rescind, retract, reverse, revoke. **antonyms** admit, own.

repudiation n abjuration, denial, disaffirmation, disavowal, disclaimer, disowning, recantation, rejection, renunciation, retraction. **antonym** acceptance.

repugnant adj abhorrent, abominable, adverse, antagonistic, antipathetic, averse, contradictory, disgusting, distasteful, foul, hateful, horrid, hostile, incompatible, inconsistent, inimical, loathsome, nauseating, objectionable, obnoxious, odious, offensive, opposed, repellent, revolting, sickening, unacceptable, vile. **antonyms** acceptable, consistent, pleasant.

repulse v beat off, check, defeat, disdain, disregard, drive back, rebuff, refuse, reject, repel, snub, spurn.

repulsive adj abhorrent, abominable, disagreeable, disgusting, distasteful, forbidding, foul, hateful, hideous, horrid, loathsome, nauseating, objectionable, obnoxious, odious, offensive, repellent, revolting, sickening, ugly, unpleasant, vile. **antonyms** friendly, pleasant.

reputable adj creditable, dependable, estimable, excellent, good, honourable, honoured, irreproachable, legitimate, principled, reliable, respectable, trustworthy, unimpeachable, upright, worthy. **antonyms** disreputable, infamous.

reputation n bad name, character, credit, distinction, esteem, estimation, fame, good name, honour, infamy, name, opinion, renown, repute, standing, stature.

repute n celebrity, distinction, esteem, estimation, fame, good name, name, renown, reputation, standing, stature. **antonym** infamy.

reputed adj accounted, alleged, believed, considered, deemed, estimated, held, ostensible, putative, reckoned, regarded, reputative, rumoured, said, seeming, supposed, thought. **antonym** actual.

request v ask, ask for, beg, beseech, demand, desire, entreat, importune, petition, pray, requisition, seek, solicit, supplicate.
n appeal, application, asking, begging, call, demand, desire, entreaty, petition, prayer, representation, requisition, solicitation, suit, supplication.

require v ask, beg, beseech, bid, command, compel, constrain, crave, demand, desire, direct, enjoin, exact, force, instruct, involve, lack, make, miss, necessitate, need, oblige, order, request, take, want, wish.

required *adj* compulsory, demanded, essential, mandatory, necessary, needed, obligatory, prescribed, recommended, requisite, set, stipulated, unavoidable, vital. *antonyms* inessential, optional.

requirement *n* demand, essential, lack, must, necessity, need, precondition, prerequisite, provision, proviso, qualification, requisite, sine qua non, specification, stipulation, term, want. *antonym* inessential.

requisite *adj* essential, imperative, indispensable, mandatory, necessary, needed, obligatory, prerequisite, required, vital. *antonyms* inessential, optional.
n condition, essential, must, necessity, need, precondition, prerequisite, requirement, sine qua non. *antonym* inessential.

requisition *v* appropriate, commandeer, confiscate, demand, occupy, put in for, request, seize, take.
n application, appropriation, call, commandeering, demand, occupation, order, request, seizure, summons, takeover, use.

requital *n* amends, compensation, indemnification, indemnity, payment, pay-off, quittance, recompense, redress, reparation, repayment, restitution, satisfaction.

requite *v* avenge, compensate, pay, reciprocate, recompense, redress, reimburse, remunerate, repay, respond, retaliate, return, reward, satisfy.

rescind *v* abrogate, annul, cancel, countermand, invalidate, negate, nullify, overturn, quash, recall, repeal, retract, reverse, revoke, void. *antonym* enforce.

rescission *n* abrogation, annulment, cancellation, invalidation, negation, nullification, recall, repeal, rescindment, retraction, reversal, revocation, voidance. *antonym* enforcement.

rescue *v* deliver, extricate, free, liberate, ransom, recover, redeem, release, salvage, save. *antonym* capture.
n deliverance, delivery, extrication, liberation, recovery, redemption, release, relief, salvage, salvation, saving. *antonym* capture.

research *n* analysis, delving, examination, experimentation, exploration, fact-finding, groundwork, inquiry, investigation, probe, quest, scrutiny, search, study.
v analyse, examine, experiment,

explore, ferret, investigate, probe, scrutinise, search, study.

resemblance *n* affinity, analogy, assonance, closeness, comparability, comparison, conformity, correspondence, counterpart, facsimile, image, kinship, likeness, parallel, parity, sameness, semblance, similarity, similitude. *antonym* dissimilarity.

resemble *v* approach, duplicate, echo, favour, mirror, parallel, take after. *antonym* differ from.

resent *v* begrudge, chafe at, dislike, grudge, grumble at, object to, take amiss, take exception to, take offence at, take the huff, take umbrage at. *antonyms* accept, like.

resentful *adj* aggrieved, angry, bitter, embittered, exasperated, grudging, huffish, huffy, hurt, incensed, indignant, irate, jealous, miffed, offended, peeved, piqued, put out, resentive, revengeful, unforgiving, wounded. *antonym* contented.

resentment *n* anger, animosity, bitterness, disaffection, discontentment, displeasure, fury, grudge, huff, hurt, ill-feeling, ill-will, indignation, ire, irritation, malice, pique, rage, rancour, umbrage, vexation, vindictiveness, wrath. *antonym* contentment.

reservation *n* condition, demur, doubt, hesitancy, hesitation, inhibition, proviso, qualification, restraint, scepticism, scruple, second thought, stipulation.

reserve[1] *v* bespeak, book, conserve, defer, delay, engage, hoard, hold, keep, postpone, prearrange, preserve, retain, save, secure, set apart, spare, stockpile, store, withhold. *antonym* use up.
n backlog, cache, capital, fund, hoard, park, preserve, reservation, reservoir, sanctuary, savings, stock, stockpile, store, substitute, supply, tract.

reserve[2] aloofness, constraint, coolness, formality, limitation, modesty, reluctance, reservation, restraint, restriction, reticence, secretiveness, shyness, silence, taciturnity. *antonyms* friendliness, informality.
adj additional, alternate, auxiliary, extra, secondary, spare, substitute.

reserved[1] *adj* booked, bound, designated, destined, earmarked, engaged, fated, held, intended, kept, meant, predestined, restricted, retained, set aside, spoken for, taken. *antonym* unreserved.

reserved[2] aloof, cautious, close-mouthed,

cold, cool, demure, formal, modest, prim, restrained, reticent, retiring, secretive, shy, silent, stand-offish, taciturn, unapproachable, uncommunicative, uncompanionable, undemonstrative, unforthcoming, unresponsive, unsociable. *antonyms* friendly, informal.

reshuffle *n* change, interchange, realignment, rearrangement, redistribution, regrouping, reorganisation, restructuring, revision, shake-up, upheaval.
v change, interchange, realign, rearrange, redistribute, regroup, reorganise, restructure, revise, shake up, shift, shuffle.

reside *v* abide, consist, dwell, exist, inhabit, inhere, lie, live, lodge, remain, settle, sit, sojourn, stay.

residence *n* abode, domicile, dwelling, habitation, home, house, household, lodging, occupation, pad, place, quarters, seat, sojourn, stay.

residual *adj* left-over, net(t), remaining, unconsumed, unused, vestigial. *antonym* core.

residue *n* balance, difference, dregs, excess, extra, left-overs, overflow, overplus, remainder, remains, remnant, residuum, rest, surplus. *antonym* core.

resign *v* abandon, abdicate, cede, forgo, forsake, leave, quit, relinquish, renounce, sacrifice, stand down, surrender, vacate, waive, yield. *antonyms* join, maintain.

resign oneself accede, accept, acquiesce, bow, comply, reconcile, submit, yield. *antonym* resist.

resignation *n* abandonment, abdication, acceptance, acquiescence, compliance, defeatism, demission, departure, endurance, forbearing, fortitude, leaving, non-resistance, notice, passivity, patience, relinquishment, renunciation, retirement, submission, sufferance, surrender. *antonym* resistance.

resigned *adj* acquiescent, compliant, defeatist, long-suffering, patient, stoical, subdued, submissive, unprotesting, unresisting. *antonym* resisting.

resilience *n* adaptability, bounce, buoyancy, elasticity, flexibility, give, hardiness, plasticity, pliability, recoil, spring, springiness, strength, suppleness, toughness, unshockability. *antonyms* inflexibility, rigidity.

resilient *adj* adaptable, bouncy, buoyant, elastic, flexible, hardy, irrepressible, plastic, pliable, springy, strong,

supple, tough, unshockable. *antonyms* downcast, rigid.

resist *v* avoid, battle, check, combat, confront, counteract, countervail, curb, defy, dispute, fight back, forbear, forgo, hinder, oppose, refuse, repel, thwart, weather, withstand. *antonyms* accept, submit.

resistance *n* combat, contention, counteraction, defiance, fight, fighting, hindrance, impedance, impediment, intransigence, obstruction, opposition, partisans, refusal, resistant, resistors, struggle, underground. *antonyms* acceptance, submission.

resistant *adj* antagonistic, combative, defiant, dissident, hard, hostile, impervious, insusceptible, intractible, intransigent, opposed, recalcitrant, stiff, strong, tough, unsusceptible, unwilling, unyielding. *antonyms* compliant, yielding.

resolute *adj* bold, constant, determined, dogged, firm, fixed, inflexible, obstinate, persevering, purposeful, relentless, set, staunch, steadfast, stout, strong-minded, strong-willed, stubborn, sturdy, tenacious, unbending, undaunted, unflinching, unshakable, unshaken, unwavering. *antonym* irresolute.

resolution *n* aim, answer, boldness, constancy, courage, decision, declaration, dedication, dénouement, determination, devotion, doggedness, earnestness, end, energy, finding, firmness, fortitude, intent, intention, judgement, motion, obstinacy, outcome, perseverance, pertinacity, purpose, relentlessness, resoluteness, resolve, settlement, sincerity, solution, solving, staunchness, steadfastness, stubbornness, tenacity, unravelling, verdict, will power, zeal. *antonym* indecision.

resolve *v* agree, alter, analyse, anatomise, answer, banish, break up, change, clear, conclude, convert, crack, decide, design, determine, disentangle, disintegrate, dispel, dissect, dissipate, dissolve, elucidate, explain, fathom, fix, intend, liquefy, melt, metamorphose, purpose, reduce, relax, remove, separate, settle, solve, transform, transmute, undertake, unravel. *antonyms* blend, waver.
n boldness, conclusion, conviction, courage, decision, design, determination, earnestness, firmness, intention, objective, project, purpose, resoluteness, resolution, sense of purpose,

steadfastness, undertaking, will power. **antonym** indecision.

resonant *adj* booming, echoing, full, resounding, reverberant, reverberating, rich, ringing, sonorous, vibrant. **antonym** faint.

resort *n* alternative, chance, course, expedient, haunt, health resort, hope, possibility, recourse, reference, refuge, retreat, spa, spot.

resort to employ, exercise, go so far as to, lower oneself to, stoop to, use, utilise.

resound *v* boom, echo, resonate, reverberate, ring, sound, thunder.

resounding *adj* booming, conclusive, crushing, decisive, echoing, full, plangent, powerful, resonant, reverberating, rich, ringing, sonorous, sounding, thorough, vibrant, vocal. **antonyms** faint, slight.

resource *n* ability, appliance, cache, capability, cleverness, contrivance, course, device, expedient, hoard, ingenuity, initiative, inventiveness, means, quick-wittedness, reserve, resort, resourcefulness, shift, source, stockpile, supply, talent. **antonym** unimaginativeness.

resourceful *adj* able, bright, capable, clever, creative, fertile, imaginative, ingenious, innovative, inventive, quick-witted, sharp, slick, talented.

respect *n* admiration, appreciation, approbation, aspect, bearing, characteristic, connection, consideration, deference, detail, esteem, estimation, facet, feature, homage, honour, matter, particular, point, recognition, reference, regard, relation, reverence, sense, veneration, way. **antonym** disrespect.
v admire, appreciate, attend, esteem, follow, heed, honour, notice, obey, observe, pay homage to, recognise, regard, revere, reverence, value, venerate. **antonym** scorn.

respectable *adj* admirable, ample, appreciable, clean-living, considerable, decent, decorous, dignified, estimable, fair, good, goodly, honest, honourable, large, passable, presentable, proper, reasonable, reputable, respected, seemly, sizable, substantial, tidy, tolerable, upright, venerable, well-to-do, worthy. **antonyms** disreputable, miserly, unseemly.

respectful *adj* civil, courteous, courtly, deferential, dutiful, filial, gracious, humble, mannerly, obedient, polite, regardful, reverent, reverential, self-effacing, solicitous, submissive, subservient, well-mannered. **antonym** disrespectful.

respecting *prep* about, concerning, considering, in respect of, regarding, with regard to, with respect to.

respective *adj* corresponding, individual, own, particular, personal, relevant, separate, several, special, specific, various.

respite *n* adjournment, break, breather, cessation, delay, gap, halt, hiatus, intermission, interruption, interval, let-up, lull, moratorium, pause, postponement, recess, relaxation, relief, remission, reprieve, rest, stay, suspension.

resplendent *adj* beaming, bright, brilliant, dazzling, effulgent, gleaming, glittering, glorious, irradiant, luminous, lustrous, radiant, refulgent, shining, splendid, splendiferous. **antonym** dull.

respond *v* acknowledge, answer, answer back, come back, counter, react, reciprocate, rejoin, reply, retort, return.

response *n* acknowledgement, answer, comeback, counterblast, feedback, reaction, rejoinder, reply, respond, retort, return, riposte. **antonym** query.

responsibility *n* accountability, amenability, answerability, authority, blame, burden, care, charge, conscientiousness, culpability, dependability, duty, fault, guilt, importance, level-headedness, liability, maturity, obligation, onus, power, rationality, reliability, sense, sensibleness, soberness, stability, trust, trustworthiness. **antonym** irresponsibility.

responsible *adj* accountable, adult, amenable, answerable, authoritative, bound, chargeable, conscientious, culpable, decision-making, dependable, duty-bound, ethical, executive, guilty, high, important, level-headed, liable, mature, rational, reliable, right, sensible, sober, sound, stable, steady, subject, trustworthy. **antonym** irresponsible.

responsive *adj* alive, awake, aware, forthcoming, impressionable, open, perceptive, reactive, receptive, sensitive, sharp, susceptible, sympathetic. **antonym** unresponsive.

rest[1] *n* base, break, breather, breathing-space, calm, cessation, cradle, doze, halt, haven, holder, holiday, idleness, inactivity, interlude, intermission, interval, leisure, lie-down, lie-in, lodging, lull, motionlessness, nap, pause, prop, refreshment, refuge, relaxation, relief, repose, retreat, shelf, shelter, shut-eye, siesta, sleep, slumber, snooze, somnolence, spell, stand, standstill, stillness, stop, support, tranquillity, trestle, vacation. *antonyms* action, activity, restlessness.

v alight, base, cease, continue, depend, desist, discontinue, doze, found, halt, hang, hinge, idle, keep, land, lay, laze, lean, lie, lie back, lie down, lie in, perch, prop, recline, relax, rely, remain, repose, reside, settle, sit, sleep, slumber, snooze, spell, stand, stay, stop, turn. *antonyms* change, continue, work.

rest² *n* balance, core, excess, left-overs, majority, others, remainder, remains, remnants, residue, residuum, rump, surplus.

restful *adj* calm, calming, comfortable, languid, pacific, peaceful, placid, quiet, relaxed, relaxing, serene, sleepy, soothing, tranquil, tranquillising, undisturbed, unhurried. *antonyms* disturbed, disturbing.

restitution *n* amends, compensation, damages, indemnification, indemnity, recompense, redress, refund, reimbursement, remuneration, reparation, repayment, requital, restoration, restoring, return, satisfaction.

restive *adj* agitated, edgy, fidgety, fractious, fretful, impatient, jittery, jumpy, nervous, obstinate, recalcitrant, refractory, restless, uneasy, unquiet, unruly. *antonyms* calm, relaxed.

restless *adj* active, agitated, anxious, bustling, changeable, disturbed, edgy, fidgety, fitful, fretful, hurried, inconstant, irresolute, jumpy, moving, nervous, nomadic, restive, roving, shifting, sleepless, transient, troubled, turbulent, uneasy, unquiet, unresting, unruly, unsettled, unstable, unsteady, wandering, worried. *antonyms* calm, relaxed.

restlessness *n* activity, agitation, anxiety, bustle, disquiet, disturbance, edginess, fitfulness, fretfulness, heebie-jeebies, hurry, hurry-scurry, inconstancy, inquietude, insomnia, instability, jitters, jumpiness, movement, nervousness, restiveness, transience, turbulence, turmoil, uneasiness, unrest, unsettledness, wanderlust, worriedness. *antonyms* calmness, relaxation.

restoration *n* instauration, kiss of life, reconstruction, recovery, re-establishment, refreshment, refurbishing,

rehabilitation, reinstallation, reinstatement, rejuvenation, renewal, renovation, repair, replacement, restitution, return, revitalisation, revival. *antonyms* damage, removal, weakening.

restore *v* fix, mend, reanimate, rebuild, recondition, reconstitute, reconstruct, recover, recruit, re-enforce, re-establish, refresh, refurbish, rehabilitate, reimpose, reinstate, reintroduce, rejuvenate, renew, renovate, repair, replace, retouch, return, revitalise, revive, revivify, strengthen. *antonyms* damage, remove, weaken.

restrain *v* arrest, bind, bit, bridle, chain, check, cohibit, confine, constrain, control, curb, curtail, debar, detain, fetter, govern, hamper, handicap, harness, hinder, hold, imprison, inhibit, jail, keep, limit, manacle, muzzle, pinion, prevent, repress, restrict, stay, subdue, suppress, tie. *antonyms* encourage, liberate.

restrained *adj* calm, controlled, discreet, low-key, mild, moderate, muted, quiet, reasonable, reticent, self-controlled, soft, steady, subdued, tasteful, temperate, undemonstrative, understated, unemphatic, unobtrusive. *antonym* unrestrained.

restraint *n* arrest, ban, bondage, bonds, bridle, captivity, chains, check, coercion, cohibition, command, compulsion, confinement, confines, constraint, control, cramp, curb, curtailment, dam, detention, embargo, fetters, grip, hindrance, hold, imprisonment, inhibition, interdict, lid, limit, limitation, manacles, moderation, pinions, prevention, rein, restriction, self-control, self-discipline, self-possession, self-restraint, stint, straitjacket, suppression, taboo, tie. *antonym* freedom.

restrict *v* astrict, bound, circumscribe, condition, confine, constrain, contain, cramp, demarcate, hamper, handicap, impede, inhibit, limit, regulate, restrain, tie. *antonyms* broaden, encourage, free.

restriction *n* check, condition, confinement, constraint, containment, control, curb, demarcation, handicap, inhibition, limitation, regulation, restraint, rule, squeeze, stint, stipulation. *antonyms* broadening, encouragement, freedom.

result *n* conclusion, consequence, decision, development, effect, end, end-product, event, fruit, issue, outcome, produce, reaction, termination, upshot. *antonyms* beginning, cause.

v appear, arise, culminate, derive, develop, emanate, emerge, end, ensue, eventuate, finish, flow, follow, happen, issue, proceed, spring, stem, terminate. *antonyms* begin, cause.

resume *v* continue, pick up, proceed, recommence, reinstitute, reopen, restart, take up. *antonym* cease.

résumé *n* abstract, digest, epitome, overview, précis, recapitulation, review, run-down, summary, synopsis.

resumption *n* continuation, re-establishment, renewal, reopening, restart, resurgence. *antonym* cessation.

resurgence *n* rebirth, re-emergence, renaissance, renascence, resumption, resurrection, return, revival. *antonym* decrease.

resurrect *v* come to life, reintroduce, renew, restore, revive. *antonyms* bury, kill off, quash.

resurrection *n* comeback, reactivation, reappearance, rebirth, renaissance, renascence, renewal, restoration, resurgence, resuscitation, return, revival. *antonyms* burying, killing off, quashing.

resuscitate *v* quicken, reanimate, reinvigorate, renew, rescue, restore, resurrect, revitalise, revive, revivify, save.

retain *v* absorb, commission, contain, detail, employ, engage, grasp, grip, hire, hold, hold back, keep, keep in mind, keep up, maintain, memorise, pay, preserve, recall, recollect, remember, reserve, restrain, save. *antonyms* release, spend.

retaliate *v* fight back, get back at, get even with, get one's own back, give as good as one gets, hit back, reciprocate, repay in kind, return like for like, revenge oneself, strike back, take revenge. *antonyms* accept, submit.

retaliation *n* a taste of one's own medicine, counterblow, counterstroke, reciprocation, repayment, reprisal, requital, retort, retribution, revenge, tit for tat, vengeance. *antonyms* acceptance, submission.

retard *v* arrest, brake, check, clog, decelerate, defer, delay, detain, encumber, handicap, hinder, impede, keep back, obstruct, slow, stall. *antonym* advance.

retardation *n* deficiency, delay, dullness, hindering, hindrance, impeding, incapability, incapacity, lag, mental handicap, obstruction, slowing, slowness. *antonym* advancement.

retch *v* disgorge, gag, heave, puke, reach, regurgitate, spew, throw up, vomit.

reticent *adj* close-lipped, close-mouthed, mum, mute, quiet, reserved, restrained, secretive, silent, taciturn, tight-lipped, uncommunicative, unforthcoming, unspeaking. *antonyms* communicative, forward, frank.

retinue *n* aides, attendants, cortège, entourage, escort, followers, following, personnel, servants, staff, suite, train.

retire *v* decamp, depart, draw back, ebb, exit, leave, recede, remove, retreat, withdraw. *antonyms* enter, join.

retired *adj* emeritus, ex-, former, past.

retirement *n* loneliness, obscurity, privacy, retiral, retreat, seclusion, solitude, withdrawal. *antonyms* company, limelight.

retiring *adj* bashful, coy, demure, diffident, humble, meek, modest, mousy, quiet, reclusive, reserved, reticent, self-effacing, shamefaced, shrinking, shy, timid, timorous, unassertive, unassuming. *antonyms* assertive, forward.

retort *v* answer, counter, rejoin, reply, respond, retaliate, return, riposte.
n answer, backword, come-back, quip, rejoinder, repartee, reply, response, riposte.

retract *v* abjure, cancel, deny, disavow, disclaim, disown, recall, recant, renounce, repeal, repudiate, rescind, reverse, revoke, unsay, unspeak, withdraw. *antonym* maintain.

retreat *v* depart, ebb, leave, quit, recede, recoil, retire, shrink, turn tail, withdraw. *antonym* advance.
n asylum, den, departure, ebb, evacuation, flight, haunt, haven, hideaway, privacy, refuge, resort, retirement, sanctuary, seclusion, shelter, withdrawal. *antonyms* advance, company, limelight.

retrench *v* curtail, cut, decrease, diminish, economise, lessen, limit, pare, prune, reduce, save, slim down, trim. *antonym* increase.

retribution *n* compensation, justice, Nemesis, payment, punishment, reckoning, recompense, redress, repayment, reprisal, requital, retaliation, revenge, reward, satisfaction, vengeance.

retrieve *v* fetch, make good, recall, recapture, recoup, recover, redeem, regain, repair, repossess, rescue, restore, return, salvage, save. *antonym* lose.

retrograde *adj* backward, declining, degenerative, denigrating, deteriorating, downward, inverse, negative, regressive, relapsing, retreating, retrogressive, reverse, reverting, waning, worsening. *antonym* progressive.

retrogress *v* backslide, decline, degenerate, deteriorate, drop, ebb, fall, recede, regress, relapse, retire, retreat, return, revert, sink, wane, withdraw, worsen. *antonym* progress.

retrogression *n* decline, deterioration, drop, ebb, fall, recidivism, regress, relapse, return, worsening. *antonyms* increase, progress.

retrospect *n* afterthought, contemplation, hindsight, recollection, re-examination, reference, regard, remembrance, reminiscence, review, survey. *antonym* prospect.

return *v* announce, answer, choose, communicate, convey, deliver, earn, elect, make, net, pick, reappear, rebound, reciprocate, recoil, recompense, recur, redound, re-establish, refund, reimburse, reinstate, rejoin, remit, render, repair, repay, replace, reply, report, requite, respond, restore, retort, retreat, revert, send, submit, transmit, volley, yield. *antonyms* leave, take.

n account, advantage, answer, benefit, comeback, compensation, form, gain, home-coming, income, interest, list, proceeds, profit, quip, reappearance, rebound, reciprocation, recoil, recompense, recurrence, redound, re-establishment, reimbursement, reinstatement, rejoinder, reparation, repayment, replacement, reply, report, requital, response, restoration, retaliation, retort, retreat, revenue, reversion, reward, riposte, statement, summary, takings, yield. *antonyms* disappearance, expense, loss, payment.

revamp *v* do up, overhaul, rebuild, recast, recondition, reconstruct, refit, refurbish, rehabilitate, renovate, repair, restore, revise.

reveal *v* announce, bare, betray, broadcast, communicate, disbosom, disclose, display, divulge, exhibit, expose, impart, leak, lift the lid off, manifest, open, proclaim, publish, show, tell, unbosom, uncover, unearth, unfold, unmask, unveil. *antonym* hide.

revel *v* carouse, celebrate, live it up, make merry, paint the town red, push the boat out, raise the roof, roist, roister, whoop it up.

n bacchanal, carousal, celebration, festivity, gala, jollification, merrymaking, party, saturnalia, spree.

revel in bask, crow, delight, gloat, glory, indulge, joy, lap up, luxuriate, rejoice, relish, savour, take pleasure, thrive on, wallow. *antonym* dislike.

revelation *n* announcement, apocalypse, betrayal, broadcasting, communication, disclosure, discovery, display, exhibition, exposé, exposition, exposure, giveaway, leak, manifestation, news, proclamation, publication, telling, uncovering, unearthing, unveiling.

revelry *n* carousal, celebration, debauch, debauchery, festivity, fun, jollification, jollity, merrymaking, party, riot, roistering, saturnalia, spree, wassail. *antonym* sobriety.

revenge *n* a dose/taste of one's own medicine, reprisal, requital, retaliation, retribution, satisfaction, vengeance, vindictiveness.

v avenge, even the score, get one's own back, get satisfaction, repay, requite, retaliate, vindicate.

revengeful *adj* bitter, implacable, malevolent, malicious, malignant, merciless, pitiless, resentful, spiteful, unforgiving, unmerciful, vengeful, vindictive. *antonym* forgiving.

revenue *n* gain, income, interest, proceeds, profits, receipts, returns, rewards, take, takings, yield. *antonym* expenditure.

reverberate *v* echo, rebound, recoil, reflect, resound, ring, vibrate.

reverberation *n* echo, rebound, recoil, reflection, resonance, resounding, ringing, vibration, wave.

revere *v* adore, defer to, exalt, honour, pay homage to, respect, reverence, venerate, worship. *antonyms* despise, scorn.

reverence *n* admiration, adoration, awe, deference, devotion, esteem, genuflection, homage, honour, respect, veneration, worship. *antonym* scorn.

v acknowledge, admire, adore, honour, respect, revere, venerate, worship. *antonyms* despise, scorn.

reverent *adj* adoring, awed, decorous, deferential, devout, dutiful, humble, loving, meek, pious, respectful, reverential, solemn, submissive. *antonym* irreverent.

reverie *n* absent-mindedness, abstraction, daydream, daydreaming, inattention, musing, preoccupation, trance, woolgathering.

reversal *n* abrogation, annulment, cancellation, countermanding, defeat, delay, difficulty, disaster, misfortune, mishap, nullification, problem, repeal, rescinding, rescission, reverse, revocation, set-back, turnabout, turnaround, turnround, upset, U-turn. **antonyms** advancement, progress.

reverse v alter, annul, back, backtrack, cancel, change, countermand, hark back, invalidate, invert, negate, overrule, overset, overthrow, overturn, quash, repeal, rescind, retract, retreat, revert, revoke, transpose, undo, up-end, upset. **antonym** enforce.
n adversity, affliction, antithesis, back, check, contradiction, contrary, converse, inverse, opposite, rear, repulse, reversal, underside, verso.
adj backward, contrary, converse, inverse, inverted, opposite, verso.

revert v backslide, lapse, recur, regress, relapse, resume, retrogress, return, reverse. **antonym** progress.

review v assess, criticise, discuss, evaluate, examine, inspect, judge, reassess, recall, recapitulate, recollect, reconsider, re-evaluate, re-examine, rehearse, remember, rethink, revise, scrutinise, study, weigh.
n analysis, assessment, commentary, criticism, critique, evaluation, examination, journal, judgement, magazine, notice, periodical, reassessment, recapitulation, recension, reconsideration, re-evaluation, re-examination, report, rethink, retrospect, revision, scrutiny, study, survey.

revile v abuse, blackguard, calumniate, defame, denigrate, libel, malign, miscall, reproach, scorn, slander, smear, traduce, vilify, vituperate. **antonym** praise.

revise v alter, amend, change, correct, edit, emend, memorise, modify, recast, reconsider, reconstruct, redo, re-examine, reread, revamp, review, rewrite, study, swot up, update.

revision n alteration, amendment, change, correction, editing, emendation, homework, memorising, modification, recast, recasting, recension, reconstruction, re-examination, rereading, review, rewriting, studying, swotting, updating.

revitalise v reactivate, reanimate, refresh, rejuvenate, renew, restore, resurrect, revive. **antonyms** dampen, suppress.

revival n awakening, quickening, reactivation, reanimation, reawakening, rebirth, renaissance, renascence, renewal, restoration, resurgence, resurrection,

resuscitation, revitalisation. **antonym** suppression.

revive v animate, awaken, cheer, comfort, invigorate, quicken, rally, reactivate, reanimate, recover, refresh, rekindle, renew, renovate, restore, resuscitate, revitalise, rouse. **antonyms** suppress, weary.

revocation n abolition, annulment, cancellation, countermanding, nullification, quashing, repeal, repealing, repudiation, rescinding, rescission, retraction, reversal, revoking, withdrawal. **antonym** enforcement.

revoke v abolish, abrogate, annul, cancel, countermand, disclaim, dissolve, invalidate, negate, nullify, quash, recall, recant, renounce, repeal, repudiate, rescind, retract, reverse, withdraw. **antonym** enforce.

revolt[1] n breakaway, defection, insurgency, insurrection, mutiny, putsch, rebellion, revolution, rising, secession, sedition, uprising.
v defect, mutiny, rebel, resist, riot, rise. **antonym** submit.

revolt[2] v disgust, nauseate, offend, outrage, repel, repulse, scandalise, shock, sicken. **antonym** please.

revolting adj abhorrent, abominable, appalling, disgusting, distasteful, fetid, foul, horrible, horrid, loathsome, nasty, nauseating, obnoxious, obscene, offensive, repellent, repugnant, repulsive, shocking, sickening, sickly. **antonym** pleasant.

revolution n cataclysm, change, circle, circuit, coup, coup d'état, cycle, gyration, innovation, insurgency, lap, metamorphosis, mutiny, orbit, putsch, rebellion, reformation, revolt, rising, rotation, round, shift, spin, transformation, turn, upheaval, uprising, volution, wheel, whirl.

revolutionary n anarchist, insurgent, insurrectionary, insurrectionist, mutineer, rebel, revolutionist.
adj anarchistic, avant-garde, different, drastic, experimental, extremist, fundamental, innovative, insurgent, insurrectionary, mutinous, new, novel, progressive, radical, rebel, seditious, subversive, thoroughgoing. **antonyms** commonplace, establishment.

revolve v circle, gyrate, orbit, rotate, spin, turn, wheel, whirl.

revulsion n abhorrence, abomination, aversion, detestation, disgust, dislike, distaste, hatred, loathing, recoil, repugnance, repulsion. **antonym** pleasure.

reward n benefit, bonus, bounty, come-up(p)ance, compensation, desert, gain, honour, meed, merit, payment, pay-off, premium, prize, profit, punishment, recompense, remuneration, repayment, requital, retribution, return, wages. **antonym** punishment.

v compensate, honour, pay, recompense, remunerate, repay, requite. **antonym** punish.

rewarding adj advantageous, beneficial, edifying, enriching, fruitful, fulfilling, gainful, gratifying, pleasing, productive, profitable, remunerative, satisfying, valuable, worthwhile. **antonym** unrewarding.

rewrite v correct, edit, emend, recast, redraft, revise, reword, rework.

rhetoric n bombast, declamation, eloquence, grandiloquence, hyperbole, magniloquence, oratory, pomposity, rant, verbosity, wordiness.

rhetorical adj artificial, bombastic, declamatory, false, flamboyant, flashy, florid, flowery, grandiloquent, high-flown, high-sounding, hyperbolic, inflated, insincere, linguistic, mag-niloquent, oratorical, over-decorated, pompous, pretentious, rhetoric, showy, silver-tongued, stylistic, verbose, windy. **antonym** simple.

rhythm n accent, beat, cadence, flow, lilt, measure, metre, movement, pattern, pulse, swing, tempo, time.

rhythmic adj cadenced, flowing, harmonious, lilting, melodious, metrical, musical, periodic, pulsating, rhythmical, throbbing. **antonym** unrhythmical.

ribald adj base, bawdy, blue, broad, coarse, derisive, earthy, filthy, foul-mouthed, gross, indecent, jeering, licentious, low, mean, mocking, naughty, obscene, off-colour, racy, risqué, rude, scurrilous, smutty, vulgar. **antonym** polite.

ribaldry n baseness, bawdiness, coarseness, derision, earthiness, filth, grossness, indecency, jeering, licentious-ness, lowness, mockery, naughtiness, obscenity, raciness, rudeness, scurrility, smut, smuttiness, vulgarity.

rich adj abounding, abundant, affluent, ample, bright, copious, costly, creamy, deep, delicious, dulcet, elaborate, elegant, expensive, exquisite, exuberant, fatty, fecund, fertile, fine, flavoursome, flush, fruitful, full, full-bodied, full-flavoured, full-toned, gay, gorgeous, heavy, highly-flavoured, humorous, in the money, intense, juicy, laughable, lavish, loaded, ludicrous, luscious, lush, luxurious, mellifluous, mellow, moneyed, opulent, palatial, pecunious, plenteous, plentiful, plutocratic, precious, priceless, productive, prolific, propertied, prosperous, resonant, ridiculous, rolling, savoury, side-splitting, spicy, splendid, strong, succulent, sumptuous, superb, sweet, tasty, valuable, vibrant, vivid, warm, wealthy, well-heeled, well-off, well-provided, well-stocked, well-supplied, well-to-do. **antonyms** harsh, miserly, plain, poor, simple, tasteless, thin, unfertile.

riches n a long purse, abundance, affluence, assets, fortune, gold, mint, money, opulence, plenty, property, resources, richness, substance, treasure, wealth. **antonym** poverty.

richly adv amply, appropriately, elaborately, elegantly, expensively, exquisitely, fully, gorgeously, lavishly, luxuriously, opulently, palatially, properly, splendidly, suitably, sumptuously, thoroughly, well. **antonyms** poorly, scantily.

rickety adj broken, broken-down, decrepit, derelict, dilapidated, feeble, flimsy, frail, imperfect, infirm, insecure, jerry-built, precarious, ramshackle, shaky, tottering, tottery, unsound, unstable, unsteady, weak, wobbly. **antonyms** stable, strong.

rid v clear, deliver, disabuse, disburden, disembarrass, disencumber, expel, free, purge, relieve, unburden. **antonym** burden.

riddance n clearance, deliverance, disposal, ejection, elimination, expulsion, extermination, freedom, purgation, release, relief, removal. **antonym** burdening.

riddle[1] n brain-teaser, conundrum, enigma, mystery, poser, problem, puzzle.

riddle[2] v corrupt, damage, fill, filter, impair, infest, invade, mar, pepper, perforate, permeate, pervade, pierce, puncture, screen, sieve, sift, spoil, strain, winnow.

ride v control, dominate, enslave, float, grip, handle, haunt, hurl, journey, manage, move, oppress, progress, sit, survive, travel, weather.

ridicule n banter, chaff, derision, irony, jeering, jeers, laughter, mockery, raillery, sarcasm, satire, scorn, sneers, taunting. **antonym** praise.

v banter, burlesque, caricature, crucify, deride, humiliate, jeer, lampoon, mock, parody, pillory, pooh-pooh, quiz, rib, satirise, scoff, send up, sneer at, take the mickey out of, taunt. **antonym** praise.

ridiculous *adj* absurd, comical, contemptible, damfool, derisory, farcical, foolish, funny, hilarious, incredible, laughable, ludicrous, nonsensical, outrageous, preposterous, silly, stupid, unbelievable. **antonym** sensible.

rife *adj* abounding, abundant, common, commonplace, current, epidemic, frequent, general, plentiful, prevailing, prevalent, raging, rampant, teeming, ubiquitous, universal, widespread. **antonym** scarce.

riff-raff *n* hoi polloi, mob, rabble, scum, undesirables.

rifle *v* burgle, despoil, gut, loot, maraud, pillage, plunder, ransack, rob, rummage, sack, strip.

rift *n* alienation, breach, break, chink, cleavage, cleft, crack, cranny, crevice, difference, disaffection, disagreement, division, estrangement, fault, flaw, fracture, gap, opening, quarrel, schism, separation, space, split. **antonym** unity.

rig¹ *v* equip, fit up, furnish, kit out, outfit, provision, supply.
n accoutrements, apparatus, ensemble, equipment, fitments, fittings, fixtures, gear, machinery, outfit, tackle.

rig out array, attire, clothe, costume, dress, dress up, equip, fit, fit out, fit up, furnish, kit out, outfit.

rig up arrange, assemble, build, construct, erect, fit up, fix up, improvise, knock up. **antonym** dismantle.

rig² *v* arrange, cook, doctor, engineer, fake, falsify, fiddle, fix, gerrymander, juggle, manipulate, tamper with, trump up.

right *adj* absolute, accurate, admissible, advantageous, appropriate, authentic, balanced, becoming, characteristic, complete, compos mentis, conservative, correct, deserved, desirable, direct, done, due, equitable, ethical, exact, factual, fair, favourable, fine, fit, fitting, genuine, good, healthy, honest, honourable, ideal, just, lawful, lucid, moral, normal, opportune, out-and-out, perpendicular, precise, proper, propitious, rational, reactionary, real, reasonable, righteous, rightful, rightist,

right-wing, sane, satisfactory, seemly, sound, spot-on, straight, suitable, thorough, thoroughgoing, Tory, true, unerring, unimpaired, upright, utter, valid, veracious, veritable, virtuous, well. **antonyms** left, left-wing, mad, unfit, wrong.

adv absolutely, accurately, advantageously, altogether, appropriate, aptly, bang, befittingly, beneficially, completely, correctly, directly, entirely, ethically, exactly, factually, fairly, favourably, fittingly, fortunately, genuinely, honestly, honourably, immediately, instantly, justly, morally, perfectly, precisely, promptly, properly, quickly, quite, righteously, rightward(s), satisfactorily, slap-bang, squarely, straight, straightaway, suitably, thoroughly, totally, truly, utterly, virtuously, well, wholly. **antonyms** incorrectly, left, unfairly, wrongly.

n authority, business, claim, due, equity, freedom, good, goodness, honour, integrity, interest, justice, lawfulness, legality, liberty, licence, morality, permission, power, prerogative, privilege, propriety, reason, rectitude, righteousness, rightfulness, rightness, title, truth, uprightness, virtue. **antonyms** depravity, wrong.

v avenge, correct, fix, rectify, redress, repair, settle, stand up, straighten, vindicate.

right away at once, chop-chop, directly, forthwith, immediately, instantly, now, promptly, right off, straight off, straightaway, this instant, without delay, without hesitation. **antonym** eventually.

righteous *adj* blameless, equitable, ethical, fair, God-fearing, good, guiltless, honest, honourable, incorrupt, just, law-abiding, moral, pure, rectitudinous, saintly, sinless, upright, virtuous. **antonym** unrighteous.

rightful *adj* authorised, bona fide, correct, due, just, lawful, legal, legitimate, licit, prescribed, proper, real, suitable, true, valid. **antonyms** incorrect, unlawful.

rightfully *adv* correctly, justifiably, justly, lawfully, legally, legitimately, properly, rightly. **antonyms** incorrectly, unjustifiably.

rigid *adj* adamant, austere, cast-iron, exact, fixed, harsh, inflexible, intransigent, invariable, rigorous, set, severe, starch(y), stern, stiff, stony, strict, stringent, tense, unalterable, unbending, uncompromising, undeviating, unrelenting, unyielding. **antonym** flexible.

rigmarole *n* bother, carry-on, hassle, palaver, performance, red tape, to-do.

rigorous *adj* accurate, austere, challenging, conscientious, demanding, exact, exacting, extreme, firm, hard, harsh, inclement, inflexible, inhospitable, meticulous, nice, painstaking, precise, punctilious, rigid, scrupulous, severe, spartan, stern, strict, stringent, thorough, tough, unsparing. **antonyms** lenient, mild.

rigour *n* accuracy, asperity, austerity, conscientiousness, exactitude, exactness, firmness, hardness, hardship, harshness, inflexibility, meticulousness, ordeal, preciseness, precision, privation, punctiliousness, rigidity, rigourousness, sternness, strictness, stringency, suffering, thoroughness, trial. **antonyms** leniency, mildness.

rig-out *n* apparel, clobber, clothing, costume, dress, ensemble, garb, gear, get-up, outfit, raiment, rig, togs, uniform.

rile *v* anger, annoy, bug, exasperate, gall, get, irk, irritate, miff, nark, nettle, peeve, pique, provoke, put out, upset, vex. **antonym** soothe.

rim *n* border, brim, brink, circumference, edge, lip, margin, skirt, verge. **antonym** centre.

ring¹ *n* annulus, arena, association, band, cabal, cartel, cell, circle, circuit, circus, clique, collar, combine, coterie, crew, enclosure, gang, group, gyre, halo, hoop, knot, loop, mob, organisation, rink, round, syndicate.

v circumscribe, encircle, enclose, encompass, gird, girdle, mark, score, surround.

ring² *v* bell, buzz, call, chime, clang, clink, peal, phone, resonate, resound, reverberate, sound, tang, telephone, ting, tinkle, tintinnabulate, toll.

n buzz, call, chime, clang, clink, knell, peal, phone-call, tang, ting, tinkle, tintinnabulation.

riot *n* anarchy, boisterousness, carousal, commotion, confusion, debauchery, disorder, display, disturbance, excess, extravaganza, festivity, flourish, fray, frolic, insurrection, jollification, lawlessness, merrymaking, quarrel, revelry, riotousness, romp, rookery, rout, row, ruction, ruffle, shindig, shindy, show, splash, strife, tumult, turbulence, turmoil, uproar. **antonyms** calm, order.

v carouse, frolic, rampage, rebel, revel, revolt, rise up, roister, romp, run riot, run wild.

riotous *adj* anarchic, boisterous, disorderly, insubordinate, insurrectionary, lawless, loud, luxurious, mutinous, noisy, orgiastic, rambunctious, rampageous, rebellious, refractory, roisterous, rollicking, rowdy, saturnalian, sidesplitting, tumultuous, ungovernable, unrestrained, unruly, uproarious, violent, wanton, wild. **antonyms** orderly, restrained.

rip *v* burst, claw, cut, gash, hack, lacerate, rend, rupture, score, separate, slash, slit, split, tear.

n cleavage, cut, gash, hole, laceration, rent, rupture, slash, slit, split, tear.

rip off cheat, con, defraud, diddle, do, dupe, exploit, filch, fleece, lift, mulct, overcharge, pilfer, pinch, rob, rogue, steal, sting, swindle, swipe, thieve, trick.

ripe *adj* accomplished, auspicious, complete, developed, favourable, finished, grown, ideal, mature, mellow, opportune, perfect, prepared, promising, propitious, ready, right, ripened, seasoned, suitable, timely. **antonyms** inopportune, untimely.

rip-off *n* cheat, con, con trick, daylight robbery, diddle, exploitation, fraud, robbery, sting, swindle, theft.

riposte *n* answer, come-back, quip, rejoinder, repartee, reply, response, retort, return.

v answer, quip, reciprocate, rejoin, reply, respond, retort, return.

rise *v* advance, appear, arise, ascend, buoy, climb, crop up, emanate, emerge, enlarge, eventuate, flow, get up, grow, happen, improve, increase, intensify, issue, kite, levitate, lift, mount, mutiny, occur, originate, progress, prosper, rebel, resist, revolt, slope, slope up, soar, spring, spring up, stand up, surface, swell, tower, volume, wax. **antonyms** descend, fall.

n advance, advancement, aggrandisement, ascent, climb, elevation, hillock, improvement, incline, increase, increment, origin, progress, promotion, raise, rising, upsurge, upswing, upturn. **antonyms** descent, fall.

rising *adj* advancing, approaching, ascending, emerging, growing, increasing, intensifying, mounting, soaring, swelling. **antonym** decreasing.

risk *n* adventure, chance, danger, gamble, hazard, jeopardy, peril, possibility,

speculation, uncertainty, venture.
antonyms certainty, safety.

v adventure, chance, dare, endanger, gamble, hazard, imperil, jeopardise, speculate, venture.

risky *adj* chancy, dangerous, dicey, dodgy, fraught, hazardous, iffy, perilous, precarious, touch-and-go, tricky, uncertain, unsafe. **antonym** safe.

risqué *adj* bawdy, blue, coarse, crude, daring, earthy, immodest, improper, indecent, indecorous, indelicate, naughty, near the knuckle, off colour, racy, ribald, suggestive. **antonym** decent.

rite *n* act, ceremonial, ceremony, custom, form, formality, liturgy, mystery, observance, office, ordinance, practice, procedure, ritual, sacrament, service, solemnity, usage, worship.

ritual *n* ceremonial, ceremony, communion, convention, custom, form, formality, habit, liturgy, mystery, observance, ordinance, practice, prescription, procedure, rite, routine, sacrament, service, solemnity, tradition, usage, wont.

adj ceremonial, ceremonious, conventional, customary, formal, formulary, habitual, prescribed, procedural, routine, stereotyped. **antonyms** informal, unusual.

rival *n* adversary, antagonist, challenger, competitor, contender, contestant, emulator, equal, equivalent, fellow, match, opponent, peer. **antonyms** associate, colleague, co-worker.

adj competing, competitive, conflicting, opposed, opposing. **antonyms** associate, co-operating.

v compete, contend, equal, match, oppose, vie with. **antonym** co-operate.

rivalry *n* antagonism, competition, competitiveness, conflict, contention, contest, duel, emulation, opposition, struggle, vying. **antonym** co-operation.

riveting *adj* absorbing, arresting, captivating, engrossing, enthralling, fascinating, gripping, hypnotic, magnetic, spellbinding. **antonym** boring.

roam *v* drift, meander, prowl, ramble, range, rove, squander, stray, stroll, travel, walk, wander. **antonym** stay.

roar *v* bawl, bay, bell, bellow, blare, clamour, crash, cry, guffaw, hoot, howl, rumble, shout, thunder, vociferate, wuther, yell. **antonym** whisper.

n bellow, belly-laugh, blare, clamour,

crash, cry, guffaw, hoot, howl, outcry, rumble, shout, thunder, yell. **antonym** whisper.

rob *v* bereave, cheat, con, defraud, deprive, despoil, dispossess, do, hold up, loot, mill, pillage, plunder, raid, ramp, ransack, reive, rifle, rip off, roll, sack, sting, strip, swindle, thieve. **antonyms** give, provide.

robust *adj* able-bodied, athletic, boisterous, brawny, coarse, down-to-earth, earthy, fit, hale, hard-headed, hardy, healthy, hearty, husky, indecorous, lusty, muscular, powerful, practical, pragmatic, raw, realistic, robustious, roisterous, rollicking, rough, rude, rugged, sensible, sinewy, sound, staunch, stout, straightforward, strapping, strong, sturdy, thick-set, tough, unsubtle, vigorous, well. **antonyms** mealy-mouthed, unhealthy, unrealistic, weak.

rock *v* astonish, astound, daze, dumbfound, jar, lurch, pitch, reel, roll, shake, shock, stagger, stun, surprise, sway, swing, tilt, tip, toss, wobble.

rogue *n* blackguard, charlatan, cheat, con man, crook, deceiver, devil, fraud, knave, miscreant, mountebank, nasty piece/bit of work, ne'er-do-well, rapscallion, rascal, reprobate, scamp, scoundrel, sharper, swindler, villain. **antonym** saint.

roguish *adj* arch, bantering, cheeky, criminal, crooked, deceitful, deceiving, dishonest, fraudulent, frolicsome, impish, mischievous, playful, puckish, raffish, shady, swindling, unprincipled, unscrupulous, villainous. **antonyms** honest, serious.

roister *v* carouse, celebrate, frolic, make merry, paint the town red, revel, roist, rollick, romp, whoop it up.

role *n* capacity, character, duty, function, impersonation, job, job of work, part, portrayal, position, post, representation, task.

roll *v* billow, bind, boom, coil, curl, drum, echo, elapse, enfold, entwine, envelop, even, flatten, flow, furl, grumble, gyrate, level, lumber, lurch, pass, peel, pivot, press, reel, resound, reverberate, revolve, roar, rock, rotate, rumble, run, smooth, spin, spread, stagger, swagger, swathe, sway, swing, swivel, thunder, toss, trundle, tumble, turn, twirl, twist, undulate, waddle, wallow, wander, welter, wheel, whirl, wind, wrap.

n annals, ball, bobbin, boom, catalogue, census, chronicle, cycle, cylinder, directory, drumming, growl, grumble, gyration, index, inventory, list, record, reel, register, resonance, reverberation, revolution, roar, roller, roster, rotation, rumble, run, schedule, scroll, spin, spool, table, thunder, turn, twirl, undulation, wheel, whirl.

roll up arrive, assemble, cluster, congregate, convene, forgather, gather. *antonyms* leave, scatter.

rollicking *adj* boisterous, carefree, cavorting, devil-may-care, exuberant, frisky, frolicsome, hearty, jaunty, jovial, joyous, lively, merry, playful, rip-roaring, roisterous, romping, spirited, sportive, sprightly, swashbuckling. *antonyms* restrained, serious.

roly-poly *adj* chubby, fat, overweight, plump, podgy, pudgy, rotund, rounded, tubby. *antonym* slim.

romance *n* absurdity, adventure, affair(e), amour, attachment, charm, colour, exaggeration, excitement, fabrication, fairy tale, falsehood, fantasy, fascination, fiction, glamour, idyll, intrigue, invention, legend, liaison, lie, love affair, love story, melodrama, mystery, novel, passion, relationship, sentiment, story, tale, tear-jerker.
v exaggerate, fantasise, lie, overstate.

romantic *adj* amorous, charming, colourful, dreamy, exaggerated, exciting, exotic, extravagant, fabulous, fairy-tale, fanciful, fantastic, fascinating, fictitious, fond, glamorous, high-flown, idealistic, idyllic, imaginary, imaginative, impractical, improbable, legendary, lovey-dovey, loving, made-up, mushy, mysterious, passionate, picturesque, quixotic, sentimental, sloppy, soppy, starry-eyed, tender, unrealistic, utopian, visionary, whimsical, wild. *antonyms* humdrum, practical, real, sober.
n Don Quixote, dreamer, idealist, sentimentalist, utopian, visionary. *antonym* realist.

Romeo *n* Casanova, Don Juan, ladies' man, lady-killer, Lothario, lover.

romp *v* caper, cavort, frisk, frolic, gambol, revel, rig, roister, rollick, skip, sport.
n caper, frolic, lark, rig, spree.

rook *v* bilk, cheat, con, defraud, diddle, do, fleece, mulct, overcharge, rip off, soak, sting, swindle.

room *n* allowance, apartment, area, capacity, chamber, chance, compartment, compass, elbow-room, expanse, extent, house-room, latitude, leeway, margin, occasion, office, opportunity, play, range, salon, saloon, scope, space, territory, volume.

roomy *adj* ample, broad, capacious, commodious, extensive, generous, large, sizable, spacious, voluminous, wide. *antonym* cramped.

root¹ *n* base, basis, beginnings, bottom, cause, core, crux, derivation, essence, foundation, fountainhead, fundamental, germ, heart, mainspring, nub, nucleus, occasion, origin, root-cause, seat, seed, source, starting point, stem.
v anchor, embed, entrench, establish, fasten, fix, ground, implant, moor, set, sink, stick.

root and branch completely, entirely, finally, radically, thoroughly, totally, utterly, wholly. *antonyms* not at all, slightly.

root² *v* burrow, delve, dig, ferret, forage, grout, hunt, nose, poke, pry, rummage.

root out abolish, clear away, destroy, dig out, discover, efface, eliminate, eradicate, erase, exterminate, extirpate, produce, remove, root up, turn up, uncover, unearth, uproot. *antonyms* cover, establish.

rooted *adj* confirmed, deep, deeply, deep-seated, entrenched, established, felt, firm, fixed, ingrained, radical, rigid, root-fast. *antonyms* superficial, temporary.

roots *n* background, beginning(s), birth-place, family, heritage, home, origins.

rope *v* bind, catch, fasten, hitch, lash, lasso, moor, pinion, tether, tie.

rope in embroil, engage, enlist, inveigle, involve, lure, persuade. *antonym* keep out.

ropy *adj* below par, deficient, inadequate, indifferent, inferior, off colour, poorly, rough, sketchy, stringy, substandard, unwell. *antonyms* good, well.

rostrum *n* dais, hustings, platform, podium, stage.

rosy *adj* auspicious, blooming, blushing, bright, cheerful, encouraging, favourable, fresh, glowing, healthy-looking, hopeful, optimistic, pink, promising, reassuring, red, reddish, rose, rose-coloured, rubicund, ruddy, sunny. *antonyms* depressed, depressing, sad.

rot *v* corrode, corrupt, crumble, decay, decline, decompose, degenerate, deteriorate, disintegrate, fester, go bad, languish, moulder, perish, putrefy, spoil, taint.

n balderdash, blight, bosh, bunk, bunkum, canker, claptrap, codswallop, collapse, corrosion, corruption, decay, decomposition, deterioration, disintegration, drivel, guff, hogwash, moonshine, mould, nonsense, poppycock, putrefaction, rubbish, tommyrot, tosh, twaddle.

rotate *v* alternate, gyrate, interchange, pirouette, pivot, reel, revolve, spell, spin, switch, swivel, turn, wheel.

rotation *n* alternation, cycle, gyration, interchanging, orbit, pirouette, reel, revolution, sequence, spin, spinning, succession, switching, turn, turning, volution, wheel.

rotten *adj* addle(d), bad, base, below par, bent, contemptible, corroded, corrupt, crooked, crumbling, crummy, decayed, decaying, deceitful, decomposed, decomposing, degenerate, deplorable, despicable, dirty, disagreeable, disappointing, dishonest, dishonourable, disintegrating, disloyal, faithless, festering, fetid, filthy, foul, grotty, ill-considered, ill-thought-out, immoral, inadequate, inferior, lousy, low-grade, manky, mean, mercenary, mouldering, mouldy, nasty, off colour, perfidious, perished, poor, poorly, putrescent, putrid, rank, regrettable, ropy, rough, scurrilous, sick, sorry, sour, stinking, substandard, tainted, treacherous, unacceptable, unfortunate, unlucky, unpleasant, unsatisfactory, unsound, untrustworthy, unwell, venal, vicious, vile, wicked. **antonyms** good, honest, practical, sensible, well.

rotter *n* bastard, blackguard, blighter, bounder, cad, cur, dastard, fink, louse, rat, scoundrel, stinker, swine. **antonym** saint.

rotund *adj* bulbous, chubby, corpulent, fat, fleshy, full, globular, grandiloquent, heavy, magniloquent, obese, orbed, plump, podgy, portly, resonant, rich, roly-poly, round, rounded, sonorous, spherical, stout, tubby. **antonyms** flat, gaunt, slim.

rough *adj* agitated, approximate, arduous, austere, basic, bearish, bluff, blunt, boisterous, bristly, broken, brusque, bumpy, bushy, cacophonous, choppy, churlish, coarse, craggy, crude, cruel, cursory, curt, discordant, discourteous, dishevelled, disordered, drastic, estimated, extreme, foggy,

formless, fuzzy, general, grating, gruff, hairy, hard, harsh, hasty, hazy, husky, ill, ill-bred, ill-mannered, imperfect, impolite, imprecise, inclement, incomplete, inconsiderate, indelicate, inexact, inharmonious, irregular, jagged, jarring, loutish, nasty, off colour, poorly, quick, rasping, raspy, raucous, raw, rocky, ropy, rotten, rough-and-ready, rowdy, rude, rudimentary, rugged, rusty, scabrous, severe, shaggy, shapeless, sharp, sick, sketchy, spartan, squally, stony, stormy, tangled, tempestuous, tough, tousled, turbulent, unceremonious, uncivil, uncomfortable, uncouth, uncultured, uncut, undressed, uneven, unfeeling, unfinished, ungracious, unjust, unmannerly, unmusical, unpleasant, unpolished, unprocessed, unrefined, unshaven, unshorn, untutored, unwell, unwrought, upset, vague, violent, wild. **antonyms** accurate, calm, harmonious, mild, polite, smooth, well.

n bruiser, bully, hooligan, mock-up, model, outline, roughneck, rowdy, ruffian, sketch, thug, tough, yob, yobbo.

rough up bash, batter, beat up, do, knock about, manhandle, mistreat, mug, thrash.

rough-and-ready *adj* adequate, approximate, crude, impoverished, makeshift, provisional, sketchy, stopgap, unpolished, unrefined. **antonyms** exact, refined.

rough-and-tumble *n* affray, barney, brawl, dust-up, fight, fracas, mêlée, punch-up, rookery, rout, ruction, ruffle, rumpus, scrap, scuffle, shindy, struggle.

roughen *v* abrade, asperate, coarsen, granulate, graze, harshen, rough, scuff. **antonym** smooth.

roughneck *n* bruiser, bully boy, hooligan, lout, rough, rowdy, ruffian, thug, tough.

round *adj* ample, annular, ball-shaped, blunt, bowed, bulbous, candid, circular, complete, curved, curvilinear, cylindrical, direct, disc-shaped, entire, fleshy, frank, full, full-fleshed, globular, mellifluous, orbed, outspoken, plain, plump, resonant, rich, ring-shaped, roly-poly, rotund, rounded, solid, sonorous, spherical, straightforward, unbroken, undivided, unmodified, whole. **antonyms** evasive, niggardly, partial, thin.

n ambit, ball, band, beat, bout, bullet, cartridge, circle, circuit, compass, course, cycle, disc, discharge, division, globe, lap, level, orb, period, ring, routine, schedule, sequence, series, session, shell, shot, sphere, stage, succession, tour, turn.

v bypass, circle, circumnavigate, encircle, flank, sail round, skirt, turn.

round off cap, close, complete, conclude, crown, end, finish, finish off, settle. *antonym* begin.

round on abuse, assail, attack, bite (someone's) head off, retaliate, snap at, turn on.

round the bend barmy, batty, bonkers, crazy, cuckoo, daft, dotty, eccentric, insane, mad, nuts, nutty, off one's rocker, screwy. *antonym* sane.

round up assemble, collect, drive, gather, gather in, group, herd, marshal, muster, rally. *antonym* disperse.

roundabout *adj* circuitous, circumlocutory, devious, discursive, evasive, indirect, meandering, oblique, periphrastic, tortuous, twisting, winding. *antonyms* direct, straight, straightforward.

roundly *adv* bluntly, completely, fiercely, forcefully, frankly, intensely, openly, outspokenly, rigorously, severely, sharply, thoroughly, vehemently, violently. *antonym* mildly.

round-up *n* assembly, collation, collection, gathering, herding, marshalling, muster, overview, précis, rally, summary, survey. *antonym* dispersal.

rouse *v* agitate, anger, animate, arouse, awaken, bestir, call, disturb, enkindle, excite, exhilarate, flush, galvanise, incite, inflame, instigate, move, provoke, rise, start, startle, stimulate, stir, suscitate, unbed, wake, whip up. *antonym* calm.

rousing *adj* brisk, electrifying, exciting, exhilarating, inflammatory, inspiring, lively, moving, spirited, stimulating, stirring, vigorous. *antonym* calming.

rout *n* beating, brawl, clamour, crowd, debacle, defeat, disturbance, drubbing, flight, fracas, fuss, herd, hiding, licking, mob, overthrow, pack, rabble, riot, ruffle, ruin, shambles, stampede, thrashing. *antonyms* calm, win.

v beat, best, chase, conquer, crush, defeat, destroy, discomfit, dispel, drub, hammer, lick, overthrow, scatter, thrash, worst.

route *n* avenue, beat, circuit, course, direction, flightpath, itinerary, journey, passage, path, road, round, run, way.

v convey, direct, dispatch, forward, send.

routine *n* act, bit, custom, formula, grind, groove, line, method, order, pattern, performance, piece, practice, procedure, programme, spiel, usage, way, wont.

adj banal, boring, clichéd, conventional, customary, day-by-day, dull, everyday, familiar, habitual, hackneyed, humdrum, mundane, normal, ordinary, predictable, run-of-the-mill, standard, tedious, tiresome, typical, unimaginative, uninspired, unoriginal, usual, wonted, workaday. *antonyms* exciting, unusual.

rove *v* cruise, drift, gallivant, meander, ramble, range, roam, stray, stroll, traipse, waltz Matilda, wander. *antonym* stay.

rover *n* drifter, gadabout, gypsy, itinerant, nomad, rambler, traveller, vagrant, wanderer. *antonym* stay-at-home.

row¹ *n* bank, colonnade, column, file, line, queue, range, rank, sequence, series, string, tier.

row² *n* altercation, brawl, castigation, commotion, controversy, dispute, disturbance, dressing-down, falling-out, fracas, fray, fuss, lecture, noise, quarrel, racket, reprimand, reproof, rollicking, rout, ruckus, ruction, ruffle, rumpus, scrap, shemozzle, shindy, slanging match, squabble, talking-to, telling-off, ticking-off, tiff, tongue-lashing, trouble, tumult, uproar. *antonym* calm.

v argue, brawl, dispute, fight, scrap, squabble, wrangle.

rowdy *adj* boisterous, disorderly, loud, loutish, noisy, obstreperous, roisterous, rough, rumbustious, stroppy, unruly, uproarious, wild. *antonyms* quiet, restrained.

n brawler, hoodlum, hooligan, lout, rough, ruffian, tearaway, tough, yob, yobbo.

royal *adj* august, grand, imperial, impressive, kinglike, kingly, magnificent, majestic, monarchical, princely, queenlike, queenly, regal, sovereign, splendid, stately, superb, superior.

rub *v* abrade, apply, caress, chafe, clean, embrocate, fray, grate, knead, massage, polish, put, scour, scrape, shine, smear, smooth, spread, stroke, wipe.

n caress, catch, difficulty, drawback, hindrance, hitch, impediment, kneading, massage, obstacle, polish, problem, shine, snag, stroke, trouble, wipe.

rub out assassinate, cancel, delete, efface, erase, expunge, kill, murder, obliterate, remove.

rub up the wrong way anger, annoy, bug, get, get one's goat, get to, get under one's skin, irk, irritate, needle, niggle, peeve, vex. **antonym** calm.

rubbish *n* balderdash, balls, baloney, bosh, bunkum, claptrap, cobblers, codswallop, crap, dead-wood, debris, drivel, dross, flotsam and jetsam, garbage, gibberish, gobbledegook, guff, hogwash, junk, kitsch, landfill, leavings, litter, moonshine, nonsense, piffle, poppycock, refuse, rot, scrap, stuff, sweepings, tommyrot, tosh, trash, twaddle, waste. **antonym** sense.

ruction *n* altercation, brawl, commotion, dispute, disturbance, fracas, fuss, quarrel, racket, rout, row, ruffle, rumpus, scrap, storm, to-do, trouble, uproar. **antonym** calm.

ruddy *adj* blooming, blushing, crimson, florid, flushed, fresh, glowing, healthy, pink, red, reddish, rosy, rosy-cheeked, rubicund, ruby, sanguine, scarlet, sunburnt. **antonyms** pale, unhealthy.

rude *adj* abrupt, abusive, artless, barbarous, blunt, boorish, brusque, brutish, cheeky, churlish, coarse, crude, curt, discourteous, disrespectful, graceless, gross, harsh, ignorant, illiterate, ill-mannered, impertinent, impolite, impudent, inartistic, inconsiderate, inelegant, insolent, insulting, loutish, low, makeshift, obscene, offhand, peremptory, primitive, raw, rough, savage, scurrilous, sharp, short, simple, startling, sudden, uncivil, uncivilised, uncouth, uncultured, uneducated, ungracious, unmannerly, unpleasant, unpolished, unrefined, untutored, violent, vulgar. **antonyms** graceful, polished, polite, smooth.

rudeness *n* abruptness, abuse, abusiveness, bad manners, barbarism, bluntness, boorishness, brusqueness, cheek, churlishness, curtness, discourtesy, disrespect, ill-manners, impertinence, impoliteness, impudence, incivility, insolence, sharpness, uncouthness, vulgarity. **antonym** politeness.

rudimentary *adj* basic, early, elementary, embryonic, fundamental, germinal, immature, inchoate, initial, introductory, primary, primitive, primordial, undeveloped, vestigial. **antonyms** advanced, developed.

rudiments *n* ABC, basics, beginnings, elements, essentials, foundation, fundamentals, principles.

rue *v* bemoan, bewail, deplore, grieve, lament, mourn, regret, repent. **antonym** rejoice.

rueful *adj* conscience-stricken, contrite, dismal, doleful, grievous, lugubrious, melancholy, mournful, penitent, pitiable, pitiful, plaintive, regretful, remorseful, repentant, sad, self-reproachful, sorrowful, sorry, woebegone, woeful. **antonym** glad.

ruffian *n* bruiser, brute, bully, bully-boy, cut-throat, hoodlum, hooligan, lout, miscreant, rascal, rogue, rough, roughneck, rowdy, scoundrel, thug, tough, villain, yob, yobbo.

ruffle *v* agitate, annoy, confuse, derange, disarrange, discompose, disconcert, dishevel, disorder, disquiet, disturb, fluster, harass, irritate, mess up, muss up, nettle, peeve, perturb, rattle, rumple, stir, torment, tousle, trouble, unsettle, upset, vex, worry, wrinkle. **antonym** smooth.

rugged *adj* arduous, austere, barbarous, beefy, blunt, brawny, broken, bumpy, burly, churlish, crabbed, craggy, crude, demanding, difficult, dour, exacting, graceless, gruff, hale, hard, hard-featured, hardy, harsh, husky, irregular, jagged, laborious, muscular, ragged, rigorous, robust, rocky, rough, rude, severe, sour, stark, stern, strenuous, strong, sturdy, surly, taxing, tough, trying, uncompromising, uncouth, uncultured, uneven, unpolished, unrefined, vigorous, weather-beaten, weathered, worn. **antonyms** easy, refined, smooth.

ruin *n* bankruptcy, breakdown, collapse, crash, damage, decay, defeat, destitution, destruction, devastation, disintegration, disrepair, dissolution, downfall, failure, fall, havoc, heap, insolvency, overthrow, ruination, subversion, undoing, Waterloo, wreck, wreckage. **antonyms** development, reconstruction.
v banjax, bankrupt, botch, break, crush, damage, defeat, demolish, destroy, devastate, disfigure, impoverish, injure, jigger, mangle, mar, mess up, overthrow, overturn, overwhelm, pauperise, raze, scupper, scuttle, shatter, smash, spoil, unmake, unshape, wreck. **antonyms** develop, restore.

ruinous *adj* baleful, baneful, broken-down, calamitous, cataclysmic, catastrophic, crippling, deadly, decrepit, deleterious, derelict, destructive, devastating, dilapidated, dire, disastrous, extravagant, fatal, immoderate, injurious, murderous, noxious, pernicious, ramshackle, ruined, shattering, wasteful, withering. **antonym** beneficial.

rule *n* administration, ascendancy, authority, axiom, canon, command, condition, control, convention, course, criterion, custom, decree, direction, domination, dominion, empire, form, formula, governance, government, guide, guideline, habit, influence, institute, jurisdiction, law, leadership, mastery, maxim, method, order, ordinance, policy, power, practice, precept, prescript, principle, procedure, regime, regulation, reign, routine, ruling, standard, supremacy, sway, tenet, way, wont.

v adjudge, adjudicate, administer, command, control, decide, decree, determine, direct, dominate, establish, find, govern, guide, judge, lead, manage, obtain, predominate, preponderate, prevail, pronounce, regulate, reign, resolve, settle.

rule out ban, debar, disallow, dismiss, eliminate, exclude, forbid, obviate, preclude, prevent, prohibit, proscribe, reject.

ruler *n* commander, controller, emperor, empress, gerent, governor, head of state, king, leader, lord, monarch, potentate, prince, princess, queen, sovereign. **antonym** subject.

ruling *n* adjudication, decision, decree, finding, judgement, pronouncement, resolution, verdict.
adj boss, chief, commanding, controlling, dominant, governing, leading, main, predominant, pre-eminent, preponderant, prevailing, prevalent, principal, reigning, supreme, upper.

rum *adj* abnormal, bizarre, curious, freakish, funny, funny-peculiar, odd, peculiar, queer, singular, strange, suspect, suspicious, unusual, weird.

rumbustious *adj* boisterous, clamorous, disorderly, exuberant, loud, noisy, obstreperous, refractory, robust, roisterous, rough, rowdy, unmanageable, unruly, uproarious, wayward, wild, wilful. **antonyms** quiet, restrained, sensible.

ruminate *v* brood, chew over, chew the cud, cogitate, consider, contemplate, deliberate, meditate, mull over, muse, ponder, reflect, revolve, think.

rummage *v* delve, examine, explore, hunt, poke around, ransack, root, rout, search.

rumour *n* breeze, bush telegraph, buzz, fame, gossip, grapevine, hearsay, news, report, story, talk, tidings, underbreath, whisper, word.
v bruit, circulate, gossip, publish, put about, report, say, tell, whisper.

rump *n* backside, bottom, bum, buttocks, croup, haunch, hindquarters, posterior, rear, seat.

rumple *v* crease, crinkle, crumple, crush, derange, dishevel, disorder, muss up, pucker, ruffle, scrunch, tousle, wrinkle. **antonym** smooth.

rumpus *n* bagarre, barney, commotion, confusion, disruption, disturbance, fracas, furore, fuss, kerfuffle, noise, rhubarb, rout, row, ruction, shemozzle, shindy, tumult, uproar. **antonym** calm.

run *v* abscond, administer, bear, beat it, bleed, bolt, boss, career, carry, cascade, challenge, circulate, clear out, climb, compete, conduct, contend, continue, control, convey, co-ordinate, course, creep, dart, dash, decamp, depart, direct, discharge, display, dissolve, drive to, escape, extend, feature, flee, flow, function, fuse, gallop, glide, go, gush, hare, hasten, head, hie, hotfoot, hurry, issue, jog, ladder, last, lead, leak, lie, liquefy, lope, manage, manoeuvre, mastermind, melt, mix, move, operate, oversee, own, pass, perform, ply, pour, print, proceed, propel, publish, race, range, reach, regulate, roll, rush, scamper, scarper, scramble, scud, scurry, skedaddle, skim, slide, speed, spill, spout, spread, sprint, stand, stream, stretch, superintend, supervise, tear, tick, trail, transport, unravel, work. **antonyms** stay, stop.
n application, category, chain, class, coop, course, current, cycle, dash, demand, direction, drift, drive, enclosure, excursion, flow, gallop, jaunt, jog, journey, joy, kind, ladder, lift, motion, movement, order, outing, passage, path, pen, period, pressure, progress, race, ride, rip, round, rush, season, sequence, series, snag, sort, spell, spin, sprint, spurt, streak, stream, stretch, string, tear, tendency, tenor, tide, trend, trip, type, variety, way.

run after chase, follow, pursue, stalk, tail. **antonym** flee.

run away abscond, beat it, bolt, clear out, decamp, elope, escape, flee, scarper, scoot, scram, skedaddle. **antonym** stay.

run down belittle, capture, criticise, curtail, cut, debilitate, decrease, decry, defame, denigrate, disparage, drop, exhaust, hit, knock, knock over, reduce, revile, run over, strike, tire, trim, vilify, weaken. **antonyms** increase, miss, praise.

run for it bolt, do a bunk, escape, flee, fly, make off, retreat, scarper, scram, skedaddle. **antonym** stay.

run in apprehend, arrest, bust, collar, feel (someone's) collar, jail, lift, nab, nick, pick up, pinch.

run into bash, encounter, hit, meet, ram, strike. **antonym** miss.

run off abscond, bleed, bolt, decamp, drain, duplicate, elope, escape, make off, print, produce, scarper, siphon, skedaddle, tap. **antonym** stay.

run out cease, close, dry up, end, expire, fail, finish, terminate.

run over hit, knock down, overflow, rehearse, reiterate, review, run down, spill, strike, survey.

run riot cut loose, go on the rampage, kick over the traces, rampage, sow one's wild oats, spread.

run through blow, check, dissipate, examine, exhaust, fritter away, pierce, practise, read, rehearse, review, spit, squander, stab, stick, survey, transfix, waste.

run together amalgamate, blend, coalesce, combine, commingle, fuse, intermingle, intermix, join, merge, mingle, mix, unite. **antonym** separate.

runaway n absconder, deserter, escapee, escaper, fugitive, refugee, truant.
adj escaped, fleeing, fugitive, loose, uncontrolled, wild.

rundown n briefing, cut, decrease, drop, lessening, outline, précis, recap, reduction, résumé, review, run-through, sketch, summary, synopsis.

run-down adj broken-down, debilitated, decrepit, dilapidated, dingy, drained, enervated, exhausted, fatigued, grotty, peaky, ramshackle, scabby, seedy, shabby, tumble-down, unhealthy, weak, weary, worn-out. **antonym** well-kept.

run-in n altercation, argument, brush, confrontation, contretemps, difference of opinion, dispute, dust-up, encounter, fight, quarrel, set-to, skirmish, tussle, wrangle.

running adj consecutive, constant, continuous, current, flowing, incessant, moving, perpetual, streaming, successive, together, unbroken, unceasing, uninterrupted. **antonyms** broken, ceased, occasional.
n administration, charge, competition, conduct, contention, contest, control, coordination, direction, functioning, going, leadership, maintenance, management, operation, organisation, pace, performance, regulation, superintendency, supervision, working.

runny adj dilute, diluted, flowing, fluid, liquefied, liquid, melted, molten, watery. **antonym** solid.

run-of-the-mill adj average, common, commonplace, everyday, fair, mediocre, middling, modest, ordinary, passable, routine, tolerable, undistinguished, unexceptional, unexciting, unimaginative, unimpressive, unremarkable. **antonym** exceptional.

rupture n altercation, breach, break, breaking, burst, bust-up, cleavage, cleft, contention, crack, disagreement, disruption, dissolution, estrangement, falling-out, feud, fissure, fracture, hernia, hostility, quarrel, rent, rift, schism, split, splitting, tear.
v break, burst, cleave, crack, disrupt, dissever, divide, fracture, puncture, rend, separate, sever, split, tear.

rural adj agrarian, agricultural, Arcadian, bucolic, countrified, country, pastoral, pr(a)edical, rustic, yokelish. **antonym** urban.

ruse n artifice, blind, deception, device, dodge, hoax, imposture, manoeuvre, ploy, sham, stall, stratagem, subterfuge, trick, wile.

rush v accelerate, attack, bolt, capture, career, charge, dart, dash, dispatch, expedite, fly, hasten, hightail it, hotfoot, hurry, hustle, overcome, press, push, quicken, race, run, scour, scramble, scurry, shoot, speed, speed up, sprint, stampede, storm, tear, wallop, w(h)oosh.
n assault, charge, dash, despatch, expedition, flow, haste, hurry, onslaught, push, race, scramble, speed, stampede, storm, streak, surge, swiftness, tear, urgency.
adj brisk, careless, cursory, emergency, expeditious, fast, hasty, hurried, prompt, quick, rapid, superficial, swift, urgent.

rush about rampage.

rust n blight, corrosion, fungus, mildew, mould, must, oxidation, patina, rot, stain, verdigris.
v atrophy, corrode, corrupt, decay, decline, degenerate, deteriorate, oxidise, rot, stagnate, tarnish.

rust-coloured *adj* auburn, chestnut, copper, coppery, ginger, gingery, red, reddish, reddish-brown, russet, rusty, sandy, tawny, titian.

rustic *adj* agrarian, Arcadian, artless, awkward, boorish, bucolic, coarse, countrified, country, crude, graceless, hick, homely, homespun, pastoral, plain, provincial, rough, rude, rural, simple, unaffected, uncouth, uncultured, unmannerly, unpolished, unrefined, unsophisticated, yokelish. *antonyms* cultivated, polished, sophisticated, urban, urbane.

n bumpkin, country cousin, hayseed, hick, hillbilly, peasant, provincial, yokel. *antonyms* dandy, man-about-town, sophisticate.

rusty *adj* ancient, antiquated, antique, corroded, creaking, creaky, croaking, croaky, dated, deficient, discoloured, dull, encrusted, hoarse, impaired, old-fashioned, outmoded, oxidised, passé, patinated, raucous, rough, rust-covered, rusted, sluggish, stagnated, stale, stiff, tarnished, time-worn, unpractised, weak.

rut *n* channel, ditch, furrow, gouge, groove, gutter, habit, indentation, pothole, routine, system, track, trough, wheelmark.

v channel, cut, furrow, gouge, groove, hole, indent, mark.

ruthless *adj* adamant, barbarous, brutal, callous, cruel, cut-throat, dog-eat-dog, ferocious, fierce, hard, hard-hearted, harsh, heartless, implacable, inexorable, inhuman, merciless, pitiless, relentless, remorseless, savage, severe, stern, stony, unfeeling, unmerciful, unpitying, unrelenting. *antonyms* compassionate, merciful.

S

sable *adj* black, coal-black, dark, dusky, ebony, inky, jet, midnight, pitch-black, pitch-dark, raven, sombre.

sabotage *v* cripple, damage, destroy, disable, disrupt, incapacitate, mar, nullify, scupper, subvert, thwart, undermine, vandalise, vitiate, wreck.

n damage, destruction, disablement, disruption, impairment, marring, subversion, treachery, treason, undermining, vandalism, vitiation, wrecking.

saccharine *adj* cloying, honeyed, maudlin, mawkish, nauseating, oversweet, schmaltzy, sentimental, sickly, sickly-sweet, sloppy, soppy, sugary, syrupy, treacly. **antonyms** bitter, tart.

sack¹ *v* axe, discharge, dismiss, fire, lay off, make redundant.

n discharge, dismissal, notice, one's books, one's cards, one's marching orders, the axe, the boot, the bum's rush, the chop, the elbow, the push.

sack² *v* demolish, depredate, desecrate, despoil, destroy, devastate, lay waste, level, loot, maraud, pillage, plunder, raid, ravage, raze, rifle, rob, ruin, spoil, strip, waste.

n depredation, desecration, despoliation, destruction, devastation, levelling, looting, marauding, pillage, plunder, plundering, rapine, ravage, razing, ruin, waste.

sacred *adj* blessed, consecrated, dedicated, devotional, divine, ecclesiastical, godly, hallowed, heavenly, holy, inviolable, inviolate, invulnerable, priestly, protected, religious, revered, sacrosanct, saintly, sanctified, secure, solemn, venerable, venerated. **antonyms** mundane, profane, temporal.

sacrifice *v* abandon, forego, forfeit, immolate, let go, lose, offer, relinquish, renounce, slaughter, surrender.

n destruction, holocaust, host, immolation, loss, offering, renunciation, surrender, victim, votive offering.

sacrificial *adj* atoning, expiatory, reparative, votive.

sacrilege *n* blasphemy, defilement, desecration, disrespect, heresy, impiety, impiousness, irreverence, mockery, outrage, profanation, profaneness, profanity, violation. **antonyms** piety, respect, reverence.

sacrilegious *adj* blasphemous, desecrating, disrespectful, godless, heretical, impious, irreligious, irreverent, profane, ungodly, unholy. **antonyms** pious, respectful, reverent.

sacrosanct *adj* hallowed, impregnable, inviolable, inviolate, sacred, sanctified, untouchable.

sad *adj* bad, blue, calamitous, cheerless, crestfallen, crushed, dark, dejected, deplorable, depressed, depressing, desolated, despondent, disastrous, disconsolate, dismal, dispirited, distressed, distressing, doleful, dolesome, doughy, dour, downcast, down-hearted, dreary, gloomy, glum, grave, grief-stricken, grieved, grieving, grievous, heart-rending, heavy, heavy-hearted, jaw-fallen, joyless, lachrymose, lamentable, long-faced, low, low-spirited, lugubrious, melancholy, miserable, mournful, moving, painful, pathetic, pensive, piteous, pitiable, pitiful, poignant, regrettable, serious, shabby, sober, sober-minded, sombre, sorrowful, sorry, stiff, tearful, touching, tragic, uncheerful, unfortunate, unhappy, unsatisfactory, upsetting, wan, wistful, woebegone, woeful, wretched. **antonyms** cheerful, fortunate, happy, lucky.

sadden *v* aggrieve, dash, deject, depress, desolate, discourage, dishearten, dispirit, distress, grieve, hurt, oppress, upset. **antonyms** cheer, delight, gratify, please.

saddle *v* burden, charge, encumber, impose, land, load, lumber, task, tax.

sadism *n* barbarity, bestiality, brutality, callousness, cruelty, heartlessness, inhumanity, malevolence, ruthlessness, sado-masochism, savagery, spite, unnaturalness, viciousness.

sadistic *adj* barbarous, bestial, brutal, cruel, heartless, inhuman, malevolent, perverted, ruthless, savage, spiteful, unnatural, vicious.

sadness *n* bleakness, cheerlessness, darkness, dejection, depression, desolation, despondency, disconsolateness, dismalness, distress, dolefulness, dolour, gloominess, glumness, gravity, grief, joylessness, low spirits, lugubriousness, melancholy, misery, misfortune, mournfulness, pain, pathos, poignancy, regret, sombreness, sorrow, sorrowfulness, tearfulness, tragedy, unhappiness, wanness, wistfulness, woe, wretchedness. **antonyms** cheerfulness, delight, happiness.

safe *adj* alive and well, all right, cautious, certain, circumspect, conservative, dependable, discreet, foolproof, guarded, hale, harmless, immune, impregnable, innocuous, intact, invulnerable, non-poisonous, non-toxic, OK, out of harm's way, protected, proven, prudent, pure, realistic, reliable, secure, sound, sure, tame, tested, tried, trustworthy, unadventurous, uncontaminated, undamaged, unfailing, unharmed, unhurt, uninjured, unscathed, wholesome. **antonyms** exposed, harmful, unsafe, vulnerable.

safeguard *v* assure, defend, guard, insure, preserve, protect, screen, secure, shelter, shield. **antonyms** endanger, jeopardise.
n armour, assurance, bulwark, convoy, cover, defence, escort, guarantee, guard, insurance, long-stop, precaution, preventive, protection, security, shield, surety.

safekeeping *n* aegis, care, charge, custody, guard, guardianship, keeping, lock and key, protection, supervision, surveillance, trust, tutelage, vigilance, ward, wardship, watch.

safety *n* assurance, cover, deliverance, dependability, harmlessness, immunity, impregnability, invulnerability, protection, refuge, reliability, safeguard, salvation, sanctuary, security, shelter, sureness. **antonyms** danger, jeopardy.
adj fail-safe, precautionary, preventative, protective.

sag *v* bag, decline, dip, drag, droop, drop, dwindle, fail, fall, flag, give, give way, hang, settle, sink, slide, slip, slump, wane, weaken, wilt. **antonyms** bulge, rise.
n decline, depression, dip, downturn, drop, dwindling, fall, low, low point, reduction, slide, slip, slump. **antonyms** peak, rise.

sagacious *adj* able, acute, apt, astute, canny, discerning, downy, far-sighted, fly, insightful, intelligent, judicious, knowing, long-headed, long-sighted, penetrating, perceptive, percipient, perspicacious, quick, sage, sapient, sharp, shrewd, smart, wary, wide-awake, wily, wise. **antonyms** foolish, obtuse, short-sighted.

sagacity *n* acumen, acuteness, astuteness, canniness, discernment, foresight, insight, judgement, judiciousness,

knowingness, penetration, percipience, perspicacity, prudence, sapience, sense, sharpness, shrewdness, understanding, wariness, wiliness, wisdom. **antonyms** folly, foolishness, obtuseness.

sage *adj* astute, canny, discerning, intelligent, judicious, knowing, knowledgeable, learned, perspicacious, politic, prudent, sagacious, sapient, sensible, wise. **antonym** foolish.
n authority, elder, expert, guru, master, oracle, philosopher, pundit, savant, teacher, wise man. **antonym** ignoramus.

sail *v* captain, cruise, drift, embark, float, fly, glide, navigate, pilot, plane, put to sea, scud, shoot, skim, skipper, soar, steer, sweep, take ship, voyage, waft, weigh anchor, wing.

sail into assault, attack, belabour, lambaste, lay into, let fly, set about, tear into, turn on.

saintliness *n* asceticism, blessedness, chastity, devoutness, faith, godliness, goodness, holiness, morality, piety, purity, righteousness, sanctity, self-denial, selflessness, self-sacrifice, spirituality, spotlessness, unselfishness, uprightness, virtue. **antonyms** godlessness, unholiness, wickedness.

saintly *adj* angelic, beatific, blameless, blessed, blest, celestial, devout, god-fearing, godly, holy, immaculate, innocent, pious, pure, religious, righteous, sainted, saintlike, seraphic, sinless, spotless, stainless, upright, virtuous, worthy. **antonyms** godless, unholy, unrighteous, wicked.

sake *n* account, advantage, aim, behalf, benefit, cause, consideration, end, gain, good, interest, motive, object, objective, principle, profit, purpose, reason, regard, respect, score, welfare, wellbeing.

salacious *adj* bawdy, blue, carnal, coarse, erotic, horny, improper, indecent, lascivious, lecherous, lewd, libidinous, lubricious, lustful, obscene, pornographic, prurient, randy, raunchy, ribald, scurrilous, smutty, steamy, wanton. **antonyms** clean, decent, proper.

salient *adj* arresting, chief, conspicuous, important, jutting, main, marked, noticeable, obvious, outstanding, principal, projecting, prominent, pronounced, protruding, remarkable, signal, significant, striking.

sallow *adj* anaemic, bilious, colourless, pale, pallid, pasty, sickly, unhealthy, wan, yellowish. **antonyms** rosy, sanguine.

salubrious *adj* beneficial, bracing, health-giving, healthy, hygienic, invigorating, refreshing, restorative, salutary, sanitary, wholesome. **antonyms** insalubrious, unwholesome.

salutary *adj* advantageous, beneficial, good, healthy, helpful, much-needed, practical, profitable, salubrious, seasonable, timely, useful, valuable, wholesome.

salutation *n* address, greeting, homage, obeisance, respects, reverence, salaam, salute, welcome.

salute *v* accost, acknowledge, address, bow, greet, hail, honour, kiss, nod, recognise, salaam, wave, welcome.
n acknowledgement, address, bow, gesture, greeting, hail, handclap, handshake, hello, kiss, nod, obeisance, recognition, reverence, salaam, salutation, salvo, tribute, wave.

salvage *v* conserve, glean, preserve, reclaim, recover, recuperate, redeem, repair, rescue, restore, retrieve, salve, save. **antonyms** abandon, lose, waste.

salvation *n* deliverance, escape, liberation, lifeline, preservation, reclamation, redemption, rescue, restoration, retrieval, safety, saving. **antonyms** damnation, loss.

same *adj* aforementioned, aforesaid, alike, analogous, changeless, comparable, consistent, corresponding, duplicate, equal, equivalent, homologous, identical, indistinguishable, interchangeable, invariable, matching, mutual, reciprocal, selfsame, similar, substitutable, synonymous, twin, unaltered, unchanged, undiminished, unfailing, uniform, unvarying, very. **antonyms** changeable, different, incompatible, inconsistent, variable.
n ditto, the above-mentioned, the above-named, the aforementioned, the aforesaid.

sample *n* cross section, demonstration, example, exemplification, foretaste, free sample, freebie, illustration, indication, instance, model, pattern, representative, sign, specimen, swatch.
v experience, inspect, investigate, sip, taste, test, try.
adj demonstration, illustrative, pilot, representative, specimen, test, trial.

sanctify *v* anoint, bless, cleanse, consecrate, dedicate, divinify, divinise, exalt, hallow, make holy, purify,

sanction. **antonyms** defile, degrade, desecrate.

sanctimonious *adj* canting, false, goody-goody, holier-than-thou, holy, hypocritical, moralising, pious, preaching, priggish, righteous, self-righteous, self-satisfied, smug, superior, unctuous. **antonym** humble.

sanction *n* agreement, allowance, approbation, approval, authorisation, authority, backing, confirmation, countenance, endorsement, go-ahead, green light, licence, OK, permission, ratification, seal, support. **antonyms** disapproval, veto.
v accredit, allow, approve, authorise, back, confirm, countenance, countersign, endorse, license, permit, ratify, support, underwrite, warrant. **antonyms** disallow, disapprove, veto.

sanctions *n* ban, boycott, embargo, interdict, penalty, prohibition, proscription, restrictions.

sanctity *n* devotion, godliness, goodness, grace, holiness, inviolability, piety, purity, religiousness, righteousness, sacredness, sacrosanctity, saintliness, saintship, solemnity, spirituality, venerableness. **antonyms** godlessness, impurity, secularity, unholiness, worldliness.

sanctuary *n* altar, ark, asylum, chancel, church, harbourage, haven, holy of holies, presbytery, protection, refuge, retreat, sanctum, sanctum sanctorum, seclusion, shelter, shrine, tabernacle, temple.

sanctum *n* cubby-hole, den, hideaway, holy of holies, refuge, retreat, sanctuary, sanctum sanctorum, shrine, snug, study.

sane *adj* all there, balanced, compos mentis, dependable, judicious, level-headed, lucid, moderate, normal, rational, reasonable, reliable, right-minded, sensible, sober, sound, stable.

sanguinary *adj* bloodied, bloodthirsty, bloody, brutal, cruel, fell, gory, grim, merciless, murderous, pitiless, ruthless, savage.

sanguine[1] *adj* animated, ardent, assured, buoyant, cheerful, confident, expectant, hopeful, lively, optimistic, over-confident, over-optimistic, spirited, unabashed, unbowed. **antonyms** cynical, depressive, gloomy, melancholy, pessimistic, realistic.

sanguine[2] *adj* florid, flushed, fresh,

fresh-complexioned, pink, red, rosy, rubicund, ruddy. **antonyms** pale, sallow.

sanitary *adj* clean, disinfected, germ-free, healthy, hygienic, pure, salubrious, uncontaminated, unpolluted, wholesome. **antonyms** insanitary, unwholesome.

sanity *n* balance of mind, common sense, dependability, judiciousness, level-headedness, lucidity, normality, rationality, reason, reasonableness, reliability, saneness, sense, soundness, stability. **antonyms** foolishness, insanity.

sap *v* bleed, deplete, devitalise, diminish, drain, enervate, exhaust, impair, reduce, rob, undermine, weaken. **antonyms** build up, increase, strengthen.

sarcasm *n* acidity, bitterness, contempt, cynicism, derision, diatribe, invective, irony, mockery, mordancy, satire, scorn, sneering, venom, vitriol.

sarcastic *adj* acerbic, acid, acrimonious, biting, caustic, contemptuous, cutting, cynical, derisive, disparaging, incisive, ironical, mocking, mordant, sardonic, sarky, satirical, scathing, sharp, sharp-tongued, sneering, taunting, withering.

sardonic *adj* biting, bitter, cynical, derisive, dry, ironical, jeering, malevolent, malicious, malignant, mocking, mordant, sarcastic, satirical, scornful, sneering, wry.

Satan *n* Beelzebub, Belial, Hornie, Lucifer, Mephistopheles, Old Nick, Prince of Darkness, The Adversary, The Devil, The Enemy, The Evil One, The Tempter.

satanic *adj* accursed, black, demonic, devilish, diabolic, diabolical, evil, fell, fiendish, hellish, infernal, inhuman, iniquitous, malevolent, malignant, Mephistophelian, wicked. **antonyms** benevolent, benign, divine, godlike, godly, heavenly, holy.

sate *v* cloy, fill, glut, gorge, gratify, overfill, satiate, satisfy, saturate, sicken, slake, surfeit, weary. **antonyms** deprive, dissatisfy, starve.

satellite *n* adherent, aide, attendant, dependant, disciple, follower, hanger-on, lackey, minion, moon, parasite, puppet, retainer, sidekick, subordinate, sycophant, tributary, vassal, votary.

satiate *v* cloy, engorge, glut, gorge, jade, nauseate, overfeed, overfill, sate, satisfy, slake, stuff, surfeit. **antonyms** deprive, dissatisfy, underfeed.

satiety *n* fullness, gratification, over-fullness, overindulgence, repleteness, repletion, satiation, satisfaction, saturation, surfeit.

satire *n* burlesque, caricature, diatribe, invective, irony, lampoon, parody, raillery, ridicule, sarcasm, send-up, skit, spoof, takeoff, travesty, wit.

satirical *adj* biting, bitter, burlesque, caustic, cutting, cynical, derisive, incisive, ironical, irreverent, mocking, mordant, pungent, sarcastic, sardonic, taunting.

satirise *v* abuse, burlesque, caricature, censure, criticise, deride, lampoon, make fun of, make sport of, mock, parody, pillory, ridicule, send up, take off. **antonyms** acclaim, celebrate, honour.

satisfaction *n* achievement, amends, appeasing, assuaging, atonement, comfort, compensation, complacency, content, contentedness, contentment, conviction, damages, ease, enjoyment, fulfilment, fullness, gratification, happiness, indemnification, justice, payment, pleasure, pride, quittance, recompense, redress, reimbursement, remuneration, reparation, repleteness, repletion, requital, resolution, restitution, reward, satiety, self-satisfaction, sense of achievement, settlement, vindication, well-being. **antonyms** discontent, displeasure, dissatisfaction, frustration.

satisfactory *adj* acceptable, adequate, all right, average, competent, fair, fit, OK, passable, proper, sufficient, suitable, tickety-boo, up to the mark. **antonyms** inadequate, unacceptable, unsatisfactory.

satisfied *adj* appeased, complacent, content, contented, convinced, full, happy, mollified, pacified, persuaded, pleased, positive, reassured, replete, sated, satiated, self-satisfied, smug, sure. **antonyms** dissatisfied, hungry, unconvinced.

satisfy *v* answer, appease, assuage, assure, atone, compensate, content, convince, delight, discharge, do, fill, fulfil, glut, gratify, indemnify, indulge, meet, mollify, pacify, pay, persuade, placate, please, qualify, quench, quiet, reassure, recompense, reimburse, remunerate, replete, requite, reward, sate, satiate, serve, settle, slake, square up, suffice, surfeit. **antonyms** disappoint, dissatisfy, fail, frustrate, thwart.

satisfying *adj* cheering, convincing, cool, filling, fulfilling, gratifying, persuasive, pleasing, pleasurable, satisfactory. **antonyms** dissatisfying, frustrating, thwarting, unsatisfactory.

saturate v douse, drench, drouk, imbue, impregnate, infuse, permeate, soak, souse, steep, suffuse, waterlog.

saturated adj drenched, dripping, droukit, imbued, impregnated, permeated, soaked, soaking, sodden, soggy, sopping, soused, steeped, suffused, waterlogged, wringing.

sauce n archness, assurance, audacity, backchat, brass, brazenness, cheek, cheekiness, disrespect, disrespectfulness, flippancy, freshness, impertinence, impudence, insolence, irreverence, lip, nerve, pertness, presumption, presumptuousness, rudeness, sass, sauciness. **antonyms** politeness, respectfulness.

saucy adj arch, audacious, cheeky, dashing, disdainful, disrespectful, flip, flippant, forward, fresh, gay, impertinent, impudent, insolent, irreverent, jaunty, lippy, natty, perky, pert, presumptuous, provocative, rakish, rude, sassy, sporty. **antonyms** polite, respectful.

saunter v amble, dacker, dally, dander, daunder, dawdle, linger, loiter, meander, mosey, perambulate, promenade, ramble, roam, rove, stroll, wander.
n airing, amble, breather, constitutional, outing, perambulation, promenade, ramble, stroll, turn, walk.

savage adj barbarous, beastly, bestial, blistering, bloodthirsty, bloody, brutal, brutish, cruel, devilish, diabolical, dog-eat-dog, fell, ferocious, fierce, harsh, immane, inhuman, merciless, murderous, pitiless, primitive, ravening, rough, rude, rugged, ruthless, sadistic, sanguinary, uncivilised, uncultivated, undomesticated, uneducated, unenlightened, unsparing, untamed, untaught, vicious, wild. **antonyms** benign, civilised, humane.
n aboriginal, aborigine, ape, barbarian, bear, beast, boor, brute, fiend, heathen, illiterate, indigene, lout, monster, native, oaf, philistine, primitive, roughneck, yobbo.
v attack, claw, hammer, lacerate, mangle, maul, pan, scarify, tear.

savagery n barbarity, bestiality, bloodthirstiness, brutality, brutishness, cruelty, ferity, ferocity, fierceness, inhumanity, mercilessness, murderousness, pitilessness, primitiveness, roughness, ruthlessness, sadism, viciousness,

wildness. **antonyms** civilisation, civility, humanity.

save v collect, conserve, cut back, deliver, economise, free, gather, guard, hinder, hoard, hold, husband, keep, lay up, liberate, obviate, preserve, prevent, protect, put aside, put by, reclaim, recover, redeem, rescue, reserve, retain, retrench, safeguard, salt away, salvage, screen, shield, spare, squirrel, stash, store. **antonyms** discard, spend, squander, waste.

saving adj careful, compensatory, economical, extenuating, frugal, mitigating, qualifying, redeeming, sparing, thrifty.
n bargain, conservation, cut, discount, economy, preservation, reclamation, redemption, reduction, rescue, retrenchment, salvage, salvation. **antonyms** expense, loss, waste.

savoir-faire n ability, accomplishment, address, assurance, capability, confidence, diplomacy, discretion, expertise, finesse, know-how, poise, tact, urbanity. **antonyms** awkwardness, clumsiness, incompetence, inexperience.

savour n excitement, fascination, flavour, interest, piquancy, relish, salt, smack, smell, spice, tang, taste, zest.
v appreciate, dwell on, enjoy, gloat over, like, luxuriate in, partake, relish, revel in. **antonyms** shrink from, wince at.

savoury adj agreeable, appetising, aromatic, dainty, decent, delectable, delicious, edifying, full-flavoured, good, honest, luscious, mouthwatering, palatable, piquant, reputable, respectable, rich, salubrious, scrumptious, spicy, tangy, tasty, wholesome. **antonyms** insipid, tasteless, unappetising.

say v add, affirm, allege, announce, answer, assert, assume, claim, comment, communicate, conjecture, convey, declare, deliver, disclose, divulge, do, enunciate, estimate, express, guess, imagine, imply, intimate, judge, maintain, mention, opine, perform, presume, pronounce, read, recite, reckon, rehearse, rejoin, remark, render, repeat, reply, report, respond, retort, reveal, rumour, signify, speak, state, suggest, surmise, tell, utter, voice.
n authority, chance, clout, crack, go, influence, power, sway, turn, voice, vote, weight, word.

saying n adage, aphorism, apophthegm, axiom, byword, dictum, gnome, maxim, motto, precept, proverb, slogan.

say-so n affirmation, agreement,

approval, assertion, asseveration, assurance, authorisation, authority, backing, consent, dictum, guarantee, OK, permission, ratification, sanction, word.

scale *n* calibration, compass, degree, degrees, extent, gamut, gradation, grading, graduation, hierarchy, ladder, measure, order, progression, proportion, range, ranking, ratio, reach, register, scope, sequence, series, spectrum, spread, steps.

v adjust, level, move, proportion, regulate, shift.

scamp *n* blighter, devil, imp, knave, mischief-maker, monkey, prankster, rascal, rogue, ruffian, scallywag, tyke, whippersnapper, wretch.

scamper *v* chevy, dart, dash, fly, frisk, frolic, gambol, hasten, hurry, pelt, romp, run, rush, scoot, scurry, scuttle, skedaddle, sprint.

scan *v* check, examine, glance through, investigate, pan, pan over, scrutinise, search, skim, survey, sweep.

n check, examination, investigation, probe, review, screening, scrutiny, search, survey.

scandal *n* abuse, aspersion, backbiting, calumniation, calumny, crime, defamation, detraction, dirt, discredit, disgrace, dishonour, embarrassment, enormity, evil, furore, gossip, gossiping, ignominy, infamy, muck-raking, obloquy, odium, offence, opprobrium, outcry, outrage, reproach, rumours, shame, sin, slander, stigma, talk, tattle, uproar.

scandalise *v* affront, appal, astound, disgust, dismay, horrify, nauseate, offend, outrage, repel, revolt, shock, sicken.

scandalous *adj* abominable, atrocious, calumnious, defamatory, disgraceful, disreputable, evil, exorbitant, extortionate, gossiping, immoderate, improper, infamous, libellous, monstrous, odious, opprobrious, outrageous, scurrilous, shameful, shocking, slanderous, unseemly, unspeakable, untrue.

scant *adj* bare, deficient, hardly any, inadequate, insufficient, limited, little, little or no, minimal, sparse. **antonyms** adequate, ample, sufficient.

scanty *adj* bare, beggarly, deficient, exiguous, inadequate, insubstantial, insufficient, light, meagre, narrow, parsimonious, poor, restricted, scant, scrimp, scrimpy, short, shy, skimped, skimpy, slender, sparing, sparse, thin. **antonyms** ample, plentiful, substantial.

scapegoat *n* fall guy, patsy, victim, whipping-boy.

scar *n* blemish, injury, lesion, mark, scar tissue, scarring, stigma, trauma, wound.
v brand, damage, disfigure, mark, stigmatise, traumatise.

scarce *adj* deficient, few, infrequent, insufficient, lacking, rare, scanty, sparse, thin on the ground, uncommon, unusual, wanting. **antonyms** common, copious, plentiful.

scarcely *adv* barely, hardly, just and no more, not readily, not willingly, only just, scarce.

scarcity *n* dearth, deficiency, infrequency, insufficiency, lack, niggardliness, paucity, poverty, rareness, rarity, scantiness, shortage, sparseness, uncommonness, want. **antonyms** abundance, enough, glut, plenty, sufficiency.

scare *v* alarm, appal, daunt, dismay, frighten, intimidate, panic, shock, startle, terrify, terrorise, unnerve. **antonym** reassure.
n agitation, alarm, alert, consternation, dismay, fright, hysteria, panic, shock, start, terror. **antonym** reassurance.

scared *adj* agitated, anxious, appalled, dismayed, fearful, frightened, nervous, panicky, panic-stricken, petrified, shaken, startled, terrified, worried. **antonyms** confident, reassured.

scarper *v* abscond, beat it, bolt, bunk off, clear off, decamp, depart, disappear, do a bunk, escape, flee, flit, go, hightail it, run away, run for it, scram, skedaddle, vamoose, vanish.

scary *adj* alarming, anxious, bloodcurdling, chilling, creepy, disturbing, frightening, hair-raising, hairy, horrendous, horrible, horrifying, intimidating, shocking, spine-chilling, spooky, terrifying, unnerving, upsetting, worrying.

scathing *adj* acid, biting, bitter, brutal, caustic, critical, cutting, harsh, lacerating, mordant, sarcastic, savage, scornful, searing, trenchant, unsparing, virulent, vitriolic, withering, wounding. **antonym** complimentary.

scatter *v* break up, broadcast, diffuse, disband, disintegrate, disject, dispel, disperse, disseminate, dissipate, disunite, divide, fling, litter, propagate, separate, shower, sow, spatter, splutter, spread, sprinkle, squander, strew. **antonyms** collect, concentrate.

scatter-brained *adj* bird-brained,

careless, dizzy, empty-headed, feather-brained, flighty, forgetful, frivolous, giddy, inattentive, irresponsible, madcap, scatty, silly, slap-happy, thoughtless, undependable, unreliable. *antonyms* careful, efficient, sensible, sober.

cattering *n* break-up, diaspora, diffusion, dispersal, dispersion, dissemination, dissipation, dissolution, few, fistful, handful, scatter, separation, smatter, smattering, sprinkling. *antonyms* abundance, mass.

cene *n* act, area, arena, backdrop, background, business, carry-on, chapter, circumstances, commotion, confrontation, display, disturbance, division, drama, environment, episode, exhibition, focus, fuss, incident, landscape, locale, locality, location, melodrama, milieu, outburst, pageant, panorama, part, performance, picture, place, position, prospect, representation, row, set, setting, show, sight, site, situation, spectacle, spot, stage, tableau, tantrum, to-do, upset, view, vista, whereabouts, world.

scenery *n* backdrop, background, décor, flats, landscape, outlook, panorama, set, setting, sight, surroundings, terrain, view, vista.

cenic *adj* awe-inspiring, beautiful, breathtaking, grand, impressive, magnificent, panoramic, picturesque, pretty, spectacular, striking, stupendous. *antonyms* dreary, dull, unspectacular.

cent *n* aroma, bouquet, fragrance, odour, perfume, redolence, smell, trace, track, trail, waft, whiff. *antonym* stink. *v* detect, discern, nose, nose out, perceive, recognise, sense, smell, sniff, sniff out.

cented *adj* aromatic, fragrant, odoriferous, perfumed, redolent, sweet-smelling. *antonyms* malodorous, stinking.

ceptic *n* agnostic, atheist, cynic, disbeliever, doubter, doubting Thomas, rationalist, unbeliever. *antonym* believer.

ceptical *adj* cynical, disbelieving, distrustful, doubtful, doubting, dubious, hesitating, incredulous, mistrustful, pessimistic, questioning, scoffing, suspicious, unbelieving, unconvinced, unpersuaded, untrustful. *antonyms* convinced, naïve, trusting.

chedule *n* agenda, calendar, catalogue, diary, form, inventory, itinerary, list, plan, programme, scheme, table, timetable. *v* appoint, arrange, book, list, organise, plan, programme, slot, table, time.

scheme *n* arrangement, blueprint, chart, configuration, conformation, conspiracy, contrivance, design, device, diagram, disposition, dodge, draft, game, idea, intrigue, lay-out, machinations, manoeuvre, method, outline, pattern, plan, plot, ploy, procedure, programme, project, proposal, proposition, racket, ruse, schedule, schema, shape, shift, stratagem, strategy, subterfuge, suggestion, system, tactics, theory. *v* collude, conspire, contrive, design, devise, frame, imagine, intrigue, machinate, manipulate, manoeuvre, mastermind, plan, plot, project, pull strings, pull wires, work out.

scheming *adj* artful, calculating, conniving, crafty, cunning, deceitful, designing, devious, duplicitous, insidious, Machiavellian, slippery, sly, tricky, underhand, unscrupulous, wily. *antonyms* artless, honest, open, transparent.

schism *n* breach, break, cleavage, discord, disunion, division, estrangement, faction, quarrel, rift, rupture, sect, separation, severance, splinter group, splintering, split.

scholarly *adj* academic, analytical, bookish, conscientious, critical, erudite, intellectual, knowledgeable, learned, lettered, scholastic, scientific, studious, well-read. *antonyms* illiterate, unscholarly.

school *n* academy, adherents, alma mater, circle, class, clique, college, creed, denomination, department, devotees, disciples, discipline, doctrine, dogma, faction, faculty, faith, followers, following, group, gymnasium, institute, institution, outlook, persuasion, pupils, sect, seminary, set, students, teaching, view, votaries. *v* coach, discipline, drill, educate, harden, indoctrinate, instruct, inure, prepare, prime, train, tutor, verse.

scientific *adj* accurate, analytical, controlled, exact, mathematical, methodical, precise, scholarly, systematic, thorough.

scintillate *v* blaze, coruscate, flash, gleam, glint, glisten, glitter, shine, spark, sparkle, twinkle, wink.

scintillating *adj* animated, blazing, blinding, bright, brilliant, coruscating, dazzling, ebullient, exciting, flashing, glittering, lively, shining, sparkling, stimulating, vivacious, winking, witty. *antonym* dull.

scoff[1] *v* belittle, deride, despise, flout, geck, gibe, jeer, knock, mock, poke fun, pooh-pooh, rail, revile, rib, ridicule, scorn, sneer, taunt. *antonyms* compliment, flatter, praise.

scoff[2] *v* bolt, consume, cram, devour, fill one's face, gobble, gulp, guzzle, pig, put away, shift, wolf. *antonym* abstain.

n chow, comestibles, commons, eatables, eats, edibles, fare, feed, fodder, food, grub, meal, nosh, nosh-up, provisions, rations, scran, tuck, victuals.

scold *v* admonish, bawl out, berate, blame, castigate, censure, chide, find fault with, lecture, nag, rate, rebuke, remonstrate, reprimand, reproach, reprove, rollick, take to task, tell off, tick off, upbraid, vituperate, wig. *antonyms* commend, praise.

n battle-axe, fishwife, harridan, nag, shrew, termagant, virago, vixen.

scolding *n* a piece of one's mind, castigation, dressing-down, earful, lecture, rebuke, reprimand, reproof, rollicking, row, talking-to, telling-off, throughgoing, ticking-off, tongue-lashing, upbraiding. *antonym* commendation.

scoot *v* beat it, bolt, bowl, career, dart, dash, hurry, run, scamper, scarper, scud, scurry, scuttle, shoot, skedaddle, sprint, tootle, vamoose, zip.

scope *n* ambit, application, area, breadth, capacity, compass, competence, confines, coverage, elbow-room, extent, freedom, latitude, liberty, opportunity, orbit, outlook, range, reach, remit, room, space, span, sphere, terms of reference.

scorch *v* blacken, blister, burn, char, parch, roast, scald, sear, shrivel, singe, sizzle, wither.

scorched *adj* arid, baked, blackened, blistered, burnt, charred, cracked, parched, sear, seared, shrivelled, torrid, withered.

scorching *adj* baking, blistering, boiling, broiling, burning, fiery, flaming, parching, red-hot, roasting, scalding, searing, sizzling, sweltering, torrid, tropical, withering.

score *n* a bone to pick, account, amount, basis, bill, cause, charge, debt, due, gash, grade, grievance, ground, grounds, grudge, injury, injustice, line, mark, notch, obligation, outcome, points, reason, reckoning, record, result, scratch, sum total, tab, tally, total, wrong.

v achieve, adapt, amass, arrange, attain, be one up, benefit, chalk up, count, cut, deface, earn, engrave, furrow, gain, gouge, grave, graze, groove, hatch, have the advantage, have the edge, impress, incise, indent, knock up, make, make a hit, mark, nick, notch, notch up, orchestrate, profit, realise, record, register, scrape, scratch, set, slash, tally, total, win.

score out cancel, cross out, delete, efface, erase, expunge, obliterate, remove, strike out. *antonyms* reinstate, restore.

scores *n* crowds, droves, hosts, hundreds, legions, lots, masses, millions, multitudes, myriads, shoals, swarms.

scorn *n* contempt, contemptuousness, derision, disdain, disgust, dismissiveness, disparagement, mockery, sarcasm, scornfulness, slight, sneer. *antonyms* admiration, respect.

v contemn, deride, despise, disdain, dismiss, flout, hold in contempt, laugh at, laugh in the face of, look down on, misprise, pooh-pooh, refuse, reject, scoff at, slight, sneer at, spurn. *antonyms* admire, respect.

scornful *adj* arrogant, contemptuous, defiant, derisive, disdainful, dismissive, disparaging, haughty, insulting, jeering, mocking, sarcastic, sardonic, scathing, scoffing, slighting, sneering, supercilious, withering. *antonyms* admiring, complimentary, respectful.

scot-free *adj* clear, ininjured, safe, undamaged, unharmed, unhurt, unpunished, unrebuked, unreprimanded, unreproached, unscathed, without a scratch.

scoundrel *n* blackguard, blighter, bounder, cheat, cur, dastard, good-for-nothing, heel, hound, knave, louse, miscreant, ne'er-do-well, rascal, rat, reprobate, rogue, rotter, ruffian, scallywag, scamp, stinker, swine, villain.

scour[1] *v* abrade, buff, burnish, clean, cleanse, furbish, polish, rub, scrape, scrub, wash.

scour[2] *v* beat, comb, drag, forage, go over, hunt, rake, ransack, search, turn upside-down.

scourge *n* affliction, bane, cat, cat o'-nine-tails, curse, evil, flagellum, infliction, lash, menace, misfortune, penalty, pest, pestilence, plague, punishment, strap, switch, terror, thong.

torment, visitation, whip. *antonyms* benefit, blessing, boon, godsend.

v afflict, beat, belt, cane, castigate, chastise, curse, devastate, discipline, excoriate, flagellate, flail, flog, harass, horsewhip, lambaste, lash, lather, leather, plague, punish, tan, terrorise, thrash, torment, trounce, wallop, whale, whip.

scout *v* case, check out, do a recce, explore, hunt, investigate, look, observe, probe, reconnoitre, search, seek, snoop, spy, spy out, survey, track, watch.

scowl *v* frown, glare, glower, grimace, lower.

n frown, glare, glower, grimace. *antonyms* beam, grin, smile.

scrabble *v* clamber, claw, dig, grope, grub, paw, root, scramble, scrape, scratch.

craggy *adj* angular, bony, emaciated, gangling, gaunt, lank, lanky, lean, meagre, rawboned, scrawny, skinny, spare, undernourished, wasted. *antonyms* plump, rounded, sleek.

cram *v* beat it, bolt, clear off, clear out, depart, disappear, do a bunk, flee, get lost, go away, leave, quit, scarper, scoot, shove off, skedaddle, take to one's heels, vamoose.

cramble *v* clamber, climb, contend, crawl, hasten, jostle, jumble, push, run, rush, scale, scrabble, shuffle, sprawl, strive, struggle, swarm, vie.

n climb, commotion, competition, confusion, contention, free-for-all, hustle, mêlée, muddle, race, rat race, rivalry, rush, strife, struggle, trek, trial, tussle.

crap¹ *n* atom, bit, bite, crumb, fraction, fragment, grain, iota, junk, mite, modicum, morsel, mouthful, part, particle, piece, portion, remnant, shard, shred, sliver, snap, snatch, snippet, trace, vestige, waste, whit.

v abandon, axe, break up, cancel, chuck, demolish, discard, ditch, drop, jettison, junk, shed, throw out, write off. *antonyms* reinstate, restore, resume.

crap² *n* argument, barney, battle, brawl, disagreement, dispute, dust-up, fight, quarrel, row, ruckus, ruction, rumpus, scuffle, set-to, shindy, squabble, tiff, wrangle. *antonyms* agreement, peace.

v argue, bicker, clash, fall out, fight, spat, squabble, wrangle. *antonym* agree.

crape *v* abrade, bark, claw, clean, erase, file, grate, graze, grind, pinch, rasp, remove, rub, save, scour, scrabble,

scratch, screech, scrimp, scuff, skimp, skin, squeak, stint.

n abrasion, difficulty, dilemma, distress, fix, graze, mess, pickle, plight, predicament, pretty kettle of fish, rub, scratch, scuff, shave, spot, trouble.

scrappy *adj* bitty, disjointed, fragmentary, incomplete, perfunctory, piecemeal, sketchy, slapdash, slipshod, superficial. *antonyms* complete, finished.

scraps *n* bits, leavings, leftovers, remains, scrapings.

scratch *v* annul, cancel, claw, curry, cut, damage, delete, eliminate, erase, etch, grate, graze, incise, lacerate, mark, race, retire, rub, scarify, score, scrab, scrabble, scrape, withdraw.

n blemish, claw mark, gash, graze, laceration, mark, race, scrape, streak.

adj haphazard, impromptu, improvised, rough, rough-and-ready, unrehearsed. *antonym* polished.

scrawny *adj* angular, bony, emaciated, gaunt, lanky, lean, rawboned, scraggy, skeletal, skinny, thin, underfed, undernourished. *antonym* plump.

scream¹ *v* bawl, clash, cry, holler, jar, roar, screech, shriek, shrill, squeal, wail, yell, yelp, yowl.

n howl, outcry, roar, screech, shriek, squeal, wail, yell, yelp, yowl. *antonym* whisper.

scream² *n* card, character, comedian, comic, hoot, joker, laugh, riot, sensation, wit. *antonym* bore.

screech *v* cry, screak, scream, shriek, squawk, squeal, yelp. *antonym* whisper.

screen *v* cloak, conceal, cover, defend, evaluate, examine, filter, gauge, grade, guard, hide, mask, process, protect, riddle, safeguard, scan, shade, shelter, shield, shroud, sieve, sift, sort, veil, vet. *antonyms* broadcast, present, show, uncover.

n awning, canopy, cloak, concealment, cover, divider, guard, hedge, hoarding, mantle, mesh, net, partition, shade, shelter, shield, shroud.

screw *v* adjust, bleed, cheat, coerce, compress, constrain, contort, contract, crumple, distort, extort, extract, fasten, force, oppress, pressurise, pucker, squeeze, tighten, turn, twist, wind, wrest, wring, wrinkle.

screw up botch, bungle, close, contort, contract, crumple, disrupt, distort, knot, louse up, make a hash of, mess up, mishandle, mismanage, pucker, queer, spoil, tighten, wrinkle. *antonyms* manage, unscrew.

screwy *adj* batty, cracked, crackers, crazy, daft, dotty, eccentric, mad, nutty, odd, queer, round the bend, round the twist, weird. *antonym* sane.

scrimmage *n* affray, bovver, brawl, disturbance, dust-up, fight, fray, free-for-all, mêlée, riot, row, scrap, scuffle, set-to, shindy, skirmish, squabble, struggle. *antonym* calmness.

scrimp *v* curtail, economise, limit, pinch, reduce, restrict, save, scrape, shorten, skimp, stint. *antonym* spend.

script *n* book, calligraphy, copy, hand, handwriting, letters, libretto, lines, longhand, manuscript, penmanship, text, words, writing.

Scrooge *n* cheapskate, meanie, miser, money-grubber, niggard, penny-pincher, skinflint, tightwad. *antonym* spendthrift.

scrounge *v* beg, bludge, bum, cadge, freeload, purloin, sponge, wheedle.

scrub *v* abandon, abolish, cancel, clean, cleanse, delete, discontinue, ditch, drop, forget, give up, rub, scour.

scruff *n* draggle-tail, ragamuffin, ragbag, scarecrow, sloven, slut, tramp.

scruffy *adj* disreputable, dog-eared, draggletailed, frowzy, grotty, ill-groomed, mangy, messy, ragged, run-down, scrubby, seedy, shabby, slatternly, slovenly, sluttish, squalid, tattered, ungroomed, unkempt, untidy. *antonyms* tidy, well-dressed.

scrumptious *adj* appetising, delectable, delicious, delightful, exquisite, luscious, magnificent, mouth-watering, succulent, yummy. *antonym* unappetising.

scrunch *v* champ, chew, crumple, crunch, crush, grate, grind, mash, squash.

scruple *v* balk at, demur at, falter, hesitate, object to, recoil from, shrink from, stick at, vacillate, waver.
n caution, compunction, difficulty, doubt, hesitation, misgiving, pang, perplexity, qualm, reluctance, squeamishness, uneasiness.

scrupulous *adj* careful, conscientious, conscionable, exact, fastidious, honourable, meticulous, minute, moral, nice, painstaking, precise, principled, punctilious, rigorous, squeaky-clean, strict, upright. *antonym* careless.

scrutinise *v* analyse, dissect, examine, explore, give a once-over, inspect, investigate, peruse, probe, scan, searc sift, study.

scrutiny *n* analysis, examinatic exploration, inquiry, inspectic investigation, once-over, perusal, searc sifting, study.

scud *v* blow, dart, fly, hasten, race, sa shoot, skim, speed.

scuff *v* abrade, brush, drag, graze, ru scratch, shuffle, skin.

scuffle *v* clash, contend, fight, grapp jostle, struggle, tussle.
n affray, barney, brawl, commotic disturbance, dog-fight, fight, ruck, ruc us, ruction, rumpus, scrap, set-to, tussl

sculpt *v* carve, chisel, cut, fashion, for hew, model, mould, represent, sculptu shape.

scum *n* crust, dregs, dross, film, fro impurities, rabble, riff-raff, rubbi spume, trash.

scupper *v* defeat, demolish, destr disable, overthrow, overwhelm, put spanner in the works, ruin, torpec wreck. *antonyms* advance, promote.

scurrility *n* abuse, abusivene coarseness, grossness, indecenc invective, nastiness, obloquy, obsceni offensiveness, rudeness, scurrilousne vituperation, vulgarity. *antony* politeness.

scurrilous *adj* abusive, coars defamatory, foul, foul-mouthed, gro indecent, insulting, low, nasty, obscer offensive, ribald, rude, salaciou scabrous, scandalous, slanderov vituperative, vulgar. *antonym* polite.

scurry *v* dart, dash, fly, hurry, rac scamper, scoot, scud, scuttle, skedadd skelter, sprint, trot, whisk. *antony* stroll.
n flurry, hustle and bustle, scamperin whirl. *antonym* calm.

scuttle *v* bustle, hare, hasten, hurry, ru rush, scamper, scoot, scramble, scu scurry, trot. *antonym* stroll.

sea *n* abundance, briny, deep, ditc drink, expanse, main, mass, multitue ocean, plethora, profusion, waves.
adj aquatic, marine, maritime, nav ocean, ocean-going, oceanic, salt, sa water, sea-going. *antonyms* air, land

seal *v* assure, attest, authenticat bung, clinch, close, conclude, confir consummate, cork, enclose, establis fasten, finalise, plug, ratify, secure, set shake hands on, shut, stamp, sto stopper, validate, waterproof. *antony* unseal.

n assurance, attestation, authentication, confirmation, insignia, notification, ratification, signet, stamp.

seal off block up, close off, cut off, fence off, isolate, quarantine, segregate, shut off. **antonym** open up.

sealed *adj* closed, corked, hermetic, plugged, shut. **antonym** unsealed.

seamy *adj* corrupt, dark, degraded, disagreeable, disreputable, low, nasty, rough, sleazy, sordid, squalid, unpleasant, unwholesome. **antonyms** pleasant, respectable.

sear *v* blight, brand, brown, burn, cauterise, desiccate, dry up, harden, scorch, seal, shrivel, sizzle, wilt, wither.

search *v* check, comb, examine, explore, ferret, forage, frisk, inquire, inspect, investigate, look, probe, pry, quest, ransack, rifle, rummage, scour, scrutinise, sift, test.

n examination, exploration, going-over, hunt, inquiry, inspection, investigation, pursuit, quest, research, rummage, scrutiny.

searching *adj* close, intent, keen, minute, penetrating, piercing, probing, quizzical, severe, sharp, thorough. **antonyms** superficial, vague.

season *n* division, interval, period, span, spell, term, time.

v acclimatise, accustom, colour, condition, discipline, enliven, flavour, habituate, harden, imbue, inure, lace, mature, mitigate, moderate, prepare, qualify, salt, spice, temper, toughen, train.

seasonable *adj* appropriate, convenient, fit, opportune, providential, suitable, timely, welcome, well-timed. **antonym** unseasonable.

seasoned *adj* acclimatised, battle-scarred, experienced, hardened, long-serving, mature, old, practised, time-served, veteran, weathered, well-versed. **antonym** novice.

seat *n* abode, axis, base, bed, bench, bottom, capital, cause, centre, chair, constituency, cradle, footing, foundation, ground, groundwork, headquarters, heart, house, hub, incumbency, location, mansion, membership, pew, place, residence, settle, shooting-stick, site, situation, source, stall, station, stool, throne.

v accommodate, assign, contain, deposit, fit, fix, hold, install, locate, place, set, settle, sit, slot, take.

secede *v* apostatise, disaffiliate, leave, quit, resign, retire, separate, split off, withdraw. **antonyms** join, unite with.

secession *n* apostasy, break, defection, disaffiliation, schism, seceding, split, withdrawal. **antonyms** amalgamation, unification.

secluded *adj* cloistered, cut off, isolated, lonely, out-of-the-way, private, reclusive, remote, retired, sequestered, sheltered, solitary, unfrequented. **antonyms** busy, public.

seclusion *n* concealment, hiding, isolation, privacy, recluseness, remoteness, retirement, retreat, shelter, solitude.

second[1] *adj* additional, alternate, alternative, double, duplicate, extra, following, further, inferior, lesser, lower, next, other, repeated, reproduction, secondary, subordinate, subsequent, succeeding, supplementary, supporting, twin.

n assistant, backer, helper, supporter.

v advance, agree with, aid, approve, assist, back, encourage, endorse, forward, further, help, promote, support.

second[2] *n* instant, jiff, jiffy, minute, mo, moment, sec, tick, trice, twinkling.

secondary *adj* alternate, auxiliary, back-up, consequential, contingent, derivative, derived, extra, indirect, inferior, lesser, lower, minor, relief, reserve, resultant, resulting, second, second-hand, second-rate, spare, subordinate, subsidiary, supporting, unimportant. **antonym** primary.

second-hand *adj* borrowed, derivative, hand-me-down, old, plagiarised, used, vicarious, worn. **antonym** new.

second-rate *adj* cheap, cheap and nasty, grotty, inferior, low-grade, mediocre, poor, rubbishy, shoddy, substandard, tacky, tawdry, undistinguished, uninspired, uninspiring. **antonym** first-rate.

secrecy *n* clandestineness, concealment, confidence, confidentiality, covertness, furtiveness, hugger-mugger, mystery, privacy, retirement, seclusion, secretiveness, silence, solitude, stealth, stealthiness, surreptitiousness. **antonym** openness.

secret *adj* abstruse, arcane, back-door, backstairs, cabbalistic(al), camouflaged, clandestine, classified, cloak-and-dagger, close, closet, concealed, conspiratorial, covered, covert, cryptic, deep, discreet, disguised, esoteric, furtive, hidden, hush-hush, mysterious, occult, out-of-the-way, private, privy, recondite, reticent, retired, secluded, secretive, sensitive, shrouded, sly, stealthy, tête-à-tête, undercover, underground, underhand, under-the-counter, undisclosed, unfrequented, unknown, unpublished, unrevealed, unseen. *antonyms* open, public.

secretary *n* assistant, clerk, girl Friday, PA, person Friday, personal assistant, stenographer, typist.

secrete¹ *v* appropriate, bury, conceal, cover, disguise, harbour, hide, screen, secure, shroud, stash away, stow, veil. *antonym* reveal.

secrete² *v* emanate, emit, extrude, exude.

secretion *n* discharge, emission, excretion, exudation.

secretive *adj* cagey, close, close-lipped, close-mouthed, cryptic, deep, enigmatic, quiet, reserved, reticent, tight-lipped, uncommunicative, unforthcoming, withdrawn. *antonyms* communicative, open.

secretly *adv* clandestinely, confidentially, covertly, furtively, in camera, in confidence, in private, in secret, on the q.t., on the quiet, on the sly, privately, quietly, stealthily, surreptitiously, unobserved. *antonym* openly.

sectarian *adj* bigoted, clannish, cliquish, doctrinaire, dogmatic, exclusive, factional, fanatic, fanatical, insular, limited, narrow, narrow-minded, parochial, partisan, rigid. *antonyms* broad-minded, cosmopolitan, non-sectarian.

section *n* area, article, component, cross section, department, district, division, fraction, fragment, instalment, part, passage, piece, portion, region, sample, sector, segment, slice, subdivision, wing, zone. *antonym* whole.

sector *n* area, category, district, division, part, quarter, region, section, stratum, subdivision, zone. *antonym* whole.

secular *adj* civil, laic, laical, lay, non-religious, profane, state, temporal, worldly. *antonym* religious.

secure *adj* absolute, assured, certain, conclusive, confident, definite, dependable, easy, fast, fastened, firm, fixed, fortified, immovable, immune, impregnable, on velvet, over-confident, protected, reassured, reliable, safe, sheltered, shielded, solid, stable, steadfast, steady, sure, tight, unassailable, undamaged, unharmed,

well-founded. *antonyms* insecure, uncertain.

v acquire, assure, attach, batten down, bolt, chain, ensure, fasten, fix, gain, get, get hold of, guarantee, insure, land, lash, lock, lock up, moor, nail, obtain, padlock, procure, rivet, seize. *antonyms* lose, unfasten.

security *n* assurance, asylum, care, certainty, collateral, confidence, conviction, cover, custody, defence, gage, guarantee, guards, hostage, immunity, insurance, pawn, pledge, positiveness, precautions, preservation, protection, refuge, reliance, retreat, safeguards, safe-keeping, safety, sanctuary, sureness, surety, surveillance, warranty. *antonym* insecurity.

sedate *adj* calm, collected, composed, cool, decorous, deliberate, demure, dignified, earnest, grave, imperturbable, middle-aged, placed, proper, quiet, seemly, serene, serious, slow-moving, sober, solemn, staid, tranquil, unflappable, unruffled. *antonyms* flippant, hasty, undignified.

sedentary *adj* desk, desk-bound, inactive, motionless, seated, sitting, stationary, still, torpid, unmoving. *antonym* active.

sedition *n* agitation, disloyalty, rabble-rousing, ruckus, rumpus, subversion, treason, tumult. *antonyms* calm, loyalty.

seditious *adj* disloyal, dissident, insubordinate, mutinous, rebellious, refractory, revolutionary, subversive, traitorous. *antonyms* calm, loyal.

seduce *v* allure, attract, beguile, betray, bewitch, corrupt, debauch, deceive, decoy, deflower, deprave, dishonour, ensnare, entice, inveigle, lure, mislead, ruin, tempt.

seduction *n* allure, allurement, come-on, corruption, enticement, lure, ruin, snare, temptation.

seductive *adj* alluring, attractive, beguiling, bewitching, captivating, come-hither, come-on, enticing, flirtatious, honeyed, inviting, irresistible, page-three, provocative, ravishing, seducing, sexy, siren, specious, tempting. *antonym* unattractive.

sedulous *adj* assiduous, busy, conscientious, constant, determined, diligent, industrious, laborious, painstaking, persevering, persistent, resolved, tireless, unflagging, unremitting, untiring. *antonym* half-hearted.

see *v* accompany, anticipate, appreciate,

ascertain, attend, behold, comprehend, consider, consult, court, date, decide, deem, deliberate, descry, determine, discern, discover, distinguish, divine, encounter, ensure, envisage, escort, espy, experience, fathom, feel, follow, foresee, foretell, get, glimpse, grasp, guarantee, heed, identify, imagine, interview, investigate, judge, know, lead, learn, look, make out, mark, meet, mind, note, notice, observe, perceive, picture, realise, receive, recognise, reflect, regard, show, sight, spot, take, understand, usher, view, visit, visualise, walk, witness.

see eye to eye accord, agree, coincide, concur, get along, get on, harmonise, speak the same language, subscribe. *antonym* disagree.

see red blow one's top, blow up, boil, go mad, go off one's head, lose one's rag, lose one's temper.

see to arrange, attend to, deal with, do, fix, look after, manage, organise, repair, sort out, take care of, take charge of.

seed *n* beginning, children, descendants, egg, embryo, germ, grain, heirs, inkling, issue, kernel, nucleus, offspring, ovum, pip, progeny, race, semen, source, spawn, sperm, start, successors, suspicion. *antonym* ancestors.

seedy *adj* ailing, crummy, decaying, dilapidated, faded, grotty, grubby, ill, mangy, manky, off-colour, old, peelie-wally, poorly, run-down, scruffy, shabby, sickly, sleazy, slovenly, squalid, tatty, unkempt, unwell, worn. *antonyms* posh, well.

seek *v* aim, ask, aspire to, attempt, beg, desire, endeavour, entreat, essay, follow, hunt, inquire, invite, petition, pursue, request, solicit, strive, try, want.

seeming *adj* apparent, appearing, illusory, ostensible, outward, pseudo-, quasi-, specious, surface. *antonym* real.

seemingly *adv* allegedly, apparently, as far as one can see, on the face of it, on the surface, ostensibly, outwardly, superficially. *antonym* really.

seemly *adj* appropriate, attractive, becoming, befitting, comely, decent, decorous, fit, fitting, handsome, maidenly, meet, nice, proper, suitable, suited. *antonym* unseemly.

seep *v* exude, leak, ooze, percolate, permeate, soak, trickle, weep, well.

seesaw *v* alternate, fluctuate, oscillate, pitch, swing, teeter.

seethe *v* boil, bubble, churn, ferment, fizz, foam, foam at the mouth, froth, fume, hotch, rage, rise, saturate, simmer, smoulder, soak, souse, steep, storm, surge, swarm, swell, teem.

see-through *adj* diaphanous, filmy, flimsy, gauzy, gossamer(y), sheer, translucent, transparent. *antonym* opaque.

segment *n* articulation, bit, compartment, division, part, piece, portion, section, slice, wedge. *antonym* whole.

segregate *v* cut off, discriminate against, dissociate, isolate, quarantine, separate, set apart. *antonym* unite.

seize *v* abduct, annex, apprehend, appropriate, arrest, capture, catch, claw, clutch, cly, collar, commander, confiscate, crimp, distrain, distress, fasten, fix, get, grab, grasp, grip, hijack, impound, nab, smug, snatch, take. *antonym* let go.

seizure *n* abduction, annexation, apprehension, arrest, attachment, attack, capture, commandeering, confiscation, convulsion, distraint, distress, fit, grabbing, paroxysm, spasm, taking. *antonym* liberation.

seldom *adv* infrequently, occasionally, rarely, scarcely. *antonym* often.

select *v* choose, cull, pick, prefer, single out.
adj choice, élite, excellent, exclusive, first-class, first-rate, hand-picked, limited, picked, posh, preferable, prime, privileged, rare, selected, special, superior, top, top-notch. *antonyms* general, second-rate.

selection *n* anthology, assortment, choice, choosing, collection, line-up, medley, miscellany, option, pick, pot-pourri, preference, range, variety.

selective *adj* careful, discerning, discriminating, discriminatory, élitist, particular. *antonym* unselective.

self-assurance *n* assurance, cockiness, cocksureness, confidence, overconfidence, positiveness, self-confidence, self-possession. *antonyms* humility, unsureness.

self-assured *adj* assured, cocksure, cocky, confident, overconfident, self-possessed, sure of oneself. *antonyms* humble, unsure.

self-centred *adj* egotistic(al), narcissistic, self-absorbed, self-interested, selfish, self-seeking, self-serving. *antonym* altruistic.

self-confident *adj* assured, confident, fearless, poised, secure, self-assured, self-collected, self-possessed, self-reliant. *antonyms* humble, unsure.

self-conscious *adj* affected, awkward, bashful, coy, diffident, embarrassed, ill at ease, insecure, nervous, retiring, self-effacing, shamefaced, sheepish, shrinking, uncomfortable. *antonyms* natural, unaffected.

self-control *n* calmness, composure, cool, coolness, discipline, encraty, restraint, self-command, self-discipline, self-government, self-mastery, self-restraint, temperance, will-power.

self-denial *n* abstemiousness, asceticism, moderation, renunciation, self-abnegation, selflessness, self-sacrifice, temperance, unselfishness. *antonym* self-indulgence.

self-esteem *n* amour-propre, dignity, pride, self-assurance, self-confidence, self-pride, self-regard, self-respect. *antonym* humility.

self-evident *adj* axiomatic, clear, incontrovertible, inescapable, manifest, obvious, undeniable, unquestionable.

self-government *n* autarchy, autonomy, democracy, home rule, independence. *antonym* subjection.

self-important *adj* arrogant, big-headed, bumptious, cocky, conceited, consequential, overbearing, pompous, pushy, strutting, swaggering, swollen-headed, vain. *antonym* humble.

self-indulgence *n* dissipation, dissoluteness, excess, extravagance, high living, incontinence, intemperance, profligacy, self-gratification, sensualism. *antonym* self-denial.

selfish *adj* egotistic, egotistical, greedy, mean, mercenary, narrow, self-centred, self-interested, self-seeking, self-serving. *antonym* unselfish.

selfless *adj* altruistic, generous, magnanimous, self-denying, self-sacrificing, ungrudging, unselfish. *antonym* selfish.

self-possessed *adj* calm, collected, composed, confident, cool, poised, self-assured, self-collected, together, unruffled. *antonym* worried.

self-possession *n* aplomb, calmness, composure, confidence, cool, coolness, poise, self-command, self-confidence, unflappability. *antonym* worry.

self-reliant *adj* independent, self-sufficient, self-supporting, self-sustaining. *antonym* dependent.

self-respect *n* dignity, pride, self-assurance, self-confidence, self-esteem,

self-pride, self-regard. *antonym* self-doubt.

self-restraint *n* abstemiousness, forbearance, moderation, patience, self-command, self-control, self-denial, self-discipline, self-government, temperance, will-power. *antonym* licence.

self-righteous *adj* complacent, goody-goody, holier-than-thou, hypocritical, pious, priggish, sanctimonious, self-satisfied, smug, superior. *antonym* understanding.

self-sacrifice *n* altruism, generosity, self-abnegation, self-denial, selflessness. *antonym* selfishness.

self-satisfied *adj* complacent, puffed up, self-congratulatory, self-righteous, smug. *antonym* humble.

self-seeking *adj* acquisitive, calculating, careerist, fortune-hunting, gold-digging, mercenary, on the make, opportunistic, self-interested, selfish, self-serving. *antonym* altruistic.

self-styled *adj* professed, pseudo, self-appointed, so-called, would-be.

sell *v* barter, cheat, convince, deal in, exchange, handle, hawk, impose on, market, merchandise, peddle, persuade, promote, retail, sell out, stock, surrender, trade, trade in, traffic in, trick. *antonym* buy.

sell out betray, double-cross, fail, fink on, rat on, sell down the river, stab in the back. *antonym* back.

semblance *n* air, apparition, appearance, aspect, bearing, façade, figure, form, front, guise, image, likeness, mask, pretence, resemblance, show, similarity, veneer.

seminal *adj* creative, formative, imaginative, important, influential, innovative, major, original, productive. *antonym* derivative.

send *v* broadcast, cast, charm, communicate, consign, convey, delight, deliver, direct, discharge, dispatch, electrify, emit, enrapture, enthrall, excite, exude, fire, fling, forward, grant, hurl, intoxicate, move, please, propel, radiate, ravish, remit, shoot, stir, thrill, titillate, transmit.

send for call for, call out, command, order, request, summon. *antonym* dismiss.

send up burlesque, imitate, lampoon, mickey-take, mimic, mock, parody, satirise, take off, take the mickey out of.

send-off *n* departure, farewell, going-

away, leave-taking, start, valediction.
antonym arrival.

send-up *n* imitation, mickey-take, mockery, parody, satire, skit, spoof, take-off.

senile *adj* decrepit, doddering, doting, failing, senescent.

senior *adj* elder, first, higher, high-ranking, major, older, superior. **antonym** junior.

seniority *n* precedence, priority, rank, standing, superiority. **antonym** juniority.

sensation *n* agitation, awareness, commotion, consciousness, emotion, excitement, feeling, furore, hit, impression, perception, scandal, sense, stir, surprise, thrill, tingle, vibes, vibrations, wow.

sensational *adj* amazing, astounding, blood-and-thunder, breathtaking, dramatic, electrifying, excellent, exceptional, exciting, fabulous, hair-raising, horrifying, impressive, lurid, marvellous, melodramatic, mind-blowing, revealing, scandalous, sensationalistic, shocking, smashing, spectacular, staggering, startling, superb, thrilling. **antonym** run-of-the-mill.

sense *n* advantage, appreciation, atmosphere, aura, awareness, brains, clear-headedness, cleverness, consciousness, definition, direction, discernment, discrimination, drift, faculty, feel, feeling, gist, good, gumption, implication, import, impression, intelligence, interpretation, intuition, judgement, logic, marbles, meaning, message, mother wit, nous, nuance, opinion, perception, point, premonition, presentiment, purport, purpose, quickness, reason, reasonableness, sagacity, sanity, savvy, sensation, sensibility, sentiment, sharpness, significance, signification, substance, tact, understanding, use, value, wisdom, wit(s), worth. **antonym** foolishness.

v appreciate, comprehend, detect, divine, feel, grasp, notice, observe, perceive, realise, suspect, understand.

senseless *adj* absurd, anaesthetised, asinine, crazy, daft, deadened, dotty, fatuous, foolish, halfwitted, idiotic, illogical, imbecilic, inane, incongruous, inconsistent, insensate, insensible, irrational, ludicrous, mad, meaningless, mindless, moronic, nonsensical, numb, numbed, out, out for the count, pointless, ridiculous, silly, simple,

stunned, stupid, unconscious, unfeeling, unintelligent, unreasonable, unwise. **antonym** sensible.

sensibility *n* appreciation, awareness, delicacy, discernment, insight, intuition, perceptiveness, responsiveness, sensitiveness, sensitivity, susceptibility, taste. **antonym** insensibility.

sensible *adj* appreciable, canny, considerable, delicate, discernable, discreet, discriminating, down-to-earth, far-sighted, intelligent, judicious, level-headed, matter-of-fact, noticeable, palpable, perceptible, practical, prudent, rational, realistic, reasonable, right-thinking, sagacious, sage, sane, shrewd, significant, sober, solid, sound, tangible, visible, well-advised, well-thought-out, wise. **antonyms** imperceptible, senseless.

sensitive *adj* acute, controversial, delicate, fine, impressionable, irritable, keen, perceptive, precise, reactive, responsive, secret, sensitised, sentient, susceptible, temperamental, tender, thin-skinned, touchy. **antonym** insensitive.

sensual *adj* animal, bodily, carnal, erotic, fleshly, lascivious, lecherous, lewd, libidinous, licentious, lustful, luxurious, physical, randy, raunchy, self-indulgent, sexual, sexy, voluptuous, worldly. **antonyms** ascetic, Puritan.

sensuality *n* animal magnetism, animalism, carnality, debauchery, eroticism, lasciviousness, lecherousness, lewdness, libertinism, libidinousness, licentiousness, lustfulness, profligacy, prurience, salaciousness, sexiness, voluptuousness. **antonyms** asceticism, Puritanism.

sensuous *adj* epicurean, gratifying, hedonistic, lush, luxurious, pleasurable, rich, sensory, sumptuous. **antonyms** ascetic, plain, simple.

sentence *n* aphorism, apophthegm, condemnation, decision, decree, doom, gnome, judgement, maxim, opinion, order, pronouncement, ruling, saying, verdict.

v condemn, doom, judge, pass judgement on, penalise, pronounce judgement on.

sententious *adj* aphoristic, axiomatic, brief, canting, compact, concise, epigrammatic, gnomic, laconic, moralising, moralistic, pithy, pointed, pompous, ponderous, preachy, sanctimonious, short, succinct, terse. **antonyms** humble, prolix.

sentient *adj* aware, conscious, live, living, reactive, responsive, sensitive. *antonym* insentient.

sentiment *n* attitude, belief, emotion, emotionalism, feeling, idea, judgement, mawkishness, maxim, opinion, persuasion, romanticism, saying, sensibility, sentimentalism, sentimentality, slush, soft-heartedness, tenderness, thought, view. *antonyms* hard-heartedness, straightforwardness.

sentimental *adj* corny, dewy-eyed, drippy, emotional, gushing, gushy, impressionable, lovey-dovey, maudlin, mawkish, mushy, nostalgic, pathetic, romantic, schmaltzy, simpering, sloppy, slushy, soft-hearted, tearful, tear-jerking, tender, touching, treacly, weepy. *antonym* unsentimental.

sentimentality *n* bathos, corniness, emotionalism, gush, mawkishness, mush, nostalgia, pulp, romanticism, schmaltz, sentimentalism, sloppiness, slush, tenderness.

separable *adj* detachable, distinguishable, divisible. *antonym* inseparable.

separate *v* abstract, bifurcate, departmentalise, detach, disaffiliate, disally, disconnect, disentangle, disjoin, dissever, distance, disunite, diverge, divide, divorce, estrange, isolate, part, part company, remove, secede, seclude, segregate, sever, shear, split, split up, uncouple, winnow, withdraw. *antonyms* join, unite.
adj alone, apart, autonomous, detached, disconnected, discrete, disjointed, disjunct, disparate, distinct, divided, divorced, independent, individual, isolated, particular, several, single, solitary, sundry, unattached, unconnected. *antonyms* attached, together.

separated *adj* apart, disassociated, disconnected, disunited, divided, isolated, parted, segregated, separate, split up. *antonyms* attached, together.

separately *adv* alone, apart, discretely, discriminately, independently, individually, severally, singly. *antonym* together.

separation *n* break, break-up, detachment, diaspora, disconnection, disengagement, disjunction, disjuncture, disseverance, dissociation, disunion, division, divorce, estrangement, farewell, gap, leave-taking, parting, rift, segregation, severance, solution, split, split-up. *antonyms* togetherness, unification.

septic *adj* festering, infected, poisoned, putrefying, putrid, suppurating.

sepulchral *adj* cheerless, deep, dismal, funereal, gloomy, grave, hollow, lugubrious, melancholy, morbid, mournful, reverberating, sad, sombre, sonorous, woeful. *antonym* cheerful.

sequel *n* conclusion, consequence, continuation, development, end, follow-up, issue, outcome, pay-off, result, upshot.

sequence *n* arrangement, chain, consequence, course, cycle, order, procession, progression, series, set, succession, track, train.

serene *adj* calm, composed, cool, halcyon, imperturbable, peaceful, placid, tranquil, unclouded, undisturbed, unflappable, unruffled, untroubled. *antonym* troubled.

serenity *n* calm, calmness, composure, cool, peace, peacefulness, placidity, quietness, stillness, tranquillity, unflappability. *antonyms* anxiety, disruption.

serious *adj* acute, alarming, critical, crucial, dangerous, deep, deliberate, determined, difficult, earnest, far-reaching, fateful, genuine, grave, grim, heavy, honest, humourless, important, long-faced, momentous, pensive, pressing, resolute, resolved, sedate, severe, significant, sincere, sober, solemn, staid, stern, thoughtful, unsmiling, urgent, weighty, worrying. *antonyms* facetious, light, slight, smiling, trivial.

seriously *adv* acutely, badly, critically, dangerously, distressingly, earnestly, gravely, grieviously, joking apart, severely, sincerely, solemnly, sorely, thoughtfully. *antonyms* casually, slightly.

seriousness *n* danger, earnestness, gravitas, gravity, humourless, importance, moment, sedateness, significance, sobriety, solemnity, staidness, sternness, urgency, weight. *antonyms* casualness, slightness, triviality.

sermon *n* address, dressing-down, exhortation, harangue, homily, lecture, talking-to.

serpentine *adj* coiling, crooked, meandering, sinuous, snakelike, snaking, snaky, tortuous, twisting, winding. *antonym* straight.

serried *adj* close, close-set, compact, crowded, dense, massed. *antonym* scattered.

servant *n* ancillary, attendant, bearer, boy, daily, day, day-woman, domestic, drudge, flunkey, footman, gentleman's gentleman, handmaid, handmaiden, help, helper, hireling, kitchen-maid, lackey, lady's maid, maid, major-domo, man, manservant, menial, retainer, scout, skivvy, slave, slavey, steward, valet, vassal, woman. **antonyms** master, mistress.

serve *v* act, aid, answer, arrange, assist, attend, avail, complete, content, dance attendance, deal, deliver, discharge, distribute, do, fulfil, further, handle, help, minister to, oblige, observe, officiate, pass, perform, present, provide, satisfy, succour, suffice, suit, supply, undergo, wait on, work for.

service *n* advantage, assistance, avail, availability, benefit, business, ceremony, check, disposal, duty, employ, employment, expediting, function, help, labour, maintenance, ministrations, observance, office, overhaul, performance, rite, servicing, set, supply, use, usefulness, utility, work, worship.

v check, maintain, overhaul, recondition, repair, tune.

serviceable *adj* advantageous, beneficial, convenient, dependable, durable, efficient, functional, hard-wearing, helpful, operative, plain, practical, profitable, simple, strong, tough, unadorned, usable, useful, utilitarian. **antonym** unserviceable.

servile *adj* abject, base, bootlicking, controlled, craven, cringing, fawning, grovelling, humble, low, mean, menial, obsequious, slavish, subject, submissive, subservient, sycophantic, toadying, toadyish, unctuous. **antonyms** aggressive, bold.

servitude *n* bondage, bonds, chains, enslavement, obedience, serfdom, slavery, subjugation, thraldom, thrall, vassalage. **antonym** freedom.

session *n* assembly, conference, discussion, get-together, go, hearing, meeting, period, semester, sitting, term, year.

set[1] *v* adjust, aim, allocate, allot, apply, appoint, arrange, assign, cake, conclude, condense, congeal, co-ordinate, crystallise, decline, decree, deposit, designate, determine, dip, direct, disappear, embed, establish, fasten, fix, fix up, gelatinise, harden, impose, install, jell, lay, locate, lodge, mount, name, ordain, park, place, plant, plonk, plump,

position, prepare, prescribe, propound, put, rectify, regulate, resolve, rest, schedule, seat, settle, sink, situate, solidify, specify, spread, stake, station, stick, stiffen, subside, synchronise, thicken, turn, vanish.

n attitude, bearing, carriage, fit, hang, inclination, position, posture, scene, scenery, setting, turn.

adj agreed, appointed, arranged, artificial, conventional, customary, decided, definite, deliberate, entrenched, established, firm, fixed, formal, hackneyed, immovable, inflexible, intentional, prearranged, predetermined, prescribed, regular, rehearsed, rigid, routine, scheduled, settled, standard, stereotyped, stock, strict, stubborn, traditional, unspontaneous, usual. **antonyms** free, movable, spontaneous, undecided.

set about assail, assault, attack, bash, beat up, begin, belabour, lambaste, mug, start, tackle, wade into.

set against alienate, balance, compare, contrast, disunite, divide, estrange, juxtapose, mix, oppose, weigh.

set apart choose, elect, peculiarise, put aside, separate.

set aside abrogate, annul, cancel, discard, dismiss, keep, keep back, lay aside, nullify, overrule, overturn, put aside, quash, reject, repudiate, reserve, reverse, save, select, separate.

set back delay, hamper, hinder, hold up, impede, interrupt, retard, slow.

set eyes on behold, clap eyes on, come across, come upon, encounter, lay eyes on, meet, meet with, notice, observe, see.

set free deliver, disentangle, emancipate, extricate, free, liberate, loose, manumit, ransom, release, rescue, rid, save, unpen. **antonyms** confine, enslave.

set off depart, detonate, display, embark, enhance, explode, ignite, leave, light, make tracks, present, sally forth, show off, touch off, trigger off.

set on assail, assault, attack, beat up, fall upon, fly at, go for, incite, instigate, lay into, mug, pitch into, sail into, set about, set upon, turn on, urge.

set out arrange, array, begin, describe, detail, display, dispose, elaborate, elucidate, embark, exhibit, explain, lay out, make a move, make tracks, present, sally forth, set off, start, start out.

set up arrange, assemble, back, begin, boost, build, cheer, compose, construct, create, elate, elevate, erect, establish, finance, form, found, gratify, inaugurate, initiate, install, institute, introduce, organise, prearrange, prepare, promote, raise, start, strengthen, subsidise.

set² *n* apparatus, assemblage, assortment, band, batch, circle, class, clique, collection, company, compendium, coterie, crew, crowd, faction, gang, group, kit, outfit, sect, sequence, series.

setback *n* blow, check, defeat, delay, disappointment, hiccup, hitch, hold-up, knock-back, misfortune, problem, rebuff, relapse, reverse, snag, throwback, upset. **antonyms** advance, advantage, boost, help.

setting *n* adjustment, backcloth, backdrop, background, context, environment, frame, locale, location, milieu, mounting, period, perspective, position, scene, scenery, set, site, surround, surroundings.

setting-up *n* creation, establishment, foundation, founding, inauguration, inception, institution, introduction, start. **antonyms** abolition, termination.

settle *v* adjust, agree, alight, appoint, arrange, bed, calm, choose, clear, colonise, compact, complete, compose, conclude, confirm, decide, decree, descend, determine, discharge, dispose, dower, drop, dwell, endow, establish, fall, fix, found, hush, inhabit, land, light, liquidate, live, lower, lull, occupy, ordain, order, pacify, pay, people, pioneer, plant, plump, populate, quell, quiet, quieten, quit, reassure, reconcile, relax, relieve, reside, resolve, sedate, sink, soothe, square, square up, subside, tranquillise.

settlement *n* accommodation, adjustment, agreement, allowance, arrangement, clearance, clearing, completion, conclusion, confirmation, decision, defrayal, diktat, discharge, disposition, establishment, income, liquidation, payment, resolution, satisfaction, termination.

set-to *n* altercation, argument, argybargy, barney, brush, conflict, contest, disagreement, dust-up, exchange, fight, fracas, quarrel, row, scrap, spat, squabble, wrangle.

set-up *n* arrangement, business, circumstances, conditions, organisation, régime, structure, system.

sever *v* alienate, bisect, cleave, cut, detach, disconnect, disjoin, dissever, dissociate, dissolve, disunite, divide, estrange, part, rend, separate, split, terminate. **antonyms** join, unite.

several *adj* assorted, different, discrete, disparate, distinct, divers, diverse, individual, many, particular, respective, separate, single, some, some few, specific, sundry, various.

severally *adv* discretely, individually, particularly, respectively, separately, specifically. **antonyms** simultaneously, together.

severe *adj* acute, arduous, ascetic, astringent, austere, biting, bitter, caustic, chaste, classic, classical, cold, critical, cruel, cutting, dangerous, demanding, difficult, disapproving, distressing, dour, Draconian, eager, exacting, extreme, fierce, flinty, forbidding, functional, grave, grim, grinding, hard, harsh, inclement, inexorable, intense, ironhanded, oppressive, pitiless, plain, punishing, relentless, restrained, rigid, rigorous, satirical, scathing, serious, shrewd, simple, sober, spartan, stern, strait-laced, strict, stringent, taxing, tight-lipped, tough, trying, unadorned, unbending, unembellished, ungentle, unrelenting, unsmiling, unsparing, unsympathetic, violent. **antonyms** compassionate, kind, lenient, mild, sympathetic.

severely *adv* acutely, austerely, badly, bitterly, coldly, critically, dangerously, disapprovingly, dourly, extremely, gravely, grimly, hard, harshly, rigorously, sharply, sorely, sternly, strictly, unsympathetically.

severity *n* acuteness, asceticism, austerity, coldness, gravity, hardness, harshness, plainness, rigour, seriousness, sharpness, sternness, stringency, strictness, toughness. **antonyms** compassion, kindness, leniency, mildness.

sex *n* coition, coitus, congress, copulation, desire, fornication, intercourse, intimacy, libido, lovemaking, nookie, reproduction, screw, sexual intercourse, sexual relations, sexuality, union, venery.

sex appeal allure, desirability, glamour, it, magnetism, nubility, oomph, seductiveness, sensuality, sexiness, voluptuousness.

sexual *adj* carnal, coital, erotic, genital, intimate, procreative, reproductive, sensual, sex, sex-related, venereal.

sexual intercourse bonk, carnal knowledge, coition, coitus, commerce, congress, consummation, copulation, coupling, fuck, fucking, mating, nookie, penetration, pussy, screw, screwing, sex, shag, shagging, tail, union.

sexuality *n* carnality, desire, eroticism, lust, sensuality, sexiness, sexual instincts, sexual urge, virility, voluptuousness.

sexy *adj* arousing, beddable, come-hither, curvaceous, erotic, flirtatious, inviting, naughty, nubile, pornographic, provocative, provoking, seductive, sensual, sensuous, slinky, suggestive, titillating, virile, voluptuous. *antonym* sexless.

shabby *adj* cheap, contemptible, dastardly, despicable, dilapidated, dingy, dirty, dishonourable, disreputable, dog-eared, down-at-heel, faded, frayed, ignoble, low, low-down, low-life, low-lived, mangy, mean, moth-eaten, neglected, paltry, poking, poky, poor, ragged, raunchy, rotten, run-down, scruffy, seedy, shameful, shoddy, tacky, tattered, tatty, threadbare, ungentlemanly, unworthy, worn, worn-out. *antonyms* honourable, smart.

shack *n* bothy, but and ben, cabin, dump, hole, hovel, hut, hutch, lean-to, shanty, shed.

shackle *v* bind, chain, constrain, embarrass, encumber, fetter, hamper, hamstring, handcuff, handicap, hobble, impede, inhibit, limit, manacle, obstruct, pinion, restrain, restrict, secure, tether, thwart, tie, trammel.

shade *n* amount, apparition, blind, canopy, colour, coolness, cover, covering, curtain, darkness, dash, degree, difference, dimness, dusk, ghost, gloaming, gloom, gloominess, gradation, hint, hue, manes, murk, nuance, obscurity, phantasm, phantom, screen, semblance, semi-darkness, shadiness, shadow, shadows, shelter, shield, shroud, spectre, spirit, stain, suggestion, suspicion, tinge, tint, tone, trace, twilight, umbra, variation, variety, veil, wraith.

v cloud, conceal, cover, darken, dim, hide, inumbrate, mute, obscure, overshadow, protect, screen, shadow, shield, shroud, veil.

shadow *n* affliction, blight, cloud, companion, cover, darkness, detective, dimness, dusk, ghost, gloaming, gloom, hint, image, inseparable, obscurity, pal, phantom, protection, representation, sadness, shade, shelter, sidekick, sleuth,

spectre, spirit, suggestion, suspicion, tenebrosity, trace, vestige.

v darken, dog, follow, obscure, overhang, overshadow, screen, shade, shield, stalk, tail, trail, watch.

shadowy *adj* crepuscular, dark, dim, dreamlike, dusky, faint, ghostly, gloomy, half-remembered, hazy, illusory, imaginary, impalpable, indistinct, intangible, murky, nebulous, obscure, shaded, shady, spectral, tenebrous, undefined, unreal, unsubstantial, vague, wraithlike.

shady[1] *adj* cool, dark, dim, leafy, shaded, shadowy, tenebrous. *antonyms* bright, sunlit, sunny.

shady[2] *adj* crooked, discreditable, dishonest, disreputable, dubious, fishy, louche, questionable, shifty, slippery, suspect, suspicious, underhand, unethical, unscrupulous, untrustworthy. *antonyms* honest, trustworthy.

shaft *n* arrow, barb, beam, cut, dart, gleam, haft, handle, missile, pole, ray, rod, shank, stem, stick, sting, streak, thrust, upright, well.

shaggy *adj* hairy, hirsute, long-haired, rough, tousled, unkempt, unshorn. *antonyms* bald, shorn.

shake *n* agitation, convulsion, disturbance, instant, jar, jerk, jiffy, jolt, jounce, moment, no time, pulsation, quaking, second, shiver, shock, shudder, tick, trembling, tremor, trice, twitch, vibration.

v agitate, brandish, bump, churn, concuss, convulse, discompose, distress, disturb, flourish, fluctuate, frighten, heave, impair, intimidate, jar, joggle, jolt, jounce, move, oscillate, quake, quiver, rattle, rock, rouse, shimmy, shiver, shock, shudder, split, stir, sway, totter, tremble, twitch, undermine, unnerve, unsettle, upset, vibrate, wag, waggle, wave, waver, weaken, wobble.

shake a leg get a move on, get cracking, hurry, look lively, step on it, stir one's stumps.

shake off dislodge, elude, get rid of, give the slip, leave behind, lose, outdistance, outpace, outstrip.

shake-up *n* disturbance, rearrangement, reorganisation, reshuffle, upheaval.

shaky *adj* dubious, faltering, inexpert, insecure, precarious, questionable, quivery, rickety, rocky, suspect, tottering, tottery, uncertain, undependable, unreliable, unsound, unstable, unsteady, unsupported, untrustworthy, weak, wobbly. *antonyms* firm, strong.

shallow *adj* empty, flimsy, foolish, frivolous, idle, ignorant, meaningless, puerile, simple, skin-deep, slight, superficial, surface, trivial, unanalytical, unintelligent, unscholarly. *antonyms* analytical, deep.

sham *n* charlatan, counterfeit, feint, forgery, fraud, hoax, humbug, imitation, impostor, mountebank, phoney, pretence, pretender, pseud.
adj artificial, bogus, counterfeit, ersatz, faked, false, feigned, imitation, mock, phoney, pinchbeck, pretended, pseudo, put-on, simulated, spurious, synthetic. *antonym* genuine.
v affect, counterfeit, fake, feign, malinger, pretend, put on, simulate.

shambles *n* anarchy, bedlam, chaos, confusion, disarray, disorder, disorganisation, havoc, madhouse, mess, muddle, pigsty, wreck.

shambling *adj* awkward, clumsy, disjointed, loose, lumbering, lurching, shuffling, unco-ordinated, ungainly, unsteady. *antonyms* agile, neat, nimble, spry.

shame *n* bashfulness, blot, chagrin, compunction, contempt, degradation, derision, discredit, disgrace, dishonour, disrepute, embarrassment, humiliation, ignominy, infamy, mortification, obloquy, odium, opprobrium, reproach, scandal, shamefacedness, stain, stigma. *antonyms* distinction, honour, pride.
v abash, blot, confound, debase, defile, degrade, discomfit, disconcert, discredit, disgrace, dishonour, embarrass, humble, humiliate, mortify, put to shame, reproach, ridicule, show up, smear, stain, sully, taint.

shamefaced *adj* abashed, apologetic, ashamed, bashful, blushing, chagrined, conscience-stricken, contrite, diffident, discomfited, embarrassed, hesitant, humiliated, modest, mortified, red-faced, remorseful, sheepish, shrinking, shy, timid, uncomfortable. *antonyms* proud, unashamed.

shameful *adj* abominable, atrocious, base, contemptible, dastardly, degrading, discreditable, disgraceful, dishonourable, embarrassing, humiliating, ignominious, indecent, infamous, low, mean, mortifying, outrageous, reprehensible, scandalous, shaming, unbecoming, unworthy, vile, wicked. *antonyms* creditable, honourable.

shameless *adj* abandoned, audacious, barefaced, blatant, brash, brazen, corrupt, defiant, depraved, dissolute, flagrant, hardened, immodest, improper, impudent, incorrigible, indecent, insolent, profligate, reprobate, unabashed, unashamed, unblushing, unprincipled, unscrupulous, wanton. *antonyms* ashamed, contrite, shamefaced.

shanty *n* bothy, cabin, hovel, hut, hutch, lean-to, shack, shed.

shape *n* apparition, appearance, aspect, build, condition, configuration, conformation, contours, cut, dimensions, fettle, figure, form, format, frame, guise, health, kilter, likeness, lines, make, model, mould, outline, pattern, physique, profile, semblance, silhouette, state, template, trim.
v accommodate, adapt, brute, construct, create, define, develop, devise, embody, fashion, forge, form, frame, girdle, guide, make, model, modify, mould, plan, prepare, produce, regulate, remodel.

shapeless *adj* amorphous, asymmetrical, battered, characterless, dumpy, embryonic, formless, inchoate, indeterminate, irregular, misshapen, nebulous, undeveloped, unformed, unshapely, unstructured. *antonym* shapely.

shapely *adj* comely, curvaceous, elegant, graceful, neat, pretty, trim, voluptuous, well-formed, well-proportioned, well-turned. *antonym* shapeless.

share *v* allot, apportion, assign, chip in, distribute, divide, divvy, divvy up, go Dutch, go fifty-fifty, go halves, muck in, partake, participate, split, whack.
n a piece of the action, allotment, allowance, contribution, cut, dividend, division, divvy, due, finger, lot, part, portion, proportion, quota, ration, snap, snip, stint, whack.

share out allot, apportion, assign, distribute, divide up, give out, parcel out. *antonym* monopolise.

sharp *adj* abrupt, acerbic, acicular, acid, acidulous, acrid, acrimonious, acute, alert, apt, artful, astute, barbed, biting, bitter, bright, burning, canny, caustic, chic, chiselled, classy, clear, clear-cut, clever, crafty, crisp, cunning, cutting, discerning, dishonest, distinct, dressy, eager, edged, excruciating, extreme, fashionable, fierce, fly, harsh, honed, hot, hurtful, incisive, intense, jagged, keen, knife-edged, knifelike, knowing, marked, natty, nimble-witted, noticing, observant, painful, penetrating, peracute,

perceptive, piercing, piquant, pointed, pungent, quick, quick-witted, rapid, razor-sharp, ready, sarcastic, sardonic, saw-edged, scathing, serrated, severe, sharpened, shooting, shrewd, sly, smart, snappy, snazzy, sour, spiky, stabbing, stinging, stylish, subtle, sudden, tart, trenchant, trendy, unblurred, undulled, unscrupulous, vinegary, violent, vitriolic, waspish, wily. **antonyms** blunt, dull, mild, obtuse, slow, stupid.
adv abruptly, exactly, on the dot, out of the blue, precisely, promptly, punctually, suddenly, unexpectedly.

sharpness *n* acuity, acuteness, astuteness, discernment, eagerness, fierceness, incisiveness, intensity, keenness, observation, penetration, perceptiveness, pungency, quickness, severity, shrewdness, whet. **antonyms** dullness, sloth.

shatter *v* blast, blight, break, burst, crack, crush, demolish, destroy, devastate, disable, dumbfound, exhaust, explode, impair, implode, overturn, overwhelm, pulverise, ruin, shiver, smash, split, stun, torpedo, undermine, upset, wreck.

shattered *adj* all in, crushed, dead beat, devastated, dog-tired, done in, exhausted, jiggered, knackered, overwhelmed, undermined, weary, worn out, zonked.

shattering *adj* crushing, damaging, devastating, overwhelming, paralysing, severe, stunning.

shave *v* barber, brush, crop, fleece, graze, pare, plane, scrape, shear, tonsure, touch, trim.

shed¹ *v* afford, cast, cast off, diffuse, discard, drop, emit, give, moult, pour, radiate, scatter, shower, slough, spill, throw.
shed light on clarify, clear up, effuse, elucidate, explain, illuminate, simplify.

shed² *n* barn, hut, lean-to, lock-up, outhouse, shack.

sheen *n* brightness, brilliance, burnish, gleam, gloss, lustre, patina, polish, shimmer, shine. **antonyms** dullness, tarnish.

sheepish *adj* abashed, ashamed, chagrined, chastened, embarrassed, foolish, mortified, self-conscious, shamefaced, silly, uncomfortable. **antonym** unabashed.

sheer¹ *adj* abrupt, absolute, arrant, complete, downright, mere, out-and-out, perpendicular, precipitous, pure, rank, steep, thorough, thoroughgoing, total,

unadulterated, unalloyed, unmingled, unmitigated, unqualified, utter, vertical.

sheer² *adj* diaphanous, fine, flimsy, gauzy, gossamer, see-through, thin, translucent, transparent. **antonyms** heavy, thick.

sheet *n* blanket, broadsheet, broadside, circular, coat, covering, expanse, film, flyer, folio, handbill, handout, lamina, layer, leaf, leaflet, membrane, nappe, news-sheet, overlay, pane, panel, piece, plate, shroud, skin, slab, stratum, surface, veneer.

shell *n* carapace, case, casing, chassis, covering, crust, frame, framework, hull, husk, pod, rind, skeleton, structure.
v attack, barrage, batter, blitz, bomb, bombard, hull, husk, strafe, strike.
shell out ante, contribute, cough up, disburse, donate, expend, fork out, give, lay out, pay out, subscribe.

shelter *v* accommodate, cover, defend, ensconce, guard, harbour, hide, protect, put up, safeguard, screen, shade, shadow, shield, shroud. **antonym** expose.
n accommodation, asylum, bunker, cover, defence, dugout, guard, harbourage, haven, lean-to, lodging, protection, refuge, retreat, roof, safety, sanctuary, screen, security, shade, shadow, umbrella. **antonym** exposure.

sheltered *adj* cloistered, cosy, hermitic, isolated, protected, quiet, reclusive, retired, screened, secluded, shaded, shielded, snug, unworldly, warm, withdrawn. **antonym** exposed.

shelve *v* defer, dismiss, freeze, halt, mothball, postpone, put aside, put in abeyance, put off, put on ice, suspend, table. **antonyms** expedite, implement.

shepherd *v* conduct, convoy, escort, guide, herd, lead, marshal, steer, usher.

shield *v* cover, defend, guard, protect, safeguard, screen, shade, shadow, shelter. **antonym** expose.

shift *v* adjust, alter, budge, change, dislodge, displace, fluctuate, manoeuvre, move, quit, rearrange, relocate, remove, reposition, rid, scoff, swallow, swerve, switch, transfer, transpose, vary, veer.
n alteration, artifice, change, contrivance, craft, device, displacement, dodge, equivocation, evasion, expedient, fluctuation, manoeuvre, modification, move, permutation, rearrangement, removal, resource, ruse, shifting, sleight, stratagem, subterfuge, switch, transfer, trick, veering, wile.

shiftless *adj* aimless, directionless,

feckless, goalless, good-for-nothing, idle, incompetent, indolent, ineffectual, inefficient, inept, irresponsible, lackadaisical, lazy, resourceless, slothful, unambitious, unenterprising. **antonyms** ambitious, aspiring, eager, enterprising.

shifty *adj* contriving, crafty, deceitful, devious, dishonest, disingenuous, dubious, duplicitous, evasive, fly-by-night, furtive, scheming, shady, slippery, tricky, underhand, unprincipled, untrustworthy, wily. **antonyms** honest, open.

shilly-shally *v* dilly-dally, dither, falter, fluctuate, haver, hem and haw, hesitate, mess about, prevaricate, seesaw, shuffle, swither, teeter, vacillate, waver.

shimmer *v* coruscate, gleam, glisten, glitter, scintillate, twinkle.
n coruscation, gleam, glimmer, glitter, glow, incandescence, iridescence, lustre, phosphorescence.

shimmering *adj* gleaming, glistening, glittering, glowing, incandescent, iridescent, luminous, lustrous, shining, shiny. **antonyms** dull, matt.

shine *v* beam, brush, buff, burnish, coruscate, effulge, excel, flash, glare, gleam, glimmer, glisten, glitter, glow, lustre, polish, radiate, scintillate, shimmer, sparkle, stand out, star, twinkle.
n brightness, burnish, effulgence, glare, glaze, gleam, gloss, glow, lambency, light, luminosity, lustre, patina, polish, radiance, sheen, shimmer, sparkle.

shining *adj* beaming, bright, brilliant, celebrated, conspicuous, distinguished, effulgent, eminent, fulgent, gleaming, glistening, glittering, glorious, glowing, illustrious, leading, luminous, outstanding, profulgent, radiant, resplendent, shimmering, sparkling, splendid, twinkling.

shiny *adj* agleam, aglow, bright, burnished, gleaming, glistening, glossy, lustrous, polished, satiny, sheeny, shimmery, sleek. **antonyms** dark, dull.

shipshape *adj* businesslike, neat, orderly, spick-and-span, spruce, tidy, trim, well-organised, well-planned, well-regulated. **antonyms** disorderly, untidy.

shirk *v* avoid, dodge, duck, duck out of, evade, funk, shun, sidestep, skive, skrimshank, slack, swing the lead.

shiver *v* palpitate, quake, quiver, shake, shudder, tremble, vibrate.
n flutter, frisson, quiver, shudder, start,

thrill, tremble, trembling, tremor, twitch, vibration.

shivery *adj* chilled, chilly, cold, fluttery, nervous, quaking, quivery, shaking, shuddery, trembly.

shoal *n* assemblage, flock, horde, mass, mob, multitude, swarm, throng.

shock *v* agitate, appal, astound, confound, disgust, dismay, disquiet, horrify, jar, jolt, numb, offend, outrage, paralyse, revolt, scandalise, shake, stagger, startle, stun, stupefy, traumatise, unnerve, unsettle. **antonyms** delight, gratify, please, reassure.
n blow, bombshell, breakdown, clash, collapse, collision, concussion, consternation, dismay, distress, disturbance, encounter, fright, impact, jarring, jolt, perturbation, prostration, stupefaction, stupor, thunderbolt, trauma, turn, upset. **antonyms** delight, pleasure.

shocking *adj* abhorrent, abominable, appalling, astounding, atrocious, deplorable, detestable, disgraceful, disgusting, disquieting, distressing, dreadful, execrable, foul, frightful, ghastly, hideous, horrible, horrific, horrifying, insufferable, intolerable, loathsome, monstrous, odious, offensive, outrageous, repugnant, repulsive, revolting, scandalous, sickening, stupefying, unbearable, unspeakable. **antonyms** acceptable, delightful, pleasant, satisfactory.

shoddy *adj* cheap, cheap-jack, flimsy, inferior, junky, poor, rubbishy, second-rate, slipshod, tacky, tatty, tawdry, trashy. **antonyms** fine, well-made.

shoot[1] *v* bag, blast, bolt, charge, dart, dash, discharge, dump, emit, film, fire, flash, gun down, hit, hurl, hurtle, kill, launch, open fire, photograph, pick off, plug, precipitate, project, propel, race, rake, rush, scoot, speed, spring, sprint, streak, take, tear, whisk, whiz, zap.

shoot[2] *v* bolt, bud, burgeon, detonate, germinate, grow, shoot up, sprout, stretch, tower.

shore[1] *n* beach, coast, foreshore, lakeside, littoral, margin, promenade, sands, seaboard, sea-front, seashore, strand, waterfront, water's edge, waterside.

shore[2] *v* brace, buttress, hold, prop, reinforce, shore up, stay, strengthen, support, underpin.

short *adj* abbreviated, abridged, abrupt, blunt, brief, brittle, brusque, compendious, compressed, concise, crisp, crumbly, crusty, curt, curtailed, deficient, diminutive, direct, discourteous, dumpy, ephemeral, evanescent, fleeting, gruff, impolite, inadequate, insufficient, lacking, laconic, limited, little, low, meagre, momentary, murly, offhand, passing, petite, pithy, poor, précised, sawn-off, scant, scanty, scarce, sententious, sharp, shortened, short-handed, short-lived, short-term, slender, slim, small, snappish, snappy, sparse, squat, straight, succinct, summarised, summary, tart, terse, tight, tiny, transitory, uncivil, understaffed, unplentiful, wanting, wee. *antonyms* adequate, ample, expansive, large, lasting, long, long-lived, polite, tall.

short of apart from, deficient in, except, lacking, less than, low on, missing, other than, pushed for, short on, wanting.

shortage *n* absence, dearth, deficiency, deficit, failure, inadequacy, insufficiency, lack, leanness, meagreness, paucity, poverty, scantiness, scarcity, shortfall, sparseness, want. *antonyms* abundance, sufficiency.

shortcoming *n* defect, drawback, failing, fault, flaw, foible, frailty, imperfection, inadequacy, weakness.

shorten *v* abbreviate, abridge, crop, curtail, cut, decrease, diminish, dock, foreshorten, lessen, lop, précis, prune, reduce, take up, telescope, trim, truncate. *antonyms* amplify, enlarge, lengthen.

shortened *adj* abbreviated, abbreviatory, abridged, abstracted, compendious, condensed, summarised. *antonym* amplified.

short-lived *adj* brief, ephemeral, evanescent, fleeting, fugacious, impermanent, momentary, passing, short, temporary, transient, transitory. *antonyms* abiding, enduring, lasting, long-lived.

shortly *adv* abruptly, anon, briefly, concisely, curtly, directly, presently, sharply, soon, succinctly, tartly, tersely.

short-sighted *adj* careless, hasty, ill-advised, ill-considered, impolitic, impractical, improvident, imprudent, injudicious, myopic, near-sighted, unimaginative, unthinking. *antonyms* far-sighted, long-sighted.

short-tempered *adj* crusty, fiery, hot-tempered, impatient, irascible, irritable, peppery, quick-tempered, ratty, testy, touchy. *antonyms* calm, patient, placid.

shot *n* attempt, ball, bash, blast, bullet, chance, conjecture, contribution, crack, discharge, dram, effort, endeavour, essay, go, guess, injection, lead, lob, marksman, opportunity, pellet, projectile, range, reach, shooter, shy, slug, spell, stab, stroke, surmise, throw, try, turn.

shot in the arm boost, encouragement, fillip, fresh talent, impetus, lift, stimulus, uplift.

shot in the dark blind guess, conjecture, guess, guesswork, speculation.

shoulder *v* accept, assume, barge, bear, carry, elbow, jostle, press, push, shove, sustain, take on, thrust.

shout *n* bay, bellow, belt, call, cheer, cry, roar, scream, shriek, yell.
v bawl, bay, bellow, call, cheer, cry, holler, roar, scream, shriek, yell.

shove *v* barge, crowd, drive, elbow, force, impel, jostle, press, propel, push, shoulder, thrust.

shove off beat it, clear off, clear out, depart, do a bunk, get lost, leave, push off, put out, scarper, scram, skedaddle, vamoose.

show *v* accompany, accord, assert, attend, attest, bestow, betray, clarify, conduct, confer, demonstrate, disclose, display, divulge, elucidate, escort, evidence, evince, exemplify, exhibit, explain, grant, guide, illustrate, indicate, instruct, lead, manifest, offer, present, prove, register, reveal, teach, usher, witness.
n affectation, air, appearance, array, dash, demonstration, display, éclat, élan, entertainment, exhibition, exhibitionism, exposition, extravaganza, façade, fair, flamboyance, illusion, indication, likeness, manifestation, ostentation, pageant, pageantry, panache, parade, performance, pizzazz, plausibility, pose, presentation, pretence, pretext, production, profession, razzle-dazzle, representation, semblance, sight, sign, spectacle, swagger, view.

show off advertise, boast, brag, brandish, demonstrate, display, enhance, exhibit, flaunt, parade, peacock, set off, strut, swagger, swank.

show up appear, arrive, come, disgrace, embarrass, expose, highlight, humiliate, lay bare, let down, mortify, pinpoint, reveal, shame, show, stand out, turn up, unmask.

show-down *n* clash, climax, confrontation, crisis, culmination, dénouement, face-off.

shower[1] *n* barrage, deluge, down-come, drift, fusillade, hail, plethora, precipitation, rain, spout, stream, torrent, volley.

v deluge, douche, douse, heap, inundate, lavish, load, overwhelm, pour, rain, sparge, spray, sprinkle.

shower[2] *n* crew, gang, mob, rabble.

showiness *n* flamboyance, flashiness, glitter, glitz, ostentation, pizzazz, razzle-dazzle, razzmatazz, swank. *antonym* restraint.

showing *n* account, appearance, display, evidence, exhibition, impression, past performance, performance, presentation, record, representation, show, staging, statement, track record.

showing-off *n* boasting, bragging, egotism, exhibitionism, peacockery, self-advertisement, swagger, swank, vainglory. *antonym* modesty.

show-off *n* boaster, braggart, egotist, exhibitionist, peacock, self-advertiser, swaggerer, swanker, vaunter.

showy *adj* euphuistic, exotic, flamboyant, flash, flashy, florid, flossy, garish, gaudy, glitzy, loud, ostentatious, pompous, pretentious, specious, swanking, swanky, tawdry, tinselly. *antonyms* quiet, restrained.

shred *n* atom, bit, fragment, grain, iota, jot, mite, piece, rag, ribbon, scrap, sliver, snippet, tatter, trace, whit, wisp.

shrew *n* bitch, dragon, harridan, nag, scold, spitfire, termagant, virago, vixen.

shrewd *adj* acute, arch, artful, astute, calculated, calculating, canny, clever, crafty, cunning, discerning, discriminating, downy, far-seeing, far-sighted, fly, intelligent, judicious, keen, knowing, observant, perceptive, perspicacious, sagacious, sharp, sly, smart, well-advised, wily. *antonyms* naïve, obtuse, unwise.

shrewdly *adv* artfully, astutely, cannily, cleverly, craftily, far-sightedly, judiciously, knowingly, perceptively, perspicaciously, sagaciously, wisely.

shrewdness *n* acumen, acuteness, astuteness, canniness, discernment, grasp, intelligence, judgement, penetration, perceptiveness, perspicacity, sagacity, sharpness, smartness, wisdom. *antonyms* foolishness, naïvety, obtuseness.

shrewish *adj* bad-tempered, captious, complaining, discontented, fault-finding, henpecking, ill-humoured, ill-natured, ill-tempered, nagging, peevish, petulant, quarrelsome, querulous, scolding, sharp-tongued, vixenish. *antonyms* affectionate, peaceable, placid, supportive.

shriek *v* bellow, caterwaul, cry, holler, howl, scream, screech, shout, squeal, wail, yell.

n bellow, caterwaul, cry, howl, scream, screech, shout, squeal, wail.

shrill *adj* acute, carrying, ear-piercing, ear-splitting, high, high-pitched, penetrating, piercing, piping, screaming, screeching, screechy, sharp, strident, treble. *antonyms* gentle, low, soft.

shrink *v* back away, balk, contract, cower, cringe, decrease, deflate, diminish, dwindle, flinch, lessen, narrow, quail, recoil, retire, shorten, shrivel, shun, shy away, wince, withdraw, wither, wrinkle. *antonyms* embrace, expand, stretch, warm to.

shrivel *v* burn, dehydrate, desiccate, dwindle, frizzle, parch, pucker, scorch, sear, shrink, wilt, wither, wizen, wrinkle.

shrivelled *adj* desiccated, dried up, dry, emaciated, puckered, sere, shrunken, withered, wizened, wrinkled.

shroud *v* blanket, cloak, conceal, cover, envelop, hide, screen, sheet, swathe, veil, wrap. *antonyms* expose, uncover.

n cloud, covering, mantle, pall, screen, veil.

shrouded *adj* blanketed, cloaked, clouded, concealed, covered, enveloped, hidden, swathed, veiled, wrapped. *antonyms* exposed, uncovered.

shrunken *adj* cadaverous, contracted, emaciated, gaunt, reduced, shrivelled, shrunk. *antonyms* full, generous, rounded, sleek.

shudder *v* convulse, heave, quake, quiver, shake, shiver, tremble.

n convulsion, frisson, horror, quiver, spasm, trembling, tremor.

shuffle[1] *v* drag, hobble, limp, scrape, scuff, shamble.

shuffle[2] *v* chop and change, confuse, disarrange, disorder, intermix, jumble, mix, rearrange, reorganise, shift, shift around, switch around.

shun *v* avoid, cold-shoulder, elude, eschew, evade, ignore, ostracise, shy away from, spurn, steer clear of. *antonyms* accept, embrace.

shut *v* bar, bolt, cage, close, fasten, latch, lock, seal, secure, slam, spar. *antonym* open.

shut down cease, close, discontinue,

halt, inactivate, shut up, stop, suspend, switch off, terminate.

shut in box in, circumscribe, confine, enclose, hedge round, hem in, imprison, incarcerate.

shut off cut off, isolate, remove, seclude, segregate, separate.

shut out banish, bar, conceal, cover, debar, exclude, hide, lock out, mask, muffle, ostracise, screen, veil.

shut up cage, clam up, confine, coop up, gag, gaol, hold one's tongue, hush up, immure, imprison, incarcerate, intern, jail, muzzle, pipe down, silence.

shy *adj* backward, bashful, cautious, chary, coy, diffident, distrustful, hesitant, inhibited, modest, mousy, nervous, reserved, reticent, retiring, self-conscious, self-effacing, shrinking, suspicious, timid, unassertive, wary. **antonyms** bold, confident.
v back away, balk, buck, flinch, quail, rear, recoil, shrink, start, swerve, wince.

shyness *n* bashfulness, constraint, coyness, diffidence, hesitancy, inhibition, modesty, mousiness, nervousness, reticence, self-consciousness, timidity, timidness, timorousness. **antonyms** boldness, confidence.

sick *adj* ailing, bored, diseased, disgusted, displeased, dog-sick, fed up, feeble, ghoulish, glutted, ill, indisposed, jaded, laid up, morbid, mortified, nauseated, pining, poorly, puking, queasy, sated, satiated, sickly, tired, under the weather, unwell, vomiting, weak, weary. **antonyms** healthy, well.

sicken *v* disgust, nauseate, put off, repel, revolt, scunner, turn off. **antonyms** attract, delight.

sickening *adj* disgusting, distasteful, foul, loathsome, offensive, putrid, repulsive, revolting, vile. **antonyms** attractive, delightful, pleasing.

sickly *adj* ailing, bilious, bloodless, cloying, delicate, faint, feeble, frail, icky, indisposed, infirm, lacklustre, languid, mawkish, nauseating, pallid, peaked, peaky, peelie-wally, pining, revolting, saccharine, sweet, syrupy, treacly, unhealthy, wan, weak, weakly. **antonyms** robust, sturdy.

sickness *n* affliction, ailment, bug, complaint, derangement, disease, disorder, ill-health, illness, indisposition, infirmity, insanity, malady, nausea, pestilence, queasiness, vomiting. **antonym** health.

side *n* airs, angle, arrogance, aspect, bank, border, boundary, brim, brink, camp, cause, department, direction, division, edge, elevation, face, facet, faction, flank, flitch, fringe, gang, hand, insolence, light, limit, margin, opinion, ostentation, page, part, party, perimeter, periphery, position, pretentiousness, quarter, region, rim, sect, sector, slant, stand, standpoint, surface, team, twist, verge, view, viewpoint.
adj flanking, incidental, indirect, irrelevant, lateral, lesser, marginal, minor, oblique, roundabout, secondary, subordinate, subsidiary.

side with agree with, befriend, favour, second, support, team up with, vote for.

sidelong *adj* covert, indirect, oblique, sideward, sideways. **antonyms** direct, overt.

sidestep *v* avoid, bypass, circumvent, dodge, duck, elude, evade, find a way round, shirk, skip, skirt. **antonym** tackle.

sidetrack *v* deflect, distract, divert, head off.

sideways *adv* askance, edgeways, edgewise, laterally, obliquely, sidelong. *adj* oblique, side, sidelong, slanted.

sidle *v* creep, edge, inch, ingratiate, insinuate, slink, sneak, steal, wriggle.

siesta *n* catnap, doze, forty winks, nap, relaxation, repose, rest, sleep, snooze.

sift *v* analyse, discuss, examine, fathom, filter, investigate, pan, part, probe, review, riddle, screen, scrutinise, separate, sieve, sort, sprinkle, winnow.
n analysis, examination, filtering, filtration, review, screening, separation, sort, sorting, straining.

sigh *n* moan, sough, wuther.
v breathe, complain, grieve, lament, moan, sorrow, sough, wuther.

sigh for grieve, lament, languish, long, mourn, pine, weep, yearn.

sight *n* appearance, apprehension, decko, display, estimation, exhibition, eye, eyes, eye-shot, eyesight, eyesore, field of vision, fright, gander, glance, glimpse, judgement, ken, look, mess, monstrosity, observation, opinion, pageant, perception, range, scene, seeing, show, spectacle, view, viewing, visibility, vision, vista.
v behold, discern, distinguish, glimpse, observe, perceive, see, spot.

sign *n* augury, auspice, badge, beck, betrayal, board, character, cipher, clue, device, emblem, ensign, evidence, figure, foreboding, forewarning, gesture, giveaway, grammalogue, hierogram, hint, indication, insignia, intimation, logo, manifestation, mark, marker, miracle, note, notice, omen, placard, pointer, portent, presage, proof, reminder, representation, rune, signal, signature, signification, signpost, suggestion, symbol, symptom, token, trace, trademark, vestige, warning.

v autograph, beckon, endorse, gesticulate, gesture, indicate, initial, inscribe, motion, signal, subscribe, wave.

sign over consign, convey, deliver, entrust, make over, surrender, transfer, turn over.

sign up appoint, contract, employ, engage, enlist, enrol, hire, join, join up, recruit, register, sign on, take on, volunteer.

signal *n* alarm, alert, beacon, beck, cue, flare, flash, gesture, go-ahead, griffin, impulse, indication, indicator, light, mark, OK, password, rocket, sign, tip-off, token, transmitter, warning, watchword.

adj conspicuous, distinguished, eminent, exceptional, extraordinary, famous, glorious, impressive, memorable, momentous, notable, noteworthy, outstanding, remarkable, significant, striking.

v beckon, communicate, gesticulate, gesture, indicate, motion, nod, sign, telegraph, wave.

significance *n* consequence, consideration, force, implication, implications, import, importance, impressiveness, interest, matter, meaning, message, moment, point, purport, relevance, sense, solemnity, weight. *antonym* unimportance.

significant *adj* critical, denoting, eloquent, expressing, expressive, important, indicative, knowing, material, meaning, meaningful, momentous, noteworthy, ominous, pregnant, serious, solemn, suggestive, symbolic, symptomatic, vital, weighty. *antonyms* meaningless, unimportant.

significantly *adj* appreciably, considerably, critically, crucially, eloquently, knowingly, materially, meaningfully, meaningly, noticeably, perceptibly, suggestively, vitally.

signify *v* announce, augur, betoken, carry weight, communicate, connote, convey, count, denote, evidence, exhibit, express, imply, indicate, intimate, matter, mean, omen, portend, presage, proclaim,

represent, show, stand for, sugges symbolise, transmit.

silence *n* calm, dumbness, hush lull, muteness, noiselessness, peac quiescence, quiet, quietness, reserv reticence, secretiveness, speechlessnes stillness, taciturnity, uncommunicative ness.

v deaden, dumbfound, extinguish, ga muffle, muzzle, quell, quiet, quieter stifle, still, strike dumb, subdu suppress.

silent *adj* dumb, hushed, idle, implici inaudible, inoperative, mum, mute muted, noiseless, quiet, reticent, shtoon soundless, speechless, still, stilly, taci taciturn, tongue-tied, uncommunicative understood, unexpressed, unforth coming, unpronounced, unsounded unspeaking, unspoken, voiceless wordless. *antonyms* loud, noisy talkative.

silently *adv* dumbly, inaudibly mutely, noiselessly, quietly, soundlessly speechlessly, tacitly, unheard wordlessly.

silky *adj* fine, satiny, silken, sleek smooth, soft, velvety.

silly *adj* absurd, addled, asinine, bird brained, brainless, childish, cuckoo daft, dazed, dopey, drippy, fatuou feather-brained, flighty, foolhardy foolish, frivolous, gaga, giddy, groggy idiotic, illogical, immature, imprudent inane, inappropriate, inept, irrational irresponsible, meaningless, mindless muzzy, pointless, preposterous, puerile ridiculous, scatter-brained, senseless stunned, stupefied, stupid, unwise witless. *antonyms* collected, mature, sane, sensible, wise.

similar *adj* alike, analogous, close comparable, compatible, congruous, corresponding, homogenous, homologous related, resembling, uniform. *antonym* different.

similarity *n* affinity, agreement, analogy, closeness, coincidence, comparability, compatibility, concordance, congruence, correspondence, equivalence, homogeneity, likeness, relation, resemblance, sameness, similitude, uniformity. *antonym* difference.

similarly *adv* by analogy, by the same token, correspondingly, likewise, uniformly.

simmer *v* boil, burn, fizz, fume, rage, seethe, smart, smoulder.

simmer down calm down, collect

oneself, contain oneself, control oneself, cool down, cool off, recollect oneself, settle down, take it easy.

simple *adj* artless, bald, basic, brainless, childlike, classic, classical, clean, clear, credulous, dense, direct, dumb, easy, elementary, feeble, feeble-minded, foolish, frank, green, guileless, half-witted, homely, honest, humble, idiot-proof, inelaborate, ingenuous, innocent, inornate, intelligible, lowly, lucid, manageable, modest, moronic, naive, naïve, naked, natural, obtuse, plain, pure, rustic, shallow, silly, sincere, single, slow, Spartan, stark, straightforward, stupid, thick, unadorned, unaffected, unalloyed, unblended, uncluttered, uncombined, uncomplicated, undeniable, understandable, undisguised, undivided, unelaborate, unembellished, unfussy, uninvolved, unmixed, unornate, unpretentious, unskilled, unsophisticated, unsuspecting, unvarnished, user-friendly. *antonyms* artful, clever, complicated, difficult, fancy, intricate.

simple-minded *adj* addle-brained, artless, backward, brainless, cretinous, dim-witted, dopey, feeble-minded, foolish, goofy, idiot, idiotic, imbecile, moronic, natural, retarded, simple, stupid, unsophisticated. *antonyms* bright, clever.

simpleton *n* blockhead, daftie, dolt, dope, dullard, dunce, dupe, flathead, fool, goon, goose, idiot, imbecile, jackass, moron, nincompoop, ninny, numskull, soft-head, stupid, twerp. *antonym* brain.

simplicity *n* artlessness, baldness, candour, clarity, classicism, clearness, directness, ease, easiness, elementariness, guilelessness, innocence, intelligibility, modesty, naïvety, naturalness, obviousness, openness, plainness, purity, restraint, simpleness, sincerity, straightforwardness, uncomplicatedness. *antonyms* difficulty, guile, intricacy, sophistication.

simplify *v* abridge, decipher, disentangle, facilitate, prune, reduce, streamline. *antonyms* complicate, elaborate.

simplistic *adj* naïve, oversimplified, schematic, shallow, simple, superficial, sweeping, unanalytical. *antonyms* analytical, detailed.

simply *adv* absolutely, altogether, artlessly, baldly, clearly, completely, directly, easily, intelligibly, just, merely, modestly, naturally, obviously, only, plainly, purely, quite, really, sincerely, solely, straightforwardly, totally, unaffectedly, undeniably, unpretentiously, unquestionably, unreservedly, utterly, wholly.

simulate *v* act, affect, assume, counterfeit, duplicate, echo, fabricate, fake, feign, imitate, mimic, parrot, pretend, put on, reflect, reproduce, sham.

simulated *adj* artificial, assumed, bogus, fake, feigned, imitation, inauthentic, insincere, make-believe, man-made, mock, phoney, pinchbeck, pretended, pseudo, put-on, sham, spurious, substitute, synthetic, ungenuine. *antonyms* genuine, real.

simultaneous *adj* accompanying, coincident, coinciding, concomitant, concurrent, contemporaneous, parallel, synchronic. *antonym* separate.

sin *n* crime, damnation, debt, error, evil, fault, guilt, impiety, iniquity, lapse, misdeed, offence, sinfulness, transgression, trespass, ungodliness, unrighteousness, wickedness, wrong, wrongdoing.
v err, fall, fall from grace, go astray, lapse, misbehave, offend, stray, transgress, trespass.

sincere *adj* artless, bona fide, candid, deep-felt, earnest, frank, genuine, guileless, heartfelt, honest, natural, open, plain-hearted, plain-spoken, pure, real, serious, simple, simple-hearted, single-hearted, soulful, straightforward, true, true-hearted, truthful, unadulterated, unaffected, unfeigned, unmixed, wholehearted. *antonym* insincere.

sincerely *adv* earnestly, genuinely, honestly, in earnest, really, seriously, simply, truly, truthfully, unaffectedly, wholeheartedly.

sincerity *n* artlessness, bona fides, candour, earnestness, frankness, genuineness, good faith, guilelessness, honesty, plain-heartedness, probity, seriousness, straightforwardness, truth, truthfulness, wholeheartedness. *antonym* insincerity.

sinecure *n* cinch, cushy job, doddle, gravy train, money for jam, picnic, plum job, soft option.

sinewy *adj* athletic, brawny, muscular, powerful, robust, stringy, strong, sturdy, vigorous, wiry.

sinful *adj* bad, corrupt, criminal, depraved, erring, fallen, guilty, immoral, impious, iniquitous, irreligious, ungodly, unholy, unrighteous, unvirtuous, wicked, wrongful. *antonyms* righteous, sinless.

sing *v* betray, blow the whistle, carol, caterwaul, chant, chirp, croon, grass, hum, inform, intone, lilt, melodise, peach, pipe, purr, quaver, rat, render, serenade, spill the beans, squeal, talk, trill, vocalise, warble, whine, whistle, yodel.

sing out bawl, bellow, call, cooee, cry, halloo, holler, shout, yell.

single *adj* celibate, distinct, exclusive, free, individual, lone, man-to-man, one, one-to-one, only, particular, separate, simple, sincere, single-minded, singular, sole, solitary, unattached, unblended, unbroken, uncombined, uncompounded, undivided, unique, unmarried, unmixed, unshared, unwed, wholehearted.

single out choose, cull, distinguish, hand-pick, highlight, isolate, pick, pinpoint, select, separate, set apart.

single-handed *adj, adv* alone, independently, solo, unaccompanied, unaided, unassisted.

single-minded *adj* dedicated, determined, dogged, fixed, hell-bent, monomaniacal, resolute, steadfast, stubborn, tireless, undeviating, unswerving, unwavering.

singular *adj* atypical, conspicuous, curious, eccentric, eminent, exceptional, extraordinary, individual, noteworthy, odd, out-of-the-way, outstanding, peculiar, pre-eminent, private, prodigious, proper, puzzling, queer, rare, remarkable, separate, single, sole, strange, uncommon, unique, unparalleled, unusual. *antonyms* normal, usual.

singularity *n* abnormality, curiousness, eccentricity, extraordinariness, idiosyncrasy, irregularity, oddity, oddness, oneness, particularity, peculiarity, queerness, quirk, strangeness, twist, uniqueness. *antonym* normality.

singularly *adv* bizarrely, conspicuously, especially, exceptionally, extraordinarily, notably, outstandingly, particularly, prodigiously, remarkably, signally, surprisingly, uncommonly, unusually.

sinister *adj* dire, disquieting, evil, inauspicious, injurious, malevolent, malign, menacing, ominous, threatening, underhand, unlucky. *antonyms* harmless, innocent.

sink *v* abandon, abate, abolish, bore, collapse, conceal, decay, decline, decrease, defeat, degenerate, degrade,

descend, destroy, dig, diminish, di disappear, drill, drive, droop, dro drown, dwindle, ebb, engulf, excavat fade, fail, fall, finish, flag, founde invest, lapse, lay, lessen, lower, merg overwhelm, pay, penetrate, plumme plunge, relapse, retrogress, ruin, sa scupper, slip, slope, slump, stoo submerge, subside, succumb, suppres weaken, worsen. *antonyms* float, ris uplift.

sinless *adj* faultless, guiltles immaculate, impeccable, innocent, pur unblemished, uncorrupted, undefile unspotted, unsullied, virtuous. *antonym* sinful.

sinner *n* backslider, evi doer, malefactor, miscreant, offende reprobate, transgressor, trespasse wrong-doer.

sinuous *adj* coiling, crooked, curve curvy, lithe, meandering, serpentine slinky, supple, tortuous, undulating winding. *antonym* straight.

sissy *n* baby, coward, milksor mummy's boy, namby-pamby, pansy softy, weakling, wet.
adj cowardly, effeminate, feeble namby-pamby, pansy, sissified, sof unmanly, weak, wet.

sit *v* accommodate, assemble, befi brood, contain, convene, deliberate, hold meet, officiate, perch, pose, preside reside, rest, seat, settle.

site *n* ground, location, lot, place, plo position, setting, spot, station.
v dispose, install, locate, place, positior set, situate, station.

situation *n* ball-game, case circumstances, condition, employmen job, kettle of fish, lie of the land locale, locality, location, office, place plight, position, post, predicament, rank scenario, seat, setting, set-up, site sphere, spot, state, state of affairs, statior status.

sizable *adj* biggish, considerable decent, decent-sized, goodly, large largish, respectable, significant substantial, tidy. *antonym* small.

size *n* amount, amplitude, bulk dimensions, extent, greatness, height hugeness, immensity, largeness magnitude, mass, measurement(s) proportions, range, vastness, volume.

size up appraise, assess, evaluate gauge, measure.

sizzle *v* crackle, frizzle, fry, hiss, scorch sear, spit, sputter.

skedaddle v abscond, beat it, bolt, decamp, disappear, do a bunk, flee, hop it, run away, scarper, scoot, scram, split, vamoose.

skeletal adj cadaverous, drawn, emaciated, fleshless, gaunt, haggard, hollow-cheeked, shrunken, skin-and-bone, wasted.

skeleton n bare bones, draft, frame, framework, outline, sketch, structure.

sketch v block out, depict, draft, draw, outline, paint, pencil, plot, portray, represent, rough out.
n design, draft, drawing, outline, plan, scenario, skeleton.

sketchy adj bitty, crude, cursory, imperfect, inadequate, incomplete, insufficient, outline, perfunctory, rough, scrappy, skimpy, slight, superficial, unfinished, vague. **antonym** full.

skilful adj able, accomplished, adept, adroit, apt, canny, clever, competent, dexterous, experienced, expert, handy, masterly, nimble-fingered, practised, professional, proficient, quick, ready, skilled, tactical, trained. **antonyms** awkward, clumsy, inept.

skill n ability, accomplishment, adroitness, aptitude, art, cleverness, competence, dexterity, experience, expertise, expertness, facility, finesse, handiness, ingenuity, intelligence, knack, proficiency, quickness, readiness, savoir-faire, savvy, skilfulness, talent, technique, touch.

skilled adj able, accomplished, crack, experienced, expert, masterly, practised, professional, proficient, schooled, skilful, trained. **antonym** unskilled.

skim v brush, coast, cream, dart, despumate, float, fly, glide, plane, sail, scan, separate, skip, soar.

skimp v conserve, cut corners, economise, pinch, scamp, scant, scrimp, stint, withhold.

skimpy adj beggarly, exiguous, inadequate, insufficient, meagre, measly, miserly, niggardly, scanty, short, sketchy, sparse, thin, tight. **antonym** generous.

skin n casing, coating, crust, epidermis, film, hide, husk, integument, membrane, outside, peel, pelt, rind.
v abrade, bark, excoriate, flay, fleece, graze, peel, scrape, strip.

skin-deep adj artificial, empty, external, meaningless, outward, shallow, superficial, surface.

skinflint n cheese-parer, meanie, miser, niggard, penny-pincher, Scrooge, tightwad.

skinny adj attenuated, emaciated, lean, scragged, scraggy, skeletal, skin-and-bone, thin, twiggy, underfed, undernourished, weedy. **antonym** fat.

skip v bob, bounce, caper, cavort, cut, dance, eschew, flisk, flit, frisk, gambol, hop, miss, omit, play truant, prance, trip.

skirmish n affair, affray, battle, brush, clash, combat, conflict, contest, dust-up, encounter, engagement, fracas, incident, scrap, scrimmage, set-to, spat, tussle.
v clash, collide, scrap, tussle.

skirt v avoid, border, bypass, circle, circumambulate, circumnavigate, circumvent, detour, edge, evade, flank, steer clear of.

skittish adj coltish, excitable, fickle, fidgety, frivolous, highly-strung, jumpy, kittenish, lively, nervous, playful, restive.

skive v dodge, idle, malinger, shirk, skrimshank, skulk, slack, swing the lead.

skiver n do-nothing, idler, loafer, malingerer, scrimshanker, shirker, slacker.

skulk v creep, lie in wait, loiter, lurk, pad, prowl, pussyfoot, slink, sneak.

slack adj baggy, dull, easy, easy-going, flaccid, flexible, idle, inactive, inattentive, lax, lazy, limp, loose, neglectful, negligent, permissive, quiet, relaxed, remiss, slow, slow-moving, sluggish, tardy. **antonyms** busy, diligent, quick, rigid, stiff, taut.
n excess, give, inactivity, leeway, looseness, play, relaxation, room.
v dodge, idle, malinger, neglect, relax, shirk, skive, slacken.

slacken off abate, decrease, diminish, fail, flag, lessen, loosen, moderate, reduce, relax, release, slow, slow down, tire. **antonyms** increase, quicken, tighten.

slacker n clock-watcher, dawdler, do-nothing, good-for-nothing, idler, layabout, loafer, malingerer, passenger, shirk(er), skiver, skrimshanker.

slag v abuse, berate, criticise, deride, insult, lambaste, malign, mock, slam, slang, slate.

slake v abate, allay, assuage, deaden, extinguish, gratify, mitigate, moderate, moisten, quench, reduce, sate, satiate, satisfy, slacken, subside.

slam v attack, bang, castigate, clap, crash, criticise, damn, dash, excoriate, fling, hurl, lambaste, pan, pillory, slate, smash, swap, swop, throw, thump, vilify.

slander *n* aspersion, backbiting, calumniation, calumny, defamation, libel, misrepresentation, muck-raking, obloquy, scandal, smear.
v asperse, backbite, calumniate, decry, defame, disparage, libel, malign, muck-rake, scandalise, slur, smear, traduce, vilify. *antonyms* glorify, praise.

slanderous *adj* abusive, calumnious, damaging, defamatory, libellous, malicious.

slang *v* abuse, berate, castigate, excoriate, insult, lambaste, malign, revile, scold, slag, vilify, vituperate. *antonym* praise.

slanging match altercation, argument, argy-bargy, barney, dispute, quarrel, row, set-to, shouting match, spat.

slant *v* angle, bend, bevel, bias, cant, colour, distort, incline, lean, list, skew, slope, tilt, twist, warp, weight.
n angle, attitude, bias, camber, declination, diagonal, emphasis, gradient, incline, leaning, pitch, prejudice, rake, ramp, slope, tilt, viewpoint.

slanting *adj* angled, askew, aslant, asymmetrical, bent, canted, diagonal, inclined, oblique, sideways, skew-whiff, slanted, slantwise, sloping, tilted, tilting. *antonym* level.

slap *n* bang, blow, clap, clout, cuff, skelp, smack, spank, wallop, whack.
v bang, clap, clout, cuff, daub, hit, plaster, plonk, skelp, spank, spread, strike, whack.
adv bang, dead, directly, exactly, plumb, precisely, right, slap-bang, smack.

slap down berate, keelhaul, rebuke, reprimand, restrain, squash, upbraid.

slap in the face affront, blow, humiliation, indignity, insult, put-down, rebuff, rebuke, rejection, repulse, snub.

slap-dash *adj* careless, clumsy, disorderly, haphazard, hasty, hurried, last-minute, messy, negligent, offhand, perfunctory, rash, slipshod, sloppy, slovenly, thoughtless, thrown-together, untidy. *antonyms* careful, orderly.

slap-up *adj* elaborate, excellent, first-class, first-rate, lavish, luxurious, magnificent, princely, splendid, sumptuous, superb, superlative.

slash *v* criticise, cut, drop, gash, hack, lacerate, lower, reduce, rend, rip, score, slit.

n cut, gash, incision, laceration, rent, rip, slit.

slate *v* abuse, berate, blame, castigate, censure, criticise, lambaste, pan, rebuke, reprimand, roast, scold, slag, slam, slang. *antonym* praise.

slatternly *adj* bedraggled, dirty, dowdy, draggle-tailed, frowzy, frumpish, frumpy, slipshod, sloppy, slovenly, sluttish, unclean, unkempt, untidy.

slaughter *n* blood-bath, bloodshed, butchery, carnage, extermination, holocaust, killing, liquidation, massacre, murder, slaying.
v butcher, crush, defeat, destroy, exterminate, hammer, kill, liquidate, massacre, murder, overwhelm, rout, scupper, slay, thrash, trounce, vanquish.

slaver *v* dribble, drivel, drool, salivate, slobber.

slavish *adj* abject, base, conventional, cringing, despicable, fawning, grovelling, imitative, laborious, literal, low, mean, menial, obsequious, servile, strict, submissive, sycophantic, unimaginative, uninspired, unoriginal. *antonyms* independent, original.

slay *v* amuse, annihilate, assassinate, butcher, destroy, dispatch, eliminate, execute, exterminate, impress, kill, massacre, murder, rub out, slaughter, wow.

sleazy *adj* crummy, disreputable, low, run-down, seedy, sordid, squalid, tacky.

sleek *adj* glossy, insinuating, lustrous, plausible, shiny, smooth, smug, well-fed, well-groomed.

sleep *v* catnap, doss (down), doze, drop off, drowse, hibernate, nod off, repose, rest, slumber, snooze, snore.
n coma, dormancy, doss, doze, forty winks, hibernation, nap, repose, rest, shut-eye, siesta, slumber(s), snooze, sopor.

sleeping *adj* asleep, becalmed, daydreaming, dormant, hibernating, idle, inactive, inattentive, off guard, passive, slumbering, unaware. *antonyms* alert, awake.

sleepless *adj* alert, disturbed, insomniac, restless, unsleeping, vigilant, wakeful, watchful, wide-awake.

sleepy *adj* drowsy, dull, heavy, hypnotic, inactive, lethargic, quiet, slow, sluggish, slumb(e)rous, somnolent, soporific, torpid. *antonyms* alert, awake, restless, wakeful.

slender *adj* faint, feeble, flimsy, fragile, inadequate, inconsiderable, insufficient, lean, little, meagre, narrow, poor, remote, scanty, slight, slim, small, spare, svelte, sylph-like, tenuous, thin, thready, weak, willowy. **antonyms** considerable, fat, thick.

sleuth *n* bloodhound, detective, dick, gumshoe, private eye, private investigator, shadow, tail, tracker.

slice *n* cut, helping, piece, portion, rasher, section, segment, share, slab, sliver, tranche, wafer, wedge, whack.
v carve, chop, cut, divide, segment, sever, whittle.

slick *adj* adroit, deft, dexterous, glib, meretricious, plausible, polished, professional, sharp, skilful, sleek, smooth, specious, trim. **antonyms** amateurish, clumsy, coarse.

slide *v* coast, glide, lapse, skate, skim, slip, slither, veer.

slight *adj* delicate, feeble, flimsy, fragile, gracile, inconsiderable, insignificant, insubstantial, meagre, minor, modest, negligible, paltry, scanty, slender, slim, small, spare, superficial, trifling, trivial, unimportant, weak. **antonyms** considerable, large, major, significant.
v affront, cold-shoulder, cut, despise, disdain, disparage, disrespect, ignore, insult, neglect, scorn, snub. **antonyms** compliment, flatter.
n affront, contempt, discourtesy, disdain, disregard, disrespect, inattention, indifference, insult, neglect, rebuff, rudeness, slur, snub.

slighting *adj* abusive, belittling, defamatory, derogatory, disdainful, disparaging, disrespectful, insulting, offensive, scornful, slanderous, supercilious, uncomplimentary. **antonym** complimentary.

slim *adj* faint, lean, narrow, poor, remote, slender, slight, svelte, sylph-like, thin, trim. **antonyms** chubby, fat, strong.
v diet, lose weight, reduce, slenderise.

slimy *adj* clammy, creeping, disgusting, glutinous, grovelling, miry, mucous, muddy, obsequious, oily, oozy, servile, smarmy, soapy, sycophantic, toadying, unctuous, viscous.

sling *v* cast, catapult, chuck, dangle, fling, hang, heave, hurl, lob, pitch, shy, suspend, swing, throw, toss.
n band, bandage, catapult, loop, strap, support.

slink *v* creep, prowl, pussyfoot, sidle, skulk, slip, sneak, steal.

slinky *adj* clinging, close-fitting, feline, figure-hugging, lean, sinuous, skin-tight, sleek.

slip[1] *v* blunder, boob, conceal, creep, disappear, discharge, dislocate, elude, err, escape, fall, get away, glide, hide, lapse, loose, miscalculate, misjudge, mistake, skate, skid, slide, slink, slither, sneak, steal, trip.
n bloomer, blunder, boob, error, failure, fault, imprudence, indiscretion, mistake, omission, oversight, slip-up.

slip[2] *n* certificate, coupon, pass, piece, sliver, strip.

slippery *adj* crafty, cunning, devious, dishonest, duplicitous, evasive, false, foxy, glassy, greasy, icy, perilous, shifty, skiddy, slippy, smooth, sneaky, treacherous, tricky, two-faced, unpredictable, unreliable, unsafe, unstable, unsteady, untrustworthy.

slippy *adj* elusive, evasive, greasy, icy, smooth, uncertain, unstable.

slipshod *adj* careless, casual, loose, negligent, slap-dash, sloppy, slovenly, unsystematic, untidy. **antonyms** careful, fastidious, neat, tidy.

slit *v* cut, gash, knife, lance, pierce, rip, slash, slice, split.
n cut, fissure, gash, incision, opening, rent, split, tear, vent.
adj cut, rent, split, torn.

slither *v* glide, skitter, slide, slink, slip, snake, undulate.

sliver *n* chip, flake, fragment, paring, shaving, shiver, shred, slip, splinter.

slob *n* boor, brute, churl, lout, oaf, philistine, yob.

slobber *v* dribble, drivel, drool, salivate, slaver, splutter, water at the mouth.

slog *v* bash, belt, hit, labour, persevere, plod, plough through, slave, slosh, slug, smite, sock, strike, thump, toil, tramp, trek, trudge, wallop, work.
n effort, exertion, grind, hike, labour, struggle, tramp, trek, trudge.

slogan *n* battle-cry, catch-phrase, catchword, chant, jingle, motto, rallying-cry, war cry, watchword.

slop *v* overflow, slobber, slosh, spatter, spill, splash, splatter, wash away.

slope *v* delve, fall, incline, lean, pitch, rise, slant, tilt, verge, weather.
n brae, cant, declivity, descent, downgrade, gradient, inclination, incline, ramp, rise, scarp, slant, tilt.

sloping *adj* bevelled, canting, inclined, inclining, leaning, oblique, slanting. **antonym** level.

sloppy *adj* amateurish, banal, careless,

clumsy, gushing, hit-or-miss, inattentive, mawkish, messy, mushy, schmaltzy, sentimental, slipshod, slovenly, sludgy, slushy, soppy, splashy, trite, unkempt, untidy, watery, weak, wet. *antonyms* careful, exact, précise.

slosh v bash, biff, flounder, hit, pour, punch, shower, slap, slog, slop, slug, sock, splash, spray, strike, swipe, thump, thwack, wade, wallop.

slot n aperture, channel, gap, groove, hole, niche, opening, place, position, slit, space, time, vacancy.
v adjust, assign, fit, insert, pigeonhole, place, position.

slouch v droop, hunch, loll, shamble, shuffle, slump, stoop.

slow adj adagio, backward, behind, behindhand, boring, conservative, creeping, dawdling, dead, delayed, deliberate, dense, dilatory, dim, dull, dull-witted, dumb, easy, gradual, inactive, lackadaisical, laggard, lagging, late, lazy, leaden, leisurely, lingering, loitering, long-drawn-out, measured, obtuse, one-horse, plodding, ponderous, prolonged, protracted, quiet, retarded, slack, sleepy, slow-moving, slow-witted, sluggardly, sluggish, stagnant, stupid, tame, tardy, tedious, thick, time-consuming, uneventful, unhasty, unhurried, uninteresting, unproductive, unprogressive, unpunctual, unresponsive, wearisome. *antonyms* active, fast, quick, rapid, swift.
v brake, check, curb, decelerate, delay, detain, draw rein, handicap, hold up, lag, relax, restrict, retard.

slowly adv adagio, gradually, inchmeal, lazily, leisurely, ploddingly, ponderously, sluggishly, steadily, unhurriedly. *antonym* quickly.

sludge n dregs, gunge, gunk, mire, muck, mud, ooze, residue, sediment, silt, slag, slime, slop, slush, swill.

sluggish adj dull, heavy, inactive, indolent, inert, lethargic, lifeless, listless, slothful, slow, slow-moving, torpid, unresponsive. *antonyms* brisk, dynamic, eager, quick, vigorous.

sluice v cleanse, drain, drench, flush, irrigate, slosh, swill, wash.

slumber v doze, drowse, nap, repose, rest, sleep, snooze.

slummy adj decayed, dirty, overcrowded, ramshackle, run-down, seedy, sleazy, sordid, squalid, wretched.

slump v bend, collapse, crash, decline, deteriorate, droop, drop, fall, hunch, loll,

plummet, plunge, sag, sink, slip, slouch worsen.
n collapse, crash, decline, depreciation, depression, downturn, drop, failure, fall, falling-off, low, recession, reverse, stagnation, trough, worsening. *antonym* boom.

slur n affront, aspersion, blot, brand, calumny, discredit, disgrace, innuendo, insinuation, insult, reproach, slander, slight, smear, stain, stigma.

sly adj arch, artful, astute, canny, clever, conniving, covert, crafty, cunning, devious, foxy, furtive, guileful, impish, insidious, knowing, mischievous, peery, roguish, scheming, secret, secretive, shifty, sleeky, stealthy, subtle, surreptitious, underhand, vulpine, wily. *antonyms* frank, honest, open, straightforward.

smack v box, clap, cuff, hit, pat, skelp, slap, sock, spank, strike, tap, thwack, whack.
n blow, box, crack, cuff, hit, pat, skelp, slap, sock, spank, strike, tap, thwack, whack.
adv directly, exactly, plumb, point-blank, precisely, right, slap, slap-bang, squarely, straight.

small adj bantam, base, dilute, diminutive, dwarf(ish), grudging, humble, illiberal, immature, inadequate, incapacious, inconsiderable, insignificant, insufficient, itsy-bitsy, lesser, limited, little, meagre, mean, mini, miniature, minor, minuscule, minute, modest, narrow, negligible, paltry, petite, petty, pint-size(d), pocket, pocket-sized, puny, scanty, selfish, slight, small-scale, tichy, tiddl(e)y, tiny, trifling, trivial, undersized, unimportant, unpretentious, wee, young. *antonyms* big, huge, large.

small-minded adj bigoted, envious, grudging, hidebound, insular, intolerant, mean, narrow-minded, parochial, petty, rigid, ungenerous. *antonyms* broad-minded, liberal, tolerant.

small-time adj inconsequential, insignificant, minor, petty, piddling, unimportant. *antonyms* important, major.

smarmy adj bootlicking, crawling, fawning, fulsome, greasy, ingratiating, obsequious, oily, servile, smooth, soapy, suave, sycophantic, toadying, unctuous.

smart[1] adj acute, adept, agile, apt, astute, bright, brisk, canny, chic, clever, cracking, dandy, effective, elegant, fashionable, fine, impertinent, ingenious, intelligent, jaunty, keen, lively, modish, natty, neat, nimble, nimble-witted, pert, pointed, quick, quick-witted, rattling, ready, ready-witted, saucy, sharp, shrewd, smart-alecky, snappy, spanking, spirited, spruce, stylish, swagger, swish, trim, vigorous, vivacious, well-appointed, witty. **antonyms** dowdy, dumb, slow, stupid, unfashionable, untidy.

smart Alec(k) clever clogs, clever dick, know-all, smart-arse, smartypants, wise guy.

smart² v burn, hurt, nip, pain, sting, throb, tingle, twinge.
adj hard, keen, nipping, nippy, painful, piercing, resounding, sharp, stinging.
n nip, pain, pang, smarting, soreness, sting, twinge.

smarten v beautify, clean, groom, neaten, polish, primp, prink, spruce up, tidy.

smash v break, collide, crash, crush, defeat, demolish, destroy, disintegrate, lay waste, overthrow, prang, pulverise, ruin, shatter, shiver, wreck.
n accident, collapse, collision, crash, defeat, destruction, disaster, downfall, failure, pile-up, prang, ruin, shattering, smash-up.

smashing adj excellent, exhilarating, fab, fabulous, fantastic, first-class, first-rate, great, magnificent, marvellous, sensational, stupendous, super, superb, superlative, terrific, tremendous, wonderful.

smattering n basics, bit, dash, elements, modicum, rudiments, smatter, soupçon, sprinkling.

smear v bedaub, besmirch, blacken, blur, calumniate, coat, cover, dab, daub, dirty, drag (someone's) name through the mud, malign, patch, plaster, rub on, smudge, soil, spread over, stain, sully, tarnish, traduce, vilify.
n blot, blotch, calumny, daub, defamation, libel, mudslinging, slander, smudge, splodge, streak, vilification, whispering campaign.

smell n aroma, bouquet, fetor, fragrance, funk, malodour, nose, odour, perfume, pong, redolence, scent, sniff, stench, stink, whiff.
v be malodorous, hum, inhale, nose, pong, reek, scent, sniff, snuff, stink, stink to high heaven, whiff.

smelly adj bad, evil-smelling, fetid, foul, foul-smelling, frowsty, high, malodorous, off, pongy, putrid, reeking, stinking, strong, strong-smelling, whiffy.

smirk n grin, leer, sneer, snigger.

smitten adj afflicted, beguiled, beset, bewitched, bowled over, burdened, captivated, charmed, enamoured, infatuated, plagued, struck, troubled.

smoke n exhaust, film, fog, fume, gas, mist, reek, smog, vapour.
v cure, dry, fumigate, reek, smoulder.

smoky adj begrimed, black, grey, grimy, hazy, murky, reeky, sooty, thick.

smooth adj agreeable, bland, calm, classy, easy, effortless, elegant, equable, even, facile, fair-spoken, flat, flowing, fluent, flush, frictionless, glassy, glib, glossy, hairless, horizontal, ingratiating, level, mellow, mild, mirror-like, peaceful, persuasive, plain, plane, pleasant, polished, regular, rhythmic, serene, shiny, silken, silky, sleek, slick, slippery, smarmy, smug, soft, soothing, steady, suave, tranquil, unbroken, unctuous, undisturbed, uneventful, uniform, uninterrupted, unpuckered, unruffled, unrumpled, untroubled, unwrinkled, urbane, velvety, well-ordered. **antonyms** coarse, harsh, irregular, rough, unsteady.
v allay, alleviate, appease, assuage, calm, dub, ease, emery, extenuate, facilitate, flatten, iron, level, levigate, mitigate, mollify, palliate, plane, polish, press, slicken, soften, unknit, unwrinkle. **antonym** roughen.

smoothly adv calmly, easily, effortlessly, equably, evenly, fluently, ingratiatingly, mildly, peacefully, pleasantly, serenely, slickly, soothingly, steadily, suavely, tranquilly.

smooth-talking adj bland, facile, glib, persuasive, plausible, slick, smooth, suave.

smother v choke, cocoon, conceal, cover, envelop, extinguish, heap, hide, inundate, muffle, overlie, overwhelm, repress, shower, shroud, snuff, stifle, strangle, suffocate, suppress, surround.

smoulder v boil, burn, fester, fume, rage, seethe, simmer, smoke.

smudge v blacken, blur, daub, dirty, mark, smear, smirch, soil, spot, stain.
n blemish, blot, blur, smear, smut, spot, stain.

smug adj cocksure, complacent, conceited, holier-than-thou, priggish, self-opinionated, self-righteous, self-satisfied, superior, unctuous. **antonym** modest.

smutty *adj* bawdy, blue, coarse, crude, dirty, filthy, gross, improper, indecent, indelicate, lewd, obscene, off colour, pornographic, prurient, racy, raunchy, ribald, risqué, salacious, suggestive, vulgar. *antonyms* clean, decent.

snag *n* bug, catch, complication, difficulty, disadvantage, drawback, hitch, inconvenience, obstacle, problem, stick, stumbling block.
v catch, hole, ladder, rip, tear.

snap *v* bark, bite, break, catch, chop, click, crack, crackle, crepitate, flash, grip, growl, nip, pop, retort, seize, separate, snarl, snatch.
n bite, break, crack, crackle, energy, fillip, flick, get-up-and-go, go, liveliness, nip, pizazz, pop, vigour, zip.
adj abrupt, immediate, instant, offhand, on-the-spot, sudden, unexpected, unpremeditated.

snap up grab, grasp, nab, pick up, pluck, pounce on, seize, snatch.

snappy *adj* brusque, chic, crabbed, cross, dapper, edgy, fashionable, hasty, ill-natured, irritable, modish, natty, quick-tempered, smart, snappish, stylish, tart, testy, touchy, trendy, up-to-the-minute, waspish.

snare *v* catch, ensnare, entrap, net, seize, trap, wire.
n catch, gin, net, noose, pitfall, trap, wire.

snarl[1] *v* complain, gnarl, growl, grumble.

snarl[2] *v* complicate, confuse, embroil, enmesh, entangle, entwine, jam, knot, muddle, ravel, tangle.

snarl-up *n* confusion, entanglement, jumble, mess, mix-up, muddle, tangle, traffic jam.

snatch *v* clutch, gain, grab, grasp, grip, kidnap, nab, pluck, pull, ramp, rap, rescue, seize, spirit, take, win, wrench, wrest.
n bit, fraction, fragment, part, piece, section, segment, smattering, snippet, spell.

snazzy *adj* attractive, dashing, fashionable, flamboyant, flashy, jazzy, raffish, ritzy, showy, smart, snappy, sophisticated, sporty, stylish, swinging, with-it. *antonyms* drab, unfashionable.

sneak *v* cower, cringe, grass on, inform on, lurk, pad, peach, sidle, skulk, slink, slip, smuggle, spirit, steal, tell tales.
n informer, snake in the grass, sneaker, telltale.
adj clandestine, covert, furtive, quick, secret, stealthy, surprise, surreptitious.

sneaking *adj* contemptible, dim, furtive, half-formed, hidden, intuitive, mean, nagging, niggling, persistent, private, secret, sly, sneaky, suppressed, surreptitious, two-faced, uncomfortable, underhand, unexpressed, unvoiced, worrying.

sneaky *adj* base, contemptible, cowardly, deceitful, devious, dishonest, disingenuous, double-dealing, furtive, guileful, low, low-down, malicious, mean, nasty, shady, shifty, slippery, sly, snide, unethical, unreliable, unscrupulous, untrustworthy. *antonyms* honest, open.

sneer *v* deride, disdain, gibe, jeer, laugh, look down on, mock, ridicule, scoff, scorn, sniff at, snigger.
n derision, disdain, gibe, jeer, mockery, ridicule, scorn, smirk, snidery, snigger.

snide *adj* base, cynical, derogatory, dishonest, disparaging, hurtful, ill-natured, insinuating, malicious, mean, nasty, sarcastic, scornful, sneering, spiteful, unkind.

sniff *v* breathe, inhale, nose, smell, snuff, snuffle, vent.

sniffy *adj* condescending, contemptuous, disdainful, haughty, scoffing, sneering, supercilious, superior.

snigger *v, n* giggle, laugh, sneer, snicker, snort, titter.

snip *v* clip, crop, cut, nick, notch, prune, shave, slit, trim.
n bargain, bit, clipping, fragment, giveaway, piece, scrap, shred, slit, snippet.

snippet *n* fragment, part, particle, piece, portion, scrap, section, segment, shred, snatch.

snivelling *adj* blubbering, crying, girning, moaning, sniffling, snuffling, weeping, whimpering, whingeing, whining.

snobbery *n* airs, arrogance, condescension, loftiness, pretension, pride, side, snobbishness, snootiness, uppishness.

snobbish *adj* arrogant, condescending, high and mighty, high-hat, hoity-toity, lofty, lordly, patronising, pretentious, snooty, stuck-up, superior, toffee-nosed, uppish, uppity.

snoop *v* interfere, pry, sneak, spy.

snooper *n* busybody, meddler, nosy parker, prodnose, pry, snoop, spy.

snooze *v* catnap, doze, drowse, kip, nap, nod off, sleep.
n catnap, doze, forty winks, kip, nap, shut-eye, siesta, sleep.

snub *v* check, cold-shoulder, cut, humble, humiliate, mortify, rebuff, rebuke, shame, slight, sneap, wither.
n affront, brush-off, check, humiliation, insult, put-down, rebuff, rebuke, slap in the face, sneap.

snug *adj* close, close-fitting, comfortable, comfy, compact, cosy, homely, intimate, neat, sheltered, trim, warm.

snuggle *v* cuddle, embrace, hug, nestle, nuzzle.

so far hitherto, thus far, till now, to date.

soak *v* bathe, damp, drench, imbue, immerse, infuse, interfuse, marinate, moisten, penetrate, permeate, saturate, souse, steep, wet.

soaking *adj* drenched, dripping, drookit, saturated, soaked, sodden, sopping, streaming, waterlogged, wringing. *antonym* dry.

soar *v* ascend, climb, escalate, fly, mount, plane, rise, rocket, tower, wing. *antonym* plummet.

sob *v* bawl, blubber, boohoo, cry, greet, howl, moan, shed tears, snivel, weep.

sober *adj* abstemious, abstinent, calm, clear-headed, cold, composed, cool, dark, dispassionate, drab, grave, level-headed, lucid, moderate, peaceful, plain, practical, quiet, rational, realistic, reasonable, restrained, sedate, serene, serious, severe, solemn, sombre, sound, staid, steady, subdued, temperate, unexcited, unruffled. *antonyms* drunk, excited, frivolous, gay, intemperate, irrational.

sobriety *n* abstemiousness, abstinence, calmness, composure, continence, coolness, gravity, level-headedness, moderation, reasonableness, restraint, sedateness, self-restraint, seriousness, solemnity, staidness, steadiness, temperance. *antonyms* drunkenness, excitement, frivolity.

so-called *adj* alleged, nominal, ostensible, pretended, professed, self-styled, supposed.

sociable *adj* accessible, affable, approachable, chummy, companionable, convivial, cordial, familiar, friendly, genial, gregarious, neighbourly, outgoing, social, warm. *antonyms* unfriendly, unsociable, withdrawn.

social *adj* collective, common, communal, community, companionable, friendly, general, gregarious, group, neighbourly, organised, public, sociable, societal.

socialise *v* entertain, fraternise, get together, go out, hang out, mix, party.

society *n* association, brotherhood, camaraderie, circle, civilisation, club, companionship, company, corporation, culture, élite, fellowship, fraternity, friendship, gentry, group, guild, humanity, institute, league, mankind, organisation, people, population, sisterhood, the nobs, the public, the smart set, the swells, the toffs, the top drawer, the world, union, upper classes, upper crust.

sodden *adj* boggy, drenched, drookit, marshy, miry, saturated, soaked, soggy, sopping, waterlogged, wet. *antonym* dry.

soft *adj* balmy, bendable, bland, caressing, comfortable, compassionate, cottony, creamy, crumby, cushioned, cushiony, cushy, daft, delicate, diffuse, diffused, dim, dimmed, doughy, downy, ductile, dulcet, easy, easy-going, effeminate, elastic, faint, feathery, feeble-minded, flabby, flaccid, fleecy, flexible, flowing, fluid, foolish, furry, gelatinous, gentle, impressible, indulgent, kind, lash, lax, lenient, liberal, light, limp, low, malleable, mellifluous, mellow, melodious, mild, mouldable, murmured, muted, namby-pamby, non-alcoholic, overindulgent, pale, pampered, pastel, permissive, pitying, plastic, pleasant, pleasing, pliable, pulpy, quaggy, quiet, restful, sensitive, sentimental, shaded, silky, silly, simple, smooth, soothing, soppy, spineless, spongy, squashy, subdued, supple, swampy, sweet, sympathetic, temperate, tender, tender-hearted, undemanding, understated, unprotected, velvety, weak, whispered, yielding. *antonyms* hard, harsh, heavy, loud, rigid, rough, severe, strict.

soft spot fondness, liking, partiality, penchant, weakness.

soften *v* abate, allay, alleviate, appease, assuage, calm, cushion, digest, diminish, ease, emolliate, lessen, lighten, lower, macerate, melt, mitigate, moderate, modify, mollify, muffle, palliate, quell, relax, soothe, still, subdue, temper.

soften up conciliate, disarm, melt, persuade, soft-soap, weaken, win over.

soft-hearted *adj* benevolent, charitable, clement, compassionate, generous, indulgent, kind, merciful, sentimental, sympathetic, tender, tender-hearted, warm-hearted. *antonym* hard-hearted.

soggy *adj* boggy, dripping, heavy, moist, mushy, pulpy, saturated, soaked, sodden, sopping, soppy, spiritless, spongy, waterlogged.

soil[1] *n* clay, country, dirt, dust, earth, ground, humus, land, loam, region, terra firma.

soil[2] *v* bedraggle, besmirch, defile, dirty, foul, muddy, pollute, smear, spatter, spot, stain, sully, tarnish.

soiled *adj* dirty, grimy, manky, polluted, spotted, stained, sullied, tarnished. *antonyms* clean, immaculate.

solace *n* alleviation, assuagement, comfort, consolation, relief, succour, support.
v allay, alleviate, comfort, console, mitigate, soften, soothe, succour, support.

sole *adj* alone, exclusive, individual, one, only, single, singular, solitary, unique. *antonyms* multiple, shared.

solecism *n* absurdity, blunder, booboo, faux pas, gaffe, impropriety, incongruity, indecorum, lapse, mistake.

solely *adv* alone, completely, entirely, exclusively, merely, only, single-handedly, singly, uniquely.

solemn *adj* august, awed, awe-inspiring, ceremonial, ceremonious, devotional, dignified, earnest, formal, glum, grand, grave, hallowed, holy, imposing, impressive, majestic, momentous, pompous, portentous, religious, reverential, ritual, sacred, sanctified, sedate, serious, sober, sombre, staid, stately, thoughtful, venerable. *antonyms* frivolous, gay, light-hearted.

solemnity *n* dignity, earnestness, grandeur, gravity, impressiveness, momentousness, portentousness, sacredness, sanctity, seriousness, stateliness. *antonym* frivolity.

solicit *v* ask, beg, beseech, canvass, crave, entreat, implore, importune, petition, pray, seek, sue, supplicate, tout.

solicitous *adj* anxious, apprehensive, ardent, attentive, careful, caring, concerned, eager, earnest, fearful, troubled, uneasy, worried, zealous.

solid *adj* agreed, compact, complete, concrete, constant, continuous, cubic, decent, dense, dependable, estimable, firm, genuine, good, hard, law-abiding, level-headed, massed, pure, real, reliable, sensible, serious, sober, sound, square, stable, stocky, strong, sturdy, substantial, trusty, unalloyed, unanimous, unbroken, undivided, uninterrupted, united, unmixed, unshakeable, unvaried, upright, upstanding, wealthy, weighty, worthy. *antonyms* broken, insubstantial, liquid.

solidarity *n* accord, camaraderie, cohesion, concord(ance), consensus, esprit de corps, harmony, like-mindedness, soundness, stability, team spirit, unanimity, unification, unity. *antonyms* discord, division, schism.

solidify *v* cake, clot, coagulate, cohere, congeal, harden, jell, set. *antonyms* dissolve, liquefy, soften.

solitary *adj* alone, cloistered, companionless, desolate, friendless, hermitical, hidden, isolated, lone, lonely, lonesome, out-of-the-way, reclusive, remote, retired, secluded, separate, single, sole, unfrequented, unsociable, unsocial, untrodden, unvisited. *antonyms* accompanied, gregarious.

solitude *n* aloneness, emptiness, isolation, loneliness, privacy, reclusiveness, retirement, seclusion, waste, wasteland, wilderness. *antonym* companionship.

solution *n* answer, blend, clarification, compound, decipherment, dénouement, disconnection, dissolution, elucidation, emulsion, explanation, explication, key, liquefaction, melting, mix, mixture, resolution, result, solvent, solving, suspension, unfolding, unravelling.

solve *v* answer, clarify, crack, decipher, disentangle, dissolve, elucidate, explain, expound, interpret, resolve, settle, unbind, unfold, unravel, work out.

sombre *adj* dark, dim, dismal, doleful, drab, dull, dusky, funereal, gloomy, grave, joyless, lugubrious, melancholy, mournful, obscure, sad, sepulchral, shadowy, shady, sober, sombrous. *antonyms* bright, cheerful, happy.

somebody *n* big noise, big shot, big wheel, bigwig, celebrity, dignitary, heavyweight, household name, luminary, magnate, mogul, name, notable, personage, star, superstar, VIP. *antonym* nobody.

somehow *adv* by fair means or foul, by hook or by crook, come hell or high water, come what may, one way or another.

sometimes *adv* at times, from time to time, now and again, now and then, occasionally, off and on, once in a while, otherwhiles. *antonyms* always, never.

somnolent *adj* comatose, dozy, drowsy, half-awake, heavy-eyed, sleepy, soporific, torpid.

song *n* air, anthem, ballad, canticle, canto, carol, chant, chorus, ditty, elegy, folk-song, hymn, lullaby, lyric, madrigal, melody, number, ode, poem, psalm, shanty, strain, tune, wassail.

song and dance ado, commotion, flap, furore, fuss, hoo-ha, kerfuffle, performance, shindy, squall, stir, tizzy, to-do, tumult.

sonorous *adj* full, full-mouthed, full-throated, full-voiced, grandiloquent, high-flown, high-sounding, loud, plangent, resonant, resounding, rich, ringing, rounded, sounding.

soon *adv* anon, betimes, in a minute, in a short time, in the near future, presently, shortly.

soothe *v* allay, alleviate, appease, assuage, calm, coax, comfort, compose, ease, hush, lull, mitigate, mollify, pacify, quiet, relieve, salve, settle, soften, still, tranquillise. **antonyms** annoy, irritate, vex.

soothing *adj* assuasive, balmy, balsamic, calming, demulcent, emollient, lenitive, palliative, relaxing, restful. **antonyms** annoying, irritating, vexing.

sophisticated *adj* advanced, citified, complex, complicated, cosmopolitan, couth, cultivated, cultured, delicate, elaborate, highly-developed, intricate, jet-set, mondain, multifaceted, refined, seasoned, subtle, urbane, worldly, worldly-wise, world-weary. **antonyms** artless, naïve, simple, unsophisticated.

sophistication *n* culture, elegance, experience, finesse, poise, savoir-faire, savoir-vivre, urbanity, worldliness. **antonyms** naïvety, simplicity.

soppy *adj* cloying, corny, daft, drippy, gushy, lovey-dovey, mawkish, mushy, pathetic, schmaltzy, sentimental, silly, slushy, soft, weepy.

sorcery *n* black art, black magic, diablerie, divination, enchantment, hoodoo, incantation, magic, necromancy, spell, voodoo, witchcraft, wizardry.

sordid *adj* avaricious, base, corrupt, covetous, debauched, degenerate, degraded, despicable, dingy, dirty, disreputable, filthy, foul, grasping, low, mean, mercenary, miserly, niggardly, rapacious, seamy, seedy, selfish, self-seeking, shabby, shameful, sleazy, slovenly, slummy, squalid, tawdry, unclean, ungenerous, venal, vicious, vile, wretched.

sore *adj* acute, afflicted, aggrieved, angry, annoyed, annoying, burning, chafed, critical, desperate, dire, distressing, extreme, grieved, grievous, harrowing, hurt, inflamed, irked, irritable, irritated, pained, painful, peeved, pressing, raw, reddened, resentful, sensitive, severe, sharp, smarting, stung, tender, touchy, troublesome, upset, urgent, vexed.
n abscess, boil, canker, carbuncle, chafe, inflammation, swelling, ulcer, wound.

sorrow *n* affliction, anguish, blow, distress, dole, grief, hardship, heartache, heartbreak, lamentation, misery, misfortune, mourning, regret, sadness, trial, tribulation, trouble, unhappiness, woe, worry. **antonyms** happiness, joy.
v agonise, bemoan, bewail, grieve, lament, moan, mourn, pine, weep. **antonym** rejoice.

sorrowful *adj* affecting, afflicted, dejected, depressed, disconsolate, distressing, doleful, grievous, heart-broken, heart-rending, heavy-hearted, lamentable, lugubrious, melancholy, miserable, mournful, painful, piteous, rueful, sad, sorry, tearful, unhappy, woebegone, woeful, wretched. **antonyms** happy, joyful.

sorry *adj* abject, apologetic, base, commiserative, compassionate, conscience-stricken, contrite, deplorable, disconsolate, dismal, distressed, distressing, grieved, guilt-ridden, mean, melancholy, miserable, mournful, moved, paltry, pathetic, penitent, piteous, pitiable, pitiful, pitying, poor, regretful, remorseful, repentant, sad, self-reproachful, shabby, shamefaced, sorrowful, sympathetic, unhappy, unworthy, vile, wretched. **antonym** glad.

sort *n* brand, breed, category, character, class, denomination, description, family, genre, genus, group, ilk, kidney, kind, make, nature, order, quality, race, species, stamp, style, type, variety.
v arrange, assort, catalogue, categorise, choose, class, classify, distribute, divide, file, grade, group, neaten, order, rank, screen, select, separate, systematise, tidy.

sort out clarify, clear up, divide, organise, resolve, segregate, select, separate, sift, tidy up.

so-so *adj* adequate, average, fair, fair to middling, indifferent, middling, moderate, neutral, not bad, OK, ordinary, passable, respectable, run-of-the-mill, tolerable, undistinguished, unexceptional.

soul *n* alma, animation, ardour, being, body, courage, creature, element, embodiment, energy, essence, feeling, fervour, force, incarnation, individual, inner man, inspiration, inspirer, intellect, leader, life, man, mind, mortal, nobility, person, personification, psyche, quintessence, reason, spirit, type, vital force, vitality, vivacity, woman.

soulful *adj* eloquent, emotional, expressive, heartfelt, meaningful, mournful, moving, profound, sensitive.

soulless *adj* callous, cold, cruel, dead, ignoble, inhuman, lifeless, mean, mean-spirited, mechanical, soul-destroying, spiritless, unfeeling, uninteresting, unkind, unsympathetic.

sound[1] *n* description, din, earshot, hearing, idea, implication, impression, look, noise, range, report, resonance, reverberation, tenor, tone, utterance, voice.

v announce, appear, articulate, chime, declare, echo, enunciate, express, knell, look, peal, pronounce, resonate, resound, reverberate, ring, seem, signal, toll, utter, voice.

sound[2] *adj* complete, copper-bottomed, correct, deep, entire, established, fair, firm, fit, hale, healthy, hearty, intact, just, level-headed, logical, orthodox, peaceful, perfect, proper, proven, prudent, rational, reasonable, recognised, reliable, reputable, responsible, right, right-thinking, robust, safe, secure, sensible, solid, solvent, stable, sturdy, substantial, thorough, tried-and-true, true, trustworthy, unbroken, undamaged, undisturbed, unhurt, unimpaired, uninjured, untroubled, valid, vigorous, wakeless, well-founded, well-grounded, whole, wise. **antonyms** shaky, unfit, unreliable, unsound.

sound[3] *v* examine, fathom, inspect, investigate, measure, plumb, probe, test.

sound out ask, canvass, examine, probe, pump, question.

sour *adj* acerbic, acetic, acid, acrid, acrimonious, bad, bitter, churlish, crabbed, curdled, cynical, disagreeable, discontented, embittered, fermented, grouchy, grudging, ill-natured, ill-tempered, inharmonious, jaundiced, off, peevish, pungent, rancid, rank, sharp, tart, turned, ungenerous, unpleasant, unsavoury, unsuccessful, unsweet, unwholesome, vinegarish, vinegary, waspish. **antonyms** good-natured, sweet.

v alienate, curdle, disenchant, embitter, envenom, exacerbate, exasperate, spoil.

source *n* author, authority, begetter, beginning, cause, commencement, derivation, fountain-head, informant, mine, origin, originator, quarry, rise, spring, water-head, well-head.

souse *v* douse, drench, dunk, immerse, marinate, pickle, plunge, soak, steep.

souvenir *n* gift, keepsake, memento, memory, relic, reminder, token.

sovereign *n* autarch, chief, dynast, emperor, empress, king, monarch, potentate, prince, queen, ruler.

adj absolute, august, chief, dominant, effectual, efficacious, efficient, excellent, imperial, kingly, majestic, monarch(ic)al, paramount, predominant, principal, queenly, regal, royal, ruling, supreme, unlimited.

sow *v* broadcast, disseminate, implant, inseminate, lodge, plant, scatter, seed, spread, strew.

space *n* accommodation, amplitude, berth, blank, capacity, chasm, distance, duration, elbow-room, expanse, extension, extent, gap, house-room, interval, lacuna, leeway, margin, omission, period, place, play, room, scope, seat, spaciousness, span, time, volume.

spacious *adj* ample, big, broad, capacious, comfortable, commodious, expansive, extensive, huge, large, roomy, sizable, uncrowded, vast, wide. **antonyms** confined, cramped, narrow, small.

spadework *n* donkey-work, drudgery, foundation, groundwork, labour, preparation.

span *n* amount, compass, distance, duration, extent, length, period, reach, scope, spell, spread, stretch, term.

v arch, bridge, cover, cross, encompass, extend, link, overarch, traverse, vault.

spank *v* belt, cane, cuff, leather, slap, slipper, smack, tan, wallop, whack.

spanking *adj* brand-new, brisk, energetic, fast, fine, gleaming, invigorating, lively, quick, smart, snappy, speedy, swift, vigorous. **antonym** slow.

spare *adj* additional, economical, emergency, extra, free, frugal, gaunt, lank, lean, leftover, meagre, modest, odd, over, remaining, scanty, slender, slight, slim, sparing, superfluous, supernumerary, surplus, unoccupied, unused, unwanted, wiry. **antonyms** corpulent, necessary, profuse.

v afford, allow, bestow, give quarter, grant, leave, let off, pardon, part with, refrain from, release, relinquish.

sparing *adj* careful, chary, cost-conscious, economical, frugal, prudent, saving, thrifty. **antonyms** lavish, liberal, unsparing.

spark *n* atom, flake, flare, flash, flicker, gleam, glint, hint, jot, scintilla, scrap, spit, trace, vestige.

v animate, cause, excite, inspire, kindle, occasion, precipitate, provoke, set off, start, stimulate, stir, trigger.

sparkle *v* beam, bubble, coruscate, dance, effervesce, fizz, fizzle, flash, gleam, glint, glisten, glister, glitter, glow, scintillate, shimmer, shine, spark, twinkle, wink.

n animation, brilliance, coruscation, dash, dazzle, effervescence, élan, emication, flash, flicker, gaiety, gleam, glint, glitter, life, panache, pizzazz, radiance, scintillation, spark, spirit, twinkle, vim, vitality, vivacity, wit, zip.

sparkling *adj* animated, bubbly, carbonated, coruscating, effervescent, fizzy, flashing, gleaming, glistening, glittering, scintillating, twinkling, witty. **antonyms** dull, flat.

sparse *adj* infrequent, meagre, scanty, scarce, scattered, sporadic. **antonyms** dense, lush, thick.

spartan *adj* abstemious, abstinent, ascetic, austere, bleak, disciplined, extreme, frugal, hardy, joyless, plain, rigorous, self-denying, severe, stern, strict, stringent, temperate, unflinching.

spasm *n* access, burst, contraction, convulsion, eruption, fit, frenzy, jerk, outburst, paroxysm, seizure, throe, twitch.

spasmodic *adj* convulsive, erratic, fitful, intermittent, irregular, jerky, occasional, sporadic. **antonyms** continuous, uninterrupted.

spate *n* deluge, epidemic, flood, flow, outpouring, rush, torrent.

spatter *v* daub, dirty, scatter, soil, speckle, splash, splodge, spray, sprinkle.

speak *v* address, allude to, argue, articulate, breathe, comment on, communicate, converse, deal with, declaim, declare, discourse, discuss, enunciate, express, harangue, lecture, mention, plead, pronounce, refer to, say, speechify, spiel, state, talk, tell, utter, voice.

speak to accost, address, admonish, bring to book, dress down, lecture, rebuke, reprimand, scold, tell off, tick off, upbraid, warn.

special *adj* appropriate, certain, characteristic, chief, choice, detailed, distinctive, distinguished, especial, exceptional, exclusive, extraordinary, festive, gala, important, individual, intimate, main, major, memorable, momentous, particular, peculiar, precise, primary, red-letter, select, significant, specialised, specific, uncommon, unique, unusual. **antonyms** common, normal, ordinary, usual.

specialist *n* adept, authority, connoisseur, consultant, expert, master, professional.

species *n* breed, category, class, collection, denomination, description, genus, group, kind, sort, type, variety.

specific *adj* characteristic, clear-cut, definite, distinguishing, especial, exact, explicit, express, limited, particular, peculiar, precise, special, unambiguous, unequivocal. **antonyms** general, vague.

specify *v* cite, define, describe, designate, detail, enumerate, indicate, individualise, itemise, list, mention, name, particularise, spell out, stipulate.

specimen *n* copy, embodiment, example, exemplar, exemplification, exhibit, illustration, individual, instance, model, paradigm, pattern, person, proof, representative, sample, type.

specious *adj* deceptive, fallacious, false, misleading, plausible, unsound, untrue. **antonym** valid.

speck *n* atom, bit, blemish, blot, defect, dot, fault, flaw, fleck, grain, iota, jot, macula, mark, mite, modicum, mote, particle, shred, speckle, spot, stain, trace, whit.

speckled *adj* brindled, dappled, dotted, flecked, fleckered, freckled, mottled, spotted, spotty, sprinkled, stippled.

spectacle *n* curiosity, display, event, exhibition, extravaganza, marvel, pageant, parade, performance, phenomenon, scene, show, sight, wonder.

spectacular *adj* amazing, breathtaking, daring, dazzling, dramatic, eye-catching, fabulous, fantastic, grand, impressive, magnificent, marked, remarkable, sensational, splendid, staggering, striking, stunning. **antonyms** ordinary, unspectacular.

n display, extravaganza, pageant, show, spectacle.

spectre *n* apparition, ghost, phantom, presence, shade, shadow, spirit, vision, wraith.

speculate *v* conjecture, consider, contemplate, deliberate, gamble, guess, hazard, hypothesise, meditate, muse, reflect, risk, scheme, suppose, surmise, theorise, venture, wonder.

speculation *n* conjecture, consideration, contemplation, deliberation, flight of fancy, gamble, gambling, guess, guesswork, hazard, hypothesis, ideology, opinion, risk, supposition, surmise, theory.

speculative *adj* abstract, academic, chancy, conjectural, dicey, hazardous, hypothetical, iffy, notional, projected, risky, suppositional, tentative, theoretical, uncertain, unpredictable.

speech *n* address, articulation, colloquy, communication, conversation, dialect, dialogue, diction, discourse, discussion, disquisition, enunciation, harangue, homily, idiom, intercourse, jargon, language, lecture, lingo, oration, parlance, parole, spiel, talk, tongue, utterance, voice.

speechless *adj* aghast, amazed, astounded, dazed, dumb, dumbfounded, dumbstruck, inarticulate, mum, mute, shocked, silent, thunderstruck, tongue-tied, wordless.

speed *n* acceleration, celerity, dispatch, expedition, fleetness, haste, hurry, lick, momentum, pace, precipitation, quickness, rapidity, rush, swiftness, tempo, velocity.
v advance, aid, assist, belt, bomb, boost, bowl along, career, dispatch, expedite, facilitate, flash, fleet, further, gallop, hasten, help, hurry, impel, lick, press on, promote, put one's foot down, quicken, race, rush, sprint, step on it, step on the gas, step on the juice, tear, urge, vroom, zap, zoom. **antonyms** delay, hamper, restrain, slow.

speedily *adv* fast, hastily, hurriedly, posthaste, promptly, quickly, rapidly, swiftly. **antonym** slowly.

speedy *adj* clipping, expeditious, express, fast, fleet, hasty, headlong, hurried, immediate, nimble, precipitate, prompt, quick, rapid, summary, swift, winged. **antonyms** dilatory, slow, tardy.

spell¹ *n* bout, course, innings, interval, patch, period, season, stint, stretch, term, time, turn.

spell² *n* allure, charm, enchantment, exorcism, fascination, glamour, hex, incantation, magic, rune, sorcery, trance.

spell³ *v* augur, herald, imply, indicate, mean, portend, presage, promise, signal, signify, suggest.
spell out clarify, elucidate, emphasise, explain, specify.

spellbound *adj* bemused, bewitched, captivated, charmed, enchanted, enthralled, entranced, fascinated, gripped, hooked, mesmerised, possessed, rapt, transfixed, transported.

spend *v* apply, bestow, blow, blue, concentrate, consume, cough up, deplete, devote, disburse, dispense, dissipate, drain, employ, empty, exhaust, expend, fill, fork out, fritter, invest, lavish, lay out, occupy, pass, pay out, shed, shell out, splash out, squander, use, use up, waste. **antonyms** hoard, save.

spendthrift *n* big spender, prodigal, profligate, spender, squanderer, waster, wastrel. **antonyms** hoarder, miser, saver.
adj extravagant, improvident, prodigal, profligate, thriftless, wasteful.

spent *adj* all in, burnt out, bushed, consumed, dead beat, debilitated, dog-tired, done in, drained, exhausted, expended, fagged (out), finished, gone, jiggered, knackered, played out, prostrate, shattered, tired out, used up, weakened, wearied, weary, whacked, worn out, zonked.

spew *v* belch, disgorge, puke, regurgitate, retch, spit out, throw up, vomit.

sphere *n* ball, capacity, circle, compass, department, domain, employment, field, function, globe, globule, milieu, orb, province, range, rank, realm, scope, station, stratum, territory.

spice *n* colour, excitement, flavouring, gusto, kick, life, pep, piquancy, relish, savour, seasoning, tang, zap, zest, zip.

spicy *adj* aromatic, flavoursome, fragrant, hot, improper, indecorous, indelicate, off-colour, piquant, pointed, pungent, racy, ribald, risqué, savoury, scandalous, seasoned, sensational, showy, suggestive, tangy, titillating, unseemly. **antonym** bland.

spike *n* barb, nail, point, prong, spine, spire.
v block, foil, frustrate, impale, reject, spear, spit, stick, thwart.

spill *v* discharge, disgorge, overflow, overturn, scatter, shed, slop, slosh, upset.

n accident, cropper, fall, overturn, tumble, upset.

spill the beans blab, blow the gaff, give the game away, grass, inform, let the cat out of the bag, rat, split, squeal, tattle.

spin *v* birl, concoct, develop, gyrate, hurtle, invent, narrate, pirouette, reel, relate, revolve, rotate, swim, swirl, tell, turn, twirl, twist, unfold, wheel, whirl.

n agitation, commotion, drive, flap, gyration, hurl, panic, pirouette, revolution, ride, roll, run, state, tizzy, turn, twist, whirl.

spin out amplify, delay, extend, lengthen, maintain, pad out, prolong, prolongate, protract, sustain.

spindly *adj* attenuated, gangling, gangly, lanky, leggy, skeletal, skinny, spidery, thin, twiggy, weedy. **antonyms** stocky, thickset.

spine-chilling *adj* bloodcurdling, eerie, frightening, hair-raising, horrifying, scary, spine-tingling, spooky, terrifying.

spineless *adj* cowardly, faint-hearted, feeble, gutless, inadequate, ineffective, irresolute, lily-livered, soft, spiritless, squeamish, submissive, vacillating, weak, weak-kneed, weak-willed, wet, wishy-washy, yellow. **antonyms** brave, strong.

spirit *n* air, animation, apparition, ardour, atmosphere, attitude, backbone, bravura, breath, brio, character, complexion, courage, dauntlessness, disposition, earnestness, energy, enterprise, enthusiasm, entrain, essence, familiar, feeling, feelings, fire, force, genius, ghost, ghoul, gist, grit, guts, humour, intent, intention, life, liveliness, meaning, mettle, mood, morale, motivation, outlook, phantom, psyche, purport, purpose, quality, resolution, resolve, revenant, sense, shade, shadow, soul, sparkle, spectre, spook, sprite, spunk, stout-heartedness, substance, temper, temperament, tenor, tone, verve, vigour, vision, vivacity, warmth, will, willpower, zest.

v abduct, abstract, capture, carry, convey, kidnap, purloin, remove, seize, snaffle, steal, whisk.

spirited *adj* active, animated, ardent, bold, courageous, energetic, game, high-spirited, lively, mettlesome, plucky, sparkling, sprightly, spunky, stomachful, vigorous, vivacious. **antonyms** lazy, spiritless, timid.

spiritless *adj* anaemic, apathetic, dejected, depressed, despondent, dispirited, droopy, dull, lacklustre, languid, lifeless, listless, low, melancholic, melancholy, mopy, torpid, unenthusiastic, unmoved, wishy-washy. **antonym** spirited.

spiritual *adj* devotional, divine, ecclesiastical, ethereal, ghostly, holy, immaterial, incorporeal, otherwordly, pure, religious, sacred, unworldly. **antonyms** material, physical.

spit *v* discharge, drizzle, eject, expectorate, hawk, hiss, spew, splutter, sputter.

n dribble, drool, expectoration, phlegm, saliva, slaver, spittle, sputum.

spite *n* animosity, bitchiness, gall, grudge, hate, hatred, ill-nature, malevolence, malice, pique, rancour, spitefulness, spleen, venom, viciousness. **antonyms** affection, goodwill.

v annoy, discomfit, gall, harm, hurt, injure, irk, irritate, needle, nettle, offend, peeve, pique, provoke, put out, vex.

spiteful *adj* barbed, bitchy, catty, cruel, ill-disposed, ill-natured, malevolent, malicious, nasty, rancorous, snide, splenetic, vengeful, venomous, vindictive, waspish. **antonyms** affectionate, charitable.

spitting image clone, dead ringer, double, likeness, lookalike, picture, replica, ringer, spit, twin.

splash *v* bathe, batter, bespatter, blazon, break, broadcast, buffet, dabble, dash, flaunt, headline, paddle, plash, plaster, plop, plunge, publicise, shower, slop, slosh, smack, spatter, splodge, spray, spread, sprinkle, squirt, strew, strike, surge, tout, trumpet, wade, wallow, wash, wet.

n burst, dash, display, effect, excitement, impact, ostentation, patch, publicity, sensation, spattering, splatter, splodge, splurge, stir, touch.

splash out invest in, lash out, push the boat out, spend, splurge.

spleen *n* acrimony, anger, animosity, animus, bad temper, bile, biliousness, bitterness, gall, hatred, hostility, ill-humour, ill-will, malevolence, malice, peevishness, petulance, pique, rancour, resentment, spite, spitefulness, venom, vindictiveness, wrath.

splendid *adj* admirable, beaming, bright, brilliant, costly, dazzling, excellent, exceptional, fantastic, fine, first-class, glittering, glorious, glowing, gorgeous, grand, great, heroic, illustrious, imposing, impressive, lavish, lustrous, luxurious, magnificent, marvellous, ornate, outstanding, radiant, rare, refulgent, remarkable, renowned, resplendent, rich, splendiferous, splend(o)rous, sterling, sublime, sumptuous, superb, supreme, tiptop, top-notch, topping, wonderful. *antonyms* drab, ordinary, run-of-the-mill.

splendour *n* brightness, brilliance, ceremony, dazzle, display, effulgence, glory, gorgeousness, grandeur, lustre, magnificence, majesty, pomp, radiance, refulgence, renown, resplendence, richness, show, solemnity, spectacle, stateliness, sumptuousness.

splenetic *adj* acid, bitchy, churlish, crabbed, crabby, cross, envenomed, fretful, irascible, irritable, morose, peevish, petulant, rancorous, sour, spiteful, sullen, testy, touchy.

splice *v* bind, braid, entwine, graft, interlace, interlink, intertwine, intertwist, interweave, join, knit, marry, mesh, plait, tie, unite, wed, yoke.

splinter *n* chip, flake, flinder, fragment, needle, paring, shaving, sliver.
  v disintegrate, fracture, fragment, shatter, smash, split.

split *v* allocate, allot, apportion, betray, bifurcate, branch, break, burst, cleave, crack, delaminate, disband, distribute, disunite, divaricate, diverge, divide, divulge, fork, gape, grass, halve, inform on, open, parcel out, part, partition, peach, rend, rip, separate, share out, skive, slash, slice up, slit, sliver, snap, splinter, squeal.
  n breach, break, break-up, cleft, crack, damage, dichotomy, difference, discord, disruption, dissension, disunion, divergence, division, estrangement, fissure, gap, partition, race, rent, rift, rip, rupture, schism, scissure, separation, slash, slit, tear.
  adj ambivalent, bisected, broken, cleft, cloven, cracked, divided, dual, fractured, ruptured, twofold.

split up break up, disband, dissolve, divorce, part, part company, separate.

spoil *v* addle, baby, blemish, bugger, butcher, coddle, cosset, curdle, damage, debase, decay, decompose, deface, despoil, destroy, deteriorate, disfigure, go bad, go off, harm, impair, indulge, injure, louse up, mar, mildew, mollycoddle, pamper, plunder, putrefy, queer, rot, ruin, screw, spoon-feed, turn, upset, wreck.

spoil-sport *n* damper, dog in the

manger, killjoy, misery, party-pooper, wet blanket.

spoken *adj* declared, expressed, oral, phonetic, said, stated, told, unwritten, uttered, verbal, viva voce, voiced. *antonyms* unspoken, written.

sponge *v* cadge, freeload, scrounge.

sponger *n* bloodsucker, cadge, cadger, freeloader, hanger-on, leech, parasite, scrounger.

sponsor *v* back, finance, fund, guarantee, promote, subsidise, underwrite.

spontaneous *adj* extempore, free, impromptu, impulsive, instinctive, natural, unbidden, uncompelled, unconstrained, unforced, unhesitating, unlaboured, unpremeditated, unprompted, unstudied, untaught, voluntary, willing. *antonyms* forced, planned, studied.

spontaneously *adv* extempore, freely, impromptu, impulsively, instinctively, of one's own accord, off the cuff, on impulse, unprompted, voluntarily, willingly.

spoof *n* bluff, burlesque, caricature, con, deception, fake, game, hoax, joke, lampoon, leg-pull, mockery, parody, prank, satire, send-up, take-off, travesty, trick.

spooky *adj* chilling, creepy, eerie, frightening, ghostly, hair-raising, mysterious, scary, spine-chilling, supernatural, uncanny, unearthly, weird.

sporadic *adj* erratic, infrequent, intermittent, irregular, isolated, occasional, random, scattered, spasmodic, uneven. *antonyms* frequent, regular.

sport *n* activity, amusement, banter, brick, buffoon, dalliance, derision, diversion, entertainment, exercise, fair game, frolic, fun, game, jest, joking, kidding, laughing-stock, merriment, mirth, mockery, pastime, play, plaything, raillery, recreation, ridicule, sportsman, teasing.
  v caper, dally, display, disport, exhibit, flirt, frolic, gambol, philander, play, romp, show off, toy, trifle, wear.

sportive *adj* coltish, frisky, frolicsome, gay, jaunty, joyous, kittenish, lively, merry, playful, rollicking, skittish, sprightly.

sporty *adj* athletic, casual, energetic, flamboyant, flashy, gay, hearty, informal, jaunty, jazzy, loud, natty, outdoor, raffish, rakish, showy, snazzy, stylish, trendy.

spot *n* bit, blemish, blot, blotch, daub,

difficulty, discoloration, flaw, little, locality, location, macula, mark, mess, morsel, pimple, place, plight, plook, point, position, predicament, pustule, quandary, scene, site, situation, smudge, speck, splash, stain, stigma, taint, trouble.
v besmirch, blot, descry, detect, dirty, discern, dot, espy, fleck, identify, mark, mottle, observe, recognise, see, sight, soil, spatter, speckle, stain, sully, taint, tarnish.

spotless *adj* blameless, chaste, faultless, flawless, gleaming, immaculate, innocent, irreproachable, pure, shining, snowy, spick and span, unblemished, unimpeachable, unstained, unsullied, untarnished, virgin, virginal, white. *antonyms* dirty, impure, spotted.

spotlight *v* accentuate, emphasise, feature, focus on, highlight, illuminate, point up, throw into relief.
n attention, emphasis, fame, interest, limelight, notoriety, public eye.

spotted *adj* brindled, dappled, dotted, flecked, mottled, pied, polka-dot, speckled. *antonym* spotless.

spout *v* declaim, discharge, emit, erupt, expatiate, gush, jet, orate, pontificate, rabbit on, ramble (on), rant, sermonise, shoot, speechify, spray, spurt, squirt, stream, surge.
n chute, fountain, gargoyle, geyser, jet, nozzle, outlet, rose, spray.

sprawl *v* flop, loll, lounge, ramble, recline, repose, slouch, slump, spread, straggle, trail.

spray *v* atomise, diffuse, douse, drench, scatter, shower, sprinkle, wet.
n aerosol, atomiser, drizzle, droplets, foam, froth, mist, moisture, spindrift, sprinkler.

spread *v* advertise, arrange, array, blazon, bloat, broadcast, broaden, cast, circulate, couch, cover, diffuse, dilate, disseminate, distribute, divulge, effuse, escalate, expand, extend, fan out, furnish, lay, multiply, mushroom, open, overlay, prepare, proclaim, proliferate, promulgate, propagate, publicise, publish, radiate, scatter, set, shed, sprawl, stretch, strew, swell, transmit, unfold, unfurl, unroll, widen. *antonyms* close, compress, contain, fold.
n advance, advancement, array, banquet, blow-out, compass, cover, development, diffusion, dispersion, dissemination, escalation, expanse, expansion, extent, feast, increase, period, proliferation, reach, span, spreading,

stretch, suffusion, sweep, term, transmission.

spree *n* bacchanalia, bender, binge, carouse, debauch, fling, jamboree, junketing, orgy, randan, razzle-dazzle, revel, splurge, tear.

sprightly *adj* active, agile, airy, alert, animated, blithe, brisk, cheerful, energetic, frolicsome, gamesome, gay, hearty, jaunty, joyous, lively, nimble, perky, playful, spirited, sportive, spry, vivacious. *antonym* inactive.

spring[1] *v* appear, arise, bounce, bound, burgeon, come, dance, derive, descend, develop, emanate, emerge, grow, hop, issue, jump, leap, mushroom, originate, proceed, rebound, recoil, shoot up, sprout, start, stem, vault.
n bounce, bounciness, bound, buck, buoyancy, elasticity, flexibility, give, hop, jump, leap, rebound, recoil, resilience, saltation, springiness, vault.

spring[2] *n* beginning, cause, eye, fountain-head, origin, root, source, well.

springy *adj* bouncy, buoyant, elastic, flexible, resilient, rubbery, spongy, stretchy. *antonyms* rigid, stiff.

sprinkle *v* dot, dredge, dust, pepper, powder, scatter, shower, spatter, spray, strew.

sprinkling *n* dash, dusting, few, handful, scatter, scattering, smattering, sprinkle, touch, trace.

sprint *v* belt, dart, dash, gallop, hare, hotfoot, race, run, scamper, shoot, tear, whiz.

sprout *v* bud, develop, germinate, grow, push, shoot, spring, vegetate.

spruce *adj* dainty, dapper, elegant, natty, neat, sleek, slick, smart, trim, well-groomed, well-turned-out. *antonyms* dishevelled, untidy.

spruce up groom, neaten, preen, smarten up, tidy, titivate.

spry *adj* active, agile, alert, brisk, energetic, nimble, nippy, peppy, quick, ready, sprightly, supple. *antonyms* doddering, inactive, lethargic.

spunk *n* backbone, bottle, chutzpah, courage, gameness, grit, guts, heart, mettle, nerve, pluck, resolution, spirit, toughness. *antonym* funk.

spur *v* animate, drive, goad, impel, incite, poke, press, prick, prod, prompt, propel, stimulate, urge. *antonym* curb.
n fillip, goad, impetus, impulse, incentive, incitement, inducement, motive, prick, rowel, stimulus. *antonym* curb.

spurious *adj* apocryphal, artificial, bogus, contrived, counterfeit, deceitful, dog, fake, false, feigned, forged, imitation, mock, phoney, pretended, pseudish, pseudo, sham, simulated, specious, suppositious, unauthentic. *antonyms* authentic, genuine, real.

spurn *v* cold-shoulder, contemn, cut, despise, disdain, disregard, rebuff, reject, repulse, scorn, slight, snub, turn down. *antonym* embrace.

spurt *v* burst, effuse, erupt, gush, jet, shoot, spew, squirt, surge. *n* access, burst, effusion, fit, rush, spate, surge.

spy *v* descry, discover, espy, glimpse, notice, observe, spot.

squabble *v* argue, bicker, brawl, clash, dispute, fall out, fight, quarrel, row, scrap, spat, tiff, wrangle. *n* argument, barney, clash, disagreement, dispute, fight, rhubarb, row, scrap, set-to, spat, tiff.

squad *n* band, brigade, company, crew, force, gang, group, outfit, team, troop.

squalid *adj* broken-down, decayed, dingy, dirty, disgusting, fetid, filthy, foul, low, nasty, neglected, poverty-stricken, repulsive, run-down, seedy, sleazy, slovenly, slummy, sordid, uncared-for, unclean, unkempt. *antonyms* clean, pleasant.

squall *n* blow, gale, gust, hurricane, storm, tempest.

squally *adj* blowy, blustery, gusty, rough, stormy, tempestuous, turbulent, wild, windy.

squalor *n* decay, dinginess, filth, foulness, meanness, neglect, sleaziness, wretchedness.

squander *v* blow, consume, dissipate, expend, fritter away, lavish, misspend, misuse, scatter, spend, splurge, throw away, waste.

square *v* accommodate, accord, adapt, adjust, agree, align, appease, balance, bribe, conform, correspond, corrupt, discharge, fit, fix, harmonise, level, liquidate, match, quit, reconcile, regulate, rig, satisfy, settle, suborn, suit, tailor, tally, true. *adj* above-board, broad, complete, conservative, conventional, decent, equitable, ethical, even, exact, fair, fitting, full, genuine, honest, just, old-fashioned, on the level, opposed, orthodox, quadrate, right-angled, satisfying, solid, straight, straightforward, strait-laced, stuffy, suitable, thick-set, traditional, true, unequivocal, unhip, upright. *n* conformer, conformist, conservative, conventionalist, die-hard, fuddy-duddy, (old) fogy, stick-in-the-mud, traditionalist.

squash *v* annihilate, compress, crowd, crush, distort, flatten, humiliate, mash, pound, press, pulp, quash, quell, silence, smash, snub, squelch, stamp, suppress, trample. *antonyms* elongate, stretch.

squat *adj* chunky, dumpy, short, stocky, stubby, stumpy, thickset. *antonyms* lanky, slender. *v* bend, camp out, crouch, hunch, hunker, settle, stoop.

squawk *v* cackle, complain, crow, cry, grouse, hoot, protest, screech, shriek, squeal, yelp.

squeak *v* peep, pipe, shrill, squeal, whine, yelp.

squeal *n* scream, screech, shriek, wail, yell, yelp, yowl. *v* betray, blab, complain, grass, inform on, moan, peach, protest, rat on, scream, screech, shout, shriek, shrill, snitch, squawk, wail, yelp.

squeeze *v* bleed, clasp, clutch, compress, cram, crowd, crush, cuddle, embrace, enfold, extort, force, grip, hug, jam, jostle, lean on, milk, nip, oppress, pack, pinch, press, pressurise, ram, scrounge, squash, strain, stuff, thrust, wedge, wrest, wring. *n* clasp, congestion, crowd, crush, embrace, grasp, handclasp, hold, hug, jam, press, pressure, restriction, squash.

squint *adj* askew, aslant, awry, cockeyed, crooked, indirect, oblique, off-centre, skew-whiff. *antonym* straight.

squirm *v* agonise, fidget, flounder, move, shift, squiggle, twist, wiggle, wriggle, writhe.

squirt *v* chirt, discharge, ejaculate, eject, emit, expel, jet, shoot, spout, spurt. *n* jet, spray, spurt.

stab *v* bayonet, cut, gore, injure, jab, knife, pierce, puncture, spear, stick, thrust, transfix, wound. *n* ache, attempt, endeavour, essay, gash, incision, jab, pang, prick, puncture, rent, thrust, try, twinge, venture, wound.

stab in the back betray, deceive, double-cross, inform on, let down, sell out, slander.

stabbing *adj* acute, piercing, shooting, stinging.

stability *n* constancy, durability, firmness, fixity, permanence, solidity, soundness, steadfastness, steadiness, strength, sturdiness. **antonyms** insecurity, instability, unsteadiness, weakness.

stable *adj* abiding, constant, deep-rooted, durable, enduring, established, fast, firm, fixed, immutable, invariable, lasting, permanent, reliable, secure, self-balanced, sound, static, steadfast, steady, strong, sturdy, sure, unalterable, unchangeable, unwavering, well-founded. **antonyms** shaky, unstable, weak, wobbly.

stack *n* accumulation, clamp, cock, heap, hoard, load, mass, mound, mountain, pile, ruck, stockpile.
v accumulate, amass, assemble, gather, load, pile, save, stockpile, store.

staff *n* crew, employees, personnel, team, workers, workforce.

stage *n* division, floor, juncture, lap, leg, length, level, period, phase, point, shelf, step, storey, subdivision, tier.
v arrange, do, engineer, give, mount, orchestrate, organise, perform, present, produce, put on, stage-manage.

stagger *v* alternate, amaze, astonish, astound, confound, dumbfound, falter, flabbergast, hesitate, lurch, nonplus, overlap, overwhelm, reel, shake, shock, step, stun, stupefy, surprise, sway, teeter, titubate, totter, vacillate, waver, wobble, zigzag.

stagnate *v* decay, decline, degenerate, deteriorate, fester, idle, languish, rot, rust, vegetate.

staid *adj* calm, composed, decorous, demure, grave, quiet, sedate, self-restrained, serious, sober, solemn, steady, Victorian. **antonyms** debonair, frivolous, jaunty, sportive.

stain *v* besmirch, blacken, blemish, blot, colour, contaminate, corrupt, defile, deprave, dirty, discolour, disgrace, dye, imbue, mark, soil, spot, sully, taint, tarnish, tinge.
n blemish, blot, discoloration, disgrace, dishonour, dye, infamy, reproach, shame, slur, smirch, soil, splodge, spot, stigma, tint.

stake[1] *n* pale, picket, pile, pole, post, spike, standard, stave, stick.
v brace, fasten, pierce, prop, secure, support, tether, tie, tie up.

stake out define, delimit, demarcate, keep an eye on, mark out, outline, reserve, stake off, survey, watch.

stake[2] *n* ante, bet, chance, claim, concern, hazard, interest, investment,

involvement, peril, pledge, prize, risk, share, venture, wager.
v ante, bet, chance, gage, gamble, hazard, imperil, jeopardise, pledge, risk, venture, wager.

stale *adj* antiquated, banal, clichéd, cliché-ridden, common, commonplace, decayed, drab, dry, effete, faded, flat, fusty, hackneyed, hard, insipid, musty, old, old hat, overused, platitudinous, repetitious, sour, stagnant, stereotyped, tainted, tasteless, threadbare, trite, unoriginal, vapid, worn-out. **antonym** fresh.

stalemate *n* deadlock, draw, halt, impasse, standstill, stop, tie. **antonym** progress.

stalk *v* approach, follow, haunt, hunt, march, pace, pursue, shadow, stride, strut, tail, track.

stall *v* delay, equivocate, hedge, obstruct, play for time, prevaricate, stonewall, temporise. **antonym** advance.

stalwart *adj* athletic, beefy, brawny, daring, dependable, determined, hefty, husky, indomitable, intrepid, lusty, manly, muscular, redoubtable, resolute, robust, rugged, sinewy, staunch, stout, strapping, strong, sturdy, valiant, vigorous. **antonyms** timid, weak.

stamina *n* energy, fibre, force, grit, indefatigability, lustiness, power, resilience, resistance, staying power, strength, vigour. **antonym** weakness.

stamp *v* beat, brand, categorise, characterise, crush, engrave, exhibit, fix, identify, impress, imprint, inscribe, label, mark, mint, mould, pound, print, pronounce, reveal, strike, trample.
n attestation, authorisation, brand, breed, cast, character, cut, description, earmark, evidence, fashion, form, hallmark, impression, imprint, kind, mark, mould, sign, signature, sort, stomp, type.

stamp out crush, destroy, eliminate, end, eradicate, extinguish, extirpate, kill, quell, quench, scotch, suppress. **antonym** encourage.

stampede *n* charge, dash, flight, rout, rush, scattering, sprint.
v charge, dash, flee, fly, gallop, hightail it, hot-foot it, run, rush, scurry, shoot, sprint, tear. **antonyms** walk, wander.

stance *n* angle, attitude, bearing, carriage, deportment, point of view, position, posture, stand, standpoint, station, viewpoint.

stand *v* abide, allow, bear, belong, brook,

continue, cost, countenance, demur, endure, erect, exist, experience, halt, handle, hold, mount, obtain, pause, place, position, prevail, put, rank, remain, rest, rise, scruple, set, stay, stomach, stop, suffer, support, sustain, take, tolerate, undergo, wear, weather, withstand. **antonym** advance.

n attitude, base, booth, determination, erection, frame, grandstand, holder, loss, opinion, place, platform, position, rack, rank, resistance, rest, stage, staging, stall, stance, standpoint, standstill, stay, stop, support, witness-box. **antonym** progress.

stand by adhere to, back, befriend, champion, defend, hold to, reiterate, repeat, speak for, stick up for, support, uphold. **antonym** let down.

stand down abdicate, cede, give away, give up, quit, resign, step down, withdraw. **antonyms** ascend, join.

stand for bear, betoken, brook, champion, countenance, denote, embody, endure, epitomise, exemplify, indicate, mean, personify, represent, signify, suffer, symbolise, tolerate, typify, wear.

stand in for cover for, deputise for, hold the fort for, replace, substitute for, understudy.

stand out bulk large, catch the eye, jut out, project, stare one in the face, stick out, stick out a mile, stick out like a sore thumb.

stand up cohere, hold up, hold water, stand, wash.

stand up for champion, defend, fight for, side with, speak for, speak up for, stick up for, support, uphold. **antonym** attack.

stand up to brave, confront, defy, endure, face, front, oppose, resist, withstand. **antonym** give in to.

standard *n* average, bench-mark, canon, criterion, example, exemplar, gauge, grade, guide, guideline, level, measure, model, norm, pattern, principle, requirement, rule, sample, specification, touchstone, type, yardstick.

adj accepted, approved, authoritative, average, basic, classic, customary, definitive, established, mainstream, normal, official, orthodox, popular, prevailing, recognised, regular, set, staple, stock, typical, usual. **antonyms** abnormal, irregular, unusual.

standardise *v* assimilate, equalise,

institutionalise, mass-produce, normalise, regiment, stereotype. **antonym** differentiate.

standards *n* ethics, ideals, morals, principles.

standing *n* condition, continuance, credit, duration, eminence, estimation, existence, experience, footing, position, prestige, rank, reputation, repute, seniority, station, status.

adj erect, fixed, lasting, on one's feet, permanent, perpendicular, perpetual, rampant, regular, repeated, up-ended, upright, vertical. **antonyms** horizontal, lying.

stand-offish *adj* aloof, cold, distant, haughty, remote, reserved, unapproachable, uncommunicative, unsociable. **antonym** friendly.

standpoint *n* angle, point of view, position, post, stance, station, vantage-point, viewpoint.

standstill *n* arrest, cessation, dead-finish, deadlock, halt, hold-up, impasse, lapse, log-jam, lull, moratorium, pause, reprieve, respite, rest, stalemate, stay, stop, stoppage, termination. **antonym** progress.

staple *adj* basic, chief, essential, fundamental, key, leading, main, major, predominant, primary, principle. **antonym** minor.

star *n* celebrity, draw, idol, lead, leading, leading lady, leading man, luminary, main attraction, name, starlet.

adj brilliant, celebrated, illustrious, leading, major, paramount, pre-eminent, principal, prominent, talented, well-known. **antonym** minor.

starchy *adj* ceremonious, conventional, formal, prim, punctilious, stiff, strait-laced, stuffy. **antonym** informal.

stare *v* gape, gawk, gawp, gaze, glare, goggle, look, watch.

stark *adj* absolute, arrant, austere, bald, bare, barren, bleak, blunt, cold, consummate, depressing, desolate, downright, dreary, entire, flagrant, forsaken, grim, harsh, out-and-out, palpable, patent, plain, pure, severe, sheer, simple, solitary, stern, stiff, strong, unadorned, unalloyed, unmitigated, unyielding, utter. **antonyms** mild, slight.

adv absolutely, altogether, clean, completely, entirely, quite, totally, utterly, wholly. **antonyms** mildly, slightly.

stark-naked *adj* in one's birthday suit,

in the altogether, in the buff, in the nude, in the raw, naked, nude, stark, starkers, stripped, undressed. *antonym* clothed.

start *v* activate, appear, arise, begin, blench, break away, commence, create, dart, depart, engender, establish, father, flinch, found, inaugurate, initiate, instigate, institute, introduce, issue, jerk, jump, kick off, launch, leave, open, originate, pioneer, recoil, sally forth, set off, set out, set up, shoot, shy, spring forward, twitch. *antonyms* finish, stop.
n advantage, backing, beginning, birth, break, chance, commencement, convulsion, dawn, edge, fit, foundation, inauguration, inception, initiation, introduction, jar, jump, kick-off, lead, onset, opening, opportunity, outburst, outset, spasm, sponsorship, spurt, twitch. *antonyms* finish, stop.

startle *v* affray, agitate, alarm, amaze, astonish, astound, electrify, flush, frighten, scare, shock, spook, start, surprise. *antonym* calm.

startling *adj* alarming, astonishing, astounding, dramatic, electric, electrifying, extraordinary, shocking, staggering, sudden, surprising, unexpected, unforeseen. *antonyms* boring, calming, ordinary.

starve *v* deny, deprive, die, diet, fast, hunger, perish, refuse. *antonym* provide.

stash *v* conceal, hide, hoard, lay up, salt away, save up, secrete, stockpile, stow. *antonyms* bring out, uncover.

state¹ *v* affirm, articulate, assert, asseverate, aver, declare, enumerate, explain, expound, express, formalise, formulate, formulise, present, propound, put, report, say, specify, voice.
n attitude, bother, case, category, ceremony, circumstances, condition, dignity, display, flap, glory, grandeur, humour, majesty, mode, mood, panic, pass, phase, plight, pomp, position, pother, predicament, shape, situation, spirits, splendour, stage, station, style, tizzy. *antonym* calmness.

state of affairs case, circumstances, condition, crisis, juncture, kettle of fish, lie of the land, plight, position, predicament, situation.

state² *n* body politic, commonwealth, country, federation, government, kingdom, land, nation, republic, territory.
adj ceremonial, ceremonious, formal, governmental, magnificent, national, official, pompous, public, solemn.

stately *adj* august, ceremonious, deliberate, dignified, elegant, grand, imperial, imposing, impressive, kingly, lofty, majestic, measured, noble, pompous, princely, queenly, regal, royal, solemn. *antonyms* informal, unimpressive.

statement *n* account, announcement, bulletin, communication, communiqué, constatation, declaration, explanation, proclamation, recital, relation, report, testimony, utterance, verbal.

static *adj* changeless, constant, fixed, immobile, inert, motionless, resting, stable, stagnant, stationary, still, unmoving, unvarying. *antonyms* active, dynamic, moving.

station *n* appointment, base, business, calling, depot, employment, grade, headquarters, location, occupation, office, place, position, post, rank, seat, situation, sphere, stance, standing, standing-place, status, stopping-place.
v appoint, assign, establish, fix, garrison, install, locate, post, send, set.

stationary *adj* fixed, inert, moored, motionless, parked, resting, settled, standing, static, stock-still, unmoving. *antonym* moving.

statuesque *adj* dignified, imposing, majestic, regal, stately. *antonym* small.

stature *n* consequence, eminence, importance, prestige, prominence, rank, size, standing, weight. *antonym* unimportance.

status *n* character, condition, consequence, degree, distinction, eminence, grade, importance, position, prestige, rank, standing, state, weight. *antonym* unimportance.

staunch *adj* constant, dependable, faithful, firm, hearty, loyal, reliable, resolute, sound, steadfast, stout, strong, sure, true, true-blue, trustworthy, trusty, watertight, zealous. *antonyms* unreliable, wavering, weak.

stave off avert, delay, evade, fend off, foil, hold off, keep at bay, keep back, parry, ward off. *antonyms* cause, encourage.

stay *v* abide, adjourn, allay, arrest, check, continue, curb, defer, delay, detain, discontinue, dwell, endure, halt, hinder, hold, hold out, hover, impede, last, linger, live, lodge, loiter, obstruct, pause, prevent, remain, reside, restrain, settle, sojourn, stand, stop, suspend, tarry, visit, wait. *antonyms* advance, leave.
n continuance, deferment, delay,

halt, holiday, pause, postponement, remission, reprieve, sojourn, stop, stopover, stopping, suspension, visit.

steadfast *adj* constant, dedicated, dependable, established, faithful, fast, firm, fixed, intent, loyal, persevering, reliable, resolute, single-minded, stable, staunch, steady, unfaltering, unflinching, unswerving, unwavering. *antonyms* unreliable, wavering, weak.

steady *adj* balanced, calm, ceaseless, confirmed, consistent, constant, continuous, dependable, equable, even, faithful, firm, fixed, habitual, immovable, imperturbable, incessant, industrious, level-headed, non-stop, persistent, regular, reliable, rhythmic, safe, sedate, sensible, serene, serious-minded, settled, sober, stable, staid, steadfast, substantial, unbroken, unchangeable, unfaltering, unfluctuating, unhasting, unhasty, unhurried, uniform, uninterrupted, unremitting, unswerving, unvarying, unwavering. *antonyms* unsteady, wavering.

v balance, brace, firm, fix, secure, stabilise, support.

steal *v* appropriate, creep, embezzle, filch, flit, half-inch, heist, knock off, lift, misappropriate, nab, nick, pilfer, pinch, plagiarise, poach, purloin, relieve someone of, rip off, shoplift, slip, snaffle, snatch, sneak, swipe, take, thieve, tiptoe. *antonym* return.

stealthy *adj* cat-like, clandestine, covert, furtive, quiet, secret, secretive, skulking, sly, sneaking, sneaky, surreptitious, underhand. *antonym* open.

steamy *adj* close, damp, gaseous, hazy, humid, misty, muggy, steaming, stewy, sticky, sultry, sweaty, sweltering, vaporous, vapoury.

steel *v* brace, fortify, harden, nerve, toughen. *antonym* weaken.

steep[1] *adj* abrupt, excessive, exorbitant, extortionate, extreme, headlong, high, overpriced, precipitous, sheer, stiff, uncalled-for, unreasonable. *antonyms* gentle, moderate.

steep[2] *v* damp, drench, fill, imbrue, imbue, immerse, infuse, marinate, moisten, permeate, pervade, pickle, saturate, soak, souse, submerge, suffuse.

steer *v* conduct, control, direct, govern, guide, pilot.

steer clear of avoid, bypass, circumvent, dodge, escape, eschew, evade, shun, skirt. *antonym* seek.

stem[1] *n* axis, branch, family, house, line, lineage, race, shoot, stalk, stock, trunk.

stem from arise from, come from, derive from, develop from, emanate from, flow from, issue from, originate in, spring from. *antonym* give rise to.

stem[2] *v* check, contain, curb, dam, oppose, resist, restrain, stanch, stay, stop, tamp. *antonyms* encourage, increase.

stench *n* odour, pong, reek, stink, whiff.

step *n* act, action, advance, advancement, deed, degree, doorstep, expedient, footfall, footprint, footstep, gait, impression, level, manoeuvre, means, measure, move, pace, phase, point, print, procedure, proceeding, process, progression, rank, remove, round, rung, stage, stair, stride, trace, track, tread, walk.

v move, pace, stalk, stamp, tread, walk.

step by step gradually, slowly.

step down abdicate, bow out, leave, quit, resign, retire, stand down, withdraw. *antonyms* ascend, join.

step up accelerate, augment, boost, build up, escalate, increase, intensify, raise, speed up, up. *antonym* decrease.

stereotype *n* convention, formula, mould, pattern.

v categorise, conventionalise, pigeon-hole, standardise, typecast. *antonym* differentiate.

stereotyped *adj* banal, clichéd, cliché-ridden, conventional, corny, hackneyed, overused, platitudinous, stale, standard, standardised, stock, threadbare, tired, trite, unoriginal. *antonyms* different, unconventional.

sterile *adj* abortive, antiseptic, bare, barren, disinfected, dry, empty, fruitless, germ-free, pointless, sterilised, unfruitful, unimaginative, unproductive, unprofitable, unprolific. *antonyms* fruitful, septic.

sterilise *v* clean, cleanse, disinfect, fumigate, purify. *antonyms* contaminate, infect.

sterility *n* barrenness, cleanness, fruitlessness, futility, impotence, ineffectiveness, inefficacy, pointlessness, purity, unfruitfulness, uselessness. *antonyms* fertility, fruitfulness.

sterling *adj* authentic, excellent, first-class, genuine, great, pure, real, sound, standard, substantial, superlative, true, worthy. *antonyms* false, poor.

stern *adj* austere, authoritarian, bitter, cruel, flinty, forbidding, frowning, grim, hard, harsh, inflexible, relentless, rigid, rigorous, serious, severe, stark, steely, strict, unrelenting, unsmiling, unsparing, unyielding. **antonym** mild.

stew v agonise, boil, braise, fret, fuss, jug, perspire, seethe, simmer, sweat, swelter, worry.

n agitation, bother, fluster, fret, fuss, pother, tizzy, worry.

stick[1] v adhere, affix, attach, bind, bond, bulge, catch, cement, cleave, cling, clog, deposit, dig, drop, endure, extend, fasten, fix, fuse, glue, gore, hold, insert, install, jab, jam, join, jut, lay, linger, lodge, obtrude, paste, penetrate, persist, pierce, pin, place, plant, plonk, poke, position, prod, project, protrude, puncture, put, put up with, remain, set, show, snag, spear, stab, stand, stay, stomach, stop, store, stuff, take, thrust, tolerate, transfix, weld. **antonym** unstick.

stick at[1] continue, hang on in, keep at, persevere in, persist, plug away at. **antonym** give up.

stick at[2] balk, demur, doubt, draw the line at, hesitate, pause, recoil, scruple, shrink from, stop at.

stick to adhere to, cleave to, honour, keep to, persevere in, stand by. **antonyms** give up, quit.

stick up for champion, defend, speak for, speak up for, stand up for, support, take the part or side of, uphold. **antonym** attack.

stick[2] n baton, birch, bludgeon, branch, cane, pole, rod, sceptre, staff, stake, stave, switch, twig, wand, whip.

stick[3] n abuse, blame, criticism, flak, hostility, punishment, reproof. **antonym** praise.

stick-in-the-mud adj conservative, fogyish, outmoded, unadventurous, Victorian. **antonyms** adventurous, modern.

stickler n fanatic, fusspot, maniac, nut, pedant, perfectionist, purist.

sticky adj adhesive, awkward, clammy, clinging, clingy, cloggy, close, delicate, difficult, discomforting, embarrassing, gluey, glutinous, gooey, gummy, hairy, humid, muggy, nasty, oppressive, painful, sultry, sweltering, syrupy, tacky, thorny, tricky, unpleasant, viscid, viscous. **antonyms** cool, dry, easy.

stiff adj arduous, arthritic, artificial, austere, awkward, brisk, brittle, ceremonious, chilly, clumsy, cold, constrained, creaky, crude, cruel, difficult, drastic, exacting, excessive, extreme, fatiguing, firm, forced, formal, formidable, fresh, graceless, great, hard, hardened, harsh, heavy, inelastic, inelegant, inexorable, inflexible, jerky, laborious, laboured, mannered, oppressive, pertinaceous, pitiless, pokerish, pompous, powerful, priggish, prim, punctilious, resistant, rheumaticky, rigid, rigorous, severe, sharp, solid, solidified, stand-offish, starch(y), stark, stilted, strict, stringent, strong, stubborn, taut, tense, tight, toilsome, tough, trying, unbending, uneasy, ungainly, ungraceful, unnatural, unrelaxed, unsupple, unyielding, uphill, vigorous, wooden. **antonyms** flexible, graceful, informal, mild.

stiffen v brace, coagulate, congeal, crystallise, harden, jell, reinforce, set, solidify, starch, tense, thicken.

stiff-necked adj arrogant, haughty, obstinate, opinionated, proud, stubborn, uncompromising. **antonyms** flexible, humble.

stifle v asphyxiate, check, choke, curb, dampen, extinguish, hush, muffle, prevent, repress, restrain, silence, smother, stop, strangle, suffocate, suppress. **antonym** encourage.

stigma n blemish, blot, brand, disgrace, dishonour, imputation, mark, reproach, shame, slur, smirch, spot, stain. **antonym** credit.

stigmatise v brand, condemn, denounce, discredit, fame, label, mark, pillory, vilify. **antonym** praise.

still adj calm, hushed, inert, lifeless, motionless, noiseless, pacific, peaceful, placid, quiet, restful, serene, silent, smooth, stagnant, stationary, tranquil, undisturbed, unruffled, unstirring. **antonyms** agitated, busy, disturbed, noisy.

v allay, alleviate, appease, calm, hold back, hush, lull, pacify, quiet, quieten, restrain, settle, silence, smooth, soothe, subdue, tranquillise. **antonyms** agitate, stir up.

n hush, peace, peacefulness, quiet, quietness, silence, stillness, tranquillity. **antonyms** agitation, disturbance, noise.

adv but, even so, even then, however, nevertheless, nonetheless, notwithstanding, yet.

stilted adj artificial, bombastic, constrained, forced, grandiloquent, high-flown, high-sounding, inflated, laboured, mannered, pedantic, pompous, pretentious, stiff, unnatural, wooden. **antonyms** flowing, fluent.

stimulate v animate, arouse, dynamise,

encourage, fan, fire, foment, get psyched
up, goad, hype up, impel, incite, inflame,
instigate, jog, prompt, provoke, psych
oneself up, quicken, rouse, spur, titillate,
urge, whet. **antonym** discourage.

stimulating *adj* exciting, exhilarating,
galvanic, inspiring, intriguing,
provocative, provoking, rousing, stirring,
thought-provoking. **antonyms** boring,
depressing, uninspiring.

stimulus *n* carrot, encouragement, fillip,
goad, incentive, incitement, inducement,
prick, provocation, spur. **antonym**
discouragement.

sting *v* anger, burn, cheat, con, defraud,
do, fleece, gall, hurt, incense, inflame,
infuriate, nettle, overcharge, pain, pique,
provoke, rile, rip off, smart, swindle,
tingle, wound. **antonym** soothe.
n agony, anguish, bite, bitterness,
distress, goad, incentive, incitement, nip,
prick, pungency, smarting, spur,
stimulus, tingle, torment, torture, woe.

stingy *adj* avaricious, cheeseparing,
close-fisted, covetous, illiberal,
inadequate, insufficient, meagre, mean,
measly, mingy, miserly, near, niggardly, parsimonious, penny-pinching,
penurious, scanty, scrimping, tightfisted,
ungenerous. **antonym** generous.

stink *v* niff, pong, reek, whiff.
n commotion, disturbance, foulness,
fuss, hubbub, malodour, niff, odour,
pong, row, rumpus, scandal, stench, stir,
to-do, uproar, upset, whiff.

stinker *n* affliction, beast, bounder,
cad, creep, cur, dastard, difficulty, fink,
heel, horror, impediment, plight, poser,
predicament, problem, rat, rotter, scab,
scoundrel, shocker, sod, swine.

stinking *adj* boozed, canned,
contemptible, disgusting, drunk, fetid,
foul-smelling, grotty, ill-smelling,
intoxicated, low, low-down, malodorous,
mean, pissed, plastered, pongy, reeking,
rotten, smashed, smelly, sozzled,
stenchy, stewed, stoned, unpleasant, vile,
whiffy, wretched. **antonyms** good,
pleasant, sober.

stint *n* assignment, bit, period, quota,
share, shift, spell, stretch, term, time,
tour, trick, turn.
v begrudge, economise, pinch, save,
scrimp, skimp on, withhold.

stipulate *v* agree, contract, covenant,
engage, guarantee, insist upon, lay down,
pledge, postulate, promise, provide,
require, settle, specify. **antonym** imply.

stipulation *n* agreement, clause,

condition, contract, engagement,
precondition, prerequisite, provision,
proviso, qualification, requirement,
restriction, settlement, sine qua non,
small print, specification, term.
antonym implication.

stir *v* affect, agitate, beat, bestir, budge,
disturb, electrify, emove, excite, fire,
flutter, hasten, inspire, look lively, mix,
move, quiver, rustle, shake, shake a leg,
thrill, touch, tremble. **antonyms** bore,
calm, stay.
n activity, ado, agitation, bustle,
commotion, disorder, disturbance,
excitement, ferment, flurry, fuss, hustle
and bustle, movement, to-do, toing and
froing, tumult, uproar. **antonym** calm.

stir up animate, arouse, awaken, excite,
incite, inflame, instigate, jog, kindle,
mix, prompt, provoke, quicken, raise,
spur, stimulate, urge. **antonyms** calm,
discourage.

stirring *adj* animating, dramatic,
emotive, exciting, exhilarating, heady,
impassioned, inspiring, intoxicating,
lively, moving, rousing, spirited,
stimulating, thrilling. **antonyms**
calming, uninspiring.

stock *n* ancestry, array, assets,
assortment, background, beasts, block,
breed, cache, capital, cattle, choice,
commodities, descent, equipment,
estimation, extraction, family, flocks,
forebears, fund, funds, goods, handle,
herds, hoard, horses, house, inventory,
investment, kindred, line, lineage,
livestock, log, merchandise, parentage,
pedigree, post, property, race, range,
repertoire, repute, reserve, reservoir,
selection, sheep, source, stem, stockpile,
store, strain, stump, supply, trunk, type,
variety, wares.
adj banal, basic, bromidic, clichéd,
commonplace, conventional, customary,
formal, hackneyed, ordinary, overused,
regular, routine, run-of-the-mill, set,
standard, staple, stereotyped, traditional,
trite, usual, worn-out. **antonym**
original.
v deal in, handle, keep, sell, supply,
trade in.

stock up accumulate, amass, equip, fill,
furnish, gather, hoard, lay in, pile up,
provision, replenish, save, store (up),
supply.

stocky *adj* blocky, chunky, dumpy,
mesomorphic, short, solid, stubby,
stumpy, sturdy, thickset. **antonyms**
skinny, tall.

stodgy *adj* boring, dull, filling, formal, fuddy-duddy, heavy, laboured, leaden, solemn, spiritless, staid, starchy, stuffy, substantial, tedious, turgid, unenterprising, unexciting, unimaginative, uninspired. *antonyms* exciting, informal, light.

stoical *adj* calm, cool, dispassionate, impassive, imperturbable, indifferent, long-suffering, patient, philosophical, phlegmatic, resigned, stoic, stolid. *antonyms* anxious, depressed, furious, irascible.

stoicism *n* acceptance, calmness, fatalism, forbearance, fortitude, impassivity, imperturbability, indifference, long-suffering, patience, resignation, stolidity. *antonyms* anxiety, depression, fury.

stolid *adj* apathetic, beefy, blockish, doltish, dull, heavy, impassive, lumpish, obtuse, po, po-faced, slow, stoic(al), stupid, unemotional, wooden. *antonyms* interested, lively.

stomach *n* abdomen, appetite, belly, bread-basket, craw, desire, gizzard, gut, inclination, inside(s), maw, mind, paunch, pot, potbelly, relish, spare tyre, taste, tummy. *v* abide, bear, endure, submit to, suffer, swallow, take, tolerate.

stony *adj* adamant, blank, callous, chilly, expressionless, frigid, hard, heartless, hostile, icy, indifferent, merciless, obdurate, pitiless, steely, stonelike, unfeeling, unforgiving, unresponsive. *antonyms* forgiving, friendly, soft-hearted.

stoop *v* bend, bow, couch, crouch, descend, duck, hunch, incline, kneel, lean, squat. *n* droop, inclination, round-shoulderedness, sag, slouch, slump.

stoop to condescend, deign, descend, go so far as, go so low as, lower oneself, resort, sink, vouchsafe.

stop *v* arrest, bar, block, break, cease, check, close, conclude, desist, discontinue, embar, end, finish, forestall, frustrate, halt, hinder, impede, intercept, intermit, interrupt, knock off, leave off, lodge, obstruct, pack (it) in, pack in, pack up, pause, plug, prevent, quit, refrain, repress, rest, restrain, scotch, seal, silence, sojourn, stall, staunch, stay, stem, stymie, suspend, tarry, terminate. *antonyms* advance, continue, start. *n* bar, block, break, bung, cessation, check, conclusion, control,

destination, discontinuation, end, finish, halt, hindrance, impediment, plug, rest, sojourn, stage, standstill, station, stay, stop-over, stoppage, termination, terminus, visit. *antonyms* continuation, start.

interj cease, cut it out, desist, easy, give over, halt, hang on, hold it, hold on, hold your horses, lay off, leave it out, refrain, stop it, wait, wait a minute, whoa.

stop-gap *n* expedient, improvisation, makeshift, resort, shift, substitute. *adj* emergency, impromptu, improvised, makeshift, provisional, rough-and-ready, temporary. *antonyms* finished, permanent.

stoppage *n* abeyance, arrest, blockage, check, close, closure, curtailment, cut-off, deduction, desistance, discontinuance, halt, hindrance, interruption, lay-off, obstruction, occlusion, shutdown, sit-in, standstill, stasis, stopping, strike, walk-out. *antonyms* continuation, start.

store *v* accumulate, deposit, garner, hive, hoard, keep, lay aside, lay by, lay up, put aside, reserve, salt away, save, stash, stock, stockpile, treasure. *antonym* use. *n* abundance, accumulation, bank, cache, cupboard, database, depository, emporium, esteem, fund, hoard, keeping, lot, market, mart, memory, mine, outlet, plenty, plethora, provision, quantity, repository, reserve, reservoir, shop, stock, stockpile, storehouse, storeroom, supermarket, supply, value, warehouse, wealth. *antonym* scarcity.

storm *n* agitation, anger, assault, attack, blast, blitz, blizzard, clamour, commotion, cyclone, disturbance, dust-devil, furore, gale, gust, hubbub, hurricane, offensive, onset, onslaught, outbreak, outburst, outcry, passion, roar, row, rumpus, rush, sandstorm, squall, stir, strife, tempest, tornado, tumult, turmoil, violence, whirlwind. *antonym* calm. *v* assail, assault, beset, bluster, charge, complain, expugn, flounce, fly, fume, rage, rampage, rant, rave, rush, scold, stalk, stamp, stomp, thunder.

stormy *adj* blustering, blustery, boisterous, choppy, dirty, foul, gustful, gusty, inclement, raging, rough, squally, tempestuous, turbulent, wild, windy. *antonym* calm.

story *n* account, ancedote, article, chronicle, episode, fable, fairy-tale, falsehood, feature, fib, fiction, history, legend, lie, myth, narration, narrative, news, novel, plot, recital, record, relation, report, romance, scoop, spiel, tale, untruth, version, yarn.

stout *adj* athletic, beefy, big, bold, brave, brawny, bulky, burly, corpulent, courageous, dauntless, doughty, enduring, fat, fearless, fleshy, gallant, hardy, heavy, hulking, husky, intrepid, lion-hearted, manly, muscular, obese, overweight, plucky, plump, portly, resolute, robust, rotund, stalwart, strapping, strong, sturdy, substantial, thick, tough, tubby, valiant, valorous, vigorous. *antonyms* slim, timid, weak.

stow *v* bundle, cram, deposit, dump, jam, load, pack, secrete, sling, stash, store, stuff, tuck. *antonym* unload.

straggle *v* amble, dilly-dally, drift, lag, loiter, ramble, range, roam, rove, scatter, spread, stray, string out, trail, wander.

straggly *adj* aimless, disorganised, drifting, irregular, loose, rambling, random, spreading, straggling, straying, strung out, untidy. *antonyms* grouped, organised, tidy.

straight *adj* accurate, aligned, arranged, authentic, balanced, blunt, candid, consecutive, conservative, continuous, conventional, decent, direct, downright, equitable, erect, even, fair, forthright, frank, honest, honourable, horizontal, just, law-abiding, level, near, neat, non-stop, normal, orderly, organised, orthodox, outright, perpendicular, plain, plumb, point-blank, pure, reliable, respectable, right, running, settled, shipshape, short, smooth, solid, square, straightforward, successive, sustained, through, tidy, traditional, true, trustworthy, unadulterated, undeviating, undiluted, uninterrupted, unmixed, unqualified, unrelieved, unswerving, upright, vertical. *antonyms* circuitous, dilute, dishonest, evasive, indirect, roundabout.
adv candidly, directly, frankly, honestly, outspokenly, point-blank, upright.

straightaway *adv* at once, directly, immediately, instantly, now, right away, there and then, this minute. *antonym* eventually.

straighten *v* arrange, neaten, order, untwist. *antonyms* bend, twist.

straighten out clear up, correct, disentangle, rectify, regularise, resolve, settle, sort out, unsnarl, work out. *antonym* muddle.

straightforward *adj* candid, clear-cut, direct, easy, elementary, forthright, genuine, guileless, honest, open, open-and-shut, routine, simple, sincere, truthful, uncomplicated, undemanding. *antonyms* complicated, devious, evasive.

strain¹ *v* compress, distend, drive, endeavour, exert, express, extend, fatigue, filter, injure, labour, overtax, overwork, percolate, pull, purify, restrain, retch, riddle, seep, separate, sieve, sift, sprain, squeeze, stretch, strive, struggle, tauten, tax, tear, tighten, tire, tug, twist, weaken, wrench, wrest, wrick.
n anxiety, burden, effort, exertion, force, height, injury, key, pitch, pressure, pull, sprain, stress, struggle, tautness, tension, wrench.

strain² *n* ancestry, blood, descent, extraction, family, humour, lineage, manner, pedigree, race, spirit, stem, stock, streak, style, suggestion, suspicion, temper, tendency, tone, trace, trait, vein, way.

strained *adj* artificial, awkward, constrained, difficult, embarrassed, false, forced, laboured, self-conscious, stiff, tense, uncomfortable, uneasy, unnatural, unrelaxed. *antonym* natural.

straitened *adj* difficult, distressed, embarrassed, impoverished, limited, poor, reduced, restricted. *antonyms* easy, well-off.

strait-laced *adj* moralistic, narrow, narrow-minded, old-maidish, prim, proper, prudish, puritanical, strict, stuffy, upright, Victorian. *antonyms* broad-minded, easy-going.

straits *n* crisis, difficulty, dilemma, distress, embarrassment, emergency, extremity, hardship, hole, mess, perplexity, plight, poverty, predicament.

stranded *adj* abandoned, aground, ashore, beached, grounded, helpless, high and dry, homeless, in the lurch, marooned, penniless, shipwrecked, wrecked.

strange *adj* abnormal, alien, astonishing, awkward, bewildered, bizarre, curious, disorientated, disoriented, eccentric, eerie, exceptional, exotic, extraordinary, fantastic(al), foreign, funny, irregular, lost, marvellous, mystifying, new, novel, odd, out-of-the-way, peculiar, perplexing, queer, rare, remarkable, remote, singular, sinister, unaccountable, unacquainted, uncanny, uncomfortable, uncommon, unexplained, unexplored, unfamiliar, unheard of, unknown, untried, unversed, weird, wonderful. **antonyms** comfortable, common, familiar, ordinary.

stranger n alien, foreigner, guest, incomer, newcomer, non-member, outlander, unknown, visitor. **antonyms** local, native.

strangle n asphyxiate, choke, constrict, gag, inhibit, repress, smother, stifle, strangulate, suffocate, suppress, throttle.

strapping adj beefy, big, brawny, burly, hefty, hulking, hunky, husky, powerful, robust, stalwart, strong, sturdy, well-built. **antonym** puny.

stratagem n artifice, device, dodge, feint, fetch, intrigue, manoeuvre, plan, plot, ploy, ruse, scheme, subterfuge, trick, wile.

strategic adj calculated, cardinal, critical, crucial, decisive, deliberate, diplomatic, important, key, planned, politic, strategetical, vital. **antonym** unimportant.

strategy n approach, design, manoeuvring, plan, planning, policy, procedure, programme, scheme, way.

stray v deviate, digress, diverge, drift, err, get lost, meander, ramble, range, roam, rove, straggle, wander (off).
adj abandoned, accidental, chance, erratic, freak, homeless, lost, odd, random, roaming, scattered, vagrant.

streak n band, dash, element, freak, layer, line, slash, smear, strain, strip, stripe, stroke, touch, trace, vein.
v band, dart, daub, flash, fleck, fly, gallop, hurtle, slash, smear, speed, sprint, striate, stripe, sweep, tear, whistle, whizz, zoom.

stream n beck, brook, burn, course, creek, current, drift, flow, gush, outpouring, rill, river, rivulet, run, runnel, rush, surge, tide, torrent, tributary.
v cascade, course, emit, flood, flow, glide, gush, issue, pour, run, shed, spill, spout, surge, well out.

streamlined adj efficient, graceful, modernised, organised, rationalised, sleek, slick, smooth, smooth-running, superior, time-saving, up-to-the-minute, well-run. **antonyms** clumsy, inefficient, old-fashioned.

strength n advantage, anchor, asset, backbone, brawn, brawniness, cogency, concentration, courage, effectiveness, efficacy, energy, firmness, force, fortitude, fushion, health, intensity, lustiness, mainstay, might, muscle, potency, power, resolution, robustness, security, sinew, spirit, stamina, stoutness, sturdiness, toughness, vehemence, vigour, virtue. **antonyms** timidness, weakness.

strengthen v bolster, brace, buttress, confirm, consolidate, corroborate, edify, encourage, enhance, establish, fortify, harden, hearten, heighten, increase, intensify, invigorate, justify, nerve, nourish, reinforce, rejuvenate, restore, steel, stiffen, substantiate, support, toughen. **antonym** weaken.

strenuous adj active, arduous, bold, demanding, determined, eager, earnest, energetic, exhausting, hard, Herculean, laborious, persistent, resolute, spirited, strong, taxing, tireless, tough, uphill, urgent, vigorous, zealous. **antonyms** easy, effortless.

stress n accent, accentuation, anxiety, beat, burden, emphasis, emphaticalness, force, hassle, importance, oppression, pressure, significance, strain, tautness, tension, trauma, urgency, weight, worry. **antonym** relaxation.
v accentuate, belabour, emphasise, repeat, strain, underline, underscore. **antonym** relax.

stretch n area, bit, distance, exaggeration, expanse, extensibility, extension, extent, period, reach, run, space, spell, spread, stint, strain, sweep, term, time, tract.
v cover, distend, elongate, expand, extend, inflate, lengthen, pull, rack, reach, spread, strain, swell, tighten, unfold, unroll. **antonyms** relax, squeeze.

stretch one's legs exercise, go for a walk, move about, stroll, take a walk, take the air.

stretch out hold out, lie down, put out, reach, relax, stretch forth. **antonym** draw back.

strew v disperse, litter, scatter, spread, sprinkle. **antonym** gather.

stricken adj affected, afflicted, expunged, hit, injured, smitten, struck, wounded. **antonym** unaffected.

strict adj absolute, accurate, austere, authoritarian, close, complete, exact, faithful, firm, harsh, meticulous, no-nonsense, particular, perfect, precise, religious, restricted, rigid, rigorous, scrupulous, severe, stern, stringent, thoroughgoing, total, true, unsparing, utter, Victorian. **antonyms** easy-going, flexible, mild.

stricture n blame, censure, criticism, flak, rebuke, reproof. **antonym** praise.

strident adj cacophonous, clamorous, clashing, discordant, grating, harsh, jangling, jarring, loud, rasping, raucous, screeching, shrill, unmusical, vociferous. **antonyms** quiet, sweet.

strife n animosity, battle, bickering, combat, conflict, contention, contest, controversy, discord, dissension, friction, quarrel, rivalry, row, squabbling, struggle, warfare, wrangling. **antonym** peace.

strike n attack, buffet, hit, mutiny, raid, refusal, stoppage, thump, walk-out, wallop, work-to-rule.

v achieve, affect, afflict, arrange, assail, assault, assume, attack, attain, bang, beat, bop, box, buff, buffet, cancel, chastise, clap, clash, clobber, clout, clump, coin, collide with, cuff, dart, dash, delete, devastate, discover, dismantle, douse, down tools, drive, dunt, effect, encounter, find, force, hammer, hit, impel, impress, interpose, invade, knock, mutiny, penetrate, pierce, pound, print, punish, ratify, reach, register, remove, revolt, seem, shoot, slap, slat, smack, smite, sock, stamp, stumble across, stumble upon, surrender, swap, swipe, swop, thrust, thump, touch, trap, turn up, uncover, unearth, walk out, wallop, whack, wham, work to rule, zap.

strike down afflict, assassinate, destroy, kill, murder, ruin, slay, smite.

strike out cancel, cross out, delete, efface, erase, excise, expunge, remove, score off, score out, strike off, strike through. **antonym** add.

striking adj arresting, astonishing, conspicuous, dazzling, extraordinary, forcible, impressive, memorable, noticeable, outstanding, salient, stunning, wonderful. **antonym** unimpressive.

string n bunch, chain, cord, fibre, file, line, number, procession, queue, row, sequence, series, strand, succession, train, twine.

v festoon, hang, link, loop, sling, stretch, suspend, thread, tie up.

string along[1] accompany, agree, assent, collaborate, co-operate, go along. **antonym** dissent.

string along[2] bluff, deceive, dupe, fool, hoax, humbug, play (someone) false, play fast and loose with, put one over on, take (someone) for a ride.

string out disperse, extend, fan ou lengthen, protract, space out, spread ou straggle, stretch out, wander. **antonym** gather, shorten.

stringent adj binding, demanding exacting, flexible, inflexible, mild, rigic rigorous, severe, strict, tight, tough.

strings n catches, condition limitations, obligations, prerequisite provisos, qualifications, requirement restrictions, stipulations.

stringy adj chewy, fibrous, gristly, rop sinewy, tough, wiry. **antonym** tender.

strip[1] v bare, clear, denude, depriv despoil, dismantle, disrobe, dives empty, excoriate, expose, gut, husk lay bare, loot, peel, pillage, plunde ransack, rob, sack, skin, spoil, unclothe uncover, undress, widow. **antonym** cover, provide.

strip[2] n band, belt, bit, lath, piece, ribbon sash, shred, slat, slip, strap, swathe, tape thong, tongue.

stripe n band, bar, belt, chevron, flash fleck, striation.

strive v attempt, compete, contend endeavour, fight, labour, push onesell strain, struggle, toil, try, work.

stroke n accomplishment, achievement apoplexy, attack, blow, clap, collapse feat, fit, flourish, hit, knock, move movement, pat, rap, seizure, shock, swap swop, thump.

v caress, clap, fondle, pat, pet rub.

stroll v amble, dander, dawdle, mose ramble, saunter, stooge, toddle, wander. n airing, constitutional, dawdle excursion, promenade, ramble, saunter toddle, turn, walk.

strong adj acute, aggressive, athletic beefy, biting, bold, brave, brawny, bright brilliant, burly, capable, clear, clear cut, cogent, compelling, competent concentrated, convincing, courageous dazzling, dedicated, deep, deep rooted, determined, distinct, drastic durable, eager, effective, efficient emphasised, excelling, extreme, fast moving, fervent, fierce, firm, forceful forcible, formidable, glaring, great grievous, gross, hale, hard, hard nosed, hard-wearing, hardy, heady healthy, hearty, heavy-duty, Herculean highly-flavoured, highly-seasoned, hot intemperate, intense, intoxicating, keen loud, lusty, marked, muscular, numerous offensive, overpowering, persuasive piquant, pithy, plucky, potent, powerful pungent, pure, rank, redoubtable, reinforced, resilient, resolute, resourceful, robust, self-assertive, severe, sharp, sinewy, sound, spicy, stalwart, stark, staunch, steadfast, stout, stouthearted, strapping, stressed, sturdy, substantial, telling, tenacious, tough, trenchant, undiluted, unmistakable, unseemly, unyielding, urgent, vehement, violent, virile, vivid, weighty, well-armed, wellbuilt, well-established, well-founded, well-protected, well-versed, zealous. *antonyms* mild, weak.

strong point advantage, aptitude, asset, bent, forte, gift, speciality, strength, talent, thing.

strongarm *adj* aggressive, bullying, coercive, forceful, intimidatory, oppressive, physical, terror, threatening, thuggish, violent. *antonym* gentle.

strong-minded *adj* determined, firm, independent, iron-willed, resolute, steadfast, strong-willed, tenacious, unbending, uncompromising, unwavering. *antonym* weak-willed.

stroppy *adj* awkward, bad-tempered, bloody-minded, cantankerous, difficult, obstreperous, perverse, quarrelsome, refractory, rowdy, unco-operative, unhelpful. *antonyms* co-operative, sweet-tempered.

structure *n* arrangement, building, configuration, conformation, construction, design, edifice, erection, fabric, form, formation, make-up, organisation, pile, set-up.
v arrange, assemble, build, construct, design, form, organise, shape.

struggle *v* agonise, battle, compete, contend, fight, grapple, labour, scuffle, strain, strive, toil, work, wrestle. *antonyms* give in, rest.
n agony, battle, brush, clash, combat, conflict, contest, effort, encounter, exertion, grind, hostilities, labour, pains, scramble, skirmish, strife, toil, tussle, work. *antonyms* ease, submission.

strut *v* cock, parade, prance, stalk, swagger.

stub *n* butt, counterfoil, dog-end, end, fag-end, remnant, stump, tail, tail-end.

stubborn *adj* bull-headed, crossgrained, difficult, dogged, dour, fixed, headstrong, inflexible, intractable, intransigent, mulish, obdurate, obstinate, opinionated, persistent, pertinacious, pig-headed, recalcitrant, refractory, rigid, self-willed, stiff, stiff-necked, tenacious, unbending, unmanageable,

unshakable, unyielding, wilful. *antonym* compliant.

stubby *adj* bristling, bristly, chunky, dumpy, knobbly, knubbly, prickly, rough, short, squat, stocky, stubbly, stumpy, thickset. *antonyms* long, tall, thin.

stuck *adj* baffled, beaten, cemented, fast, fastened, firm, fixed, glued, joined, nonplussed, stumped, stymied. *antonym* loose.

stuck on crazy about, dotty about, enthusiastic about, infatuated with, keen on, mad on, nuts on, obsessed with, wild about. *antonym* indifferent to.

stuck-up *adj* arrogant, big-headed, conceited, condescending, exclusive, haughty, high and mighty, hoitytoity, overweening, patronising, prideful, proud, snobbish, snooty, swollenheaded, toffee-nosed, uppish, uppity. *antonym* humble.

studied *adj* calculated, conscious, deliberate, forced, intentional, over-elaborate, planned, premeditated, purposeful, unnatural, wilful. *antonyms* natural, unplanned.

studious *adj* academic, assiduous, attentive, bookish, careful, diligent, eager, earnest, hard-working, heedful, intellectual, intent, meditative, reflective, scholarly, sedulous, serious, solicitous, thoughtful. *antonym* lazy.

study *v* analyse, consider, contemplate, cram, deliberate, dig, examine, investigate, learn, meditate, mug up, peruse, ponder, pore over, read, read up, research, scan, scrutinise, survey, swot.
n analysis, application, attention, cogitation, consideration, contemplation, cramming, critique, examination, inclination, inquiry, inspection, interest, investigation, learning, lessons, monograph, prolusion, reading, report, research, reverie, review, scrutiny, survey, swotting, thesis, thought, zeal.

stuff *v* binge, compress, cram, crowd, fill, force, gobble, gorge, gormandise, guzzle, jam, load, overindulge, pack, pad, push, ram, sate, satiate, shove, squeeze, stodge, stow, wedge. *antonyms* nibble, unload.
n belongings, clobber, cloth, effects, equipment, essence, fabric, furniture, gear, goods, impedimenta, junk, kit, luggage, material, materials, matter, objects, paraphernalia, pith, possessions, provisions, quintessence, staple, substance, tackle, textile, things, trappings.

stuffy *adj* airless, close, conventional, deadly, dreary, dull, fetid, fogyish, frowsty, fusty, heavy, humourless, muggy, musty, old-fashioned, oppressive, pompous, priggish, prim, staid, stale, stifling, stilted, stodgy, strait-laced, suffocating, sultry, uninteresting, unventilated, Victorian. **antonyms** airy, informal, interesting, modern.

stultify *v* blunt, dull, invalidate, negate, nullify, numb, smother, stifle, stupefy, suppress, thwart. **antonyms** prove, sharpen.

stumble *v* blunder, fall, falter, flounder, fluff, hesitate, lurch, reel, slip, stagger, stammer, stutter, titubate, trip.

stumble on blunder upon, chance upon, come across, discover, encounter, find, happen upon, light upon.

stumbling-block *n* bar, barrier, crux, difficulty, hindrance, hurdle, impediment, obstacle, obstruction, snag. **antonym** boost.

stump *v* baffle, bamboozle, bewilder, clomp, clump, confound, confuse, defeat, dumbfound, flummox, foil, mystify, nonplus, outwit, perplex, plod, puzzle, stamp, stomp, stop, stymie, trudge. **antonym** assist.

stump up contribute, cough up, donate, fork out, hand over, pay, pay out, pay up, shell out. **antonym** receive.

stumped *adj* baffled, bamboozled, floored, flummoxed, nonplussed, perplexed, stuck, stymied.

stumpy *adj* chunky, dumpy, dwarf, dwarfish, heavy, short, squat, stocky, stubby, thick, thickset. **antonyms** long, tall, thin.

stun *v* amaze, astonish, astound, bewilder, confound, confuse, daze, deafen, dumbfound, flabbergast, overcome, overpower, shock, stagger, stupefy.

stung *adj* angered, bitten, exasperated, goaded, hurt, incensed, irked, needled, nettled, peeved, piqued, resentful, roused, wounded. **antonym** soothed.

stunned *adj* astounded, dazed, devastated, dumbfounded, flabbergasted, floored, numb, shocked, staggered, stupefied. **antonym** indifferent.

stunner *n* beauty, charmer, dazzler, dish, dolly, eye-catcher, eyeful, femme fatale, good-looker, heart-throb, honey, knock-out, looker, lovely, peach, sensation, siren, smasher. **antonym** dog.

stunning *adj* beautiful, brilliant, dazing, dazzling, devastating, gorgeous, great, heavenly, impressive, lovely, marvellous, ravishing, remarkable, sensational, smashing, spectacular, striking, wonderful. **antonyms** poor, ugly.

stunt[1] *n* act, campaign, deed, enterprise, exploit, feat, feature, performance, tour de force, trick, turn.

stunt[2] *v* arrest, check, dwarf, hamper, hinder, impede, restrict, slow, stop. **antonym** promote.

stupefy *v* amaze, astound, baffle, bewilder, confound, daze, drowse, dumbfound, numb, shock, stagger, stun.

stupendous *adj* amazing, astounding, breathtaking, colossal, enormous, fabulous, fantastic, gigantic, huge, marvellous, mind-blowing, mind-boggling, overwhelming, phenomenal, prodigious, staggering, stunning, superb, tremendous, vast, wonderful. **antonym** unimpressive.

stupid *adj* asinine, beef-brained, boring, brainless, clueless, cretinous, cuckoo, damfool, dazed, deficient, dense, dim, doltish, dopey, dozy, drippy, dull, dumb, foolish, futile, gaumless, glaikit, gormless, groggy, gullible, half-baked, half-witted, idiotic, ill-advised, imbecilic, inane, indiscreet, insensate, insensible, irrelevant, irresponsible, laughable, ludicrous, meaningless, mindless, moronic, naïve, nonsensical, obtuse, pointless, puerile, punch-drunk, rash, semiconscious, senseless, short-sighted, simple, simple-minded, slow, slow-witted, sluggish, stolid, stunned, stupefied, thick, thick-headed, thick-witted, trivial, unintelligent, unthinking, vacuous, vapid, witless, wooden-headed. **antonyms** alert, clever.

stupor *n* coma, daze, inertia, insensibility, lethargy, numbness, stupefaction, torpor, trance, unconsciousness, wonder. **antonym** alertness.

sturdy *adj* athletic, brawny, determined, durable, firm, flourishing, hardy, hearty, husky, muscular, obstinate, powerful, resolute, robust, secure, solid, stalwart, staunch, steadfast, stout, strong, substantial, vigorous, well-built, well-made. **antonyms** decrepit, puny.

stutter *v* falter, hesitate, mumble, splutter, stammer, stumble.

style *n* affluence, appearance, approach, category, chic, comfort, cosmopolitanism, custom, cut, dash, design, diction, dressiness, dress-sense, ease, élan, elegance, expression, fashion fashionableness, flair, flamboyance, form, genre, grace, grandeur, hand, kind, luxury, manner, method, mode, panache, pattern, phraseology, phrasing, pizzazz, polish, rage, refinement, savoir-faire, smartness, sophistication, sort, spirit, strain, stylishness, taste, technique, tenor, tone, treatment, trend, type, urbanity, variety, vein, vogue, way, wording. *antonym* inelegance.

v adapt, address, arrange, call, christen, create, cut, denominate, design, designate, dress, dub, entitle, fashion, label, name, shape, tailor, term, title.

stylish *adj* à la mode, chic, classy, dapper, dressy, fashionable, in vogue, modish, natty, polished, smart, snappy, snazzy, trendy, urbane, voguish. *antonym* unstylish.

stymie *v* baffle, balk, bamboozle, confound, defeat, flummox, foil, frustrate, hinder, mystify, nonplus, puzzle, snooker, stump, thwart. *antonym* assist.

suave *adj* affable, agreeable, bland, charming, civilised, courteous, diplomatic, gracious, obliging, pleasing, polite, smooth, smooth-tongued, soft-spoken, sophisticated, unctuous, urbane, worldly. *antonym* unsophisticated.

subconscious *adj* hidden, inner, innermost, intuitive, latent, repressed, subliminal, suppressed, unconscious. *antonym* conscious.

n id, super-ego, unconscious.

subdue *v* allay, break, check, conquer, control, crush, damp, dampen, daunt, defeat, discipline, humble, master, mellow, moderate, overcome, overpower, overrun, quell, quieten, reduce, repress, soften, soft-pedal, subact, subject, suppress, tame, trample, vanquish. *antonym* arouse.

subdued *adj* abated, chastened, crestfallen, dejected, dim, downcast, grave, hushed, low-key, muted, quiet, repentant, repressed, restrained, sad, serious, shaded, sober, soft, solemn, sombre, subtle, unobtrusive. *antonyms* aroused, lively.

subject *n* affair, business, case, chapter, citizen, client, dependant, ground, issue, matter, mind, national, object, participant, patient, point, question, subordinate, substance, theme, topic, victim. *antonym* master.

adj answerable, captive, conditional, contingent, dependent, disposed, enslaved, exposed, inferior, liable,

obedient, open, prone, subjugated, submissive, subordinate, subservient, susceptible, vulnerable. *antonyms* free, insusceptible, superior.

v expose, lay open, subdue, submit, subordinate, treat.

subjective biased, emotional, idiosyncratic, individual, instinctive, introspective, intuitive, personal, prejudiced. *antonym* objective.

subjugate *v* conquer, crush, defeat, enslave, master, overcome, overpower, overthrow, quell, reduce, subdue, suppress, tame, vanquish. *antonym* free.

sublime *adj* elevated, eminent, exalted, glorious, grand, great, high, imposing, lofty, magnificent, majestic, noble, transcendent. *antonym* lowly.

submerge *v* deluge, dip, drown, duck, dunk, engulf, flood, immerse, implunge, inundate, overflow, overwhelm, plunge, sink, submerse, swamp. *antonym* surface.

submerged *adj* concealed, drowned, hidden, immersed, inundated, obscured, submarine, submersed, sunk, sunken, swamped, undersea, underwater, unseen.

submission *n* acquiescence, argument, assent, capitulation, compliance, contention, deference, docility, entry, meekness, obedience, passivity, presentation, proposal, resignation, submissiveness, submitting, suggestion, surrender, tendering, tractability, yielding. *antonym* intractability.

submissive *adj* abject, accommodating, acquiescent, amenable, biddable, bootlicking, complaisant, compliant, deferential, docile, dutiful, humble, ingratiating, malleable, meek, obedient, obsequious, passive, patient, pliant, resigned, subdued, subservient, supine, tractable, uncomplaining, unresisting, yielding. *antonym* intractable.

submit *v* accede, acquiesce, advance, agree, argue, assert, bend, bow, capitulate, claim, commit, comply, contend, defer, endure, knuckle under, move, present, proffer, propose, propound, put, refer, state, stoop, succumb, suggest, surrender, table, tender, tolerate, volunteer, yield. *antonym* struggle.

subnormal *adj* cretinous, ESN, feeble-minded, imbecilic, inferior, low, moronic, retarded, slow, unteachable. *antonym* gifted.

subordinate *adj* ancillary, auxiliary,

dependent, inferior, junior, lesser, lower, menial, minor, secondary, servient, subject, subservient, subsidiary, supplementary. **antonym** superior.

n adjunct, aide, assistant, attendant, dependant, inferior, junior, second, sub, subaltern, underling. **antonym** superior.

subscribe *v* acquiesce, advocate, agree, approve, consent, contribute, cough up, countenance, donate, endorse, fork out, give, offer, pledge, promise, shell out, support.

subsequent *adj* after, consequent, consequential, ensuing, following, later, resulting, succeeding. **antonym** previous.

subsequently *adv* after, afterwards, consequently, later. **antonym** previously.

subservient *adj* abject, accessory, ancillary, auxiliary, bootlicking, cringing, deferential, inferior, obsequious, serviceable, servile, slavish, subject, submissive, subordinate, subsidiary, sycophantic. **antonyms** domineering, rebellious.

subside *v* abate, collapse, decline, decrease, descend, diminish, drop, dwindle, ease, ebb, fall, lessen, lower, moderate, quieten, recede, settle, sink, slacken, slake, wane. **antonym** increase.

subsidence *n* abatement, decline, decrease, descent, diminution, ebb, lessening, settlement, settling, sinking, slackening. **antonym** increase.

subsidiary *adj* adjective, aiding, ancillary, assistant, auxiliary, branch, contributory, co-operative, helpful, lesser, minor, secondary, serviceable, subordinate, subservient, supplementary, useful. **antonym** chief.

n affiliate, branch, division, offshoot, part, section.

subsidise *v* aid, back, finance, fund, promote, sponsor, support, underwrite.

subsidy *n* aid, allowance, assistance, backing, contribution, finance, grant, help, sponsorship, subvention, support.

subsist *v* continue, endure, exist, hold out, inhere, last, live, remain, survive.

subsistence *n* existence, food, keep, livelihood, living, maintenance, nourishment, provision, rations, support, survival, sustenance, upkeep, victuals.

substance *n* actuality, affluence, assets, body, burden, concreteness, consistence, element, entity, essence, estate, fabric, force, foundation, gist, ground, import,

material, matter, meaning, means, nitty-gritty, pith, property, reality, resources, significance, solidity, stuff, subject, subject-matter, texture, theme, wealth.

substandard *adj* damaged, imperfect, inadequate, inferior, poor, second-rate, shoddy, tawdry, unacceptable. **antonym** first-rate.

substantial *adj* actual, ample, big, bulky, considerable, corporeal, durable, enduring, essential, existent, firm, full-bodied, generous, goodly, hefty, important, large, massive, material, positive, real, significant, sizable, solid, sound, stout, strong, sturdy, tidy, true, valid, weighty, well-built, worthwhile. **antonyms** insignificant, small.

substantiate *v* affirm, authenticate, confirm, corroborate, embody, establish, prove, support, validate, verify. **antonym** disprove.

substitute *v* change, commute, exchange, interchange, replace, subrogate, swap, switch.

n agent, alternate, depute, deputy, equivalent, ersatz, locum, makeshift, proxy, relief, replacement, replacer, reserve, stand-by, stop-gap, sub, supply, surrogate, temp.

adj acting, additional, alternative, ersatz, proxy, replacement, reserve, second, surrogate, temporary, vicarious.

substitute for act for, cover for, deputise, double for, fill in for, relieve, stand in for, sub.

substitution *n* change, exchange, interchange, replacement, swap, swapping, switch, switching.

subterfuge *n* artifice, deception, deviousness, dodge, duplicity, evasion, expedient, machination, manoeuvre, ploy, pretence, pretext, ruse, scheme, shift, stall, stratagem, trick. **antonyms** honesty, openness.

subtle *adj* artful, astute, crafty, cunning, deep, delicate, designing, devious, discriminating, elusive, faint, fine, drawn, impalpable, implied, indirect, ingenious, insinuated, intriguing, keen, nice, obtuse, over-refined, penetrating, profound, rarefied, refined, scheming, shrewd, slight, sly, sophisticated, tenuous, understated, wily. **antonyms** open, unsubtle.

subtlety *n* acumen, acuteness, artfulness, astuteness, cleverness, craftness, cunning, delicacy, deviousness, discernment, discrimination, finesse, guile, intricacy, nicety, openness penetration, refinement, sagacity, skill, slyness, sophistication, unsubtlety, wiliness.

subtract *v* debit, deduct, detract, diminish, remove, withdraw. *antonyms* add, add to.

subversive *adj* destructive, disruptive, incendiary, inflammatory, insurrectionary, overthrowing, perversive, riotous, seditious, treasonous, underground, undermining. *antonym* loyal.
n dissident, fifth columnist, freedom fighter, insurrectionary, quisling, saboteur, terrorist, traitor.

subvert *v* confound, contaminate, corrupt, debase, demolish, demoralise, deprave, destroy, disrupt, invalidate, overturn, pervert, poison, raze, ruin, sabotage, undermine, upset, vitiate, wreck. *antonyms* boost, uphold.

succeed *v* arrive, ensue, flourish, follow, make good, make it, prosper, result, supervene, thrive, triumph, work. *antonyms* fail, precede.

succeeding *adj* coming, ensuing, following, later, next, subsequent, successive, to come. *antonym* previous.

success *n* ascendancy, bestseller, celebrity, eminence, fame, fortune, happiness, hit, luck, prosperity, sensation, somebody, star, triumph, winner. *antonym* failure.

successful *adj* acknowledged, bestselling, booming, efficacious, favourable, flourishing, fortunate, fruitful, lucky, lucrative, moneymaking, paying, profitable, prosperous, rewarding, satisfactory, satisfying, thriven, thriving, top, unbeaten, victorious, wealthy. *antonym* unsuccessful.

succession *n* accession, assumption, chain, concatenation, continuation, course, cycle, descendants, descent, elevation, flow, inheritance, line, lineage, order, procession, progression, race, run, sequence, series, train.

successive *adj* consecutive, following, in succession, sequent, succeeding.

succinct *adj* brief, compact, compendious, concise, condensed, pithy, short, summary, terse. *antonym* wordy.

succour *v* aid, assist, befriend, comfort, encourage, foster, help, help out, nurse, relieve, support. *antonym* undermine.
n aid, assistance, comfort, help, helping hand, ministrations, relief, support.

succulent *adj* fleshy, juicy, luscious, lush, moist, mouthwatering, rich, sappy. *antonym* dry.

succumb *v* capitulate, collapse, deteriorate, die, fall, give in, knuckle under, submit, surrender, yield. *antonym* overcome.

suck *v* absorb, drain, draw in, extract, imbibe.

sucking-up *n* arse-licking, bootlicking, currying favour, fawning, flattering, ingratiating, toadying.

sudden *adj* abrupt, hasty, hurried, impulsive, prompt, quick, rapid, rash, snap, startling, swift, unexpected, unforeseen, unusual. *antonym* slow.

sue *v* apply, beg, beseech, charge, entreat, indict, petition, plead, prosecute, solicit, summon, supplicate.

suffer *v* ache, agonise, allow, bear, brook, deteriorate, endure, experience, feel, grieve, hurt, let, permit, sorrow, support, sustain, tolerate, undergo.

suffering *n* ache, affliction, agony, anguish, discomfort, distress, hardship, martyrdom, misery, ordeal, pain, pangs, torment, torture.

suffice *v* answer, content, do, measure up, satisfy, serve.

sufficiency *n* adequacy, adequateness, competence, conceit, enough, plenty, quantum sufficit, satiety, sufficience. *antonym* insufficiency.

sufficient *adj* adequate, competent, effective, enough, satisfactory, sufficing, well-off, well-to-do. *antonyms* insufficient, poor.

suffocate *v* asphyxiate, choke, smother, stifle, strangle, throttle.

suffuse *v* bathe, colour, cover, flood, imbue, infuse, permeate, pervade, redden, steep, transfuse.

suggest *v* advise, advocate, connote, evoke, hint, imply, indicate, innuendo, insinuate, intimate, move, propose, recommend. *antonyms* demonstrate, order.

suggestion *n* breath, hint, incitement, indication, innuendo, insinuation, intimation, motion, plan, proposal, proposition, recommendation, suspicion, temptation, trace, whisper. *antonyms* demonstration, order.

suggestive *adj* bawdy, blue, evocative, expressive, immodest, improper, indecent, indelicate, indicative, insinuating, meaning, off-colour, page-three, provocative, prurient, racy, redolent, reminiscent, ribald, risqué, rude, smutty, spicy, titillating, unseemly. *antonyms* clean, unevocative.

suit *v* accommodate, adapt, adjust, agree,

answer, become, befit, correspond, do, fashion, fit, gratify, harmonise, match, modify, please, proportion, satisfy, tailor, tally. *antonyms* clash, displease.

n action, addresses, appeal, attentions, case, cause, clothing, costume, courtship, dress, ensemble, entreaty, get-up, habit, invocation, kind, lawsuit, outfit, petition, prayer, proceeding, prosecution, request, rig-out, series, trial, type.

suitable *adj* acceptable, adequate, applicable, apposite, appropriate, apt, becoming, befitting, competent, conformable, congenial, congruent, consonant, convenient, correspondent, due, fit, fitting, opportune, pertinent, proper, relevant, right, satisfactory, seemly, square, suited. *antonym* unsuitable.

suitably *adv* acceptably, accordingly, appropriately, fitly, fittingly, properly, quite. *antonym* unsuitably.

sulk *v* brood, grouch, grump, mope, pet, pout.

sulky *adj* aloof, churlish, cross, disgruntled, grouty, ill-humoured, moody, morose, perverse, pettish, petulant, put out, resentful, sullen. *antonym* cheerful.

sullen *adj* baleful, brooding, cheerless, cross, dark, dismal, dull, gloomy, glowering, glum, heavy, lumpish, moody, morose, obstinate, perverse, silent, sombre, sour, stubborn, sulky, surly, unsociable. *antonym* cheerful.

sully *v* besmirch, blemish, contaminate, darken, defile, dirty, disgrace, dishonour, distain, mar, pollute, spoil, spot, stain, taint, tarnish. *antonyms* cleanse, honour.

sultry *adj* close, come-hither, erotic, hot, humid, indecent, lurid, muggy, oppressive, passionate, provocative, seductive, sensual, sexy, sticky, stifling, stuffy, sweltering, torrid, voluptuous. *antonyms* cold, cool.

sum *n* aggregate, amount, completion, culmination, entirety, height, quantity, reckoning, result, score, substance, sum total, summary, tally, total, totality, whole.

sum up close, conclude, précis, recapitulate, review, summarise.

summarily *adv* abruptly, arbitrarily, expeditiously, forthwith, hastily, immediately, peremptorily, promptly, speedily, swiftly.

summarise *v* abbreviate, abridge, condense, encapsulate, epitomise, outline, précis, review, shorten, sum up. *antonym* expand (on).

summary *n* abridgement, abstract, compendium, digest, epitome, essence, extract, outline, précis, recapitulation, résumé, review, rundown, summation, summing-up, synopsis.

adj arbitrary, brief, compact, compendious, concise, condensed, cursory, expeditious, hasty, perfunctory, pithy, short, succinct. *antonym* lengthy.

summit *n* acme, apex, apogee, crown, culmination, head, height, peak, pinnacle, point, top, vertex, zenith. *antonyms* bottom, nadir.

summon *v* arouse, assemble, beckon, bid, call, convene, convoke, gather, hist, invite, invoke, mobilise, muster, rally, rouse. *antonym* dismiss.

sumptuous *adj* costly, dear, expensive, extravagant, gorgeous, grand, lavish, luxurious, magnificent, opulent, plush, posh, princely, rich, ritzy, splendid, superb. *antonym* mean.

sundry *adj* a few, assorted, different, divers, miscellaneous, separate, several, some, varied, various.

sunk *adj* done for, doomed, finished, lost, ruined, up the creek, up the spout.

sunken *adj* buried, concave, depressed, drawn, emaciated, gaunt, haggard, hollow, hollowed, immersed, lower, recessed, submerged.

sunless *adj* bleak, cheerless, cloudy, dark, depressing, dismal, dreary, gloomy, grey, hazy, overcast, sombre. *antonym* sunny.

sunny *adj* beaming, blithe, bright, brilliant, buoyant, cheerful, cheery, clear, cloudless, fine, genial, happy, joyful, light-hearted, luminous, optimistic, pleasant, radiant, smiling, summery, sun-bright, sunlit, sunshiny. *antonym* gloomy.

sunrise *n* aurora, cock-crow, crack of dawn, dawn, daybreak, daylight, sun-up.

sunset *n* dusk, evening, eventide, gloaming, nightfall, sundown, twilight.

super *adj* excellent, glorious, incomparable, magnificent, marvellous, matchless, outstanding, peerless, sensational, smashing, superb, terrific, top-notch, wizard, wonderful. *antonym* poor.

superb *adj* admirable, breathtaking, choice, clipping, excellent, exquisite, fine, first-rate, gorgeous, grand, magnificent, marvellous, splendid, superior, unrivalled. *antonym* poor.

supercilious *adj* arrogant, condescending, contemptuous, disdainful, haughty, hoity-toity, imperious, insolent, lofty, lordly, overbearing, patronising, proud, scornful, snooty, snotty, stuck-up, toffee-nosed, uppish, uppity. *antonym* humble.

superficial *adj* apparent, casual, cosmetic, cursory, desultory, empty, empty-headed, evident, exterior, external, frivolous, hasty, hurried, lightweight, nodding, ostensible, outward, passing, perfunctory, peripheral, seeming, shallow, silly, sketchy, skin-deep, slapdash, slight, surface, trivial. *antonym* detailed.

superfluous *adj* excess, excessive, extra, needless, otiose, pleonastic, redundant, remaining, spare, superabundant, supernumerary, surplus, uncalled-for, unnecessary, unneeded, unwanted. *antonym* necessary.

superhuman *adj* divine, great, herculean, heroic, immense, paranormal, phenomenal, prodigious, stupendous, supernatural, valiant. *antonyms* average, ordinary.

superior *adj* admirable, airy, better, choice, condescending, de luxe, disdainful, distinguished, excellent, exceptional, exclusive, fine, first-class, first-rate, good, grander, greater, haughty, high-class, higher, hoity-toity, lofty, lordly, par excellence, patronising, preferred, pretentious, prevailing, respectable, snobbish, snooty, snotty, stuck-up, supercilious, surpassing, top-notch, unrivalled, upper, uppish, uppity. *antonyms* humble, inferior.
n boss, chief, director, foreman, gaffer, manager, principal, senior, supervisor. *antonyms* inferior, junior.

superiority *n* advantage, ascendancy, edge, excellence, lead, predominance, pre-eminence, preponderance, prevalence, supremacy. *antonym* inferiority.

superlative *adj* consummate, crack, excellent, greatest, highest, magnificent, matchless, outstanding, peerless, supreme, surpassing, unbeatable, unbeaten, unparalleled, unrivalled, unsurpassed. *antonym* poor.

supernatural *adj* abnormal, dark, ghostly, hidden, metaphysical, miraculous, mysterious, mystic, occult, paranormal, phantom, psychic, spectral, spiritual, uncanny, unearthly, unnatural. *antonym* natural.

supernumerary *adj* excess, excessive, extra, extraordinary, redundant, spare, superfluous, surplus. *antonym* necessary.

supersede *v* annul, displace, oust, overrule, remove, replace, succeed, supplant, supplement, suspend, usurp.

superstition *n* delusion, fable, fallacy, illusion, myth, old wives' tale.

superstitious *adj* delusive, fallacious, false, groundless, illusory.

supervise *v* administer, conduct, control, direct, general, handle, inspect, keep tabs on, manage, oversee, preside over, run, superintend.

supervision *n* administration, auspices, care, charge, control, direction, guidance, instruction, leading-strings, management, oversight, stewardship, superintendence, surveillance.

supplant *v* displace, dispossess, oust, overthrow, remove, replace, supersede, topple, undermine, unseat.

supple *adj* bending, double-jointed, elastic, flexible, limber, lithe, loose-limbed, plastic, pliable, pliant, whippy, willowy. *antonym* rigid.

supplement *n* addendum, addition, appendix, codicil, complement, extra, insert, postscript, pull-out, rider, sequel, supplemental, supplementary.
v add, add to, augment, complement, extend, fill up, reinforce, supply, top up. *antonym* deplete.

supplementary *adj* accompanying, additional, ancillary, auxiliary, complementary, extra, secondary. *antonym* core.

supplication *n* appeal, entreaty, invocation, petition, plea, pleading, prayer, request, solicitation, suit.

supplies *n* equipment, food, foodstuffs, materials, necessities, provender, provisions, rations, stores, victuals, vittles.

supply *v* afford, contribute, endow, equip, fill, furnish, give, grant, minister, outfit, produce, provide, purvey, replenish, satisfy, stock, store, victual, yield. *antonym* take.
n cache, fund, hoard, materials, necessities, provender, provisions, quantity, rations, reserve, reservoir, service, source, stake, stock, stockpile, store, stores. *antonym* lack.

support *v* advocate, aid, assist, authenticate, back, bear, bolster, brace, brook, buttress, carry, champion, cherish, confirm, corroborate, countenance, crutch, defend, document, endorse, endure, finance, foster, fund, help, hold, keep, maintain, nourish, promote, prop, rally round, reinforce, second, stand (for), stay, stomach, strengthen, strut, submit, subsidise, substantiate, succour, suffer, sustain, take (someone's) part, tolerate, underpin, underwrite, uphold, verify. **antonyms** contradict, oppose.

n aid, approval, assistance, back, backbone, backer, backing, blessing, brace, championship, comfort, comforter, crutch, encouragement, foundation, friendship, furtherance, help, jockstrap, keep, lining, livelihood, loyalty, mainstay, maintenance, patronage, pillar, post, prop, protection, relief, second, stanchion, stay, stiffener, subsistence, succour, supporter, sustenance, underpinning, upkeep. **antonym** opposition.

supporter *n* adherent, advocate, ally, apologist, champion, co-worker, defender, fan, follower, friend, helper, patron, seconder, sponsor, upholder, well-wisher. **antonym** opponent.

supportive *adj* attentive, caring, encouraging, helpful, reassuring, sympathetic, understanding. **antonym** discouraging.

suppose *v* assume, believe, calculate, conceive, conclude, conjecture, consider, expect, fancy, guess, hypothesise, hypothetise, imagine, infer, judge, opine, posit, postulate, presume, presuppose, pretend, surmise, think. **antonym** know.

supposed *adj* accepted, alleged, assumed, conjectured, hypothetical, imagined, presumed, presupposed, professed, putative, reported, reputed, rumoured. **antonym** known.

supposed to expected to, intended to, meant to, obliged to, required to.

supposedly *adv* allegedly, assumedly, avowedly, hypothetically, ostensibly, presumably, professedly, purportedly, theoretically. **antonym** really.

supposition *n* assumption, conjecture, doubt, guess, guesstimate, guesswork, hypothesis, idea, notion, opinion, postulate, presumption, speculation, surmise, theory. **antonym** knowledge.

suppress *v* censor, check, conceal, conquer, contain, crush, extinguish, muffle, muzzle, overpower, overthrow, quash, quell, repress, restrain, silence, smother, snuff out, squelch, stamp out, stifle, stop, strangle, subdue, submerge,

vote down, withhold. **antonyms** encourage, incite.

suppression *n* censorship, check, clampdown, crackdown, crushing, dissolution, elimination, extinction, inhibition, prohibition, quashing, quelling, smothering, termination. **antonyms** encouragement, incitement.

supremacy *n* ascendancy, dominance, domination, dominion, hegemony, lordship, mastery, predominance, pre-eminence, primacy, sovereignty, sway.

supreme *adj* cardinal, chief, consummate, crowning, culminating, extreme, final, first, foremost, greatest, head, highest, incomparable, leading, matchless, paramount, peerless, predominant, pre-eminent, prevailing, prime, principal, second-to-none, sovereign, superlative, surpassing, top, ultimate, unbeatable, unbeaten, unsurpassed, utmost, world-beating. **antonyms** lowly, poor, slight.

sure *adj* accurate, assured, bound, certain, clear, confident, convinced, decided, definite, dependable, effective, fast, firm, fixed, foolproof, guaranteed, honest, indisputable, ineluctable, inescapable, inevitable, infallible, irrevocable, persuaded, positive, precise, reliable, safe, satisfied, secure, solid, stable, steadfast, steady, sure-fire, trustworthy, trusty, undeniable, undoubted, unerring, unfailing, unmistakable, unswerving, unwavering. **antonyms** doubtful, unsure.

surely *adv* assuredly, certainly, confidently, definitely, doubtlessly, firmly, indubitably, inevitably, inexorably, safely, undoubtedly, unquestionably.

surface *n* covering, day, exterior, façade, face, facet, outside, plane, side, skin, top, veneer, working-surface, worktop. **antonym** interior.

adj apparent, exterior, external, outer, outside, outward, superficial. **antonym** interior.

v appear, come to light, emerge, materialise, rise, transpire. **antonyms** disappear, sink.

surfeit *n* bellyful, excess, glut, overindulgence, plethora, satiety, superabundance, superfluity. **antonym** lack.

v cram, fill, glut, gorge, overfeed, overfill, satiate, stuff.

surge *v* billow, eddy, gush, heave, rise, roll, rush, seethe, swell, swirl, tower, undulate.

n flood, flow, gush, intensification, outpouring, rush, swell, uprush, upsurge, wave.

urly *adj* bearish, brusque, chuffy, churlish, crabbed, cross, crusty, curmudgeonly, grouchy, gruff, grum, ill-natured, morose, perverse, sulky, sullen, testy, uncivil, ungracious. **antonym** pleasant.

urmise *v* assume, conclude, conjecture, consider, deduce, fancy, guess, imagine, infer, opine, presume, speculate, suppose, suspect. **antonym** know.

n assumption, conclusion, conjecture, deduction, guess, hypothesis, idea, inference, notion, opinion, possibility, presumption, speculation, supposition, suspicion, thought. **antonym** certainty.

urmount *v* conquer, exceed, get over, master, overcome, surpass, triumph over, vanquish.

urpass *v* beat, best, eclipse, exceed, excel, outdo, outshine, outstrip, override, overshadow, surmount, top, tower above, transcend.

urpassing *adj* exceptional, extraordinary, incomparable, inimitable, matchless, outstanding, phenomenal, rare, supreme, unrivalled, unsurpassed. **antonym** poor.

urplus *n* balance, excess, remainder, residue, superabundance, superfluity, surfeit. **antonym** lack.

adj excess, extra, odd, redundant, remaining, spare, superfluous, unused. **antonym** essential.

urprise *v* amaze, astonish, astound, bewilder, confuse, disconcert, dismay, flabbergast, nonplus, stagger, startle, stun.

n amazement, astonishment, bewilderment, bombshell, dismay, eye-opener, incredulity, jolt, revelation, shock, start, stupefaction, wonder. **antonym** composure.

urprised *adj* amazed, astonished, confounded, disconcerted, incredulous, nonplussed, open-mouthed, shocked, speechless, staggered, startled, thunderstruck. **antonym** composed.

urprising *adj* amazing, astonishing, astounding, extraordinary, incredible, marvellous, remarkable, staggering, startling, stunning, unexpected, unlooked-for, unusual, unwonted, wonderful. **antonym** expected.

urrender *v* abandon, capitulate, cede, concede, forego, give in, give up, quit, relinquish, remise, renounce, resign,

submit, succumb, waive, yield. **antonym** fight on.

n appeasement, capitulation, déchéance, delivery, relinquishment, renunciation, resignation, submission, white flag, yielding.

surreptitious *adj* clandestine, covert, fraudulent, furtive, secret, sly, sneaking, stealthy, unauthorised, underhand, veiled. **antonym** open.

surrogate *n* deputy, proxy, representative, stand-in, substitute.

surround *v* besiege, compass, encase, encircle, enclose, encompass, envelop, girdle, ring.

surrounding *adj* adjacent, adjoining, ambient, bordering, circumambient, circumjacent, encircling, enclosing, nearby, neighbouring.

surroundings *n* ambience, background, environment, environs, locale, location, milieu, neighbourhood, setting, vicinity.

surveillance *n* care, charge, check, control, direction, guardianship, inspection, monitoring, observation, regulation, scrutiny, stewardship, superintendence, supervision, vigilance, watch.

survey *v* appraise, assess, consider, contemplate, estimate, examine, inspect, measure, observe, peruse, plan, plot, prospect, reconnoitre, research, review, scan, scrutinise, study, supervise, surview, view.

n appraisal, assessment, conspectus, examination, geodesy, inquiry, inspection, measurement, overview, perusal, review, sample, scrutiny, study.

survive *v* endure, exist, last, last out, live, live out, live through, outlast, outlive, ride, stay, subsist, weather, withstand. **antonym** succumb.

susceptible *adj* defenceless, disposed, given, impressible, impressionable, inclined, liable, open, predisposed, prone, receptive, responsive, sensitive, subject, suggestible, tender, vulnerable. **antonyms** impregnable, resistant.

suspect *v* believe, call in question, conclude, conjecture, consider, distrust, doubt, fancy, feel, guess, infer, mistrust, opine, speculate, suppose, surmise.

adj debatable, dodgy, doubtful, dubious, fishy, questionable, suspicious, unauthoritative, unreliable. **antonyms** acceptable, innocent, straightforward.

suspend *v* adjourn, append, arrest, attach, cease, dangle, debar, defer, delay, disbar, discontinue, dismiss, expel, freeze, hang, hold off, interrupt, postpone, shelve, sideline, stay, swing, withhold. **antonyms** continue, expedite, reinstate, restore.

suspense · n anticipation, anxiety, apprehension, doubt, excitement, expectancy, expectation, incertitude, indecision, insecurity, irresolution, tension, uncertainty, wavering. **antonyms** certainty, knowledge.

suspension n abeyance, adjournment, break, cessation, deferment, deferral, delay, disbarment, discontinuation, intermission, interruption, moratorium, postponement, remission, respite, standstill, stay. **antonyms** continuation, reinstatement, restoration.

suspicion n apprehension, chariness, conjecture, distrust, doubt, glimmer, guess, hint, hunch, idea, impression, intuition, jealousy, misgiving, mistrust, notion, presentiment, qualm, scepticism, shade, shadow, soupçon, strain, streak, suggestion, supposition, surmise, suspiciousness, tinge, touch, trace, wariness. **antonym** trust.

suspicious adj apprehensive, chary, distrustful, dodgy, doubtful, dubious, fishy, incredulous, irregular, jealous, louche, mistrustful, peculiar, queer, questionable, sceptical, shady, suspect, suspecting, unbelieving, uneasy, wary. **antonyms** innocent, trustful, unexceptionable.

sustain v aid, approve, assist, bear, carry, comfort, confirm, continue, endorse, endure, experience, feel, foster, help, hold, keep going, maintain, nourish, nurture, prolong, protract, provide for, ratify, relieve, sanction, stay, suffer, support, survive, undergo, uphold, validate, verify, withstand.

sustained adj constant, continuous, long-drawn-out, non-stop, perpetual, prolonged, protracted, steady, unremitting. **antonyms** broken, intermittent, interrupted, occasional, spasmodic.

svelte adj lissom, lithe, shapely, slender, slinky, smooth, streamlined, sylphlike, willowy. **antonyms** bulky, ungainly.

swagger v bluster, boast, brag, cock, crow, parade, prance, roister, strut, swank.
n arrogance, bluster, boastfulness, boasting, display, ostentation, show, showing off, swank, vainglory. **antonyms** diffidence, modesty, restraint.

swallow v absorb, accept, assimilate, believe, buy, consume, devour, down, drink, eat, engulf, gulp, imbibe, ingest, knock back, quaff, stifle, suppress, swig, swill, wash down.

swallow up absorb, consume, deplete, dissipate, drain, eat up, engulf, envelop, exhaust, gobble up, guzzle, overrun, overwhelm, use up, waste.

swamp v beset, besiege, capsise, deluge, drench, engulf, flood, inundate, overload, overwhelm, saturate, sink, submerge, waterlog.

swank v attitudinise, boast, parade, posture, preen oneself, show off, strut, swagger.
n boastfulness, conceit, conceitedness, display, ostentation, pretentiousness, self-advertisement, show, showing-off, swagger, vainglory. **antonyms** modesty, restraint.

swanky adj de luxe, exclusive, expensive, fancy, fashionable, flash, flashy, glamorous, grand, lavish, luxurious, ostentatious, plush, posh, pretentious, rich, ritzy, showy, smart, stylish, sumptuous, swish. **antonyms** discreet, unobtrusive.

swap, swop v bandy, barter, exchange, interchange, substitute, switch, trade, traffic, transpose.

swarm n army, bevy, concourse, crowd, drove, flock, herd, horde, host, mass, mob, multitude, myriad, shoal, throng.
v congregate, crowd, flock, flood, mass, stream, throng.

swarm with abound, bristle, crawl, hotch, teem.

swarthy adj black, brown, dark, dark-complexioned, dark-skinned, dusky. **antonyms** fair, pale.

swathe v bandage, bind, cloak, drape, envelop, fold, furl, lap, sheathe, shroud, swaddle, wind, wrap. **antonyms** unwind, unwrap.

sway v affect, bend, control, direct, divert, dominate, fluctuate, govern, guide, incline, induce, influence, lean, lurch, oscillate, overrule, persuade, rock, roll, swerve, swing, titter, veer, wave.
n ascendency, authority, cloud, command, control, dominion, government, hegemony, influence, jurisdiction, leadership, power, predominance, preponderance, rule, sovereignty, sweep, swerve, swing.

swear[1] v affirm, assert, asseverate, attest, avow, declare, insist, promise, testify, vow, warrant.

swear[2] v blaspheme, blind, curse, cuss, eff, imprecate, maledict, take the Lord's name in vain, turn the air blue.

swearing n bad language, blasphemy, cursing, cussing, effing and blinding, expletives, foul language, imprecations, profanity.

sweat n agitation, anxiety, chore, dew, distress, drudgery, effort, flap, labour, panic, perspiration, strain, worry.
v agonise, chafe, exude, fret, glow, perspirate, perspire, swelter, worry.

sweep v brush, career, clean, clear, dust, flounce, fly, glance, glide, hurtle, pass, remove, sail, scud, skim, tear, whisk, zoom.
n arc, bend, clearance, compass, curve, expanse, extent, gesture, impetus, move, movement, onrush, range, scope, span, stretch, stroke, swing, vista.

sweeping adj across-the-board, all-embracing, all-inclusive, blanket, broad, comprehensive, exaggerated, extensive, far-reaching, global, indiscriminate, oversimplified, radical, simplistic, thoroughgoing, unqualified, wholesale, wide, wide-ranging.

sweet adj affectionate, agreeable, amiable, appealing, aromatic, attractive, balmy, beautiful, beloved, benign, charming, cherished, cloying, darling, dear, dearest, delightful, dulcet, engaging, euphonious, fair, fragrant, fresh, gentle, gracious, harmonious, honeyed, kin, lovable, luscious, mellow, melodious, melting, mild, musical, perfumed, pet, precious, pure, redolent, saccharine, sickly, silver-toned, silvery, soft, suave, sugary, sweetened, sweet-smelling, sweet-sounding, sweet-tempered, syrupy, tender, treasured, tuneful, unselfish, wholesome, winning, winsome. **antonyms** acid, bitter, cacophonous, discordant, malodorous, salty, sour, unpleasant.
n afters, dessert, pudding, second course, sweet course.

sweeten v alleviate, appease, cushion, dulcify, honey, mellow, mollify, pacify, soften, soothe, sugar, take the sting out of, temper. **antonyms** aggravate, embitter, jaundice.

swell¹ v aggravate, augment, balloon, belly, billow, bloat, bulb, bulge, dilate, distend, enhance, enlarge, expand, extend, fatten, grow, heave, heighten, increase, intensify, louden, mount, protrude, reach a crescendo, rise, surge. **antonyms** contract, dwindle, shrink.
n bulge, distension, enlargement, loudening, rise, surge, swelling, undulation, wave.

swell² adj de luxe, exclusive, fashionable, flashy, grand, posh, ritzy, smart, stylish, swanky. **antonyms** seedy, shabby.

swelling n blister, bruise, bulb, bulge, bump, dilation, distension, enlargement, gathering, gout, inflammation, lump, protuberance, puffiness, tumour.

sweltering adj airless, baking, broiling, burning, hot, humid, oppressive, perspiring, scorching, steamy, stifling, suffocating, sultry, sweating, torrid, tropical. **antonyms** airy, breezy, chilly, cold, cool, fresh.

swerve v bend, carve, deflect, deviate, diverge, incline, sheer, shift, stray, sway, swing, turn, veer, wander, warp, wind.

swift adj abrupt, agile, expeditious, express, fast, fleet, fleet-footed, flying, hurried, limber, nimble, nimble-footed, nippy, precipitate, prompt, quick, rapid, ready, short, spanking, speedy, sudden, winged. **antonyms** slow, sluggish, tardy.

swiftly adj at full tilt, double-quick, expeditiously, express, fast, hotfoot, hurriedly, instantly, posthaste, promptly, quickly, rapidly, speedily. **antonyms** slowly, tardily.

swill v consume, drain, drink, gulp, guzzle, imbibe, knock back, quaff, swallow, swig.
swill out cleanse, drench, flush, rinse, sluice, wash down, wash out.

swindle v bilk, cheat, con, deceive, defraud, diddle, do, dupe, fleece, grift, hand someone a lemon, overcharge, rip off, rook, trick.
n chicanery, con, deceit, deception, double-dealing, fiddle, fraud, grift, racket, rip-off, scam, sharp practice, shenanigans, skin-game, swizz, swizzle, trickery.

swine n beast, boar, boor, brute, cad, heel, pig, reptile, rotter, scoundrel.

swing v arrange, brandish, control, dangle, fix, fluctuate, hang, hurl, influence, oscillate, rock, suspend, sway, swerve, vary, veer, vibrate, wave, whirl.
n fluctuation, impetus, motion, oscillation, rhythm, scope, stroke, sway, swaying, sweep, sweeping, vibration, waving.
swing round curve, gyrate, pivot, revolve, rotate, spin, swivel, turn, twirl, wheel.

swingeing adj Draconian, drastic, excessive, extortionate, harsh, heavy, huge, oppressive, punishing, severe, stringent, thumping. **antonym** mild.

swinging *adj* contemporary, dynamic, fashionable, fast, hip, jet-setting, lively, modern, stylish, trendy, up-to-date, up-to-the-minute, with it. **antonyms** old-fashioned, square.

swipe *v* appropriate, clip, filch, half-inch, hit, lift, pilfer, pinch, purloin, slap, snaffle, snitch, sock, steal, strike, thwack, wallop, whack.
n blow, clip, clout, cuff, slap, smack, thwack, wallop, whack.

swirl *v* agitate, boil, churn, eddy, scud, spin, surge, swish, twirl, twist, wheel, whirl.

swish[1] *v* birch, brandish, flog, flourish, lash, rustle, swing, swirl, swoosh, thrash, twirl, wave, whip, whirl, whisk, whistle, whiz(z), whoosh.

swish[2] *adj* de luxe, elegant, exclusive, fashionable, flash, grand, plush, posh, ritzy, smart, sumptuous, swanky, swell. **antonyms** seedy, shabby.

switch *v* change, change course, change direction, chop and change, deflect, deviate, divert, exchange, interchange, put, rearrange, replace, shift, substitute, swap, trade, turn, veer.
n about-turn, alteration, change, change of direction, exchange, interchange, shift, substitution, swap.
switch off inactivate, put off, turn off.

swivel *v* gyrate, pirouette, pivot, revolve, rotate, spin, swing round, turn, twirl, wheel.

swollen *adj* bloated, bulbous, distended, enlarged, inflamed, puffed up, puffy. **antonyms** contracted, emaciated, shrunken.

swoop *v* descend, dive, drop, fall, lunge, pounce, rush, stoop, sweep.
n attack, descent, drop, lunge, onslaught, plunge, pounce, rush, stoop, sweep.

swop *see* **swap**.

sworn *adj* attested, confirmed, devoted, eternal, implacable, inveterate, relentless.

swot *v* bone up, burn the midnight oil, cram, learn, memorise, mug up, pore over, revise, study, work.

sycophancy *n* adulation, arse-licking, backscratching, bootlicking, fawning, flattery, grovelling, kowtowing, obsequiousness, servility, slavishness, toadyism.

sycophant *n* arse-licker, backscratcher, bootlicker, fawner, flatterer, groveller,

lickspittle, parasite, slave, sponger, toady, yes-man.

sycophantic *adj* arse-licking, backscratching, bootlicking, fawning, flattering, grovelling, ingratiating, obsequious, servile, slavish, slimy, smarmy, toadying, unctuous.

sylph-like *adj* elegant, graceful, lithe, slender, slight, slim, streamlined, svelte, willowy. **antonyms** bulky, plump.

symbol *n* badge, character, emblem, figure, ideogram, image, logo, mark, representation, rune, sign, token, type.

symbolic *adj* allegorical, allusive, emblematic, figurative, metaphorical, representative, ritual, significant, token, typical.

symbolise *v* allude to, betoken, connote, denote, emblemise, exemplify, mean, personate, personify, represent, signify, typify.

symmetrical balanced, corresponding, isometric, parallel, proportional, regular, well-balanced, well-proportioned. **antonyms** asymmetrical, irregular.

symmetry *n* agreement, balance, correspondence, evenness, form, harmony, order, parallelism, proportion, regularity. **antonyms** asymmetry, irregularity.

sympathetic *adj* affectionate, agreeable, appreciative, caring, comforting, commiserating, companionable, compassionate, compatible, concerned, congenial, consoling, empathetic, feeling, friendly, interested, kind, kindly, like-minded, pitying, responsive, supportive, tender, understanding, warm, warm-hearted, well-intentioned. **antonyms** antipathetic, callous, indifferent, unsympathetic.

sympathetically *adv* appreciatively, comfortingly, compassionately, consolingly, feelingly, kindly, pityingly, responsively, sensitively, supportively, understandingly, warm-heartedly, warmly.

sympathise *v* agree, commiserate, empathise, feel for, identify with, pity, respond to, side with, understand. **antonyms** disapprove, dismiss, disregard, ignore, oppose.

sympathiser *n* adherent, admirer, backer, fan, fellow-traveller, friend in need, partisan, supporter, well-wisher. **antonyms** enemy, opponent.

sympathy *n* affinity, agreement, comfort, commiseration, compassion, condolence, condolences, congeniality, correspondence, empathy, fellow-feeling, harmony, pity, rapport, responsiveness, tenderness, thoughtfulness, understanding, warmth. *antonyms* callousness, disharmony, incompatibility, indifference.

symptom *n* evidence, expression, feature, indication, manifestation, mark, note, sign, syndrome, token, warning.

syndicate *n* alliance, bloc, cartel, combination, combine, group, ring.

synonymous *adj* comparable, corresponding, equal, equivalent, exchangeable, identical, identified, interchangeable, parallel, similar, substitutable, tantamount, the same. *antonyms* antonymous, dissimilar, opposite.

synopsis *n* abridgement, abstract, compendium, condensation, digest, epitome, outline, précis, recapitulation, résumé, review, run-down, sketch, summary, summation.

synthesis *n* alloy, amalgam, blend, combination, composite, compound, fusion, integration, union, welding.

synthesise *v* amalgamate, blend, coalesce, combine, compound, fuse, integrate, manufacture, merge, unify, unite, weld. *antonyms* analyse, resolve, separate.

synthetic *adj* artificial, bogus, ersatz, fake, imitation, man-made, manufactured, mock, pseudo, put-on, sham, simulated. *antonyms* genuine, real.

system *n* arrangement, classification, co-ordination, logic, method, methodology, mode, modus operandi, orderliness, organisation, plan, practice, procedure, process, regularity, routine, rule, scheme, set-up, structure, systematisation, taxonomy, technique, theory, usage.

systematic *adj* businesslike, efficient, habitual, intentional, logical, methodical, ordered, orderly, organised, planned, precise, standardised, well-ordered, well-planned. *antonyms* disorderly, inefficient, unsystematic.

T

table *n* agenda, altar, bench, board, catalogue, chart, counter, diagram, diet, digest, fare, flat, food, graph, index, inventory, list, paradigm, plain, plan, plateau, record, register, roll, schedule, slab, spread, stall, stand, syllabus, synopsis, victuals.

v postpone, propose, put forward, submit, suggest.

taboo *adj* banned, forbidden, inviolable, outlawed, prohibited, proscribed, sacrosanct, unacceptable, unmentionable, unthinkable. **antonym** acceptable.

n ban, disapproval, interdict, interdiction, prohibition, proscription, restriction.

tabulate *v* arrange, catalogue, categorise, chart, classify, codify, index, list, order, range, sort, systematise, table.

tacit *adj* implicit, implied, inferred, silent, ulterior, undeclared, understood, unexpressed, unprofessed, unspoken, unstated, unuttered, unvoiced. **antonyms** explicit, express, spoken, stated.

taciturn *adj* quiet, reserved, reticent, silent, tight-lipped, uncommunicative, unforthcoming, withdrawn. **antonyms** communicative, forthcoming, sociable, talkative.

tack *n* approach, attack, bearing, course, direction, drawing-pin, heading, line, loop, method, nail, path, pin, plan, procedure, route, staple, stitch, tactic, thumb-tack, tin-tack, way.

v add, affix, annex, append, attach, baste, fasten, fix, join, nail, pin, staple, stitch, tag.

tackle¹ *n* accoutrements, apparatus, equipment, gear, harness, implements, outfit, paraphernalia, rig, rigging, tools, trappings.

tackle² *n* attack, block, challenge, interception, intervention, stop.

v attempt, begin, block, challenge, clutch, confront, deal with, embark upon, encounter, engage in, essay, face up to, grab, grapple with, grasp, halt, intercept, seize, set about, stop, take on, throw, try, undertake, wade into. **antonyms** avoid, side-step.

tacky *adj* adhesive, cheap, gluey, gummy, messy, nasty, scruffy, seedy, shabby, shoddy, sleazy, sticky, tasteless, tatty, tawdry, vulgar, wet.

tact *n* address, adroitness, consideration, delicacy, diplomacy, discernment, discretion, finesse, grace, judgement, perception, prudence, savoir-faire, sensitivity, skill, thoughtfulness, understanding. **antonyms** clumsiness, indiscretion, tactlessness.

tactful *adj* careful, considerate, delicate, diplomatic, discerning, discreet, graceful, judicious, perceptive, polished, polite, politic, prudent, sensitive, skilful, subtle, thoughtful, understanding. **antonym** tactless.

tactic *n* approach, course, device, line, manoeuvre, means, method, move, ploy, policy, ruse, scheme, shift, stratagem, subterfuge, tack, trick, way.

tactical *adj* adroit, artful, calculated, clever, cunning, diplomatic, judicious, politic, prudent, shrewd, skilful, smart, strategic. **antonym** impolitic.

tactics *n* approach, campaign, game plan, line of attack, manoeuvres, moves, plan, plan of campaign, plans, ploys, policy, procedure, shifts, stratagems, strategy.

tactless *adj* blundering, boorish, careless, clumsy, discourteous, gauche, hurtful, ill-timed, impolite, impolitic, imprudent, inappropriate, inconsiderate, indelicate, indiscreet, inept, insensitive, rough, rude, thoughtless, uncivil, undiplomatic, unfeeling, unkind, unsubtle. **antonym** tactful.

tag *v* add, adjoin, affix, annex, append, call, christen, designate, dub, earmark, fasten, identify, label, mark, name, nickname, style, tack, term, ticket.

tag along accompany, attend, dog, follow, hang round, shadow, tail, trail.

tail *n* appendage, backside, behind, bottom, bum, buttocks, conclusion, croup, detective, end, extremity, file, follower, fud, line, posterior, queue, rear, rear end, retinue, rump, scut, suite, tailback, tailpiece, tailplane, train.

v dog, follow, keep with, shadow, spy on, stalk, track, trail.

tail off decrease, die, die out, drop, dwindle, fade, fail, fall away, peter out, tail away, taper off, wane. **antonyms** grow, increase.

tailor *v* accommodate, adapt, adjust, alter, convert, cut, fashion, fit, modify, mould, shape, style, suit, trim.

takings

tailor-made *adj* bespoke, custom-built, custom-made, fitted, ideal, made-to-measure, perfect, right, suitable, suited. *antonyms* ill-adapted, unsuitable.

taint *v* adulterate, besmirch, blacken, blemish, blight, blot, brand, contaminate, corrupt, damage, defile, deprave, dirty, disgrace, dishonour, foul, infect, muddy, poison, pollute, ruin, shame, smear, smirch, soil, spoil, stain, stigmatise, sully, tarnish, vitiate.

take *v* abduct, abide, abstract, accept, accommodate, accompany, acquire, adopt, appropriate, arrest, ascertain, assume, attract, bear, believe, bewitch, blight, book, brave, bring, brook, buy, call for, captivate, capture, carry, cart, catch, charm, clutch, conduct, consider, consume, contain, convey, convoy, deduct, deem, delight, demand, derive, detract, do, drink, eat, effect, eliminate, enchant, endure, engage, ensnare, entrap, escort, execute, fascinate, ferry, fetch, filch, gather, glean, grasp, grip, guide, haul, have, have room for, hire, hold, imbibe, ingest, inhale, lead, lease, make, measure, misappropriate, necessitate, need, nick, observe, obtain, operate, perceive, perform, photograph, pick, pinch, please, pocket, portray, presume, purchase, purloin, receive, regard, remove, rent, require, reserve, secure, seize, select, stand, steal, stomach, strike, subtract, succeed, suffer, swallow, swipe, tolerate, tote, transport, undergo, understand, undertake, usher, weather, win, withstand, work.

n catch, gate, haul, income, proceeds, profits, receipts, return, revenue, takings, yield.

take aback astonish, astound, bewilder, disconcert, dismay, flabbergast, floor, nonplus, stagger, startle, stun, surprise, upset.

take apart analyse, disassemble, dismantle, resolve, take down, take to pieces.

take back deny, disavow, disclaim, eat one's words, recant, reclaim, regain, renounce, repossess, repudiate, retract, unsay, withdraw.

take down deflate, demolish, disassemble, dismantle, humble, humiliate, level, lower, minute, mortify, note, put down, raze, record, reduce, set down, strike, transcribe, write.

take effect be effective, become operative, begin, come into force, work.

take heart brighten up, buck up, cheer up, perk up, rally, revive. *antonym* despond.

take in absorb, accommodate, admit, annex, appreciate, assimilate, bamboozle, bilk, bluff, cheat, comprehend, comprise, con, contain, cover, cozen, deceive, digest, do, dupe, embrace, enclose, encompass, fool, furl, grasp, gull, hoodwink, imagine, include, incorporate, kid, mislead, realise, receive, shelter, subdue, swindle, tighten, trick, understand.

take issue call in question, challenge, disagree, dispute, object, oppose, quarrel, question, take exception.

take off beat it, bloom, burgeon, caricature, decamp, depart, disappear, discard, divest, doff, drop, expand, flourish, go, imitate, lampoon, leave, mimic, mock, parody, remove, satirise, scarper, send up, soar, spoof, strip, take wing, travesty, vamoose.

take offence be miffed, miff, sulk, take it ill, take the huff.

take on accept, acquire, assume, complain, contend with, employ, engage, enlist, enrol, face, fight, grieve, hire, lament, oppose, retain, tackle, undertake, vie with.

take part associate oneself, be instrumental, be involved, join, partake, participate, play a part, share, take a hand.

take pity on feel compassion for, forgive, give quarter, have mercy on, melt, pardon, pity, relent, reprieve, show mercy, spare.

take place befall, betide, come about, come off, come to pass, fall, happen, occur.

take stock appraise, assess, estimate, size up, survey, weigh up.

take the plunge commit oneself, cross the Rubicon, decide, pop the question.

take to task blame, censure, criticise, lecture, rebuke, reprimand, reproach, reprove, scold, tell off, tick off, upbraid. *antonyms* commend, praise.

take up absorb, accept, adopt, affect, arrest, assume, begin, borrow, carry on, consume, continue, cover, engage in, engross, fasten, fill, interrupt, lift, monopolise, occupy, proceed, raise, recommence, restart, resume, secure, start, use up.

take-off *n* burlesque, caricature, imitation, lampoon, mickey-take, mimicry, parody, spoof, travesty.

takings *n* earnings, emoluments, gain, gate, haul, income, pickings, proceeds, profits, receipts, returns, revenue, take, yield.

tale *n* account, anecdote, fable, fabrication, falsehood, fib, fiction, legend, lie, myth, narration, narrative, old wives' tale, relation, report, romance, rumour, saga, spiel, story, superstition, tall story, tradition, untruth, yarn.

talent *n* ability, aptitude, bent, capacity, endowment, faculty, feel, flair, forte, genius, gift, knack, long suit, nous, parts, power, strength. **antonyms** inability, ineptitude, weakness.

talented *adj* able, accomplished, adept, adroit, apt, artistic, brilliant, capable, clever, deft, gifted, ingenious, inspired, well-endowed. **antonyms** clumsy, inept.

talk *v* articulate, blab, blether, chat, chatter, chinwag, commune, communicate, confabulate, confer, converse, gab, gossip, grass, inform, jaw, natter, negotiate, parley, prate, prattle, rap, say, sing, speak, squeak, squeal, utter, verbalise, witter.
n address, blether, chat, chatter, chinwag, chitchat, colloquy, confab, confabulation, conference, consultation, conversation, crack, dialect, dialogue, discourse, discussion, disquisition, dissertation, gab, gossip, harangue, hearsay, jargon, jaw, jawing, language, lecture, lingo, meeting, natter, negotiation, oration, parley, patois, rap, rumour, seminar, sermon, slang, speech, spiel, symposium, tittle-tattle, utterance, words.

talk big bluster, boast, brag, crow, exaggerate, swank, vaunt.

talk into bring round, coax, convince, encourage, overrule, persuade, sway, win over. **antonym** dissuade.

talk out of caution, deter, discourage, dissuade, expostulate, head off, protest, put off, remonstrate, urge against.

talkative *adj* chatty, communicative, conversational, conversative, effusive, expansive, forthcoming, gabby, garrulous, gossipy, long-tongued, long-winded, loquacious, prating, prolix, unreserved, verbose, vocal, voluble, wordy. **antonyms** reserved, taciturn.

talking-to *n* criticism, dressing-down, earful, jaw, lecture, rebuke, reprimand, reproach, reproof, row, scolding, slating, telling-off, ticking-off. **antonyms** commendation, congratulation, praise.

tall *adj* absurd, big, dubious, elevated, embellished, exaggerated, far-fetched, giant, grandiloquent, great, high, implausible, improbable, incredible, lanky, leggy, lofty, overblown, preposterous, remarkable, soaring, steep, topless, towering, unbelievable, unlikely. **antonyms** low, reasonable, short, small.

tally *v* accord, agree, coincide, compute, concur, conform, correspond, figure, fit, harmonise, jibe, mark, match, parallel, reckon, record, register, square, suit, tie in, total. **antonyms** differ, disagree.
n account, count, counterfoil, counterpart, credit, duplicate, label, mark, match, mate, notch, reckoning, record, score, stub, tab, tag, tick, total.

tame *adj* amenable, biddable, bland, boring, broken, compliant, cultivated, disciplined, docile, domesticated, dull, feeble, flat, gentle, humdrum, insipid, lifeless, manageable, meek, obedient, prosaic, spiritless, subdued, submissive, tedious, tractable, unadventurous, unenterprising, unexciting, uninspired, uninspiring, uninteresting, vapid. **antonyms** exciting, rebellious, unmanageable, wild.
v break in, bridle, calm, conquer, curb, discipline, domesticate, enslave, gentle, house-train, humble, master, mellow, mitigate, mute, pacify, quell, repress, soften, subdue, subjugate, suppress, temper, train.

tamper *v* alter, bribe, cook, corrupt, damage, fiddle, fix, influence, interfere, intrude, juggle, manipulate, meddle, mess, rig, tinker.

tang *n* aroma, bite, flavour, hint, kick, overtone, piquancy, pungency, reek, savour, scent, smack, smell, suggestion, taste, tinge, touch, trace, whiff.

tangible *adj* actual, concrete, corporeal, definite, discernible, evident, manifest, material, objective, observable, palpable, perceptible, physical, positive, real, sensible, solid, substantial, tactile, touchable. **antonym** intangible.

tangle *n* complication, confusion, convolution, embroglio, embroilment, entanglement, fix, imbroglio, jam, jumble, jungle, knot, labyrinth, mass, mat, maze, mesh, mess, mix-up, muddle, raffle, snarl, snarl-up, twist, web.
v catch, coil, confuse, convolute, embroil, enmesh, ensnare, entangle, entrap, hamper, implicate, interlace, interlock, intertwine, intertwist, interweave, involve, jam, knot, mat,

mesh, muddle, snarl, trap, twist. **antonym** disentangle.

tangled *adj* complex, complicated, confused, convoluted, dishevelled, entangled, intricate, involved, jumbled, knotted, knotty, matted, messy, mixed-up, scrambled, snarled, tortuous, tousled, twisted. **antonyms** clear, free.

tangy *adj* biting, bitter, fresh, gamy, piquant, pungent, savoury, sharp, spicy, strong, tart. **antonym** insipid.

tantalise *v* baffle, bait, entice, frustrate, lead on, play upon, provoke, taunt, tease, titillate, torment, torture. **antonym** satisfy.

tantamount *adj* as good as, commensurate, equal, equivalent, synonymous, the same as, virtually.

tantrum *n* fit, flare-up, fury, hysterics, outburst, paroxysm, rage, scene, storm, temper.

tap¹ *v* beat, chap, drum, knock, pat, rap, strike, tat, touch.
n beat, chap, knock, pat, rap, rat-tat, touch.

tap² *n* bug, bung, faucet, plug, receiver, spigot, spout, stop-cock, stopper, valve.
v bleed, broach, drain, exploit, milk, mine, open, pierce, quarry, siphon, unplug, use, utilise.

tape *n* band, binding, magnetic tape, riband, ribbon, strip, tape-measure.
v assess, bind, measure, record, seal, secure, stick, tape-record, video, wrap.

taper *v* attenuate, decrease, die away, die out, dwindle, fade, lessen, narrow, peter out, reduce, slim, subside, tail off, thin, wane, weaken. **antonyms** increase, swell, widen.

tardily *adv* at the eleventh hour, at the last minute, belatedly, late, late in the day, slowly, sluggishly, unpunctually. **antonyms** promptly, punctually.

tardy *adj* backward, behindhand, belated, dawdling, delayed, dilatory, eleventh-hour, lag, last-minute, late, loitering, overdue, procrastinating, retarded, slack, slow, sluggish, unpunctual. **antonyms** prompt, punctual.

target *n* aim, ambition, destination, end, goal, intention, mark, object, objective, prey, purpose, quarry, scapegoat, victim.

tariff *n* assessment, bill of fare, charges, customs, duty, excise, impost, levy, menu, price list, rate, schedule, tax, toll.

tarnish *v* befoul, blacken, blemish, blot, darken, dim, discolour, dislustre, dull, mar, rust, soil, spoil, spot, stain, sully, taint. **antonyms** brighten, enhance, polish up.
n blackening, blemish, blot, discoloration, film, patina, rust, spot, stain, taint. **antonyms** brightness, polish.

tarry *v* abide, bide, dally, dawdle, delay, dwell, lag, linger, loiter, pause, remain, rest, sojourn, stay, stop, wait.

tart¹ *adj* acerbic, acid, acidulous, acrimonious, astringent, barbed, biting, bitter, caustic, cutting, incisive, piquant, pungent, sardonic, scathing, sharp, short, sour, tangy, trenchant, vinegary.

tart² *n* broad, call girl, fallen woman, floosie, harlot, hooker, prostitute, slut, street-walker, strumpet, trollop, whore.

task *n* assignment, burden, business, charge, chore, duty, employment, enterprise, exercise, imposition, job, job of work, labour, mission, occupation, toil, undertaking, work.
v burden, charge, commit, encumber, entrust, exhaust, load, lumber, oppress, overload, push, saddle, strain, tax, test, weary.

taste *n* appetite, appreciation, bent, bit, bite, choice, correctness, cultivation, culture, dash, decorum, delicacy, desire, discernment, discretion, discrimination, drop, elegance, experience, fancy, finesse, flavour, fondness, grace, inclination, judgement, leaning, liking, morsel, mouthful, nibble, nicety, nip, palate, partiality, penchant, perception, polish, politeness, predilection, preference, propriety, refinement, relish, restraint, sample, sapor, savour, sensitivity, sip, smack, smatch, soupçon, spoonful, style, swallow, tact, tactfulness, tang, tastefulness, titbit, touch.
v assay, differentiate, discern, distinguish, encounter, experience, feel, know, meet, nibble, perceive, relish, sample, savour, sip, smack, test, try, undergo.

tasteful *adj* aesthetic, artistic, beautiful, charming, correct, cultivated, cultured, delicate, discreet, discriminating, elegant, exquisite, fastidious, graceful, handsome, harmonious, judicious, polished, refined, restrained, smart, stylish, well-judged. **antonym** tasteless.

tasteless *adj* barbaric, bland, boring, cheap, coarse, crass, crude, dilute, dull, flashy, flat, flavourless, garish, gaudy, graceless, gross, improper, inartistic, indecorous, indelicate, indiscreet, inelegant, inharmonious, insipid, low, mild, naff, rude, stale, tacky, tactless, tame, tatty, tawdry, thin, uncouth, undiscriminating, uninspired, uninteresting, unseemly, untasteful, vapid, vulgar, watered-down, watery, weak. *antonym* tasteful.

tasty *adj* appetising, delectable, delicious, flavorous, flavourful, flavoursome, luscious, mouthwatering, palatable, piquant, savoury, scrumptious, succulent, yummy. *antonyms* disgusting, insipid, tasteless.

tattered *adj* frayed, in shreds, ragged, raggy, rent, ripped, tatty, threadbare, torn. *antonyms* neat, trim.

taunt *v* bait, deride, fleer, flout, gibe, insult, jeer, mock, provoke, reproach, revile, rib, ridicule, sneer, tease, torment, twit.

n barb, catcall, censure, cut, derision, dig, gibe, insult, jeer, poke, provocation, reproach, ridicule, sarcasm, sneer, teasing.

taut *adj* contracted, rigid, strained, stressed, stretched, tense, tensed, tight, tightened, unrelaxed. *antonyms* loose, relaxed, slack.

tautological *adj* otiose, pleonastic, redundant, repetitious, repetitive, superfluous, truistic. *antonyms* economical, succinct.

tautology *n* duplication, otioseness, pleonasm, redundancy, repetition, repetitiousness, repetitiveness, superfluity. *antonyms* economy, succinctness.

tawdry *adj* cheap, cheap-jack, flashy, garish, gaudy, glittering, meretricious, pinchbeck, plastic, raffish, showy, tacky, tasteless, tatty, tinsel, tinselly, vulgar. *antonyms* excellent, fine, superior.

tax *n* assessment, burden, charge, contribution, customs, demand, drain, duty, excise, imposition, levy, load, pressure, rate, scot, strain, tariff, tithe, toll.

v accuse, arraign, assess, blame, burden, censure, charge, demand, drain, enervate, exact, exhaust, extract, impeach, impose, impugn, incriminate, load, overburden, overtax, push, rate, reproach, sap, strain, stretch, task, tithe, try, weaken, weary.

taxing *adj* burdensome, demanding, draining, enervating, exacting, exhausting, heavy, onerous, punishing, stressful, tiring, tough, trying, wearing, wearisome. *antonyms* easy, gentle, mild.

teach *v* accustom, advise, coach, counsel, demonstrate, direct, discipline, drill, edify, educate, enlighten, ground, guide, impart, implant, inculcate, inform, instil, instruct, school, show, train, tutor, verse.

teaching *n* didactics, doctrine, dogma, education, gospel, grounding, indoctrination, instruction, pedagogy, precept, principle, schooling, tenet, training, tuition.

team *n* band, body, bunch, company, crew, gang, group, line-up, pair, set, shift, side, span, squad, stable, troupe.

v combine, couple, join, link, match.

team up band together, combine, co-operate, join, unite.

teamwork *n* collaboration, co-operation, co-ordination, esprit de corps, fellowship, joint effort, team spirit. *antonyms* disharmony, disunity.

tear *v* belt, bolt, career, charge, claw, dart, dash, divide, drag, fly, gallop, gash, grab, hurry, lacerate, mangle, mutilate, pluck, pull, race, rend, rip, rive, run, rupture, rush, scratch, seize, sever, shoot, shred, snag, snatch, speed, split, sprint, wrench, wrest, yank, zoom.

n hole, laceration, rent, rip, run, rupture, scratch, snag, split.

tearaway *n* delinquent, good-for-nothing, hoodlum, hooligan, hothead, madcap, rascal, rough, roughneck, rowdy, ruffian, tough.

tearful *adj* blubbering, crying, distressing, dolorous, emotional, lachrymose, lamentable, maudlin, mournful, pathetic, pitiable, pitiful, poignant, sad, sobbing, sorrowful, upsetting, weeping, weepy, whimpering, woeful.

tears *n* blubbering, crying, distress, lamentation, mourning, pain, regret, sadness, sobbing, sorrow, wailing, waterworks, weeping, whimpering, woe.

tease *v* aggravate, annoy, badger, bait, bedevil, chaff, gibe, goad, irritate, josh, mock, needle, pester, plague, provoke, rag, rib, ridicule, take a rise out of, tantalise, taunt, torment, twit, vex, worry.

technique *n* address, adroitness, approach, art, artistry, course, craft, craftsmanship, delivery, execution, expertise, facility, fashion, knack, know-how, manner, means, method, mode, modus operandi, performance, procedure, proficiency, skill, style, system, touch, way.

tedious *adj* annoying, banal, boring, deadly, drab, draggy, dreary, dreich, dull, fatiguing, humdrum, irksome, laborious, lifeless, long-drawn-out, monotonous, prosaic, prosy, soporific, tiring, unexciting, uninteresting, vapid. **antonyms** exciting, interesting.

tedium n banality, boredom, drabness, dreariness, dullness, lifelessness, monotony, prosiness, routine, sameness, tediousness, vapidity.

teem v abound, bear, brim, bristle, burst, increase, multiply, overflow, overspill, produce, proliferate, pullulate, swarm. **antonyms** lack, want.

teeming adj abundant, alive, brimming, bristling, bursting, chock-a-block, chock-full, crawling, fruitful, full, numerous, overflowing, packed, pregnant, proliferating, pullulating, replete, swarming, thick. **antonyms** lacking, rare, sparse.

teeny adj diminutive, microscopic, miniature, minuscule, minute, teensy-weensy, teeny-weeny, tichy, tiny, tottie, wee.

teeter v balance, lurch, pitch, pivot, rock, seesaw, stagger, sway, titubate, totter, tremble, waver, wobble.

telepathy n clairvoyance, ESP, mind-reading, sixth sense, thought transference.

telephone n blower, dog and bone, handset, line, phone.
v buzz, call, call up, contact, dial, get in touch, get on the blower, give someone a tinkle, phone, ring (up).

television n goggle-box, idiot box, receiver, set, small screen, telly, the box, the tube, TV, TV set.

tell v acquaint, announce, apprise, authorise, bid, calculate, chronicle, command, communicate, comprehend, compute, confess, count, depict, describe, differentiate, direct, discern, disclose, discover, discriminate, distinguish, divulge, enjoin, enumerate, express, foresee, identify, impart, inform, instruct, mention, militate, narrate, notify, number, order, portray, predict, proclaim, reckon, recount, register, rehearse, relate, report, require, reveal, say, see, speak, state, summon, tally, understand, utter, weigh.

tell off bawl out, berate, censure, chide, dress down, lecture, objurgate, rebuke, reprimand, reproach, reprove, scold, take to task, tear off a strip, tick off, upbraid.

telling-off n bawling-out, castigation, dressing-down, lecture, rebuke, reprimand, reproach, reproof, row, scolding, tongue-lashing.

temerity n audacity, boldness, brass neck, chutzpah, daring, effrontery, forwardness, gall, heedlessness, impudence, impulsiveness, intrepidity, nerve, rashness, recklessness. **antonym** caution.

temper n anger, annoyance, attitude, calm, calmness, character, composure, constitution, cool, coolness, disposition, equanimity, fury, heat, humour, ill-humour, irascibility, irritability, irritation, mind, moderation, mood, nature, passion, peevishness, pet, petulance, rage, resentment, sang-froid, self-control, surliness, taking, tantrum, temperament, tenor, tranquillity, vein, wrath.
v allay, anneal, assuage, calm, harden, lessen, mitigate, moderate, modify, mollify, palliate, restrain, soften, soothe, strengthen, toughen.

temperament n anger, bent, character, complexion, constitution, crasis, disposition, excitability, explosiveness, hot-headedness, humour, impatience, make-up, mettle, moodiness, moods, nature, outlook, personality, petulance, quality, soul, spirit, stamp, temper, tendencies, tendency, volatility.

temperamental adj capricious, emotional, erratic, excitable, explosive, fiery, highly-strung, hot-headed, hypersensitive, impatient, inconsistent, irritable, mercurial, moody, neurotic, over-emotional, petulant, sensitive, touchy, unpredictable, unreliable, volatile, volcanic. **antonyms** calm, serene, steady.

temperance n abstemiousness, abstinence, continence, discretion, forbearance, moderation, prohibition, restraint, self-abnegation, self-control, self-denial, self-discipline, self-restraint, sobriety, teetotalism. **antonyms** excess, intemperance.

temperate adj abstemious, abstinent, agreeable, balanced, balmy, calm, clement, composed, continent, controlled, cool, dispassionate, equable, even-tempered, fair, gentle, mild, moderate, pleasant, reasonable, restrained, sensible, sober, soft, stable. **antonyms** excessive, extreme, intemperate.

tempest n commotion, cyclone, disturbance, ferment, furore, gale, hurricane, squall, storm, tornado, tumult, typhoon, upheaval, uproar.

tempestuous adj agitated, blustery, boisterous, breezy, emotional, excited, feverish, furious, gusty, heated, hysterical, impassioned, intense, passionate, raging, squally, stormy, troubled, tumultuous, turbulent, uncontrolled, violent, wild, windy. **antonyms** calm, quiet.

tempo n beat, cadence, measure, metre, pace, pulse, rate, rhythm, speed, time, velocity.

temporal adj carnal, civil, earthly, evanescent, fleeting, fleshly, fugacious, fugitive, impermanent, lay, material, momentary, mortal, mundane, passing, profane, secular, short-lived, temporary, terrestrial, transient, transitory, unspiritual, worldly. **antonym** spiritual.

temporarily adv briefly, fleetingly, for the time being, in the interim, momentarily, pro tem, transiently, transitorily. **antonym** permanently.

temporary adj brief, ephemeral, evanescent, fleeting, fugacious, fugitive, impermanent, interim, makeshift, momentary, passing, pro tem, pro tempore, provisional, short-lived, stop-gap, transient, transitory. **antonyms** everlasting, permanent.

temporise v delay, equivocate, hang back, hum and haw, pause, play for time, procrastinate, stall.

tempt v allure, attract, bait, coax, dare, decoy, draw, enamour, entice, incite, inveigle, invite, lure, provoke, risk, seduce, tantalise, test, try, woo. **antonyms** discourage, dissuade.

temptation n allurement, appeal, attraction, attractiveness, bait, blandishments, coaxing, come-on, decoy, draw, enticement, fascination, forbidden fruit, inducement, invitation, lure, persuasion, pull, seduction, snare.

tempting adj alluring, appetising, attractive, enticing, inviting, mouthwatering, seductive, tantalising. **antonyms** unattractive, uninviting.

tenable adj arguable, believable, credible, defendable, defensible, justifiable, maintainable, plausible, rational, reasonable, sound, supportable, viable. **antonyms** indefensible, unjustifiable, untenable.

tenacious adj adamant, backboned, clinging, coherent, cohesive, determined, dogged, fast, firm, forceful, inflexible, intransigent, obdurate, obstinate, persistent, pertinacious, resolute, retentive, single-minded, solid, staunch, steadfast, strong, strong-willed, stubborn, sure, tight, tough, unshakeable, unswerving,

unwavering, unyielding. **antonyms** loose, slack, weak.

tend¹ v affect, aim, bear, bend, conduce, contribute, go, gravitate, head, incline, influence, lead, lean, move, point, trend, verge.

tend² v attend, comfort, control, cultivate, feed, guard, handle, keep, maintain, manage, minister to, nurse, nurture, protect, serve, succour. **antonym** neglect.

tendency n bearing, bent, bias, course, direction, disposition, drift, drive, heading, inclination, leaning, liability, movement, partiality, penchant, predilection, predisposition, proclivity, proneness, propensity, purport, readiness, susceptibility, tenor, thrust, trend, turning.

tender¹ adj aching, acute, affectionate, amorous, benevolent, breakable, bruised, callow, caring, chary, compassionate, complicated, considerate, dangerous, delicate, difficult, emotional, evocative, feeble, fond, fragile, frail, gentle, green, humane, immature, impressionable, inexperienced, inflamed, irritated, kind, loving, merciful, moving, new, painful, pathetic, pitiful, poignant, raw, risky, romantic, scrupulous, sensitive, sentimental, smarting, soft, soft-hearted, sore, sympathetic, tender-hearted, ticklish, touching, touchy, tricky, vulnerable, warm, warm-hearted, weak, young, youthful. **antonyms** callous, chewy, hard, harsh, rough, severe, tough.

tender² v advance, extend, give, offer, present, proffer, propose, submit, suggest, volunteer.
n bid, currency, estimate, medium, money, offer, payment, proffer, proposal, proposition, specie, submission, suggestion.

tender-hearted adj affectionate, benevolent, benign, caring, compassionate, considerate, feeling, fond, gentle, humane, kind, kind-hearted, kindly, loving, merciful, mild, pitying, responsive, sensitive, sentimental, soft-hearted, sympathetic, warm, warm-hearted. **antonyms** callous, cruel, hard-hearted, unfeeling.

tenderness n ache, aching, affection, amorousness, attachment, benevolence, bruising, callowness, care, compassion, consideration, delicateness, devotion, discomfort, feebleness, fondness, fragility, frailness, gentleness, greenness, humaneness, humanity, immaturity, impressionableness, in-experience, inflammation, irritation, kindness, liking, love, loving-kindness, mercy, pain, painfulness, pity, rawness, sensitiveness, sensitivity, sentimentality, soft-heartedness, soft-ness, soreness, sweetness, sympathy, tender-heartedness, vulnerability, warm-heartedness, warmth, weakness, youth, youthfulness. **antonyms** cruelty, hardness, harshness.

tenet *n* article of faith, belief, canon, conviction, credo, creed, doctrine, dogma, maxim, opinion, precept, principle, rule, teaching, thesis, view.

tenor *n* aim, course, direction, drift, essence, evolution, gist, intent, meaning, path, point, purport, purpose, sense, spirit, substance, tendency, theme, trend, way.

tense *adj* anxious, apprehensive, edgy, electric, exciting, fidgety, jittery, jumpy, moving, nerve-racking, nervous, overwrought, restless, rigid, strained, stressful, stretched, strung up, taut, tight, uneasy, uptight, worrying. **antonyms** calm, lax, loose, relaxed.
v brace, contract, strain, stretch, tighten. **antonyms** loosen, relax.

tension *n* anxiety, apprehension, edginess, hostility, nervousness, pressure, restlessness, rigidity, stiffness, strain, straining, stress, stretching, suspense, tautness, tightness, tone, unease, worry. **antonyms** calm(ness), laxness, looseness, relaxation.

tentative *adj* cautious, conjectural, dif-fident, doubtful, experimental, faltering, hesitant, indefinite, provisional, specu-lative, timid, uncertain, unconfirmed, undecided, unformulated, unsettled, unsure. **antonyms** conclusive, decisive, definite, final.

tenuous *adj* delicate, doubtful, dubious, fine, flimsy, gossamer, insignificant, insubstantial, nebulous, questionable, rarefied, shaky, sketchy, slender, slight, slim, thin, weak. **antonyms** significant, strong, substantial.

tenure *n* incumbency, occupancy, occupation, possession, proprietorship, residence, tenancy, term, time.

tepid *adj* apathetic, cool, half-hearted, indifferent, lukewarm, unenthusiastic, warmish. **antonyms** animated, cold, hot, passionate.

term¹ *n* appellation, denomination, designation, epithet, expression, locution, name, phrase, title, word.

v call, denominate, designate, dub, entitle, label, name, style, tag, title.

term² *n* bound, boundary, close, conclusion, confine, course, culmination, duration, end, finish, fruition, half, interval, limit, period, season, session, space, span, spell, terminus, time, while.

terminal *adj* bounding, concluding, deadly, desinential, extreme, fatal, final, incurable, killing, last, lethal, limiting, mortal, ultimate, utmost. **antonym** initial.
n boundary, depot, end, extremity, limit, termination, terminus.

terminate *v* abort, cease, close, complete, conclude, cut off, discontinue, drop, end, expire, finish, issue, lapse, result, stop, wind up. **antonyms** begin, initiate, start.

termination *n* abortion, cessation, close, completion, conclusion, conse-quence, dénouement, discontinuation, effect, end, ending, expiry, finale, finish, issue, result. **antonyms** beginning, initiation, start.

terminology *n* argot, cant, jargon, language, lingo, patois, phraseology, terms, vocabulary, words.

terminus *n* boundary, close, depot, destination, end, extremity, furthermost point, garage, goal, limit, station, target, termination.

terms *n* agreement, charges, compro-mise, conditions, fees, footing, language, particulars, payment, phraseology, position, premises, price, provisions, provisos, qualifications, rates, relations, relationship, specifications, standing, status, stipulations, terminology, understanding.

terrible *adj* abhorrent, appalling, awful, bad, beastly, dangerous, desperate, dire, disgusting, distressing, dread, dreaded, dreadful, extreme, fearful, foul, frightful, god-awful, gruesome, harrowing, hateful, hideous, horrendous, horrible, horrid, horrific, horrifying, loathsome, monstrous, obnoxious, odious, offensive, outrageous, poor, repulsive, revolting, rotten, serious, severe, shocking, unpleasant, vile. **antonyms** great, pleasant, superb, wonderful.

terribly *adv* awfully, decidedly, desperately, exceedingly, extremely, frightfully, gravely, greatly, much, seriously, shockingly, thoroughly, very.

terrific *adj* ace, amazing, awesome, awful, breathtaking, brilliant, dreadful, enormous, excellent, excessive, extreme, fabulous, fantastic, fearful, fierce, fine, gigantic, great, harsh, horrific, huge, intense, magnificent, marvellous, monstrous, outstanding, prodigious, sensational, severe, smashing, stupendous, super, superb, terrible, tremendous, wonderful.

terrified *adj* alarmed, appalled, awed, dismayed, frightened, horrified, horror-struck, intimidated, panic-stricken, petrified, scared.

terrify *v* alarm, appal, awe, dismay, frighten, horrify, intimidate, petrify, scare, shock, terrorise.

territory *n* area, bailiwick, country, dependency, district, domain, jurisdiction, land, park, preserve, province, region, sector, state, terrain, tract, zone.

terror *n* alarm, anxiety, awe, bogeyman, bugbear, consternation, devil, dismay, dread, fear, fiend, fright, horror, intimidation, monster, panic, rascal, rogue, scourge, shock, tearaway.

terrorise *v* alarm, awe, browbeat, bully, coerce, dismay, frighten, horrify, intimidate, menace, oppress, petrify, scare, shock, strongarm, terrify, threaten.

terse *adj* abrupt, aphoristic, brief, brusque, clipped, compact, concise, condensed, crisp, curt, economical, elliptical, epigrammatic, gnomic, incisive, laconic, neat, pithy, sententious, short, snappy, succinct. *antonyms* long-winded, prolix, repetitious.

test *v* analyse, assay, assess, check, examine, experiment, investigate, prove, screen, try, verify.
n analysis, assessment, attempt, catechism, check, evaluation, examination, hurdle, investigation, moment of truth, ordeal, probation, proof, trial, try-out.

testament *n* attestation, demonstration, devise, earnest, evidence, exemplification, proof, testimony, tribute, will, witness.

testicles *n* balls, bollocks, goolies, knackers, nuts, pills, stones.

testify *v* affirm, assert, asseverate, attest, avow, certify, corroborate, declare, depone, depose, evince, show, state, swear, vouch, witness.

testimonial *n* certificate, character, commendation, credential, endorsement, gift, memorial, plug, recommendation, reference, tribute.

testimony *n* affidavit, affirmation, asseveration, attestation, avowal, confirmation, corroboration, declaration,

demonstration, deposition, evidence, indication, information, manifestation, profession, proof, statement, submission, support, verification, witness.

testy *adj* bad-tempered, cantankerous, captious, carnaptious, crabbed, cross, crusty, fretful, grumpy, impatient, inflammable, irascible, irritable, peevish, peppery, petulant, quarrelsome, quick-tempered, short-tempered, snappish, snappy, splenetic, tetchy, touchy, waspish. *antonyms* even-tempered, good-humoured.

tether *n* bond, chain, cord, fastening, fetter, halter, lead, leash, line, restraint, rope, shackle.
v bind, chain, fasten, fetter, lash, leash, manacle, picket, restrain, rope, secure, shackle, tie.

texture *n* character, composition, consistency, constitution, fabric, feel, grain, quality, structure, surface, tissue, weave.

thankful *adj* appreciative, beholden, contented, grateful, indebted, obliged, pleased, relieved. *antonyms* thankless, unappreciative, ungrateful.

thankless *adj* fruitless, unappreciated, ungrateful, unprofitable, unrecognised, unrequited, unrewarding, useless. *antonym* rewarding.

thanks *n* acknowledgement, appreciation, credit, gratefulness, gratitude, recognition, thanksgiving.
interj cheers, ta.

thanks to as a result of, because of, by reason of, due to, in consequence of, on account of, owing to, through.

thaw *v* defrost, dissolve, liquefy, melt, soften, unbend, uncongeal, unfreeze, unthaw, warm. *antonym* freeze.

the end beyond endurance, enough, insufferable, intolerable, the final blow, the last straw, the limit, the worst, too much, unbearable, unendurable.

the limit enough, it, the end, the final blow, the last straw, the worst.

the masses hoi polloi, the common people, the commonalty, the crowd, the majority, the many, the multitude, the people, the plebs, the proles, the proletariat, the rank and file.

theatrical *adj* affected, artificial, ceremonious, dramatic, exaggerated, extravagant, hammy, histrionic, mannered, melodramatic, ostentatious, overdone, pompous, scenic, showy, stagy, stilted, Thespian, unreal.

theft *n* abstraction, embezzlement, fraud,

heist, larceny, pilfering, purloining, rip-off, robbery, stealing, thievery, thieving.

theme *n* argument, composition, dissertation, essay, exercise, idea, keynote, leitmotiv, matter, motif, subject, subject-matter, topic.

theorem *n* dictum, formula, hypothesis, postulate, principle, proposition, rule, statement, thesis.

theoretical *adj* abstract, academic, conjectural, doctrinaire, doctrinal, hypothetical, ideal, impractical, on paper, pure, speculative. **antonyms** applied, concrete, practical.

theorise *v* conjecture, formulate, guess, hypothesise, postulate, project, propound, speculate, suppose.

theory *n* abstraction, assumption, conjecture, guess, hypothesis, ism, philosophy, plan, postulation, presumption, proposal, scheme, speculation, supposition, surmise, system, thesis. **antonyms** certainty, practice.

therapeutic *adj* beneficial, corrective, curative, good, healing, recuperative, remedial, restorative, salubrious, salutary, tonic. **antonym** harmful.

therefore *adv* accordingly, as a result, consequently, ergo, for that reason, hence, so, then, thence, thus.

thesaurus *n* dictionary, lexicon, synonymicon, vocabulary, wordbook.

thesis *n* argument, assumption, composition, contention, disquisition, dissertation, essay, hypothesis, idea, monograph, opinion, paper, postulate, premiss, proposal, proposition, statement, supposition, surmise, theory, tract, treatise, view.

thick *adj* abundant, brainless, brimming, bristling, broad, bulky, bursting, chock-a-block, chock-full, chummy, close, clotted, coagulated, compact, concentrated, condensed, confidential, covered, crawling, crowded, decided, deep, dense, devoted, dim-witted, distinct, distorted, dopey, dull, excessive, familiar, fat, foggy, frequent, friendly, full, gross, guttural, heavy, hoarse, husky, impenetrable, inarticulate, indistinct, insensitive, inseparable, intimate, marked, matey, moronic, muffled, numerous, obtuse, opaque, packed, pally, pronounced, replete, rich, slow, slow-witted, solid, soupy, squabbish, strong, stupid, substantial, swarming, teeming, thick-headed, throaty, turbid, wide. **antonyms** brainy, clever, slender, slight, slim, thin, watery.

thing *n* centre, focus, heart, hub, middle, midst.

thicken *v* cake, clot, coagulate, condense, congeal, deepen, gel, jell, set. **antonym** thin.

thickhead *n* blockhead, bonehead, chump, clot, dimwit, dolt, dope, dullard, dummy, dunce, dunderhead, fathead, fool, idiot, imbecile, moron, nitwit, numskull, pinhead, twit.

thickness *n* body, breadth, bulk, bulkiness, density, diameter, layer, ply, stratum, viscosity, width. **antonym** thinness.

thickset *adj* beefy, brawny, bulky, burly, dense, heavy, muscular, nuggety, powerful, solid, squat, stocky, strong, stubby, sturdy, thick, well-built. **antonym** lanky.

thick-skinned *adj* callous, case-hardened, hard-boiled, hardened, impervious, insensitive, inured, obdurate, stolid, tough, unfeeling. **antonym** thin-skinned.

thieve *v* abstract, cheat, embezzle, filch, half-inch, heist, knock off, lift, misappropriate, nick, pilfer, pinch, plunder, poach, purloin, rip off, rob, steal, swindle, swipe.

thieving *n* banditry, burglary, crookedness, embezzlement, larceny, mugging, pilfering, piracy, plundering, robbery, shop-lifting, stealing, theft, thievery.

thin *adj* attenuated, bony, deficient, delicate, diaphanous, dilute, diluted, emaciated, feeble, filmy, fine, fine-drawn, flimsy, gaunt, gossamer, inadequate, insubstantial, insufficient, lanky, lean, light, meagre, narrow, poor, rarefied, runny, scant, scanty, scarce, scattered, scragged, scraggy, scrawny, see-through, shallow, sheer, skeletal, skimpy, skinny, slender, slight, slim, spare, sparse, spindly, superficial, tenuous, translucent, transparent, unconvincing, undernourished, underweight, unsubstantial, washy, watery, weak, wishy-washy, wispy. **antonyms** broad, dense, fat, solid, strong, thick.
v attenuate, dilute, diminish, emaciate, extenuate, prune, rarefy, reduce, refine, trim, water down, weaken, weed out.

thing *n* act, action, affair, apparatus, article, aspect, attitude, being, body, circumstance, concept, contrivance, creature, deed, detail, device, dislike, entity, event, eventuality, facet, fact, factor, feat, feature, fetish, fixation, gadget, hang-up, happening, idée fixe, implement, incident, instrument, item, liking, machine, mania, matter, means, mechanism, monomania, object, obsession, occurrence, part, particular, phenomenon, phobia, point, portion, possession, preoccupation, problem, proceeding, quirk, something, statement, substance, thought, tool.

things *n* baggage, belongings, bits and pieces, clobber, clothes, effects, equipment, gear, goods, junk, luggage, odds and ends, paraphernalia, possessions, stuff, utensils.

think *v* anticipate, be under the impression, believe, brood, calculate, cerebrate, cogitate, conceive, conclude, consider, contemplate, deem, deliberate, design, determine, envisage, esteem, estimate, expect, foresee, hold, imagine, intellectualise, judge, meditate, mull over, muse, ponder, presume, purpose, reason, recall, reckon, recollect, reflect, regard, remember, revolve, ruminate, suppose, surmise.

n assessment, cogitation, consideration, contemplation, deliberation, meditation, reflection.

think much of admire, esteem, prize, rate, respect, set store by, think highly of, value. *antonym* abominate.

think over chew over, consider, contemplate, meditate, mull over, ponder, reflect upon, ruminate, weigh up.

think up conceive, concoct, contrive, create, design, devise, dream up, imagine, improvise, invent, visualise.

thinking *n* assessment, cogitation, conclusions, conjecture, idea, judgement, opinion, outlook, philosophy, position, reasoning, theory, thoughts, view.

adj analytical, cerebral, contemplative, cultured, intelligent, meditative, philosophical, rational, reasoning, reflective, sophisticated, thoughtful.

thin-skinned *adj* hypersensitive, irascible, irritable, sensitive, snappish, soft, susceptible, tender, testy, touchy, vulnerable. *antonym* thick-skinned.

third-rate *adj* bad, cheap and nasty, cheap-jack, duff, indifferent, inferior, low-grade, mediocre, poor, ropy, shoddy.

thirst *n* appetite, craving, desire, drought, drouth, drouthiness, dryness, eagerness, hankering, hunger, keenness, longing, lust, passion, thirstiness, yearning, yen.

thirsty *adj* appetitive, arid, avid, burning, craving, dehydrated, desirous, drouthy, dry, dying, eager, greedy, hankering, hungry, itching, longing, lusting, parched, thirsting, yearning.

thorny *adj* awkward, barbed, bristly, difficult, fraught, harassing, hard, irksome, pointed, prickly, problematic, sharp, spiky, spiny, sticky, ticklish, tough, troublesome, trying, unpleasant, upsetting, vexatious, vexed, worrying.

thorough *adj* absolute, all-embracing, all-inclusive, arrant, assiduous, careful, complete, comprehensive, conscientious, deep-seated, downright, efficient, entire, exhaustive, full, in-depth, intensive, meticulous, out-and-out, painstaking, perfect, pure, root-and-branch, scrupulous, sheer, sweeping, thoroughgoing, total, unmitigated, unqualified, utter. *antonyms* careless, haphazard, partial.

though *conj* albeit, allowing, although, even if, granted, notwithstanding, while. *adv* all the same, even so, for all that, however, in spite of that, nevertheless, nonetheless, notwithstanding, still, yet.

thought *n* aim, anticipation, anxiety, aspiration, assessment, attention, attentiveness, belief, brainwork, care, cerebration, cogitation, compassion, concept, conception, concern, conclusion, conjecture, considerateness, consideration, contemplation, conviction, deliberation, design, dream, estimation, expectation, heed, hope, idea, intention, introspection, jot, judgement, kindness, little, meditation, muse, musing, notion, object, opinion, plan, prospect, purpose, reflection, regard, resolution, rumination, scrutiny, solicitude, study, sympathy, thinking, thoughtfulness, touch, trifle, view.

thoughtful *adj* absorbed, abstracted, astute, attentive, canny, careful, caring, cautious, circumspect, considerate, contemplative, deliberate, deliberative, discreet, heedful, helpful, introspective, kind, kindly, meditative, mindful, musing, pensive, prudent, rapt, reflective, ruminative, serious, solicitous, studious, thinking, unselfish, wary, wistful. *antonym* thoughtless.

thoughtless *adj* absent-minded, careless, foolish, heedless, ill-considered, impolite, imprudent, inadvertent, inattentive, inconsiderate, indiscreet, injudicious, insensitive, mindless, neglectful, negligent, rash, reckless, regardless, remiss, rude, selfish, silly, stupid, tactless, uncaring, undiplomatic, unkind, unmindful, unobservant, unreflecting, unthinking. **antonym** thoughtful.

thrash v beat, belt, birch, cane, chastise, clobber, crush, defeat, drub, flagellate, flail, flog, hammer, heave, horse-whip, jerk, lam, lambaste, lather, lay into, leather, maul, overwhelm, paste, plunge, punish, quilt, rout, scourge, slaughter, spank, squirm, swish, tan, thresh, toss, towel, trim, trounce, wallop, whap, whip, writhe.

thrash out debate, discuss, negotiate, resolve, settle, solve.

thread n cotton, course, direction, drift, fibre, filament, line, plot, story-line, strain, strand, string, tenor, theme, yarn. v ease, inch, meander, pass, string, weave, wind.

threadbare adj clichéd, cliché-ridden, commonplace, conventional, corny, down-at-heel, frayed, hackneyed, moth-eaten, old, overused, overworn, ragged, scruffy, shabby, stale, stereotyped, stock, tattered, tatty, tired, trite, used, well-worn, worn, worn-out. **antonyms** fresh, luxurious, new, plush.

threat n danger, foreboding, foreshadowing, frighteners, hazard, menace, omen, peril, portent, presage, risk, sabre-rattling, warning.

threaten v browbeat, bully, cow, endanger, forebode, foreshadow, impend, imperil, intimidate, jeopardise, menace, portend, presage, pressurise, terrorise, warn.

threatening adj baleful, bullying, cautionary, grim, inauspicious, intimidatory, menacing, minatory, ominous, sinister, terrorising, warning.

threshold n beginning, brink, dawn, door, entrance, inception, minimum, opening, outset, sill, start, starting-point, verge.

thrift n carefulness, conservation, economy, frugality, parsimony, prudence, saving, thriftiness. **antonyms** profligacy, waste.

thrifty adj careful, conserving, economical, frugal, parsimonious, provident, prudent, saving, sparing. **antonyms** prodigal, profligate, thriftless, wasteful.

thrill n adventure, buzz, charge, flutter, fluttering, frisson, glow, kick, pleasure, quiver, sensation, shudder, stimulation, throb, tingle, titillation, tremble, tremor, vibration. v arouse, electrify, excite, flush, flutter, glow, move, quake, quiver, send, shake,

shudder, stimulate, stir, throb, tingle, titillate, tremble, vibrate, wow.

thrilling adj electrifying, exciting, exhilarating, gripping, hair-raising, heart-stirring, quaking, rip-roaring, riveting, rousing, sensational, shaking, shivering, shuddering, soul-stirring, stimulating, stirring, trembling, vibrating.

thrive v advance, bloom, blossom, boom, burgeon, develop, flourish, gain, grow, increase, profit, prosper, succeed, wax. **antonyms** die, fail, languish, stagnate.

thriving adj affluent, blooming, blossoming, booming, burgeoning, comfortable, developing, flourishing, growing, healthy, prosperous, successful, wealthy, well. **antonyms** ailing, dying, failing, languishing, stagnating.

throaty adj deep, gruff, guttural, hoarse, husky, low, rasping, raucous, thick.

throb v beat, palpitate, pound, pulsate, pulse, thump, vibrate. n beat, palpitation, pounding, pulsating, pulsation, pulse, thump, thumping, vibration.

throe n convulsion, fit, paroxysm, seizure, spasm.

throes n agony, anguish, distress, pain, suffering, torture.

throng n assemblage, bevy, congregation, crowd, crush, flock, herd, horde, host, mass, mob, multitude, pack, press, swarm. v bunch, congregate, converge, cram, crowd, fill, flock, herd, mill around, pack, press, swarm.

throttle v asphyxiate, choke, control, gag, inhibit, silence, smother, stifle, strangle, strangulate, suppress.

through prep as a result of, because of, between, by, by means of, by reason of, by virtue of, by way of, during, in, in and out of, in consequence of, in the middle of, past, thanks to, throughout, using, via. adj completed, direct, done, ended, express, finished, non-stop, terminated. **through and through** altogether, completely, entirely, from top to bottom, fully, thoroughly, to the core, totally, unreservedly, utterly, wholly.

throughout adv everywhere, extensively, ubiquitously, widely.

throw v astonish, baffle, bemuse, bring down, cast, chuck, confound, confuse, defeat, discomfit, disconcert, dislodge, dumbfound, elance, execute, fell, fling, floor, heave, hurl, launch, lob, overturn, perform, perplex, pitch, produce, project,

propel, put, send, sling, slug, toss, unhorse, unsaddle, unseat, upset, whang.
n attempt, cast, chance, essay, fling, gamble, hazard, heave, lob, pitch, projection, put, sling, spill, toss, try, venture, wager.

throw away blow, cast off, discard, dispense with, dispose of, ditch, dump, fritter away, jettison, lose, reject, scrap, squander, waste. **antonyms** keep, preserve, rescue, salvage.

throw off abandon, cast off, confuse, discard, disconcert, disturb, drop, shake off, throw, unsaddle, unseat, unsettle, upset.

throw out confuse, diffuse, discard, disconcert, dismiss, disseminate, disturb, ditch, dump, eject, emit, evict, expel, give off, jettison, radiate, reject, scrap, throw, turf out, turn down, unhouse, unsettle, upset, utter.

throw over abandon, chuck, desert, discard, drop, finish with, forsake, jilt, leave, quit, reject.

throw up abandon, chuck, disgorge, give up, heave, jack in, leave, produce, puke, quit, regurgitate, relinquish, renounce, resign, retch, reveal, spew, vomit.

throwaway *adj* careless, casual, offhand, passing.

thrust *v* bear, butt, drive, force, impel, intrude, jab, lunge, pierce, plunge, poke, press, prod, propel, push, ram, shove, stab, stick, urge, wedge.

thud *n* clonk, clump, clunk, crash, knock, smack, thump, thwack, wallop, wham.
v bash, clonk, clump, clunk, crash, knock, smack, thump, thunder, thwack, wallop, wham.

thug *n* animal, assassin, bandit, bruiser, bully-boy, cut-throat, gangster, goon, gorilla, heavy, hood, hoodlum, hooligan, killer, mugger, murderer, robber, ruffian, tough.

thumb one's nose at cock a snook at, deride, flout, guy, jeer at, laugh at, mock, ridicule, scoff.

thumb through browse through, flick through, flip through, glance at, leaf through, peruse, scan, skim.

thumbnail *adj* brief, compact, concise, miniature, pithy, quick, short, small, succinct.

thumbs down disapproval, negation, no, rebuff, refusal, rejection. **antonym** thumbs up.

thumbs up acceptance, affirmation, approval, encouragement, go-ahead, green light, OK, sanction, yes. **antonym** thumbs down.

thump *n* bang, blow, box, clout, clunk, crash, cuff, knock, rap, smack, thud, thwack, wallop, whack.
v bang, batter, beat, belabour, box, clout, crash, cuff, daud, ding, dunt, dush, hit, knock, lambaste, pound, rap, smack, strike, thrash, throb, thud, thwack, wallop, whack.

thumping *adj* big, colossal, enormous, excessive, exorbitant, gargantuan, gigantic, great, huge, immense, impressive, mammoth, massive, monumental, terrific, thundering, titanic, towering, tremendous, whooping. **antonyms** insignificant, petty, piddling, trivial.

thunder *n* boom, booming, clap, cracking, crash, crashing, detonation, explosion, pealing, roll, rumble, rumbling.
v bark, bellow, blast, boom, clap, crack, crash, curse, declaim, denounce, detonate, explode, fulminate, inveigh, peal, rail, resound, reverberate, roar, rumble, shout, threaten, yell.

thunderous *adj* booming, deafening, ear-splitting, loud, noisy, resounding, reverberating, roaring, stentorian, tumultuous.

thunderstruck *adj* agape, aghast, amazed, astonished, astounded, dazed, dumbfounded, flabbergasted, floored, flummoxed, nonplussed, open-mouthed, paralysed, petrified, shocked, staggered, stunned.

thus *adv* accordingly, as follows, consequently, ergo, hence, in this way, like so, like this, so, then, therefore.

thwart *v* baffle, balk, check, defeat, foil, frustrate, hinder, impede, obstruct, oppose, outwit, prevent, spite, stop, stymie, traverse. **antonyms** abet, aid, assist.

tick *n* clack, click, clicking, flash, instant, jiffy, mark, minute, moment, sec, second, shake, stroke, tap, tapping, tick-tick, tick-tock, trice, twinkling.
v beat, choose, clack, click, indicate, mark (off), select, tally, tap.

tick off bawl out, berate, censure, chide, haul over the coals, keelhaul, lecture, rebuke, reprimand, reproach, reprove, scold, take to task, tear off a strip, tell off, upbraid. **antonym** praise.

ticket *n* card, certificate, coupon, docket, label, marker, pass, slip, sticker, tab, tag, token, voucher.

tickle v amuse, cheer, delight, divert, enchant, entertain, excite, gratify, please, thrill, titillate.

ticklish adj awkward, critical, delicate, difficult, dodgy, hazardous, nice, precarious, risky, sensitive, thorny, touchy, tricky, uncertain, unstable, unsteady. **antonyms** easy, straightforward.

tide n course, current, direction, drift, ebb, flow, flux, movement, stream, tendency, tenor, trend.

tidy adj ample, clean, considerable, fair, generous, good, goodly, handsome, healthy, large, largish, methodical, neat, ordered, orderly, respectable, shipshape, siz(e)able, spick, spick-and-span, spruce, substantial, systematic, trim, uncluttered, well-groomed, well-kept. **antonyms** disorganised, untidy.
v arrange, clean, groom, neaten, order, spruce up, straighten.

tie v attach, bind, confine, connect, draw, equal, fasten, hamper, hinder, hold, interlace, join, knot, lash, limit, link, match, moor, oblige, restrain, restrict, rope, secure, strap, tether, truss, unite.
n affiliation, allegiance, band, bond, commitment, connection, contest, cord, dead heat, deadlock, draw, duty, encumbrance, fastening, fetter, fixture, game, hindrance, joint, kinship, knot, liaison, limitation, link, match, obligation, relationship, restraint, restriction, rope, stalemate, string.
tie up attach, bind, conclude, end, engage, engross, finish off, lash, moor, occupy, pinion, restrain, rope, secure, settle, terminate, tether, truss, wind up, wrap up.

tier n band, belt, echelon, floor, layer, level, line, rank, row, stage, storey, stratification, stratum, zone.

tiff n barney, difference, disagreement, dispute, falling-out, quarrel, row, scrap, set-to, spat, squabble, words.

tight¹ adj close, close-fitting, compact, constricted, cramped, dangerous, difficult, even, evenly-balanced, fast, firm, fixed, grasping, harsh, hazardous, hermetic, impervious, inflexible, mean, miserly, narrow, near, niggardly, parsimonious, penurious, perilous, precarious, precise, problematic, proof, rigid, rigorous, sealed, secure, severe, snug, sound, sparing, stern, sticky, stiff, stingy, stretched, strict, stringent, taut, tense, ticklish, tight-fisted, tough, tricky, troublesome, uncompromising, unyielding, watertight. **antonyms** lax, loose, slack.

tight² adj blotto, drunk, half cut, half-seas-over, inebriated, intoxicated, pickled, pie-eyed, pissed, plastered, smashed, sozzled, stewed, stoned, three sheets in the wind, tiddly, tipsy, under the influence. **antonym** sober.

tighten v close, constrict, constringe, cramp, crush, fasten, fix, narrow, screw, secure, squeeze, stiffen, stretch, tense. **antonyms** loosen, relax.

tight-fisted adj cheese-paring, close, close-fisted, grasping, mean, mingy, miserly, niggardly, parsimonious, penny-pinching, penurious, sparing, stingy, tight. **antonym** generous.

tight-lipped adj mum, quiet, reserved, reticent, secretive, silent, taciturn, uncommunicative, unforthcoming. **antonyms** garrulous, talkative.

time n age, beat, chronology, date, day, duration, epoch, era, generation, heyday, hour, instance, interval, juncture, life, lifespan, lifetime, measure, metre, occasion, peak, period, point, rhythm, season, space, span, spell, stage, stretch, tempo, term, tide, while.
v clock, control, count, judge, measure, meter, regulate, schedule, set.
time and again frequently, many times, often, on many occasions, over and over again, recurrently, repeatedly, time after time.

time-honoured adj accustomed, age-old, ancient, conventional, customary, established, fixed, historic, long-established, old, traditional, usual, venerable.

timeless adj abiding, ageless, ceaseless, changeless, deathless, endless, enduring, eternal, everlasting, immortal, immutable, imperishable, indestructible, lasting, permanent, perpetual, persistent, undying.

timely adj appropriate, convenient, judicious, opportune, prompt, propitious, punctual, seasonable, suitable, well-timed. **antonyms** ill-timed, inappropriate, unfavourable.

time-worn adj aged, ancient, broken-down, bromidic, clichéd, dated, decrepit, dog-eared, hackneyed, hoary, lined, old hat, out of date, outworn, passé, ragged, ruined, run-down, shabby, stale, stock, threadbare, tired, trite, weathered, well-worn, worn, wrinkled. **antonyms** fresh, new.

timid adj afraid, apprehensive,

bashful, cowardly, coy, diffident, faint-hearted, fearful, irresolute, modest, mousy, nervous, pusillanimous, retiring, shrinking, shy, spineless, timorous. *antonyms* audacious, bold, brave.

timorous *adj* afraid, apprehensive, bashful, cowardly, coy, diffident, faint-hearted, fearful, inadventurous, irresolute, modest, mousy, nervous, pusillanimous, retiring, shrinking, shy, tentative, timid, trembling. *antonyms* assertive, assured, bold.

tinge *n* bit, cast, colour, dash, drop, dye, flavour, pinch, shade, smack, smattering, sprinkling, stain, suggestion, tint, touch, trace, wash.

v colour, dye, imbue, shade, stain, suffuse, tint.

tingle *v* itch, prickle, ring, sting, thrill, throb, tickle, vibrate.

n frisson, gooseflesh, goose-pimples, itch, itching, pins and needles, prickling, quiver, shiver, stinging, thrill, tickle, tickling.

tinker *v* dabble, fiddle, meddle, monkey, play, potter, toy, trifle.

tinsel *adj* cheap, flashy, gaudy, meretricious, ostentatious, pinchbeck, plastic, sham, showy, specious, superficial, tawdry, trashy.

n artificiality, display, flamboyance, garishness, gaudiness, glitter, insignificance, ostentation, pinchbeck, pretension, sham, show, spangle, triviality, worthlessness.

tint *n* cast, colour, dye, hint, hue, rinse, shade, stain, streak, suggestion, tinge, tone, touch, trace, wash.

v affect, colour, dye, influence, rinse, stain, streak, taint, tinge.

tiny *adj* diminutive, dwarfish, infinitesimal, insignificant, itsy-bitsy, Lilliputian, little, microscopic, mini, miniature, minute, negligible, petite, pint-size(d), pocket, puny, slight, small, teensy, teeny, teeny-weeny, tiddl(e)y, tottie, totty, trifling, wee, weeny. *antonyms* big, immense.

tip¹ *n* acme, apex, cap, crown, end, extremity, ferrule, head, nib, peak, pinnacle, point, summit, top.

v cap, crown, finish, pinnacle, prune, surmount, top.

tip² *v* cant, capsize, ditch, dump, empty, heel, incline, lean, list, overturn, pour out, slant, spill, tilt, topple over, unload, up-end, upset.

n coup, dump, midden, refuse-heap, rubbish-heap, slag-heap.

tipple *v* drink, imbibe, indulge, quaff swig, tope.

n alcohol, booze, drink, liquor, poison.

tipsy *adj* a peg too low, cockeyed, drunk fuddled, happy, mellow, merry, nappy slewed, squiff(y), tiddley, tiddly, tight. *antonym* sober.

tirade *n* abuse, denunciation, diatribe fulmination, harangue, invective, lecture outburst.

tire *v* annoy, bore, drain, droop, enervate exasperate, exhaust, fag, fail, fatigue flag, harass, irk, irritate, jade, knacker sink, weary. *antonyms* energise enliven, exhilarate, invigorate, refresh.

tired *adj* all in, beat, bone-weary, bushed clapped-out, clichéd, conventional corny, dead-beat, dog-tired, drained drooping, drowsy, enervated, exhausted fagged, familiar, fatigued, flagging hackneyed, jaded, knackered, old outworn, shagged, shattered, sleepy spent, stale, stock, threadbare, trite weary, well-worn, whacked, worn out. *antonyms* active, energetic, fresh, lively rested.

tireless *adj* determined, diligent, energetic, indefatigable, industrious resolute, sedulous, unflagging, untiring unwearied, vigorous. *antonyms* tired, unenthusiastic, weak.

tiresome *adj* annoying, boring, bothersome, dull, exasperating fatiguing, flat, irksome, irritating, laborious, monotonous, pesky, tedious, troublesome, trying, uninteresting, vexatious, wearing. *antonyms* easy, interesting, stimulating.

tiring *adj* arduous, demanding, draining, enervating, enervative, exacting, exhausting, fagging, fatiguing, laborious, strenuous, tough, wearing, wearying.

tissue *n* accumulation, agglomeration, collection, combination, concatenation, conglomeration, fabric, fabrication, gauze, mass, mesh, network, pack, paper, series, structure, stuff, texture, tissue-paper, web.

titanic *adj* colossal, enormous, giant, gigantic, herculean, huge, immense, jumbo, mammoth, massive, mighty, monstrous, monumental, mountainous, prodigious, stupendous, towering, vast. *antonyms* insignificant, small.

titillating *adj* arousing, captivating, exciting, interesting, intriguing, lewd, lurid, provocative, sensational, stimulating, suggestive, teasing, thrilling.

titivate *v* doll up, make up, prank, preen,

primp, prink, refurbish, smarten up, tart up, touch up.

title *n* appellation, caption, championship, claim, crown, denomination, designation, entitlement, epithet, handle, heading, inscription, label, laurels, legend, letter-head, moniker, name, nickname, nom de plume, ownership, prerogative, privilege, pseudonym, right, soubriquet, style, term.
v call, christen, designate, dub, entitle, label, name, style, term.

titter *v* chortle, chuckle, giggle, laugh, mock, snigger, tee-hee.

titular *adj* formal, honorary, nominal, puppet, putative, so-called, token.

to a fault excessively, immoderately, in the extreme, needlessly, out of all proportion, over the top, overly, overmuch, preposterously, ridiculously, to extremes, unduly.

to a man bar none, every one, one and all, unanimously, without exception.

to a turn correctly, exactly, perfectly, precisely, to perfection.

to all intents and purposes as good as, practically, pretty much, pretty well, virtually.

to be reckoned with consequential, considerable, formidable, important, influential, powerful, significant, strong, weighty.

to the full completely, entirely, fully, thoroughly, to the utmost, utterly.

to the hilt absolutely, completely, entirely, fully, totally, wholly.

to the letter accurately, exactly, literally, precisely, spot on, strictly, word for word.

to the point applicable, apposite, appropriate, apropos, apt, brief, fitting, germane, pertinent, pithy, pointed, relevant, short, suitable, terse. *antonym* irrelevant.

toady *n* arse-licker, bootlicker, crawler, creep, flatterer, flunky, groveller, hanger-on, lackey, lickspittle, minion, nark, parasite, sycophant, yes-man.
v bootlick, bow and scrape, butter up, crawl, creep, curry favour, fawn, flatter, grovel, kiss the feet, kowtow, suck up.

to-do *n* agitation, bother, bustle, commotion, disturbance, excitement, flap, flurry, furore, fuss, hoo-ha, performance, pother, quarrel, ruction, rumpus, stew, stir, tumult, turmoil, unrest, uproar.

together *adv* all at once, arranged, as one, as one man, at the same time, cheek by jowl, closely, collectively, concurrently, consecutively, contemporaneously, continuously, en masse, hand in glove, hand in hand, in a row, in concert, in co-operation, in succession, in unison, jointly, mutually, on end, settled, shoulder to shoulder, side by side, simultaneously, sorted out, straight, successively. *antonym* separately.
adj calm, commonsensical, composed, cool, down-to-earth, level-headed, sensible, stable, well-adjusted, well-balanced, well-organised.

toil *n* application, donkey-work, drudgery, effort, elbow grease, exertion, graft, industry, labour, pains, slog, sweat, travail.
v drudge, graft, grind, grub, labour, persevere, plug away, slave, slog, strive, struggle, sweat, work.

toilet *n* ablutions, bathing, bathroom, bog, can, closet, comfort station, convenience, gents', john, karsey, kazi, ladies', latrine, lavatory, loo, outhouse, powder-room, privy, rest-room, smallest room, thunder-box, urinal, washroom, water closet, WC.

token *n* badge, clue, demonstration, evidence, expression, index, indication, keepsake, manifestation, mark, memento, memorial, note, pledge, proof, remembrance, reminder, representation, sign, souvenir, symbol, testimony, voucher, warning.
adj emblematic, hollow, inconsiderable, minimal, nominal, perfunctory, superficial, symbolic.

tolerable *adj* acceptable, adequate, all right, allowable, average, bearable, endurable, fair, fair to middling, indifferent, liv(e)able, mediocre, middling, not bad, OK, ordinary, passable, run-of-the-mill, so-so, sufferable, supportable, unexceptional. *antonym* intolerable.

tolerance *n* allowance, broad-mindedness, charity, endurance, fluctuation, forbearance, fortitude, hardiness, hardness, indulgence, magnanimity, open-mindedness, patience, permissiveness, play, resilience, resistance, rope, stamina, sufferance, swing, sympathy, toughness, variation. *antonyms* bigotry, intolerance, narrow-mindedness, prejudice.

tolerant *adj* biddable, broad-minded, catholic, charitable, complaisant, compliant, easy-going, fair, forbearing, indulgent, kind-hearted, latitudinarian, lax, lenient, liberal, long-suffering, magnanimous, open-minded, patient, permissive, soft, sympathetic, understanding, unprejudiced. **antonyms** biased, bigoted, intolerant, prejudiced, unsympathetic.

tolerate v abear, abide, accept, admit, allow, bear, brook, condone, connive at, countenance, endure, indulge, permit, pocket, put up with, receive, sanction, stand, stomach, suffer, swallow, take, turn a blind eye to, undergo, wear, wink at.

toll[1] v announce, call, chime, clang, knell, peal, ring, send, signal, sound, strike, summon, warn.

toll[2] n assessment, charge, cost, customs, damage, demand, duty, fee, levy, loss, payment, penalty, rate, tariff, tax, tithe.

tomb n burial-place, catacomb, cenotaph, crypt, grave, mausoleum, sepulchre, vault.

tomfoolery n buffoonery, childishness, clowning, foolishness, horseplay, larking about, larks, messing about, nonsense, silliness, skylarking.

tone n accent, air, approach, aspect, attitude, cast, character, colour, drift, effect, emphasis, feel, force, frame, grain, harmony, hue, inflection, intonation, manner, modulation, mood, note, pitch, quality, shade, spirit, strength, stress, style, temper, tenor, timbre, tinge, tint, tonality, vein, volume.
v blend, harmonise, intone, match, sound, suit.

tone down alleviate, assuage, dampen, dim, mitigate, moderate, modulate, palliate, play down, reduce, restrain, soften, soft-pedal, subdue, temper.

tone up brighten, freshen, invigorate, limber up, shape up, sharpen up, touch up, trim, tune up.

tongue n argot, articulation, dialect, discourse, idiom, language, lingo, parlance, patois, speech, talk, utterance, vernacular, voice.

tongue-tied adj dumb, dumbstruck, inarticulate, mute, silent, speechless, voiceless. **antonyms** garrulous, talkative, voluble.

tonic n boost, fillip, inspiration, livener, pick-me-up, refresher, restorative, shot in the arm, stimulant.

too[1] adv also, as well, besides, further, in addition, into the bargain, likewise, moreover, to boot, what's more.

too[2] adv excessively, exorbitantly, extremely, immoderately, inordinately,

over, overly, ridiculously, to excess, to extremes, unduly, unreasonably, very.

tool n agency, agent, apparatus, appliance, contraption, contrivance, creature, device, dupe, flunkey, front, gadget, hireling, implement, instrument, intermediary, jackal, lackey, machine, means, medium, minion, pawn, puppet, stooge, toady, utensil, vehicle, weapon.

top n acme, apex, apogee, cap, cop, cork, cover, crest, crown, culmination, head, height, high point, lead, lid, peak, pinnacle, stopper, summit, upside, vertex, zenith. **antonyms** base, bottom, nadir.
adj best, chief, crack, crowning, culminating, dominant, élite, finest, first, foremost, greatest, head, highest, lead, leading, pre-eminent, prime, principal, ruling, sovereign, superior, topmost, upmost, upper, uppermost.
v ascend, beat, best, better, cap, climb, command, cover, crest, crown, decorate, eclipse, exceed, excel, finish, finish off, garnish, head, lead, outdo, outshine, outstrip, roof, scale, surmount, surpass, tip.

topic n issue, matter, point, question, subject, subject-matter, talking-point, theme.

topical adj contemporary, current, familiar, newsworthy, popular, relevant, up-to-date, up-to-the-minute.

topmost adj dominant, foremost, highest, leading, loftiest, maximum, paramount, principal, supreme, top, upper, uppermost. **antonyms** bottom, bottommost, lowest.

topple v capsize, collapse, oust, overbalance, overthrow, overturn, totter, tumble, unseat, upset.

topsy-turvy adj backside-foremost, chaotic, confused, disarranged, disorderly, disorganised, inside-out, jumbled, messy, mixed-up, untidy, upside-down. **antonyms** ordered, tidy.

torment v afflict, agitate, agonise, annoy, bedevil, bother, chivvy, crucify, devil, distort, distress, excruciate, harass, harrow, harry, hound, irritate, nag, pain, persecute, pester, plague, provoke, rack, tease, torture, trouble, vex, worry, wrack.
n affliction, agony, angst, anguish, annoyance, bane, bother, distress, harassment, hassle, hell, irritation, misery, nag, nagging, nuisance, pain, persecution, pest, plague, provocation, scourge, suffering, torture, trouble, vexation, worry.

orn *adj* cut, dithering, divided, havering, irresolute, lacerated, ragged, rent, ripped, slit, split, swithering, uncertain, undecided, unsure, vacillating, wavering.

orpid *adj* apathetic, dormant, drowsy, inactive, indolent, inert, lackadaisical, languid, languorous, lazy, lethargic, listless, motionless, numb, passive, slothful, slow, slow-moving, sluggish, somnolent, stagnant. *antonyms* active, lively, vigorous.

orpor *n* apathy, dormancy, drowsiness, dullness, inactivity, indolence, inertia, inertness, languor, laziness, lethargy, listlessness, numbness, passivity, sloth, sluggishness, somnolence, stagnancy, stupidity, stupor, torpidity. *antonyms* activity, animation, vigour.

orrent *n* barrage, cascade, deluge, downpour, effusion, flood, flow, gush, outburst, rush, spate, stream, tide, volley.

orrid *adj* ardent, arid, blistering, boiling, broiling, burning, dried, dry, emotional, erotic, fervent, fiery, hot, intense, parched, parching, passionate, scorched, scorching, sexy, sizzling, steamy, stifling, sultry, sweltering, tropical. *antonym* arctic.

ortuous *adj* ambiguous, bent, circuitous, complicated, convoluted, crooked, cunning, curved, deceptive, devious, indirect, involved, mazy, meandering, misleading, roundabout, serpentine, sinuous, tricky, twisted, twisting, winding, zigzag. *antonyms* straight, straightforward.

orture *v* afflict, agonise, crucify, distress, excruciate, harrow, lacerate, martyr, pain, persecute, rack, torment, wrack.
n affliction, agony, anguish, distress, gyp, hell, laceration, martyrdom, misery, pain, pang(s), persecution, rack, suffering, torment.

toss *v* agitate, cant, cast, chuck, disturb, fling, flip, heave, hurl, jiggle, joggle, jolt, labour, launch, lob, lurch, pitch, project, propel, rock, roll, shake, shy, sling, thrash, throw, tumble, wallow, welter, wriggle, writhe.
n cast, chuck, fling, lob, pitch, shy, sling, throw.

tot *n* baby, bairn, child, dram, finger, infant, measure, mite, nip, shot, slug, snifter, toddler, wean.

tot up add (up), calculate, compute, count (up), reckon, sum, tally, total.

total *n* aggregate, all, amount, ensemble, entirety, lot, mass, sum, totality, whole.

adj absolute, all-out, complete, comprehensive, consummate, downright, entire, full, gross, integral, out-and-out, outright, perfect, root-and-branch, sheer, sweeping, thorough, thoroughgoing, unconditional, undisputed, undivided, unmitigated, unqualified, utter, whole, whole-hog. *antonyms* limited, partial, restricted.
v add (up), amount to, come to, count (up), reach, reckon, sum (up), tot up.

totalitarian *adj* authoritarian, despotic, dictatorial, monocratic, omnipotent, one-party, oppressive, tyrannous, undemocratic. *antonym* democratic.

totality *n* aggregate, all, completeness, cosmos, entireness, entirety, everything, fullness, sum, total, universe, whole, wholeness.

totally *adv* absolutely, completely, comprehensively, consummately, entirely, fully, perfectly, quite, thoroughly, unconditionally, undisputedly, undividedly, unmitigatedly, utterly, wholeheartedly, wholly. *antonym* partially.

totter *v* falter, lurch, quiver, reel, rock, shake, stagger, stumble, sway, teeter, titter, tremble, waver.

touch *n* ability, acquaintance, adroitness, approach, art, artistry, awareness, bit, blow, brush, caress, characteristic, command, communication, contact, correspondence, dash, deftness, detail, direction, drop, effect, facility, familiarity, feel, feeling, flair, fondling, hand, handiwork, handling, hint, hit, influence, intimation, jot, knack, manner, mastery, method, palpation, pat, pinch, push, skill, smack, smattering, soupçon, speck, spot, stroke, style, suggestion, suspicion, tap, taste, technique, tinge, trace, trademark, understanding, virtuosity, way, whiff.
v abut, adjoin, affect, attain, border, brush, caress, cheat, compare with, concern, consume, contact, converge, disturb, drink, eat, equal, feel, finger, fondle, graze, handle, hit, hold a candle to, impress, influence, inspire, interest, mark, match, meet, melt, move, palp, palpate, parallel, pat, pertain to, push, reach, regard, rival, soften, stir, strike, stroke, tap, tinge, upset, use, utilise.

touch on allude to, broach, cover, deal with, mention, refer to, remark on, speak of.

touch up arouse, brush up, enhance, finish off, fondle, improve, patch up, perfect, polish up, renovate, retouch, revamp, stimulate, titivate.

touch-and-go *adj* close, critical, dangerous, dodgy, hairy, hazardous, near, nerve-racking, perilous, precarious, risky, sticky, tricky.

touched *adj* affected, barmy, batty, bonkers, crazy, cuckoo, daft, disturbed, dotty, eccentric, impressed, mad, melted, moved, nuts, nutty, softened, stirred, swayed, upset.

touchiness *n* bad temper, captiousness, crabbedness, grouchiness, grumpiness, irascibility, irritability, peevishness, pettishness, petulance, surliness, testiness, tetchiness.

touching *adj* affecting, emotional, emotive, heartbreaking, melting, moving, pathetic, piteous, pitiable, pitiful, poignant, sad, stirring, tender.

touchstone *n* bench-mark, criterion, gauge, measure, norm, proof, standard, yardstick.

touchy *adj* bad-tempered, captious, crabbed, cross, feisty, grouchy, grumpy, huffy, irascible, irritable, miffy, peevish, pettish, petulant, querulous, quick-tempered, sensitive, sore, splenetic, surly, testy, tetchy, thin-skinned. *antonyms* calm, imperturbable, serene, unflappable.

tough *adj* adamant, arduous, bad, baffling, brawny, butch, callous, cohesive, difficult, durable, exacting, exhausting, firm, fit, hard, hard-bitten, hard-boiled, hardened, hard-nosed, hardy, herculean, inflexible, intractable, irksome, knotty, laborious, lamentable, leathery, merciless, obdurate, obstinate, perplexing, pugnacious, puzzling, refractory, regrettable, resilient, resistant, resolute, rigid, rough, rugged, ruthless, seasoned, severe, solid, stalwart, stern, stiff, stout, strapping, strenuous, strict, strong, stubborn, sturdy, tenacious, thorny, troublesome, unbending, unforgiving, unfortunate, unlucky, unyielding, uphill, vicious, vigorous, violent. *antonyms* brittle, delicate, fragile, liberal, soft, tender, vulnerable, weak.

n bruiser, brute, bully, bully-boy, droog, gorilla, hooligan, rough, roughneck, rowdy, ruffian, thug, yob, yobbo.

tour *n* circuit, course, drive, excursion, expedition, jaunt, journey, outing, ride, round, trip.

v drive, explore, journey, ride, sightsee, travel, visit.

tousled *adj* disarranged, dishevelled, disordered, messed up, ruffled, rumpled, tangled, tumbled.

tow *v* drag, draw, haul, lug, pull, tote, trail, transport, trawl, tug, yank.

towards *prep* a little short of, about, almost, approaching, close to, coming up to, concerning, for, getting on for, in the direction of, in the vicinity of, just before, nearing, nearly, on the way to, regarding to, -wards, with regard to, with respect to.

tower *v* ascend, dominate, exceed, loom, mount, overlook, overtop, rear, rise, soar, surpass, top, transcend, uprise.

towering *adj* colossal, elevated, excessive, extraordinary, extreme, gigantic, great, high, immoderate, imposing, impressive, inordinate, intemperate, lofty, magnificent, mighty, monumental, outstanding, overpowering, paramount, prodigious, soaring, sublime, superior, supreme, surpassing, tall, vehement, violent. *antonyms* minor, small, trivial.

town *n* borough, burgh, city, metropolis, municipality, settlement, township. *antonym* country.

toxic *adj* baneful, deadly, harmful, lethal, noxious, pernicious, poisonous, septic, unhealthy. *antonym* harmless.

toy *n* bauble, knick-knack, plaything, trifle, trinket.

v dally, fiddle, flirt, play, potter, sport, tinker, trifle.

trace *n* bit, dash, drop, evidence, footmark, footprint, footstep, hint, indication, iota, jot, mark, path, record, relic, remains, remnant, scintilla, shadow, sign, smack, soupçon, tinge, suggestion, survival, suspicion, tinge, token, touch, track, trail, trifle, vestige, whiff.

v ascertain, chart, copy, delineate, depict, detect, determine, discover, draw, find, follow, map, mark, outline, pursue, record, seek, shadow, show, sketch, stalk, track, trail, traverse, unearth, write.

track *n* course, drift, footmark, footprint, footstep, line, mark, orbit, path, pathway, piste, rail, rails, ridgeway, road, scent, sequence, slot, tack, trace, trail, train, trajectory, wake, wavelength, way.

v chase, dog, follow, hunt, pursue, shadow, spoor, stalk, tail, trace, trail, travel, traverse.

track down apprehend, capture, catch, dig up, discover, expose, ferret out, find, hunt down, locate, run to earth, sniff out, trace, unearth.

trade *n* avocation, barter, business,

calling, clientele, commerce, commodities, custom, customers, deal, dealing, employment, exchange, job, line, market, métier, occupation, profession, public, pursuit, shopkeeping, skill, swap, traffic, transactions, truck.

v bargain, barter, commerce, deal, do business, exchange, peddle, swap, switch, traffic, transact, truck.

trademark *n* badge, brand, crest, emblem, hallmark, identification, insignia, label, logo, name, sign, symbol.

tradition *n* convention, custom, customs, folklore, habit, institution, lore, praxis, ritual, usage, way.

traditional *adj* accustomed, ancestral, conventional, customary, established, fixed, folk, historic, long-established, new, old, oral, time-honoured, unconventional, unwritten, usual.

traduce *v* abuse, blacken, calumniate, decry, defame, denigrate, deprecate, disparage, knock, malign, misrepresent, revile, run down, slag, slander, smear, vilify.

traffic *n* barter, business, commerce, communication, dealing, dealings, doings, exchange, freight, intercourse, movement, passengers, peddling, relations, toing and froing, trade, transport, transportation, truck, vehicles.

v bargain, barter, deal, do business, exchange, intrigue, market, merchandise, peddle, trade, truck.

tragedy *n* adversity, affliction, blow, calamity, catastrophe, disaster, misfortune, unhappiness. **antonyms** prosperity, success, triumph.

tragic *adj* anguished, appalling, awful, calamitous, catastrophic, deadly, dire, disastrous, doleful, dreadful, fatal, grievous, heartbreaking, heart-rending, ill-fated, ill-starred, lamentable, miserable, mournful, pathetic, pitiable, ruinous, sad, shocking, sorrowful, unfortunate, unhappy, woeful, wretched. **antonyms** comic, successful, triumphant.

trail *v* chase, dangle, dawdle, drag, draw, droop, extend, follow, hang, haul, hunt, lag, linger, loiter, pull, pursue, shadow, stalk, straggle, stream, sweep, tail, tow, trace, track, traipse.

n appendage, drag, footpath, footprints, footsteps, mark, marks, path, road, route, scent, stream, tail, trace, track, train, wake, way.

trail away decrease, die away, diminish, disappear, dwindle, fade

(away), fall away, lessen, peter out, shrink, sink, subside, tail off, taper off, trail off, weaken.

train *v* aim, coach, direct, discipline, drill, educate, exercise, focus, guide, improve, instruct, lesson, level, point, prepare, rear, rehearse, school, teach, tutor.

n appendage, attendants, caravan, chain, choo-choo, column, concatenation, convoy, cortège, course, court, entourage, file, followers, following, household, lure, order, process, procession, progression, retinue, sequence, series, set, staff, string, succession, suite, tail, trail.

training *n* coaching, discipline, dressage, education, exercise, grounding, guidance, instruction, practice, preparation, schooling, teaching, tuition, tutelage, upbringing, working-out.

traipse *v* plod, slouch, trail, tramp, trudge.

trait *n* attribute, characteristic, feature, idiosyncrasy, mannerism, peculiarity, quality, quirk.

traitor *n* back-stabber, betrayer, deceiver, defector, deserter, double-crosser, fifth columnist, informer, Judas, miscreant, quisling, rebel, renegade, turncoat.

traitorous *adj* dishonourable, disloyal, double-crossing, double-dealing, faithless, false, perfidious, renegade, seditious, treacherous, treasonable, unfaithful, untrue. **antonyms** faithful, loyal, patriotic.

trajectory *n* course, flight, line, path, route, track, trail.

trammel *n* bar, block, bond, chain, check, clog, curb, fetter, hamper, handicap, hindrance, impediment, obstacle, rein, shackle, stumbling-block.

v bar, block, capture, catch, check, clog, curb, enmesh, ensnare, entrap, fetter, hamper, handicap, hinder, impede, inhibit, restrain, restrict, shackle, snag, tie.

tramp *v* crush, footslog, hike, march, plod, ramble, range, roam, rove, slog, stamp, stomp, stump, toil, traipse, trample, tread, trek, trudge, walk, yomp.

n derelict, dosser, down-and-out, drifter, footfall, footstep, hike, hobo, march, plod, ramble, slog, stamp, toe-rag, tread, trek, vagabond, vagrant.

trample *v* crush, flatten, hurt, infringe, insult, squash, stamp, tread, violate.

trance *n* abstraction, catalepsy,

daze, dream, ecstasy, muse, rapture, reverie, spell, stupefaction, stupor, unconsciousness.

tranquil *adj* at peace, calm, composed, cool, dispassionate, pacific, peaceful, placid, quiet, reposeful, restful, sedate, serene, still, undisturbed, unexcited, unperturbed, unruffled, untroubled. *antonyms* agitated, disturbed, noisy, troubled.

tranquillity *n* calm, calmness, composure, coolness, equanimity, hush, imperturbability, peace, peacefulness, placidity, quiet, quietness, repose, rest, restfulness, sedateness, serenity, silence, stillness. *antonyms* agitation, disturbance, noise.

transact *v* accomplish, carry on, carry out, conclude, conduct, discharge, dispatch, do, enact, execute, handle, manage, negotiate, perform, prosecute, settle.

transaction *n* action, affair, arrangement, bargain, business, coup, deal, deed, enterprise, execution, negotiation, proceeding, undertaking.

transcend *v* eclipse, exceed, excel, outdo, outrival, outshine, outstrip, overleap, overstep, overtop, surmount, surpass.

transcendent *adj* exceeding, extraordinary, foremost, incomparable, matchless, peerless, pre-eminent, sublime, superior, transcendental, unequalled, unparalleled, unrivalled, unsurpassed.

transcribe *v* copy, engross, exemplify, interpret, note, record, render, reproduce, rewrite, take down, tape, tape-record, transfer, translate, transliterate.

transcript *n* carbon, copy, duplicate, manuscript, note, notes, record, recording, reproduction, transcription, translation, transliteration, version.

transfer *v* carry, cede, change, consign, convey, decal, decant, demise, displace, grant, hand over, move, relocate, remove, second, shift, translate, transmit, transplant, transport, transpose.
n change, changeover, crossover, displacement, handover, move, relocation, removal, shift, switch, switch-over, transference, translation, transmission, transposition.

transfigure *v* alter, change, convert, exalt, glorify, idealise, metamorphose, transform, translate, transmute.

transfix *v* engross, fascinate, fix, hold, hypnotise, impale, mesmerise, paralyse, petrify, pierce, puncture, skewer, spear, spellbind, spike, spit, stick, stun. *antonym* bore.

transform *v* alter, change, convert, metamorphose, reconstruct, remodel, renew, revolutionise, transfigure, translate, transmogrify, transmute, transverse. *antonym* preserve.

transformation *n* alteration, change, conversion, metamorphosis, renewal, revolution, sea-change, transfiguration, translation, transmogrification, transmutation. *antonym* preservation.

transgress *v* breach, break, contravene, defy, disobey, encroach, err, exceed, infringe, lapse, misbehave, offend, overstep, sin, trespass, violate. *antonym* obey.

transgression *n* breach, contravention, crime, debt, encroachment, error, fault, infraction, infringement, iniquity, lapse, misbehaviour, misdeed, misdemeanour, offence, peccadillo, sin, trespass, violation, wrong, wrongdoing.

transient *adj* brief, ephemeral, evanescent, fleeting, flying, fugacious, fugitive, impermanent, momentary, passing, short, short-lived, short-term, temporary, transitory. *antonym* permanent.

transit *n* alteration, carriage, change, changeover, conversion, conveyance, crossing, haulage, motion, movement, passage, shift, shipment, transfer, transition, transport, transportation, travel, traverse.

transition *n* alteration, change, changeover, conversion, development, evolution, flux, metamorphosis, passage, passing, progress, progression, shift, transformation, transit, transmutation, upheaval. *antonyms* beginning, end.

transitional *adj* changing, developmental, fluid, intermediate, passing, provisional, temporary, transition, unsettled. *antonyms* final, initial.

transitory *adj* brief, ephemeral, evanescent, fleeting, flying, fugacious, fugitive, impermanent, momentary, passing, short, short-lived, short-term, temporary, transient, vanishing. *antonym* lasting.

translate *v* alter, carry, change, construe, convert, convey, decipher, decode, elucidate, explain, interpret, metamorphose, move, paraphrase, render, simplify, spell out, transcribe, transfer, transfigure, transform, transliterate, transmogrify, transmute, transplant, transport, transpose, turn.

translucent *adj* clear, diaphanous, limpid, transparent. *antonym* opaque.

transmission *n* broadcast, broadcasting, carriage, communication, conveyance, diffusion, dispatch, dissemination, passage, programme, relaying, remission, sending, shipment, show, showing, signal, spread, trajection, transfer, transference, transit, transport, transportation. *antonym* reception.

transmit *v* bear, broadcast, carry, communicate, convey, diffuse, dispatch, disseminate, forward, impart, network, radio, relay, remit, send, spread, traject, transfer, transport. *antonym* receive.

transmute *v* alter, change, convert, metamorphose, remake, transfigure, transform, translate, transmogrify. *antonym* retain.

transparent *adj* apparent, candid, clear, crystalline, diaphanous, direct, distinct, easy, evident, explicit, filmy, forthright, frank, gauzy, ingenuous, limpid, lucid, manifest, obvious, open, patent, plain, plain-spoken, recognisable, see-through, sheer, straight, straightforward, translucent, unambiguous, understandable, undisguised, unequivocal, visible. *antonyms* ambiguous, opaque, unclear.

transpire *v* appear, arise, befall, betide, chance, come out, come to light, emerge, happen, leak out, occur, take place, turn up.

transplant *v* displace, relocate, remove, resettle, shift, transfer, uproot. *antonym* leave.

transport *v* banish, bear, bring, captivate, carry, carry away, convey, delight, deport, ecstasise, electrify, enchant, enrapture, entrance, exile, fetch, haul, move, remove, run, ship, spellbind, take, transfer, waft. *antonyms* bore, leave.

n bliss, carriage, conveyance, delight, ecstasy, enchantment, euphoria, happiness, haulage, heaven, rapture, removal, shipment, shipping, transference, transportation, vehicle. *antonym* boredom.

transpose *v* alter, change, exchange, interchange, move, rearrange, relocate, reorder, shift, substitute, swap, switch, transfer. *antonym* leave.

transverse *adj* cross, crossways, crosswise, diagonal, oblique, transversal.

trap *n* ambush, artifice, bunker, danger, deception, device, gin, hazard, net, noose, pitfall, ruse, snare, spring, strategem, subterfuge, toils, trap-door, trick, trickery, wile.

v ambush, beguile, catch, corner, deceive, dupe, enmesh, ensnare, entrap, inveigle, lime, snare, take, tangle, trick.

trapped *adj* ambushed, beguiled, caught, cornered, deceived, duped, ensnared, inveigled, netted, snared, stuck, surrounded, tricked. *antonym* free.

trappings *n* accompaniments, accoutrements, adornments, clothes, decorations, dress, equipment, finery, fittings, fixtures, furnishings, gear, ornaments, paraphernalia, things, trimmings.

trash *n* balderdash, dregs, drivel, dross, garbage, hogwash, inanity, junk, kitsch, litter, nonsense, refuse, rot, rubbish, sweepings, tripe, twaddle, waste. *antonym* sense.

trashy *adj* catchpenny, cheap, cheap-jack, flimsy, grotty, inferior, kitschy, meretricious, pinchbeck, rubbishy, shabby, shoddy, tawdry, third-rate, tinsel, worthless. *antonym* first-rate.

trauma *n* agony, anguish, damage, disturbance, hurt, injury, jolt, lesion, ordeal, pain, scar, shock, strain, suffering, torture, upheaval, upset, wound. *antonyms* healing, relaxation.

traumatic *adj* agonising, damaging, distressing, disturbing, frightening, hurtful, injurious, painful, scarring, shocking, unpleasant, upsetting, wounding. *antonyms* healing, relaxed, relaxing.

travel *v* carry, commute, cross, go, journey, move, proceed, progress, ramble, roam, rove, tour, traverse, trek, voyage, walk, wander, wend. *antonym* stay.

travelling *adj* itinerant, migrant, migratory, mobile, movable, moving, nomadic, on the move, peripatetic, roaming, roving, touring, vagrant, wandering, wayfaring. *antonyms* fixed, stay-at-home.

traverse *v* balk, bridge, check, consider, contradict, contravene, counter, counteract, cover, cross, deny, dispute, examine, eye, frustrate, hinder, impede, inspect, investigate, move, negotiate, obstruct, oppose, ply, range, review, roam, scan, scrutinise, span, study, swing, thwart, turn, wander. *antonyms* aid, confirm.

travesty *n* apology, burlesque, caricature, distortion, lampoon, mockery, parody, perversion, send-up, sham, take-off.

v caricature, deride, distort, lampoon, mock, parody, pervert, pillory, ridicule, send up, sham, spoof, take off.

treacherous *adj* dangerous, deceitful, deceptive, disloyal, double-crossing, double-dealing, duplicitous, faithless, false, hazardous, icy, perfidious, perilous, precarious, risky, slippery, slippy, traitorous, treasonable, tricky, unfaithful, unreliable, unsafe, unstable, untrue, untrustworthy. **antonyms** dependable, loyal.

tread *v* crush, hike, march, oppress, pace, pad, plod, press, quell, repress, squash, stamp, step, stride, subdue, subjugate, suppress, tramp, trample, trudge, walk, walk on.

n footfall, footstep, gait, pace, step, stride, walk.

tread on someone's toes affront, annoy, bruise, discommode, disgruntle, hurt, inconvenience, infringe, injure, irk, offend, upset, vex. **antonym** soothe.

treason *n* disaffection, disloyalty, duplicity, lese-majesty, mutiny, perfidy, sedition, subversion, traitorousness, treachery. **antonym** loyalty.

treasure *n* cash, darling, flower, fortune, funds, gem, gold, jewel, jewels, money, paragon, pearl, precious, pride and joy, prize, riches, valuables, wealth.

v adore, cherish, esteem, idolise, love, preserve, prize, revere, value, venerate, worship. **antonym** disparage.

treat *n* banquet, celebration, delight, enjoyment, entertainment, excursion, feast, fun, gift, gratification, joy, outing, party, pleasure, refreshment, satisfaction, surprise, thrill. **antonym** drag.

v attend to, bargain, care for, confer, consider, contain, deal with, discourse upon, discuss, doctor, entertain, feast, give, handle, manage, negotiate, nurse, provide, regale, regard, stand, use.

treatment *n* care, conduct, cure, deal, dealing, discussion, handling, healing, management, manipulation, medication, medicine, prescript, reception, regimen, remedy, surgery, therapeutics, therapy, usage, use.

treaty *n* agreement, alliance, bargain, bond, compact, concordat, contract, convention, covenant, entente, negotiation, pact.

treble *adj* high, high-pitched, piping, sharp, shrill, threefold, triple. **antonym** deep.

trek *n* expedition, footslog, hike, journey, march, migration, odyssey, safari, slog, tramp, walk.

v footslog, hike, journey, march, migrate, plod, range, roam, rove, slog, traipse, tramp, trudge, yomp.

tremble *v* oscillate, quake, quiver, rock, shake, shiver, shudder, teeter, totter, vibrate, wobble.

n oscillation, quake, quiver, shake, shiver, shudder, tremor, vibration. **antonym** steadiness.

trembling *n* oscillation, quaking, quavering, quivering, rocking, shakes, shaking, shivering, shuddering, trepidation, vibration. **antonym** steadiness.

tremendous *adj* ace, amazing, appalling, awe-inspiring, awesome, awful, colossal, deafening, dreadful, enormous, excellent, exceptional, extraordinary, fabulous, fantastic, fearful, formidable, frightful, gargantuan, gigantic, great, hell of a, herculean, huge, immense, incredible, mammoth, marvellous, monstrous, prodigious, sensational, spectacular, stupendous, super, terrible, terrific, titanic, towering, vast, whopping, wonderful. **antonyms** boring, dreadful, run-of-the-mill, tiny.

tremor *n* agitation, earthquake, quake, quaking, quaver, quavering, quiver, quivering, shake, shaking, shiver, shock, thrill, tremble, trembling, trepidation, vibration, wobble. **antonym** steadiness.

tremulous *adj* afraid, agitated, agog, anxious, dithery, excited, fearful, frightened, jittery, jumpy, nervous, quavering, quivering, quivery, scared, shaking, shivering, timid, trembling, vibrating, wavering. **antonyms** calm, firm.

trench *n* channel, cut, ditch, drain, earthwork, excavation, furrow, gutter, pit, rill, trough, waterway.

trenchant *adj* acerbic, acid, acidulous, acute, astringent, biting, caustic, clear, clear-cut, cogent, crisp, cutting, distinct, driving, effective, effectual, emphatic, energetic, explicit, forceful, forthright, hurtful, incisive, keen, mordant, penetrating, piquant, pointed, potent, powerful, pungent, sarcastic, scratching, severe, sharp, strong, tart, unequivocal, vigorous. **antonym** woolly.

trend *n* bias, course, crazed, current, direction, drift, fad, fashion, flow, inclination, leaning, look, mode, rage, style, tendency, thing, vogue.

trendy *adj* fashionable, funky, groovy,

hip, in, latest, modish, stylish, up to the minute, voguish, with it. *antonym* unfashionable.

repidation *n* agitation, alarm, anxiety, apprehension, butterflies, cold sweat, consternation, dismay, disquiet, disturbance, dread, emotion, excitement, fear, fright, jitters, misgivings, nervousness, palpitation, perturbation, qualms, quivering, shaking, trembling, tremor, unease, uneasiness, worry. *antonym* calm.

respass *v* encroach, err, infringe, injure, intrude, invade, obtrude, offend, poach, sin, transgress, violate, wrong. *antonyms* keep to, obey.
n breach, contravention, crime, debt, delinquency, encroachment, error, evil-doing, fault, infraction, infringement, iniquity, injury, intrusion, invasion, misbehaviour, misconduct, misdeed, misdemeanour, offence, poaching, sin, transgression, wrong-doing.

rial *n* adversity, affliction, assay, attempt, audition, bane, bother, burden, check, contest, crack, distress, effort, endeavour, examination, experience, experiment, go, grief, hardship, hassle, hearing, irritation, litigation, load, misery, nuisance, ordeal, pain, pest, plague, proof, shot, sorrow, stab, suffering, taster, temptation, test, testing, tribulation, tribunal, trouble, try, trying, unhappiness, venture, vexation, woe, worry, wretchedness. *antonyms* happiness, rest.
adj dry, dummy, experimental, exploratory, pilot, probationary, provisional, testing.

ribe *n* blood, branch, caste, clan, class, division, dynasty, family, group, house, ilk, nation, people, race, stock.

ribulation *n* adversity, affliction, blow, burden, care, curse, distress, grief, heartache, misery, misfortune, ordeal, pain, reverse, sorrow, suffering, travail, trial, trouble, unhappiness, vexation, woe, worry, wretchedness. *antonyms* happiness, rest.

ribute *n* accolade, acknowledgement, applause, commendation, compliment, credit, encomium, esteem, eulogy, first-fruits, gift, gratitude, homage, honour, laudation, offering, praise, recognition, respect, testimonial, testimony. *antonym* blame.

trice *n* flash, instant, jiff, jiffy, minute, moment, sec, second, shake, tick, twinkling, whiff.

trick *n* antic, art, artifice, caper, characteristic, chicane, command, con, deceit, deception, device, dodge, expedient, expertise, feat, feint, foible, fraud, frolic, gag, gambol, gift, gimmick, habit, hang, hoax, idiosyncrasy, jape, joke, josh, knack, know-how, leg-pull, mannerism, manoeuvre, peculiarity, ploy, practical joke, practice, prank, put-on, quirk, ruse, secret, skill, stratagem, stunt, subterfuge, swindle, technique, trap, wile.
adj artificial, bogus, counterfeit, ersatz, fake, false, feigned, forged, imitation, mock, pretend, sham. *antonym* genuine.
v bamboozle, beguile, cheat, con, cozen, deceive, defraud, delude, diddle, dupe, fool, gull, hoax, hoodwink, lead on, mislead, outwit, pull a fast one on, pull someone's leg, sell, swindle, trap.

trick out adorn, array, attire, bedeck, decorate, do up, doll up, dress up, ornament, prank, prink, spruce up, tart up, trick up.

trickery *n* cheating, chicanery, con, deceit, deception, dishonesty, double-dealing, dupery, fraud, funny business, guile, hoax, hocus-pocus, jiggery-pokery, monkey business, pretence, shenanigans, skulduggery, swindling. *antonym* honesty.

trickle *v* dribble, drip, drop, exude, filter, gutter, leak, ooze, percolate, run, seep. *antonyms* gush, stream.
n drib, dribble, driblet, dribs and drabs, drip, seepage. *antonyms* gush, stream.

tricky *adj* artful, complicated, crafty, cunning, deceitful, deceptive, delicate, devious, difficult, knotty, problematic, risky, scheming, slippery, sly, sticky, subtle, thorny, ticklish, touch-and-go, wily. *antonyms* easy, honest.

trifle *n* bagatelle, bauble, bit, dash, drop, foolishness, jot, knick-knack, little, nonsense, nothing, pinch, plaything, spot, touch, toy, trace, trinket, triviality, whim-wham.
v dabble, dally, flirt, fool, fritter, idle, meddle, play, play with, sport, toy, waste.

trifling *adj* empty, frivolous, idle, inconsiderable, insignificant, minuscule, negligible, paltry, petty, piddling, piffling, puny, shallow, silly, slight, small, tiny, trivial, unimportant, valueless, worthless. *antonym* important.

trigger *v* activate, actuate, cause,

elicit, generate, initiate, produce, prompt, provoke, set off, spark off, start.

trill v cheep, chirp, chirrup, sing, tweet, twitter, warble, whistle.

trim adj compact, dapper, natty, neat, orderly, shipshape, slender, slim, smart, spick-and-span, spruce, streamlined, svelte, well-dressed, well-groomed, willowy. **antonym** scruffy.

v adjust, adorn, arrange, array, balance, barb, barber, beautify, bedeck, clip, crop, curtail, cut, decorate, distribute, dock, dress, embellish, embroider, garnish, lop, order, ornament, pare, prepare, prune, settle, shave, shear, tidy, trick.

n adornment, array, attire, border, clipping, condition, crop, cut, decoration, disposition, dress, edging, embellishment, equipment, fitness, fittings, form, frill, fringe, garnish, gear, health, humour, nick, order, ornament, ornamentation, piping, pruning, repair, shape, shave, shearing, situation, state, temper, trappings, trimming.

trimmings n accessories, accompaniments, additions, clippings, cuttings, ends, extras, frills, garnish, ornaments, paraphernalia, parings, remnants, shavings, trappings.

trinket n bagatelle, bauble, knick-knack, nothing, ornament, toy, trifle.

trip n blunder, boob, errand, error, excursion, expedition, fall, faux pas, foray, indiscretion, jaunt, journey, lapse, outing, ramble, run, skip, slip, step, stumble, tour, travel, voyage.

v activate, blunder, boob, caper, confuse, dance, disconcert, engage, err, fall, flip, flit, frisk, gambol, go, hop, lapse, miscalculate, pull, ramble, release, set off, skip, slip, slip up, spring, stumble, switch on, throw, tip up, tour, trap, travel, tumble, unsettle, voyage.

tripe n balderdash, balls, bosh, bullshit, bunkum, claptrap, drivel, garbage, guff, hogwash, inanity, nonsense, poppycock, rot, rubbish, tosh, trash, twaddle. **antonym** sense.

trite adj banal, bromidic, clichéd, common, commonplace, corny, dull, hack, hackneyed, ordinary, overworn, pedestrian, routine, run-of-the-mill, stale, stereotyped, stock, threadbare, tired, uninspired, unoriginal, well-worn, worn, worn out. **antonym** original.

triumph n accomplishment, achievement, ascendancy, attainment, conquest, coup, elation, exultation, feat, happiness, hit, joy, jubilation, masterstroke, mastery, pride, rejoicing, sensation, smash, smash-hit, success, tour de force, victory, walk-over, win. **antonym** disaster.

v best, celebrate, crow, defeat, dominate, exult, gloat, glory, have the last laugh, humble, humiliate, overcome, overwhelm, prevail, prosper, rejoice, revel, subdue, succeed, swagger, vanquish, win. **antonym** fail.

triumphant adj boastful, celebratory, cock-a-hoop, conquering, dominant, elated, exultant, gloating, glorious, joyful, jubilant, proud, rejoicing, successful, swaggering, triumphal, undefeated, victorious, winning. **antonyms** defeated, humble.

trivia n details, irrelevancies, minutiae, trifles, trivialities. **antonym** essentials.

trivial adj commonplace, everyday, frivolous, incidental, inconsequential, inconsiderable, insignificant, little, meaningless, minor, negligible, nugatory, paltry, petty, piddling, piffling, puny, slight, small, trifling, trite, unimportant, valueless, worthless. **antonym** significant.

trivialise v belittle, depreciate, devalue, minimise, play down, scoff at, underestimate, underplay, undervalue. **antonym** exalt.

troop n assemblage, band, body, bunch, company, contingent, crew, crowd, division, drove, flock, gang, gathering, group, herd, horde, multitude, pack, squad, squadron, swarm, team, throng, trip, unit.

v crowd, flock, go, march, pack, parade, stream, swarm, throng, traipse, turn.

tropical adj equatorial, hot, humid, lush, luxuriant, steamy, stifling, sultry, sweltering, torrid. **antonyms** arctic, cold, cool, temperate.

trot v bustle, canter, jog, pace, run, scamper, scurry, scuttle.

n canter, jog, jog-trot, run.

trouble n affliction, agitation, ailment, annoyance, anxiety, attention, bother, care, commotion, complaint, concern, danger, defect, difficulty, dilemma, disability, discontent, discord, disease, disorder, disquiet, dissatisfaction, distress, disturbance, effort, exertion, failure, grief, heartache, illness, inconvenience, irritation, labour, malfunction, mess, misfortune, nuisance, pain, pains, pest, pickle, predicament, problem, row, scrape, shtook, solicitude, sorrow, spot, strife, struggle, suffering, thought, torment, travail, trial, tribulation, tumult, uneasiness, unrest, upheaval, upset, vexation, woe, work, worry. *antonyms* calm, peace.

v afflict, agitate, annoy, bother, burden, discomfort, discommode, discompose, disconcert, disquiet, distress, disturb, fash, fret, grieve, harass, incommode, inconvenience, pain, perplex, perturb, pester, plague, sadden, torment, upset, vex, worry. *antonyms* help, reassure.

troublemaker *n* agent provocateur, agitator, bovver boy, firebrand, instigator, meddler, mischief-maker, rabble-rouser, ringleader, stirrer, tub-thumper. *antonym* peace-maker.

troublesome *adj* annoying, arduous, bothersome, burdensome, demanding, difficult, disorderly, harassing, hard, importunate, inconvenient, insubordinate, irksome, irritating, laborious, oppressive, plaguesome, poxy, rebellious, recalcitrant, refractory, rowdy, spiny, taxing, thorny, tiresome, tricky, trying, turbulent, unco-operative, undisciplined, unruly, upsetting, vexatious, violent, wearisome, worrisome, worrying. *antonyms* easy, helpful, polite.

trough *n* back, channel, conduit, crib, depression, ditch, duct, flume, furrow, gully, gutter, hollow, manger, trench, tub.

trounce *v* beat, best, censure, clobber, crush, drub, hammer, lick, overwhelm, paste, punish, rebuke, rout, slaughter, thrash, whitewash.

trousers *n* bags, bloomers, breeches, breeks, culottes, denims, flannels, jeans, knickerbockers, lederhosen, pantaloons, pants, plus-fours, shorts, slacks, trews.

truce *n* armistice, break, cease-fire, cessation, intermission, interval, let-up, lull, moratorium, peace, respite, rest, stay, suspension, treaty. *antonym* hostilities.

truculent *adj* aggressive, antagonistic, bad-tempered, bellicose, belligerent, combative, contentious, cross, defiant, fierce, hostile, ill-tempered, obstreperous, pugnacious, quarrelsome, savage, scrappy, sullen, violent. *antonyms* co-operative, good-natured.

trudge *v* clump, footslog, hike, labour, lumber, march, mush, plod, slog, stump, traipse, tramp, trek, walk.
n footslog, haul, hike, march, mush, slog, traipse, tramp, trek, walk.

true *adj* absolute, accurate, actual, authentic, bona fide, confirmed, conformable, constant, correct, corrected, dedicated, devoted, dutiful, exact, factual, faithful, fast, firm, genuine, honest, honourable, legitimate, loyal, natural, perfect, precise, proper, pure, real, right, rightful, sincere, spot-on, square, staunch, steady, true-blue, trustworthy, trusty, truthful, typical, unerring, unswerving, upright, valid, veracious, veritable. *antonyms* faithless, false, inaccurate.
adv accurately, correctly, exactly, faithfully, honestly, perfectly, precisely, properly, rightly, truly, truthfully, unerringly, veraciously, veritably. *antonyms* falsely, inaccurately.

true-blue *adj* card-carrying, committed, confirmed, constant, dedicated, devoted, dyed-in-the-wool, faithful, loyal, orthodox, staunch, true, trusty, uncompromising, unwavering. *antonyms* superficial, wavering.

truism *n* axiom, bromide, cliché, commonplace, platitude, truth.

truly *adv* accurately, authentically, constantly, correctly, devotedly, dutifully, exactly, exceptionally, extremely, factually, faithfully, firmly, genuinely, greatly, honestly, honourably, in reality, in truth, indeed, indubitably, legitimately, loyally, precisely, properly, really, rightly, sincerely, staunchly, steadfastly, steadily, truthfully, undeniably, veraciously, verily, veritably, very. *antonyms* faithlessly, falsely, incorrectly, slightly.

trumped-up *adj* concocted, contrived, cooked-up, fabricated, fake, faked, false, falsified, invented, made-up, phoney, spurious, untrue. *antonym* genuine.

truncate *v* abbreviate, clip, crop, curtail, cut, cut short, lop, maim, pare, prune, shorten, trim. *antonym* lengthen.

trust *n* assurance, belief, care, certainty, certitude, charge, confidence, conviction, credence, credit, custody, duty, expectation, faith, fidelity, guard, guardianship, hope, obligation, protection, reliance, responsibility, safekeeping, trusteeship. *antonym* mistrust.
v assign, assume, bank on, believe, command, commit, confide, consign, count on, credit, delegate, depend on, entrust, expect, give, hope, imagine, presume, rely on, suppose, surmise, swear by. *antonym* mistrust.

trusting *adj* confiding, credulous,

gullible, innocent, naïve, optimistic, simple, trustful, unguarded, unquestioning, unsuspecting, unsuspicious, unwary. **antonyms** cautious, distrustful.

trustworthy *adj* authentic, dependable, ethical, honest, honourable, mature, principled, reliable, responsible, righteous, sensible, steadfast, true, trusty, truthful, upright. **antonym** unreliable.

trusty *adj* dependable, faithful, firm, honest, loyal, reliable, responsible, solid, staunch, steady, straightforward, strong, supportive, true, trustworthy, upright. **antonym** unreliable.

truth *n* accuracy, actuality, axiom, candour, certainty, constancy, dedication, devotion, dutifulness, exactness, fact, facts, faith, faithfulness, fidelity, frankness, genuineness, honesty, integrity, law, legitimacy, loyalty, maxim, naturalism, precision, realism, reality, truism, truthfulness, uprightness, validity, veracity, verity. **antonym** falsehood.

truthful *adj* accurate, candid, correct, exact, faithful, forthright, frank, honest, literal, naturalistic, plain-spoken, precise, realistic, reliable, sincere, straight, straightforward, true, trustworthy, veracious, veritable. **antonym** untruthful.

truthfulness *n* candour, frankness, honesty, openness, righteousness, sincerity, straightness, uprightness, veracity. **antonym** untruthfulness.

try *v* adjudge, adjudicate, afflict, aim, annoy, appraise, attempt, catechise, endeavour, essay, evaluate, examine, experiment, hear, inconvenience, inspect, investigate, irk, irritate, pain, plague, prove, sample, seek, strain, stress, strive, struggle, taste, tax, test, tire, trouble, undertake, upset, venture, vex, wear out, weary.
n appraisal, attempt, essay, evaluation, effort, endeavour, essay, evaluation, experiment, fling, go, inspection, sample, shot, stab, taste, taster, test, trial, whack.
try out appraise, check out, evaluate, inspect, sample, taste, test, try on.

trying *adj* aggravating, annoying, arduous, bothersome, difficult, distressing, exasperating, fatiguing, hard, irksome, irritating, searching, severe, stressful, taxing, testing, tiresome, tough, troublesome, upsetting, vexing. **antonym** calming.

tubby *adj* chubby, corpulent, fat, obese, overweight, paunchy, plump,

podgy, portly, roly-poly, stout, well-upholstered. **antonym** slim.

tube *n* channel, conduit, cylinder, duct, hose, inlet, main, outlet, pipe, shaft, spout, trunk.

tuck[1] *v* cram, crease, fold, gather, insert, push, stuff.
n crease, fold, gather, pinch, pleat, pucker.

tuck[2] *n* comestibles, eats, food, grub, nosh, scoff, victuals, vittles.
tuck in devour, dine, eat, eat up, feast, gobble, gorge, scoff.

tug *v* drag, draw, haul, heave, jerk, lug, pluck, pull, tow, wrench, yank.
n drag, haul, heave, jerk, pluck, pull, tow, traction, wrench, yank.

tuition *n* education, instruction, lessons, pedagogy, schooling, teaching, training, tutelage, tutoring.

tumble *v* disorder, drop, fall, flop, jumble, overthrow, pitch, plummet, roll, rumple, stumble, topple, toss, trip up.
n collapse, drop, fall, flop, plunge, roll, spill, stumble, toss, trip.

tumbledown *adj* broken-down, crumbling, crumbly, decrepit, dilapidated, disintegrating, ramshackle, rickety, ruined, shaky, tottering. **antonym** well-kept.

tumid *adj* affected, bloated, bombastic, bulbous, bulging, distended, enlarged, euphuistic, flowery, fulsome, grandiloquent, grandiose, high-flown, inflated, magniloquent, overblown, pompous, pretentious, protuberant, puffed up, puffy, stilted, swollen, turgid. **antonyms** flat, simple.

tumult *n* ado, affray, agitation, altercation, bedlam, brawl, bustle, clamour, coil, commotion, din, disorder, disturbance, excitement, fracas, hubbub, hullabaloo, pandemonium, quarrel, racket, riot, rout, row, ruction, ruffle, stir, strife, turmoil, unrest, upheaval, uproar. **antonym** calm.

tumultuous *adj* agitated, boisterous, clamorous, confused, disorderly, disturbed, excited, fierce, hectic, irregular, lawless, noisy, obstreperous, passionate, raging, restless, riotous, rowdy, rumbustious, stormy, tempestuous, troubled, turbulent, unrestrained, unruly, uproarious, violent, vociferous, wild. **antonym** calm.

tune *n* agreement, air, attitude, concert, concord, consonance, demeanour, disposition, euphony, frame of mind, harmony, melody, mood, motif, pitch,

song, strain, sympathy, temper, theme, unison.
v adapt, adjust, attune, harmonise, pitch, regulate, set, synchronise, temper.

tuneful *adj* catchy, euphonious, harmonious, mellifluous, mellow, melodic, melodious, musical, pleasant, sonorous. **antonym** tuneless.

tuneless *adj* atonal, cacophonous, clashing, discordant, dissonant, harsh, unmelodic, unmelodious, unmusical. **antonym** tuneful.

tunnel *n* burrow, channel, chimney, drift, flue, gallery, hole, passage, passageway, shaft, subway, underpass.
v burrow, dig, excavate, mine, penetrate, undermine.

turbid *adj* clouded, cloudy, confused, dense, dim, disordered, foggy, foul, fuzzy, hazy, impure, incoherent, muddled, muddy, murky, opaque, thick, unclear, unsettled. **antonym** clear.

turbulent *adj* agitated, anarchic, blustery, boiling, boisterous, choppy, confused, disordered, disorderly, foaming, furious, insubordinate, lawless, mutinous, obstreperous, raging, rebellious, refractory, riotous, rough, rowdy, seditious, stormy, tempestuous, tumultuous, unbridled, undisciplined, ungovernable, unruly, unsettled, unstable, uproarious, violent, wild. **antonym** calm.

turf *n* clod, divot, grass, green, sod.
 turf out banish, bounce, chuck out, discharge, dismiss, dispossess, eject, elbow, evict, expel, fire, fling out, give the elbow to, kick out, oust, sack, throw out, turn out.

turgid *adj* affected, bloated, bombastic, bulging, congested, dilated, distended, extravagant, flowery, fulsome, grandiloquent, grandiose, high-flown, inflated, magniloquent, ostentatious, overblown, pompous, pretentious, protuberant, puffy, stilted, swollen, windy. **antonyms** flat, simple.

turmoil *n* agitation, bedlam, bustle, chaos, combustion, commotion, confusion, disorder, disquiet, disturbance, dust, ferment, flurry, hubbub, noise, pandemonium, pother, rout, row, ruffle, stir, strife, trouble, tumult, turbulence, uproar, violence, welter. **antonym** calm.

turn *v* adapt, alter, appeal, apply, approach, become, change, circle, construct, convert, corner, curdle, defect, deliver, depend, desert, divert, double, execute, fashion, fit, form, frame, go, gyrate, hang, hinge, infatuate, influence, issue, look, make, metamorphose, mould, move, mutate, nauseate, negotiate, pass, perform, persuade, pivot, prejudice, remodel, renege, resort, retract, return, reverse, revolve, roll, rotate, shape, shift, sicken, sour, spin, spoil, swerve, switch, swivel, taint, transfigure, transform, translate, transmute, twirl, twist, upset, veer, wheel, whirl, write.
n act, action, airing, aptitude, bend, bent, bias, bout, cast, chance, change, circle, circuit, constitutional, crack, crankle, crisis, culmination, curve, cycle, deed, departure, deviation, direction, distortion, drift, drive, excursion, exigency, fashion, favour, fling, form, format, fright, gesture, go, guise, gyration, heading, innings, jaunt, make-up, manner, mode, mould, occasion, opportunity, outing, performance, performer, period, pivot, promenade, reversal, revolution, ride, rotation, round, saunter, scare, service, shape, shift, shock, shot, spell, spin, start, stint, stroll, style, succession, surprise, swing, tendency, time, trend, trick, try, turning, twist, U-turn, vicissitude, walk, warp, way, whack, whirl.

turn away avert, deflect, depart, deviate, discharge, dismiss. **antonym** accept.

turn back beat off, drive back, drive off, force back, go back, rebuff, repel, repulse, resist, retrace one's steps, return, revert. **antonyms** go on, stay.

turn down decline, diminish, fold, invert, lessen, lower, muffle, mute, quieten, rebuff, refuse, reject, repudiate, soften, spurn. **antonyms** accept, turn up.

turn in deliver, enter, give back, give up, go to bed, hand in, hand over, hit the sack, register, retire, return, submit, surrender, tender. **antonyms** get up, give out, keep.

turn of phrase diction, expression, idiom, locution, metaphor, phraseology, saying, style.

turn off alienate, bore, branch off, cut out, depart from, deviate, discourage, disenchant, disgust, dismiss, displease, divert, irritate, kill, leave, nauseate, offend, put off, put out, quit, repel, shut, shut down, sicken, stop, switch off, turn out, unplug. **antonym** turn on.

turn on activate, arouse, assail, assault, attack, attract, balance, depend, energise, excite, expose, fall on, hang, hinge, ignite, inform, initiate, introduce, pivot, please, rest, round on, rouse, show, start, start up, stimulate, switch on, thrill, titillate, trip, turn against, work up. **antonym** turn off.

turn out appear, assemble, attend, attire, banish, become, cashier, clean out, clear, clothe, come, come about, crop up, deport, develop, discharge, dismiss, dispossess, dress, drive out, drum out, emerge, empty, end up, eventuate, evict, evolve, expel, fabricate, finish, fire, fit, gather, go, happen, kick out, make, manufacture, muster, oust, outfit, process, produce, result, sack, show up, switch off, throw out, transpire, turf out, turn off, turn up, unplug, unseat. **antonyms** stay away, turn on.

turn over activate, assign, break up, capsize, commend, commit, consider, contemplate, crank, deliberate, deliver, dig, examine, give over, give up, hand over, keel over, mull over, overturn, pass on, plough, ponder, reflect on, render, reverse, revolve, rob, ruminate, start up, surrender, switch on, think about, think over, transfer, upend, upset, yield. **antonym** stand firm.

turn over a new leaf amend, begin anew, change, change one's ways, improve, mend one's ways, reform. **antonym** persist.

turn tail escape, flee, hightail it, make off, retreat, run away, run for it, run off, scarper, skedaddle, take off, take to one's heels, vamoose. **antonym** stand firm.

turn up amplify, appear, arrive, attend, boost, come, crop up, dig up, disclose, discover, disgust, expose, find, increase, intensify, invert, pop up, raise, reveal, show, show up, transpire, unearth. **antonyms** stay away, turn down.

turncoat n blackleg, defector, deserter, fink, rat, renegade, scab, traitor.

turning-point n change, crisis, crossroads, crux, moment of truth, watershed.

turn-out n array, assembly, attendance, attire, audience, company, congregation, costume, crowd, dress, equipment, gate, gear, get-up, number, outfit, output, outturn, product, production, productivity, rig-out, team, throng, turnover, volume, yield.

turnover n business, change, flow, income, movement, output, production, productivity, profits, replacement, volume, yield.

turpitude n badness, baseness, corruption, corruptness, criminality, degeneracy, depravity, evil, flagitiousness, foulness, immorality, iniquity, nefariousness, rascality, sinfulness, viciousness, vileness, villainy, wickedness. **antonym** honour.

tussle v battle, brawl, compete, contend, fight, grapple, scramble, scrap, scuffle, struggle, vie, wrestle.
n battle, bout, brawl, competition, conflict, contention, contest, dust-up, fight, fracas, fray, mêlée, punch-up, race, scramble, scrap, scrimmage, scrum, scuffle, set-to, struggle.

twaddle n balderdash, balls, blether, bunk, bunkum, chatter, claptrap, drivel, garbage, gobbledegook, gossip, guff, hogwash, hot air, nonsense, piffle, poppycock, rot, rubbish, stuff, tattle, tosh, trash, waffle. **antonym** sense.

tweak v, n jerk, nip, pull, punch, snatch, squeeze, tug, twist, twitch.

twee adj affected, cute, cutesy, dainty, kitschy, precious, pretty, quaint, sentimental, sweet.

twiddle v adjust, fiddle, finger, jiggle, juggle, swivel, turn, twirl, twist, wiggle.

twig v catch on, comprehend, cotton on, fathom, get, grasp, rumble, savvy, see, tumble to, understand.

twilight n decline, dimness, dusk, ebb, evening, eventide, gloaming, half-light, sundown, sunset.
adj crepuscular, darkening, declining, dim, dying, ebbing, evening, final, last, shadowy.

twin n clone, corollary, counterpart, doppelgänger, double, duplicate, fellow, likeness, lookalike, match, mate, ringer.
adj balancing, corresponding, double, dual, duplicate, identical, matched, matching, paired, parallel, symmetrical, twofold.
v combine, couple, join, link, match, pair, yoke.

twine v bend, braid, coil, curl, encircle, entwine, interlace, interweave, knit, loop, meander, plait, snake, spiral, splice, surround, tie, twist, weave, wind, wrap, wreathe, wriggle, zigzag.

twinge n bite, gripe, pain, pang, pinch, prick, qualm, spasm, stab, stitch, throb, throe, tweak, twist, twitch.

twinkle v blink, coruscate, flash, flicker, gleam, glint, glisten, glitter, scintillate, shimmer, shine, sparkle, vibrate, wink.
n amusement, blink, coruscation, flash, flicker, gleam, glimmer, glistening,

glitter, glittering, light, quiver, scintillation, shimmer, shine, spark, sparkle, wink.

twinkling n flash, instant, jiff, jiffy, mo, moment, no time, sec, second, shake, tick, trice, twinkle, two shakes.

twirl v birl, coil, gyrate, pirouette, pivot, revolve, rotate, spin, swivel, turn, twist, wheel, whirl, wind.

n coil, convulution, gyration, helix, pirouette, revolution, rotation, spin, spiral, turn, twist, whirl, whorl.

twist v alter, change, coil, contort, corkscrew, crinkle, crisp, curl, distort, encircle, entangle, entwine, garble, intertwine, misquote, misrepresent, pervert, pivot, revolve, rick, screw, spin, sprain, squirm, strain, swivel, turn, tweak, twine, warp, weave, wind, wrap, wreathe, wrench, wrick, wriggle, wring, writhe.

n aberration, arc, bend, bent, braid, break, change, characteristic, coil, confusion, contortion, convolution, curl, curve, defect, deformation, development, distortion, eccentricity, entanglement, fault, flaw, foible, idiosyncrasy, imperfection, jerk, kink, knot, meander, mess, mix-up, nuance, oddity, peculiarity, plug, pull, quirk, revelation, roll, screw, slant, snarl, spin, sprain, squiggle, surprise, swivel, tangle, turn, twine, undulation, variation, warp, wind, wrench, wrest, zigzag.

twist someone's arm bulldoze, bully, coerce, dragoon, force, intimidate, lean on, persuade, pressurise.

twisted adj bent, biased, bitter, coiled, contorted, convoluted, curled, deformed, deviant, devious, distorted, garbled, intertwined, jaundiced, misshapen, perverse, perverted, quirky, torqued, tortuous, unnatural, warped, wound, woven, wry. **antonyms** straight, straightforward.

twit n ass, blockhead, buffoon, chump, clot, clown, dope, fool, halfwit, idiot, muggins, nerd, nincompoop, ninny, nitwit, nurd, silly ass, simpleton, twerp.

twitch v blink, flutter, jerk, jump, pinch, pluck, pull, snatch, tug, tweak.

n blink, convulsion, flutter, jerk, jump, pluck, pull, tremor, tweak, twinge.

twitter v chatter, cheep, chirp, chirrup, giggle, prattle, sing, snigger, titter, trill, tweet, warble, whistle.

n agitation, anxiety, call, chatter, cheeping, chirping, chirruping, cry, dither, excitement, flurry, fluster, flutter, nervousness, song, tizz, tizzy, trill, tweeting, warble.

two-faced adj deceitful, deceiving, devious, dissembling, double-dealing, duplicitous, false, hypocritical, insincere, lying, mendacious, perfidious, treacherous, untrustworthy. **antonyms** candid, frank, honest.

tycoon n baron, big cheese, big noise, big shot, capitalist, captain of industry, entrepreneur, fat cat, industrialist, magnate, mogul, potentate, supremo.

type n archetype, breed, category, class, classification, description, designation, emblem, embodiment, epitome, essence, example, exemplar, form, genre, group, ilk, insignia, kidney, kind, mark, model, order, original, paradigm, pattern, personification, prototype, quintessence, sort, species, specimen, stamp, standard, strain, subdivision, variety.

typical adj archetypal, average, characteristic, classic, conventional, distinctive, essential, illustrative, indicative, model, normal, orthodox, quintessential, representative, standard, stock, symptomatic, usual, vintage. **antonyms** atypical, untypical.

typify v characterise, embody, encapsulate, epitomise, exemplify, illustrate, personify, represent, symbolise.

tyrannical adj absolute, arbitrary, authoritarian, autocratic, coercive, despotic, dictatorial, domineering, high-handed, imperious, iron-handed, magisterial, oppressive, overbearing, overpowering, peremptory, ruthless, severe, tyrannous, unjust, unreasonable. **antonyms** liberal, tolerant.

tyrannise v browbeat, bully, coerce, crush, dictate, domineer, enslave, intimidate, lord it, oppress, subjugate, terrorise.

tyranny n absolutism, authoritarianism, autocracy, coercion, despotism, dictatorship, harshness, high-handedness, imperiousness, injustice, oppression, peremptoriness, relentlessness, ruthlessness. **antonyms** democracy, liberality.

tyrant n absolutist, authoritarian, autocrat, bully, despot, dictator, Hitler, martinet, monarch, oppressor, slave-driver, sovereign, taskmaster.

U

ubiquitous *adj* all-over, common, commonly-encountered, ever-present, everywhere, frequent, global, omnipresent, pervasive, universal. **antonym** rare.

ugliness *n* danger, deformity, disgrace, enormity, evil, frightfulness, heinousness, hideousness, homeliness, horridness, horror, menace, monstrosity, monstrousness, nastiness, offensiveness, plainness, repulsiveness, unattractiveness, unpleasantness, unsightliness, vileness. **antonyms** beauty, charm, goodness, pleasantness.

ugly *adj* angry, bad-tempered, dangerous, dark, disagreeable, disgusting, distasteful, evil, forbidding, frightful, hagged, haggish, hard-favoured, hard-featured, hideous, homely, horrid, ill-favoured, malevolent, menacing, misshapen, monstrous, nasty, objectionable, offensive, ominous, plain, repugnant, repulsive, revolting, shocking, sinister, spiteful, sullen, surly, terrible, threatening, truculent, unattractive, unlovely, unpleasant, unprepossessing, unsightly, vile. **antonyms** beautiful, charming, good, pretty.

ulterior *adj* concealed, covert, hidden, personal, private, secondary, secret, selfish, undisclosed, unexpressed. **antonyms** declared, overt.

ultimate *adj* basic, conclusive, consummate, decisive, elemental, end, eventual, extreme, final, fundamental, furthest, greatest, highest, last, maximum, paramount, perfect, primary, radical, remotest, superlative, supreme, terminal, topmost, utmost.
n consummation, culmination, daddy of them all, epitome, extreme, granddaddy, greatest, height, peak, perfection, summit.

ultimately *adv* after all, at last, basically, eventually, finally, fundamentally, in origin, in the end, originally, primarily, sooner or later.

ultra *adj* avant-garde, excessive, extravagant, extreme, fanatical, immoderate, rabid, radical, revolutionary, way-out.

ultra- *adv* especially, exceptionally, excessively, extra, extraordinarily, extremely, remarkably, unusually.

umbrage *n* anger, chagrin, disgruntlement, displeasure, grudge, high dudgeon, huff, indignation, offence, pique, resentment, sulks.

umbrella *n* aegis, agency, brolly, cover, gamp, mushroom, parasol, patronage, protection, sunshade, umbel.

umpire *n* adjudicator, arbiter, arbitrator, judge, linesman, mediator, moderator, ref, referee.
v adjudicate, arbitrate, call, control, judge, moderate, ref, referee.

umpteen *adj* a good many, a thousand, considerable, countless, innumerable, millions, n, numerous, plenty, uncounted. **antonym** few.

unabashed *adj* blatant, bold, brazen, composed, confident, unawed, unblushing, unconcerned, undaunted, undismayed, unembarrassed. **antonym** sheepish.

unable *adj* impotent, inadequate, incapable, incompetent, ineffectual, powerless, unequipped, unfit, unfitted, unqualified.

unabridged *adj* complete, entire, full, full-length, uncondensed, uncut, unexpurgated, unshortened, whole.

unacceptable *adj* disagreeable, displeasing, distasteful, improper, inadmissible, insupportable, objectionable, offensive, ugly, undesirable, unpleasant, unsatisfactory, unwelcome.

unaccommodating *adj* disobliging, inflexible, intransigent, obstinate, perverse, rigid, stubborn, unbending, uncomplaisant, uncompromising, uncooperative, unyielding. **antonyms** flexible, obliging.

unaccompanied *adj* a cappella, alone, lone, solo, unattended, unescorted.

unaccountable *adj* astonishing, baffling, extraordinary, impenetrable, incomprehensible, inexplicable, inscrutable, mysterious, odd, peculiar, puzzling, singular, strange, uncommon, unexplainable, unfathomable, unheard-of, unintelligible, unusual, unwonted. **antonym** explicable.

unaccustomed *adj* different, green, inexperienced, new, remarkable, special, strange, surprising, unacquainted, uncommon, unexpected, unfamiliar, unpractised, unprecedented, unused, unusual, unwonted. **antonyms** accustomed, customary.

unadorned *adj* austere, outright, plain, restrained, severe, simple, stark, straightforward, undecorated, unembellished, unornamented, unvarnished. *antonyms* decorated, embellished, ornate.

unaffected[1] *adj* aloof, impervious, naïve, natural, spontaneous, unaltered, unchanged, unimpressed, unmoved, unresponsive, untouched. *antonym* unnatural.

unaffected[2] *adj* artless, blasé, genuine, honest, indifferent, ingenuous, naïve, plain, simple, sincere, straightforward, unassuming, unconcerned, unpretentious, unsophisticated, unspoilt, unstudied. *antonyms* impressed, moved.

unafraid *adj* confident, daring, dauntless, fearless, imperturbable, intrepid, unshakeable.

unalterable *adj* final, fixed, immutable, inflexible, invariable, permanent, rigid, steadfast, unchangeable, unchanging, unyielding. *antonym* flexible.

unanimity *n* accord, agreement, chorus, concert, concord, concurrence, consensus, consent, correspondence, harmony, like-mindedness, unison, unity. *antonyms* disagreement, disunity.

unanimous *adj* agreed, common, concerted, concordant, harmonious, in accord, in agreement, joint, united. *antonyms* disunited, split.

unanimously *adv* at one man, by common consent, conjointly, in concert, unopposed, without exception, without opposition.

unanswerable *adj* absolute, conclusive, final, incontestable, incontrovertible, indisputable, irrefutable, unarguable, undeniable. *antonym* refutable.

unappetising *adj* disagreeable, distasteful, insipid, off-putting, tasteless, unappealing, unattractive, unexciting, uninteresting, uninviting, unpalatable, unpleasant, unsavoury.

unapproachable *adj* aloof, distant, forbidding, formidable, frigid, godforsaken, inaccessible, remote, reserved, stand-offish, unbending, unfriendly, unget-at-able, unreachable, unsociable, withdrawn.

unarmed *adj* assailable, defenceless, exposed, helpless, open, unarmoured, unprotected, vulnerable, weak, weaponless.

unashamed *adj* impenitent, open, shameless, unabashed, unconcealed, undisguised, unrepentant.

unasked *adj* gratuitous, spontaneous, unbidden, uninvited, unprompted, unrequested, unsolicited, unsought, unwanted, voluntary. *antonyms* invited, solicited.

unassailable *adj* absolute, conclusive, impregnable, incontestable, incontrovertible, indisputable, invincible, inviolable, invulnerable, irrefutable, positive, proven, sacrosanct, secure, sound, undeniable, well-armed, wellfortified.

unassertive *adj* backward, bashful, diffident, meek, mousy, quiet, retiring, self-effacing, shy, timid, timorous, unassuming.

unassuming *adj* diffident, humble, meek, modest, natural, quiet, restrained, retiring, self-effacing, simple, unassertive, unobtrusive, unostentatious, unpresuming, unpretentious. *antonyms* presumptuous, pretentious.

unattached *adj* autonomous, available, fancy-free, footloose, free, independent, non-aligned, single, unaffilated, uncommitted, unengaged, unmarried, unspoken for. *antonyms* committed, engaged.

unattended *adj* abandoned, alone, disregarded, ignored, unaccompanied, unescorted, unguarded, unsupervised, unwatched. *antonym* escorted.

unattractive *adj* disagreeable, disgusting, distasteful, homely, illfavoured, objectionable, offensive, off-putting, plain, repellent, ugly, unappealing, unappetising, uncomely, undesirable, unexciting, uninviting, unlovely, unpalatable, unpleasant, unprepossessing, unsavoury, unsightly, unwelcome.

unauthorised *adj* illegal, illicit, irregular, unlawful, unofficial, unsanctioned, unwarranted.

unavailing *adj* abortive, barren, bootless, fruitless, futile, idle, ineffective, ineffectual, inefficacious, pointless, unproductive, unprofitable, unsuccessful, useless, vain. *antonyms* productive, successful.

unavoidable *adj* certain, compulsory, fated, ineluctable, inescapable, inevitable, inexorable, mandatory, necessary, obligatory.

unaware *adj* blind, deaf, forgetful, heedless, ignorant, incognisant, oblivious, unconscious, unenlightened, uninformed, unknowing, unmindful, unsuspecting, unsuspicious.

unawares *adv* aback, abruptly, accidentally, by surprise, imperceptibly, inadvertently, insidiously, mistakenly, off guard, on the hop, suddenly, unconsciously, unexpectedly, unintentionally, unknowingly, unprepared, unthinkingly, unwittingly.

unbalanced *adj* asymmetrical, biased, crazy, demented, deranged, disturbed, eccentric, erratic, inequitable, insane, irrational, irregular, lopsided, lunatic, mad, off-balance, off-centre, one-sided, partial, partisan, prejudiced, shaky, touched, unequal, uneven, unfair, unhinged, unjust, unsound, unstable, unsteady, wobbly.

unbearable *adj* insufferable, insupportable, intolerable, outrageous, unacceptable, unendurable, unspeakable. *antonym* acceptable

unbeatable *adj* indomitable, invincible, matchless, supreme, unconquerable, unstoppable, unsurpassable. *antonyms* inferior, weak.

unbeaten *adj* supreme, triumphant, unbowed, unconquered, undefeated, unsubdued, unsurpassed, unvanquished, victorious, winning. *antonyms* defeated, vanquished.

unbecoming *adj* discreditable, dishonourable, ill-suited, improper, inappropriate, incongruous, indecorous, indelicate, offensive, tasteless, unattractive, unbefitting, unfit, unflattering, unmaidenly, unseemly, unsightly, unsuitable, unsuited. *antonym* seemly.

unbelievable *adj* astonishing, far-fetched, implausible, impossible, improbable, inconceivable, incredible, outlandish, preposterous, questionable, staggering, unconvincing, unimaginable, unlikely, unthinkable. *antonym* credible.

unbending *adj* aloof, distant, firm, forbidding, formal, formidable, hard-line, inflexible, intransigent, reserved, resolute, rigid, severe, stiff, strict, stubborn, tough, uncompromising, unyielding. *antonyms* approachable, friendly, relaxed.

unbiased *adj* disinterested, dispassionate, equitable, even-handed, fair, fair-minded, impartial, independent, just, neutral, objective, open-minded, uncoloured, uninfluenced, unprejudiced.

unbidden *adj* free, spontaneous, unasked, unforced, uninvited, unprompted, unsolicited, unwanted, unwelcome, voluntary, willing. *antonyms* invited, solicited.

unbind *v* free, liberate, loose, loosen, release, unchain, undo, unfasten, unfetter, unloose, unloosen, unshackle, untie, unyoke. *antonym* restrain.

unblemished *adj* clear, flawless, immaculate, irreproachable, perfect, pure, spotless, unflawed, unimpeachable, unspotted, unstained, unsullied, untarnished. *antonyms* flawed, imperfect.

unblinking *adj* assured, calm, composed, cool, emotionless, fearless, impassive, imperturbable, steady, unafraid, unemotional, unfaltering, unflinching, unshrinking, unwavering. *antonyms* cowed, faithful, fearful.

unblushing *adj* amoral, blatant, bold, brazen, immodest, shameless, unabashed, unashamed, unembarrassed. *antonyms* abashed, ashamed.

unborn *adj* awaited, coming, embryonic, expected, foetal, future, hereafter, in utero, later, subsequent, succeeding.

unbosom *v* admit, bare, confess, confide, disburden, disclose, divulge, lay bare, let out, pour out, reveal, tell, unburden, uncover. *antonyms* conceal, suppress.

unbounded *adj* absolute, boundless, endless, immeasurable, infinite, lavish, limitless, prodigal, unbridled, unchecked, unconstrained, uncontrolled, unlimited, unrestrained, vast. *antonym* limited.

unbreakable *adj* armoured, durable, indestructible, infrangible, lasting, permanent, proof, resistant, rugged, shatter-proof, solid, strong, tough, toughened. *antonyms* breakable, fragile.

unbridled *adj* excessive, immoderate, intemperate, licentious, profligate, rampant, riotous, unchecked, unconstrained, uncontrolled, uncurbed, ungovernable, ungoverned, unrestrained, unruly, violent, wanton.

unbroken *adj* ceaseless, complete, constant, continuous, endless, entire, incessant, intact, integral, perpetual, progressive, serried, solid, successive, total, unbowed, unceasing, undivided, unimpaired, uninterrupted, unremitting, unsubdued, untamed, whole. *antonyms* cowed, fitful, intermittent.

unburden *v* confess, confide, disburden, discharge, disclose, disencumber, empty, lay bare, lighten, offload, pour out, relieve, reveal, tell all, unbosom, unload. *antonyms* conceal, hide, suppress.

uncalled-for *adj* gratuitous, inappropriate, needless, undeserved, unheeded, unjust, unjustified, unmerited, unnecessary, unprovoked, unwanted, unwarranted, unwelcome. *antonym* timely.

uncanny *adj* astonishing, astounding, bizarre, creepy, eerie, exceptional, extraordinary, fantastic, incredible, inspired, miraculous, mysterious, prodigious, queer, remarkable, scary, singular, spooky, strange, supernatural, unaccountable, unearthly, unheard-of, unnatural, unusual, weird.

uncaring *adj* callous, inconsiderate, indifferent, negligent, unconcerned, unfeeling, uninterested, unmoved, un-responsive, unsympathetic. *antonyms* concerned, solicitous.

unceasing *adj* ceaseless, constant, continual, continuing, continuous, endless, incessant, never-ending, non-stop, perpetual, persistent, relentless, unbroken, unending, unfailing, uninterrupted, unrelenting, unremitting. *antonyms* intermittent, spasmodic.

uncertain *adj* ambiguous, ambivalent, chancy, changeable, conjectural, dicky, dithery, doubtful, dubious, erratic, fitful, hazardous, hazy, hesitant, iffy, in the lap of the gods, incalculable, inconstant, indefinite, indeterminate, indistinct, insecure, irregular, irresolute, precarious, problematic, questionable, risky, shaky, slippy, speculative, unclear, unconfirmed, undecided, undetermined, unfixed, unforeseeable, unpredictable, unreliable, unresolved, unsettled, unsure, vacillating, vague, variable, wavering.

uncertainty *n* ambiguity, bewilderment, confusion, diffidence, dilemma, doubt, dubiety, hesitancy, hesita-tion, incalculability, inconclusiveness, indecision, insecurity, irresolution, misgiving, perplexity, puzzlement, qualm, quandary, risk, scepticism, unpredictability, vagueness. *antonym* certainty.

unchallengeable *adj* absolute, conclusive, final, impregnable, incon-testable, incontrovertible, indisputable, irrefutable. *antonyms* contestable, inconclusive.

unchangeable *adj* changeless, eternal, final, immutable, irreversible, permanent, unchanging.

unchanging *adj* abiding, changeless, constant, continuing, enduring, eternal, fixed, immutable, imperishable, lasting, permanent, perpetual, phaseless, steadfast, steady, unchanged, unfading, unvarying. *antonyms* changeable, changing.

uncharitable *adj* callous, captious, cruel, hard-hearted, hypercritical, inhumane, insensitive, mean, merciless, pitiless, stingy, unchristian, unfeeling, unforgiving, unfriendly, ungenerous, unkind, unsympathetic. *antonym* charitable.

uncharted *adj* foreign, mysterious, new, novel, strange, undiscovered, unexplored, unfamiliar, unknown, unplumbed, virgin. *antonyms* familiar, well-known.

uncivil *adj* abrupt, bad-mannered, bearish, boorish, brusque, churlish, curt, discourteous, disrespectful, gruff, ill-bred, ill-mannered, impolite, rude, surly, uncouth, ungracious, unmannerly.

uncivilised *adj* antisocial, barbarian, barbaric, barbarous, boorish, brutish, churlish, coarse, gross, heathenish, ill-bred, illiterate, philistine, primitive, savage, uncouth, uncultivated, uncultured, uneducated, unpolished, unsophisticated, untamed, vulgar, wild.

unclean *adj* contaminated, corrupt, defiled, dirty, evil, filthy, foul, impure, insalubrious, nasty, polluted, soiled, spotted, stained, sullied, tainted, unhygienic, unwholesome.

unclear *adj* ambiguous, as clear as mud, dim, doubtful, dubious, equivocal, hazy, indefinite, indiscernible, indistinguishable, obscure, uncertain, vague.

unclothed *adj* bare, disrobed, in one's birthday suit, in the altogether, in the buff, naked, nude, stark naked, starkers, stripped, undressed. *antonym* dressed.

uncomfortable *adj* awkward, bleak, confused, conscience-stricken, cramped, disagreeable, discomfited, discomposed, disquieted, distressed, disturbed, embarrassed, hard, ill-fitting, incommodious, irritating, painful, poky, self-conscious, sheepish, troubled, troublesome, uneasy. *antonym* easy.

uncommitted *adj* available, fancy-free, floating, free, neutral, non-aligned, non-partisan, unattached, undecided, uninvolved.

uncommon *adj* abnormal, atypical, bizarre, curious, distinctive, exceptional, extraordinary, incomparable, infrequent, inimitable, notable, noteworthy, novel, odd, outstanding, peculiar, queer, rare, recherché, remarkable, scarce, singular, special, strange, superior, unfamiliar, unparalleled, unprecedented, unusual, unwonted.

uncommonly *adv* abnormally, exceptionally, extremely, infrequently, occasionally, outstandingly, particularly, peculiarly, rarely, remarkably, seldom, singularly, strangely, unusually, very. *antonym* frequently.

uncommunicative *adj* brief, close, curt, guarded, reserved, reticent, retiring, secretive, short, shy, silent, taciturn, tight-lipped, unforthcoming, unresponsive, unsociable, withdrawn.

uncompromising *adj* decided, die-hard, firm, hard-core, hard-line, inexorable, inflexible, intransigent, obdurate, obstinate, rigid, steadfast, strict, stubborn, tough, unaccommodating, unbending, unyielding. *antonyms* flexible, open-minded.

unconcealed *adj* admitted, apparent, blatant, conspicuous, evident, frank, ill-concealed, manifest, naked, noticeable, obvious, open, overt, patent, self-confessed, unashamed, undistinguished, visible. *antonyms* hidden, secret.

unconcerned *adj* aloof, apathetic, blithe, callous, carefree, careless, complacent, composed, cool, detached, dispassionate, distant, easy, incurious, indifferent, nonchalant, oblivious, pococurante, relaxed, serene, uncaring, uninterested, uninvolved, unmoved, unperturbed, unruffled, unsympathetic, untroubled, unworried.

unconditional *adj* absolute, categorical, complete, downright, entire, full, implicit, out-and-out, outright, plenary, positive, thoroughgoing, total, unequivocal, unlimited, unqualified, unreserved, unrestricted, utter, whole-hearted.

uncongenial *adj* antagonistic, antipathetic, disagreeable, discordant, displeasing, distasteful, incompatible, unappealing, unattractive, uninviting, unpleasant, unsavoury, unsuited, unsympathetic.

unconnected *adj* detached, disconnected, disjointed, divided, illogical, incoherent, independent, irrational, irrelevant, separate, unattached, unrelated. *antonym* relevant.

unconquerable *adj* enduring, indomitable, ingrained, insuperable,

insurmountable, inveterate, invincible, irrepressible, irresistible, overpowering, unbeatable, undefeatable, unyielding. *antonyms* weak, yielding.

unconscionable *adj* amoral, criminal, excessive, exorbitant, extravagant, extreme, immoderate, inordinate, outrageous, preposterous, unethical, unjustifiable, unpardonable, unprincipled, unreasonable, unscrupulous, unwarrantable.

unconscious *adj* accidental, automatic, blind to, comatose, concussed, deaf to, heedless, ignorant, inadvertent, innate, insensible, instinctive, involuntary, knocked out, latent, oblivious, out, out cold, out for the count, reflex, repressed, senseless, stunned, subconscious, subliminal, suppressed, unaware, unintended, unintentional, unknowing, unmindful, unsuspecting, unwitting.

uncontrollable *adj* frantic, furious, intractable, irrepressible, irresistible, irrestrainable, mad, recalcitrant, refractory, strong, ungovernable, unmanageable, unruly, violent, wild. *antonym* manageable.

uncontrolled *adj* boisterous, furious, rampant, riotous, unbridled, unchecked, uncurbed, undisciplined, ungoverned, unhindered, unrestrained, unruly, untrammelled, violent, wild. *antonym* contained.

unconventional *adj* abnormal, alternative, atypical, bizarre, bohemian, different, eccentric, freakish, idiosyncratic, individual, individualistic, informal, irregular, nonconformist, odd, offbeat, original, unorthodox, unusual, way-out, wayward.

unconvincing *adj* doubtful, dubious, feeble, fishy, flimsy, implausible, improbable, inconclusive, lame, questionable, specious, suspect, tall, thin, unlikely, unpersuasive, weak. *antonym* plausible.

unco-ordinated *adj* awkward, bumbling, clodhopping, clumsy, desultory, diffuse, disjointed, disorganised, graceless, inept, lumbering, unconcerted, ungainly, ungraceful. *antonyms* concerted, graceful, systematic.

uncouth *adj* awkward, barbarian, barbaric, boorish, clownish, clumsy, coarse, crude, gauche, gawky, graceless, gross, ill-mannered, loutish, lubberly, oafish, rough, rude, rustic, uncivilised, uncultivated, ungainly, unrefined, unseemly, vulgar. *antonyms* polished, polite, refined, urbane.

uncover *v* bare, detect, disclose, discover, dismask, disrobe, divulge, exhume, expose, leak, lift the lid off, open, reveal, show, strip, unearth, unmask, unveil, unwrap. *antonyms* conceal, suppress.

uncritical *adj* accepting, credulous, indiscriminate, naïve, non-judgemental, superficial, trusting, undiscerning, undiscriminating, unexacting, unfussy, unscholarly, unselective, unthinking. *antonyms* discriminating, sceptical.

unctuous *adj* fawning, glib, greasy, gushing, ingratiating, insincere, obsequious, oily, plausible, religiose, sanctimonious, slick, smarmy, smooth, suave, sycophantic.

uncultured *adj* awkward, boorish, coarse, crude, hick, raw, rustic, uncivilised, uncouth, uncultivated, unrefined, unsophisticated.

undaunted *adj* bold, brave, courageous, dauntless, fearless, gallant, indomitable, intrepid, resolute, steadfast, unbowed, undashed, undeterred, undiscouraged, undismayed, unfaltering, unflinching, unperturbed, unshrinking. *antonyms* cowed, timorous.

undecided *adj* ambivalent, debatable, dithering, doubtful, dubious, hesitant, in two minds, indefinite, irresolute, moot, open, pending, swithering, tentative, torn, uncertain, uncommitted, unconcluded, undetermined, unfixed, unsettled, unsure, vague, vexed, wavering. *antonyms* certain, decided, definite.

undefended *adj* defenceless, exposed, naked, open, unarmed, unfortified, unguarded, unprotected, vulnerable. *antonyms* armed, defended, fortified.

undefiled *adj* chaste, clean, clear, flawless, immaculate, intact, inviolate, pure, sinless, spotless, unblemished, unsoiled, unspotted, unstained, unsullied, virginal.

undefined *adj* formless, hazy, ill-defined, imprecise, indefinite, indeterminate, indistinct, inexact, nebulous, shadowy, tenuous, unclear, unexplained, unspecified, vague, woolly. *antonyms* definite, precise.

undemonstrative *adj* aloof, cold, contained, cool, distant, formal, impassive, reserved, restrained, reticent, stiff, stolid, unbending, uncommunicative, unemotional, unresponsive, withdrawn.

undeniable *adj* certain, clear, evident, incontestable, incontrovertible, indisputable, indubitable, irrefutable, manifest, obvious, patent, proven, sound, sure, unassailable, undoubted, unmistakable, unquestionable.

undependable *adj* capricious, changeable, erratic, fair-weather, fickle, inconsistent, inconstant, irresponsible, mercurial, treacherous, uncertain, unpredictable, unreliable, unstable, untrustworthy, variable. *antonyms* dependable, reliable.

under *prep* belonging to, below, beneath, governed by, included in, inferior to, junior to, lead by, less than, lower than, secondary to, subject to, subordinate to, subservient to, underneath.
adv below, beneath, down, downward, less, lower.

under an obligation beholden, bound, duty-bound, grateful, honour-bound, in debt to, in honour bound, indebted, obligated, obliged, thankful.

under the weather ailing, below par, groggy, hung over, ill, indisposed, nauseous, off-colour, out of sorts, peeliewally, poorly, queer, seedy, sick, squeamish, the worse for wear.

under way afoot, begun, going, in motion, in operation, in progress, launched, moving, on the go, on the move, started.

undercover *adj* clandestine, concealed, confidential, covert, furtive, hidden, hush-hush, intelligence, private, secret, spy, stealthy, surreptitious, underground. *antonyms* open, unconcealed.

undercurrent *n* atmosphere, aura, cross-current, drift, eddy, feeling, flavour, hint, movement, murmur, overtone, rip, riptide, sense, suggestion, tendency, tenor, tide, tinge, trend, underflow, undertone, undertow, vibes, vibrations.

undercut *v* excavate, gouge out, hollow out, mine, sacrifice, scoop out, underbid, undercharge, undermine, underprice, undersell.

underestimate *v* belittle, dismiss, fail to appreciate, minimise, miscalculate, sell short, underrate, undervalue. *antonyms* exaggerate, overestimate.

undergo *v* bear, brook, endure, experience, run the gauntlet, stand, submit to, suffer, sustain, weather, withstand.

underground *adj* alternative, avant-garde, buried, clandestine, concealed, covered, covert, experimental, hidden, radical, revolutionary, secret, subterranean, subversive, surreptitious, undercover.

underhand *adj* clandestine, crafty, crooked, deceitful, deceptive, devious, dishonest, dishonourable, fraudulent, furtive, immoral, improper, shady, shifty, sly, sneaky, stealthy, surreptitious, treacherous, underhanded, unethical, unscrupulous. **antonym** above board.

underline *v* accentuate, emphasise, highlight, italicise, labour, mark, point up, press, reiterate, stress, underscore, urge. **antonyms** play down, soft-pedal.

underling *n* flunkey, hireling, inferior, lackey, menial, minion, nobody, nonentity, servant, slave, subordinate, weakling. **antonyms** boss, leader, master.

underlying *adj* basic, concealed, elementary, essential, fundamental, hidden, intrinsic, latent, lurking, primary, prime, root, veiled.

undermine *v* debilitate, disable, erode, excavate, impair, mar, mine, sabotage, sap, subvert, threaten, tunnel, undercut, vitiate, weaken, wear away. **antonyms** fortify, strengthen.

underprivileged *adj* deprived, destitute, disadvantaged, impecunious, impoverished, needy, poor, poverty-stricken. **antonyms** affluent, fortunate.

underrate *v* belittle, depreciate, discount, dismiss, disparage, underestimate, undervalue. **antonyms** exaggerate, overrate.

undersell *v* cut, depreciate, disparage, mark down, play down, reduce, slash, undercharge, undercut, understate.

undersized *adj* dwarfed, dwarfish, miniature, minute, puny, pygmy, runtish, small, stunted, tiny, underdeveloped, underweight. **antonyms** big, oversized, overweight.

understand *v* accept, appreciate, apprehend, assume, believe, commiserate, comprehend, conceive, conclude, cotton on, discern, fathom, follow, gather, get, get the message, get the picture, grasp, hear, know, learn, penetrate, perceive, presume, realise, recognise, savvy, see, see daylight, suppose, sympathise, think, tolerate, tumble, twig. **antonym** misunderstand.

understanding *n* accord, agreement, appreciation, awareness, belief, comprehension, conclusion, discernment, estimation, grasp, idea, impression, insight, intellect, intellection, intelligence, interpretation, judgement, knowledge, notion, opinion, pact, penetration, perception, reading, sense, view, viewpoint, wisdom.

adj accepting, compassionate, considerate, discerning, forbearing, forgiving, kind, kindly, loving, patient, perceptive, responsive, sensitive, sympathetic, tender, tolerant. **antonyms** impatient, insensitive, intolerant, unsympathetic.

understate *v* belittle, dismiss, make light of, make little of, minimise, play down, soft-pedal, underplay, undersell.

understatement *n* dismissal, litotes, meiosis, minimisation, restraint, underplaying.

understood *adj* accepted, assumed, axiomatic, implicit, implied, inferred, presumed, tacit, unspoken, unstated, unwritten.

undertake *v* accept, agree, assume, attempt, bargain, begin, commence, contract, covenant, embark on, endeavour, engage, guarantee, pledge, promise, shoulder, stipulate, tackle, try.

undertaking *n* adventure, affair, assurance, attempt, business, commitment, effort, endeavour, enterprise, game, operation, pledge, project, promise, task, venture, vow, word.

undertone *n* atmosphere, current, feeling, flavour, hint, murmur, suggestion, tinge, touch, trace, undercurrent, whisper.

undervalue *v* depreciate, discount, dismiss, disparage, minimise, misjudge, underestimate, underrate. **antonyms** exaggerate, overrate.

underwear *n* frillies, lingerie, smalls, underclothes, underclothing, undergarments, undies, unmentionables.

underworld *n* criminal fraternity, gangland, Hades, hell, nether world, the Inferno.

underwrite *v* approve, authorise, back, consent, countenance, countersign, endorse, finance, fund, guarantee, initial, insure, okay, sanction, sign, sponsor, subscribe, subsidise, validate.

undesirable *adj* disagreeable, disliked, disreputable, distasteful, dreaded, objectionable, obnoxious, offensive, repugnant, unacceptable, unattractive, unpleasant, unpopular, unsavoury, unsuitable, unwanted, unwelcome, unwished-for.

undeveloped *adj* dwarfed, embryonic, immature, inchoate, latent, potential, stunted, unformed. **antonym** mature.

indignified *adj* foolish, improper, inappropriate, indecorous, inelegant, infra dig, petty, unbecoming, ungentlemanly, unladylike, unrefined, unseemly, unsuitable.

indisciplined *adj* disobedient, disorganised, obstreperous, uncontrolled, unpredictable, unreliable, unrestrained, unruly, unschooled, unsteady, unsystematic, untrained, wayward, wild, wilful.

indisguised *adj* apparent, blatant, confessed, evident, explicit, frank, genuine, ill-concealed, manifest, naked, obvious, open, out-and-out, outright, overt, patent, stark, thoroughgoing, transparent, unadorned, unashamed, unconcealed, unmistakable, utter, whole-hearted. *antonyms* concealed, hidden, secret.

indisputed *adj* accepted, acknowledged, certain, conclusive, incontestable, incontrovertible, indisputable, irrefutable, recognised, sure, unchallenged, uncontested, undeniable, undoubted, unequivocal, unmistakable, unquestioned. *antonyms* dubious, uncertain.

indistinguished *adj* banal, commonplace, everyday, indifferent, inferior, mediocre, ordinary, pedestrian, prosaic, run-of-the-mill, so-so, unexceptional, unexciting, unimpressive, unremarkable. *antonym* exceptional.

indisturbed *adj* calm, collected, composed, equable, even, motionless, placid, quiet, serene, tranquil, unaffected, unconcerned, uninterrupted, unperturbed, unruffled, untouched, untroubled. *antonym* interrupted.

individed *adj* combined, complete, concentrated, concerted, entire, exclusive, full, individuate, solid, thorough, tight-knit, unanimous, unbroken, united, whole, whole-hearted.

undo *v* annul, cancel, defeat, destroy, disengage, invalidate, loose, loosen, mar, neutralise, nullify, offset, open, overturn, quash, reverse, ruin, separate, shatter, spoil, subvert, unbutton, undermine, unfasten, unlock, unloose, unloosen, untie, unwind, unwrap, upset, vitiate, wreck. *antonym* fasten.

undoing *n* besetting sin, blight, collapse, curse, defeat, destruction, disgrace, downfall, humiliation, misfortune, overthrow, overturn, reversal, ruin, ruination, shame, tragic fault, trouble, weakness.

undone[1] *adj* betrayed, destroyed, lost, ruined.

undone[2] *adj* forgotten, incomplete, left, neglected, omitted, outstanding, unaccomplished, uncompleted, unfinished, unfulfilled, unperformed. *antonyms* accomplished, complete.

undone[3] *adj* loose, open, unbraced, unbuttoned, unfastened, unlaced, unlocked, untied. *antonyms* fastened, secured.

undoubted *adj* acknowledged, certain, definite, evident, incontrovertible, indisputable, indubitable, obvious, patent, sure, unchallenged, undisputed, unquestionable, unquestioned.

undoubtedly *adv* assuredly, certainly, definitely, doubtless, indubitably, of course, surely, undeniably, unmistakably, unquestionably.

undreamed-of *adj* astonishing, inconceivable, incredible, miraculous, undreamt, unexpected, unforeseen, unheard-of, unhoped-for, unimagined, unsuspected.

undress *v* disrobe, divest, peel off, remove, shed, strip, take off.
n disarray, nakedness, nudity.

undressed *adj* disrobed, naked, nude, stark naked, starkers, stripped, unclad, unclothed.

undue *adj* disproportionate, excessive, extravagant, extreme, immoderate, improper, inordinate, intemperate, needless, overmuch, uncalled-for, undeserved, unnecessary, unreasonable, unseemly, unwarranted. *antonym* reasonable.

undulating *adj* billowing, rippling, rolling, sinuous, undate, wavy. *antonym* flat.

unduly *adv* disproportionately, excessively, extravagantly, immoderately, inordinately, over, overly, overmuch, too, unjustifiably, unnecessarily, unreasonably. *antonym* reasonably.

undutiful *adj* careless, defaulting, delinquent, disloyal, neglectful, negligent, remiss, slack, unfilial.

undying *adj* abiding, constant, continuing, deathless, eternal, everlasting, immortal, imperishable, indestructible, inextinguishable, infinite, lasting, perennial, permanent, perpetual, undiminished, unending, unfading. *antonyms* impermanent, inconstant.

unearth *v* detect, dig up, discover, disinter, dredge up, excavate, exhume, expose, ferret out, find, reveal, uncover.

unearthly *adj* abnormal, eerie, ethereal, extraordinary, ghostly, haunted, heavenly, nightmarish, other-worldly, phantom, spectral, spine-chilling, strange, sublime, supernatural, uncanny, ungodly, unreasonable, weird.

uneasiness *n* agitation, alarm, anxiety, apprehension, apprehensiveness, disquiet, doubt, misgiving, nervousness, perturbation, qualms, suspicion, unease, worry. *antonyms* calm, composure.

uneasy *adj* agitated, anxious, apprehensive, awkward, constrained, discomposed, disquieting, disturbed, disturbing, edgy, impatient, insecure, jittery, nervous, niggling, on edge, perturbed, precarious, restive, restless, shaky, strained, tense, troubled, troubling, uncomfortable, unsettled, unstable, upset, upsetting, worried, worrying. *antonyms* calm, composed.

uneconomic *adj* loss-making, non-profit-making, uncommercial, unprofitable. *antonym* profitable.

uneducated *adj* benighted, ignorant, illiterate, low-brow, philistine, uncultivated, uncultured, uninstructed, unlettered, unread, unschooled, untaught.

unemotional *adj* apathetic, cold, cool, dispassionate, impassive, indifferent, laid-back, low-key, objective, passionless, reserved, undemonstrative, unexcitable, unfeeling, unimpassioned, unresponsive. *antonym* excitable.

unemployed *adj* idle, jobless, on the dole, out of work, redundant, resting, unoccupied.

unending *adj* ceaseless, constant, continual, endless, eternal, everlasting, incessant, interminable, never-ending, perpetual, unceasing, undying, unrelenting, unremitting. *antonyms* intermittent, transient.

unendurable *adj* insufferable, insupportable, intolerable, overwhelming, shattering, unbearable. *antonym* bearable.

unenthusiastic *adj* apathetic, blasé, bored, cool, half-hearted, indifferent, lukewarm, neutral, nonchalant, unimpressed, uninterested, unmoved, unresponsive.

unenviable *adj* disagreeable, painful, thankless, uncomfortable, uncongenial, undesirable, unpalatable, unpleasant, unsavoury. *antonym* desirable.

unequal *adj* asymmetrical, different, differing, disparate, disproportionate, dissimilar, ill-equipped, ill-matched, inadequate, incapable, incompetent, insufficient, irregular, unbalanced, uneven, unlike, unmatched, variable, varying.

unequalled *adj* exceptional, incomparable, inimitable, matchless, paramount, peerless, pre-eminent, supreme, surpassing, unmatched, unparalleled, unrivalled, unsurpassed.

unequivocal *adj* absolute, certain, clear, clear-cut, crystal-clear, decisive, definite, direct, distinct, evident, explicit, express, incontrovertible, indubitable, manifest, plain, positive, straight, unambiguous, uncontestable, unmistakable. *antonyms* ambiguous, vague.

unerring *adj* accurate, certain, dead, exact, faultless, impeccable, infallible, perfect, sure, uncanny, unfailing. *antonym* fallible.

unethical *adj* dirty, discreditable, dishonest, dishonourable, disreputable, illegal, illicit, immoral, improper, shady, underhand, unfair, unprincipled, unprofessional, unscrupulous, wrong.

uneven *adj* asymmetrical, broken, bumpy, changeable, desultory, disparate, erratic, fitful, fluctuating, ill-matched, inconsistent, intermittent, irregular, jerky, lopsided, odd, one-sided, patchy, rough, spasmodic, unbalanced, unequal, unfair, unsteady, variable.

uneventful *adj* boring, commonplace, dull, humdrum, monotonous, ordinary, quiet, routine, tame, tedious, unexceptional, unexciting, uninteresting, unmemorable, unremarkable, unvaried. *antonym* memorable.

unexceptional *adj* average, commonplace, conventional, indifferent, insignificant, mediocre, normal, ordinary, pedestrian, run-of-the-mill, typical, undistinguished, unimpressive, unmemorable, unremarkable, usual. *antonym* impressive.

unexcitable *adj* calm, composed, contained, cool, dispassionate, easy-going, impassive, imperturbable, laid-back, passionless, relaxed, self-possessed, serene, unimpassioned.

unexpected *adj* abrupt, accidental, amazing, astonishing, chance, fortuitous, startling, sudden, surprising, unaccustomed, unanticipated, unforeseen, unlooked-for, unpredictable, unusual, unwonted. *antonyms* normal, predictable.

unexpectedly *adv* abruptly, by chance, fortuitously, out of the blue, suddenly, surprisingly, unpredictably, without warning.

unexpressive *adj* blank, dead-pan, emotionless, expressionless, immobile, impassive, inexpressive, inscrutable, vacant. *antonym* mobile.

unfailing *adj* certain, constant, dependable, faithful, infallible, loyal, reliable, staunch, steadfast, steady, sure, true, undying, unfading. *antonyms* fickle, impermanent, transient.

unfair *adj* arbitrary, biased, bigoted, crooked, discriminatory, dishonest, dishonourable, inequitable, one-sided, partial, partisan, prejudiced, uncalled-for, undeserved, unethical, unjust, unmerited, unprincipled, unscrupulous, unsporting, unwarranted, wrongful.

unfairness *n* bias, bigotry, discrimination, inequity, injustice, one-sidedness, partiality, partisanship, prejudice. *antonym* equity.

unfaithful *adj* adulterous, deceitful, dishonest, disloyal, faithless, false, false-hearted, fickle, godless, inconstant, perfidious, traitorous, treacherous, treasonable, two-timing, unbelieving, unchaste, unreliable, untrue, untrustworthy. *antonym* loyal.

unfaltering *adj* constant, firm, fixed, indefatigable, pertinacious, resolute, steadfast, steady, tireless, unfailing, unflagging, unflinching, unswerving, untiring, unwavering. *antonyms* uncertain, wavering.

unfamiliar *adj* alien, curious, different, foreign, new, novel, out-of-the-way, strange, unaccustomed, unacquainted, uncharted, uncommon, unexplored, unknown, unpractised, unskilled, unusual, unversed. *antonym* customary.

unfashionable *adj* antiquated, dated, obsolete, old hat, old-fashioned, out, out of date, outmoded, passé, square, unpopular.

unfasten *v* detach, disconnect, loosen, open, separate, uncouple, undo, unlace, unlock, unloose, unloosen, untie.

unfathomable *adj* abstruse, baffling, bottomless, deep, esoteric, fathomless, hidden, immeasurable, impenetrable, incomprehensible, indecipherable, inexplicable, mysterious, profound, unplumbed, unsounded. *antonyms* comprehensible, explicable, penetrable.

unfavourable *adj* adverse, bad, contrary, critical, disadvantageous, discouraging, hostile, ill-suited, inauspicious, infelicitous, inimical, inopportune, low, negative, ominous, poor, threatening, uncomplimentary, unfortunate, unfriendly, unlucky, unpromising, unseasonable, unsuited, untimely, untoward.

unfeeling *adj* apathetic, callous, cold, cruel, hard, hardened, hard-hearted, harsh, heartless, inhuman, insensitive, pitiless, soulless, stony, uncaring, unsympathetic. *antonym* concerned.

unfettered *adj* free, unbridled, unchecked, unconfined, unconstrained, unhampered, unhindered, uninhibited, unrestrained, unshackled, untrammelled. *antonym* constrained.

unfinished *adj* bare, crude, deficient, half-done, imperfect, incomplete, lacking, natural, raw, rough, rude, sketchy, unaccomplished, uncompleted, undone, unfulfilled, unpolished, unrefined, wanting. *antonyms* polished, refined.

unfit *adj* debilitated, decrepit, feeble, flabby, flaccid, ill-adapted, ill-equipped, inadequate, inappropriate, incapable, incompetent, ineffective, ineligible, unequal, unhealthy, unprepared, unqualified, unsuitable, unsuited, untrained, useless. *antonyms* competent, suitable.

unflagging *adj* constant, fixed, indefatigable, never-failing, persevering, persistent, single-minded, staunch, steady, tireless, unceasing, undeviating, unfailing, unfaltering, unremitting, unswerving, untiring. *antonyms* faltering, inconstant.

unflappable *adj* calm, collected, composed, cool, equable, impassive, imperturbable, level-headed, phlegmatic, self-possessed, unexcitable, unruffled, unworried. *antonyms* excitable, nervous, temperamental.

unflinching *adj* bold, constant, determined, firm, fixed, resolute, stalwart, staunch, steadfast, steady, sure, unblinking, unfaltering, unshaken, unshrinking, unswerving, unwavering. *antonyms* cowed, scared.

unfold *v* clarify, describe, develop, disclose, disentangle, divulge, elaborate, evolve, expand, explain, flatten, grow, illustrate, mature, open, present, reveal, show, spread, straighten, stretch out, uncoil, uncover, undo, unfurl, unravel, unroll, unwrap. *antonyms* fold, suppress, withhold, wrap.

unforeseen *adj* abrupt, accidental, fortuitous, startling, sudden, surprise, surprising, unanticipated, unavoidable, unexpected, unheralded, unlooked-for, unpredicted. **antonyms** expected, predictable.

unforgettable *adj* exceptional, extraordinary, historic, impressive, memorable, momentous, notable, noteworthy. **antonyms** unexceptional, unmemorable.

unforgivable *adj* deplorable, disgraceful, indefensible, inexcusable, reprehensible, shameful, unconscionable, unjustifiable, unpardonable, unwarrantable. **antonym** venial.

unfortunate *adj* adverse, calamitous, cursed, deplorable, disastrous, doomed, hapless, hopeless, ill-advised, ill-fated, ill-timed, inappropriate, infelicitous, inopportune, lamentable, luckless, poor, regrettable, ruinous, star-crossed, tactless, unbecoming, unfavourable, unhappy, unlucky, unprosperous, unsuccessful, unsuitable, untimely, untoward, wretched.

unfortunately *adv* regrettably, sad to relate, sad to say, sadly, unhappily, unluckily, worse luck.

unfounded *adj* baseless, fabricated, false, gratuitous, groundless, idle, spurious, trumped-up, unjustified, unmerited, unproven, unsubstantiated, unsupported. **antonym** justified.

unfriendly *adj* alien, aloof, antagonistic, chilly, cold, critical, disagreeable, distant, hostile, ill-disposed, inauspicious, inhospitable, inimical, quarrelsome, sour, stand-offish, surly, unapproachable, unbending, uncongenial, unfavourable, unneighbourly, unsociable, unwelcoming. **antonyms** agreeable, amiable.

unfruitful *adj* arid, barren, exhausted, fruitless, impoverished, infertile, sterile, unproductive, unprofitable, unprolific, unrewarding.

ungainly *adj* awkward, clumsy, gangling, gauche, gawky, inelegant, loutish, lubberly, lumbering, slouching, unco-ordinated, uncouth, unwieldy. **antonyms** elegant, graceful.

ungodly *adj* blasphemous, corrupt, depraved, dreadful, godless, horrendous, immoral, impious, intolerable, irreligious, outrageous, profane, sinful, unearthly, unreasonable, unseasonable, unseemly, unsocial, vile, wicked.

ungovernable *adj* disorderly, rebellious, refractory, uncontrollable, ungoverned, unmanageable, unrestrainable, unruly, wild.

ungracious *adj* bad-mannered, boorish, churlish, discourteous, disrespectful, graceless, ill-bred, impolite, offhand, rude, uncivil, unmannerly. **antonym** polite.

ungrateful *adj* heedless, ill-mannered, selfish, thankless, unappreciative, ungracious, unmindful.

unguarded[1] *adj* careless, foolhardy, foolish, heedless, ill-considered, impolitic, imprudent, incautious, indiscreet, rash, thoughtless, undiplomatic, unheeding, unthinking, unwary. **antonym** cautious.

unguarded[2] *adj* defenceless, exposed, undefended, unpatrolled, unprotected, vulnerable. **antonym** protected.

unhappy *adj* awkward, blue, clumsy, contentless, crestfallen, cursed, dejected, depressed, despondent, disconsolate, dismal, dispirited, down, downcast, gloomy, hapless, ill-advised, ill-chosen, ill-fated, ill-omened, ill-timed, inappropriate, inapt, inept, infelicitous, injudicious, long-faced, luckless, lugubrious, melancholy, miserable, mournful, sad, sorrowful, sorry, tactless, uneasy, unfortunate, unlucky, unsuitable, wretched. **antonym** fortunate.

unharmed *adj* intact, safe, scot-free, sound, undamaged, unhurt, unimpaired, uninjured, unscarred, unscathed, untouched, whole. **antonyms** damaged, impaired.

unhealthy *adj* ailing, bad, baneful, corrupt, corrupting, degrading, deleterious, delicate, demoralising, detrimental, feeble, frail, harmful, infirm, insalubrious, insalutary, insanitary, invalid, morbid, noxious, polluted, poorly, sick, sickly, undesirable, unhygienic, unsound, unwell, unwholesome, weak. **antonyms** hygienic, robust, salubrious.

unheard-of *adj* disgraceful, extreme, inconceivable, new, novel, obscure, offensive, out of the question, outrageous, preposterous, shocking, singular, unacceptable, unbelievable, undiscovered, undreamed-of, unexampled, unfamiliar, unimaginable, unique, unknown, unprecedented, unregarded, unremarked, unsung, unthinkable, unthought-of, unusual. **antonyms** famous, normal, usual.

unheeded *adj* disobeyed, disregarded, forgotten, ignored, neglected, overlooked, unnoticed, unobserved, unremarked. *antonyms* noted, observed.

unhesitating *adj* automatic, immediate, implicit, instant, instantaneous, prompt, ready, resolute, spontaneous, steadfast, unfaltering, unquestioning, unreserved, unswerving, unwavering, whole-hearted. *antonyms* hesitant, tentative, uncertain.

unhinge *v* confuse, craze, derange, disorder, distract, drive mad, madden, unbalance, unnerve, unsettle, upset.

unholy *adj* appalling, base, corrupt, depraved, dishonest, evil, heinous, immoral, iniquitous, irreligious, outrageous, profane, shocking, sinful, taboo, unconscionable, unearthly, ungodly, unnatural, unreasonable, vile, wicked. *antonyms* godly, pious, reasonable.

unhoped-for *adj* incredible, surprising, unanticipated, unbelievable, undreamed-of, unexpected, unforeseen, unimaginable, unlooked-for.

unhurried *adj* calm, deliberate, easy, easy-going, laid-back, leisurely, relaxed, sedate, slow. *antonym* hasty.

unidentified *adj* anonymous, incognito, mysterious, nameless, unclaimed, unclassified, unfamiliar, unknown, unmarked, unnamed, unrecognised, unspecified. *antonyms* known, named.

unification *n* alliance, amalgamation, coalescence, coalition, combination, confederation, federation, fusion, incorporation, merger, union, uniting. *antonyms* separation, split.

uniform *n* costume, dress, garb, gear, habit, insignia, outfit, regalia, rig, robes, suit.
adj alike, consistent, constant, equable, equal, even, homogenous, identical, like, montonous, of a piece, regular, same, selfsame, similar, smooth, unbroken, unchanging, undeviating, unvarying. *antonyms* changing, colourful, varied.

uniformity *n* constancy, drabness, dullness, evenness, flatness, homogeneity, invariability, monotony, regularity, sameness, similarity, tedium. *antonyms* difference, dissimilarity, variation.

unify *v* amalgamate, bind, combine, confederate, consolidate, federate, fuse, join, marry, merge, unite, weld. *antonyms* separate, split.

unimaginable *adj* fantastic, impossible, inconceivable, incredible, indescribable, ineffable, mind-boggling, unbelievable, undreamed-of, unheard-of, unhoped-for, unthinkable.

unimaginative *adj* banal, barren, blinkered, commonplace, derivative, dry, dull, hackneyed, lifeless, matter-of-fact, myopic, ordinary, pedestrian, predictable, prosaic, routine, short-sighted, tame, uncreative, uninspired, unoriginal. *antonym* original.

unimpeachable *adj* blameless, faultless, immaculate, impeccable, irreproachable, perfect, spotless, unassailable, unblemished, unchallengeable, unexceptionable, unquestionable. *antonyms* blameworthy, faulty.

unimpeded *adj* all-round, clear, free, open, unblocked, unchecked, unconstrained, unhampered, unhindered, uninhibited, unrestrained, untrammelled. *antonym* hampered.

unimportant *adj* immaterial, inconsequential, insignificant, irrelevant, low-ranking, minor, minuscule, negligible, off the map, paltry, petty, slight, small-time, trifling, trivial, worthless.

unimpressive *adj* average, commonplace, dull, indifferent, mediocre, undistinguished, unexceptional, uninteresting, unremarkable, unspectacular. *antonyms* memorable, notable.

uninhibited *adj* abandoned, candid, emancipated, frank, free, informal, instinctive, liberated, natural, open, relaxed, spontaneous, unbridled, unchecked, unconstrained, uncontrolled, uncurbed, unrepressed, unreserved, unrestrained, unrestricted, unselfconscious. *antonyms* constrained, repressed.

uninspired *adj* boring, commonplace, dull, humdrum, indifferent, ordinary, pedestrian, prosaic, stale, stock, trite, undistinguished, unexciting, unimaginative, uninspiring, uninteresting, unoriginal. *antonym* original.

unintelligent *adj* brainless, dense, dull, dumb, empty-headed, fatuous, foolish, gormless, half-witted, obtuse, silly, slow, stupid, thick, unreasoning, unthinking.

unintelligible *adj* double Dutch, garbled, illegible, inapprehensible, inarticulate, incoherent, incomprehensible, indecipherable, indistinct, jumbled, meaningless, muddled, unfathomable.

unintentional *adj* accidental, fortuitous, inadvertent, involuntary, unconscious, unintended, unpremeditated, unthinking, unwitting. *antonym* deliberate.

uninterested *adj* apathetic, blasé, bored, distant, impassive, incurious, indifferent, listless, unconcerned, unenthusiastic, uninvolved, unresponsive. *antonyms* concerned, enthusiastic, responsive.

uninteresting *adj* boring, commonplace, drab, dreary, dry, dull, flat, humdrum, monotonous, tame, tedious, tiresome, uneventful, unexciting, unimpressive, uninspiring, *antonym* exciting.

uninterrupted *adj* constant, continual, continuous, non-stop, peaceful, prolonged, quiet, steady, sustained, unbroken, undisturbed, unending. *antonyms* broken, intermittent.

uninvited *adj* unasked, unbidden, unsolicited, unsought, unwanted, unwelcome. *antonym* solicited.

uninviting *adj* disagreeable, distasteful, offensive, off-putting, repellent, repulsive, unappealing, unappetising, unattractive, undesirable, unpleasant, unsavoury, unwelcoming. *antonym* welcome.

union *n* accord, agreement, alliance, amalgam, amalgamation, association, blend, coalition, coitus, combination, compact, concord, concrescence, concurrence, confederacy, confederation, conjugation, conjunction, copulation, coupling, federation, fusion, harmony, intercourse, junction, juncture, league, marriage, matrimony, mixture, synthesis, unanimity, unison, uniting, unity, wedlock. *antonyms* alienation, disunity, estrangement, separation.

unique *adj* incomparable, inimitable, lone, matchless, one-off, only, peerless, single, singular, sole, solitary, unequalled, unexampled, unmatched, unparalleled, unprecedented, unrivalled. *antonym* commonplace.

unison *n* accord, accordance, agreement, concert, concord, co-operation, harmony, unanimity, unity. *antonym* disharmony.

unit *n* ace, assembly, component, constituent, detachment, element, entity, group, item, measure, measurement, member, module, one, part, piece, portion, quantity, section, segment, system, whole.

unite *v* accrete, ally, amalgamate, associate, band, blend, coalesce, combine, confederate, conjoin, conjugate, consolidate, cooperate, couple, fuse, incorporate, join, join forces, league, link, marry, merge, pool, splice, unify, wed. *antonyms* separate, sever.

united *adj* affiliated, agreed, allied, collective, combined, concerted, concordant, conjoined, corporate, in accord, in agreement, leagued, likeminded, one, pooled, unanimous, unified. *antonyms* differing, disunited, separated, unco-ordinated.

unity *n* accord, agreement, community, concord, concurrence, consensus, entity, harmony, integrity, oneness, peace, singleness, solidarity, unanimity, unification, union, wholeness. *antonyms* disagreement, disunity.

universal *adj* across-the-board, all-embracing, all-inclusive, all-round, catholic, common, ecumenical, entire, general, global, omnipresent, total, ubiquitous, unlimited, whole, widespread, worldwide.

universe *n* cosmos, creation, firmament, heavens, macrocosm, nature, world.

unjust *adj* biased, gratuitous, groundless, inequitable, one-sided, partial, partisan, prejudiced, undeserved, unethical, unfair, unjustified, unmerited, wrong, wrongful.

unjustifiable *adj* excessive, immoderate, indefensible, inexcusable, outrageous, steep, unacceptable, unforgivable, unjust, unpardonable, unreasonable, unwarrantable, wrong.

unkempt *adj* bedraggled, blowsy, disarranged, dishevelled, disordered, frowsy, messy, rumpled, scruffy, shabby, shaggy, slatternly, sloppy, slovenly, sluttish, tousled, uncombed, ungroomed, untidy. *antonyms* neat, tidy.

unkind *adj* callous, cruel, disobliging, hard-hearted, harsh, inconsiderate, inhuman, inhumane, insensitive, malevolent, malicious, mean, nasty, spiteful, thoughtless, uncaring, uncharitable, unchristian, unfeeling, unfriendly, unsympathetic. *antonym* considerate.

unknown *adj* alien, anonymous, concealed, dark, foreign, hidden, humble, incognito, mysterious, nameless, new, obscure, secret, strange, uncharted, undisclosed, undiscovered, undistinguished, unexplored, unfamiliar, unheard-of, unidentified, unnamed, unrecognised, unsung, untold. *antonym* familiar.

unlawful *adj* actionable, banned,

criminal, forbidden, illegal, illegitimate, illicit, outlawed, prohibited, unauthorised, unconstitutional, unlicensed, unsanctioned.

unleash v free, loose, release, unloose, untether, untie. **antonym** restrain.

unlike adj contrasted, different, disparate, dissimilar, distinct, divergent, diverse, ill-matched, incompatible, opposed, opposite, unequal, unrelated. **antonyms** related, similar.

unlikely adj doubtful, dubious, faint, implausible, improbable, incredible, questionable, remote, slight, suspect, suspicious, tall, unbelievable, unconvincing, unexpected, unimaginable. **antonym** plausible.

unlimited adj absolute, all-encompassing, boundless, complete, countless, endless, extensive, full, great, illimitable, immeasurable, immense, incalculable, infinite, limitless, total, unbounded, unconditional, unconstrained, unfettered, unhampered, unqualified, unrestricted, vast. **antonym** circumscribed.

unload v discharge, disencumber, dump, empty, offload, relieve, unburden, unpack.

unlock v bare, disengage, free, open, release, unbar, unbolt, undo, unfasten, unlatch. **antonym** fasten.

unlooked-for adj chance, fortuitous, fortunate, lucky, surprise, surprising, unanticipated, undreamed-of, unexpected, unforeseen, unhoped-for, unpredicted, unthought-of. **antonyms** expected, predictable.

unloved adj detested, disliked, forsaken, hated, loveless, neglected, rejected, spurned, uncared-for, uncherished, unpopular, unwanted. **antonym** beloved.

unlucky adj cursed, disastrous, doomed, hapless, ill-fated, ill-omened, inauspicious, jinxed, luckless, miserable, ominous, unfavourable, unfortunate, unhappy, unsuccessful, untimely, wretched.

unmanageable adj awkward, bulky, cumbersome, difficult, disorderly, fractious, inconvenient, intractable, obstreperous, recalcitrant, refractory, stroppy, uncontrollable, unco-operative, unhandy, unruly, unwieldy, wild. **antonym** docile.

unmannerly adj badly-behaved, bad-mannered, boorish, discourteous, disrespectful, graceless, ill-bred, ill-mannered, impolite, rude, uncivil, uncouth, ungracious. **antonym** polite.

unmarried adj available, bachelor, fancy-free, footloose, maiden, single, unattached, unwed, unwedded. **antonym** married.

unmask v bare, detect, disclose, expose, reveal, show, uncover, unveil.

unmatched adj beyond compare, incomparable, matchless, paramount, peerless, supreme, unequalled, unexampled, unparalleled, unrivalled, unsurpassed.

unmentionable adj abominable, disgraceful, disreputable, immodest, indecent, scandalous, shameful, shocking, taboo, unnameable, unspeakable, unutterable.

unmethodical adj confused, desultory, disorderly, haphazard, illogical, irregular, muddled, random, unco-ordinated, unorganised, unsystematic.

unmistakable adj certain, clear, conspicuous, crystal-clear, decided, distinct, evident, explicit, glaring, indisputable, manifest, obvious, palpable, patent, plain, positive, pronounced, sure, unambiguous, undeniable, undisputed, unequivocal, unquestionable. **antonyms** ambiguous, unclear.

unmitigated adj absolute, arrant, complete, consummate, downright, grim, harsh, intense, oppressive, out-and-out, outright, perfect, persistent, pure, rank, relentless, sheer, thorough, thoroughgoing, unabated, unalleviated, unbroken, undiminished, unmodified, unqualified, unredeemed, unrelenting, unrelieved, unremitting, utter.

unmoved adj adamant, cold, determined, dispassionate, dry-eyed, fast, firm, impassive, indifferent, inflexible, obdurate, phlegmatic, resolute, resolved, steadfast, steady, unaffected, unchanged, undeviating, unfeeling, unimpressed, unresponsive, unshaken, untouched, unwavering. **antonyms** affected, shaken.

unnatural adj aberrant, abnormal, affected, anomalous, artificial, assumed, bizarre, brutal, callous, cataphysical, cold-blooded, contrived, cruel, evil, extraordinary, factitious, false, feigned, fiendish, forced, freakish, heartless, inhuman, insincere, irregular, laboured, mannered, monstrous, odd, outlandish, perverse, perverted, phoney, queer, ruthless, sadistic, savage, self-conscious, stagy, stiff, stilted, strained, strange, studied, supernatural, theatrical, unaccountable, uncanny, unfeeling, unspontaneous, unusual, wicked. *antonyms* acceptable, normal.

unnecessary *adj* dispensable, expendable, inessential, needless, nonessential, otiose, pleonastic, redundant, superfluous, supernumerary, tautological, uncalled-for, unjustified, unneeded, useless. *antonym* indispensable.

unnerve *v* confound, daunt, demoralise, disconcert, discourage, dishearten, dismay, dispirit, fluster, frighten, intimidate, rattle, scare, shake, unhinge, unman, upset, worry. *antonyms* brace, steel.

unnoticed *adj* disregarded, ignored, neglected, overlooked, passed over, unconsidered, undiscovered, unheeded, unobserved, unperceived, unrecognised, unrecorded, unremarked, unseen. *antonyms* noted, remarked.

unobtrusive *adj* humble, inconspicuous, low-key, meek, modest, quiet, restrained, retiring, self-effacing, subdued, unassertive, unassuming, unemphatic, unnoticeable, unostentatious, unpretentious. *antonym* ostentatious.

unobtrusively *adv* inconspicuously, modestly, on the q.t., on the quiet, quietly, surreptitiously, unostentatiously. *antonym* ostentatiously.

unoccupied *adj* empty, free, idle, inactive, jobless, unemployed, uninhabited, untenanted, vacant. *antonym* busy.

unofficial *adj* backyard, confidential, illegal, informal, personal, private, ulterior, unauthorised, unconfirmed, undeclared, wildcat.

unoriginal *adj* cliché-ridden, copied, cribbed, derivative, derived, secondhand, stale, trite, unimaginative, uninspired. *antonym* imaginative.

unorthodox *adj* abnormal, alternative, fringe, heterodox, irregular, nonconformist, unconventional, unusual, unwonted. *antonym* conventional.

unpaid *adj* due, free, honorary, outstanding, overdue, owing, payable, unremunerative, unsalaried, unsettled, voluntary.

unpalatable *adj* bitter, disagreeable, displeasing, distasteful, inedible, insipid, offensive, repugnant, unappetising, unattractive, uneatable, unenviable, unpleasant, unsavoury. *antonym* pleasant.

unparalleled *adj* exceptional, incomparable, matchless, peerless, rare, singular, superlative, supreme, surpassing, unequalled, unexampled, unique, unmatched, unprecedented, unrivalled, unsurpassed.

unpardonable *adj* deplorable, disgraceful, indefensible, inexcusable, outrageous, scandalous, shameful, shocking, unconscionable, unforgivable. *antonyms* forgivable, understandable.

unperturbed *adj* calm, collected, composed, cool, impassive, placid, poised, self-possessed, serene, tranquil, undisturbed, unexcited, unflinching, unflustered, unruffled, untroubled, unworried. *antonyms* anxious, perturbed.

unpleasant *adj* abhorrent, bad, disagreeable, distasteful, god-awful, ill-natured, irksome, nasty, objectionable, obnoxious, poxy, repulsive, rocky, sticky, traumatic, troublesome, unattractive, unpalatable.

unpleasantness *n* annoyance, bother, embarrassment, furore, fuss, ill-feeling, nastiness, scandal, trouble, upset.

unpopular *adj* avoided, detested, disliked, hated, neglected, rejected, shunned, undesirable, unfashionable, unloved, unsought-after, unwanted, unwelcome. *antonym* fashionable.

unprecedented *adj* abnormal, exceptional, extraordinary, freakish, new, novel, original, remarkable, revolutionary, singular, unexampled, unheard-of, unknown, unparalleled, unrivalled, unusual.

unpredictable *adj* chance, changeable, doubtful, erratic, fickle, fluky, iffy, in the lap of the gods, inconstant, random, scatty, unforeseeable, unreliable, unstable, variable.

unprejudiced *adj* balanced, detached, dispassionate, enlightened, even-handed, fair, fair-minded, impartial, just, non-partisan, objective, open-minded, unbiased, uncoloured. *antonym* narrow-minded.

unpremeditated *adj* extempore, fortuitous, impromptu, impulsive, offhand, off-the-cuff, spontaneous, spur-of-the-moment, unintentional, unplanned, unprepared, unrehearsed.

unprepared *adj* ad-lib, extemporaneous, half-baked, ill-considered, improvised, incomplete, napping, off-the-cuff, spontaneous, surprised, unawares, unfinished, ungirded, unplanned, unready, unrehearsed, unsuspecting. **antonym** ready.

unpretentious *adj* homely, honest, humble, modest, natural, plain, simple, straightforward, unaffected, unassuming, unimposing, unobtrusive, unostentatious, unpretending, unsophisticated, unspoiled.

unprincipled *adj* amoral, corrupt, crooked, deceitful, devious, discreditable, dishonest, dishonourable, immoral, underhand, unethical, unprofessional, unscrupulous. **antonym** ethical.

unproductive *adj* arid, barren, bootless, dry, fruitless, futile, idle, ineffective, inefficacious, infertile, otiose, sterile, unavailing, unfruitful, unprofitable, unprolific, unremunerative, unrewarding, useless, vain, valueless, worthless. **antonym** fertile.

unprofessional *adj* amateur, amateurish, improper, inadmissible, incompetent, inefficient, inexperienced, inexpert, lax, negligent, unacceptable, unbecoming, unethical, unfitting, unprincipled, unseemly, unskilled, untrained, unworthy. **antonym** skilful.

unpromising *adj* adverse, depressing, discouraging, dispiriting, doubtful, gloomy, inauspicious, ominous, unfavourable, unpropitious.

unprotected *adj* defenceless, exposed, helpless, liable, naked, open, unarmed, unattended, undefended, unfortified, unguarded, unsheltered, unshielded, unvaccinated, vulnerable. **antonyms** immune, safe.

unqualified *adj* absolute, categorical, complete, consummate, downright, ill-equipped, incapable, incompetent, ineligible, out-and-out, outright, thorough, thoroughgoing, total, uncertificated, unconditional, unfit, unmitigated, unmixed, unprepared, unreserved, unrestricted, untrained, utter, whole-hearted. **antonyms** conditional, tentative.

unquestionable *adj* absolute, certain, clear, conclusive, definite, faultless, flawless, incontestable, incontrovertible, indisputable, indubitable, irrefutable, manifest, obvious, patent, self-evident, sure, unchallenged, undeniable, unequivocal, unmistakable. **antonym** dubious.

unquestioning *adj* implicit, questionless, unconditional, unhesitating, unqualified, whole-hearted. **antonym** doubtful.

unravel *v* disentangle, explain, extricate, figure out, free, interpret, penetrate, puzzle out, resolve, separate, solve, sort out, undo, unknot, untangle, unwind, work out. **antonyms** complicate, tangle.

unreal *adj* academic, artificial, chimerical, fabulous, fairy-tale, fake, false, fanciful, fantastic, fictitious, hypothetical, illusory, imaginary, immaterial, impalpable, insincere, insubstantial, intangible, made-up, make-believe, mock, mythical, nebulous, ostensible, phantasmagorical, pretended, seeming, sham, storybook, synthetic, vaporous, visionary. **antonym** genuine.

unrealistic *adj* half-baked, idealistic, impracticable, impractical, improbable, quixotic, romantic, starry-eyed, theoretical, unworkable. **antonym** pragmatic.

unreasonable *adj* absurd, arbitrary, biased, blinkered, capricious, erratic, excessive, exorbitant, extortionate, extravagant, far-fetched, foolish, froward, headstrong, illogical, immoderate, inconsistent, irrational, mad, nonsensical, opinionated, perverse, preposterous, quirky, senseless, silly, steep, stupid, uncalled-for, undue, unfair, unjust, unjustifiable, unjustified, unwarranted. **antonyms** moderate, rational.

unrefined *adj* boorish, coarse, crude, imperfect, inelegant, raw, rude, uncultivated, uncultured, unfinished, unperfected, unpolished, unpurified, unsophisticated, untreated, vulgar. **antonym** finished.

unrelated *adj* different, disparate, dissimilar, distinct, extraneous, inapplicable, inappropriate, irrelevant, unassociated, unconnected, unlike. **antonym** similar.

unrelenting *adj* ceaseless, constant, continual, continuous, cruel, endless, implacable, incessant, inexorable, insistent, intransigent, merciless, perpetual, pitiless, relentless, remorseless, ruthless, steady, stern, tough, unabated, unalleviated, unbroken, unceasing, uncompromising, unmerciful, unremitting, unsparing. **antonyms** intermittent, spasmodic.

unreliable *adj* deceptive, delusive, disreputable, erroneous, fair-weather, fallible, false, implausible, inaccurate, inauthentic, irresponsible, mistaken, specious, uncertain, unconvincing, undependable, unsound, unstable, untrustworthy.

unremitting adj assiduous, ceaseless, conscientious, constant, continual, continuous, diligent, incessant, indefatigable, perpetual, relentless, remorseless, sedulous, tireless, unabated, unbroken, unceasing, unrelenting. **antonym** spasmodic.

unrepentant adj callous, hardened, impenitent, incorrigible, obdurate, shameless, unabashed, unashamed, unregenerate, unremorseful, unrepenting. **antonym** penitent.

unreserved adj absolute, candid, complete, demonstrative, direct, entire, extrovert, forthright, frank, free, full, open, open-hearted, outgoing, outspoken, total, unconditional, unhesitating, uninhibited, unlimited, unqualified, unrestrained, whole-hearted. **antonyms** inhibited, tentative.

unresolved adj doubtful, indefinite, moot, pending, problematic, unanswered, undecided, undetermined, unsettled, unsolved, up in the air, vague, vexed. **antonyms** definite, determined.

unresponsive adj aloof, apathetic, cool, indifferent, unaffected, uninterested, unmoved, unsympathetic. **antonym** sympathetic.

unrest n agitation, anxiety, apprehension, disaffection, discontent, discord, disquiet, dissatisfaction, dissension, distress, perturbation, protest, rebellion, restlessness, sedition, strife, tumult, turmoil, unease, uneasiness, worry. **antonyms** calm, peace.

unrestrained adj abandoned, boisterous, free, immoderate, inordinate, intemperate, irrepressible, natural, rampant, unbounded, unbridled, unchecked, unconstrained, uncontrolled, unhindered, uninhibited, unrepressed, unreserved, uproarious. **antonym** inhibited.

unrestricted adj absolute, all-round, clear, free, free-for-all, free-wheeling, open, public, unbounded, unconditional, unhindered, unimpeded, unlimited, unobstructed, unopposed, unregulated. **antonym** limited.

unrivalled adj incomparable, inimitable, matchless, peerless, superlative, supreme, surpassing, unequalled, unmatched, unparalleled, unsurpassed, without equal.

unruffled adj calm, collected, composed, cool, even, imperturbable, level, peaceful, placid, serene, smooth, tranquil, unbroken, undisturbed, unflustered, unmoved, unperturbed, untroubled. **antonyms** anxious, troubled.

unruly adj disobedient, disorderly, fractious, headstrong, insubordinate, intractable, lawless, mutinous, obstreperous, rebellious, refractory, riotous, rowdy, ruleless, turbulent, uncontrollable, ungovernable, unmanageable, wayward, wild, wilful. **antonym** manageable.

unsafe adj dangerous, exposed, hazardous, insecure, perilous, precarious, risky, threatening, treacherous, uncertain, unreliable, unsound, unstable, vulnerable. **antonym** secure.

unsaid adj undeclared, unexpressed, unmentioned, unpronounced, unspoken, unstated, unuttered, unvoiced. **antonym** spoken.

unsatisfactory adj deficient, disappointing, displeasing, dissatisfying, frustrating, inadequate, inferior, insufficient, leaving a lot to be desired, mediocre, poor, rocky, thwarting, unacceptable, unsatisfying, unsuitable, unworthy, weak.

unsavoury adj disagreeable, distasteful, nasty, nauseating, objectionable, obnoxious, offensive, repellent, repugnant, repulsive, revolting, sickening, sordid, squalid, unappetising, unattractive, undesirable, unpalatable, unpleasant. **antonyms** palatable, pleasant.

unscathed adj intact, safe, scot-free, sound, unharmed, unhurt, uninjured, unmarked, unscarred, unscratched, untouched, whole. **antonyms** harmed, injured.

unscrupulous adj corrupt, crooked, cynical, discreditable, dishonest, dishonourable, immoral, improper, ruthless, shameless, unethical, unprincipled.

unseasonable adj ill-timed, inappropriate, inopportune, intempestive, mistimed, unsuitable, untimely. **antonym** timely.

unseat v depose, dethrone, discharge, dismiss, dismount, displace, oust, overthrow, remove, throw, topple, unhorse, unsaddle.

unseemly adj discreditable, disreputable, improper, inappropriate, indecorous, indelicate, shocking, unbecoming, unbefitting, undignified, undue, ungentlemanly, unladylike, unrefined, unsuitable. **antonym** decorous.

unseen *adj* concealed, hidden, invisible, lurking, obscure, overlooked, undetected, unnoticed, unobserved, unobtrusive, unperceived, veiled. **antonyms** observed, visible.

unselfish *adj* altruistic, charitable, dedicated, devoted, disinterested, generous, humanitarian, kind, liberal, magnanimous, noble, philanthropic, self-denying, selfless, self-sacrificing, single-eyed, ungrudging, unstinting. **antonym** selfish.

unsentimental *adj* cynical, hard as nails, hard-headed, level-headed, practical, pragmatic, realistic, shrewd, tough. **antonym** soft.

unsettled *adj* agitated, anxious, changeable, changing, confused, debatable, disorderly, disoriented, disturbed, doubtful, due, edgy, flustered, iffy, inconstant, insecure, moot, open, outstanding, overdue, owing, payable, pending, perturbed, problematic, restive, restless, shaken, shaky, tense, troubled, uncertain, undecided, undetermined, uneasy, unnerved, unpredictable, unresolved, unstable, unsteady, upset, variable. **antonyms** certain, composed, settled.

unshakable *adj* absolute, adamant, constant, determined, firm, fixed, immovable, resolute, stable, staunch, steadfast, sure, unassailable, unswerving, unwavering, well-founded. **antonym** insecure.

unsightly *adj* disagreeable, hideous, horrid, off-putting, repellent, repugnant, repulsive, revolting, ugly, unattractive, unpleasant, unprepossessing. **antonym** pleasing.

unsociable *adj* aloof, chilly, cold, distant, hostile, inhospitable, introverted, reclusive, reserved, retiring, stand-offish, taciturn, uncommunicative, uncongenial, unforthcoming, unfriendly, unneighbourly, unsocial, withdrawn. **antonym** friendly.

unsolicited *adj* gratuitous, spontaneous, unasked, uncalled-for, unforced, uninvited, unrequested, unsought, unwanted, unwelcome, voluntary. **antonym** invited.

unsophisticated *adj* artless, childlike, guileless, hick, homespun, inexperienced, ingenuous, innocent, naïve, natural, plain, simple, small-town, straightforward, unaffected, uncomplicated, uninvolved, unpretentious, unrefined, unspecialised, unspoilt,

untutored, unworldly. **antonyms** complex, pretentious.

unsparing *adj* abundant, bountiful, generous, hard, harsh, implacable, inexorable, lavish, liberal, merciless, munificent, open-handed, plenteous, prodigal, profuse, relentless, rigorous, ruthless, scathing, severe, stern, stringent, uncompromising, unforgiving, ungrudging, unmerciful, unstinting. **antonyms** forgiving, mean.

unspeakable *adj* abhorrent, abominable, appalling, dreadful, evil, execrable, frightful, heinous, horrible, inconceivable, indescribable, ineffable, inexpressible, loathsome, monstrous, odious, overwhelming, repellent, shocking, unbelievable, unimaginable, unutterable, wonderful.

unspoilt *adj* artless, innocent, intact, natural, perfect, preserved, unaffected, unaltered, unassuming, unblemished, unchanged, undamaged, unharmed, unimpaired, unscathed, unsophisticated, unspoiled, unstudied, untouched, wholesome. **antonym** affected.

unspoken *adj* assumed, implicit, implied, inferred, mute, silent, speech-less, tacit, undeclared, understood, unexpressed, unsaid, unstated, unuttered, voiceless, wordless. **antonym** explicit.

unstable *adj* capricious, changeable, erratic, fitful, fluctuating, inconsistent, inconstant, insecure, irrational, precarious, rickety, risky, shaky, slippy, ticklish, tottering, unpredictable, unsettled, unsteady, untrustworthy, vacillating, variable, volatile, wobbly. **antonym** steady.

unsteady *adj* changeable, dicky, erratic, flickering, flighty, fluctuating, frail, inconstant, infirm, insecure, irregular, precarious, reeling, rickety, shaky, skittish, tottering, treacherous, tremulous, unreliable, unsafe, unstable, vacillating, variable, volatile, wavering, wobbly. **antonym** firm.

unstinting *adj* abounding, abundant, ample, bountiful, full, generous, large, lavish, liberal, munificent, plentiful, prodigal, profuse, ungrudging, unsparing. **antonyms** grudging, mean.

unsubstantiated *adj* debatable, dubious, questionable, unattested, unconfirmed, uncorroborated, un-established, unproved, unproven, unsupported, unverified. **antonyms** proved, proven.

unsuccessful *adj* abortive, failed,

foiled, fruitless, frustrated, futile, ill-fated, inadequate, ineffective, ineffectual, losing, luckless, otiose, sterile, thwarted, unavailing, unfortunate, unlucky, unproductive, unsatisfactory, useless, vain. **antonym** effective.

unsuitable *adj* improper, inapposite, inappropriate, inapt, incompatible, incongruous, inconsistent, indecorous, ineligible, infelicitous, unacceptable, unbecoming, unbefitting, unfitting, unlikely, unseasonable, unseemly, unsuited. **antonym** seemly.

unsullied *adj* clean, immaculate, intact, perfect, pristine, pure, spotless, stainless, unblackened, unblemished, uncorrupted, undefiled, unsoiled, unspoiled, unspotted, unstained, untarnished, untouched. **antonyms** dirty, stained.

unsung *adj* anonymous, disregarded, forgotten, neglected, obscure, overlooked, unacknowledged, uncelebrated, unhailed, unhonoured, unknown, unnamed, unrecognised, unrenowned. **antonyms** famous, renowned.

unsure *adj* agnostic, distrustful, doubtful, dubious, hesitant, insecure, irresolute, mistrustful, sceptical, suspicious, tentative, uncertain, unconvinced, undecided, unpersuaded. **antonym** resolute.

unsurpassed *adj* consummate, exceptional, incomparable, matchless, paramount, peerless, sublime, superlative, supreme, unequalled, unexcelled, unparalleled, unrivalled.

unsuspecting *adj* childlike, confiding, credulous, green, gullible, inexperienced, ingenuous, innocent, naïve, trusting, unconscious, uncritical, unsuspicious, unwary, unwitting. **antonyms** conscious, knowing.

unswerving *adj* constant, dedicated, devoted, direct, firm, fixed, immovable, resolute, single-minded, staunch, steadfast, steady, sure, true, undeviating, unfaltering, unflagging, untiring, unwavering. **antonyms** irresolute, tentative.

unsympathetic *adj* antagonistic, antipathetic, callous, cold, compassionless, cruel, hard, hard as nails, hard-hearted, harsh, heartless, indifferent, inhuman, insensitive, soulless, stony, uncharitable, uncompassionate, unconcerned, unfeeling, unkind, unmoved, unpitying, unresponsive. **antonym** compassionate.

unsystematic *adj* chaotic, confused, desultory, disorderly, disorganised, haphazard, illogical, indiscriminate, irregular, jumbled, muddled, random, shambolic, slapdash, sloppy, uncoordinated, unmethodical, unorganised, unplanned, untidy. **antonym** logical.

untamed *adj* barbarous, fierce, haggard, savage, unbroken, undomesticated, unmellowed, untameable, wild. **antonyms** domesticated, tame.

untangle *v* disentangle, explain, extricate, resolve, solve, undo, unravel, unsnarl. **antonym** complicate.

untarnished *adj* bright, burnished, clean, glowing, immaculate, impeccable, intact, polished, pristine, pure, shining, spotless, stainless, unblemished, unimpeachable, unsoiled, unspoilt, unspotted, unstained, unsullied. **antonym** blemished.

untenable *adj* fallacious, flawed, illogical, indefensible, insupportable, rocky, shaky, unmaintainable, unreasonable, unsound, unsustainable. **antonyms** sound, tenable.

unthinkable *adj* absurd, illogical, implausible, impossible, improbable, inconceivable, incredible, insupportable, outrageous, preposterous, shocking, unbelievable, unheard-of, unimaginable, unlikely, unreasonable.

unthinking *adj* automatic, careless, heedless, impulsive, inadvertent, incautious, inconsiderate, indiscreet, insensitive, instinctive, mechanical, negligent, oblivious, rash, rude, selfish, senseless, tactless, thoughtless, unconscious, undiplomatic, unguarded, vacant, witless. **antonyms** conscious, deliberate, witting.

untidy *adj* bedraggled, chaotic, cluttered, dishevelled, disorderly, higgledy-piggledy, jumbled, littered, messy, muddled, raunchy, rumpled, scruffy, shambolic, slatternly, slipshod, sloppy, slovenly, topsy-turvy, unkempt, unsystematic. **antonym** systematic.

untie *v* free, loosen, release, unbind, undo, unfasten, unknot, unlace, unloose, unloosen, untether. **antonym** fasten.

untimely *adj* awkward, early, illtimed, inappropriate, inauspicious, inconvenient, inopportune, mistimed, premature, unfortunate, unseasonable, unsuitable. **antonyms** opportune, timely.

untold *adj* boundless, countless, hidden, incalculable, indescribable, inexhaustible, inexpressible, infinite, innumerable, measureless, myriad, numberless, private, secret, uncountable, uncounted, undisclosed, undreamed-of, unimaginable, unknown, unnumbered, unpublished, unreckoned, unrecounted, unrelated, unrevealed, unthinkable, unutterable.

untouched *adj* indifferent, intact, safe, unaffected, unaltered, unconcerned, undamaged, unharmed, unhurt, unimpaired, unimpressed, uninjured, unmoved, unscathed, unstirred. *antonyms* affected, impaired, moved.

untoward *adj* adverse, annoying, awkward, contrary, disastrous, ill-timed, improper, inappropriate, inauspicious, inconvenient, indecorous, inimical, inopportune, irritating, ominous, troublesome, unbecoming, unexpected, unfavourable, unfortunate, unlucky, unpropitious, unseemly, unsuitable, untimely, vexatious, worrying. *antonyms* auspicious, suitable.

untried *adj* experimental, exploratory, innovative, new, novel, unestablished, unproved, untested. *antonyms* proven, tested.

untroubled *adj* calm, composed, cool, impassive, peaceful, placid, serene, steady, tranquil, unconcerned, undisturbed, unexcited, unflappable, unflustered, unperturbed, unruffled, unstirred, unworried. *antonym* anxious.

untrue *adj* deceitful, deceptive, deviant, dishonest, disloyal, distorted, erroneous, faithless, fallacious, false, fraudulent, inaccurate, inauthentic, inconstant, incorrect, lying, mendacious, misleading, mistaken, perfidious, sham, specious, spurious, traitorous, treacherous, two-faced, unfaithful, untrustworthy, untruthful, wrong. *antonym* honest.

untrustworthy *adj* capricious, deceitful, devious, dishonest, disloyal, dubious, duplicitous, fair-weather, faithless, false, fickle, fly-by-night, shady, slippery, treacherous, tricky, two-faced, undependable, unfaithful, unreliable, unsafe, untrue, untrusty. *antonym* reliable.

untruth *n* deceit, deceitfulness, duplicity, fabrication, falsehood, falsification, falsism, falsity, fib, fiction, inexactitude, invention, lie, lying, mendacity, perjury, prevarication, story, tale, trick, truthlessness, untruthfulness, whopper.

untutored *adj* artless, ignorant, illiterate, inexperienced, inexpert, simple, uneducated, unlearned, unpractised, unrefined, unschooled, unsophisticated, untrained, unversed. *antonyms* educated, trained.

unused *adj* available, extra, fresh, idle, intact, left, left-over, new, pristine, remaining, unaccustomed, unconsumed, unemployed, unexploited, unfamiliar, untouched, unutilised.

unusual *adj* abnormal, anomalous, atypical, bizarre, curious, different, eccentric, exceptional, extraordinary, odd, phenomenal, queer, rare, remarkable, singular, strange, surprising, uncommon, unconventional, unexpected, unfamiliar, unwonted. *antonym* normal.

unutterable *adj* egregious, extreme, indescribable, ineffable, overwhelming, unimaginable, unspeakable.

unveil *v* bare, disclose, discover, divulge, expose, reveal, uncover, unfold, unshroud. *antonyms* cover, hide.

unwanted *adj* extra, otiose, outcast, rejected, superfluous, surplus, unasked, undesired, uninvited, unnecessary, unneeded, unrequired, unsolicited, unwelcome, useless. *antonyms* necessary, needed.

unwarranted *adj* baseless, gratuitous, groundless, indefensible, inexcusable, uncalled-for, unjust, unjustified, unprovoked, unreasonable, vain, wrong. *antonym* justifiable.

unwavering *adj* consistent, dedicated, determined, resolute, single-minded, staunch, steadfast, steady, sturdy, tenacious, undeviating, unfaltering, unflagging, unquestioning, unshakable, unshaken, unswerving, untiring. *antonym* fickle.

unwelcome *adj* disagreeable, distasteful, excluded, rejected, thankless, unacceptable, undesirable, uninvited, unpalatable, unpleasant, unpopular, unwanted, upsetting, worrying. *antonym* desirable.

unwell *adj* ailing, ill, indisposed, off-colour, poorly, sick, sickly, unhealthy. *antonyms* healthy.

unwholesome *adj* bad, corrupting, degrading, deleterious, demoralising, depraving, evil, harmful, immoral, insalubrious, insalutary, insanitary, junk, noxious, pale, pallid, pasty, perverting, poisonous, sickly, tainted, unhealthy, unhygienic, wan, wicked. *antonym* salubrious.

unwieldy *adj* awkward, bulky, burdensome, clumsy, cumbersome, gangling, hefty, hulking, inconvenient, massive, ponderous, ungainly, unhandy, unmanageable, weighty. *antonyms* dainty, neat, petite.

unwilling *adj* averse, disinclined, grudging, indisposed, loath, opposed, reluctant, resistant, slow, unenthusiastic. *antonym* enthusiastic.

unwind *v* calm down, disentangle, quieten down, relax, slacken, uncoil, undo, unravel, unreel, unroll, untwine, unwrap, wind down. *antonym* twist.

unwise *adj* foolhardy, foolish, ill-advised, ill-considered, ill-judged, impolitic, improvident, imprudent, inadvisable, indiscreet, inexpedient, injudicious, irresponsible, rash, reckless, senseless, short-sighted, silly, stupid, thoughtless, unintelligent. *antonym* prudent.

unwitting *adj* accidental, chance, ignorant, inadvertent, innocent, involuntary, unaware, unconscious, unintended, unintentional, unknowing, unmeant, unplanned, unsuspecting, unthinking. *antonyms* conscious, deliberate, knowing.

unworldly *adj* abstract, celestial, ethereal, extra-terrestrial, idealistic, impractical, inexperienced, innocent, metaphysical, naïve, otherworldly, religious, spiritual, transcendental, unearthly, unsophisticated, visionary. *antonyms* materialistic, practical.

unworthy *adj* base, contemptible, degrading, discreditable, disgraceful, dishonourable, disreputable, ignoble, improper, inappropriate, ineligible, inferior, shameful, unbecoming, unbefitting, undeserving, unfitting, unprofessional, unseemly, unsuitable, unsuited. *antonym* commendable.

unwritten *adj* accepted, conventional, customary, implicit, oral, recognised, tacit, traditional, understood, unformulated, unrecorded, verbal, vocal, word-of-mouth. *antonym* recorded.

unyielding *adj* adamant, determined, firm, hardline, immovable, implacable, inexorable, inflexible, intractable, intransigent, obdurate, obstinate, relentless, resolute, rigid, solid, staunch, steadfast, stubborn, tough, unbending, uncompromising, unrelenting, unwavering. *antonym* flexible.

up to one's eyes busy, engaged, inundated, overwhelmed, preoccupied, tied up. *antonyms* free, idle.

up to scratch acceptable, adequate,

capable, competent, OK, satisfactory, sufficient. *antonym* unsatisfactory.

up-and-coming ambitious, assertive, eager, enterprising, go-getting, promising, pushing.

upbeat *adj* bright, bullish, buoyant, cheerful, cheery, encouraging, favourable, forward-looking, heartening, hopeful, optimistic, positive, promising, rosy. *antonyms* down-beat, gloomy.

upbraid *v* admonish, berate, blame, carpet, castigate, censure, chide, condemn, criticise, dress down, jaw, lecture, rate, rebuke, reprimand, reproach, reprove, scold, take to task, tell off, tick off. *antonyms* commend, praise.

upbringing *n* breeding, care, cultivation, education, instruction, parenting, raising, rearing, tending, training.

upgrade *v* advance, ameliorate, better, elevate, enhance, gentrify, improve, promote, raise. *antonyms* degrade, downgrade.

upheaval *n* cataclysm, chaos, confusion, disorder, disruption, disturbance, earthquake, eruption, overthrow, revolution, shake-up, turmoil, upset.

uphill *adj* arduous, ascending, climbing, difficult, exhausting, gruelling, hard, laborious, mounting, punishing, rising, strenuous, taxing, tough, upward, wearisome. *antonyms* downhill, easy.

uphold *v* advocate, aid, back, champion, countenance, defend, encourage, endorse, fortify, hold to, justify, maintain, promote, stand by, stengthen, support, sustain, vindicate.

upkeep *n* care, conservation, expenditure, expenses, keep, maintenance, oncosts, operating costs, outgoing, outlay, overheads, preservation, repair, running, running costs, subsistence, support, sustenance. *antonym* neglect.

uplift *v* advance, ameliorate, better, boost, civilise, cultivate, edify, elate, elevate, enlighten, exalt, heave, hoist, improve, inspire, lift, raise, refine, upgrade.
n advancement, betterment, boost, cultivation, edification, enhancement, enlightenment, enrichment, improvement, lift, refinement.

upper *adj* elevated, eminent, exalted, greater, high, higher, important, loftier, senior, superior, top, topmost, uppermost. *antonyms* inferior, junior, lower.

upper hand advantage, ascendancy, control, dominance, domination, dominion, edge, mastery, superiority, supremacy, sway.

upper-class *adj* aristocratic, blue-blooded, educated, élite, exclusive, gentle, high-born, high-class, noble, patrician, swanky, top-drawer, tweedy, well-born, well-bred. **antonyms** humble, working-class.

uppermost *adj* chief, dominant, first, foremost, greatest, highest, leading, loftiest, main, paramount, predominant, pre-eminent, primary, principal, prominent, supreme, top, topmost, upmost. **antonyms** bottommost, lowest.

uppish *adj* affected, arrogant, big-headed, bumptious, cocky, conceited, hoity-toity, impertinent, overweening, presumptuous, self-important, snobbish, stuck-up, supercilious, swanky, toffee-nosed, uppity. **antonyms** diffident, unassertive.

upright *adj* bluff, conscientious, erect, ethical, faithful, good, high-minded, honest, honourable, incorruptible, just, noble, perpendicular, principled, righteous, straight, straightforward, true, trustworthy, unimpeachable, upstanding, vertical, virtuous. **antonyms** dishonest, flat, horizontal, prone, supine.

uprising *n* insurgence, insurgency, insurrection, mutiny, putsch, rebellion, revolt, revolution, rising, sedition, upheaval.

uproar *n* brawl, clamour, commotion, confusion, din, disorder, furore, hubbub, hullabaloo, hurly-burly, noise, outcry, pandemonium, racket, riot, ruckus, ruction, rumpus, tumult, turbulence, turmoil.

uproarious *adj* boisterous, clamorous, confused, convulsive, deafening, disorderly, gleeful, hilarious, hysterical, killing, loud, noisy, rib-tickling, riotous, rip-roaring, roistering, rollicking, rowdy, side-splitting, tempestuous, tumultuous, turbulent, unrestrained, wild. **antonym** sedate.

uproot *v* deracinate, destroy, disorient, displace, eliminate, eradicate, exile, exterminate, extirpate, grub up, remove, rip up, root out, weed out, wipe out.

upset *v* agitate, bother, capsize, change, conquer, defeat, destabilise, discompose, disconcert, dismay, disorder, disorganise, disquiet, distress, disturb, fluster, grieve, overcome, overset, overthrow, overturn, perturb, ruffle, shake, spill, spoil, tip, topple, trouble, unnerve, unsteady.

n agitation, bother, bug, complaint, defeat, disorder, disruption, disturbance, illness, indisposition, malady, reverse, shake-up, shock, sickness, surprise, trouble, upheaval, worry.

adj agitated, bothered, capsized, chaotic, choked, confused, disconcerted, dismayed, disordered, disquieted, distressed, disturbed, frantic, grieved, hurt, ill, messed up, muddled, overturned, overwrought, pained, poorly, queasy, ruffled, shattered, sick, spilled, toppled, topsy-turvy, troubled, tumbled, worried.

upshot *n* conclusion, consequence, culmination, end, event, finale, finish, issue, outcome, pay-off, result.

upside down at sixes and sevens, chaotic, confused, disordered, higgledy-piggledy, inverted, jumbled, muddled, overturned, topsy-turvy, upset, upturned, wrong side up. **antonym** shipshape.

upstanding *adj* erect, ethical, firm, good, hardy, healthy, hearty, honest, honourable, incorruptible, moral, principled, robust, stalwart, strong, sturdy, true, trustworthy, upright, vigorous. **antonyms** puny, untrustworthy.

upstart *n* arriviste, mushroom, nobody, nouveau riche, parvenu, social climber.

uptight *adj* anxious, edgy, hung-up, irritated, nervy, prickly, tense, uneasy. **antonyms** calm, cool, relaxed.

up-to-date *adj* all the rage, contemporary, current, fashionable, in, latest, modern, newest, now, popular, smart, stylish, swinging, trendy, up-to-the-minute, vogue, with it. **antonym** old-fashioned.

upturn *n* advancement, amelioration, boost, improvement, increase, recovery, revival, rise, upsurge, upswing. **antonyms** downturn, drop, setback.

urban *adj* built-up, city, civic, inner-city, metropolitan, municipal, town, urbanised. **antonyms** country, rural, rustic.

urbane *adj* civil, civilised, cosmopolitan, courteous, cultivated, cultured, debonair, easy, elegant, mannerly, polished, refined, smooth, sophisticated, suave, well-bred, well-mannered. **antonyms** gauche, uncouth.

urge *v* advise, advocate, beg, beseech, champion, compel, constrain, counsel, drive, emphasise, encourage, entreat, exhort, force, goad, hasten, hist, impel, implore, incite, induce, instigate, nag, plead, press, propel, push, recommend, solicit, spur, stimulate, support, underline, underscore. **antonyms** deter, dissuade.

n compulsion, desire, drive, eagerness, fancy, impulse, inclination, itch, libido, longing, wish, yearning, yen. **antonym** disinclination.

urgency *n* exigence, exigency, extremity, gravity, hurry, imperativeness, importance, importunity, necessity, need, pressure, seriousness, stress.

urgent *adj* clamorous, cogent, compelling, critical, crucial, eager, earnest, emergent, exigent, immediate, imperative, important, importunate, insistent, instant, intense, persistent, persuasive, pressing, top-priority.

urinate *v* ease oneself, leak, make water, micturate, pass water, pee, piddle, piss, relieve oneself, spend a penny, tinkle, wee, wee-wee.

usable *adj* available, current, exploitable, functional, operating, operational, practical, serviceable, utilisable, valid, working. **antonyms** unusable, useless.

usage *n* application, control, convention, custom, employment, etiquette, form, habit, handling, management, method, mode, operation, practice, procedure, protocol, régime, regulation, routine, rule, running, tradition, treatment, use, wont.

use *v* apply, bring, consume, employ, enjoy, exercise, exhaust, expend, exploit, handle, manipulate, misuse, operate, ply, practise, spend, treat, utilise, waste, wield, work.

n advantage, application, avail, benefit, call, cause, custom, employment, end, enjoyment, exercise, good, habit, handling, help, meaning, mileage, necessity, need, object, occasion, operation, point, practice, profit, purpose, reason, service, treatment, usage, usefulness, utility, value, way, wont, worth.

use up absorb, consume, deplete, devour, drain, eat into, exhaust, finish, fritter, sap, squander, swallow, waste.

used *adj* accustomed, cast-off, dog-eared, familiar, hand-me-down, nearly new, reach-me-down, second-hand, shop-soiled, soiled, worn. **antonyms** fresh, new, unused.

useful *adj* advantageous, all-purpose,

beneficial, convenient, effective, fruitful, general-purpose, handy, helpful, practical, productive, profitable, salutary, serviceable, valuable, worthwhile. **antonym** useless.

useless *adj* clapped-out, disadvantageous, effectless, feckless, fruitless, futile, hopeless, idle, impractical, incompetent, ineffective, ineffectual, inefficient, inept, naff, of no use, pointless, profitless, stupid, unavailing, unproductive, unworkable, vain, valueless, weak, worthless. **antonym** useful.

uselessness *n* futility, hopelessness, idleness, impracticality, incompetence, ineffectiveness, ineffectuality, ineptitude. **antonyms** effectiveness, usefulness.

usher *v* conduct, direct, escort, guide, lead, shepherd, steer.

usher in announce, herald, inaugurate, initiate, introduce, launch, precede, ring in.

usual *adj* accepted, accustomed, common, constant, conventional, customary, everyday, expected, familiar, fixed, general, habitual, normal, ordinary, recognised, regular, routine, standard, stock, typical, unexceptional, wonted. **antonyms** unheard-of, unusual.

usually *adv* as a rule, by and large, chiefly, commonly, customarily, generally, generally speaking, habitually, in the main, mainly, mostly, normally, on the whole, ordinarily, regularly, routinely, traditionally, typically. **antonym** exceptionally.

usurp *v* annex, appropriate, arrogate, assume, commandeer, seize, steal, take, take over, wrest.

utilise *v* adapt, appropriate, employ, exploit, make use of, put to use, resort to, take advantage of, turn to account, use.

utilitarian *adj* convenient, down-to-earth, effective, efficient, functional, lowly, practical, pragmatic, sensible, serviceable, unpretentious, useful. **antonyms** decorative, impractical.

utility *n* advantage, avail, benefit, convenience, efficacy, expedience, fitness, point, practicality, profit, service, use, usefulness, value. **antonym** inutility.

utmost *adj* extreme, farthest, final, first, greatest, highest, last, maximum, outermost, paramount, remotest, supreme, ultimate.

Utopian *adj* airy, chimerical, dream, Elysian, fanciful, fantastic, ideal, idealistic, illusory, imaginary, impractical, perfect, romantic, unworkable, visionary, wishful.

utter¹ *adj* absolute, arrant, complete, consummate, dead, downright, entire, out-and-out, perfect, sheer, stark, thorough, thoroughgoing, total, unmitigated, unqualified.

utter² *v* articulate, declare, deliver, divulge, enunciate, express, proclaim, promulgate, pronounce, publish, reveal, say, sound, speak, state, tell, verbalise, vocalise, voice.

utterance *n* announcement, articulation, comment, declaration, delivery, ejaculation, expression, gift of tongues, glossolalia, opinion, pronouncement, remark, speaking with tongues, speech, statement, verbalisation, vocalisation.

utterly *adv* absolutely, completely, dead, diametrically, entirely, extremely, fully, perfectly, thoroughly, totally, wholly.

U-turn *n* about-turn, backtrack, reversal, volte-face.

V

vacancy *n* accommodation, emptiness, gap, job, opening, opportunity, place, position, post, room, situation, space, void.

vacant *adj* absent, absent-minded, abstracted, available, blank, dreaming, dreamy, empty, expressionless, free, idle, inane, inattentive, incurious, thoughtless, to let, unemployed, unengaged, unfilled, unoccupied, untenanted, unthinking, vacuous, void. **antonyms** engaged, occupied.

vacate *v* abandon, depart, evacuate, leave, quit, withdraw.

vacillate *v* fluctuate, haver, hesitate, oscillate, shilly-shally, sway, swither, temporise, waver.

vacillation *n* fluctuation, hesitancy, hesitation, inconstancy, indecision, indecisiveness, irresolution, shilly-shallying, temporisation, unsteadiness, wavering.

vacuity *n* apathy, blankness, emptiness, inanity, incomprehension, nothingness, space, vacuum, void.

vacuous *adj* apathetic, blank, empty, idle, inane, stupid, uncomprehending, unfilled, unintelligent, vacant, void.

vacuum *n* chasm, emptiness, gap, nothingness, space, vacuity, void.

vagabond *n* beggar, bum, down-and-out, hobo, itinerant, migrant, nomad, outcast, rover, runabout, tramp, vagrant, wanderer, wayfarer.

vagrant *n* beggar, bum, hobo, itinerant, rolling stone, stroller, tramp, wanderer. *adj* footloose, homeless, itinerant, nomadic, roaming, rootless, roving, travelling, vagabond, wandering.

vague *adj* amorphous, blurred, dim, doubtful, evasive, fuzzy, generalised, hazy, ill-defined, imprecise, indefinite, indeterminate, indistinct, inexact, lax, loose, misty, nebulous, obscure, shadowy, uncertain, unclear, undefined, undetermined, unknown, unspecific, unspecified, woolly. **antonyms** certain, clear, definite.

vaguely *adv* absent-mindedly, dimly, faintly, imprecisely, inexactly, obscurely, slightly, vacantly.

vagueness *n* ambiguity, amorphousness, dimness, faintness, fuzziness, haziness, imprecision, inexactitude, looseness, obscurity, uncertainty, woolliness. **antonyms** clarity, precision.

vain *adj* abortive, affected, arrogant, baseless, bigheaded, conceited, egotistical, empty, fruitless, futile, groundless, hollow, idle, inflated, mindless, narcissistic, ostentatious, overweening, peacockish, pointless, pretentious, proud, purposeless, self-important, self-satisfied, senseless, stuck-up, swaggering, swollen-headed, time-wasting, trifling, trivial, unavailing, unimportant, unproductive, unprofitable, unsubstantial, useless, vainglorious, vaporous, worthless. **antonyms** modest, self-effacing.

valediction *n* adieu, farewell, godspeed, goodbye, leave-taking, send-off. **antonyms** greeting, welcome.

valetudinarian *adj* delicate, feeble, frail, hypochondriac, infirm, invalid, neurotic, sickly, weakly. **antonym** stoical.

valiant *adj* bold, brave, courageous, dauntless, doughty, fearless, gallant, heroic, indomitable, intrepid, plucky, redoubtable, stalwart, staunch, stout, stout-hearted, valorous, worthy. **antonym** cowardly.

valid *adj* approved, authentic, binding, bona fide, cogent, conclusive, convincing, efficacious, efficient, genuine, good, just, lawful, legal, legitimate, logical, official, potent, powerful, proper, rational, reliable, sound, substantial, telling, weighty, well-founded, well-grounded. **antonym** invalid.

validate *v* attest, authenticate, authorise, certify, confirm, corroborate, endorse, legalise, ratify, substantiate, underwrite.

validity *n* authority, cogency, force, foundation, grounds, justifiability, lawfulness, legality, legitimacy, logic, point, power, soundness, strength, substance, weight. **antonym** invalidity.

valley *n* coomb, cwm, dale, dell, den, depression, dingle, glen, gulch, hollow, strath, vale.

valorous *adj* bold, brave, courageous, dauntless, doughty, fearless, gallant, hardy, heroic, intrepid, lion-hearted, mettlesome, plucky, redoubtable, stalwart, valiant. **antonyms** cowardly, weak.

valour *n* boldness, bravery, courage, derring-do, doughtiness, fearlessness, fortitude, gallantry, hardiness, heroism, intrepidity, lion-heartedness, mettle, spirit. *antonyms* cowardice, weakness.

valuable *adj* advantageous, beneficial, blue-chip, cherished, costly, dear, esteemed, estimable, expensive, fruitful, handy, helpful, high-priced, important, invaluable, precious, prized, productive, profitable, serviceable, treasured, useful, valued, worthwhile, worthy. *antonyms* useless, valueless.

value *n* account, advantage, avail, benefit, cost, desirability, equivalent, good, help, importance, merit, price, profit, rate, significance, use, usefulness, utility, worth.
v account, appraise, appreciate, assess, cherish, compute, esteem, estimate, evaluate, hold dear, price, prize, rate, regard, respect, survey, treasure. *antonyms* disregard, neglect, undervalue.

valued *adj* beloved, cherished, dear, esteemed, highly regarded, loved, prized, respected, treasured.

values *n* ethics, morals, principles, standards.

vamoose *v* clear off, decamp, disappear, do a bunk, make oneself scarce, quit, scarper, scram, skedaddle, vanish.

vanish *v* dematerialise, depart, die out, disappear, disperse, dissolve, evanesce, evaporate, exit, fade, fizzle out, melt, peter out. *antonyms* appear, materialise.

vanity *n* affectation, airs, arrogance, bigheadedness, conceit, conceitedness, egotism, emptiness, frivolity, fruitlessness, futility, hollowness, idleness, inanity, narcissism, ostentation, peacockery, pointlessness, pretension, pride, self-admiration, self-conceit, self-love, self-satisfaction, swollen-headedness, triviality, unreality, uselessness, vainglory, worthlessness. *antonyms* modesty, worth.

vanquish *v* beat, confound, conquer, crush, defeat, humble, master, overcome, overpower, overwhelm, quell, reduce, repress, rout, subdue, subjugate, triumph over.

vapid *adj* banal, bland, bloodless, boring, colourless, dead, dull, flat, flavourless, insipid, lifeless, limp, stale, tame, tasteless, tedious, tiresome, trite, uninspiring, uninteresting, watery, weak, wishy-washy. *antonyms* interesting, vigorous.

vaporous *adj* chimerical, fanciful, flimsy, foggy, fumy, gaseous, insubstantial, misty, steamy, vain. *antonym* substantial.

vapour *n* breath, brume, damp, dampness, exhalation, fog, fumes, haze, miasma, mist, reek, smoke, steam.

variable *adj* capricious, chameleonic, changeable, fickle, fitful, flexible, fluctuating, inconstant, mercurial, moonish, mutable, protean, shifting, temperamental, unpredictable, unstable, unsteady, vacillating, varying, wavering. *antonym* invariable.

variance *n* difference, disagreement, discord, discrepancy, disharmony, dissension, dissent, divergence, division, inconsistency, quarrelling, strife, variation. *antonyms* agreement, harmony.

variant *adj* alternative, derived, deviant, different, divergent, exceptional, modified. *antonyms* normal, standard, usual.

variation *n* alteration, change, departure, deviation, difference, discrepancy, diversification, diversity, elaboration, inflection, innovation, modification, modulation, novelty, variety. *antonyms* monotony, similitude, uniformity.

varied *adj* assorted, different, diverse, heterogeneous, manifold, miscellaneous, mixed, motley, multifarious, sundry, various. *antonyms* similar, uniform.

variety *n* array, assortment, brand, breed, category, change, class, collection, difference, discrepancy, diversification, diversity, intermixture, kind, make, manifoldness, many-sidedness, medley, miscellany, mixture, multifariousness, multiplicity, order, pot-pourri, range, sort, species, strain, type, variation. *antonyms* monotony, similitude, uniformity.

various *adj* assorted, different, differing, disparate, distinct, divers, diverse, diversified, heterogeneous, many, many-sided, miscellaneous, multifarious, several, sundry, varied, variegated, varying.

vary *v* alter, alternate, change, depart, differ, disagree, diverge, diversify, fluctuate, inflect, intermix, modify, modulate, permutate, reorder, transform.

vast *adj* astronomical, boundless, capacious, colossal, enormous, extensive, far-flung, fathomless, gigantic, great, huge, illimitable, immeasurable, immense, limitless, mammoth, massive, measureless, monstrous, monumental, never-ending, prodigious, stupendous, sweeping, tremendous, unbounded, unlimited, voluminous, wide.

vault[1] v bound, clear, hurdle, jump, leap, leap-frog, spring.

vault[2] n arch, cavern, cellar, crypt, depository, mausoleum, repository, roof, span, strongroom, tomb, wine-cellar.

vaunt v blazon, boast, brag, crow, exult in, flaunt, parade, show off, trumpet. **antonyms** belittle, minimise.

veer v change, sheer, shift, swerve, tack, turn, wheel.

vegetate v degenerate, deteriorate, go to seed, idle, languish, moulder, rust, stagnate.

vehemence n animation, ardour, eagerness, earnestness, emphasis, energy, enthusiasm, fervency, fervour, fire, force, forcefulness, heat, impetuosity, intensity, keenness, passion, urgency, verve, vigour, violence, warmth, zeal. **antonym** indifference.

vehement adj animated, ardent, eager, earnest, emphatic, enthusiastic, fervent, fervid, fierce, forceful, forcible, heated, impassioned, impetuous, intense, passionate, powerful, strong, urgent, violent, zealous. **antonyms** apathetic, indifferent.

veil v cloak, conceal, cover, dim, disguise, dissemble, dissimulate, hide, mantle, mask, obscure, screen, shade, shadow, shield. **antonyms** expose, uncover.
n blind, cloak, cover, curtain, disguise, film, mask, screen, shade, shroud.

vein n blood vessel, course, current, frame of mind, hint, humour, mode, mood, note, seam, strain, stratum, streak, stripe, style, temper, tenor, thread, tone, trait.

velocity n celerity, fleetness, impetus, pace, quickness, rapidity, rate, speed, swiftness.

venal adj bent, bribable, buyable, corrupt, corruptible, mercenary, purchasable. **antonym** incorruptible.

veneer n appearance, coating, façade, front, gloss, guise, layer, mask, pretence, semblance, show, surface.

venerable adj aged, august, dignified, esteemed, grave, honoured, respected, revered, reverenced, reverend, sage, venerated, wise, worshipful.

venerate v adore, esteem, hallow, honour, respect, revere, reverence,

worship. **antonyms** anathematise, disregard, execrate.

veneration n adoration, awe, deference, devotion, esteem, respect, reverence, worship.

vengeance n avengement, reprisal, requital, retaliation, retribution, revenge, tit for tat. **antonym** forgiveness.

vengeful adj avenging, implacable, punitive, rancorous, relentless, retaliatory, retributive, revengeful, spiteful, unforgiving, vindictive. **antonym** forgiving.

venial adj excusable, forgivable, insignificant, minor, negligible, pardonable, slight, trifling, trivial. **antonyms** mortal, unforgivable, unpardonable.

venom n acrimony, bane, bitterness, gall, grudge, hate, hatred, ill-will, malevolence, malice, maliciousness, poison, rancour, spite, spitefulness, spleen, toxin, vindictiveness, virulence, virus.

venomous adj baleful, baneful, envenomed, hostile, malicious, malign, malignant, noxious, poison, poisonous, rancorous, savage, spiteful, toxic, vicious, vindictive, virulent, vitriolic.

vent n aperture, blowhole, duct, hole, opening, orifice, outlet, passage, split.
v air, discharge, emit, express, let fly, release, unloose, utter, voice.

ventilate v air, broadcast, debate, discuss, examine, expound, express. **antonym** suppress.

venture v advance, adventure, chance, dare, endanger, hazard, imperil, jeopardise, make bold, presume, put forward, risk, speculate, stake, suggest, take the liberty, volunteer, wager.
n adventure, chance, endeavour, enterprise, fling, gamble, hazard, operation, project, risk, speculation, undertaking.

venturesome adj adventurous, audacious, bold, courageous, daredevil, daring, dauntless, doughty, enterprising, fearless, intrepid, plucky, spirited. **antonyms** pusillanimous, unenterprising.

veracious adj accurate, credible, dependable, exact, factual, faithful, frank, genuine, honest, reliable, straightforward, true, trustworthy, truthful, veridical. **antonym** untruthful.

veracity n accuracy, candour, credibility, exactitude, frankness, honesty, integrity, precision, probity, rectitude, trustworthiness, truth, truthfulness, verity. **antonym** untruthfulness.

verbatim *adv* exactly, literally, precisely, to the letter, word for word.

verbose *adj* circumlocutory, diffuse, garrulous, long-winded, loquacious, periphrastic, phrasy, prolix, windy, wordy. **antonyms** economical, succinct.

verbosity *n* garrulity, long-windedness, loquaciousness, loquacity, prolixity, verbiage, windiness, wordiness. **antonyms** economy, succinctness.

verdant *adj* fresh, grassy, green, leafy, lush.

verdict *n* adjudication, assessment, conclusion, decision, finding, judgement, opinion, sentence.

verdure *n* foliage, grass, greenery, greenness, meadows, pasture, verdancy.

verge *n* border, boundary, brim, brink, edge, edging, extreme, limit, lip, margin, roadside, threshold.

verge on approach, border on, come close to, near.

verification *n* attestation, authentication, checking, confirmation, corroboration, proof, substantiation, validation.

verify *v* attest, authenticate, check, confirm, corroborate, prove, substantiate, support, testify, validate. **antonyms** discredit, invalidate.

verisimilitude *n* authenticity, colour, credibility, likeliness, plausibility, realism, resemblance, ring of truth, semblance. **antonym** implausibility.

verity *n* actuality, authenticity, factuality, soundness, truth, truthfulness, validity, veracity. **antonym** untruth.

vernacular *adj* colloquial, common, endemic, indigenous, informal, local, mother, native, popular, vulgar.
n argot, cant, dialect, idiom, jargon, language, lingo, parlance, patois, speech, tongue.

versatile *adj* adaptable, adjustable, all-round, flexible, functional, general-purpose, handy, many-sided, multifaceted, multipurpose, protean, resourceful, variable. **antonym** inflexible.

versed *adj* accomplished, acquainted, au fait, competent, conversant, experienced, familiar, knowledgeable, learned, practised, proficient, qualified, seasoned, skilled.

version *n* account, adaptation, design, form, interpretation, kind, model, paraphrase, portrayal, reading, rendering, rendition, style, translation, type, variant.

vertex *n* acme, apex, apogee, crown, culmination, extremity, height, peak, pinnacle, summit, top, zenith. **antonym** nadir.

vertical *adj* erect, on end, perpendicular, upright, upstanding. **antonym** horizontal.

vertigo *n* dizziness, giddiness, light-headedness.

verve *n* animation, brio, dash, élan, energy, enthusiasm, force, gusto, life, liveliness, pizzazz, punch, relish, sparkle, spirit, vigour, vim, vitality, vivacity, zeal, zip. **antonym** apathy.

very *adv* absolutely, acutely, awfully, decidedly, deeply, dogged, eminently, exceeding(ly), excessively, extremely, greatly, highly, jolly, noticeably, particularly, passing, rattling, really, remarkably, superlatively, surpassingly, terribly, truly, uncommonly, unusually, wonderfully. **antonyms** hardly, scarcely, slightly.
adj actual, appropriate, bare, exact, express, identical, mere, perfect, plain, precise, pure, real, same, selfsame, sheer, simple, unqualified, utter.

vestibule *n* anteroom, entrance, entrance-hall, foyer, hall, lobby, porch.

vestige *n* evidence, glimmer, hint, indication, print, relic, remainder, remains, remnant, residue, scrap, sign, suspicion, token, trace, track, whiff.

vet *v* appraise, audit, check, examine, inspect, investigate, review, scan, scrutinise, survey.

veteran *n* master, old hand, old soldier, old stager, old-timer, pastmaster, pro, trouper, war-horse. **antonyms** novice, recruit.
adj adept, battle-scarred, experienced, expert, long-serving, masterly, old, practised, professional, proficient, seasoned. **antonyms** inexperienced, raw.

veto *v* ban, blackball, disallow, forbid, interdict, kill, prohibit, reject, rule out, turn down. **antonyms** approve, sanction.
n ban, embargo, interdict, prohibition, rejection, thumbs down. **antonyms** approval, assent.

vex *v* afflict, aggravate, agitate, annoy, bother, bug, displease, distress, disturb, exasperate, fret, gall, get (to), harass, irritate, molest, needle, nettle, offend, peeve, perplex, pester, pique, plague, provoke, rile, spite, tease, torment, trouble, upset, worry. **antonym** soothe.

vexatious *adj* afflicting, aggravating, annoying, bothersome, burdensome, disagreeable, disappointing, distressing, doggone, exasperating, harassing, infuriating, irksome, irritating, nagging, pesky, provoking, teasing, tormenting, troublesome, trying, unpleasant, upsetting, worrisome, worrying. **antonyms** pleasant, soothing.

vexed *adj* afflicted, aggravated, agitated, annoyed, bedevilled, bored, bothered, confused, contested, controversial, deaved, displeased, disputed, distressed, disturbed, exasperated, harassed, irritated, miffed, moot, nettled, peeved, perplexed, provoked, put out, riled, ruffled, tormented, troubled, upset, worried.

viable *adj* achievable, applicable, feasible, operable, possible, practicable, usable, workable. **antonyms** impossible, unworkable.

vibes *n* ambience, atmosphere, aura, emotions, feel, feelings, reaction, response, vibrations.

vibrant *adj* alive, animated, bright, colourful, dynamic, electric, electrifying, jazzy, oscillating, palpitating, peppy, pulsating, quivering, responsive, sensitive, sparkling, spirited, trembling, vivacious, vivid.

vibrate *v* fluctuate, judder, oscillate, pendulate, pulsate, pulse, quiver, resonate, reverberate, shake, shiver, shudder, sway, swing, throb, tremble, undulate.

vicarious *adj* acting, commissioned, delegated, deputed, empathetic, indirect, second-hand, substituted, surrogate.

vice *n* bad habit, besetting sin, blemish, corruption, defect, degeneracy, depravity, evil, evil-doing, failing, fault, immorality, imperfection, iniquity, profligacy, shortcoming, sin, venality, weakness, wickedness. **antonym** virtue.

vicinity *n* area, district, environs, locality, neighbourhood, precincts, propinquity, proximity.

vicious *adj* abhorrent, atrocious, backbiting, bad, barbarous, bitchy, brutal, catty, corrupt, cruel, dangerous, debased, defamatory, depraved, diabolical, fiendish, foul, heinous, immoral, infamous, malicious, mean, monstrous, nasty, perverted, profligate, rancorous, savage, sinful, slanderous,

spiteful, unprincipled, venomous, vile, vindictive, violent, virulent, vitriolic, wicked, worthless, wrong. **antonyms** gentle, good, virtuous.

vicissitude *n* alteration, alternation, change, deviation, divergence, fluctuation, mutation, revolution, shift, turn, twist, variation.

victim *n* casualty, dupe, fall guy, fatality, innocent, mark, martyr, sacrifice, scapegoat, sitting target, sucker, sufferer.

victimise *v* bully, cheat, deceive, defraud, discriminate against, dupe, exploit, fool, gull, hoodwink, oppress, persecute, pick on, prey on, swindle, use.

victorious *adj* champion, conquering, first, prize-winning, successful, top, triumphant, unbeaten, winning. **antonyms** losing, unsuccessful.

victory *n* conquest, laurels, mastery, prize, subjugation, success, superiority, triumph, vanquishment, win. **antonyms** defeat, loss.

vie *v* compete, contend, contest, fight, rival, strive, struggle.

view *n* aspect, attitude, belief, contemplation, conviction, display, estimation, examination, feeling, glimpse, impression, inspection, judgement, landscape, look, notion, opinion, outlook, panorama, perception, perspective, picture, prospect, scan, scene, scrutiny, sentiment, sight, spectacle, survey, viewing, vision, vista. *v* behold, consider, contemplate, deem, examine, explore, eye, inspect, judge, observe, perceive, read, regard, scan, speculate, survey, watch, witness.

viewpoint *n* angle, attitude, feeling, opinion, perspective, position, slant, stance, standpoint.

vigil *n* lookout, sleeplessness, stake-out, wakefulness, watch.

vigilant *adj* alert, attentive, careful, cautious, circumspect, guarded, on one's guard, on one's toes, on the alert, on the lookout, sleepless, unsleeping, wakeful, watchful, wide-awake. **antonyms** careless, forgetful, lax, negligent.

vigorous *adj* active, brisk, dynamic, effective, efficient, energetic, enterprising, flourishing, forceful, forcible, full-blooded, hale, hardy, healthy, hearty, intense, lively, mettlesome, powerful, red-blooded, robust, sound, spanking, spirited, stout, strenuous, strong, virile, vital. **antonyms** feeble, lethargic, weak.

vigorously *adv* briskly, eagerly, energetically, forcefully, hard, heartily, powerfully, strenuously, strongly. *antonyms* feebly, weakly.

vigour *n* activity, animation, dash, dynamism, energy, force, forcefulness, gusto, health, liveliness, might, oomph, pep, potency, power, punch, robustness, snap, soundness, spirit, stamina, strength, verve, vim, virility, vitality, zip. *antonyms* impotence, sluggishness, weakness.

vile *adj* abject, appalling, bad, base, coarse, contemptible, corrupt, debased, degenerate, degrading, depraved, despicable, disgraceful, disgusting, evil, foul, horrid, humiliating, ignoble, impure, loathsome, low, mean, miserable, nasty, nauseating, nefarious, noxious, offensive, perverted, repellent, repugnant, repulsive, revolting, scabby, scandalous, shocking, sickening, sinful, ugly, vicious, vulgar, wicked, worthless, wretched.

vileness *n* baseness, coarseness, corruption, degeneracy, depravity, dreadfulness, enormity, evil, foulness, meanness, noxiousness, offensiveness, outrage, profanity, ugliness, wickedness.

vilification *n* abuse, aspersion, calumniation, calumny, criticism, defamation, denigration, disparagement, invective, mud-slinging, revilement, scurrility, vituperation.

vilify *v* abuse, asperse, bad-mouth, berate, calumniate, criticise, debase, decry, defame, denigrate, denounce, disparage, malign, revile, slander, smear, stigmatise, traduce, vituperate. *antonyms* adore, compliment, eulogise, glorify.

villain *n* anti-hero, baddy, blackguard, criminal, devil, evil-doer, heavy, knave, malefactor, miscreant, profligate, rapscallion, rascal, reprobate, rogue, scoundrel, wretch. *antonyms* angel, goody, hero, heroine.

villainous *adj* atrocious, bad, base, blackguardly, criminal, cruel, debased, degenerate, depraved, detestable, diabolical, disgraceful, evil, fiendish, hateful, heinous, ignoble, infamous, inhuman, malevolent, mean, nefarious, opprobrious, outrageous, sinful, terrible, vicious, vile, wicked. *antonyms* angelic, good, heroic.

vindicate *v* absolve, acquit, advocate, assert, clear, defend, establish, exculpate, excuse, exonerate, justify, maintain, rehabilitate, support, uphold, verify. *antonyms* accuse, convict.

vindication *n* apology, assertion, defence, exculpation, excuse, exoneration, extenuation, justification, maintenance, plea, rehabilitation, substantiation, support, verification. *antonyms* accusation, conviction.

vindictive *adj* implacable, malevolent, malicious, merciless, punitive, rancorous, relentless, resentful, retributive, revengeful, spiteful, unforgiving, unrelenting, vengeful, venomous. *antonyms* charitable, forgiving, merciful.

vintage *n* collection, crop, epoch, era, generation, harvest, origin, period, year. *adj* best, choice, classic, fine, mature, old, prime, quintessential, rare, ripe, select, superior, venerable, veteran.

violate *v* abuse, assault, befoul, break, contravene, debauch, defile, desecrate, dishonour, disobey, disregard, flout, infract, infringe, invade, outrage, pollute, profane, rape, ravish, transgress. *antonyms* obey, observe, uphold.

violation *n* abuse, breach, contravention, defilement, desecration, disruption, encroachment, infraction, infringement, offence, profanation, rapine, sacrilege, spoliation, transgression, trespass. *antonyms* obedience, observance.

violence *n* abandon, acuteness, bestiality, bloodshed, bloodthirstiness, boisterousness, brutality, conflict, cruelty, destructiveness, ferocity, fervour, fierceness, fighting, force, frenzy, fury, harshness, hostilities, intensity, murderousness, passion, power, roughness, savagery, severity, sharpness, storminess, terrorism, thuggery, tumult, turbulence, vehemence, wildness. *antonyms* passivity, peacefulness.

violent *adj* acute, agonising, berserk, biting, bloodthirsty, blustery, boisterous, brutal, cruel, destructive, devastating, excruciating, extreme, fiery, forceful, forcible, furious, harsh, headstrong, homicidal, hot-headed, impetuous, intemperate, intense, maddened, maniacal, murderous, outrageous, painful, passionate, powerful, raging, riotous, rough, ruinous, savage, severe, sharp, strong, tempestuous, tumultuous, turbulent, uncontrollable, ungovernable, unrestrained, vehement, vicious, wild. *antonyms* calm, gentle, moderate, passive, peaceful.

VIP *n* big cheese, big name, big noise, big shot, bigwig, celebrity, dignitary, heavyweight, lion, luminary, notable, personage, somebody, star. *antonyms* nobody, nonentity.

virago *n* battle-axe, dragon, fury, gorgon, harridan, hell-cat, scold, shrew, tartar, termagant, vixen.

virginal *adj* celibate, chaste, fresh, immaculate, maidenly, pristine, pure, spotless, stainless, uncorrupted, undefiled, undisturbed, untouched, vestal, virgin, white.

virile *adj* forceful, husky, lusty, macho, male, man-like, manly, masculine, potent, red-blooded, robust, rugged, strong, vigorous. *antonyms* effeminate, impotent, weak.

virility *n* huskiness, machismo, manhood, manliness, masculinity, potency, ruggedness, vigour. *antonyms* effeminacy, impotence, weakness.

virtual *adj* effective, essential, implicit, implied, indirect, potential, practical, tacit. *antonym* actual.

virtually *adv* almost, as good as, effectively, effectually, in effect, in essence, nearly, practically, to all intents and purposes.

virtue *n* advantage, asset, attribute, chastity, credit, excellence, goodness, high-mindedness, honour, incorrupt-ibility, innocence, integrity, justice, merit, morality, plus, probity, purity, quality, rectitude, redeeming feature, righteousness, strength, uprightness, virginity, worth, worthiness. *antonym* vice.

virtuosity *n* bravura, brilliance, éclat, expertise, finesse, finish, flair, mastery, panache, polish, skill, wizardry.

virtuoso *n* ace, artist, genius, maestro, magician, master, prodigy, whiz, wizard. *adj* bravura, brilliant, dazzling, expert, masterly, wizard.

virtuous *adj* blameless, celibate, chaste, clean-living, ethical, excellent, exemplary, good, high-principled, honest, honourable, incorruptible, innocent, irreproachable, moral, praiseworthy, pure, righteous, spotless, squeaky-clean, unimpeachable, upright, virginal, worthy. *antonyms* bad, dishonest, immoral, vicious, wicked.

virulence *n* acrimony, antagonism, bitterness, deadliness, harmfulness, hatréd, hostility, hurtfulness, infectious-ness, malevolence, malice, malignancy, poison, rancour, resentment, spite, spleen, toxicity, venom, viciousness, vindictiveness, vitriol.

virulent *adj* acrimonious, baneful, bitter, deadly, envenomed, hostile, infective, injurious, lethal, malevolent, malicious, malignant, noxious, pernicious, poisonous, rancorous, resentful, septic, spiteful, splenetic, toxic, venomous, vicious, vindictive, vitriolic.

viscous *adj* adhesive, clammy, gelatinous, gluey, glutinous, gooey, gummy, mucilaginous, mucous, sticky, syrupy, tacky, tenacious, thick, treacly, viscid. *antonyms* runny, thin, watery.

visible *adj* apparent, clear, conspicuous, detectable, discernible, discoverable, distinguishable, evident, manifest, noticeable, observable, obvious, open, palpable, patent, perceptible, plain, unconcealed, undisguised, unmistakable. *antonym* invisible.

vision *n* apparition, chimera, concept, conception, construct, daydream, delusion, discernment, dream, eyes, eyesight, fantasy, far-sightedness, foresight, ghost, hallucination, idea, ideal, illusion, image, imagination, insight, intuition, mirage, penetration, perception, phantasm, phantom, picture, prescience, revelation, seeing, sight, spectacle, spectre, view, wraith.

visionary *adj* chimerical, delusory, dreaming, dreamy, fanciful, fantastic, ideal, idealised, idealistic, illusory, imaginary, impractical, prophetic, quixotic, romantic, speculative, starry-eyed, unreal, unrealistic, unworkable, utopian.

n daydreamer, Don Quixote, dreamer, enthusiast, fantasist, idealist, mystic, prophet, rainbow-chaser, romantic, seer, theorist, utopian. *antonym* pragmatist.

visit *v* afflict, assail, attack, befall, call in, call on, drop in on, haunt, inspect, look in, look up, pop in, punish, see, smite, stay at, stay with, stop by, take in, trouble.

n call, excursion, sojourn, stay, stop.

visitation *n* appearance, bane, blight, calamity, cataclysm, catastrophe, disaster, examination, infliction, inspection, manifestation, ordeal, punishment, retribution, scourge, trial, visit.

vista *n* panorama, perspective, prospect, view.

visual *adj* discernible, observable, optic, optical, perceptible, visible.

visualise *v* conceive, envisage, imagine, picture.

vital *adj* alive, animate, animated, animating, basic, cardinal, critical, crucial, decisive, dynamic, energetic, essential, forceful, fundamental, generative, imperative, important, indispensable, invigorating, key, life-giving, life-or-death, live, lively, living, necessary, quickening, requisite, significant, spirited, urgent, vibrant, vigorous, vivacious, zestful. **antonyms** inessential, peripheral, unimportant.

vitality n animation, energy, exuberance, go, life, liveliness, lustiness, oomph, pep, robustness, sparkle, stamina, strength, vigour, vim, vivacity.

vitiate v blemish, blight, contaminate, corrupt, debase, defile, deprave, deteriorate, devalue, harm, impair, injure, invalidate, mar, nullify, pervert, pollute, ruin, spoil, sully, taint, undermine. **antonym** purify.

vitriolic adj acerbic, acid, bitchy, biting, bitter, caustic, destructive, envenomed, malicious, sardonic, scathing, venomous, vicious, virulent, withering.

vituperation n abuse, blame, castigation, censure, diatribe, fault-finding, flak, invective, objurgation, obloquy, rebuke, reprimand, reproach, revilement, scurrility, stick, vilification. **antonyms** acclaim, eulogy, praise.

vivacious adj animated, bubbling, bubbly, cheerful, chipper, ebullient, effervescent, frisky, frolicsome, gay, high-spirited, jolly, light-hearted, lively, merry, scintillating, sparkling, spirited, sportive, sprightly, vital. **antonym** languid.

vivacity n animation, brio, bubbliness, ebullience, effervescence, energy, friskiness, gaiety, high spirits, jollity, life, liveliness, pep, quickness, sparkle, spirit, sprightliness. **antonym** languor.

vivid adj active, animated, bright, brilliant, clear, colourful, distinct, dramatic, dynamic, energetic, expressive, flamboyant, glowing, graphic, highly-coloured, intense, lifelike, lively, memorable, powerful, quick, realistic, rich, sharp, spirited, stirring, striking, strong, telling, vibrant, vigorous. **antonyms** dull, lifeless.

vixen n bitch, fury, harpy, harridan, hell-cat, scold, shrew, spitfire, termagant, virago.

vocabulary n dictionary, glossary, idiom, language, lexicon, lexis, thesaurus, word-book, words.

vocal adj articulate, clamorous, eloquent, expressive, forthright, frank, free-spoken, noisy, oral, outspoken, plain-spoken, said, shrill, spoken, strident, uttered, vociferous, voiced. **antonyms** inarticulate, quiet.

vocation n business, calling, career, employment, job, métier, mission, niche, office, post, profession, pursuit, role, trade, work.

vociferous adj clamorous, loud, loud-mouthed, noisy, obstreperous, ranting, shouting, shrill, stentorian, strident, thundering, uproarious, vehement, vocal. **antonyms** quiet, silent.

vogue n acceptance, craze, currency, custom, day, fashion, fashionableness, favour, last word, mode, popularity, prevalence, style, the latest, the rage, the thing, trend, usage, use.
adj current, fashionable, in, now, popular, prevalent, stylish, trendy, up-to-the-minute, with it.

voice n agency, articulation, decision, expression, inflection, instrument, intonation, language, medium, mouthpiece, organ, part, say, sound, speech, spokesman, spokesperson, spokeswoman, tone, utterance, vehicle, view, vote, will, wish, words.
v air, articulate, assert, bruit, convey, declare, disclose, divulge, enunciate, express, say, speak of, utter, ventilate.

void adj bare, blank, cancelled, clear, dead, drained, emptied, empty, free, inane, ineffective, ineffectual, inoperative, invalid, null, unenforceable, unfilled, unoccupied, useless, vacant, vain, worthless. **antonyms** full, valid.
n blank, blankness, cavity, chasm, emptiness, gap, hiatus, hollow, lack, opening, space, vacuity, vacuum, want.
v abnegate, annul, cancel, defecate, discharge, drain, eject, elimate, emit, empty, evacuate, invalidate, nullify, rescind. **antonyms** fill, validate.

volatile adj changeable, erratic, explosive, fickle, flighty, hot-headed, hot-tempered, inconstant, lively, mercurial, temperamental, unsettled, unstable, unsteady, variable, volcanic. **antonyms** constant, steady.

volition n choice, choosing, determination, discretion, election, option, preference, purpose, resolution, taste, velleity, will.

volley n barrage, blast, bombardment, burst, discharge, explosion, hail, salvo, shower.

voluble adj articulate, fluent, forthcoming, garrulous, glib, loquacious, talkative. **antonym** pauciloquent.

volume n aggregate, amount, amplitude,

bigness, body, book, bulk, capacity, compass, dimensions, mass, part, publication, quantity, tome, total, treatise.

voluminous *adj* abounding, ample, big, billowing, bulky, capacious, cavernous, commodious, copious, full, large, massive, prolific, roomy, vast. *antonyms* scanty, slight.

voluntarily *adv* by choice, consciously, deliberately, freely, intentionally, of one's own accord, of one's own free will, on one's own initiative, purposely, spontaneously, willingly. *antonyms* involuntarily, unwillingly.

voluntary *adj* conscious, deliberate, discretional, free, gratuitous, honorary, intended, intentional, optional, purposeful, spontaneous, unconstrained, unforced, unpaid, volunteer, wilful, willing. *antonyms* compulsory, forced, involuntary, unwilling.

volunteer *v* advance, communicate, extend, offer, present, proffer, propose, put forward, step forward, suggest, tender.

voluptuous *adj* ample, buxom, curvaceous, enticing, erotic, hedonistic, licentious, luscious, pleasure-loving, provocative, seductive, self-indulgent, sensual, shapely. *antonym* ascetic.

vomit *v* barf, boak, boke, bring up, cat, chunder, disgorge, eject, emit, heave, puke, regurgitate, retch, sick up, spew out, spew up, throw up.

voracious *adj* acquisitive, avid, devouring, gluttonous, greedy, hungry, insatiable, omnivorous, prodigious, rapacious, ravening, ravenous, uncontrolled, unquenchable.

vortex *n* eddy, maelstrom, whirl, whirlpool, whirlwind.

vote *n* ballot, election, franchise, plebiscite, poll, referendum, show of hands, suffrage.
v ballot, choose, declare, elect, judge, opt, plump for, pronounce, propose, recommend, return, suggest.

voucher *n* certificate, check, coupon, ticket, token, warrant.

vouch for affirm, assert, asseverate, attest to, back, certify, confirm, endorse, guarantee, support, swear to, uphold.

vouchsafe *v* accord, bestow, cede, confer, deign, grant, impart, yield.

vow *v* affirm, consecrate, dedicate, devote, maintain, pledge, profess, promise, swear.
n oath, pledge, promise, troth.

vulgar *adj* blue, boorish, cheap and nasty, coarse, common, crude, dirty, flashy, gaudy, general, gross, ill-bred, impolite, improper, indecent, indecorous, indelicate, low, low-life, low-minded, naff, nasty, naughty, ordinary, plebby, plebeian, ribald, risqué, rude, suggestive, tacky, tasteless, tawdry, uncouth, unmannerly, unrefined, vernacular. *antonyms* correct, decent, elegant, noble, polite, refined.

vulgarity *n* coarseness, crudeness, crudity, dirtiness, gaudiness, grossness, indecency, indecorum, indelicacy, ribaldry, rudeness, suggestiveness, tastelessness, tawdriness. *antonyms* decency, politeness.

vulnerable *adj* accessible, assailable, defenceless, exposed, sensitive, susceptible, tender, thin-skinned, unprotected, weak, wide open. *antonyms* protected, strong.

W

wacky *adj* crazy, daft, eccentric, erratic, goofy, irrational, loony, loopy, nutty, odd, screwy, silly, unpredictable, wild, zany. *antonym* sensible.

wad *n* ball, block, bundle, chunk, hunk, mass, plug, roll.

waddle *v* rock, shuffle, sway, toddle, totter, wiggle, wobble.

waffle *v* fudge, jabber, prate, prattle, prevaricate, rabbit on, spout, witter on.
n gobbledegook, guff, jabber, nonsense, padding, prating, prattle, prolixity, verbiage, verbosity, wordiness.

waft *v* bear, carry, convey, drift, float, ride, transmit, transport.
n breath, breeze, current, draught, puff, scent, whiff.

wag *n* card, clown, comedian, comic, droll, fool, humorist, jester, joker, wit.

wage *n* allowance, compensation, earnings, emolument, fee, hire, pay, payment, recompense, remuneration, reward, salary, screw, stipend, wage-packet, wages.
v carry on, conduct, engage in, practise, prosecute, pursue, undertake.

wager *n* bet, flutter, gage, gamble, hazard, pledge, punt, speculation, stake, venture.
v bet, chance, gamble, hazard, lay, lay odds, pledge, punt, risk, speculate, stake, venture.

waggle *v* bobble, flutter, jiggle, oscillate, shake, wag, wave, wiggle, wobble.
n bobble, flutter, jiggle, oscillation, shake, wag, wave, wiggle, wobble.

wail *v* bemoan, complain, cry, deplore, grieve, howl, keen, lament, moan, weep, yowl.
n caterwaul, complaint, cry, grief, howl, lament, lamentation, moan, weeping, yowl.

wait *v* abide, dally, delay, hang fire, hesitate, hold back, hover, linger, loiter, mark time, pause, remain, rest, stay, tarry. *antonyms* depart, go, leave.
n delay, halt, hesitation, hiatus, hold-up, interval, pause, rest, stay.

waive *v* abandon, defer, disclaim, forgo, postpone, relinquish, remit, renounce, resign, surrender. *antonyms* claim, maintain.

waiver *n* abandonment, abdication, deferral, disclaimer, postponement, relinquishment, remission, renunciation, resignation, surrender.

wake¹ *v* activate, animate, arise, arouse, awake, awaken, bestir, enliven, excite, fire, galvanise, get up, kindle, provoke, quicken, rise, rouse, stimulate, stir. *antonyms* relax, sleep.
n death-watch, funeral, vigil, watch.

wake² *n* aftermath, backwash, path, rear, track, trail, train, wash, waves.

wakeful *adj* alert, alive, attentive, heedful, insomniac, observant, restless, sleepless, unblinking, unsleeping, vigilant, wary, watchful. *antonyms* inattentive, sleepy, unwary.

waken *v* activate, animate, arouse, awake, awaken, enliven, fire, galvanise, get up, ignite, kindle, quicken, rouse, stimulate, stir, whet.

walk *v* accompany, advance, amble, convoy, escort, go by Shanks's pony, hike, hoof it, march, move, pace, perambulate, plod, saunter, step, stride, stroll, take, traipse, tramp, tread, trek, trog, trudge.
n aisle, alley, avenue, carriage, constitutional, esplanade, footpath, gait, hike, lane, march, pace, path, pathway, pavement, perambulation, promenade, ramble, saunter, sidewalk, step, stride, stroll, trail, traipse, tramp, trek, trudge, turn.

walk of life activity, area, arena, calling, career, course, field, line, métier, profession, pursuit, sphere, trade, vocation.

walk-out *n* industrial action, protest, rebellion, revolt, stoppage, strike.

walk-over *n* child's play, cinch, doddle, picnic, piece of cake, pushover.

wallop *v* batter, beat, belt, best, buffet, clobber, crush, defeat, drub, hammer, hit, lambaste, lick, paste, pound, pummel, punch, rout, slug, smack, strike, swat, swipe, thrash, thump, thwack, trounce, vanquish, whack, worst.
n bash, belt, blow, hit, kick, punch, slug, smack, swat, swipe, thump, thwack, whack.

wallow *v* bask, delight, enjoy, glory, indulge, lie, lurch, luxuriate, relish, revel, roll, splash, stagger, stumble, tumble, wade, welter.

wan *adj* anaemic, ashen, bleak, bloodless, cadaverous, colourless, dim, discoloured, faint, feeble, ghastly, lurid, mournful, pale, pallid, pasty, sickly, waxen, weak, weary, whey-faced, white.

wander v aberrate, babble, cruise, depart, deviate, digress, divagate, diverge, drift, err, lapse, meander, mill around, peregrinate, ramble, range, rave, roam, rove, saunter, squander, straggle, stray, stroll, swerve, traipse, veer.

wanderer n drifter, gypsy, itinerant, nomad, rambler, rolling stone, rover, straggler, stray, stroller, traveller, vagabond, vagrant, voyager.

wandering adj aberrant, drifting, homeless, itinerant, migratory, nomadic, peregrinatory, peripatetic, rambling, rootless, roving, strolling, travelling, vagabond, vagrant, voyaging, wayfaring.

wane v abate, atrophy, contract, decline, decrease, dim, diminish, droop, drop, dwindle, ebb, fade, fail, lessen, shrink, sink, subside, taper off, weaken, wither. **antonyms** increase, wax.

n abatement, atrophy, contraction, decay, decline, decrease, diminution, drop, dwindling, ebb, fading, failure, fall, lessening, sinking, subsidence, tapering off, weakening. **antonym** increase.

wangle v arrange, contrive, engineer, fiddle, fix, manage, manipulate, manoeuvre, pull off, scheme, work.

want v call for, covet, crave, demand, desire, fancy, hanker after, hunger for, lack, long for, miss, need, pine for, require, thirst for, wish, yearn for, yen.

n absence, appetite, craving, dearth, default, deficiency, demand, desire, destitution, famine, fancy, hankering, hunger, indigence, insufficiency, lack, longing, necessity, need, neediness, paucity, pauperism, penury, poverty, privation, requirement, scantiness, scarcity, shortage, thirst, wish, yearning, yen. **antonyms** abundance, plenty, riches.

wanton adj abandoned, arbitrary, careless, coltish, cruel, dissipated, dissolute, evil, extravagant, fast, gratuitous, groundless, heedless, immoderate, immoral, intemperate, lavish, lecherous, lewd, libertine, libidinous, licentious, loose, lubricious, lustful, malevolent, malicious, motiveless, needless, outrageous, promiscuous, rakish, rash, reckless, senseless, shameless, spiteful, uncalled-for, unchaste, unjustifiable, unjustified, unprovoked, unrestrained, vicious, wicked, wild, wilful.

war n battle, bloodshed, combat, conflict, contention, contest, enmity, fighting, hostilities, hostility, strife, struggle, warfare. **antonym** peace.

v battle, clash, combat, contend, contest, fight, skirmish, strive, struggle, take up arms, wage war.

war cry battle cry, rallying-cry, slogan, war-song, war-whoop, watchword.

warble v chirp, chirrup, quaver, sing, trill, twitter, yodel.

n call, chirp, chirrup, cry, quaver, song, trill, twitter.

ward n apartment, area, care, charge, custody, dependant, district, division, guardianship, keeping, minor, precinct, protection, pupil, quarter, room, safe-keeping, vigil, watch, zone.

ward off avert, avoid, beat off, block, deflect, disperse, evade, fend off, forestall, parry, repel, repulse, stave off, thwart, turn aside, turn away.

wares n commodities, goods, lines, manufactures, merchandise, produce, products, stock, stuff.

warfare n arms, battle, blows, combat, conflict, contention, contest, discord, fighting, hostilities, passage of arms, strife, struggle, war. **antonyms** harmony, peace.

warily adv apprehensively, cagily, carefully, cautiously, charily, circumspectly, distrustfully, gingerly, guardedly, hesitantly, suspiciously, uneasily, vigilantly, watchfully. **antonyms** heedlessly, recklessly, thoughtlessly, unwarily.

warlike adj aggressive, antagonistic, bellicose, belligerent, bloodthirsty, combative, hawkish, hostile, inimical, jingoistic, martial, militaristic, military, pugnacious, sabre-rattling, truculent, unfriendly. **antonym** peaceable.

warm adj affable, affectionate, amiable, amorous, animated, ardent, balmy, cheerful, cordial, dangerous, disagreeable, earnest, effusive, emotional, enthusiastic, excited, fervent, friendly, genial, glowing, happy, hazardous, hearty, heated, hospitable, impassioned, intense, irascible, irritable, keen, kindly, lively, loving, lukewarm, passionate, pleasant, quick, sensitive, short, spirited, stormy, sunny, tender, tepid, thermal, touchy, tricky, uncomfortable, unpleasant, vehement, vigorous, violent, zealous. **antonyms** cool, indifferent, unfriendly.

v animate, awaken, excite, heat, heat up, interest, melt, mull, put some life into, reheat, rouse, stimulate, stir, thaw, turn on. **antonym** cool.

warm-hearted *adj* affectionate, ardent, compassionate, cordial, generous, genial, kind-hearted, kindly, loving, sympathetic, tender, tender-hearted. **antonyms** cold, unsympathetic.

warmth *n* affability, affection, amorousness, animation, ardour, cheerfulness, cordiality, eagerness, earnestness, effusiveness, enthusiasm, excitement, fervency, fervour, fire, happiness, heartiness, heat, hospitableness, intensity, kindliness, love, passion, spirit, tenderness, vehemence, vigour, violence, zeal, zest. **antonyms** coldness, coolness, unfriendliness.

warn *v* admonish, advise, alert, apprise, caution, counsel, forewarn, inform, notify, put on one's guard, tip off.

warning *n* admonishment, admonition, advance notice, advice, alarm, alert, augury, caution, caveat, forenotice, foretoken, forewarning, hint, lesson, notice, notification, omen, premonition, presage, sign, signal, siren, threat, tip, tip-off, token, word, word to the wise.
adj admonitory, cautionary, ominous, premonitory, threatening.

warp *v* bend, contort, deform, deviate, distort, kink, misshape, pervert, twist. **antonym** straighten.
n bend, bent, bias, contortion, deformation, deviation, distortion, irregularity, kink, perversion, quirk, turn, twist.

warrant *n* authorisation, authority, commission, guarantee, licence, permission, permit, pledge, sanction, security, voucher, warranty.
v affirm, answer for, approve, assure, attest, authorise, be bound, call for, certify, commission, declare, demand, empower, entitle, excuse, guarantee, justify, license, necessitate, permit, pledge, require, sanction, secure, underwrite, uphold, vouch for.

warrantable *adj* accountable, allowable, defensible, excusable, justifiable, lawful, legal, necessary, permissible, proper, reasonable, right. **antonyms** indefensible, unjustifiable, unwarrantable.

warranty *n* assurance, authorisation, bond, certificate, contract, covenant, guarantee, justification, pledge.

warring *adj* at daggers drawn, at war, belligerent, combatant, conflicting, contending, embattled, fighting, hostile, opposed, opposing.

wary *adj* alert, apprehensive, attentive, cagey, careful, cautious, chary, circumspect, distrustful, guarded, hawk-eyed, heedful, on one's guard, on the lookout, prudent, suspicious, vigilant, watchful, wide-awake. **antonyms** careless, foolhardy, heedless, reckless, unwary.

wash¹ *v* bath, bathe, clean, cleanse, launder, moisten, rinse, scrub, shampoo, shower, sluice, swill, wet.
n a lick and a promise, ablution, bath, bathe, cleaning, cleansing, coat, coating, ebb and flow, film, flow, laundering, layer, overlay, rinse, roll, screen, scrub, shampoo, shower, souse, stain, suffusion, surge, sweep, swell, washing, wave.

wash one's hands abandon, abdicate responsibility, give up on, have nothing to do with, leave to one's own devices.

wash² *v* bear examination, bear scrutiny, carry weight, hold up, hold water, pass muster, stand up, stick.

washed-out *adj* all in, blanched, bleached, colourless, dead on one's feet, dog-tired, drained, drawn, exhausted, faded, fatigued, flat, haggard, knackered, lacklustre, pale, pallid, peelie-wally, spent, tired-out, wan, weary, worn-out.

wash-out *n* disappointment, disaster, failure, fiasco, flop, lead balloon, lemon, loser, mess. **antonyms** success, triumph, winner.

waste *v* atrophy, blow, consume, corrode, crumble, debilitate, decay, decline, deplete, despoil, destroy, devastate, disable, dissipate, drain, dwindle, eat away, ebb, emaciate, enfeeble, exhaust, fade, fritter away, gnaw, lavish, lay waste, misspend, misuse, perish, pillage, prodigalise, rape, ravage, raze, ruin, sack, sink, spend, spoil, squander, throw away, undermine, wane, wear out, wither.
n debris, desert, desolation, destruction, devastation, dissipation, dregs, dross, effluent, expenditure, extravagance, garbage, havoc, leavings, leftovers, litter, loss, misapplication, misuse, offal, prodigality, ravage, refuse, rubbish, ruin, scrap, slops, solitude, spoilage, squandering, sweepings, trash, void, wastefulness, wasteland, wild, wilderness.
adj bare, barren, desolate, devastated, dismal, dreary, empty, extra, left-over, superfluous, supernumerary,

uncultivated, uninhabited, unproductive, unprofitable, unused, unwanted, useless, wild, worthless.

wasted *adj* abandoned, atrophied, cadaverous, debauched, depleted, dissipated, dissolute, emaciated, exhausted, finished, gaunt, profligate, shrivelled, shrunken, spent, wanton, war-worn, washed-out, withered. *antonyms* healthy, robust.

wasteful *adj* extravagant, improvident, lavish, prodigal, profligate, ruinous, spendthrift, thriftless, uneconomical, unthrifty. *antonyms* economical, frugal, thrifty.

waster *n* good-for-nothing, idler, layabout, loafer, lounger, malingerer, ne'er-do-well, profligate, shirker, skiver, spendthrift, wastrel. *antonym* worker.

watch *v* attend, contemplate, eye, gaze at, guard, keep, keep an eye open, look, look after, look at, look on, look out, mark, mind, note, observe, ogle, pay attention, peer at, protect, regard, see, spectate, stare at, superintend, take care of, take heed, tend, view, wait.

n alertness, attention, eye, heed, inspection, lookout, notice, observation, supervision, surveillance, vigil, vigilance, wake, watchfulness.

watch out have a care, keep a weather eye open, keep one's eyes open, keep one's eyes peeled, keep one's eyes skinned, mind oneself.

watch over defend, guard, keep an eye on, look after, mind, preserve, protect, shelter, shield, stand guard over, tend.

watchful *adj* alert, attentive, cautious, circumspect, guarded, heedful, observant, on one's guard, on the lookout, on the watch, suspicious, vigilant, wary, wide awake. *antonym* inattentive.

watchfulness *n* alertness, attention, attentiveness, caution, cautiousness, circumspection, heedfulness, suspicion, suspiciousness, vigilance, wariness. *antonym* inattention.

watchword *n* battle-cry, buzz-word, byword, catchphrase, catchword, magic word, maxim, motto, password, rallying-cry, signal, slogan.

water *n* Adam's ale, Adam's wine, aqua, lake, ocean, rain, river, saliva, sea, stream, sweat, tears, urine.

v adulterate, damp, dampen, dilute, douse, drench, drink, flood, hose, irrigate, moisten, soak, souse, spray, sprinkle, thin, water down, weaken. *antonyms* dry out, purify, strengthen.

water down adulterate, dilute, mitigate, mix, qualify, soften, thin, tone down, water, weaken. *antonyms* purify, strengthen.

waterproof *adj* damp-proof, impermeable, impervious, proofed, rubberised, water-repellent, water-resistant. *antonym* leaky.

watertight *adj* airtight, firm, flawless, foolproof, hermetic, impregnable, incontrovertible, sound, unassailable, waterproof. *antonyms* leaky, unsound.

watery *adj* adulterated, aqueous, damp, dilute, diluted, flavourless, fluid, humid, insipid, liquid, marshy, moist, poor, rheumy, runny, soggy, squelchy, tasteless, tear-filled, tearful, thin, washy, watered-down, waterish, weak, weepy, wet, wishy-washy. *antonyms* solid, strong.

wave¹ *v* beckon, brandish, direct, flap, flourish, flutter, gesticulate, gesture, indicate, oscillate, quiver, ripple, shake, sign, signal, stir, sway, swing, undulate, waft, wag, waver, weave, wield.

wave² *n* billow, breaker, current, drift, flood, ground swell, movement, outbreak, rash, ripple, roller, rush, stream, surge, sweep, swell, tendency, tidal wave, trend, undulation, unevenness, upsurge, white horse.

waver *v* blow hot and cold, dither, falter, flicker, fluctuate, haver, hesitate, hum and haw, quiver, reel, rock, seesaw, shake, shilly-shally, sway, swither, totter, tremble, undulate, vacillate, vary, waffle, wave, weave, wobble. *antonyms* decide, stand.

wavering *adj* dithering, dithery, doubtful, doubting, havering, hesitant, in two minds, shilly-shallying. *antonym* determined.

wavy *adj* curly, curvy, ridged, ridgy, rippled, ripply, sinuous, undulated, winding, wrinkled, zigzag. *antonyms* flat, smooth.

wax *v* become, develop, dilate, enlarge, expand, fill out, grow, increase, magnify, mount, rise, swell. *antonym* wane.

waxen *adj* anaemic, ashen, bloodless, colourless, ghastly, livid, pale, pallid, wan, white, whitish. *antonym* ruddy.

way *n* access, advance, aim, ambition, approach, aspect, avenue, channel, characteristic, choice, circumstance, condition, conduct, course, custom, demand, desire, detail, direction, distance, elbow-room, fashion, feature, fettle, gate, goal, habit, headway, highway, idiosyncrasy, journey, lane, length, manner, march, means, method, mode, movement, nature, opening, particular, passage, path, pathway, personality, plan, pleasure, point, practice, procedure, process, progress, respect, road, room, route, scheme, sense, shape, situation, space, state, status, street, stretch, style, system, technique, thoroughfare, track, trail, trait, usage, will, wish, wont.

wayfarer *n* bird of passage, globetrotter, gypsy, itinerant, journeyer, nomad, rover, traveller, trekker, voyager, walker, wanderer. *antonyms* resident, stay-at-home.

waylay *v* accost, ambush, attack, buttonhole, catch, hold up, intercept, lie in wait for, seize, set upon, surprise.

way-out *adj* advanced, amazing, avant-garde, bizarre, crazy, eccentric, excellent, experimental, fantastic, far-out, freaky, great, marvellous, off-beat, outlandish, progressive, satisfying, tremendous, unconventional, unorthodox, unusual, weird, wild, wonderful. *antonym* ordinary.

wayward *adj* capricious, changeable, contrary, disobedient, erratic, fickle, flighty, headstrong, inconstant, incorrigible, insubordinate, intractable, mulish, obdurate, obstinate, perverse, rebellious, refractory, self-willed, stubborn, undependable, ungovernable, unmanageable, unpredictable, unruly, uppity, wilful. *antonyms* complaisant, good-natured.

weak *adj* anaemic, cowardly, debilitated, decrepit, defenceless, deficient, delicate, diluted, dull, effete, enervated, exhausted, exposed, faint, faulty, feeble, fibreless, flimsy, fragile, frail, helpless, hollow, imperceptible, impotent, inadequate, inconclusive, indecisive, ineffective, ineffectual, infirm, insipid, invalid, irresolute, lacking, lame, languid, low, milk-and-water, muffled, namby-pamby, pathetic, poor, powerless, puny, quiet, runny, shaky, shallow, sickly, slight, small, soft, spent, spineless, substandard, tasteless, tender, thin, timorous, toothless, unconvincing, under-strength, unguarded, unprotected, unresisting, unsafe, unsatisfactory, unsound, unsteady, unstressed, untenable, vulnerable, wanting, wasted,

watery, weak-hearted, weak-kneed, weakly, weak-minded, weak-spirited, wishy-washy. *antonym* strong.

weaken *v* abate, adulterate, craze, cut, debase, debilitate, depress, dilute, diminish, droop, dwindle, ease up, emasculate, enervate, enfeeble, fade, fail, flag, give way, impair, invalidate, lessen, lower, mitigate, moderate, reduce, sap, soften up, temper, thin, tire, undermine, wane, water down. *antonym* strengthen.

weakness *n* Achilles' heel, blemish, debility, decrepitude, defect, deficiency, enervation, enfeeblement, failing, faintness, fault, feebleness, flaw, foible, fondness, fragility, frailty, imperfection, impotence, inclination, infirmity, irresolution, lack, liking, passion, penchant, powerlessness, predilection, proclivity, proneness, shortcoming, soft spot, soft underbelly, underbelly, vulnerability, weakpoint, weediness. *antonyms* dislike, strength.

weak-willed *adj* faint-hearted, pliable, pusillanimous, spineless, submissive, weak-hearted, weak-kneed, weak-minded. *antonym* strong-willed.

wealth *n* abundance, affluence, assets, bounty, capital, cash, copiousness, cornucopia, estate, fortune, fullness, funds, golden calf, goods, lucre, mammon, means, money, opulence, plenitude, plenty, possessions, profusion, property, prosperity, resources, riches, richness, store, substance. *antonym* poverty.

wealthy *adj* affluent, comfortable, easy, filthy rich, flush, living in clover, loaded, moneyed, opulent, prosperous, rich, rolling in it, well-heeled, well-off, well-to-do. *antonym* poor.

wear *v* abrade, accept, allow, annoy, bear, bear up, believe, brook, carry, consume, corrode, countenance, deteriorate, display, don, drain, dress in, endure, enervate, erode, exasperate, exhibit, fall for, fatigue, fly, fray, grind, harass, have on, hold up, irk, last, permit, pester, put on, put up with, rub, show, sport, stand for, stand up, stomach, swallow, take, tax, tolerate, undermine, use, vex, waste, weaken, weary.

n abrasion, apparel, attire, attrition, clothes, corrosion, costume, damage, depreciation, deterioration, dress, durability, employment, erosion, friction, garb, garments, gear, habit, mileage, outfit, service, things, use, usefulness, utility, wear and tear.

wear down abrade, chip away at, consume, corrode, diminish, erode, grind down, lessen, macerate, overcome, reduce, rub away, undermine.

wear off abate, abrade, decrease, diminish, disappear, dwindle, ebb, efface, fade, lessen, peter out, subside, wane, weaken. **antonym** increase.

wear out consume, deteriorate, enervate, erode, exhaust, fag out, fatigue, fray, impair, knacker, prostrate, rub through, sap, tire (out), use up, wear through, weary. **antonyms** refresh, replenish.

weariness n drowsiness, enervation, exhaustion, fatigue, languor, lassitude, lethargy, listlessness, prostration, sleepiness, tiredness. **antonym** freshness.

wearing adj abrasive, exasperating, exhausting, fatiguing, irksome, oppressive, taxing, tiresome, tiring, trying. **antonym** refreshing.

weary adj all in, arduous, beat, bored, browned-off, dead beat, dead on one's feet, discontented, dog-tired, drained, drooping, drowsy, enervated, exhausted, fagged, fatigued, fed up, flagging, impatient, indifferent, irksome, jaded, knackered, laborious, sick, sick and tired, sleepy, spent, taxing, tired, tiresome, tiring, wayworn, wearied, wearing, whacked, worn out. **antonyms** excited, fresh, lively.

v annoy, bore, bug, burden, debilitate, drain, droop, enervate, exasperate, fade, fag, fail, fatigue, irk, irritate, jade, plague, sap, sicken, tax, tire, tire out, wear out.

wearying adj exhausting, fatiguing, taxing, tiring, trying, wearing, wearisome. **antonym** refreshing.

weather n climate, conditions, rainfall, temperature.

v brave, come through, endure, expose, harden, live through, overcome, pull through, resist, ride out, rise above, season, stand, stick out, suffer, surmount, survive, toughen, weather out, withstand. **antonym** succumb.

weave v blend, braid, build, construct, contrive, create, criss-cross, entwine, fabricate, fuse, incorporate, intercross, interlace, intermingle, intertwine, introduce, knit, make, mat, merge, plait, put together, spin, twist, unite, wind, zigzag.

web n interlacing, lattice, mesh, meshwork, net, netting, network, screen, snare, tangle, texture, trap, weave, webbing.

wed v ally, blend, coalesce, combine, dedicate, espouse, fuse, get hitched, interweave, join, jump the broomstick, link, marry, merge, splice, tie the knot, unify, unite, yoke. **antonym** divorce.

wedge n block, chock, chunk, lump, wodge.

v block, cram, crowd, force, jam, lodge, pack, push, ram, squeeze, stuff, thrust. **antonyms** dislodge, space out, take out.

wee adj diminutive, insignificant, itsy-bitsy, Lilliputian, little, microscopic, midget, miniature, minuscule, minute, negligible, small, teeny, teeny-weeny, tiny, weeny. **antonym** large.

weed v hoe.

weed out eliminate, eradicate, extirpate, get rid of, purge, remove, root out. **antonyms** add, fix, infiltrate.

weedy adj feeble, frail, ineffectual, insipid, puny, skinny, thin, undersized, ungainly, weak, weak-kneed, wet, wimpish. **antonym** strong.

weep v bemoan, blub, blubber, boo-hoo, bubble, complain, cry, drip, exude, greet, keen, lament, leak, moan, mourn, ooze, pour forth, pour out, rain, snivel, sob, whimper, whinge. **antonym** rejoice.

n blub, bubble, cry, greet, lament, moan, snivel, sob.

weigh v bear down, burden, carry weight, consider, contemplate, count, deliberate, evaluate, examine, give thought to, impress, matter, meditate on, mull over, oppress, ponder, prey, reflect on, study, tell, think over. **antonyms** cut no ice, hearten.

weigh down afflict, bear down, burden, depress, get down, load, oppress, overburden, overload, press down, trouble, weigh upon, worry. **antonyms** hearten, lighten, refresh.

weigh up assess, chew over, cogitate, consider, contemplate, deliberate, discuss, examine, mull over, perpend, ponder, ruminate on, think over.

weight n authority, ballast, burden, clout, consequence, consideration, efficacy, emphasis, force, gravity, heaviness, heft, impact, import, importance, impressiveness, influence, load, mass, millstone, moment, onus, oppression, persuasiveness, poundage, power, preponderance, pressure, significance, strain, substance, tonnage, value. *antonym* lightness.

v ballast, bias, burden, charge, encumber, freight, handicap, hold down, impede, keep down, load, oppress, overburden, slant, unbalance, weigh down. *antonym* lighten.

weighty *adj* backbreaking, burdensome, consequential, considerable, critical, crucial, crushing, cumbersome, demanding, dense, difficult, exacting, forcible, grave, heavy, hefty, important, leading, massive, momentous, onerous, oppressive, ponderous, portentous, respected, revered, serious, significant, solemn, substantial, taxing, worrisome, worrying. *antonyms* trivial, unimportant.

weird *adj* bizarre, creepy, eerie, freakish, ghostly, grotesque, mysterious, odd, outlandish, queer, spooky, strange, supernatural, uncanny, unearthly, unnatural, witching. *antonym* normal.

weirdo *n* crackpot, crank, eccentric, freak, fruitcake, loony, nut, nutcase, nutter, oddball, queer fish.

welcome *adj* able, acceptable, accepted, agreeable, allowed, appreciated, delightful, desirable, entitled, free, gratifying, permitted, pleasant, pleasing, refreshing. *antonym* unwelcome.

n acceptance, greeting, hospitality, reception, red carpet, salaam, salutation.

v accept, approve of, embrace, greet, hail, meet, receive, roll out the red carpet for. *antonyms* reject, snub.

weld *v* bind, bond, cement, connect, fuse, join, link, seal, solder, unite. *antonym* separate.

n bond, joint, seal, seam.

welfare *n* advantage, benefit, good, happiness, health, interest, profit, prosperity, success, well-being. *antonym* harm.

well *adv* ably, abundantly, accurately, adeptly, adequately, admirably, agreeably, amply, approvingly, attentively, capitally, carefully, clearly, closely, comfortably, completely, conscientiously, considerably, correctly, deeply, easily, effectively, efficiently, expertly, fairly, famously, favourably, fittingly, flourishingly, fully, glowingly, graciously, greatly, happily, heartily, highly, intimately, justly, kindly, nicely, personally, pleasantly, possibly, proficiently, profoundly, properly, prosperously, readily, rightly, satisfactorily, skilfully, smoothly, splendidly,

substantially, successfully, sufficiently, suitably, thoroughly, warmly. *antonym* badly.

adj A1, able-bodied, advisable, agreeable, bright, fine, fit, fitting, flourishing, fortunate, good, great, hale, happy, healthy, hearty, in fine fettle, in good health, lucky, on the top of the world, pleasing, profitable, proper, prudent, right, robust, satisfactory, sound, strong, thriving, up to par, useful. *antonyms* bad, ill.

well-balanced *adj* graceful, harmonious, judicious, level-headed, nutritious, proportional, rational, reasonable, sane, sensible, sober, sound, symmetrical, together, well-adjusted, well-proportioned. *antonym* unbalanced.

well-being *n* comfort, contentment, good, happiness, prosperity, welfare. *antonyms* discomfort, harm.

well-bred *adj* aristocratic, blue-blooded, civil, courteous, courtly, cultivated, cultured, gallant, genteel, gentle, gentlemanly, ladylike, mannerly, noble, patrician, polished, polite, refined, titled, upper-crust, urbane, well-brought-up, well-mannered. *antonym* ill-bred.

well-deserved *adj* appropriate, condign, deserved, due, just, justified, meet, merited, rightful. *antonym* undeserved.

well-disposed *adj* agreeable, amicable, favourable, friendly, sympathetic, well-arranged, well-minded, well-placed. *antonym* ill-disposed.

well-dressed *adj* dapper, natty, neat, smart, spruce, tidy, trim, well-groomed. *antonym* scruffy.

well-known *adj* celebrated, famed, familiar, famous, illustrious, notable, noted, popular, renowned. *antonym* unknown.

well-off *adj* affluent, comfortable, flourishing, flush, fortunate, in the money, loaded, lucky, moneyed, prosperous, rich, successful, thriving, warm, wealthy, well-heeled, well-to-do. *antonym* poor.

well-thought-of *adj* admired, esteemed, highly regarded, honoured, reputable, respected, revered, venerated, weighty. *antonym* despised.

well-to-do *adj* affluent, comfortable, flush, loaded, moneyed, prosperous, rich, warm, wealthy, well-heeled, well-off. *antonym* poor.

well-worn *adj* commonplace,

hackneyed, overused, stale, stereotyped, threadbare, timeworn, tired, trite. *antonym* original.

welsh v cheat, defraud, diddle, do, swindle, welch.

wet *adj* boggy, clammy, damp, dank, drenched, dripping, drizzling, effete, feeble, foolish, humid, ineffectual, irresolute, misty, moist, moistened, namby-pamby, pouring, raining, rainy, saturated, showery, silly, sloppy, soaked, soaking, sodden, soft, soggy, sopping, soppy, soused, spineless, spongy, teeming, timorous, waterlogged, watery, weak, weedy, wimpish, wimpy. *antonyms* dry, resolute, strong.

n clamminess, condensation, damp, dampness, drip, drizzle, humidity, liquid, milksop, moisture, rain, rains, sap, water, weakling, weed, wetness, wimp. *antonym* dryness.

v damp, dampen, dip, douse, drench, humidify, imbue, irrigate, moisten, saturate, sluice, soak, splash, spray, sprinkle, steep, water. *antonym* dry.

wet behind the ears callow, green, immature, inexperienced, innocent, naïve, new, raw, untrained. *antonym* experienced.

wetness n clamminess, condensation, damp, dampness, dankness, humidity, liquid, moisture, soddenness, sogginess, water, wet. *antonym* dryness.

whack v bang, bash, beat, belabour, belt, biff, box, buffet, clobber, clout, cuff, hit, lambaste, rap, slap, slug, smack, sock, strike, thrash, thump, thwack, wallop, whale, whang.

n allotment, attempt, bang, bash, belt, biff, bit, blow, box, buffet, clout, crack, cuff, cut, go, hit, part, portion, quota, rap, share, shot, slap, slug, smack, sock, stab, stroke, thump, thwack, try, turn, wallop, wham, whang.

wham n bang, bash, blow, clout, concussion, hit, impact, slam, smack, splat, thump, thwack, wallop, whack, whang.

what's-its-name n doodah, thingumajig, thingumabob, thingummy, what-d'ye-call-it, whatsit, what-you-may-call-it.

wheedle v cajole, charm, coax, court, draw, entice, flatter, importune, inveigle, persuade. *antonym* force.

wheel n birl, circle, gyration, pivot, revolution, roll, rotation, spin, turn, twirl, whirl.

v birl, circle, gyrate, orbit, pirouette, revolve, roll, rotate, spin, swing, swivel, turn, twirl, whirl.

wheeze¹ v cough, gasp, hiss, rasp, whistle.

n cough, gasp, hiss, rasp, whistle.

wheeze² n anecdote, catch-phrase, chestnut, crack, expedient, gag, idea, joke, one-liner, plan, ploy, practical joke, prank, ruse, scheme, story, stunt, trick.

whereabouts n location, place, position, site, situation, vicinity.

wherewithal n capital, cash, funds, means, money, necessary, readies, resources, supplies.

whet v arouse, awaken, file, grind, hone, incite, increase, kindle, pique, provoke, quicken, rouse, sharpen, stimulate, stir, strop, titillate. *antonyms* blunt, dampen.

whiff n aroma, blast, breath, draught, gale, gust, hint, niff, odour, pong, puff, reek, scent, smell, sniff, stench, stink.

whim n caprice, chimera, craze, fad, fancy, freak, humour, impulse, notion, quirk, sport, urge, vagary, whims(e)y.

whimper v blub, blubber, cry, girn, moan, pule, snivel, sob, weep, whine, whinge.

n girn, moan, snivel, sob, whine.

whimsical *adj* capricious, chimeric(al), curious, dotty, droll, eccentric, fanciful, fantastic(al), freakish, funny, mischievous, odd, peculiar, playful, quaint, queer, singular, unusual, weird. *antonym* sensible.

whine n beef, belly-ache, complaint, cry, girn, gripe, grouch, grouse, grumble, moan, sob, wail, whimper.

v beef, belly-ache, carp, complain, cry, girn, gripe, grizzle, grouch, grouse, grumble, moan, sob, wail, whimper, whinge.

whinge v beef, belly-ache, carp, complain, gripe, grouse, grumble, moan.

n beef, belly-ache, complaint, gripe, grouse, grumble, moan.

whip v agitate, beat, best, birch, cane, castigate, clobber, compel, conquer, dash, defeat, dive, drive, drub, flagellate, flash, flit, flog, flounce, fly, foment, goad, hammer, hound, incite, instigate, jambok, jerk, lash, leather, lick, outdo, overcome, overpower, overwhelm, paddle, prick, prod, produce, provoke, pull, punish, push, quirt, remove, rout, rush, scourge, shoot, snatch, spank, spur, stir, strap, switch, tan, tear, thrash, trounce, urge, whisk, whop.

whip up agitate, arouse, excite, foment, incite, inflame, instigate, kindle, provoke, psych up, stir up, work up. *antonyms* dampen, deter.

whipping *n* beating, belting, birching, caning, castigation, flagellation, flogging, hiding, lashing, leathering, punishment, spanking, tanning, thrashing.

whirl *v* birl, circle, gyrate, gyre, pirouette, pivot, reel, revolve, roll, rotate, spin, swirl, swivel, turn, twirl, twist, wheel.
n agitation, birl, bustle, circle, commotion, confusion, daze, dither, flurry, giddiness, gyration, hubbub, hurly-burly, merry-go-round, pirouette, reel, revolution, roll, rotation, round, series, spin, stir, succession, swirl, tumult, turn, twirl, twist, uproar, vortex, wheel, whorl. *antonym* calm.

whirling *adj* birling, gyral, gyrating, pirouetting, pivoting, reeling, revolving, rotating, spinning, turning, twirling, vertiginous, vorticular, wheeling. *antonym* stationary.

whirlwind *n* cyclone, dust-devil, tornado, vortex, waterspout.
adj hasty, headlong, impetuous, impulsive, lightning, precipitate, quick, rapid, rash, short, speedy, split-second, swift. *antonyms* deliberate, slow.

whisk *v* beat, brush, dart, dash, flick, fly, grab, hasten, hurry, race, rush, scoot, shoot, speed, sweep, swipe, tear, twitch, whip, wipe.

whisper *v* breathe, buzz, divulge, gossip, hint, hiss, insinuate, intimate, murmur, rustle, sigh, sough. *antonym* shout.
n breath, buzz, gossip, hint, hiss, innuendo, insinuation, murmur, report, rumour, rustle, shadow, sigh, sighing, soughing, soupçon, suggestion, suspicion, swish, tinge, trace, underbreath, undertone, whiff, word. *antonym* roar.

whistle *n* call, cheep, chirp, hooter, siren, song, warble.
v call, cheep, chirp, pipe, sing, warble, wheeze.

whit *n* atom, bit, crumb, damn, dash, drop, fragment, grain, hoot, iota, jot, little, mite, modicum, particle, piece, pinch, scrap, shred, speck, tittle, trace. *antonym* lot.

white *adj* ashen, auspicious, bloodless, bright, Caucasian, clean, colourless, favourable, ghastly, grey, grizzled, hoar, hoary, honest, immaculate, innocent, pale, pallid, pasty, pure, purified, reliable, silver, snowy, spotless, stainless, unblemished, unsullied, wan, waxen, whey-faced. *antonyms* black, dark, dishonest, ruddy, unclean, unreliable.

white-collar *adj* clerical, executive, non-manual, office, professional, salaried. *antonyms* blue-collar, manual.

whiten *v* blanch, bleach, blench, etiolate, fade, pale, whitewash. *antonyms* blacken, colour, darken.

whitewash[1] *n* camouflage, concealment, cover-up, deception, extenuation. *antonym* exposure.
v camouflage, conceal, cover up, euphemise, extenuate, gloss over, make light of, suppress. *antonym* expose.

whitewash[2] *v* beat, best, clobber, crush, drub, hammer, lick, paste, thrash, trounce, whale.

whittle *v* carve, consume, cut, destroy, diminish, eat away, erode, hew, pare, reduce, scrape, shape, shave, trim, undermine, wear away.

whole *adj* better, complete, cured, entire, faultless, fit, flawless, full, good, hale, healed, healthy, in one piece, intact, integral, integrate, inviolate, mint, perfect, recovered, robust, sound, strong, total, unabbreviated, unabridged, unbroken, uncut, undamaged, undivided, unedited, unexpurgated, unharmed, unhurt, unimpaired, uninjured, unmutilated, unscathed, untouched, well. *antonyms* damaged, ill, partial.
n aggregate, all, ensemble, entirety, entity, everything, fullness, lot, piece, total, totality, unit, unity. *antonym* part.

whole-hearted *adj* committed, complete, dedicated, determined, devoted, earnest, emphatic, enthusiastic, genuine, heartfelt, hearty, passionate, real, sincere, true, unfeigned, unqualified, unreserved, unstinting, warm. *antonym* half-hearted.

wholesale *adj* broad, comprehensive, extensive, far-reaching, indiscriminate, mass, massive, sweeping, total, wide-ranging. *antonym* partial.
adv comprehensively, en bloc, extensively, indiscriminately, massively, totally. *antonym* partially.

wholesome *adj* advantageous, beneficial, clean, decent, edifying, exemplary, good, healthful, health-giving, healthy, helpful, honourable, hygienic, improving, innocent, invigorating, moral, nice, nourishing, nutritious, propitious, pure, respectable, righteous, salubrious, salutary, sanitary, squeaky-clean, uplifting, virtuous, worthy. **antonym** unwholesome.

wholly *adv* absolutely, all, altogether, completely, comprehensively, entirely, exclusively, fully, in toto, only, perfectly, solely, thoroughly, through and through, totally, utterly. **antonym** partly.

whoop *v, n* cheer, cry, holler, hoop, hoot, hurrah, roar, scream, shout, shriek, yell.

whopper *n* colossus, cracker, fable, fabrication, fairy story, falsehood, giant, lie, monster, tall story, untruth.

whopping *adj* big, enormous, extraordinary, giant, gigantic, great, huge, large, mammoth, massive, mighty, monstrous, monumental, prodigious, staggering, tremendous, whacking. **antonym** tiny.

whore *n* call girl, courtesan, fallen woman, harlot, hooker, prostitute, scarlet woman, street-walker, strumpet, tart, tramp, trollop, wench, woman of the town, working girl.

whorehouse *n* bawdy-house, bordello, brothel, cat-house, house of ill repute, knocking-shop.

wicked *adj* abandoned, abominable, acute, agonising, amoral, arch, atrocious, awful, bad, black-hearted, bothersome, corrupt, debased, depraved, destructive, devilish, difficult, dissolute, distressing, dreadful, egregious, evil, fearful, fiendish, fierce, flagitious, foul, galling, guilty, harmful, heinous, immoral, impious, impish, incorrigible, inexpiable, iniquitous, injurious, intense, irreligious, mighty, mischievous, nasty, naughty, nefarious, offensive, painful, roguish, scandalous, severe, shameful, sinful, spiteful, terrible, troublesome, trying, ungodly, unpleasant, unprincipled, unrighteous, vicious, vile, villainous, worthless. **antonyms** good, harmless, modest, upright.

wickedness *n* abomination, amorality, atrocity, corruption, corruptness, depravity, devilishness, dissoluteness, enormity, evil, fiendishness, foulness, heinousness, immorality, impiety, iniquity, pravity, reprobacy, shamefulness, sin, sinfulness, unrighteousness, vileness, villainy. **antonym** uprightness.

wide *adj* ample, baggy, broad, capacious, catholic, commodious, comprehensive, diffuse, dilated, distant, distended, encyclopaedic, expanded, expansive, extensive, far-reaching, full, general, immense, inclusive, large, latitudinous, loose, off, off-course, off-target, outspread, outstretched, remote, roomy, spacious, sweeping, vast. **antonyms** limited, narrow.
adv astray, off course, off target, off the mark, out. **antonym** on target.

wide-awake *adj* alert, astute, aware, conscious, fully awake, heedful, keen, observant, on one's toes, on the alert, on the ball, quick-witted, roused, sharp, vigilant, wakened, wary, watchful. **antonym** asleep.

widely *adv* extensively, generally, universally.

widen *v* broaden, dilate, distend, enlarge, expand, extend, open out, splay, spread, stretch. **antonym** narrow.

wide-open *adj* defenceless, expansive, exposed, gaping, indeterminate, open, outspread, outstretched, splayed, spread, susceptible, uncertain, unfortified, unpredictable, unprotected, unsettled, vulnerable, wide. **antonyms** closed, narrow.

widespread *adj* broad, common, epidemic, extensive, far-flung, far-reaching, general, pervasive, popular, prevailing, prevalent, rife, sweeping, universal, unlimited, wholesale. **antonyms** limited, uncommon.

width *n* amplitude, beam, breadth, compass, diameter, extent, girth, measure, range, reach, scope, span, thickness, wideness.

wield *v* brandish, command, control, employ, exercise, exert, flourish, handle, have, hold, maintain, manage, manipulate, ply, possess, swing, use, utilise, wave, weave.

wiggle *v, n* jerk, jiggle, shake, shimmy, squirm, twist, twitch, wag, waggle, wriggle, writhe.

wild *adj* barbaric, barbarous, berserk, blustery, boisterous, brutish, chaotic, choppy, crazed, crazy, daft, delirious, demented, desert, deserted, desolate, dishevelled, disordered, disorderly, eager, empty, enthusiastic, excited, extravagant, fantastic, ferocious, fierce, flighty, foolhardy, foolish, frantic, free, frenzied, furious, giddy, god-forsaken, howling, hysterical, ill-considered, impetuous, impracticable, imprudent, inaccurate, indigenous, intense, irrational, lawless, mad, madcap, maniacal, native, natural, noisy, nuts, outrageous, potty, preposterous, primitive, rabid, raging, rash, raving, reckless, riotous, rough, rowdy, rude, savage, self-willed, tempestuous, tousled, turbulent, unbridled, unbroken, uncheated, uncivilised, uncontrollable, uncontrolled, uncultivated, undisciplined, undomesticated, unfettered, ungovernable, uninhabited, unjustified, unkempt, unmanageable, unpopulated, unpruned, unrestrained, unruly, unsubstantiated, untamed, untidy, uproarious, violent, virgin, wayward, woolly. *antonyms* civilised, peaceful, sane, sensible, tame, unenthusiastic.

wilderness *n* clutter, confusion, desert, jumble, jungle, mass, maze, muddle, tangle, waste, wasteland, wild.

wile *n* artfulness, artifice, cheating, chicanery, contrivance, craft, craftiness, cunning, deceit, device, dodge, expedient, fraud, guile, hanky-panky, imposition, lure, manoeuvre, ploy, ruse, slyness, stratagem, subterfuge, trick, trickery. *antonym* guilelessness.

wilful *adj* adamant, bloody-minded, bull-headed, conscious, deliberate, determined, dogged, headstrong, inflexible, intended, intentional, intractable, intransigent, mulish, obdurate, obstinate, persistent, perverse, pig-headed, purposeful, refractory, self-willed, stubborn, uncompromising, unyielding, volitional, voluntary. *antonyms* complaisant, good-natured.

will *n* aim, attitude, choice, command, decision, declaration, decree, desire, determination, discretion, disposition, fancy, feeling, inclination, intention, mind, option, pleasure, preference, prerogative, purpose, resolution, resolve, testament, volition, will-power, wish, wishes.
v bequeath, bid, cause, choose, command, confer, decree, desire, determine, devise, direct, dispose of, elect, give, leave, opt, ordain, order, pass on, resolve, transfer, want, wish.

willing *adj* agreeable, amenable, biddable, compliant, consenting, content, desirous, disposed, eager, enthusiastic, favourable, game, happy, inclined, pleased, prepared, ready, so-minded. *antonym* unwilling.

willingly *adv* by choice, cheerfully, eagerly, freely, gladly, happily, readily, unhesitatingly, voluntarily. *antonym* unwillingly.

willingness *n* agreeableness, agreement, complaisance, compliance, consent, desire, disposition, enthusiasm, favour, inclination, volition, will, wish. *antonym* unwillingness.

willowy *adj* graceful, gracile, limber, lissom, lithe, lithesome, slender, slim, supple, svelte, sylph-like. *antonym* buxom.

will-power *n* determination, drive, grit, resolution, resolve, self-command, self-control, self-discipline, self-mastery, single-mindedness.

wilt *v* atrophy, diminish, droop, dwindle, ebb, fade, fail, flag, flop, languish, melt away, sag, shrivel, sink, wane, weaken, wither. *antonym* perk up.

wily *adj* arch, artful, astute, cagey, crafty, crooked, cunning, deceitful, deceptive, designing, fly, guileful, intriguing, Machiavellian, scheming, sharp, shifty, shrewd, sly, streetwise, tricky, underhand. *antonym* guileless.

win *v* accomplish, achieve, acquire, attain, bag, capture, catch, collect, come away with, conquer, earn, gain, get, net, obtain, overcome, pick up, prevail, procure, receive, secure, succeed, sweep the board, triumph. *antonym* lose.
n conquest, mastery, success, triumph, victory. *antonym* defeat.

win over allure, attract, carry, charm, convert, convince, disarm, dissuade, induce, influence, persuade, prevail upon, sway, talk round.

wince *v* blench, cower, cringe, draw back, flinch, funk, jerk, quail, recoil, shrink, start.
n cringe, flinch, jerk, start.

wind[1] *n* air, air-current, babble, blast, bluster, boasting, breath, breeze, clue, current, cyclone, draught, flatulence, gab, gale, gas, gust, hint, hot air, humbug, hurricane, idle talk, inkling, intimation, monsoon, notice, puff, report, respiration, rumour, suggestion, talk, tidings, tornado, warning, whisper, windiness, zephyr.

wind[2] *v* bend, coil, curl, curve, deviate, encircle, furl, loop, meander, ramble, reel, roll, serpent, snake, spiral, turn, twine, twist, wreath, zigzag.
n bend, curve, meander, turn, twist, zigzag.

wind down decline, diminish, dwindle, lessen, quieten down, reduce, relax, slacken off, slow, slow down, subside, unwind. *antonyms* increase, tense.

wind up close, close down, coil, conclude, crank up, end, end one's days, end up, excite, finalise, find oneself, finish, finish up, hoist, liquidate, raise, settle, terminate, tighten, work up, wrap up. *antonym* begin.

windfall *n* bonanza, find, godsend, jackpot, manna, pennies from heaven, stroke of luck, treasure-trove.

winding *adj* bending, circuitous, convoluted, crooked, curving, indirect, meandering, roundabout, serpentine, sinuous, spiral, tortuous, turning, twisting. *antonym* straight.

windy *adj* blowy, blustering, blustery, boastful, boisterous, bombastic, breezy, changeable, conceited, diffuse, empty, flatulent, flatuous, garrulous, gusty, long-winded, loquacious, meandering, pompous, prolix, rambling, squally, stormy, tempestuous, timid, turgid, verbose, wild, windswept, wordy. *antonyms* calm, modest.

wing *n* adjunct, annexe, arm, branch, circle, clique, coterie, extension, faction, flank, group, grouping, protection, section, segment, set, side.
v clip, fleet, flit, fly, glide, hasten, hit, hurry, move, nick, pass, race, soar, speed, travel, wound, zoom.

wink *v* bat, blink, flash, flicker, flutter, gleam, glimmer, glint, sparkle, twinkle.
n blink, flash, flutter, gleam, glimmering, glint, hint, instant, jiffy, moment, second, sparkle, split second, twinkle, twinkling.

winning *adj* alluring, amiable, attractive, bewitching, captivating, charming, conquering, delectable, delightful, disarming, enchanting, endearing, engaging, fascinating, fetching, lovely, on top, pleasing, prepossessing, successful, sweet, taking, triumphant, unbeaten, undefeated, victorious, winsome. *antonyms* losing, unappealing.

winnow *v* comb, cull, diffuse, divide, fan, part, screen, select, separate, sift, waft.

winsome *adj* agreeable, alluring, amiable, attractive, bewitching, captivating, charming, cheerful, comely, delectable, disarming, enchanting, endearing, engaging, fair, fascinating, fetching, graceful, pleasant, pleasing, prepossessing, pretty, sweet, taking, winning. *antonym* unattractive.

wintry *adj* bleak, cheerless, chilly, cold, desolate, dismal, freezing, frosty, frozen, gelid, harsh, icy, Siberian, snowy, winterly. *antonym* summery.

wipe *v* brush, clean, clear, dry, dust, erase, mop, remove, rub, sponge, swab, take away, take off.

wipe out abolish, annihilate, blot out, destroy, efface, eradicate, erase, expunge, exterminate, extirpate, massacre, obliterate, put paid to, raze. *antonym* establish.

wisdom *n* astuteness, circumspection, comprehension, discernment, enlightenment, erudition, foresight, intelligence, judgement, judiciousness, knowledge, learning, prudence, reason, sagacity, sapience, sense, understanding. *antonym* folly.

wise *adj* aware, clever, discerning, enlightened, erudite, informed, intelligent, judicious, knowing, long-headed, long-sighted, perceptive, politic, prudent, rational, reasonable, sagacious, sage, sapient, sensible, shrewd, sound, understanding, well-advised, well-informed. *antonym* foolish.

wish *v* ask, aspire, bid, command, covet, crave, desire, direct, greet, hanker, hope, hunger, instruct, long, need, order, require, thirst, want, whim, yearn, yen. *antonyms* dislike, fear.
n aspiration, bidding, command, desire, hankering, hope, hunger, inclination, intention, liking, order, request, thirst, urge, voice, want, whim, will, yearning, yen. *antonyms* dislike, fear.

wishy-washy *adj* bland, feeble, flat, ineffective, ineffectual, insipid, namby-pamby, tasteless, thin, vapid, watered-down, watery, weak. *antonym* strong.

wisp *n* lock, piece, shred, snippet, strand, thread, twist.

wispy *adj* attenuated, delicate, diaphanous, ethereal, faint, fine, flimsy, flyaway, fragile, frail, gossamer, insubstantial, light, thin. *antonym* substantial.

wistful *adj* contemplative, disconsolate, dreaming, dreamy, forlorn, longing, meditative, melancholy, mournful, musing, pensive, reflective, sad, soulful, thoughtful, wishful, yearning.

wit *n* acumen, banter, brains, card, cleverness, comedian, common sense, comprehension, conceit, discernment, drollery, facetiousness, fun, humorist, humour, ingenuity, insight, intellect, intelligence, jocularity, joker, judgement, levity, mind, nous, perception, pleasantry, raillery, reason, repartee, sense, understanding, wag, wisdom, wordplay. *antonyms* seriousness, stupidity.

witchcraft *n* black magic, conjuration, divination, enchantment, incantation, magic, necromancy, occultism, sorcery, spell, the black art, the occult, voodoo, wizardry.

with it fashionable, groovy, hep, hip, in, modern, modish, progressive, trendy, up-to-date, up-to-the-minute, vogue. *antonym* out-of-date.

withdraw *v* abjure, absent oneself, back out, depart, disavow, disclaim, disengage, disinvest, draw back, draw out, drop out, extract, fall back, go, go away, hive off, leave, pull back, pull out, recall, recant, remove, repair, rescind, retire, retract, retreat, revoke, secede, subtract, take away, take back, take off, unsay, waive. *antonyms* advance, deposit, persist.

withdrawal *n* abjuration, departure, disavowal, disclaimer, disengagement, disinvestment, exit, exodus, extraction, recall, recantation, removal, repudiation, retirement, retraction, retreat, revocation, secession, waiver. *antonyms* advance, deposit, persistence.

withdrawn *adj* detached, distant, hidden, introvert, isolated, out-of-the-way, private, quiet, remote, reserved, retiring, secluded, shrinking, shy, silent, solitary, taciturn, uncommunicative, unforthcoming, unsociable. *antonym* outgoing.

wither *v* blast, blight, decay, decline, desiccate, disintegrate, droop, dry, fade, humiliate, miff, mortify, perish, put down, shame, shrink, shrivel, snub, wane, waste, welt, wilt. *antonyms* boost, thrive.

wither away decrease, die, die off, disappear, dwindle, fade away, miff, shrink, shrivel, wilt.

withering *adj* deadly, death-dealing, destructive, devastating, humiliating, killing, mortifying, murderous, scathing, scornful, searing, slaughterous, snubbing, wounding. *antonym* supportive.

withhold *v* check, conceal, deduct, detain, hide, keen, keep back, refuse, repress, reserve, resist, restrain, retain, sit on, suppress, suspend. *antonyms* accord, give.

without delay at once, immediately,

pronto, right away, straight away, there and then.

without doubt certainly, doubtless, no doubt, questionless, unquestionably.

without fail conscientiously, constantly, dependably, faithfully, like clockwork, predictably, punctually, regularly, reliably, religiously, unfailingly, without exception. *antonyms* unpredictably, unreliably.

withstand *v* bear, brave, combat, confront, cope with, defy, endure, face, grapple with, hold off, hold one's ground, hold out, last out, oppose, put up with, resist, stand, stand fast, stand one's ground, stand up to, survive, take, take on, thwart, tolerate, weather. *antonyms* collapse, yield.

witness *n* attestant, beholder, bystander, corroborator, eye-witness, looker-on, observer, onlooker, spectator, testifier, viewer, watcher.
v attend, attest, bear out, bear witness, confirm, corroborate, countersign, endorse, look on, mark, note, notice, observe, perceive, see, sign, testify, view, watch.

wits *n* acumen, astuteness, brains, cleverness, comprehension, faculties, gumption, ingenuity, intelligence, judgement, marbles, nous, reason, sense, understanding. *antonym* stupidity.

witty *adj* amusing, brilliant, clever, comic, droll, facetious, fanciful, funny, humorous, ingenious, jocular, lively, original, piquant, salty, sparkling, waggish, whimsical. *antonyms* dull, unamusing.

wizard¹ *n* conjurer, enchanter, mage, magician, magus, necromancer, occultist, sorcerer, warlock, witch.

wizard² *n* ace, adept, expert, genius, hotshot, maestro, master, prodigy, star, virtuoso, whiz. *antonym* duffer.
adj ace, brilliant, enjoyable, fab, fantastic, good, great, marvellous, sensational, smashing, super, superb, terrif, terrific, tiptop, top-hole, topping, tremendous, wonderful. *antonym* rotten.

wizened *adj* dried up, gnarled, lined, shrivelled, shrunken, thin, weazen, weazened, withered, worn, wrinkled. *antonyms* plump, smooth.

wobble *v* dither, dodder, fluctuate, haver, heave, hesitate, oscillate, quake, rock, seesaw, shake, shilly-shally, sway, swither, teeter, totter, tremble, vacillate, vibrate, waver.

n oscillation, quaking, rock, shake, tremble, tremor, unsteadiness, vibration.

wobbly *adj* doddering, doddery, rickety, shaky, teetering, tottering, unbalanced, uneven, unsafe, unstable, unsteady, wonky. *antonym* stable.

woe *n* adversity, affliction, agony, anguish, burden, curse, dejection, depression, disaster, distress, dolour, gloom, grief, hardship, heartache, heartbreak, melancholy, misery, misfortune, pain, sadness, sorrow, suffering, tears, trial, tribulation, trouble, unhappiness, wretchedness. *antonym* joy.

woebegone *adj* blue, crestfallen, dejected, disconsolate, dispirited, doleful, down in the mouth, downcast, downhearted, forlorn, gloomy, grief-stricken, hangdog, long-faced, lugubrious, miserable, mournful, sad, sorrowful, tearful, tear-stained, troubled, wretched. *antonym* joyful.

woeful *adj* agonising, appalling, awful, bad, calamitous, catastrophic, cruel, deplorable, disappointing, disastrous, disconsolate, disgraceful, distressing, doleful, dreadful, feeble, gloomy, grieving, grievous, heartbreaking, heart-rending, hopeless, inadequate, lamentable, lousy, mean, miserable, mournful, paltry, pathetic, piteous, pitiable, pitiful, plaintive, poor, rotten, sad, shocking, sorrowful, sorry, terrible, tragic, unhappy, wretched. *antonym* joyful.

womaniser *n* Casanova, Don Juan, ladies' man, lady-killer, Lothario, philanderer, Romeo, seducer.

wonder *n* admiration, amaze, amazement, astonishment, awe, bewilderment, curiosity, fascination, marvel, miracle, phenomenon, portent, prodigy, rarity, sight, spectacle, stupefaction, surprise, wonderment. *antonyms* disinterest, ordinariness.

v ask oneself, boggle, conjecture, doubt, gape, gaup, gawk, inquire, marvel, meditate, ponder, puzzle, query, question, speculate, stare, think.

wonderful *adj* ace, admirable, amazing, astonishing, astounding, awe-inspiring, awesome, brilliant, excellent, extraordinary, fab, fabulous, fantastic, great, incredible, magnificent, marvellous, miraculous, outstanding, peculiar, phenomenal, remarkable, sensational, smashing, staggering, startling, strange, stupendous, super,

superb, surprising, terrif, terrific, tiptop, topping, tremendous, wizard, wondrous. *antonyms* ordinary, rotten.

wonky *adj* amiss, askew, awry, groggy, infirm, shaky, skew-whiff, squint, unsound, unsteady, weak, wobbly, wrong. *antonyms* stable, straight.

wont *adj* accustomed, given, habituated, used.

n custom, habit, practice, routine, rule, use, way.

wonted *adj* accustomed, common, conventional, customary, daily, familiar, frequent, habitual, normal, regular, routine, usual. *antonym* unwonted.

woo *v* chase, court, cultivate, importune, look for, pay court to, pursue, seek, seek the hand of.

wooden *adj* awkward, blank, clumsy, colourless, deadpan, dense, dim, dim-witted, dull, dull-witted, emotionless, empty, expressionless, gauche, gawky, glassy, graceless, inelegant, inflexible, lifeless, ligneous, muffled, oaken, obstinate, obtuse, rigid, slow, spiritless, stiff, stupid, thick, timber, unbending, unemotional, ungainly, unresponsive, unyielding, vacant, woody. *antonyms* bright, lively.

woolly *adj* blurred, clouded, confused, fleecy, foggy, frizzy, fuzzy, hairy, hazy, ill-defined, indefinite, indistinct, muddled, nebulous, shaggy, unclear, vague, woollen, woolly-haired.

woozy *adj* befuddled, bemused, blurred, confused, dazed, dizzy, fuddled, nauseated, pickled, rocky, tipsy, unsteady, vague, wobbly, woolly. *antonyms* alert, sober.

word *n* account, advice, affirmation, assertion, assurance, bidding, bulletin, chat, colloquy, command, commandment, comment, communication, communiqué, confab, confabulation, consultation, conversation, declaration, decree, dicky-bird, discussion, dispatch, edict, expression, go-ahead, green light, guarantee, hint, information, intelligence, interlocution, intimation, locution, mandate, message, news, notice, oath, order, parole, password, pledge, promise, remark, report, rescript, rumour, sign, signal, slogan, talk, term, tête-à-tête, tidings, undertaking, utterance, vocable, vow, war-cry, watch-word, will.

v couch, explain, express, phrase, put, say, write.

wording *n* choice of words, diction,

language, phraseology, phrasing, style, terminology, words.

wordy *adj* diffuse, discursive, garrulous, long-winded, loquacious, phrasy, pleonastic, prolix, rambling, verbose, windy. **antonym** concise.

work *n* achievement, art, assignment, book, business, calling, chore, commission, composition, craft, creation, deed, doings, drudgery, duty, effort, elbow grease, employ, employment, exertion, graft, grind, handiwork, industry, job, labour, line, livelihood, métier, occupation, oeuvre, office, opus, performance, piece, play, poem, production, profession, pursuit, service, skill, slog, stint, sweat, task, toil, trade, undertaking, workload, workmanship. **antonyms** hobby, play, rest.

v accomplish, achieve, act, arrange, beaver, bring about, bring off, cause, contrive, control, create, cultivate, dig, direct, drive, drudge, effect, encompass, execute, exploit, farm, fashion, fiddle, fix, force, form, function, go, graft, handle, implement, knead, labour, make, manage, manipulate, manoeuvre, mould, move, operate, perform, ply, process, progress, pull off, run, shape, slave, slog, sweat, swing, till, toil, twitch, use, wield, writhe. **antonyms** fail, play, rest.

work on butter up, cajole, coax, dissuade, influence, inveigle, persuade, soft-soap, sweet-talk, talk round, wheedle.

work out accomplish, achieve, add up to, amount to, arrange, attain, calculate, clear up, come out, come to, construct, contrive, develop, devise, drill, effect, elaborate, evolve, excogitate, exercise, exhaust, expiate, figure out, flourish, form, formulate, go, happen, pan out, plan, practise, prosper, put together, puzzle out, reach, resolve, result, solve, succeed, train, turn out, win, worry out.

work up agitate, animate, arouse, elaborate, enkindle, excite, expand, foment, generate, incite, increase, inflame, instigate, move, rouse, spur, stir up, wind up.

workaday *adj* common, commonplace, dull, everyday, familiar, humdrum, labouring, mundane, ordinary, practical, prosaic, routine, run-of-the-mill, toiling, working. **antonym** exciting.

workforce *n* employees, hands, labour, labour force, personnel, shop-floor, staff, workers.

working *n* action, functioning, manner, method, operation, routine, running.
adj active, employed, functioning, going, labouring, operational, operative, running. **antonyms** idle, inoperative, retired, unemployed.

workmanlike *adj* adept, careful, efficient, expert, masterly, painstaking, professional, proficient, satisfactory, skilful, skilled, thorough, workmanly. **antonym** amateurish.

workmanship *n* art, artistry, craft, craftsmanship, execution, expertise, handicraft, handiwork, manufacture, skill, technique, work.

world *n* age, area, class, creation, days, division, domain, earth, environment, epoch, era, existence, field, globe, human race, humanity, humankind, kingdom, life, man, mankind, men, na ure, people, period, planet, province, public, realm, society, sphere, star, system, times, universe.

worldly *adj* ambitious, avaricious, blasé, carnal, cosmopolitan, covetous, earthly, experienced, fleshly, grasping, greedy, knowing, lay, materialistic, mundane, physical, politic, profane, secular, selfish, sophisticated, temporal, terrestrial, unspiritual, urbane, worldly-wise. **antonym** unworldly.

worn *adj* careworn, clichéd, drawn, exhausted, fatigued, frayed, hackneyed, haggard, jaded, lined, pinched, played-out, ragged, shabby, shiny, spent, tattered, tatty, threadbare, tired, trite, wearied, weary, wizened, worn-out. **antonyms** fresh, new.

worn out all in, clapped out, clapped-out, dead on one's feet, decrepit, dog-tired, done, done in, exhausted, fatigued, finished, fit to drop, frayed, jiggered, knackered, moth-eaten, on its last legs, played-out, prostrate, ragged, shabby, spent, tattered, tatty, threadbare, tired, tired out, used, useless, warby, weary, worn, zonked. **antonym** fresh.

worried *adj* afraid, agonised, anxious, apprehensive, bothered, concerned, distracted, distraught, distressed, disturbed, fearful, fretful, frightened. ill at ease, nervous, on edge, overwrought, perturbed, strained, tense, tormented, troubled, uneasy, unquiet, upset. **antonyms** calm, unconcerned, unworried.

worry *v* agonise, annoy, attack, badger, bite, bother, brood, disquiet, distress, disturb, fret, get one's knickers in a twist, gnaw at, go for, harass, harry, hassle, hector, importune, irritate, kill, lacerate, nag, perturb, pester, plague, savage, tantalise, tear, tease, torment, trouble, unsettle, upset, vex. **antonyms** comfort, reassure.

n agitation, annoyance, anxiety, apprehension, care, concern, disturbance, fear, irritation, misery, misgiving, perplexity, pest, plague, problem, stew, tew, tizz, tizzy, torment, trial, trouble, unease, vexation, woe. **antonyms** comfort, reassurance.

worrying *adj* anxious, disquieting, distressing, disturbing, harassing, nail-biting, perturbing, troublesome, trying, uneasy, unsettling, upsetting. **antonym** reassuring.

worsen *v* aggravate, damage, decay, decline, degenerate, deteriorate, disimprove, exacerbate, go downhill, retrogress, sink, take a turn for the worse. **antonym** improve.

worship *v* adore, adulate, deify, exalt, glorify, honour, idolatrise, idolise, laud, love, praise, pray to, respect, revere, reverence, venerate. **antonym** despise.
n adoration, adulation, devotion(s), exaltation, glorification, glory, homage, honour, image-worship, laudation, love, praise, prayer(s), regard, respect, reverence. **antonym** vilification.

worth *n* aid, assistance, avail, benefit, cost, credit, desert(s), excellence, goodness, help, importance, merit, price, quality, rate, significance, use, usefulness, utility, value, virtue, worthiness. **antonym** worthlessness.

worthless *adj* abandoned, abject, base, beggarly, contemptible, depraved, despicable, futile, good-for-nothing, grotty, ignoble, ineffectual, insignificant, meaningless, miserable, naff, no use, no-good, paltry, pointless, poor, rubbishy, scabby, trashy, trifling, trivial, unavailing, unimportant, unusable, useless, valueless, vile, wretched. **antonym** valuable.

worthwhile *adj* beneficial, constructive, gainful, good, helpful, justifiable, productive, profitable, useful, utile, valuable, worthy. **antonym** useless.

worthy *adj* admirable, appropriate, commendable, creditable, decent, dependable, deserving, estimable, excellent, fit, good, honest, honourable, laudable, meritorious, praiseworthy, reliable, reputable, respectable, righteous, suitable, upright, valuable, virtuous, worthwhile. **antonyms** disreputable, unworthy.
n big cheese, big noise, big shot, big-wig, dignitary, luminary, name, notable, personage.

wound *n* anguish, cut, damage, distress, gash, grief, harm, heartbreak, hurt, injury, insult, laceration, lesion, offence, pain, pang, scar, shock, slash, slight, torment, torture, trauma.
v annoy, bless, cut, cut to the quick, damage, distress, gash, grieve, harm, hit, hurt, injure, irritate, lacerate, mortify, offend, pain, pierce, shock, slash, sting, traumatise.

wrangle *n* altercation, argument, argy-bargy, barney, bickering, brawl, clash, contest, controversy, dispute, quarrel, row, set-to, slanging match, squabble, tiff, tussle. **antonym** agreement.
v altercate, argue, bicker, brawl, contend, disagree, dispute, fall out, fight, quarrel, row, scrap, squabble. **antonym** agree.

wrap *v* bind, bundle up, cloak, cocoon, cover, encase, enclose, enfold, envelop, fold, immerse, muffle, pack, package, roll up, sheathe, shroud, surround, swathe, wind. **antonym** unwrap.
n cape, cloak, mantle, robe, shawl, stole.

wrap up[1] bring to a close, complete, conclude, end, finish off, pack up, package, parcel, round off, terminate, wind up. **antonym** begin.

wrap up[2] be quiet, hold one's tongue, hold one's wheesht, put a sock in it, shoosh, shut it, shut one's cakehole, shut one's face, shut one's mouth, shut one's trap, shut up, wheesht.

wrath *n* anger, bitterness, displeasure, exasperation, fury, indignation, ire, irritation, passion, rage, resentment, spleen, temper. **antonyms** calm, pleasure.

wreak *v* bestow, bring about, carry out, cause, create, effect, execute, exercise, express, inflict, perpetrate, unleash, vent, visit, work.

wreck *v* break, demolish, destroy, devastate, play havoc with, ravage, ruin, shatter, smash, spoil, torpedo, write off. **antonyms** repair, save.
n derelict, desolation, destruction, devastation, disruption, hulk, mess, overthrow, ruin, ruination, shipwreck, undoing, write-off.

wrench *v* distort, force, jerk, pull, rick, rip, sprain, strain, tear, tug, twist, wrest, wring, yank.

n ache, blow, jerk, monkey-wrench, pain, pang, pliers, pull, sadness, shock, sorrow, spanner, sprain, tear, tug, twist, upheaval, uprooting.

wrestle *v* battle, combat, contend, contest, fight, grapple, scuffle, strive, struggle, tussle, vie.

wretch *n* blackguard, cad, cur, good-for-nothing, miscreant, no-good, outcast, profligate, rapscallion, rascal, rat, rogue, rotter, ruffian, scoundrel, swine, villain, worm.

wretched *adj* abject, base, broken-hearted, calamitous, cheerless, comfortless, contemptible, crestfallen, dejected, deplorable, depressed, despicable, disconsolate, distressed, doggone, doleful, downcast, forlorn, gloomy, grotty, hapless, hopeless, inferior, low, low-down, mean, melancholy, miserable, paltry, pathetic, pesky, pitiable, pitiful, poor, ratty, scurvy, shabby, shameful, sorry, unfortunate, unhappy, vile, woebegone, woeful, worthless. **antonyms** excellent, happy.

wriggle *v* crawl, dodge, edge, extricate, jerk, jiggle, manoeuvre, sidle, slink, snake, sneak, squiggle, squirm, talk one's way out, turn, twist, wag, waggle, wiggle, worm, writhe, zigzag.

n jerk, jiggle, squirm, turn, twist, twitch, wag, waggle, wiggle.

wring *v* coerce, distress, exact, extort, extract, force, hurt, lacerate, mangle, pain, pierce, rack, rend, screw, squeeze, stab, tear, torture, twist, wound, wrench, wrest.

wrinkle *n* corrugation, crease, crinkle, crow's-foot, crumple, fold, furrow, gather, line, pucker, rumple.

v corrugate, crease, crinkle, crumple, fold, furrow, gather, line, pucker, rivel, ruck, rumple, runkle, shrivel.

wrinkled *adj* creased, crinkled, crinkly, crumpled, furrowed, puckered, ridged, rivelled, rumpled, wrinkly. **antonym** smooth.

write *v* compose, copy, correspond, create, draft, draw up, inscribe, jot down, pen, record, scribble, set down, take down, tell, transcribe.

write off cancel, crash, cross out, destroy, disregard, scrub, smash up, wreck.

writhe *v* coil, contort, jerk, squirm, struggle, thrash, toss, twist, wiggle, wriggle.

wrong *adj* abusive, amiss, askew, awry, bad, blameworthy, criminal, crooked, defective, dishonest, dishonourable, erroneous, evil, fallacious, false, faulty, felonious, funny, illegal, illicit, immoral, improper, in error, in the wrong, inaccurate, inappropriate, inapt, incongruous, incorrect, indecorous, infelicitous, iniquitous, inner, inside, inverse, misinformed, mistaken, off base, off beam, off target, opposite, out, out of commission, out of order, reprehensible, reverse, sinful, unacceptable, unbecoming, unconventional, undesirable, unethical, unfair, unfitting, unhappy, unjust, unlawful, unseemly, unsound, unsuitable, untrue, wicked, wide of the mark, wrongful. **antonym** right.

adv amiss, askew, astray, awry, badly, erroneously, faultily, improperly, inaccurately, incorrectly, mistakenly, wrongly. **antonym** right.

n abuse, crime, error, grievance, immorality, inequity, infraction, infringement, iniquity, injury, injustice, misdeed, offence, sin, sinfulness, transgression, trespass, unfairness, wickedness, wrong-doing. **antonym** right.

v abuse, cheat, discredit, dishonour, harm, hurt, ill-treat, ill-use, impose on, injure, malign, misrepresent, mistreat, oppress, traduce.

wrong-doer *n* criminal, culprit, delinquent, evil-doer, felon, law-breaker, malefactor, miscreant, offender, sinner, transgressor, trespasser.

wrongful *adj* blameworthy, criminal, dishonest, dishonourable, evil, felonious, illegal, illegitimate, illicit, immoral, improper, reprehensible, unethical, unfair, unjust, unlawful, wicked, wrong. **antonym** rightful.

wrongly *adv* badly, by mistake, erroneously, in error, inaccurately, incorrectly, mistakenly. **antonym** rightly.

wry *adj* askew, aslant, awry, contorted, crooked, deformed, distorted, droll, dry, ironic, mocking, perverse, sarcastic, sardonic, twisted, uneven, warped. **antonym** straight.

X,Y,Z

xenophobia n ethnocentrism, racialism, racism. *antonym* xenomania.

ya(c)k v blather, chatter, gab, gossip, jabber, jaw, prattle, run on, witter on, yap, yatter.
n chat, chinwag, confab, gossip, hot air, jaw, prattle, ya(c)kety-ya(c)k, yatter.

yank v, n haul, heave, jerk, pull, snatch, tug, wrench.

yap v babble, blather, chatter, go on, gossip, jabber, jaw, prattle, talk, ya(c)k, yammer, yatter, yelp, yip.

yardstick n benchmark, comparison, criterion, gauge, measure, standard, touchstone.

yarn n anecdote, cock-and-bull story, fable, fabrication, story, tale, tall story.

yawning adj cavernous, gaping, huge, vast, wide, wide-open. *antonym* narrow.

yearn for ache for, covet, crave, desire, hanker for, hunger for, itch for, languish for, long for, lust for, pant for, pine for, want, wish for, yen for. *antonym* dislike.

yell v bawl, bellow, holler, howl, roar, scream, screech, shout, shriek, squawl, squeal, whoop, yelp, yowl. *antonym* whisper.
n bellow, cry, holler, howl, roar, scream, screech, shriek, squawl, whoop, yelp. *antonym* whisper.

yelp v bark, bay, cry, yap, yell, yip, yowl.
n bark, cry, yap, yell, yip, yowl.

yen n craving, desire, hankering, hunger, itch, longing, lust, passion, thing, yearning. *antonym* dislike.

yes interj absolutely, affirmative, agreed, aye, quite, right, uh-huh, yea, yeah, yep. *antonym* no.

yes-man n arse-licker, bootlicker, crawler, lackey, minion, sycophant, toady.

yield¹ v abandon, abdicate, accede, acquiesce, admit defeat, agree, allow, bow, capitulate, cave in, cede, comply, concede, consent, give, give in, give way, go along with, grant, knuckle under, part with, permit, relinquish, resign, resign oneself, submit, succumb, surrender, throw in the towel. *antonym* withstand.

yield² v afford, bear, bring forth, bring in, earn, furnish, generate, give, net, pay, produce, provide, return, supply.

n crop, earnings, harvest, income, output, proceeds, produce, product, profit, return, revenue, takings.

yielding adj accommodating, acquiescent, amenable, biddable, complaisant, compliant, docile, easy, elastic, flexible, obedient, obliging, pliable, pliant, resilient, soft, spongy, springy, submissive, supple, tractable, unresisting. *antonyms* obstinate, solid.

yobbo n hoodlum, hooligan, lager lout, lout, rough, rowdy, ruffian, thug, tough, yob.

yoke n bond, bondage, burden, chain, coupling, enslavement, link, oppression, service, servility, servitude, slavery, subjugation, tie.
v bracket, connect, couple, enslave, harness, hitch, join, link, tie, unite. *antonym* unhitch.

yokel n boor, bumpkin, corn-ball, country cousin, hick, hillbilly, peasant, rustic. *antonyms* sophisticate, towny.

young adj adolescent, baby, callow, cub, early, fledgling, green, growing, immature, infant, junior, juvenile, little, new, recent, unfledged, youthful. *antonym* old.

youngster n boy, girl, juvenile, kid, lad, laddie, lass, lassie, nipper, shaver, teenybopper, young pup, youth. *antonym* oldie.

youth n adolescence, adolescent, boy, boyhood, colt, girlhood, immaturity, juvenescence, juvenile, kid, lad, salad days, stripling, teenager, the young, young man, young people, younger generation, youngster. *antonyms* old age, oldie.

youthful adj active, boyish, childish, fresh, girlish, immature, inexperienced, juvenescent, juvenile, lively, pubescent, puerile, sprightly, spry, vigorous, vivacious, well-preserved, young. *antonyms* aged, languorous.

yowl v bay, caterwaul, cry, howl, screech, squall, wail, yell, yelp.
n cry, howl, screech, wail, yell, yelp.

yucky adj beastly, dirty, disgusting, filthy, foul, grotty, horrible, messy, mucky, revolting, saccharine, sentimental, sickly, unpleasant. *antonym* nice.

zany adj amusing, clownish, comical, crazy, daft, droll, eccentric, funny, goofy, kooky, loony, madcap, nutty, screwy, wacky. **antonym** serious.

n buffoon, card, clown, comedian, fool, jester, joker, laugh, nut, nutcase, nutter, screwball, wag.

zeal *n* ardour, dedication, devotion, eagerness, earnestness, enthusiasm, fanaticism, fervour, fire, gusto, keenness, militancy, passion, spirit, verve, warmth, zest. **antonym** apathy.

zealous *adj* ardent, burning, devoted, eager, earnest, enthusiastic, fanatical, fervent, fervid, fired, gung-ho, impassioned, keen, militant, passionate, rabid, spirited. **antonym** apathetic.

zenith *n* acme, apex, apogee, climax, culmination, height, high point, peak, pinnacle, summit, top, vertex. **antonym** nadir.

zero *n* bottom, cipher, duck, goose-egg, love, nadir, naught, nil, nothing, nought.

zero in on aim for, concentrate on, converge on, direct at, fix on, focus on, head for, home in on, level at, pinpoint, train on.

zest *n* appetite, charm, delectation, élan, enjoyment, flavour, gusto, interest, joie de vivre, keenness, kick, peel, piquancy, pungency, relish, rind, savour, smack, spice, tang, taste, zeal, zing. **antonym** apathy.

zigzag *v* meander, snake, wind.

adj meandering, serpentine, sinuous, zigzagging, zigzaggy. **antonym** straight.

zing *n* animation, brio, dash, élan, energy, go, joie de vivre, life, liveliness, oomph, pizazz, sparkle, spirit, vigour, vitality, zest, zip. **antonym** listlessness.

zip *n* brio, drive, élan, energy, enthusiasm, get-up-and-go, go, gusto, life, liveliness, oomph, pep, pizzazz, punch, sparkle, spirit, verve, vigour, vim, vitality, zest, zing. **antonym** listlessness.

v dash, flash, fly, gallop, hurry, race, rush, scoot, shoot, speed, tear, whiz, whoosh, zoom.

zone *n* area, belt, district, region, section, sector, sphere, territory, tract.

zoom *v* buzz, dash, dive, flash, fly, gallop, hare, hurtle, pelt, race, rush, scoot, shoot, speed, streak, tear, whirl, whiz, whoosh, zip.

Appendices

Appendices

Classified word-lists

air and space vehicles

aerobus
aerodrome
aerodyne
aerohydroplane
aeroplane
aerostat
air-ambulance
air-bus
airship
all-wing aeroplane
amphibian
autogiro
balloon
biplane
blimp
bomber
cable-car
camel
canard
chopper
comsat
convertiplane
crate
delta-wing
dirigible
dive bomber
fan-jet
fighter
fire-balloon
flying boat
flying saucer
flying wing
glider
gondola
gyrocopter
gyroplane
helibus
helicopter
hoverbus
hovercar
hovercraft
hovertrain
hydro-aeroplane
hydrofoil
hydroplane
intercepter
jet

jetliner
jetplane
lem
microlight
module
monoplane
multiplane
plane
rocket
rocket-plane
runabout
sailplane
satellite
seaplane
space platform
space probe
space shuttle
spacecraft
spaceship
spitfire
sputnik
step-rocket
stol
strato-cruiser
stratotanker
swingtail cargo aircraft
swing-wing
tanker
taube
téléférique
tow-plane
tractor
triplane
troop-carrier
tube
tug
turbojet
turbo-jet
twoseater
UFO
warplane
zeppelin

alphabets, writing systems

Chalcidian alphabet
cuneiform
cyrillic

devanagari
estrang(h)elo
finger-alphabet
futhark
Glagol
Glossic
Greek
Gurmukhi
hieroglyphs
hiragana
ideograph
kana
katakana
Kufic
linear A
linear B
logograph
nagari
naskhi
og(h)am
pictograph
Roman
runic
syllabary

art

abstract
abstraction
action painting
anaglyph
anastasis
anastatic
anthemion
aquarelle
bas relief
Bauhaus
camaieu
cire perdue
dadaism
decal
decoupage
Der Blaue Reiter
diaglyph
Die Brücke
diptych
dry-point
duotone
écorché
enamel

art *(contd.)*
encaustic
engraving
etch
etchant
faience
fashion-plate
Fauve
Fauvism
fête champêtre
figurine
filigree
flambé
flannelgraph
Flemish
flesh-tint
Florentine
free-hand
fresco
fret
frit
futurism
futurist
gadroon
genre
gesso
glyptics
glyptography
Gobelin
gouache
graphic
graphics
graphium
graticulation
gravure
grecque
grisaille
gumption
hachure
hatch
hatching
haut relief
herm(a)
historiated
hound's-tooth
intaglio
linocut
literalism
litho
lithochromatic(s)
lithochromy
lithograph
lithoprint
lost wax
mandorla
meander
monotint
monotype
morbidezza

Parian
paysage
phylactery
pietra-dura
piqué
pochoir
pompier
putto
quattrocento
relievo
repoussage
repoussé
reserved
retroussage
rilievo
sculp(t)
scumble
sea-piece
seascape
secco
serigraph
statuary
stipple
stylus
surrealism
symbolism
tachism(e)
tempera
tenebrism
tessellated
tessera
tondo
trecento
triptych
ukiyo-e
velatura
Venetian mosaic
Venetian red
verditer
verism
vermiculate(d)
versal
vitrail
vitraillist
vitrifacture
vitrine
vitro-di-trina
volute
vorticism
woodblock
wood-carving
woodcut
wood-engraving
xoanon
zoomorphic

chemical elements

actinium

aluminium
americium
antimony
argon
arsenic
astatine
barium
berkelium
beryllium
bismuth
boron
bromine
cadmium
caesium
calcium
californium
carbon
cerium
chlorine
chromium
cobalt
copper
curium
dysprosium
einsteinium
erbium
europium
fermium
fluorine
francium
gadolinium
gallium
germanium
gold
hafnium
hahnium
helium
holmium
hydrogen
indium
iodine
iridium
iron
krypton
lanthanum
lawrencium
lead
lithium
lutetium
magnesium
manganese
mendelevium
mercury
molybdenum
neodymium
neon
neptunium
nickel
niobium

chemical elements
(contd.)

nitrogen
nobelium
osmium
oxygen
palladium
phosphorus
platinum
plutonium
polonium
potassium
praseodymium
promethium
protoactinium
radium
radon
rhenium
rhodium
rubidium
ruthenium
rutherfordium
samarium
scandium
selenium
silicon
silver
sodium
strontium
sulphur
tantalum
technetium
tellurium
terbium
thallium
thorium
thulium
tin
titanium
tungsten
uranium
vanadium
xenon
ytterbium
yttrium
zinc
zirconium

coins, currencies

agora
antoninianus
as
asper
aureus
baht
balboa
bawbee

bekah
belga
bezant
bit
bod(d)le
bolivar
boliviano
bonnet-piece
broad(piece)
buck
cardecu(e)
Carolus
cash
cent
centavo
centime
chiao
colon
conto
cordoba
couter
crown
crusado
cruzeiro
dam
daric
deaner
décime
denarius
denier
Deutschmark
didrachm(a)
dime
dinar
dirham
doit
dollar
double
doubloon
drachma
ducat
dupondius
duro
eagle
écu
eighteen-penny piece
ekuele
escudo
farthing
fen
fifty-pence piece
fifty-penny piece
five-pence piece
five-penny piece
florin
forint
franc
geordie
gerah

gourde
groat
groschen
guinea
gulden
haler
half-crown
half-dollar
halfpenny
half-sovereign
heller
jacobus
jane
jiao
jitney
joe
joey
jo(h)annes
kina
knife-money
koban(g)
kopeck
koruna
kreutzer
krona
krone
Krugerrand
kwacha
kyat
lek
lempira
leone
lepton
leu
lev
lilangeni
lion
lira
litre
livre
louis
louis-d'or
mag
maik
make
manch
mancus
maravedi
mark
markka
mawpus
merk
metical
mil
millième
millime
milreis
mina
mite

coins, currencies
(contd.)

mna
mohur
moidore
mopus
naira
napoleon
(naya) paisa
(new) cedi
ngwee
nickel
nicker
obang
obol
obolus
öre
øre
Paduan
pagoda
pänga
paolo
para
pataca
patrick
paul
peseta
pesewa
peso
pfennig
piastre
picayune
pice
piece of eight
pine-tree money
pistareen
pistole
pistolet
plack
portague
portcullis
pound
pula
punt
qintar
quetzal
quid
rag
rand
real
red
red cent
reichsmark
reis
renminbi
rial
rider
riel
ringgit

rix-dollar
riyal
rose-noble
r(o)uble
royal
ruddock
ruddy
rupee
rupiah
ryal
saw-buck
sceat(t)
schilling
scudo
semis
semuncia
sen
sequin
sesterce
sestertium
sextans
shekel
shilling
silverling
sixpence
skilling
smacker
sol
soldo
solidus
sou
sovereign
spade-guinea
spur-royal
stater
sterling
stiver
sucre
sword-dollar
sycee
tael
taka
talent
tanner
tenner
tenpence
ten-pence piece
ten-penny piece
tester(n)
testo(o)n
testril(l)
tetradrachm
thaler
thick'un
thin'un
three-farthings
three-halfpence
threepence
threepenny bit/piece

tical
tick(e)y
tizzy
toman
turner
twenty-pence piece
twenty-penny piece
two bits
twopence
two-pence piece
two-penny piece
unicorn
ure
vellon
wakiki
wampum
won
xerafin
yen
yuan
zack
zaire
zecchino
zimbi
zloty
zuz
zwanziger

collective nouns

building of rooks
cast of hawks
cete of badgers
charm of goldfinches
chattering of choughs
clamour of rooks
clowder of cats
company of widgeon
covert of coots
covey of partridges
down of hares
drift of swine
drove of cattle
dule of doves
exaltation of larks
fall of woodcock
fesnyng of ferrets
gaggle of geese
gam of whales
gang of elks
grist of bees
husk of hares
kindle of kittens
leap of leopards
leash of bucks
murder of crows
murmuration of starlings
muster of peacocks

collective nouns
(contd.)

mute of hounds
nide of pheasants
pace of asses
pod of seals
pride of lions
school of porpoises
siege of herons
skein of geese
skulk of foxes
sloth of bears
sounder of boars
spring of teals
stand of plovers
stud of mares
team of ducks
tok of capercailzies
troop of kangaroos
unkindness of ravens
walk of snipe
watch of nightingales

collectors, enthusiasts

abolitionist
ailurophile
antiquary
antivaccinationist
antivivisectionist
arachnologist
arctophile
audiophil(e)
balletomane
bibliolatrist
bibliomane
bibliopegist
bibliophagist
bibliophile
bibliophilist
bicameralist
campanologist
canophilist
cartophile
cartophilist
cheirographist
coleopterist
conservationist
cynophilist
Dantophilist
deltiologist
discophile
dog-fancier
ecclesiologist
egger
entomologist
environmentalist

ephemerist
epicure
ex-librist
feminist
Francophile
Gallophile
gastronome
gemmologist
Germanophil(e)
gourmet
herpetologist
hippophile
homoeopathist
iconophilist
incunabulist
Kremlinologist
lepidopterist
medallist
miscegenationist
monarchist
myrmecologist
negrophile
negrophilist
notaphilist
numismatist
oenophile
oenophilist
ophiophilist
orchidomaniac
ornithologist
orthoepist
orthographist
ostreiculturist
pangrammatist
Panhellenist
panislamist
Pan-Slavist
paragrammatist
paroemographer
perfectionist
philanthrope
philatelist
philhellene
phillumenist
philogynist
philologist
philologue
prohibitionist
pteridophilist
reincarnationist
Russophile
Russophilist
scripophile
scripophilist
sericulturist
Sinophile
Slavophile
spelaeologist
steganographist

stegophilist
supernaturalist
tege(s)tologist
timbrologist
timbromaniac
timbrophilist
tulipomane
tulipomaniac
Turcophile
ufologist
ultramontanist
vexillologist
virtuoso
vulcanologist
xenophile
zoophile
zoophilist

dog breeds

affenpinscher
badger-dog
basenji
basset(-hound)
Bedlington (terrier)
Blenheim spaniel
boar-hound
Border terrier
borzoi
Boston terrier
Briard
Brussels griffon
bull mastiff
bulldog
bull-terrier
cairn terrier
Cavalier King Charles
 spaniel
chihuahua
chow
clumber spaniel
coach-dog
cocker spaniel
collie
corgi
dachshund
Dalmatian
Dandie Dinmont
Dane
deerhound
dhole
dingo
Doberman(n) pinscher
elkhound
Eskimo dog
foxhound
fox-terrier
German police dog
German Shepherd dog

dog breeds (contd.)
Great Dane
greyhound
griffon
harlequin
(Irish) water-spaniel
Jack Russell
keeshond
King Charles spaniel
Labrador
laika
lhasa apso
lurcher
lyam-hound
malemute
Maltese
mastiff
peke
Pekin(g)ese
pinscher
pointer
Pomeranian
poodle
pug
pug-dog
retriever
Rottweiler
saluki
Samoyed(e)
sausage-dog
schipperke
schnauzer
Scotch-terrier
Sealyham
setter
sheltie
Shetland sheepdog
shih tzu
shough
Skye (terrier)
spaniel
Spartan
spitz
St Bernard
staghound
Sussex spaniel
talbot
teckel
terrier
vizsla
volpino
warragal
water-dog
Weimaraner
whippet
wire-hair(ed terrier)
wolf-dog
wolf-hound
Yorkshire terrier

zorro

minerals

adularia
aegirine
aegirite
alabandine
almandine
alum-shale
alum-slate
alum-stone
alunite
amazonite
amazon-stone
amianthus
amosite
amphibole
analcime
anatase
andesine
aplite
argil
arkose
asbestos
asparagus-stone
asphalt(um)
aventurine
baetyl
balas
Barbados earth
barilla
baryta
barytes
basalt
Bath stone
bath-brick
bezoar
bitter-earth
bitter-spar
bitumen
blackjack
blacklead
blaes
blende
bloodstone
blue ground
blue John
blue vitriol
bluestone
Bologna phosphorus
borane
borax
borazon
boride
bornite
boulder-clay
breccia
Bristol-brick

Bristol-diamond
brown spar
brownstone
buhrstone
cacholong
caen-stone
cairngorm
calamine
calc-sinter
calcspar
calc-tuff
caliche
calp
Carborundum®
cat's-eye
cat-silver
cauk
celestine
cement-stone
ceruse
chalcedony
chalcedonyx
chalk
chert
Chile saltpetre
china clay
china stone
chrome-alum
chrome-spinel
chrysoberyl
chrysocolla
chrysoprase
chrysotile
cinnabar
cinnamon-stone
cipollino
corundum
cryolite
cymophane
dacite
dendrite
Derbyshire spar
diabase
diallage
dialogite
diaspore
diatomite
dice-coal
diopside
dioptase
diorite
dogger
dogtooth-spar
dolerite
dolomite
dopplerite
dropstone
dunite
dyscrasite

minerals (contd.)

dysodyle
eagle-stone
earthflax
earthwax
eclogite
electric calamine
elvan
emery
encrinite
enhydrite
enhydros
epidiorite
epidosite
epidote
epistilbite
epsomite
erinite
erionite
erubescite
erythrite
euclase
eucrite
eudialyte
eutaxite
euxenite
fahlerz
fahlore
fakes
fayalite
fel(d)spar
felsite
felstone
flint
fluorite
fluorspar
franklinite
French chalk
fuchsite
fulgurite
fuller's earth
gabbro
gadolinite
gahnite
galena
galenite
gangue
gan(n)ister
garnet-rock
gibbsite
glance
glauberite
glauconite
glimmer
gmelinite
gneiss
goldstone
goslarite
gossan

göthite
granite
granitite
granodiorite
granophyre
granulite
graphic granite
graphite
green earth
greenockite
greensand
greenstone
greisen
greywacke
gummite
gypsum
haematite
hälleflinta
halloysite
harmotome
hatchettite
haüyne
heavy spar
hedyphane
hemimorphite
hepatite
hercynite
(h)essonite
heulandite
hiddenite
honey-stone
hornblende
hornfels
hornstone
horseflesh ore
humite
hyacinth
hyalophane
hypersthene
ice-spar
ice-stone
idocrase
ironstone
jacinth
keratophyre
kermes
kermesite
kieselguhr
knotenschiefer
kunkur
kupferschiefer
lamprophyre
lapis lazuli
lepidomelane
limestone
lithomarge
marlstone
meerschaum
mellite

mica
microlite
microlith
mispickel
morion
moss-agate
mundic
nail-head-spar
needle-tin
nepheline
nickel-bloom
nickel-ochre
Norway saltpetre
nosean
noselite
obsidian
omphacite
onyx
onyx-marble
ophiolite
orthoclase
orthophyre
ottrelite
ozokerite
peacock-ore
pencil-ore
pencil-stone
peperino
periclase
pericline
petuntse
piedmontite
pipeclay
pipestone
plagioclose
pleonaste
porphyry
potstone
prase
protogine
pyrites
quartz
realgar
rock-oil
rubicelle
ruby-spinel
rutile
saltpetre
sandstone
sanidine
sapphire
sapphire-quartz
sapphirine
sard
sardonyx
satin-spar
satin-stone
scaglia
scawtite

minerals (contd.)
schalstein
schiller-spar
schist
schorl
serpentine
serpentine(-rock)
shale
shell-limestone
shell-marl
silica
silver-glance
sinter
slate
soapstone
spar
speiss-cobalt
spelter
sphene
spiegeleisen
spinel
spinel-ruby
spodumene
stinkstone
strontian(ite)
sunstone
surturbrand
swinestone
sylvine
tabular spar
tachylyte
talc
talc-schist
terne
terpene
terpineol
terra alba
terracotta
terra-japonica
terramara
terra-rossa
terra-sigillata
terts
thulia
tiger(s)-eye
till
tin-stone
toad-stone
tombac
touchstone
tourmaline
trass
travertin(e)
tripoli
troutstone
tufa
tuff
Turkey hone
Turkey stone

turquoise
tutty
uinta(h)ite
umber
Uralian emerald
uralite
uraninite
uranite
uvarovite
vanadinite
variolite
variscite
veinstone
veinstuff
Venice talc
verd-antique
vesuvianite
vitrain
vivianite
vulpinite
wacke
wad(d)
wallsend
wavellite
Wernerite
whet-slate
whewellite
whinstone
white pyrites
willemite
witherite
wolfram
wollastonite
wood-coal
wulfenite
wurtzite
zaratite
zarnich
zeolite
zeuxite
zinkenite
zircon
zoisite
zorgite

musical instruments

aeolian harp
aerophone
alpenhorn
alphorn
althorn
alto
Amati
American organ
apollonicon
archlute
arpeggione
atabal

autoharp
balalaika
bandore
bandura
banjulele
baryton(e)
bass clarinet
bass drum
bass fiddle
bass horn
bass tuba
bass viol
basset horn
bazooka
bombard
bombardon
bongo (drum)
bouzouki
buccina
bugle
buglet
bull fiddle
calliope
castanets
celeste
cello
cembalo
chair-organ
chalumeau
chamber organ
chikara
Chinese pavilion
chitarrone
chordophone
cinema-organ
cithara
cither(n)
citole
cittern
clarichord
clarinet
clarino
clarion
clarsach
clave
clavichord
cornet
cornettino
crwth
cymbal
cymbalo
decachord
dichord
didgeridoo
digitorium
double bass
drum
dulcimer
Dulcitone®

musical instruments
(contd.)
dumb-piano
echo
electric guitar
electric organ
euphonium
fagotto
fife
fipple-flute
flageolet
flügel
flügelhorn
flute
flûte-à-bec
flutina
French horn
gamba
gamelan
German flute
gimbard
gittern
glass harmonica
glockenspiel
grand piano
gu
guiro
guitar
gusla
Hammerklavier
hand-horn
hand-organ
harmonica
harmonicon
harmoniphone
harmonium
harp
harpsichord
hautboy
heckelphone
heptachord
horn
hornpipe
humstrum
hunting-horn
hurdy-gurdy
idiophone
jingling Johnny
kantele
kazoo
kent-bugle
keyboard(s)
keybugle
klavier
koto
krummhorn
Kuh-horn
langsp(i)el
lituus

lur(e)
lyra-viol
lyre
mandola
mandolin(e)
mandora
manzello
maraca
marimba
marimbaphone
marine trumpet
melodeon
metallophone
mirliton
monochord
Moog synthesiser
mouth-harp
mouth-organ
mridangam
musette
musical glasses
naker
nose-flute
nun's-fiddle
oboe
oboe d'amore
oboe di caccia
ocarine
octachord
octave-flute
ophicleide
organ-harmonium
orpharion
orpheorion
pandora
panharmonicon
Pan-pipes
Pan's pipes
pantaleon
pianette
pianino
piano
piano-accordion
pianoforte
Pianola®
piano-organ
piffero
pipe
pipeless organ
pipe-organ
player piano
polyphon(e)
poogye
posaune
psaltery
pyrophone
quena
quint(e)
racket(t)

rebec(k)
regal
rote
sackbut
salpinx
sambuca
sancho
sang
santir
sarangi
sarod
sarrusophone
sausage-bassoon
saxhorn
saxophone
seraphine
serinette
serpent
s(h)amisen
shawm
side-drum
sitar
small-pipes
sourdeline
sousaphone
spinet(te)
squeeze-box
squiffer
steeldrum
sticcado
stock-and-horn
strad
Stradivari(us)
string bass
sultana
symphonion
symphony
synthesiser
syrinx
tabla
tabor
tabo(u)rin
tabret
tambour
tamboura
tambourine
tam-tam
testudo
tetrachord
theatre organ
theorbo
timbal
timbrel
timpano
tin whistle
traps
triangle
trichord
tromba marina

tools *(contd.)*

auger-bit
awl
boaster
bodkin
bolster
bradawl
broach
bucksaw
burin
burr
buzz-saw
card
caschrom
caulking-iron
celt
centre-bit
chaser
chisel
chopper
clamp
cleaver
cold-chisel
cradle-scythe
crosscut-saw
crown-saw
diamond-drill
dibble
dividers
dolly
drawing-knife
draw-knife
drill
drove
els(h)in
extirpator
fillister
float
forceps
forfex
fork
fraise
frame-saw
fretsaw
gad
gang-saw
gavelock
gimlet
gouge
grapnel
grapple
graver
gurlet
hacksaw
hammer
handsaw
hawk
hay fork
hay knife

helve-hammer
hod
hoe
holing-axe
jackhammer
jack-plane
jointer
laster
level
levelling-rod
levelling-staff
loy
mace
madge
maker
mall
mallet
mattock
maul
monkey
moon-knife
mortar
muller
oliver
oustiti
pachymeter
pad-saw
palstave
panel saw
panga
paper-cutter
paper-knife
pattle
pecker
peel
pestle
pick
pickaxe
pincers
pinch
pinking-shears
piolet
pitchfork
plane
planer
plessor
plexor
pliers
plough
plow
plugger
plumb
plumb-line
plumb-rule
plummet
pocket-knife
pointel
pricker
priest

priming-iron
priming-wire
probang
probe
probing-scissors
prod
prog
pruning-bill
pruning-hook
pruning-knife
pruning-shears
prunt
punch
puncheon
punty
quadrant
quannet
rabble
rake
raspatory
reed-knife
repositor
retractor
ricker
rickstick
riddle
riffle
ripper
ripping-saw
ripple
rip-saw
risp
router
rule
ruler
sash-tool
saw
sax
scalpel
scauper
scissors
scoop
scooper
scorper
scraper
screwdriver
screwjack
screw-wrench
scribe(r)
scutch(er)
scythe
seam-set
serving-mallet
shave
shears
shovel
sickle
slane
slate-axe

tools *(contd.)*

slater
slicker
smoother
snap
snarling-iron
snarling-rod
snips
soldering-bolt
soldering-iron
spade
spanner
spider
spokeshave
spud
squeegee
stadda
stake
stapler
stapling-machine
steel
stithy
stone-hammer
stretching-iron
strickle
strigil
stubble-rake
style
stylet
swage
swingle(-hand)
switch
tedder
tenon-saw
threshel
thresher
thrust-hoe
tint-tool
tongs
trepan
trowel
T-square
turfing-iron
turf-spade
turning-saw
tweezers
twist drill
upright
van
vice
vulsella
waster
whip-saw
widener
wimble
wood-shears
wortle
xyster
Y-level

weapons, armour

A-bomb
ack-ack
aerodart
ailette
air rifle
amusette
an(e)lace
arbalest
arblast
Archibald
Archie
arcubalist
armet
arquebus(e)
baldric(c)
ballista
ballistic missile
bandolier
basilisk
baton gun
bazooka
beaver
bill
Biscayan
blackjack
blowgun
blowpipe
bludgeon
blunderbuss
boarding-pike
bodkin
Bofors gun
bolas
bomb
bombard
boomerang
bowie knife
brassard
breastplate
breech-loader
Bren (gun)
bricole
brigandine
broadsword
brown Bess
brown bill
buckler
buckshot
bulldog
bullet
bundook
Bungalore torpedo
burganet
byrnie
caltrop
cannon
carbine

carronade
casque
cataphract
catapult
chain-armour
chain-mail
chamfrain
Chassepot
chausses
cheval-de-frise
chokebore
claymore
cluster-bomb
coal-box
co(e)horn
Colt
Congreve
corium
dag
dagger
dah
Damascus blade
Damascus sword
demi-cannon
demi-culverin
demi-lance
depth-bomb
depth-charge
dirk
dragoon
elephant gun
épée
escopette
Exocet®
express rifle
falchion
falconet
field gun
fire-arm
fire-arrow
firebomb
firelock
firepot
fission bomb
flail
flame-thrower
flick-knife
flintlock
foil
fougade
fougasse
four-pounder
fusee
fusil
Garand rifle
gatling-gun
gavelock
genouillère
gisarme

weapons, armour
(contd.)
gladius
gorget
grapeshot
greave
Greek fire
grenade
gun
habergeon
hackbut
hacqueton
hailshot
halberd
half-pike
hand-grenade
hand-gun
han(d)jar
handstaff
harquebus
hauberk
H-bomb
heaume
helm
helmet
hielaman
howitzer
jack
jamb(e)
jazerant
jesserant
Jethart staff
kalashnikov
katana
kirpan
kris
lamboys
lame
lance
Lochaber-axe
Long Tom
machete
machine-gun
mangonel
martel
Martini (-Henry)
matchlock
Mauser
Maxim(-gun)
mesail
Mills bomb
Mills grenade
mine
mine-thrower
mine-rocket launcher
minnie
mitrailleur
mitrailleuse
morgenstern

morglay
morning-star
mor(r)ion
mortar
musket
musketoon
nulla-nulla
oerlikon
panga
partisan
Patriot
pauldron
pavis(e)
pederero
pelican
pelta
perrier
petrary
petronel
pickelhaube
pike
pilum
pistol
pistolet
placket
plastron
plate-armour
pocket-pistol
poitrel
pole–ax(e)
poleyn
pompom
poniard
potgun
quarter-staff
queen's-arm
rapier
rerebrace
rest
revolver
rifle
rifle-grenade
sabaton
sabre
saker
sallet
saloon-pistol
saloon-rifle
sap
sarbacane
schiavone
schläger
scimitar
scorpion
Scud
scutum
serpentine
sharp

shell
shield
shillela(g)h
shortsword
shotgun
shrapnel
siege-artillery
siege-gun
siege-piece
singlestick
six-gun
six-shooter
skean(dhu)
sling
slung-shot
small-arm
small-sword
smoke-ball
smoke-bomb
snickersnee
spadroon
sparth(e)
spear
spear gun
splint-armour
spontoon
spring-gun
squid
steel
sten gun
Sterling
stern-chaser
stiletto
stone axe
stone-bow
stylet
submachine-gun
sumpit(an)
switch-blade (knife)
swivel-gun
sword
sword bayonet
sword-cane
sword-stick
tace
targe
target
taslet
tasse
tasset
testudo
three-pounder
threshel
throw-stick
time-bomb
toc emma
toggle-iron
tomahawk
Tomahawk

weapons, armour
(contd.)
tomboc
tommy-gun
tormentum
torpedo
tortoise
trecento
trench-mortar
trident
truncheon
tuille
tuillette
tulwar
turret-gun
twibill
vambrace
vamplate
V-bomb
visor

vou(l)ge
war-wolf
waster
water-cannon
water-pistol
Welsh hook
white-arm
Winchester (rifle)
wind-gun
wo(o)mera(ng)
yatag(h)an
zumbooruk

wine-bottle sizes

baby
balthaser
jeroboam
magnum
Methuselah

nebuchadnezzar
nip
rehoboam
salmanazar

zodiac signs

Aquarius
Aries
Cancer
Capricorn
Gemini
Leo
Libra
Pisces
Sagittarius
Scorpio
Taurus
Virgo